Track & Field

In memory of Ulrich Jonath and Univ.-Prof. Dr. Dr. Wildor Hollmann

Univ.-Prof. Dr. Heiko K. Strüder | Ulrich Jonath | Kai Scholz

Track & Field

Training & Movement Science – Theory and Practice for All Disciplines

In cooperation with:
Univ.-Prof. Dr. Dr. Wildor Hollmann
Dr. Axel Knicker
Dr. Wolfgang Ritzdorf
Dr. Jürgen Schiffer
Dr. Norbert Stein

MEYER & MEYER SPORT

British Library of Cataloguing in Publication Data
A catalogue record for this book is available from the British Library

Original title: *Leichtathletik: Trainings- und Bewegungswissenschaft – Theorie und Praxis aller Disziplinen*, © 2017 by SPORTVERLAG *Strauß*
Translation provided by World Athletics.
Translators: Dr. Jürgen Schiffer, Dr. Patrick Labriola

Track & Field
Maidenhead: Meyer & Meyer Sport (UK) Ltd., 2023
ISBN: 978-1-78255-222-2

© 2023 by Meyer & Meyer Sport (UK) Ltd.
Aachen, Auckland, Beirut, Dubai, Hägendorf, Hong Kong, Indianapolis, Cairo, Cape Town,
Manila, Maidenhead, New Delhi, Singapore, Sydney, Tehran, Vienna

 Member of the World Sport Publishers' Association (WSPA), www.w-s-p-a.org
Printed by Print Consult GmbH, Munich, Germany
Printed in Hungary

MIX
Paper from
responsible sources
FSC
www.fsc.org   FSC® C084279

ISBN: 978-1-78255-222-2
Email: info@m-m-sports.com
www.thesportspublisher.com

Credits
Cover design: Hannah Park
Interior design: Anja Elsen
Interior layout: Guido Maetzing, www.mmedia-agentur.de
Interior images: Courtesy of Heiko K. Strüder, Ulrich Jonath, Kai Scholz
Managing editor: Elizabeth Evans
Copy editor: Anne Rumery
Indexer: Rebecca McCorkle, prairieindexing10@gmail.com

CONTENTS

FOREWORD

Whatever your ability and aspirations, whether an elite athlete or a recreational runner, if you want to improve, then coaching competence is the key to development.

At national level you can invest in all the talent-spotting, athletics grassroots and development programmes you like, but if you don't have qualified coaches, and they aren't delivering high-quality coaching based on comprehensive coach education, it's just a happy accident if anything happens.

This is why *Track & Field: Training and Movement Science – Theory and Practice for All Disciplines* is such an important publication. Within its more than 1,000 pages, authors Univ.-Prof. Dr. Heiko K. Strüder, Ulrich Jonath and Kai Scholz illustrate and explain established training knowledge and techniques and detail how the latest discoveries of sport science impact coaching.

World Athletics is immensely proud to be associated with the publishers. Together our aim is to disseminate to the athletics community the commanding repository of knowledge which is contained within this book and encourage the engagement and progression of more coaches across the globe.

Extensively illustrated with more than 240 charts, 150 graphics and 470 photographs, *Track & Field* appeals not just to coaches and athletes, but also to teachers, lecturers and academics. As part of our ambition to grow the coaching community across the world, World Athletics has translated the original German edition into Arabic, Chinese, French, English, Russian and Spanish and will use parts of the book on our eLearning platform and via our worldwide Coaches Education and Certification System (CECS).

I am grateful for the time, dedication and vast experience that has gone into writing and editing this publication. Its legacy will be the contribution to the further advancement of our CECS system and the increase of talented coaches worldwide.

–Sebastian Coe

World Athletics President

PREFACE

This book is meant for coaches, athletes, physical education teachers, sport students, and sport scholars who wish to acquire comprehensive knowledge of the entire field of athletics.

As early as 1995, three textbooks on athletics: "Running" (vol. 1), "Jumping" (vol. 2), and "Throwing and the Combined Events" (vol. 3) were published by Jonath, Krempel, Haag, and Müller. Due to a recommendation by World Athletics (formerly "International Association of Athletics Federations" (IAAF)) and the translation of the work into several languages, a great number of these books were sold. However, progress and modern knowledge of the various fields of sport science required extensive editing and revision of these three volumes. The present comprehensive textbook on athletics succeeds these books. The first edition published in German by Strauß in 2013 already included extensive changes and additions to the content, and was based on an entirely new concept. In 2016, the book was selected as the official textbook of the IAAF and translated by the IAAF into Arabic, Chinese, English, French, Portuguese, Russian and Spanish. As a result, the textbook has become an important foundation of the World Athletics' educational materials, and many parts are used on their e-learning platform for coaches. This World Athletics certified textbook, *Track & Field*, is the only available translation that contains the entire contents of the original edition.

Modern athletics training is characterised by two factors: first, experience and opinions— therefore also training methods and contents of successful coaches—are passed on to the next generation of coaches. Second, the current findings in sport science have a great impact on training. Both of these factors are closely linked and have their own advantages and disadvantages. This textbook attempts to represent athletics in all its complexity and as the symbiotic interaction between training science and practice. In terms of practical training, an individual coach's experience as well as intuition and know-how are as important as a sound scholarly foundation.

This edition includes a general section which deals with the following topics:

- types of motor stress;
- adaptation and performance capacity;
- training control;
- training methods; and
- general training contents.

The Olympic disciplines of athletics are dealt with in the discipline-specific sections. In each case, the respective discipline is introduced from an anecdotal and historical perspective. Then, the following aspects are covered:

- competition rules;
- technique;
- strategy;
- didactics; and
- training planning.

The latest findings from training practice are presented while taking into consideration comprehensive national and international training literature. The photo sequences illustrating the technique of each discipline show top athletes and are accompanied by expert commentary. The various examples of training planning can be used as guidelines by interested individuals in various age groups. Recent findings in training and movement science are documented for the individual disciplines, taking into account the requirement profile of the athletes and the diagnostic methods to organise and improve training processes.

The results of the biomechanical studies on world-class athletes and the precise representation of the parameters determining performance are a useful addition to the technical features. The sections on training were deliberately written in a more extensive manner to illustrate the modern state of training methodology. The length of this book may be explained by the complexity of the topics presented in the texts, diagrams, and figures.

Our thanks go to Prof. Dr. Dr. Wildor Hollmann (general section), Dr. Norbert Stein (running events), Dr. Wolfgang Ritzdorf (jumping events), and Dr. Axel Knicker (throwing events) for the expert revision of the manuscript. We would also like to thank the German Athletics Association, Philippka Publishing House, and Helmar Hommel for making the photo sequences of top athletes available. Very helpful assistance for the original edition of the book was also provided by Dr. Frank Scholz for proofreading the book, by Ulrike Jonath who designed the cover, and by Horst Jonath (pictograms). Special thanks go to Dr. Jürgen Schiffer for his valuable assistance in obtaining current literature as well as for the final editing and the creation of an index. We also thank World Athletics for providing the excellent translation of the book by Dr. Jürgen Schiffer together with Dr. Patrick Labriola, and we look forward to the further development of the content and its continued success. Finally, we greatly appreciate the commitment of Martin Meyer, Robert Meyer, and Liz Evans from Meyer & Meyer Sport to this project, making the publication of the English edition of the textbook possible.

We wish the book a wide, varied, and interested audience.

–Heiko K. Strüder, Ulrich Jonath, Kai Scholz

TEST AND TRAINING FORMS IN THIS BOOK

All the forms of games, exercise, and tests used in the book are numbered. When first presented, each form of games and exercises is provided with a bold blue number and is described in detail. The same applies to the test and control procedures which are marked with a "T" in front of the number. The numbers (blue, not in bold) are used in many places in the book (e.g., in connection with another discipline or in the "Errors – Causes – Corrections" chapters) to refer to the (description of) forms of games and exercises or test and control procedures. In some exceptional cases, there is a number reference before the detailed description. This is when an exercise is a core exercise in discipline 3, while it is only an auxiliary exercise in disciplines 1 and 2, but discipline 3 occurs later in the book. The 5-box system (see figure 1) shows for whom a certain form of game or exercise is suitable and refers to the age and performance categories described in chapter II–3.1.1. Depending on the shading in the box, the game or exercise form is more or less suitable for the appropriate age and performance category.

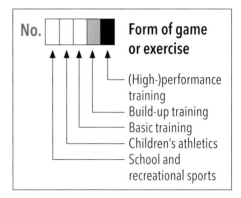

Figure 1: Explanation of the 5-box system.
This sample exercise is especially suitable for (high-)performance sport. In some instances, the box is filled with diagonal lines (e.g., when in the general part an exercise is presented which is often used differently in various disciplines).

Table 1: Overview of the numbering of the forms of games and exercises and the test forms

Chapter		Forms of games and exercises	Test forms
I	General chapter	1-96	T1-T11
II-1.3	100 m	101-145	T21-T26
II-1.5	400 m	151-160	T31-T33
II-1.6	4 x 100 m	161-165	T41-T44
II-1.7	4 x 400 m	171-174	
II-1.8	100- and 110-meter hurdles	181-208	T51-T54
II-1.9	400-m hurdles	211-217	
II-1.10	Common features: middle and long distances	221-234	T61-T66
II 1:11	800 and 1500 m		T71-T73
II 1:12	3000 m steeplechase	241-248	T81-T82
II 1:13	5000 m, 10,000 m, and marathon		T91-T92
II 1:14	Race walking	251-256	
II-2.2	Long jump	261-291	T101-T104
II-2.3	Triple jump	301-312	T111-T115
II-2.4	High jump	321-343	T121-T125
II-2.5	Pole vault	351-374	T131-T135
II-3.2	Javelin throw	381-399	T141-T145
II-3.3	Discus throw	401-417	T151-T155
II-3.4	Shot put	421-439	T161-T165
II-3.5	Hammer throw	441-453	T171-T174

PART I

GENERAL ASPECTS
OF ATHLETICS TRAINING

1 MAJOR TYPES OF MOTOR STRESS

In order to carry out optimal training, the following questions must be answered:

- Which factors have an effect that limits performance in specific sports?
- Which available measurements can accurately determine the current situation and the effects of training?
- Which training methods work best for individual athletes?

As a basis to answering these questions, Hollmann introduced the concept of major types of motor stress to training theory in 1967. These include:

- coordination,
- flexibility,
- strength,
- speed, and
- endurance.

Of course, there are smooth transitions and overlapping areas between these various categories. Nevertheless, a conceptual distinction is helpful to develop a precise understanding of factors which limit performance and specific training adaptations as well as the required training stimuli. In particular, specific factors pertaining to age and gender must be considered. A detailed presentation of the major types of motor stress and additional reference works can be found in Hollmann and Strüder (2009).

1.1 COORDINATION

(Movement) coordination is defined as the interaction of the central nervous system (CNS; the brain and spinal cord) and the skeletal muscles within a specific sequence of movements. *Intramuscular* coordination (IC) refers to the interaction between nerves and muscles within a specific sequence of movements in a single muscle, while *intermuscular* coordination is the interaction of various muscles during a specific sequence of movements. The term *technique* is often used when coordination is meant during specific movements in sports. However, the individual technique

specific to a sport is also limited by the other major types of motor stress. For example, the technical behaviour of a jumper during the flight phase depends significantly on the time available, which is determined by the vertical velocity of departure as a result of jumping strength.

The neuromuscular function provides the physiological basis for coordination. All muscle groups in the body are represented in the cerebral cortex. Voluntary movements are based on the integration of the motor and sensory

DISCOURSE I:
IMPORTANT TERMS TO UNDERSTAND THE MOTOR SYSTEM

Fibre, afferent/efferent

Afferent: conducting inwards; afferent nerve fibres transmit information (impulses) taken from the periphery to the CNS.

Efferent: conducting outward; efferent nerve fibres transmit information from the CNS to the executive organs in the periphery; in the case of motor-efferent fibres, the muscles are the effector organs.

Fibre, extrafusal/intrafusal

Extrafusal muscle fibres make up the bulk of the skeletal muscles and cannot be found within the sensory muscle spindle.

Intrafusal muscle fibres can be found in the muscle spindle; their contraction initiates or modulates the sensory discharge.

Golgi tendon organ

Sensory element in the tendons of muscles, which is activated by elongation or contraction of the muscle; an important receptor type in the muscle; it consists primarily of an afferent nerve fibre whose endings are located in the tendons between the muscle and the bone; these nerve fibres have many ramifications among the individual tendon fibres near the muscular origin of the tendon.

Motor neurone

One of the three major functional types of neurones, a motor neurone is a nerve cell which is involved in movement processes; motor neurones form synapses with muscle cells, transmit information from the CNS, and translate them into muscle movement. Alpha motor neurones regulate the length of the extrafusal fibres in the muscle (also called skeletomotor system), alpha motor neurones innervate the intrafusal muscle fibres of the muscle spindle and, using the proprioceptive reflex arc, trigger a contraction of the striated muscles. The muscle length during a contraction of the muscle is influenced by the gamma efferences; the gamma motor system adjusts the threshold and sensitivity of the stretch receptor.

Muscle spindle

A spindle-shaped structure in the skeletal muscle which contains small muscle fibres and receptors, the muscle spindles are activated by stretching.

Neurite (axon)/dendrite

A long/short extension of the neurones (nerve cells).

Proprioception

Deep sensitivity; perception of the position and movement of the body in space; through specific receptors (proprioceptors), information is registered about muscle tension, muscle length, and joint position or movement.

Reflex

Involuntary movement or other response which is caused by the activation of sense organs and is conducted via one or more synapses in the CNS.

Spinal ganglion

Thickening of nerve cells in the posterior root of the spinal cord; contains cell bodies.

Synapse

Point of contact between nerve cells or nerve cells and muscle cells or nerve cells and sensory cells; the intermediate space between the membranes of the pre-synaptic and the post-synaptic cell in a chemical synapse through which the transmitter (messenger substance) diffuses is referred to as synaptic cleft; monosynaptic means a connection with only one synapse.

system (see figure 2). Here, the cerebellum and the basal ganglia (a collection of nerve cell bodies) play an important role. In particular, the cerebellum receives sensory information and then modulates the temporal interaction and the direction of movements. The basal ganglia are primarily responsible for the regulation of movement speed. The brain stem and the motor nuclei in the thalamus control the functions of the cerebellum and the basal ganglia. This occurs in contrast to the motor part of the cerebral cortex, which initiates movements by planning which motor neurones (nerve cells) shall be used. A portion of the pre-frontal cortex, the pre-motor strip, is specifically used for the design of actions. From here, complex sequences of motor actions are controlled. The excitation of the motor centres in the cerebrum increases the impulses of the gamma system and prepares the pre-start state. This includes an increase in muscle tone (basic tension of the muscle) with a sensitivity increase of mechanoreceptors and proprioceptors. The latter include the muscle spindles, the Golgi tendon organs, and the joint receptors. This will allow smooth and properly dosed movements.

At the beginning of the motion sequence, the muscle spindles provide the target value of muscle length necessary to solve the motor task. In addition, the muscle spindles continuously measure the length of the muscle during movement execution. Only the simultaneous action in the antagonistic muscles allows for movements which are most finely graded in terms of force. The two muscle groups that enable movements in opposite directions at a joint are called **agonists and antagonists**.

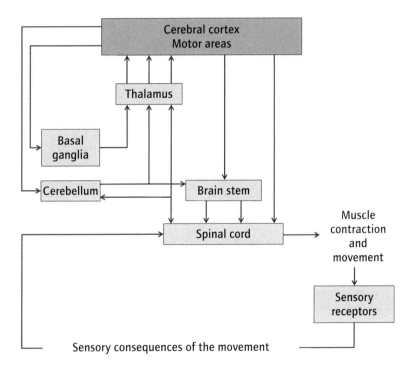

*Figure 2: **Motor areas of the cerebral cortex.** These affect the motor spinal nerves both directly and through the brain stem. All three levels of the system receive sensory information and are affected by the mutually independent systems of the basal ganglia and the cerebellum (modified on the basis of Hollmann and Strüder, 2009, p. 21).*

The following factors are crucial for the quality of coordination:

- consideration of the physical laws that are relevant for the respective motion;
- degree of exercise of the agonist-antagonist muscles active during the respective motion; and
- adaptation state of the vestibular system (vestibular apparatus).

Depending on preliminary training as well as the type and frequency of stress on the muscle groups, the optimal level of coordination for each individual is reached at different ages. In men and women, movements which are not specifically trained may likely reach their individually optimal quality at about the age of 20. Accelerated growth and an early start of specific practice can lead to achieving an optimal level of coordination at a much earlier age. The more complicated the movements in a discipline, the more emphasis should be placed on starting coordination training as early as possible. If specific coordination exercises are started at an early age, optimal coordination can already be achieved by the age of 12 or 13. Disturbances in the longitudinal growth of young people (ratio of trunk to leg length), which during certain developmental phases are caused by accelerated growth and which have adverse effects on coordination, deserve special attention. Without special exercises there is a decline in the quality of coordination at old age. Improvement in the quality of coordination through practising the respective movement sequence is primarily achieved by facilitating (ingraining) the corresponding specific movement pattern. The better the quality of coordination, the more straightforward, effortless, and precise the movement goal is achieved. The movement sequences become more fluent and economic, and the superfluous luxury movements, typical for beginners, disappear. This leads to a decrease in energy expenditure and thus the demand for oxygen during a given muscular activity. Due to the improvement in coordination, a conscious action, which is controlled by the cerebral cortex, is turned into an unconsciously executed action, whose automatism is controlled by subordinate centres of the brain. This relieves the cerebral cortex, and the movement sequence is mastered more safely and accurately than before. Economising movements, which is the result of improving coordination, also reduces the risk of injury, which is counteracted by an improved coordination of muscles while avoiding unnecessary innervation.

Especially when the body is set in rotary motion, for example in the hammer throw, the state of adaptation of the vestibular system plays an important role for coordination performance. The vestibular response to an appropriate stimulus is a complex sum of peripheral excitability and adaptation status of the entire vestibular apparatus. Through appropriate exercises, the intensity of the vestibular reaction can be reduced, and thereby the coordination can be improved. Four stages can be distinguished from the beginner stage to optimally developed quality in coordination:

- visual presentation in the cortex of the beginner, derived from the theoretical explanation and practical demonstration of the respective motion sequence;
- own experience in the motor process with a corresponding reduction in the extent of propagation (irradiation) of the stimulus processes;

- elimination of superfluous associated movements of other muscle groups; and
- automation and thus stabilisation of coordination with optimal intra- and intermuscular coordination.

DISCOURSE II: CATEGORIES OF COORDINATION REQUIREMENTS

The categories of coordination requirements and the concept of the Coordination Requirement Controller (CRC) derived from this by Neumaier et al. (2009) have also proved to be relevant to practising (see figure 3). In this approach it is assumed that there is a difference between the coordination requirements in terms of the afferent sensory information and pressure (constraint) conditions inherent to the movement task. The information requirements are divided into **optical** (o), **acoustic** (a), **kinesthetic** (k), **vestibular** (v), **tactile** (t), and "integrative sensory abilities to cope with the **equilibrium requirements**" (E). The pressure (constraint) conditions are divided into the following areas:

- **Precision constraints** (P): requirements concerning movement accuracy
- **Time constraints** (T): requirements concerning the available movement time and/or movement speed
- **Complexity constraints**: requirements concerning simultaneous coordination (C_1; concurrent movement parts), successive coordination (C_2; successive moving parts) and muscle selection (C_3; amount of the muscle groups to be included)
- **Situation constraints**: requirements concerning the environment and situation variability (S_1) and situation complexity (S_2)
- **Stress constraints**: requirements concerning physical stress (St_1) and mental stress (St_2).

Practical relevance arises in particular from the fact that during training the different areas can be up-regulated or down-regulated in a manner oriented toward an objective (see chapter I-4.1).

In this book, the requirement profiles for the individual disciplines are based on a simplified form of the CRC. This means that the superordinate equilibrium requirements are not assessed separately, and both the complexity constraints and the situation constraints are reduced to one controller each. The psychological stress constraints are not assessed, since these can differ from person to person and from one competition to the next one due to different circumstances.

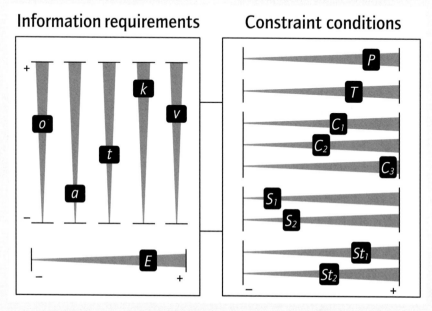

Figure 3: **Coordination Requirement Controller** (modified on the basis of Neumaier, 2009, p. 134).

However, the objective of practice and training is not only the ingraining of an optimal motor-dynamic stereotype, but during movement and technique training the task must often be varied, so that during competition the athlete can optimally adapt to constantly changing situations (variable availability of the movement sequence). In most cases, the ingraining of certain (always identical) movement programmes and the associated perception make it more difficult to change movements once learned than to learn a new movement sequence.

The observation that when exceeding a certain number of exercise movements per day the exercise effect no longer increases but decreases is also very important particularly for athletic training. The probable cause of this is the onset of fatigue, which impairs coordination and no longer guarantees optimal movements.

1.2 FLEXIBILITY

Flexibility (mobility) is defined as the possible range of movement that can be voluntarily achieved in one or more joints. The larger this range, the greater the flexibility. Factors limiting flexibility are:

- joint structure;
- amount of muscle mass;
- stretchability of the muscle;
- stretchability of the tendons, ligaments, and joint capsules as well as the skin; and
- tonus/pre-excitation.

These factors are of a mechanical nature, whereby a distinction must be made between non-controllable and controllable factors. The former pertain to the respective joint structure and the muscle mass. Flexibility is the only major type of motor stress whose maximum value is already achieved during the transition from childhood to adolescence and which then decreases. The age of greatest flexibility-related development dynamics is 10 years of age at the latest. Women have a greater flexibility than men and reach the corresponding maximum values earlier.

In training practice, a distinction is often made between **active** and **passive flexibility**. Active flexibility, which is brought about by the antagonists of the stretched muscle, is less than passive flexibility, which is caused by an external resistance. This is especially true for slow movement speeds. At high speeds, the antagonist can produce a correspondingly greater moment of inertia of the moving body segments, which then, so to speak, becomes the external force and stretches the agonist passively. For example, when standing on one leg and moving slowly one cannot raise the heel of the free leg all the way up to the buttocks. Causes of this *active insufficiency* are the decreasing force with decreasing muscle length and the mass of the contracted calf and hamstring muscles. However, when moving quickly with enough momentum (moment of inertia) it is possible to raise one's heel all the way up to the buttocks. Other examples of additional external forces which enable the athlete to reach greater passive movement amplitudes are the inertia of a throwing device, one athlete stretching another, or the resistance of the ground.

In respect to flexibility, joints can only be viewed in connection with one another if the muscle and tendon units extend over more than one joint. For example, some thigh muscles extend both over the knee and the hip joint. Some parts of the hamstring muscle group work as hip extensors and knee flexors at the same time. Some finger and foot muscles as well as certain parts of trunk muscles even span over a greater number of joints. Active insufficiency occurs especially in these muscles. Since a muscle cannot shorten indefinitely, a maximum range of motion is not possible in all joints simultaneously. The stretchability of a muscle is primarily determined by the properties of the elastic component of the muscle and tendon unit. Stretchability is required especially in a stretching position and is responsible for the resistance to stretching. In addition to active insufficiency, there is also the *passive insufficiency* of multi-joint muscles. Stretchability is too limited to achieve a maximum range of motion in all joints. Therefore, a multi-joint muscle more easily reaches the limit of its stretchability and is thus more susceptible to injury. When performing stretching training, one should keep in mind that the position of all the joints spanned is crucial when stretching a multi-joint muscle.

To understand the use of stretching exercises, knowledge of some basics of neurology is helpful. Among the reflex arcs involved in controlling motor function, the monosynaptic *stretch reflex* is of particular importance. The muscle spindle is the receptor organ of this reflex arc (see figure 4). In the muscle, thinner and shorter muscle fibres are positioned in the shape of spindles parallel to the "normal" muscle fibres. They are called intrafusal muscle fibres and have their own motor innervation, the gamma-fibres. In addition to motor innervation, the muscle spindles also have sensory innervation. These afferent fibres wrap themselves around the centre of the intrafusal muscle fibres several times. In respect to their function, they are stretch receptors. Simultaneous stretching of the muscle and the muscle spindle causes the spindle to send action potentials to the CNS, with the pulse frequency being proportional to the extent of the stretch. By stretching the extrafusal or contracting the intrafusal muscle fibres, the muscle spindle can trigger afferent impulses. These pulses are conducted to the spinal ganglion, whose neurit initiates synaptic contact with the alpha motor neuron. From this point, a contraction of extrafusal muscle fibres can be triggered. Both triggering processes are complementary in their effect or attenuate each other. Thus, an intrafusal contraction with simultaneous stretching of the muscle leads to a particularly strong activation of the stretch receptor, while extrafusal contraction and intrafusal relaxation relax the stretch receptor. In this way, the threshold value, and thus sensitivity, can be set anywhere between these extremes. An optimum setting is achieved by repeatedly performing the stretching of relevant muscles, which results in an increase in movement speed. Some athletes make use of these physiological principles when preparing for a sprint, jump, throw, etc. However, there is also fear that, in particular when stretching statically, reactive force is reduced and therefore performance decreased.

In addition to muscle spindles, there are also stretch receptors in tendons. These tendon spindles (Golgi tendon organs) act contrary to the muscle spindles, thus leading to an inhibition of the alpha motor neurones, which excite the stretched muscle. This behaviour is termed *inverse stretch reflex*. It only occurs at a significantly greater elongation than caused by the stretch reflex induced by muscle spindle.

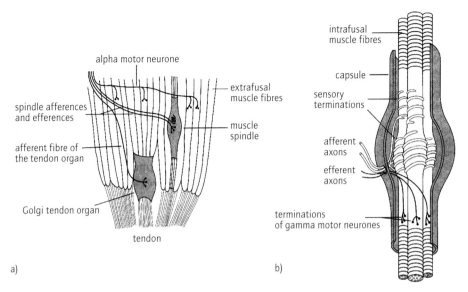

intrafusal
muscle fibres

alpha motor neurone

capsule

extrafusal
muscle fibres

sensory
terminations

spindle afferences
and efferences

muscle
spindle

afferent fibre of
the tendon organ

afferent
axons

efferent
axons

Golgi tendon organ

terminations
of gamma motor neurones

tendon

a)   b)

Figure 4a: **Sensory receptors in the muscle**; *b:* **Muscle spindle** *(modified on the basis of Kandel et al., 1995, p. 519). The muscle spindle is excited by both afferent and efferent fibres (gamma motor neurones). The muscle spindle consists of intrafusal fibres, sensory terminations and motor axons. The Golgi tendon organ is connected to the muscle fibres through collagen fibres.*

1.3 STRENGTH

Force can be defined in physical and biological terms. From a physical point of view, forces deform bodies or change their states of motion. Without force effects, a body remains in its state of uniform motion due to its inertia (Newton's first law). Apart from rest, two main states of motion can be distinguished: rotation, in which all points of a body rotate on concentric circles around the centre of mass (centre of gravity = CG) of a body, and translation, in which all points of a body move on parallel paths. The change of the state of motion (i.e., the magnitude of acceleration [a]) of a body with the mass m is proportional to the force causing this change (a = F/m; Newton's second law). Each force

produces an equal counterforce (action = reaction; Newton's third law). Therefore, if one pushes against a wall with a force of 100 Newtons (N), the wall pushes back with 100N. However, these statements about physical force cannot be so easily applied to force in the field of biology.

A muscle develops force through tension. The main manifestations of force in humans are static and dynamic strength. **Static strength** is understood as the muscle tension which in a given position can be voluntarily exerted against a fixed resistance. **Dynamic strength** is the force developed within a specific sequence of movements. Dynamic strength in the form of so-called strength endurance also occurs in the context of endurance which is one of the major types of motor stress. All types of endurance will be discussed together in chapter I-1.5. There, strength endurance loads will be dealt with under the name of local or general anaerobic endurance.

Dynamic strength is divided into movements occurring with muscle shortening (**concentric strength**) and muscle lengthening (**eccentric strength**). Maximum strength is defined as the highest possible strength that can be voluntarily produced by the nerve and muscle system. Maximum strength is less than absolute strength, which also includes autonomously protected reserves (see discourse III). The difference is referred to as strength deficit. Furthermore, **absolute maximum strength** must be distinguished from **relative maximum strength**, which is related to body mass. Since the acceleration achieved also depends on the mass of the accelerated body (a = F/m; see above), good relative maximum strength (in N/kg) is of decisive importance when a person's body must be moved, for example, especially in the athletics jumps. **Reactive strength**, which occurs in stretch-shortening cycles, is rather independent of maximum strength. Within a cycle, first a rapid eccentric contraction (stretch) occurs; immediately afterwards the movement direction is reversed and a concentric contraction (shortening) of the same muscles occurs. This results in increased force production during the concentric phase, since during the eccentric phase energy was stored in

the elastic structures and certain reflexes were triggered. In athletics, stretch-shortening cycles and thus reactive-strength loads occur especially in take-offs, but also during every sprint stride. In throws, stretch-shortening cycles are also specifically triggered by clever strategies used by the athlete. Reactive-strength loads in stretch-shortening cycles are almost characteristic of most highly dynamic athletic movements.

The amount of maximum static strength is determined by the following factors:
* muscle fibre cross-section,
* number of muscle fibres,
* muscle structure (including the proportion of fast and slow muscle fibres),
* muscle-fibre length and angle of traction,
* coordination, and
* motivation.

In contrast, the following factors are important for the effect of dynamic strength:
* static strength,
* mass to be moved (weight and form),
* contraction velocity of the muscles,
* coordination,
* observation of the relevant physical laws and anthropometric (body-structural) properties, and
* muscle pre-stretching,

and especially in connection with reactive strength:
* current muscle length and previous movement and
* structure of the passive elements of the muscle-tendon unit.

In human muscles, there are type I and type II fibres. Type II fibres are divided into two subgroups: type IIa and type IIx (the latter were formerly known as IIb fibres). The different *fibre types* are characterised by sometimes large differences in their metabolic and contractile properties. Type I fibres contract slower, type II fibres contract faster, and type IIx fibres contract fastest. Type IIx fibres are about 10 times and type IIa fibres approximately three to five times faster than type I fibres. In comparison to type I fibres, type IIx fibres can develop tension which is about 15–20% greater. Type I fibres have far more capillaries, a larger mitochondrial volume, a greater capacity to metabolise fat, and a higher insulin sensitivity than the other fibre types. In this respect, the performance of the IIx fibres is the lowest. It can be assumed that in average people about 50% of all muscle fibres in the body belong to the fast type, while the remaining 50% are slow fibres. There is a statistically high correlation in percentage between the cross-sectional area ratio of fast fibres in a muscle and the maximum speed strength of this muscle, but hardly a statistically significant correlation with static maximum strength. There are also extremely significant correlations between speed strength per kg body weight and the percentage of fast-fibre area.

The amount of force a muscle can produce depends on the joint angle. In the event of a stronger stretch, the actin and myosin filaments of the muscle fibre overlap only a short distance, some myosin heads cannot attach, and muscle strength decreases (see figure 5). If, however, the muscle, and thus the individual sarcomeres, have already shortened significantly, the myosin filaments even touch the Z-disks and muscle strength also decreases. This means that the muscle generates the greatest force at a medium length. This effect is enhanced by the following biomechanical phenomenon: Most tendons of muscles attach to the bone in such a way that the effective lever arm is the greatest in a medium joint position, since the torque generated in a joint not only depends on the strength of the muscle but also on the effective lever arm. The effective lever arm is the distance between the axis of rotation of the joint and the point where the tendon attaches to the bone, at right angles to the pulling direction of the tendon. The corresponding bell-shaped curve of the active force determines, together with the stretch resistance of the connective tissue, the typical *length-tension relationship*. The sliding filament theory described above applies to concentric loads, and even during static movements the muscle belly shortens to a certain extent, while the tendon is stretched accordingly. The process during eccentric muscle work, in which the muscle is extended despite tension, is not yet fully understood. Since the tilting movement of the myosin heads is possible in only one direction, it is assumed that individual sarcomeres are torn apart and that tension at these points is transmitted only via passive elastic filament structures such as titins and desmins.

DISCOURSE III: FUNDAMENTALS OF MUSCLE CONTRACTION

The central nervous system controls muscle force through the number of muscle fibres activated simultaneously (recruitment) and the frequency at which it sends impulses to the muscle fibres (frequencing or rate coding). A central nervous protection mechanism ensures that maximum muscle excitation is possible only in panic situations and under drugs, hypnosis, or electric stimulation. The highest level of performance unable to be activated under normal circumstances is called autonomously protected reserve. This can be reduced by training. Each alpha motor neurone coming from the spinal cord branches out in the muscle and simultaneously excites (innervates) 5 to approximately 2000 muscle fibres. An alpha motor neurone and the muscle fibres excited by it are called motor unit. If any excitation (action potential) reaches a muscle fibre, Ca^{++} ions are released in the muscle, allowing for the contraction of the muscle (sliding action of the actin and myosin filaments). If no further excitation occurs, the contraction is deactivated quickly, since Ca^{++} ions are continually pumped out of the muscles. However, if several action potentials reach the muscle in rapid succession, the amount of Ca^{++} ions adds up inside the cell and the muscle force increases. Thus, it is only in the case of maximum excitation frequency that a maximum force development of the individual muscle fibre takes place. If the recruitment is also optimal, the whole muscle develops its maximum force. During muscle contraction, the heads of the myosin molecules attach to contact sites on the actin molecules, which were exposed by the influx of Ca^{++} ions. After forming these cross-bridges the myosin heads perform a tilting movement and the myosin filament slides a little way along the actin filament. Then the myosin heads detach again from the actin. This process goes hand in hand with a breakdown of ATP. Provided there are still Ca^{++} ions inside the cell, the grip-release cycle (ratchet mechanism) can begin anew. When the actin and myosin filament slide into each other, the Z-disks approach each other, the sarcomere shortens, and the whole muscle shortens by multiplying this process.

Inside and outside the muscle fibre, there are lots of *passive elastic structures*. Outside the muscle fibre, these are the structures of the connective tissue of the muscles consisting of the collagen protein: Individual muscle fibres are surrounded by the so-called endomysium. Groups of muscle fibres (muscle bundles/fascicles) are surrounded by the firmer perimysium. The entire muscle is surrounded by the epimysium. At the ends of the muscles, the membranes of the muscle fibres, the perimysium and the endomysium, merge into the connective tissue fibres of the tendon or aponeurosis. Since all these components are positioned either

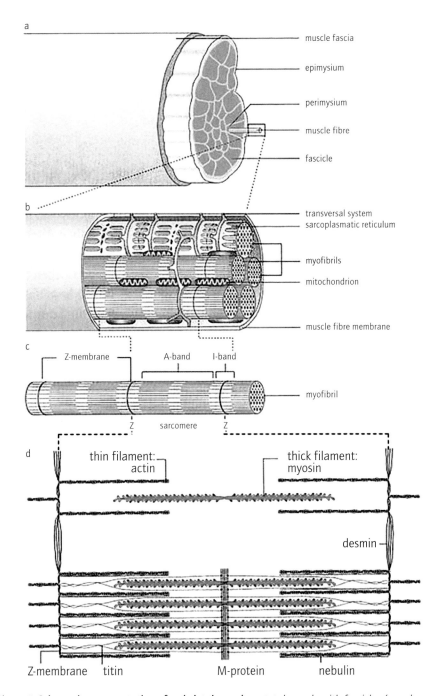

*Figure 5: **Schematic representation of a skeletal muscle**, a: total muscle with fascicles (muscle bundles), b: muscle fibre (muscle cell) with five myofibrils, c: myofibril with 2½ sarcomeres, d: sarcomere with filamentary structure (modified on the basis of De Morree, 2001, pp. 126–127).*

parallel or in series to the contractile components, a distinction is made between serial- and parallel-elastic components. These components are used for force transmission, protection against over-stretching of the muscle, and energy storage. The latter is especially interesting in the context of reactive strength. During reactive-strength exercise, the power output during the concentric phase is not only increased through reflex activity but also by storing energy in elastic structures. This energy was previously stored during the concentric phase as in a rubber band. The more a muscle is stretched during tension, the more its strength depends on passive elastic components.

The CNS, however, not only affects strength through the above-mentioned mechanisms of recruitment and frequencing (rate coding) of muscle fibres, but also by another trick. During the highest strength loads (e.g., during a long-jump take-off or a maximum squat), the CNS triggers strength-increasing exhalation against closed air passages (Valsalva manoeuvre). In this case, all trunk muscles (abdominal, back, intercostal, diaphragmatic muscle, etc.) contract simultaneously, so that the trunk is formed into a compact unit. Only with a compact trunk is a maximum momentum transfer possible. This way, during maximum exercise, strength can be increased by about 10%. The hypertensive effect of the Valsalva manoeuvre and the associated risk for cardiovascular patients have been frequently pointed out. An extended pressing power can even lead to orthostatic collapse. For healthy athletes, however, forced breathing is a natural and sensible phenomenon—no one should try to exhale during a long-jump take-off! The phrase *pressing means power* has always been an old weightlifter's rule.

In strength development, there are not only inter-individual but also intra-individual muscle-specific differences. As far as the forearm flexor muscles are concerned, girls reach maximum values by the age of 16 years, whereas boys only do so between the age of 18 and 20. In women, the former also applies to the lower leg extensor muscles. As far as these muscles are concerned, maximum values can also be measured in boys by the age of 16. In men, maximum strength is on average 30–40% higher than in women. The main reason for sex-related differences in strength is the smaller muscle fibre cross-section in women. At the same time, women generate less explosive and dynamic power per cm^2 muscles, which is possibly caused by higher intramuscular fat content. If there is still not a sufficiently high testosterone level in the muscle cell, structural strength trainability is limited. Nevertheless, in both sexes strength training before the age of 10 cannot only result in highly significant strength gains but also in an increase in muscle fibre size (hypertrophy). During specific movement sequences, increased strength is caused especially by improved quality in coordination (i.e., through the interaction between the central nervous system and the skeletal muscles).

The immobilisation of a muscle group (e.g., resulting from a plaster cast) can lead to a reduction in maximum static strength by about 20% even after eight days and by almost 30% after 14 days. In the course of the ageing process, strength is also reduced, with leg strength being reduced faster than arm strength. In men, the loss of muscle strength takes place more rapidly than in women. Clear reductions in static muscle strength occur after the age of 60 on average. Healthy people in the 7th and 8th decades of life exhibit on average 20–40% less static and dynamic muscle strength than young people; in the 9th and 10th decade of their lives, the reduction amounts to 50% and more. Age-related decline in muscle strength is mainly due to a reduction in the number of muscle fibres. One can roughly assume that beyond 30 years of age about 6% of the muscle fibres perish per decade of life. The cause of this is still scientifically unclear. At the same time, a regression of the cross-sectional size of the individual muscle fibre can be observed (atrophy). This loss can be counteracted, at least partially, by suitable strength training.

When maximum strength is related to kg body weight, sex differences become much greater. This applies even more when regarding the relationship of static strength to fat-free body mass. The percentage increase in static muscle strength due to training is about the same in both sexes. Unlike static measurements, isokinetic measurements at low speeds of movement (30°/sec) can lead to greater differences than at high speeds. Eccentric strength exercise causes the least sex-based strength differences.

The distribution of the number of muscle fibres in terms of slow and fast fibres is also about the same in both sexes, with a greater interindividual variation in males. The exercise-induced increase in muscle-fibre cross-section per unit of time does not vary in female and male people.

Although strength training alters the percentages of muscle-fibre distribution only to a small extent, it can change the magnitude of the cross-sectional area of the available types of muscle fibre. The genome plays a crucial role for the percentage composition of muscle fibre. Although the 110m hurdles world record was held by an Asian athlete until recently and, for example, with Kim Gevaert and Matic Osovnikar one female and one male athlete of Caucasian origin qualified for the 100m World Cup final in 2007, a large proportion of Africans, Afro-Americans, -Jamaicans, and -Britons among the world-class sprinters, which is unexpectedly high in comparison to the world population, is striking. Apart from diverse social influences, causal factors of this can be particularly genetic factors, for example a genetically determined higher proportion of fast-twitch muscle fibres.

Connective tissue (cells and substances which are located between the body cells) is strengthened by weight training. Thus, tendon and ligament damage can be remedied faster by performing specific strength training than by immobilisation. There are close links between the development of strength and bone structure and density. According to longitudinal studies conducted over several decades, strength training during youth or early adulthood as well as the associated pressure and tensile loads on the bones can lead to significant increases in bone density, which later may be beneficial when getting older. Thereby, the probability of osteoporosis (degenerative reduction of bone density) is reduced. Former world-class long-distance runners, whose physical activity did only include low strength loads, barely show significant differences in bone density between the age of 50–60 when compared with same-aged men and women with a sedentary lifestyle. Unlike endurance athletes, former female and male gymnasts between 50 and 60 show superior bone density values. Strength training can increase the diameter of long bones (e.g., in the thigh) to a highly significant degree. There is also an increase in the outer layer, bone density, and the bone projections of the muscle-tendon attachments. Such changes are evident as early as after three to five years of systematic strength training. The resulting changes are retained to a certain degree even after prolonged interruption of training. The articular cartilage is also positively affected by strength training, to the extent that an increase in thickness can be detected. Conversely, a prolonged immobilisation has a negative effect on bone strength and elasticity.

1.4 SPEED

Speed of athletic movements is the ability to respond to a stimulus as fast as possible and/or to carry out movements at the highest speed. The following four motor characteristics can be dealt with in the context of speed:

- reaction time,
- speed of a single movement,
- movement frequency, and
- locomotion speed.

Reaction time is defined as the time which elapses from the point of giving a signal until the start of voluntary reaction. A distinction is made between single and choice reactions. In the former, there is only one possible stimulus followed by a previously fixed response. In choice reactions there are at least two possible stimuli (signals). Each signal is followed by a different action. Furthermore, reactions can be distinguished by the nature of the stimulus. In athletics, there are reactions to acoustic stimuli (e.g., the starting signal in a crouch start), visual stimuli (e.g., during the outgoing runner's start in the 4 x 100m relay), and tactile stimuli (e.g., when touching an obstacle or an opponent).

- The simpler the stimulus (auditory stimuli are simpler than visual stimuli),
- the simpler the required motor action (pressing a key vs. crouch start),
- the more clearly defined the task (the CNS can then prepare the required motor programme even before the appearance of the stimulus), and

- the more previous experience with the required motion available,
- the lower the reaction time will be.

If the movements are simple (e.g., pressing a key), or if the influence of the movement is reduced (e.g., when measuring the first detectable movement during the crouch start by sensors in the starting block), results show that the (pure) reaction time – after a short initial period of adaptation – is hardly trainable and subject to fluctuations from trial to trial. The objective of training is therefore to optimise the quality of the prepared motor programme and the training of concentration to stabilise the reaction times (selective attention).

The repetitive movements of running are called cyclic movements. Therefore, in terms of an athletics sprint, people often talk of **cyclic speed**. In contrast, **acyclic speed** is the speed in non-cyclic movements, such as putting, throwing and jumping movements. Basic speed is defined as the maximum achievable speed of movement. The following factors limit performance:

- the dynamic strength of the working muscles,
- coordination,
- contraction velocity,
- muscle viscosity,
- anthropometric characteristics, and
- flexibility.

Some of these factors overlap one another since coordination already affects the force developed; viscosity (i.e., the frictional resistance within a muscle during movements) is also of importance for contraction velocity. The most important factors are undoubtedly the dynamic strength of the working muscles and coordination. For contraction velocity, besides the size of the cross-sectional area of faster muscle fibres, muscle elasticity is also of importance, among other things. This applies equally to the agonistic and antagonistic muscles. Furthermore, the extensive relaxation of the muscles not currently active is also a requirement for high contraction velocity. Nervousness or exaggerated pre-start tension with resultant muscle tension can have a negative impact on contraction velocity. Anthropometric characteristics can also affect the basic speed in physical terms. Studies have shown that somatometric (involving body measurement) dimensions of body weight, pelvic width, thigh length (lever arm), and circumference (muscle strength) influence sprinting time.

The velocity of individual movements can differ from one person to another. An athlete may have fast legs, but slow arm movements. Conversely, one also speaks of the fast arm of the otherwise rather slow javelin thrower. The speed of individual movements, for example at a joint, also determines the frequency of movement. The maximum values of movement frequency are considerably different at the various joints. During concentric contractions, force decreases in relation to increasing speed, while the opposite behaviour is observed in an eccentric contraction, when the active muscle is lengthened. Here, the maximum eccentric force attained is higher than the concentric force at all comparable speeds. Elastic structures are of considerable importance in this context.

The structure of a muscle determines the maximum attainable speed of movement. If a muscle contains a large number of sarcomeres connected in series, it can attain higher maximum shortening speeds than a muscle containing a low number of sarcomeres. Force (also the possible force per unit of time) increases with the number of sarcomeres connected in parallel. Moreover, a high percentage or a particularly large cross-sectional area of fast-twitch muscle fibres improves the

capacity to generate a high acceleration and speed. The concentration of the myosin ATPase enzyme in the muscle cell, which determines the rate of myosin cross-bridge formation, is also crucial for the development of an explosive strength effort. The contractile properties of the muscle can be changed in two ways through training. One involves fibre conversion, the other a selective hypertrophy of a specific fibre type. Fast fibres contain predominantly myosin heavy chains and other fast contractile protein isoforms. Specific stimuli addressing the relevant genes cause specific changes in the muscles. The precise cellular signals for the individual muscle gene are still largely unknown.

1.5 ENDURANCE

Endurance is characterised by the ability to maintain a given performance over a period as long as possible. Thus, endurance is identical with fatigue resistance. Depending on the quality and quantity of physical work per unit of time, morphological (amount of muscle mass used), biochemical (aerobic/

anaerobic metabolism) and biophysical aspects (dynamic/static stress) need to be distinguished (see figure 6). The most important types of endurance will be discussed below.

Local muscle endurance is defined as the endurance of a muscle mass, which is

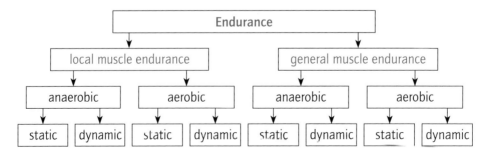

Figure 6: *Scheme of the different types of endurance performance capacity* (according to Hollmann, 1967).

less than 1/7–1/6 of the total skeletal muscles (roughly equivalent to the muscles of one leg). Factors **limiting local aerobic dynamic endurance** are:

- the amount of intracellular oxygen supply per unit of time, which in turn is dependent on cardiac output, the sum of the vessel cross-sections in the working muscles (vascularisation or capillarisation and collaterals), the economy of intramuscular blood distribution, and myoglobin concentration,
- capacity of the mitochondrial metabolism (mitochondrial volume),
- size of local carbohydrate depots,
- quality of metabolic processes (high or low fatty acid metabolism), and
- coordination (fatigue).

This type of muscular endurance is of great importance for performance sport. Here, important haemodynamic and metabolic mechanisms occur. An exercise-induced improvement of local dynamic aerobic endurance affects haemodynamics and metabolism qualitatively and quantitatively. The backlash involves increased performance capacity even in the case of unchanged cardiopulmonary capacity. As far as percentage is concerned, this type of endurance is the most trainable type of motor stress, since its initial value can be improved far more than tenfold.

An improvement in local dynamic aerobic endurance is at least as important for increasing overall physical performance as training-induced cardiopulmonary adaptations. The physiological fundamentals for improvement are the following haemodynamic and metabolic changes:

Haemodynamic changes
- Improved vascularisation (enlargement of the cross section of vessels, development of collaterals and capillarisation)
- Improved intramuscular blood distribution

Metabolic changes
- Increase in the concentration of intramuscular glycogen
- Enlargement and proliferation of mitochondria
- Increase in the activity of anaerobic and aerobic enzymes
- Percentage increase in fat metabolism in comparison with carbohydrate metabolism during submaximal exercise

There is also an increase in the quality of coordination. The end result of these adaptations is an increase in peripheral haemodynamic, metabolic, and physical performance with retroactions on central control.

Local anaerobic static muscle endurance, for example, is addressed when a weight of more than approximately 15%, specifically when higher than 50% of the maximum static strength, is held in a fixed position (static work). Here, increasing the

DISCOURSE IV: FUNDAMENTALS OF ENERGY SUPPLY

The basis of each muscle contraction is the breakdown of adenosine triphosphate (ATP) to adenosine diphosphate (ADP) and phosphate (P_i) with the release of energy. ATP is the only form of energy which can be used directly by cells. The quickest way to resynthesise ATP is from creatine phosphate stored in the muscle cell. However, the creatine phosphate store, and thus anaerobic-alactacid metabolism, fulfils the energy requirements only during the first few seconds of exercise. The resynthesis of ATP must occur continuously and without interruption. The metabolic processes using oxygen and occurring in the mitochondria are called aerobic, while anaerobic metabolism occurs outside the mitochondria without oxygen consumption. The important difference between these metabolic processes is based essentially on the fact that, unlike carbon dioxide (CO_2) and water (H_2O), which are generated during aerobic metabolism, the lactate produced during anaerobic metabolism can only leave the cell with difficulty and very slowly. The result is an accumulation of intracellular lactate with an appropriate acidification of the cell milieu (i.e., a decrease in pH value). This has a negative effect on performance capacity.

In summary, the most important energy-providing metabolic processes are:

anaerobic:
- ATP ↔ ADP + P_i + free energy
- creatine phosphate + ADP ↔ creatine + ATP
- glycogen/glucose + P_i + ADP ↔ lactate + ATP

aerobic:
- glycogen/glucose/fatty acids + P_i + ADP + O_2 ↔ CO_2 + H_2O + ATP

The kind of nutrient metabolised depends on the quality and quantity of work, diet, and the training state. During the first minutes of work and at a high exercise intensity, the main focus is on carbohydrate metabolism, while fat oxidation becomes increasingly important during prolonged submaximal exercise. The intracellular stores are used first. The fat reserves are practically inexhaustible, because fatty acids can be supplied in sufficient amounts via the blood, whereas this applies to glucose only to a limited extent through the mobilisation of liver glycogen (glycogen = storage form of carbohydrates).

load causes a reduction of the oxygen supply due to the reduced blood flow in the muscles. The following factors limit general performance:

- amount of anaerobic energy to be developed and
- local and central fatigue.

Local anaerobic static muscle endurance is increased in particular by training leading to an increase in the maximum static strength of relevant muscles.

General aerobic dynamic endurance is defined as aerobic endurance exercise consisting of dynamic work by using a muscle mass greater than 1/7–1/6 of the entire skeletal muscles. Factors limiting **general dynamic aerobic endurance** are:

- maximum oxygen uptake or maximum oxygen uptake/kg body weight,
- height of the aerobic-anaerobic threshold,
- size of the glycogen store,
- quality of metabolic processes, and
- the brain (see also chapter I-2.5).

Maximum oxygen uptake is regarded as the major criterion of cardiopulmonary capacity. Oxygen uptake provides information about the amount of energy supplied aerobically over a period of a few minutes. The following factors can limit maximum oxygen uptake:

- ventilation,
- lung diffusion,
- cardiac output,
- total haemoglobin content,
- nutritional status, and

- dynamic performance capacity of the working muscles,

as well as the following external factors:

- mode of exercise,
- size and type of muscles used,
- body position,
- partial pressure of oxygen in the inspired air (altitude), and
- climate (heat, cold, humidity).

The old statement that the magnitude of the maximum oxygen uptake corresponds to the endurance capacity is not correct. Such a substantive connection only applies to short-term aerobic endurance (3–10 min). The longer the general aerobic endurance load, the more significant the metabolic processes in the muscles for the maintenance of the prescribed exercise intensity. Here, endurance performance primarily depends on:

- extent of the aerobic-anaerobic threshold,
- amount of glycogen stored in the muscles, and
- the quality of the oxidation processes (percentage proportion of carbohydrate and fat oxidation).

One can therefore assume that an increase in the world records in endurance competitions in recent years is due less to an increase in maximum oxygen uptake than rather to the quantitative and qualitative improvement of the metabolic processes occurring in the muscles. In summary, the following factors are therefore crucial for running endurance:

- extent of oxygen consumption at certain running speeds,
- percentage of maximum oxygen uptake, which can be sustained over the entire race distance,
- percentage of maximum oxygen uptake (or running speed) at which lactic acid concentration begins to rise (aerobic-anaerobic threshold);
- the absolute level of lactic acid concentration at certain running speeds, or the angle of increase in lactic acid concentration per unit of time during exercise;
- and individual maximum oxygen uptake as an indicator of maximum aerobic metabolism.

The mechanical efficiency is hardly improved in the course of the running training of an already good runner. However, the level of the aerobic-anaerobic threshold at which a long-term load can be sustained can be trained in larger percentages.

General anaerobic endurance is characteristic of the endurance exercise of large muscle masses, whose performance is limited by anaerobic metabolic processes. This means that the exercise-induced oxygen requirements cannot be satisfied during the exercise itself. During anaerobic metabolic processes lactic acid (lactate) is formed as compensation, leading to a decrease in pH value. Therefore, with increasing exercise duration, there is increased acidity which impairs performance. However, lactate is not only a waste product; as an intermediate product and signalling molecule it is also very

important for metabolism. For example, many tissues—for example the heart and skeletal muscles—satisfy their energy requirements by metabolising lactate while reducing glucose oxidation at the same time. Lactate transporters and metabolic processes are of central significance in this context and can apparently be positively influenced by exercise.

General anaerobic dynamic endurance is also called *speed endurance*. If the resistances overcome are greater, one speaks of *strength endurance*, which is also a form of general anaerobic dynamic endurance. Factors which limit performance are:

- dynamic strength of muscles used,
- coordination,
- contraction velocity,
- muscle viscosity,
- anthropometric characteristics,
- flexibility, and
- the ability to release a large amount of energy per unit of time and to maintain a high level of performance despite a large oxygen debt (motivation).

Girls achieve their maximum oxygen uptake/min by the age of 16 on average, while boys typically achieve it by the age of 19. The same applies to maximum respiratory minute volume in the range of maximum oxygen uptake. Vital capacity and maximal breathing capacity as an expression of the maximum ventilatory capacity of the lungs may reach maximum values in girls by the age of 13 and in boys

DISCOURSE V: IMPORTANT CONCEPTS FOR UNDERSTANDING ENDURANCE PERFORMANCE CAPACITY

Aerobic-anaerobic threshold

Highest load level or highest oxygen (O_2) uptake value/min, which can be achieved without disproportionate increase in arterial lactate concentration and respiratory minute volume in relation to the level of work; the better the aerobic dynamic performance capacity, the later the onset of the disproportionate increase of respiratory minute volume and arterial lactate concentration.

Arteriovenous oxygen difference

Difference in O_2 content of the blood in the pulmonary artery (= mixed venous blood) and in arterial blood; the increase of the arterio-venous O_2 difference attained by endurance training enables a correspondingly higher O_2 uptake in the lungs.

Maximal breathing capacity

Maximum amount of air that can be inhaled and exhaled through a voluntary increase in respiration within a minute; trained endurance athletes may exceed the values of untrained people by 100%; maximal breathing capacity can be used for making a statement about maximum ventilatory capacity.

Respiratory minute volume

Product of tidal volume and respiratory rate; the better the endurance training state, the lower the respiratory minute volume at given submaximal levels of exercise.

Respiratory equivalent

Respiratory minute volume in ml/min, divided by O_2 uptake in ml/min during the same minute; indicator of breathing economy; the lower the value, the better the economy; the better the endurance training state, the later and lower the incremental value of the respiratory equivalent; with increasing exercise intensity, the tendency of the rising leg of the respiratory equivalent is generally identical with that of respiratory minute volume, arterial lactate concentration and—in the opposite direction—arterial pH value.

Glycogen

High-molecular intracellular storage form of glucose; the glycogen content in muscle is a co-determinant of endurance performance capacity and fatigue; carbohydrate diet leads to a rapid replenishment of glycogen.

Cardiac output

Amount of blood which is conveyed by the heart per unit of time, expressed in l/min.

Capillarisation

Functional opening and expansion of existing capillaries; enlargement of the capillary bed, associated with a slowing of blood flow velocity and thus more economic utilisation of available O_2.

Maximum oxygen uptake

Largest amount of O_2 that can be absorbed by the entire body per minute during dynamic work using muscle groups as large as possible; even an additional increase in exercise intensity does not lead to a further change of the value—the athlete has reached the levelling-off phenomenon; relative maximum O_2 uptake is the maximum amount of O_2 absorbed per kg body weight.

Mitochondria

Cell organelle made up of a highly folded outer and an inner membrane which is responsible for the molecular organisation of the conversion of ADP to ATP; aerobic metabolic processes take place inside the mitochondria, whereas anaerobic processes occur outside the mitochondria; endurance training leads to an increase in mitochondrial surface and volume.

Myoglobin

Related to haemoglobin as an O_2 carrier, but located inside the plasma of the muscle cell; carries oxygen from the cell membrane to the mitochondrion.

Respiratory Quotient (RQ)

Indicator of the ratio of the volume of carbon dioxide (CO_2) eliminated (VCO_2) to the volume of oxygen (O_2) consumed (VO_2); RQ = CO_2 output (l/min)/O_2 consumption (l/min); the exclusive metabolism of fatty acids results in an RQ of 0.70, with protein metabolism the RQ is 0.81, and when only carbohydrates (e.g., glucose) are metabolised the RQ is 1.00.

Vital capacity

Consists of tidal volume, inspiratory reserve volume, and expiratory reserve volume; total volume of exchangeable air; endurance training may lead to an increase in vital capacity by 15–30%.

by the age of 18. Thus, maximum lung capacity is achieved earlier than maximum cardiovascular capacity in both males and females. The growth of the heart occurs strictly parallel to an increase in maximum oxygen uptake. Heart volume per kg body weight ratio remains constant from childhood to old age, which is a sign of the fundamentally harmonious development of the heart size and body weight. At given submaximal exercise levels, the pulse rate decreases in the course of childhood and adolescence (which is an expression of the higher stroke volume and thus of sufficient cardiac output during physical work), while systolic blood pressure rises. It can be proven that there is a strictly harmonious enlargement of all cardiac sections in connection with the development of the whole organism. It is remarkable that in so-called accelerated as well as in adolescents behind in physical development, there is always a harmonious growth of organic performance, organ dimensions, and the skeletal system. Basically, accelerated boys and girls exhibit a better performance capacity and load tolerance with respect to endurance than normally developed and boys and girls behind in physical development.

Then, until about the age of 30, maximum oxygen uptake/min is consistent before it starts to decline due to aging. In the third decade of life, the difference in the magnitude of the cardiopulmonary performance is about 30% between the sexes. With increasing age, the differences between men and women are getting smaller. Sex differences in terms of maximum aerobic performance in the third decade of life also become smaller when calculating the relative maximum oxygen uptake (i.e., per kilogram of body weight). In men, the physiological standard value of relative maximum oxygen uptake from childhood to old age appears to be in a range between 40 and 55 ml/kg/min. This requires the maintenance of a normal body weight and an average state of performance capacity. The corresponding values for women in the third decade of life are 32 to 38 ml/kg/min. If maximum oxygen uptake per kilogram is related to fat-free body weight, there are only small differences between normal male and female subjects. On average, the values for men are 46–49 ml/kg/min and 44–48 ml/kg/min for women. Top female athletes can have maximum oxygen uptake values between 5000 and 5500 ml/min, while top male athletes can achieve values up to 7000 ml/min. The associated relative oxygen uptake values amount to 80–85 ml/kg/min in men and to 60–75 ml/kg/min in women.

In terms of the aerobic-anaerobic threshold, the age-related decline in maximum cardiopulmonary performance capacity occurs slower than the decline of maximum oxygen uptake. Within the energy-supplying elements of the muscle cell, women have a greater percentage of lipid droplets than men, possibly associated with a greater activity of some enzymes of lipid metabolism. Women are apparently particularly suited for endurance exercise. Fat metabolism can be better mobilised and thus the glycogen store be spared.

However, mitochondrial volume is about 20% lower than in comparable men. The absolute lower aerobic endurance capacity of women is caused by their lower heart rate, total haemoglobin, and blood volume. There are close correlations between body weight on the one hand and other above-mentioned parameters on the other hand. Regardless, there is a sex-related difference of the haemoglobin concentration in the blood (13.8 g/dl in women versus 15.6 g/dl in men). The lower haemoglobin levels of women are partly due to a combination of menstrual-related blood loss, lower blood levels of androgenic steroids, and possibly dietary restrictions. For every litre of blood pumped by the heart, approximately 13% more oxygen can be transported to the working muscles in men's bodies than in women's. Finally, the size of the arterial cross-section is smaller in women than in men and may also limit performance.

The development of maximum lactate formation is largely parallel in both sexes from 6 to 18 years of age. In later life, the maximum lactate concentrations in the blood, which vary from sport to sport, are largely independent of sex. Both in women and in men, there is a strictly linear relationship between the production of lactic acid and pH-value. Women do not seem to be able to exploit intramuscular glycogen reserves as completely as men. Here, however, differences in the amount of carbohydrates taken in and in the timing of the intake might be of significance. As already mentioned, the capacity of fat metabolism is better in women. At a given submaximal exercise level, women have a lower respiratory quotient. However, this finding does not apply at high exercise intensities. During physical work, women also catabolise less protein than men. The most striking sex differences can be found in the behaviour of hormones. Oestrogens have a profound influence on metabolic activity, both at rest and during physical work. They promote subcutaneous fat deposition (subcutaneous fat tissue) and stimulate gluconeogenesis, whereby glucose tolerance is enhanced, and increase the lipolysis in fat cells, which is stimulated by catecholamines. Due to their greater subcutaneous fat layer, women are at an advantage compared to men in cold conditions. The same applies to running exercise in cold and wet conditions. However, this advantage is partially reduced by their greater body surface area/body mass ratio and lower heat production capacity. In hot environments, women are therefore at a disadvantage. Men also tend to have greater sweat production than women. In terms of percentage, training-induced improvements in performance are identical in women and men. This is true for both heart dimensions and cardiac function (stroke volume), maximum achievable arteriovenous O_2 difference, and an increase in the number of capillaries in trained muscles.

DISCOURSE VI: ATHLETE'S HEART

Endurance training causes functional and structural cardiac adaptations. The so-called athlete's heart is an enlarged, although healthy heart of a performance or high-performance endurance athlete. The normal heart size of a man is 750–800 ml, while endurance athletes exhibit sizes of 900–1700 ml. The heart of women, which is 200 ml smaller on average, can also be enlarged by about 100% due to endurance sports. The cardiac enlargement is mainly due to an expansion of the cavities of the heart, and to a lesser extent to an increase in the wall thickness of the left ventricle in particular (about 30%). Characteristic of an athlete's heart is low resting heart rates, possibly even with values between 28–35 beats/min. Because of individual variations, however, one cannot draw conclusions about the endurance capacity from the resting heart rate. However, athletes with the highest maximum oxygen uptake/min values also have the largest athlete's hearts. Whereas during exercise the average heart of a man pumps a maximum of about 20 l/min, the athlete's heart achieves an output of 40–45 l/min. The physiological significance of cardiac hypertrophy is to maintain increased heart work for a long time without exerting the heart muscle to the limit of its capacity. A negative aspect of the large athlete's heart is the fact that a twofold increase in the diameter of the muscle fibre leads to an eightfold increase in volume, whereas the oxygen tension decreases with the square of the distance. But the findings obtained both at rest and at the limits of performance clearly show that this negative factor for O_2 supply is more than offset by a variety of favourable aspects. However, it seems that only athletes who are genetically preferred in this respect are capable of developing larger than average hearts through appropriate training. After the termination of a sports career, an athlete's heart regresses although there are big individual differences. Therefore, an athlete's heart does not constitute a health hazard.

2 ADAPTATION AND PERFORMANCE CAPACITY

2.1 TRAINING AND LOAD ORGANISATION

As early as 1895, Roux wrote that individual functional changes have a specific effect on organic form. This is the basis of adapting organisms to changing environmental conditions – a prerequisite for survival. Specific stimuli always lead to specific adaptations. This specificity of reaction and adaptation is also the basis of physical training. It extends from the macroscopic to the intracellular and ultra-structural area.

Training is commonly defined as the sum of all steps leading to a systematic increase or the maintenance of physical fitness. This includes not only the related muscular stresses, but also nutrition and the entire way of life. More precisely, Hollmann (Hollmann & Strüder, 2009) defines training as a systematic repetition of target-oriented, above-threshold muscle tensions resulting in morphological and functional adaptations for the purpose of performance enhancement. This definition refers to muscular stress itself. Training must take into account individual performance and motivation. These two factors together largely determine performance capacity. Performance capacity itself is a cumulative value, which is composed of individual variables such as physical abilities, specific intelligence, technical and tactical ability,

and individual experience. Performance readiness is based on exogenous and endogenous factors, such as motivation.

There is a relationship between the quantity and quality of training and the quantity and quality of its impact. Exceeding a critical threshold and thus a sufficiently high load intensity per unit of time is a prerequisite. A load is primarily characterised by loading intensity and loading volume. The duration and the frequency of loading as well as the rest intervals between the loading intervals are secondary characteristics. However, the threshold of the training stimulus not only depends on intensity, duration, and the number of repetitions, but also on the individual athlete's state of performance. The relations between stress and adaptation have already been mentioned. Below, important principles of load organisation will be presented.

PRINCIPLE OF THE RELATIONSHIP BETWEEN STRESS AND RECOVERY

Stress and recovery (regeneration) must correspond to each other. High loads require long recovery periods and vice versa.

PRINCIPLE OF EFFECTIVE TRAINING STIMULUS

Below-threshold stimuli result in negative adaptation (atrophy); neutral stimuli do not result in a change; above-threshold stimuli result in positive adaptation (hypertrophy); and extremely above-threshold stimuli may result in overstraining and injury. Since (high-)performance athletes operate at the limit of their maximum capacity, it is particularly difficult to achieve adequate above-threshold stimuli.

PRINCIPLE OF CONTINUOUS LOADING

Rest intervals that are too long between loads (e.g., due to irregular training) are synonymous with prolonged periods of below-threshold stimuli. The resulting negative adaptation again destroys the positive adaptation to training and should therefore be avoided. Long-term and continuous training results in a slower decrease in performance during training breaks (see figure 7).

PRINCIPLE OF INCREASING LOADING

If performance is increased by means of above-threshold stimuli and positive adaptation, the stimuli must also be increased to remain above the threshold. An increase in loading can be achieved through intensity or volume. For young athletes, the increase in loading should first occur by means of the volume. Nevertheless, technically correct and intensive loads (which are adjusted to the stage of growth) are possible and necessary even in children's athletics when performing training which is aimed at speed, reactive strength, and coordination.

PRINCIPLE OF VARYING LOAD

Similar training contents also lead to similar adjustments. However, the factors

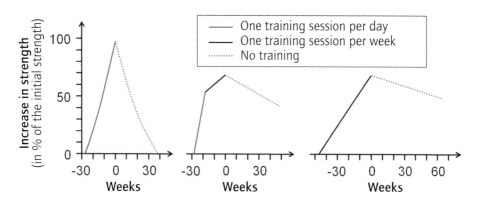

Figure 7: **Effect of training frequency and the long-term nature of training on muscle strength and a decrease in muscle strength after the end of training.** *A daily training session for 30 weeks results in a greater increase in muscle strength than one training session per week over 45 weeks. However, in the first example, strength decreases at the end of training much faster than with continuous training over an extended period.*

which determine performance and the development of the (athletics) competition performance through training are very complex. Avoiding monotony in training with constant variation of the game, exercise, and training forms are therefore of great importance to develop versatile athletes.

PRINCIPLE OF INDIVIDUALISED AND TARGET-ORIENTED LOADING

Loads must be adapted to the current physical and mental fitness and load tolerance of the individual athlete, and therefore also to his/her age and objectives. Loads must also correspond to the factors which determine performance in the target discipline and the emphasis placed on them.

PRINCIPLE OF THE PLANNED DEVELOPMENT OF FORM

Various individual aspects of training can influence one another. For example, endurance training can improve regeneration ability. However, in respect to speed and reactive-strength disciplines, endurance training can also have a negative effect on muscle fibre structure. Therefore, athletes cannot maintain their personal best shape all year round. The purpose of the training plan is to control the development of form so that top form is achieved during peak competition in the season. Therefore, long before the peak competition, more general, versatile, non-specific, and volume-oriented training contents should be

included. The last is especially true for lower levels of performance. Then, close to major competition, there is an increase in the proportion of special, specific, and intensity-oriented contents. This is also expressed in the classic maxims for training planning:

- from general to specific (from non-specific to specific);
- from volume to intensity (from easy [weight] to heavy [weight]).

PRINCIPLE OF PROPER LOADING SEQUENCE

If training contents are addressed in one or consecutive training sessions in terms of various aspects of the major types of motor stress, the order of training stimuli must be taken into consideration. In the majority of cases, the following sequence is most suitable:

1. coordination or technique training, speed training, reactive-strength training, or strength training focusing on intramuscular coordination,
2. strength training to achieve hypertrophy or eccentric strength training,
3. anaerobic (strength- or speed-)endurance training,
4. aerobic endurance training, and
5. flexibility training.

However, in respect to certain objectives—especially in connection with utilisation (see chapter I-5.5)—athletes and coaches often deviate from this sequence.

2.2 SUPER-COMPENSATION AND OVERSTRAINING

In classical training theory, based on Yakovlev (1977) and Harre (1970), it is assumed that improving athletic performance is the result of the interaction of the following three steps: stress, recovery (compensation), and super-compensation. Figures 8a–c illustrate this idea in more detail.

However, the various recovery times for different biological sub-systems should be noted. While acidosis due to lactacid exercise is again reduced after a few minutes or hours, and depleted energy stores are replenished after adequate food supply after one to two days, the full restoration of structural proteins (e.g., actin, myosin) or cell organelles (e.g., mitochondria) may take several days to weeks. In addition, there are intra- and inter-individual temporal variations. Finding the optimal length of rest intervals for achieving an increase in performance capacity is therefore extremely difficult.

The principle of super-compensation, originally based on observations of glycogen concentration in the muscle cell, falsely implies the possibility of an infinite and/or linear increase in performance. Mader (1990) therefore introduced a biological and mathematical model as an alternative to the super-compensation theory (see figure 9). This theory of active stress adaptation and regulation of protein synthesis at the cellular level extends Roux's original principle of the organic form being a result of function.

Proteins are the building blocks of all organic structures. Their specific composition is encoded in the genes of every living being depending on the respective tasks. As with all organs, increased wear and degradation of structural proteins is also the result of functional muscle overload. It is believed that relatively short-lived protein-specific fragments are created in the process of the degradation of the old proteins, which activate the transcription rate of the respective gene. The transcription rate of the gene is defined as the frequency of how often a gene code is read for the production of a new protein. According to Mader, it is destruction by stress which indirectly causes increased formation of structural proteins. Up to a certain genetically limited maximum performance capacity (maximum functional capacity) the organism responds to a load with positive adaptation. This is applicable provided that the stimulus is high enough (higher than the athlete's current functional capacity) but not too high (loaded functional capacity <15%). This means that there is an increase in transcription rate, a positive relationship between protein formation and degradation, thus an increase in protein mass (hypertrophy), and as a result, an increase in performance capacity. However, this only works to a certain extent. If more than approximately 15% of the structures are destroyed through stress and protein formation can no longer compensate for protein degradation, the body reacts to rising loads with negative adaptation from that

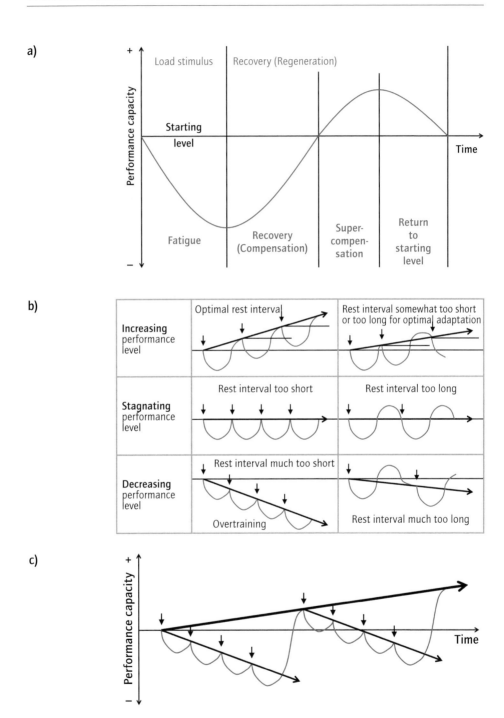

Figure 8a: *Principle of super-compensation; b: Possible tendencies and reasons for development; c: Principle of increasing fatigue (modified on the basis of Blum & Friedmann, 1997).*

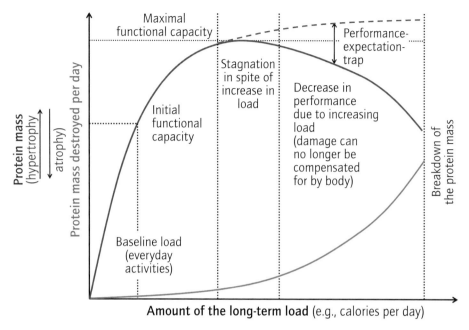

*Figure 9: **Simulated connection between exercise-induced protein consumption and functional capacity** (protein mass; modified on the basis of Mader, 2002). The interrupted blue line illustrates the increase in performance capacity (functional capacity) which is expected by coaches and/or athletes who apply extremely above-threshold stimuli.*

point on (i.e., with decreased performance). It is understandable that the recognisable symptoms are different depending on the structure loaded. The decisive factor is the realisation that ***stress should be optimal instead of maximal***. In performance sport, current performance capacity (average functional capacity) comes closer and closer to individual maximum capacity (maximum functional capacity). However, this also results in a reduction of the area in which hypertrophy can occur—and, of course, the danger of overloading is correspondingly greater.

2.3 OVERTRAINING SYNDROME

Overtraining syndrome refers to the ongoing decline of sport-specific performance (despite carrying out systematic training), combined with anomalous symptoms of subjective and objective nature (reviewed in Hollmann & Strüder, 2009; Hollmann et al., 2007). The occurrence of overtraining results from an incompatibility between psycho-physical stress on the one hand and ability to regenerate on the other. Many symptoms of overtraining were described many decades ago. Major symptoms of overtraining are decline in performance, depression, loss of motivation, insomnia, loss of appetite, weight loss, irritability, impaired coordination, increased oxygen consumption and increased respiratory minute volume at given submaximal exercise levels, cardiac arrhythmias, rapid onset of fatigue, chronic fatigue and complaints about heavy legs, and increased susceptibility to infections and injuries. Due to the various diagnostic findings, a differentiation in basedowide overtraining (primarily excitation processes) and addisonoid overtraining (primarily inhibition processes) has been proposed. The sympathicotonic form of overtraining is more often found in speed and strength athletes, whereas the parasympathicotonic reaction is assumed to be typical of endurance athletes. Especially during the past two decades, numerous authors have dealt with the relationship between overtraining and hormonal changes. In this respect, malfunctions of the hormones ACTH, cortisol, and testosterone hormones, for example, have been described. Dysregulations in the interaction between building and degrading processes have been observed.

However, the variety of symptoms associated with overtraining syndrome can only be explained as a functional disturbance in the brain as the central governing body of the entire human organism. Accordingly, it is believed that central neurotransmitters (chemical messengers in the nervous system) may play a crucial role in the process.

Serotonin, dopamine, noradrenalin, and glutamate are, like endogenous opioid peptides, centrally regulating substances. A strong imbalance in the serotonergic neurotransmitter system may trigger depression, even suicide. Neurones using serotonin as neurotransmitter are located both in the medulla oblongata as well as in the raphe nuclei and in the pons. There are connections to the cortex, the limbic system, hippocampus, and hypothalamus up to the dorsal root ganglia in the periphery of the body. It is conceivable that the overtraining symptoms mentioned are associated with disorders in this serotonergic system. The excitability of motor neurones is increased by descending serotonin neurones, with corresponding effects on monosynaptic reflexes including a decrease in the excitability of polysynaptic reflexes. Serotonin may also influence the secretion of numerous hormones. Furthermore, sympathetic afferent cardiac nerves are stimulated by serotonin, while the vasoconstrictor effect of noradrenalin is reduced in peripheral vessels. The results of these reactions frequently correspond to overtraining symptoms.

In over-trained athletes, the main cause of this imbalance in the serotonergic system is probably not the exercise-induced increase in serotonergic activity during training and competition. Rather, the great flood of serotonergic signals is based on the additional enhancement of serotonergic activity caused by the raphe nuclei, the actual pacemakers of the serotonergic system. In overtrained athletes, the raphe nuclei are characterised by a stress setting triggered by other cortical structures, leading to excessive activation of the serotonergic system. This does not need to be physical stress but may also be psychosocial stress (family problems, experience of failure in other areas, etc.). This then leads to an excessive serotonergic impulse, which is exacerbated further by a usual increase in serotonin release during physical stress. This serotonergic disturbance always impairs the function of other neurotransmitters and neuropeptide systems. In affected athletes—especially when associated with pathological leanness (anorexia) in women—this can even take life-threatening forms. It is clear how important it is to take a holistic view of athletes including all biological, psychological, and social factors.

A regular examination of the psychological well-being of athletes who have an open mind to corresponding methods may be a simple but very useful method for early detection of overtraining syndrome.

2.4 HIERARCHY AND BRAIN PLASTICITY

The brain is characterised by a hierarchical structure. In the spinal cord, groups of motor neurones represent movements of the muscles; in the primary motor cortex, movement directions are encoded, regardless of which muscles perform the respective movement. Finally, in the pre-motor cortex, complete actions instead of individual movements are represented in such a way that they are encoded in a coordinate system in terms of an objective. Activity can be located in the pre-motor cortex when new motor tasks are learned, however, this activity is reduced during the learning process. The highest level of hierarchy is ultimately represented by the pre-frontal cortex. This is used when a time delay is bridged between a stimulus and an associated response. During this process, there are close connections between the pre-frontal area and the entire post-central cortex. They run in both directions. Interneurones are by far the greatest number of all nerve cells in the brain. They establish connections within the brain so that an afferent signal is divided into diverse branches leading to many nerve cells, before a motor response is triggered. This interneural network has a crucial influence on the result (see chapter I–1.1).

An image of the muscles in the cortex (somatotopy) displays a high structural variability (plasticity) and can be changed in a very short time through practice and training on the one hand and lack of exercise and injuries on the other. This is due to changes in the synapses. More specifically, changes occur with respect to the neurotransmitters released there and, in particular, the receptors to which the neurotransmitters attach. The somatotopic organisation of the cortex can be constantly varied according to this. This plasticity remains throughout life Continuously, new connections are formed between nerve cells; new nerve cells are activated, while old connections disappear. The quality and quantity of the respective brain activity is critical to this process. Since each sensory signal reaching the cortex is divided into diverse branches across the interneurones before a motor response is given, the quality of this neural network is more important than the sensory input for the later result.

At the point of contact between two nerve cells, the spine (dendritic spinous process) may change morphologically within minutes to hours and may even split in several spines. At the same time, dendrites and axons may grow, and the formation of new blood vessels (angiogenesis) is promoted. The eventual results are macroscopic reorganisations ranging up to the centimetres. Reduced muscular stress results in reduced activation of the relevant cortical representation area. Then, the affected area is soon involved in the information processing occurring in adjacent areas. It is believed that overstrain, which is caused in particular by exercise monotony, can induce expansions of cortical brain areas. This initially results in positive effective adaptation, but later trigger negative biochemical reactions as a result of structural overlays. This applies especially to the functions of the pre-frontal cortex.

In summary, it should be noted that structural and biochemical adaptations to physical training extend up into the controlling regions of the brain.

2.5 THE BRAIN AS A FACTOR LIMITING PERFORMANCE

The brain is the command centre for the quality, quantity, and intensity of physical stress. Functions such as the development of intentions, steering, execution, and control of muscle movements are the primary tasks of the frontal lobe. The front part of the cortex is the pre-frontal cortex, which is also referred to as the seat of the executive branch, since it is interconnected with many other brain regions. It is the only neocortical region that communicates directly with the hypothalamus, responsible for the hormonal control of the organism. All sensory and motor modalities are integrated in the pre-frontal cortex. Moreover, close links to the basal ganglia exist.

After having resolved to perform a motor task, the command runs from the motor cortex through the pyramidal tract to selected neurones, which depolarise the motor endplates, trigger the muscle action potential and release calcium (see also discourse III). As already mentioned, cross-bridges then form and the myofibrils are shortened. The magnitude of the central impulse grows parallel to the force exerted. However, it will also increase if the reaction of the motor neurones or muscle cells subsides due to fatigue. In a fresh muscle, maximum central command intensity may activate motor units by 100 percent. Central and peripheral fatigue factors may decrease the muscular response. This process is triggered by reflexes via the dorsal root ganglion and by receptor stimulation in the muscles. Stimulation of tendon organs and free nerve endings in the muscles reduces the response of the motor neurones. An increase in potassium and hydrogen ion concentrations in the interstitial fluid (tissue fluid outside the cells) as well as an increase in body temperature hinder the reflexes of the motor neurones. Finally, the excitation-contraction coupling is disabled to the extent that an increase in intracellular inorganic phosphor in particular causes muscle fatigue due to the obstruction of bridge formation. The reduction of intracellular potassium and also an increase in extracellular potassium decrease the charging of the membrane and thus muscle action potentials (see figure 10 in chapter 3).

For decades, the concept of motivation has been mentioned as a factor that limits physical and sporting performance. Motivation is defined as the intensity of the drive to perform a particular task. As early as the beginning 1960s, one observed the performance-limiting role of the brain for the development of static strength. At this time, however, it was scientifically very controversial to research the extent in which the will is linked to biochemical and biophysical processes in the brain. Based on scientific progress during the past two decades, it can be assumed that the will is the expression of structural, biochemical, and biophysical conditions in certain regions of the brain. Ultimately the will determines the maximum number of motor units activated within a muscle and the firing rate at which this occurs. Intramuscular biochemical metabolic processes have a modifying effect on the will. Therefore, leading brain researchers now assume that there is a central governor (i.e., a brain region which receives all the inputs and outputs from the body and integrates the modes of behaviour based on this). Previous ideas about the limitations of performance by the cardiovascular system and muscular metabolism are therefore no longer pursued and attention now focuses more on the brain and its role of limiting performance. One can even assume that vital organs such as the heart and the brain itself send sensory signals to the pre-frontal cortex, among other areas, which through the central governor in the pre-frontal cortex trigger a protective response in terms of no longer being able to continue the physical activity (see table 2).

Table 2: **Relationships between physiological systems and functions, taking into account the exercise intensity perceived** *(according to Hollmann et al., 2008). PFC = pre-frontal cortex, ADP = adenosine diphosphate, ATP = adenosine triphosphate, FFA = free fatty acids.*

System	Function	Perception
Brain (PFC)	PFC command	Exertion
CNS	Excitement – Contraction $(Na^+ - K^+)$	Weak
Skeletal muscle	Cross-bridge formation (Ca^{2+}) Energy development $(ATP \rightarrow ADP)$	Exertion
Metabolism	Glycogen + ADP $\rightarrow$ ATP + Laktat + H^+ Glycogen + ADP + O_2 $\rightarrow$ ATP + CO_2 FFA + ADP + O_2 $\rightarrow$ ATP + CO_2	
Cardiovascular system	Haemodynamics	Fatigue
Lungs	Respiration O_2 CO_2	

3 TRAINING CONTROL

Training control (as an element of coaching) includes all steps which change (athletic) performance. This includes an analysis of the current situation and the target situation (diagnostics), setting goals and training planning, and corrective intervention in training execution, as well as training documentation. Although the terminology and the wording in the following chapters often imply control by a coach, in practice it is also the athlete who often intervenes in training through corrective steps.

3.1 TARGET ANALYSIS

3.1.1 AGE OR TRAINING LEVELS AND SCHOOL SPORTS

Training control starts with target analysis (i.e., with the question: "What should my athlete be able to achieve at the present and in the future?"). The answer to this question will differ depending on the athlete's age and level of training. Although in the following, age and training levels are sometimes used interchangeably, a 16-year-old newcomer, for example, should of course first begin with basic training.

CHILDREN'S ATHLETICS

Regular training usually begins with children's athletics. The term is not only a designation of age, but also a synonym for the term *playful athletics*. It expresses a certain orientation of training which has been used increasingly in everyday training since the beginning of the 1990s. Given the fact that at that time more and more children opted for team or trendy or fun sports, it was critically questioned whether children under 10 years of age (see table 3) should already learn specific athletics techniques, or whether there was more attractive and child-oriented content for this age group. Starting with this question, many games and playful training forms have been developed to practice the core elements of athletics, such as jumping, sprinting, throwing, etc., which focus on coordination, versatility, and fun. In this respect, many expensive (e.g., Aero howlers) or simple, creatively re-purposed motivational training devices (e.g., tennis ball with fluttering ribbons) were developed. Moreover, numerous alternative competition exercises and programmes, mostly designed as team rather than individual competition exercises, were designed. The IAAF and the German Athletics Association (DLV) have presented these competition programmes under the umbrella of Kids' Athletics and Fun in Athletics and are also part of the new concept of the German Federal Youth Games (see chapter II–4.1.7). Children's athletics training should ideally begin before school age. Initially, this training is versatile, consisting of athletics, gymnastics, and playful elements in virtually equal amounts. Basic training starts approximately at the time of transition into the U14 age category.

BASIC TRAINING

In contrast to children's athletics, basic training is characterised by a slow increase in the amount of training; in addition to playful exercises, classic exercise sequences are used. This is especially true for the development of the various techniques of as many athletics disciplines as possible. Basic training is versatile and thus geared more toward combined events. However, strength, speed, and endurance are also developed by means of age-appropriate forms of games and exercises. The first emphasis should be established relatively

Table 3: **Official age categories in the German Athletics Association (DLV)***. The transition from one age category to the next takes place at the beginning of each new year. For example, this means that for the entire year in which the adolescent turns 14 years of age, he/she belongs to the w14 or m14 category and thus at the same time to the U16 category. The designation "–" indicates common rating, while "/" represents separate rating. Up to the U16 category, the two cohorts are combined only for relays and team competitions.*

Age	Age category (old terminology)		Age category (new terminology since 2012)
6/7	---		w/m U8
8/9	Boys/Girls D	Children	w/m U10
10/11	Boys/Girls C		w/m U12
12/13	Boys/Girls B		w/m U14
14/15	Boys/Girls A	Youth	w/m U16
16-17	Female/Male Youth B		w/m U18
18-19	Female/Male Youth A		w/m U20
20-22	Female/Male Juniors		Female Juniors/ Male Juniors
20 and older	Women/Men		
30-34	Female Seniors W30/ Male Seniors M30	Adults	
35-39	Female Seniors W35/ Male Seniors M35		Women/Men
40-44	Female Seniors W40/ Male Seniors M40		W40/ M40
45-49	Female Seniors W45/ Male Seniors M45	Seniors	W45/ M45
	etc. every five years		

early on (i.e., at the transition to the U16 age category). First, one training session in the respective athlete's special discipline (possibly with a specialist coach) is added to the combined-event-oriented training sessions. Instead of a special discipline, such as pole vault, hammer throw, or walking, this may also involve a special block such as sprinting, jumping, throwing, or middle- and long-distance running. Over the years, the number of special sessions is then increased until final specialisation takes place at the end of youth. Within this period (i.e., around the time of transition to the U18 age category), athletes start with build-up training.

BUILD-UP TRAINING

Build-up training is characterised by an increase in specialisation. This coincides with the introduction of more specific training methods and contents. Extending the total amount of training is also based on the greater volume of basic strength and endurance training. The fact that the term *basic* is still used here indicates that some very special content is still reserved for (high-)performance training. Only at the approximate time of entering the junior age category will the transition to performance training take place.

(HIGH-)PERFORMANCE TRAINING

The term *performance training* may seem surprising at first, since even in the younger age categories the objective is to increase physical performance capacity. The difference is that during performance training the objective is actually the maximisation of performance by taking advantage of all available training methods and contents. In contrast, at all previous stages some methods and contents are always held back to first fully exploit adaptation to versatile and general or basic training stimuli. This means that at these stages and under these conditions, performance is only optimised, not maximised. High-performance training is characterised by a very high-performance capacity, which is identical with international or at least national top-level performances. It is also characterised by an immense training volume and by stagnating or only slightly increasing performances. This usually goes hand in hand with at least partial professionalisation, which is a prerequisite for such extensive training.

In this respect, coaches and athletes in particular should also reflect on whether they want to carry out performance sport in which only measurable performance and its usefulness count, or whether they want to establish themselves in sport especially by performance-oriented sportsmanlike thinking and behaviour. Performance-oriented sportsmanlike thinking and behaviour is characterised as follows:

- Sport is the highest priority in life in addition to school, education, studies, or job.
- Like school, education, studies, and job, performance-oriented sport is based on the principle of achievement. This involves exertion, asceticism, often lack of understanding by others,

and the postponement of a reward, which is not guaranteed in any case.

» Exertion: Every competitive athlete should enjoy testing and expanding his/her (physical and mental) performance limits.

» Asceticism: In order to have enough time and energy for training and recovery, athletes must forgo other activities.

» Lack of understanding by others: Exertion and asceticism may appear an unnecessary self-limitation to some friends and relatives.

» Postponement of a reward, which is not guaranteed in any case: "Hard work guarantees you nothing, but without it you will not accomplish anything" is a statement by basketball coaching legend Chuck Daly. An athlete is personally responsible for ensuring that he/she performs this hard work on the long road to the goal.

• Increasing one's own best performance, pride in what has been accomplished, the feeling of physical fitness, the fun of training and competing with others, and motivating oneself to give everything, recognition by friends who also believe in performance, and lessons for one's personal and professional life are good objectives and rewards. In contrast, placement in competitions, positions on the top ranking lists, public recognition, and money are significantly less suitable motivators. They depend on many external factors and are only of secondary importance. They should never be the main motivators for performance-oriented athletics because an athlete cannot influence the performance of his/her opponents (along with many other factors).

Such performance-oriented thinking and behaviour is independent of one's actual performance capacity. Moreover, it should be developed during the stages of training prior to performance training.

SCHOOL AND RECREATIONAL SPORTS

The training stages presented so far are part of a performance-oriented career in athletics. In practice, however, recreational and performance sport are neither separated in children's athletics nor in basic training. This applies even to some build-up training groups. This means that recreational and fitness-oriented athletes often train in performance-oriented training groups. Unlike performance athletes, recreational athletes perform athletics for rather self-indulgent reasons (i.e., for fun). In addition to improving their health, fitness athletes are also interested in enhancing their physical performance capacity. However, they do not want to maximise their performance. Particularly in the adult and senior category, there should be special athletics training groups for each target group.

At the same time, school sport is a fundamental part of (motor) education and an important provider of club sports. Depending on the curriculum, school sport should be designed in such a way that the following six educational principles are taken into consideration. The main criteria are (see MSW NRW, 2001, pp 34–39)

- to improve one's perception capability and to enhance one's motor experience;
- to express oneself physically and to deal with movement creatively;
- to risk doing something and to accept responsibility;
- to experience, understand, and evaluate achievement;

- to cooperate, compete, and communicate; and
- to promote fitness and to develop health awareness.

These educational principles can also be taken into consideration in club sports, although in performance-oriented sports the focus is on experiencing, understanding, and evaluating achievement. However, in school sports, the six factors should be regarded as being equally important.

DISCOURSE VII: THE CONCEPT OF TALENT

In retrospect, evaluation is simple: Athletes who are successful as adults or on a high-performance level were talented as children or adolescents, and the support they received was correct or at least adequate. But how do you discover which young athlete is talented and deserves special attention? Talent is usually understood as a snapshot (i.e., it does not only mean a genetic predisposition, but also the present state of development which is geared toward an objective (here peak athletic performance) and the related development potential). In addition to hereditary factors, an athlete's past experience also plays a role (e.g., in sports or society). In terms of statistics, one only speaks of a talented athlete if the state and potential of development show an extreme (positive) deviation from the mean value of the population. However, the prognosis of future development on the basis of previous development is difficult in many respects.

In terms of talent selection, the phenomena of acceleration and retardation are major problems. In some children, physical development occurs earlier, whereas in others it occurs later. Whether a present lower physical performance capacity indicates a generally lower development potential or only a temporarily retarded physical development can hardly be reliably diagnosed. Many tests used for talent selection prefer accelerated individuals, although some individuals are later surpassed by athletes, who at the time of the test were behind in physical development and only showed a mediocre performance capacity. Therefore, a talented athlete is often understood as someone with superior coordination skills and good motor-learning ability. However, ultimately, outstanding coordination alone without proper strength, speed, or endurance skills does not help to win (athletics) competitions. Generally, the range of talent criteria includes more than the major types of motor stress. First, mental skills such as motivation and willingness to perform as well as load tolerance in terms of injury resistance should be mentioned in this respect. At a young age, load tolerance in particular is even more difficult to predict than the development of motor performance capacity. However, some talent criteria (such as anticipated growth) should be qualified in respect to their significance. These talent criteria were often considered in the past due to the fact that they can be identified with relative ease.

In this respect, the movement from the system in the former German Democratic Republic (GDR) to the current heterogeneous screening system, which according to some German experts is seen as a step backward, is probably also an expression of the impossibility of the reliable talent diagnosis described above. The greatest advantage of the screening and promotion system used in the former GDR was most likely its comprehensive nature and the fact that it helped sport to play a very important role in both school and society. If a large number of children receive special training, some of them will certainly be able to withstand extreme training loads. These children then deserve to be classified as special talents. However, even in the former GDR system, some athletes were not identified as talented during childhood and only managed to reach their designated sport by chance or because of their perseverance. The more liberal (Western) system probably places greater emphasis on the athlete's personal interests which are ultimately crucial for motivation and hence success in sports.

An optimal and, for the most part, consistent approach to talent identification and promotion does not currently exist. In most cases, promotion and squad nomination depend on an athlete's actual competition performance. Even at a young age, top athletes always achieve perhaps not the best, but relatively good performances, and with increasing age the competition performance becomes a more reliable talent criterion. In the lower age categories in particular, this means that proper training for all children interested in athletics must be provided so that children behind in physical development will also be supported. Afterwards, the objective must be that promotion is based on a large pool of athletes to select from. In this respect, it is unavoidable that not every supposed talent reaches the top level. All children who could potentially have talent should receive optimal support in terms of general conditions and high-quality training.

3.1.2 FACTORS WHICH DETERMINE PERFORMANCE

General aspects have already been dealt with in the discussion on the major types of motor stress (see chapter I–1). Moreover, the respective factors determining performance in different disciplines will be covered in the second part of this book. Therefore, in the following, only the fundamentals of movement technique will be addressed.

Answers to the question about the expected skill level raised in the process of target analysis, primarily depend on the particular discipline. Different disciplines have different factors which determine performance and very different requirement profiles. For example, in the 100m sprint, performance is determined by the technique of toe push-off sprinting and grasping/pulling sprinting, by maximum strength, speed strength or reactive strength (especially of the legs), reaction speed as well as acyclic and cyclic speed, and anaerobic endurance. Moreover, the factors which determine performance must be assessed in terms of their importance. The technique of grasping/pulling sprinting, reactive power, and cyclic speed are more important for the 100m performance than reaction speed and anaerobic endurance.

Generally, the purpose of optimal technique in performance sport is to enable the optimal working of all elements involved in terms of physiology, biomechanics, and functional anatomy. However, when teaching technique, coaches should always consider that the different physiques of various athletes always allow for, or even require, individual variations of technique. The objective is not the imitation of world-best athletes, but to move within a standard range of biomechanically and technically correct alternatives and to find the best alternative. Biomechanical studies show that identical world-class performances can be achieved by using very different movement techniques. Several explanations of this are possible. These technical alternatives may, for example, be individually optimal solutions with inverse advantages and disadvantages, or solutions which best fit the individual athlete's anthropometric characteristics. Technically inferior athletes can also compensate for this disadvantage, for example through superior strength. However, there is usually a mutual influence of strength and technique: For example, certain features of the target technique can only be implemented using certain strength capacities. At the same time, only an individually optimal technique enables the effective use of one's own strength. From a health perspective, there is the additional consideration that individually optimal mechanical solutions can be stressful or harmful in different ways. This may also require changes in technique.

On the one hand, knowledge of a technical model based on high-performance sport (variations included) is important when training young athletes. On the other hand, as mentioned above, the techniques of the world-best athletes can often only be imitated on the basis of extreme strength capacities and must therefore be adapted to young athletes. For this reason,

when dealing with individual disciplines, it is important to identify those elements of technique which should be learned very early.

3.1.3 GENERAL CONDITIONS

The target values also include general conditions. If these are inadequate, they can have a negative effect on training and performance.

TRAINING VENUES AND EQUIPMENT

Athletics disciplines differ greatly in terms of cost. While a recreational runner only needs a forest, a pole vaulter, for example, requires very expensive training facilities and equipment. In general, the quality of training or school teaching increases depending on how many of the following questions can be answered affirmatively: Is an athletics training facility available? Does it have a synthetic floor covering? Are a 400m track and facilities available for all throwing and jumping disciplines? Is a training gym available? Is there a special athletics gym? Can this be used often enough or even without restrictions? Is it big enough? Is it close to the outdoor facilities? Are important training devices, such as hurdles, throwing implements, etc. available in good quality and sufficient quantity? Is a set of vaulting poles, for example, available which meet the needs of both beginners and advanced athletes? Are additional items of equipment available, such as gym mats and boxes, mini hurdles, foam blocks, etc.? Are special equipment items available, such

as a Speedy for assisted sprints? Is there a weight room? Is this near the outdoor facility/gym? Are necessary devices for weight training available? Are there any special devices? Does the facility include a suitable course for long-distance runs, a long, approximately ten percent gradient for uphill or downhill runs, long stairs, a cross-country running course, a large sand area, massage rooms, etc.? Are these facilities near other training venues?

TRAINING GROUP

First, certain harmony in the training group is crucial. The coach can influence this by taking certain steps. Second, the size of the training group is very important. The smaller the training group, the better the coach can provide for individual details. In general, it is believed that the group size should decrease in relationship to an increase in the performance level of the athletes. In high-performance sports, technique training should be performed on a ratio of 1:1, whereas in other types of training the group is still a key motivator.

COACH OR COACHING STAFF

The home coach is the most important contact person for an independent athlete. The home coach should have the best possible training of sport science, as much coaching experience as possible, and a knack for dealing with athletes. As a rule, the coach prepares the training plan, supervises the main part of the training, corrects an athlete's movement techniques, etc. In (high-)performance sports, the coach also coordinates cooperation with squad coaches and special coaches and should be involved in communication and collaboration with parents, therapists, doctors, managers, sponsors, etc. Squad and special coaches have a specific expertise, which home coaches and athletes can benefit from. Although the problems of cooperation between home, squad, and special coaches will not be dealt with in detail here, such cooperation is certainly required.

MEDICAL AND THERAPEUTIC SUPPORT

An optimal care team includes physicians and therapists. Physiotherapeutic, osteopathic, psychological, and sports-medicine support is optimal. Therapy should be applied only when needed, even if in high-performance sports a permanent concomitant therapy may sometimes be necessary.

REGENERATION, OTHER FORMS OF STRESS, AND NUTRITION

In sports, an optimal relationship between stress and recovery is crucial. A training plan provides no information about whether an athlete actually regenerates during non-training time. One of the most important factors for good recovery is regular and restful sleep. However, the body should be given sufficient time to regenerate not only at night. Recreational time outside of training should also include as little physical stress as possible. However, unavoidable physical stress (e.g., school sport) and physical activities which are not relinquished in spite of sport (hobby) must be taken into account in training documentation and the individual training plan. In addition, a healthy and balanced diet is essential for regeneration and performance.

FAMILY, PEER GROUP, AND SCHOOL/JOB

Last, but not least, a non-athletic social environment has an influence on athletic development. The classical socialisation entities such as family (especially parents) and peer groups (i.e., a group of friends of the same age) mainly affect attitudes such as motivation and willingness to perform in general and specifically in sports. For children and adolescents involved in performance-oriented training, the training group, or part of it, is often identical with the peer group. School, education, studies, and job, which are also important socialisation entities, often limit the time available for sport. School in general, and especially the current trend toward all-day schools, should be taken into consideration since this could pose a potential risk for the development of a performance athlete if sport is not integrated adequately into these schools.

3.2 ANALYSIS OF THE CURRENT SITUATION AND TEST AND CONTROL PROCEDURES

In the analysis of the current situation, a comparison is made using the values found in the target analysis. While age and general conditions are obvious, the state of performance in respect to the factors determining performance must be measured by means of specific tests and control procedures. Competition results alone do not provide sufficient data about the reasons for improvements or declines in performance. By using test and control procedures, factors which determine performance in terms of the major types of motor stress or aspects of technique are measured. The quality of test and control procedures depends primarily on how accurately the scientific quality criteria are met. The major quality criteria are the following:

- **Validity:** To what extent does a test really measure what it claims to measure? Of course, the jump-and-reach test measures jumping strength. However, this test has relatively little to do with reactive one-legged jumping strength within short stretch-shortening cycles. Its validity for the measurement of jumping strength in athletics is therefore very low.
- **Reliability:** How accurate are the measuring instruments? How great is the potential measurement error relative to the parameter measured? Manual time measurement can be sufficiently reliable for a 400m tempo run, whereas this is not true for a flying 20m sprint. The possible error relative to the possible change in performance is too great. In respect to reliability, the question whether the conditions are always the same is also important.
- **Objectivity:** Is the result of the test independent of the examiner? This is usually not the case with the previously mentioned manual time measurement.

The quality of a test also depends on how accurately the secondary quality criteria are met:

- **Standardisation:** Are individual or general standard values, which are specific to age, gender, and performance, available for estimating performance?
- **Usefulness:** Does the test provide results which in terms of their importance go beyond the observations of a trained coach's eye?
- **Economy:** Is the test feasible and financially viable? Is it worth the time spent?

Below, examples of general test and control procedures shall be presented. They differ in their quality (i.e., to the extent in which they meet the quality criteria listed). Sport-motor tests, which can be performed using simple materials at a training location, are often characterised by a poorer fulfilment of the quality criteria than, for example, biomechanical laboratory tests. However, the tests mentioned here are valid at least in terms of certain performance categories. More specific control procedures are explained in connection with the individual disciplines. Accordingly, the test and control procedures for cyclic speed will be dealt with in connection with the 100m sprint, the tests for anaerobic endurance in connection with the 400m sprint, and the tests for aerobic endurance in connection with middle- and long-distance running (see chapters II-1.3, II-1.4 and II-1.10).

Test: Ability/skill tested	Execution/comments
T1 **Analysis of video recordings:** coordination/technique	Modern video recorders come with a small built-in screen from which coaches and athletes can view the recorded motion directly after the attempt, often even in slow motion. Although in competition it is not permitted to show video recordings to athletes, many coaches deliberately watch the original motion only through the viewfinder of their video recorder and afterwards watch it repeatedly. For optimal video analysis in training, it is advantageous if a TV, laptop or tablet computer is used to present enlarged and thus more detailed images. Analysis should preferably occur directly between two attempts since athletes can then distinctly remember their previous attempt, and, if necessary, corrections can be made immediately. More accurate analysis can be carried out by using specific computer programmes. Such analysis, for example, enables a better comparison of different attempts, the creation of picture sequences, the setting of markers, the measurement of angles, etc. Most of these functions require some follow-up time. However, more and more functions have been developed which facilitate immediate evaluation in training and in this respect offer new possibilities.
T2 **General flexibility tests:** flexibility	In daily training, even stretching exercises performed in flexibility training are often used as test and control procedures. The range of motion achieved during a stretching exercise provides information about an athlete's flexibility. Even if one only wants to analyse and/or quantify the lack of flexibility more accurately, specific tests are necessary. Figures 10a–e show a small selection of flexibility tests. For additional test and control procedures on the topic of flexibility, see Weineck (2007), etc.

(continued)

71

(continued)

Test: Ability/skill tested	Execution/comments

Fig. 10:

a: **Stretchability of the hip flexors:** If an athlete is forced to lift his/her knee when pulling his/her opposite knee maximally to his/her chest, the hip flexors are shortened (iliopsoas, tensor fascia latae, rectus femoris); if only the lower leg is not hanging down, the biarticular rectus femoris is shortened.

b: **Estimation of the stretchability of the hamstrings** on the basis of the angle between both legs.

c: **Functional test of the stretchability of the soleus:** If this muscle is shortened, the athlete will fall over backward.

d: **Bending forward (reaching-down test):** Quantification of the stretchability of the hip and back extensors by affixing a carpenter's ruler to the front of the box the athlete is standing on; how far can the athlete reach down with his/her fingertips?

e: **Stretchability test of the shoulder and chest muscles:** How close can the athlete grip the javelin and still move it to his/her buttocks with arms extended?

T3	**Body-weight and body-fat measurement:** (which in combination with the following tests results in) **relative strength**	This test shall help to avoid inappropriate increases or decreases in body weight and fat. Unlike simple weight measurement, an additional body-fat measurement enables a more accurate assessment of possible changes. Various methods are available (e.g., measurement of skinfold thickness and bioelectrical impedance analysis). The latter is being used in standard body-fat scales, but can be prone to error. Often, body weight is related to body height. The body mass index, for example, is very popular (body mass index = body mass/(body height^2), measured in kg/m^2). In performance sport, body weight and fat must be considered in relation to the requirement profile of each discipline.

Test: Ability/skill tested	Execution/comments
T4 **One repetition maximum (1RPM): concentric maximal strength**	The one repetition maximum (1RPM) is defined as the maximum weight which in a particular exercise can be moved by the athlete one time over a given distance.
T5 **Squat jump and similar procedures: concentric maximal strength (speed strength) of the extensor loop of the legs**	If the weight to be managed is below 1RPM, movement velocity must be measured to make a statement about concentric maximum strength (speed strength). However, continuous velocity measurement is only possible if the latest diagnostic training devices are used. Therefore, speed strength is usually neither measured for one movement direction in a joint, nor for a muscle or muscle group. It is typically measured within certain specific multi-joint movements. The speed strength of the extensor loop of the lower extremities is usually measured by jumping from a squatting position on a force plate or contact mat. The simpler measurement on the contact mat, which is also much cheaper and easier to transport, is also inaccurate since the force is not measured directly, but calculated from the flight time. However, the flight time can be manipulated by the landing method. Therefore, the movement sequence must be accurately standardised and controlled. In the squat jump, the athlete initially stays in the squat position for a short time before vigorously jumping from this position and generating a maximum amount of speed strength. To minimise the effect of the arms as swinging elements, the athlete must support his/her hands during the whole movement at his/her hips. To get closer to the 1RPM range, the squat and counter-movement jump (T8) can also be performed with an additional external load on the shoulders, such as a barbell weighing 50/75/ ...% of the athlete's body weight.
T6 **Isokinetic (or desmodromic) strength measurement:** concentric and eccentric maximal strength	Another possibility of dynamic strength measurement is the use of so-called (usually computer-controlled) isokinetic or desmodromic strength-training devices. With these devices, the person tested applies force against a resistance moving at a prescribed, usually constant, speed. The device then continuously measures the force generated during this process. Depending on whether the resistance of the device moves in or opposite to the desired direction of movement, the load is concentric or eccentric. However, this force measurement has two major drawbacks: First, athletic movements are not isokinetic (i.e., the movement velocity at a joint constantly varies). Second, isokinetic or desmodromic machines are rarely available in daily training.

(continued)

(continued)

Test: Ability/skill tested	Execution/comments
T7 **Static strength measurement:** static maximum strength, as well as start-, explosive-, and speed-strength index	Although static force measurement is less specific for most athletic movements, it is much simpler than dynamic force measurement. Therefore, it has been used in sports science for a much longer time. In the simplest case, static force measurement can be conducted using a simple spring (scale). Isometric (static) strength can also be measured at various angles (constant velocity = 0) with the isokinetic strength-training devices described above.

Due to the simpler technical feasibility, start-, explosive-, and speed-strength indexes are often calculated on the basis of the rate of force development against an unmovable (static) resistance. Figure 11 illustrates this method in more detail.

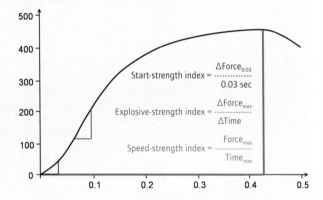

$$\text{Start-strength index} = \frac{\Delta \text{Force}_{0.03}}{0.03 \text{ sec}}$$

$$\text{Explosive-strength index} = \frac{\Delta \text{Force}_{max}}{\Delta \text{Time}}$$

$$\text{Speed-strength index} = \frac{\text{Force}_{max}}{\text{Time}_{max}}$$

Figure 11: **Start-, explosive- and speed-strength index,** defined by using the rate-of-force development curve in the force-time diagramme (modified on the basis of Bührle, 1985).

T8 **Counter-movement and drop jump:** reactive strength of the extensor loop of the legs	Like speed strength, reactive strength can normally only be measured when performing a specific movement. Depending on the movement complexity, the result is also strongly dependent on movement technique. Counter-movement and drop jumps are related to the squat jump (see T5 for measurement, standardisation, arm position, and additional load). In the counter-movement jump, the athlete tested moves from a standing position to the crouch position before taking off vigorously after a movement reversal which is performed as quickly as possible. The drop jump is a standardised two-legged depth jump (85) onto a force plate or contact mat.

	Test: Ability/skill tested	Execution/comments
T9	**3-, 5- or 10-stride bounding run or hop with distance maximisation:** reactive strength of the legs	For a description of this movement, see bounding run (88) and one-legged jumps (= hops, 89). In general, the last jump is performed by using a long jump which lands in the pit. On the one hand, these tests are clearly much more specific to athletics than counter-movement and drop jumps, but on the other hand they are more dependent on technique. Nevertheless, they should be performed by jumpers and sprinters alike, and even by throwers and distance runners.
T10	**30m bounding run with time minimisation:** reactive strength of the legs	A distance of 30m must be covered as quickly as possible using a bounding run (88). If possible, this should be done using photoelectric measurement.
T11	**Strength-endurance tests:** especially anaerobic strength endurance	There are various methods of strength-endurance measurement. The time and/or number of repetitions until exhaustion using a given weight and a given range of movement can be taken as quantities to be measured; other possible measurement categories can be the maximum weight possible for a set time, number of repetitions, and movement amplitude. In desmodromic/isokinetic or static strength measurement, the impulse sum (i.e., the average force applied multiplied by the time tested) can be taken as an indicator. In athletics, primarily multi-joint (whole-body) exercises are selected (e.g., 1-min squats).

At the end of each training phase, the current state should be measured again. At the end of a mesocycle, a standardised test battery is performed. In shorter training phases, tests are often performed only by observation. The control of the actual state and training documentation (see chapter I–3.4) are the basis of the final analysis. This is a new comparison between the current and the target state in terms of cause. The analysis leads directly to the setting of goals and the planning of training for the new training phase, and possibly to the adjustment of long-term goals and plans.

Instead of arriving at an objective analysis (i.e., an analysis based on facts), athletes in particular, as well as some coaches, perform subjective analysis. In general, an analysis which is as realistic, multi-faceted (never only negative), and objective as possible is always recommended. Both athletes and coaches should arrive at the same results as independently of each other as possible. In the long term, subjective analysis usually leads to false self-images and a (permanently) incorrect estimation of reality (see Eberspächer, 2004).

3.3 TRAINING PLANNING

3.3.1 GOAL SETTING

The training objectives to be achieved should be set based on a comparison between the target values and the current values (i.e., How close can I get to the target values starting with my current values?). In the final analysis, the fulfilment or non-fulfilment of the objectives set at the beginning is crucial for the success or failure of the training. Every person acts in a goal-oriented manner by continuously setting new objectives. Sometimes this even occurs unconsciously. However, in sports, it is recommended to do so consciously and explicitly. Athletes should establish long- and medium-term objectives at the beginning of a training phase in consultation with their coach. Long-, medium-, and short-term goals should all be pursued with the same commitment. If an athlete is much better than expected or if an objective is not achieved, the training process and/or the objectives must be adjusted accordingly if possible. Therefore, goals should be realistic. This means that although success is supposed to be more probable, failure should not be entirely impossible. Ultimately, the experienced feeling of success results from the possibility of failure, even from temporary failure. This means that goals which can be reached too easily make success worthless. However, objectives that are too challenging lead to constant failure and disappointment. When setting goals, athletes should also consider what they are willing to do to achieve their goals. Objectives require effort; achieving goals is not possible without commitment, even when success cannot be guaranteed. Objectives can be formulated in the form of an athlete-coach contract, in which responsibilities, goals, and the like are written down (as a symbolic gesture). In the younger age groups and in school sports, the objectives are usually set by the coach or teacher. However, educational scientists keep recommending that students actively participate in defining the objectives and thus also the content of lessons.

3.3.2 PERIODISATION PHASES

According to the long-, medium-, and short-term objectives, training is also planned by using periodisation phases of different length.

SEVERAL YEARS

Multi-year plans usually extend over four years. Not only the Olympic cycle, but also basic and build-up training are of this (approximate) duration.

MACROCYCLE (SEASON/YEAR)

A macrocycle is defined as the planned development of athletic form toward the peak of the season. Depending on whether *single or double periodisation* is used, the length of a macrocycle in athletics is either a whole or half year. There are very few competitions in winter especially for the so-called long throws (javelin, discus, hammer) and in combined events. Here, planning sometimes occurs in the form of single periodisation with only one performance peak in the summer and a long period of preparatory and basic training in winter. However, double periodisation is far more common, with two performance peaks and competition phases in summer and winter. The competition phase in summer is considerably longer than that in winter. Between the national championships, which are generally used as a qualification for international championships (Olympic Games, world championships, and continental championships), and the international championships themselves,

there are often another six or seven weeks. Most athletes must be in top form to qualify even at the national championships. Then the question arises whether one should try to maintain one's form or start a new build-up toward a new peak. The latter alternative is characteristic of the classical *direct competition preparation* (DCP), which once again includes fundamental and extensive training contents. Today, the former strategy of planning DCP is also used very often. Although there are other reasons why many athletes fall significantly short of their seasonal best at international championships, the problem is still relevant.

PERIOD/PHASE

A macrocycle is often roughly divided into a preparation and *a competition period or phase*. The preparation period can be further divided *into a general and a specific preparation period or phase*. In double periodisation, the general preparation period (phase) is often much longer in the winter than in the summer season. Both the transition from the general to the specific preparation period and the transition from the preparation to the competition period are fluid. For example, even in the competition period, athletes still perform specific preparatory training. Between the peak of the season and the start of training in the next macrocycle, there is usually *a transition period or phase*. During this phase, the training loads used have little or nothing to do with athletics. The objective of this phase is physical and mental regeneration. In (high-)performance training, this phase usually lasts only one to two weeks between the winter and summer seasons, and at least three weeks before the start of the winter season. With athletes of a lower performance level or with younger athletes this phase is often longer.

Within the competition period or phase, the important question arises about how training immediately before an important competition should be organised. For example, it has been demonstrated that following reactive-strength training the performance peak probably will be delayed for several weeks after ceasing training. Therefore, only training stimuli requiring very short regeneration and adaptation time can be meaningful. However, an optimal rest interval is not possible before each competition. Before preparatory competitions, there are often much shorter breaks and some of them are often considered to be rather intense workouts. The results achieved during these competitions must be assessed accordingly.

MESOCYCLE

Detailed training planning occurs in the form of so-called mesocycles. This term is used differently in various literary sources and sometimes is regarded as identical with the terms *period* or *phase*. Mesocycles usually last about a month or 4–7 weeks (see table 4). Within double periodisation, a season is often divided

into four mesocycles. The competition period or phase most often occurs in the fourth mesocycle, but it can already begin near the end of the third mesocycle by the athlete taking part in certain preparatory competitions. In each mesocycle, the focus of training is on different major types of motor stress or training contents. Respective tables can be found in the discipline-specific part of this book in each chapter dealing with training planning in individual disciplines.

MICROCYCLE

Within a mesocycle, identical or similar training contents are repeated at certain intervals. These repetitive intervals are called microcycles. A microcycle often lasts one week. In high-performance training, with training twice per day, half-week microcycles are even possible. In children's athletics and in basic training, a two-week microcycle can also be used. In addition to microcycles, in which actual training is performed, the last microcycle of a mesocycle has a special function. Its main objectives are regeneration as well as conducting test and control procedures (regeneration and testing week). During a mesocycle, the training loads, which are repeated in the form of successive microcycles, can be organised in three ways:

- *Increasing load volume:* Due to adaptation to training, a higher load volume is possible and necessary to trigger new adaptation processes. The organisation of load is mainly used in volume-oriented training during the general preparation phase.

- *Constant load volume:* Due to adaptation to training, a higher intensity level is possible and necessary to trigger new adaptation processes. This organisation of load is mainly used in intensity-oriented training during the specific preparation phase.
- *Pyramidal load volume:* Such an organisation with first increasing and then decreasing load volume can be used as an intended combination of the two forms previously described. However, it can also become necessary if the total load at the beginning of the mesocycle was too high and there is the risk of decreasing intensity.

Macro-, meso-, and microcycles are organised similarly in certain respects. Macrocycles end with the transition phase, which is for regeneration, whereas mesocycles end with a regeneration (and test) week, and microcycles usually also end with a recovery day (Sunday).

TRAINING SESSION

The sub-units of a microcycle are the various training sessions. Determining their number and duration is one of the most important decisions to be made at the beginning of training planning. The total training volume established in this way should continuously increase from children's athletics via basic and build-up training to (high-)performance training.

MODULE/CONTENT

Both training sessions and school lessons are divided into multiple modules. First, they are basically divided into the warm-up, the main part, and the follow-up. But even these parts consist of various components or contents which must be distributed in the microcycle training plan according to the principle of proper loading sequence and in consideration of specific regeneration times.

Table 4: Annual training planning in high-performance sport with double and single periodisation (abbreviations: R/Reg.: regeneration, Te: test and control procedures, Trai: training, Nat: national peak, Int.: international peak, DCP: direct competition preparation, TP: transition period).

Double periodisation

Month	October				November				December					January					February				March						April				May				June					July				August				September				
Cal.-week	40	41	42	43	44	45	46	47	48	49	50	51	52	01	02	03	04	05	06	07	08	09	10	11	12	13	14	15	16	17	18	19	20	21	22	23	24	25	26	27	28	29	30	31	32	33	34	35	36	37	38	39
Competitions																	X	X	X	X	Nat		Int									X	X				X	X X	X X		Nat			X	X	X		Int	(X)			
Macrocycle													1																									2														
Period	Preparation period I <= general I special =>													Competition period I									TP		Preparation period II <= general I special =>										Competition period II								Direct competition preparation (DCP)				Transition period				
Mesocycle	1				2				3										4								1				2				3					4				5				6				
Load/Reg./Tests	Training			R/Te	Training			R/Te	Training			R/Te	Training			R/Te	Training		R		Trai		R		Training				R/Te	Training		R/Te	Training		R/Te	Training		R/Te		R		R/Te	Training			R		Te	R/ Training			
Microcycle	1	2	3	4	5	6	1	2	3	4	5	6	1	2	3	4	5	1	2	3	4	5	6	7	1	2	3	4	5	1	2	3	4	5	1	2	3	4	5	1	2	3	4	5	1	2	3	4	5	6	1	2

Single periodisation

Month	October				November				December					January					February				March						April				May				June					July				August				September				
Competitions																														X				X	X	X	X	X	X	Nat				X	X		Int	(X)	(X)			
Macrocycle																			1																																	
Period	TP	Preparation period <= general I special =>																													Competition period														Direct competition preparation (DCP)				Transition period				
Mesocycle	8	1				2				3								4								5				6				7				8														
Load/Reg./Tests	Te	R/Te	Training			R/Te	Training			R/Te	Training			R/Te	Training			R/Te	Training			R/Te	Training			R/Te	Training			R/Te	Training			R/Te	Training			R	R/ Training			
Microcycle	5	6	1	2	3	4	5	6	7	1	2	3	4	5	6	7	1	2	3	4	5	6	7	1	2	3	4	5	6	7	1	2	3	4	5	1	2	3	4	5	6	1	2	3	4	5	6	1	2	3	4	

3.3.3 PERIODISATION MODELS

Four different approaches to training planning can be distinguished although they are rarely implemented in their exact form and have diverse effects on each individual athlete.

TRADITIONAL PERIODISATION MODEL

Training planning according to traditional periodisation has two major features:

- usually only one type of content for each session; and
- consistent development from high training volumes and low intensities at the beginning of the general preparation phase toward high intensities and low volumes during specific preparation.

COMPLEX TRAINING

The model of complex training must be seen primarily as an alternative to the first-mentioned feature of the traditional periodisation model. To obtain optimal adaptation in a major area, the interval between two training stimuli sometimes appears too long, and the objective is therefore to practice this area several times a week. In addition, numerous factors determining performance must be taken into consideration in the training plan. Therefore, one is forced to structure individual training sessions in a more complex way even when carrying out more than six training sessions per week. Several major training contents (such as stabilisation training, technique training,

and jumping-strength training, speed training and strength training, and aerobic endurance training and flexibility training) are then performed one after the other in one training session. In combined-event training in particular, this approach is unavoidable and should integrate the principle of proper loading sequence.

HIGH INTENSITIES ALL YEAR-ROUND

The model of high intensities all year-round is primarily inconsistent with the second-mentioned feature of the traditional periodisation model. In speed- and reactive-strength dominated disciplines in particular (short sprints, jumps, throws), it is doubtful whether it is sensible to initially slow athletes down through extensive (speed- or strength-) endurance training at the beginning of the preparation period. Does one really need such an extensive basis (of endurance) for subsequent training so that the consequences of converting fast into slow muscle fibres must be put up with? In these disciplines, training may be organised in such a way that the athlete can deliver relatively good performances throughout the year. Although basic training would not completely disappear, it would be used less frequently and would be distributed over a longer period.

BLOCK TRAINING

Block training is in contrast to the previously presented periodisation models. These models embody the following problem: Speed, reactive-strength, maximum-strength, strength-endurance, speed-endurance, aerobic-endurance, and flexibility training designate somewhat similar, but at times also very different and even opposing adaptation stimuli for the organism. However, training in these areas is carried out within a short time of one another. In block training, one tries to circumvent this disadvantage by placing extreme emphasis on only one type of motor stress in (sometimes relatively short) mesocycles. In such a mesocycle or block, approximately 80% of the training contents are used exclusively for the development of only one component determining performance. For example, the preparation of a jumper could begin with an anaerobic (speed- and strength-) endurance block and then include a muscle-building, a reactive-strength, a speed, and finally a block for developing technique. Since the contents of the first blocks practically do not occur in the subsequent blocks, the question, however, is whether the results still last until the competition period. A proponent of block training would dismiss these concerns as follows: First, the training contents of the first mesocycles are the least important for competition performance. Second, block training develops better adaptations in certain areas than would be possible in conventional training. Even if some of these adaptations are lost again, there is still an advantage. Third, although some adaptations (e.g., the hypertrophy achieved during the second block) are perhaps not further developed in other contents, they are still maintained. On the whole, block training is expected to work well particularly with top athletes whose fundamentals are already very well developed through training. In double periodisation, it is also possible to use block training only during one of the two preparation phases.

3.3.4 SAMPLE TRAINING PLANS FOR CHILDREN'S ATHLETICS AND BASIC TRAINING

Many sample training plans for build-up and high-performance training can be found in the discipline-specific part of this book. The suggested training plans are to be understood as part of a double periodisation, represent a mix of the traditional periodisation model and complex training, and include approaches pertaining to year-round high intensities. Numerous coaches have achieved optimal results using this system. Block training and a more thorough implementation of year-round high intensities is incompatible with this and would lead to completely different training plans. However, this does not mean that the training suggested here would generally be superior to training based on the latter periodisation models. Thus, the potential benefits of a more consistent implementation of year-round high intensities and training blocks must certainly be considered.

Sample training plans for children's athletics and basic training (see tables 5–7) have already been presented here since training does not focus on specific events at this age. In the training plans suggested, the amount of training is increased according to age by extending the duration of the training sessions. An increase based on the frequency of training sessions is also possible. An extension of the microcycles to two weeks may also be beneficial. The training plans show the above-mentioned development of very general, often non-athletics training contents to increasingly specialised, but still combined-event-oriented contents. Here, the training plan for U16 athletes attempts to do justice to the conflicting requirements for versatile basic training on the one hand and early specialisation on the other hand by placing emphasis at an early stage.

Table 5: Children's athletics: sample microcycle for the U10 category

Monday	Tuesday	Wednesday	Thursday	Friday	Saturday	Sunday
Focus: *Sprinting*	Focus: *Throwing*	Focus: *Jumping*	Focus: *Gymnastics*	Focus: *Major games*	Rest	Rest
Chain catching (5 min) alternatively: shadow running	**Spider football** (5 min) forward; alternatively: fistball on all fours backwards	**Jump garden** (10 min) crisscross over banana boxes, small boxes, gym mats mini hurdles, etc.	**Move like** (5 min) ... a creeping cat, a racing dog, a bird, etc.	(this week: basketball)		
Black and white (5 min) different starting positions	**Target-throwing game(s)** (5 min) tennis balls into large wall bars, bicycle tubes over traffic cones, and/or similar game	**ABCs of sprinting/ jumping** (15 min) knee lifts, heel kicks, running backward, simple skipping variations, pop-up jumps onto gymnastics boxes, etc.	**Learning at stations** (40 min) station cards show picture sequences for target and graded preliminary exercises (e.g., balancing; rolling about one's longitudinal axis; forward and backward roll; crouch turn; handstand; swinging on rings; curl, inverted hang, and over-rotation on the rings; rope climbing; underswing dismount on the horizontal bar; over the trampette onto soft ground)	**Ten successful passes within a team for one point** (5 min) 2 teams with one basketball		
Pendulum relay over banana boxes, sprint over hurdles (10 min) 2 teams, 3 run-throughs, varying set-up: uniform or varying distances	**Aero-howler competition** (10 min) simultaneous throwing side by side (e.g., from the lawn edge); each child marks his/her own best distance with a cone	**Long-jump competition into zones** (10 min) limited run-up (10-15 m), 3 trials		**Dribbling obstacle course** (10 min) left and right, forward and backward, slow and fast, slalom, etc.		
Rounders (15 min) teams as above; alternatively: tagging the team	**Dodgeball** (15 min) alternatively: Zombie ball	**Pendulum sack race relay** (10 min) 2 run-throughs		**Dribbling relay** (5 min) 2 run-throughs		
Collecting cards (10 min) 4 teams				**Passing and catching** (15 min) simple exercises against the wall, with a partner or in small groups, different pass variations		
				Ball over the cord (10 min)		

Table 6: Basic training: sample microcycle from the first mesocycle in the U14 category

Monday	Tuesday	Wednesday	Thursday	Friday	Saturday	Sunday
Focus: *Sprinting*	Focus: *Throwing*	Focus: *Gymnastics*	Focus: *Jumping*	Focus: *Running*	Rest	Rest
Baton exchange (10 min) while sitting and jogging	**Ten successful passes within a team for one point** (5 min) 2 teams with one 1kg medicine ball	**Warm-up jogging** (5 min) with circling one's arms or doing something similar	**Warm-up jogging** (5 min) stairs included	**Trunk stabilisation exercises and belly crunches** (10 min) with dynamic variations		
ABCs of sprinting (15 min)	**Stabilisation exercises for the trunk, belly crunches, and foot strengthening** (15 min)	**Floor exercises** (15 min) exercises already mastered (rolls, cartwheel, handstand) as special warm-up	**ABCs of jumping** (15 min) on the lawn	**ABCs of walking/running** (10 min)		
Acceleration runs (5 min) 2-3 repetitions	**Fundamentals of shot putting** (30 min) tossing, chest passes, frontal puts, and puts of a 2kg medicine ball from a standing position toward a partner, two rows of children facing each other	**Learning at stations** (60 min) in groups of 3, preliminary exercises and methods of assisting with the exercises shown on station cards (e.g., round-off, handspring, roll backward to handstand; squat vault; upstart, hip circle, and underswing dismount on the horizontal bar; swinging in full support on the parallel bars; swinging rings)	**Slalom sprints** (5 min) 3 repetitions	**Sprints with varied arm exercises** (5 min) 4 repetitions		
Hurdles sprint (25 min) from sprints over gymnastics mats to sprints over obstacles of gradually increasing height	**Game** (20 min) football or field/indoor hockey		**Basics of the flop high jump** (40 min) falling exercises, pop-up jumps from a curved run-up, pop-up jumps with initiating the rotation, jump onto a pile of mats	**Biathlon relay** (20 min) organisation: big lap (ca. 150 m), throwing station, if necessary, small penalty lap, big lap, exchange; 3-4 children per team, each child runs three times		
Relay around turning marks (15 min) with passing the baton from behind, 2-3 teams against one another, 2-3 run-throughs	**Stretching** (10 min) the upper body		**Passing and Catching** (10 min) a handball for specific warming-up	**Continuous run** (20 min) e.g., as orientation run		
Stretching (10 min) hurdle seat variations			**Throws from a jump** (10 min) toward the handball goal, high throws possibly over an elastic cord	**Stretching** (15 min) whole body		

85

Tab. 7: Basic training: sample microcycle from the third mesocycle in the U16 category

Monday	Tuesday	Wednesday	Thursday	Friday	Saturday	Sunday
Trunk stabilisation exercises and belly crunches (15 min) with numerous dynamic variations	**Low intensity (LI) warm-up runs** (5 min) 5 x 80m, rest: 20 sec.	**Warm-up running** (5 min) including arm circling, rotations, etc.	Rest	**Warm-up running** (5 min) back and forth across the whole area	*Training in the individual athlete's major discipline*	Rest
Acceleration runs (5 min) 2 repetitions barefoot	**Practising the shot-put technique** (45 min) including specific warm-up, puts from a standing position, establishment of competition technique (glide technique, scissor-step technique, or rotational technique)	**Practising the discus-throw or javelin-throw technique** (45 min) including specific warm-up, standing throws, development of 6/4 turn or long run-up		**Acceleration runs** (5 min) 3 repetitions	**LI warm-up runs** (5 min) 6 x 60m, rest: 15 sec., with vaulting pole	*For Saturday, a sample training for the pole vault/combined events as major disciplines was presented. Alternative major disciplines could be short sprint/hurdles; long sprint/hurdles; middle-distance running/steeplechase; walking; sprint/horizontal jumps; high jump/javelin throw; discus/shot put/hammer throw.*
ABCs of sprinting (15 min)				**Practising the hurdling technique** (50 min) including specific warm-up (e.g., ABCs of hurdling, and slow running over hurdles at 5-stride rhythm), distance shortened by one foot in length, competition height, up to the third hurdle	**Practising the pole-vault technique** (55 min) including specific warm-up (vaults with straight pole, vaults with rockback, Jagodin exercises), finding the preliminary competition technique, run-up length 8–12 strides depending on the individual athlete's technical skills	
Acceleration runs (5 min) 2 repetitions wearing spikes	**Practising the high-jump technique** (45 min) including specific warm-up (e.g., skipping, slalom sprints), scissors, and flop jumps from competition run-up	**Weightlifting techniques** (20 min) technical development with broomstick or very light barbell; whereas in previous mesocycles the focus was on the squat and the clean, the focus is now on the snatch				
Ankle jumps (5 min) 5 x 6 repetitions		**Fartlek** (15 min) extreme variations of intensity, high stress		**Practising the long-jump technique** (40 min) including specific warm-up (e.g., pop-up jumps), finding a competition run-up, complete jumps from a slightly shortened run-up, stride-jump technique	**Gymnastics** (40 min) (e.g., development of a backward somersault on a trampoline)	
Sprints from the starting block (35 min) 3 x 10m with individual correction, as well as maximal sprints over 20, 30, 40, 50, and 30m against each other	**LI tempo run** (5 min) 1 x 120m at maximal speed	**Stretching** (15 min) whole body				
Game (20 min) e.g., soccer or basketball						

3.4 IMPLEMENTING AND DOCUMENTING TRAINING

Training is done according to the training plan. Due to illness, injury, unavoidable appointments, etc., it is sometimes inevitable to switch or even cancel training sessions. Often coaches and athletes spontaneously decide to increase or decrease training based on mutual feedback. All this makes individual training documentation essential, beginning with the start of build-up training at the latest. This is especially true if training plans relate to entire groups instead of to individuals. There is much to be said for athletes performing the documentation themselves. First, the coach is normally very busy with the training plan, other organisational activities, and, if he/she is not a full-time coach, also with his/her job outside of training. Second, it is easier for athletes themselves to document their physical or mental states and physically stressful activities outside of athletics training. Third, such an approach strengthens the athlete's sense of responsibility for his/her training. However, the athlete should send a copy of the documentation to his/her coach as a fax or email. Athletes' files on the Internet with definable access options are another possibility. Tables 8a and b show examples of documentation sheets which might be distributed by the coaches.

Table 8a: **Simple training documentation sheet;** b: **Complex training documentation** (see next page) for a combined-event athlete: Depending on the athlete's major discipline, as well as personal preferences and needs, the left column may vary.

Training documentation for _____ for week from _____ to _____			
	Training contents including volume (duration/repetitions) and intensity; also results if possible (such as times, weights, etc.)	Assessments, comments, peculiarities (e.g., newly-learned element, strikingly good/bad results, physical and mental state, injuries)	Other sports or stressful activities, such as school/ recreational sports, disco night (including volume/ intensity)
MONDAY			
TUESDAY			

(continued)

(continued)

Training documentation	Week from ___ to ___														Major discipline: ___	Performance goal for the season: ___	
	Monday		Tuesday		Wednesday		Thursday		Friday		Saturday		Sunday		Weekly sum
	1.TS	2.TS	1.TS	2.TS	1.TS	2.TS	1.TS	2.TS	1.TS	2.TS	1.TS	2.TS	1.TS	2.TS	
Name:															
Game (min)															
Warm-up/Warm-down/reg. jog (min)															
Continuous run (min)															
Tempo-endurance run (min)															
Minute runs/1000s/2000s/usw. (min)															
Tempo runs at LI (low intensity) (km)															
I3 tempo runs (km)															
I2 tempo runs (km)															
I1 tempo runs, over 60m (km)															
I1 tempo runs for speed up to 60m, also over hurdles (km)															
ABCs of sprinting/hurdling, Coord./acceleration runs (km)															
ABCs of jumping, coordinative/foot-strengthening jumps (min)															
Multiple reactive horizontal jumps (km)															
Multiple strength-oriented vertical jumps (number)															
Take-offs from a short run-up (number)															
Take-offs from a long run-up (number)															
Strength-oriented throws (number)															
Technique-oriented throws (number)															
Maximal throws (number)															
Arm strength (IC, ecc.) (number)															
Arm strength (muscle build-up) (number)															
Trunk strength (IC, ecc.) (min or number)															
Trunk strength (stabilisation, muscle build-up) (min or number)															
Leg strength (IC, ecc.) (number)															
Leg strength (muscle build-up, stabilisation) (number)															
Strength-endurance training (min or number)															
Gymnastics (min)															
Technique training in which discipline?															
Additional training contents, competition results, findings, assessments, peculiarities, stressful activities, mental and physical state, injuries, illnesses															

4 TRAINING METHODS

The training methods shown below apply to all sports and disciplines. Some of them cannot be attributed only to a single major type of motor stress. Nevertheless, they are described under the major type of motor stress with which they are primarily associated in training practice. For example, the repetition method is primarily associated with (speed-)endurance training. Nevertheless, in practice 5 x 1000m with 3 min jog intervals and 5 x 50m with 10 min walk/sit-down intervals would both be referred to as the repetition method although the former training programme is part of aerobic endurance training, whereas the latter belongs to speed training. The term repetition should be explained for another reason: A repetition in weight training is more comparable to a stride in running training, while a repetition in running training corresponds more to a set or series in strength training. In respect to strength training, specific terms are commonly used, although the terms *interval* and *repetition method* could be used here in a similar manner.

4.1 COORDINATION TRAINING

A high quality of coordination is specific and not general in nature. Therefore, in coordination training, the focus is on requirements specific to athletics (techniques). Coordination and technique training should adhere to the following general principles:

- from the known to the unknown,
- from the simple to the complex, and
- from few to many.

Exercises should only include as many new elements as can be implemented by athletes. Since the attention for coordination requirements is limited, new, unfamiliar, more difficult and complex requirements can often only be implemented if the basic movements have been sufficiently automated.

Regardless of the discipline, general approaches to technique training, or teaching and learning methods in technique training, can be distinguished from one another. For example, the question of whether in hurdling one should start directly with sprinting over obstacles or with isolated training of the trailing and swing leg illustrates the difference between the **whole- and the part-learning method**. While athletes involved with hurdles are usually first confronted with low obstacles which they are told to sprint over (confrontation method), throws and jumps are normally introduced using the part-learning method, which means that their most important element (the release or take-off) is taught first. Only then are the complexity of the movement, the time constraints, and the strength requirements increased by increasing the pre-acceleration of the athlete (and the device). The term **whole-part-whole method** illustrates the strategy of practising movements first and mainly as a whole. However, occasionally partial movements are practised and improved in isolation and in a goal-oriented manner. This is probably the most promising strategy for all disciplines, at least after leaving the immediate beginner stage. If technical errors occur during technique training while using these methods, one tries to correct them.

This can either occur through the specific use of the above-mentioned auxiliary exercises or by means of **verbal, acoustic, visual, or tactile correction or assistance**. In addition to the verbal explanation of what the athlete should correct during his/her next attempt, acoustic assistance (e.g., by verbal accompaniment and rhythmisation of motion) can be provided (e.g., leeeft – right-left with the 3-step rhythm in the javelin throw). Visual correction is performed through the personal demonstration of a movement or by showing pictures, videos, etc. This not only helps beginners to create the idea of the movement, but if it involves a video recording of the athlete himself or herself, for example, it can even help advanced athletes whose subjective perception of motion may possibly differ greatly from the objective external view. If this is the case, the **over-correction or the contrast method** in the form of verbal correction is often used. Here, the athlete is either asked to exaggerate the desired change

or to perform the opposite of the desired change. Tactile correction is usually performed by an assistant who, during the imitation or the actual movement, moves a body part in the right direction at the right time.

Another approach to motor learning is the method of **differential learning** developed by Schöllhorn (2003), which assumes that athletes learn fastest by performing specific variations of movements. Without ever explicitly correcting errors or providing a clear idea of motion, it is the coach's task to teach the athlete an effective and variable technique in the target discipline through specific variations of the initial situation and task. The variation of the initial situation can be achieved by varying the starting position, by using different throwing weights, changing the run-up length, restricting the sensory input (see below), etc. Variation of the task occurs by means of the repeated use of over-correction and the contrast method while trying to deliberately deviate from the target movement in as many ways as possible. Here, a great deal of creativity and very good intuition by the coach are required.

Moreover, **mental rehearsal** can support motor practice or training. Mental rehearsal is defined as the intense visualisation or perception of movements without actually performing them. The basis of mental rehearsal is the so-called ideomotor response. Studies have shown that both ideas of motion, and movement perceptions and thinking of the movement, trigger responses in resting muscles. Mental rehearsal is therefore particularly suitable for improving and stabilising coordination. Thus, a distinction can be made between practical training methods (training by performing the movement) and training methods focusing on speech, thought, and imagination processes. The latter group is divided into training by means of communication and training by means of internal realisation. Internal realisation is one of the basic forms of mental rehearsal by using imagination and observation. Ultimately, internal realisation is therefore physiologically an improvement to coordination and technique due to the ingrained mental image.

In addition to the general methods of coordination training, the following **general tips and suggestions** can be provided:

- training with a variation of the sensory input
  - » visual: training with closed eyes;
  - » vestibular: with additional∕ modified movements of the head;
  - » kinesthetic: on various surfaces; and
  - » tactile: assistance and guided movements;
- training with different constraint situations
  - » increased situation constraints: competition simulation;
  - » increased time constraints;
  - » increased precision constraints: e.g., throwing the javelin toward targets; and

- » increased complexity constraints: with additional tasks;
- bilateral training, not only to avoid imbalances in muscle strength, but also because athletes who use the nondominant side of their bodies are forced to think quite differently about the movement, and it is assumed that when training the nondominant side of the body the coordination of the dominant side is always trained simultaneously; and
- versatile training to not only master movements in their ideal form but to make them variably available in all (weather) conditions.
- The closer one gets to the peak of the season, the more specific the training exercises should become in terms of movement form and dynamics.
- With experienced athletes, ingrained technical errors should be dealt with at the beginning of the preparation period. Only one error should be dealt with at a time, and the most important error should be dealt with first. The objective should be to create conditions in training that allow the athlete to perform the movement correctly in at least 80% of all attempts. Nevertheless, experienced coaches report that such a relearning of a single technique detail can take up to two years.

4.2 FLEXIBILITY TRAINING

During **active-static stretching**, the stretch is produced by the antagonist of the stretched muscle (e.g., when drawing back both extended arms at shoulder level to stretch the chest muscle [pectoralis]). In this case, there is only a very slight strain. Therefore, this method is rarely performed in flexibility training. It corresponds to natural stretching which both people and animals perform quite unconsciously after having remained in one position for a long time (e.g., after sleeping). This short stretching of the flexor muscles seems to have an acute performance-enhancing effect after periods of rest.

In **dynamic stretching**, the muscles are also stretched actively most of the time. To avoid overstraining, athletes should only perform slight bouncing movements (i.e., they should not work with too much momentum). If an athlete wants to stretch his/her chest muscles, he/she will move his/her arms back and forth several times in a bouncing manner. However, there are variations of dynamic and passive stretching in which the muscle is also stretched by external forces. For example, one athlete could move his/her partner's arms backward in a bouncing way, or the athlete could use gravity by lying on his/her back. In dynamic stretching, the momentum (inertia) results in a wider range of motion than in active-static stretching. The rapid combination of muscle stretching and contraction, in which the respective monosynaptic proprioceptive reflexes are triggered, corresponds more to actions during athletic movements than is the case with the following two methods.

In contrast to the very general use of the term *stretching* in English, *stretching* in German has established itself as a short term for the method of **passive-static stretching**. In the previous example with the chest muscle, a partner could again move the athlete's arms backward and now hold them there, or the athlete could place his/her hand on a wall and twists his/her body in such a way that the chest muscle is stretched. Due to the continuous stimulus caused by the lack of movement, the stretch receptors (muscle spindles) and pain receptors in the muscles become tired, and, after a few seconds, no additional proprioceptive reflexes are triggered. Now the stretch can be intensified. Thus, the athlete achieves a wider stretching position than in active-static and bouncing-dynamic stretching. For this purpose, however, a certain holding time is necessary. In many cases, 3 sets of 20 to 30 seconds are recommended. Due to the wider stretching position, there is also an increased strain on the stretched structures. The effect on the muscle spindles lasts for some time and is also expressed after stretching in reduced muscle tone and reflex activity. Although this second effect can be undone by some contractions of the stretched muscles, passive-static stretching has no acute performance-enhancing effect. To have a long-term performance-enhancing effect, flexibility training must therefore be performed at the end of a training session and not during the warm-up. There should be a sufficiently long time interval between stretching and competition or other maximum reactive-strength or speed loads.

The **contract-relax method** of flexibility training is another passive stretching method. Here, 3–4 periods of passive-static stretching of about 10 sec duration each are interrupted by periods of maximum-static contraction in (or near) the stretching position of 3–7 sec duration each. The contraction triggers an inverse

stretching reflex via the tendon spindles, which even reinforces the relaxation effect due to the fatigue of the muscle spindle. Moreover, during the passive-static stretching phases, the antagonist of the stretched muscle can also be contracted to achieve a reciprocal inhibition. Thus, compared to the other stretching methods, during contract-relax stretching the widest range of motion is achieved. It is also the most intense, structurally stressful, and therefore to some extent most effective method of flexibility training. The restrictions already mentioned in respect to passive-static stretching apply here all the more.

4.3 STRENGTH TRAINING

Hypertrophy-oriented strength training (muscle build-up training) is primarily multi-set training on strength-training machines or with free weights although other training methods also have a muscle-building effect. Hypertrophy training typically consists of 3–5 series or sets of 8–12 repetitions. Load intensity (weight moved) is about 70–85% of the one-repetition maximum (T4, see table 9). Between series or sets, rest intervals of 3–5 min are common. To make training performances comparable, the range of motion and the duration of repetitions, and thus the speed of movement, should also be defined during each strength training. The extent to which differences in these parameters also influence the training effect is still scientifically unclear. In general, the weight is moved over the

entire range of the motion at a medium speed and in a controlled way. If the movement is too fast, there will no longer be adequate stress at all joint positions due to the exploitation of the swing.

In addition to the classical *multi-set training* described above, it has also been proposed to perform hypertrophy training as *single-set training*. In the version proclaimed by Kieser (2003), each repetition lasts 10 sec: 4 sec for the concentric phase, 2 sec static tension in the maximum contraction position, and 4 sec for the eccentric phase. For muscle building, a set of 6–9 repetitions per exercise is recommended for each exercise. However, the same muscles are sometimes stressed several times by different exercises. The criterion for terminating the set during

*Table 9: **Table of standard values for the weights** (in kg) **used in strength training**, corresponding with the one repetition-maximum (T4, left column) and the exercise intensity desired (upper line).*

%:	100	95	90	85	80	75	70	65	60	55	50	45	40	35	30
5.0	4.8	4.5	4.3	4.0	3.8	3.5	3.3	3.0	2.8	2.5	2.3	2.0	1.8	1.5
7.5	7.1	6.8	6.4	6.0	5.6	5.3	4.9	4.5	4.1	3.8	3.4	3.0	2.6	2.3
10.0	9.5	9.0	8.5	8.0	7.5	7.0	6.5	6.0	5.5	5.0	4.5	4.0	3.5	3.0
12.5	11.9	11.3	10.6	10.0	9.4	8.8	8.1	7.5	6.9	6.3	5.6	5.0	4.4	3.8
15.0	14.3	13.5	12.8	12.0	11.3	10.5	9.8	9.0	8.3	7.5	6.8	6.0	5.3	4.5
17.5	16.6	15.8	14.9	14.0	13.1	12.3	11.4	10.5	9.6	8.8	7.9	7.0	6.1	5.3
20.0	19.0	18.0	17.0	16.0	15.0	14.0	13.0	12.0	11.0	10.0	9.0	8.0	7.0	6.0
25.0	23.8	22.5	21.3	20.0	18.8	17.5	16.3	15.0	13.8	12.5	11.3	10.0	8.8	7.5
30.0	28.5	27.0	25.5	24.0	22.5	21.0	19.5	18.0	16.5	15.0	13.5	12.0	10.5	9.0
35.0	33.3	31.5	29.8	28.0	26.3	24.5	22.8	21.0	19.3	17.5	15.8	14.0	12.3	10.5
40.0	38.0	36.0	34.0	32.0	30.0	28.0	26.0	24.0	22.0	20.0	18.0	16.0	14.0	12.0
45.0	42.8	40.5	38.3	36.0	33.8	31.5	29.3	27.0	24.8	22.5	20.3	18.0	15.8	13.5
50.0	47.5	45.0	42.5	40.0	37.5	35.0	32.5	30.0	27.5	25.0	22.5	20.0	17.5	15.0
55.0	52.3	49.5	46.8	44.0	41.3	38.5	35.8	33.0	30.3	27.5	24.8	22.0	19.3	16.5
60.0	57.0	54.0	51.0	48.0	45.0	42.0	39.0	36.0	33.0	30.0	27.0	24.0	21.0	18.0
65.0	61.8	58.5	55.3	52.0	48.8	45.5	42.3	39.0	35.8	32.5	29.3	26.0	22.8	19.5
70.0	66.5	63.0	59.5	56.0	52.5	49.0	45.5	42.0	38.5	35.0	31.5	28.0	24.5	21.0
75.0	71.3	67.5	63.8	60.0	56.3	52.5	48.8	45.0	41.3	37.5	33.8	30.0	26.3	22.5
80.0	76.0	72.0	68.0	64.0	60.0	56.0	52.0	48.0	44.0	40.0	36.0	32.0	28.0	24.0
85.0	80.8	76.5	72.3	68.0	63.8	59.5	55.3	51.0	46.8	42.5	38.3	34.0	29.8	25.5
90.0	85.5	81.0	76.5	72.0	67.5	63.0	58.5	54.0	49.5	45.0	40.5	36.0	31.5	27.0
95.0	90.3	85.5	80.8	76.0	71.3	66.5	61.8	57.0	52.3	47.5	42.8	38.0	33.3	28.5
100.0	95.0	90.0	85.0	80.0	75.0	70.0	65.0	60.0	55.0	50.0	45.0	40.0	35.0	30.0
105.0	99.8	94.5	89.3	84.0	78.8	73.5	68.3	63.0	57.8	52.5	47.3	42.0	36.8	31.5
110.0	104.5	99.0	93.5	88.0	82.5	77.0	71.5	66.0	60.5	55.0	49.5	44.0	38.5	33.0
115.0	109.3	103.5	97.8	92.0	86.3	80.5	74.8	69.0	63.3	57.5	51.8	46.0	40.3	34.5
120.0	114.0	108.0	102.0	96.0	90.0	84.0	78.0	72.0	66.0	60.0	54.0	48.0	42.0	36.0
125.0	118.8	112.5	106.3	100.0	93.8	87.5	81.3	75.0	68.8	62.5	56.3	50.0	43.8	37.5
130.0	123.5	117.0	110.5	104.0	97.5	91.0	84.5	78.0	71.5	65.0	58.5	52.0	45.5	39.0
135.0	128.3	121.5	114.8	108.0	101.3	94.5	87.8	81.0	74.3	67.5	60.8	54.0	47.3	40.5
140.0	133.0	126.0	119.0	112.0	105.0	98.0	91.0	84.0	77.0	70.0	63.0	56.0	49.0	42.0
145.0	137.8	130.5	123.3	116.0	108.8	101.5	94.3	87.0	79.8	72.5	65.3	58.0	50.8	43.5
150.0	142.5	135.0	127.5	120.0	112.5	105.0	97.5	90.0	82.5	75.0	67.5	60.0	52.5	45.0
155.0	147.3	139.5	131.8	124.0	116.3	108.5	100.8	93.0	85.3	77.5	69.8	62.0	54.3	46.5
160.0	152.0	144.0	136.0	128.0	120.0	112.0	104.0	96.0	88.0	80.0	72.0	64.0	56.0	48.0
165.0	156.8	148.5	140.3	132.0	123.8	115.5	107.3	99.0	90.8	82.5	74.3	66.0	57.8	49.5
170.0	161.5	153.0	144.5	136.0	127.5	119.0	110.5	102.0	93.5	85.0	76.5	68.0	59.5	51.0
175.0	166.3	157.5	148.8	140.0	131.3	122.5	113.8	105.0	96.3	87.5	78.8	70.0	61.3	52.5
180.0	171.0	162.0	153.0	144.0	135.0	126.0	117.0	108.0	99.0	90.0	81.0	72.0	63.0	54.0

%:	100	95	90	85	80	75	70	65	60	55	50	45	40	35	30
	185.0	175.8	166.5	157.3	148.0	138.8	129.5	120.3	111.0	101.8	92.5	83.3	74.0	64.8	55.5
	190.0	180.5	171.0	161.5	152.0	142.5	133.0	123.5	114.0	104.5	95.0	85.5	76.0	66.5	57.0
	195.0	185.3	175.5	165.8	156.0	146.3	136.5	126.8	117.0	107.3	97.5	87.8	78.0	68.3	58.5
	200.0	190.0	180.0	170.0	160.0	150.0	140.0	130.0	120.0	110.0	100.0	90.0	80.0	70.0	60.0
	205.0	194.8	184.5	174.3	164.0	153.8	143.5	133.3	123.0	112.8	102.5	92.3	82.0	71.8	61.5
	210.0	199.5	189.0	178.5	168.0	157.5	147.0	136.5	126.0	115.5	105.0	94.5	84.0	73.5	63.0
	215.0	204.3	193.5	182.8	172.0	161.3	150.5	139.8	129.0	118.3	107.5	96.8	86.0	75.3	64.5
	220.0	209.0	198.0	187.0	176.0	165.0	154.0	143.0	132.0	121.0	110.0	99.0	88.0	77.0	66.0
	225.0	213.8	202.5	191.3	180.0	168.8	157.5	146.3	135.0	123.8	112.5	101.3	90.0	78.8	67.5
	230.0	218.5	207.0	195.5	184.0	172.5	161.0	149.5	138.0	126.5	115.0	103.5	92.0	80.5	69.0
	235.0	223.3	211.5	199.8	188.0	176.3	164.5	152.8	141.0	129.3	117.5	105.8	94.0	82.3	70.5
	240.0	228.0	216.0	204.0	192.0	180.0	168.0	156.0	144.0	132.0	120.0	108.0	96.0	84.0	72.0
	245.0	232.8	220.5	208.3	196.0	183.8	171.5	159.3	147.0	134.8	122.5	110.3	98.0	85.8	73.5
	250.0	237.5	225.0	212.5	200.0	187.5	175.0	162.5	150.0	137.5	125.0	112.5	100.0	87.5	75.0

single-set training is not the completion of a certain number of repetitions, but rather absolute exhaustion. Muscle build-up training in general and in particular forms with slower movement execution is considered to be relatively non-specific for highly dynamic athletics disciplines and is therefore used mainly in the general preparation period.

Jumps, throws, etc. are of course also included in **intramuscular coordination training (IC training)**. Nevertheless, this term usually refers to multi-set training on strength-training machines or with free weights. Such training usually consists of 3–5 series or sets of 1–5 repetitions. Stress intensity (weight moved) here is about 90–100% of the one-repetition maximum. Between series or sets, rest intervals of 3–5 min duration are common. To enable the athlete to overcome the reversal point, movement speed should be relatively slow during the eccentric phase. For the concentric phase, an explosive strength effort is often demanded. In spite of this, visible movement speed remains quite low due to the high resistance.

Pyramid training is a mixed form, in which primarily muscle build-up training and IC training are combined. This training method is often used to make training more variable or to gradually become accustomed to higher weights. Some examples of such pyramids can be found in table 10.

Isometric strength training, in which a weight is statically held several times (3–5 series) for a certain time (5–30 sec depending on the training goal), is of minor importance in athletics. Nevertheless, in strength training for the trunk, static holding exercises are sporadically used, which, however, are increasingly modified through dynamic variations and are performed as stabilisation exercises. An important application of this form of training is, for example, during rehabilitation after injury.

Table 10: **Sample strength-training sets according to the pyramid principle.**

65%	70%	75%	80%	85%	90%	95%	100%	
12x →	10x →	8x →	6x →	4x				complete pyramid, very high number of sets
12x ←	10x ←	8x ←	6x ←	4x ↵				
				3x →	2x →	1x ↵		complete pyramid, normal number of sets
				3x ←	2x			
			7x →	5x →	3x →	2x ←	1x ↵	almost complete pyramid, high number of sets
			7x	←	3x	←		
15x →	12x →	10x →	8x					In each case:
	12x →	10x →	8x →	6x				half pyramid, normal number of sets
		10x →	8x →	6x →	4x			
			8x →	6x →	4x →	2x (2x)		
			8x →	5x →	3x →	2x → 1x		

Stabilisation training can be called a method of its own to the extent that its objective is to hold the position of a joint as constant as possible despite multiple displacements or excursions. Athletics movements are dynamic, not static. Nevertheless, in many athletic movements the described behaviour (i.e., isometric contraction despite the fact that the movement as a whole is dynamic) is particularly characteristic of the trunk muscles and occurs in stabilisation exercises with a great number of dynamic movement variations of the limbs. The limb movements ensure that the trunk muscles, in stabilising the spine, are exposed to continuously changing and higher strength requirements. Instead of statically holding each position for 3 x 30 sec, an athlete can, for example, carry out 6–10 sets of 10 sec duration using dynamic variations.

The same procedure is also often used to stabilise the foot (and knee) joint. Here, the athlete is, for example, asked to remain standing on one leg despite multiple displacements (e.g., when catching a ball). This task is often made more difficult by a wobbly stance (on sand, wobble board, gel pads, etc.).

The term **sensorimotor training**, which in training practice is often used for this training method, expresses that this training is performed primarily because it is good for general coordination. The objective is to practise the motor response to sensory stimuli, which is coordinated by the CNS. Since it is, for example, important that the muscles are tense even before contact with the ground to prevent twisting one's ankle, the absorption of (depth) jump landings is sometimes practised on unstable surfaces. However, sensorimotor training not only pursues such preventive medical objectives, but in addition always constitutes a versatile strength training of the muscles involved.

In the classic **speed-strength method**, the athlete tries to accelerate a relatively low resistance from rest or from an isometric/static pre-tension as quickly as possible. However, this method has become less important in athletics because muscle-building, IC, eccentric-strength, and reactive-strength training seem to promise better adaptations and because purely powerful movements are rare in athletics. The crouch start and the initiating movement in the glide technique of the shot put are exceptions here. Exercises, which are typically carried out by using the speed-strength method, are two-legged jumps onto an object (91).

All of the above methods of strength training focus on the concentric (or isometric) phase since maximum strength is much higher for eccentric loads. A constant weight is a relatively heavier weight in the concentric phase than in the eccentric phase when expressed as a percentage of maximum strength. However, in the reactive-strength loads which occur in athletics, the eccentric phase is at least as important as the concentric phase. The adaptation potential of maximum strength seems to be even greater in the eccentric area than in the concentric area. Therefore, specific **eccentric strength training** should also be carried out when preparing for reactive-strength loads. Eccentric

loads also seem to represent an excellent stimulus for the elastic component and thus to improve energy storage and to reduce susceptibility to injury. However, since this adaptation is due to tissue damage, there should be a sufficiently long interval between eccentric training (particularly if it is recently introduced) and high-intensity speed and reactive-strength training.

Maximum-eccentric strength training has not yet been used very much in athletics. This is a training which uses resistances that are supramaximal in terms of static and concentric maximum strength. During training, these stresses can be generated in several ways. The most versatile and most practical way to do this is through manual resistances. Manual resistance of a partner or a coach can be combined with the resistance of devices, making the eccentric phase more difficult or facilitating the concentric phase. Second, when training the extremities, the concentric phase can be carried out bilaterally (e.g., both legs), whereas the eccentric phase is carried out unilaterally. A variation of the first two options are so-called negatives at the end of a set. These are a mixture of muscle-building and IC training on the one hand, and maximum-eccentric strength training on the other. If, at the end of a set, the athlete's concentric strength is no longer sufficient, the concentric phase will be supported by a partner or the free extremity, and only the eccentric phase will be performed without support. Third, changes in the effective load arm can be used to generate a maximum-eccentric

Table 11: **Load increase in strength training** (according to Boeckh-Behrens & Buskies, 2001, pp. 64–65).

Load increase during single repetition and set/series	
End contractions	static hold for 1-3 sec or bouncing 1-3 times at the point of the greatest stress, either at the point of maximal contraction (particularly in pulling exercises) or in the maximal stretch position (particularly in pressing exercises)
Slow-motion or stutter repetitions	The complete range of movement is performed very slowly, with short holding phases or even short phases of movement reversal.
Partial movements	Training only in the most stressful section of the whole range of movement
Last-possible contraction	each set/each series up to the last-possible repetition
Cheating, forced repetitions and burning series/sets	If no more repetition over the whole range of movement is possible, the athlete will cheat (e.g., by using momentum, changing his/her initial position, etc.), is assisted by his/her partner, uses his/her other extremity to help with the movement, or continues exercising only within the still possible range of movement.

Load increase during single repetition and set/series	
	2-3 exercises for the same muscle or the same muscle group
a: Agonist-super-sets or combined sets/series (pre-/post-fatigue)	a: There is an alternation of sets of different exercises (possibly after only a short rest interval)
b: Selection principle	b: first, all sets of the most important exercise, then the second most-important exercise, etc.
	In the rest intervals between the sets of one and the same exercise, the athlete
a: Antagonist-super-sets/ series	a: either trains the antagonist
b: Interrupted sets/series	b: or performs another exercise for a muscle not involved.

Load increase through the general organisation of the training	
Isolation or complex training	To apply the highest possible stimulus to a muscle it should be trained in isolation. To train the weakest part of a muscle loop (e.g., the extensor loop including the ankle, knee, hip and back extensors) and thus achieve an optimal effect on sports performance, complex whole-body exercises should be chosen (e.g., squat).
Principle of priority	The weakest or most important muscle is trained first.
Split principle	To highly stress individual muscles and then give them a sufficiently long time to recover, the body is divided into certain regions (e.g., arms, trunk, legs), which are trained on different days.

load for a few degrees of the joint angle. The fourth way to generate maximum-eccentric resistances are so-called isokinetic (or desmodromic) strength-training machines. However, these are very expensive, very complicated to operate, and therefore rarely available in everyday training. For maximum-eccentric strength training, 1–3 sets of 1–8 repetitions are recommended, with the athlete defending himself or herself from a maximal isometric pre-innervation against a superior external resistance.

Absorbing movements are another form of eccentric strength training closer to reactive strength. Examples are absorbing the landing after a depth jump (92) by performing a squat, or absorbing the forward tilt from a (knee) stand by falling into the push-up position (48). Here again, the load volume should be relatively low due to the high intensity.

Other forms of training, such as eccentric or vibration-strength training, also have an effect on reactive strength. However, reactive strength is trained specifically in the stretch-shortening cycles of jumping and throwing exercises. Depending on the volume and intensity, **pure reactive-strength/plyometric training** or **reactive strength-endurance training** must be distinguished from one another here. Associated exercises range from a few single jumps, for example take-offs or drop jumps with shorter or longer rest intervals, to highly intensive multiple jumps over 20 to 40m with long rest intervals, to multiple jumps over distances of up to 100 or even

200m with relatively short rest intervals. The training plans in the discipline-specific part of this book provide deeper insight into the matter. A transitional form between classic muscle-building and IC training on the one hand and reactive-strength training on the other hand is strength training with free weights or work on strength-training machines with low resistance and at high movement speed. In each instance, the reversal points are overcome as quickly as possible by using a stretch-shortening cycle.

High stimuli, particularly on the nervous system and elastic components, are provided by **vibration-strength training**. In most cases, the respective exercises are performed on a platform which moves up and down. This results in a variety of impacts on the trained muscles, which each time must be compensated for by the nervous and muscle system. Athletes can perform both (quasi-)static and dynamic exercises for the arms, trunk, and leg muscles on a vibrating platform. For safety reasons, it should be ensured that only small vibrations are transmitted to the head and that the selected vibration frequency does not correspond to the resonance frequency of organs. If an exercise, as is typically done in muscle-building training, is performed on a vibrating plate, the training volume must be considerably lower. The stress is usually much higher than felt acutely by the exercising athlete. Moreover, adaptations to vibration-strength training seem to be very individual. Thus, the risk of overloading is very high in vibration-strength training. This is all the more true because exact details of the optimal load dosage are not yet available. Another strength-training method is **electrical stimulation**. Here, the excitation of the muscle does not occur via the central nervous system, but electronically via adhesive electrodes on the skin. The positive success of electrical stimulation as a training measure is probably due to the fact that hereby a high-intensity muscle contraction with correspondingly large adaptations can be achieved. Moreover, it is assumed that mainly fast muscle fibres are stimulated, while it is difficult to only recruit them during voluntary contractions. The volume and structure of training also depend on the type of device used and the selected innervation programme. The advantages of electrical stimulation compared with voluntary muscle contractions are the activation of the entire contractile apparatus, the longer duration of muscle contractions due to the elimination of the effects of fatigue processes in the central nervous system, and the possibility of specific training of individual and especially important muscles (direct stimulation) or whole muscle groups (indirect stimulation), which are possibly difficult to reach through voluntary exercises. Such training in which coordinative control components do not exist can certainly not replace active training, but can possibly add to it. The primary role of electrical stimulation is the rehabilitation of muscle atrophy. Here, the rapid training effect is possible due to very specific (selective) stimulation.

4.4 SPEED TRAINING

In **reaction-speed training**, reactions must be trained especially in direct connection with subsequent movements which are specific to athletics. In children's athletics, however, game forms should also be used with a range of different choice and multiple reactions.

Due to the maximum nature of speed loads, pure **speed training** must be performed at an intensity of about 100%. A lower-intensity workout becomes speed-endurance training. An intensity of about 100% is only possible on the basis of a rested state. Therefore, speed training should occur at the beginning of a workout, if possible even after a day of rest. The rest intervals between repetitions must be very long, and there should only be a relatively small number of repetitions. In addition, supra-maximal intensities are often the objective: In comparison to competition exercises, they are carried out at a speed of over 100% and are achieved through appropriate methods of support.

To ensure high intensity when **training cyclic speed**, one can use the following rules of thumb: The sprinting distance should not exceed 60 m; for each 10m sprinted there should be a rest interval of 2 min. Based on the use of support methods, stride frequency is increased, for example, in towed sprints (139), downhill sprints (140), tapping (134), and frequency coordination (135). In particular, these exercises are also used if athletes have developed a so-called speed barrier due to multiple sprinting at the same intensity.

Training of acyclic speed is performed in particular by means of exercises which are similar to competition and are carried out at the highest intensity. In the throwing events, training with low-weight implements ensures that high-speed loads are achieved.

Many other discipline-specific methods and contents of speed training will be presented in the discipline-specific part of this book.

4.5 ENDURANCE TRAINING

The **continuous method** is characterised by training without a break (see figure 12). The amount of stress (expressed in exercise duration or distance covered) is high and intensity is low. Nevertheless, a distinction is made between long and slow, short and fast, and short and slow (= regenerative) exercise.

The special features of the **interval method** are the two types of rest intervals: short rest intervals within a series, and longer rest intervals between the series (see figure 13). Depending on the number of runs or series, extensive and intensive interval methods can be distinguished from one another. Intensive interval training is characterised by relatively low volumes and high intensities, while in extensive interval training the volume is high and the intensity is lower. In intensive interval training, the number of repetitions is consequently lower, and the fatigue after each single stimulus is higher than in extensive interval training.

In the **repetition method**, no distinction is made in respect to rest intervals (see figure 14). The rest intervals are either always of the same length or correspond with the different distances covered. Due to the high intensity of the exercise, the number of repetitions is low.

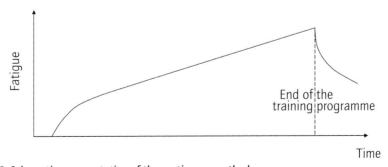

*Figure 12: **Schematic representation of the continuous method.***

a)

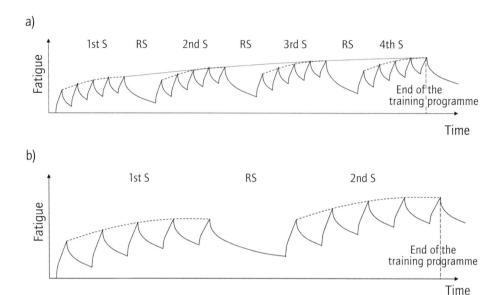

Figure 13: **Schematic representation of** a: **extensive, and** b: **intensive interval method** (S = series, RS = rest interval between series).

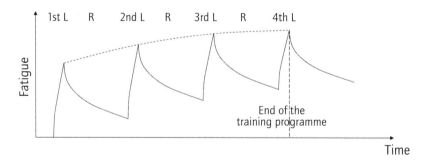

Figure 14: **Schematic representation of the repetition method** (L = Load interval, R = Rest interval).

The **competition method** is characterised by exercise of the highest intensity, whether it is a real or a training competition. Due to the fact that competitions, tests, etc. exert stress on the body, they also have a training effect. When using this method, the psychological requirements of the competition are also trained.

The continuous method and extensive interval method are mainly associated with aerobic-endurance training. Although there is an accumulation of lactate even during extensive intervals, the focus is clearly on aerobic metabolism. The intensive interval method, repetition method, and competition method, however, are associated with a decreasing total volume of training (in particular fewer repetitions) and usually with increasingly higher intensities, longer rest intervals, and anaerobic speed-endurance training.

In **speed-endurance training**, the intensity (i.e., the average running speed or time for a certain distance) is divided into four zones (see table 12). The basis of the calculation is either the best performance from the previous season or the target time for the next season. If electronic competition times are used, 0.6 sec must be subtracted before the calculation, which corresponds with the time measured manually in training at the release of the rear foot. Runs can be organised either in series of the same running distance or with increasing and/or decreasing length of the distance. The series principle is widely used in the interval method, while the pyramid principle is used more in the repetition method. However, this assignment is not mandatory. In anaerobic endurance training with strength exercises, usually 3–5 sets/series of 15–60 repetitions each are carried out. The intensity level is at 30–65% of the one-repetition maximum.

Load control is also possible on the basis of exercise duration and is sometimes even more accurate (e.g., 1-min squats). Strength-endurance training according to the single-set principle is also possible. Here, for example, 9–12 repetitions of 10 sec each can be performed. **Strength-endurance training** is often organised as circuit training, in which all exercises are completed in a kind of rotation. A strength-endurance circle often consists of whole-body or at least complex exercises. In addition to exercises on apparatuses and with free weights, stabilisation exercises, multiple jumps, and throws are often included. Since identical muscle groups are often trained in the various exercises, it is difficult to determine the duration of the rest interval. To ensure high stress on the cardiovascular system without endangering the feasibility of the muscle exercise, a short rest-interval duration (10–60 sec) is chosen, whereas the interval between exercises for the same muscle group is as long as possible.

Table 12: *Intensity zones in speed-endurance training.*

Intensity zone corresponding to …	… average maximal velocity	… Best time/Target time
Low intensity (LI)	50-75%	200-134%
Intensity 3 (I3)	75-90%	133-112%
Intensity 2 (I2)	91-95%	111-105%
Intensity 1 (I1)	96-100%	104-100%

5 GENERAL TRAINING CONTENTS

The following sections present training contents which are used in all athletics disciplines. All discipline-specific games and forms of exercise are found in the discipline chapters themselves. For an explanation of the numbers and the five-box system, as noted in the Test and Training Forms section at the beginning of the book.

5.1 PREPARING FOR EXERCISE

Warming up is defined as all steps toward the acute psycho-physical preparation of a training session or competition. Its goal comprises an acute increase in performance and the prevention of injury. Usually, a distinction is made between general and (discipline-)specific warm-ups. Both components together can take approximately 10–90 minutes, depending on the subsequent exercise. In practice, one often witnesses warm-up programmes with unnecessary contents that are too long (such as intensive stretching programmes) which waste valuable training time and are not relevant. In disciplines such as the pole vault, however, it is sometimes necessary to start warming-up more than 90 minutes before a competition if, for example, several athletes can only use one pole-vault facility for the special part of warm-up vaulting. Moreover, the duration of the warm-up increases, according to various situations such as age, colder temperatures, and earlier times of the day. The warm-up on the competition day must be organised individually. Often, athletes tend to perform a particularly extensive warm-up before a competition because they would like to make sure that they are fully prepared. Although this idea may seem correct, there is nonetheless the danger of doing too much of a good thing. It usually helps athletes to develop a set ritual and to warm up identically in training and competition so as not to cause even more nervousness due to a modified procedure. In exceptional situations, an athlete's attention can also be increased by means of a pre-competition warm-up unlike the one used in training. Of course, the warm-up must be adjusted depending on the weather conditions, and the number of attempts or heats in the competition, etc. In general, the following sub-goals are aimed at in warming up, typically in the order presented.

INCREASING THE BODY'S TEMPERATURE

Warming up usually takes place in the form of general aerobic endurance exercises while using large muscle groups. During muscle exercise, heat is generated as a by-product due to internal friction. There is an increase in the body's core temperature to approximately 38.5°C, the blood flow of the muscles by up to six times, and the temperature of the muscles (slightly slower) to about 37.5° C. Many physiological processes, which are crucial for athletic performance and are based on chemical or physical reactions, occur better, faster, and more efficiently under these conditions. These include metabolic processes (e.g., oxygen supply and enzyme activity), neuronal processes (e.g., nerve conduction velocity or sensitivity of the muscle spindles), and mechanical properties (e.g., the internal friction [viscosity] of muscles and tendons). In particular, the change in the mechanical properties results in a reduced risk of injury during the subsequent exercise. This means that light endurance exercises not only forestall the partially specific adaptation processes at the beginning of an endurance exercise, but also have positive preparatory effects on subsequent strength, speed, flexibility, and coordination exercises. Ambient temperature is also an important factor for endurance performance. Due to thermoregulation and a rise in the body's core temperature, it is true (to a certain extent) that the lower the optimal ambient temperature, the longer the exercise should be. While in a marathon the optimal ambient temperature is only 10–12°C, it increases with the decreasing length of the distance and is 28°C for the 400 and 800m races. Studies also show that a 20- to 35-minute endurance exercise at high ambient temperatures (30°C) after a 20-minute pre-cooling period by means of a 1–4°C cooling vest could be sustained longer while having lower body temperature and heart rate values than after a 20-minute warm-up at 70% of maximum heart rate.

CONTENTS

If the purpose of warm-ups is to reduce acute susceptibility to injury, the warm-up activities themselves must not be potentially dangerous, which means that their intensity must not be too high. Typically, a warm-up includes an easy jog of 6- to 20-minute duration. Instead, endurance games (221–225) without intense load peaks may also be performed. However, athletes are often too cautious in terms of intensity and waste a lot of time with slow jogging which has negative effects on the neuronal processes during subsequent speed exercises. That is why it has often recently been suggested to select more specific exercises of medium intensity. The warm-up for sprints or jumps can, for example, include several LI-runs (see table 12; 142) over 60–100m with very short rest intervals and increasing intensity, or run-throughs of the ABCs of sprinting/jumping over a fixed distance with the athlete jogging back to the starting point (83–88 and 112–121). Other alternatives are jumping-rope exercises (80) or little jumps (81), and other coordination exercises on the spot. Even stabilisation exercises (41–47), which are performed without rest intervals and with a great deal of dynamic variation, can be used at the very beginning of a training session for general warm-up. The latter contents in particular always meet other objectives of warming up described below.

MOBILISATION

Highly intensive stretching in terms of flexibility training should not be used as part of the warm-up. This is particularly true for passive-static stretching and contract-relax stretching. The term mobilisation is difficult to define, but it is probably best described as loose, extensive movements in all directions of the joints required during the subsequent exercise. The main purpose of mobilisation is the loosening of tension within the muscles. Moreover, the articular cartilage is better supplied with synovial fluid through the wide movements. Moreover, mobilisation exercises sometimes result in a better feel for one's own body.

CONTENTS

The following contents can be used to mobilise: loose, circular, and/or wide swinging movements of the large joints, such as an arm or forearm circling (384), swinging at the hip joint (205), or circling or flexion and extension of the feet (52 & 74), shot habituation (427), and similar exercises; the spine may be mobilised by means of controlled rotation, or switching between arching one's back like a cat or forming a hollow back like a horse (23); forms of active-static stretching, such as animals do after having remained in one position for a long time, as well as light forms of bouncing-dynamic stretching.

FACILITATION, INCITING, AND PRE-LOADING

The three concepts of facilitation, inciting, and pre-loading mean different contents although there are clear overlaps. Facilitation means the pre-activation of specific neuronal processes. By performing certain movement elements, the subsequent associated exercise programmes are supposed to be more readily available. If these exercises are rather maximum speed or strength exercises than (submaximal) coordination exercises, one also speaks of inciting. It has been demonstrated, for example, that in maximum strength exercises it is not the first, but the third or fourth attempt which provides the best result. The term inciting, however, still emphasises the neuronal component of this pre-load. Especially in endurance training, there are also intensive pre-loads, which are determined more by metabolic processes. The associated activation of energy provision is much higher than activation through general warming up.

CONTENTS

Often, coordination exercises, for example from the ABCs of sprinting/jumping or throwing imitations, are performed during the warm-up. However, caution should be taken when these are fixed rituals without any supervision by the coach. The risk that technical errors will creep in is very high. If the coach only supervises the main training contents, but not the warm-up, coordination exercises should be kept to the (necessary) minimum in the warm-up and should rather be performed as one of the main training contents. To increase muscle tone, some coaches recommend pre-loading with light weights during the morning of the competition day. Maximum exercise is mainly performed before the competition if there is only one attempt (e.g., in the running events). For example, many 100m sprinters finish their warm-up 10–15 min before the start with a maximum 60m sprint, which is only followed by the direct start preparation. The 400m world record holder Michael Johnson is said to have completed two near maximum 300m runs before a race, which is certainly a load that would be too tiring even for many good athletes. For them, 1–2 150m sprints would be sufficient. Moreover, for throws and horizontal jumps, especially when the competition consists of only three attempts, 1–3 maximum attempts are performed for the purpose of inciting even before the competition. Strength exercises which have a close affinity to the target movement are also used. For example, many shot putters perform a few reactive push-ups (38), explosive squat-extension jumps (82), or, if possible, even some maximum bench-press or squat repetitions (54 & 62). To take advantage of inciting effects in further training, it is also useful to integrate stabilisation exercises or part of the trunk-strength training (41–47) in the warm-up.

PSYCHO-COGNITIVE PREPARATION

The warm-up alone has an effect on the central nervous system. Usually it results in an increased state of wakefulness, but may also have a positive effect on over-excitation and states of inhibition. Increased alertness (vigilance) fosters technical learning processes and coordination performances. Special psychoregulatory assistance can also be used in the warm-up.

5.2 COORDINATION: FORMS OF GAMES AND EXERCISES

5.2.1 GAMES AND SKILL EXERCISES

Major games (also called sports games or game sports) are games with strict rules prescribed by a governing body and performed within a league system. In athletics training, they are used for the versatile and playful improvement of coordination, endurance, speed, strength, and flexibility.

Minor games are simple games with variable rules. Many of them are also mentioned in the discipline-specific part of this book. Especially in children's athletics, they are an excellent form of exercise to develop the fundamentals of athletics. Often, they can also be used in many ways for coordination training.

---

1 **Major games: Football, field/indoor hockey, volleyball, etc.**

Execution/Variations: Besides the game itself, non-athletics prerequisites, such as catching, dribbling (with one's hand, one's foot, or a racket), should be practised in a playful manner to improve general playing ability; for rules, execution, variations, lead-up games, and exercises, etc., please see the respective special literature.

---

2  **Skill relays**

Execution/Variations: All relay forms, in which, for example, an object is carried and balanced (e.g., a ball on a spoon); a ball is dribbled, the athlete crawls or climbs over, under or through something; gymnastics elements and many other skills may also be included.

If exercises from the ABCs of sprinting or jumping (see chapters I–5.4.6 and II–1.3.8) are greatly varied, they will promote coordination in a versatile way:

- with circling one arm forward while circling the other one backward; with moving one arm up and down while moving the other one back and forth; with changing the position of one's arm as indicated by the coach;
- moving forward/backward; also in rapid succession: three steps or jumps backward, three steps sideways, three steps forward, etc.;
- throwing balls to each other while performing partner exercises;
- with eyes closed; or
- to the beat of different music.

3 Pirouettes and rotational jumps

Execution/Variations: Pirouettes on one's heel or on the ball of one's foot; rotational jumps with one- or two-legged take-off; from or onto a trampoline; with quarter, half, three-quarter, complete, or even more turns; landing with both legs if possible; rotations while running; rotations and straight-line sprint alternately; all variations while holding something in one's hands or with eyes closed.

5.2.2 GYMNASTICS AND CLIMBING

4 Balancing

Execution/Variations: On all fours, while walking, running or sprinting; on a line, a jumping rope, balance beam, one or two bars, and on a normal standing, inverted, inclined, declined, and/or on a gym bench standing on a soft floor mat (wobbly ground), etc.; with additional tasks: climbing over something, throwing the ball high into the air or dribbling it, eliminating arm actions (e.g., by holding a ball above one's head.), with turns, small jumps, with eyes closed, with head movements, with oncoming traffic on the bench, etc. (see also sensorimotor strength training in chapter I–4.3 and wobbly stands, 50).

5 Side vaults, leapfrogs, tuck jump, and split jump

Execution/Variations: Side vaults over a gym bench; leapfrogs over small boxes, over partners, or over a vaulting buck; rabbit hops (two-legged take-off from the squat position to a position supported by the arms, lifting of the legs and moving them forward in a tucked position between the hands); at first side vault over, then jumping onto and landing on a transversely positioned large gym box in a tucked or split-leg position; at first from a standing position, then from a run-up over a springboard, then tuck jump and split jump over a large gym box (for the tuck jump initially transversely, then longitudinally positioned; for the split jump initially longitudinally, then transversely positioned); assistance: supporting grip on the upper arm by two helpers behind the box.

6 **Rolling about one's longitudinal axis**

Execution/Variations: For strengthening the trunk with raised arms and legs; also as so-called tree-trunk rolling: several teammates lie side by side, while another teammate lies crosswise on the first ones, the lower teammates roll in one direction transporting the upper one.

7 **Rolling forward and backward about the transverse axis**

Execution/Variations: Back swing as a preparatory exercise for both rolls: in a squat position, head toward chest ("look at your belly") and hold knees, roll back over round back onto shoulders and forward again into squat stand (for backward roll also with slight hand support during the backward swing, as well as start from a standing position and sitting down backward); forward roll initially in slow motion: put hands onto the ground, move head toward chest and put head onto the ground, extend legs, roll; then faster up into a standing position; later as jump roll (from springboard/ trampoline; over an object or through tires); backward roll initially on an inclined surface downward, later with stronger push of the arms, initially into squat support, later up into handstand (8).

8 Handstand (and walking in handstand position)

Execution/Variations: Initially from a squatting position into a fleeting squat handstand; then handstand against wall with belly facing the wall followed by a short-time push-off of the feet from the wall into handstand.

From a large gym box (see picture) swing up a leg, followed by the other leg into handstand; handstand with two helpers (bracket-grip on the thigh); for learning the downward roll: swing up into the shoulder stand, then roll downward into the squat stand; perform handstand in front of a soft floor mat and roll downward onto the mat; perform handstand and slow downward roll assisted by teammate.

Handstand from a walking approach, from a squat or from a split position; walking in handstand position on the partner's feet; walking in handstand position with slight assistance; later forward or backward, as well as uphill or downhill; rotations about the longitudinal body axis while in the handstand position.

9 Cartwheel and round-off

Execution: In the cartwheel, both hands and both legs are put onto the ground one after the other (verbal accompaniment: "cher-ry ice-cream"), the legs remain spread in the air and the movement ends in the stride position; in the round-off, both hands and the feet are each put onto the ground almost simultaneously, the legs are brought together in the air for a fleeting handstand, and the movement ends in a standing position with closed legs.

Variations: Preliminary exercises: Scissors handstand (handstand with [repeated] scissoring movements of the legs), scissors handstand with ¼ rotation about the longitudinal axis, scissoring handstand with hand support similar to that in the cartwheel; cartwheel on a line (along an upright positioned gym mat), cartwheel from a run-up and preliminary skip; initially slow round-off with hand support on the upper element of a gym box with deliberate closing of the legs and rotation of the hips in the handstand position (with securing/assistance at the hip); increase in the dynamics of the round-off; round-off with subsequent reactive and powerful take-off from both feet; later, for example, followed by flic-flac (see also round-off over bar specific to the pole vault, 368).

End of round-off with transition to flic-flac (14):

10 Underswing (glide and shoot) on the horizontal bar

Execution/Variations: Underswing initially with preliminary swing of one leg (and closing the legs in the air) for distance over a low rope, then over a high rope, finally from the stand with both feet side by side; assistance: carrying grip under the shoulder blade and the thigh, during the landing, the helper quickly moves his/her hand from the thigh to the belly or upper arm to prevent the exerciser from falling forward.

11 Upswing and circle on the horizontal bar/parallel bars

Execution: The upswing (onto the chin-high horizontal bar) is performed from a standing position, while the circle is performed after a backswing from the support.

Variations: A prerequisite for the upswing and circle is the over-rotation (40); upswing with the assistance of a partner and/or the assistance of a device: a small or large gym box is placed in front of the gymnast, who with one leg pushes himself/herself upward off of this box; initially upswing with preliminary swing of one leg and bending of the legs when rotating around the bar; later with straight legs and/or as a pull-up from the parallel stand without preliminary swing; initially circle with rope assistance, then also with bent legs and assistance.

Upswing:

Circle:

Hand support

Sit on the rope on the bottom seam of your pants

12   Forward turn and backward turn on the parallel bars

Execution: The forward turn is performed after a forward swing while the backward turn is performed after a backward swing.

Variations: A prerequisite of the turn is swinging on parallel bars (39); preliminary exercise for the forward turn: scissoring to the sitting position on the bar; preliminary exercises for the backward turn: backward tucked turn from the half-high box into the space between the bars, then backward turn at the end of the parallel bar over a loose cord extending from the bar, then backward turn over the declined bar (both bars are lower behind the athlete's back); assistance on the landing side: the assistant grips the exerciser's upper arm on the landing side and also supports him/her below the centre of gravity; both exercises are first performed with intermediate tucking movement, later with straight legs.

Forward turn:

Backward turn:

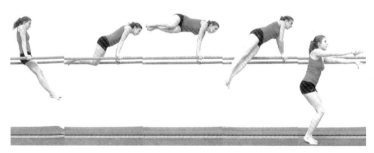

13  **Backward roll into the handstand**

Execution/Variations: Preliminary exercise: rolling backward from the squat into the shoulder stand and placing the hands onto the ground; then from the squat into the handstand with assistance by two strong partners; reduce assistance, increase the active stretching of the hip and trunk, and start from a standing position; later as straight arm backward roll with arms placed on the ground.

14 ▮▯▮▯ Front handspring and back flip

Assistance during front handspring:

Assistance during back flip:

Execution/Variations: For learning the front handspring, the exerciser first swings upward into the handstand, and then two helpers slowly carry him/her through the flip; handspring from a walking approach on a gym box onto a soft floor mat assisted by two helpers; then increasingly faster and from an initial skip; gradual reduction of box height and assistance; for learning the back flip, the exerciser is initially assisted while lowering down from the sitting position on a large gym box backward into the handstand; then he/she is slowly carried through the flip by two helpers; preliminary exercises for the backward lowering down: arm swing and backward take-off with whole-body (over)extension (e.g., vertical jump backward with landing in supine position on a high soft floor mat); then back flip assisted by two helpers from a slightly heightened inclined surface (e.g., inclined trampette) onto a soft floor mat; then back flip on a long, slightly inclined surface; finally, back flip on flat surface with gradually reduced assistance; later as part of movement combinations (following a round-off) and increasingly faster; assistance in the form of a carrying grip each at the thigh and back (with the front handspring, the grip is rather at the shoulders, with the back flip rather at the lumbar spine).

Front handspring:

Back flip (here following a round-off, 9):

15 ▮▮▮▮ Upstarts (kips) on the horizontal bar, uneven bars, and parallel bars

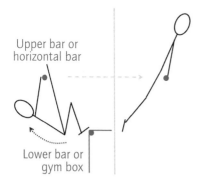

Upper bar or
horizontal bar

Lower bar or
gym box

Execution/Variations: Preliminary exercise: First two-legged, then one-legged cast forward (see sketch on the left); first as upstart from hanging and lying position under the bar with a great deal of assistance (e.g., from a lying starting position on the lower bar of the uneven bars while gripping the upper bar, shins to the upper bar, and with a great deal of assistance through the upstart movement); possibly with a great deal of assistance as a running upstart on shoulder-high parallel bars or the horizontal bar; then as a floating upstart; reduce assistance; later as long-hang upstart from swinging on the high bar; additional assistance on the other side of the horizontal bar for better support of the final phase of the upstart.

Start of the running upstart
on the horizontal bar:

Assistance:

Floating upstart on parallel bars:

16   Forward and backward somersault

Forward somersault from run-up
over a springboard:

Execution/Variations: Forward somersault: At first, dive forward roll from run-up, over trampette onto mat pile; then somersault from a standing position with the assistance of two helpers: rotation-bracket grip on upper arm close to the shoulder (in the starting position, the exerciser's arms are behind his/her body); then from dive forward, roll onto mat pile to somersault onto increasingly low, soft floor mat; replacement of trampette with springboard (possibly with assistance: two helpers are placed at the beginning of the landing mat facing each other, they support the exerciser's belly with their near hand while supporting the rotation with the other hand at the backside of the shoulder; to secure the landing, they switch their hands: from belly to lumbar spine and from shoulder to belly);

119

finally without supporting the take-off; backward somersault: initially backward-curl and extension exercises (e.g., backward and downward roll from the supine position on a box, or backward rotational swing, over-rotation, and return on the rings, 40); then (wall) somersault from a standing position with two helpers: rotation-bracket grip on upper arm close to the shoulder; then from a standing position downward from a trampette, with two helpers: waistband grip (an elastic band, which is wrapped around the exerciser's hips, may be gripped); then backward somersault dismount from swinging rings (see also 35); then reduction of take-off support and assistance during the backward somersault from a standing position; initially from slight elevation (caution: beware of the habit of jumping backward); later, following a round-off or back flip; both somersaults also on trampoline.

Assistance for the backward somersault:

Rotation-bracket grip on the upper arm:

Waistband grip:

Carrying grip:

Backward somersault dismount from swinging rings: Assistance:

Backward somersault from a standing position: Assistance:

For pole vaulters, the development of gymnastics skills must be considerably more extensive. See the special gymnastics literature for further methodical assistance with the exercises described and specifically for the development of the free circle and giant circle for pole vaulters.

17 ▮▮▯▯ Climbing and skill course

Execution/Variations: As early as in mother-child sports, varied obstacle courses offer opportunities to gain a great deal of experience with movement and to improve perception ability; the possibilities are almost endless: onto an object, through an object, under an object, over an object, down from an object, etc.

18  **Parkour/freerunning**

Execution/Variations: The objective of this modern trend sport is to get from A to B as quickly or with as much style as possible by clearing various obstacles; elements of parkour/freerunning can be very useful additions not only to coordination, but also to strength and endurance training.

19 **(Sport) climbing**

Execution/Variations: In nature (e.g., on trees), on a climbing frame, or on a climbing wall; during leisure time or in training; as a day trip or in a training camp; mutual securing as a team-building measure.

5.3 FLEXIBILITY: FORMS OF EXERCISES

20 **Hand between shoulder blades**

Muscles: Broad back muscle (latissimus dorsi) and elbow extensor (triceps brachii)

Execution: The supporting arm pulls the other arm into the stretch position.

Variations: Shaking hands behind one's back (one upper arm is pointing upward, whereas the other one is pointing downward); when using the active-dynamic alternative, the arm is swung freely to the position at the back of the head.

21 Chest exercises

Muscles: Chest muscles (pectoralis) and the front part of the delta muscle (deltoideus); in the exercise presented in the middle also broad back muscle (latissimus dorsi)

Execution/Variations: The chest muscles are moved into a stretched position with the assistance of a partner or through passive resistance; active, free (slightly bouncing), backward movement of the arms at shoulder height while standing.

22 Lateral trunk flexion

Muscles: Lateral abdominal muscles, broad back muscle (latissimus dorsi), and other muscles

Execution/Variations: Also with legs uncrossed or in a knee-stand position.

23 Back exercises

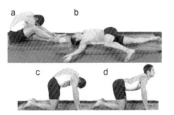

Muscles: Different parts of the back extensor (erector spinae), and other muscles

Execution/Variations: a: hunchback; b: twisting of the hip and shoulder axis (also see hurdle-specific variation, 204); c: arched back, for mobilisation alternating with d: hollow back.

24 Glute exercises

Muscles: Mainly uni-articular hip extensors (glutes)

Execution/Variations: Exercise on the right can also be performed in a standing or one-sided knee-stand position (25).

25   One-sided knee stand

Muscles: Mainly uni-articular hip flexors (iliopsoas and tensor fasciae latae)

Execution: Push your hips forward and downward while avoiding hollow back.

Variations: Also with lifted rear knee (lunge; see 26).

26   Exercises for the front-thigh muscles

Muscles: Muscles of the front side of the thigh (mainly quadriceps)

Execution/Variations: In a standing position, one-sided knee-stand position, or lying position; if possible, use both hands to move your foot into the stretched position; brace your abdominal muscles.

27   Exercises for the back side of the thigh muscles

Muscles: Muscles of the back side of the thigh (hamstrings)

Execution/Variations: In a standing or lying position; with maximal flexion at the hip joint (see second picture from the right), or maximal extension at the knee joint; also with the assistance of a partner who fixes the lower leg to the ground while moving the upper leg into the stretched position.

28  **Adductor exercises**

Muscles: Adductors of the hip joint
Execution/Variations: While standing, squatting, or sitting; the back is kept straight.

29  **Calf-muscle exercises**

Muscles: Calf muscles (triceps surae); with bent legs, mainly soleus muscle
Execution/Variations: The rear leg, which is either in bent or extended position, is stretched.

5.4 STRENGTH: FORMS OF GAMES AND EXERCISES

5.4.1 PLAYFUL STRENGTH TRAINING IN CHILDREN'S TRAINING AND BASIC TRAINING

30 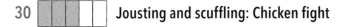 **Jousting and scuffling: Chicken fight**

Muscles: Leg extensors and trunk muscles
Execution: Limping on one leg, push one's opponent out of a certain zone; using one's arms is not allowed.
Variations: Hands behind one's back or crossed in front of one's chest.

31 Jousting and scuffling: Medicine-ball wrestling

Muscles: Leg extensors, trunk, and arm-pull muscles

Execution: Draw one's opponent out of a certain zone, or take the ball away from him.

Variations: While gripping hands, pulling on a rope, etc.

32 Wheelbarrowing

Muscles: Wheelbarrow: Chest muscles (pectoralis), elbow extensor (triceps brachii), front part of the delta muscle (deltoideus), and abdominal muscles; pusher: extensor loop, grip muscles, and other muscles

Execution/Variations: Carrying the thighs makes running on hands easier; over obstacles, for time/speed, by bouncing up from the ground with two hands simultaneously.

33 Building pyramids

Muscles: Various, depending on the type of pyramid

Execution/Variations: Observe falling height and injury risk (but don't use a soft floor mat due to instability); possibilities increase with improving gymnastics skills and holding strength.

34 Bench carrying

Muscles: Delta muscle (deltoideus), elbow extensor (triceps), trunk muscles, and other muscles
Execution/Variations: Move bench from one side to the other; lying back, getting up, sitting down, running, etc., with bench over head.

The forms of brachiating, climbing, swinging, etc. presented in the following may also be playfully integrated as simple strength exercises into (children's) training.

5.4.2 STRENGTH EXERCISES USING ONE'S OWN BODY WEIGHT

35 Hanging and swinging

Muscles: Elbow flexors (biceps brachii), large back muscle (latissimus dorsi), hand muscles
Execution/Variations: Also on horizontal bar, trapeze, or the rings (here also with half or full turn at the end of the forward and/or backward swing); also in the inverted hanging position (angled or extended); swinging from box to box, also as part of a story ("Over the shark or crocodile pool", "Board the pirate ship!").

36 | Rope climbing and pull-ups

Muscles: Elbow flexors (biceps brachii), large back muscle (latissimus dorsi), hand muscles, and other muscles

Execution/Variations: Also on climbing pole or horizontal bar; climbing in inverted hanging position, particularly for pole vaulters; pull-up on the horizontal bar, etc.

37 | Brachiating

Muscles: Large back muscle (latissimus dorsi), chest muscles (pectoralis), hand muscles, and other muscles

Execution/Variations: Later omit several bars during brachiating; brachiating also on the horizontal bar or high parallel bars; brachiating in the inverted hanging position (for advanced athletes; see picture on the right).

38  Push-ups

Muscles: Chest muscles (pectoralis), elbow extensors (triceps), front part of the delta muscle (deltoideus), abdominal muscles, and other muscles

Execution: Ankle joint, knee, hips, shoulder and head form a line; no hollow back.

Variations: Hands close together or far apart; make it easier by placing knees on the ground and bending the knees, or standing tilted forward against the wall; on fingertips for finger strengthening for the crouch start; with very dynamic push-off from the ground and clapping of the hands; with hands on vibration platform.

39  Supporting and swinging on the parallel bars

Muscles: Chest muscles (pectoralis), broad back muscle (latissimus dorsi), delta muscle (deltoideus), elbow extensor (triceps), and other muscles

Execution/Variations: Initially move forward with the arms in supported position (above right picture), move hands forward alternately or by small jumps; move forward in the supported position while swinging the legs: push up on the bar, swing forward, place feet onto the bars in front of you, shift support of the hands forward over the support of the legs, swing forward again, etc.; swing forward and backward (see pictures on the left), initially with breaks in the push-up position (feet on the bars); swinging is done from the shoulders (hip is kept straight); later: backswing up to handstand; move vertically up and down in the arm-support position (dips; below right), initially also supported on a small box behind your back or with hands on a vibration platform; also possible on a specific strength-training machine.

40  **Backward rotation to tucked inverse hang, over-rotation, and return on rings, parallel bars, and horizontal bar**

Muscles: Chest muscles (pectoralis), broad back muscle (latissimus dorsi), delta muscle (deltoideus), hand muscles, and other muscles

Execution/Variations: Rings, parallel bars and horizontal bars initially just below reaching height; Backward rotation from a standing position is easier than from a hanging position; slow movement execution during the over-rotation (only so far that the return is still possible) and return; start backward rotation from a hanging position with a counter-swing.

Here, rockbacks (366) and cloud shifters (367) should also be mentioned, which are specific exercises for the pole vault. Nevertheless, these exercises are good whole-body strengthening exercises for jumpers, throwers, and sprinters, too.

41 **Stable prone position**

Muscles: Abdominal muscles, and other muscles

Execution/Variations: For all stable positions: Lift your foot; move raised leg upward, downward, to the left, and/or to the right, pull up your leg to the side, or circle it; move your hips up and down or to the left and to the right; while doing all this, vary or increase the speed of movement; support yourself on your hands; with feet on fitness ball or vibration platform; with hands on medicine ball or vibration platform; as so-called sling training with feet or hands in loops on ropes; move into the other stable positions without a break; in the stable prone (and supine) position: arms and legs further apart; lift your arm (and move it); run with your legs to the right and left, open and close your legs by performing a jumping movement, or jump to the right and left with closed legs; combine with push-ups.

42 Stable position on the side

Muscles: Abdominal and back muscles, abductors and adductors (depending on the variation), and other muscles

Execution/Variations: See 41; also with hand on the hip or extended toward your head; only upper or lower foot on the ground; bend your free leg and swing it back and forth, or perform gripping running movements with it; also opposite to arm movement: arm over head and knee to the back, knee forward, and elbow to knee.

43 Stable position on the back

Muscles: Back muscles, hip extensors, and other muscles

Execution/Variations: See 41; also inward and outward rotated foot; place shoulders on the ground and lift hips with knees bent at right angles, straighten legs alternately; place shoulders on the ground and lift hips with straight knees, while doing so also lift one leg and move it into the take-off position.

44 Abdominal crunches

Muscles: Abdominal muscles, hip flexors, and other muscles

Execution: Lift your shoulders and pelvis while lying on your back (see below on the right); when performing this exercise dynamically within one set, do not move your shoulders or hips completely to the ground if possible.

Variations: The further the arms are away from the pelvis, the higher the intensity; elevating the legs excludes hip flexors; possibly deliberate fixation of the feet to also train the hip flexors as synergists; also belly punches with tense abdominals to increase intensity (77).

131

45   █ **Lumborum exercise**

Muscles: Square lumbar muscle (quadratus lumborum), back and oblique abdominal muscles, and other muscles

Execution/Variations: Perform exercise on a mat or on a large box; the further the arms are away from the pelvis, the higher the intensity; with rotation (see pictures below); particularly when lying on a large box, advanced athletes can use additional weights.

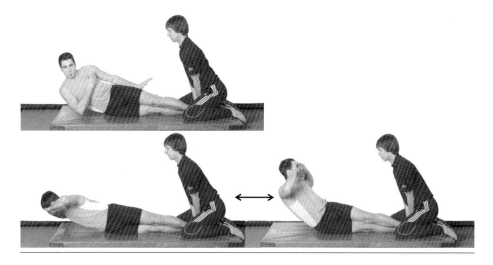

46 Back exercise on a box

Muscles: Back extensors (erector spinae), hip extensors (glutaeus and hamstrings), and other muscles

Execution/Variations: The further the arms are away from the pelvis, the higher the intensity (figures a–c); move your extended trunk up and down at the hip joint (not completely down to maintain tension) or roll it up vertebra by vertebra (figure e); keep your trunk lifted and rotate your shoulders about your body's longitudinal axis (figure d) or bend it to the left and right; hold your extended arms horizontally and form circles with a small weight, which you keep in your hands (move it from one hand to the other in front of your head and behind your back; figure f); fix only one leg to increase intensity (figure a).

47 Additional hip- and back-extensor exercises

Muscles: Back extensor (erector spinae) and hip extensors (glutes and hamstrings), and other muscles

Execution/Variations: While in prone position, lift your extended arms and legs and open and close them; while in prone or quadruped position, simultaneously lift one arm and the diagonally opposite leg (alternately; also with partner exerting pressure to increase intensity (77)); similar on a large box: alternate lifting and stretching of a leg (with or without additional weights); while in prone position on a large box: lifting of the extended or bent legs from the hip joint; while holding the back as flat as a table in knee-stand position; in quadruped position also raise leg to the side for strengthening the glutes (for intensification extend your leg at the highest point).

48   Flexors by frontward tilt

Muscles: Knee flexors (hamstrings and gastrocnemius), hip extensors (hamstrings and glutes), and back extensor (erector spinae)

Execution/Variations: Tilt slowly forward (at the knee joint), keep your hips straight, either reverse the movement as late as possible, or continue the tilt movement as slowly as possible and catch yourself with your hands.

49   Walking lunges and jumping lunges

Muscles: Knee extensors (quadriceps), hip extensors (hamstrings and glutes), and other muscles

Execution/Variations: Initially without, later with weight; on different surfaces (e.g., sand); walking lunges: while rising, lift the foot of the swinging leg over the knee of the supporting leg; tilt forward and perform a wide reaching-out movement with your lower leg into the next lunge (without pushing your knee over the tip of your foot); lateral variations (e.g., stepping sideways in the deep squat position); jumping lunges: either by jumping upwards over the front leg forward or in place: jump out of the lunge upwards, perform one ankle jump (84), and jump into the next lunge (switching legs); skating jumps: while moving forward on the 100m straight, the athlete jumps diagonally forward to the left and to the right between the boundary lines.

Just as the intensity of the walking lunge and other exercises can be increased by an additional weight, some of the barbell exercises, such as squats, can initially be performed without weight, particularly during the technical development.

50  Unstable ground

Muscles: Foot and calf muscles, and other muscles
Execution/Variations: Knee-lift stand or, for example, squat (62) on a gel pad, wobble board, Posturomed, soft floor mat, etc.; ABCs of sprinting/jumping, slalom runs, or tag games in the sand or on a soft floor mat.

51 Walking variations

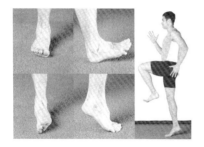

Muscles: Foot and calf muscles, and other muscles.
Execution/Variations: Walking on the heels, the balls of the feet, the outer or inner edges of the foot; with pronounced rolling-off (and rising up onto the toes); with rolling-off up to the knee-lift stand on the tip of the toe; on different surfaces (Tartan, grass, sand, etc.).

52 Toe exercises

Muscles: Toe muscles
Execution/Variations: Grab various objects; alternately clench and extend your toes; crawl with your toes in the sand.

5.4.3 TRAINING WITH A BARBELL OR DUMBBELL

53 ▢▢▨▨ Hand and forearm strengthening

Muscles: Finger and arm muscles (especially for throwing events and pole vault)
Execution/Variations: Lifting a barbell using the under- or overgrip; squeezing a tennis ball or a hand strengthening device.

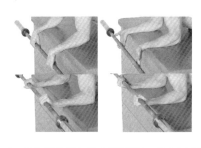

54 ▢▢▨■ (Inclined) bench press

Muscles: Chest muscles (pectoralis), elbow extensor (triceps brachii), front (and the higher the bank at the top end, the more also the upper) portion of the deltoid muscle
Execution/Variations: Lower the barbell to the chest (without touching it) and lift it up just before your elbows are straight (no full extension with loss of tension); later also as inclined bench press with the top end of the bench elevated (shot-put-specific) or with the top end of the bench lowered (declined bench; maximal stress on the chest muscles); if performed with dumbbells, the demands on coordination and shoulder stabilization are increased; also on specific strength-training machines.

55 ▢▢▨■ Butterfly

Muscles: Chest muscles (pectoralis), anterior portion of the deltoid muscle, elbow flexor (biceps brachii)

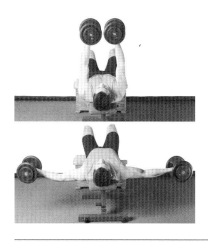

Execution/Variations: Do not lift your arms all the way up to the vertical position; also on specific strength-training machines.

56  Shoulder press

Muscles: Elbow extensor (triceps brachii), deltoid muscle, upper portion of the trapezius muscle
Execution/Variations: Lower the barbell to the chest (see pictures on the left) or to the neck (see picture on the right), lift the barbell until your elbows are almost straight (no complete extension with loss of tension); if performed with dumbbells, the demands on coordination and shoulder stabilisation are increased; also on specific strength-training machines; training of the deltoid also by lateral lifting of the arms or on a special deltoid machine.

57 Pull-overs

Muscles: Mainly broad back muscle (latissimus dorsi) and elbow extensor (triceps brachii)
Execution/Variations: If possible, do not perform the movement in such a way that you reach a vertical upper-arm and extended elbow position in order to maintain the tension of the muscles involved during the whole range of motion; also without barbell but with weight plate between

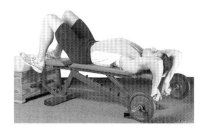

hands; to make training more specific for the javelin throw (and more complex), the buttocks can be slightly lifted during the backswing; for pole vault work with straight arms; very specific for the javelin or pole vault also with dumbbell in one hand and/or without support surface for the (upper part) of the trunk; also on special strength-training machines.

58 Bench pull

Muscles: Trapezius, rhomboid muscle, broad back muscle (latissimus dorsi), back portion of the deltoid muscle; if performed without support surface for the trunk (see pictures on the right), also back extensor (erector spinae), and hip extensor (glutes and hamstrings)

Execution/Variations: Lower the barbell until your elbows are almost straight (no complete extension with loss of tension); if performed with dumbbells, the demands on coordination and shoulder stabilization are increased.

59 Reverse butterfly

Muscles: Trapezius, rhomboid muscle, broad back muscle (latissimus dorsi), back portion of the deltoid muscle, elbow extensor (triceps brachii)

Execution/Variations: Lateral raising of the arms in prone position; also with inward rotated palms; also on a special strength-training machine.

60 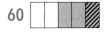 Running arm swing

Muscles: Mainly muscles of the shoulder joint
Execution/Variations: Also while holding rounders balls, nockenballs, or similar objects in one's hands.

61  Calf exercise

Muscles: Calf muscles (triceps surae)
Execution/Variations: On one or on two legs; initially without weight; on the balls of the feet, for example, on a bench, the top element of a box, or at wall bars; also on a special strength-training machine; also with bent legs on the appropriate machine (or with weights, or with partner on knees) to specifically train the uni-articular area (soleus).

62  Squats

a   b

c   d

Muscles: Knee extensor (quadriceps), hip extensor (glutes and hamstrings), back extensor (erector spinae), and other muscles
Execution/Variations: Squats differ in terms of holding the barbell [a: standard squat; b: frontal squat, resulting in slightly less stress on the lower back muscles; c: deadlift, with additional stress on the arms, shoulders, and neck; d: snatch squat as a preparation for the snatch (64), cannot be performed with very heavy loads], in terms of lowering depth [a, b, and d: full squat; c and h: half squat; e and f: quarter squat; a small box or the like (see e), can be used to standardise the lowering depth and increase security], and

139

whether they are performed with both legs (a-e) or one leg (f: stride squat; g and h: one-legged squat with free leg in front of or behind one's body; i: step-up, also with moving the swinging leg at increased horizontal speed forward against a wall; one-legged squats place increased demands on the stabilisation of the pelvis, especially g and h); also as a guided one- or two-legged leg press (j; backrest reduces stress on the lower back, but at the same time makes the exercise more non-specific); also with isolated hip extension as so-called "good mornings" (k: high stress on the lower back and hamstrings; [lower] spine is always kept straight).

63 Weightlifting techniques: clean and jerk

Muscles: Complete extensor loop, as well as many other muscles of the shoulder girdle

Execution: At first, clean (see the first five pictures below), then jerk (see the last four pictures below): from the lunge (next-to-last picture below), the front leg is extended and moved backward, only then the rear leg is moved forward; with low weights, the barbell can be lowered and caught at the waist, with high weights, the barbell is dropped from the high holding position in a controlled way.

Variations: Clean and jerk are also trained individually, performing several repetitions without rest; to work only at the joint angles typical for athletics, the movement is often begun only above the knee; as a preliminary exercise (narrow pull), the movement is only up to the third picture below, after which the barbell is caught at the hip; also as neck jerk with ankle jumps in stride position (see left).

64 ▭▨▨■ Weightlifting techniques: snatch

Muscles: Complete extensor loop, as well as many other muscles of the shoulder girdle; since in the snatch lighter weights are moved across a greater amplitude, this exercise is more speed-strength-oriented than the clean (63).

Execution: After the fourth picture, the athlete extends from the squat, and the lowering and catching or dropping of the barbell are performed from the high holding position (see clean and snatch, 63).

Variations: The movement is often begun only above the knees; as a preliminary exercise (snatch initiation or wide pull), the movement is carried out so far as shown in the right picture below, after which the barbell is caught at the hip; also as snatch into the lunge.

The techniques of weightlifting should be developed early in basic training. This is done by practising the movements at first with a broomstick or similar object.

5.4.4 MACHINE-SUPPORTED STRENGTH TRAINING

In many weight rooms, besides the machines shown in the following, there are also other machines which imitate the free-weight exercises mentioned above. These are not presented here. The guided movements on the machines are often safer and thus allow higher weights, but they are also significantly less challenging in respect to coordination. Therefore, the free-weight exercises should be introduced earlier, but initially only focusing on technique and without high loads.

65  **Lat-pull**

Muscles: Large chest muscle (latissimus dorsi), elbow flexor (biceps brachii), and other muscles
Execution/Variations: Pull toward the neck or chest; when pulling toward the chest, lean the trunk back for additional training of the erector spinae; undergrip or more narrow overgrip; some strength-training machines allow unilateral training (see picture on the right), which means more intense training of the trunk muscles.

66 **Abdominal machine**

Muscles: Straight and oblique abdominal muscles (abdomini), and other muscles
Execution/Variations: One hand or both hands on handles and one or both feet behind the pad; if only a foot and a hand exert force, then usually the diagonally opposite limbs (right picture).

67 ▢▢▢■ Hip-shoulder twist

Muscles: Oblique abdominal muscles (obliqui abdomini), and diagonal portions of the back extensor (erector spinae)

Execution/Variations: Also possible with a barbell: standing upright with a barbell on one's shoulders, knees are slightly flexed, shoulder axis is twisted away from the hip axis, and with fast reversal in the other direction; or place the barbell upright in front of your body, grasp it with your arms extended in front of your body, and tilt the barbell with straight arms alternately to the left and right.

68 ▢▢▨■ Flexor exercises

Muscles: Knee flexors (hamstrings and gastrocnemius), and other muscles

Execution/Variations: With one leg (see top picture on the left) or with two legs (see middle picture on the left); with knees on the pad or lifted from the pad (see bottom picture on the left); also as flexor sliding (see bottom pictures on the right), with the foot being placed on a mobile object (e.g., on a weight plate on smooth surface) and drawn under one's body; when lifting the knee and during flexor sliding, the hamstrings are stressed in respect to their two functions: hip extension and knee flexion.

69 **Extensor exercise**

Muscles: Knee extensors (quadriceps)
Execution/Variations: One- or two-legged knee extension.

70 **Adductor exercises**

Muscles: Hip adductors
Execution/Variations: On a special machine or cable machine (with pull in front of or behind one's support leg).

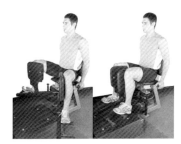 

71 **Abductor exercises**

Muscles: Hip abductors
Execution/Variations: On a special machine or cable machine (with pull in front of or behind one's support leg).

72 Glute exercises

Muscles: Mainly hip extensors (glutes, etc.)
Execution/Variations: On a special machine or (rather stabilising and as imitation) on the cable machine.

73 Hip-flexor exercise

Muscles: Hip flexors (iliopsoas and tensor fasciae latae), and many other muscles as stabilisers
Execution/Variations: On special machine or cable machine.

74 Foot-lifting exercise

Muscles: Front muscles of the tibia (tibialis anterior), and other muscles
Execution/Variations: With one leg or with two legs, lifting the feet alternately or simultaneously; initially also without elastic band; also circling the feet while sitting or standing.

75 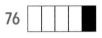 **Jump- and sprint-specific strength training** (according to Hutt [1992])

Muscles/*Execution/Variations:* Strength in sprint- and jump-specific joint angles, body positions and movements, depending on the respective exercise.

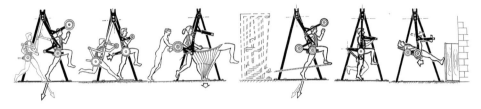

76 **Sprint-strength training** (according to Tidow & Wiemann [1994])

Muscles: Hip flexors (iliopsoas, etc.) and hip extensors (glutes and hamstrings)
Execution/Variations: One machine is for training hip extension on the left side and hip flexion on the right side, while another machine is for training hip extension on the right side and hip flexion on the left side.

5.4.5 STRENGTH TRAINING AGAINST PARTNER RESISTANCE

77 **Partner exercises**

Execution: During eccentric training, the partner or coach should countdown "2-1-Go", and the exerciser should try to contract the respective muscles maximally and isometrically already during this phase.
Muscles/Variations: a–c: stabilisation exercises (41–43) with partner exerting pressure; d: lifting opposite upper and lower limbs while in

prone position with partner exerting pressure (back extensors, hip extensors, and shoulder muscles); e: abdominals (as well as hip flexors and shoulder muscles); f–g: belly punches with tense abdominals; h–j: hamstrings (h: with co-contractions of the hip flexors, knee placed on the mat; i–j: with co-contractions of the hip extensors; i: knees lifted); k–m: hip abductors; n–o: hip adductors; p: hip flexors; q: dorsal flexors of the foot; r: toe extensors; s: chest muscles.

Examples of strictly manual resistances:

Examples of combined resistances (for intensifying the eccentric phase):

5.4.6 FORMS OF JUMPING

78  **Hopping, limping, and jumping games: French skipping, hopscotch, etc.**

Muscles: Extensor loop, and other muscles
Execution: Children often invent their own rules for hopping and limping games; the line drawings should be understood only as suggestions.
Variations: Many of the games mentioned in the running section of this book can be varied as one- or two-legged limping or hopping games (e.g., relays).

---

79 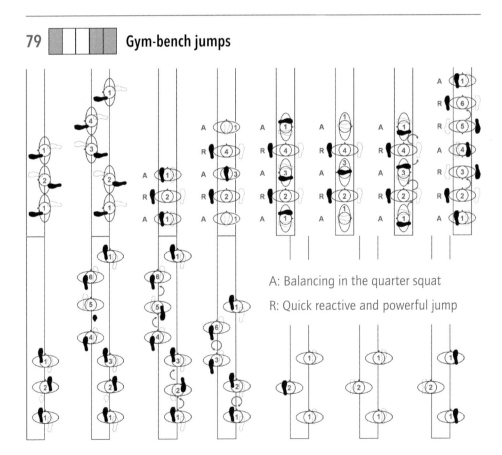 **Gym-bench jumps**

A: Balancing in the quarter squat

R: Quick reactive and powerful jump

Muscles: Complete extensor loop

Execution/Variations: Quick reactive jumps at a gym bench, on the spot, or while moving forward along the bench; the jumping sequences should be performed increasingly faster with time.

80  Rope jumping

Muscles: Calf muscles (triceps surae), knee extensors (quadriceps), muscles of the lower arm, and other muscles

Execution/Variations: With one leg and with both legs; with the focus on jumping frequency or jumping height; while crossing one's arms and return; with intermediate hop; while swinging the rope through twice per jump; while running; partners swing a long rope.

81 Small jumps for strengthening the feet

Muscles: Mainly calf muscles and other foot (joint) muscles

Execution/Variations: Small jumps forward and backward, to the left and to the right, by opening and closing the legs, in the triangle, rectangle, and pentagon, with inward or outward rotated foot position, with quarter or half turns (forward and backward), with one leg or two legs, on various surfaces, etc.

82 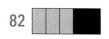 Squat-extension jumps, start jumps, and Tscherbakis (split jumps)

Muscles: Complete extensor loop (see above)

Execution/Variations: Squat jumps (see left two pictures): forward and backward, for distance or height, with intermediate static holding phase (speed strength), or with quick reversal (reactive

strength); start jumps (see right two pictures): with switch of legs in the air so that when landing the other leg is in front; Tscherbakis: the athlete takes off from both legs, splits his/her legs in the air like after a take-off from one leg, and lands again on both legs side by side (see line drawing); for performance athletes also with additional load (weighted vest, sandbag, or barbell on one's shoulders).

A part of the ABCs of jumping shall be presented only in the chapter on jumps (see II-2). Those forms of jumping which, as reactive multi-jumps are the main element of the reactive-strength training of all sprints, jumps, and throws, are described here.

83 ABCs of jumping: Galloping sideways

Muscles: Mainly calf muscles and other foot and ankle joint muscles; adductors and abductors of the hip

Execution: Keep legs as straight as possible; pull up your toes in the air; arms swing outwards during a jump and during the next jump, they swing inward again.

Variations: For distance, height, or speed; with or without armswing.

84 ABCs of jumping: Ankle jumps

Muscles: Calf muscles (triceps surae), knee extensors (quadriceps)

Execution: Knees and hips as fixed as possible, short ground contact; pull up your toes in the air.

Variations: On the spot, forward, backward, and sideways; with quarter-turns; with and without the use of the arms; for height or frequency; with the support of the hands on a large gym box (and bending at the hip) to increase the height; the partner or coach can grasp the forearms of the athlete and cause the athlete to land with higher vertical velocity by intensifying the downward or upward movement.

85 ABCs of jumping: Tuck jumps and depth jumps

Muscles: Compare ankle jumps, with tuck jumps also hip flexors and extensors

Execution: When doing tuck jumps, lift knees in front of your body instead of under your body.

Variations: When performing depth jumps, the intensity is determined by the height of the take-off which should correspond to the jumper's abilities so that there is still brief ground contact; the similar is applicable to the hurdle height when performing tuck jumps (i.e., the hurdles should only be so high that the ground contact is brief enough); sprinters in particular should also increase the distance between the hurdles with time.

86   ABCs of jumping: Skipping with two-legged landing

Muscles: Compare above, complete extensor loop of the trunk and of the lower extremities, and other muscles

Execution: As with ankle jumps, the landing occurs on both feet, but alternately one leg breaks contact with the ground earlier so that the reactive take-off ends in the take-off position which is typical of one-legged take-offs.

Variations: For height or distance; forward, backward, or sideways.

87   ABCs of jumping: Skipping (with one-legged landing)

Muscles: All sprinting and jumping muscles

Execution: One-legged take-offs from the whole foot with landing on the take-off leg, in each case followed by a stride and take-off from the other leg.

Variations: For height, distance, or speed; while stressing the left or right leg; with deliberately gripping touchdown of the foot; forward, backward, or sideways; straight, through the curve, or in slalom fashion; with or without the use of arms; with double armswing.

88 ABCs of jumping: Bounding run

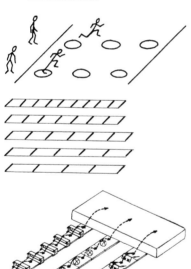

Muscles: All sprinting and jumping muscles

Execution: Each stride as longest jump possible with touchdown of the whole foot (some coaches demand an exclusive ball contact specific to sprinting; in any case, the touchdown must be performed actively from the previously flexed tip of the foot).

Variations: (Initially) over mats, medicine balls, mini hurdles, with markings, or through hoops placed on the ground for setting the stride length, etc.; in competitive game form ("Who can cover a fixed distance with the fewest jumps?"); first from a standing position, then from several preliminary walking steps, later from a run-up; with deliberately gripping touchdown of the foot; with emphasis on one side; with a slight pulling resistance (see 137).

89 ▢▢▢▰▰ **ABCs of jumping: One-legged jumps (hops) and rhythm jumps**

Muscles: All sprinting and jumping muscles

Execution/Variations: As in the bounding run, each ground contact is performed with a take-off as powerful as possible from the entire foot (flex tip of the foot before the touchdown); for one-legged jumps exclusively on one leg (for advanced triple jumpers also with extended swing leg during its backward movement); rhythm jumps are a combination of bounding runs and one-legged jumps which are performed with a certain rhythm (e.g., l-r-l-l-r, r-r-l-l-r-r-l-l, r-r-r-l-l-r-r-r-l-l, or r-r-r-l-l-l-r-r-r-l-l-l, etc.; for intensity control, see table 13).

90 ▢▢▢▢▢ **Jumps on various surfaces**

Execution/Variations: Barefoot, in running shoes or spikes; on sand, mat path, grass, synthetic surface, etc.: the softer the ground, the less reactive and powerful is the load; the stress on the elastic component is lower on soft ground, resulting in the possibility of performing more jumps, however, the stress on the elastic component is often desirable to trigger respective adaptations; the coordination demands and adaptations also differ depending on the surface (see details in chapter II-2.1.4).

91 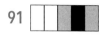 Uphill jumps and jumps onto a box

Muscles: Extensor loop (emphasis on the concentric phase)

Execution/Variations: Vertical jumps, usually with both legs, onto a box or in a staircase [see squat-extension jumps (82), or ankle jumps (84)] must be distinguished from more horizontally oriented uphill jumps [see skipping (87), bounding runs (88), one-legged and rhythm jumps (89)]; the latter ones can also be performed on stairs consisting of longitudinally placed boxes instead of on a rising slope.

92 Downhill jumps and depth jumps

Muscles: Extensor loop (emphasising the eccentric phase)

Execution/Variations: The absorption of depth jumps (e.g., from a box) must be distinguished from horizontally oriented multiple jumps (e.g., skipping [87], bounding runs [88], one-legged and rhythm jumps [89]) on a descending slope; the absorption of depth jumps is also performed after a previous jump onto a box/after previous jumps onto boxes.

Table 13: **Classification of multiple jumping forms:** *With children, the less intensive forms are first introduced.*

Low intensity (less stressful for structures) higher volume = more metres and/or repetitions		High intensity (more stressful for structures) lower volume = fewer metres and/or repetitions
on soft surface		on hard surface
from the stand	from a walk-up	from a run-up
uphill/jumps onto a box	on level ground	downhill/depth jumps
without additional load		with additional load
with leg switch (bounding run	rhythm jumps	without leg switch one-legged jumps)

5.4.7 THROWS

Many throws from speed-strength, reactive-strength, and technique training of the throwing events are presented only in the second part of this book with the appropriate disciplines. However, the throwing forms that are crucial for speed-strength, reactive-strength, and stabilisation training for all athletes have already been presented here.

93 Tossing

Muscles: Complete extensor loop, delta muscle (deltoideus), and other muscles

Execution/Variations: Forward, upward, or backward; with medicine ball, shot, stone, etc.; with powerful take-off forward or backward and landing on a soft floor mat.

94 Goalkeeper throws

Muscles: Abdominal muscles (abdominis), chest muscles (pectoralis), broad back muscle (latissimus dorsi), and other muscles

Execution: Ball is thrown by a partner, caught by

the athlete over his/her head, and returned as quickly as possible, powerfully and flat.
Variations: Slightly diagonal throws.

95  **Rotation throws**

Muscles: Straight and oblique abdominal muscles (abdominis), delta muscle (deltoideus), and other muscles
Execution: The ball thrown by a partner or rebounded from a wall is caught above the knees; then the athlete reaches out (approximately 90° about the longitudinal axis of his/her body, looking at the ball), reverses the direction of his/her movement, and throws the ball back.
Variations: With legs on the ground or raised: In the first instance, there is less stress on the straight abdominal muscles and the hip flexors; however, the oblique abdominal and back muscles can apply more force due to the abutment.

96 **Forward throws from a prone position**

Muscles: Back extensor and backward shoulder muscles
Execution: The partner rolls balls toward the exerciser; the exerciser must throw each ball over the next ball rolling toward him/her.
Variations: Legs are fixed or not fixed (by fixing the legs, the hip extensors can also be used).

5.5 FOLLOWING UP ON EXERCISE

UTILISATION, WARM-DOWN JOGGING, AND/OR FLEXIBILITY TRAINING

Utilisation refers to terminating each training session with reactive and powerful stress, speed, or high-intensity stress which is very similar to the target technique to remind the CNS of the coordination and speed of the target movement. It is also recommended to perform flexibility training at the end of a training session (rather than as a part of the warm-up). Traditionally, however, at the end of the training session, most athletes go for a warm-down jog. Through this relaxed, regenerative, endurance run, which can also be interrupted by some walking breaks, the cardiopulmonary activity is maintained slightly longer or triggered again. Due to an increase in blood flow to the muscles, regeneration is accelerated. Moreover, the muscles are loosened up, and the muscle tone is reduced. Often, an increase in the general well-being is also observed.

But how can the three subjects mentioned in the title be best used and combined? After coordination, reactive and powerful (or speed) exercises, which (at least to some extent) are aimed at causing adaptations of the nervous system, it often appears to be most sensible to keep the stimulus on the muscles. Utilisation is unnecessary, and warm-down jogging and flexibility training would destroy this effect. For the same reason, warm-down jogging and flexibility training are not recommended after utilisation. Utilisation and warm-down jogging appear to be especially useful after extensive strength and endurance exercise. Flexibility training should be performed mainly in the general preparation phase. Since both the main training content as well as intensive flexibility training can possibly destroy tissue structures, there may be too much risk of injury when this training is followed by utilisation using reactive and powerful or speed exercises. Thus, the combination of the three contents is not consistently possible all the time. However, the training plans presented in the discipline-specific part of this book provide some examples of how these contents can be incorporated into training.

PASSIVE REGENERATIVE MEASURES

Due to the great amount of training performed by performance athletes, it is often necessary to support recovery through additional passive measures. Here, for example, self-massage, hot baths, sauna rounds, etc. should be mentioned. In high-performance sports, often more costly measures, such as massage, electrical stimulation, and other physiotherapy and osteopathy methods are also applied. However, even for these measures there are good days and bad days within the training week since they may have an influence on the next training session or on the desired effects of the previous session. Last, but not least, sleep and nutrition also determine the regeneration process.

6 BIBLIOGRAPHY - PART I

Bundesministerium für Familie, Senioren, Frauen und Jugend & Deutsche Sportjugend (Hrsg.). (2009). *Vielseitigkeitswettbewerb der Grundsportart Leichtathletik*. Zugriff am 18.04.2011 unter http://www.bundesjugendspiele.de/cgi-bin/showcontent. asp?ThemaID=4528.

Blum, I & Friedmann K. (1997). *Trainingslehre. Sporttheorie für die Schule*. Pfullingen: Promos.

Boeckh-Behrends, W.-U. & Buskies, W. (2001). *Fitness-Krafttraining: Die besten Übungen und Methoden für Sport und Gesundheit*. Reinbek: Rowohlt.

Bührle, M. (Hrsg.). (1985). *Grundlagen des Maximal- und Schnellkrafttrainings*. Schorndorf: Hoffmann.

Bauersfeld, K. H. & Schröter, G. (1998). *Grundlagen der Leichtathletik*. Berlin: Sportverlag.

De Marées, H. (2003). *Sportphysiologie*. Köln: Sport und Buch Strauß.

De Morree, J. J. (2001). *Dynamik des menschlichen Bindegewebes: Funktion, Schädigung und Wiederherstellung*. München: Urban & Fischer.

Deutscher Leichtathletikverband & Internationaler Leichtathletikverband (Hrsg.). (2004). *Fun & Kids' athletics*. Zugriff am 01.03.2008 unter http://www.kidsathletics.de.

Eberspächer, H. (2004). *Mentales Training: Ein Handbuch für Trainer und Sportler*. München: Stiebener.

Ehlenz, H., Grosser, M. & Zimmermann, E. (2003). *Krafttraining: Grundlagen, Methoden, Übungen, Leistungssteuerung, Trainingsprogramme*. München: BLV.

Gerling, I. E. (2007). *Basisbuch Gerätturnen* (5. Aufl.). Aachen: Meyer & Meyer.

Grosser, M. & Starischka, S. (1998). *Das neue Konditionstraining*. München: BLV.

Güllich, A. (1996). *Schnellkraftleistungen im unmittelbaren Anschluss an maximale und submaximale Krafteinsätze* (Berichte und Materialien des Bundesinstitut für Sportwissenschaft, 14). Köln: Sport und Buch Strauß.

Harre, D. (1970). *Trainingslehre*. Berlin: Sportverlag.

Hill, A. V. (1951). The mechanics of voluntary muscle. *Lancet 261*, 947.

Hohmann, A., Lames, M. & Letzelter, M. (2003). *Einführung in die Trainingswissenschaft*. Wiebelsheim: Limpert.

Hollmann, W. (1967). Zur Trainingslehre: Muskuläre Beanspruchungsformen und ihre leistungsbegrenzenden Faktoren. *Sportarzt und Sportmedizin 11*, 443-452.

Hollmann, W. (Hrsg.). (1995). *Lexikon der Sportmedizin*. Heidelberg: Johann Ambrosius Barth.

Hollmann, W. & Strüder, H. K. (2009). *Sportmedizin. Grundlagen für körperliche Aktivität, Training und Präventivmedizin*. Stuttgart: Schattauer.

Hollmann, W., Strüder, H. K., Predel, H. G. & Tagarakis, C. (2006). *Spiroergometrie – Kardiopulmonale Leistungsdiagnostik des Gesunden und Kranken*. Stuttgart: Schattauer.

Hollmann, W., Strüder, H. K., Rojas Vega, S., Tagarakis, C. V. & Diehl, J. (2007). Gehirn – körperliche Aktivität und ihre Bedeutung für die Gehirngesundheit und -leistungsfähigkeit. *Österreichisches Journal für Sportmedizin 4*, 6-24.

Hollmann, W., Strüder, H. K. & Tagarakis, C. V. M. (2005). Gehirn und körperliche Aktivität. *Sportwissenschaft 35*, 3-14.

Hollmann, W., Strüder, H. K. & Tagarakis, C. V. M. (2003). Übertraining – ein Resultat der Hirnplastizität? *Deutsche Zeitschrift für Sportmedizin 54*, 25-26.

Hollmann, W., Strüder, H. K., Tagarakis, C. V. M., King, G. & Diehl, J. (2006). Das Gehirn – der leistungsbegrenzende Faktor bei Ausdauerbelastungen? *Deutsche Zeitschrift für Sportmedizin 57*, 155-160.

Hutt, E. (1992). Dreisprung für Praktiker II: Das Training. *Die Lehre der Leichtathletik 31* (21), 15-18, (22), 15-18 & (24), 15-16.

Jakowlew, N. N. (1977). *Sportbiochemie*. Leipzig: Barth.

Kandel, E. R., Schwartz, J. H. & Jessell, T. M. (Hrsg.). (1995). *Neurowissenschaften*. Heidelberg: Spektrum Akademischer.

Kieser, W. (2003). *Ein starker Rücken kennt keinen Schmerz: Gesundheitsorientiertes Krafttraining nach der Kieser-Methode*. München: Heyne.

Killing, W. (2008). Besonderheiten im Training von Frauen. *Leistungssport 38* (1), 6-12.

Mader, A. (1990). Aktive Belastungsadaptation und Regulation der Proteinsynthese auf zellulärer Ebene. Ein Beitrag zum Mechanismus der Trainingswirkung und der Kompensation von funktionellen Mehrbelastungen von Organen. *Deutsche Zeitschrift für Sportmedizin 41*, 40.

Mader, A. (2002). Die Zeit im Sport – Die Geburt und Herrschaft eines Prinzips des Hochleistungssport, in den Sportwissenschaften und in der Gesellschaft aus der

Sicht der eigenen überschaubaren Zeit. In B. Ränsch-Trill, *Zeit und Geschwindigkeit: Sportliches Erleben in beschleunigten Prozessen* (Brennpunkt der Sportwissenschaften, 24) St. Augustin: Academia.

Martin, D., Carl, K. & Lehnertz, K. (1991). *Handbuch Trainingslehre*. Schorndorf: Hofmann.

Meinel, K. & Schnabel, G.(1998). *Bewegungslehre*. Berlin: Sportverlag.

Ministerium für Schule und Weiterbildung des Landes Nordrhein-Westfalen (MSW NRW, Hrsg.). (2001). *Sekundarstufe I. Gymnasium. Sport. Richtlinien und Lehrpläne* (Schule in NRW, Nr. 3426, 1. Aufl.). Frechen: Ritterbach.

Nett, T. (1960). *Das Übungs- und Trainingsbuch der Leichtathletik, Bd. 1: Der Lauf*. Berlin: Bartels und Wernitz.

Neumaier, A., Mechling, H. & Strauß, R. (2002). *Koordinative Anforderungsprofile ausgewählter Sportarten. Analyse, Variationsprinzipien, Trainingsbeispiele zu Leichtathletik, Fußball, Judo, Alpiner Skilauf, Rudern* (Training der Bewegungskoordination). Köln: Sport und Buch Strauß.

Nicholls, J. G., Martin, A. R. & Wallace, B. G. (1995). *Vom Neuron zum Gehirn*. Stuttgart: Gustav Fischer.

Boss, N. (Hrsg.) (1993). *Roche-Lexikon Medizin* (3. Aufl.). München: Urban und Schwarzenburg.

Roux, W. (1895). *Gesammelte Abhandlungen über Entwicklungsmechanik der Organismen: Erster Band: Abhandlungen I-XII, vorwiegend über Functionelle Anpassung*. Leipzig: Wilhelm Engelmann.

Schlumberger, A. (2000): *Optimierung von Trainingsstrategien im Schnellkrafttraining* (Bundesinstitut für Sportwissenschaften, Wissenschaftliche Berichte und Materialien 6). Köln: Sport und Buch Strauß.

Schmidtbleicher, D. (1985). Klassifizierung der Trainingsmethoden im Krafttraining. *Lehre der Leichtathletik 24*, 25-30.

Schnabel, G., Harre, D., Krug, J. & Borde, A. (2002). *Trainingswissenschaft*. Berlin: Sportverlag.

Schöllhorn, W. (2003). *Eine Sprint- und Laufschule für alle Sportarten*. Aachen: Meyer & Meyer.

Schöllhorn, W. (2005). Differenzielles Lehren und Lernen von Bewegung - Durch veränderte Annahmen zu neuen Konsequenzen. In H. Gabler, U. Göhner & F. Schiebl (Hrsg.), *Zur Vernetzung von Forschung und Lehre in Biomechanik, Sportmotorik und Trainingswissenschaft* (S. 125-135). Hamburg: Czwalina.

Scholz, K.: Ein "Leistungsport-Manifest". *Leichtathletiktraining 18 (7)*, 36-39.

Strüder, H. K. (2003). The serotonergic system: implications for overtraining and exercise-induced eating disorders. *European Journal of Sport Science 3* (1), 1-21.

Strüder, H. K. (Gast-Hrsg.). (2001). "Gehirn und körperliche Aktivität". *Deutsche Zeitschrift für Sportmedizin 12*.

Tepper, E. & Czingon, H. (Red.). (1995). *Rahmentrainingsplan für das Aufbautraining Sprint* (Edition Leichtathletik, 2). Aachen: Meyer & Meyer.

Thompson, R. F. (1992). *Das Gehirn*. Heidelberg: Spektrum Akademischer.

Tidow, G. & Wiemann, K. (1994). Zur Optimierung des Sprintlaufs – leistungsdiagnostische Aspekte und trainingspraktische Folgerungen. *Leistungssport 24* (6), 11-16.

Vonstein, W. & Massin, D. (2001). *Fun in Athletics*. Aachen: Meyer & Meyer.

Überkert, S. & Joch, W. (2007). The effects of warm-up and pre-cooling on endurance performance in high ambient temperatures. *New Studies in Athletics 22*, 33-39.

Weineck, J. (2007). *Optimales Training*. Balingen: Spitta.

PART II

EVENT-SPECIFIC ASPECTS OF ATHLETICS

1 RUNNING

1.1 COMMON FEATURES AND COMPARISON OF RUNNING DISCIPLINES

1.1.1 THE MOST IMPORTANT GENERAL COMPETITION RULES

The following abridged and simplified International Competition Rules comprise the framework for the techniques and strategy, as well as the organisation of running events:

- Running events should usually be performed on a 400m circular arc track with an artificial surface.
- The track consists of two parallel straight lines and two bends with equal radii.
- The field-event area is on the left in relation to the running direction.
- Boundary lines in athletics are normally 5cm wide, which also applies to the boundary lines of the lanes, the start lines, and finish lines.
- The length of the track is measured from the edge of the start line away from the finish to the edge of the finish line near the start. The measurement is taken 30cm outward from the inner kerb and, in the other lanes, 20cm from the line marking the inside of the track.
- The competitors may participate in all competitions barefoot or with footwear on one or both feet. They are allowed to wear spikes, each shoe with

up to 11 spikes up to 9mm in length. The organising committee, however, may limit the length of the spikes to 6mm.

- All runs are started by a shot from a starting gun (or by another approved starting signal). A false start is signalled by a second shot.
- The time is recorded at the moment in which a competitor crosses the perpendicular plane of the finish line with any part of his/her trunk.
- Three alternative methods of keeping time are recognised as being official:
  - » Hand timing: The timekeepers start their watches when they see the start signal (flash or smoke emission from the starting gun). The time is rounded up to the next higher tenth of a second (e.g., 10.11 => 10.2).
  - » Fully automatic timing with finish photo: If possible, this should always be used. The starting signal is recorded automatically. The finish camera should record at least 100 frames per second. The time is usually rounded up to the next higher hundredth of a second.
  - » Fully automatic timing with

transponder system: Only for races that do not take place entirely in a stadium. The starting signal is recorded automatically. The transponder is attached to the shirt or shoes of the runner. The system detects the crossing of the finish line fully automatically by means of the transponder. The time from crossing the starting line to the finish line of the event may be announced to the runner, but is not officially required.
- A runner is disqualified,
  » if he/she initiates the starting motion after taking his/her final

starting position and before the shot, or if he/she touches the ground in the running direction beyond the starting line; or
  » if he/she bumps into or hinders another runner.
- According to the number of participants, there may be heats as well as intermediate runs and semi-finals. The International Competition Rules specify guidelines for the number of runs and the number of participants, which runners are to participate in these runs, and who will qualify for the next round (time or place).

1.1.2 SPORT-SCIENCE FINDINGS, PHASE STRUCTURE, AND TECHNIQUE

HOW TO DISTINGUISH BETWEEN SPRINTING, MIDDLE- AND LONG-DISTANCE RUNNING, AND WALKING

In the title of chapter 1, running is used as a general term for sprinting, middle and long distances, and the walking disciplines. However, in other instances, running is used in a narrow sense especially for endurance running as opposed to sprinting and/or walking.

The distinction between sprinting and middle- and long-distance running on the one hand, and walking on the other is simple. While in sprinting and endurance running, there is a flight phase between the one-legged support phases; this must not be true for walking. The occurrence of flight phases during walking is prohibited in the official competition rules of athletics

and is punishable by disqualification (see chapter II-1.14).

The difference between the (long) sprint and (middle-distance) running is defined by the IAAF as follows: All runs, including the 400m race, which are started from starting blocks are sprints, whereas all longer runs which are started from a standing position are part of middle- and long-distance running. From the point of view of sport science, the distinction is more difficult. For example, from a specific point of view, the 800m race can also be defined as a long sprint. A possible distinction is based on technique: When running (in the narrow sense), the whole foot touches the ground during ground contact, whereas when sprinting only the ball of the foot touches the ground. However, so-called "front-foot runners" exist both among elite 10,000m runners and among recreational joggers. While in the case of joggers this should be regarded as uneconomic and as a technical error which places too much stress on the passive structures, it is a worthwhile technique for elite 10,000m runners due to their high average speed.

Therefore, the technique criterion described for the distinction between running and sprinting cannot be fully maintained. A distinction in terms of physiology is more adequate. Whereas during sprinting, the energy is drawn primarily from anaerobic metabolism, middle- and long- distance running is primarily dependent on aerobic energy provision (see chapter I–1.5). *Since the proportions of the energy supply routes continuously change, the transition from sprinting to (endurance) running is also fluent* (see figure 1).

GENERAL PHASE STRUCTURE OF THE RUNNING STRIDE

FLIGHT AND SUPPORT PHASES

The support phase is that period in which the athlete touches the ground with one foot. As described above, there is a flight phase between the individual support phases both when sprinting and running for endurance. Thus, phases without drive (flight phases) and those in which propulsive forces can be exchanged with the ground (support phases) can be distinguished.

FRONT AND REAR SUPPORT AND SWING PHASE

A rather technical distinction between phases is based on the movement cycle of one leg (see figure 2). The actions of the rest of the body, especially of the arms and of the other leg, are then described with reference to the leg considered.

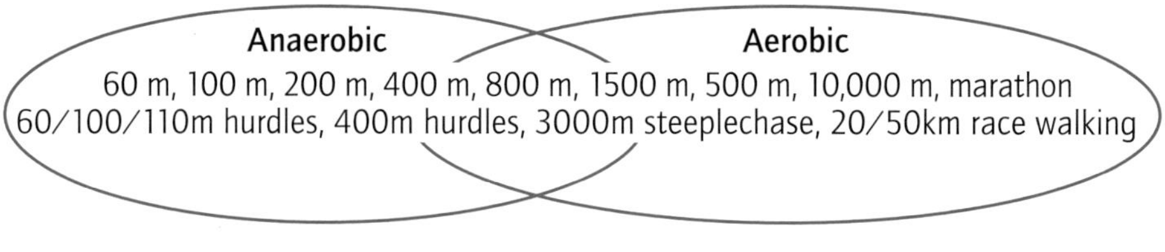

Anaerobic ⟶⟵ Aerobic
60 m, 100 m, 200 m, 400 m, 800 m, 1500 m, 500 m, 10,000 m, marathon
60/100/110m hurdles, 400m hurdles, 3000m steeplechase, 20/50km race walking

*Figure 1: **Simplified presentation of the overlapping anaerobic and aerobic performance zones** (modified on the basis of Jonath et al., 1995, p. 167).*

*Table 1: **Best times of the former world-class 400m hurdler Harald Schmid** (best time in the hurdles: 47.48 sec), with very good performances throughout the anaerobic performance range, **and of the former 2000, 3000, and 5000m world-record holder Said Aouita** (additional best times of Aouita: 1000 m: 2:15.78 min, mile: 3:46.76 min, 2000 m: 4:50.81 min, 3000 m: 7:29.45 min, 3000m steeplechase: 8:13.21 min) with very good performances throughout the aerobic performance range (and still respectable performances in the anaerobic performance range).*

	100 m	200 m	400 m	800 m	1500 m	5000 m	10,000 m
H. S.	10.30 sec	20.68 sec	44.92 sec	1:44.83 min			
S. A.	10.80 sec	21.23 sec	45.85 sec	1:43.86 min	3:29.46 min	12:58.39 min	27:26.11 min

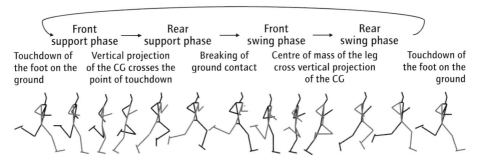

*Figure 2: **Phases of the running stride and their transitions** (CG = centre of gravity or centre of mass; picture sequence of a 10,000m runner, modified on the basis of Enomoto et al., 2008).*

Although the technique of the individual phases in the sprint as well as in the middle- and long-distance events is different, the phase structure remains always the same. Although the athlete can produce propulsion only during the support phase (see ground reaction forces below), it should be noted from the point of view of training methodology that no phase enjoys a priority. In each phase errors may occur, which in most cases also have a negative effect on the next phase. *The generation of propulsion during the support phase is only successful if it is usefully prepared in the swing phase.* Moreover, an optimal technical execution of all phases is based on the principle of economy (see below).

RUNNING VELOCITY = STRIDE FREQUENCY X STRIDE LENGTH

The duration of one stride results from the duration of a support phase plus the duration of a flight phase. Stride frequency is the reciprocal value of stride duration (i.e., one divided by the stride duration in seconds). Stride length is the distance in the direction of running from the tip of the foot during a support phase up to the tip of the foot during the next support phase. Running velocity results from the product of stride frequency and stride length or just from stride length divided by stride duration.

However, stride frequency and stride length are not independent variables. In the short term, the improvement of one of these quantities causes the deterioration of the other. Longer and slower strides require a longer (i.e., higher) flight phase which in turn requires a stronger push-off in the vertical direction. Moreover, the higher drop height must also be absorbed in the next front support. This exertion of force perpendicular to the main direction of movement, which in extreme form can result in a sort of jumping stride, can be regarded as an unnecessary use of energy. However, the ground contact time is also shorter in the event of shorter and faster strides, and thus there is less time to produce force in the main horizontal movement direction. *It is therefore important to find an individually optimal ratio of the two quantities.* In the long term, an improvement of both variables is desired to increase running velocity—or at least the improvement of one of the two quantities without being (too much) at the expense of the other.

GENERAL CHARACTERISTICS OF GROUND REACTION FORCES

Ground reaction forces (i.e., the force exerted by the athlete onto the ground) can be measured by running over measuring plates placed in the ground. Looking at the ground reaction forces during the support phases of a running stride, clear similarities can be observed which also occur similarly in the jumps. The generalised presentation of the ground reaction forces in figure 3 can be supplemented by the following general description:

- The ground contact time (= duration of the support phase = width of the curves in the direction of the time axis) is shorter when sprinting at high

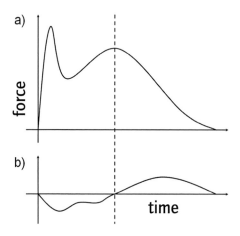

Figure 3: Generalised presentation of a) vertical and b) horizontal ground reaction forces during running.

speed than in jumping, after a crouch start, or during running.

- The vertical ground reaction forces are much higher than the horizontal ones. This applies both to the force maxima as well as to the whole force impulse (area under the curve). This is, for example, extreme in world-class sprinters during the maximum-velocity phase: In a study, their vertical peak value (approx. 4500 N) was about nine times as high as the peak value in the horizontal direction (approx. 500 N). Thus, despite a very flat angle of departure (3° during the phase of maximum velocity in the 100m sprint), the runner is more concerned with overcoming gravity than with generating propulsion.
- The forces in the horizontal direction are initially negative (projection below the time axis in the lower diagram) and then positive (projection above the time axis). This means that the athlete initially decelerates and then accelerates during the support phase. This phase boundary can be roughly equated with the relative position of the foot touchdown to the vertical projection of the CG. As long as the point of touchdown (centre of pressure) of the foot is in front of the body, more precisely in front of the vertical projection of the CG, the athlete decelerates. If the point of touchdown is behind the body or behind the vertical projection of CG, the athlete can accelerate. This is also a more detailed explanation of the previously established distinction

between the front and rear support phase (figure 2). In figure 3, the transition between the front and rear support phase is marked by the dashed line.

- If the athlete runs at a constant speed, the area of the negative projection in the diagram of horizontal ground reaction forces is approximately the same as the area of the positive projection above the time axis. This is actually true, however, only to a certain extent since in the rear support phase the athlete is not only forced to compensate for the loss of speed from the front support phase, but also for the loss of speed caused by air resistance. Therefore, the negative phase is particularly slightly shorter than the positive one.

- If the runner accelerates, the positive projection in the diagram of horizontal ground reaction forces is higher and longer than the negative projection (i.e., its area is larger). Since during start acceleration in sprinting there is initially no front support phase (see chapter II–1.3), the negative projection is almost completely eliminated. Conversely, the negative projection is larger and longer if the athlete slows down. With take-offs, the negative projection is much larger and has a clear impact force peak (see next point).

- The ground reaction forces in the vertical direction are also characterised by a very typical course: After the touchdown of the foot, there is initially a conspicuous force peak,

which is also called impact. After the decline of this first force peak, the vertical ground reaction forces rise again until the CG is approximately vertically above the point of foot touchdown. This can be seen in the upper diagram by the interrupted line which marks the transition between front and rear support phase and passes through the peak of the curve of the vertical ground reaction forces.

- The maximum forces in the vertical direction are larger in jumping than in sprinting, and larger in sprinting than in running. This does not mean that the impulse (= area under the curve = force • time) in the vertical direction and thus the flight height while sprinting is also greater than in running, since the ground contact time is longer when running. The relative magnitude of the impact force peak compared to the second force peak decreases in the following order: jump, sprint, endurance running. Within a sprint, the relative magnitude of the impact force peak as compared to the second force peak is smaller during start acceleration than in the free sprint. With jumpers, an only minimal decrease in the vertical ground reaction force between the force maxima is considered as a sign of superior reactive-strength capabilities.

MOVEMENT ECONOMY

In the running events, technique must primarily lead to economy. Economy primarily means to save energy, especially in walking and endurance running, and to maximise the power output in the desired direction of movement, particularly in sprinting. Movements become economic through the effective rhythmic interaction of agonists and antagonists, the avoidance of unnecessary movements, and by taking advantage of physical aids such as gravity, inertia, or the elastic energy stored in passive structures.

The measurable external force (or the measurable external torque) depends not only on the force of the agonist, but also on the relaxation of the antagonist. This is challenging in respect to the cyclic movement of running since the tension and relaxation phases of the individual muscles change very quickly (i.e., a muscle is agonist, antagonist, and then again agonist in rapid succession: hip flexion follows hip extension, hip extension follows hip flexion, etc). Coaches often address this problem indirectly when they speak of athletes being too tense or ask them to relax It is often said that sprinting means maximal tension in spite of maximal relaxation. This sentence, which at first seems to be a contradiction, expresses exactly the fact mentioned: maximal tension of the agonists, maximal relaxation of the antagonists and the uninvolved muscles, as well as efficient and fast switching between the agonist and antagonist roles. The demand for relaxation is often difficult to implement voluntarily. Natural relaxation in spite of high tension can be described as a downright talent criterion. The requirement for relaxation can be fulfilled best in uninvolved muscles, and it is hoped

that this helps the athlete to also become generally more relaxed. Therefore, coaches, for example, tell athletes to run with their mouths open, to relax facial muscles, and to loosen hands. Tasks which distract the athlete's attention from the running movement can also promote relaxation: turning one's head alternately to the left and right, counting silently backward by threes, etc. (see exercise 130).

An unnecessary movement, which should be avoided in terms of economy, is an excessive heel lift during the first strides after the crouch start for example. Instead, the athlete should show a flat foot-movement curve to be able to push himself/herself off from the ground quickly again (see chapter II-1.3). An excessive lifting of one's heels in this phase represents an unnecessary, time-consuming luxury movement.

Inertia and gravity, which should be exploited to achieve an economic running motion, are, for example, largely sufficient to explain the action of the lower leg (i.e., the movement of the knee joint during the swing phase). Coaches often require athletes to run from the hip with relaxed knees. This means that the movement of the lower leg at the knee joint should be performed naturally and rather passively from the active movement of the upper leg at the hip joint.

THE IMPORTANCE OF ARM MOTION

The arms set the pace for the legs or, as a coach saying goes: "You run with your arms and throw with your legs." In terms of biomechanics, the contralateral arm work counteracts the rotational momentum about the longitudinal body axis, which the legs produce with every stride. Thus, the arm swing and its amplitude and velocity are related to the action of the legs. If one runs faster or at a higher frequency, then one must also (be able to) move one's arms faster and at a higher frequency. If one runs faster and with longer strides, then the amplitude of the arm swing will also be larger. If an athlete moves his/her arms asymmetrically, there will also be another asymmetry. If, for example in training, an athlete runs with unusual arm movements (e.g., deliberately asymmetrically, exaggeratedly, or without arm movements, see 131), it quickly becomes clear how much the arm swing influences the movements of the legs.

It can be said that in terms of correct technique, the arm swing should be generated mainly in the shoulders. The elbow joint is either fixed approximately at a right angle (90°) or moved only slightly about this angle (i.e., it is slightly opened during the backswing and slightly closed during the forward swing). The wrist is loosely fixed in a central position, and the hand is also slightly opened in a central position. The amplitude of the arm swing depends, as mentioned, on the amplitude of the stride and the running velocity. However, in no case should the fingertips be moved higher than the nose at the end of the forward swing. At the end of the backswing, the forearm should not be moved beyond the vertical. From the front view, a largely parallel arm swing should

be identifiable. In front of the body, the hands may move slightly inside, without, however, exceeding the centre axis of the body. Moreover, the arms and forward swinging leg act as swing elements (see chapter II–2.1.2).

THE IMPORTANCE OF THE TRUNK MUSCLES

When hearing or reading about the trunk muscles, it is mostly about their importance in terms of injury prevention. They stabilise the spine in particular and thus prevent injuries to these structures, resulting from excessive or faulty loads.

Much rarer, however, the performance-determining role of the trunk muscles is mentioned: If the arm movements, as mentioned, counteract the rotational momentum of the legs, this can only work if these two sub-systems (arms and legs) are also coupled. This coupling occurs via the tendons, muscles, and connective tissues of the trunk muscles. Only if the trunk muscles are contracted (at the right moment), the momentum transfer (or the momentum trade-off) will occur efficiently, quickly, and directly.

However, this signifies a much more fundamental role of the trunk muscles: Their tension is a prerequisite for the upright body position, which makes running possible in the first place. However, the trunk muscles make running not only possible, they also contribute to an increase in performance if they stabilise the trunk in a particularly favourable position. For example, how a pelvis which is erect due to strong abdominal muscles contributes to an optimal sprint technique is described in the chapter about the 100m sprint (see II–1.3). Here, the strength requirements are significantly higher than the everyday stresses of walking and standing. Thus, a specific strength training for the trunk should be a standard element of training for each running discipline.

1.1.3 BIBLIOGRAPHY

Enomoto, Y., Kadano, H., Suzuki, Y., Chiba, T. & Koyama, K. (2008). Biomechanical analysis of the medalists in the 10,000 metres at the 2007 World Championships in Athetics. *New Studies in Athletics 23* (3), 61-66.

Jonath, U., Krempel, R., Haag, E. & Müller, H. (1995). *Leichtathletik 1: Laufen.* Reinbek bei Hamburg: Rowohlt Taschenbuch.

Regelkommissionen des DLV, FLA, ÖLV und SLV (Hrsg.). (2008). *Internationale Wettkampfregeln.* Waldfischbach: Hornberger.

1.2 SPRINT: COMMON FEATURES AND COMPARISON OF DISCIPLINES

1.2.1 THE MOST IMPORTANT COMPETITION RULES

The following abridged and simplified International Competition Rules comprise the framework for the techniques and strategy, as well as the organisation of sprint competitions:

- In all races up to and including 400 m, each athlete shall have a separate lane, with a maximum width of 1.22 m ± 0.01 m. The lanes are numbered from the inside to the outside. For international competitions, eight individual lanes must be available.
- Starting blocks shall be used for all races up to and including 400 m (and the first sections of the corresponding sprint relays); for all other races they are not permitted (see figure 1).
- In most cases, the starting blocks provided by the organising committee of the competition organiser must be used. At international championships, these must be linked to a World

Athletics-approved false-start-control apparatus. If the reaction time is less than 100 msec (= 0.1 sec = one tenth of a second), the start is considered a false start.

- In all races which are started out of the blocks, the starter, before the start, gives the following commands in the national language or in English or French: "On your marks" and "Set."
- A runner who commits a false start is disqualified. In the combined events, the first false start per race does not result in disqualification. Any combined-event athlete responsible for an additional false start in the race must be disqualified.
- In the 100m, 200m, and short hurdles, there must be wind measurement (by ultrasound at national and international championships). The wind gauge is placed in the interior area, 50m from the finish line, not

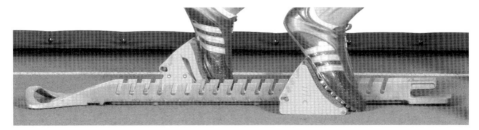

Figure 1: **Starting block:** *Various versions are possible if they comply with the specifications prescribed by World Athletics. The rail is fixed to the ground by spikes. The possibilities of adjustment in the running direction as well as in respect to the slope of the foot plates are clearly visible.*

more than 2m from the first lane at a height of 1.22m. In the 100m and the short hurdles, measurement begins with the starting signal, while in the 200m measurement commences when the leader enters the straight. In the 100 and 200m, the wind velocity is measured for a period of 10 seconds; in the short hurdles it is measured for a period of 13 seconds. Records (and qualification performances) achieved with a tailwind of more than 2.0 m/s are not accepted.

- A runner shall be disqualified if he/she voluntarily leaves his/her lane to the inside in the curve. If he/she leaves his/her lane to the outside in the curve or on the straight, he/she shall only be disqualified if he/she obstructs another athlete.

Otherwise, the general competition rules for running apply (see chapter II-1.1).

1.2.2 DISTINCTIONS BETWEEN SHORT SPRINTS AND LONG SPRINTS

Short-sprint disciplines include 100m, 100m hurdles, and 110m hurdles (and the corresponding 60m distances indoor), and the 4x100m relay. The classic long-sprint events are 400m, 400m hurdles, and the 4x400m. The 200m race is between the short and the long sprints. For some, this is rather a short sprint; for others, it is a long sprint. In addition to a number of sprinters who run 100 and 200m, there are also some who prefer 200 and 400m (e.g., Michael Johnson, ex-world record holder over 200m), as well as many 200m specialists, who are clearly better over 200m than over the other two distances.

VELOCITIES
Figure 2 shows the 50m average velocities of world-class sprinters over the various distances (for more detailed velocity curves over 100 and 200m see figures 1 and 3 in chapter II-1.3 and figure 2 in Chapter II-1.4). Due to the flying start, 200m sprinters regularly achieve times better than the 100m world record over the second 100m, showing that there are similarities between 100 and 200m. The distinct and long-lasting loss of speed in the 200m as compared to the 100m indicates a higher importance of speed endurance and similarities to the 400m sprint.

PHYSIOLOGICAL ASPECTS
The velocity curves in figure 2 alone provide an idea of what can be seen in figure 3 and table 1. The importance of anaerobic-lactacid energy supply increases along with the length of the sprint distance, or (more precisely) the duration of the load. The 400m is the distance at which the anaerobic-lactacid energy supply, and especially the lactate tolerance of low pH values induced by lactate, are of paramount importance. However, it is also important to note that in the 400m race even about 45% of the energy is provided aerobically (for more details see discourse I in chapter II-1.5.3).

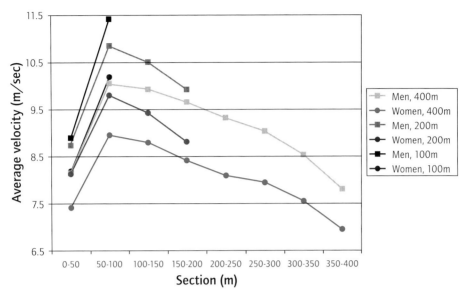

*Figure 2: **Velocity curves of world-class athletes in the three sprints:** 100m (modified on the basis of Letzelter & Letzelter, 2005, p. 74; average time for women: 11.03 sec (n = 20), average time for men: 10.00 sec (n = 20)), 200m (modified on the basis of Letzelter & Letzelter, 2005, p. 124; women's average time: 22.41 sec (n = 32), men's average time: 20.31 sec (n = 32)), and 400m (modified on the basis of Letzelter & Eggers, 2003, p. 40; female finalists (n = 12), and male finalists (n = 11) at the 1997 and 1999 World Championships): It should be noted that the actual maximum speed is still above the fastest average speed for a section.*

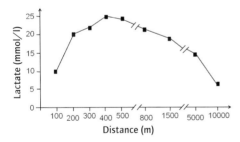

*Figure 3: **Lactate concentration after test runs over the given distances** (modified on the basis of Keul, 1975, p. 161).*

*Table 1: **Proportions of energy supply over various running distances** (according to Hartmann, 2004, based on Mader and Bompa).*

Distance	Anaerobic-alactacid (%)	Anaerobic-lactacid (%)	Aerobic (%)
100m	25	70	<5
200m	15	60	25
400m	12	43	45
800m	10	30	60
1500m	8	20	72
3000m	5	15	80
5000m	4	10	86
10,000m	3–2	12–8	85–90
42.195 m	0	5–2	95–98

TECHNIQUE

The techniques of the crouch start and toe push-off sprinting described in connection with the 100m race (see II–1.3.3) are important common features of sprinting. The technique of grasping/ pulling sprinting also described there is one important commonality at least of the flat sprints.

Apart from relays, sprinters must sprint through curves only from the 200m distance onward. In chapter II–1.4.3, it is described how this affects the technique of the crouch start and the sprint. However, short sprinters must master curve running in the 4x100m relay. Therefore, it is not possible to define curve sprinting as a typical feature of long sprints and thus to call the 200m race a long sprint.

STRATEGIES

From a physical point of view, it must be the goal both in the long and the short sprint to quickly achieve high speed and to reduce one's pace as late and as slowly as possible. However, for reasons of economy, the 400m distances are not started at maximum speed (also see chapters II–1.5.6

and II–1.9.6). In contrast, short sprinters run from start to finish as fast as possible. With this in mind, it is controversial whether the 200m sprint is a short or a long sprint. This question is discussed in more detail in chapter II–1.4.6.

Since short sprinters cover the entire distance with maximum effort, it is generally assumed that strategy does not count in the short sprint. Many sprinters often confirm this statement themselves. However, coaches ask athletes with a rather tense running style (even in competition) to run in a relaxed and technically correct manner instead of with maximum effort. Is this a technical correction, psychoregulatory help, or even strategy? One can only speak clearly of strategy if the athlete is given a detailed race model which he should adhere to during the race (see chapter II–1.3.6 and II–1.8.6).

Strategy has a very different, supplemental, and unique meaning in relays. Chapters II–1.6.6 and II–1.7.5 show which aspects must be considered when establishing a relay team.

1.2.3 BIBLIOGRAPHY

Duffield, R. & Dawson, B. (2003). Energy system contribution in track running. *New Studies in Athletics 18* (4), 47-56.

Hartmann, U. (2004). *Grundlagen der Energiebereitstellung* (Materialien zur A-Trainer-Ausbildung). Mainz: Deutscher Leichtathletik Verband.

Keul, J. (1975). Kohlenhydrate zur Leistungsbeeinflussung in der Sportmedizin. *Nutrition and Metabolism: Journal of Nutrition, Metabolic Diseases and Dietetics 18* (Supplement 1), 157-170.

Letzelter, S. & Eggers, R. (2003). Geschwindigkeitsverlauf über 400 m in der Weltklasse. *Leistungsport 33* (6), 40-45.

Letzelter, S. & Letzelter, M. (2005). *Der Sprint: Eine Bewegungs- und Trainingslehre* (Mainzer Studien zur Sportwissenschaft, 21). Niedernhausen: Schors.

Regelkommissionen des DLV, FLA, ÖLV und SLV (Hrsg.). (2008). *Internationale Wettkampfregeln.* Waldfischbach: Hornberger.

Spencer, M. R. & Gastin, P. B. (2001). Energy system contribution during 200- to 1500-m running in highly trained athletes. *Medicine and Science in Sports and Exercise 33* (1), 157-162.

1.3 100M RACE

1.3.1 DOUBLE WORLD RECORDS

When you think of speed, the fastest 100m sprinters in the world are the first to come to mind. Even if technical disciplines also include a variety of speed requirements, the 100m sprint is the typical speed discipline.

On 21 June of the Olympic year 1960, the German sprinter Armin Hary competed in Zurich Letzigrund Stadium on what was then allegedly the fastest cinder track in the world. When the timekeepers looked at their three precision Swiss watches, they saw times of 10.0, 10.0, and 9.9 seconds, which raised considerable doubt for the judges. Therefore, they construed a false start, which had not been sanctioned by the starter, and annulled the mythical time of 10.0 seconds. However, the judges allowed Hary's request to be allowed to repeat the race after approximately half an hour. Hurriedly, four runners were found to participate in a second race. With a tailwind of 0.9 m/sec, the three stopwatches this time showed 10.0, 10.0, and 10.1 sec for Hary. The world record of 10.0 seconds was complete.

It took four years until the American Bob Hayes was able to equal this time. The first 100m sprint below 10.0 sec was achieved by the American Jim Hines, again four years later, when at the U.S. Trials he improved the world record to 9.9 sec.

The 1968 Olympic Games ushered in a new era in the sprint. For the first time, the sprint times benefitted from all-weather tracks. Initially, the sprinters ran in brush spikes (i.e., shoes with short claw-like spikes, which were later banned by the IAAF). Slightly lower gravity at 2,200m above sea level in Mexico City further promoted the sprint times. Moreover, electronic timing was used for the first time, which resulted in slower times than manual timing. The IAAF regulations first assumed a bonus of 0.05 sec. Only at the 1972 Olympic Games in Munich did detailed experiments show that manual timing provides results which are 0.24 sec better on average than electronic timing (10.0 sec measured manually = 10.24 sec measured electronically).

The Olympic final of 1968, in which Hines improved the world record to 9.95 sec measured electronically, was also the first instance in which only sprinters of African descent took part (see section I–1.3.). In subsequent years, almost everyone was interested in even faster times. The number of sub-10-sec sprinters, almost all of whom are of African descent, has now exceeded one hundred.

While the U.S. was initially the leading sprint nation, Jamaica has taken over this role since the Olympic Games in 2008.

While Jamaican men collected more medals at the London Olympic Games in 2012, Jamaican women had previously done so in 2008. In London, the men, who were led by superstar Usain Bolt (see chapter II–1.4.1) won all three medals over 200m. The same feat had been achieved four years earlier by the women, led by Shelly-Ann Fraser, in the 100m race. In addition to two other medals over 200 and 400m, the success of Jamaican women was complete in 2008 by Veronica Campbell-Brown, who managed to repeat her 2004 Olympic victory over 200m. But even the Jamaican women will probably always remain behind the mythical world records of Florence Griffith Joyner (USA; 100m: 10.49 sec, and 200m: 21.34 sec) which are regarded with scepticism among experts.

1.3.2 THE MOST IMPORTANT COMPETITION RULES

The most important competition rules have been presented in their entirety in the general running and sprinting rule chapters (see chapters II–1.1.1 and II–1.2.1). In the U14 category, the sprinting distance is 75m, while in the lower age categories it is 50m.

1.3.3 SPORT-SCIENCE FINDINGS, PHASE STRUCTURE, AND TECHNIQUE

Figures 1 and 3 represent the velocity curve in the 100m sprint. As mentioned above (see chapter II–1.1.2), this results from the course of the stride frequency and stride length which can be seen in figures 2 and 3. Stride frequency is based on flight and support times, whose course is shown in figures 3 and 4. The 100m sprint begins with the crouch start. This is followed by three phases which are distinguished by their velocity curve (see figure 1). Accordingly, the 100m and all other flat sprint events are described in terms of the following four (main) phases:

* crouch start,
* positive acceleration,
* maximal velocity, and
* negative acceleration.

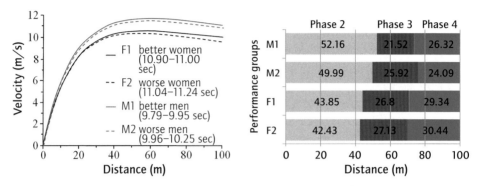

Figure 1: *Velocity characteristics and phases in the 100m with world-class athletes (modified on the basis of Letzelter & Letzelter, 2005, pp. 80 & 83): Delimitation of the maximum-velocity phase (phase 3): acceleration < ± 0.1 m/sec2. This is a mathematical modelling, starting from 10m intermediate times. In comparison to figure 3, the development of speed during the first metres appears to be too slow. As early as at the end of the push-off from the block, the CG of the expert has achieved a horizontal start velocity of nearly 4 m/s (p. 243).*

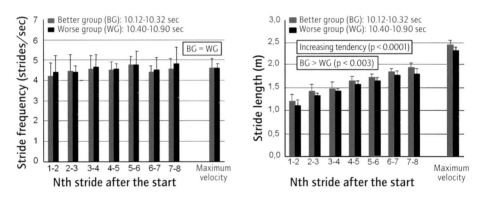

Figure 2: *Stride-frequency and stride-length development at the start of the 100m compared to the maximum velocity phase at the 2005 World Championships (modified on the basis of Ito et al., 2006, p. 37).*

Table 1: *Average stride frequencies and stride lengths (Türk-Noack, 2006).*

Men	Women		
100m average values	10.05 sec (9.84-10.19)	10.36 sec (10.23-10.49)	11.06 sec (10.94-11.18)	11.36 (11.21-11.51)
Number	n=13	n=18	n=10	n=11
Stride frequency (sec-1)	4.52 (4.32-4.72)	4.51 (4.19-4.89)	4.49 (4.30-4.61)	4.52 (4.15-4.89)
Stride length (m)	2.20 (2.09-2.29)	2.14 (1.95-2.33)	2.02 (1.96-2.13)	1.94 (1.86-2.12)

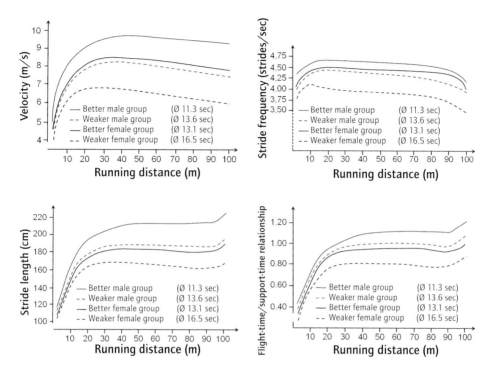

Figure 3: **Velocity, stride-length, and stride-frequency curves, as well as the curve concerning the relationship between flight and support times in the 100m race** *in heterogeneous groups with a relatively low performance level (modified on the basis of Gundlach, 1963, pp. 347, 349, 352 & 421). These rather old studies still provide the most comprehensive and meaningful data. Studies of world-class female and male runners also confirm the trends found here (see figures 1, 2 and 4, as well as Ae et al., 1992). Individual curves are less smooth than the group averages shown here.*

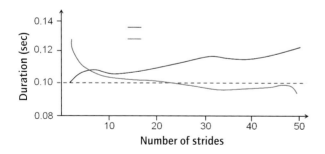

Figure 4: **Support-time (t$_{St}$) and flight-time (t$_{Fl}$) curves during** *an 11.03 sec sprint of Annegret Richter (modified on the basis of Baumann et al., 1986, p. 6).*

PHASE 1: CROUCH START

After setting the starting blocks, the crouch start is performed in the following three sub-phases:

- on-your-marks position,
- set position, and
- start reaction.

The first two sub-phases are only indirectly relevant to performance since time is recorded from the beginning of the third sub-phase (i.e., the starting signal).

SETTING OF THE STARTING BLOCKS

The terms narrow, medium, and wide starting position denote the distance between the two starting blocks in the direction of the run. The medium starting position is defined as a distance of one to one and a half feet (30–45cm). A shorter distance is called narrow starting position, while a longer distance is called a wide starting position.

Figure 5 shows that with good sprinters, the push-off usually is produced first by the rear leg. An excessively wide starting position can cause the rear leg to be already (almost) extended in the set position and thus the rear leg cannot or can hardly contribute to the push-off. In the event of a too narrow starting position, the knee and hip angle of the rear leg is possibly too small for a maximum initial force impulse. Thus, the medium starting position has prevailed with most good sprinters.

Another very important factor is the distance between the blocks and the starting line. *Many world-class sprinters prefer a distance of 1.5–2 feet in length between the starting line and the bottom edge of the front block in combination with a medium starting position.*

The incline of the foot plates must be adapted to the starting position. *The rear foot plate is set at a steeper angle than the front one* with the four-notch blocks used mostly in Germany (0, 1st, 2nd, and 3rd notch), for example, 0 notch (about 50° to the floor) for the front block and 2nd notch (about 70° to the floor) for the rear block.

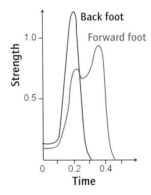

*Figure 5: **Force-time curve of the push-off out of the blocks** (modified on the basis of Van Coppenolle et al., 1988, p. 84.) The better the athlete, the shorter (less wide curve) and stronger (higher curve) the starting action will be.*

ON-YOUR-MARKS POSITION

To take the on-your-marks position, the athlete first puts his/her hands on the ground beyond the starting line, then he/she first places his/her front foot and thereafter his/her rear foot against the foot plates. In general, the feet are pressed

*Figure 6: **On-your-marks position.***

against the foot plates in such a manner that the toes still touch the ground. Only then is the knee of the rear leg placed on the ground, while the hands are placed behind the line (see figure 6). Until the "set" command, the sprinter continues breathing at his/her normal rhythm.

SET POSITION

The set position is determined in part by the setting of the block (see above). At the "set" command, the athlete is supposed to take his/her final starting position as soon as possible and stay there. Thus, he/she is not in danger of not yet having reached his/her final position when the starter fires the starting gun. For this purpose, he/she raises his/her hips and also the rear knee off the ground.

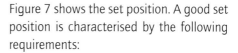

Figure 7 shows the set position. A good set position is characterised by the following requirements:

- In contrast to handedness, the stronger leg is not always the more skilful one. Mostly, however, *it is the take-off leg used in the jumps which is in the front starting block*.
- *The shoulders should be in front of the hands.* This influences the position of the CG and thus the direction of the force impulse during extension from the block. If the shoulders are further back, the CG will also be further back and the push-off will be too upward instead of forward. This results in the weight being placed mostly on the hands (70–80%).
- *The front knee should be bent at approximately a right angle, while the bend of the rear knee should be approximately 120–130°.* Since the knee angle of one leg also determines the angle of the other leg in the case of a fixed block setting (see above), the coach can use the right angle of the front knee joint, which is much easier to estimate,

*Figure 7: **Set position***

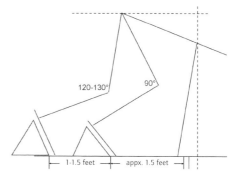

120-130°   90°

1-1.5 feet   appx. 1.5 feet

as a control criterion. In respect to the optimal acceleration of the total body, the angles mentioned seem to guarantee the optimum ratio between a maximum (velocity of) force development and the maximally possible acceleration path since the former becomes larger in the direction of the extension, whereas the latter becomes shorter.

- *The hip should be clearly above shoulder height* (for reasons see "Discourse 1").

- To raise the hip to this level, it is important to look between or slightly before one's hands. *The head remains aligned with the trunk.*

- During the set position, the athlete should try to push the ground forward away from himself/herself with his/her hands. By so doing, he/she generates a pre-tension of his/her extensor muscles which are responsible for the full body extension after the starting signal. Using this pre-tension, it is also possible to place the heels (especially the heel of the rear foot) against the blocks (*pressure against the block*). Thus, the sprinter is provided with a fixed abutment immediately after the starting signal and can begin to push off without delay.

- To increase the development of force during the first strides, the athlete should hold his/her breath already in the set position (forced breathing; see chapter I–1.3; for the topic of breathing during the 100m sprint, see also chapter II–1.3.6).

START REACTION

The extremely short sub-part of the initial reaction phase begins with the starting signal and ends with the onset of detectable movement. At (inter)national championships, this is usually measured by means of sensors in the starting block. This means that performance in this phase is exclusively influenced by reaction speed (see chapter I–1.4). The reaction time for female and male world-class sprinters is on average 0.13–0.17 sec (see also table 1 in chapter II–1.5.3), with women reacting on average approximately three hundredths of a second slower than men (see the false start rule in chapter II–1.2.1). Differences of hundredths of a second may be crucial in close championship races. In particular, when considering a heterogeneous population and given the poor trainability of reaction speed, the reaction time has a fairly insignificant influence on sprinting time (influence below 1%).

Since a movement is already prepared in the brain before the final decision to perform this movement is undertaken, sprinters should focus less on the signal and more on the subsequent actions (namely the push-off, the forward pull of the rear knee, and the arm action), while holding the set position.

PHASE 2: POSITIVE ACCELERATION

The phase of positive acceleration is divided into two sections or sub-phases:

- start acceleration, and
- pick-up acceleration.

DISCOURSE I: ARGUMENTS FOR GETTING CLOSE TO THE STARTING LINE

Some coaches recommend getting close to the starting line with a medium starting position. The advantage of this position (lower edge of the front block only 1.2–1.5 feet in length away from the starting line) is the distance thereby gained. The farther forward the front block is, the closer to the finish line are the first, second, third, etc. foot touchdowns after leaving the blocks. The disadvantage of this block setting is the more acute angle of the knee and hip (especially of the front leg). These more acute angles could have a negative effect on the speed of force development during the first extension in the start. However, these disadvantages can be compensated for as follows: If the sprinter combines the forward-shifted starting position with a stronger lift of his/her hips in the set position, the knee-joint angle will be slightly larger (and therefore more favourable) again; the hip-joint angle, however, will be even smaller than before (and thus unfavourable). However, through a rather close placement of the hands (only a little more than shoulder width apart), a high hand support (only on the fingertips) and stretched arms, the athlete will also be able to raise his/her shoulders slightly and thus to slightly increase the thigh-torso angle again. Moreover, the increased hip and shoulder position also result in raising the CG, which means that it must not be raised too much during the initial start extension. However, in order not to produce a too vertical push-off, the shoulders must be simultaneously positioned farther forward. Such a block setting is easy to implement especially by strong athletes.

These two sub-phases can be distinguished kinematically: First, the acceleration is high, then lower. But the sprinter can still increase his/her speed in the second sub-phase (i.e., pick up speed). However, from a practical point of view, a technical and functional difference is crucial.

START ACCELERATION: TOE PUSH-OFF SPRINTING

Start acceleration is characterised by a sprinting technique of its own. It is referred to as toe push-off sprinting because during start acceleration the sprinter pushes off strongly with his/her extensor muscles in a forward and upward direction. If one ignores the occurring rotation impulses, the athlete will, at any given time, push off in the direction of a line passing through the point of foot touchdown and the centre of gravity (CG). The idea that the push-off occurs along a line reaching from the touchdown to the hips is simpler and useful in training. As long as the CG is in front of the touchdown point of the foot (i.e., the athlete is in the back-support phase), he/she can accelerate his/her body forward (see chapter II–1.1.2). This situation is provided by the crouch-start position right from the beginning.

Throughout the start acceleration, the athlete runs with a forward lean of his/her body. This should always be as great as possible to work as much as possible in the back support to direct as much of the push-off force as possible horizontally to the rear. If the forward lean is too great, the athlete will push himself/herself off too flat and he/she will not be able to move the other leg forward again on time. The CG becomes too low, and the starting situation for the next fast stride becomes unfavourable. With increasing speed, it becomes more and more difficult to prevent this, and the athlete must gradually raise his/her trunk towards a vertical position. Throughout this process, the CG is raised higher and higher. If, however, the sprinter straightens up his/her body too early (without being forced to do so), he/she will miss out on his/her potential for accelerating forward.

As in any sport, the position of the whole body is also influenced by head and eye movements. Therefore, to achieve an optimal forward lean of the body, the view should be directed to the ground only a few metres forward and should only be lifted slowly while raising one's body.

TECHNICAL CHARACTERISTICS OF THE START ACCELERATION

First, the athlete should push off powerfully from the starting block with both feet.

Due mainly to the longer duration (t), two-thirds of the impulse ($p = F \cdot t$) are created by the front leg (see figure 5). Weaker sprinters tend to overemphasise the push-off from the front block. Nevertheless, even the rear leg of top sprinters is released from the block before it is completely straight and is rapidly moved forward with a pronounced knee lift (see figure 8) to prepare the first foot touchdown on time. This should be done in the most direct manner (i.e., with a flat foot-movement curve and without raising one's heels to the buttocks during the first strides). The heel lift will only increase with the aforementioned rising from the forward lean of the body and during the transition to pick-up acceleration (see below). Not only the knee lift, but also the arms act as swing elements and should therefore be used powerfully (see chapter II-2.1.2). Figure 9 shows the push-off extension during the first stride/s. In poor sprinters with worse force ratios, the angle to the ground will be greater, and thus the push-off will be more vertically directed.

This is followed by the foot touchdown which occurs during the first three to four touchdowns initially behind and then on the vertical projection of the CG. Thus, during these strides, the front support phase is completely eliminated. A prerequisite for this is that the lower leg is directed backward and downward

*Figure 8: **Crouch start and start acceleration** (toe push-off sprinting).*

(see figures 9 and 10) already during the knee lift and also before and during the foot touchdown. Thus, a grasping movement, in which the lower leg is temporally directed forward and downward (see phase 3), does not occur during the first strides in favour of the preparation of an optimal next push-off. But even during start acceleration, the athlete tries to touch down his/her foot backward at the greatest possible speed. The following idea is helpful: "The push-off begins before the foot touchdown." During the entire support phase, the knee and hip joints are then extended. An amortisation (i.e., a flexion of the knee joint) is not visible. Throughout the run, the ankle is first dorsiflexed (lifting of the tip of the foot) before the touchdown. However, due to the forward lean, the foot is touched down with a much higher heel than during grasping/pulling sprinting (see phase 3). Unlike in the knee and hip joints, a certain, albeit as slight as possible amortisation, and thus reactive and powerful action, can be seen in the ankle joint even in top sprinters. During the subsequent strides, the front support phase is added and the raising of the body is continued. Nevertheless, the first sprinting strides are performed focusing on the push-off.

STRIDE FREQUENCY, LENGTH, AND WIDTH

Figures 2 and 3 show the variation of stride frequency and length at the start. Stride frequency is already very high during the first strides (>4 strides/sec) and increases only slightly up to its maximum value at about 20 m. At that point, world-class men and women achieve on average 4.80–4.70 strides/sec. Absolute peak values in both men and women are just over 5 strides/sec. The proportion of the support phases of the total stride duration during the first strides is greater than during the later stages of a sprint (see figures 3 and 4).

The increase in stride length is clearer and continues until reaching maximum velocity. Faster sprinters run with longer strides from the start. The stride lengths of world-class women during start acceleration are 20–40cm shorter than those of world-class men, which is caused by the women's lower body height and poorer force conditions. Figure 11 shows that the stride width also characteristically changes during the first strides. Better sprinters make wider strides than poorer sprinters.

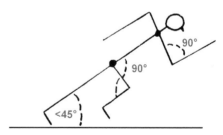

Figure 9: **First extension from the blocks.**

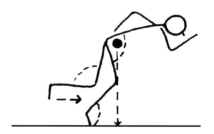

Figure 10: **The foot touchdown upon the first ground contact** occurs behind the vertical projection of the CG

Figure 12 shows the changes in the model technique associated with this finding.

PICK-UP ACCELERATION

How long the start acceleration lasts depends on the athlete's performance. For better athletes the start acceleration is longer (in metres, not necessarily in seconds or strides). However, for world-class athletes, too, the values vary between 20 and 35m (not least because there is a fluent transition to the pick-up acceleration). Analyses of 10m interval times have shown that the main difference between the world-record holder Joyner and the former German champion Paschke was the pick-up acceleration and that the difference in start acceleration was significantly less and that there was no difference in reaction time.

Due to their good maximum-strength capacity in the extensor muscles, throwers are often equal to sprinters in terms of start acceleration. In the transition to pick-up acceleration they then quickly lose ground

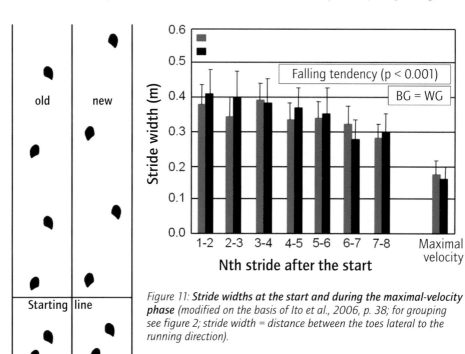

*Figure 11: **Stride widths at the start and during the maximal-velocity phase** (modified on the basis of Ito et al., 2006, p. 38; for grouping see figure 2; stride width = distance between the toes lateral to the running direction).*

*Figure 12: **Possible variation of the technique model in respect to the first strides:** "Coach instruction in the past: Stride width: narrow; stride frequency: high; Coach instruction in the future: Stride width: wide; stride frequency: high, but with emphasis on long strides" (modified on the basis of Ito et al, 2006, p. 39). This behaviour is similar to that of a weightlifter who also places the feet a little apart for the maximal and vigorous use of the extensor muscles. Consequently, there are also findings which indicate that a somewhat wider positioning of the feet in the starting blocks (as permitted by the starting blocks currently in use) would lead to faster starting times. Note also that during the first step the touchdown occurs about a foot beyond the starting line.*

due to different requirements. However, when observing a large heterogeneous group, this is no longer valid and instead the following applies: Athletes with better start acceleration also have better pick-up acceleration and accelerate longer. Better sprinters gain a lead in both sections.

Based on investigations of muscle activity (electromyography = EMG), a functional-anatomical difference between start and pick-up acceleration was observed. During start acceleration, the extensor loop, including the muscles of the front thigh, determines performance (see above). After the sprinter straightens up from his/her forward lean, there is, however, a change of function. From now on until the finish, primarily the hip extensors including the muscles of the posterior thigh (hamstrings) are of importance. *The transition from start to pick-up acceleration is equal to the transition from toe push-off sprinting to grasping/pulling sprinting* (see phase 3). Correlation studies on performances during pick-up acceleration and those in the maximum-velocity phase show that there is a close correlation due to the same technique.

PHASE 3: MAXIMUM VELOCITY
Figures 1 and 3 show the position of the maximum-velocity phase. However, some absolute top sprinters reach their top speed even later. Carl Lewis, for example, is said to have reached his top speed of about 11.8 m/sec between 80 and 90m into his race at the 1987 World Championships (however, problems in measurement accuracy must be taken into

account). In general, 12 m/sec (which, with the conversion factor of 3.6, is the equivalent of 43.2 km/h) is considered the magical speed limit in the men's 100m sprint, which so far has only been exceeded by very few sprinters. Similarly, this applies to 11m/sec for women. Weaker sprinters not only have a lower maximal speed, but cannot accelerate over such a long distance either. Thus, they also reach their maximum velocity after fewer metres (not necessarily after fewer seconds or strides).

Maximal sprinting speed (like the so-called acceleration ability) is a complex skill which is affected by several types of motor stress. These are mainly reactive strength and maximum cyclic speed (see chapters I–1.3 and I–1.4).

STRIDE FREQUENCIES AND STRIDE LENGTHS
Figure 3 shows that the stride length increases until maximum velocity is almost achieved and then remains about the same. Male world-class sprinters run at an average maximum stride length between 2.40 and 2.50m. While there are extreme individual values of up to 2.70m, most lower-level world-class sprinters are approximately 10cm below these values on average. The corresponding values for women are approximately 20cm shorter.

Figure 3 shows that on the group average, stride frequency, after having reached its maximum value at approximately 20m (see phase 2), remains approximately the same or only decreases very slowly until just before the finish.

MORE DETAILED BIOMECHANICAL ANALYSIS

As described in chapter II–1.1.2, a runner loses horizontal velocity (or accelerates negatively) at every stride during the flight and the front support phase before he/she is able again to accelerate (positively) in the rear support phase. This applies to all phases of the 100m sprint alike. However, the total acceleration per stride in the horizontal direction, which consists of these three stride phases, is positive during the second phase of 100 m, equal to zero during the third phase, and negative during the fourth phase.

Table 2: Flight and support times of good, medium, and poor world-class sprinters (according to Mann 1999, p. 27).

	good	medium	poor
Flight times	approx. 123 msec		
Support times	approx. 85 msec	approx. 100 msec	approx. 110 msec

The impulse (p), which is calculated on the basis of the mean force (F) exerted over a certain time (t), is crucial for the change in velocity (Δv) of a body of mass m ($\Delta v \cdot m = p = F \cdot t$). Due to the shorter ground contact times (see table 2), or in order to achieve these, better sprinters must produce significantly higher forces to achieve the same impulse in the vertical direction. In respect to the horizontal direction, the analysis is more difficult. Since the drag-induced loss of velocity is difficult to influence, the sprinter is either forced to minimise the time and/or the forces occurring during the front support

phase or maximise the time and/or the forces occurring during the rear support phase.

GRASPING/PULLING SPRINTING

The technical behaviour during the front swing and support phase and that during the rear support and swing phase are not independent from one another. A maximisation of the push-off results in a forward tilting of the pelvis and an elevated heel lift behind the body (see below) and ultimately in problems when preparing the next foot touchdown, and thus in increased braking forces during the front support phase. Therefore, a rethinking has been going on for some time now: Toe push-off sprinting is only predominant during the starting phase (see above). In all subsequent phases, *the technical model of grasping/pulling sprinting is predominant to minimise time and force generation in the front support and to emphasise the front swing phase to the detriment of the rear support and rear swing phase (front-side technique).*

A strategy of athletes to reduce braking forces is *the attempt to synchronise the velocity of the foot before touchdown with the relative velocity of the ground by means of a grasping, ground-contacting movement.* The following comparison illustrates this idea: Imagine cycling past a tree and stretching your arm out to the side. Depending on your speed, contact with the tree may well hurt and your bike will slow down a little. If, however, you first move your arm forward and then backward as quickly as possible while cycling past

DISCOURSE II: ABOUT THE PRIMACY OF STRIDE LENGTH OR STRIDE FREQUENCY

Stride frequency is usually attributed to coordination skills. This is supported by the fact that girls achieve stride frequencies of 4.0 as early as ten years of age, while boys of the same age achieve 4.4 strides/sec. The fact that women and men achieve very similar maximum stride frequencies also seems to show the influence of coordination.

Stride length, however, is explained on the one hand as being influenced by (the development of) body length, and on the other hand as being mainly dependent on strength capacities. In this respect, men have natural advantages and the percentage difference between world-class male sprinters and world-class female sprinters is larger than the difference in terms of stride frequency.

In the 1970s, the East German female sprinters Göhr and Stecher, who attracted much attention because of their extremely frequency-oriented sprinting, contributed to the theory that the focus of training with women should mainly be on stride frequency, whereas with men, the emphasis should be on stride length or strength. This theory, however, has not held, primarily due to the fact that the entire stride structure (i.e., stride frequency and stride length), like any movement, is based on the development of force by the muscles. The (amount of) force development is significantly based on neural processes. The simple equations described (stride frequency = coordination; stride length = force) are therefore not sustainable.

In practice, both stride length and frequency should be trained (even in their extreme forms) to find an individually optimal ratio of both variables for competition. This also means that there may be significant differences in and among individuals although the finishing times are similar. With beginners in particular, the emphasis on stride frequency often leads to the misconception that "when I move my legs fast, I will also run fast." This should be avoided.

the tree, then maybe you would even be able to pull yourself forward and push off the tree and thus accelerate your bike.

To prepare an optimal grasping/pulling foot touchdown, good sprinters relinquish something in the rear support phase: The knees and hips are not fully extended until the end of the push-off. Thus, the backward follow-through of the leg in the air is shortened; the whole leg does not get so far behind the body and can be brought forward again faster and earlier. To move the leg even faster forward during the swing phase, a more acute knee-joint angle is crucial, since if one assumes that the hip flexors (particularly the iliopsoas) can produce a certain torque at the hip joint, the rotational velocity will be greater the closer the mass of the leg is to the hip joint. The heel lift is due less to the active contraction of the knee flexors than to the laxity of the knee extensors. The lower leg follows the thigh and its own inertia. The early dissolution of the push-off and the erect pelvis should ensure that the heel lift will occur below rather than behind the body.

Hip flexion leads to the knee lift. The thigh should be brought forward almost to the horizontal. Toward the end of this movement, the knee joint angle already opens again slightly. The quickest possible hip flexion is followed by the reactive and powerful contraction of the pre-strained hip extensors. These are mainly the glutes and the hamstrings. Due to its inertia, the lower leg continues swinging forward in the direction of extension, which is accelerated by the movement of the thigh downward and backward. Just before the touchdown of the foot, the leg is almost straight and the foot moves backward as quickly as possible.

The sprinter tries to place his/her foot as close as possible to the vertical projection of the centre of gravity. While Mann (1999) showed a distance of 20cm between the toes and the vertical projection of the CG for the best world-class sprinters, Ito et al. (2008) measured a distance of 31cm in two sub-ten-second sprinters. It is assumed that

the front support is shortened by a small touchdown distance, not only spatially, but also in terms of time. The shorter time and the steeper touchdown angle of the leg result in a smaller braking (or negative) impulse. Moreover, the sprinter tries to place his/her foot on the ground with a small stride width (see figure 11) to avoid wasting power in the lateral direction.

During the support phase, the hip extensors pull the hips and the trunk further forward beyond the touchdown point. At the same time, the tension of the knee extensors during the front support phase ensures that the yield (amortisation) at the knee joint is as little as possible. Kersting (1999, pp. 30 and 40) measured an amortisation at the knee joint of 8.3° in world-class female sprinters (n = 3) and of 14.0° in world-class male sprinters (n = 6). In the rear support phase, the reactive and powerful contraction of the knee extensors results in the extension of the knee joint, which, however, remains incomplete (see above). The hip extensors support the knee extension by moving the knee backward, while the foot is fixed to the ground. In world-class sprinters, the push-off is performed at an angle of approximately 3° to the horizontal. Thus, during the sprint, the hips and the centre of gravity remain at almost identical height.

The results of Ae et al. (1992) and Ito et al. (2008) are a good summary of the importance of the grasping style of sprinting: Below-ten-second sprinters differ from mediocre sprinters (10.60 to 11.50 sec) by a smaller minimum knee angle during

Figure 13: *Grasping/pulling sprinting.*

the swing phase, a higher grasping velocity of the foot backward before the touchdown, a faster hip extension, and a slower knee extension during ground contact.

LOOSENESS, TRUNK POSITION, ARM MOVEMENTS, AND FOOT TOUCHDOWN

In order to achieve the above-mentioned knee lift (thigh almost to the horizontal), the sprinter must run with an upright trunk or a minimal forward lean of the trunk and an erect pelvis. Kersting (1999, pp. 30 and 40) measured the forward lean of the trunk at foot touchdown between 3° and 14° to the vertical in world-class female and male sprinters (n = 9). At the end of the support phase or at the beginning of the flight phase, the trunk position is usually even more upright. Figure 14 shows how the position of the pelvis affects the cycle of leg movements (illustrated here by the trajectory of one foot). One should

keep in mind during strength training that the pelvis is held erect by the abdominal muscles.

In connection with the model of the grasping/pulling technique, many coaches emphasise that the backswing of the arm in particular should be performed actively, quickly, and powerfully to support and stabilise the pulling action of the contralateral leg.

In order to ensure a safe and direct force transmission between the foot and the running track, track runners (as well as jumpers and javelin throwers) wear spikes (i.e., shoes with spikes under the front sole). The ideal sprint-appropriate action of the ankle before and during the foot touchdown is shown in figure 15. Before touchdown of the foot, the ball of the foot and the toes are pulled inward and forward to achieve a pre-tension of the calf muscles

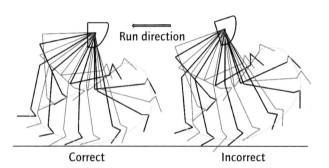

Correct   Incorrect

Figure 14: **The influence of the pelvis position on the action of the legs** (modified on the basis of Tepper & Czingon, 1995, p. 161).

193

DISCOURSE III: DISCUSSION OF SELECTED ASPECTS OF THE MODEL OF THE GRASPING/PULLING TECHNIQUE

Touchdown with straight leg?

In this book (see above) as well as elsewhere, grasping/pulling sprinting is associated with the touchdown of an almost straight leg. In the process, it is often forgotten that the extension of the knee joint is not an active (kicking) movement triggered by the knee extensors. Throughout the entire swing phase, the lower leg follows the movements of the upper leg and its own inertia (see above) almost passively. *The sprinting action should be initiated by the hips, not the knee joints.* This is not only a statement pertaining to technique, but also one with implications for strength training. In coordination training, the touchdown with a nearly straight leg is even practised individually by using exercises like the goose step (116). In both world-class and poorer sprinters, the actual knee-joint angle during foot touchdown is on average approximately 150°. Lehmann and Voss (1997, p. 25) observed that top sprinters slightly bend their knee joints again just before touchdown from 160 to 155°, while up-and-coming young German sprinters extend their legs further from 160 to 164°. The behaviour of top sprinters could be a sign that the hamstrings, which shortly before were responsible for slowing down the (passive) extension movement of the knee, are now reactively contracted. This would also be beneficial to the extent that at least the biarticular parts of the hamstrings are simultaneously, and in the following support phase significantly involved in supporting the rapid hip extension. This could also explain why Ito et al. (2008) pointed out that some sub-ten-second sprinters bend their knee joints in the rear support phase instead of straightening it (as would be expected).

Knee lift up to the horizontal?

That the knee lift up to the horizontal is questionable is also evident from the fact that very successful frequency-oriented short and long sprinters (e.g., the 100m Olympic champion Renate Stecher and the 400m world-record holder Michael Johnson) and very strong sprinters (e.g., the 100m world champion Lauryn Williams) sprint with a significantly lower amplitude of the front swing phase. In fact, at its highest point, the upper leg of world-class sprinters is on average 16° to the horizontal (n = 9; Kersting, 1999). While Ae et al. (1992), Ito et al. (2008), and Korneljuk (1982) did not consider the height of the knee lift as relevant to performance, Armstrong and Cooksey (1983) as well as Mann (1999, p. 29) believed that better world-class sprinters sprint with a higher knee lift than inferior sprinters.

Pelvis rotation about the longitudinal axis?

Too little attention is paid to the fact that there is a slight rotation of the pelvis about the longitudinal axis of the body during each sprinting stride, and that this results in a slight shoulder-hip separation. On the one hand, this separation caused by a lack of trunk strength is inconvenient for many beginners. On the other hand, there are very special coordination exercises (especially in parts of the Russian school of sprinters) for learning the appropriate rotation of the pelvis. The basis of this is that if the hip is moved backward by the trunk muscles during the support phase, the forward pull or push-off could be reinforced.

Neglected muscles

In connection with investigations on muscle activity in the sprint, which have decisively influenced the model of grasping/pulling sprinting techniques, the importance not only of the hamstrings but also of the muscles on the inside of the upper leg (adductors) has been re-evaluated. The adductors are involved in both the forward return of the leg (hip flexion) at the beginning of the swing phase and in the grasping movement (hip extension) at the end of the swing phase. In the past, strength training focused almost exclusively on the extensor loop (i.e., the anti-gravity muscles of the calf, front thigh, buttocks and the back extensors) which are responsible for a powerful push-off action. The continued high frequency of injuries of the hamstrings in sprinters gives reason to believe that even today there are still deficits in many sprinters, such as weak connective tissue, lack of hypertrophy, or bad innervation abilities. Many exercises (e.g., squats, weightlifting exercises, or multiple reactive jumps) are available to prepare the extensor loop for stress during sprinting. The hamstrings and adductors, however, are often trained only by concentric exercises on strength-training machines. However, to prepare these muscles for the high stress in sprinting it is absolutely necessary to also perform maximal-eccentric strength training. Moreover, special exercises on a vibration strength-training machine or exercises from the ABCs of sprinting should be considered for the muscles mentioned. For the hamstrings, resisted sprints with low weights and a conscious grasping/pulling action, as well as horizontally oriented multiple jumps with a grasping foot touchdown should be added (prerequisite: correct technique).

(supination and dorsiflexion). A drop foot in this situation is always associated with a foot touchdown far in front of the body, which results in a too long amortisation at the ankle and increased braking forces (see above). The push-off triggered by the calf muscles begins right before the ground contact. The tip of the foot moves down a bit so that the foot touchdown is performed over the outside of the ball of the foot. Nevertheless, the foot is put on the ground with a fairly low heel. During the entire ground contact, the foot rests on the ball. The foot should be firm and yield only very little. Nevertheless, there will be a slight yield (= amortisation), while the foot is forced to absorb the weight of the body before the (already initiated) push-off (triggered by the calf muscles) can be continued reactively and powerfully. However, there is no correlation between the sprint performance and the extension velocity of the ankle.

Figure 15: Ideal foot touchdown during the sprint.

According to Seagrave (2008), the desire to run with a firm foot and a low heel (despite high hips) although still on the balls of the feet is called the credit card rule. This means that one should still be able to insert a credit card between the heel and the ground, without being able to insert something thicker between the heel (at the lowest point) and the ground.

The low heel results in a long path of acceleration when pushing off from the ground.

PHASE 4: NEGATIVE ACCELERATION

The phase of negative acceleration can be further divided into (at least) two sections or sub-phases:

- speed-endurance section; and
- attacking the finish line.

Deceleration behind the finish line can be considered as the third sub-phase. However, this phase is no longer relevant to performance since the recording of time is completed once crossing the finish line.

SPEED-ENDURANCE SECTION

The speed-endurance section begins with the first measurable loss of velocity due to fatigue. Figures 1 and 3 show the distance in metres at which this section begins. A late transition to the speed-endurance section may indicate a good 200m sprinter. However, a division into phases according to metres can be misleading since a top sprinter is forced to enter the phase of negative acceleration after 75 metres, whereas a novice sprinter has perhaps covered only 50m during this same time. The loss of velocity is due to two factors. The phase transition corresponds to the maximum duration of the anaerobic-alactacid energy supply at maximum intensity, which is approximately 7 sec. 3 to 7 min after the race; 100m sprinters (men: 10.54–10.69 sec; women: 11.65–12.01 sec) have blood lactate levels of 13–16 mmol/l. Better athletes have higher lactate levels which indicates the importance of anaerobic energy supply even in the 100m sprint. Other authors attribute the loss of velocity to neural fatigue processes which lead to impaired excitation of the muscles. Despite fatigue, the athlete must try to maintain an optimal sprint technique.

ATTACKING THE FINISH LINE
In figure 3 it can be seen that during the last metres there is once again a significant decrease in stride frequency while stride length increases. Other data of world-class sprinters does not confirm these findings. A possible change of stride length and frequency is probably due less to physiological reasons than to the psychological anticipation of the finish line. Figures 1 and 3 show that this does not lead to a dip in the velocity curve.

If the race is close, one can often see sprinters trying to throw forward their chests just before crossing the finish line (see rule in chapter II–1.1.1). On the one hand, the athlete thereby tries to shift his/her chest forward relative to his/her

DISCOURSE IV: IMPLICATIONS FOR TRAINING

In order to shift the transition from the phase of maximum velocity to the phase of negative acceleration backward, sprinters in the past often performed interval sprints over 60–80m with relatively short rest intervals. There was no evidence that this resulted in an increase in the creatine phosphate storage (Mader, 2002, p. 80). However, sets of 60 or 80m sprints can be highly useful for other reasons (e.g., for making sprinting technique more economic).

In the phase of negative acceleration, the decrease in speed or the fatigue-induced loss of time is extremely low, especially in some top male sprinters. Results are affected only to a very small extent by individual differences in this area. Accordingly, the training of the acceleration abilities and of maximal sprinting speed is much more important for top sprinters. Although they cannot afford extreme weaknesses in speed endurance either, one can state that the better the 100m sprinter, the less important is the training of speed endurance. One of the reasons why this statement makes sense is that the speed-endurance section does not start after a certain distance, but rather after a certain time, and therefore better sprinters spend a shorter period of time in this section.

This means that in the training of young athletes, speed-endurance training provides a greater potential for improvement. However, it may for example have a negative long-term impact on the muscle fibre structure and thus on acceleration and maximum velocity. Therefore, young sprinters in particular or their coaches should avoid premature and excessive speed-endurance training.

centre of gravity by keeping his/her arms, buttocks, and upper head backward. On the other hand, he/she can also shift his/her centre of gravity forward relative to the touchdown point of his/her feet for a short time. However, he/she then runs the risk of falling forward or, to prevent this, unintentionally decelerating before reaching the finish line. Thus, a good crossing of the finish line must be practised, even if it might only lead to an improvement of a hundredth of a second.

DECELERATION BEHIND THE FINISH LINE

Behind the finish line, the athlete must reduce his/her velocity without running the risk of injury. To achieve this, he/she should continue running with tension (in the legs, trunk, and arms) and shift his/her trunk, and thus also his/her centre of gravity slightly backward. He/she now intentionally emphasises the front support phase in which the horizontal velocity is reduced mainly by the extensor muscles.

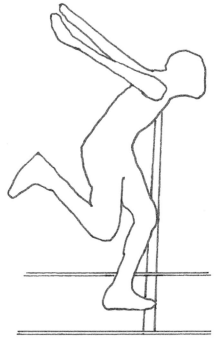

Figure 16: **Attacking the finish line.**

*Table 3: **Requirement profile for the 100m race:** The suggested rough estimate of the values of selected factors determining performance is based on the importance for the overall performance and the percentage of time spent training (IR: information requirements, constr.: constraints; see chapter I–1.1).*

Factors determining 100m performance	Estimate of value	Notes
Coordination	+ + +	optical IR: low, acoustic IR: at the start medium, then low, tactile IR: low, kinaesthetic IR: medium, vestibular IR: low; precision constr.: high, time constr.: high, complexity constr.: low, situation constr.: medium, physical stress constr.: low
Flexibility	+ +	no extreme movement amplitudes required
Strength		particular importance of the hamstrings; extensor loop (glutes, quadriceps, triceps surae, erector spinae), iliopsoas, abdominus, adductors, shoulder and upper-arm muscles
Maximal strength	+ + + +	during start acceleration and as a basis
Reactive strength	+ + + + +	within various stretch-shortening cycles
Speed	+ + + + +	primarily cyclic; acyclic aspects at the start and when attacking the finish line; reaction speed at the start (can be decisive for winning the race; however, relatively insignificant in terms of percentage; hardly improvable through training)
Endurance (general dynamic) Anaerobic endurance		
Strength endurance	+	as a basis of speed endurance
Speed endurance	+ + +	long maintenance of maximal velocity and only slight velocity loss at the end of the race
Aerobic endurance	+ +	particularly as a basis of training
Psychological and cognitive abilities	+ + + + +	concentration ability (on the point; there is no possibility to compensate for errors); performance-oriented thinking and behaviour (see chapter I–3.1.1)
Anthropometric and primarily genetically determined characteristics	+ + + + +	high proportion of fastest muscle fibres; connective tissue with optimal energy-storing capacities; medium body height; low percentage of body fat

1.3.4 SUMMARY OF THE MOST IMPORTANT TECHNICAL
CHARACTERISTICS = TECHNIQUE-ANALYSIS SHEET

CROUCH START

ON-YOUR-MARKS POSITION

- The front block is approximately 1½ feet from the starting line, approximately 50° to the ground; the rear block is approximately 1–1½ feet further back, approximately 70° to the ground.
- Hands are initially placed in front of the starting line; only then is the (long-jump) take-off leg placed against the front block, then the other leg is placed against the rear block.
- The rear knee is placed onto the ground.
- The hands are placed behind the line, just shoulder width apart; high hand support on fingertips; the arms are extended.
- The head is aligned with the trunk; the view is directed between the hands.
- Quiet breathing; relaxation.

SET POSITION

- Rapid settling into the final starting position by lifting one's pelvis (lifting one's rear knee from the ground).
- The shoulders are in front of the hands (arm position as before).
- The pelvis is higher than the shoulders.
- The front knee is at a right angle; the rear knee is at an angle of approximately 120–130°.
- The head is aligned with the trunk; the view is directed between the hands.
- Pressure is applied against the block: The hands try to push the ground forward; pre-tension of the extensor muscles; the heels are pressed backward against the blocks.
- Inhaling, holding breath (forced breathing).
- Focus on the subsequent movement (not on the acoustic signal).

TOE PUSH-OFF SPRINTING

- The push-off is performed by the extensor muscles of both legs; the push-off by the rear leg is more intense and shorter (1/3 of the pressure), whereas the push-off by the front leg is longer (2/3 of the pressure).
- Due to the stretching of the legs and the trunk, the arms are lifted from the ground (no push-off by the arms); direct start of the first energetic arm swing.
- The rear leg is the first to break contact with the block, and the hip flexion starts immediately (forward swing).
- In each stride, the push-off results in the extension of the whole body so that the head, shoulder, hip, knee, and foot are on one line, which initially is only at approximately 45° to the ground (forward lean of the body); the view is directed to the ground a few feet in front of the runner.
- In each instance, the swing leg is quickly moved forward until the angle between the thigh and the trunk is 90° (knee lift); the foot movement curve is flat (initially the heels are not raised behind the body).
- The knee lift and arm swing (from the shoulder; elbows at 90°) are used as swing elements.
- After the knee lift, the hips and knees are extended again (the next push-off starts already during the swing phase).
- The lower legs are pointed backward and downward throughout the movement (initially there is no grasping movement).
- The tip of the foot is raised before the touchdown (dorsiflexion).
- The touchdown with the balls of the feet is behind the vertical projection of the CG during the first strides, then it is on the vertical projection of the CG, and finally it is in front of the projection of the CG.
- The foot touchdown is initially a bit wider and placed to the outside.
- During the touchdown, the foot is fixed (no yielding).
- An increase in stride length and stride frequency.
- Only slow rising from the forward body lean and thus smooth transition to grasping/pulling sprinting.

GRASPING/PULLING SPRINTING

- Upright trunk or minimum forward lean; erect pelvis (contracted abdominals).
- The view is directed to the finish line; the facial muscles are relaxed.

- Incomplete extension at the knee and hip joint during the push-off.
- Sprinting from the hips (during the swing phase, the lower leg follows the movements of the upper leg and its own inertia mostly passively).
- Marked heel rise under the body, not behind the body (heel is never as high as the buttocks), then the knee joint angle is opened.
- Rapid hip flexion so that the knee is raised in front of the body until the thigh is (almost) horizontal.
- Subsequent fast, reactive, and powerful extension of the hips.
- Shortly before touchdown, the knee joint is almost straight, and the tip of the foot is raised (dorsiflexed and supinated).
- The knee flexors contract reactively; before touchdown they bend the knee slightly again and (partially) support the extension of the hip.
- The foot is placed on the ground over the outside of the ball of the foot, with fixed foot as close to the vertical projection of the CG as possible.
- Small stride width.
- Continuation of the hip extension; the muscles of the front thigh stabilise the knee; the calf muscles stabilise the ankle joint; the bending of the leg following the touchdown (amortisation) is as minimal as possible.
- Reactive and powerful extension of the hip, knee, and ankle joints during the rear support phase; the extension remains incomplete so that the next stride can be prepared quickly.
- The contralateral arm swing is initiated by the shoulder and is performed almost parallel to the running direction; the backswing is emphasised; elbow angle approximately 90°, only slight opening during the backward swing and closing during the forward swing; hands are kept loose in the central position; hands are moved forward up to chin level, backward to just behind the hips (forearm not exceeding the vertical).

ATTACKING THE FINISH LINE AND SUBSEQUENT DECELERATION

- Shifting of the chest and trunk to the front relative to the arms, upper head, and legs as close to the finish line as possible; also slight shifting forward of the CG relative to the touchdown point.
- Maintenance of tension in order to decelerate without running the risk of injury; shifting backward of the trunk and thus the CG.

1.3.5 PHOTO SEQUENCES

**CROUCH START AND
START ACCELERATION**

Data about the photo sequence

Athlete:	Leena Günther (born: 16 April 1991, Germany)
Height/weight:	1.63 m/54 kg
Best performance:	11.46 sec (wind: +1.0 m/sec; 5 June 2010, Regensburg)
Greatest success:	Fifth place over 100m and second place over 4 x 100m at the 2010 U20 World Championships in 2010, fifth place over 4 x 100m at the 2012 Olympic Games

COMMENTARY

Filming a 100m sprint competition from the front is nearly impossible due to the camera position required. Therefore, the photo sequence shows a training run of the three-time German A-Junior Champion (100, 200, and 4 x 100m) filmed in 2010.

Picture 1 shows a relaxed and largely appropriate on-your-marks position. The distance of the blocks to the line (not shown here) is 1½–1¾ feet in length for the front, plus almost another foot in length to the rear block. The front block is set in the 0 notch, while the rear block is set in the second notch. The relatively close positioning of the hands, the high support of the fingers, and the extended arms result in the highest possible position of the shoulders and thus a maximum hip angle. It is striking that the left hand is further to the outside than the right hand, or (in other words) that the hand support seems to be offset to the left. Günther overextends her left arm, while she keeps her right elbow in a minimally bent position. In terms of optimum pre-tension, the position of the right elbow seems to be more appropriate. The different positions of the arms can be interpreted as compensation for the displaced hand position, whereby the shoulders are again slightly pushed back to the right.

In the set position (picture 2), the displaced hand position results in a shift of the pelvis to the right and a shift of the head to the left in front of the rear leg. Otherwise, the set position seems appropriate: The athlete's view is directed between her hands. Most of her weight seems to rest on her arms. Her pelvis is significantly higher than her shoulders and the angle at the front knee seems to be approximately 90°. Her foot position indicates that there is good pressure against the blocks and that she has placed her feet relatively high against the blocks. This appears to be quite useful for achieving a high CG position and a flat push-off in spite of her rather small feet.

Pictures 3 and 4 are the last photos, each before the two feet are released from the blocks. Although Günther might exert pressure against the block with her rear leg for a moment longer, this leg is released in accordance with the target technique considerably prior to full knee extension. The push-off of the front leg leads to a good, complete, and flat extension with ideal arm movements.

The other pictures are the first and last shots of the first ground contact phases. Günther's first foot touchdown occurs slightly outward, as is usual. However, at the second touchdown (right foot), she continues to place her foot on the left side of the track with only a narrow stride width and thereafter she also remains on this side of the track. In other start attempts (possibly due to a stronger push-off of the front leg), all ground contacts continue to be further to the left. Her coach explains this by pointing to strength deficits in her left leg (up to -11%) because of which it is impossible for her to sufficiently compensate for her drift to the left during the first ground contact. A more powerful push-off of her left leg from the block and an attempt to run straight out of the blocks could also be possible approaches to solving this problem. However, an attempt to run straight out of the blocks could lead to a weaker push-off of the right leg. A more promising approach seems to be shifting the support points of both hands approximately 3–10cm to the right. Since the greatest part of the push-off out of the blocks is performed by the front leg, the shoulders and thus the CG should be at least in the middle in front of the legs or even somewhat further on the side of the front leg.

The pictures show a technique which is largely in accordance with the target technique, including a slow raising of the head and straightening up from the forward lean.

FREE SPRINT
AT MAXIMUM
VELOCITY

Data about the photo sequence

Athlete:	Usain Bolt (born: 21 August 1986, Jamaica)
Height/weight:	1.94 m/93 kg
Performance:	9.69 sec (wind: ± 0.0 m/sec; 16 August 2008, Beijing, world record)
Personal best:	9.58 sec (wind: +0.9 m/sec; 16 August 2009, Berlin, world record)
Greatest successes:	Olympic champion over 100, 200, and 4 x 100m in 2008 and 2012, world champion over 100, 200, and 4 x 100m in 2009, as well as over 200 and 4 x 100m in 2011

COMMENTARY

Usain Bolt's victory in Beijing has become known as the most relaxed Olympic victory and world record ever. More than 30 metres from the finish, Bolt glanced to the left and right several times. Approximately 15 metres before the finish line, he even rejoiced by stretching his arms sideward and downward and by hitting his chest with his right hand even before reaching the finish line. Consequently, he was able to improve the world record exactly one year later to 9.58 sec. Although in this race he celebrated his victory not before the finish line, his running style and his whole manner were still extremely relaxed.

In the Olympic final in Beijing, Usain Bolt took only 41.2 strides. This number is extremely low and synonymous with a superior average stride length of 2.43 m. Although outstanding, these values can be expected with such a finishing time and his body height. At 1.94 m, Bolt is remarkably tall for a sprinter. An examination of the entire run shows that Bolt was not in the lead from the start, which is also quite typical of tall 100m sprinters. At 20 metres, he was just behind the eventual runner-up Richard Thomson (Trinidad & Tobago, 9.89 sec). Only at the transition to the pick-up acceleration phase, or to grasping/pulling sprinting, did Bolt begin to overtake Thomson before clearly pulling away in the maximum-velocity phase between 50 and 60 m. This photo sequence made by ZDF television images in Germany shows Bolt at a distance between 75 and 80 m.

Bolt keeps his pelvis stable and upright so that at the moment of maximum hip extension his knees are not fully extended (pictures 5–6 and 16–17). In the subsequent swing phase, he raises his heels in an exemplary relaxed manner from his hips until he has achieved a maximally flexed position under his body (pictures 2 and 13). As a result, he is already able to move the knee of his swing leg alongside the knee of his support leg at the moment of the touchdown of the support leg (pictures 1 and 12). Thus, an actively grasping front swing phase is possible, during which the thigh swings almost up to the horizontal (pictures 6 and 17) while the lower leg swings loosely forward. Shortly before his pulling touchdown, his leg is almost extended (pictures 11 and 23). The high hips enable Bolt to perform the touchdown close to the vertical projection of his CG (pictures 12 and 23–24). In the short support phase, there is only a slight yield at the knee of the support leg (the maximum knee bend can be seen in pictures 3 and 13–14), so that the variation of the CG height remains low. Bolt keeps his heel low at the moment of touchdown (pictures 2 and 13), the work of his ankle is active (raised tip of the foot before touchdown [Pictures 10 and 21]), and there is ankle extension during the push-off from the ground [pictures 6 and 17]).

In this phase, Bolt is sprinting with a fairly clear forward lean of his trunk. This is partly due to his arm work, which for the most part occurs behind his body in an unusually pronounced manner. By striking his hands backward and by achieving the maximum elbow angle already in the middle of the backswing (pictures 13–14), he well supports the pull-through movement of the opposite support leg. Subsequently, the angle of the elbow is already reduced while he swings his elbow unusually high up to almost shoulder height (pictures 7 and 17). During the forward swing, Bolt strongly flexes his elbow. His upper arm remains almost vertical. All these movements are criticised by some people since it results in a rocking movement of his shoulders (brief pulling up and twisting about the longitudinal body axis).

1.3.6 STRATEGY

The race model by Seagrave (2008, p. 7) can be understood as a possible strategy for the 100m race. Seagrave proposes dividing the 100m distance into five sections with four breaths. According to Seagrave, athletes have 5 metres time for each breath. Each breath consists of very quickly exhaling and inhaling. During the five major sections, each of which is 15–20m long, the athlete is supposed to hold his breath and focus on a specific technical feature. Each technical feature is represented by a keyword that the athlete shall repeat in mind during the corresponding phase.

On your marks: After the signal and before crouching down, the athlete can still perform some reactive and powerful ankle jumps to incite the muscles (see chapter I–5.1).

0–15 m: The mental command "push" represents the described technique of toe push-off sprinting (see chapter II–1.3.3). The athlete should focus on hip and knee extension with an optimum forward lean of his/her body.

20–35 m: The mental command "drive taller" helps the athlete to keep in mind that he/she shall now increasingly straighten up his/her body to be able to change into the grasping/pulling sprinting phase (see chapter II–1.3.3). The athlete slowly directs his/her view toward the finish. He/she is now running with increasingly high hips. The pelvis is kept upright by the abdominal muscles.

40–60 m: The mental command "step over" represents the idea that the athlete should lift his foot during each swing over the height of the knee of his/her supporting leg. This shall help to emphasise the heel kick and the knee lift (i.e., hip flexion) and thus the preparation of the grasping sprinting action.

65–80 m: The mental command "grab back" (= grip and pull) is supposed to direct the athlete's focus to the immediate preparation of the ground contact. An aggressive hip extension (i.e., the rapid movement just before the touchdown of the almost straight leg) shall be the focus of attention.

85-100 m: In front of the finish line, the mental command "hot track" is once again supposed to focus the sprinter's attention on the hip flexion and stride frequency. The sprinter imagines running on a hot plate.

15-20, 35-40, 60-65, and 80-85 m: In the athlete's imagination, the breaths are comparable to shifting from a lower gear to a higher gear in a race car.

To actually be able to implement this racing model in competition, it must first be intensively practised in training. For example, the different sections can be marked by cones in training, and the various tasks can initially be performed on the coach's command.

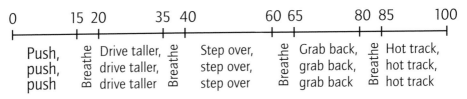

Figure 17: **Race model** with keywords (modified on the basis of Seagrave, 2008, p. 7)

1.3.7 DIDACTICS: SUPERORDINATE LONG-TERM OBJECTIVES AND GENERAL METHODOLOGY

Sprint training should be started with sprinting games. In addition to a number of major and minor games, relays are especially important in playful sprint training. The challenging nature of games and relays, and the idea of team spirit, have a motivating effect, and the competitive character ensures the necessary high intensity. Not only versatile and coordinative aspects of reacting, starting, accelerating, and free sprinting, but also the required (acyclic) speed and strength capacities can be trained in a playful manner. Depending on the organisation of games and relays, the focus can be on (maximum) cyclic

(sprinting) speed or speed endurance. *The length of the sprints and the relationship between stress and recovery for each individual determine the effects.* Each of these playful training forms should be carried out only as long as the intensity is high and the participants are having fun. The high intensity also requires a thorough prior warm-up, which means conversely that games are unsuitable at least for the first phase of the warm-up.

Exercises from the ABCs of sprinting should also be included very early in training. This can even be done first in connection with minor games and relays. Apart from the general and coordinative effects, exercises utilising the ABCs of sprinting force athletes to focus especially on certain **elements of sprinting techniques**. Certain technical features (e.g., the grasping foot strike) are isolated and sometimes performed in an exaggerated way. In particular, the various techniques of toe push-off and grasping/pulling sprinting should be practised very early. Exercises from the ABCs of sprinting are often integrated into later phases of the warm-up. However, this should be done as rarely as possible without the supervision of a coach especially at a young age. Otherwise, there is the risk that there will not be multifaceted technique training with corresponding improvements, but rather ingrained errors. The individual exercises should also be performed more than once so that the coach has the possibility for correction. However, if the athlete performs too many repetitions (more than three or four per exercise), the training progress is threatened by the athlete's decreasing attention.

The ABCs of jumping and multiple jumps (see chapter I–5.4.6) are crucial for sprinters when training reactive strength, and their technique should also be developed early on. Some coaches believe that sprinters should even perform jumps which are typically performed with a touchdown of the entire foot (e.g., bounding runs, 88) with a touchdown with only the ball of the foot. Regardless, the foot strike should be active in any case (i.e., it should be performed based on the previously raised tip of the foot).

Between the ABCs of sprinting, which divides the sprinting stride into its elements, and the holistic training of the complete sprinting action, there are exercises in technique training from basic training onward which focus particularly on the various phases of a sprint. There are exercises exclusively for the start (e.g., 127) and exercises for practising specifically the start and toe push-off sprinting (e.g., 128). In respect to the slightly longer runs, the focus might then be on the transition to pick-up acceleration. Flying sprints (132) are performed specifically for practising grasping/pulling sprinting in the pick-up acceleration and maximum-velocity phase. Tempo runs (e.g., 143) are finally performed to improve the speed-endurance phase. In sprint training, particular attention is paid to avoiding so-called motor-dynamic stereotypes or neural barriers. This negative adaptation to certain constantly identical movement patterns must be prevented by versatile sprinting, different intensities and, in high-performance training, by supramaximal loads.

With advanced athletes, strength, speed, and (speed-)endurance training is based much more on the requirements of the 100m sprint listed in table 3 and on the corresponding training objectives and methods already listed in the general part of this book.

1.3.8 TRAINING CONTENTS: FORMS OF GAMES AND EXERCISES

101 Shadow running

Possible objectives: Warming up; versatile sprinting technique; (speed) endurance; leg strength.

Execution: Two partners one after the other; the follower must imitate the leader's movements.

Variations: As many changes of direction as possible; integration of exercises taken from the ABCs of sprinting (see below); on the coach's signal, the follower must catch the leader.

Typical load standards: See chapter II-1.3.7 in respect to the following game forms.

102 Catching games (e.g.: Tagging the team)

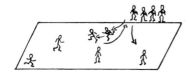

Possible objectives: Versatile sprinting technique; reaction, acyclic and cyclic speed, speed and reactive strength of the legs.

Execution: Team A is in a marked-off field; the members of team B are standing outside this field in a row; player X from team B tries to tag players from team A; if he/she succeeds, the player from team A tagged must squat down, and player X sprints back to player Y from team B, who also tries to tag someone; if a player from team B cannot tag anyone, he/she may decide himself/ herself the time when he/she will run back and pass on the task to the next teammate in the row; which team will take longer to tag all players of the other team?

Variations: Various types of movement (limping, skipping (87), etc.).

103 Rounders/Softball/Baseball and other major games

Possible objectives: Reaction speed, acyclic and cyclic speed; speed and reactive strength; hitting and throwing technique and strength.

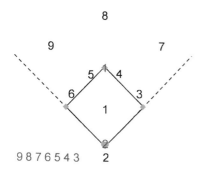

Execution: Player X of team A (e.g., the blue 2 in the picture) throws or kicks a ball onto the field, where team B is the defending team; player X runs from safe base to safe base until the ball has been taken to a certain spot by team B; if team B succeeds in this, while X is between two bases, player X is out; however, if X is standing on a safe base, he/she can continue to run when player Y of team A throws or kicks the ball; for each player who reaches the goal, team A is awarded one point; task switching between teams after a certain time.

Variations: Clearing an obstacle during the sprint (is the sprint character maintained?); different ways of movement (limping, running backward ...).

---

104   ▮▮▯▯   Sprint through a swinging rope

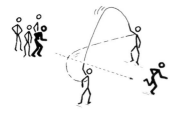

Possible objectives: Reaction speed, acyclic, and cyclic speed; speed and reactive strength of the legs.

Execution: The athlete tries to sprint through the rope without touching it.

Variations: With verbal commands: "On your marks – Set – Go"

---

105   ▮▯▯▯   Blue and red and other reaction games

Possible objectives: Reaction speed with subsequent action similar to sprinting.

Execution: Supine position; arms at the sides of the body; on the command "blue," left hand to the right knee; on the command "red," right hand to left knee.

Variations: Other reaction games.

106 Come along - run away!

Possible objectives: Versatile sprinting technique (curve technique); reaction speed; acyclic and cyclic speed; speed strength and reactive strength; depending on the organisation also speed endurance.

Execution: One player runs around groups of three players who are sitting on the ground and calls to one of them: "Come along" or "run away"; depending on the command, everyone tries to reach their sitting place again after running a full circle (in the same or opposite direction as the caller); the player who is last, tags the next group.

Variations: From a squatting position, lying position, push-up position; different types of movement (hopping, limping, running backward, walking like a crab, etc.).

107 Inner circle catches outer circle

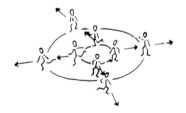

Possible objectives: Versatile sprinting technique; reaction speed; acyclic and cyclic speed; speed strength and reactive strength; depending on the organisation also speed endurance.

Execution: An identical number of players runs in two concentric circles in opposite directions; on the command, all of them sprint away to the outside and every player from the inner circle must chase a player from the outer circle.

Variations: Types of movement (see 106).

108 Numbers race

Possible objectives: Versatile sprinting technique; reaction speed; acyclic and cyclic speed; speed strength and reactive strength; depending on the organisation also speed endurance.

Execution: Depending on the number called, the

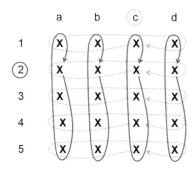

horizontal rows run around the vertical rows.

Variations: Additional letters for vertical rows, which then run around the horizontal rows; integrate code words (instead of numbers and letters) into a story; different types of movement (see 106).

---

109  Black and white

Possible objectives: Versatile sprinting technique; reaction speed; acyclic and cyclic speed; speed strength and reactive strength; depending on the organisation also speed endurance.

Execution: The colour called decides the direction of the sprint and who chases whom.

Variations: (See 106 in respect to types of movement); different starting positions (sitting, prone position, supine position, push-up, etc.).

---

110 ▮▮▮ Starting from various positions

Possible objectives: Versatile sprinting technique; reaction speed; acyclic and cyclic speed; speed strength and reactive strength; depending on the organisation also speed endurance.

Execution: In contrast to "black and white" (109), the running direction is now pre-determined (simple reaction).

Variations: Two runners in one lane, one leader and one chaser, or against opponents in other lanes; starting positions (see 109).

111 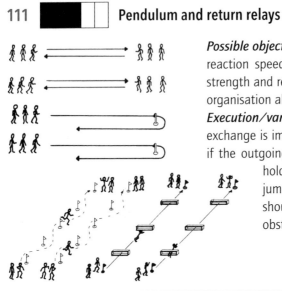 Pendulum and return relays

Possible objectives: Versatile sprinting technique; reaction speed; acyclic and cyclic speed; speed strength and reactive strength; depending on the organisation also speed endurance.

Execution/variations: In pendulum relays, a fair exchange is important; this can be accomplished if the outgoing runner takes over the baton by holding his/her arm around a high-jump post; the sprinting character should be maintained in spite of the obstacles.

See also the forms of games and exercises presented in connection with the 4x100m relay (see chapter II–1.6.8), particularly in respect to children's training, and the playful speed-endurance training forms for the 400m sprint and the 4x400m relay (see chapter II–1.5.8 and II–1.7.7).

112 ABCs of sprinting: high-knee run (one-legged or double contact)

Possible objectives: Technique of toe push-off sprinting; leg strength; stride-length training.

Execution: In contrast to step-over exercises (117), the foot should be raised on a relatively straight-line path during high-knee running movements; the knee should be raised up to the horizontal (no less and no more); the hip and knee of the supporting leg are fully extended; low support-leg heel.

Variations: (See 120, 121, 130, 131, and 135); in a standing position with forward lean of the whole body and hands supported against a wall as an imitation of the start acceleration.

Typical load standards: 2–4 reps of 20–30m each.

High-knee run:

One-legged high-knee run (limping run):

Double-contact high-knee run (Frankies):

---

113  **ABCs of sprinting: Running with knees raised to half the horizontal position**

Possible objectives: Technique of toe push-off sprinting; reactive strength; stride-frequency training; fixed foot.

Execution: Knees half as high as in high-knee running (see 112).

Variations: Mostly with an emphasis on frequency (see 120, 121, 130, 131, & 135).

Typical load standards: 2–4 reps of 10–20m each.

---

114 ▮▮▮ **ABCs of sprinting: Imitation of grasping movements in a standing position**

Possible objectives: Technique of grasping/pulling sprinting.

Execution: Standing on one leg (possibly on an elevation, possibly while holding on to something with one's hands on the sides; possibly easier in running shoes); the other leg performs grasping movements (from the hips).

Variations: A quick grasping movement on command from various starting positions.

Typical load standards: 2–3 sets of 10 reps each per side.

---

115 ▮▮▮ **ABCs of sprinting: Heel kicks**

Possible objectives: Technique of grasping/pulling sprinting; strength of the flexor muscles.

Execution: Heel kicks should not be performed behind, but under the body (from below up to the buttocks).

Variations: Sideward and backward (see also 120, 121, 130, 131, and 135); as limping run comparable to the one-legged high-knee run (112).

Typical load standards: 2–4 reps of 20–30m each.

116 ABCs of sprinting: Pulling stride

Possible objectives: Technique of grasping/pulling sprinting; leg strength.

Execution: Task: "Pull your hip with extended leg over the touchdown point."

Variations: (See 120, 121, 130, and 131).

Typical load standards: 2–4 reps of 20–30m each.

117 ABCs of sprinting: Step-over (with pulling)

Possible objectives: Technique of grasping/pulling sprinting; leg strength.

Execution: "Try each time to lift the foot of your swing leg over the knee of your support leg!" (see photo sequence below).

Variations: Later also with earlier grasping movement and stronger pulling action (see photo sequence on the left; see also 120, 121, 130, and 131); as limping run comparable to the one-legged high-knee run (112).

Typical load standards: 2–4 reps of 20–30m each.

118 ABCs of sprinting: Skipping with grasping action (specific to sprinting)

Possible objectives: Technique of grasping/pulling sprinting.

Execution: (Relaxed) skipping (87) on the balls of the feet with grasping movements during the swinging phase.

Variations: Grasping with only one leg.

Typical load standards: 2–4 reps of 20–30m each.

119 ABCs of sprinting: Can-can exercise

Possible objectives: Technique of toe push-off and/or grasping/pulling sprinting (depending on the execution); leg strength.

Execution: Similar to the can-can dance: Push-off from both legs side by side, then one leg performs heel kick or knee lift (see photo sequence below) or step-over movement (see photo below right); while this leg is at its highest point, the other leg is placed down and pushes off again; then touchdown and push-off with both legs side by side again.

Variations: The free leg changes each time, or not at all, or after every third time, etc.; with arm action (e.g., each time when the left knee is lifted, clap your hands with your arms extended once below the knee, once in front of your chest, and once over your head, then switch to right knee lift, and clap your hands three times as before).

Typical load standards: 2–4 reps of 10–20m each.

120   ABCs of sprinting: Quick leg

Possible objectives: Technique of toe push-off and/or grasping/pulling sprinting (depending on the execution); leg strength.

Execution/variations: Relaxed running with knees raised to half the horizontal position (113); in the process, every 5th, 4th, or 3rd stride maximally fast high-knee movement (112); also with jogging and heel kicks (115), or with pulling strides (116), and with step-overs with grasping action (117).

Typical load standards: 2–3 reps of 20–30m each for each variation.

121 **ABCs of sprinting: Combination and transitions**

Possible objectives: Technique of toe push-off and/or grasping/pulling sprinting (depending on the execution); leg strength.

Execution/variations: From heel kicks (115), or pulling strides (116), to step-overs (117); alternation between powerful high-knee running (112) and frequency-focused running with knees raised to half the horizontal position (113); high-knee run, then increase forward body lean up to toe push-off sprinting; heel kicks, step-overs (with grasping action) or pulling strides, then increase locomotion velocity and (fluent) transition to grasping/pulling sprinting; one and the same exercise forward, backward, and sideward.

Typical load standards: 2–3 reps of 20–70m each for each variation.

All forms of jumping (78–92, and 261–270) also play a crucial role for the sprint. From children's training on, and even more so in basic training, the technique of the simpler exercises of the ABCs of jumping should be developed.

122  **Falling starts**

Possible objectives: Correct forward lean of the body during toe push-off sprinting (during start acceleration).

Execution: Both feet side by side on the balls (low heel); stand upright and extended; tilt slowly forward, start running as late as possible, but extend your body during all following strides (the hips should not be lowered too much).

Variations: As chain reaction: Athletes stand side by side and start shortly one after the other; also through the curve.

Typical load standards: 2–5 reps of 10–40m each.

123　　Starts from a standing position

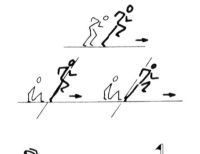

Possible objectives: Technique of toe push-off sprinting, speed strength, and reactive strength of the legs; acyclic and cyclic speed.

Execution: Feet offset by one foot length in running direction (tip of one foot on a line with the heel end of the other foot); standing on the balls of the feet (low heel); legs are bent (front knee approximately 90°); trunk (almost) horizontal; arms contralateral to leg position with bent elbows; let yourself tilt forward; the rear leg is the first to be moved forward; pay attention to forward body lean and extension (see falling start, 122).

Variations: Chain reaction (see 122); three-point start: hand is placed on the ground at the side of the rear leg (1½–2 feet in front of the front foot); partner's feet under the heels to imitate blocks for better push-off; also focusing on the transition to pick-up acceleration or to grasping/pulling sprinting; also through the curve.

Typical load standards: 2–5 reps of 20–50m each.

124　Four-point start with elevated hand support

Possible objectives: Technique of the crouch start (with facilitation).

Execution: Elevated hand support on two laterally placed boxes (facilitation of initial extension).

Variations: From blocks or from the partner's feet as block imitation (see starts from a standing position, 123); also through the curve.

Typical load standards: 2–4 reps of 20–40m each.

125 Crouch start and acceleration

Possible objectives: Training of the target technique; speed strength and reactive strength of the legs; acyclic and cyclic speed.

Execution: (See technique chapter II–1.3.3).

Variations: With and without command (if without command, do not take a preliminary swing, but start from static set position); alone or against one another (also with handicap bonus for individual sprinters); from blocks or in children's training from the partner's feet as block imitation; also focusing on the transition to pick-up acceleration or to grasping/pulling sprinting; also through the curve.

Typical load standards: 3–8 reps of 20–50m each; in pyramids: 20, 30, 40, 50, 40, 30, and 20m; rest interval: running distance divided by 5 in min.

126 Multiple hip raises into the set position and return

Execution: From the on-your-marks position rapidly to the set position; correction and return.

Variations: With subsequent start.

Typical load standards: 2–4 x raising and lowering, 3–6 reps (starts in between).

127 Jump from the starting block

Possible objectives: Push off of both legs from the blocks.

Execution: The starting blocks are placed in front of the soft floor mat; on command: maximal extension out of the set position into a 45°-angle position (caution: the important, partially overlaid follow-up movement of the first knee lift is neglected here).

Typical load standards: 2–4 reps, possibly several sets with crouch starts in between.

128   Sprints into or under a finish tape

Possible objectives: Correct forward lean of the body during start acceleration.

Execution: Caution: no forward lean of the trunk with bent hips, but forward lean of the whole body.

Typical load standards: 2–4 reps of 10–20m each.

129   Acceleration and coordination runs

Possible objectives: Technique of (grasping/pulling) sprinting; special warm-up; reactive strength of legs; cyclic speed.

Execution: Submaximal acceleration up to (sub-)maximal pace and maintenance of pace (in most cases, the runner decelerates before he/she reaches the speed-endurance zone); focusing on technique, playing with technique.

Variations: (See versatile sprinting, 130).

Typical load standards: 2–6 reps of 50–70m each.

130   Versatile sprinting

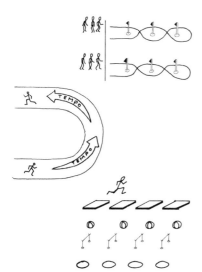

Possible objectives: Versatile sprinting technique (toe push-off and grasping/pulling sprinting); special warm-up; speed strength and reactive strength particularly of the legs; acyclic and cyclic speed.

Execution/variations: Sprinting in slalom, in a circle, through a curve (curve technique), over obstacles, at a different pace, backward (with heels high), with eyes closed, with head movements (looking upward, downward, to the left, and to the right); with slight forward and backward lean of the trunk; with additional tasks (e.g., counting backward from 100 in steps of three); on synthetic track, lawn, sand, etc. (immediately before the competition only on synthetic track); etc.

Typical load standards: depending on the task; 1–3 reps.

---

131  Sprinting with varying arm actions

Possible objectives: Demonstration and training of the arm action and trunk stabilisation in sprinting.

Execution/variations: Sprinting with the arms extended upward, downward, forward, backward, and sideward, with loosely dangling arms, with arms folded behind the head or in front of the chest; with medicine ball in one arm, in front of the chest, over the head, behind the back; with relay batons, weights (≤ 2 kg) or similar objects in the hands; without or with exaggerated, correct, or false arm action; arm action (with weights) also when standing.

Typical load standards: 2–10 reps of 40–80m each, variation of tasks (even within a sprint).

---

132 Flying sprints

Possible objectives: Technique of grasping/pulling sprinting; reactive strength; cyclic speed.

Execution: (Mostly maximal) sprint over a fixed distance from (submaximal) pre-acceleration.

Variations: Often also as test (T24) through light barriers; through a curve.

Typical load standards: 20–30m flying after 20–50m acceleration; at maximum intensity mostly no more than 3 reps; rest interval: running distance (run-up and flying) divided by 5 in min.

---

133 Alternating-pace sprints (ins and outs)

Possible objectives: Technique of grasping/pulling sprinting; reactive strength; cyclic

speed; depending on load standards also speed endurance.

Execution: Alternating phases of maximal (i.e., faster) and submaximal/technical (i.e., slower) sprinting.

Variations: Without fixed points of change or with points of change marked by traffic cones; through the curve; change of stride frequency.

Typical load standards: Total distance 60–120 m, phases 10–25 m; considerably varying depending on the objective; even within tempo runs (143 and 144).

---

134   Tappings

Possible objectives: Cyclic speed (with reduced loading).

Execution/variations: Trampling or treading of feet with maximum frequency.

Typical load standards: 2–5 reps of 5–7 sec each (do not forget rest intervals!).

a   b   c   d

---

135   Frequency sprints and coordination

Possible objectives: Cyclic speed (stride-frequency training), reactive strength, versatile sprinting technique.

Execution: (ABCs of) sprinting with increased stride frequency.

Variations: Indication of stride-length shortening by means of hurdle boards, ropes, foam blocks, cones, tyres, bicycle tubes, medicine balls, mats, and mini-hurdles; at the start also with increasing distances; possibly from a run-up.

Typical load standards: 3–8 reps of 10–30m each.

136 Stride-length training

Possible objectives: Speed and reactive strength of the extensor loop in particular; versatile sprinting technique.

Execution: Sprinting with longer strides.

Variations: Lengthening of strides by using hurdle boards, etc. (see 135); at the start also with increasing distances; from bounding run (88), from step-overs (with grasping movement, 117) to sprinting.

Typical load standards: 3–6 reps of 40–60m each.

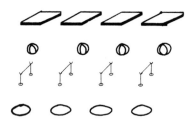

After playful strengthening exercises in children's athletics (e.g., see 30, 33, and 78), one should begin with foot- and trunk-stabilisation exercises as early as in basic training (41–47, and 50–52). For advanced 100m sprinters, the following strength exercises are of increasing importance: 48–49, 60–64, 66–77 and 79–96.

137 (Pull-)resisted sprints

Possible objectives: (a) Technique of toe push-off sprinting; maximal strength and speed strength of the extensor loop in particular; (b) technique of grasping/pulling sprinting; speed strength and reactive strength of the hamstrings in particular.

Execution/variations: (a) Resistance through partner from the front and from behind (by grasping the hips or with rope or elastic band); pushing of gym mat transporter or (upside down) large gym box; pulling of car tyres, tractor tyres, or heavy, weighted sleds on a rope (> 5 kg, for top athletes up to 60 kg; hip belt is better than shoulder belt; the rope should be long; in this case

start from starting blocks is also possible; the blocks should be removed by partner immediately after the start to create space for the sled); (b) with parachute, paraglide chute, or light pulling sled (< or = 5 kg); with some systems it is possible to release the resistance so that the athlete can then sprint freely; also against strong headwind; also through the curve.

Typical load standards: (a) 10–40 m, (b) 50–120 m; the number of runs depends on the intensity (see 125 and 143–145); with younger athletes, only playful partner exercises; with older athletes, higher loads (as target-oriented strength training); often alternated with normal sprints.

---

138  Uphill and stair sprints

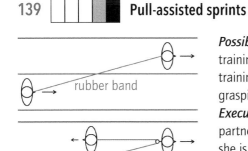

Possible objectives: Concentric strength of the extensor loop; technique of toe push-off sprinting.

Execution: (e.g., in open terrain).

Variations: Depending on the incline and number of repetitions, the focus is on speed, speed strength, or speed endurance.

Typical load standards: (See crouch start and acceleration (125) or tempo runs (143–145)).

---

139  Pull-assisted sprints

rubber band

pulley

Possible objectives: Eccentric reactive-strength training of the legs; cyclic speed (stride-frequency training, breaking of speed barriers); technique of grasping/pulling sprinting.

Execution: The sprinter is pulled by his/her partner using a pulley or rubber band so that he/she is able to run faster than without assistance.

Variations: Rubber bands should be used with not-so-advanced athletes; if pulleys are used, there will be a greater assistance during the maximum-velocity phase; the time is measured by means of light barriers (the objective is to reach a faster time than in a flying sprint, 132); also with continuing to sprint as fast as possible after the towing rope has been released.

Typical load standards: 2–3 reps of 30–50m each; rest interval: running distance divided by 5 in min.

140 Downhill or tailwind sprints

Possible objectives: Eccentric reactive-strength training of the legs; cyclic speed (stride-frequency training, breaking of speed barriers).

Execution/variations: Downhill sprints or sprints with strong tailwind (wind sprints).

Typical load standards: 2–5 reps of 40–80m each at maximum intensity; rest interval: running distance divided by 5 in min.

141 ABCs of endurance

Possible objectives: (Variation in) speed-endurance training and (reactive) strength-endurance training.

Execution/variations: ABCs of sprinting/jumping over considerably longer distances and/or duration; possibly with weighted sleeves on the feet.

Typical load standards: for example, 100m bounding run or 20 sec step-overs; in long sprint and middle-distance running even considerably longer.

142 LI tempo runs for short-distance sprinters and jumpers

Possible objectives: Aerobic endurance; speed endurance; movement economy; warm-up.

Execution: Runs at low intensity (LI; see table 12 in chapter I–4.5) in accordance with pre-set

guiding times (see tempo table in chapter II–1.5.8); in spite of pre-set times the runs should be performed at even pace (the first ones not too fast), but the total time of all runs should be as fast as possible; if possible, they should be performed in groups, from standing start on the command of one of the sprinters: "forward – backward – go" and corresponding forward and backward movements of the body.

Variations: Curve plus straight or straight plus curve; in the wrong direction; on varying surfaces: synthetic track, lawn, forest track, etc.; mostly wearing running shoes; as (endless) relay (173); also as runs with pre-set running times (seconds) and intensity control by varying the distance to be run in this time.

Typical load standards: For example:

a) According to the extensive interval method: 3 sets of 4–5 reps of 150–200m each; walking interval: 90 sec, rest interval between sets: 5–8 min.

b) For sprint-specific warm-up: 6–10 reps of 60–100m each; walking interval: 15–30 sec.

---

143 **I3 tempo runs for short-distance sprinters and jumpers**

Possible objectives: Speed endurance; movement economy (= coordination); reactive strength.

Execution: Runs at intensity level 3 (I3, see table 12 in chapter I–4.5, tempo table in chapter II–1.5.8, as well as LI tempo runs, 142); if possible in groups, but in individual lanes; usually wearing spikes.

Variations: (See LI tempo runs, 142); each athlete should run once in each lane: once in the inside lane, once in the outside lane; also in combination with light pulling resistance (137), uphill (138), with changes of pace (133), or over hurdles (207).

Typical load standards: For example:

a) Over-distance runs according to the intensive interval method as sets: 2 sets of 4–5 reps of 150 m; walking interval: 5 min; rest interval between sets: 10 min.

b) According to the intensive interval method in pyramids: 80, 100, 120, 150, 180, 150, 120, 100, and 80 m; rest intervals: 2, 3, 4, 5, 10, 6, 5, and 4 min.

c) Under-distance runs according to the extensive interval method as sets: 4 sets of 5 reps of 60 m, or 4 reps of 80 m; walking interval: 90–120 sec; rest interval between sets: 8 min.

---

144 ▯▯▮ **I2 Tempo runs for short-distance sprinters and jumpers**

Possible objectives: Speed endurance (at higher intensity); movement economy; reactive strength.

Execution: Runs at intensity level 2 (I2, see table 12 in chapter I–4.5, tempo table in chapter II–1.5.8, as well as I3 tempo runs, 143).

Variations: (See I3 tempo runs, 143).

Typical load standards: For example:

a) According to the repetition method as sets: 3–4 reps of 100m each, 4–5 reps of 80m each or 6 reps of 60m each; rest intervals: running distance divided by 10 in min.

b) According to the intensive interval method as sets: 3 sets of 3 reps of 60m each, or 2 sets of 3 reps of 80m each, walking interval: 4 or 6 min, rest interval between sets: 12 or 15 min.

c) According to the repetition method in pyramids: 80, 120, 150, 120, and 80 m, or 150, 120, 100, and 80m (or in reverse order); rest intervals: running distance divided by 10 in min.

---

145 ▯▯▮ **I1 Tempo runs for short-distance sprinters and jumpers**

Possible objectives: Speed endurance (at maximum intensity); movement economy; reactive strength.

Execution: Runs at intensity level 1 (I1, see table 12 in chapter I–4.5, tempo table in chapter II–1.5.8, as well as I3 tempo runs, 143).

Variations: On the straight, through a curve, or both; in training or (preparatory) competition.

Typical load standards: According to the competition or repetition method as sets: 1–3 runs, often slightly longer than the competition distance (e.g., 2 reps of 120m each); rest intervals: 20–30 min.

At the beginning of general preparation, even short-distance sprinters should perform aerobic endurance training (besides 142 see also 227–231; for reasons see chapter I-1.5).

1.3.9 SPECIAL TEST AND CONTROL PROCEDURES

Test: Ability/skill tested	Execution/comments
T21 **60m analysis:** Sprinting technique	Maximal sprint from the blocks (125; with or without starting signal); judging on the basis of technique (see chapter II-1.3.4), possibly by means of video (T1), and picture sequences made thereof.
T22 **Crouch-start reaction test:** Reaction speed	Only possible by means of sensors in the starting blocks (rarely available in training).
T23 **Crouch start and acceleration up to 20 m:** a) Reaction speed and start acceleration; b) Start acceleration without reaction speed	Start and sprint from the starting blocks (see exercise 125): **a)** electronic time measurement (very complex; with manual time measurement; the possible error may be as great as possible improvements). **b)** 1. with light barriers at 1 and 20 (or 21) m; 2. with special systems; time is started when the hand or the foot leaves a contact surface; at the finish, the athlete runs through light barriers; 3. with LAVEG measurement (see next page).
T24 **30m flying sprint:** Maximum sprinting speed	Running over a 30m distance after an arbitrarily long run-up (see exercise 132); measurement by means of light barriers (with manual time measurement; the possible error may be as great as possible improvements).
T25 **20m frequency test:** Cyclic speed	Running over foam blocks at 1m distances; arbitrarily long run-up; if possible, measurement by means of light barriers.

(continued)

(continued)

Test: Ability/skill tested	Execution/comments
T26 **Short-sprint tempo-run programmes:** Anaerobic speed endurance and aerobic endurance	For example, standardised programmes can be as follows: a) LI: 3 x 5 x 200 m; rest intervals: 90 sec; rest intervals between sets: 6 min b) I3: 2 x 4 x 150 m; rest intervals: 5 min; rest intervals between sets: 10 min c) I2: 4 x 120 m; rest intervals: 15 min The (average) times achieved and the post-exercise lactate values are used as test criteria.
T4 **1RPM:** Maximal strength	Squat (62), clean (63), snatch (64), flexor (68), extensor (69), arm exercises, etc. (if possible, also eccentric maximal strength measurement).
T5 **Squat jump, and T8 counter-movement and drop jump:** Two-legged speed strength and reactive strength of the extensor loop	As simpler test, the forward and/or backward toss of the shot (93) can be performed for distance.
T9 **5-stride hops with distance maximisation:** Reactive strength of the legs in comparison to one another	Test should be performed on both sides.
T10 **30m bounding run with time minimisation:** Reactive strength of the legs	
T44 **130m test:** Specific speed endurance	30m curve + 100m straight.
T66 **Graded field test:** Basic aerobic endurance	With lactate withdrawal (and spirometry; for young athletes also Cooper test, T65, which is easy to perform but inaccurate).
T2 **Flexibility tests:** General flexibility	
T3 **Body weight and body fat measurement:** Relative strength	Inappropriate upward and downward deflections should be avoided.

Moreover, for all sprint events, especially when dealing with specific issues, additional sports-medicine (e.g., blood tests), biomechanical, sport-psychology, nutritional, etc. tests, are recommended).

*Table 4: **Basic performances of 100m sprinters** (according to Tepper & Czingon, 1995, p. 44)*

	Women			Men		
100m target time (sec)	11.95	11.60	11.20	10.90	10.60	10.20
30m from the starting blocks (sec)	4.40	4.38	4.18	4.15	4.11	3.82
30m flying (sec)	3.19	3.05	2.86	2.88	2.74	2.70
200m (sec)	24.60	23.20	22.60	21.95	20.95	20.45
10-stride bounding run (m)	22-25	24-28	26-30	32-34	35-38	37-40
½ squat (barbell weight = body weight x factor)	1.5-1.8	1.7-2.0	1.8-2.1	2.2-2.6	2.4-2.8	2.5-2.9
Running velocity at 4 mmol/l measured in graded lactate field test (m/sec)	3.4-3.7	3.7-3.9	3.9-4.1	3.8-4.0	3.8-4.0	3.8-4.1

LAVEG VELOCITY MEASUREMENT

For a long time, sprint velocity in certain sections of a sprinting distance have been measured by means of light barriers and by evaluating (high-speed) videos filmed from the side. The latter are also used for the measurement of stride length and stride frequency. To effectively calculate stride lengths and section velocities, there must be either markings on the track, or the video recordings must be calibrated accordingly. On a computer, the video recordings are transformed into two-dimensional space, or, if at least two cameras are used which are placed at right angles to each other, a three-dimensional space is created in which also joint angles (and angular velocities), etc. can be measured.

Since 1993, it has been possible to measure horizontal velocity more easily (especially in linear sprints, also occurring in the long jump, triple jump, and pole vault), namely by means of laser measurement using the LAVEG device (LAser VElocity Guard), which was originally developed for military purposes. In sports, the runner is traced by looking through a sight and targeted from the front or rear. A laser beam is emitted and reflected by the athlete 50 (or 100) times per second. By using the established speed of light (c) and the time (t) between emitting and receiving the beam, the distance ($d = c/t$) between the device and the athlete can be calculated. By using the change in this distance ($\Delta d = d_2 - d_1$) and the time elapsed between measurements ($\Delta t = t_2 - t_1$), the runner's velocity can be calculated ($v = \Delta d / \Delta t$). Due to the short measurement intervals, one can speak of an analogous measurement of the instantaneous velocity which can be immediately displayed and analysed on a connected computer.

233

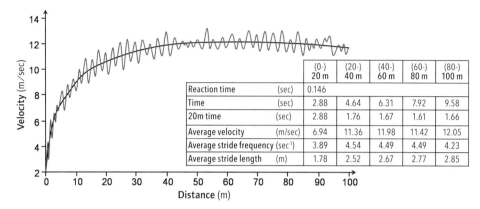

Figure 17: *LAVEG curve and smoothed velocity curve as well as supplementary data on Usain Bolt during his world-record run of 9.58 sec on 16 August 2010 at the World Championships in Berlin (modified on the basis of DLV, 2009). Although the oscillation of the curve reflects Bolt's stride frequency, it cannot be equated with the velocity changes of his CG from stride to stride since these are distorted by several error sources: fluttering of clothes, movement of the targeted point relative to the CG, etc.*

1.3.10 ERRORS - CAUSES - CORRECTIONS

In all disciplines, coaches should not stand too close to the action and should vary their observation point or angle of view to actually detect all errors effectively. Errors and their detection are always individual. Nevertheless, some errors can be identified which are particularly common or important for beginners. Of these errors, up to six are highlighted in blue for each discipline.

Error	Causes	Corrections
Hips too low in the "set" position (e.g., at shoulder height).	• The athlete is looking toward the finish with his/her head thrown back. • Athlete makes insufficient effort to raise his/her CG, since he/she has not yet experienced the benefits thereof.	✔ The athlete should look between his/her hands. ✔ Repeated lifting of the hips into the "set" position and back (126). ✔ Experimenting with different "set" positions.
In the "set" position, the athlete's shoulders and CG are too far back or the support of his/her hands is not high enough.	• Lack of strength in the fingers, arms, and shoulders. • Athlete makes insufficient effort to achieve a high and forward shifted CG position, since he/she has not yet experienced the benefits thereof.	✔ Appropriate strength games and exercises: 31, 32, 35-38, and 53. ✔ Repeated lifting of the hips into the "set" position and back (126). ✔ Experimenting with different "set" positions.

Error	Causes	Corrections
Otherwise inappropriate "set" position.	• Inappropriate block setting. • Inappropriate narrow or wide positioning of the hands.	✔ Front block approximately 1½ feet away from the finish line, approximately 50° to the ground; rear block approximately 1–1½ feet further back, approximately 70° to the ground. ✔ Hands only slightly further apart than shoulder width.
Frequent false starts.	• Too little competition simulation in training. • Too monotonous starting commands in training. • Restless "set" position: twitching or slow lowering of the hips. • Nervousness.	✔ Crouch start and acceleration (125): often on command (against each other). ✔ Advise to keep still in the "set" position. ✔ Constant variation of the pauses between the "set" command and the starting signal. ✔ Sanctioning of false starts even in training (e.g., by making the athlete perform extra tasks). ✔ Psychoregulatory assistance.
After the starting signal, the heels (especially the rear one) are initially moved backward (loss of time).	• Lack of pressure against the block (see chapter II–1.3.3).	✔ In the "set" position, the athlete should try to push the ground forward with his/her hands, which results in (pre-)tension of the extensor muscles so that the heels can be pushed backward.
Hips too low during the first strides so that the athlete appears to be falling forward on the first strides.	• Hips too low in the "set" position and its causes (see above). • Too much forward lean of the body, possibly because the shoulders are too far forward in the "set" position, so that • The push-off angle is too flat. • Lack of extension force.	✔ See corrections of "Hips too low in the 'set' position". ✔ Crouch starts and acceleration (125) with correction of technique. ✔ Maximal-strength training for the knee, hip, and trunk extensors.
Too upright or insufficient forward lean during the first strides.	• In the "set" position, the shoulders and the CG are too far backward and its causes (see above). • In the ("on your marks" and) "set" position, the athlete looks back or at his/her legs, which initially results in a hanging head and then in an exaggerated upward jerk of the head and straightening up during the start (the fast rotation of the head disturbs the vestibular system in the ear). • The athlete looks at the finish too early. • The athlete makes insufficient effort to attain a flat push-off position.	✔ Repeated lifting of the hips into the "set" position and back (126). ✔ At all times, the head should be aligned with the trunk. ✔ Sprints into or under a finish tape (128). ✔ Marking of points to look at 5, 10, and 20m after the start. ✔ Versatile technique training of the correct forward lean of the body and head position using exercises 122-124, and 137.

(continued)

(continued)

Error	Causes	Corrections
Lack of hip extension (hip bend) during start acceleration.	• The forward lean of the body is misunderstood as a forward lean of the trunk. • The athlete looks down too much (head on the chest during start acceleration).	✔ Versatile technique training (122-125, and 137), focusing on hip extension and head aligned with the trunk.
Too short strides, too high stride frequency, and lack of whole-body extension during start acceleration.	• False interpretation of the stride-frequency behaviour of top sprinters. Although the stride frequency reaches its maximum soon after the start, it should not be increased as fast as possible. • Lack of leg-extension force.	✔ Versatile, powerful start acceleration training using exercises 123-125, and 136-138. ✔ Bounding run (88) out of the blocks with forward body lean, touchdown on the balls of the feet, and focusing on extension. ✔ Maximal-strength training for knee, hip, and trunk extensors.
Exaggerated heel raise (behind the body) during the first strides.	• The athlete is unable to distinguish between grasping/pulling and toe push-off sprinting.	✔ High-knee run with forward body lean against wall (see 112). ✔ Transitions (121) from high-knee run or running with knees raised to half the horizontal position (113) to toe push-off sprinting. ✔ Versatile practising of start acceleration (123-125, and 136-138) with corresponding corrections (e.g., flat curve of foot movement).
Too small or too large stride width during the first strides.	• Too small: outdated model technique (see figure 12). • Too large: • Unsuitable imitation of top athletes. • Diagonal arm action.	✔ Experimenting with different stride width and corresponding tests (T21 and T23). ✔ Sprinting with corrected or varied arm action (125).
Static plantar flexion before foot touchdown (drop foot); often in connection with foot touchdown too far in front of the body.	• Muscles of the lower leg (dorsal and plantar flexion) and foot are too weak. • Athlete makes insufficient effort to raise the tip of his/her foot to initiate (from this position) an active foot touchdown to avoid braking forces during the front support.	✔ Strengthening the muscles in the lower leg and foot using exercises 50-52, 61, and 74. ✔ ABCs of sprinting as well as acceleration and coordination runs (129) with correction of the foot touchdown (see figure 15).
The heel touches the track (at foot touchdown or during the subsequent ground contact in toe push-off or grasping/pulling sprinting).	• Calf and foot muscles are too weak. • Too long strides and its causes (see below). • Athlete makes insufficient effort to attain a high running position.	✔ Strengthening the calf muscles using exercises 30, 50-52, and 74. ✔ See corrections of "too long strides" below. ✔ ABCs of sprinting as well as acceleration and coordination runs (129) focusing on correct foot touchdown and high running position (as though someone were pulling you up by the hair).

Error	Causes	Corrections
Too weak or wrong arm movements (e.g., diagonal, with too much movement at the elbow, too small or too large elbow angle).	• Weak coordination. • Lack of shoulder strength. • Often related to errors in leg action and their causes (see below).	✔ ABCs of sprinting/jumping and sprints with a focus on correct, energetic, and sometimes exaggerated arm actions. ✔ Training of shoulder strength, especially sprint arm swing with dumbbells (60).
Restless and/or swaying trunk.	• Incorrect arm action and its causes (see above), especially unsymmetrical and/or diagonal arm actions. • Weak trunk muscles. • Restless head posture. • Too large stride width and its causes (see below).	✔ See corrections of "too weak or wrong arm movements" above, and "too large stride width" below. ✔ Sprinting with varied arm actions (131; e.g., with objects in hands) and appropriate corrections in technique training. ✔ Training the trunk muscles using exercises 41–47. ✔ During toe push-off sprinting, the athlete should look at his/her own lane; during grasping/pulling sprinting, he/she should look at the finish concentrating on one point.
Hollow back resulting in forward tilted pelvis during grasping/pulling sprinting (often more pronounced at the end of the 100m race).	• Too weak or non-activated abdominal muscles. • Fatigue.	✔ Strength(-endurance) training for the abdominal muscles using exercises 41, 44, and 45. ✔ ABCs of sprinting as well as acceleration and coordination runs with deliberately upright pelvis and contracted abdominal muscles.
Excessive forward lean of the trunk and/ or forward tilted pelvis during grasping/pulling sprinting (often even more pronounced at the end of the 100m race).	• The athlete has the correct technique of grasping/pulling sprinting not yet sufficiently internalised. • Lack of strength abilities. • Fatigue. • Psychological anticipation of the finish.	✔ ABCs of sprinting as well as acceleration and coordination runs (129) with deliberately upright trunk. ✔ Strength training, especially of the hip extensors (e.g., 46, 49, 62–64, 72, 75, and 76). ✔ Speed-endurance training focusing on deliberately correct technique, even if it is difficult.
Heel kick with heel raised as high as the buttocks behind the body, usually accompanied by insufficient knee lift and lacking grasping/pulling foot touchdown.	• Forward tilted pelvis due to hollow back and/or forward lean of the trunk and its causes (see above). • Insufficient knee lift, possibly also due to too weak hip flexors (especially too weak iliopsoas).	✔ See corrections of hollow back and forward lean of the trunk above. ✔ Strength training for the hip flexors using exercises 73, 76, and 112.

(continued)

(continued)

Error	Causes	Corrections
Lower leg kick instead of grasping during forward swing phase.	• Athlete makes insufficient effort to sprint from the hips (instead of from the knee).	✔ During the swing phase, the lower leg follows the movements of the legs more or less passively (loose knee). ✔ Grasping exercises when standing (114), step-overs with grasping (117), as well as acceleration and coordination runs (129).
Too high stride frequency (in general).	• Error in perception: "If I move my legs quickly back and forth, I will sprint fast."	✔ Focusing on perception as a topic of discussion. ✔ Stride-length training (136). ✔ Bounding runs (88).
Too long strides (jump-like sprinting = push-off too vertical).	• False perception of the optimal relationship between stride length and stride frequency and optimal push-off angle.	✔ Frequency sprints and frequency coordination (135). ✔ Tappings (134). ✔ "Sprint forward"; "pull your hips forward with every stride."
Too small stride width (sprinting on a line or even cross-over sprinting), or too large stride width (broad-gauge running) during free sprinting.	• Athlete makes insufficient effort to use the available force in the main movement direction.	✔ Frequent use of over-correction and the contrast method (e.g., in coordination runs [129]).
Too tense and thus uneconomic sprinting.	• Tension is caused by unnecessary muscle contractions (i.e., muscles actually not involved), as well as by simultaneous contraction of agonists and antagonists interfering with each other.	✔ Sprinting consists of rhythmic maximum contractions on the basis of an otherwise maximal relaxation. ✔ Often to be corrected by deliberately relaxed face muscles, slightly open mouth, and loose fingers in middle position when performing exercises of the ABCs of sprinting, accelerations and coordination runs (129), and versatile sprints (130).
Reduced knee lift and hence reduced grasping/pulling on the last 20m (increased braking forces during the front support phase).	• Fatigue (of the hip flexors, especially the iliopsoas). • Forward lean of the trunk and its causes (see above).	✔ Speed-endurance training. ✔ With deliberately correct technique, even if difficult. ✔ Strength-endurance training of the hip flexors: exercise 73, and ABCs of endurance (141) with high-knee run (112).
Considerable slowing down even before reaching the finish.	• Premature initiation of attacking the finish line: chest too early or too far forward (possibly even falling down) with touchdown of the foot too far ahead of the hip. • Psychological anticipation of the finish.	✔ Practising attacking the finish line and its correct timing during training. ✔ The finish is five metres behind the line, even in training.

1.3.11 TRAINING PLANNING

Relay training is the best sprint training because it is a so-called enforcing aid. The maximum intensity, which is necessary in speed training, is enforced to the extent that the incoming runner does not want the outgoing runner to outrun him, while the outgoing runner does not want to be overtaken. Moreover, relay training is very motivating and makes sprint training more versatile. Therefore, no training plans are presented here, but readers should view the chapter on the 4 x 100m relay (II–1.6.11). Many contents can be performed even if the training group consists of fewer than four sprinters. These will be well prepared if there are four athletes available for a relay team. However, the relay-specific contents in the training plans can also be easily translated into purely sprint-specific contents.

1.3.12 BIBLIOGRAPHY

Armstrong, L. E. & Cooksey, S. M. (1983). Biomechanical changes in selected collegiate sprinters due to increased velocity. *Track and Field Quarterly Review 83* (2), 10-14.

Bartionetz, K. & Güllich, A. (1992). Die Bedeutung der Pick-up-Beschleunigung bei Höchstleistungen im 100-m-Sprint. *Die Lehre der Leichtathletik 31* (10), 17-18 & (11), 15-18.

Baumann, W. (1985). Biomechanische Analyse des 100m-Sprints der Frauen. In N. Müller, D. Augustin & B. Hunger (Red.), *Frauenleichtathletik* (S. 203-210). Niedernhausen: Schors.

Baumann, W., Schwirtz, A. & Gross, V. (1986). Biomechanik des Kurzstreckenlaufs. In R. Ballreich & A Kuhlow (Hrsg.), *Biomechanik der Leichtathletik* (Biomechanik der Sportarten, 1, S. 1-15). Stuttgart: Enke.

Čoh, M., Milanović, D. & Dolenec, A. (1999). Biomechanische Merkmale des Sprintschritts von Sprinterinnen der Spitzenklasse. *Leistungssport 29* (5), 41-46.

Deutscher Leichtathletikverband (DLV, Hrsg.). (2009). *Biomechanical Analysis of selected events at the 12th IAAF World Championships in Athletics, Berlin 15-23 August 2009*. Zugriff am 20.04.2010 unter http://www.iaaf.org/mm/Document/Development/Research/05/64/57/20100415075418_httppostedfile_1-BiomechanicsReportWC Berlin2009_Sprint_Men_19905.pdf

Gundlach, H. (1963). Laufgeschwindigkeit und Schrittgestaltung im 100-m-Lauf. *Theorie und Praxis der Körperkultur 12* (3), 254-262, (4), 346-359 & (5), 418-425.

Heß, W.-D., Gundlach, H., Bosse, T., Federle, R., Gohlitz, D., Jung, K. & Scholich, M. (1991). *Leichtathletik: Sprint – Lauf – Gehen* (Technik der Top-Athleten, 3). Berlin: Sportverlag.

Heynen, M. (2001). Hamstring injuries in sprinting. *New Studies in Athletics 16* (3), 43-48.

Hollmann, W. & Strüder, H. K. (2009). *Sportmedizin: Grundlagen für körperlicher Aktivität, Training und Präventivmedizin*. Stuttgart: Schattauer.

Ito, A., Fukuda, K. & Kijima, K. (2008). Mid-phase movements of Tyson Gay and Asafa Powell in the 100 metres at the 2007 World Championships in Athletics. *New Studies in Athletics 23* (2), 39-43.

Ito, A., Ishikawa, M., Isolehto, J. & Komi, P. V. (2006). Changes in the step width, step length, and step frequency of the world´s top sprinters during the 100 meters. *New studies in Athletics 21* (3), 35-39.

Kersting, U. G. (1999). Biomechanical Analysis of the Sprinting Events. In G.-P. Brüggemann, D. Koszewski & H. Müller (eds.), *Biomechanical Research Project Athens 1997: Final Report.* Oxford: Meyer & Meyer.

Korneljuk, A. O. (1982). Scientific basis of sprinting speed development. *Track and Field Quarterly Review 82* (2), 6-9.

Letzelter, S. & Letzelter, M. (2005). *Der Sprint: Eine Bewegungs- und Trainingslehre* (Mainzer Studien zur Sportwissenschaft, 21). Niedernhausen: Schors.

Locatelli, E. & Arsac, L. (1995). The mechanics and energetics of the 100 m sprint. *New Studies in Athletics* 10 (1), 81-87.

Mader, A. (2002). Die Zeit im Sport – Die Geburt und Herrschaft eines Prinzips im Hochleistungssport, in den Sportwissenschaften und in der Gesellschaft aus der Sicht der eigenen überschaubaren Zeit. In B. Ränsch-Trill, *Zeit und Geschwindigkeit: Sportliches Erleben in beschleunigten Prozessen* (Brennpunkt der Sportwissenschaft, 24). St. Augustin: Academia.

Mann, R. (1999). Biomechanische Grundlagen des Kurzsprints. *Leichtathletiktraining 10* (12), 24-31.

Mendoza, L. & Schöllhorn, W. (1993). Training of the sprint start technique with biomechanical feedback. *Journal of Sport Science 11* (1), 25-29.

Mero, A., Luthanen, P. & Komi, P. V. (1983). A biomechanical study of the sprint start. *Scandinavian Journal of Sport Sciences 5* (1), 20-28.

Mouchbahani, R., Gollhofer, A. & Dickhuth, H. (2004). Pulley systems in sprint training. *Modern Athlete and Coach 42* (3), 14-17.

Parry, E., Hensen, P. & Cooper, J. (2003). Lateral foot placement analysis of the sprint start. *New Studies in Athletics 18* (1), 13-22.

Qing, L. & Krüger, A. (1995). Die Beschleunigungsphase im Sprint ist nicht ein-, sondern zweiteilig. *Leistungssport 25* (3), 39-45.

Schölhorn, W. (2003). *Eine Sprint- und Laufschule für alle Sportarten.* Aachen: Meyer & Meyer.

Schrader, A., Müller, F. & Killing, W. (2008). Jamaikas ‚Lightning-Bolt'. *Leichtathletiktraining 19* (12), 4-11.

Seagrave, L. (2008). *Race Model Sprints & Hurdles* (Power-Point-Präsentation: Coaches Education and Certification System: Level IV: Sprints and Hurdles). Monaco: International Association of Athletics Federations (IAAF).

Sebestyen, E. (1996). Speed improvements with the Speedy-System. *New Studies in Athletics 11* (2-3), 149-154.

Stanton, P. & Purdam, C. (1989). Hamstring Injuries in Sprinting – The Role of Eccentric Exercise. *The Journal of Orthopaedic and Sports Physical Therapy 10* (9), 343-349.

Tepper, E. & Czingon, H. (Red.) (mit Keydel, H.). (1995). Rahmentrainingsplan für das *Aufbautraining Sprint* (4. Aufl.) (Edition Leichtathletik, 2). Aachen: Meyer und Meyer.

Tidow, G. & Wiemann, K. (1994). Zur Optimierung des Sprintlaufs – bewegungsanalytische Aspekte. *Leistungssport 24* (5), 14-19.

Türk-Noack, U. (2006). LAVEG-Analyse zum 100m-Sprint (OS, Atlanta 1996). In Wohlgefahrt, K. & Michel, S. (Hrsg.), *Beiträge zur Speziellen Trainingswissenschaft Leichtathletik: Symposium der dvs-kommission Leichtathletik vom 10.-11.10.2002 in Bad Blankenburg* (Schriften der Deutschen Vereinigung für Sportwissenschaften, 153). Hamburg: Czwalina.

Türk-Noack, U. (2006). Lasergeschwindigkeitsmessung zur Analyse translatorischer Bewegungsabläufe. In Wohlgefahrt, K. & Michel, S. (Hrsg.), *Beiträge zur Speziellen Trainingswissenschaft Leichtathletik: Symposium der dvs-kommission Leichtathletik vom 10.-11.10.2002 in Bad Blankenburg* (Schriften der Deutschen Vereinigung für Sportwissenschaften, 153). Hamburg: Czwalina.

Van Coppenolle, H., Delecluse, C., Goris, M., Bohets, W. & Vanden Eynde, E. (1988). Technology and the development of speed: Evaluation of the start, sprint and body composition of Pavoni, Cooman and Desruelles. *Athletics Coach 23* (1), 82-90.

Wiemann, K. & Tidow, G. (1994). Die Adduktoren beim Sprint – bisher vernachlässigt? *Die Lehre der Leichtathletik 33* (7), 15-18 & (8), 15-18.

Zatsiorsky, V. M. (1996). *Krafttraining: Praxis und Wissenschaft*. Aachen: Meyer und Meyer.

1.4 200M RACE

1.4.1 THE MOST IMPORTANT SPRINTING DISTANCE

In contrast to the 100 and 400m race, the 200m race has often received less attention. However, the simple stadium race in ancient Olympia, which was 192.72m long, was more of a 200m race. This race is considered the origin of the Olympic Games. The Olympiad (i.e., the four-year period leading up to the next Olympics) was named after the winner of the stadium run who was allowed to light the Olympic flame at the next Games.

Even in modern times, 200m sprinters repeatedly achieve high social and political esteem. At the Olympic Games in 1936, the Black American quadruple winner (100, 200, 4 x 100m, and long jump) Jesse Owens challenged Hitler's racial propaganda. The gold and bronze medal winners over 200m in 1968 protested against discrimination against the Black community in the United States and for the Black Power movement. The then new world-record holder Tommie Smith and John Carlos raised a fist to the sky clad with a black glove and lowered their heads when the national anthem was played during their victory ceremony. Less attention was paid to the fact that both also took a shoe with them on the podium to protest against increasing commercialisation. Prior to the Olympic Games, athletes were forbidden to use their traditional shoe brands because other manufacturers were the official suppliers.

Commercialisation has continuously and fundamentally changed sports, which is considered positive by some and negative by others. The 150m duel in June 1997 was one of the highlights. The then world champion, Olympic champion, and world-record holder over 100m, Donavan Bailey, and the former 200m world champion, Olympic winner and world-record holder, Michael Johnson, competed against each other. Clearly behind, Johnson suffered an injury, and Bailey won $1.5 million dollars in prize money and the title of "fastest man in the world."

At the Olympic Games in 2008, Jamaica's Usain Bolt won the 100 and 200m in world-record time, with 9.69 and 19.30 sec respectively. Although these were considered mythical world records, Bolt improved the times of both races a year later at the World Championships in Berlin to 9.58 and 19.19 sec. In 2008, 2009, and at the 2012 Olympics, Bolt even achieved a triple by winning in the 4 x 100m relay. In 2008 and 2012, the 4 x 100m time was also a new world record. At the 2011 World Championship, a spectacular false start over 100m prevented this success. Prior to Usain Bolt, the last athlete to achieve triple success had been Carl Lewis. Like Owens at the 1936 Olympics, Lewis was successful in the 100 and 200m races and in the long jump at the 1984 Olympics in the absence of East Bloc countries.

It was speculated whether Bolt would also try to beat Johnson's world record over 400m. He would have then dominated nearly the entire primarily anaerobic performance area (see figure 1 in chapter II–1.1.2), an objective which many sprinters, who possibly concentrate too much on only one distance, do not seem to pursue any longer even at national championships.

1.4.2 THE MOST IMPORTANT COMPETITION RULES

The most important competition rules have been presented in their entirety in the general running and sprinting rules chapters (see II–1.1.1 and II–1.2.1). It only remains to be mentioned that the 200m sprint is only a part of the competition programme beginning with the U18 age category.

1.4.3 SPORT-SCIENCE FINDINGS, PHASE STRUCTURE, AND TECHNIQUE

The phase structure of the 200m sprint is identical with that of the 100m race (see chapter II–1.3.3). The technique is also nearly the same. However, the following differences should be noted.

PHASE 1: CROUCH START
The crouch start in the 200m (and 400m) race takes place in the curve. Most sprinters place their blocks slightly outwards within their lane and so diagonal that they point tangentially to the inside of the track (see figure 1). This starting position enables athletes to make their first strides on a straight line and then immediately use the shortest path on the inside of the lane. In this starting position, the left (inner) hand is often somewhat set back from the starting line, so that the connecting line between the hands is still perpendicular to the mounting rail of the blocks.

(For reaction times, see chapter II–1.5.3.)

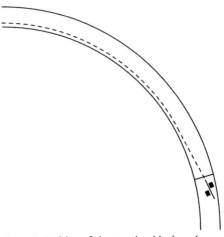

Figure 1: *Position of the starting block and tangential run toward the inward side of the lane* in the crouch start in the curve.

PHASE 2: POSITIVE ACCELERATION
According to the starting position, start and pick-up acceleration also take place in the curve. With increasing speed, the athlete must therefore lean more and more into the curve. (The biomechanical special features of the curve sprint are described in phase 3.)

PHASE 3: MAXIMUM VELOCITY

In various studies it is pointed out that there is an average difference of 0.177 to 0.4 sec between a maximum 100m race on the straight and in the curve. However, figure 2 in chapter II-1.2.2 shows that despite the **biomechanical special features of the curve** sprint the maximum-velocity phase in the 200m sprint already takes place in the curve.

In the sprint on the straight, the sprinter must work up power in the horizontal direction for propulsion with each ground contact and must also work up power in the vertical direction to overcome the force of gravity. In addition to this, the curve runner must overcome the centrifugal forces which act on his/her body in the lateral direction. To be able to apply force in the lateral direction (i.e., toward the inside of the curve), the runner is forced to lean toward the inside of the curve like a motorcyclist, and even more so the faster the speed. Furthermore, the necessary inward lean increases with the decreasing radius of the curvature. A runner in lane 1 must therefore lean more into the curve than a runner in lane 8. Not only is the runner forced to use a part of the total (resultant) force for lateral force development, he/she is also forced to change his/her sprinting technique due to the inward lean into the curve. As if running in the track left by a motorcycle, the sprinter runs with a smaller stride width than in the sprint on the straight (see figure 11 in chapter II-1.3.3). By so doing, the runner is able to counteract the centrifugal forces to an equal extent with each ground contact (and not only while his/her right outer foot is on the ground). Due to the inward lean, the distance from the hip joint to the touchdown point of the foot is longer on the outside than on the inside. As a result, it is likely that the angular positions and paths of the foot, knee, and/or hip joint of both legs may differ, and that they may also differ from the sprint on the straight and may be less favourable. Findings that injuries to the hamstrings and hip muscles are more than twice as likely on the left side than on the right side are an indication that training on the oval running track results in different loads on the two legs.

Table 1 shows that athletes actually achieve better times in the outer lane at championships. Table 2 provides a more accurate idea of how the curve radius alters biomechanical parameters and performance.

Table 1: **Average times (sec) in the 200m races** of the 2nd, 3rd, and 4th round at Olympic Games and World Championships (according to Ryan & Harrison, 2003, p. 58).

Lane	1996	2000	2001
1	20.91	20.66	20.64
2	20.66	20.77	20.61
7	20.56	20.62	20.50
8	20.57	20.47	20.58

*Table 2: **Average values and standard deviation of biomechanical parameters depending on the lane when sprinting in the curve** (according to Ryan & Harrison, 2003, p. 64; group of 8 men [best times over 200 m: 20.67–22.10 sec] and 5 women [best times over 200 m: 24.06–24.50 sec]).*

Lane		Velocity (m/sec)	Stride length (m)	Stride frequency (Hz)	Contact time (sec)
Indoors	1	8.14 ± 0.830	1.82 ± 0.081	4.47 ± 0.412	0.113 ± 0.015
	4	8.44 ± 0.872	1.89 ± 0.098	4.48 ± 0.429	0.104 ± 0.016
Outdoors	1	8.70 ± 0.775	1.99 ± 0.118	4.37 ± 0.339	0.097 ± 0.016
	8	9.08 ± 0.818	2.00 ± 0.092	4.51 ± 0.445	0.097 ± 0.015

Since the radius of the curvature of a 200m indoor running track is much smaller, the runner is forced to lean inward even more. The curves are banked (i.e., higher on the outside) so that the difference described in the distance between the hip and the touchdown point and the lateral force component does not become too large. Although the sprinter must in fact apply less force toward the inside of the curve as a result, he/she is nevertheless forced to exert more force perpendicularly to the track as if he/she were heavier. Due to the inclination of the indoor curve, runners in the outer lanes are forced to run uphill at the beginning of the curve and downhill at the end of the curve. The staggered start means that although runners in the outer lanes start out with a pronounced inward lean, they run (almost) only downhill through the first curve. In general, it is estimated that the benefit to the runner in the outer lane is even more evident indoors than outdoors. However, due to the smaller radius of curvature the running times are still usually slower than on a 400m oval track with flat curves. As a result of the large differences between inner and outer lanes, especially at high speeds, there are no longer any competitions over 200m at international indoor championships (world and European championships).

PHASE 4: NEGATIVE ACCELERATION

As expected, the section of negative acceleration is significantly longer in the 200m sprint than in the 100m sprint. This points to the respective greater importance of speed endurance. However, in good sprinters, overall 200m performance (like the 100m performance) depends on acceleration capability and maximum sprinting speed to a great extent. The loss of velocity on the finishing straight of a 200m race not only depends on energy parameters (lactate tolerance), but also on reactive-strength parameters (muscle stiffness). A lower loss of velocity is associated with better results (height of flight and contact time) in reactive vertical-jump tests (see ankle jumps, 84).

Figure 2 shows the velocity profile in the speed-endurance section. Comparing the 50m average speeds in figure 2 in chapter II–1.2.2, it can be seen that in the fourth 50m segment women achieve 90% of the velocity which they achieve in the second and fastest 50m segment. Men achieve a similar value of 91%.

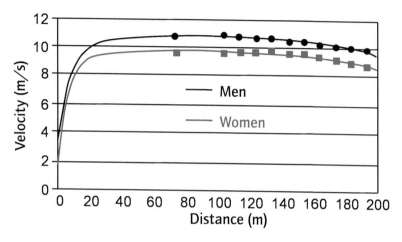

*Figure 2: **Velocity curve of the 200m finalists** at the Olympic Games in 1987 (modified on the basis of Letzelter et al., 1995): Since 10m intervals were measured only in the finishing straight, the figure illustrates the negative acceleration particularly well; the velocity curve before this section was estimated and modelled mathematically.*

*Table 3: **Requirement profile for the 200m race:** The suggested rough estimate of the value of selected factors determining performance is based on the importance of overall performance and the percentage of time spent training (IR: information requirements, constr.: constraints; see chapter I–1.1).*

Factors determining 200m performance	Estimate of value	Notes
Coordination	+ + +	optical IR: low, acoustic IR: at the start medium, then low, tactile IR: low, kinaesthetic IR: medium, vestibular IR: low–medium; precision constr.: high, time constr.: high, complexity constr.: low, situation constr.: medium–low, physical stress constr.: low–medium
Flexibility	+ +	no extreme movement amplitudes required
Strength		particular importance of the hamstrings; extensor loop (glutes, quadriceps, triceps surae, erector spinae), iliopsoas, abdominus, adductors, shoulder and upper-arm muscles
Maximal strength	+ + + +	during start acceleration and as a basis
Reactive strength	+ + + + +	within various stretch-shortening cycles
Speed	+ + + + +	primarily cyclic; acyclic aspects at the start and when attacking the finish line; reaction speed at the start (can be decisive for winning the race; however, relatively insignificant in terms of percentage; hardly improvable through training)
(General dynamic) Anaerobic endurance		
Strength endurance	+ +	as a basis of speed endurance
Speed endurance	+ + + +	long maintenance of maximal velocity and only slight loss of velocity thereafter
Aerobic endurance	+ + +	particularly as a basis of training
Psychological and cognitive abilities	+ + + + +	concentration ability (on the point; there is no possibility to compensate for faults); performance-oriented thinking and behaviour (see Chapter I–3.1.1)
Anthropometric and primarily genetically determined characteristics	+ + + + +	e.g.: high proportion of fast muscle fibres; connective tissue with optimal energy-storing capacities; medium body height; low percentage of body fat

1.4.4 SUMMARY OF THE MOST IMPORTANT TECHNICAL CHARACTERISTICS = TECHNIQUE-ANALYSIS SHEET

See chapter II–1.5.4.

1.4.5 PHOTO SEQUENCE

CROUCH START AND START ACCELERATION

Data about the photo sequence

Athlete: Usain Bolt (born: 21 August 1986, Jamaica)

Height/weight: 1.94 m/93 kg

Performance: 20.08 sec (wind: ± 0,0 m/sec; 19 August 2009, Berlin)

Personal best: 19.19 sec (wind: +0.9 m/sec; 20 August 2009, Berlin, world record)

Greatest successes: Olympic champion over 100, 200, and 4 x 100m in 2008 and 2012, world champion over 100, 200, and 4 x 100m in 2009, as well as over 200 and 4 x 100m in 2011

COMMENTARY

With his first world record over 200m in 19.30 sec at the 2008 Olympic Games in Beijing, Usain Bolt is said to have been the first man to sprint 100m from a starting block through a curve under 10 sec. Table 4 shows that he was again able to beat the time of 9.98 sec measured in Beijing when he set a new world record in 2009. The photo sequence presented shows Bolt's semi-final run, one day before his mythical world record in 2009. The partial times show that the clear difference between both final times is due mainly to the last 50 metres, probably because in the semi-final Bolt imagined himself to be sufficiently in the lead. He ran the first 50 metres 14 hundredths slower than in the final. Of this total, 4 hundredths can be attributed to a longer reaction time. Significant technical differences between these two races, which are visible in the photo sequence of the start, are not to be expected.

The distance between Bolt's starting blocks is on the brink of what can be described as a medium setting of the starting blocks. In comparison to his body height, one can even speak of a surprisingly narrow setting of the starting blocks. The distance between the front block and the starting line appears quite long. The rail of his starting block is only slightly tangential to the inside of his lane. That is why he places his inner hand slightly back from the line (picture 1). In the set position, the typical features such as right-angled anterior knee, shoulders in front of hands, hip significantly above shoulder height, etc. are clearly visible. Whether there is really insufficient pressure on the rear block is difficult to detect. Due to the long distance between the blocks and the starting line, the position of the CG is, on the one hand, slightly set back, but, on the other hand, the CG is further in front of the

*Table 4: **Partial times, average stride lengths and frequencies of Usain Bolt** in the semi-final and the final at the 2009 World Championships (according to DLV [German Athletics Federation], 2009, pp. 11–12).*

Final time (sec) (run)	Partial times (sec) in the section between			
	0–50m (reaction time)	50–100m	100–150m	150–200m
	Average stride lengths (m) and stride frequencies (strides/sec)			
20.08 (semi-final)	5.74 (0.177)	4.40	4.72	5.22
19.19 (final)	5.60 (0.133) 2.14; 4.17	4.32 2.61; 4.43	4.52 2.66; 4.16	4.75 2.69; 3.91

contact points of the feet with the ground. The latter enables an extremely flat push-off forward, which, however, seems to be generated almost exclusively by the front leg. The rear leg is moved forward with an exemplary flat foot-movement curve. The tip of the foot seems almost to drag on the ground. In picture 5, Bolt achieves an optimal push-off extension, with the line including the foot, knee, hip and shoulder reaching an angle to the ground of even less than 45°. Due to his commendable first arm action, Bolt's arms reach a reversal point, which allows an ideal arm swing. Between pictures 6 and 7, there is the first foot touchdown with the lower leg clearly forward and far behind the vertical projection of the CG. With his ankle fixed, Bolt pushes himself into the next stride, which is as good as the first one. In pictures 9 (or shortly thereafter) and 15, Bolt again achieves ideal push-off extensions as a result of the quality of his strides. Bolt straightens himself up only slowly, while initially still looking downward.

In general, Bolt's powerful starting acceleration seems to be completely free of unnecessary movements and is thus extremely dynamic and directed straight forward.

1.4.6 STRATEGY

During the first 100 metres, 200m world-class sprinters are 1–5 tenths of a second slower than their 100m times. Whether this is because they consciously or unconsciously save their energy at the start of the race like 400m sprinters (see chapter II–1.5.6) is difficult to answer. The time difference mentioned could also be mostly due to the difficulty of sprinting through the curve (see chapter II–1.4.3). Since the second 100 metres of a 200m sprint are covered flying, particularly world-class male sprinters run faster than their 100m best time on the second 100 metres. While they are approximately 0.35 sec faster on average, world-class female sprinters, on average, run as fast as their 100m personal best. Therefore, the men's 200m time is often exactly twice their 100m time, while women remain on average approximately three tenths of a second below their double 100m time. The difference between 200m time and the double 100m time is also referred to as the speed-endurance index. However, it is too inexact to derive a comparative statement from this about the speed-endurance capabilities of the different sexes. Illustrations in figure 2 (and figure 2 in chapter II–1.2.2) provide more precise information about the velocity curve of male and female 200m runners.

While it is possible that top athletes run the entire 200m distance at maximum effort, the following guideline may be helpful for less advanced athletes:

- First 50 m: maximal start and acceleration;

- Second 50 m: try to achieve an economic and fast sprinting rhythm;
- Third 50 m: try to maintain your velocity and economic sprinting stride

- on the finishing straight; and
- Fourth 50 m: try to run as fast as possible; give your best effort.

1.4.7 DIDACTICS: SUPERORDINATE LONG-TERM OBJECTIVES AND GENERAL METHODOLOGY

In children's athletics and in basic training, the 200m race is prepared by using the methods described in the chapter on 100m (see II–1.3.7). However, in respect to the 200m race (and 400m race), an effective and economic curve-sprinting technique should be practised even in these early years by versatile, often playful, curve, slalom, and circular sprinting. Speed-endurance training should be emphasised only at later training stages.

1.4.8 TRAINING CONTENTS: FORMS OF GAMES AND EXERCISES

See chapter II–1.3.8, and II–1.5.8.

1.4.9 SPECIAL TEST AND CONTROL PROCEDURES

See chapter II–1.5.9.

1.4.10 ERRORS – CAUSES – CORRECTIONS

See chapter II–1.3.10, and II–1.5.10.

1.4.11 TRAINING PLANNING

Special training plans for 200m sprinters are not shown here. On the one hand, a specific 200m plan can be relatively simply developed as a mixture of the training plans for the (4x)100m and (4x)400m races (see chapter II–1.6.11, and II–1.7.10). On the other hand, athletes who train according to the suggested (4x)100m or the (4x)400m plan will be able to also perform very good 200m sprints.

1.4.12 BIBLIOGRAPHY

Ayres, T. R. & Gottlieb, M. S. (2006). Occurrence of right vs. left side injury location in elite sprinters who train on an oval 400m track. *New Studies in Athletics 21* (4), 51-56.

Deutscher Leichtathletik-Verband (DLV, Hrsg.). (2009). *Scientific Research Project. Biomechanical Analysis at the 12th IAAF World Championships in Athletics. Berlin 2009, August 15-23. Final Report. Sprint Men.* Zugriff am 20.10.2010 unter http://www.iaaf.org/mm/Document/Development/Research/05/64/57/20100415075418_httppostedfile_1-BiomechanicsReportWC Berlin2009_Sprint_Men_19905.pdf

Letzelter. H., Letzelter M. & Fuchs, P. (1995). Geschwindigkeitsgestaltung im 200m-Lauf. In D. Böhmer & N. Müller (Hrsg.), *Leben in Bewegung* (S. 207-224). Niederhausen: Schors.

Letzelter, S. & Letzelter, M. (2005). *Der Sprint: Eine Bewegungs- und Trainingslehre* (Mainzer Studien zur Sportwissenschaft, 21). Niederhausen: Schors.

Locatelli, E. (1996). The importance of anaerobic glycolysis and stiffness in the sprints (60, 100 and 200 metres). *New Studies in Athletics 11* (2-3), 121-125.

Ryan, G. J. & Harrison, A. J. (2003). Technical adaptations of competitive sprinters induced by bend running. *New Studies in Athletics 18* (4), 57-67.

Vonstein, W. (2010). Immer wieder Jamaika! Teil 1. *Leichtathletiktraining 21* (1), 26-31

1.5 400M RACE

1.5.1 PROGRESS OR STAGNATION?

At the 14th Olympic Games in 724 B.C., the race over two stadium lengths (Diaulus: approximately 385 m) was also introduced besides the stadium race over one length. At that time, runners started from a standing position with their toes placed in the grooves of a stone starting block. False starts were punished by caning. In modern times, the start was performed from holes which the sprinter dug into the cinder track for a better push-off in the crouch-start position. In 1921, the Australian Charles Booth experimented with the first primitive starting block. Today, starting blocks measure the reaction times at major championships and are equipped with loudspeakers so that the starting signal is heard at the same time in the outer and inner lane in spite of the staggered start.

Despite progress in technology and training science, there are 400m sprinters who would have qualified for the final at the London Olympics in 2012 with the times they achieved on a cinder track at the 1960 Olympics. Although the German Carl Kaufmann set a world record with 44.9 sec in the Roman Stadio Olimpico in 1960, he was still beaten by the equally fast American Otis Davis based on a photo-finish decision. This drama was repeated two days later, when Kaufmann as the anchor had to surrender the Olympic gold medal in the 4 x 400m relay to the American anchor Davis. After Kaufmann,

there has never been another European to establish a 400m world record. All of his successors and most of his predecessors were from the U.S. In terms of Olympic medals, the dominance of U.S. men is fascinating: They have won gold medals in 20 out of 28 Olympic 400m finals. In 1904, 1968, 1988, 2004, and 2008, they even won all three medals. In 2012, however, the otherwise less successful women had to step up with two medals, while the men were unsuccessful for the first time since 1920 (with the exception of the boycott year 1980).

Due to frequent injuries in the 1958/59 season, Kaufmann, an outstanding athlete, was forced to switch to the long sprint which he did with amazing success. Although he had been strictly a short-distance sprinter until then, he became one of the world's best quarter milers after a very short transition phase. His training at that time may surprise many experts even today. "The 300 metres remained my longest training run," said Kaufmann. His coach confirmed this statement: "Even in winter, Karl never ran long distances." This method used half a century ago does not seem to be the same method used by today's leading American 400m runners. For example, Friedlander (2005) describes the training devised by Clyde Hart, the successful coach of world-record holder Michael Johnson and Olympic champion

Jeremy Wariner, with the words, "Train slower to race faster" (see discourse I).

In 2008, the South African Oscar Pistorius, born without both his lower legs, fought for 400m Olympic qualification. A study conducted at the German Sport University in Cologne set out to clarify whether his advanced carbon-fibre prostheses should be considered an impairment or bionic doping. A final decision could not be made. While the prostheses may be helpful on the straights, they are likely to be a hindrance at the start and in the curves. In 2011, Pistorius qualified for the world championships and reached the semi-final despite many protests. He was also allowed to start in the 2012 Olympics.

1.5.2 THE MOST IMPORTANT COMPETITION RULES

The most important competition rules for the 400m sprint have been presented in their entirety in the general running and sprinting rules chapters (see II–1.1.1 and II–1.2.1). In Germany, the long sprint is introduced to the U16 age group in form of the 300m race. The 400m is part of the competition programme beginning with the U18 age category.

1.5.3 SPORT-SCIENCE FINDINGS, PHASE STRUCTURE, AND TECHNIQUE

The phase structure of the 400m sprint is identical with that of the 100m race (see chapter II–1.3.3). The technique is also nearly the same. However, the differences presented in the chapter on the 200m (see chapter II–1.4.3) and below should be taken into consideration.

PHASE 1: CROUCH START
In the long sprint, average reaction times are longer than in the short sprint (see table 1). This is attributed to the largely unconscious, but accurate opinion of athletes that the reaction time in the long sprint has an even lower percentage influence on the final time than in the short sprint. However, reaction time can decide victory or defeat even in the long sprint. This can be proven with an example

from the hurdles. In the 400m hurdle final at the 1987 World Championships in Rome, third-place Harald Schmid, who lost by 2 hundredths of a second, would have won if he had had the same reaction time as the winner Edwin Moses. Another reason for the longer reaction times could be submaximal acceleration behaviour (see chapter II–1.5.6).

PHASE 2: POSITIVE ACCELERATION
The recording of biomechanical data such as velocity, stride length, and stride frequency is technically more difficult in the long sprint. Therefore, only average values for 50m segments are available for the 400m sprint. Figure 2 in chapter II–1.2.2 shows that the average velocity over the first 50m segment is much slower

*Table 1: **Average reaction times** of male sprinters at world championships and the Olympic Games (according to Collet, 1999, p. 69).*

	100 m	200 m	400 m
Number of subjects	102	32	64
Ø reaction time (sec)	0.148 ± 0.025	0.173 ± 0.039	0.203 ± 0.057

than the average velocity over the second 50m segment due to reaction time and acceleration from a resting position.

As a result of the lower acceleration and velocity in the long sprint, the sprinter must straighten up as earlier than in the short sprint. Thus, the transition from toe push-off sprinting in the start-acceleration phase to grasping/pulling sprinting in the pick-up acceleration phase occurs after fewer metres in contrast to the 100m and 200m sprint. It is believed that the maximum-velocity phase (i.e., the end of the pick-up acceleration phase) is also reached after fewer metres in the long sprint than in the short sprint. However, a clear statement on this cannot be made based on 50m segment times.

PHASE 3: MAXIMUM VELOCITY
The mean velocity over 400m is about 94% of the mean velocity achieved by athletes in the 200m race. Despite the aforementioned biomechanical special features of the sprint through the curve, 400m sprinters reach their maximum mean velocity over the second 50m segment (i.e., in the starting curve). Although this is below the maximum velocity attained in the 100m and 200m sprints, **400m runners must be sprinters for the most part.**

In a 400m competition, they achieve only about 90% of the maximum velocity achieved in a 100m race. However, the ability to achieve a correspondingly higher maximum sprinting speed is necessary since sub-maximum sprinting is more economic than maximum sprinting.

Table 2 provides information on the stride pattern in the 400m sprint (also compare the values for the 100m sprint shown in chapter II–1.3.3). For women, the quotient of average stride length divided by body height is approximately 1.2, while for men it is approximately 1.3. Compared to athletes of national and regional class, world-class athletes achieve a higher velocity mainly by longer strides. The fact that maximum velocity is achieved in the curve mainly by high stride frequency could be attributed to flight phases being shortened in the process and the sprinter being carried less outward in each flight phase. On the straight, however, slightly longer strides are still considered more economic by many coaches. Conversely, world-record holder M. Johnson and other successful American long sprinters have been noted to use relatively short strides with a low knee lift. Ultimately, economy is the top priority for long-sprint techniques. In terms of the long sprint, economy means

*Table 2: **Stride parameters of world-class 400m sprinters:** maximum mean values in 50m sections (according to Gajer et al., 2007)..*

	maximum stride frequency	maximum stride length
Men	4.12 ± 0.19 sec	2.53 ± 0.08 m
Women	3.99 ± 0.13 sec	2.29 ± 0.04 m
50m segment	Second	Third

increased endurance by saving energy through superior sprinting techniques (for more details see chapter II–1.1.2). The technique of grasping/pulling sprinting, whose objective is to avoid braking forces, is the model technique even in long sprint. This technique should be used beginning with the pick-up acceleration segment (see chapter II–1.3.3).

PHASE 4: NEGATIVE ACCELERATION

Figure 2 in chapter II–1.2.2 shows that even in 400m world-class runners the third 50m section is significantly slower than the second one. Afterwards, velocity decreases more and more. The loss of velocity on the finishing straight is the greatest especially on the last 50 metres. Here it is particularly difficult to continue with an economic style of grasping/pulling sprinting, which is especially due to the increasing acidification of the muscles.

Within heterogeneous ability groups (e.g., as shown by comparing world-class women with world-class men), overall faster runners are in the lead from the start onwards and continue to increase their lead because of their higher velocity. However, the loss of velocity in the third to eighth 50m section in world-class 400m

men and women is almost identical in terms of percentage of the maximum (average) velocity achieved. In respective groups of world-class male and female 400m sprinters, the average velocity in the eighth 50m corresponded to 78% of the average velocity in the second 50m section (see figure 2 in chapter II–1.2.2).

Within homogeneous groups (e.g., in the final races at the world championships), superior runners achieve their lead mainly in the second half of the race, which emphasises the importance of speed endurance. In a group of world championships finalists (n = 12), the overall faster half of the group is even slower over the first three 50m sections than the other half of the group which is slower at the finish (see figure 2 in chapter II–1.2.2). It is also observed with 400m women and men that those who are the fastest over the first 50m section tend to be slower in the last section. However, it is difficult to interpret individual differences in the velocity curves and variations in the times over various sections despite identical or similar final times. This may be due to strategy (see chapter II–1.5.6) as well as various distinct and contrary capabilities in terms of the major types of

DISCOURSE I: ENERGY SUPPLY

Information on the distribution of the aerobic and anaerobic energy supply in the 400m sprint were presented in table 1 in chapter II–1.2.2. In actuality, various studies have arrived at very different results. A meta-analysis of 11 studies showed that the values found for the aerobic portion of energy supply during a 400m sprint vary between 28.0 and 71.2%. Arcelli et al. (2008) provide several reasons for this:

- With identical absolute performance (e.g., 48 sec), men are supplied with a greater proportion of energy aerobically. If the performance is comparable (which means that it would, for example, result in identical placements in the world ranking list), women receive approximately 1–4% more energy from aerobic metabolism.
- Among 400m runners, there are those who can be described as sprinter types (e.g., world record holder M. Johnson) and likely achieve similar positive results in the 200m race. Others can be called endurance types. They are in the minority and are increasingly disappearing. Endurance-type runners prefer the 800m (e.g., A. Juantorena, the 400m and 800m double Olympic champion in 1976) and receive 3–8% more energy from aerobic metabolism than sprinter types.
- Different research methods as well as diverging mathematical calculation models lead to dissimilar results. A simulated run on the treadmill might not lead to the same physical exertion as a sprint race.
- Figure 1 shows a possible connection between the 400m time and the percentages of energy supply. As expected, these percentages are dependent less on the length of the racing distance and more on the duration of the load.

The differences shown also result in uncertainties in training planning. The speed of the anaerobic and aerobic energy supply and the lactate tolerance (acidosis tolerance) are of crucial importance in the 400m sprint. All relevant aspects should be taken into consideration in training. When emphasising the various training contents, an athlete's strengths and weaknesses must also be considered.

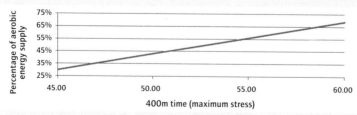

Figure 1: *Possible correlation between the percentage of energy supply in the 400m sprint and the 400m time achieved by male runners (modified on the basis of Arcelli et al., 2008, p. 21).*

motor stress (e.g., particularly good or bad curve-running techniques, cyclic speed, or speed endurance).

Attacking the finish line and deceleration behind the finish line are generally the same as in the 100m sprint. However, the majority of long sprinters rarely throw themselves over the finish line due to their great fatigue and the reduced importance of this finishing technique for the final time. Deceleration after crossing the finish line is also not performed in a controlled manner due to excessive acidity. However, the risk of injury attributed to the lower speed is also lower.

Table 3: **Requirement profile for the 400m race:** *The suggested rough estimate of the value of selected factors determining performance is based on the importance of the overall performance and the percentage of time spent training. (IR: information requirements, constr.: constraints; see chapter I–1.1).*

Factors determining 400m performance	Estimate of value	Notes
Coordination	+ + +	optical IR: low, acoustic IR: at the start medium, then low, tactile IR: low, kinaesthetic IR: medium, vestibular IR: low–medium; precision constr.: high, time constr.: medium–high, complexity constr.: low, situation constr.: medium–low, physical stress constr.: high
Flexibility	+ +	no extreme movement amplitudes required
Strength		particular importance of the hamstrings; extensor loop (glutes, quadriceps, triceps surae, erector spinae), iliopsoas, abdominus, adductors, shoulder and upper-arm muscles
Maximal strength	+ + +	during start acceleration and as a basis
Reactive strength	+ + + +	within various stretch-shortening cycles
Speed	+ + + +	primarily cyclic; acyclic aspects at the start and when attacking the finish line; reaction speed at the start (can be decisive for winning the race; however, extremely insignificant in terms of percentage; hardly improvable through training)
Endurance (general dynamic) Anaerobic endurance		
Strength endurance	+ + +	as a basis of speed endurance
Speed endurance	+ + + + +	long maintenance of maximal velocity and slight and slow velocity loss thereafter
Aerobic endurance	+ + + +	for energy supply during the race as well as the basis of training
Psychological and cognitive abilities	+ + + + +	feel for pace and correct strategy (initial pace); ability to deliberately achieve low pH values (lactate acidosis) and to tolerate these values; performance-oriented thinking and behaviour (see chapter I–3.1.1)
Anthropometric and primarily genetically determined characteristics	+ + + +	high proportion of fast muscle fibres; connective tissue with optimal energy-storing capacities; medium body height; low percentage of body fat

1.5.4 SUMMARY OF THE MOST IMPORTANT TECHNICAL CHARACTERISTICS = TECHNIQUE-ANALYSIS SHEET

CROUCH START

"ON-YOUR-MARKS" POSITION

- Blocks are placed slightly outwards and so diagonal that they point tangentially to the inside of the track.
- The front block is approximately 1½ feet from the starting line, approximately 50° to the ground; the rear block is approximately 1–1½ feet further back, approximately 70° to the ground.
- Hands are initially placed in front of the starting line, only then is the (long-jump) take-off leg placed against the front block, then the other leg is placed against the rear block.
- The rear knee is placed onto the ground.
- The hands are placed behind the line, just shoulder width apart; high hand support on fingertips; the arms are extended.
- Quiet breathing, relaxation.

"SET" POSITION

- Quickly taking the final starting position by lifting one's pelvis (lifting one's rear knee from the ground).
- The shoulders are in front of the hands (arm position as before).
- The pelvis is higher than the shoulders.
- The front knee is at a right angle; the rear knee is at an angle of approximately 120–130°.
- The head is aligned with the trunk; the view is directed between the hands.
- Pressure is applied against the block: The hands try to push the ground forward; pre-tension of the extensor muscles; the heels are pressed backward against the blocks.
- Inhaling, holding breath (forced breathing).
- Focus on the subsequent movement (not on the acoustic signal).

TOE PUSH-OFF SPRINTING

- The push-off is performed by the extensor muscles of both legs; the push-off by the rear leg is more intense and shorter (1/3 of the pressure), whereas the push-off by the front leg is longer (2/3 of the pressure).
- Due to the stretching of the legs and the trunk, the arms are lifted from the ground (no push-off by the arms); direct start of the first energetic arm swing.
- The rear leg is the first to break contact with the block, and the hip flexion starts immediately (forward swing).
- The push-off by each leg results in the extension of the whole body so that the head, shoulders, hips, knees, and feet are on one line, which initially is only at approximately 45° to the ground (forward lean of the body); the look is directed to the ground a few feet in front of the runner.
- In each instance, the swing leg is quickly moved forward until the angle between the thigh and the trunk is 90° (knee lift); the foot movement curve is flat (initially the heels are not raised behind the body).
- The knee lift and arm swing (from the shoulder; elbows at 90°) are used as swing elements.
- After the knee lift, the hips and knees are extended again (the next push-off is begun as early as in the swing phase).
- The lower legs are pointed backward and downward at any time (initially there is no grasping movement).
- The tip of the foot is raised before touchdown (dorsiflexion).
- The touchdown with the balls of the feet is behind the vertical projection of the CG during the first strides, then it is on the vertical projection of the CG, and finally it is in front of the projection of the CG.
- The foot touchdown is initially a bit wider and placed to the outside.
- Upon touchdown, the foot is fixed (no yielding).
- An increase in stride length and stride frequency.
- Increasing inward lean into the curve as the velocity increases.
- Only slow rising from the forward body lean and thus smooth transition to grasping/pulling sprinting.

GRASPING/PULLING SPRINTING

- Economic sprinting style.
- Upright trunk or minimum forward lean; erect pelvis (contracted abdominals).
- The athlete's view is directed to the finish line, the end of the straight, or the further path of the curve; facial muscles are relaxed.
- Sprinting from the hips (during the swing phase, the lower leg follows the movements of the upper leg and its own inertia mostly passively).
- Noticeable heel rise under the body, not behind the body (heel is never as high as the buttocks), then the knee joint angle is opened.
- Rapid hip flexion so that the knee is raised in front of the body until the thigh is (almost) horizontal.
- Subsequent fast reactive and powerful extension of the hips.
- Shortly before touchdown, the knee joint is almost straight, and the tip of the foot is raised (dorsiflexed and supinated).
- Knee flexors contract reactively; they bend the knee slightly again before touchdown and support (to some extent) the extension of the hip.
- The foot is placed on the ground over the outside of the ball of the foot, with fixed foot as close to the vertical projection of the CG as possible.
- Small stride width; in the curve even smaller than on the straight.
- Continuation of the hip extension; the muscles of the front thigh stabilise the knee; the calf muscles stabilise the ankle joint; the bending of the leg following the touchdown (amortisation) is as minimal as possible.
- Extension of the hip, knee, and ankle joint during the rear support phase.
- The contralateral arm swing is initiated by the shoulder and is performed almost parallel to the running direction; the backward swing is emphasised; elbow angle approximately 90°, only slight opening during the backward swing and closing during the forward swing; hands are kept loose in the central position; hands are moved forward up to chin level, backward to just behind the hips (forearm not exceeding the vertical).
- Particularly tall sprinters should possibly run with a higher stride frequency in the curve and with a longer strides on the straight.
- The athlete must try to maintain his/her optimal technique as well as possible in spite of increasing acidification.

ATTACKING THE FINISH LINE AND SUBSEQUENT DECELERATION

- Shifting of the chest and trunk to the front relative to the arms, head, and legs as close to the finish line as possible; also slight shifting forward of the CG relative to the touchdown point.
- Maintenance of tension in order to decelerate without running the risk of injury; shifting backward of the trunk and thus the CG.

1.5.5 PHOTO SEQUENCE

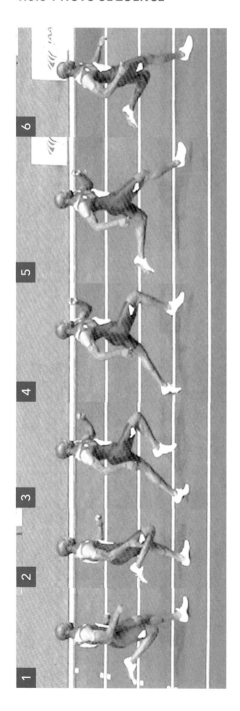

Data about the photo sequence

Athlete:	LaShawn Merritt (born: 27 June 1986, USA)
Height/weight:	1.88 m/82 kg
Performance:	45.23 sec (18 August 2009, Berlin)
Best performance:	43.75 sec (21 August 2008, Beijing)
Greatest success:	Double Olympic champion in 2008 and world champion over 400m and 4 x 400m in 2009

COMMENTARY

Before the World Championship final in Berlin 2009, there were indications that there would be a duel between the two Americans, Jeremy Wariner and LaShawn Merritt, just like a year before in Beijing. Merritt had inflicted a crushing defeat on Wariner in Beijing who was the 400m Olympic champion of 2004 and world champion of 2005 and 2007. While third-place athlete Renny Quow started the first 200m of the final in Berlin too slowly (see half-race difference in table 4), Wariner and Merritt ran head to head until they reached the finishing straight. Merritt, however, covered the finishing straight more than half a second faster than Wariner and thus once again secured a clear victory. Accordingly, loneliness is the impression which Merritt conveys in the depicted picture sequence which was recorded approximately 30 metres in front of the finish line.

While Merritt ran with significant forward lean of his upper body on the back straight, his body is upright near the finish line. However, his running style is characterised by a slight swayback posture. This is also expressed in the position of his head, which is slightly tilted backward, the low knee lift (pictures 4 and 9), and the high position of the foot behind his body (pictures 1, 6, 7, and 12). In many 400m sprinters, a swayback posture on the finishing straight frequently results in a significant loss of speed and thus represents a weakness (see figure 14 in chapter II–1.3.3). Merritt, however, runs the entire distance in his personal style which fulfils the main criteria for a good 400m technique. He powerfully accelerates his foot backward before touchdown (pictures 5, 6, 10, and 11) and, while keeping his hips high, he places his almost straight leg at a relatively short distance in front of his body. Afterwards, he flexes his support leg only slightly before extending it completely (on the right clearer than on the left; pictures 3, 4, 8, and 9). It is probably due to fatigue that Merritt places his left foot on the ground with the entire sole of the foot. Simultaneously, he moves his swing leg forward at an exemplary acute knee angle (pictures 2 and 7) in order to move it quickly to the front of his body.

Merritt's arm action shows few anomalies. Although he moves his arms slightly diagonally (his elbows are slightly splayed to the side, and his hands swing forward and inward and backward and outward so that there is a slight shoulder rotation and shoulder-hip separation [picture 4]), his arm actions appear rhythmic and his shoulders sufficiently fixed in the respective video.

*Table 4: **Interval and split times of the top three finishers at the 2009 World Championships** in Berlin in the final race (in sec; according to Graubner et al., 2009, p. 14).*

	Reaction time	Interval times					Difference between the two halves of the race	Split and final times		
		0-100	100-200	200-300	300-400	200-400		0-200	0-300	0-400
LaShawn Merritt (USA)	0.161	11.14	10.35	10.83	11.74	22.57	1.08	21.49	32.32	44.06
Jeremy Wariner (USA) 0.162		10.98	10.43	10.93	12.26	23.19	1.78	21.41	32.34	44.60
Renny Quow (TRI) 0.195		11.70	10.73	10.89	11.70	22.59	0.16	22.43	33.32	45.20

1.5.6 STRATEGY

After almost maximal acceleration over the first 50 metres, the 400m sprinter tries to run with relaxed and loose but fast sprinting strides. On the first 200m, 400m sprinters lag behind their 200m times. ***They save their reserves for reasons of economy*** because if they exert too much energy in the beginning, they will suffer excessively in the end. Conversely, it is impossible to compensate at the end of the race for time lost at the beginning. The objective is therefore to find an optimum balance which is not always an easy task. There is evidence that not only different sprinters, but also one and the same sprinter, use a different strategy in different races depending on the situation. If a more sophisticated analysis (50 or 100m split times) is not possible, the time for the half race is often used for strategic analysis. While T. Matthews, 400m Olympic champion from 1972, was only 0.5 sec slower over the first 200m than his fastest 200m time, M. Johnson was almost

2 sec behind his 200m world record when he ran his 400m world record. The average speed reserve of the world-leading runners over the first 200m is about 1 sec. The speed reserve of beginners is greater.

*Table 5: **Exemplary calculations for the distribution of the race** for two 400m runners with different qualifications.*

200m best time	23.2 sec
+ speed reserve	1.4 sec
= 1st 200m of a 400m race	24.6 sec
+ fatigue-induced time difference	2.8 sec
= 2nd 200m of a 400m race	27.4 sec
Final time of a 400m race (1st 200m + 2nd 200m =)	52.0 sec
200m best time	20.7 sec
+ speed reserve	1.0 sec
= 1st 200m in 400m race	21.7 sec
+ fatigue-induced time difference	1.6 sec
= 2nd 200m of a 400m race	23.3 sec
Final time of a 400m race (1st 200m + 2nd 200m =)	45.0 sec

The *relation between the first and second half of the distance* is the second criterion (see table 5). As a rule of thumb, the difference between the first and the second half of the distance is 2 sec for 400m world-class runners, with women remaining on average slightly above this time and the men remaining slightly below. During his winning race at the 1993 World Championships, world-record holder M. Johnson, who often started the race at a relatively slow pace, ran the second half of the race approximately 35 hundredths of a second slower than the first one. However, the difference between the first and the second half of the race as well as the complete race distribution depend on the athlete's skill level (tables 6 and 7 include corresponding guiding values).

Table 6: Split and interval times (in sec) for optimal speed distribution in women's 400m sprint, based on analyses conducted at the 1988 Olympic Games (Sušanka & Moravec, 1988).

400m	0-100m	0-200m	0-300m	100-200m	200-300m	300-400m	200-400m	2nd-1st 200m
47.00	12.01	23.12	34.31	11.11	11.19	12.69	23.88	0.76
47.50	12.05	23.21	34.62	11.16	11.41	12.88	24.29	1.08
48.00	12.10	23.30	34.92	11.20	11.62	13.08	24.70	1.40
48.50	12.14	23.38	35.22	11.24	11.84	13.28	25.12	1.74
49.00	12.23	23.50	35.53	11.27	12.03	13.47	25.50	2.00
49.50	12.33	23.70	35.87	11.37	12.17	13.63	25.80	2.10
50.00	12.43	23.89	36.22	11.46	12.33	13.78	26.11	2.22
50.50	12.53	24.09	36.56	11.56	12.47	13.94	26.41	2.32
51.00	12.62	24.28	36.90	11.66	12.62	14.10	26.72	2.44
51.50	12.72	24.48	37.25	11.76	12.77	14.25	27.02	2.54
52.00	12.82	24.67	37.59	11.85	12.92	14.41	27.33	2.66
52.50	12.91	24.86	37.93	11.95	13.07	14.57	27.64	2.78
53.00	13.01	25.05	38.29	12.04	13.24	14.71	27.94	2.90
53.50	13.11	24.24	38.65	12.13	13.41	14.85	28.26	3.02
54.00	13.20	24.43	39.02	12.23	13.59	14.98	28.57	3.14

*Table 7: **Intermediate and interval times (in sec) for optimal speed distribution in men's 400m sprint**, based on analyses conducted at the 1988 Olympic Games (Sušanka & Moravec, 1988).*

400m	0-100m	0-200m	0-300m	100-200m	200-300m	300-400m	200-400m	2nd-1st200m
45.00	11.32	21.67	32.74	10.35	11.07	12.26	23.33	1.66
45.50	11.42	21.87	33.09	10.45	11.22	12.41	23.63	1.76
46.00	11.52	22.07	33.43	10.55	11.36	12.57	23.93	1.86
46.50	11.62	22.27	33.78	10.65	11.51	12.72	24.23	1.96
47.00	11.72	22.46	34.13	10.74	11.67	12.87	24.54	2.08
47.50	11.82	22.66	34.47	10.84	11.81	13.03	24.84	2.18
48.00	11.92	22.86	34.82	10.94	11.96	13.18	25.14	2.28
48.50	12.01	23.05	35.17	11.04	12.12	13.33	25.45	2.40
49.00	12.11	23.25	35.53	11.14	12.28	13.47	25.75	2.50
49.50	12.21	23.44	35.89	11.23	12.45	13.61	26.06	2.62
50.00	12.30	23.63	36.25	11.33	12.62	13.75	26.37	2.74
50.50	12.40	23.82	36.61	11.42	12.79	13.89	26.68	2.86
51.00	12.50	24.01	36.98	11.51	12.97	14.02	26.99	2.98
51.50	12.59	24.20	37.34	11.61	13.14	14.16	27.30	3.10
52.00	12.68	24.39	37.70	11.71	13.31	14.30	27.61	3.22

1.5.7 DIDACTICS: SUPERORDINATE LONG-TERM OBJECTIVES AND GENERAL METHODOLOGY

In children's athletics and in basic training, the 400m sprint is prepared in particular by means of the short sprint (see chapter II–1.3.7) and aerobic running (see chapter II–1.10.5). In coordination training, an economic sprinting stride should be developed as early as possible. Although the predominantly anaerobic games presented in connection with the 400m race (see chapter II–1.5.8) should be included sporadically in training, the emphasis on special training should only begin with build-up training. The amount of tempo-run training is then gradually increased beginning with the U18 age category. The fact that the long sprint is only a part of the competition programme beginning with the 15-year age group illustrates that the German Athletics Association tries to prevent misdirected ambition which possibly results in too early inclusion of extremely strenuous anaerobic loads in training. These often monotonous loads are considered especially mentally stressful and can therefore have a discouraging effect on children.

At a later point in time, a competitive-sport attitude is characterised especially by the desire to test one's physical limitations (see chapter I–3.1.1). Tempo runs and long-sprint competitions in adulthood are excellent means to do so. Thus, the high intrinsic motivation of the performance athlete and the ability to deal cognitively with one's own sport is a special requirement for long-sprint training.

COMPLEX TRAINING

Table 3 illustrates the diversity of the requirement profile for the 400m sprint. Reactive power, speed, anaerobic and aerobic endurance, etc. must each be trained specifically. Such a versatile and thus varied training to improve the whole complex of abilities required in competition is referred to as complex training. Such training is frequently performed according to the periodisation model of complex training (see chapter I–3.3.3) and often includes versatile training methods such as fartlek (230) with its varying intensities. Complex training should also help 400m sprinters to master longer distances (800m) and especially shorter distances (100 and 200m) so that the total anaerobic performance area (see figure 1 in chapter II–1.1.2) is well mastered in competition.

1.5.8 TRAINING CONTENTS: FORMS OF GAMES AND EXERCISES

Below, forms of anaerobic speed-endurance training are presented especially for the long sprint. Some of the forms of games and exercises presented below also improve aerobic endurance by using the extensive interval method. However, most forms of games and exercises for aerobic endurance training are presented in connection with middle- and long-distance running in chapter II–1.10.6. However, they are also important contents for long-sprint training. Moreover, all forms of coordination, speed, and strength training mentioned in connection with the 100m sprint (see chapter II–1.3.8) are also contents of (200 and) 400m training. However, 400m runners perform coordination- and speed-training exercises particularly often on curved and slalom courses. Long sprinters perform strength exercises more often than short sprinters in the form of strength-endurance training (see chapter I–4.5).

151 ▯▯▮ Crouch start and acceleration in the curve

Possible objectives: Training of the target technique; speed strength and reactive strength of the legs; acyclic and cyclic speed.
Execution: See chapter II–1.4.3.
Variations: With and without command (if without

command, do not take a preliminary swing, but start from a static set position); also holding a relay baton in the right hand; also focusing on the transition to pick-up acceleration.

Typical load standards: 3–8 reps of 20-50m each; as acceleration training (e.g., in pyramid form): 20, 30, 40, 50, 40, 30, and 20m, rest interval: running distance divided by 5 (or 10) in min.

In many cases, it is not the forms of games and exercises which determine the training effect, but rather the duration of the rest interval and the length of the distance. If forms of games mentioned in connection with the short sprint (e.g., black and white [109] or the number race [108]) are performed with correspondingly short rest intervals and over long distances, they train primarily anaerobic speed endurance. Many games (basketball [324], handball [325], soccer, hockey [1], etc.) and their simplified preparatory forms and variations are characterised by an interval-like alternation between fast sprints and low-intensity activities and improve anaerobic and aerobic endurance while the athletes have a lot of fun.

152 Chasing games (e.g., flag chasing)

Possible objectives: Versatile sprinting technique; reaction speed, acyclic, and cyclic speed; speed strength and reactive strength of the legs; speed endurance.

Execution: Each participant places one or two flags in his/her waistband and tries to catch the flags of the other players.

Variations: Various types of movement (e.g., limping).

Typical load standards: See chapter II–1.3.7.

153 Collecting cards

Possible objectives: The winner is not only the one with the best speed endurance, but luck is also important.

Execution: Four (or two) teams are formed and assigned the playing card suits: clubs, spades,

hearts, and diamonds (or the colours red and black). The mixed cards are placed face down at one end of the 30–40m long playing field. At the other end, the teams position themselves. One player of each team runs to the cards, turns over one card, takes it with him/her if it is the correct colour, or otherwise puts it back again face down, and sprints back to his/her team to tag the next player and send him/her on the way to the cards. *Typical load standards:* determined by the number of cards.

---

154 ▢ **Beat the 5,000/10,000m world record!**

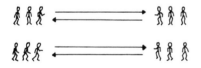

Possible objectives: Anaerobic speed endurance; aerobic endurance; cognitive involvement with the sport.

Execution/variations: 5,000 or 10,000m are run by one team or training group in the form of a pendulum relay (111) (e.g., in 100m sections).

Typical load standards: 5,000m world record: 12:37.35 min (100m average time: 15.1 sec); 10,000m world record: 26:17.53 min (100m average time: 15.8 sec); if a group of 10 runners wants to beat the 10,000m world record, each member of this group must run 10 times and there will be a rest interval of approx. 2:22 min.

Like many game forms in anaerobic speed-endurance training, the two forms mentioned above are so-called endless relays. It is absolutely necessary to also consider performing the playful relay forms in chapter II–1.7.7!

---

155 ▢ **Square runs**

Possible objectives: Anaerobic speed endurance; aerobic endurance; development of the feel for pace.
Execution/variations: around a 24 x 24m square

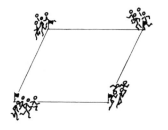

(approx. 100 m) on the lawn; at each corner, there is a runner or group; who can reach the pre-set time most exactly?

Typical load standards: The pace varies between relaxed continuous-run pace (6 min/km = 36 sec/100 m) and 10,000m pace (16 sec/100 m; see 154).

156 Line pendulum

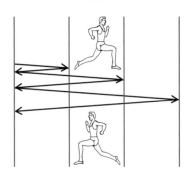

Possible objectives: Speed-endurance training on a small area (e.g., in the gym); high strength-endurance and eccentric loads through stopping and new acceleration.

Execution/variations: Without rest interval from the starting line to the first line, back to the starting line, to the second line, back to the starting line, etc.

Typical load standards: The number of repetitions and total distance or duration of a pendulum are very variable (see tempo runs below).

157 LI tempo runs for long sprinters (and middle- and long-distance runners)

Possible objectives: Aerobic endurance; anaerobic speed endurance; economy (coordination); feel for pace.

Execution: Runs at low intensity (LI; see table 12 in chapter I-4.5) in accordance with pre-set guiding times (see tables 8–10 below); in spite of pre-set times, the runs should be performed at an even pace (the first ones not too fast), but the total time of all runs should be as fast as possible; if possible, they should be performed in groups, from a standing start on the command of one of the sprinters: "forward – backward – go" and corresponding forward and backward movements of the body.

Variations: In the wrong direction (clockwise on a 400m track); on varying grounds: synthetic track, lawn, forest track, etc., also in profiled terrain; usually wearing running shoes; also barefoot as diagonal sprints on the lawn (diagonal sprints: sprint on the diagonal – walk or jog on the short [or long] side – sprint on the diagonal); as (endless) relays (173); also as runs according to pre-set running times (seconds) and with intensity control by varying the distance to be run.

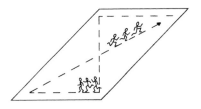

Typical load standards: according to the extensive interval method:

a) 2–3 series of 6–10 lawn diagonals or reps of 100m each, walking or jogging intervals: 30–45 sec, rest intervals between the series: 5–8 min;

b) 3–5 series of 4–5 reps of 200m each, walking or jogging intervals: 90 sec, rest intervals between the series: 5–8 min;

c) 2 series of 4–6 reps, or 1 series of 6–10 reps of 400m each, walking or jogging intervals: 3 min, rest intervals between the series: 5–8 min;

d) with series of varying distances: e.g., 4 reps of 300m each, 5 reps of 250m each, and 6 reps of 200m each, walking or jogging intervals: 150, 120, and 90 sec, rest intervals between the series: 5–8 min;

e) according to the pyramid principle within a series: e.g., 3–4 series of 180, 220, 250, 200, and 150m, walking or jogging intervals: 90 sec, rest intervals between the series: 5–8 min.

158 I3 tempo runs for long sprinters (and middle- and long-distance runners)

Possible objectives: Anaerobic speed endurance; economy (coordination); feel for pace.

Execution: Runs at intensity level 3 (I3; see table 12 in chapter I-4.5, tables 8–10 below, as well as LI tempo runs, 157); if possible, they should

be performed in groups, but in individual lanes; usually wearing spikes.

Variations: (See Ll tempo runs, 157); each athlete once in each lane: once in the inner lane, once in the outer lane; also in combination with light pull-resistance (137), uphill (138), at alternating pace (133), or over hurdles (214–217).

Typical load standards: e.g.:

a) under-distance runs according to the intensive interval method in series: 2 series of 4–5 reps of 150m each, walking interval: 4–5 min, rest interval between the series: 10 min;

b) relatively short tempo runs according to the intensive interval method in pyramids: 120, 150, 180, 220, 250, 220, 180, 150, and 120m, walking intervals: 3, 4, 5, 6, 10, 8, 6, and 5 min;

c) over-distance runs according to the repetition method: 4–5 reps of 500m each, walking intervals: 5–8 min;

d) combined programmes according to the repetition method in pyramids: 200, 400, 600, 500, 300, and 100m, and walking intervals: 4, 6, 10, 8, and 6 min;

e) combined programmes according to the intensive interval method with varying distances within the series: slow I3: 3 series of 200, 300, and 500m, walking intervals: 3, 5, and 10 min; fast I3: 2–3 series of 150, 150, and 500m, walking intervals: 5, 5, and 12–15 min.

---

159 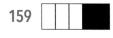 **I2 tempo runs for long sprinters (and middle- and long-distance runners)**

Possible objectives: Anaerobic speed endurance; economy (coordination); feel for pace.

Execution/variations: Runs at intensity level 2 (I2; see table 12 in chapter I-4.5, tables 8-10 below as well as I3 tempo runs, 158).

Typical load standards: e. g.:

a) under-distance runs according to the repetition method in pyramids: 120, 150, 180, 150, and 100m, or 180, 150, 120, and 100m (or in reverse order), walking intervals: running distance divided by 10 in min;

b) under-distance runs according to the intensive interval method in series: 2 series of 3 reps of 150m each, walking interval: 8 min, rest interval between series: 12–15 min;

c) medium distances according to the repetition method: 3–4 reps of 300m each, walking intervals: 15–25 min;

d) over-distance runs according to the repetition method: 2–3 reps of 500m each, walking intervals: 20–30 min;

e) combined programmes according to the repetition method in pyramids: 150, 500, 300, and 200m, walking intervals: 15, 25, and 20 min;

f) double runs: 300 + 150, 250 + 150, and 200 + 150m, walking intervals after each individual run: 2, 30, 2, 25, and 2 min;

g) competition simulations: 1–2 reps of 350m each at the aimed desired 50m split times; 3 reps of 300m each: 50m at maximum speed, 150m relaxed and fast, 100m at maximum speed.

160   I1 tempo runs for long sprinters

Possible objectives: Anaerobic speed endurance; economy (coordination); feel for pace.

Execution/variations: Runs at intensity level 1 (I1; see table 12 in chapter I-4.5, tables 8-10 below as well as I3 tempo runs, 158); also in competition.

Typical load standards: According to the repetition or competition method: e.g.:

a) 150, 150, and 300m, walking intervals: 15 min;

b) 2 reps of 200–300m each, minimum walking interval: running distance divided by 10 in min;

c) 1 rep of 400–600m (possibly b and c with 150m pre-load, walking interval: 15 min).

The specific anaerobic endurance training of long sprinters also includes more extreme variants of the ABCs of endurance (141, e.g., 300m bounding run [88] or 60 sec step-overs [117]) than in the short sprint.

Table 8: **Tempo table for the distances from 60 to 120 m,** on the basis of the 100m best times (mathematically modelled in accordance with Tepper & Czingon, 1992, pp. 104–105): It is assumed that the best time was measured with fully automatic equipment at a competition, while in training the times are measured manually upon the release of the rear foot.

100m best time	60m				80m				100m					120m				
	100%	95%	90%	85%	100%	95%	90%	85%	100%	95%	90%	80%	70%	100%	95%	90%	80%	70%
9.90	5.8	6.1	6.5	6.8	7.6	7.9	8.4	8.9	9.3	9.8	10.3	11.6	13.3	11.2	11.7	12.4	14.0	15.9
10.00	5.9	6.2	6.5	6.9	7.6	8.0	8.5	9.0	9.4	9.9	10.4	11.8	13.4	11.3	11.9	12.5	14.1	16.1
10.10	5.9	6.3	6.6	7.0	7.7	8.1	8.6	9.1	9.5	10.0	10.6	11.9	13.6	11.4	12.0	12.7	14.3	16.3
10.20	6.0	6.3	6.7	7.1	7.8	8.2	8.7	9.2	9.6	10.1	10.7	12.0	13.7	11.5	12.1	12.8	14.4	16.5
10.30	6.1	6.4	6.7	7.1	7.9	8.3	8.8	9.3	9.7	10.2	10.8	12.1	13.9	11.6	12.3	12.9	14.6	16.6
10.40	6.1	6.4	6.8	7.2	8.0	8.4	8.9	9.4	9.8	10.3	10.9	12.3	14.0	11.8	12.4	13.1	14.7	16.8
10.50	6.2	6.5	6.9	7.3	8.0	8.5	9.0	9.5	9.9	10.4	11.0	12.4	14.1	11.9	12.5	13.2	14.9	17.0
10.60	6.3	6.6	6.9	7.4	8.1	8.5	9.0	9.6	10.0	10.5	11.1	12.5	14.3	12.0	12.6	13.3	15.0	17.1
10.70	6.3	6.6	7.0	7.4	8.2	8.6	9.1	9.6	10.1	10.6	11.2	12.6	14.4	12.1	12.8	13.5	15.2	17.3
10.80	6.4	6.7	7.1	7.5	8.3	8.7	9.2	9.7	10.2	10.7	11.3	12.8	14.6	12.2	12.9	13.6	15.3	17.5
10.90	6.4	6.8	7.2	7.6	8.4	8.8	9.3	9.8	10.3	10.8	11.4	12.9	14.7	12.4	13.0	13.7	15.5	17.7
11.00	6.5	6.8	7.2	7.6	8.4	8.9	9.4	9.9	10.4	10.9	11.6	13.0	14.9	12.5	13.1	13.9	15.6	17.8
11.10	6.6	6.9	7.3	7.7	8.5	9.0	9.5	10.0	10.5	11.1	11.7	13.1	15.0	12.6	13.3	14.0	15.8	18.0
11.20	6.6	7.0	7.4	7.8	8.6	9.1	9.6	10.1	10.6	11.2	11.8	13.3	15.1	12.7	13.4	14.1	15.9	18.2
11.30	6.7	7.0	7.4	7.9	8.7	9.1	9.6	10.2	10.7	11.3	11.9	13.4	15.3	12.8	13.5	14.3	16.1	18.3
11.40	6.8	7.1	7.5	7.9	8.8	9.2	9.7	10.3	10.8	11.4	12.0	13.5	15.4	13.0	13.6	14.4	16.2	18.5
11.50	6.8	7.2	7.6	8.0	8.9	9.3	9.8	10.4	10.9	11.5	12.1	13.6	15.6	13.1	13.8	14.5	16.4	18.7
11.60	6.9	7.2	7.6	8.1	8.9	9.4	9.9	10.5	11.0	11.6	12.2	13.8	15.7	13.2	13.9	14.7	16.5	18.9
11.70	6.9	7.3	7.7	8.2	9.0	9.5	10.0	10.6	11.1	11.7	12.3	13.9	15.9	13.3	14.0	14.8	16.7	19.0
11.80	7.0	7.4	7.8	8.2	9.1	9.6	10.1	10.6	11.2	11.8	12.4	14.0	16.0	13.4	14.1	14.9	16.8	19.2
11.90	7.1	7.4	7.8	8.3	9.2	9.7	10.1	10.7	11.3	11.9	12.6	14.1	16.1	13.6	14.3	15.1	17.0	19.4
12.00	7.1	7.5	7.9	8.4	9.3	9.7	10.2	10.8	11.4	12.0	12.7	14.3	16.3	13.7	14.4	15.2	17.1	19.5
12.10	7.2	7.6	8.0	8.5	9.3	9.8	10.3	10.9	11.5	12.1	12.8	14.4	16.4	13.8	14.5	15.3	17.3	19.7
12.20	7.3	7.6	8.1	8.5	9.4	9.9	10.4	11.0	11.6	12.2	12.9	14.5	16.6	13.9	14.7	15.5	17.4	19.9
12.30	7.3	7.7	8.1	8.6	9.5	10.0	10.5	11.1	11.7	12.3	13.0	14.6	16.7	14.0	14.8	15.6	17.6	20.1
12.40	7.4	7.8	8.2	8.7	9.6	10.1	10.6	11.2	11.8	12.4	13.1	14.8	16.9	14.2	14.9	15.7	17.7	20.2
12.50	7.4	7.8	8.3	8.7	9.6	10.2	10.6	11.3	11.9	12.5	13.2	14.9	17.0	14.3	15.0	15.9	17.9	20.4
12.60	7.5	7.9	8.3	8.8	9.7	10.3	10.7	11.4	12.0	12.6	13.3	15.0	17.1	14.4	15.2	16.0	18.0	20.6
12.70	7.6	8.0	8.4	8.9	9.8	10.3	10.8	11.5	12.1	12.7	13.4	15.1	17.3	14.5	15.3	16.1	18.2	20.7
12.80	7.6	8.0	8.5	9.0	9.9	10.4	10.9	11.6	12.2	12.8	13.6	15.3	17.4	14.6	15.4	16.3	18.3	20.9
12.90	7.7	8.1	8.5	9.0	10.0	10.5	11.1	11.7	12.3	12.9	13.7	15.4	17.6	14.8	15.5	16.4	18.5	21.1
13.00	7.7	8.2	8.6	9.1	10.1	10.6	11.2	11.8	12.4	13.1	13.8	15.5	17.7	14.9	15.7	16.5	18.6	21.3

*Table 9: **Tempo table for the distances from 150 to 250m,** on the basis of the 200m best time (mathematically modelled in accordance with Tepper & Czingon, 1992, pp. 106-107); for further details see the explanation for table 8.*

200m best time	150m 100%	150m 95%	150m 90%	150m 80%	150m 70%	150m 50%	180m 100%	180m 95%	180m 90%	180m 80%	180m 70%	180m 50%	200m 100%	200m 95%	200m 90%	200m 80%	200m 70%	200m 50%	220m 100%	220m 95%	220m 90%	220m 80%	220m 70%	220m 50%	250m 100%	250m 95%	250m 90%	250m 80%	250m 70%	250m 50%
19.80	14.2	15.0	15.8	17.8	20.3	28.4	17.2	18.1	19.1	21.5	24.5	34.3	19.2	20.2	21.3	24.0	27.4	38.4	21.3	22.4	23.7	26.6	30.4	42.6	24.8	26.2	27.6	31.1	35.5	49.7
20.00	14.4	15.1	16.0	17.9	20.5	28.7	17.3	18.3	19.3	21.7	24.8	34.7	19.4	20.4	21.6	24.3	27.7	38.8	21.5	22.6	23.9	26.9	30.7	43.0	25.1	26.4	27.9	31.4	35.9	50.2
20.20	14.5	15.3	16.1	18.1	20.7	29.0	17.5	18.4	19.5	21.9	25.0	35.0	19.6	20.6	21.8	24.5	28.0	39.2	21.7	22.9	24.2	27.2	31.1	43.5	25.4	26.7	28.2	31.7	36.2	50.7
20.40	14.7	15.4	16.3	18.3	20.9	29.3	17.7	18.6	19.7	22.1	25.3	35.4	19.8	20.8	22.0	24.8	28.3	39.6	22.0	23.1	24.4	27.4	31.4	43.9	25.6	27.0	28.5	32.0	36.6	51.2
20.60	14.8	15.6	16.4	18.5	21.1	29.6	17.9	18.8	19.9	22.4	25.5	35.8	20.0	21.1	22.2	25.0	28.6	40.0	22.2	23.3	24.6	27.7	31.7	44.4	25.9	27.2	28.8	32.4	37.0	51.8
20.80	14.9	15.7	16.6	18.7	21.4	29.9	18.1	19.0	20.1	22.6	25.8	36.1	20.2	21.3	22.4	25.3	28.9	40.4	22.4	23.6	24.9	28.0	32.0	44.8	26.1	27.5	29.0	32.7	37.3	52.3
21.00	15.1	15.9	16.8	18.9	21.6	30.2	18.2	19.2	20.3	22.8	26.1	36.5	20.4	21.5	22.7	25.5	29.1	40.8	22.6	23.8	25.1	28.3	32.3	45.2	26.4	27.8	29.3	33.0	37.7	52.8
21.20	15.2	16.0	16.9	19.1	21.8	30.5	18.4	19.4	20.5	23.0	26.3	36.8	20.6	21.7	22.9	25.8	29.4	41.2	22.8	24.0	25.4	28.6	32.6	45.7	26.7	28.1	29.6	33.3	38.1	53.3
21.40	15.4	16.2	17.1	19.2	22.0	30.8	18.6	19.6	20.7	23.2	26.6	37.2	20.8	21.9	23.1	26.0	29.7	41.6	23.1	24.3	25.6	28.8	33.0	46.1	27.0	28.3	29.9	33.6	38.5	53.8
21.60	15.5	16.4	17.3	19.4	22.2	31.1	18.8	19.8	20.9	23.5	26.8	37.5	21.0	22.1	23.3	26.3	30.0	42.0	23.3	24.5	25.9	29.1	33.3	46.6	27.2	28.6	30.2	33.8	38.8	54.3
21.80	15.7	16.5	17.4	19.6	22.4	31.4	19.0	20.0	21.1	23.7	27.1	37.9	21.2	22.3	23.6	26.5	30.3	42.4	23.5	24.7	26.1	29.4	33.6	47.0	27.4	28.9	30.5	34.0	39.2	54.9
22.00	15.8	16.7	17.6	19.8	22.6	31.7	19.1	20.1	21.3	23.9	27.3	38.3	21.4	22.5	23.8	26.8	30.6	42.8	23.7	25.0	26.4	29.7	33.9	47.5	27.7	29.1	30.8	34.3	39.6	55.4
22.20	16.0	16.8	17.8	20.0	22.8	32.0	19.3	20.3	21.5	24.1	27.6	38.6	21.6	22.7	24.0	27.0	30.9	43.2	24.0	25.2	26.6	29.9	34.2	47.9	28.0	29.4	31.1	34.6	40.0	55.9
22.40	16.1	17.0	17.9	20.2	23.0	32.3	19.5	20.5	21.7	24.4	27.8	39.0	21.8	22.9	24.2	27.3	31.1	43.6	24.2	25.4	26.9	30.2	34.5	48.4	28.2	29.7	31.3	34.9	40.3	56.4
22.60	16.3	17.1	18.1	20.4	23.3	32.6	19.7	20.7	21.9	24.6	28.1	39.3	22.0	23.2	24.4	27.5	31.4	44.0	24.4	25.7	27.1	30.5	34.9	48.8	28.5	30.0	31.6	35.3	40.7	56.9
22.80	16.4	17.3	18.3	20.5	23.5	32.9	19.8	20.9	22.1	24.8	28.4	39.7	22.2	23.4	24.7	27.8	31.7	44.4	24.6	25.9	27.4	30.8	35.2	49.2	28.7	30.2	31.9	35.6	41.0	57.5
23.00	16.6	17.4	18.4	20.7	23.7	33.2	20.0	21.1	22.3	25.0	28.6	40.1	22.4	23.6	24.9	28.0	32.0	44.8	24.8	26.1	27.6	31.1	35.5	49.7	29.0	30.5	32.2	35.9	41.4	58.0
23.20	16.7	17.6	18.6	20.9	23.9	33.4	20.2	21.3	22.4	25.3	28.9	40.4	22.6	23.8	25.1	28.3	32.3	45.2	25.1	26.4	27.8	31.3	35.8	50.1	29.2	30.8	32.5	36.2	41.8	58.5
23.40	16.9	17.8	18.7	21.1	24.1	33.7	20.4	21.5	22.6	25.5	29.1	40.8	22.8	24.0	25.3	28.5	32.6	45.6	25.3	26.6	28.1	31.6	36.1	50.6	29.5	31.1	32.8	36.6	42.1	59.0
23.60	17.0	17.9	18.9	21.3	24.3	34.0	20.6	21.6	22.8	25.7	29.4	41.1	23.0	24.2	25.6	28.8	32.9	46.0	25.5	26.8	28.3	31.9	36.4	51.0	29.8	31.3	33.1	36.9	42.5	59.5
23.80	17.2	18.1	19.1	21.5	24.5	34.3	20.7	21.8	23.0	25.9	29.6	41.5	23.2	24.4	25.8	29.0	33.1	46.4	25.7	27.1	28.6	32.2	36.8	51.5	30.0	31.6	33.4	37.2	42.9	60.0
24.00	17.3	18.2	19.2	21.6	24.7	34.6	20.9	22.0	23.2	26.1	29.9	41.8	23.4	24.6	26.0	29.3	33.4	46.8	26.0	27.3	28.8	32.4	37.1	51.9	30.3	31.9	33.6	37.5	43.3	60.6
24.20	17.5	18.4	19.4	21.8	24.9	34.9	21.1	22.2	23.4	26.4	30.1	42.2	23.6	24.8	26.2	29.5	33.7	47.2	26.2	27.5	29.1	32.7	37.4	52.3	30.5	32.1	33.9	37.8	43.6	61.1
24.40	17.6	18.5	19.6	22.0	25.2	35.2	21.3	22.4	23.6	26.6	30.4	42.6	23.8	25.1	26.4	29.8	34.0	47.6	26.4	27.8	29.3	33.0	37.7	52.8	30.8	32.4	34.2	38.2	44.0	61.6
24.60	17.8	18.7	19.7	22.2	25.4	35.5	21.5	22.6	23.8	26.8	30.7	42.9	24.0	25.3	26.7	30.0	34.3	48.0	26.6	28.0	29.6	33.3	38.0	53.2	31.1	32.7	34.5	38.5	44.4	62.1
24.80	17.9	18.9	19.9	22.4	25.6	35.8	21.6	22.8	24.0	27.0	30.9	43.3	24.2	25.5	26.9	30.3	34.6	48.4	26.8	28.3	29.8	33.5	38.3	53.7	31.3	33.0	34.8	38.8	44.7	62.6
25.00	18.1	19.0	20.1	22.6	25.8	36.1	21.8	23.0	24.2	27.3	31.2	43.6	24.4	25.7	27.1	30.5	34.9	48.8	27.1	28.5	30.1	33.8	38.7	54.1	31.6	33.2	35.1	39.1	45.1	63.1
25.20	18.2	19.2	20.2	22.8	26.0	36.4	22.0	23.1	24.4	27.5	31.4	44.0	24.6	25.9	27.3	30.8	35.1	49.2	27.3	28.7	30.3	34.1	39.0	54.6	31.8	33.5	35.4	39.5	45.5	63.7
25.40	18.4	19.3	20.4	22.9	26.2	36.7	22.2	23.3	24.6	27.7	31.7	44.3	24.8	26.1	27.6	31.0	35.4	49.6	27.5	29.0	30.6	34.4	39.3	55.0	32.1	33.8	35.7	39.8	45.8	64.2
25.60	18.5	19.5	20.6	23.1	26.4	37.0	22.4	23.5	24.8	27.9	31.9	44.7	25.0	26.3	27.8	31.3	35.7	50.0	27.7	29.2	30.8	34.7	39.6	55.5	32.4	34.1	35.9	40.1	46.2	64.7
25.80	18.6	19.6	20.7	23.3	26.6	37.3	22.5	23.7	25.0	28.2	32.2	45.1	25.2	26.5	28.0	31.5	36.0	50.4	27.9	29.4	31.1	34.9	39.9	55.9	32.6	34.3	36.2	40.4	46.6	65.2
26.00	18.8	19.8	20.9	23.5	26.9	37.6	22.7	23.9	25.2	28.4	32.4	45.4	25.4	26.7	28.2	31.8	36.3	50.8	28.2	29.7	31.3	35.2	40.2	56.3	32.9	34.6	36.5	40.8	47.0	65.7

*Table 10: **Tempo table for the distances from 300 to 600m**, on the basis of the 400m best times (mathematically modelled in accordance with Tepper & Czingon, 1992, pp. 108-109); for further details see the explanation for table 8.*

400m best time	300m						350m						400m						500m						600m					
	100%	95%	90%	80%	70%	50%	100%	95%	90%	80%	70%	50%	100%	95%	90%	80%	70%	50%	100%	95%	90%	80%	70%	50%	100%	95%	90%	80%	70%	50%
44.50	31.2	32.9	34.7	39.0	44.6	62.5	36.9	38.8	41.0	46.1	52.7	73.8	43.9	46.2	48.8	54.9	62.7	87.8	58.5	61.6	65.0	73.1	83.6	117.0	73.6	77.5	81.8	92.0	105.2	147.2
45.00	31.6	33.3	35.1	39.5	45.2	63.2	37.3	39.3	41.5	46.7	53.3	74.7	44.4	46.7	49.3	55.5	63.4	88.8	59.1	62.3	65.7	73.9	84.5	118.3	74.5	78.4	82.8	93.1	106.4	149.0
45.50	32.0	33.7	35.5	40.0	45.7	64.0	37.8	39.8	42.0	47.2	54.0	75.6	44.9	47.3	49.9	56.1	64.1	89.8	59.8	62.9	66.4	74.7	85.4	119.5	75.4	79.4	83.8	94.3	107.7	150.8
46.00	32.4	34.1	36.0	40.5	46.2	64.7	38.2	40.2	42.5	47.8	54.6	76.5	45.4	47.8	50.4	56.8	64.9	90.8	60.4	63.6	67.1	75.5	86.3	120.8	76.3	80.3	84.8	95.4	109.0	152.6
46.50	32.8	34.5	36.4	40.9	46.8	65.5	38.7	40.7	43.0	48.3	55.3	77.4	45.9	48.3	51.0	57.4	65.6	91.8	61.0	64.3	67.8	76.3	87.2	122.1	77.2	81.3	85.8	96.5	110.3	154.4
47.00	33.1	34.9	36.8	41.4	47.3	66.3	39.1	41.2	43.5	48.9	55.9	78.2	46.4	48.8	51.6	58.0	66.3	92.8	61.7	64.9	68.5	77.1	88.1	123.3	78.1	82.2	86.8	97.6	111.6	156.2
47.50	33.5	35.3	37.2	41.9	47.9	67.0	39.6	41.7	44.0	49.5	56.5	79.1	46.9	49.4	52.1	58.6	67.0	93.8	62.3	65.6	69.2	77.9	89.0	124.6	79.0	83.1	87.8	98.7	112.8	158.0
48.00	33.9	35.7	37.7	42.4	48.4	67.8	40.0	42.1	44.5	50.0	57.2	80.0	47.4	49.9	52.7	59.3	67.7	94.8	62.9	66.2	69.9	78.7	89.9	125.9	79.9	84.1	88.8	99.9	114.1	159.8
48.50	34.3	36.1	38.1	42.8	49.0	68.6	40.5	42.6	45.0	50.6	57.8	80.9	47.9	50.4	53.2	59.9	68.4	95.8	63.6	66.9	70.6	79.5	90.8	127.1	80.8	85.0	89.8	101.0	115.4	161.6
49.00	34.7	36.5	38.5	43.3	49.5	69.3	40.9	43.1	45.4	51.1	58.4	81.8	48.4	50.9	53.8	60.5	69.1	96.8	64.2	67.6	71.3	80.3	91.7	128.4	81.7	86.0	90.8	102.1	116.7	163.4
49.50	35.0	36.9	38.9	43.8	50.1	70.1	41.3	43.5	45.9	51.7	59.1	82.7	48.9	51.5	54.3	61.1	69.9	97.8	64.8	68.2	72.0	81.0	92.6	129.7	82.6	86.9	91.8	103.2	118.0	165.2
50.00	35.4	37.3	39.4	44.3	50.6	70.8	41.8	44.0	46.4	52.2	59.7	83.6	49.4	52.0	54.9	61.8	70.6	98.8	65.5	68.9	72.7	81.8	93.5	130.9	83.5	87.9	92.8	104.4	119.3	167.0
50.50	35.8	37.7	39.8	44.8	51.1	71.6	42.2	44.5	46.9	52.8	60.3	84.5	49.9	52.5	55.4	62.4	71.3	99.8	66.1	69.6	73.4	82.6	94.4	132.2	84.4	88.8	93.8	105.5	120.5	168.8
51.00	36.2	38.1	40.2	45.2	51.7	72.4	42.7	44.9	47.4	53.4	61.0	85.4	50.4	53.1	56.0	63.0	72.0	100.8	66.7	70.2	74.1	83.4	95.3	133.5	85.3	89.8	94.8	106.6	121.8	170.6
51.50	36.6	38.5	40.6	45.7	52.2	73.1	43.1	45.4	47.9	53.9	61.6	86.3	50.9	53.6	56.6	63.6	72.7	101.8	67.4	70.9	74.9	84.2	96.2	134.7	86.2	90.7	95.7	107.7	123.1	172.3
52.00	36.9	38.9	41.1	46.2	52.8	73.9	43.6	45.9	48.4	54.5	62.3	87.2	51.4	54.1	57.1	64.3	73.4	102.8	68.0	71.6	75.6	85.0	97.1	136.0	87.1	91.7	96.7	108.8	124.4	174.1
52.50	37.3	39.3	41.5	46.7	53.3	74.7	44.0	46.3	48.9	55.0	62.9	88.0	51.9	54.6	57.7	64.9	74.1	103.8	68.6	72.2	76.3	85.8	98.0	137.3	88.0	92.6	97.7	110.0	125.7	175.9
53.00	37.7	39.7	41.9	47.1	53.9	75.4	44.4	46.8	49.3	55.6	63.5	88.9	52.4	55.2	58.2	65.5	74.9	104.8	69.3	72.9	77.0	86.6	98.9	138.5	88.9	93.5	98.7	111.1	127.0	177.7
53.50	38.1	40.1	42.3	47.6	54.4	76.2	44.9	47.3	49.9	56.1	64.2	89.8	52.9	55.7	58.8	66.1	75.6	105.8	69.9	73.6	77.7	87.4	99.9	139.8	89.8	94.5	99.7	112.2	128.2	179.5
54.00	38.5	40.5	42.7	48.1	55.0	76.9	45.4	47.7	50.4	56.7	64.8	90.7	53.4	56.2	59.3	66.8	76.3	106.8	70.5	74.2	78.4	88.2	100.8	141.1	90.7	95.4	100.7	113.3	129.5	181.3
54.50	38.9	40.9	43.2	48.6	55.5	77.7	45.8	48.2	50.9	57.3	65.4	91.6	53.9	56.7	59.9	67.4	77.0	107.8	71.2	74.9	79.1	89.0	101.7	142.3	91.6	96.4	101.7	114.5	130.8	183.1
55.00	39.2	41.3	43.6	49.0	56.0	78.5	46.3	48.7	51.4	57.8	66.1	92.5	54.4	57.3	60.4	68.0	77.7	108.8	71.8	75.6	79.8	89.7	102.6	143.6	92.5	97.3	102.7	115.6	132.1	184.9
55.50	39.6	41.7	44.0	49.5	56.6	79.2	46.7	49.2	51.9	58.4	66.7	93.4	54.9	57.8	61.0	68.6	78.4	109.8	72.4	76.2	80.5	90.5	103.5	144.9	93.4	98.3	103.7	116.7	133.4	186.7
56.00	40.0	42.1	44.4	50.0	57.1	80.0	47.1	49.6	52.4	58.9	67.3	94.3	55.4	58.3	61.6	69.3	79.1	110.8	73.1	76.9	81.2	91.3	104.4	146.1	94.3	99.2	104.7	117.8	134.7	188.5
56.50	40.4	42.5	44.9	50.5	57.7	80.8	47.6	50.1	52.9	59.5	68.0	95.2	55.9	58.8	62.1	69.9	79.9	111.8	73.7	77.6	81.9	92.1	105.3	147.4	95.2	100.2	105.7	118.9	135.9	190.3
57.00	40.8	42.9	45.3	50.9	58.2	81.5	48.0	50.6	53.4	60.0	68.6	96.1	56.4	59.4	62.7	70.5	80.6	112.8	74.3	78.2	82.6	92.9	106.2	148.6	96.1	101.1	106.7	120.1	137.2	192.1
57.50	41.1	43.3	45.7	51.4	58.8	82.3	48.5	51.0	53.9	60.6	69.3	97.0	56.9	59.9	63.2	71.1	81.3	113.8	75.0	78.9	83.3	93.7	107.1	149.9	96.9	102.1	107.7	121.2	138.5	193.9
58.00	41.5	43.7	46.1	51.9	59.3	83.0	48.9	51.5	54.4	61.2	69.9	97.8	57.4	60.4	63.8	71.7	82.0	114.8	75.6	79.6	84.0	94.5	108.0	151.2	97.8	103.0	108.7	122.3	139.8	195.7
58.50	41.9	44.1	46.6	52.4	59.9	83.8	49.3	52.0	54.9	61.7	70.5	98.7	57.9	60.9	64.3	72.4	82.7	115.8	76.2	80.2	84.7	95.3	108.7	152.4	98.7	103.9	109.7	123.4	141.1	197.5
59.00	42.3	44.5	47.0	52.9	60.4	84.6	49.8	52.4	55.3	62.3	71.2	99.6	58.4	61.5	64.9	73.0	83.4	116.8	76.9	80.9	85.4	96.1	109.8	153.7	99.6	104.9	110.7	124.6	142.3	199.3
59.50	42.7	44.9	47.4	53.3	60.9	85.3	50.3	52.9	55.8	62.8	71.8	100.5	58.9	62.0	65.4	73.6	84.1	117.8	77.5	81.6	86.1	96.9	110.7	155.0	100.5	105.8	111.7	125.7	143.6	201.1
60.00	43.0	45.3	47.8	53.8	61.5	86.1	50.7	53.4	56.3	63.4	72.4	101.4	59.4	62.5	66.0	74.3	84.9	118.8	78.1	82.2	86.8	97.7	111.6	156.2	101.4	106.8	112.7	126.8	144.9	202.9

1.5.9 SPECIAL TEST AND CONTROL PROCEDURES

	Test: Ability/skill tested	Execution/comments
T31	**Wingate Test:** Anaerobic endurance	All-out exercise on a bicycle ergometer for 30 sec (see below).
T32	**Under- and over-distance tests:** Anaerobic speed endurance	Maximum sprint from standing start over 150m, 300m, or 500m; manual time measurement upon the release of the rear foot is usually sufficiently accurate.
T33	**Long-sprint tempo-run programmes:** Anaerobic speed endurance and aerobic endurance	For example, standardised programmes can be as follows: a) LI: 2 x 5 x 400m, rest intervals: 3 min, rest intervals between sets: 6 min; b) I3: 2 x 3 x 400m, rest intervals: 8 min, rest intervals between sets: 15 min; c) I2: 3 x 400m, rest intervals: 20 min. Test criteria are the (average) times achieved and the post-exercise lactate values.
T4	**1 RPM:** Maximal strength	Squat (62), clean (63), snatch (64), flexors (68), extensors (69), arm exercises, etc. (if possible, also eccentric maximal-strength measurement).
T5	**Squat jump and T8 counter-movement and drop jump:** Two-legged speed strength and reactive strength of the extensor loop	As a simpler test, the forward and/or backward toss of the shot (93) for distance may be performed instead of counter-movement jumps.
T9	**5-stride hops with distance maximisation:** Reactive strength of the legs in comparison to one another	Test should be performed on both sides.
T10	**30m bounding run with time minimisation:** Reactive strength of the legs	
T11	**Strength-endurance tests:** Anaerobic strength endurance	e.g., squats for 1 min, or 200m bounding run.
T21	**60m analysis:** Sprint technique	See technique analysis sheet in chapter II-1.5.4; test should also be performed in the curve.
T22	**Crouch-start reaction test:** Reaction speed	

(continued)

(continued)

	Test: Ability/skill tested	Execution/comments
T23	**Crouch start and acceleration up to 20m:** Start acceleration with and without reaction speed	Test should also be performed in the curve.
T24	**30m flying sprint:** Maximum sprinting speed	Test should also be performed in the curve.
T25	**20m frequency test:** Cyclic speed	Test should also be performed in the curve.
T66	**Graded field test:** Aerobic endurance	With lactate withdrawal (and spirometry; for young athletes also Cooper test, T65, which is easy to perform but inaccurate).
T2	**Flexibility tests:** General flexibility	
T3	**Body weight and body fat measurement:** Relative strength	Inappropriate upward and downward deflections should be avoided.

WINGATE TEST

The Wingate Test (T31), which was developed at the Israeli Coaches Academy, may be used as a general under-distance test which is not specific to any discipline. This test is probably one of the most commonly performed tests for anaerobic endurance. Due to its easy measurement of physical power output (in watts), it is performed on a bicycle ergometer. During this test, the athlete pedals with maximum effort against a high resistance for 30 seconds. In the process, talented athletes display typical load curves for the long sprint, middle distance, and long distance (see table 11).

*Table 11: **Typical results in the Wingate Test** (modified on the basis of Ijzerman et al., 2008, p. 41).*

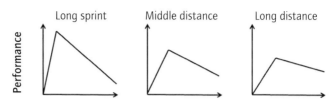

	Long sprint	Middle distance	Long distance
maximum power output (= mp)	high	high	low
time to mp (= ttmp)	short	short	long
mp/ ttmp	high	medium	low
decline in power output	high	medium	low
maximum lactate value	high	high	low
area under the curve	large	large	small

*Table 12: **Basic performances of 400m sprinters** (according to Tepper & Czingon, 1995, p. 45). Although the lengths of the rest intervals are not indicated in the tempo-run test programmes, they should be approx. 20 min in the I2 zone and 5–8 min in the I3 zone.*

	Women			Men		
400m target time (sec)	56.00	54.50	51.00	48.50	47.00	45.30
30m from the starting blocks (sec)	4.74	4.70	4.44	4.23	4.22	4.13
30m flying (sec)	3.27	3.20	3.09	2.91	2.89	2.84
10-stride bounding run (m)	20–23	22–26	22–29	29–32	32–35	33–36
half squat (multiple of body weight)	1.3–1.6	1.5–1.7	1.6–1.9	1.9–2.2	2.1–2.3	2.2–2.5
100m (sec)	12.50	12.30	11.75	11.05	10.95	10.75
200m (sec)	24.75	24.35	23.00	22.10	21.60	21.15
300m (sec)	39.50	39.00	36.80	34.70	33.50	32.75
3x400m/3x300m average time (I2) (sec)	59.5/45.0	58.0/42.5	54.5/–	50.5/–	59.0/–	47.5/–
6x400m/6x300m average time (I3) (sec)	66.5/48.5	65.0/45.0	61.5/–	56.5/–	55.0/–	54.0/–
Running velocity at 4 mmol/l measured in graded lactate field test (m/sec)	3.6–3.9	3.8–4.0	4.0–4.2	4.1–4.3	4.3–4.5	4.5–4.8

1.5.10 ERRORS – CAUSES – CORRECTIONS

Error	Causes	Corrections
Disqualification for stepping on the inner boundary when running in the curve (shortly after the start).	• False placement of the blocks: pointing too much to the inside or placed too much to the left. • Balance problems when straightening up and simultaneous initiation of curve running. • Trying to achieve a running path as short as possible. • Reduction of velocity in the last curve before the finish. • Coordination problems.	✔ Emphasising the importance of the rules (see chapter II–1.2.1). ✔ Development of an appropriate crouch start in the curve (see chapter II–1.4.3 and 151) ✔ Versatile sprinting through the curve while adhering to the rules on the one hand, and keeping a running path as short as possible on the other hand. ✔ If the velocity decreases, the inward lean must also be reduced.
When running in the curve, the sprinter runs too far to the outside of the lane.	• Inappropriate inward lean into the curve. • Insufficient strength (e.g., of the trunk muscles) to counteract the centrifugal forces or compression in the curve. • Athlete makes insufficient effort to achieve a running path as short as possible.	✔ Maximum sprints in lane 1 through the curve, with deliberate inward lean. ✔ If possible, special strength training (e.g., lumborum exercise [45]). ✔ Demonstration of the optimal running path.
The sprinter is able to increase his/her speed at the end of the race (i.e., to accelerate shortly in front of the finish), or he/she runs identical halves or even a faster second half.	• False strategy (sprinter is too slow at the start of the race). • The sprinter orientates himself/herself to slower sprinters in next higher lanes in the starting curve. • The sprinter is not willing to take risks (fear of over-acidification or of wearing himself/herself out too much).	✔ Training the feel for pace (e.g., by performing the exercises 154–155 and 157–160). ✔ 100–200m tempo runs at 400m competition pace (see tables 8 and 9; also with runners in the other lanes who run at their own pace; each runner once in each lane). ✔ Talk and psychological intervention if necessary.
Wearing oneself out: excessive decrease in velocity on the last 50 or 100m, or too great time difference between the two halves of the race.	• False strategy (sprinter is too fast at the start). • The sprinter orientates himself/herself to faster sprinters in the next higher lanes in the starting curve. • Insufficient speed endurance.	✔ Training the feel for pace (e.g., by performing the exercises 154–155 and 157–160). ✔ 100–200m tempo runs at 400m competition pace (see tables 8 and 9; also with runners in the other lanes who run at their own pace; each runner once in each lane). ✔ More aerobic and anaerobic endurance training.
Knees too low on the finishing straight (resulting in bad preparation of foot touchdown).	• Lacking strength endurance of the hip flexors and/or the abdominal muscles (sprinter adopts a sway-back posture). • Abandonment of upright running posture (head or chest want to reach the finishing line).	✔ ABCs of endurance (141) with step-overs (117), or high-knee run (112, also with weighted sleeves on the ankles). ✔ Strength-endurance training for the abdominal muscles. ✔ Deliberately upright posture when performing tempo runs.

In addition to the errors listed in this table, all other errors, causes, and corrections listed for the 100m race (see chapter II–1.3.10) also occur in the 400m race.

1.5.11 TRAINING PLANNING

As in the 100m sprint (see chapter II–1.3.11) and the 4 x 100m relay, the 4 x 400m relay training can be regarded as the best 400m training. A corresponding training plan can therefore be found in chapter II–1.7.10. In terms of young athletes in the U18 and U20 age groups, 400m and 400m hurdle training may also be regarded as identical since hurdle training makes long-sprint training more versatile and focusing on a special discipline early on is not necessary.

1.5.12 BIBLIOGRAPHY

Arcelli, E., Mambretti, M., Cimadoro, G. & Alberti, G. (2008). The aerobic mechanism in the 400 metres. *New Studies in Athletics 23* (2), 15-23.

Collet, C. (1999). Strategic aspects of reaction time in world-class sprinters. *Perceptual and motor Skills 88* (1), 65-75.

Friedlander, A. (2005). Clyde Hard on the 400: Train S-L-O-W-E-R to Race Faster. American Track & Field (Merit Rankings Issue), 60-62.

Gajer, B., Hanon, C. & Thepaut-Mathieu, C. (2007). Velocity and stride parameters in the 400 Metres. *New Studies in Athletics 22* (3), 39-46.

Graubner, R., Buckwitz, R., Landmann, M. & Starke, A. (2009). Final Report Sprint Men. In Deutscher Leichtathletikverband (Hrsg.), *Biomechanical Analysis of selected events at the 12th IAAF World Championships in Athletics, Berlin 15-23 August 2009*. Zugriff am 20.04.2010 unter http://www.iaaf. org/mm/Document/ Development/Research/05/64/57/20100415075418_httppostedfile_1- BiomechanicsReportWCBerlin2009_ Sprint_Men_19905.pdf

Ijzerman, J., Damen, T., Koens, G. & Collée T. (2008). Improving talent identification and development in young distance runners. *New Studies in Athletics 23* (3), 35-48.

Letzelter, S. & Eggers, R. (2003). Geschwindigkeitsverlauf über 400 m in der Weltklasse. *Leistungsport 33* (6), 40-45.

Schiffer, J. (2008). The 400 metres. *New Studies in Athletics 23* (2), 7-13.

Tepper, E. & Czingon, H. (Red.) (mit Keydel, H.). (1995). *Rahmentrainingsplan für das Aufbautraining Sprint* (4. Aufl.) (Edition Leichtathletik, 2). Aachen: Meyer und Meyer.

Vonstein, W. (2008). Eine Runde sprinten. Leichtathletiktraining 19 (11), 12-17.

1.6 4 X 100M

1.6.1 WAVES OF EXCITEMENT AND SUDDEN HORROR

Short sprinters are hot-blooded athletes whose coaches and fellow athletes often find their inflated egos difficult to bear. However, sometimes these egos seem to be the reason for their success. At the most, spectators notice no more than the battle of words before the race, the posing behind the starting blocks, and the show at the finish. Uniting these athletes in the relay, the one genuine team competition in athletics, is like trying to fit a square into a circle.

But this is not the only reason why the relays are highlights of athletics events. They are also the climax of sporting dramatics. What is striking is the frequent failure of highly favoured relay teams whose members are unable to exploit their running potential. The reason for this is often a lack of specific relay qualities of the sprinters: concentration, reaction, and a perfect exchange technique to ensure that the baton is exchanged at the highest possible sprinting speed with optimum utilisation of the exchange zone. A lack of fine-tuning among the runners, mostly due to a lack of training, may have been the reason for some relay tragedies in the past. The 4 x 100m relay for women and men was held for the first time at the Olympic Games in 1912. The German runner Rau ran over the exchange mark and relinquished his team's chance to win the gold medal.

At the 1936 Olympics in Berlin, the German women's 4 x 100m relay team set a new world and Olympic record in 46.4 sec. Therefore, the Germans were the clear favourites for the final. In the final, the lead of the German runner at the third exchange was approximately 10 metres. Then it happened: Ilse Dörffeldt, who received the baton from Marie Dollinger, did not hold the baton firmly enough, and it fell on the cinder track. The seemingly safe gold medal was lost. At the 1960 Olympic Games in Rome, the U.S. relay team, whose members were clearly champion runners, shocked the spectators in the stadium by getting disqualified after the first exchange. The German relay team, with 100m Olympic champion Hary as the anchor runner, won the gold medal. The British team was lucky since it won the silver medal only because the exchange judges did not see that their first handover had taken place outside the exchange zone.

A positive result of the relay drama in Rome was a rule change by the IAAF: In front of the 20m exchange zone, a 10m acceleration zone was established. Since then, the receiver has had the possibility of a longer acceleration before taking over the baton, preferably only after 25–28m in the exchange zone. The fact that even this relief is not always used by many relay teams is demonstrated by the results of the sprint relays at the 2008 Olympic Games: The strong U.S. sprinters failed in their semi-final race. The Jamaican women runners were not better in the final and lost the gold medal which they were sure to win. The British and Polish women made the ultimate drama perfect with their disqualifications. The medals were won by Russia, Belgium, and Nigeria. The men were comparable to the women. The former leading relay nation USA was forced to watch helplessly as the Jamaicans pulverised their existing world record from 1993, which at that time was run without optimal handovers, by an enormous three tenths of a second. They themselves had been disqualified like the British in the semi-final. The disqualifications of China and the Netherlands completed the disaster of the Olympic sprint relays. Bad luck for the relay teams? No, rather relay dilettantism!

1.6.2 THE MOST IMPORTANT COMPETITION RULES

The following abridged and simplified International Competition Rules comprise the framework for the technique and strategy, as well as for the organisation of 4 x 100m competitions:

- Each exchange zone is 30m long with a scratch line 20m from the start of the zone. The scratch line marks the end of each 100m section and is thereby identical with the white starting line for the 300m at the first handover and with the white starting line for the 200m at the second handover. In the curve near the 100m start, the scratch line of the third exchange zone is marked by a short white line.
- The beginning of the exchange zone is marked by a yellow "1", while the end is marked by a yellow mirror-inverted "1" (viewing direction in each case from the interior field).
- In accordance with their sprinting distance, U14 athletes run 4 x 75m. The exchange zones are similarly marked. In the U12 age group and the lower age groups, 4 x 50m are run. For the 4 x 50m, no exchange zones are marked. The receivers must position themselves at the start of their 50m leg.

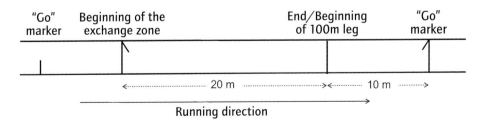

*Figure 1: **Markings of the exchange zone.***

- The receivers are allowed to attach an adhesive tape (maximum 5 x 40cm) onto their lane, which they use as a "go" or "coincidence" marker (see figure 1 and chapter II–1.6.3).
- The relay baton is a smooth hollow tube, with a round circumference, made of wood, metal, or any other rigid material in one piece, the length of which is 28–30cm. The circumference of the baton is 12–13cm and the weight is not less than 50g. The baton is coloured.
- The relay baton is carried by hand throughout the race. Athletes are not permitted to wear gloves or to have materials or substances in their hands in order to get a better grip on the baton. If dropped, the baton may be recovered, but only by the athlete who dropped it and only if no other athlete is impeded.
- Not the sprinters, but the baton must be within the exchange zone during the handover, which is the period in which both sprinters have contact with the baton.
- If leaving the lane before, during, or after the exchange results in an advantage for the receiving sprinter or impedes other sprinters, there will be a disqualification.
- Assistance to the receiver by pushing or by any other method shall result in disqualification.

Apart from that, the general competition rules for running and sprinting apply (see chapters II–1.1.1 and II–1.2.1).

1.6.3 SPORT-SCIENCE FINDINGS, PHASE STRUCTURE, AND TECHNIQUE

In the following, only those technical elements of the 4 x 100m relay are described and discussed which were not discussed in previous chapters. Thus, the start with the relay baton and the handover will be dealt with here. The handover will be described and discussed in terms of the following four phases:

- preparation of the exchange;
- start and approximation;
- handing over the baton; and
- conclusion of the exchange.

CROUCH START WITH THE BATON

The problem for the first runner is to hold the baton while supporting himself/herself on his/her hands. There are two main possible solutions. Either the athlete grips the baton with his/her index finger while the other fingers provide support as usual, or the baton is gripped with the middle, ring, and little fingers, while the thumb and forefinger provide support as usual.

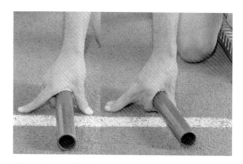

*Figure 2: **Possible finger position at the relay start.***

In addition, the sprinter supports himself/ herself on the middle phalanges of the fingers gripping the baton (see figure 2).

PHASE 1: PREPARATION OF THE EXCHANGE

INSIDE EXCHANGE AND OUTSIDE EXCHANGE

The exchange is always performed from the left to the right hand or from the right to the left hand, but never from the right to the right or from the left to the left hand. If one did the latter, the incoming sprinter would run directly behind the outgoing sprinter and thus there would be the risk of stepping on the front sprinter's heels and causing him/her to fall. An exchange from the right to the left hand is called an inside exchange since the incoming sprinter runs on the inside (i.e., on the left side of the lane), while the outgoing sprinter looks to the inside and takes the baton with his/ her inner hand. Accordingly, an exchange from the left to the right hand is called an outside exchange (see figure 3).

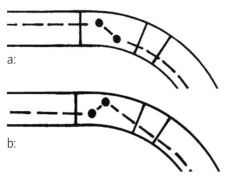

Figure 3a: **Inside exchange;** *b: Outside exchange*

ALTERNATE EXCHANGE OR FRANKFURT EXCHANGE

Although performing the 4 x 100m relay with only inside or outside exchanges would facilitate the organisation of training, it is not advisable. For example, if the baton were always passed from the right to the left hand, the second and third sprinter would be forced to take the baton back from the left to the right hand.

The concomitant stopping of arm work costs time. Therefore, in 4 x 100m relay teams a particular combination of inside and outside exchange has established itself, which is called the Frankfurt exchange (see figure 4). The first runner carries the baton in his/her right hand and runs as far inside or on the left side of his/her lane as possible, since the smaller the radius of curvature, the shorter the distance. The second runner stands on the outside or right side of the lane and stays on the outside half of the lane during the approximation (see phase 2). Thus, there is an inside exchange to the left hand of the second sprinter. This sprinter keeps the baton in his/her left hand and continues to run on the outside or right side of the lane. On the straight, the distance on the inside and on the outside is the same length. The second exchange is an outside exchange to the right hand of the third runner standing and accelerating on the inside or on the left side of the lane. This sprinter can again run through the curve along the shortest path inside and keep the baton in his/her right hand before passing it into the left hand of the anchor runner standing outside or on the right. In

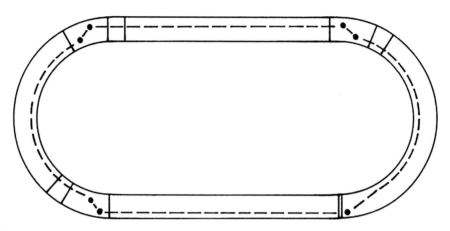

*Figure 4: **Frankfurt exchange**, consisting of one inside, one outside, and again one inside exchange.*

short, the curve sprinters carry the baton in their right hand, whereas the sprinters on the straight carry it in their left hand.

"GO" MARKER

The receiver is usually positioned as close to the beginning of the exchange zone (see chapter II–1.6.2). The runner attaches the "go" marker (also called "coincidence" marker) a few metres before the exchange zone. Since the tape used for this must not be longer than 40cm, the runner attaches it to the side of the lane on which the incoming runner will arrive (see above). The distance between the "go" marker and the receiver's starting position must be tested individually in training and competition (see chapter II–1.6.7). The following values can serve as a guide:

Men: 6.80–8.80 m
Women and male U18/20: 6.30–6.80 m
Female U18/20: 5.30–6.30 m.

According to other sources, the distance should be 25 feet in length for equally good runners. If a sprinter with a fast finish passes the baton to a sprinter with a weak start, the distance will be longer. Conversely, the distance will be shorter if a sprinter who is slow (especially toward the end of the 100m) passes the baton to someone who is fast at the start. It is suggested to add or subtract half a foot per tenth of a second difference in the 100m personal best. Sometimes, a strong wind must also be taken into consideration. Headwind affects the incoming runner (due to the greater relative speed difference between wind and runner) more than the outgoing runner. In the event of tailwind, a recommendation for strategy is more difficult. Although the relative velocity difference between wind and runner is higher for the outgoing runner, he/she also has a smaller attack area due to the forward lean of his/her body. The distance of the "go" marker is also influenced by the starting position, the starting reaction, as well as considerations for optimising the exchange (see below).

OUTGOING POSITIONS: STANDING START, RELAY THREE-POINT START, OR CROUCH START

By the time the passing sprinter has completed half of his/her distance, the receiving sprinter should have taken his/her outgoing position and looked back at the "go" marker. Particular difficulties may occur during the first exchange. Due to the staggered start, the contesting athletes in the more inside lanes are usually positioned in such a way that the incoming sprinter of one's own team cannot be seen for a period of time. This should be particularly noted and practised in training (see 164–165).

There are three different outgoing positions used by relay runners. All these positions have in common that the runner, who receives the baton with his/her left hand, positions himself/herself on the right side of the lane with his/her right foot forward and his/her left foot backward. He/she turns to the left or looks to the left past his/her body. Accordingly, the runner who receives the baton with his/her right hand stands on the left side of the lane with his/her left foot forward and turns to the right or looks to the right past his/her body. The outgoing positions differ mainly by the number of limbs placed on the ground (2, 3, or all 4). In the standing start, the receiver looks over his/her shoulder or sideways past his/her shoulder back to the "go" marker. The advantage of the standing start is the high position of the eyes, which allows for a favourable angle of view to the incoming runner and the "go" marker. This advantage is possibly increased by a trunk position which is more upright than in a conventional standing start (123). The disadvantage of the standing start position is that shifting one's centre of gravity forward in order to achieve the forward lean of the body which is necessary for acceleration is relatively difficult and takes a long time after the starting reaction. Since it is also difficult to perform this procedure in always the same manner, the standing start position can also lead to inaccuracies at the start. This disadvantage cannot be adequately compensated for by a slightly wider spacing of the feet in the running direction. The advantages and disadvantages of starting from a crouch position are precisely the opposite. Here, the athlete looks under his/her shoulder past his/her legs back to the "go" marker and the incoming runner. A disadvantage of the crouch start is the deep position of the eyes, which makes it very difficult to estimate the remaining distance between the incoming runner and the "go" marker.

However, the centre of gravity is already shifted forward relative to the touchdown point of the feet and the start is fast and constant. Starting from a three-point support (see figure 5) is a compromise to be recommended. Here, only the hand on the side of the front foot is placed on the ground 1½ to 2 feet in length in front of this foot. Due to the additional slight rotation of his/her upper body about the longitudinal axis, the sprinter is now able to look from a medium-high position sideways past his/her shoulder back to the "go" marker. Since his/her weight rests on the supporting hand, the CG is also shifted forward.

*Figure 5: **Three-point outgoing position**.*

PHASE 2: START AND APPROXIMATION

START REACTION

As soon as the passer runs over the "go" marker, the receiver starts. This statement sounds a lot easier than it is in practice. Does the receiver anticipate this moment or does he/she wait until he/she actually sees the passer running over the marker? The solution and recommendation for the receiver is that no matter how he/she reacts, it is important that he/she always reacts in an identical manner. In any case, however, the second method results in a more distant "go" marker than the first one (see phase 1). Even if the second option may seem a bit more accurate, it raises a new question: Does the receiver start when he/she thinks that the trunk of the passer is over the "go" marker or when he/she sees the first foot contact of the passer beyond the "go" marker? Due to the high speed and the spatial distance between the trunk and the "go" marker, it is difficult to estimate whether the passer's trunk is over the marker. However, the identification of the first foot contact beyond the marker is also inexact since the first ground contact may be either a few centimetres or approximately two metres beyond the line due to the individual stride length.

NON-VISUAL EXCHANGE OF THE BATON

Two different types of exchange should be distinguished: In the 4 x 400m relay, a visual exchange is performed (see chapter II–1.7.3), while in the 4 x 100m relay a so-called non-visual exchange (i.e., an exchange without sight) is performed. In the latter exchange, the receiver looks forward after the start reaction and does not turn around during his/her maximum acceleration (to look at the passer or the baton). The quick rotation of the head about the longitudinal and/or transverse axis directly after the start reaction disturbs the vestibular organ in the inner ear. To maintain one's balance in spite of this and to place the first strides of the acceleration sprint correctly, the relay start, which is demanding in terms of coordination, must be specifically practised (see 163).

For the passer, it is crucial that he/she continues sprinting at the highest possible speed before and during the approximation.

PHASE 3: PASSING THE BATON

OPTIMAL DISTANCE AND COMMAND

The optimal distance between the trunk of the passer and the receiver when exchanging the baton is approximately two arm lengths. This means that the baton should be passed with arms outstretched over the largest possible distance, since this extra space simultaneously means gaining time.

During his/her acceleration, the receiver initially sprints with normal sprint-like arm movements. As soon as or shortly before the aforementioned optimum distance for the handover has been reached, the passer gives a short and loud monosyllabic command (such as "now"). On this command, the receiver stretches his/her arm backward and upward. It is optimal when the passer gives this command when the baton is just in front of his/her body. While the passer swings back his/her arm with the baton again, the receiver moves his/her arm upward, so that the passer may pass the baton at the end of the subsequent forward movement of his/her arm.

To insure against any mishaps, it should be agreed that the receiver automatically raises his/her arm 5–8m before the end of the exchange zone if by then no command has been given. In extreme emergency situations in competitions, when the passer has the impression that the receiver has started too early, he/she may possibly interrupt the arm action of the receiver by a premature command and thus slow him/her down a little. If the receiver seems to be even more difficult to reach, a loud "stop" may even be necessary. However, if things have gone this far, it is clear that it is impossible to achieve a new personal best time in this race.

DOWNWARD OR UPWARD HANDOVER TECHNIQUES

There are two specific techniques to hand over the baton. The passer either hands over the baton from above (downward pass) or from below (upward pass) to the receiver (see figure 6).

In the two types of baton exchanges, the receiving hand should be aligned with the forearm (or slightly dorsiflexed), the fingers should be closed, and the thumb should be abducted. The hand should be kept as still as possible to make it easier for the passer to hit the receiver's hand correctly. Even if the receiver perceives that the passer has not hit his/her hand on the first try (e.g., by a touch), he/she should not make grasping movements to find the baton but should wait until the passer places the baton into his/her hand. Especially when handing over the baton from above, it is crucial that the receiving arm is raised (almost) horizontally. This is facilitated by the forward lean of the body during the acceleration or by a slight additional forward lean of the trunk. When passing the baton from the top, the passer stretches his/her arm forward at the end of the forward swinging movement and bends his/her wrist forward and downward in such a way that he/she can pass the baton almost horizontally. When passing the baton from below, the passer stretches his/her arm even earlier during the forward swinging movement. The wrist is bent downward in the same manner, and the baton is placed into the receiving hand from below during the upward swing. In response to the baton hitting the middle of the hand (downward pass) or the area between the thumb and index finger (upward pass), the receiver closes his/her hand. As soon as the receiver holds the baton securely, the passer must let go of the baton on time to avoid pulling the baton out of the hand of the receiver. In general, the handover should be performed as quickly as possible. The interruption of the receiver's arm action due to the backward arm extension, which has a negative effect on acceleration, should not last more than 2–3 strides.

Both handover techniques are performed by world-class relay sprinters. However, the upward pass has two small drawbacks: First, figure 7 shows that when performing the Frankfurt exchange combined with a pass from below, there may be too little room on the baton. While during the pass from above the two exchanging sprinters can grab the respective ends of the baton (see figure 6a), the hands must be as close together as possible during the pass from below. If the pass from below is not performed correctly and the second or third sprinter grabs at the end of the baton, he/she must briefly press the "bottom" of the baton against his/her hip to slide the baton through his/her hand. This interruption of arm work may cost a little time. Secondly, due to the higher arm position and the aforementioned manner of grasping the baton, the pass from above can generally be performed with a larger distance between the sprinters. As already mentioned, this gain in space also means a gain in time. A relay team, a training group, or a club should agree on

a:

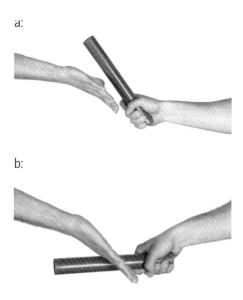

b:

Figure 6: *Passing the baton a: downward, and b: upward.*

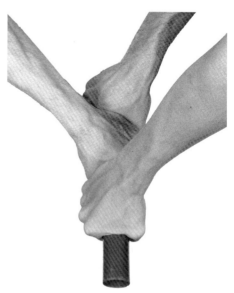

Figure 7: *Problems of space on the baton in the Frankfurt exchange using the upward pass.*

one handover technique so that there is no confusion about the exchange technique (e.g., in the event of a reshuffling of the relay team).

EXCHANGE IN THE LAST FOURTH OF THE EXCHANGE ZONE

It is crucial in a good exchange that the speed of the baton is as fast as possible and remains so. For this reason, the exchange should occur as late as possible (i.e., in the 10, or better yet, in the last 7m of the exchange zone). It is only sensible to hand over the baton to the receiver when he/she has reached his/her highest possible speed (provided that the passer sprints at almost constant, high speed; see figure 8). Therefore, the distance of the "go" marker should be as far as possible. However, with increasing distance the risk of exceeding the end of the exchange zone also increases. If a poor sprinter hands over the baton to a good one, there is even the risk that after an initial approximation the receiver will run away from the passer when reaching the end of the exchange zone. Therefore, good relay results require extensive training and testing in training and competition.

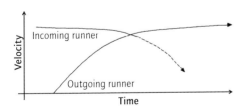

*Figure 8: **Velocity-time curve of the incoming and outgoing sprinters** during the baton exchange.*

EXCHANGE GAIN AND TWO-SECOND RULE

Since the second, third, and fourth sprinters run their 100m leg from a flying start, the 4 x 100m time is better than the sum of the 100m individual times of the four sprinters. For good athletes, the relay time should be at least 2 sec faster (see table 1).

*Table 1: **Table for assessing the quality of the exchange** (according to Mallett & Connor, 2004, p. 29).*

Assessment	Gain in time over the addition of the individual times (sec)	
	Adult elite	Youth teams
Excellent	>3.00	>2.5
Very good	2.75–3.00	2.3–2.5
Good	2.50–2.74	2.0–2.2
Moderate	2.00–2.49	1.5–1.9
Poor	<2.00	<1.5

PHASE 4: COMPLETION OF THE EXCHANGE

Studies conducted during strength training show that motivating shouts may increase athletic performance by up to 10%. Therefore, the passer usually cheers on the receiver before attempting to slow down his/her speed in a controlled manner (see chapter II–1.3.3). The passer may only leave his/her lane after having made sure that nobody will be impeded.

*Table 2: **Requirement profile for the 4 x 100m relay race:** The suggested rough estimate of values of selected factors determining performance is based on the importance for the overall performance and the percentage of time spent training (IR: information requirements, constr.: constraints; see chapter I-1.1).*

Factors determining 4 x 100m performanceEstimate of value Notes	Estimate of value	Notes
Coordination	+ + + +	optical IR: high, acoustic IR: medium, then low, tactile IR: medium, kinaesthetic IR: medium, vestibular IR: medium; precision constr.: high, time constr.: high, complexity constr.: medium, situation constr.: medium–high, physical stress constr.: low
Flexibility	+ +	no extreme movement amplitudes required
Strength		particular importance of the hamstrings; extensor loop (glutes, quadriceps, triceps surae, erector spinae), iliopsoas, abdominus, adductors, shoulder and upper-arm muscles
Maximal strength	+ + + +	during start acceleration and as a basis
Reactive strength	+ + + + +	within most various stretch-shortening cycles
Speed	+ + + + +	primarily cyclic; acyclic aspects at the start, during the exchange, and when attacking the finish line; reaction speed on acoustic signal (start, raising of the receiving hand), visual (start when passer runs over the "go" marker, hitting the receiving hand), and tactile stimulus (grasping the baton)
Endurance (general dynamic) Anaerobic endurance		
Strength endurance	+	as a basis of speed endurance
Speed endurance	+ + +	long maintenance of maximal velocity and slight and slow velocity loss at the end of the race
Aerobic endurance	+ +	primarily as training basis
Psychological and cognitive abilities	+ + + + +	ability to concentrate (on the point; there is no possibility to compensate for errors); performance-oriented thinking and behaviour (see chapter I-3.1.1)
Anthropometric and primarily genetically determined characteristics	+ + + + +	high proportion of the fastest muscle fibres; connective tissues with optimal energy-storing capacities; medium body height; low percentage of body fat

1.6.4 SUMMARY OF THE MOST IMPORTANT TECHNICAL CHARACTERISTICS = TECHNIQUE-ANALYSIS SHEET

CROUCH START WITH RELAY BATON

- For crouch start in the curve, see the technique analysis sheet in chapter II–1.5.4.
- The athlete grips the baton either with the index finger, or with the middle, ring, and little fingers of his/her right hand.

PREPARATION OF THE EXCHANGE

PASSER

- Sprint at the highest possible speed.

RECEIVER

- Attaching the "go" marker at the correct distance and on the correct side of the lane.
- Timely positioning for the start: The heel of the foot on the side of the receiving hand is placed at the beginning of the exchange zone, while the other foot is placed forward by one foot length; in the three-point start, the weight is also on the non-receiving hand 1½ to 2 feet in length in front of the front foot.
- The athlete looks back at the incoming runner and the "go" marker.
- The second and fourth sprinters stand on the outer or right side, while the third sprinter stands on the inner or left side.

START AND APPROXIMATION

PASSER

- Sprint at the highest possible speed.
- The first and third sprinters run on the inner or left side, while the second sprinter runs on the outer or right side.

RECEIVER

- Exact (i.e., always identical) reaction and start as soon as the incoming runner runs over the "go" marker.
- Maximal acceleration (see chapter II–1.3.4) while performing sprint-like arm movements and looking toward the front.
- The second and fourth sprinters run on the outer or right side, while the third sprinter runs on the inner or left side.

PASSING THE BATON

- Handover if possible in the last fourth of the exchange zone.

PASSER

- Highest possible speed and correct side of the lane.
- Loud, monosyllabic command (e.g., "now") as soon as or shortly before the optimum distance for the handover has been reached (two arm lengths).
- Continuation of normal actions (at least one swing-back movement) until the receiver has raised his/her hand.
- Downward pass: The arm is stretched at the end of the forward swinging movement, the wrist is bent downward, and the baton is horizontally placed into the receiving hand from above.
- Upward pass: The arm is already stretched in the middle of the forward swinging movement, and the baton is placed into the receiving hand from below.
- Letting go of the baton on time.

RECEIVER

- Maximal acceleration and correct side of the lane.
- Backward and upward arm movement immediately after the command.
- Fingers together, thumb abducted, hand still and in alignment with the forearm or slightly dorsiflexed.
- Active grasping movement as a response to the baton hitting the hand.
- Interruption due to the extended arm maximally 2–3 strides.

COMPLETION OF THE EXCHANGE

PASSER

- Motivating shouts to the outgoing runner; injury-free deceleration; stepping out of the lane only after all exchanges have been completed.

RECEIVER

- Maximal acceleration.

1.6.5 PHOTO SEQUENCE

NON-VISUAL
EXCHANGE OF
THE BATON

COMMENTARY

The picture sequence displays the third exchange of a U.S. relay team in the inner lane and a relay team of the former U.S.S.R. in the outer lane. Both teams take advantage of the Frankfurt exchange and accordingly demonstrate the inside exchange. The U.S. team demonstrates the downward pass, while the Soviet-Russian sprinters pass the baton from below. The two handovers do not occur simultaneously. The exchange of the U.S. team is shown in pictures 4–6, while the exchange of the U.S.S.R. team is shown in pictures 7–10. Both handovers seem to occur without any major problems. All sprinters maintain their lane correctly. It cannot be seen whether the exchanges occur in the last fourth of the exchange zone as required by the target technique.

Figure 1 shows that the passer of the U.S. team is running much too early with a high outstretched arm before the receiver raises her arm. The behaviour of the receiving U.S. sprinter, however, largely corresponds to the target technique. She raises her extended receiving arm almost horizontally, and her hand is aligned with her arm while the thumb is abducted.

Therefore, the Americans are able to pass the baton at the optimum, largest possible distance of two arm lengths (picture 4). However, if the significant size difference between the two American sprinters is taken into account, the receiver raises her arm too high. This means that the passer must raise her arm (which she raised too early anyway) also very high. This considerably upsets her sprinting rhythm. Therefore, if she had not hit the receiver's hands directly, it could have well happened that she would have run away from her.

The handover of the Soviet sprinters corresponds to the target technique. The effort to push the baton as far as possible into the hands of the receiver is clearly visible (see pictures 7–10). Although this is of crucial importance in the first handovers of the Frankfurt exchange with an upward pass of the baton, it would have been no longer necessary here in the third exchange. It can be clearly seen that the sprinters from the U.S.S.R. must get closer to each other due to the narrow grip of their hands and the somewhat lower arm position, which is typical of the upward pass of the baton.

1.6.6 STRATEGY

Strategy in the 4 x 100m relay focuses primarily on the following question. Which sprinter should be used in which position? In respect to this question, the following factors must be considered.

TOTAL LENGTH OF DISTANCES

The maximum possible distances that each of the four relay sprinters must run are not all the same. The first runner must sprint a maximum of 110m (0–110 m) at full speed, while the second and third sprinter must run up to 130m (80–210m, and 180–310m), and the fourth sprinter must run 120m (280–400m). Therefore, not only the 100m competition time, but also a 130m test (T44) should be decisive for choosing the relay team. The athletes with the best speed-endurance capabilities (i.e., typically good 200m sprinters) should therefore run the second and third leg.

LENGTH OF THE DISTANCE RUN WITH THE BATON AND PSYCHOLOGICAL EFFECTS

A different conclusion may be reached when one only considers the length of the distance covered while carrying the baton. If one assumes that it is optimal to perform each exchange in the last fourth of the exchange zone, the first leg is the longest (about 105 m) and the last one is the shortest (about 95 m). Therefore, the fastest sprinter should run the first leg.

This is also supported by the effect on the psyche. Each sprinter knows that it is easier to run ahead of the other runners than to follow behind them. Therefore, even the first athlete should try to gain a lead. According to this logic, the second best sprinter should run the second leg, etc.

From a psychological perspective, the last leg is probably also very important. Coaches often use particularly experienced athletes or those with the best fighting spirit for this leg, athletes who are able to get tough and to secure the team's victory.

CROUCH START, START ACCELERATION, AND START ACCURACY

However, it should be noted that the fastest athlete is not necessarily the one with the fastest reaction out of the crouch start or with the best start acceleration. If this is not the case, the athlete with the best crouch start should run the first leg. However, start acceleration is also crucial for the subsequent legs. Although it is not necessary for the sprinters running the second, third, and fourth legs to react quickly but only to react accurately, it is important that they are able to achieve the highest possible speed after approximately 25m at the moment of the handover. There are always some athletes who, despite extensive training, are not able to react consistently on the passer passing the "go" marker, to keep their hand still at the moment of the handover, etc. If there are no adequate substitutes, these athletes should run the first leg, for better or for worse.

SPRINTING IN THE CURVE VERSUS SPRINTING ON THE STRAIGHT

Some athletes are better in the curve, others are faster on the straight. For example, pure 100m sprinters often have more difficulties running in the curve than athletes who are also experienced 200m sprinters. Moreover, heavier athletes when running in the curve are subjected to centrifugal forces to a greater extent than lighter athletes, and tall sprinters who usually run with longer strides are taken outward at each stride in the curve. Therefore, they are often better on the straight, whereas smaller and lighter athletes often sprint faster and at a higher stride frequency through the curve. To determine which athletes are better in the curve or on the straight, the 130m test (T44) should also be performed in the curve.

1.6.7 DIDACTICS: SUPERORDINATE LONG-TERM OBJECTIVES AND
GENERAL METHODOLOGY

From an educational perspective, relay running plays a prominent role in the sport of athletics. Although there are team competitions in which points are assigned for each individual performance, the relay is ultimately the only real team competition in athletics. Thus, relay running helps to develop social skills and there is more to it than simply the educational principle of achievement (see chapter I-3.1.1). The educational principles of cooperation, competition, and communication and of taking risks and accepting responsibility are essential to relay running.

These are also reasons why relays are extremely popular training methods even in the earliest years of children's athletics and in basic training. In the beginning, the motor fundamentals of relay sprinting, especially of the baton exchange, should be trained in a playful manner. The chasing games already listed in association with the sprint (see chapter II-1.3.8) as well as the pendulum and return relays are only suitable to some extent for this purpose. The specific coordinative requirements of the 4 x 100m relay should be trained by more specific relay forms in which the passer runs to the receiver from behind and hands the baton to him/her. Here, the exchange zones and the "go" markers can initially be dispensed with. It is more important that children get a feel for the visual and the non-visual exchange. The primary objective is to learn to estimate

their partner's velocity and to relate it to their own starting behaviour. All playful forms of training should only be performed as long as the intensity is high and the participants enjoy doing them. The high intensity also requires a thorough prior warm-up, which means that these games are not suitable for the first part of the warm-up.

Only later is the training of starting accuracy and the optimal handover technique, etc. introduced. The handover technique is initially practised in a resting position (e.g., with the children sitting behind one another) or at a slower pace (see 161). Finally, during fine tuning to improve performance, the focus is on finding the optimal distance of the "go" marker for two specific exchange partners. During this process, which is inevitably performed by using the trial-and-error approach, the following aspects should be considered. Due to the onset of fatigue, the passer is unable to run at maximum speed in competition at the end of his/her leg. This submaximal speed is difficult to imitate in training. Therefore, sprinters often run too fast into the exchange zone during training. However, efforts by the receiver and the passer may also be reduced during training due to lack of motivation. Moreover, some athletes generally react sooner or later to the visual stimulus of the passer passing the "go" marker in competition than in training. All this suggests that competition simulations in training and test competitions are absolutely necessary. When forming the relay team and choosing the runners for the different legs, coaches should proceed with the utmost transparency and fairness. To avoid disputes, decisions should be based on announced and objective tests and should be explained to the relay team aspirants in personal talks.

1.6.8 TRAINING CONTENTS: FORMS OF GAMES AND EXERCISES

In general, all forms of games and exercises which were listed for the 100m (see chapter II–1.3.8) are also contents of 4 x 100m training. In addition, the crouch start in the curve (151) must be practised for the relay. In respect to games, all catching and chasing games, and even the pendulum and return relay with handover from the front, have already been mentioned in connection with the 100m race. These games and exercises are supplemented here by forms of games and exercises for the specific practice of the handover from behind. Some other games which may also be used for this, but which may be primarily used to improve speed endurance, are listed in the corresponding 4 x 400m relay chapter (see chapter II–1.7.7). However, the latter games are also good warm-up games for 4 x 100m training.

161 **Handovers when sitting, standing, jogging, or sprinting at submaximal pace**

Possible objectives: Handover technique; warm-up.

Execution: Two, four, or more relay sprinters sit (with legs stretched out), stand, jog, or sprint (at submaximal pace) in a row staggered depending on their respective handover hand and at a distance of two arm lengths from one another; their arms swing in a sprint-like manner (even when sitting or standing); command (the passer continues swinging his/her arms); the receiving hand is raised; the handover is performed; when the baton reaches the athlete at the front of the row, it is handed back (in a manner similar to the handover typical of the relay), or the athlete carrying the baton is overtaken by the athlete(s) behind him/her.

Variations: Training should be done on both sides. Each athlete must be able to receive and to hand over the baton with both hands; while seated, several relay teams, athletes swing their arms, the coach gives only one command, upon which all athletes who are not carrying the baton raise their handover hand to the back; which team is the first to hand over the baton to the athlete at the front?; several handovers to the front during an acceleration run and handing back the baton.
Typical load standards: 5–10 run-throughs each, during warm-up even more.

162 Relay races around turning marks with handover from behind

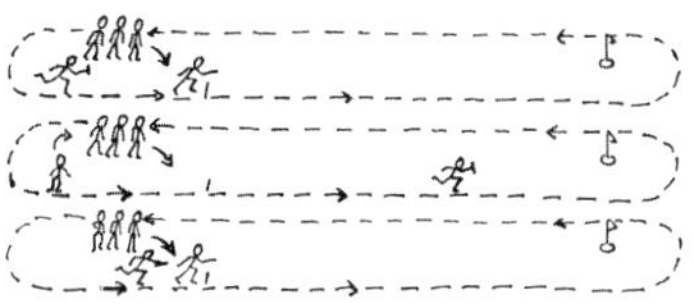

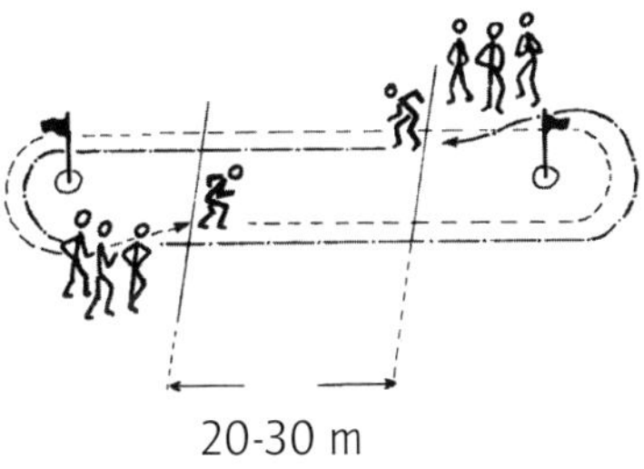

Possible objectives: Introduction of the handover from behind; acyclic and cyclic speed; speed strength and reactive strength; possibly also speed endurance.
Execution: (See pictures).
Variations: With one or two handovers per lap; with or without fixed exchange zones; as an endless relay (see 173) from various starting positions (see chapter II–1.6.3); over low obstacles, running slalom, etc.; with clear instruction (initially possibly only to the weaker team) that a team can achieve a lead by skilfully approaching the receiver; to illustrate the advantages of a relay team, it may also be helpful to have a (good) individual runner competing against a whole relay team.
Typical load standards: As long as the children have fun, or according to the criteria of speed-endurance training (see 142–145).

163  Relay starts (with increasingly specific start stimulus)

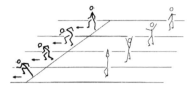

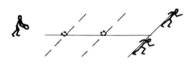

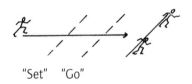

"Set" "Go"

Possible objectives: Starting behaviour specific to the exchange; reaction to increasingly complex visual stimuli; maintenance of balance in spite of turning one's head; acyclic and cyclic speed; speed strength and reactive strength.

Execution: Start from one of the three-point starting positions for the relay; first look to the back, then to the front; start with arm action; stay on a particular side of the lane.

Variations: With individual starters for each lane; with reaction when a ball rolls over the line or the sprinter crosses the line; possibly "set" line in addition to the "go" line; the incoming sprinter must tag the outgoing sprinter (in spite of the increasing distance between the "go" line from the outgoing sprinter); also on the straight, but especially in the curve.

Typical load standards: 3–5 reps on each side of the lane.

164  Exchange training as sprint training

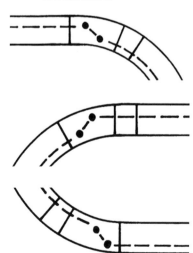

Possible objectives: Exchange technique; individual approximate adjustment of the "go" marker; technique of toe push-off and grasping/pulling sprinting; acyclic and cyclic speed; speed strength and reactive strength.

Execution: See technique chapter II–1.6.3; maximal effort; 30–40m approach of the passer; receiver continues running up to at least 5m behind the exchange zone; caution: the distance to the "go" marker will be farther than in competition.

Variations: Training both sides during the general preparation period; after having established the relay, the sequence is usually as follows: 1 hands over to 2, 3 hands over to 4, substitute runner hands over to 1, 2 hands over to 3, and 4 hands over to substitute runner (the handovers to the substitute runner are practised as an outside exchange at the place of the second exchange); the lane which is used for training should be switched (once inner lane, once outer lane).

Typical load standards: 3-6 handovers per position.

---

165 ▮▮ Position-specific exchange training

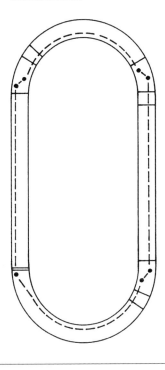

Possible objectives: Exchange technique; individual fine tuning of the "go" marker; primarily cyclic speed; speed strength and reactive strength; speed endurance.

Execution: (See 164); during the first attempts 100m approach of the passer up to the acceleration mark at maximal speed; during the last attempts perhaps only 50m in order to run into the exchange zone each time at a realistic speed.

Variations: (See 164); during the first exchange, athletes can be placed into the inner lanes, imitating receivers blocking the sight as in competition; also completely as competition simulation; depending on age or also fatigue with shortened distances (4 x 75m and 4 x 50m).

Typical load standards: 2–5 exchanges per position, or 2-3 competition simulations with long rest intervals.

1.6.9 SPECIAL TEST AND CONTROL PROCEDURES

Test: Ability/skill tested	Execution/comments
T41 **Exchange analysis:** Exchange technique	Exchange at maximal speed (164 or 165); assessment using technique analysis sheet (see chapter II–1.6.4), possibly with the assistance of video (T1) and picture sequences made thereof.
T42 **30m exchange test:** Exchange technique and sprinting speed	Exchange at maximal speed with 100m approach of the passer up to the acceleration mark; measurement of the 30m time by means of light barriers placed at the beginning of the exchange zone (triggered by the passer) and at the end of the exchange zone (triggered by the receiver); time measurement also by detecting those frames of a (competition) video in which the baton passes the beginning and the end of the exchange zone (see figure 9); with manual time measurement, the possible error may be as great as the potential improvements (even if, like in figure 9, ranging poles are used for the beginning-of-exchange and end-of-exchange mark).
T43 **Split times for the partial distances:** Performances of the individual runners	In a 4 x 100m or 4 x 400m (test) competition (165), the split times are taken when the baton crosses the middle line of the exchange zone, no matter which sprinter is carrying it at this moment; when interpreting the data, it must be considered that the times of the second, third, and fourth runners were from a flying start, the location in the exchange zones where the baton was handed over, and how well the handovers were performed.
T44 **130m test:** Relay-specific speed endurance	Maximal sprint from a standing start (123 or 145): a) on the straight (80–210m); b) in the curve (180–310m). Manual time measurement upon the release of the rear foot is usually sufficiently accurate.

All test and control procedures used for the 100m sprint (see chapter II–1.3.9) are also used for the 4 x 100m relay.

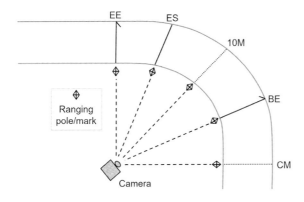

*Figure 9: **Use of ranging poles** when evaluating an exchange by means of video (modified on the basis of Jacobs, 2005, p. 38):*

EE: End of exchange zone

ES: end of 100m section

10M: 10m after the beginning of the exchange zone
BE: Beginning of exchange zone

CM: Coincidence mark/ "go" marker

1.6.10 ERRORS – CAUSES – CORRECTIONS

Error	Causes	Corrections
Inconstant starting behaviour (too early or too late).	• Start from a standing position; different lengths of time in shifting one's weight forward. • Sometimes anticipation by the athlete, sometimes not (see chapter II–1.6.3). • Problems with visual assessment. • Nervousness (especially in competition).	✔ Choosing a wider stride position when starting from a standing position or choosing a different starting position (three- or four-point start). ✔ Establishing standardised reaction behaviour. ✔ Intensive start and exchange training using exercises 163–165. ✔ Psychoregulatory assistance.
Incorrect first strides of the outgoing runner (e.g., stumbling, low hips, zigzag run while leaving (correct half of) the lane).	• The fast turn of the gaze from back to front and the associated rotation of the head disturb the vestibular organ in the inner ear and impair coordination.	✔ Start training using exercise 163 and its variations.
Deceleration of the passer even before the handover.	• Fear of overtaking the receiver and its causes (see below) or of stationary or too slow obstacle. • Incorrect visual estimation of the distance. • Underestimation of the capabilities of the receiver. • "Go" marker too close.	✔ Development of a feel for the exchange through playful relay forms without "go" marker (see chapter II–1.6.7). ✔ Intensive exchange training using exercises 162, 164, and 165, and possibly adjustment of the "go" marker.
The passer steps on the heels of the receiver (or is forced to swerve or slow down in order to avoid this).	• Leaving the running path within the lane.	✔ Intensive exchange training using exercises 162, 164, and 165. ✔ The first and third runner sprint on the inside of the lane; the second and fourth runner sprint on the outside.

(continued)

(continued)

Error	Causes	Corrections
Turning around, raising the receiving arm backward and upward before the command, and/or grasping movements to find the baton.	• General insecurity and insufficient automation of the correct technique. • Negative influence of visual exchange.	✔ Intensive exchange training using exercises 161–165, and explanatory illustration of the target technique (in particular of the differences between the visual and non-visual exchange).
The passer's hand is already forward and upward before the receiver's hand has been moved upward.	• Too late command. • Impatience. • Insufficient automation of the correct technique.	✔ Intensive exchange training using exercises 161, 162, 164, and 165, and explanatory illustration of the correct sequence of actions (see chapter II–1.6.3).
During downward exchange: excessive semi-circle movement of the giving arm above or at head height before the handover.	• Insufficient automation of the efficient target technique.	✔ Intensive exchange training using exercises 161, 162, 164, and 165, and explanatory illustration of the arm extension movement and the bending-down movement of the wrist.
Loss of the baton during the exchange.	• Most often as the result of the three last-mentioned errors. • The passer does not let go of the baton on time. • Insufficient automation of the correct technique.	✔ Intensive exchange training using exercises 161, 162, 164, and 165, and explanatory illustration of the target technique.
The passer does not reach the receiver (before the end of the exchange zone).	• The "go" marker is too far away from the start position. • Too early start of the receiver and its causes (see above). • In training, the passer always hands over the baton at maximum speed (too short run-up, no fatigue). • Lack of maximal effort of the outgoing runner in training.	✔ Intensive start and exchange training using exercises 162–165, and adjustment of the "go" marker. ✔ Making sure that the run-up of the passer is sufficiently long (see 164) since he/she does not reach the receiver at maximum velocity in competition either. ✔ Making sure that the receiver demonstrates maximum effort in training.
The passer runs close to the receiver (closer than the optimal distance of two arm lengths) or even surpasses him/her.	• The "go" marker is too close to the starting position. • Too late start or incorrect first strides and their causes (see above). • Lack of maximal effort of the passer in training.	✔ Intensive start and exchange training using exercises 162–165, and adjustment of the "go" marker. ✔ Making sure that the receiver demonstrates maximum effort in training.
The passer leaves the lane too early after completion of the exchange.	• Lack of rule knowledge. • Lack of attention to this error in training. • Lack of commitment, no cheering for the outgoing runner. • Lacking or too early drop in concentration.	✔ Explaining the rules and making sure that the exchange is performed according to the rules in training; demanding concentration on conformity to the rules. ✔ Checking whether the athletes are motivated for the relay in talks.

See also the "Errors – Causes – Corrections" chapter in the 100m section (chapter II–1.3.10).

1.6.11 TRAINING PLANNING

The training planning for 100m and 4 x 100m sprinters is done in accordance with recommendations in the general part of this book (see chapter I–3.3). In particular, the training plans suggested here are based on the training plans for children's athletics and basic training presented in the general part.

AMOUNT OF TRAINING AND INTENSITY

With the increasing age of the athletes, the training frequency also increases and the individual training sessions become longer. For the build-up training of a 17-year-old, six training sessions per week are assumed. To ensure that the individual sessions are not too long and certain training modules can be performed with the athlete as rested and focused as possible, nine training sessions per microcycle (= week) are suggested for the first two mesocycles of high-performance training. Since one day remains completely free for regeneration (usually Sunday) as in build-up training, the athlete performs two daily sessions on three days of the week. In high-performance training, especially in the first mesocycles, the amount of training performed within individual training modules (e.g., tempo runs) tends to be greater than during build-up training.

When one compares the total amount of training with other disciplines (e.g.,

middle- and long-distance running, pole vaulting, and combined events), the amount of training for the short sprint can be described as relatively low. In respect to high-performance training, this is all the more true for the third and fourth mesocycles. Here, there is not only a reduction in the amount of training within individual workouts and training modules, but training frequency is also reduced to once a day or even less. The main reason for this is the very high intensity which short sprinters want to achieve, which is only possible in a rested state. A week with competition (in the fourth mesocycle) usually includes significantly fewer than six training sessions per week, both during build-up and high-performance training. A model microcycle in the competition period will be described in the triple jump chapter (see chapter II–2.3.10).

*Table 3: **Training emphasis in the various mesocycles** for 4 x 100m training in build-up and high-performance training.*

1st mesocycle	basic aerobic and anaerobic endurance training; hypertrophy-oriented maximal-strength training, especially for the legs and the trunk; basic reactive-strength training for the legs; flexibility training; general (e.g., hurdle training), and special (e.g., ABCs of sprinting) coordination training
2nd mesocycle	basic anaerobic (speed-) endurance training; hypertrophy-, IC- and connective-tissue-oriented maximal- and reactive-strength training, especially for the legs and the trunk; sprinting-speed training; special coordination training: techniques of toe push-off and grasping/pulling sprinting; exchange technique
3rd mesocycle	special speed-endurance training at high intensity; IC- and connective-tissue-oriented maximal- and reactive-strength training, especially for the legs and the trunk; sprinting-speed and acceleration training at maximum intensity; exchange technique
4th mesocycle	competitions and corresponding regeneration; IC- and connective-tissue-oriented maximal- and reactive-strength training, especially for the legs and the trunk; sprinting-speed and acceleration training at maximum intensity; exchange technique; maintenance stimuli

DIFFERENCES BETWEEN BUILD-UP AND HIGH-PERFORMANCE TRAINING IN TERMS OF CONTENT

When one compares the training plans for build-up and high-performance training, it is not only the different amount of training (see above) which is noticeable, but also different training content or different emphases placed on the various training content. Strength training, for example, is much more important in high-performance training since it is regarded as an important reserve for increased performance. This is especially true for leg-strength training, while strength training for the trunk in build-up training, which also has a preventive purpose, is almost identical in volume as strength training for the trunk in high-performance training. At the beginning of build-up training, the weight-lifting techniques of the squat (62), clean (63), and snatch (64) must still be performed under precise technical supervision due to their potential dangers for the passive movement apparatus. However, the process of their technical development should have already started during the second half of basic training. Similarly, this is true for many other high-intensity training contents and methods. Due to its preventive effect, maximal-eccentric strength training should already be used during build-up training, but more sporadically than regularly. (Pull-)resisted sprints (137) and pull-assisted sprints (139, using a rubber band) are also used in the build-up training rather sporadically for reasons of versatility. (Pull-)resisted sprints are also very suitable to demonstrate how the same content can be used with different objectives. In basic and build-up training, (pull-)resisted sprints are rather used for developing the technique of toe push-off sprinting, whereas in high-performance training they are used for very specific speed-strength training. Similarly, high-intensity rhythm jumps are prepared more technically during the build-up training of a sprinter before they are used systematically as part of reactive-strength training in high-performance training.

Even at the beginning of build-up training, there will not necessarily be a complete specialisation. This means that athletes should still be able to perform a quadrathlon or pentathlon (i.e., the first day of a heptathlon or decathlon). Especially the hurdles, long jump, and triple jump (and to some extent also the long sprint) are closely related disciplines, which are continued to be practised for reasons of versatility. It is still conceivable that athletes will ultimately choose one of these events as his/her major competition discipline.

SUGGESTED TRAINING PLANS
Below, there are exemplary microcycles for the

- second mesocycle of a 17-year-old athlete in build-up training (table 4);
- first mesocycle of an athlete in high-performance training (table 5); and
- third mesocycle of an athlete in high-performance training (table 6).

At the beginning of build-up training, short sprinters, long jumpers, and triple jumpers still train very similarly. Thus, the training plan presented here is supplemented by the exemplary microcycles for the

- first mesocycle of a 17-year-old athlete in the long jump (see chapter II–2.2.10); and
- third mesocycle of a 17-year-old athlete in the triple jump (see chapter II–2.3.10).

In respect to high-performance training, advice for the planning of the mesocycles not elaborated here may be derived in particular from the exemplary microcycles for the

- second mesocycle in the short hurdles and the triple jump; and
- fourth mesocycle in the short hurdles and the triple jump (see chapters II–1.8.11 and II–2.3.10)

Table 4: Build-up training: sample microcycle for a 17-year-old athlete in the second mesocycle.

Monday	Tuesday	Wednesday	Thursday	Friday	Saturday	Sunday
Trunk stabilisation exercises and abdominal crunches (20 min) with a lot of dynamic variation	**Foot strengthening** (10 min)	**Baton handovers** (25 min) while sitting/standing, jogging, and sprinting at submaximal speed	**Continuous run** (30 min)	**Ll runs** (6 x 80m, rest intervals: 20 sec)	**Baton handovers** (25 min) while sitting/standing, jogging, and sprinting at submaximal speed	Rest
Baton handovers (3 run-throughs) at submaximal sprinting speed	**Acceleration runs** (3 reps) barefoot	**Training hurdling technique** (30 min) especially using 3- and 4-stride rhythm over up to 3 hurdles, from the starting blocks	**Contract-relax stretching** (15 min)	**ABCs of jumping** (8–10 run-throughs)	**ABCs of sprinting** (15–20 run-throughs)	*On Saturdays before the tempo runs possibly also train the technique of one event of the quadrathlon or pentathlon.*
ABCs of sprinting (10–15 run-throughs)	**ABCs of jumping** (10–15 run-throughs) galloping sideways, ankle jumps, skipping with two-legged landing, skipping variations, etc.	**I2 tempo runs** (2 x 3 x 60 m; rest intervals: 2–3 min; intervals between sets: 10 min)	Two out of the following: **Strength training** for the trunk on apparatus and/or for the arms, **medicine-ball work, gymnastics, technique training for the throwing events, boxing,** etc. (30 min each) e.g., goalkeeper throws, rotational throws, throws from a prone position, and tossing, using a medicine ball	**Practising the long-jump technique** (40 min) medium run-up lengths, take-offs from the left and right leg, additional tasks (e.g., development of the running-in-the-air technique of long jumping)	**Acceleration runs** (2 reps)	
Technique sprints (4–6 reps) sprints with additional tasks such as varied arm actions, alternating-pace sprints, with pre-set stride lengths, etc.	**Bounding runs and/or rhythm jumps** (6–8 run-throughs)			**Strength training** (40 min) according to the pyramid principle or maximal-eccentrically: hamstrings, quadriceps, adductors, hip flexors and extensors	**I3 tempo runs** (100, 150, 200, 180, 120, and 80m; rest intervals: 3, 5, 7, 6, and 4 min)	
Exchange training (30 min) as maximum sprinting-speed training; each athlete receives and passes the baton 3 times	**Strength training** (30 min) according to the pyramid principle: clean and snatch (the coach must continue to supervise the technique attentively)		**Tappings** (8 x 5 sec) or frequency coordination (10 min), e.g., over foam blocks	**Foot strengthening** (10 min) in the sand	**Contract-relax stretching** (15 min)	
	Game (20 min) basketball or handball			**Acceleration runs** (3 x 60m)	**Warm-down jogging** (10 diagonals on the lawn)	
					Relay starts (3 x 30m) against each other	

Table 5: High-performance training: sample microcycle in the first mesocycle.

	Monday	Tuesday	Wednesday	Thursday	Friday	Saturday	Sunday
Morning	Trunk stabilisation exercises and abdominal crunches (20 min) Acceleration runs (3 reps) ABCs of hurdling (15 min) Hurdle sprints (40 min) versatile, bilateral, low hurdles, shortened spacing between hurdles, etc.	I runs (8 x 80m; rest intervals: 20 sec)	Foot strengthening (10 min) Acceleration runs ABCs of sprinting (10–15 run-throughs) Muscle build-up training (45 min) adductors, quadriceps, hip flexors, full squat Crouch starts (4–6 focusing on technique and 2 at maximal effort)		LI runs (6 x 100 m; rest intervals: 30 sec) as warm-up ABCs of jumping (10–15 run-throughs) Skipping, pop-up jumps, and squat-extension jumps (5–7 run-throughs each) start jumps and jumps onto a box Tappings (8 x 5 sec)	Baton handovers (6 min) while jogging and at submaximal sprinting speed LI tempo runs (3 x 5 x 200m; rest intervals: 1.5–2 min; rest intervals between sets: 6–8 min) in running shoes; possibly as endless relay Contract-relax stretching (15 min)	Rest
Afternoon	Rope jumping (5 min) ABCs of sprinting (10–15 run-throughs) Technique sprints (4–6 reps) Muscle build-up training (50 min) hamstrings, adductors, hip/back extensors and clean High-knee run (5 x 20 sec) with weighted sleeves	Baton handovers (10 min) while sitting/standing ABCs of jumping (10–15 run-throughs) Bounding runs and/or rhythm jumps (2 x 5 x 50m) Medicine-ball work (30 min) Game (30 min) basketball or handball	Baton handovers While jogging and at submaximal sprinting speed I3 tempo runs (5 x 60m, 4 x 80m, 5 x 60m, 4 x 80m; rest interval: walking back; rest interval between sets: 6–8 min), possibly including pull-resisted runs, uphill runs, or runs over hurdles Contract-relax stretching (15 min) Warm-down jogging Relay starts	Continuous run (40 min) Contract-relax stretching (15 min) Muscle build-up training (35 min) trunk on apparatus plus (35 min) arms Frequency coordination (10 min) over foam blocks	Warm-up jogging (8 min) Acceleration runs (3 reps) ABCs of sprinting (10–15 run-throughs) Muscle build-up training (45 min) hamstrings, adductors and lunges Foot strengthening- (15 min) in the sand Alternating-pace sprints (6 x 80m)	Warm-down jogging (10 diagonals on the lawn) Relay starts (3 reps) against each other, as utilisation	

Table 6: High-performance training: sample microcycle in the third mesocycle.

Monday	Tuesday	Wednesday	Thursday	Friday	Saturday	Sunday
Baton handovers (6 min) while jogging	**LI runs** (6 x 100m; rest intervals: 30 sec) as warm-up	**Warm-up** (6 min)	**Baton handovers** (25 min) while sitting/ standing, jogging, and at submaximal sprinting speed	**Foot strengthening** (10 min)	**Warm-up jogging** (6 min)	Rest
Maximal-eccentric strength training (15 min) trunk stabilisation, lifting opposite upper and lower limbs while in prone position, belly punches with tense abdominals, raising the foot/toes	**Tuck jumps** (3 x 3 run-throughs over 5 hurdles each)	**Strength training for the trunk, medicine-ball work or gymnastics** (45 min) e.g., abdominal machine, hip-shoulder twist, lumborum, and hip/ back extensors	**Depth jumps** (5 x 10) from box to box, or ankle jumps with pushing downward and lifting upward	**Frequency coordination** (3x submaximal and 5x maximal) over foam blocks	**ABCs of jumping** (8–10 run-throughs)	
High-intensity strength training (15 min) snatch	**ABCs of jumping** (8–10 run-throughs)	**High-intensity strength training** (45 min) bench press, lat pull, and two more varying arm exercises	**Exchange training** (30 min) each athlete receives and hands over the baton 4x each, or 2–3 competition simulations	**Acceleration runs/ standing starts** (3–4 reps)	**Acceleration runs** (3 reps)	
ABCs of sprinting (8–10 run-throughs)	**Jumping test** (20–30 min) after specific warm-up each week a different test (e.g., 10-stride bounding run or 5-stride hops)		**High-intensity strength training** (25 min) clean and quarter split squat	**Pull-resisted starts alternating with crouch starts** (40–50 min: altogether 8–12 sprints of 10–40m each) against each other; the shorter the distances, the higher the loading of the sled (up to 60kg)	**Rhythm jumps** (5–7 x 30m) high intensity	
Acceleration runs/ standing starts (4–5 reps)	**II tempo runs** (2 x 120m; rest interval: 20 min)		**Technique sprints** (3–4 reps) with additional tasks	**Maximal-eccentric strength training** (30 min) hamstrings, adductors, etc.	**I2 tempo runs** (80, 120, 150, 120, and 80m; rest intervals: 8, 12, 15, and 12 min)	
Pull-assisted sprints (2–3 reps) with pulley, release of the assistance 10m in front of the second light barrier				**Alternating-pace sprints** (3 x 60m)		
Flying sprints (1–2 x 30m + 30–40m run-up) through light barriers						

1.6.12 BIBLIOGRAPHY

Hücklekemkes, J. (2000). Staffellaufen leicht gemacht. *Leichtathletiktraining 11* (7), 4-9.

Jacobs, K. (2005). Schnelles Raumüberwinden mit dem Stab: Die Kennzeichen schneller und erfolgreicher Staffelteams! *Leichtathletiktraining 16* (4), 34-35 & 38-39.

Mallett, C. & Connor, K. (2004). The what, why and how of the push pass. *Modern Athlete and Coach 42* (2), 25-30.

Regelkommissionen des DLV, FLA, ÖLV und SLV (Hrsg.). (2008). *Internationale Wettkampfregeln*. Waldfischbach: Hornberger.

Rotter, D. (2004). Erfolgreich Staffellaufen trainieren! *Leichtathletiktraining 15* (5), 26-27.

Sanderson, L. (1997). Some thoughts on sprint relay racing from a Canadian perspective. *New Studies in Athletics 12* (4), 49-52.

Sugiura, Y., Numazawa, H. & Ae, M. (1995). Time analysis of elite sprinters in the 4x100 metres relay. *New Studies in Athletics 10* (3), 45-49.

Vonstein, W. (1988). Die Entwicklung der Leistungsfähigkeit einer 4x100-m-Staffel. *Die Lehre der Leichtathletik 27* (43-44), 1528 & (45-46), 1553-1555.

1.7 4 X 400M

1.7.1 GRAND FINALE OF TOP EVENTS

Relay races originated from a division of labour whenever a message was to be delivered beyond the strength of one individual, as was the case with the Incas, Mayas, and Aztecs. In ancient Greece there were torch relays associated with the cult of the dead and passing on the sacred fire to the colonies. The Olympic flame, which was first carried from Olympia to Berlin by relay runners in 1936, also had its roots in ancient Greek traditions.

At the 1908 Olympic Games, the Olympic relay race (800, 200, 200, and 400m) was first introduced for men. Today, this relay race is still run at some regional championships. In addition, various long relays are still run today (see chapter II–1.10.5) including the Swedish relay (400, 300, 200 and 100m) which is seldom held. Since 1912, men have run 4 x 400m at the Olympic Games. The women, however, had to wait until 1972 when the East German women in the 4 x 400m won Olympic gold ahead of the third-place West German women, while it was the other way round in the 4 x 100m event (gold: FRG, silver: GDR). Today, the 4 x 400m relay races are often contested as the final events of the Olympic Games, world championships, and European championships and have thereby become very special highlights.

1.7.2 THE MOST IMPORTANT COMPETITION RULES

The following abridged and simplified International Competition Rules comprise the framework for the technique and strategy, as well as for the organisation of 4 x 400m competitions:

- The 4 x 400m are started from a three-turn staggered start in individual lanes. The starting lines in lanes 2–8 are white with a 40cm wide blue area in the middle.
- The exchange zone is 20m long and begins 10m before the end of the leg.
- In contrast with the 4 x 100m, the receiver must take his/her starting position within the exchange zone.
- The first exchange is performed in lanes. In each lane, the beginning of the exchange zone is marked with a blue "1", while the end is marked by a blue mirror-inverted "1."
- After his/her first curve, the second runner moves to the inside lane. The breakline is the green line for the 800m (see chapter II–1.11.2).
- Thus, the second and third exchanges occur in the inner lane(s). In the first five lanes, the beginning and end of the exchange zones are marked by 80cm long blue stripe marks parallel to the finish line.

- At the second and third exchange, the receivers line up from the inside to the outside in the order of the incoming runners' places at the 200m mark. If a receiver tries to change the positioning order thereafter, his/her team will be disqualified. However, after the completion of the exchanges of the better placed teams, the receivers may move to the inside while maintaining their order.

- A max. 40cm wide "go" marker may only be attached to the assigned lane at the first exchange.

Otherwise, the general competition rules for running, the short sprint, and the 4 x 100m apply (see chapters II–1.1.1, II–1.2.1, and II–1.6.2).

1.7.3 SPORT-SCIENCE FINDINGS, PHASE STRUCTURE AND TECHNIQUE

In the following, only those technical elements of the 4 x 400m relay are described and discussed which have not been sufficiently discussed in previous chapters. In particular, this involves the visual exchange which is very different from the (non-visual) exchange in the 4 x 100m due to the rules, the slower running velocity, and the great fatigue. The division into phases is similar to the 4 x 100m exchange.

PHASE 1: PREPARATION OF THE EXCHANGE

INSIDE EXCHANGE OR OUTSIDE EXCHANGE

It is ultimately a question of agreement among runners whether in the 4 x 400m relay, the Frankfurt exchange, or only the inside or outside exchange (see chapter II–1.6.3), after which the receiver changes the baton from one hand to the other, is performed. It is commonly observed that there are some reasons why only the inside exchanges is performed in the

4 x 400m (i.e., handovers from the right to the left hand). This is primarily due to the competition rules and the nature of the exchanges resulting from them. If the receiver takes the baton with his/her left hand, he/she can turn around to the left (i.e. inward and backward to the incoming passer). Due to the remaining turn stagger, the first exchange occurs in the curve (with the possible exception of lane 1 and 2). Looking back to the left on the inside makes it much easier for the receiver to keep sight of both the passer and his/her own running path. If he/she turns in the other direction, he/she will have to control a field of view of more than 180°. At the second and third exchanges, the runner receiving the baton with his/her left hand can also better observe the incoming passers in the inside lane, and possibly the team(s) placed in front of him/her, and may move to the inside lane.

START FROM A STANDING POSITION

Starting from a standing position is recommended since the start of the outgoing runner is not at a maximal speed, but rather adapted to the velocity of the incoming runner. The starting position during the second and third exchanges must be adjusted on short notice by moving up to the inside. At the first exchange, as with any inside exchange, the receiver takes his/her position on the right side of the lane and subsequently stays there until the handover is completed. In the starting position for the inside exchange, the right foot is placed in front, while the heel of the rear left foot is as close as possible to the beginning of exchange mark, and the receiver looks backward over his/her left shoulder to the passer (see figure 1). This also applies to the third and fourth sprinters who otherwise take their starting positions according to the rules.

*Figure 1: **Starting position in the 4 x 400m relay.***

PHASE 2: START AND APPROXIMATION

START REACTION

According to the rules, a "go" marker may only be used at the first exchange. At the second and third exchanges, the receivers must estimate the distance and speed of the passer without additional aids. However, other markers on the track (e.g., hurdle markers) can provide some orientation. But even a "go" marker would only be a rough aid, since the passer's speed before the exchange may vary greatly depending on the race distribution and his/her physical condition and therefore must be reassessed before each start reaction.

VISUAL EXCHANGE OF THE BATON

Contrary to the (non-visual) 4 x 100m exchange, the view of the 4 x 400m receiving sprinter remains directed backward during the approximation so that he/she is able to continuously assess the passer's speed and distance and is in a position to adjust his/her own speed. While the passer continues to run at the highest possible speed, the receiver accelerates submaximally along the lane markings with his/her upper body (slightly) turned sideways. This behaviour is problematic for the receiver during the narrow and busy second and third exchanges because he/she always runs the risk of running into passers stopping in front of him/her or into receivers of other teams cutting to the inside lane. It is difficult for the receiver to see peripherally or to perceive intuitively what is happening in front of him/her, and this skill can almost only be improved through competition experience. The risk of being involved in a frequently observed collision or fall in the 4 x 400m exchange increases when one's own relay team is behind and the passers of the leading relay teams slow down or stop on the track.

PHASE 3: PASSING THE BATON

HANDOVER TECHNIQUE

Contrary to the 4 x 100m, there is no need for a command to lift the receiving arm when performing the visual exchange. During the visual exchange, the handover starts with the passer stretching out his/her arm while holding the baton to the front just before he/she reaches the optimum distance for the handover of about two arm lengths. Contrary to the non-visual exchange, it is not the passer who places the baton into the receiver's hand, but rather the receiver who looks at the baton and reaches for it. This can be performed as a kind of downward or upward exchange (see figure 6 in chapter II–1.6.3), with the opening between the thumb and forefinger of the receiving hand pointing downward in each case. The third possibility is that the receiver may reach upward for the vertically held baton with the opening between his/her thumb and index finger. The active grasping movement with one hand must be practised frequently in training, especially as the receiver is usually forced to grasp the baton with his/her less skilful left hand for the reasons stated above. Grasping the baton with both hands, which is done by some relay teams for reasons of caution, is not recommended. In the process, the

upper body becomes too twisted and disturbs the start considerably.

HANDOVER IN THE MIDDLE OF THE EXCHANGE ZONE

As in the non-visual exchange, it must be the objective of a good visual exchange to pass the baton through the exchange zone as quickly as possible. Since the speed of the passer decreases and is significantly slower than in the 4 x 100m relay and at the beginning of the stadium lap, the 4 x 400m exchange is performed in the middle of the exchange zone, despite the fact that the run-up of the receiver is 10m shorter than in 4 x 100m. Even with world-class 4 x 400m relay teams, the handover often takes place even before the middle of the exchange zone is reached, which means that the receiver's run-up consists of only a few strides.

PHASE 4: COMPLETION OF THE EXCHANGE

Immediately after the handover, the receiver turns his/her glance to the front. The second runner does so to stay in his/her lane, while the third and fourth runners want to avoid collisions and to find the fastest path to the inside lane. The receiver accelerates now (almost) maximally. If, as described above, all exchanges in the 4 x 400m occur from the right to the left hand, the second and third sprinters need to take the baton from their left to their right hands after the exchange.. The disadvantage of the slight velocity loss due to this interruption of the running rhythm seems to be significantly outweighed by the benefits of only using inside exchanges. To keep the velocity loss as minimal as possible, the changing of hands should occur as soon as possible after the handover, still at a relatively low speed and in a non-fatigued state.

However, during the second and third exchanges the runner should already have cut to the inside lane and should have left the exchange jostle behind before he/she changes hands.

Table 1: Requirement profile for the 4 x 400m relay race: The suggested rough estimate of the values of selected factors determining performance is based on the importance for the overall performance and the percentage of time spent training (IR: information requirements, constr.: constraints; see chapter I-1.1).

Factors determining 4 x 400m performance	Estimate of value	Notes
Coordination	+ + +	optical IR: high, acoustic IR: medium, then low, tactile IR: low–medium, kinaesthetic IR: medium, vestibular IR: medium; precision constr.: high, time constr.: medium–high, complexity constr.: medium, situation constr.: high, physical stress constr.: high
Flexibility	+ +	no extreme movement amplitudes required
Strength		particular importance of the hamstrings; extensor loop (glutes, quadriceps, triceps surae, erector spinae), iliopsoas, abdominus, adductors, shoulder and upper-arm muscles
Maximal strength	+ + +	during start acceleration and as a basis
Reactive strength	+ + + +	within various stretch-shortening cycles
Speed	+ + + +	primarily cyclic; acyclic aspects at the start, during the exchange, and when attacking the finish line; reaction speed on acoustic (start), and visual stimulus (approaching baton)
Endurance (general dynamic) Anaerobic endurance		
Strength endurance	+ + +	as a basis of speed endurance
Speed endurance	+ + + + +	long maintenance of maximal velocity and slight and slow velocity loss at the end of the race
Aerobic endurance	+ + + +	for energy supply during the run and as a training basis
Psychological and cognitive abilities	+ + + + +	feel for pace and correct strategy (initial speed); ability to deliberately achieve low pH values (lactate acidosis) and to tolerate them; performance-oriented thinking and behaviour (see chapter I-3.1.1)
Anthropometric and primarily genetically determined characteristics	+ + + +	high proportion of fast muscle fibres; connective tissue with optimal energy-storing capacities; medium body height; low percentage of body fat

1.7.4 SUMMARY OF THE MOST IMPORTANT TECHNICAL CHARACTERISTICS = TECHNIQUE-ANALYSIS SHEET

(For crouch start with baton, see chapter II–1.6.4.)

PREPARATION OF THE EXCHANGE

PASSER

- Sprint at the highest possible speed.
- Baton in his/her right hand.

RECEIVER

- The first sprinter may attach a "go" marker (at the correct distance and on the left side of the lane).
- Timely positioning for the start: The heel of the rear left foot is placed at the beginning of exchange mark, while the other foot is placed forward approximately two feet in length.
- The receiver looks at the incoming runner with his/her trunk (slightly) turned sideways.
- The second sprinter stands on the outside of the lane; the third and fourth sprinters stand in the inner lanes according to the rules and move to the inside if required.

START AND APPROXIMATION

PASSER

- Sprint at the highest possible speed.
- The first sprinter runs on the inside of the lane, while the second and third sprinters run toward the receiver on a path slightly set off to the left.

RECEIVER

- The start (reaction) is adapted to the passer's speed and distance.
- Submaximal acceleration, still with trunk slightly turned sideways and looking back to the passer.

- The second sprinter runs on the outside or on the right, while the third and fourth sprinters run parallel to the lane markings.

PASSING THE BATON

- The handover takes place roughly in the middle of the exchange zone.

PASSER

- Sprint at the highest possible speed on the same running path as above.
- Shortly before reaching the optimal distance of two arm lengths, the passer stretches out his/her arm to the front.
- Release of the baton on time.

RECEIVER

- The second sprinter runs on the outside or on the right, while the third and fourth sprinters run parallel to the lane markings.
- Submaximal acceleration, still with trunk turned slightly sideways and looking back at the baton.
- Active grasping movement toward the baton using some kind of downward or upward pass or with thumb and index finger pointing upward.

COMPLETION OF THE EXCHANGE

PASSER

- Injury-free deceleration without impeding other teams if possible.

RECEIVER

- Turns glance to the front.
- Maximal acceleration.
- If necessary, cutting in to the inner lane.
- Immediate change of the baton from the right to the left hand.

1.7.5 STRATEGY

TOP SPRINTERS ON THE FIRST POSITION

For several reasons, it usually makes sense to place the best sprinters on positions 1 and 2 in a 4 x 400m relay. The primary objective is to be in the lead when the runners cut to the inside lane after the third curve. It is assumed that overtaking runners later on takes time and costs a lot of energy. Additionally, the probability of making tactical mistakes is greater the further back a runner is placed in the race. For example, sprinters tend to tense up more, the further back they are in the race. Moreover, runners who are behind start with a fast pace since they want to catch up with the leading runners as quickly as possible. At the second and third exchange, the hustle and bustle is also greater for the teams further behind.

Alternatively, it may also make sense to put athletes wearing glasses on the first position since they have more problems with running and performing the exchange in the pack, especially when it is raining. It may also be useful to place unassertive sprinters on position 1 since there is no physical contact between the runners during the first exchange.

STRONG-WILLED AND ASSERTIVE SPRINTERS WITH A GOOD FEELING FOR PACE AND SAVE EXCHANGE TECHNIQUE ON THE LAST POSITIONS

Based on the possible errors mentioned above, athletes on the third and fourth positions should be sprinters who have a reliable feel for pace and are not tempted to start too fast. They should also be able to correctly estimate the passer's pace during the exchange, master the 4 x 400m exchange proficiently, and be able to use their elbows during the exchange while also observing the rules of fairness. These are often the most experienced 4 x 400m sprinters. Often there are very strong-willed long sprinters who are able to mobilise enormous strength on the fourth position particularly in the final sprint and are therefore ideal on this position. In some situations, this may lead to ignoring the first principle (top sprinters in the starting position).

On positions two to four, the important strategic principle of not overtaking an opponent in the curve because of the longer path on the outside should also be observed if possible. However, if the runner in the back is much faster, exceptions to this principle are certainly possible.

1.7.6 DIDACTICS: SUPERORDINATE LONG-TERM OBJECTIVES AND GENERAL METHODOLOGY

The special significance of the relays as the only real team competitions in the sport of athletics has already been pointed out in the chapter on the short-sprint relay. This also applies to the 4 x 400m relay although this is a part of the training and competition programme at a later stage because of the high psycho-physical stress in the long sprint (see chapter II–1.5.7). However, long-relay training (e.g., in combination with the tempo-run training in the form of an endless relay [173]) is a relief to the otherwise often monotonous speed-endurance training. The 4 x 400m exchange technique is also introduced to training later on. On the one hand, this technique is easier to learn than the 4 x 100m exchange. On the other hand, the primary objective when teaching the non-visual exchange to young athletes is to get them out of the habit of looking back. However, sending 4 x 400m sprinters into competition entirely without specific exchange training may result in a loss of performance potential. It requires special preparation to anticipate the speed of the passer and to deal with jostle during the exchange.

1.7.7 TRAINING CONTENTS: FORMS OF GAMES AND EXERCISES

In addition to the forms of games and exercises listed below, 4 x 400m training includes all the games and training forms listed in connection with the 400m race and some games and exercises listed for the 4 x 100m relay (see chapters II–1.5.8 and II–1.6.8).

171 Trailer relay

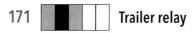
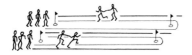

Possible objectives: Anaerobic and/or aerobic endurance; warm-up (lower intensity due to the trailers); hold hands as preparation for the exchange.
Execution: One more runner is taken along on each lap of the track.
Variations: Always only two or three runners; this means that runners who have already run two or three laps may stop running.
Typical load standards: Depending on the objective; during the warm-up shorter or fewer repetitions; avoid monotony: alternate with other game forms.

172 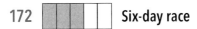 Six-day race

Possible objectives: Anaerobic and/or aerobic endurance; visual exchange technique.

Execution: Relatively small teams (2–4); athletes run an endless relay around a demarcated field; which team can run the most laps in a certain time or a certain number of laps in the shortest time?; the teams themselves decide on the distance to be covered before a (visual) exchange is performed; for example, a better runner sometimes may run more laps.

Variations: Over hurdles; good teams are formed by putting the fastest and slowest, the second-fastest and second-slowest, etc. runners together.

Typical load standards: Depends on the training goal and the children's ages.

173 Endless relays on the oval track

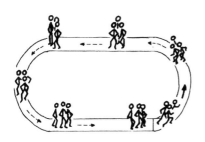

Possible objectives: Anaerobic and/or aerobic endurance; exchange technique; alternative tempo-run training.

Execution/variations: On a 400m oval track; usually visual exchange, with short individual distances (e.g., 50m) and few repetitions as non-visual exchange; in each relay team, the starting position must be occupied by an additional runner.

Typical load standards: Determined by the distance of the segment, the number of the runners per relay team (determines the rest interval), and the number of repetitions or the total duration.

174 ⬜⬜⬛ **4 x 400m exchange training**

Possible objectives: Technique of the visual exchange.

Execution: In accordance with the second and third exchange in the 4 x 400m relay, 3–8 passers start in the inside lane at a distance of 1–5m between the runners; there is the same number of receivers at the beginning of the exchange; they start, receive the baton with their left hand and change the baton from their left to their right hands.

Variations: The passers should vary the starting pace and order; partners should often be changed as long as the positions are not yet fixed.

Typical load standards: 3–5 reps each as passer and receiver.

1.7.8 SPECIAL TEST AND CONTROL PROCEDURES

In addition to the test and control procedures used in 400m training (see chapter II–1.5.9), the technique of the visual exchange can also be checked using the technique analysis sheet presented in chapter II–1.7.4. The examination of the time between those frames of a (competition) video in which the baton passes the beginning and the end of the exchange zone (see test T42) may also provide important information, even though the time is not as important as in the 4 x 100m exchange.

1.7.9 ERRORS – CAUSES – CORRECTIONS

Error	Causes	Corrections
The passer runs too close to the receiver (closer than the optimal distance of two arm lengths), or even surpasses him/her.	• The receiver has incorrectly estimated the passer's distance and velocity and has started too late or too slowly. • False strategy of the passer: started too slowly.	✔ Training the visual 4 x 400m exchange using exercises 173 and 174. ✔ Checking the passer's individual strategy.

Error	Causes	Corrections
Handover only at the end of the exchange zone or even behind the exchange zone (the passer does not reach the receiver).	• The receiver has incorrectly estimated the passer's distance and velocity and has started too early or too quickly. • Hyperacidity of the passer (false strategy: started too fast).	✔ Training of the visual 4 x 400m exchange using exercises 173 and 174. ✔ Checking the passer's individual strategy.
The passer changes the baton from his/her left to his/her right hand too late, perhaps only shortly before the exchange, or even hands over the baton from his/her left hand to the receiver's left hand.	• The passer has not yet realised that changing the baton from the left to the right hand is part of the exchange.	✔ Training the visual 4 x 400m exchange using exercises 173 and 174 as well as explicit advice to change the baton from the left to the right hand immediately after the exchange.
Considerable loss of velocity on the finishing straight.	• Sprinter was over-motivated and wanted to catch up with the runner(s) in front of him/her (too early).	✔ Focusing on strategies as a topic of discussion. ✔ Training the feel for pace through tempo runs (157-160). ✔ Having the athlete run in the 4 x 400m relay more often in competition than 400m individually; gaining experience.

The errors, causes, and corrections listed in connection with the 400m race should also be observed (see chapter II–1.5.10).

1.7.10 TRAINING PLANNING

Compared to short-sprint training (see chapter II–1.6.11), long-sprint training is characterised by an increase in aerobic and anaerobic endurance training. This also results in overall increased training volume, measured not only by the kilometres run per week but also by the frequency of training. In contrast to basic training (see chapter I–3.3.4), the training frequency of seven sessions in the first two mesocycles, six sessions in the third mesocycle, and 4–6 sessions in the fourth mesocycle is suggested here for a 17-year-old athlete. For high-performance athletes, two training sessions per day are suggested initially. Only on Sunday is there no training so that athletes may regenerate mentally and physically. To enable a higher training frequency in the third mesocycle, the training frequency is reduced to nine training sessions before it is further decreased in the competition phase.

SUGGESTED TRAINING PLANS

Below, there are exemplary microcycles for the

- first mesocycle of a 17-year-old athlete in build-up training (table 3);
- first mesocycle of an athlete in high-performance training (table 4); and

- third mesocycle of an athlete in high-performance training (table 5).

Since young long sprinters do not need to specialise in either the flat or hurdle distances, the suggested training plan for the third mesocycle of a 17-year-old athlete in build-up training presented in connection with the 400m hurdles (see chapter II–1.9.11) is designed for the same athlete as in this chapter.

The suggested training plans for the

- second mesocycle of an athlete in high-performance training, and
- fourth mesocycle of an athlete in high-performance training

presented in connection with the 400m hurdles may in some respects at least be compared to the plans presented in this chapter.

*Table 2: **Training emphasis in the various mesocycles** for 4 x 400m training in build-up and high-performance training*

1st mesocycle	aerobic endurance training; (partly reactive) strength-endurance training for the legs and the trunk; hypertrophy-oriented maximal-strength training especially for the legs and the trunk; basic reactive-strength training for the legs; flexibility training; general (e.g., hurdle training), and special (e.g., ABCs of sprinting) coordination training
2nd mesocycle	aerobic endurance training; anaerobic endurance training; (reactive) strength endurance and speed endurance training; hypertrophy-, IC- and connective-tissue-oriented maximal- and reactive-strength training, especially for the legs and the trunk; special coordination training: grasping/pulling sprinting and exchange technique
3rd mesocycle	maintenance of aerobic endurance; special speed-endurance training at increased intensity; IC- and connective-tissue-oriented maximal- and reactive-strength training, especially for the legs and the trunk; speed training at maximum intensity
4th mesocycle	competitions and corresponding regeneration; speed-endurance training at maximum intensity; IC- and connective-tissue-oriented maximal- and reactive-strength training, especially for the legs and the trunk; speed and acceleration training at maximum intensity; maintenance stimuli

Table 3: Build-up training: sample microcycle for a 17-year-old athlete in the first mesocycle

Monday	Tuesday	Wednesday	Thursday	Friday	Saturday	Sunday
Trunk stabilisation exercises and abdominal crunches (20 min) with a lot of dynamic variation	Foot strengthening (10 min)	Warm-up jogging (15 min)	Continuous run (50 min)	LI runs (6 x 80m, rest intervals: 20 sec) for warming up	*Morning:* Baton handovers (25 min) while sitting/standing, jogging, and sprinting at submaximal speed	Rest
Acceleration runs (2 reps) barefoot	Acceleration runs (3 reps) barefoot	4 x 400m exchange training (approach and start, 4 times each)	Contract-relax stretching (15 min) primarily specific to the hurdles	ABCs of jumping (10–15 run-throughs)	ABCs of sprinting (10–15 run-throughs)	*On Saturdays before the tempo runs possibly also training the technique of one event of the quadrathlon or pentathlon.*
ABCs of hurdling and hurdling imitation (25 min)	ABCs of sprinting (15–20 run-throughs) heel kicks, pulling strides, step-overs, etc.	ABCs of jumping (15–20 run-throughs) galloping sideways, ankle jumps, skipping with two-legged landing, etc.	Two out of the following:	Skipping, pop-up jumps, and squat-extension jumps (4 run-throughs each) or start jumps and jumps onto a box	Acceleration runs (3 reps) barefoot	
Acceleration runs (2 reps) wearing spikes	Muscle build-up training (30 min) full squat and clean (careful supervising of technique)	Strength-endurance circuit (2–3 run-throughs, 40 sec loading, rest interval: 30 sec) trunk strength, leg strength, multiple jumps, hurdle circuit	Muscle build-up training for the trunk on apparatus and/or for the arms, medicine-ball work, gymnastics, technique training for the throwing events, boxing, etc. (30 min each) e.g., goalkeeper throws, rotational throws, throws from a prone position, and tossing, using a medicine ball	Muscle build-up training (40 min; e.g., 15, 12, 10, and 7 reps each) hamstrings, quadriceps, adductors, abductors, hip flexors and extensors	LI tempo runs (Frinolli runs: 3 x 3 x 2 laps of 120m each; rest intervals: 90 sec; rest interval between sets: 8 min)	
Practising the hurdling technique (40 min) after specific warm-up: 4, 5, 6, or 7-step rhythm; also at varying rhythms; long-hurdle-specific distances between hurdles	Fartlek or minute runs 1, 2, 3, 2, and 1 min fast; jog interval of same length	Relay race around turning marks (2–3 run-throughs) with handover from behind	Tappings (8 x 5 sec)	Foot strengthening (10 min) in the sand	Warm-down jogging (diagonals on the lawn)	
Game (30 min) e.g., basketball or soccer ball	Contract-relax stretching (15 min)			Technique sprints (4–6 reps) sprints with additional tasks	*Afternoon:* Continuous run (30 min) relaxed	
	Warm-down jogging (5 laps on the lawn)				Contract-relax stretching (15 min)	
	Relay starts (3 x 30m) against each other				Rhythm or frequency coordination (10 min)	

Table 4: High-performance training: sample microcycle in the first mesocycle.

	Monday	Tuesday	Wednesday	Thursday	Friday	Saturday	Sunday
Morning	Trunk stabilisation exercises and abdominal crunches (20 min) Acceleration runs Muscle build-up training (50 min) hamstrings, quadriceps, adductors and abductors, hip extensors, full squat Crouch starts (4–6 focusing on technique, and 2 at maximum intensity)	LI runs (8 x 80m; rest intervals: 20 sec) for warming up ABCs of hurdling (15 min) Hurdle sprints (40 min) versatile, low hurdles, shorter distances between hurdles, etc., weekly variation	Foot strengthening (10 min) Acceleration runs (3 reps) Strength-endurance circuit (3–4 run-throughs, 1 min loading, 30 sec rest) trunk strength, leg strength, ABCs of sprinting/jumping Alternating-pace sprints (4 x 80m)	LI runs (6 x 100m; rest intervals: 30 sec) for warming up ABCs of jumping (10–15 run-throughs) Skipping, pop-up jumps, and squat-extension jumps (5 run-throughs each) or start jumps and onto a box; possibly also as stair jumps	Continuous run (60 min) first 15 min including ABCs of sprinting/jumping with varying arm actions Foot strengthening (10 min) in the sand using an elastic band ABCs of sprinting (10–15 run-throughs) Frequency coordination (10 min)	Warm-up jogging (15 min) Acceleration runs (3 reps) LI tempo runs (2 x 5 x 400m; walk intervals: 3 min; rest intervals between sets: 5–6 min) wearing running shoes; if possible as endless relay Warm-down jogging (10 diagonals on the lawn)	Rest
Afternoon	Rope jumping (5 x 1 min) Acceleration runs (3 reps) ABCs of jumping (10–15 run-throughs) Bounding runs (2 x 3 x 100m; rest intervals: walking back; rest interval between sets: 10 min) Game (30 min) e.g., basketball or soccer ball	Warm-up jogging (6 min) ABCs of sprinting (10–15 run-throughs) Technique sprints (4–6 reps) Fartlek or minute runs (5 min warm-up jog; 1, 2, 3, 2, and 1 min fast; jog interval of same length; 5 min warm-down jog) Contract-relax stretching (15 min) Tappings (8 x 5 sec)	Continuous run (45 min) Muscle build-up training (35 min) e.g., bench press, lat pull, and two other varying arm exercises; alternatively: boxing Frequency coordination (10 min) over foam blocks	Warm-up jogging (15 min) 4 x 400m exchange training (15 min) approach and start, 4 times each LI tempo runs (5 x 1000m; walk intervals: 3 min) Contract-relax stretching (15 min) Warm-down jogging (10 diagonals on the lawn) Standing starts (3 x 30m) against each other	Warm-up jogging (6 min) Muscle build-up training (35 min) trunk strength at machines; alternatively: boxing Strength-endurance training 13 x 13 reps; 3 sec eccentrically, 3 sec concentrically; rest intervals: 1 min) full squats Contract-relax stretching (15 min) Acceleration runs	Continuous run (30 min) for regeneration; alternatively and imperatively also cycling, swimming, inline skating, cross-country skiing, etc. Contract-relax stretching (15 min) Standing starts (3 x 30m) against each other	

Table 5: High-performance training: sample microcycle in the third mesocycle.

	Monday	Tuesday	Wednesday	Thursday	Friday	Saturday	Sunday
Morning	**Warm-up jogging** (6 min) **Maximal-eccentric strength training** (15 min) trunk stabilisation, lifting opposite upper and lower limbs while in prone position, belly punches with tense abdominals, raising the foot/toes **High-intensity strength training** (15 min) snatch	**LI runs** (6 × 100m; rest intervals: 30 sec) **Tuck jumps** (3 × 3 run-throughs over 5 hurdles each) **ABCs of jumping** (8–10 run-throughs) **Jumping test** (20–30 min) a different test each week (e.g., 10-stride bounding run or 5-stride hops)	**Continuous run** (35 min) **Strength training** for the trunk, **medicine-ball work,** or **gymnastics** (45 min) e.g., abdominal machine, hip-shoulder twist, lumborum, hip/back extensors **High-intensity strength training** (45 min) bench press, lat pull, and two more varying arm exercises **Frequency coordination** (10 min) over foam blocks	**Warm-up jog** (6 min) **Acceleration runs** (2 reps) **ABCs of sprinting** (8–10 run-throughs) **Depth jumps** (5 × 10) from box to box **Acceleration runs** (2 reps) **Flying sprints** (3 × 30m + 30–40m run-up) through light barriers	**Foot strengthening** (10 min) **Acceleration runs/standing starts** (4–5 reps) **Pull-resisted runs** and **crouch starts** alternately (40–50 min; altogether 8–12 sprints of 10–40m each) against each other; the shorter the distance, the higher the sled loading	**Warm-up jogging** (15 min) **ABCs of jumping** (8–10 run-throughs) **Acceleration runs** (3 reps) **Rhythm jumps** (5–7 × 30m) at high intensity **I2 tempo runs** (e.g., 4 × 300m; walk intervals: 20 min) **Warm-down jogging** (10 diagonals on the lawn)	Rest
Afternoon	**Acceleration runs/relay starts** (4–5 reps) **Pull-assisted sprints** (2–3 reps) with pulley, release of the resistance 10m in front of the second light barrier **Flying sprints** (1–2 × 30m + 30–40m run-up) through light barriers	**Warm-up jogging** (15 min) **ABCs of sprinting** (8–10 run-throughs) **Acceleration runs** (3 reps) **I3 tempo runs** (3 sets of 150, 150, and 500m each; walk interval: 5, 5, and 15 min each) **Warm-down jog** (10 diagonals on the lawn) **Standing starts** (3 × 30m) against each other		**High-intensity strength training** (40 min) hamstrings, adductors, clean, quarter split squat; perhaps also maximal-eccentric strength training	**Warm-up jogging** (6 min) **Acceleration runs/technique sprints** (5–6 reps) with additional tasks **Alternating-pace sprints** (4 × 80m; rest intervals: 6 min) **LI tempo runs** (2 sets of 150, 200, 250, 200, and 150m each; rest intervals: 90 sec; rest intervals between sets: 6 min) **Standing starts** (3 × 30m)	**Continuous run** (20 min) for regeneration After rest interval: **Standing starts** (3 × 30m) against each other	

1.8 100 AND 100M HURDLES

1.8.1 UNFINISHED EMANCIPATION

About 150 years ago, British college students were no longer content to test their strength in the sprint over distances with flat surfaces. They began to leap over obstacles placed on the track in more a jumping than a running style. The obstacles used were three and a half feet (1.067m) high and were similar to the sheepfolds used in sheep raising. For male runners, the sheepfold height is still used today. The distance of ten yards (9.14m) at that time between the hurdles and the first running distance of 120 yards (109.98m) have not changed either since establishing the first standards at Oxford and Cambridge in 1864. However, in 1895 hurdles with a T-foot, which allowed obstacles to be knocked over more easily, and in 1935 hurdles with the currently used L-foot were introduced. At the time of the T-foot hurdles, runners were disqualified if they knocked over more than three hurdles. A record was only recognised if all hurdles remained standing.

The first modern attempt at hurdling was demonstrated by the double Olympic winner over the 110 and 200m hurdles, Alvin Kraenzlein (USA), at the 1900 Olympic Games. The technique used was characterised by a flat run over the hurdles, a deep forward lean of the upper body, and 3-stride rhythm between the hurdles. The 200m hurdles were part of the competition at the 1900 and 1904 Olympic Games in addition to the 110m and 400m hurdles. The IAAF recognized world records for the 200m hurdles (which were also performed over 10 obstacles) until 1960. The fastest time in the curve together with the straight was 22.5 sec, achieved by the American Glenn Davis and recorded in Bern on 20 August 1960.

Women have been sprinting over hurdles since the Olympic Games in Berlin in 1936. Their hurdle height was initially set at 2.5 ft (76.2cm). The sprinting distance was 80 metres; the distance from the starting line to the first hurdle was 12m; and the distance between the hurdles was 8m. In 1969, the hurdle height and distances between hurdles were changed to today's current standards. Sport-science findings (see chapter II–1.8.3) convincingly show that women's and men's short hurdles still differ more clearly than is justified by their biological differences. Female hurdle sprinters run differently and look different than male hurdlers. They are often quite small and powerful. Male hurdlers are tall, have long legs, and are less muscular than flat sprinters. Their greatest enemy is the tailwind in extremely short running segments between the hurdles. In addition to the combined events, the hurdle race is one of the few athletics events in which there is still no full equalisation of men and women. It is hoped that it will not take another 40, 70, or even 150 years until comparable conditions are created in the hurdles. After 28 years, Jordana Dankova's world record (12.21 sec) was broken in 2016 by the American Kendra Harrison, who was one-hundredth of second faster. The current world record was set by Tobi Amusan (USA) in 2022. In 2008, Dayron Robles (12.87 sec) from the jumping nation of Cuba broke the men's record of the Chinese runner Liu Xiang, who disappointed his entire country when he failed to defend his Olympic title at home after an injury. In 2012, Aries Merritt (USA), who shortly afterwards set a new world record in 12.80 sec, won the Olympic gold medal.

1.8.2 THE MOST IMPORTANT COMPETITION RULES

The following abridged and simplified International Competition Rules comprise the framework for the technique and strategy, as well as for the organisation of short hurdle competitions:

- The specifications of a hurdle can be found in figure 1. The general requirements of the short hurdle sprint for the various age groups (height, distance, etc.) are shown in table 1.
- Each hurdle is placed on the track in such a way that the feet of the hurdle are on the side of the approach so that the hurdle may fall in the running direction. In height-adjustable hurdles, there must be sliding weights at the feet of the hurdle so that the same force is required to overturn the hurdle regardless of the hurdle height. The horizontal force which must be applied to the central edge of the top bar to tilt the hurdle must equal the weight of 3.6–4.0 kg.
- Touching and overturning the hurdles is allowed (for exceptions see below).

- A runner is disqualified if he/she
  - » does not clear each hurdle;
  - » his/her foot or leg is, at the moment of clearance, beside the hurdle (on either side), below the horizontal plane of the top of any hurdle;
  - » does not clear each hurdle in his/ her assigned lane;
  - » in the opinion of the referee, deliberately knocks down a hurdle.

Otherwise, the general competition rules for running and sprinting apply (see chapter II–1.1.1 and II–1.2.1).

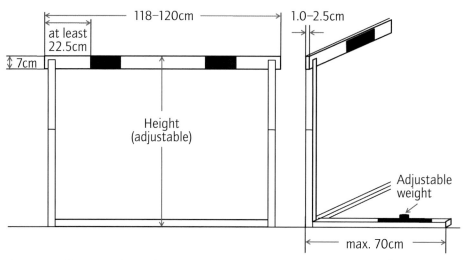

Figure 1: **Hurdle construction and specifications** (modified on the basis of DLV, FLA, ÖLV, and SLV, 2010, p. 80): The total weight of a hurdle may not be less than 10 kg.

Table 1: **Overview of the general requirements of the short hurdle sprint for the various age groups** valid for the German Athletics Association (DLV).

Age group		Distance	Number of hurdles	Height of hurdle	Distance from start line to first hurdle	Distance between hurdles	Distance from last hurdle to finish line
Men, Juniors		110m	10	106.7cm	13.72m	9.14m	14.02m
Male U20,	M40–45	110m	10	99.0cm	13.72m	9.14m	14.02m
Male U18		110m	10	91.4cm	13.72m	8.90m	16.18m
M50–55		100m	10	91.4cm	13.00m	8.50m	10.50m
M60–65		100m	10	84.0cm	16.00m	8.00m	12.00m
Women, Female Juniors,	Female U20	100m	10	84.0cm	13.00m	8.50 m	10.50m
Female U18		100m	10	76.2cm	13.00m	8.50m	10.50m
Male U16		80m	7	84.0cm	13.50m	8.60m	14.90m
Female U16,	W40–45	80m	7	84.0cm	13.50m	8.60m	14.90m
W50–55,	M70–75	80m	8	76.2cm	12.00m	7.00m	19.00m
W60 and older	M80 and older	80m	8	68.6cm	12.00m	7.00m	19.00 m
U14		60m	6	76.2cm	11.50m	7.50m	11.00m

1.8.3 SPORT-SCIENCE FINDINGS, PHASE STRUCTURE, AND TECHNIQUE

DIFFERENCES BETWEEN WOMEN'S AND MEN'S SHORT HURDLES

Both the 100 and 110m hurdles can be described by using the following phase structure:

- crouch start;
- acceleration to the first hurdle;
- hurdle stride;
- sprint between the hurdles; and
- finish.

The women's and men's short hurdles (as well as the long hurdles and the steeplechase) may be described as a *constrained run* and are therefore fundamentally different from the free sprint over flat distances. The running pattern (stride rhythm, etc.) is enforced by the general requirements set by the rules (distances between the hurdles, etc., see table 1). However, these are so different in the 100m and 110m hurdles that *the women's and the men's short hurdles must be described as disciplines of a significantly different character.* The men's hurdle is a disproportionate 22.7cm higher than the women's hurdle. Considering the average leg length, men are still forced to jump approximately 17cm higher than women. Therefore, the technique of clearing the hurdle (and body height) is more important for men than for women. This is also the reason why more scientific data is available for the men's short hurdles. The distance between the hurdles is slightly longer for men than for women, but only disproportionately so.

This means that in comparison to the flat sprint, men need to clearly shorten their strides to a greater extent than women. Overall, the women's 100m hurdles race is much more similar to the flat sprint. This is confirmed not least of all by the fact that (even on the world-class level) there are some female athletes who are similarly good flat sprinters as well as hurdlers. This is never the case with men. To equalise the conditions, it has repeatedly been suggested to increase the height of the women's hurdle to 91.4cm and to extend the distance between the men's hurdles to 9.50 metres (as well as to increase the hurdle height in women's long hurdles to 84.0cm). As long as these necessary changes are not finalised, *the women's and the men's target technique will be different.*

TECHNIQUE INDEX

The technique index is a rough scale to assess hurdling technique. It is the quotient of the flat sprint and the hurdle time. If one wants to get a similar index for men and women, the index for men must be multiplied by 1.1 due to the longer distance of their hurdle race.

Technique index for women
= 100m flat time/100m hurdles time
Technique index for men
= (100m flat time/110m hurdles time) · 1.1

When the respective world records are used in these formulas, one arrives at a technique index of 0.86 for women. If one took the annual world-best performances of recent years, the index would even improve to 0.87. For the men's world records, the index only comes to 0.83. This confirms the above-mentioned theory that under current competition rules clearing the hurdles is more difficult for men. For female hurdle specialists, the *time difference* is about 1.1–1.5 sec (100m flat versus 100m hurdles), which means good index values, whereas for male hurdlers the running time difference is 2.5–3.4 sec (100m flat versus 110m hurdles).

PHASE 1: CROUCH START

The start of the short hurdles is fundamentally similar to the 100m crouch start (see chapter II–1.3.3). Only two differences must be considered: The front and rear leg in the starting block must be chosen in accordance with the number of strides to the first hurdle and the push-off leg in front of the hurdle. However, an adjustment to the starting position is usually not required since the take-off leg (e.g., in the long jump) is mostly chosen as the front leg in the crouch start and the push-off leg in front of the hurdle and since there are usually eight strides to the first hurdle.

If athletes in the competition period continue to run too close to the first hurdle, they may move the position of the blocks and, accordingly, also the supporting position of their fingers by 10–50cm away from the starting line in the hope that a smoother run over the first hurdle will more than compensate for this loss of distance.

However, this behaviour may only be tolerated in basic training (for combined athletes possibly slightly longer).

PHASE 2: ACCELERATION TO THE FIRST HURDLE

The acceleration to the first hurdle resembles the start acceleration in the 100m sprint. Most hurdle sprinters require eight strides to reach the first hurdle. In exceptional situations, very tall male athletes require seven strides, while some beginners require nine strides. The length of the individual strides do not necessarily correspond to those in the acceleration phase of the 100m flat sprint, but must be adapted to the pre-set distance to the first hurdle. The stride length is usually shorter than in the 100m sprint (see figure 2 in chapter II–1.3.3, and table 2 below). The penultimate stride is often somewhat longer than the last stride before the hurdle.

*Table 2: **Stride lengths when approaching the first hurdle** (according to Schmolinsky, 1980, pp. 192–193).*

Stride	1	2	3	4	5	6	7	8
110 m	0.60	1.10	1.35	1.50	1.65	1.80	1.90	1.80
100 m	0.65	1.05	1.35	1.40	1.50	1.65	1.75	1.70

From about the fourth stride on (i.e., much earlier than in the flat sprint), an athlete directs his/her glance to the front in order to target the hurdle. In addition, an athlete must straighten himself/herself up (and thus raise his/her CG) more quickly. The first hurdle and each of the subsequent hurdles should be attacked from an

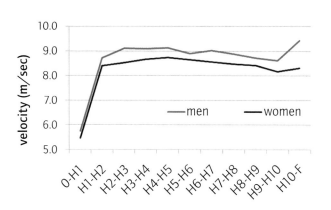

Figure 2: **Curves of the interval velocities in the short hurdles:** mean values of 7 finalists each over 100m and 110m hurdles at the 1997 World Championships in Athens (based on data provided by Hommel & Koszewski, 1999, pp. 70–71).

upright and high running position. In order to sprint with the highest possible position of the CG, short male hurdlers in particular are often advised to run with heels high, which is not the case in the flat sprint.

The sprint to the first hurdle is crucial as the hurdler performs most of his acceleration work during this segment of the race. With top hurdle sprinters, the average speed in the segment between the first and second hurdle is only slightly lower than in the segment between the second and third and between the third and fourth hurdles (see figure 2). In individual cases, there are very slight increases in speed up to the sixth hurdle. Due to the fact that the 100m hurdle race is more similar to the flat sprint, some world-class female hurdlers are able to accelerate a little longer than men. However, beginners reach their maximum velocity in front of the first hurdle and then continuously become slower.

PHASE 3: HURDLE STRIDE

The **swing leg** is the leg which clears the hurdle and is brought back to the ground behind the hurdle first. The **trail leg** is identical with the **push-off leg**, which after the push-off in front of the hurdle is spread to the side and moved over the hurdle into a high-knee position. The arm on the side of the trail leg is called the **counter-arm.**

GENERAL BIOMECHANICAL OBJECTIVES

The ultimate objective of a good hurdle stride must be to lose as little velocity through the stride as possible. Even in 110m hurdlers of higher qualification, the loss of velocity due to the hurdle stride is up to 10% (see figure 8). The loss of velocity is caused by the braking forces occurring during the front support (see chapters II–1.1.2 and II–1.3.3). Both during the push-off in front of the hurdle and the touchdown behind the hurdle, this loss of velocity is lower, the flatter an athlete runs over a hurdle or the less he/she has to jump over a hurdle. The latter is equivalent to only a minimal excursion of the CG upward due to a push-off angle as flat as possible. For a given hurdle and body height, an athlete must pursue two main objectives to keep the excursion of the CG or the push-off angle as minimal as possible:

- If the position of the CG is already high in front of the hurdle, the CG must be less raised above the hurdle (see figure 3).
- Using an optimal technique, the sprinter over the hurdle attempts to move his/her body parts in a vertical direction so close to the CG that he/she can shift his/her CG as low as possible over the upper edge of the hurdle bar (see figure 4). With top 110m hurdlers, the highest point of the CG trajectory is only about 25–35cm above the top edge of the hurdle bar.

Another key objective of the hurdle stride is to minimise whole-body rotation about the lateral and longitudinal axis of the body. This whole-body rotation would impede a continuation of running at the fastest possible speed in the inter-hurdle segments (see phase 4), as the sprinter

*Figure 3: **Favourable and unfavourable curve of the CG** depending on body height and run-up behaviour.*

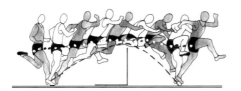

*Figure 4: **Approximation of the body parts to the CG** curve during the hurdle stride.*

would have to exert (much) force upon the first contacts after the hurdle to counteract it again. The rapid return to an upright and frontal running position after the hurdle would be difficult.

LENGTH OF THE HURDLE STRIDE

Table 3 shows key biomechanical data of the hurdle stride. The 60/40 ratio described and the fact that the peak of the CG trajectory is even about 15cm in front of the hurdle are primarily due to the fact that the hurdle sprinter needs room for the swing leg (see below).

Beginners usually run too close to the hurdle, then take off steeply upwards, are forced to perform evasive movements while clearing the hurdle and land passively too far behind the hurdle in relation to the push-off point (see table 4). On an overall high level of performance,

*Table 3: **Hurdle-stride length of world-class hurdlers** (Coh, 1996, 2003; Mann, 2000; Schwirtz et al., 1986): In each case, the values in metres are measured from the tip of one foot to the tip of the other foot. Table 2 in chapter II–1.3.3 shows corresponding data for the flat sprint.*

Hurdle-stride length	Women: 3.00-3.25m		Men: 3.40-3.70m	
Flight time	0.29-033 sec		0.31-0.36 sec	
Distance	in front of the hurdle		behind the hurdle	
	60%		40%	
	Women:	Men:	Women:	Men:
	1.90-2.00m	2.00-2.15m	1.10-1.25m	1.40-1.55m

110m H. time in group average	n	Distance in front of the hurdle	Distance behind hurdle
14.6 sec	10	2.22m	1.45m
15.1 sec	10	2.11m	1.49m
17.4 sec	10	2.02m	1.67m

there is an average decrease in the length of the hurdle stride, a reduction in the distance in front of and behind the hurdle, and less flight time with increasing levels of performance. This is possible for the better hurdle sprinters due to their superior technical and/or strength abilities.

PUSH-OFF INTO THE HURDLE

The claims made about biomechanical objectives have already indicated that the push-off in front of the hurdle is between the normal sprint stride and the take-off for the long jump in respect to its biomechanical characteristics. This applies to the ground contact time before the hurdle (0.11–0.13 sec), the angle of departure (about 15° in the 110m hurdles), and the size of ground reaction forces (cf. chapter II–1.1.2, II–1.3.3, and table 1 in II–2.1.2). The foot strike during the push-off also takes place more in front of the vertical projection of the CG than in the flat-sprint stride. The best hurdle sprinters place their foot closer to the vertical projection of their CG (approx. 30cm) than poorer hurdle sprinters (approx. 40cm; while in the sprint the distance is 20–28cm). This means that hurdlers brace more than sprinters, but less than jumpers.

As in the jumps, the slight bracing results in a conversion of a part of the horizontal velocity into vertical push-off velocity (see loss of horizontal velocity in figure 8). In spite of this, the foot strike should still be performed over the ball of the foot, as in the sprint, and the heel should not be lowered to the ground at any time during the push-off. However, even many world-class athletes do not succeed in performing this action since they place the entire foot on the ground as in the jump.

During the ground contact of the push-off leg, the swing leg is brought forward and upward. At the end of the push-off, the thigh of the swing leg should be (almost) horizontal. The knee-joint angle is still less than 90°. To counteract the moment of inertia of the swing leg, which is pulled upward, and to avoid a reverse rotation about the lateral axis of the body, the upper body is leaned forward at the end of the push-off.

The curve of the foot movement of the swing leg must be observed from the front. In general, hurdlers should try to achieve a straight curve of the foot movement without lateral evasion (see figure 5) as this favours an optimal hip extension and a straightforward continuation of running after the hurdle.

Even with world-class, short-hurdle sprinters, the push-off extension at the knee and the hip joint is often incomplete during the push-off into the hurdle. This is due to the generally shorter stride length in the inter-hurdle sprint (see below) and the high knee lift of the swing leg. Nevertheless, superior hurdle sprinters extend their hips during the rear support of the push-off better than poor hurdle sprinters. This means that their total loss of velocity during the last ground contact is not only smaller due to a shorter front support, but also to a longer rear support.

HURDLE CLEARANCE (FLIGHT PHASE)

While the trail leg is still directed backward to the push-off point, the swing leg and trunk perform a jackknife motion at the start of the flight phase. The vertical velocity of departure, hip and trunk flexion, and the continued extension of the swing-leg knee cause the upper body to be lowered and the swing-leg foot to be raised above the height of the hurdle. While the jackknife position is assumed, the arm on the swing-leg side is kept in a sprint-like angled position and remains laterally behind or close to the body.

While the foot of the swing leg is raised, the counter-arm is extended forward and downward to the swing-leg foot.

From the widest spread position of both thighs after the push-off, the movement of the trail leg is initiated through the reactive and powerful contraction of the hip flexors and an additional abduction at the hip joint. Thus, the knee of the trail leg is moved around on the outside to the front and top. The high lateral lifting of the trail leg is facilitated through the forward tilt of the pelvis in the jackknife position. To minimise the moment of inertia of the trail leg and thus to bring forward the trail leg more quickly, it is closely bent at the knee joint. The foot is pronated (externally rotated) to avoid the contact of the tip of the foot with the hurdle. The trail leg and foot clear the hurdle at about the same height as the hip. This means that during the hurdle clearance, the lower part of the

*Figure 5: **Hurdle stride from the front view.***

*Figure 6: **Hurdle stride from the side view.***

DISCOURSE I:
DISCUSSION OF SELECTED ASPECTS OF THE SWING-LEG ACTION

It is often recommended to bring forward the swing leg with a knee-joint angle as acutely as possible and then to extend the lower leg forward using a relaxed pendulum movement. Mann (2000, p. 27), however, criticises the **relaxed forward pendulum movement of the lower swing leg** as it renders the movement uncontrollable and thus makes the clearing of the hurdle and the landing difficult. He observed that better hurdle sprinters already have a larger knee-joint angle than poorer hurdle sprinters at the moment of the push-off.

In connection with the action described above, the following tendency, which can be observed especially in the **women's hurdles**, should be considered. **The swing leg is deliberately not brought up to full extension.** Instead, the knee is raised a little higher. The movement is therefore not only more controlled, but the upper body can also remain more upright since the moment of inertia of the swing leg is smaller. The moment of inertia is smaller since the mass of the leg is closer to the pivot point (i.e., the hip). If it is assumed that the hip flexors and extensors can produce an equal force and can thus generate a constant torque, the rotating velocity at the hip will also be greater with a smaller moment of inertia. Thus, a bent knee allows a more rapid hip flexion in front of the hurdle and a more rapid hip extension after the hurdle.

In particular, when athletes get too close to a hurdle, they tend to perform an **outward or inward sickle movement**. Intuitively, most hurdlers are more inclined to bring their foot to the front using an outward curved movement. However, this usually goes hand in hand with a tilt of the pelvis about the depth (sagittal) body axis. The hip on the side of the swing leg is raised, while the hip on the side of the trail leg is lowered. This increases the risk of banging the trail leg against the hurdle so that the athlete is forced to jump higher over the hurdle. On the contrary, it may be concluded that a slight inward sickle movement is consistent with an effective hurdle technique since the hip on the side of the trail leg is slightly raised in this case.

trail leg is almost horizontal. Nevertheless, to prepare an optimal knee lift during the first inter-hurdle stride, the knee is kept higher than the foot during the entire trail-leg movement.

For example, if the right leg were the trail leg, the outward curved movement of this leg to the front would actually result in a clockwise rotation of the trunk about the longitudinal axis of the body. To compensate for this angular momentum, the counter-arm is moved externally around the trail leg. In the process, the greater range of motion of the arm is intended to compensate for the greater mass of the leg. To examine this, the coach should watch the hip and shoulder axis which should remain in frontal position throughout the hurdle stride to achieve a linear hurdle sprint.

Ultimately, within this system of balanced rotations, the actions occurring on the swing-leg side, which overlap the movements of the trail leg, must also be considered. Immediately after the swing-leg foot has cleared the hurdle, the hip on the side of the swing leg is extended in a reactive and powerful manner (reflexively). The downward movement of the swing-leg foot, the raising of the upper body, and the forward swing of the arm on the swing-leg side begin simultaneously.

TOUCHDOWN AFTER THE HURDLE

The sprinter already directs his/her glance to the next hurdle while he/she is still over the hurdle. Coaches talk about the "starting signal" over the hurdle, which the athletes should give themselves. When still being over the hurdle, the sprint toward the next hurdle begins.

There is a fluent transition from the straightening up of the body and the downward and backward movement of the swing leg to the preparation of the touchdown of the foot behind the hurdle. As in the flat sprint, the foot must be synchronised with the relative movement

velocity of the ground (see chapter II–1.3.3). The better the hurdler, the closer the touchdown of his/her foot will be to the vertical projection of his/her CG. With the best hurdle sprinters, the tip of the foot is even directly under the CG at touchdown.

The front support phase and the braking forces produced during this phase are minimised by this behaviour, and there is very short ground contact time (about 0.08 sec; compare the push-off described above and the values presented for the flat sprint). This also corresponds with the fact that better hurdlers place their foot down with an already more extended swing-leg hip and that the hip passes through a smaller angle during ground contact than with poorer hurdle sprinters. In the process, the best hurdlers achieve a much faster hip-

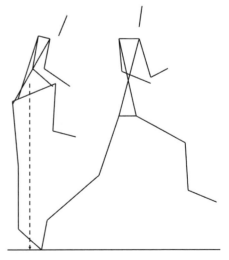

*Figure 7: **Body positions of a 110m hurdle sprinter during landing after the hurdle,** moment of the first and last ground contact (modified on the basis of Coh, 2003, p. 41).*

extension velocity (approximately 830°/ sec). Better hurdle sprinters extend their knee joint more before touchdown, bend it slightly prior to touchdown, and then bend it more and faster than poorer hurdle sprinters during the ground contact. While the exclusive work during the rear support and the rapid hip extension result in an optimum increase of the horizontal velocity of the CG, the quicker and stronger flexion of the knee joint results in an extremely short first stride after the hurdle (see phase 4). Moreover, the hip extension, in combination with the simultaneous knee flexion during ground contact, results in a further straightening of the upper body (see figure 7).

During the downward movement of the swing leg and the first support phase after the hurdle, the swing leg is still brought forward at a narrow angle. The trail-leg movement is finished at the end of the first ground contact by achieving a high-knee running position. The thigh should point (almost) horizontally in the running direction; the upper body should be almost completely upright again; and the knee angle should now be slightly opened up to about 90°.

PHASE 4: INTER-HURDLE SPRINT

3-STRIDE RHYTHM

The short hurdle sprint is run using a 3-stride rhythm. This means that an athlete makes three strides between the hurdles. The fact that there is an even number of four steps in total including the hurdle stride means that the swing and trail leg are always identical at every hurdle.

As in phase 2, the strides are shorter in the upper performance categories than in the flat sprint due to the distances between the hurdles. Thus, the inter-hurdle sprint is a stride-frequency sprint. This is especially true for tall world-class men. However, due to their smaller body size and lower horizontal velocity, beginners rather have the problem of reaching the next hurdle although the distances between the hurdles are shorter (and the hurdle heights are lower). They also have difficulties realising that extending their strides results in a further reduction of their horizontal velocity and therefore is only helpful until they have reached the next hurdle if at all (see further information in chapter II–1.8.7).

INTER-HURDLE STRIDES IN DETAIL

The first stride of the 3-stride rhythm is still greatly influenced by the hurdle stride. The goal of the above-mentioned behaviour of world-class hurdle sprinters during the first ground contact after the hurdle is to make the first stride after the hurdle as short as possible. Empirical data confirms that the first stride is the shortest of the three inter-hurdle strides even in the women's short hurdles (see figure 8). However, this is also related to the fact that the behaviour described during the first ground contact leads to virtually two ground contacts used for landing after the hurdle, and the lowest point of the CG is at the end of the amortisation of the second support.

Despite all attempts to achieve a linear hurdle sprint to avoid and compensate for rotation, there is usually a slight twisting of the upper body to the swing-leg side during the first support and stride after the hurdle and a longer back swing of the arm on the swing-leg side than is usual in the sprint. During the second ground contact, the hurdle sprinter should be able to compensate for this with an intensive arm swing and by returning to a frontal and upright or minimally bent forward position of his/her trunk and by resuming a sprint-like arm movement.

Hurdle sprinters are able to accelerate not only during the first ground contact after the hurdle, but also during the second and third ground contacts between the hurdles (see figure 8). During the second and third ground contacts, the hurdle sprinter also attempts to return to the highest possible

running position and to ensure an upright trunk position and an erect pelvis to be able to optimally attack the next hurdle (see phase 2).

Due to the short stride length, the inter-hurdle sprint can be compared to a high-knee run focusing on stride frequency (112) or to running with knees raised to half the horizontal position (113). The knee lift, the grasping action, and the push-off extension are reduced compared to the sprint.

ABILITY TO ESTABLISH RHYTHM
Due to the various make-ups of individual strides, the short hurdle sprint must first be described as a non-cyclic movement. The only cyclic aspect of the hurdling motion is

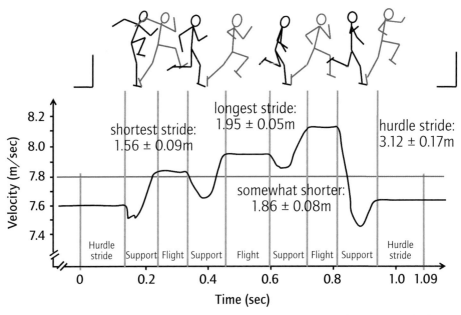

Figure 8: Velocity curve and stride lengths in (women's) hurdle sprint (modified on the basis of Schwirtz et al., 1986, p. 22); the stride lengths and inter-hurdle strides of men are approximately 1.55m, 2.10m, and 2.00m (Schmolinsky, 1980, p. 192).

the nine- or ten-fold repetition of phases 3 and 4 at an optimal high-frequency rhythm which should be as identical as possible. The ability to establish rhythm as one aspect of coordination skills needs to be practised for and by hurdling (see chapter II–1.8.7). The hurdle stride requires complex coordination skills which make hurdle sprinters typically very skilful athletes. Various forms of rhythmic hurdle sprints improve coordination, speed, strength, and flexibility in such a versatile way that they are some of the most important training contents in children's athletics, in basic training, and in build-up training of almost every athletics discipline.

SPLIT TIMES

Tables 5 and 6 show the split times at the individual hurdles. The split times designate the times between the starting signal and the moment of the foot touchdown after each hurdle. Together with figure 2, the tables show that in the short hurdle sprint there is a speed-endurance segment with decreasing running speed as one also finds in the flat sprint.

PHASE 5: RUN TOWARD THE FINISH LINE

During the run toward the finish line, which is 3.5m longer for men (14.02m) than for women (10.50m), hurdle sprinters are able to accelerate again (see figure 2). Since there is no longer the necessity to prepare for a hurdle stride, sprinters may once again lean their trunk forward similar to the start acceleration, which means that they shift their CG forward and use rather the toe push-off technique of sprinting. The forward lean of the body, and eventually

the additional forward lean of the trunk, also result in a more effective crossing of the finish line.

(For deceleration behind the finish line, see chapter II–1.3.3.)

Table 5: **Typical intermediate and interval times** (in sec) in the 100m hurdle sprint with specific finishing times (second and third columns in italics: measured individual run according to Schwirtz et al., 1986, p. 20; 4th–11th column: guiding values, modified according to Tepper & Czingon, 1995, p. 46).

First hurdle	2.60		2.58		2.62		2.70		2.77	
Second hurdle	3.62	(1.02)	3.61	(1.03)	3.67	(1.05)	3.80	(1.10)	3.90	(1.13)
Third hurdle	4.59	(0.97)	4.60	(0.99)	4.69	(1.02)	4.86	(1.06)	4.97	(1.07)
Fourth hurdle	5.55	(0.96)	5.58	(0.98)	5.69	(1.00)	5.91	(1.05)	6.05	(1.08)
Fifth hurdle	6.52	(0.97)	6.56	(0.98)	6.68	(0.99)	6.96	(1.05)	7.13	(1.08)
Sixth hurdle	7.49	(0.97)	7.52	(0.96)	7.67	(0.99)	8.02	(1.06)	8.21	(1.08)
Seventh hurdle	8.45	(0.96)	8.49	(0.97)	8.67	(1.00)	9.09	(1.07)	9.31	(1.10)
Eighth hurdle	9.44	(0.99)	9.46	(0.97)	9.67	(1.00)	10.18	(1.09)	10.43	(1.12)
Ninth hurdle	10.42	(0.98)	10.48	(1.02)	10.71	(1.04)	11.29	(1.11)	11.59	(1.16)
Tenth hurdle	11.44	(1.02)	11.50	(1.02)	11.75	(1.04)	12.40	(1.11)	12.75	(1.16)
Finishing time	**12.55**	(1.11)	**12.60**	(1.10)	**12.90**	(1.15)	**13.65**	(1.25)	**14.10**	(1.35)

Table 6: **Typical intermediate and interval times** (in sec) in the 110m hurdle sprint with specific finishing times (second and third columns in italics: values measured in Colin Jackson's world-record sprint according to Jonath et al., 1995, p. 314; 4th–11th column: guiding values, modified according to Tepper & Czingon, 1995, p. 46).

First hurdle	2.56		2.55		2.61		2.67		2.74	
Second hurdle	3.54	(0.98)	3.62	(1.07)	3.70	(1.09)	3.80	(1.13)	3.90	(1.16)
Third hurdle	4.52	(0.98)	4.64	(1.02)	4.74	(1.04)	4.87	(1.07)	5.01	(1.11)
Fourth hurdle	5.50	(0.98)	5.65	(1.01)	5.77	(1.03)	5.93	(1.06)	6.13	(1.12)
Fifth hurdle	6.48	(0.98)	6.65	(1.00)	6.79	(1.02)	6.99	(1.06)	7.25	(1.12)
Sixth hurdle	7.46	(0.98)	7.64	(0.99)	7.82	(1.03)	8.06	(1.07)	8.38	(1.13)
Seventh hurdle	8.48	(1.02)	8.64	(1.00)	8.86	(1.04)	9.14	(1.08)	9.52	(1.14)
Eighth hurdle	9.48	(1.00)	9.65	(1.01)	9.91	(1.05)	10.23	(1.09)	10.68	(1.16)
Ninth hurdle	10.50	(1.02)	10.68	(1.03)	10.98	(1.07)	11.35	(1.12)	11.87	(1.19)
Tenth hurdle	11.52	(1.02)	11.72	(1.04)	12.06	(1.08)	12.48	(1.13)	13.06	(1.19)
Finishing time	**12.91**	(1.39)	**13.10**	(1.38)	**13.50**	(1.44)	**14.10**	(1.62)	**14.80**	(1.74)

*Table 7: **Requirement profile for the 100m and 110m hurdles race:** The suggested rough estimate of the values of selected factors determining performance is based on the importance for the overall performance and the percentage of time spent training (IR: information requirements, constr.: constraints; see chapter I–1.1).*

Factors determining 100m and 110m hurdles performance	Estimate of value	Notes
Coordination	+ + + + +	optical IR: high, acoustic IR: medium, then low, tactile IR: medium-low, kinaesthetic IR: high, vestibular IR: medium; precision constr.: high, time constr.: high, complexity constr.: high, situation constr.: medium-high, physical stress constr.: low
Flexibility	+ + + (+ +)	While the men's hurdle sprint requires great flexibility (particularly in terms of hip flexion and also the adductors of the trail leg), the women's hurdle sprint requires only moderate flexibility
Strength		extensor loop (glutes, quadriceps, triceps surae, erector spinae), iliopsoas, hamstrings; special importance of the adductors and abductors of the trail leg as well as the abdominal muscles; shoulder and upper-arm muscles
Maximal strength	+ + + +	during start acceleration and as basis
Reactive strength	+ + + + +	within various stretch-shortening cycles
Speed	+ + + + +	ten-fold (rhythmic and cyclic) repetition of an acyclic movement; additional acyclic aspects at the start and when attacking the finish line; reaction speed at the start (can be decisive for winning the race; however, relatively insignificant in terms of percentage; hardly improvable through training)
Endurance (general dynamic) Anaerobic endurance		
Strength endurance	+ +	as basis of speed endurance and specific for hurdle clearance
Speed endurance	+ + +	long maintenance of maximal velocity and only slight velocity loss at the end of the race
Aerobic endurance	+ +	particularly as basis of training
Psychological and cognitive abilities	+ + + + +	courage ("aggressive" attacking of the hurdle); concentration ability (on the point; there is no possibility to compensate for errors); performance-oriented thinking and behaviour (see chapter I-3.1.1)
Anthropometric and primarily genetically determined characteristics	+ + + + +	high proportion of fastest muscle fibres; connective tissue with optimal energy-storing capacities; while in the men's hurdle sprint a certain body height and long legs are positive for performance, this is hardly the case in the women's hurdle sprint; low percentage of body fat

1.8.4 SUMMARY OF THE MOST IMPORTANT TECHNICAL CHARACTERISTICS = TECHNIQUE-ANALYSIS SHEET

CROUCH START

- See chapter II–1.3.4.
- Push-off leg (= trail leg) in the front block (prerequisite: 8 strides to the first hurdle).

RUN-UP TO THE FIRST HURDLE

- See chapter II–1.3.4.
- Usually 8 strides to the first hurdle, for very tall men possibly 7, with beginners possibly 9.
- With advanced athletes usually shorter stride length and higher stride frequency than in the flat sprint.
- Slightly longer penultimate stride.
- Slightly shorter last stride.
- More rapid and earlier straightening of the body than in the flat sprint.
- Attacking the hurdle from a high running position (high hips and heels high) and with upright trunk.

HURDLE STRIDE

PUSH-OFF

- Push-off point far in front of the hurdle: women: approx. 1.90–2.00m; men: approx. 2.00–2.15m (approx. 60% of the hurdle stride in front of the hurdle).
- Foot touchdown close to the vertical projection of the CG (due to the short front-support phase; the bracing movement is less pronounced).
- The complete push-off is performed with the ball of the foot (greater push-off height).
- Result: flat push-off (no take-off).

- Emphasised push-off into the hurdle with the extension of the foot, knee, and hip joint of the push-off leg.
- The swing leg is raised up to the horizontal, linear to the running direction (or with a slight inward sickle movement).
- At the moment of the last ground contact, the knee of the swing leg is still at an acute angle.
- Beginning forward lean of the trunk at the end of the push-off.

FLIGHT

- Continued raising and extension of the swing leg and lowering of the trunk in the form of a jackknife movement (women demonstrate a less pronounced jackknife movement and knee extension than men).
- The arm on the trail-leg side is extended in the direction of the swing-leg foot, while the other arm is kept at the side of the body.
- Due to the hip flexion and abduction, the knee of the trail leg is moved outward and upward.
- The downward movement of the swing leg and the straightening up of the trunk (hip extension) begin reactively immediately after the swing-leg foot has cleared the hurdle.
- At the same time, the athlete directs his/her glance to the next hurdle.
- At the same time, the backward swing of the (so-called) counter-arm on the outer circle around the trail leg is started.
- The lower trail leg is almost horizontal during hurdle clearance although the knee is still higher than the foot.
- The foot of the trail leg is pronated during hurdle clearance.
- The forward swing of the arm on the side of the swing leg is started.
- During the complete hurdle stride, the shoulder and pelvis axis are kept in a position as frontal as possible.
- The upward straightening of the trunk and the downward and backward movement of the swing leg are continued in the direction of the grasping touchdown of the foot.
- The trail leg is moved forward and inward in the direction of the high-knee running position, while the counter-arm is moved backward and inward.

LANDING

- The touchdown of the (almost) straight leg is performed on the ball of the foot; during the entire ground contact, the heel does not touch the ground.
- At touchdown, the CG is as vertical as possible above the tip of the foot.
- The rapid extension of the hip joint and rapid flexion of the knee joint result in a further straightening of the upper body and a short first stride behind the hurdle.
- At the end of the first ground contact behind the hurdle, the thigh of the trail leg points almost horizontally in the running direction; the knee joint is slightly opened again (approx. 90°).

INTER-HURDLE SPRINT

- The first stride is the shortest, the second stride the longest, and the third stride is approx. 10cm shorter than the second stride.
- High stride frequency, shortened strides, and a smaller swinging amplitude at the hip joint to achieve sufficient distance to the next hurdle; sprinting similar to running with knees raised to half the horizontal position (113).
- Maintenance of or return to an upright, frontal and high running position with upright pelvis, heels high and sprint-like arm action.

RUN TOWARD THE FINISH LINE AND SUBSEQUENT DECELERATION

- After the last hurdle, the hurdle sprinter accelerates again by shifting his/her CG forward and by using the toe push-off technique of sprinting.
- After crossing the finish line, the hurdle sprinter maintains his/her tension and shifts his/her trunk and CG backward to decelerate without running the risk of injury.

1.8.5 PHOTO SEQUENCES

RUN-UP TO THE FIRST HURDLE

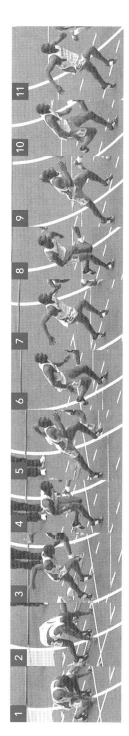

Data about the photo sequence

Athlete:	Ryan Brathwaite (born: 1 June 1988, Barbados)
Performance:	13.35 sec (wind: +0.5 m/sec; 19 August 2009, Berlin)
Best performance:	13.14 sec (wind: +0.1 m/sec; 20 August 2009, Berlin)
Greatest success:	World champion 2009

COMMENTARY

The men's 110m hurdles final at the 2009 World Championships was certainly one of the closest races in history (see table 8). The three leading sprinters crossed the finish line within a hundredth of a second, and the analysis shows that even during the race they were never more than 4 hundredths of a second apart.

Each photo presented shows the moment of foot touchdown or foot push-off of each of Brathwaite's eight steps to the first hurdle of his preliminary heat at the 2009 World Championships. Although the diagonal front perspective is not typical for such photo sequences, it is the only possibility to present the start acceleration of a short-hurdle sprinter (not running in lane 8).

Brathwaite's starting-block setting, "on-your-marks", and "set" position correspond to the recommendations made in discourse I in chapter II–1.3.3. The setting is characterised by a short distance between the front block and starting line (less than 1.5 feet in length), a medium distance between the blocks (about 1.5 feet in length), a relatively narrow and high hand support, and high hips in the "set" position (picture 2). The push-off extension from the block with very active arm action results in a typical extended position with the push-off leg and trunk at an angle of 45° to the ground (picture 3). Very early (i.e., even during the second stride, pictures 4–6), Brathwaite lifts his glance toward the first hurdle. The subsequent movements of his very muscular arms

result in a considerable rotation of the shoulder axis about the longitudinal axis of the body. This is continued beyond the first hurdle (not shown here).

His starting position results in a long first stride over the starting line. Brathwaite is forced to make his next seven strides with a high stride frequency in order to attack the first hurdle from a sufficient distance. This often results in an incomplete extension of the push-off leg. This incomplete extension is also the reason for the rapid straightening up of the trunk immediately after the start, which is necessary in the hurdles but not in the flat sprint. Upon the foot touchdown for the push-off into the hurdle (picture 18), Brathwaite has reached an almost upright trunk position before he lowers his trunk again forward to clear the hurdle. Immediately before clearing the hurdle, the angle of his knee is very narrow (picture 19). However, he subsequently does not extend his swing leg completely (picture 20), which is nowadays more often observed in the men's hurdle sprint. The foot touchdown behind the hurdle is performed in accordance with the target technique with an extended leg directly under the body (picture 21).

Table 8: **Reaction times** *(RT),* **intermediate, final, and interval times** *(the interval times in brackets)* **of the top three finishers at the 2009 World Championships in Berlin** *(in sec; according to Graubner et al., 2009, p. 5).*

	RT	1st hurdle	2nd hurdle	3rd hurdle	4th hurdle	5th hurdle	6th hurdle	7th hurdle	8th hurdle	9th hurdle	10th hurdle	Finish
Ryan Brathwaite (BAR)	0.157	2.54	3.60 (1.06)	4.61 (1.01)	5.60 (0.99)	6.59 (0.99)	7.60 (1.01)	8.62 (1.02)	9.65 (1.03)	10.70 (1.05)	11.74 (1.04)	13.14 (1.40)
Terrence Trammell (USA)	0.122	2.54	3.58 (1.04)	4.61 (1.03)	5.61 (1.00)	6.62 (1.01)	7.64 (1.02)	8.66 (1.02)	9.69 (1.03)	10.74 (1.05)	11.78 (1.04)	13.15 (1.37)
David Payne (USA)	0.141	2.56	3.60 (1.04)	4.61 (1.01)	5.60 (0.99)	6.60 (1.00)	7.62 (1.02)	8.63 (1.01)	9.66 (1.03)	10.71 (1.05)	11.77 (1.06)	13.15 (1.38)

HURDLE STRIDE AND INTER-HURDLE SPRINT

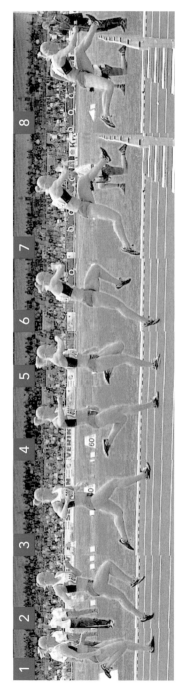
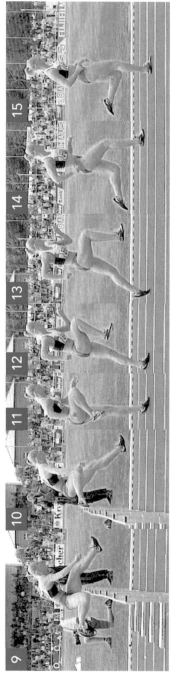
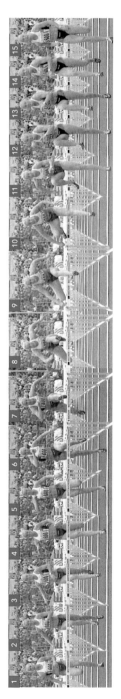

Data about the photo sequence
Athlete: Kirsten Bolm (born: 4 March
                1975, Germany)
Height/weight: 1.81 m/74 kg
Performance:
    Side view: 13.08 sec (wind: +0.9 m/sec)
    Front view: 13.03 sec (wind: -0.6 m/
                sec, both: 7 July 2002,
                Wattenscheid)
Best performance: 12.59 sec (22 July 2005,
                London)
Greatest success: Fourth place at the 2005
                World Championships,
                European vice-champion
                2006)

COMMENTARY

In the pictures from the side view, Bolm is seen at the 8th hurdle of her preliminary heat at the German Championships. The pictures from the front view show her at the 10th hurdle during the final. At the time of the competition, Bolm suffered pain from her sciatic nerve and was treated with several injections. This may well be the reason why she remained behind her season best of 12.84 sec. Nevertheless, one can still clearly see her good basic technique training.

When examining the photo sequence, it is striking that Kirsten Bolm stays on the ball of her foot only during the foot touchdown behind the hurdle (pictures 11–12). Upon all other ground contacts, the entirely sole of her foot briefly touches the ground (pictures 15, 1, and 4). Despite numerous recommendations to the contrary by coaches, this phenomenon is observed with relative frequency in world-class hurdlers. A counter-example is Carolin Nytra, Bolm's successor as the German and a European top hurdler. A photo sequence with the slightly smaller athlete shows that she stays on the ball of her foot during all ground contacts.

Bolm attacks the hurdle from a good upright, high, and frontal sprint position. What is striking is her preparation for hurdle clearance by moving her extended right arm to the outside and then to the front. Although a straighter movement of the counter-arm to the swing-leg foot is usually recommended, Bolm's action is not uncommon among top female hurdlers. The claim that Bolm compensates for an outward sickle movement through this wide arm movement cannot be completely supported. From a considerably angled position (picture 5), she is able to move her swing leg quickly and almost straight over the hurdle (picture 6). It is typical for modern female hurdle sprinters not to extend their swing legs over the hurdle (picture 8), but only when preparing the touchdown behind the hurdle (picture 10).

Bolm's distance to the hurdle is within the lower normal range. With a little more distance to the hurdle she would possibly have been able to push herself off even more aggressively into the hurdle and to extend herself more (picture 6). However, this is difficult for an athlete of her height.

From the side view, her position over the hurdle also seems to be suitable for her height (picture 9). Men and smaller women must lower their upper body to a greater extent. Bolm's vertical distance to the obstacle may seem far, but even with a body height of 1.81m the CG must be shifted a little upward to be able to perform a 3m stride and to have enough time for the leg movement. This means that a flatter clearance hardly seems possible. Her trail leg is at a good acute angle, its forward and upward movement is delayed, and the movement of her opposite arm around her trail leg is purposeful. However, the shot from the front shows a lateral, hardly desirable bending of her upper body.

The landing is performed in accordance with the target technique with an actively pulled and extended swing leg exactly on the vertical projection of the CG. Toward the push-off, the support leg is bent slightly, the upper body is straightened, and a fast first stride is initiated through the high-knee position of the swing leg. In the image from the side, the twisting of the shoulder axis still remains within a tolerance range, while in the picture from the front it is much too pronounced at the last hurdle before the finish. Although the reasons for this cannot be conclusively identified on the basis of this photo sequence, they may have begun in front of the hurdle.

1.8.6 STRATEGY

Chapter II–1.2.2 points out the limited importance of strategy in the short sprint. Nevertheless, Seagrave (2008, p. 9) proposed that (extremely) advanced short hurdle sprinters should divide the sprint distance into different phases which are similar to the 100m flat sprint through breathing (see chapter II–1.3.6). The athlete must learn to breathe in and out quickly when clearing the first, fourth, seventh, and tenth hurdle clearing (i.e., when clearing the "money hurdles"). During these five segments, the sprinter should focus on different technique features which can be verbalised through certain keywords. Interestingly, these technique features do not relate to the hurdle stride, but to the inter-hurdle sprint. Seagrave is referring explicitly to the women's 100m hurdle sprint which is more similar to the flat sprint and for which he chooses similar keywords like for the 100m flat sprint.

One must examine in detail whether this strategy helps female (or even male) sprinters or disturbs their concentration which is needed in clearing the hurdles.

Toward the first hurdle: The mental command "push, push, push" is supposed to remind the sprinter of the described technique of toe push-off sprinting during the start acceleration phase (see chapter II–1.3.3).

Toward the second, third, and fourth hurdles: The mental command "drive taller, drive taller, drive taller" is supposed to motivate the sprinter to fully straighten up between the hurdles. As during the first phase, the hip extension and foot touchdown are thus stressed.

Toward the fifth, sixth, and seventh hurdles: The mental command "step over, step over, step over" is supposed to direct the sprinter's focus to a stride frequency as high as possible during the phase of maximum rhythm velocity when sprinting between the hurdles. The concentration should be primarily directed to the rapid flexion of the hips and a fast movement of the leg to the front.

Toward the eighth, ninth, and tenth hurdles: The mental command "grab

back, grab back, grab back" draws the sprinter's attention once again to the hip extension and the preparation of the foot touchdown.

Toward the finish: The mental command "hot track, hot track, hot track" is supposed to invoke the idea of a hot stove and emphasise again stride frequency, hip flexion, and the movement of the leg to the front.

1.8.7 DIDACTICS: SUPERORDINATE LONG-TERM OBJECTIVES AND GENERAL METHODOLOGY

Generally, sprinting over various obstacles and the versatile training of rhythmic sprinting and running should be dealt with early on and extensively in children's athletics. As in the flat sprint, a variety of games and playful exercise forms can be used which include different forms of relay races. On the one hand, the obstacles should be broad rather than high (see 183) to motivate athletes to sprint rather than jump over them, and on the other hand, to help them to avoid errors such as the outward sickle movement of the swing leg. If the hurdle height is then raised slowly while taking the children's height into account, it is essential to ensure that the run remains a sprint. If there is an age- and skill-appropriate inter-hurdle distance of 5–6.5m, children will automatically sprint over the obstacles at a 3-stride rhythm without the coach instructing them to do so. It may be helpful to emphasise intra-group differentiation by using multiple lanes with different distances. However, it is

also absolutely necessary to use distances which require the children to deliberately run at a 2-, 4-, or 6-stride rhythm in order to promote bilateral hurdling. It is also extremely useful to employ rules according to which the children are supposed to run at a 3-, 5-, or 7-stride rhythm once with the left and once with the right leg as swing legs. As a result, beginners are taught using the whole method, which can be described by the phrase:

FROM SPRINT TO HURDLE SPRINT
When using this teaching method, introducing a correct trail leg technique (i.e., spreading it to the side) is a particular problem that can be solved by using u-shaped obstacles (see 184).

In basic training which is generally geared toward combined events (see chapter I–3.1.1 and I–3.3.4), the hurdle race plays a pivotal role in technique training. No other discipline is trained more often since the transfer effect of this highly demanding discipline on the other technical disciplines is so versatile (see chapter II–1.8.3).

The whole method is later extended to the whole-part-whole method, and special technique exercises are incorporated into the training. At least some workouts are now also performed according to this methodology:

FROM TECHNIQUE TO HURDLE SPRINT

Special (imitation) exercises for the swing and trail leg, as well as runs at a reduced speed and with a consciously controlled technique are characteristic of this teaching method. It is absolutely necessary that the exercises are performed on both sides. This is also particularly important for a possible change to the 400m hurdles in the future. To prepare for the 400m hurdles, hurdle sprints should also be performed in the curve from time to time.

CONCERNING THE PROBLEM OF COMPETITION DISTANCE

Beginning with the U14 age group, the short hurdle race is part of the competition programme. Although the competition distances between the hurdles are roughly adapted to the height of the developing athletes, the various skills and abilities of young athletes, retarded growth and abrupt changes in the transition from one age category to the next sometimes result in problems with the competition distance. The question arises whether it is absolutely necessary to teach athletes the 8-stride run-up and 3-stride rhythm. Since high-performance athletes run at a high stride frequency, it may be helpful to use a high-frequency 9-stride run-up and 4-stride rhythm. This should be easy to achieve for bilaterally trained athletes, and such a procedure would also be useful for continued versatility training.

A NOTE ON SAFETY

For reasons of safety and to avoid that athletes jump too high over the hurdles out of fear, rigid and immovable obstacles such as long benches, large gym boxes, toppled hurdles, etc. should not be used. Athletes should also be strictly forbidden from running over hurdles from the wrong direction. Wide and long trousers reduce the mobility of the legs and should therefore be avoided. However, full-length tights and socks prevent abrasions when a hurdle is touched.

1.8.8 TRAINING CONTENTS: FORMS OF GAMES AND EXERCISES

All training contents for the 100m sprint (see chapter II–1.3.8) are also contents for short hurdle-sprint training. Some training forms mentioned in connection with the 400m hurdles (see chapter II–1.9.8) may also be suitable for the short hurdles.

181 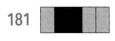 **Rhythm sprints, rhythm coordination, and rhythm relays**

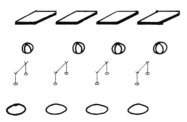

Possible objectives: Ability to establish rhythm; stride frequency (also see frequency sprints and frequency coordination, 135); speed; reactive strength.

Execution/variations: 1, 2, 3, 4 … contacts between hurdles (see frequency sprints and frequency coordination, 135); also with exercises from the ABCs of sprinting; also combinations without hurdles: e.g. 3 knee lifts – 4 heel kicks – 3 knee lifts – … (see Quick leg, 120); also as a pendulum and return relay (111).

Typical load standards: 2–4 reps for each task, 20–40m each (rest intervals guarantee maximum intensity).

182 ▨▨ **Hurdle relays**

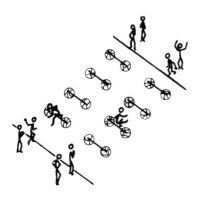

Possible objectives: Hurdle technique; ability to establish rhythm; stride frequency; speed; reactive strength.

Execution/variations: As a pendulum and return relay (111); using varying distances between hurdles (see chapter II–1.8.7), varying hurdle heights, and varying setup (see 183); also u-shaped obstacles (see 184).

Typical load standards: 1–3 reps of each task, 30–40m each, rest interval: running distance divided by 10 in min.

183 Maximal sprints over broad and low obstacles

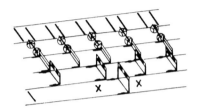

Possible objectives: Hurdle technique: flat push-off, running over the hurdles at high speed; ability to establish rhythm; stride frequency; speed; reactive strength.

Execution: The maintenance of a high sprinting velocity is of crucial importance.

Variations: Also gym mats as broad obstacles and/or banana boxes as hurdles (the height of these boxes varies depending on the side they are placed on; on gym mats, the banana boxes should be placed at the end of the mat to prompt a wide push-off); usually using a 3-stride rhythm (see chapter II–1.8.7, as well as 186).

Typical load standards: 4–12 reps of 30–40m each (using various setups), rest intervals: running distance divided by 10 in min.

184 Maximal sprints over u-shaped obstacles

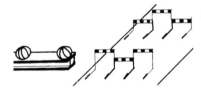

Possible objectives: Hurdle technique: spreading the trail leg to the side and straight-lined use of the swing leg; (as above).

Execution/variations: The swing leg is moved straight through the gap in the middle, while the trail leg is spread to the side and moved over the high hurdle; bilateral practice (see setup on the right).

Typical load standards: 3–4 reps per side, 30–40m each.

185 Maximal hurdle sprints using assisting markers

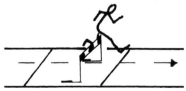

Possible objectives: Hurdle technique: linear sprinting and correct distance to the hurdle; speed; reactive strength.

Execution/variations: Distance markers (e.g., adhesive tape, foam block, or possibly also

jumping ropes, which should be placed in such a way that the athletes do not step on them); the correct landing on the push-off point in front of the hurdle is particularly important; also running along the side of the hurdles focusing on landing on the push-off point.

Typical load standards: See 183–184.

186   Maximal hurdle sprints using 4-, 5-, 6-, and 7-stride rhythm

Possible objectives: Hurdle technique: versatility, running over the hurdles at a high speed; speed; reactive strength; possibly also speed endurance.

Execution: Possibly lowering the height of the hurdles (particularly in the case of uneven rhythms and to prepare for the 400m hurdle race); distances (4-, 5-, 6-, 7-stride rhythm): women: 9–11m, 11–12.5m, 13–15m, 15–17m; men: 10–12m, 12–14m, 14–16m, 17–19m.

Variations: Also through the curve; also against each other; possibly using different rhythms for sprinters competing against each other.

Typical load standards: 5–9 reps (possibly using varying setup) of 40–100m each, rest intervals: running distance divided by 5 or 10 in min.

187   Maximal hurdle sprints up to the 2nd–6th hurdle

Possible objectives: Hurdle technique; speed; reactive strength; sprints over relatively high hurdles always improve specific flexibility, too.

Execution: Hurdles at competition height; the distance to the first hurdle should be the competition distance as long as the athlete has

the impression that this distance is rather long, later the distance should be reduced by ½–1 foot in length; in training, the inter-hurdle distance should be reduced by one foot in length since the intensity is higher in competition (also see hurdle sprints with shorter inter-hurdle distances, 190); silent sprinting (to avoid a "take-off").

Variations: Bilateral practice; verbal accompaniment of the running rhythm: "ta-tam-ta-tap," or "ta-ta-ta-boom."

Typical load standards: 5–9 reps (also with increasing running distance or using the pyramid method up to the 2nd, 3rd, 4th, 5th, 4th, 3rd, and 2nd hurdle), rest intervals: running distance divided by 5 in min.

188   Maximal hurdle sprints up to the 1st hurdle

Possible objectives: Hurdle technique: run-up to the first hurdle; reactive strength; speed; (acceleration ability).

Execution: See maximal hurdle sprints up to the 2nd–6th hurdle, 187; first run-up possibly along the side of the hurdle: The coach or a partner checks whether the number of strides, the stride length, and the take-off point are correct.

Variations: Bilateral practice; lengthening the run-up by 2–4 strides.

Typical load standards: 3–7 reps, rest intervals: 3 min each.

189   Maximal hurdle sprints through the finishing tape

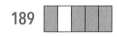

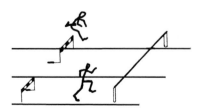

Possible objectives: Hurdle technique; acceleration after the (last) hurdle and run toward the finish; reactive strength; speed (ability to accelerate).

Execution: See chapter II–1.8.3.

Variations: To improve the inter-hurdle sprint; running away from the hurdle should be practised

using an upright trunk position and without finishing tape.
Typical load standards: See 188.

---

190  **Maximal hurdle sprints using shorter inter-hurdle distances**

Possible objectives: Hurdle technique: shorter distances for adaption to the individual athlete's skill level or for special stride-frequency training; speed, speed strength, and reactive strength.
Execution/variations: 3-stride rhythm maximally up to the 6th hurdle (but also using different rhythms); shortening of inter-hurdle distances by up to 20%, possibly also increasingly shorter distance from hurdle to hurdle; possibly slightly lower hurdle height; full run-up or run-up to the first hurdle reduced to 6 strides.
Typical load standards: See 187.

---

191 **Maximal hurdle sprints over increasing or decreasing hurdle heights**

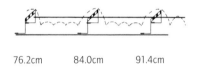

76.2cm   84.0cm   91.4cm

Possible objectives: Hurdle technique: versatility; making sure that the velocity of running over the hurdle is high; speed; reactive strength.
Execution/variations: The height of the hurdle is decreased or increased after the first hurdle; (see also sprints over wide and low obstacles, 183).
Typical load standards: See 187.

---

192 **Maximal hurdle sprints at varying rhythms**

Possible objectives: Hurdle technique: versatility; ability to adapt; making sure that the run-up velocity to the hurdle is high; speed; reactive strength; possibly also speed endurance.
Execution/variations: In the setup presented in the picture (alternation between 3-stride and

7-stride rhythm), the 3rd (later the 4th or 5th instead) hurdle is left out; however, almost every other combination of rhythms is possible (see guiding values for distances in 186); also against each other with the runners being forced to run a different rhythms.

Typical load standards: See 186.

193 Maximal hurdle sprints at 1- or 2-stride rhythm

Possible objectives: Hurdle technique: as many hurdle strides as possible; special flexibility; speed and reactive strength (hurdle-stride specific).

Execution/variations: Considerably increased demands since there is hardly any possibility for correction and for velocity development between the hurdles; athletes should jump as little as possible; bilateral training; run-up from standing start (see 123) reduced to 6 strides; lower hurdle height; distances (1-stride and 2-stride rhythm): 3.5–4m, 4.5–6m, 3.5–4.5m, 5–6.5m.

Typical load standards: 3–7 reps on each side, 4–8 hurdles each, rest intervals: running distance divided by 10 in min.

194 Maximal hurdle sprints over oxer

Possible objectives: Hurdle technique: correct distance to the hurdle, early raising of the swing leg; speed; reactive strength.

Execution/variations: Special setup can be combined with many other exercises.

Typical load standards: 2–5 reps of 3–5 hurdles each, rest intervals: running distance divided by 5 in min.

The forms of games and exercises described until now follow the methodology from the sprint to the hurdle sprint (see chapter II-1.8.7). However, the training sessions and teaching sessions which are more inclined to begin with the exercises below and therefore adhere to the principle from technique to the hurdle sprint usually end with the so-called complex exercises mentioned above.

---

195 ▢▢■▢▢ **Hurdle imitation using the gym box**

Possible objectives: Hurdle-stride technique (imitation).
Execution: Slow, detailed imitation (no running over gym boxes for the safety reasons mentioned; see chapter II–1.8.7).
Variations: Bilateral training.
Typical load standards: 1–3 sets of 5–8 reps each.

---

196 ▢▢■ **Trail-leg exercises with hands supported**

Possible objectives: Trail-leg technique (imitation).
Execution: Hip and shoulder axis remain as parallel to the wall and the floor as possible.
Variations: Slow and controlled with rest intervals or rapid without interruptions; without hand support.
Typical load standards: 1–3 sets of 10 reps each.

---

197 ▢▢■ **Swing-leg exercises**

Possible objectives: Swing-leg technique (imitation).
Execution/variations: Frontal position of the push-off foot, the hips, and the shoulder axis.
Typical load standards: 1–3 sets of 10 reps each.

---

198 ABCs of hurdling: walking over hurdles

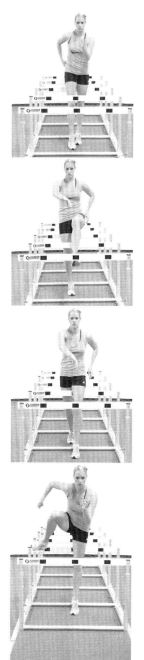

Possible objectives: Hurdle-stride technique (imitation).

Execution: Lower hurdle height; the hip and shoulder axis remain as frontal and parallel to the ground as possible; a: two contacts between the hurdles; the swing and trail leg are identical at every hurdle; the swing leg is moved over the hurdle on a straight line or by using a slight inward sickle movement; the trail-leg movement and the arm action are in accordance with the target technique (see chapter II–1.8.3); b: only one contact between the hurdles; only trail-leg movements.

Variations: Bilateral training; the imitation is usually as slow as possible, but now and again the movement speed is also faster; without arm movements: for example, arms folded in front of one's chest, extended to the side, or clasped behind one's back; touching the swing-leg foot and trail-leg knee at their highest points with the opposite hand; performance of the movement also backward (e.g., two hurdles forward, one hurdle backward); to improve general agility also over a hurdle, under a hurdle; three contacts between the hurdles to alternate swing and trail leg (with a slightly greater distance between the hurdles).

Typical load standards: 2–5 run-throughs over 5–10 hurdles each.

199 **ABCs of hurdling: skipping over hurdles**

Possible objectives: Hurdle-stride technique (imitation); special strength and flexibility.

Execution: Over hurdles or not (for movement execution see "walking over hurdles," 198).

Variations: See "walking over hurdles", 198; also as fast as possible (for time).

Typical load standards: 2–5 run-throughs over 5–10 hurdles each.

---

200 **ABCs of hurdling: skipping over hurdles sideways**

Possible objectives: Swing-leg technique; special strength and flexibility.

Execution: Sideward skipping movement over hurdles.

Variations: Also forward and backward; also for time.

Typical load standards: 2–5 run-throughs over 5–10 hurdles each.

---

201 **Submaximal technique runs**

Possible objectives: Hurdle-stride technique; special warm-up.

Execution/variations: Over hurdles placed at competition distance using a 5-stride rhythm; inter-hurdle sprint with knees raised to half the horizontal position or with high knees; deliberate check of technique; bilateral training; with variation of arm actions as in walking over hurdles (198); with beginners with two assistants running alongside the exerciser and holding his/ her hands.

Typical load standards: 3–6 run-throughs over 3–6 hurdles each.

202 | Running past hurdles

Possible objectives: Hurdle technique: isolation of trail-leg (or also swing-leg) technique at higher velocity.

Execution: Only trail-leg movement over the hurdle or only with forward extension of the swing leg over the hurdle (or even only on the side of the hurdle); in the picture, a 4-stride rhythm would require a trail-leg movement at the next hurdle, while a 3-stride rhythm would require a swing-leg movement.

Variations: At maximal or submaximal intensity, or by running with knees raised to half the horizontal position (113), or from high-knee run (112); to make the exercise easier, the hurdles should initially be set up only on one side.

Typical load standards: 2–5 run-throughs over 3–6 hurdles each.

On the one hand, all exercises already mentioned in connection with the 100m sprint are also used in strength, endurance, and flexibility training (see chapter II–1.3.8). On the other hand, the following exercises as well as some exercises already described in the general part of this book should be added: one-sided jackknife (44), flexor sliding with extended swing leg (68), etc.

203 | Hurdle seat variations

Possible objectives: (Dynamic) flexibility (training), mobilisation, imitation, and strength training (in each case specific to hurdles).

Execution/variations: Alternating several times between the positions presented; also imitation of hurdle arm actions in the hurdle-seat position.

Typical load standards: 1–3 sets of 10 reps each.

204 Hurdle exercises in lying position

Possible objectives: (Dynamic) flexibility (training), mobilisation and strength training (in each case specific to hurdles).

Execution/variations: While in supine position, alternately bring left foot toward right hand, then right foot toward left hand (shoulders remain on the ground if possible), or alternate between the positions presented below.

Typical load standards: 1–3 sets of 10 reps each.

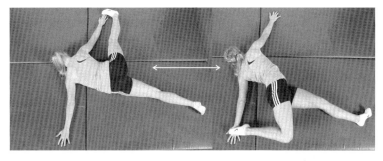

205 Hurdle swing exercises

Possible objectives: (Dynamic) flexibility (training) and mobilisation (in each case specific to hurdles).

Execution/variations: Controlled rhythmic swinging movements; with or without supporting oneself on a wall.

Typical load standards: 1–3 sets of 10 reps each.

206  **Swing- and trail-leg movement with additional resistance**

Possible objectives: Hurdle-specific strength; illustration of the movement direction.

Execution/variations: With elastic band, cable-pull strength-training machine, or with weighted sleeves on the feet; with or without supporting oneself on a wall.

Typical load standards: 1–3 sets of 10 reps each.

A certain amount of velocity is necessary to perform the specific short-hurdle technique. Therefore there are no specific low-intensity runs for the short hurdles (see chapter II–1.3.8).

---

207 **I3 tempo runs: hurdle Z (or hurdle set)**

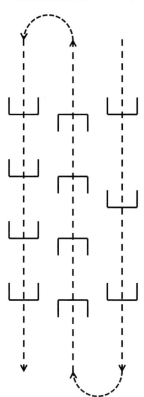

Possible objectives: Hurdle-specific speed endurance and strength endurance.

Execution/variations: It is characteristic of hurdle Zs that several flights of hurdles are run through (in both directions) almost without rest; due to the submaximal intensity, the distances between the hurdles, and possibly also the height of the hurdles must be reduced; the tasks during each run-through can vary: 50m at 4-stride rhythm, after deceleration immediately to the start of the next flight leading back again, 50m using the 3-stride rhythm and the weak leg, after deceleration immediately to the start of the next flight leading back again, 50m using the 3-stride rhythm and the strong leg.

Typical load standards: in accordance with the intensive interval method using sets (see chapter I–4.5): 2 sets of 4 Zs of 3 run-throughs each of 50m each; walking intervals after Z: 4 min; rest intervals between sets: 10 min.

208  **l2 tempo runs over (up to 12) hurdles**

Possible objectives: Hurdle-specific speed endurance and strength endurance.

Execution: As always in training, the distances between the hurdles are reduced by one foot in length; in the 100m or 110m hurdle sprint, the distances between the last four hurdles (at least beginning with the second run) are even reduced by two feet in length; thus, there is room for an eleventh hurdle placed at the same distance.

Variations: If the distances between the hurdles are reduced by 1–2 foot lengths, there is enough space for a twelfth hurdle immediately in front of the finish line in the men's 110m, while this hurdle must be placed immediately behind the finish line in the women's 100m; in the event of 4 or 5 run-throughs, a reduction by 2–3 foot lengths is also conceivable.

Typical load standards: In accordance with the repetition method: 3–5 reps of 100 or 110m each, walking intervals: 10–12 min.

1.8.9 SPECIAL TEST AND CONTROL PROCEDURES

	Test: Ability/skill tested	Execution/comments
T51	**Test over flat course:** Hurdle technique	Maximal flat sprint under competition conditions (100 or 200m, see technique index in chapter II–1.8.3).
T52	**60m hurdles:** a) hurdle technique; b) all factors determining performance (with the exception of speed endurance)	Maximal hurdle sprint under competition conditions (hurdle height, distance, etc.; a) possible without starting signal): a) evaluation with the help of the technique analysis sheet (see chapter II–1.8.4), possibly on the basis of video (T1) and photo sequences made thereof; b) with electronic time measurement (very complex, or possible only at indoor competitions); manual timing is also possible, but significantly less accurate.
T53	**Interval times:** Strengths and weaknesses in the course of the race	Maximal hurdle sprint under competition conditions (hurdle height, distance, etc.). Upon the touchdown of the swing leg a) behind each hurdle (see tables 5 and 6), b) behind the first, fourth, seventh, and tenth hurdle, split times are recorded and the corresponding inter-hurdle times are calculated; measurement also performed by the exact evaluation of each frame of a video; manual timing is very inaccurate and may only be used with b).
T54	**I1 test over 11 hurdles:** Hurdle-specific speed endurance	Maximal hurdle sprint over 100 or 110m (208); there is an additional eleventh hurdle placed at the same distance (it is also possible for the sprinter to run up to the twelfth hurdle placed immediately behind the finish line); manual timing is normally sufficiently accurate.
T4	**1 RPM:** Maximal strength	Squat (62), clean (63), snatch (64), hip and trunk flexors (68), extensors (69), arm exercises, etc. (if possible, also eccentric maximal-strength measurement).
T5	**Squat jump and T8 Counter-movement and drop jump:** Two-legged speed strength and reactive strength of the extensor loop	Possibly tossing the shot instead (93).

	Test: Ability/skill tested	Execution/comments
T9	**5-stride hops with distance maximisation:** Reactive strength of the legs in comparison to one another	Test should be performed on both sides.
T10	**30m bounding run with time minimisation:** Reactive strength of the legs	
T22	**Crouch-start reaction test:** Reaction speed	
T23	**Crouch start and acceleration up to 20m:** Start acceleration without hurdles	
T24	**30m flying sprint:** Maximal sprinting speed	
T25	**20m frequency test:** Cyclic speed	
T26	**Short-sprint tempo-run programmes as test:** Anaerobic speed endurance and aerobic endurance	Also over hurdles as an alternative.
T66	**Graded field test:** Aerobic basic endurance	With lactate withdrawal (and spirometry; for young athletes also Cooper test, T65, which is easy to perform but inaccurate).
T2	**Flexibility tests:** General flexibility and flexibility specific to the hurdles	using exercises 203–205.
T3	**Body weight and body fat measurement:** Relative strength	Inappropriate upward and downward deflections should be avoided.

*Table 9: **Basic performances of 100m or 110m hurdle sprinters** (according to Tepper & Czingon, 1995, p. 46).*

	Women			Men		
Hurdle target time (sec)	**14.10**	**13.65**	**12.90**	**14.80**	**14.10**	**13.50**
30m from the starting blocks (sec)	4.72	4.70	4.46	4.28	4.19	4.09
30m flying (sec)	3.26	3.20	3.10	3.05	2.89	2.74
60m hurdles (sec)	n.s.	8.50	8.03	8.31	7.94	7.71
100m flat (sec)	12.60	12.30	11.80	11.40	10.95	<10.55
200m flat (sec)	25.80	24.50	23.40	22.95	21.70	<21.00
Difference = hurdle time – 100m time	1.50	>1.35	>1.10	3.40	>3.15	>2.75
10-stride bounding run (m)	19-23	22-26	24-25	32-35	35-38	36-39
½ squat (with multiple body weight)	1.2-1.5	1.7-2.0	1.8-2.1	2.2-2.5	2.4-2.7	2.5-2.8
Running velocity at 4 mmol/l measured in graded lactate field test (m/sec)	3.5-3.9	3.7-3.9	3.8-4.0	3.5-3.8	3.7-3.9	3.8-4.0

1.8.10 ERRORS - CAUSES - CORRECTIONS

Error	Causes	Corrections
Too fast or too early straightening of the trunk after the crouch start.	• The athlete directs his/her glance too early to the hurdle (even before his/her fourth stride).	✔ The fourth stride should be marked; the athlete should not direct his/her glance to the hurdle before this mark and should also straighten his/her trunk only when at this mark.
Too slow or too late straightening of the trunk after the crouch start.	• Lack of differentiation between the sprint and short-hurdle start. • Lack of attempt to create an optimal starting position for the jackknife movement over the hurdle.	✔ Focusing on the difference between the acceleration in the flat sprint and the hurdle sprint as a topic of discussion. ✔ The fourth stride should be marked; the athlete should direct his/her glance to the hurdle already at this mark and should also straighten his/her trunk when at this mark. ✔ Exaggeration of the forward lean followed by a reduction of the forward lean (contrast method).

Error	Causes	Corrections
Submaximal or generally insecure and hesitant run-up to the first or to the second to tenth hurdle.	• Insecurity in respect to the number of strides. • Lack of experience and thus lack of rhythm. • Fear of the hurdle.	✔ If the athlete requires 8 strides to reach the first hurdle, the push-off leg should be in the front block; if he/she requires (7 or) 9 strides, the swing leg should be in the front block. ✔ With small youths, the 4-stride rhythm should be used temporarily as the competition standard. ✔ Verbal accompaniment of the rhythm: with 8 strides: "and-1-and-2-and-3-and-push(-off)," with 3-stride rhythm: "ta-tam-ta-tap" or "ta-ta-ta-boom." ✔ Marking the strides. ✔ Increase in the amount of short-hurdle training. ✔ Maximal sprints over wide and low obstacles (183); slow increase of the hurdle height. ✔ Possibly initial sprinting over equally high, less painful obstacles (caution: not for too long; avoid habituation effect).

Running too close to the first or to the second to tenth hurdle.	• Too many strides to the first hurdle (9 instead of 8, or in exceptional cases even 8 instead of 7 strides).
	• Too long strides or too low stride frequency due to
	  » lacking or wrong stride rhythm (often automated at a time when strength and speed were worse and the distances between the hurdles appeared to be too long); in particular, the penultimate or medium stride is too long (too pronounced short-long-short rhythm);
	  » lacking differentiation between the sprint and short-hurdle start.
	• The sprinter intends to jump over the hurdle (for causes see below).
		✔ In the case of 8 strides to the first hurdle: push-off leg in the front block; in the case of 7 strides: swing leg in the front block.
		✔ The starting block and the support position of the hands should possibly be set backward for a limited period (see chapter II-1.3.8).
		✔ Verbal accompaniment of the running rhythm (see above).
		✔ Maximum hurdle sprints in training from a run-up and with distances between the hurdles reduced by one foot length (see 187); the hurdle distance may even be reduced more (190).
		✔ Markers for strides and/or push-off point (185) while running over the hurdles or landing on the correct push-off point when sprinting past the hurdle.
		✔ Hurdles as oxer (194).
		✔ General training of the ability to establish a certain rhythm (181).

(continued)

Track & Field

(continued)

Error	Causes	Corrections
Take-off instead of push-off in front of the hurdle (too great loss of horizontal velocity).	• Last foot touchdown too far in front of the vertical projection of the CG, resulting in the development of too much force during the front support (bracing; mostly in association with a touchdown of the whole sole of the foot): in most cases caused by: » running too close to the hurdle (for causes see above), » too low running position when approaching the hurdle, or » fear of the hurdle. • Lack of technical skills concerning hurdle clearance which requires greater height above the hurdle, possibly due to lack of flexibility.	✔ Maximum sprints over wide and low obstacles (183); slow increase in the height of the hurdle while maintaining maximum velocity when running over the hurdle. ✔ Running with knees raised to half the horizontal position (113), high-knee run (112), ABCs of hurdling (198-200) with heels high, hips high, and upright trunk. ✔ Possibly initially sprinting over equally high, less painful obstacles (caution: not for too long; avoid habituation effect). ✔ Technique training using exercises 185 and 195-202. ✔ Flexibility training using exercises 27-28 and 203-205.
Creation of too much forward rotation when pushing off in front of the hurdle.	• The shoulder is moved forward too early when attacking the hurdle. • Too pronounced forward lean of the trunk while sprinting between the hurdles (or during the run-up to the first hurdle). • Too pronounced shortening of the last stride due to a too short distance to the hurdle.	✔ Practising the upright trunk position in the ABCs of sprinting (112-121). ✔ Illustrating the alternation between the upright trunk position during the inter-hurdle sprint at a high stride frequency and the forward lean of the trunk over the hurdle (e.g., within exercises 198-201), and subsequently practising this alternation while sprinting over the hurdles at maximal speed.
No straight movement of the swing leg (outward sickle or pronounced inward sickle).	• (Habit of) running too close to the hurdle (for causes see above).	✔ See corrections of running too close to the hurdle above. ✔ Straight swinging of the leg toward a mark in the middle of the hurdle (coach checks from the front). ✔ Imitation exercises (197-202). ✔ U-shaped obstacles (184).
Frequent contact with the hurdle by the swing-leg foot.	• Running too close to the hurdle (for causes see above). • In the jackknife position, the athlete is bent too far forward due to the creation of too much forward rotation while pushing off in front of the hurdle and its contributing factors. • Too little pronounced jackknife position (for causes see below).	✔ See corrections of running too close to the hurdle, creation of too much forward rotation while pushing off in front of the hurdle, and too little pronounced jackknife position over the hurdle.

Error	Causes	Corrections
Too little pronounced jackknife position over the hurdle.	• Lack of flexibility (particularly of the hamstrings). • Lack of strength of the abdominal muscles and hip flexors. • Lack of attempt to achieve a flat CG curve over the hurdle.	✔ Stretching using exercises 27, 203, and 205. ✔ Strengthening using exercises 44 and 73. ✔ Versatile technique training including respective corrections.
Drawing the trail leg forward too early.	• Lack of push-off into the hurdle (i.e., lack of extension of the hip, knee, and foot of the push-off leg).	✔ Strong push-off into the hurdle from running with knees raised to half the horizontal position at a high stride frequency but slow speed (113), or from running with high knees (112); one-stride rhythms (193).
The trail leg is not abducted enough (i.e., moved outward and upward) and/or touches the hurdle.	• Lack of hip flexibility. • Lack of forward lean of the body or jackknife position over the hurdle.	✔ Flexibility training using exercises 28, 195-196, 198-200, and 203-205. ✔ Versatile technique training, including instruction on leaning forward with one's trunk.
The trail leg is moved to the front too late or too slowly.	• Fear of touching the hurdle with the trail leg (however, paradoxically the probability of touching the hurdle is increased all the more by this behaviour). • Lack of attempt to perform a fast and active first stride after the hurdle.	✔ Running at a submaximal pace by using a 3-stride rhythm (201), and maximal running over high hurdles using a 5- or 7-stride rhythm (186) enables the hurdler to focus more on his/her trail leg. ✔ Versatile technique training, including corresponding instructions. ✔ Focusing on fear as a topic of discussion. ✔ Setting the following objective: Try to place both legs down after the hurdle in a stride position nearly simultaneously.
Lifting the arms to the side, particularly on the side of the swing leg.	• A strong compensation of the rotation through the arms is required » since the opposite arm is not moved to the front enough while attacking the hurdle; » since the knee of the trail leg is not bent enough or is opened too early; and » since the shoulder and pelvic axis are not kept frontal (i.e., parallel to the hurdle bar) during the push-off or a rotation about the longitudinal axis of the body is initiated differently.	✔ Since the arm movement should rather be regarded as a compensatory movement, one must look especially for other faults (see causes). ✔ Making the athlete aware of his/her arm actions (e.g., by temporary elimination): walking over hurdles (198) or skipping over hurdles (199) with folded arms or arms fixed differently. ✔ Submaximal technique runs (201), and maximal hurdle sprints (e.g., 187), walking or skipping over hurdles with deliberate arm actions: in particular, extending the opposite arm forward toward the swing leg and temporarily resting the other arm on the body.

(continued)

377

(continued)

Error	Causes	Corrections
Insufficient or no gain of velocity upon the first support after the hurdle (mostly accompanied by the tip of the foot being in front of the CG instead of on the vertical projection of the CG during the touchdown).	• Lack of hip extension (downward and backward movement of the swing leg and straightening up of the trunk) when preparing for and during the first support after the hurdle. • Take-off instead of push-off in front of the hurdle (for causes see above). • Backward lean during the landing (for causes see below).	✔ Practise preparing for the touchdown and running from the hurdle using exercises 199-200 and subsequent practice of the touchdown and running from the hurdle while sprinting over hurdles. ✔ See corrections of take-off instead of push-off above and the backward lean during the landing behind the hurdle corrections below.
Backward lean during the landing behind the hurdle; too deep amortisation of the landing leg with a resulting loss of horizontal velocity.	• Lack of forward movement of the shoulder or forward lean of the trunk during the push-off, resulting in the initiation of a backward rotation about the transverse axis of the body. • Running too close to the hurdle (for causes see above).	✔ Practising the correct attack of the hurdle (from an upright body position to the jackknife position) using exercises 198, 199, and 201, and subsequent performance of the correct attack at higher velocities. ✔ See corrections of running too close to the hurdle above.
Still pronounced forward lean of the trunk upon the first ground contact and falling onto the second support after the hurdle (i.e., long contact time, deep amortisation at the knee joint and loss of horizontal velocity).	• Creation of too much forward rotation while pushing off in front of the hurdle (for causes see above).	✔ See corrections of creation of too much forward rotation while pushing off in front of the hurdle.
Pronounced twist about the longitudinal axis of the body at the first and/or second support after the hurdle (mostly in combination with a lack of sprint-like arm actions during the inter-hurdle sprint and a corresponding loss of velocity).	• The athlete tries to compensate for the rotation (see causes of lifting of the arms toward the side).	✔ See corrections of lifting of the arms toward the side.

With respect to the crouch start and the first strides, one should also observe the errors connected with the 100m race as well as their causes and corrections (see chapter II–1.3.10).

1.8.11 TRAINING PLANNING

Due to many of the same requirements, the training plans for the short sprint and horizontal jumps are similar. Compared to (4x)100m training, 100m- and 110m-hurdle training must be supplemented by training hurdling technique. However, in short-hurdle training, grasping/pulling sprinting requires less emphasis since the inter-hurdle sprint is rather similar to frequency-oriented running with knees raised to half the horizontal position (113) or to frequency-oriented high-knee running (112). The special strength and flexibility requirements in the short-hurdle sprint require a great deal of specific training. Speed endurance should be trained both generally (without hurdles) and specifically (over hurdles).

SUGGESTED TRAINING PLANS

Below, there are exemplary microcycles for the

• first mesocycle of a 17-year-old athlete in build-up training (table 11);
• second mesocycle of an athlete in high-performance training (table 12); and

• fourth mesocycle of an athlete in high-performance training (table 13).

Due to similarities between the disciplines mentioned above, the suggested training plans for the

• second mesocycle of a 17-year-old athlete in build-up training presented in connection with the 4 x 100m (see chapter II–1.6.11);
• third mesocycle of a 17-year-old athlete in build-up training presented in connection with the triple jump (see chapter II–2.3.10);
• first mesocycle of an athlete in high-performance training presented in connection with the 4 x 100m; and
• third mesocycle of an athlete in high-performance training presented in connection with the 4 x 100m

may be used as a basis when supplementing the mesocycles not presented in this chapter.

Table 10: **Training emphasis in the various mesocycles** *for short-hurdle training in build-up and high-performance training.*

1st Mesocycle	basic aerobic and anaerobic endurance training (in speed-endurance training also over hurdles); hypertrophy-oriented maximal-strength training especially for the legs and the trunk; basic reactive-strength training for the legs; flexibility training; versatile and general coordination training (e.g., ABCs of sprinting/jumping) and versatile hurdle-technique training
2nd Mesocycle	basic speed-endurance training with and without hurdles; hypertrophy-, IC- and connective-tissue-oriented maximal- and reactive-strength training, especially for the legs and the trunk; (particularly special) flexibility training; more special (3-stride rhythm) as well as versatile hurdle-technique training
3rd Mesocycle	(special) speed-endurance training at high intensity; IC- and connective-tissue-oriented maximal- and reactive-strength training, especially for the legs and the trunk; speed, acceleration, and technique training at maximum intensity
4th Mesocycle	competitions and corresponding regeneration; IC- and connective-tissue-oriented maximal- and reactive-strength training, especially for the legs and the trunk; speed, acceleration, and technique training at maximum intensity; maintenance stimuli

Table 11: Build-up training: sample microcycle for a 17-year-old athlete in the first mesocycle.

Monday	Tuesday	Wednesday	Thursday	Friday	Saturday	Sunday
Trunk stabilisation exercises and abdominal crunches (20 min) with a lot of dynamic variation	Foot strengthening (10 min)	Warm-up jogging (6 min)	Continuous run (40 min)	LI runs (6 x 80m, rest intervals: 20 sec) for warming up	Baton handovers (25 min) while sitting/standing, jogging, and sprinting at submaximal speed	Rest
Acceleration runs (2 reps) barefoot	Acceleration runs (3 reps) barefoot	Mobilisation (10 minutes) specific to hurdles	Contract-relax stretching (15 min) primarily hurdle-specific	ABCs of jumping (10–15 run-throughs)	ABCs of sprinting (15–20 run-throughs)	*On Saturdays before the tempo runs possibly also training the techniques of one event for the quadrathlon or pentathlon.*
ABCs of hurdling and hurdle imitation (25 min)	ABCs of jumping (10–15 run-throughs) galloping sideways, ankle jumps, skipping with two-legged landing, skipping variations, etc.	Acceleration runs (3 reps)	Two out of the following:	Skipping, pop-up jumps, and squat-extension jumps (4 run-throughs each) or start jumps or jumps onto a box	Acceleration runs (3 reps)	
Acceleration runs (2 reps) wearing spikes	Bounding runs and/or rhythm jumps (6–8 run-throughs)	Hurdle preparation (10 min) relaxed running over hurdles	Muscle build-up training for the trunk and/or for the arms, medicine-ball work, gymnastics, technique training for the throwing events, boxing, etc. (30 min each) goalkeeper throws, rotational throws, throws from a prone position, tossing, etc., using a medicine ball	Muscle build-up training (40 min; e.g., 15, 12, 10, and 7 reps each) hamstrings, quadriceps, adductors, abductors, hip flexors and extensors	LI tempo runs (3 x 300m, 4 x 200m, and 3 x 300m; rest intervals: 3, 3, 6–8, 2, 2, 2, 6–8, 3, and 3 min) wearing running shoes	
Practising the hurdling technique (40 min) after specific warm-up: 4, 5, 6, or 7-stride rhythm; also at varying rhythms; short-hurdle-specific distances between hurdles	Muscle build-up training (30 min) e.g., full squat and clean (coach must still supervise the athlete's technique carefully), possibly interspersed with abdominal exercises	Hurdle Zs (2 sets of 4 Zs each of 2 run-throughs over 4 hurdles each; rest intervals: 3 min; rest intervals between sets: 10 min) e.g., out in a 3-stride rhythm with the weak side, back with the strong side	Tappings (8 x 5 sec)	Foot strengthening (10 min) in the sand	Contract-relax stretching (15 min)	
Relay around turning marks (2–3 run-throughs) with handover from behind	Game (30 min) e.g., basketball or soccer	Contract-relax stretching (15 min)		Technique sprints (4–6 reps) sprints with additional tasks	Warm-down jogging (10 diagonals on the lawn)	
		Warm-down jogging (diagonals on the lawn)			Rhythm or frequency coordination (10 min)	
		Relay starts (3 x 30m) against each other				

Table 12: High-performance training: sample microcycle in the second mesocycle.

	Monday	Tuesday	Wednesday	Thursday	Friday	Saturday	Sunday
Morning	Trunk stabilisation exercises and abdominal crunches (20 min) Acceleration runs Strength training (50 min) pyramid principle: hamstrings, quadriceps, adductors/abductors, snatch Skipping over hurdles (3x per variation and push-off leg) as utilisation	LI runs (10 x 60m, rest intervals: 15 sec)	Foot strengthening (10 min) Hurdle imitation and ABCs of hurdling (20 min) Rhythm coordination (20 min) Strength training (30 min, e.g., 4 x 6 reps each) clean and full squat Uphill sprints (6 x 60m, rest intervals: 5–8 min)		Warm-up jogging (6 min) Acceleration runs (3 reps) Ankle jumps (5 x 15) or skipping with two-legged landing Practising the hurdling technique (45 min; after specific warm-up, 8–12 x up to 60m) versatile, bilateral	Rope jumping (5 min) Acceleration runs (3 reps) barefoot ABCs of sprinting (12–15 run-throughs) I3 tempo runs (e.g., 80, 100, 120, 150, 180, 150, 120, 100, and 80m; rest intervals: 2, 3, 4, 5, 10, 6, 5, and 4 min)	Rest
Afternoon	Warm-up jogging (6 min) Acceleration runs/standing starts (5–6 reps) Flying sprints (2 x 30m with individual run-up length; rest intervals: 10 min) Practising the hurdling technique (specific warm-up, 3x up to the 1st hurdle, 8x up to the 2nd–6th hurdle) distance: reduced by 3 foot lengths High-knee run	Tuck jumps (5 x 2 run-throughs over 10 hurdles each) Bounding runs and/or rhythm jumps (2 x 3 x 40m; rest intervals between sets: 4 min) high intensity Game (30 min) e.g., basketball or soccer	Warm-up jogging (6 min) Mobilisation (10 minutes) specific to hurdles Hurdle preparation (10 min) I2 tempo runs (5 x 100/110m up to and over the 11th hurdle) distance: reduced by 2–3 foot lengths Contract-relax stretching (15 min) Warm-down jogging Standing starts (3 x 30m)	Continuous run (30 min) Contract-relax stretching (15 min) Strength training (35 min) trunk exercises on apparatus, or with medicine ball, or gymnastics plus (35 min) arms, possibly also boxing Frequency coordination (10 min)	LI runs (6 x 80m, rest intervals: 20 sec) Pop-up jumps using a 1- or 3-stride rhythm and bounding runs (2 x 3 run-throughs each) Maximal-eccentric strength training (30 min) hamstrings, adductors, belly punches with tense abdominals, lunges, etc. Alternating-pace sprints (4 x 60m)	Acceleration runs (3 reps) barefoot ABCs of sprinting (12–15 run-throughs) Contract-relax stretching (15 min) specific to hurdles Warm-down jogging (10 diagonals on the lawn) Rhythm or frequency coordination (10 min)	

Table 13: High-performance training: sample microcycle in the fourth mesocycle.

Monday	Tuesday	Wednesday	Thursday	Friday	Saturday	Sunday
Warm-up jogging (6 min)	**LI runs** (8 x 80m, rest intervals: 20 sec) as warm-up	**Warm-up jogging** (6 min)	Rest	**Warm-up jogging** (6 min)	Rest	*Preparatory competition* • Warm-up jogging or LI runs • Inciting (trunk and foot) • 2 acceleration runs • ABCs of sprinting/hurdling • 5-stride rhythm over hurdles • 2 standing starts • 5–6 runs out of the block up to the 1st-3rd hurdle
Maximal-eccentric strength training (15 min) trunk stabilisation, lifting opposite upper and lower limbs while in prone position, belly punches with tense abdominals, raising the foot/toes	**ABCs of jumping** (8–10 run-throughs)	**ABCs of sprinting** (8–10 run-throughs)		**Belly punches with tense abdominals** (4 x 5 sec)		**100m/110m hurdles heat** Short re-warm-up
Acceleration runs (3 reps)	**Practising the hurdling technique** (45 min) after specific warm-up: from the starting block over 1–6 hurdles as in competition, distance: reduced by 1 foot length	**Depth jumps** or **tuck jumps** (approx. 20 jumps)		**Strength training at high intensity** (15 min) snatch		**100m/110m hurdles final** Short re-warm-up
Strength training at high intensity (45 min) clean and quarter split squat, bench press, lat pull, and double arm swing with dumbbells	**Rhythm jumps** (4 x 30m) maximum intensity	**Acceleration runs** (3 reps)		**Acceleration runs** (2 reps)		**200m best-time final**
Alternating-pace sprints (4 x 60m)		**Flying sprints** (3 x 20m with individual run-up length; rest intervals: 10 min) through light barriers		**Practising the hurdling technique** (35 min) after specific warm-up: only few hurdles and runs at maximum intensity		
		LI tempo run (150m) maximal				

In the competition phase, the training plan must be adapted to the (irregular) competition calendar. In this plan, it can be assumed that the athlete took part in a preparatory competition with two 100m races on the previous Sunday. If there are no other competitions for one and a half weeks (or more) between two preparatory competitions, the athlete should perform more training, and his/her training should be of a more basic nature. Before the main competition, the athlete should not take part in any competition for two weeks and should train even less than shown here.

1.8.12 BIBLIOGRAPHY

Bauersfeld, K.-H. & Schröter, G. (mit Lohmann, W., Löffler, H.-P., Scholich, M., Lenz, G., Losch, M. & Fritzsch, W.). (1998). *Grundlagen der Leichtathletik* (5., überarb. Aufl.). Berlin: Sportverlag.

Coh, M. (2003). Biomechanical analysis of Colin Jackson's hurdle clearance technique. *New Studies in Athletics 18* (1), 37-45.

Čoh, M. & Dolenec, A. (1996). Three-dimensional kinematic analysis of the hurdles technique used by Brigita Bukovec. *New Studies in Athletics 11* (1), 63-69.

Ellrott, *J. & Harksen R. (2002).* Die richtige Technik im Kurzhürdensprint. *Leichtathletiktraining 13* (12), 18-23.

Graubner, R., Buckwitz, R., Landmann, M. & Starke, A. (2009). Final Report Hurdles Men. In Deutscher Leichtathletikverband (Hrsg.), *Biomechanical Analysis of selected events at the 12th IAAF World Championships in Athletics, Berlin 15-23 August 2009.* Zugriff am 20.04.2010 unter http://www.iaaf.org/mm/Document/Development/Research/05/64/44/20100415081724_httppostedfile_2-BiomechanicsReportWCBerlin2009_Hurdles_Men_19921.pdf

Hommel, H. & Koszewski, D. (1999). 110 and 100m Hurdles. In G.-P. Brüggemann, D. Koszewski & H. Müller (Hrsg.), *Biomechanical Research Project Athens 1997: Final Report.* Oxford: Meyer & Meyer.

Iskra, J. (1995). The most effective technical training for the 110 metres hurdles. *New Studies in Athletics 10* (3), 51-55

Jonath, U., Krempel, R., Haag, E. & Müller, H. (1995). *Leichtathletik 1: Laufen.* Reinbek bei Hamburg: Rowohlt Taschenbuch.

Mann, R. (1996). Rules-related limiting factors in hurdling. *Track Coach 136*, 4335-4337.

Mann, R. (2000). Biomechanische Grundlagen des Hürdensprints. *Leichtathletiktraining 11* (5), 25-30.

Regelkommissionen des DLV, FLA, ÖLV und SLV (Hrsg.). (2010). *Internationale Wettkampfregeln.* Waldfischbach: Hornberger.

Schmolinski, G. (Red.). (1980). *Leichtathletik.* Berlin: Sportverlag.

Schwirtz, A., Groß, V., Baumann, W. & Kollath, E. (1986). Biomechanik des Hürdenlaufs. In R. Ballreich & A. Kuhlow, *Biomechanik der Leichtathletik* (Biomechanik der Sportarten, 1, S. 16-17). Stuttgart: Ferdinand Enke.

Seagrave, L. (2008). *Race Model Sprints & Hurdles* (Power-Point-Präsentation: Coaches Education and Certification System: Level IV: Sprints and Hurdles). Monaco: International Association of Athletics Federations (IAAF).

Stein, N. (2000). Reflections on a change in the height of the hurdles in the women's sprint hurdles event. *New Studies in Athletics 15* (2), 15-19.

Tepper, E. & Czingon, H. (Red.) (mit Keydel, H.). (1995). *Rahmentrainingsplan für das Aufbautraining Sprint* (4. Aufl.) (Edition Leichtathletik, 2). Aachen: Meyer und Meyer.

Willimczik, K. (1972). *Leistungsbestimmende Bewegungsmerkmale der 110-m-Hürdentechnik*: Ein Beitrag zur Bewegungslehre und Trainingslehre der Leibesübungen (Sportwissenschaftliche Arbeiten, 6). Berlin: Bartels & Wernitz.

1.9 400M HURDLES

1.9.1 FROM A NOBODY TO AN OLYMPIC CHAMPION IN ONE SEASON

Even in the mid-19th century when the first obstacle races over long distances such as the 440 yards (about 402 m) were held, hurdles were often three feet/one yard (= 91.4cm) high. At the Olympic Games in 1968, the German Gerhard Hennige came up short of the then world record of 48.8 seconds in the intermediate heat by 0.3 sec. Clearly in the lead, he jogged the last 40m to the finish line in 5.6 sec. In the final race, he ran the same distance in 5.0 sec and realised that he had given away a world record. However, the British hurdler Dave Hemery set a new world record of 48.1 sec in the final race and was significantly faster than Hennige.

In 1972, John Aki Bua from Uganda was the first runner of African descent to win the 400m hurdle race at the Olympic Games. Subsequently, the American Edwin Moses dominated the long hurdle distance for more than a decade. In 1975, he made his first attempt over the 400m hurdles in 52.0 sec. In 1976 he won the Olympic final in the world-record time of 47.63 sec. Experts were puzzled about how an athlete could ascend from a nobody to a world-record holder in only one season. One contributing factor was that he covered the entire hurdle distance in a 13-stride rhythm with his long legs. For a very long time, Moses' last world record (47.02 sec, 1983)

was only surpassed by Kevin Young (USA, 46.78 sec, 1992). Moses achieved an incredible series of 122 consecutive wins and was beaten only four times in his career. Once he was defeated by his biggest adversary at that time, the German Harald Schmid. Schmid achieved his greatest triumph at the European Cup in Turin in 1979 when he set a new European record over 400m hurdles in 47.85 sec and won the 400m flat in 45.31 sec. He opted for both distances, which he ran within 55 minutes when only a few days before he had run a 600m training run in an unofficial world record of 1:14.0 min. Schmid's secret to success: fast tempo toughness due to diligent training.

After Norway's Karsten Warholm had already run a world record a month earlier, no fewer than three athletes remained under Young's world record in the Tokyo 2021 Olympic final. At the top, Warholm broke the 46-sec barrier and ran 45.94 sec. Something similar happened in the women's final. After the US athlete Sydney McLaughlin had become the first woman to stay under the 52-sec mark just over a month before the Games, she ran another world record in Tokyo with 51.46 sec. Only one year later, at the World Championships in Eugene, she even stayed below 51 sec and ran 50.68 sec.

1.9.2 THE MOST IMPORTANT COMPETITION RULES

The technique and strategies of the long hurdle sprint are primarily determined by the framework conditions presented in table 1. Otherwise, the general competition rules for running, sprinting, and the short hurdle sprint apply (see chapter II–1.1.1, II–1.2.1 and II–1.8.2).

Table 1: **Overview of the general requirements for the long hurdle sprint for the various age groups in the German Athletics Association (DLV).**

Age group		Distance	Number of hurdles	Height of hurdle	Distance from start line to first hurdle	Distance between hurdles	Distance from last hurdle to finish line
Men, Juniors, Male U20,	M40–45	400m	10	91.47cm	45.00m	35.00m	40.00m
Male U18,	M50–55	400m	10	84.0cm	45.00m	35.00m	40.00m
Women, Female Juniors, Female U20 and U18,	W40–45	400m	10	76.2cm	45.00m	35.00m	40.00m
Male U16		300m	7	84.0cm	50.00m	35.00m	40.00m
Female U16,	W50–55, M60–65	300m	7	76.2cm	50.00m	35.00m	40.00m
	W60 and older, M70 and older	300m	7	68.6cm	50.00m	35.00m	40.00m

1.9.3 SPORT-SCIENCE FINDINGS, PHASE STRUCTURE, AND TECHNIQUE

The phase structure and a presentation of technique are based on the description of the short hurdles (see chapter II–1.8.3). The special features of the crouch start in the curve are discussed in chapter II–1.4.3.

PHASE 1: CROUCH START
Like the short hurdles, the 400m hurdles is not a free, but rather a constrained sprint in which the running rhythm, especially the stride length, is adapted to the hurdler's distance to each subsequent hurdle. If

the number of strides to the first hurdle is even, the push-off or trail leg is in the front starting block, whereas the swing leg is in the front block if the number of strides is odd. Most hurdle sprinters attempt to sprint over the first hurdle using either their usual (or better) side (which they also use in the short hurdles) or specifically with the right leg as their push-off leg. (The long-hurdle-specific advantages of a push-off from the right leg are explained in phase 3.) This may require changing the start leg (front leg) in the starting block, such as in the short hurdles. However, if a hurdler is not able to cope at all with a starting position which differs from that used in the flat sprint, there are still alternatives to changing the starting position in the long hurdles (which is not the case in the short hurdles). For example, the run-up to the first hurdle with one stride more or less than usual can be equally fast and economic. When looking at the total distance of the race, runners who perform an even number of strides between the hurdles (14-stride or 16-stride rhythm; see phase 4) and thus change the push-off, swing, and trail leg at each hurdle may just as well or should even start with the unpopular swing and trail leg at the first hurdle.

PHASE 2: ACCELERATION TO THE FIRST HURDLE

Figure 1 shows that at the Olympic Games in 2000, half of the men evaluated ran to the first hurdle with 21 strides; fewer athletes (n = 22) ran to the first hurdle with 22 strides; only very few athletes (n = 7) ran with 20 strides. The former world-record holder and double Olympic gold medallist Edwin Moses even sprinted to the first hurdle with only 19 strides. World-class women run to the first hurdle with 22–24 strides. However, in groups with very heterogeneous performances the number of strides decreases during both the run to the first hurdle and between the hurdles depending on the final times. This means that faster sprinters make longer strides. However, in groups with homogeneous performance, these findings are impossible to prove since they greatly

depend on individual running technique and anthropometric characteristics such as body height and leg length. For example, in the Olympic final in Sydney in 2000, most sprinters (n = 4) even ran to the first hurdle with 22 strides; including the winner, three ran with 21 strides, and one hurdler even ran with only 20 strides.

When choosing the number of strides to the first hurdle (see also phase 1), athletes should make sure that their running rhythm and sprint technique are designed similar to the flat sprint, so that only minimal changes in stride length and stride frequency must be made to reach the optimum distance for the push-off in front of the first hurdle. If minimal changes are necessary, the adaptation must be distributed throughout the entire 45m run-up to the first hurdle. A shortening or lengthening of the final strides before the hurdle must be absolutely avoided since in both cases the result would be a reduction of running velocity, mainly through increased braking forces during the front support. On competition day, the wind must also be observed before the race. Headwind may require a little more emphasis on the push-off, whereas in the case of a tailwind the emphasis should be on stride frequency.

Figure 1 shows that 400m hurdlers (both male and female) achieve the highest average velocity between the first two hurdles. The average velocity from the start to the first hurdle is generally lower than between the first and the second hurdle due to acceleration from zero speed. Nevertheless, long hurdlers probably reach their maximum velocity even before the first hurdle. Since the long distances between the hurdles disturb sprinting between the hurdles less, *the peak velocity in the long hurdles is well above that in the short hurdles* (see figure 2 in chapter II–1.8.3). Women reach up to 8.5 m/sec, men up to 9.5 m/sec.

PHASE 3: HURDLE STRIDE

In general, the long-hurdle stride is similar to the short-hurdle stride, especially for women. The hurdle stride varies much more during the race than in the short hurdles since the velocity in the 400m hurdles decreases more clearly during the race than in the short hurdles, and since toward the end of the race athletes struggle with high acidification and are therefore frequently even forced to change their stride rhythm between the hurdles. Claims about biomechanical standard values, such as the length of the hurdle stride, are therefore difficult to make and have not often been investigated. The fact that the speed of approaching the hurdles is higher at least at the beginning of the race speaks in favour of a longer hurdle stride, whereas the lower hurdle height speaks in favour of a shorter hurdle stride. In any case, the correct distance of about 2m from the hurdle, which depends on the quality of the run-up to the first hurdle

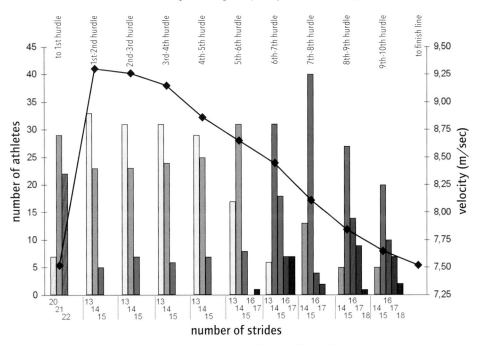

Figure 1: *Number of strides used in the run-up to the first hurdle and in the segments between the hurdles* for all participants in the 2000 Olympics in Sydney, and the *average velocities in the relevant segments* as mean value of the eight finalists (according to data by Ditroilo & Marini, 2001, pp. 23 and 29): different total number of athletes in the various inter-hurdle segments may be explained by the dropout rate of runners and the limited camera angle for the TV footage.

and the inter-hurdle sprint, is crucial for the fastest possible hurdle clearance. In general, one often has the impression that long hurdlers jump too high over their low hurdles and perhaps thereby lose too much horizontal speed (since upon each take-off horizontal velocity is converted to vertical velocity). However, hurdle sprinters require a certain amount of time to move their legs in the air when performing the hurdle stride, and the flight duration is determined solely by the flight height. Moreover, the relatively high run over the hurdle enables them to perform the hurdle stride in a less extreme manner. They must raise their swing and trail leg, extend their swing-leg knee, and lean forward with their upper body less and therefore are able to save energy (see chapter II–1.1.2).

THE HURDLE STRIDE IN THE CURVE

A specific requirement in the 400m hurdles is sprinting over the hurdles in the curve. Here, it is advantageous to use the right leg for the push-off and trail leg, and the left leg as the swing leg. Thus, an athlete with a normal inward lean may choose the shortest path on the inside of his/her lane. During the longer flight phase, long hurdlers are driven more to the outside by centrifugal forces than would be the case with a normal sprint stride. This can be better counteracted by pushing off with the right leg toward the inside of the curve rather than by pushing off with the left leg. Due to the inward lean, the trail leg on the outside has to be raised less. If, on the contrary, the left leg is the trail leg and thus on the inside, it must be raised more in the event of a normal inward lean. If the 400m hurdler sprints far to the inside in the curve, he/she also runs the risk of drawing the foot of the trail leg inside, alongside and below the upper edge of the hurdle bar and consequently being disqualified. In order to solve these problems and not to be forced to jump higher over the hurdle, it is recommended to cut the hurdle tangentially if the right leg is the swing leg in the curve. This means that the sprinter should leave the favoured inside path in his lane. Four or five strides before the hurdle he/she should be in the middle of the lane, then he/she should run from there straight to the inside to be able to sprint over the hurdle, as on the straight, with no or at least less inward lean. An advantage of the left push-off and trail leg, however, is that the rotational momentum about the longitudinal axis of the body initiated by the trail leg, which is pulled laterally forward, is smaller. The sprinter must counteract the longer path of the right trail leg around the outside in the curve by means of the even more noticeable movement of his/her right arm toward the foot of the swing leg and the subsequent swing of the same arm far backward around the outside of the acutely angled trail leg.

TECHNIQUE INDEX

As in the short hurdles, the quotient of the 400m and 400m hurdle time can be used as an index of the quality of the technique in general (i.e., not only of the technique for the hurdle stride). If the technique index is established on the basis of respective world records, one arrives at a value of 0.94 for both men and women.

Analysing the best performances of recent years also leads to similar values for men and women. The fact that the technique index is higher for the long hurdles than for the short hurdles shows that the same number of lower hurdles on the 400m course does not inhibit sprinters as much as in the short hurdles. Both women and men achieve good technique indexes in the long hurdles with running-time differences of 2.5–4 sec.

PHASE 4: INTER-HURDLE SPRINT

As in the run-up to the first hurdle, the inter-hurdle sprint must be adapted to the distances between the hurdles. Figure 1 shows that the majority (n = 33) of world-class male hurdle sprinters start the race with a 13-stride rhythm (i.e., with 13 strides between the hurdles) and maintain this rhythm up to the fifth or sixth hurdle; six of the sprinters even continue this stride to the seventh hurdle. In the past, top 400m hurdle sprinters such as Edwin Moses or Harald Schmid managed to maintain the 13-stride rhythm even up to the tenth hurdle. However, at the 2000 Olympic Games, a considerable number of sprinters (n = 23) began their races with a 14-stride rhythm, which requires a change of the swing and trail-leg at each hurdle. These sprinters seemed to be able to maintain this rhythm 1–2 hurdles longer than those who started with a 13-stride rhythm. In the inter-hurdle sprint to the eighth hurdle, most sprinters (n = 40 of 59) then changed to a 15-stride rhythm. Even in the last two inter-hurdle sprints, the 15-stride rhythm was still most commonly used. In these inter-hurdle segments, considerably more

sprinters than in the previous segments even required 16 or 17 strides.

The most common rhythm for women is the 15-stride rhythm, with which most women also start their races. Only a few tall world-class female athletes start their races with a 14-stride rhythm. Toward the end of the race, the women switch to the 16- or 17-stride rhythm more often than men.

The stride rhythm determines the technique in the inter-hurdle sprint and should be planned strategically (see chapter II–1.9.6). As during the run-up to the first hurdle, stride length and stride frequency should correspond as much as possible to the flat sprint at any time of the race. If one assumes that the economic technique of grasping/pulling sprinting was sufficiently developed in and for the flat sprint, a similar stride pattern should also be the most economic technique in the long hurdles. Table 6 provides an overview of which rhythm corresponds to which stride length. The potential (average) stride lengths in the long-hurdle sprint are thus graded, whereas the stride lengths in the flat sprint change (or can be changed) on a continuum. This shows that the hurdle sprint is a constrained run and points to the necessary adjustments of the sprint technique during the race. If, for example, a sprinter maintains the 14-stride rhythm up to the seventh hurdle, he/she will most likely deliberately use short strides during the first inter-hurdle segments and (due to his/her reduced velocity) will try to make his/her strides a little longer during the last inter-hurdle segments covered with

14 strides. As in front of the first hurdle, these adjustments should be distributed evenly among all inter-hurdle strides and should not lead to shortening or lengthening one's strides in front of the hurdle. The demand for a sprint technique which is as similar as possible to the flat sprint also includes the requirement that the number of strides between the hurdles should always be increased by only one stride (if possible) in the event of a rhythm change. Nevertheless, the first inter-hurdle segment which is covered with more strides—typical of the sixth or seventh inter-hurdle segment—is usually much slower disproportionally than the previous ones. For example, this is confirmed by the sharp drop in the average speed in the segment between the seventh and eighth hurdle shown in figure 1. In this inter-hurdle segment, five of the eight finalists at the 2000 Olympics switched to a higher rhythm. However, from an economic point of view, this reduction of velocity should not necessarily be judged negatively. This means that in individual cases it is not absolutely certain that the lower rhythm should be maintained longer at any cost in the next race. Maintaining the lower rhythm may require so much energy that exactly this causes the subsequent velocity drop or has dire consequences at the end of the race. Psychological reasons may also be decisive for the drop in speed. Whereas before the change of rhythm the long hurdler was forced to exert himself/herself more and make his/her steps longer to reach the next hurdle, the athlete now knows that he/she will easily get to the next hurdle. This relaxation can be extremely

useful from the perspective of economy. However, if it results in excessive speed reduction, special exercises to practise the rhythm change must be used in training.

Similar to the short hurdles, the first and last step of the inter-hurdle sprint are usually slightly shorter than the values presented in table 6. This is true even though long hurdlers try to move the trail leg as far forward as possible to achieve a long first stride instead of making a stride as short as possible like short hurdlers.

PHASE 5: RUN TOWARD THE FINISH LINE
The average velocity during the 40m free sprint to the finish line is generally lower than the average speed during the last inter-hurdle segment. While a few athletes, such as A. Taylor, winner of the 2000 Olympic Games, are able to mobilise their last reserves despite acidification and to achieve an even higher average speed than during the last inter-hurdle segment, other athletes use all their strength to maintain the rhythm up to the last hurdle. Overall, the reduction in speed in the 400m hurdles final in the 2000 Olympics is slightly lower than for world-class 400m flat sprinters as is shown in figure 2 in chapter II-1.2.2. The average velocity over the last 40m segment of the race is 7.52 m/sec. This is 80.9% of the fastest inter-hurdle segment with approximately 9.30 m/sec. In comparison, the average speed of the male and female finalists at the 1997 and 1999 World Championships over the last 50m segment of the 400m flat race is 78% of the average speed over the second 50m segment. However,

it would surely be too simple to deduce from this that flat sprinters start too fast and hurdle sprinters too slowly.

For suggestions on the technique of attacking the finish line and subsequent deceleration see chapter II–1.5.3.

Table 2: **Requirement profile for the 400m hurdles:** *The suggested rough estimate of the value of selected factors determining performance is based on the importance for the overall performance and the percentage of time spent training (IR: information requirements, constr.: constraints; see chapter I–1.1).*

Factors determining 400m hurdle performance	Estimate of value	Notes
Coordination	+ + +	optical IR: high, acoustic IR: medium, then low, tactile IR: low-medium, kinaesthetic IR: high, vestibular IR: medium; precision constr.: high, time constr.: medium-high, complexity constr.: medium, situation constr.: low-medium, physical stress constr.: high
Flexibility	+ + (+)	While the men's long hurdle sprint requires some specific flexibility, this hardly applies to the women's long hurdle sprint
Strength		extensor loop (glutes, quadriceps, triceps surae, erector spinae), iliopsoas, hamstrings; special importance of the adductors and abductors of the trail leg as well as the abdominal muscles; shoulder and upper-arm muscles
Maximal strength	+ + +	during start acceleration and as a basis
Reactive strength	+ + + +	within various stretch-shortening cycles
Speed	+ + + +	mainly cyclic; acyclic aspects at the start, during hurdle clearance and when attacking the finish line; reaction speed at the start (can be decisive for winning the race; however, relatively insignificant in terms of percentage; hardly improvable through training)
Endurance (general dynamic) Anaerobic endurance		
Strength endurance	+ + + +	as a basis of speed endurance and specific for hurdle clearance
Speed endurance	+ + + + +	long maintenance of maximal velocity and only slight and slow velocity loss afterwards
Aerobic endurance	+ + + +	for energy supply during the run and as a basis of training
Psychological and cognitive abilities	+ + + + +	feel for pace and rhythm and correct strategy (initial pace and choice of the respective correct number of inter-hurdle strides); ability to deliberately achieve low pH values (lactate acidosis) and to tolerate them; performance-oriented thinking and behaviour (see chapter I–3.1.1)
Anthropometric and primarily genetically determined characteristics	+ + + +	high proportion of the fastest muscle fibres; connective tissue with optimal energy-storing capacities; medium (with men possibly above-average) body height; low percentage of body fat

1.9.4 SUMMARY OF THE MOST IMPORTANT TECHNICAL CHARACTERISTICS = TECHNIQUE-ANALYSIS SHEET

CROUCH START

- See chapter II–1.5.4.
- If the number of strides to the first hurdle is even, the push-off (trail leg) is in the front starting block; if the number of strides is odd, the swing leg is in the front block.

RUN-UP TO THE FIRST HURDLE

- See chapter II–1.5.4.
- Men: 19–22 strides to the first hurdle, usually 21 or 22; women: 22–24 strides to the first hurdle, usually 22 or 23.
- The stride frequency and stride length should be as similar to the 400m flat sprint as possible.
- The last stride is slightly shortened.
- The hurdle is attacked from a high running position (high hips) and with upright upper body.
- If the push-off in front of the hurdle is performed with the right leg, then the hurdle is cut: When approaching the hurdle, the sprinter should run in the middle of the lane, then he/she runs from there straight to the inside and clears the hurdle without or with only little inward lean.

HURDLE STRIDE

PUSH-OFF

- In the curve, using the right leg as the push-off and trail leg is beneficial.
- The point of push-off is far in front of the hurdle (approximately 60% of the hurdle stride in front of the hurdle).
- The foot touchdown is close to the vertical projection of the CG (short front support => little bracing).

- The ground contact is performed only with the ball of the foot (high push-off height).
- Result: flat push-off (no take-off).
- Noticeable push-off into the hurdle with extension of the foot, knee, and hip of the push-off leg.
- The swing leg is raised up to the horizontal, straight in the running direction (or with a slight inward sickle).
- At the moment of the last ground contact, the knee of the swing leg is still acutely angled.
- Beginning forward lean of the upper body at the end of the push-off.

FLIGHT

- Further raising and extension of the swing leg and lowering of the trunk (the forward lean of the upper body and extension of the swing-leg knee is less than in the short hurdle sprint).
- The arm on the trail-leg side is extended in the direction of the swing-leg foot, while the other arm is kept at the side of the body.
- Due to the hip flexion and abduction, the knee of the trail leg is moved outward and upward (less abduction than in the short hurdle sprint).
- The downward movement of the swing leg and the straightening of the trunk (hip extension) begin reactively immediately after the swing-leg foot has cleared the hurdle.
- Simultaneously, the athlete directs his/her view to the next hurdle.
- Simultaneously, the back swing of the (so-called) counter-arm is started on an outer circle around the trail leg.
- The lower trail leg is nearly horizontal during hurdle clearance although the knee is still higher than the foot.
- The foot of the trail leg is pronated during hurdle clearance.
- The forward swing of the arm on the side of the swing leg is started.
- Throughout the hurdle stride, the shoulder and pelvis axis are kept in a position as frontal as possible.
- The upward straightening of the trunk and the downward and backward movement of the swing leg lead to the grasping touchdown of the foot.
- The trail leg is moved forward and inward in the direction of the high-knee running position to perform a long first stride, while the counter-arm is moved backward and inward.

LANDING

- The touchdown of the (nearly) straight leg is performed on the ball of the foot; during the entire ground contact, the heel does not touch the ground.
- At touchdown, the CG is approximately vertical above the tip of the foot.
- The rapid extension of the hip joint results in a further straightening of the upper body.
- At the end of the first ground contact behind the hurdle, the thigh of the trail leg points nearly horizontally in the running direction; the knee joint is slightly opened again (approx. 90°).

INTER-HURDLE SPRINT

- The first and last strides are shorter than the other inter-hurdle strides.
- Men: mostly 13–15 strides between the hurdles (most often 14-stride rhythm); women: 14–17 strides (most often 15-stride rhythm).
- Throughout the race, the stride frequency and stride length are as similar to the 400m flat sprint as possible; in most cases, this requires a change of rhythm.
- If in the curve the push-off in front of the hurdle is performed with the right leg, then the hurdle is cut: When approaching the hurdle, the sprinter runs in the middle of the lane, then he/she runs from there straight to the inside and clears the hurdle without or with only little inward lean.

RUN TOWARD THE FINISH LINE, ATTACKING THE FINISH LINE, AND SUBSEQUENT DECELERATION

- Free sprint toward the finish line while mobilising all reserves.
- As close to the finish line as possible, the sprinter shifts his/her chest forward relative to his/her arms, head, and legs; in addition, the CG is shifted a little forward relative to the point of foot touchdown.
- After crossing the finish line, the hurdle sprinter maintains his/her tension and shifts his/her trunk and CG backward to decelerate without running the risk of injury.

1.9.5 PHOTO SEQUENCE

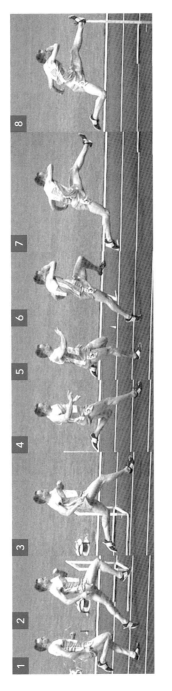
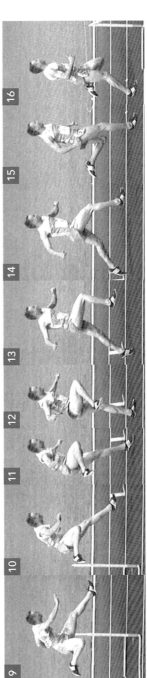

Data about the photo sequence

Athlete:	Louis Jacob van Zyl (born: 20 July 1985, South Africa)
Height/weight:	1.86 m/75 kg
Performance:	49.48 sec (15 August 2009, Berlin)
Best performance:	47.66 (25 February 2011, Pretoria)
Greatest success:	2nd in the 2009 world-ranking list, 3rd place at the 2011 World Championships

COMMENTARY

When van Zyl travelled to the 2009 World Championships in Berlin, he led the world-ranking list as the top favourite with a time of 47.94 sec. However, he failed in the semi-finals in which he placed sixth with a time of 48.80 sec. Nevertheless, in the 2009 world ranking list van Zyl was only outranked by Kerron Clement (USA), who won the final in Berlin in 47.91 sec.

The video recordings of the semi-final show that van Zyl started with the right (push-off) leg in the front starting block, covered the distance to the first hurdle with 22 strides, and thereby cleared this hurdle with his left leg as the swing leg. Then he covered five inter-hurdle segments using a 14-stride rhythm before he changed to a 15-stride rhythm (right swing leg). The change in rhythm is associated with a great decrease in inter-hurdle time (see table 3). Van Zyl lost the crucial tenths of a second to the future medallists on the back straight and in the second curve. In the first curve and down the finishing straight, he ran at the same speed or even faster. Except for a slightly braced touchdown after the last hurdle (perhaps the distance in front of the hurdle was a bit too long),

no major stride adjustments in front of the hurdles or problems with hurdle clearances can be witnessed.

The photo sequence shows van Zyl at the 5th hurdle of his heat in Berlin, which he finished in second place in 49.48 sec. He attacks the hurdle from a good upright running position with high hips (pictures 1–4). The push-off occurs far in front of the hurdle (well over 2m), so that he is able to perform a very active push-off forward into the hurdle (picture 6). His swing-leg action is characterised by a very high position of the heel (picture 5) and a negligible outward sickle (picture 6), a thigh position slightly above the horizontal (picture 7), and finally nearly full extension (picture 8). Zyl moves his right arm to the front of his body using an abnormally flexed position of his elbow and a too high lateral lift (picture 7). From the aggressive push-off extension, the trail leg movement to the front is slightly delayed (pictures 7 and 8). When clearing the hurdle, the trail leg is at an acute angle and spread to the side over the hurdle (pictures 9 and 10). The hurdle clearance appears to be perfectly flat. There is only a slight lowering of the upper body, which is typical for the long hurdles (picture 8). After his foot has cleared the hurdle, a downward grasping movement of the extended swing leg and a straightening up of the upper body can be seen. While the swing leg is being placed on the ground only slightly in front of the CG, the trail leg is moved to the front of the body using a high knee position (pictures 11–13). Zyl swings his right arm horizontally backward. As a result of the push-off far in front of the hurdle, the landing occurs close behind the hurdle. Both the push-off in front of the hurdle and the landing behind the hurdle are performed on the entire sole of the foot. Due to the movement of his right arm close to his body in front of the hurdle, Zyl is then forced to move this arm and his right shoulder a little too far to the rear (picture 14). However, the shoulder-hip separation seems to be just tolerable since he is able to quickly resume inter-hurdle sprinting.

Table 3: **Split times and inter-hurdle times** (in sec) of Louis Jacob van Zyl's semi-final at the 2009 World Championships in Berlin (Graubner et al., 2009, p. 7).

Reaction	1st hurdle	2nd hurdle	3rd hurdle	4th hurdle	5th hurdle	6th hurdle	7th hurdle	8th hurdle	9th hurdle	10th hurdle	Finish
0.168	5.96	9.70	13.46	17.34	21.36	25.54	29.92	34.30	38.70	43.34	**48.80**
		(3.74)	(3.76)	(3.88)	(4.02)	(4.18)	(4.38)	(4.38)	(4.40)	(4.64)	(5.46)

1.9.6 STRATEGY

As in the 400m flat, a simple method for estimating race strategy is possible on the basis of the 200m split time. On the one hand, this time is compared with the 200m flat sprint time, and on the other hand with the time for the second half of the course. The difference between the personal 200m best time and the 200m split time is likely to be greater in the long hurdles than the time of 0.5 to a maximum of 2.0 sec in the 400m flat sprint (see chapter II–1.5.6). The average value here can be assumed to be 2.0 sec. Table 4 illustrates the differences between the times for the first and second 200m of the race.

Thus, the following example calculation can be made: A 400m hurdler with a personal best time of 46.00 sec for the 400m flat and a corresponding personal best over 200m of 21.00 sec should run the first 200m in the 400m hurdles in 23.0 sec. If he runs the second 200m 3 sec slower, he will reach an end time of 49 sec. The time difference of 3 sec between the flat and the hurdle sprint results in quite a good technique index (see chapter II–1.9.3). The values for a similarly good female runner are:

Table 4: **Final times and differences between the second and first 200m** in the men's 400m hurdle sprint in the semi-final and final at the 2000 Olympics in Sydney (based on data provided by Ditroilo & Marini, 2001, pp. 21–23). In some finals in the past, there were considerably less differences between the two halves of the race (e.g., in Rome in 1987: women: 1.72 sec; men: 2.05 sec).

	Semi-final (n = 22; sec)	Final (n = 8; sec)
Final times Average	48.14–50.52 49.04	47.50–49.01 48.18
2nd minus 1st 200 m Average	1.56–4.53 3.02	1.85–3.10 2.56

400m best time:	52.0 sec.
200m best time:	24.0 sec.
1st 200m in 400m hurdles:	26.0 sec.
2nd 200m in 400m hurdles:	29.0 sec.
400m hurdle time:	55.0 sec.

Two indications show that even with world-class athletes strategy can vary greatly and that therefore a significantly more economic race distribution is possible at least with some sprinters. In the 2000 Olympics, a comparison of the ranking after the fifth hurdle with the placement at the finish showed that the correlation coefficient was only approximately 0.5; this means that the two rankings correspond only approximately 25%. At the 1987 World Championships, it was discovered that Busch, the female world champion, ran the same time over the final 40m segment to the finish as the male world champion Moses.

This requires more detailed analysis which is relatively easy in the long hurdles and sufficiently accurate at the same time. Since the course is divided into equal intervals by the hurdles, the velocity profile can usually be established on the basis of the foot touchdowns after the hurdles by simple manual time measurement or (even better) by using the time code of a conventional camcorder (see T1). Respective guiding values are included in table 5.

The guiding values presented depend largely on the stride rhythm between the hurdles. Many considerations regarding the stride rhythm have already been mentioned in connection with technique. Technique and stride rhythm should be varied according to a plan of strategy. In this plan, for each inter-hurdle segment the rhythm should be chosen which ensures the optimum ratio of economy and speed.

Table 5: **Typical split and inter-hurdle times** (in sec) with a given final time in the 400m hurdle sprint (modified on the basis of Tepper & Czingon, 1995, p. 47).

	Men				Women			
1st H.	5.97	6.10	6.15	6.23	6.50	6.61	6.90	7.10
2nd H.	9.73 (3.8)	9.92 (3.8)	10.00 (3.9)	10.16 (3.9)	10.69 (4.2)	10.80 (4.2)	11.20 (4.3)	11.64 (4.5)
3rd H.	13.55 (3.8)	13.82 (3.9)	14.00 (4.0)	14.24 (4.1)	14.93 (4.2)	15.04 (4.2)	15.65 (4.5)	16.48 (4.8)
4th H.	17.45 (3.9)	17.80 (4.0)	18.10 (4.1)	18.50 (4.3)	19.25 (4.3)	19.37 (4.3)	20.30 (4.7)	21.50 (5.0)
5th H.	21.44 (4.0)	21.88 (4.1)	22.30 (4.2)	22.94 (4.4)	23.69 (4.4)	23.85 (4.5)	25.05 (4.8)	26.55 (5.1)
6th H.	25.54 (4.1)	26.06 (4.2)	26.60 (4.3)	27.52 (4.6)	28.25 (4.6)	28.46 (4.6)	30.04 (5.0)	31.70 (5.2)
7th H.	29.77 (4.2)	30.37 (4.3)	31.00 (4.4)	32.31 (4.8)	32.93 (4.7)	33.23 (4.8)	35.10 (5.1)	37.05 (5.4)
8th H.	34.12 (4.4)	34.81 (4.4)	35.60 (4.6)	37.17 (4.9)	37.70 (4.8)	38.23 (5.0)	40.30 (5.2)	42.50 (5.5)
9th H.	38.62 (4.5)	39.40 (4.6)	40.44 (4.8)	42.13 (5.0)	42.64 (4.9)	43.36 (5.1)	45.60 (5.3)	48.10 (5.6)
10th H.	43.28 (4.7)	44.15 (4.8)	45.52 (5.1)	47.29 (5.2)	47.70 (5.1)	48.68 (5.3)	51.10 (5.5)	53.90 (5.8)
Finish	**48.50** (5.2)	**49.50** (5.4)	**51.00** (5.5)	**53.00** (5.7)	**53.20** (5.5)	**54.50** (5.8)	**57.50** (6.4)	**60.60** (6.7)

The question of "What is fast?" is much easier to answer than the question "What is economic?" For beginners, the question of with which swing leg the athlete achieves a better and more secure hurdle clearance is also a part of these considerations. For advanced athletes, however, the hurdle clearance with both legs should be fast and economic enough that considerations should focus mainly on the question of which stride rhythm in the inter-hurdle sprint most closely matches the running technique at this point in the 400m flat sprint. Rhythm training can be supported by loud counting (verbal accompaniment).

1.9.7 DIDACTICS: SUPERORDINATE LONG-TERM OBJECTIVES AND GENERAL METHODOLOGY

Like the flat long sprint, the long hurdle sprint is included in the competition programme beginning in the second year of the U16 in the form of the 300m distance. In terms of training, the long hurdle sprint is already prepared in children's athletics and in basic training through short hurdles, short sprints, and endurance training (see chapters II–1.3.7, II–1.8.7, and II–1.10.5). Highly lactacid loads are included for the first time in build-up training. From then on, the lactacid capacity is regularly and increasingly trained by means of appropriate tempo runs (see chapter II–1.5.7).

BILATERALITY AND HURDLES IN THE CURVE

The ability to sprint over hurdles equally well with both the left and right leg as swing legs is of particular importance for long hurdlers. This is perhaps even more important for athletes who in the short hurdle sprint choose the left leg as the push-off and trail leg and the right leg as the swing leg, since the hurdles placed in the curve can be cleared better when using the right leg as the push-off leg. Important contents of children's athletics and basic training in preparation for a possible long-sprint career are hurdle sprints in the curve, hurdle sprints with an odd number of strides between hurdles (3-, 5-, and 7-stride rhythms; no switch of the push-off leg), hurdle sprints with the weak side, and hurdle sprints with an even number of inter-hurdle strides (4-, 6-, and 8-stride; switch of the push-off leg). However, from the point of view of learning theory, the training of bilaterality is not only useful for the long hurdle sprint but also for the short hurdles since it is assumed that training the weaker side of one's body always leads to improvements on the strong side.

1.9.8 TRAINING CONTENTS: FORMS OF GAMES AND EXERCISES

In general, almost all contents of the 100m, the short-hurdle and the 400m training (see chapter II–1.3.8, II–1.5.8, and II–1.8.8) are also used in long-hurdle training. In addition, forms of aerobic endurance training (see chapter II–1.10.6) and the special training forms described below are used.

211  **Chase over hurdles**

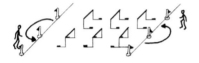

Possible objectives: Playful speed-endurance training over hurdles.

Execution: Two runners start at the same time at identical distance from each other on a circular course and try to catch up with each other.

Variation: In the form of a relay (e.g., six-day race, 172).

Typical load standards: Max. 1 min.

In addition to the hurdling technique exercises mentioned in chapter II–1.8.8, which for the long sprint are most often performed with the weaker side, with odd stride rhythms, and through the curve, the following exercises are added especially for the long hurdle sprint.

212 **Hurdle sprints with increasing rhythms**

Possible objectives: Becoming accustomed to longer distances between the hurdles.

Execution/variation: for example, 4-stride rhythm between the first and second hurdle, 6-stride rhythm before the third hurdle, 8-stride rhythm before the fourth hurdle, and 10-stride rhythm before the fifth hurdle; also with uneven rhythms (3-, 5-, 7-, and 9-stride rhythm); see table 6 for orientation.

Typical load standards: 3-6 reps per task.

213  **Hurdle sprints using arbitrary inter-hurdle distances**

Possible objectives: Earliest possible adjustment of the stride length for the remaining distance to the hurdle and correspondingly free choice of the push-off leg; speed endurance.

Execution/variation: During short tempo runs, the athlete sprints over hurdles placed at relatively long, but random distances.

Typical load standards: Change of set-up after 3 runs (also see 158–159).

Generally, long hurdlers perform the same (speed-)endurance training as 400m flat sprinters. If the tempo runs are performed over hurdles, an almost equal stress is achieved through the addition of 0.3 seconds per cleared hurdle to the values listed in the tempo tables (see table 8–10 in chapter II–1.5.8). In addition to the hurdle-Zs (207) already mentioned in connection with the short hurdle sprint, the following specific training forms may be used:

214 **LI tempo runs: Frinolli runs**

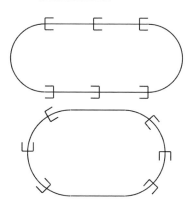

Possible objectives: Speed endurance specific to long hurdles.

Execution/variation: Circular runs on the lawn; distances between hurdles: 15–17m, reduced hurdle height.

Typical load standards: for example:
a) 4 sets of 6 reps for every 1 lap, walking interval: 45 sec, rest interval between sets: 5–8 min;
b) 3 sets of 4 reps for every 2 laps, walking interval: 90 sec, rest interval between sets: 5–8 min;
c) 2 sets of 4 reps for every 3 laps, walking interval: 2:30 min, rest interval between sets: 5–8 min; shorter programme for young athletes.

In order to practise the right stride rhythm, in the 3rd (or 7th), and 4th (or 8th) mesocycle, tempo runs over hurdles should only be performed at race pace. However, this is only possible over relatively short running distances with long rest intervals and/or few reps.

215 ▯▯▮ **(Tempo) runs at competition pace using shorter rhythms**

Possible objectives: Rhythm-specific stride-length training; speed endurance specific to long hurdles; hurdle technique.

Execution/variations: For the set-up of hurdles see table 6; as I2 or fast I3 under-distance tempo runs (158–159) up to 150m over hurdles using the 7- or 8- stride rhythm; also with change of distance and rhythm in one run to practise the change from even to uneven rhythm (or vice versa).

Typical load standards: Depending on the objective; not fewer than 4 hurdles (see tempo-run programme, 158–159).

216 ▯▯▮ **Runs using competition distances**

Possible objectives: Rhythm-specific stride-length training; speed endurance specific to long hurdles.

Execution/variations: From the starting block over hurdles placed as in competition, possibly with strategically planned rhythm variations.

Typical load standards: for example:

a) 2–4 runs up to the 8th hurdle, walking interval: 20–30 min;

b) 4–6 runs up to the 6th hurdle, walking interval: 10–15 min;

c) 6–9 runs up to the 4th hurdle, walking interval: 5–8 min

in the form of under-distance I3/I2 tempo runs (158–159).

217 ▯▯▮ **Flat distance plus hurdle distance**

Possible objectives: Speed endurance specific to long hurdles.

Execution/variations:

a) 400m from the start; however, only the 3rd

to 10th, 4th to 10th, or 5th to 10th hurdles are placed on the track, plus an 11th hurdle 5m before the finish.

b) Approx. 500m: 200m flat sprint and then over the 3rd to 10th hurdle.

Typical load standards: Due to the necessary high intensity, there can only be very few runs in the I1 zone (see 160).

Table 6: **Hurdle distances** *(in m)* **using various training rhythms depending on the target rhythm** *(modified on the basis of Boyd, 2001, pp. 4825 and 4830): A prerequisite for applying the table is the sprint at 400m hurdles race pace. This could be particularly difficult with the short rhythms. At a lower speed, the distances must be respectively shorter. The calculation is based on the following assumptions:*

• *The hurdle stride for men, most of whom use a 13- to 15-stride rhythm, is approximately 3.20m long.*

• *The hurdle stride for women, most of whom use a 15- to 18-stride rhythm, is approximately 3.00m long. The correction value of 40cm is taken into consideration since the last stride before and the first stride after the hurdle are shorter than the other inter-hurdle strides.*

• *Inter-hurdle stride length = (35m − hurdle stride length + 0.40m)/target rhythm.*
  Hurdle distance in training = training rhythm x inter-hurdle stride length + hurdle stride length − 0.40m

Target rhythm		13-stride	14-stride	15-stride	16-stride	17-stride	18-stride
Hurdle stride length		3.20	3.20	3.10	3.00	3.00	3.00
Inter-hurdle stride length		2.48	2.30	2.15	2.03	1.91	1.80
Training rhythm	5-stride	15.18	14.30	13.47	12.73	12.13	11.60
	6-stride	17.66	16.60	15.62	14.75	14.04	13.40
	7-stride	20.14	18.90	17.77	16.78	15.94	15.20
	8-stride	22.62	21.20	19.93	18.80	17.85	17.00
	9-stride	25.09		22.08		19.75	
	10-stride		25.80		22.85		20.60
	11-stride	30.05		26.39		23.56	
	12-stride		30.40		26.90		24.20
	13-stride	35.00		30.69		27.38	
	14-stride		35.00		30.95		27.80
	15-stride			35.00		31.19	
	16-stride				35.00		31.40
	17-stride					35.00	
	18-stride						35.00

1.9.9 SPECIAL TEST AND CONTROL PROCEDURES

The test and control procedures in the long hurdles are the same as those mentioned for the short hurdles and the 400m sprint (see chapter II–1.5.9 and II–1.8.9). In particular, recording split times, as described in test T53 and for the long sprint in the strategy chapter (chapter II–1.9.6), is one of the most important controlling methods. Table 5 shows the crucial guideline values for the long sprint.

*Table 7: **Basic performances of 400m hurdle sprinters** (according to Tepper & Czingon, 1995, p. 47): Although the rest interval lengths are not indicated in the tempo-run test programmes, they are likely to be approx. 20 min with the I2 zone and 5–8 min with the I3 zone*

	Women			Men		
Hurdle target time (sec)	60.60	57.20	54.50	53.00	51.00	49.50
30m from the starting blocks (sec)	4.75	4.70	4.54	4.36	4.26	4.15
30m flying (sec)	3.26	3.20	3.14	3.04	2.92	2.87
10-stride bounding run (m)	20–23	22–26	26–29	29–32	32–35	33–35
½ squat (with multiple body weight)	1.3–1.6	1.5–1.7	1.7–1.9	1.9–2.2	2.1–2.3	2.2–2.5
100m flat (sec; electron.)	12.60	12.30	12.00	11.45	11.10	10.85
200m flat (sec; electron.)	25.00	24.50	24.00	22.75	21.90	21.45
300m flat (sec; electron.)	40.00	39.0–39.9	38.0–39.0	35.7–36.5	33.9–34.8	32.9–33.5
400m flat (sec; electron.)	56.8–57.5	53.7–54.7	51.5–52.5	49.5–50.5	47.5–48.5	46.0–47.0
3x400m/3x300m average time (I2) (sec)	59.5/45.0	58.0/42.0	56.5/-	53.0/-	51.0/-	49.0/-
6x400m/6x300m average time (I3) (sec)	66.5/48.5	65.0/45.0	60.0/-	59.5/-	57.5/-	55.0/-
Running velocity at 4 mmol/l measured in graded lactate field test (m/sec)	3.6–3.9	3.8–4.0	3.9–4.1	4.1–4.3	4.3-4.5	4.4–4.6

1.9.10   ERRORS – CAUSES – CORRECTIONS

Error	Causes	Corrections
Too short strides in front of the hurdle result in velocity loss.	• The planned number of strides to the first hurdle or between the hurdles is too high. • The planned number of strides to the first hurdle or between the hurdles is too low: the sprinter must take (an) additional stride(s). • Incorrect estimation of the required stride length: the strides at the start of the run-up to the first hurdle or the strides of the inter-hurdle sprint are too long (sprinting with too noticeable push-off). • Insecurity when sprinting over the hurdle with the weaker swing leg: the sprinter takes an additional stride to run over the hurdle with the strong swing leg.	✔ General long-hurdle specific rhythm and stride-length training using exercise 215. ✔ Adaptation of race strategy as well as its preparation using exercise 216. ✔ Training sprinting over the hurdle with the weaker side or with the side not normally used; first only with the weaker side, then alternating, and with arbitrary distances between the hurdles (213).
Bounding run (too long strides) in front of the hurdle results in velocity loss.	• The planned number of strides to the first hurdle or between the hurdles is too low. • Incorrect estimation of the required stride length for the planned number of strides: the strides at the start of the run-up to the first hurdle or the strides of the inter-hurdle sprint are too short (too high stride frequency). • Insecurity when sprinting over the hurdle with the weaker swing leg: the sprinter avoids an additional stride to sprint over the hurdle with the strong swing leg.	✔ General long-hurdle specific rhythm and stride-length training using exercise 215. ✔ Adaptation of race strategy as well as its preparation using exercise 216. ✔ Training sprinting over the hurdle with the weaker side or with the side not normally used; first only with the weaker side, then alternating, and with arbitrary distances between the hurdles (213).
High jump over the hurdle (with great loss of velocity during the front support of the push-off; results in take-off instead of push-off).	• Too short strides in front of the hurdle and the reasons which have caused it (see above). • Push-off point too close in front of the hurdle. • Correct rhythm, but too long last strides in front of the hurdle due to a poor estimation of the distance to the hurdle.	✔ See corrections of too short strides in front of the hurdle above. ✔ Sprinting over the hurdle using distance markers (185). ✔ Hurdle sprints using arbitrary distances between the hurdles (213) for improving the estimation of distance and situational adjustment of stride length.

(continued)

(continued)

Error	Causes	Corrections
Long jump over the hurdle (with great loss of velocity during the front support of the landing after the hurdle).	• Bounding run in front of the hurdle and the reasons which have caused it (see above). • Push-off point too far in front of the hurdle. • Correct rhythm, but too short last strides in front of the hurdle due to a poor estimation of the distance to the hurdle.	✔ See corrections of bounding run in front of the hurdle above. ✔ Hurdle sprints using arbitrary distances between the hurdles (213) for improving the estimation of distance and situational adjustment of stride length.
Extreme loss of velocity on the finishing straight (often in combination with problems in clearing the last hurdle(s)).	• The sprinter is too fast at the beginning of the race. • Too few strides to the first hurdles. • Poorly developed speed endurance.	✔ Adjustment of race strategy as well as reinforcement of this strategy in training using exercise 216 and willingness to test the new strategy in competition. ✔ More speed-endurance training (e.g., 214).
Hardly any velocity loss on the finishing straight or fast final spurt on the final 40m.	• The sprinter was too slow at the beginning of the race. • Too many strides to the first hurdles.	✔ Adjustment of race strategy as well as reinforcement of this strategy in training using exercise 216 and willingness to test the new strategy in competition.

One should also observe the errors, causes, and corrections mentioned in connection with the 100m race, the short hurdle sprint, and the 400m race (see chapters II–1.3.10, II–1.5.10, and II–1.8.10).

1.9.11   TRAINING PLANNING

400m hurdles training is ultimately a mixture of long-sprint training (see chapter II–1.7.10) and hurdle training (see chapter II–1.8.11). The preliminary remarks made in these chapters also apply here.

SUGGESTED TRAINING PLANS
Below, there are exemplary microcycles for the

• third mesocycle of a 17-year-old athlete in build-up training (table 9);

• second mesocycle of an athlete in high-performance training (table 10); and

• fourth mesocycle of an athlete in high-performance training (table 11).

Since young long sprinters should not specialise in the flat or hurdle sprint, the suggested training plan for the first mesocycle of a 17-year-old athlete in build-up training presented in connection with the 4 x 400m (see chapter II–1.7.10) is intended for the same athlete as in this chapter.

The suggested training plans for the

- first mesocycle of an athlete in high-performance training; and

- third mesocycle of an athlete in high-performance training presented for the 4 x 400m may in some respects at least be compared to the plans presented here.

*Table 8: **Training emphasis in the various mesocycles** of 400m hurdle training in build-up and high-performance training.*

1st mesocycle	aerobic endurance training; (reactive) strength-endurance training for the legs and the trunk; hypertrophy-oriented maximal-strength training especially for the legs and the trunk; basic reactive-strength training for the legs; flexibility training; coordination (ABCs of sprinting/jumping) and technique training specific to the long hurdles
2nd mesocycle	aerobic endurance training; anaerobic endurance training; (reactive) strength-endurance and speed-endurance training; hypertrophy-, IC- and connective-tissue-oriented maximal- and reactive-strength training, especially for the legs and the trunk; flexibility training specific to the hurdles; special coordination training: grasping/pulling sprinting and long-hurdle technique
3rd mesocycle	maintenance of aerobic endurance; special speed-endurance training at increased intensity; IC- and connective-tissue-oriented maximal- and reactive-strength training, especially for the legs and the trunk; speed training at maximum intensity; Practising the hurdling technique and specific rhythm training
4th mesocycle	competitions and corresponding regeneration; speed-endurance training at maximum intensity; IC- and connective-tissue-oriented maximal- and reactive-strength training, especially for the legs and the trunk; speed and acceleration training at maximum intensity; maintenance stimuli

Table 9: Build-up training: sample microcycle for a 17-year-old athlete in the third mesocycle.

Monday	Tuesday	Wednesday	Thursday	Friday	Saturday	Sunday
Baton handovers (6 min) while jogging	**LI runs** (6 x 80m, rest intervals: 20 sec) as warm-up	**Continuous run** (30 min)	**Warm-up jogging** (8 min)	**Foot strengthening** (10 min)	**LI runs** (8 x 60m; rest intervals: 15 sec)	Rest
Maximal-eccentric strength training (15 min) trunk stabilisation, lifting opposite upper and lower limbs while in prone position, belly punches with tense abdominals, raising the foot/toes	**Tuck jumps** (2 x 3 run-throughs over 5 hurdles each)	Two of the following: **Strength training** for the trunk on apparatus and/or for the arms	**Acceleration runs** (3 reps)	**Acceleration runs** (3 reps)	**Acceleration runs** (3 reps) barefoot	
	Rhythm and frequency coordination (8–10 run-throughs)	**Medicine-ball work, gymnastics, technique training for the throwing events, boxing, etc.** (30 min each) for example, hip-shoulder twists, abdominal machine, lumborum and back extensors using a big box for strengthening the trunk; or goalkeeper throws, rotational throws, throws from a prone position, tossing, etc, using a medicine ball	**ABCs of hurdling** (15 min)	**ABCs of sprinting** (8–10 run-throughs)	**ABCs of sprinting/ hurdling** (15 run-throughs)	
Acceleration runs (2 reps) barefoot	**ABCs of jumping** (6–8 run-throughs) for example, galloping sideways, ankle jumps, and skipping with two-legged landing		**Practising the hurdling technique** (45 min) after specific warm-up: long-hurdle-specific: for example, 6–8 x 60–80m using a 7- or 8-stride rhythm at competition pace; alternatively: short-hurdle-specific	**Depth jumps** (3 x 10) from box to box	**Practising the hurdling technique** (20 min) 4–5 x 80m using arbitrary distances between the hurdles as specific warm-up	
ABCs of sprinting (6–8 run-throughs)	**Skipping and bounding runs** (2 x 2 run-throughs of 30m each) maximum intensity			**Practising the long-jump technique** (35 min) or high jump		
Standing starts (2 reps)	**I2/I1 tempo runs** (e.g. 2 x 300m, 1st run: 90–95%, 2nd run: 100%; rest interval: 15 min)		**LI tempo runs** (2 x 5 x 200m; walking intervals: 90 sec; rest intervals between sets: 6 min) 5 athletes as endless relay with 4 x 400m exchanges	**Strength training** (40 min) pyramid principle at high intensity and/or maximal-eccentric strength training: hamstrings, quadriceps, adductors, abductors, quarter split squat	**I2/I3 tempo runs** (4–5 x 210m; rest intervals: 10–15 min) from the starting block up to the 6th hurdle	
Crouch starts (e.g., 20, 30, 40, 50, and 30m, long rest intervals) 2x alone with correction, 3x against each other	**Warm-down jogging** (10 diagonals on the lawn)	**Tappings** (8 x 5 sec)	**Warm-down jogging** (5 laps on the lawn)		**Contract-relax stretching** (15 min) specific to hurdles	
Flying sprints (3 x 30m, run-up: 20–30m; rest intervals: 4 x 10 min) alternatively: 4 x 100m exchange training			**Standing starts** (3 x 30m at maximum pace)	**Rhythm and frequency coordination** (5–6 run-throughs)	**Warm-down jogging** (10 diagonals on the lawn)	
					Standing starts (3 x 30m) against each other	

Table 10: High-performance training: sample microcycle in the second mesocycle.

	Monday	Tuesday	Wednesday	Thursday	Friday	Saturday	Sunday
Morning	Trunk stabilisation exercises and abdominal crunches (20 min) Acceleration runs Strength training (50 min) pyramid principle: hamstrings, quadriceps, adductors, abductors, snatch Alternating-pace sprints (4 x 80m)	LI runs (10 x 60m, rest intervals: 15 sec) as warm-up Tuck jumps (5 x 2 run-throughs over 10 hurdles each) ABCs of sprinting (15–20 run-throughs) Technique sprints (8 x 60–80m) varying arm actions, stride lengths, etc.	Foot strengthening (10 min) Acceleration runs (3 reps) Strength-endurance circuit (3–4 run-throughs; loading: 45 sec; rest interval: 45 sec) trunk strength, leg strength, ABCs of sprinting/ jumping Acceleration runs (4 x 80m)	Warm-up jogging (6 min) Acceleration runs (3 reps) barefoot ABCs of hurdling and hurdle imitation (20 min) Practising the hurdling technique (45 min) weekly variation, also in the curve, primarily long-hurdle specific, but also short-hurdle specific	Warm-up jogging (6 min) Acceleration runs (3 reps) barefoot Ankle jumps (5 x 15 jumps) alternatively: skipping with two-legged landing ABCs of jumping (6–8 run-throughs) Skipping, pop-up jumps and rhythm jumps (4 run-throughs of 40m each)	Warm-up jogging (15 min) Acceleration runs (3 reps) I3 tempo runs (3 sets of 200, 300, and 500m; walking intervals: 3, 5, and 10, respectively), now and again 200 and 300m over hurdles Warm-down jogging (10 diagonals on the lawn)	Rest
Afternoon	Warm-up jogging (6 min) Acceleration runs (3 reps) Flying sprints (2 x 30m with individual run-up length; rest intervals: 10 min) Crouch starts (60, 50, 40, 30, and 20m, long rest intervals) in the curve Bounding run and step-overs (3 x 1 min each, alternately; rest intervals: 6 min)	Warm-up jogging (15 min) Mobilisation (10 min) specific to hurdles Acceleration runs LI tempo runs (Frinolli runs: 3 x 4 x 2 laps of 240m each; rest intervals: 90 sec; rest intervals between sets: 5–6 min) Contract-relax stretching (15 min) Warm-down jogging (15 min) Tappings (8 x 5 sec)	Continuous run (45 min) Muscle build-up training (35 min) bench press, lat pull, and 2 other varying arm exercises; alternatively: boxing Rhythm and frequency coordination (6–8 run-throughs)	Warm-up jogging (15 min) Acceleration runs (3 reps) I3 tempo runs (2 x 5 x 150m; walking intervals: 4–5 min; rest interval between sets: 10 min) now and again as alternating-pace sprints or using a parachute Contract-relax stretching (15 min) Warm-down jogging (15 min) Standing starts (3 x 30m)	LI runs (8 x 80m; rest intervals: 20 sec) Medicine-ball work (30 min) alternatively: gymnastics Maximal-eccentric strength training (40 min) hamstrings, adductors, abductors, hip flexors and extensors, belly punches with tense abdominals Game (30 min) for example, soccer	Continuous run (30 min) for regeneration; alternatively and imperatively also cycling, swimming, inline skating, cross-country skiing, etc. Contract-relax stretching (15 min) Rhythm and frequency coordination	

Table 11: High-performance training: sample microcycle in the fourth mesocycle.

Monday	Tuesday	Wednesday	Thursday	Friday	Saturday	Sunday
Warm-up jogging (6 min)	Warm-up jogging (6 min)	Continuous run (25 min)	Warm-up jogging (6 min)	Rest	*Preparatory competition* • Warm-up jogging • Inciting (trunk and foot muscles) • Three acceleration runs • ABCs of sprinting/jumping • Three crouch starts • Pre-loading: 60m • Rest interval and relaxed ABCs of sprinting	Rest
Maximal-eccentric strength training (15 min) trunk and foot	Acceleration runs (2 reps)	ABCs of sprinting (10–15 run-throughs)	Belly punches with tense abdominals (4 x 5 sec)			*If there is no short-distance competition before the 400m race, the athlete may perform maximal 1–2 150m sprints as pre-loading on the warm-up field.*
Acceleration runs	Depth jumps (3 x 6) from box to box	Acceleration runs (3 reps)	Strength training at high intensity (15 min) snatch		100m competition	
Strength training at high intensity (20 min) hamstrings and quarter squat	Practising the hurdling technique (40 min) after specific warm-up: as in competition, long-hurdle specific, now and again short-hurdle specific	Rhythm jumps (4 x 30m) maximum intensity	Acceleration runs (2 reps)		If necessary, re-warm-up: 4–5 sprints from the block up to the 1st–3rd hurdle	
Crouch starts (e.g., 20, 30, 40, 30, and 20m, long rest intervals) 2 x alone with correction, 3–4 x against each other	I1 tempo runs (2 x 210m; rest interval: 15 min) from the starting block up to the 6th hurdle	I1 tempo runs (2 x 5 x 200m; walking interval: 90 sec; rest interval between sets: 5 min)	Tuck jumps (3 x 2 run-throughs over 3 hurdles each)		400m hurdles competition	
Flying sprints (2 x 30m with individual run-up length; rest intervals: 10 min)		Warm-down jogging (5 laps on the lawn)	Standing starts (2 reps)		Warm-down jogging	
		Standing starts (3 x 30m) maximal, against each other	Crouch starts (20, 30, 40, and 60m, long rest intervals) against each other			

In the competition phase, the training plan must be adapted to the (irregular) competition calendar. In this plan, it may be assumed that the athlete took part in a preparatory competition over 100m/110m hurdles and 400m (flat) on the previous Saturday. As preparation for major championships with heats, a semi-final, and a final, the athlete should now and again perform two 400m (hurdle) races on two consecutive days. After this, two rest days are advisable. If there are no other competitions for one and a half weeks (or more) between two preparatory competitions, the athlete once again performs more training and his/her training is of a more basic nature. Before the main competition, the athlete should not take part in any 400m competition for two weeks and should train even less than shown here.

1.9.12   BIBLIOGRAPHY

Boyd, R. (2000). Components of The 400m Hurdles. *Track Coach* (151), 4822-4830.

Ditroilo, M. & Marini, M. (2001). Analysis of the race distribution for male 400m hurdlers competing at the 2000 Sydney Olympic Games. *New Studies in Athletics 16* (3), 15-30.

Graubner, R., Buckwitz, R., Landmann, M. & Starke, A. (2009). 400m Hurdles Men. In Deutscher Leichtathletikverband (Hrsg.), *Biomechanical Analysis of selected events at the 12th IAAF World Championships in Athletics, Berlin 15-23 August 2009*. Zugriff am 20.04.2010 unter http://www.iaaf. org/mm/Document/ Development/Research/05/64/44/20100415081724_httppostedfile_2- BiomechanicsReportWCBerlin2009_ Hurdles_Men_19921.pdf.

Lindemann, R. (1995). 400-meter hurdle theory. *Track Technique* 4169-4171.

Regelkommissionen des DLV, FLA, ÖLV und SLV (Hrsg.). (2008). *Internationale Wettkampfregeln*. Waldfischbach: Hornberger.

Vonstein, W. (1995). Zur technischen Entwicklung des 400-m-Hürdenlaufs. Die Lehre der Leichtathletik 34, 60-62.

Tepper, E. & Czingon, H. (Red.) (mit Keydel, H.). (1995). *Rahmentrainingsplan für das Aufbautraining Sprint* (4. Aufl.) (Edition Leichtathletik, 2). Aachen: Meyer und Meyer.

1.10 MIDDLE- AND LONG-DISTANCE RUNNING: COMMON FEATURES OF THE DISCIPLINES

1.10.1 THE MOST IMPORTANT COMPETITION RULES

The following abridged and simplified International Competition Rules comprise the framework for the technique and strategy, as well as the organisation of middle- and long-distance competitions:

- In all runs that are not started in single lanes (longer than 800m), runners start from an arced line (see figure 1). This arc is created so that all runners have the same distance to the finish. With many participants in a 1000, 2000, 3000, 5000, or 10,000m race (the race must start at the beginning of a curve), a smaller group including the strongest runners may start from a second arced line on the outer half of the track (typically lanes 5–8). After the curve, the runners then cut to the inside lane as in the 800m race (see chapter II–1.11.2).

- In all races longer than 400m, the runners start from a standing position. Before the starting signal, the starter

*Figure 1: **Arced starting line and finish line:** The blue arrows indicate the arced line for the 2000m and 10,000m start. The solid straight line is the finish line. The small black markings, where the finish line and the lane lines meet, are used for the automatic timing with finish photo (see chapter II–1.1.1). Finish line photos are created by taking up to 1000 photos per second of the finish line as a narrow strip and by displaying these strips side by side. Therefore, the final image shows a solid white background, while the boundary lines between the lanes are black, advancing body parts appear narrow, and backward moving body parts appear wider.*

gives the command "On your marks" in the language of the country or in English or French.

Otherwise, the general competition rules for running apply (see chapter II–1.1.1).

Some remarks about road races may be found in the chapter on marathons (see chapter II–1.13.2). Cross-country and mountain races are other areas of competitive athletics not further discussed here.

1.10.2   SPORT-SCIENCE FINDINGS, PHASE STRUCTURE, AND TECHNIQUE

The middle- and long-distance events constitute those running disciplines which depend primarily on aerobic energy availability (see chapter II–1.1.2 and table 2 in chapter II–1.2.2). Whereas in middle-distance running there is an increase in lactate over the entire distance, anaerobic energy supply plays a much less significant role in long-distance running (see figure 2). In the final sprint, however, lactate tolerance may be important.

Apart from endurance capabilities, middle- and long-distance runners also require a certain amount of strength. While in the past emphasis was placed on strength endurance, recent studies tend to emphasise the importance of IC or reactive strength training to improve running economy (for improved coordination and energy storage in passive elastic elements see chapter I–1.3). In middle-distance running, cyclic speed is also an important factor determining performance. The relatively low level of flexibility of (middle- and) long-distance runners is often criticised. However, an active range of motion that only slightly exceeds the movement amplitude required by the target movement might facilitate

the storage of much kinetic energy in passive elastic structures. An excessive increase of flexibility is therefore not

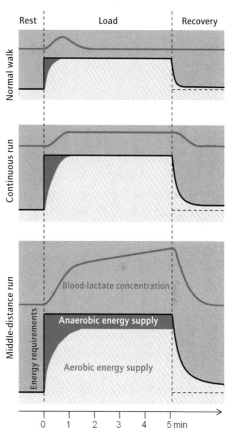

*Figure 2: **Energy supply during different types of exercise** (modified on the basis of Markworth, 2007, p. 254).*

appropriate. Moreover, it is assumed that with increasing running distance those psychological abilities which are crucial for the extent to which the athlete is able to mobilise his/her existing performance reserves become increasingly important.

Below, the technical similarities of middle- and long-distance running are described in reference to the following three phases:

* standing start;
* start acceleration; and
* main phase of the race.

(Please observe the general comments about running in chapter II–1.1.2.)

PHASE 1: STANDING START

Unlike the sprint, middle- and long-distance running is performed from a standing start. In contrast to the crouch start, there is no setting of the starting blocks, neither is there, according to the rules, the command "set" (see chapter II–1.10.1). Consequently, the standing start can be divided into two sub-phases:

* on-your-marks position; and
* start reaction.

The first sub-phase is only indirectly relevant to performance since the time begins to run only at the beginning of the second sub-phase (i.e., with the starting signal).

(For a detailed description of the relevant aspects of the start reaction see the previous chapters.)

ON-YOUR-MARKS POSITION

On the command "on your marks," the runners step to the starting line and take the position shown in figure 3, which shows the final position of the standing start in middle- and long-distance running. As in the crouch start, the stronger leg (in terms of jumping power) is usually the front leg. Alternatively, the "on your marks" position may be taken in such a way that the choice of the front arm depends on the side where the stronger competitor stands next to you. The backswing of the arm can be effective protection against jostling during the start. This is especially true when one is positioned more inward, specifically the left foot and right arm should be in a front position with the same logic in mind, as the other runners cut from the outside to the inside lane. To shift the CG as far forward as possible even in the "on your marks" position, the majority of body weight rests on the front leg. However, due to the lack of support of the hands it is not possible to

Figure 3: **On-your-marks position** during the standing start.

shift the vertical projection of the CG ahead of the contact point of the feet already in this position without falling forward.

PHASE 2: START ACCELERATION

TOE PUSH-OFF RUNNING

Like sprinters, even middle- and long-distance runners run with a toe push-off during the initial start acceleration (see description in chapter II–1.3.3). In order to be able to immediately take a good running position and quickly reach racing pace, the runners sprint with a touchdown on the ball of the foot and a toe push-off.

A characteristic feature of toe push-off sprinting or running is the forward shifted CG or the forward lean of the entire body. The runner can only push himself/herself forward (off the ground) during the rear support (see chapter II–1.1.2) when the vertical projection of the CG is in front of the touchdown point of the foot. With respect to the front leg in the standing start position, this situation must be created only after the starting signal. This is done primarily through a strong short push-off of the rear leg. For some athletes, the push-off of the rear leg is so strong that they raise the front leg a little and sometimes even put it slightly forward. This means that the first small stride is performed with the front leg.

During the subsequent strides, toe push-off running strongly resembles the technical behaviour described for the 100m. However, there is only little forward lean of the body from the start onward

and the transition to the grasping style of running occurs after fewer metres than in the sprint.

JOSTLING AT THE START

Usually, runners are not only forced to secure a good and appropriate position in the field during start acceleration, but are also forced to run to the inside lane on the most direct path. Only then do they run the shortest possible distance (see chapter II–1.10.4). One exception is the 800m race in which the runners cut to the inside lane only after the first curve. In a way, this is also true of the 1500m race. In both events, the runners have a distance of 100m to run straight to the inside lane. The jostling is greater when in the 1000, 2000, 3000, 5000, or 10,000m race the runners run to the inside lane in the curve. Here, they must keep (their trunk) stable and use their elbows (while observing the rules of fairness) to prevent them from being pushed aside or locked in.

PHASE 3: MAIN PHASE OF THE RACE

In contrast to the sprint, the remainder of the race after the start acceleration cannot be divided into a phase of maximum velocity and a phase of negative acceleration. During the major part of middle- and long-distance races, the velocity profile is characterised by strategy and is described in more detail in the relevant chapters.

In respect to the running technique, there is no fundamental difference between the sprint and middle- and long-distance running. Even between middle-distance running on the one hand and long-distance running on the other hand, there is no fundamental difference in technique. *The basic principle of grasping/pulling running, which was described in detail in connection with the 100m race, also applies to middle- and long-distance running* (see chapter II−1.3.3). However, in spite of this, there is a change in the running technique from the shortest to the longest distances (see also figure 4). The following trends may be identified:

STRIDE LENGTH AND STRIDE FREQUENCY

Depending on the running velocity (see also table 1), there is also a change in its basic influencing factors: stride length and stride frequency (see chapter II−1.1.2). In groups with heterogeneous ability or if there is a strong variation in running velocity, stride frequency and stride length decrease with decreasing speed or increasing distance. However, stride length decreases to a higher degree than stride frequency. But it depends entirely on individual variation (which is not least determined by anthropometric factors) whether a higher stride frequency or a larger stride length is responsible for a runner running faster in one race than in another race, or whether he/she, in one

and the same race, runs faster than an equally good competitor.

OTHER VELOCITY-DEPENDENT CHANGES

In contrast to the 100m sprint, there is usually a full extension of the feet, knees, and hips at the end of the push-off in middle- and long-distance running. This also results in a more noticeable rear swing phase, and the pelvis is often less erect than in the 100m sprint. Nevertheless, in the subsequent forward swing phase, runners should try to achieve a pulling foot touchdown by using a relaxed grasping movement.

Moreover, the following may be stated. The slower the speed,

- the more to the rear is that point on the outer edge of the foot with which the runner makes the first ground contact during the touchdown of the foot;
- the more likely it is that the runner touches the ground with the entire sole of his/her foot during the mid-support phase;
- the longer are the ground contact phases;
- the smaller is the flight phase/support phase ratio;

Figure 4: Running stride in middle- and long-distance running

- the lower is the knee lift;
- the smaller is the amplitude of the arm swing; and
- the larger is the smallest knee-joint angle during the swing phase.

BREATHING TECHNIQUE

An optimal breathing rhythm is usually established unconsciously and automatically. Trying to consciously control one's breathing rhythm usually only results in a deterioration of breathing economy and in problems such as so-called side stitches. However, if the runner suffers from side stitches without deliberately changing of his/her breathing rhythm, a conscious, calm, and steady breathing rhythm in connection with a reduction in running pace may bring about relief. Usually, the same number of strides is performed while inhaling and exhaling again. The number of strides taken depends on the running intensity and the runner's physique and must be tested individually if not left to unconscious control. The general recommendation for continuous running (227-228) is a 3:3 breathing rhythm, which means three strides for breathing in and three strides for breathing out. Inhaling and exhaling should be done through the mouth and nose at the same time. Some authors recommend inhaling only through the nose since the air is then better purified, moistened, and warmed. However, breathing (in) through the nose is not possible even at moderate intensities since the flow resistance in nasal breathing is too great.

Table 1: **World records in the Olympic running events, arranged by average speed:** *Since the velocity profile is not uniform, the maximum velocities achieved during the race are higher than the values presented for each event.*

	Men					Women				
Distance	World record (h:min:sec)	Time (sec)	100m ø time (sec)	ø velocity (m/sec, **km/h**)		World record (h:min:sec)	Time (sec)	100m ø time (sec)	ø velocity (m/sec, **km/h**)	
100m	9.58	9.58	9.58	10.43	**37.6**	10.49	10.49	10.49	9.53	**34.3**
200m	19.19	19.19	9.60	10.42	**37.5**	21.34	21.34	10.67	9.37	**33.7**
400m	43.03	43.03	10.76	9.29	**33.5**	47.60	47.60	11.90	8.40	**30.2**
100m/110m hurdles	12.80	12.80	11.64	8.59	**30.9**	12.12	12.12	12.12	8.25	**29.7**
400m hurdles	45.94	45.94	11.49	8.71	**31.3**	50.68	50.68	12.67	7.89	**28.4**
800m	1:40.91	100.91	12.61	7.92	**28.5**	1:53.28	113.28	14.16	7.06	**25.4**
1500m	3:26.00	206.00	13.73	7.28	**26.2**	3:50.07	230.07	15.34	6.52	**23.5**
5000m	12:35.36	755.36	15.11	6.62	**23.8**	14:06.62	846.62	16.93	5.91	**21.3**
10,000m	26:11.00	1571.00	15.71	6.37	**22.9**	29:17.45	1757.45	17.57	5.69	**20.5**
3000m steeplechase	7:53.63	473.63	15.79	6.33	**22.8**	8:44.32	514,32	17.14	5.83	**21.0**
Marathon	2:01:39	7299.00	17.30	5.78	**20.8**	2:14:04	8044.00	19.06	5.25	**18.9**
20km race walking	1:16:36	4596.00	22,98	4.35	**15.7**	1:24:38	5078.00	25.39	3.94	**14.2**
50km race walking	3:32:33	12753.00	25.51	3.92	**14.1**	4:04:36	14676.00	29.35	3.41	**12.3**

In respect to the finish of a race and deceleration after crossing the finish line, there are no fundamental technique differences between middle- and long- distance running and the long sprint. It is only the initial velocity which is lower in middle- and long-distance races (see chapter II–1.5.3).

1.10.3 SUMMARY OF THE MOST IMPORTANT TECHNICAL CHARACTERISTICS = TECHNIQUE-ANALYSIS SHEET

STANDING START

ON-YOUR-MARKS POSITION

- On the command, the runners step to the starting line.
- The front leg is usually the stronger leg, or specifically the left leg, or either leg depending on which side the weaker competitor stands.
- The opposite arm is in front; the elbow is at a 90° angle.
- Only the balls of the feet are placed on the ground; approx. two feet apart.
- Both knees are bent; the front knee at an angle of approx. 120–130°.
- The trunk is bent forward at an angle of approx. 45° (to the vertical).
- The weight is placed on the front foot.
- The athlete inhales and holds his/her breath (forced breathing).
- The focus is on the subsequent movement (not on the starting signal).

TOE PUSH-OFF RUNNING

- The short, powerful push-off performed by the extensor muscles of the rear leg leads to assuming the forward body lean.
- Beginning of the powerful first arm swing.
- Powerful push-off with the front leg.
- The rear leg releases contact with the ground, and the hip flexion starts immediately (forward swing to the high knee position).
- Each push-off results in the extension of the entire body (ankle, knee hip, trunk) so that, viewed from the side, the head, shoulders, hips, knees, and feet are in one line, which is clearly inclined forward (forward lean of the body).

- In each case, the swing leg is moved quickly forward with noticeable knee lift and flat foot movement curve (initially there is only a slight heel lift behind the body).
- The knee lift and arm swing (from the shoulder; elbows at approx. 90°) are used as swing elements.
- After the knee lift, the hips and knees are extended again (the next push-off already starts during the swing phase).
- The lower legs are pointed backward and downward throughout the movement (initially there is no grasping movement).
- The tip of the foot is raised before the touchdown (dorsiflexion).
- The touchdown with the balls of the feet is initially approximately on the vertical projection of the CG; fixed foot during touchdown (hardly any yielding).
- High, rather sprint-like acceleration to secure a good running position.
- Increasing stride length and stride frequency.
- Slow straightening up from the forward body lean and thus smooth transition to grasping/pulling running.
- If the start is from the arced line in the curve, taking the inward lean into the curve when reaching the inside lane; increasing the inward lean with increasing velocity.

GRASPING/PULLING RUNNING

- Economic running style.
- Upright, still head position; relaxed facial muscles.
- Upright trunk or minimum forward lean.
- Erect pelvis (contracted abdominals), but less than in the sprint.
- Running from the hips (during the swing phase, the lower leg follows the movements of the upper leg and its own inertia mostly passively).
- Noticeable heel lift under rather than behind the body (heel is never raised as high as the buttocks; when the pace is very slow, the minimal knee angle becomes larger); then the knee joint angle is opened.
- The hip flexion leads to the knee lift (the thigh is not raised up to the horizontal; the height of the knee lift decreases with decreasing running

velocity); subsequently reactive hip extension, while the lower leg continues its pendulum movement to the front.

- Before touchdown the foot performs a (pulling) movement downward and backward.
- The foot is placed on the ground with an almost extended knee, close to the vertical projection of the CG, over the outside of the ball of the foot (the slower the running velocity, the further to the rear of the foot the first ground contact occurs, and the more likely it is that the ground contact is performed with the entire sole of the foot).
- Small stride width (foot touchdown almost on a straight line); in the curve, the stride width is narrower than on the straight.
- Minimal amortisation at the knee joint (high hips).
- Complete extension of the hip, knee, and ankle joints during the rear support phase (therefore larger rear swing phase than in the sprint).
- The contralateral arm swing is initiated by the shoulder and is performed almost parallel to the running direction (possibly the hands are moved slightly to the middle of the body when in front); elbow angle approx. 90°, only very slight opening during the backward swing and closing during the forward swing; hands are kept loose in the middle position; the amplitude of the arm swing gets smaller as the running velocity decreases.

CROSSING THE FINISH LINE AND SUBSEQUENT DECELERATION

- In the case of a close finish: Shifting of the chest and trunk to the front relative to the arms, head and legs as close to the finish line as possible; also slight forward shift of the CG.
- Maintenance of tension in order to decelerate without running the risk of injury, shifting backward of the trunk and thus the CG.

1.10.4 STRATEGY

Generally, one must distinguish between two strategies:

- running to achieve a good time; and
- running for victory, place, or qualification.

The following remarks about strategy primarily involve the first strategy. The second strategy is mainly found at championships. At commercial meetings, an attempt is made to prevent pure running to win by using a pacemaker (rabbit) and performance-related bonuses.

Moreover, at championships, the second strategy should only be applied by superior runners or runners who are able to produce a strong (final) spurt. Often, the race is slow at the beginning while the final spurt is faster and/or longer. Mentioning all the possibilities associated with the second strategy, including opponents, helpers, individual strengths and weaknesses, weather conditions, race courses (for road races and marathons), would go far beyond the scope of this chapter.

TUB SHAPE

In all middle- and long-distance events, the velocity curve during the race should be characterised by a tub shape. This means that the first (100–200) metres and the final spurt should be run faster than the main part of the race. The fact that the start is slightly faster can first be explained by the jostling for the best running position. Another reason is that a high oxygen uptake is quickly activated in this way. Conversely, a start that is too fast can also prevent a runner from accelerating at the end of the race so that he/she misses optimal results. If an over-aggressive race is expected, it may therefore be wise to stay out of the jostling at the start, to save energy and then to work one's way gradually to the front. Supplying energy in the main part of the race is primarily aerobic. During the final spurt to the finish line, all performance reserves are mobilised and there is an increasing lactate accumulation in the muscles and blood.

Recording significant split times is possible in middle- and long-distance running simply through manual time measurement. Depending on the length of the race, the time is usually taken every 100, 400, or 1000 metres. An individual race strategy should be prepared in detail and tested in training and competition. A good feel for pace (i.e., the ability to estimate one's own race pace as objectively as possible) is an important factor contributing to performance in middle- and long-distance running.

ADDITIONAL TECHNICAL AND STRATEGIC PRINCIPLES

In order to always take the shortest path, a runner should run on the inside of the inner lane if possible. If a runner must leave this inside lane to overtake a competitor, this should happen on the straight. However, toward the end of a race (for a middle-distance race of 800m perhaps during most of the race) a runner should also make sure that he/she is not locked in on the inside of the track contrary to the suggestion above. If a runner is running with another runner directly in front of him/her and another runner next to him/her, it may not be possible to pursue the runners further ahead if there is an increase in pace. It may then be useful to leave the inside lane early and to choose the longer path in the curve.

For psychological reasons and to improve running economy, a runner should never look back. The runner's view and orientation should be directed to the finish, the beginning of the next bend, the course of the bend, the leading runner, or the runner running in front of him/her.

1.10.5 DIDACTICS: SUPERORDINATE LONG-TERM OBJECTIVES AND GENERAL METHODOLOGY

Endurance running (mostly in playful forms) is part of the general training in children's athletics and basic training. However, the length of the competition courses offered for the different age groups should only increase gradually. Too early and too monotonous endurance training should be avoided. Even with future middle- (and long-) distance runners, playful training for speed and the versatile development of coordination should be the first priorities. As part of endurance training, the focus should be predominantly on aerobic training in the beginning. This does not mean that loads (e.g., in games or in fartlek [230]) may not be of an interval character. However, high lactacid and monotonous tempo-run programmes should not be introduced before build-up training.

IMPROVEMENT OF RUNNING TECHNIQUE
Important performance gains at the beginning of systematic training are made through an improvement in running economy as a result of the (unconscious) improvement of coordination. A variable and economic running technique should be practised in a versatile way at all running paces and in all situations (when running on the straight or in a curve, uphill or downhill, etc.). Changes in the running circumstances also help to prevent imbalances, pain, and injuries which typically occur primarily in the lower legs and feet. Therefore, runners should alternately run on synthetic or cinder tracks, on forest and meadow paths, on a flat beach or through the dunes, on the right and left side of paths that are higher in the middle, etc. However, every deliberate change in running technique initially results in a deterioration of running economy especially for advanced athletes. Nevertheless, running technique should be specifically varied in practice to train neglected or weak muscles and to create variations in terms of (unconscious) differential learning. The change from deliberately controlled to unconsciously relaxed running should be systematically practised.

CROSS-COUNTRY RUNS
On the one hand, cross-country runs and forest runs are a separate discipline for more or less specialised runners. On the other hand, they are an important part of both competition and training with many advantages for the development of children and adolescents and for the general preparation of adult track runners. The normally softer ground protects the joints. Hills, ditches, tight curves, uneven and varying surfaces place many demands on coordination and develop not only aerobic endurance, but also the specific strength abilities of both the legs and the trunk. In addition, running on a varied course in nature is less monotonous than running laps in a stadium. In competition, non-standard distances and varied terrains make recorded times unimportant and thus

reduce the mental stress for an athlete. In lower age groups, cross-country runs are often the longest races in the competition calendar and therefore prepare athletes for long-distance running in a manner suitable for children. Versatile obstacle courses, which not only prepare runners for the steeplechase, are perhaps even more enjoyable (see chapter II–1.12.7).

LONG RELAYS

Long relay runs have an equally high motivational importance for middle- and long-distance running, in particular for children and youths. Although not included in the Olympic programme, 3 x 800m or 3 x 1000m relays are regularly performed. Cross-country, forest, and road races are also run as relays with varying length. Marathons are usually divided into the following six sections: 5, 10, 5, 10, 5, and 7.195km.

1.10.6   TRAINING CONTENTS: FORMS OF GAMES AND EXERCISES

In middle- and long-distance training almost all forms of games and exercises presented in connection with the long sprint are also used (although with less emphasis; see chapters II–1.5.8, II–1.7.7, and II–1.9.8). Since in middle-distance running, maximum sprinting speed is also of crucial importance (for reasons, see chapter II–1.11.3), the training forms mentioned in connection with the short sprint are also important for this discipline (see chapter II–1.3.8, II–1.6.8, and II–1.8.8). In children's athletics and in basic training, even future long-distance runners should perform the games and playful exercise forms of speed training mentioned in the respective chapters. Since there is no fundamental difference between sprint technique and running technique, the exercises to improve technique mentioned in connection with the 100m are also performed by middle- and long-distance runners. Here, the focus should be on the exercises in the ABCs of sprinting, which is largely identical with the ABCs of running. In the following, training forms to improve aerobic endurance are specifically listed. Many of these training forms are also used by all other disciplines.

221 ▮▮▮▯ Estimating time

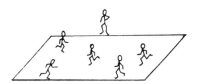

Possible objectives: Aerobic endurance; warm-up.
Execution: Without looking at a watch, players should sit down after a pre-set time (between 1 and 5 min); the coach, who has a watch, checks how well they estimated the time.

Variations: Rewards for the best players; running to the rhythm of music.
Typical load standards: Total running time: 6–15 min.

---

222 Traffic policeman

Possible objectives: Aerobic endurance; warm-up.
Execution: Children run around a marked circle or square; the instructor turns (slowly or quickly) with extended arms, thus indicating running velocity and direction; change in running direction (slow (turning) velocity and certain duration to achieve an endurance stimulus).
Variations: Each child may be the traffic policeman once.
Typical load standards: Total running time: 6–15 min.

---

223 The last runner overtakes the other runners!

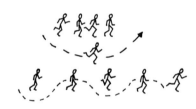

Possible objectives: Aerobic endurance; warm-up.
Execution: The group runs at a slow pace, while the last runner overtakes the other runners and takes the lead until all members of the group have taken the lead once.
Variations: Track, lawn, cross-county, etc.
Typical load standards: Total running time: 6–15 min.

---

224 Biathlon competition

Possible objectives: Aerobic and anaerobic endurance; straight throw.
Execution: In addition to covering a running distance or an obstacle course, an athlete must throw at targets at a separate station; for each target he misses, he must run a short penalty lap.
Typical load standards: Total running time: 6–15 min.

225  **Chain catching**

Possible objectives: Anaerobic and aerobic endurance; reaction, start, and acceleration.

Execution: Two athletes holding each other's hands starts as the catchers; anyone who has been tagged, must join the chain; as soon as a chain consists of 4 players, it is separated into 2 chains of two players; who is the last one to be tagged?

Typical load standards: Total running time: 6–15 min.

---

226 **Warm-up running/warm-down running/regenerative run (slow, short continuous run)**

Possible objectives: Warm-up, regeneration.

Execution: Running according to the continuous method (see chapter I-4.5); slow pace, on no account until complete exhaustion; usually on flat terrain.

Variations: Including the coordinative exercises in the ABCs of sprinting or running; also see 223.

Typical load standards: 5–30 min (for pace distribution in continuous runs see table 4).

---

227  **(Slow, long) continuous run**

Possible objectives: Aerobic endurance (relatively low intensity).

Execution: Running according to the continuous method; the intensity should be adapted to the individual athlete, not to the group.

Variations: Including coordination exercises in the ABCs of sprinting or running; flat or hilly course; varying surfaces (road, forest floor, etc.); also as cross-country run (see 244).

Typical load standards: 30–120 min, the duration increases with age and the distance of the competition course; in marathon training up to 30km.

DISCOURSE I: CONTROLLING CONTINUOUS RUNNING PACE BY MEANS OF HEART RATE

The following rules of thumb provide a rough guideline for controlling velocity using heart rate (HR). HR should be measured using a chest belt:

- For fitness athletes, particularly over 50 years of age, the following formula for determining training intensity has proven worthwhile (Hollmann & Strüder, 2009, p. 411):

$$HR_{Training} = 180 - age$$

- A more complex formula (Karvonen et al., 1957) is based on heart rate at rest (HR_{Rest}) and maximum heart rate (HR_{max}) and takes an intensity factor (F) into consideration:

$$HR_{Training} = HR_{Rest} + [(HR_{max} - HR_{Rest}) \cdot F]$$

Since determining HR_{max} is difficult and for non-performance athletes can be dangerous to their health, it is often suggested to use the following formula:

$HR_{max} = 220 - (age / 2)$; therefore the following formula is applicable:

$$HR_{Training} = HR_{Rest} + [(220 - (age / 2) - HR_{Rest}) \cdot F]$$

Depending on the state of training, the following factors are recommended for tempo runs (228):

$F_{untrained} = 0.60$; $F_{moderately\ trained} = 0.65$; $F_{endurance\text{-}trained} = 0.70$; $F_{performance\ athletes} = 0.75$

During long continuous runs, heart rate should be lower by approx. 10 beats/min.

- Thibault (2003, p. 50) mentions the following heart rates as guidelines for adult elite runners (HR_{max}: 180 beats/min, $\dot{V}O_2max$: approx. 70 ml/kg/min):

% of maximum aerobic performance ability: 95 90 85 80 75 70 65
Heart rate (beats/min):   174 168 161 155 149 143 136

- Sometimes certain percentages of HR_{max} are mentioned for certain training forms: continuous run (227): 70–85%, tempo-endurance run (228): 85–90 %, interval runs: 90–100%.

228   ⬜⬜⬜⬛   **Tempo-endurance run (fast, short continuous run)**

Possible objectives: Aerobic endurance (relatively high intensity).

Execution: Running according to the continuous method; the intensity should be adapted to the individual athlete, not to the group.

Variations: See 227; crescendo run with increasing pace as a mixture of 227 and 228.
Typical load standards: 20–45 min.

---

229   Tempo-endurance run at alternating pace

Possible objectives: Aerobic and anaerobic endurance.

Execution: Running velocity is varied according to a certain pattern (e.g., 5 min warm-up run, 5 min faster, 5 min slower, 5 min faster, 5 min slower, 5 min fast run, and 5 min warm-down run); the transition to the minute runs described under 232 is smooth: in 232 the velocity difference between the fast-run interval and the jogging interval is greater than the difference between the intervals of varying running paces in this training form; a pacing watch may be used for stride-frequency modulation.

Variations: In contrast to the example mentioned above, the phases of high and low stress do not have to be equally long; (see also 227).

Typical load standards: 20–40 min.

---

230   Fartlek (tempo-endurance run at a varying pace depending on the terrain)

Possible objectives: Aerobic and anaerobic endurance; versatile running-specific coordination and strength endurance.

Execution: Play with pace; the pace is varied (mostly in an unplanned and therefore irregular way); in addition to the athlete's subjective feeling, the terrain often determines the pace; in most cases, the variation of pace is greater than during a tempo-endurance run at alternating pace (229); intermediate sprints, walking and jogging intervals.

Variations: An intermediate sprint where the road

is well paved, before running cross-country at a slower pace (see also cross-country runs, 244); an intermediate sprint uphill and running downhill at slow pace or vice versa; with climbing and jumping over tree trunks, etc.; inclusion of coordination exercises of the ABCs of sprinting or running.
Typical load standards: 15–45 min.

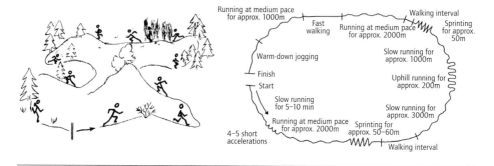

231   Orienteering run

Possible objectives: Aerobic endurance, navigation abilities, game or competition form for loosening up continuous-run training.

Execution: Using a map, the runners must find various check points/stations, where they must possibly solve additional tasks (possibly cross-country, see 244).

Variations: See also 224.

Typical load standards: See 227–228.

Non-specific endurance training for runners may (or should) also be performed in the form of *aqua jogging, swimming, cycling, cross-country skiing, inline skating, etc.* according to the principles of the above-mentioned exercises. Even *major games* (see 1) including interval-like loads may contribute to an improvement in endurance in a versatile way.

232 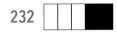 **LI (and I3) tempo runs for middle- and long-distance runners (and long sprinters)**

Possible objectives: Aerobic and anaerobic endurance; feel for pace.

Execution: Runs at low intensity (LI; see table 12 in chapter I–4.5); as in all tempo runs, the following rule holds true: run as fast and at as even a pace as possible; often with jogging intervals (very slow running instead of walking intervals).

Variations: On the track, for example as sets of 1000 or 2000m runs, cross-county as second or minute runs; flat or hilly course (fast uphill, slow downhill, or vice versa); on different surfaces (forest path, grass, road, dunes, etc.); rest interval possibly based on heart rate: incomplete or rewarding rest interval (in 1/3 of the time required for complete recovery 2/3 of the recovery take place, decrease of heart rate down to 120–130 beats/min).

Typical load standards: (Extensive) interval method; since training is performed mostly on cross-country courses, intensity is controlled rather via time: Figure 5 represents a possible system of interval training; additional programmes for example are

a) 3–6 reps of 2000m each, walking or jogging interval: 3–6 min

b) 4–8 reps of 1000m each, walking or jogging interval: 3–6 min

c) Running for 3, 4, 5, 4, and 3 min, jogging interval: 2 min

d) Running for 1, 2, 3, 4, 3, 2, and 1 min, jogging interval = running time

e) Running for 30, 45, 60, 75, 90, 75, 60, 45, and 30 sec, jogging interval = double running time.

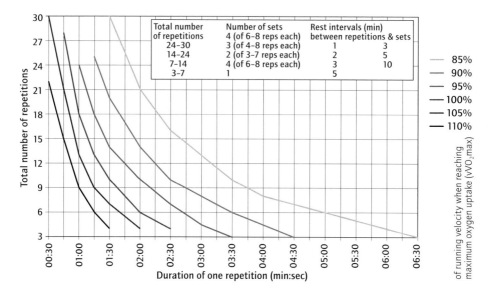

Total number of repetitions	Number of sets	Rest intervals (min) between repetitions & sets	
24–30	4 (of 6–8 reps each)	1	3
14–24	3 (of 4–8 reps each)	2	5
7–14	2 (of 3–7 reps each)	3	10
3–7	4 (of 6–8 reps each)	5	
	1		

*Figure 5: **Possible system of interval training in middle- and long-distance running** (modified on the basis of Thibault, 2003, p. 51): The system allows simple and endless variation possibilities in interval training. The desired (average) running velocity, which is represented by the six lines, is the automatic result of the pre-set training programme and maximum effort. In the course of the preparation period, either the running velocity can be increased (85% => 90% => ...), or the number of runs may be reduced with variable training in all velocity zones, or the total duration of the training programmes can be successively increased.*

The aforementioned long-time intervals (232) are primarily important for training aerobic endurance. However, middle- and long-distance runners, especially middle-distance runners, and here primarily 800m runners, also perform the middle- and short-time intervals (see 157, 159) mentioned in connection with the long sprint to greatly improve speed endurance.

233 Under-distance runs at competition pace

Possible objectives: Feel for pace, rehearsing tactical behaviour, aerobic and anaerobic endurance.

Execution: Maintaining planned intermediate times for competition , but not running the full competition distance.

Variations/Typical load standards: for 800m: 1–4 reps of 400–600m each, rest interval:

3–15 min; for 1500m: 1–4 reps of 800–1200m, rest interval: 3–10 min; for 5000 or 10000m: 1–4 reps of 2000–3000m, rest interval: 3–6 min; or as pyramid including a central (longest) run at competition pace.

234 Simulation of competition situations

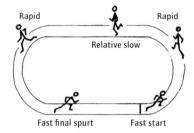

Rapid
Rapid
Relative slow
Fast final spurt   Fast start

Possible objectives: Technical and strategic training specific to middle- and long-distance running; anaerobic and aerobic endurance.

Execution/***Variations:*** Fast starts by several runners from a standing position and acceleration up to a target pace; many changes of pace, intermediate spurts, and overtaking manoeuvres (on the straight); with focus on the final spurt, possibly several final or intermediate spurts as a competition, similar to a points race in cycling; as variation within tempo runs.

Typical load standards: Very variable.

In addition, there are (preparatory) competitions for under-distances (I1 runs) as well as for over-distances particularly for middle-distance runners. In practice, the athletes often perform strength-endurance training as well. However, this should be done by using uphill and downhill runs (138 and 140) rather than by using bars and other devices. Moreover, IC, reactive-strength and maximal-eccentric training should be performed to improve running economy (see chapter II-1.10.2). Appropriate exercises are primarily 48–49, 60–64, and 77–88. Furthermore, strength(-endurance) training for the trunk (41–47 and 66–67) and foot-stabilisation training (50–52 and 74) should be performed.

1.10.7   SPECIAL TEST AND CONTROL PROCEDURES

Test: Ability/skill tested	Execution/comments
T61 **Standing start and acceleration:** Start and start acceleration	A maximum sprint over 21m is performed from a standing start. The standing start is initiated on a command which should be variable and delayed for a long time to prevent the athlete from tilting forward in anticipation or from taking a preliminary swing. The measurement is performed using a light barrier at the 1 and 21m point. Manual timing would be too inaccurate. With some systems it is also possible to record the time at the moment when the foot releases contact with the contact area. The test should be performed both in the curve and on the straight.
T62 **Technique analysis:** Running technique	The running technique (during a competition) is assessed by using a technique-analysis sheet (see chapter II–1.10.3); possibly using video recordings (T1) or photo sequences made thereof.
T63 **Measurement of stride frequency and lengths:** Technique and special strength endurance	The average stride frequency and stride length may be calculated by using time measurement and counting the strides over a certain distance. A comparison of stride frequency and stride length in different training periods, in the starting, middle, and final segments of a race, as well as with deliberate variation may provide valuable clues for technique and strength training.
T64 **Tactical analysis:** Racing strategy	From the intermediate times recorded during a competitive race or the time-code of a corresponding video recording, the interval times for certain partial distances are calculated and compared with the pre-set times in the respective strategy chapters.
T65 **Minute tests (8-, 12-, 15-, 30-, 45-, or 60-min run):** Aerobic endurance in running	Ultimately, every middle- and long-distance run is a running-specific endurance test. As a test and control procedure in training, the distance covered in a given time is often measured instead of the time for a given distance. The most well-known minute test is the 12-minute Cooper test. Table 2 helps to assess the results of young athletes. For adults, the distance covered can be used to roughly estimate the $\dot{V}O_2max$ (see chapter I–1.5 as well as the measurement methods below; see table 3). However, the results in the Cooper test are influenced by a variety of factors such as

Test: Ability/skill tested	Execution/comments
	competitors and sense of time. Therefore, minute tests do not reach the accuracy of sports-medical tests (especially spiroergometry).

Table 2: **Estimation of the results achieved in the Cooper test** *(according to Grosser et al., 1986, p. 129): The values presented are for boys; for the girls, 200m should be subtracted in each case.*

	Age (years)	11	12	13	14	15	16	17	
Assessment of aerobic endurance	Excellent	2800	2850	2900	2950	3000	3050	3100	Distance (m)
	Very good	2600	2650	2700	2750	2800	2850	2900	
	Good	2200	2250	2300	2350	2400	2450	2500	
	Satisfactory	1800	1850	1900	1950	2000	2050	2100	
	Poor	1200	1250	1300	1350	1400	1450	1500	
	Insufficient				less than poor				

Table 3: **Estimation of the maximum oxygen uptake** *($\dot{V}O_2$max) of men using the distance covered in the Cooper test (according to Cooper, 1970, p. 29).*

Distance covered (km)	<1.6	1.6–2	2–2.4	2.4–2.8	>2.8
$\dot{V}O_2$max (ml/kg/min)	<25	25–34	34–43	43–52	>52

Variations of the Cooper test are the 8-min run for children and the 15-min run, which is supposed to reduce the influence of anaerobic endurance. The influence of anaerobic endurance is even less in the 30-, 45-, and 60-min tests, which are mainly used in (highly) competitive long-distance training. Table 4 shows how training speeds can be derived from a 30-min test. In the hours run even world records are listed by the WA:

Women:	18,930 m, Sifan Hasan, Netherlands (04 September 2020, Brussels);
Men:	21,330 m, Mo Farah, United Kingdom (04 September 2020, Brussels).

(continued)

435

Track & Field

(continued)

Test: Ability/skill tested	Execution/comments
T66 **Graded (field) or ramp tests:** Anaerobic and aerobic running endurance	Graded tests are endurance tests in which the load increases in standardised steps. Tests with many small short steps or with a rapid continuous increase in intensity are also called ramp tests. They can either be performed on ergometers (e.g., on a treadmill) or as (graded) field tests on a 400m track. In the latter tests, the intensity (i.e., the running speed) is checked at regular intervals by means of acoustic signals. On each signal, the subjects must have covered a certain marked distance (usually 50 m). The result of each graded test (lactate values, spiroergometric measuring values, etc.) also depends on the length and height of the steps. To compare the tests of one and the same athlete in the course of a season, the test protocols must be accurately standardised (i.e., the tests must be conducted under identical conditions, including nutrition before the test, treadmill type, or running surface, etc.).

Moreover, additional sport-medicine tests (e.g., blood tests), biomechanical tests, sport-psychology tests, nutritional tests, etc. may be necessary, especially to answer specific questions.

Table 4: **Derivation of training interval times from a 30-min endurance test.**
(Caution: The percentage values relate to the 30-min test. This means that this intensity neither corresponds with the values presented in figure 5 nor with those in table 12 in chapter I–4.5.)

30-min test				Training					
Distance	Velocity		Time/400 m			Time (in min:sec) per km			
(m)	(m/sec)	(km/h)	100%	100%	95%	90%	85%	70%	>110%
				Tempo-endurance run (228)		Continuous run (227)		Recovery run (226)	Long-time intervals (232)
10.000	5.56	20.0	1:12.0	3:00	3:09	3:20	3:32	4:17	<2:44
9867	5.48	19.7	1:13.0	3:02	3:12	3:23	3:35	4:21	<2:46
9733	5.41	19.5	1:14.0	3:05	3:15	3:25	3:38	4:24	<2:48
9600	5.33	19.2	1:15.0	3:08	3:17	3:28	3:41	4:28	<2:50
9467	5.26	18.9	1:16.1	3:10	3:20	3:31	3:44	4:32	<2:53
9333	5.19	18.7	1:17.1	3:13	3:23	3:34	3:47	4:36	<2:55
9200	5.11	18.4	1:18.3	3:16	3:26	3:37	3:50	4:40	<2:58
9067	5.04	18.1	1:19.4	3:19	3:29	3:41	3:54	4:44	<3:00
8933	4.96	17.9	1:20.6	3:21	3:32	3:44	3:57	4:48	<3:03
8800	4.89	17.6	1:21.8	3:25	3:35	3:47	4:01	4:52	<3:06
8667	4.81	17.3	1:23.1	3:28	3:39	3:51	4:04	4:57	<3:09
8533	4.74	17.1	1:24.4	3:31	3:42	3:54	4:08	5:01	<3:12
8400	4.67	16.8	1:25.7	3:34	3:46	3:58	4:12	5:06	<3:15
8267	4.59	16.5	1:27.1	3:38	3:49	4:02	4:16	5:11	<3:18
8133	4.52	16.3	1:28.5	3:41	3:53	4:06	4:20	5:16	<3:21
8000	4.44	16.0	1:30.0	3:45	3:57	4:10	4:25	5:21	<3:25
7867	4.37	15.7	1:31.5	3:49	4:01	4:14	4:29	5:27	<3:28
7733	4.30	15.5	1:33.1	3:53	4:05	4:19	4:34	5:33	<3:32
7600	4.22	15.2	1:34.7	3:57	4:09	4:23	4:39	5:38	<3:35
7467	4.15	14.9	1:36.4	4:01	4:14	4:28	4:44	5:44	<3:39
7333	4.07	14.7	1:38.2	4:05	4:18	4:33	4:49	5:51	<3:43
7200	4.00	14.4	1:40.0	4:10	4:23	4:38	4:54	5:57	<3:47
7067	3.93	14.1	1:41.9	4:15	4:28	4:43	5:00	6:04	<3:52
6933	3.85	13.9	1:43.8	4:20	4:33	4:48	5:05	6:11	<3:56
6800	3.78	13.6	1:45.9	4:25	4:39	4:54	5:11	6:18	<4:01
6667	3.70	13.3	1:48.0	4:30	4:44	5:00	5:18	6:26	<4:05
6533	3.63	13.1	1:50.2	4:36	4:50	5:06	5:24	6:34	<4:10
6400	3.56	12.8	1:52.5	4:41	4:56	5:13	5:31	6:42	<4:16
6267	3.48	12.5	1:54.9	4:47	5:02	5:19	5:38	6:50	<4:21
6133	3.41	12.3	1:57.4	4:53	5:09	5:26	5:45	6:59	<4:27
6000	3.33	12.0	1:50.0	5:00	5:16	5:33	5:53	7:09	<4:33
5867	3.26	11.7	2:02.7	5:07	5:23	5:41	6:01	7:18	<4:39
5733	3.19	11.5	2:05.6	5:14	5:30	5:49	6:09	7:29	<4:45
5600	3.11	11.2	2:08.6	5:21	5:38	5:57	6:18	7:39	<4:52
5467	3.04	10.9	2:11.7	5:29	5:47	6:06	6:27	7:50	<4:59
5333	2.96	10.7	2:15.0	5:38	5:55	6:15	6:37	8:02	<5:07

METHODS OF MEASURING PHYSIOLOGICAL ENDURANCE PARAMETERS

LACTATE DIAGNOSTICS

In the graded (field) test (see T66) including lactate diagnostics, capillary blood is taken from the subject after each load step (usually from the earlobe). If such a test is carried out during running, running has to be interrupted for a standardised time (usually 30 seconds) for blood sampling after each stage. Although this disadvantage does not exist in a graded step test on a bicycle ergometer, a precise derivation of training speeds is not possible from this test due to the different form of movement. The respective lactate levels in the blood are measured using laboratory analysis. This results in the typical lactate performance curve (see figure 6). The training of aerobic endurance leads to a shift to the right in the lactate performance curve. In addition to the state of training, the test make-up and analysis devices, the state of exhaustion (e.g., caused by training on the day before), and the previous diet (poor or rich in carbohydrates) may modify the test results.

The blood lactate value is influenced by both the lactate formation rate (anaerobic metabolism) and the lactate removal rate (aerobic metabolism). In performance diagnostics, various lactate threshold concepts are used.

In competitive long-sprint and middle-distance training (T33, T72, and T92),

lactate values are also often measured as part of (test) tempo-run programmes. They help to interpret the times achieved and indicate whether the training is performed within the desired intensity zone.

SPIROERGOMETRY

Spiroergometry is the measurement of respiratory gases while controlling the athlete's applied energy at the same time. Using a mask through which the subject breathes in and out, not only the respiratory rate and the amount of inhaled air (tidal and minute ventilation), but also the proportions of gases contained therein can be analysed. Of the latter, oxygen (O_2) and carbon dioxide (CO_2) shed light on physiological performance parameters.

Maximum oxygen uptake ($\dot{V}O_2$max, see chapter I–1.5) is the classic spiroergometric performance parameter of endurance capacity. It is measured in millilitres of oxygen per minute and relates to the athlete's body weight as relative oxygen uptake (ml/kg/min). (Relative) $\dot{V}O_2$max

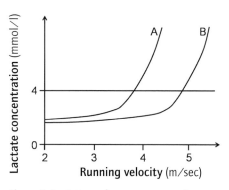

Figure 6: *Lactate-performance curve* of an athlete before (A) and after (B) a training period to improve aerobic endurance (modified on the basis of Janssen, 1989, p. 128).

is achieved in ramp tests with very short exercise steps. During these tests, there is an initial linear increase in oxygen uptake with exercise intensity (running velocity). After that, the curve flattens and the (maximum) oxygen uptake (achieved) remains constant even in the case of a further increase in intensity. In heterogeneous performance groups,

$\dot{V}O_2$max correlates with middle- and long-distance running performance. The correlations are higher in men than in women. In a homogeneous group of elite marathon runners there is only a low correlation. Table 5 shows the average $\dot{V}O_2$max values of athletes in different athletics disciplines.

Table 5: **Maximum oxygen uptake of highly trained runners** (according to Legaz-Arrese et al., 2005, p. 7): during a graded treadmill test; within the period of two months before the seasonal best performance.

Event	n	Age	Men Performance (h:min:sec)	$\dot{V}O_2$max (ml/kg/min)	n	Age	Women Performance (h:min:sec)	$\dot{V}O_2$max (ml/kg/min)
100m	18	21.4	10.70	61.9 ± 6.5	5	24.9	12.18	48.2 ± 5.6
400m	22	23.9	47.77	62.5 ± 6.2	9	22.3	55.23	56.6 ± 4.4
800m	24	21.7	1:50.07	68.5 ± 5.0	7	22.8	2:07.13	63.4 ± 6.6
1500m	18	24.2	3:42.08	73.9 ± 5.7	9	24.8	4:19.65	61.7 ± 5.8
3000m	3	26.9	7:45.53	77.6 ± 4.4	6	21.7	9:11.61	69.2 ± 5.3
3000m-Hi.	9	21.8	8:38.90	79.9 ± 5.5				
5000m	7	25.1	13:45.49	78.9 ± 8.5	2	26.6	15:13.88	69.8 ± 11.5
10,000m	17	26.1	28:58.75	77.1 ± 5.6	5	24.6	33:54.77	71.1 ± 8.3
Marathon	19	30.4	2:13:21	80.1 ± 4.0	10	30.8	2:35:50	73.7 ± 6.7

Table 6: **Maximum duration** of the maintenance of an intensity corresponding to a certain percentage of the performance at the moment when reaching maximum oxygen uptake in a runner with poor aerobic endurance (A) and in a runner with good aerobic endurance (B) (according to Thibault, 2003, p. 50; 2006, 14).

% of vVO₂max	110	105	100	95	90	85	80	75	70	65
A	3:00	4:00	7:00	11:00	17:00	26:00	40:00	1:02:00	2:27:00	3:47:00
B	3:00	4:00	7:00	15:13	32:54	1:10:55	2:33:00	5:30:00	very long	very long

1.10.8 ERRORS – CAUSES – CORRECTIONS

In all disciplines, coaches should not stand too close to the action and should vary their angle of observation to detect all errors effectively. Errors and their detection are always individual. Nevertheless, some errors can be identified which are particularly common or important for beginners. Of these errors, up to six are highlighted in blue for each discipline.

Error	Causes	Corrections
Running style appears tense (e.g., high shoulders, movements which are not round and smooth, etc.).	• Unnecessary contraction of not involved muscles (waste of energy). • Co-contraction (simultaneous contraction) of antagonist muscles (see chapter II–1.1.2).	✔ The athlete should try to achieve a general looseness through relaxation of his/her facial muscles (mouth slightly opened, cheeks relaxed) and hand muscles (neither clenched nor fingers spread); now and again the athlete should hold his/her arms dangling downward in a relaxed manner. ✔ Versatile exercises of the ABCs of sprinting or running (see chapter II–1.3.8) as well as relaxed acceleration runs (129).
Incomplete leg extension during the rear support phase (too short strides).	• Unfavourable relationship of stride length and stride frequency. • Lack of relaxation or too tense running style and its causes (see above). • Lack of leg extension strength. • Too short hip flexors.	✔ Deliberate variation of stride length and stride frequency in training. ✔ See corrections of running style appears tense above.) ✔ Continuous runs (227 and 228) and fartlek (230) in hilly terrain, hill runs (138), and jumps (86–88). ✔ Flexibility training for the hip flexors (25).
Jumping strides (too long strides).	• Unfavourable relationship of stride length and stride frequency. • Too vertical push-off.	✔ Deliberate variation of stride length and stride frequency in training. ✔ Shorter strides at faster pace.
Foot touchdown over the heel.	• Exaggerated kicking movement of the lower leg during the front swing phase. • Deliberately long strides.	✔ Grasping imitations (114), goose steps (116), step-overs (117), and skipping with grasping action (118), in each case with deliberate foot touchdown over the outside close to the vertical projection of the CG. ✔ Deliberate variation of stride length and stride frequency in training.
Lowering of the foot onto the entire sole even when running at fast pace.	• Too weak calf muscles or too low reactive strength endurance of the calf muscles.	✔ Specific strength (-endurance) training for the calf muscles: calf exercise (61), ankle jumps (84), ABCs of endurance (141), etc.

Error	Causes	Corrections
Overpronation.	• Too weak foot (joint) stabilising muscles. • Weak ligament apparatus, bony deformations.	✔ Exercises on unstable ground (50), walking variations (51), etc. ✔ Possibly switch to another shoe brand. ✔ If the connective-tissue problem is too great (e.g., flat foot), one should possibly advise against an (extensive) running training.
Too little, too extensive, or otherwise wrong use of arm actions (e.g., diagonal, with too much movement at the elbow, with too small or too large angle at the elbow).	• Fatigue and lack of strength endurance of the arm and shoulder muscles. • Athlete makes insufficient effort to run economically.	✔ Deliberate variation of arm actions as well as strength-endurance training using exercise 60 (also running while carrying weights in one's hands). ✔ Demonstration and imitation.
Restless and/or swinging upper body (exaggerated shoulder-hip separation).	• Unsymmetrical and/or diagonal arm actions (transverse arm actions). • Too marked flexion of the arms at the elbow joint. • Lack of trunk stability. • Restless head.	✔ Deliberate variation of arm actions as well as strength-endurance training using exercise 60 (also running while carrying weights in one's hands). ✔ Demonstration and imitation. ✔ Strength-endurance training of the trunk muscles using exercises 41–47 and 66 and 67. ✔ Control of the viewing direction (straight ahead; see chapter 1.10.4).
Frequent looking back during running in competition (disturbs the running rhythm).	• For most runners this indicates a lack of self-confidence (i.e., they do not look back for orientation).	✔ Directing one's focus on one's own performance capacity. ✔ Encouragement. ✔ Psychological counselling.
The runner leaves the inside lane for too long or too often and overtakes others in the curve.	• Athlete makes insufficient effort to find the shortest running path. • Lack of experience. • Over-motivation.	✔ Discussion, as well as variation and (careful) testing of tactical behaviour in many competitions.
Uneven split times, deviation from the tub shape or from the racing plan.	• Lack of feel for pace. • Running for victory instead of for time (caution: uneven split times are also dangerous when running for victory). • Can be caused during road races by terrain, wind, etc.	✔ Training of general feel for pace using tempo runs (232, use of many different distances), or similar exercises (221, and 154 and 155). ✔ Runs at competition pace (233). ✔ Using rewards (and punishment) to force the runner to concentrate on the exact keeping of pre-set split times.

1.10.9 BIBLIOGRAPHY

Ascensão, A., Santos, P., Magalhães, J., Oliveira, J., Krüger, J. & Soares, J. (2002a). Maximal lactate steady state in young male athletes. *New Studies in Athletics 17* (1), 25-33.

Ascensão, A., Santos, P., Magalhães, J., Oliveira, J., Maia, J. A. & Soares, J. M. C. (2002b). Blood lactate concentrations during a constant load at an intensity corresponding to the aerobic-anaerobic threshold in young athletes. *New Studies in Athletics 17* (2), 29-35.

Baum, K. (2005). Die optimale Vorbereitung, um 42,195 km durchzustehen. *Condition 36* (10), 5-12.

Belz, V. (2006). Deep Water Running. *Leichtathletiktraining 17* (2+3), 52-57.

Benson, T. (1993). Steeplechasing – the art of interrupted running. *Modern Athlete and Coach 31* (1), 15-18.

Benson, T. (1998). Accumulated volume – the forgotten factor. *Modern Athlete and Coach 36* (2), 30-33.

Camus, G. (1992). Relationship between record time and maximal oxygen consumption in middle-distance running. *European Journal of Applied Physiology and Occupational Physiology 64*, 534-537.

Canova, R. (1998). Can cross-country running be considered an athletics event in its own right? *New Studies in Athletics 13* (4), 13-19.

Cavanag, P. R. & Williams, K. R. (1982). The effect of stride length variation on oxygen uptake during distance running. *Medicine & Science in Sport & Exercise 14*, 30-35.

Conconi, F., Ferrari, M., Ziglio, P. G., Droghetti, P. & Codeca, L. (1982). Determination of the anaerobic threshold by a non-invasive field test in runners. *Journal of Applied Physiology 52* (4), 869-873.

Cooper, K. H. (1970). *The new aerobics.* New York: Bantam Books.

Coyle, E. F. (2005). Very intense exercise-training is extremely potent and time efficient: a reminder. *Journal of Applied Physiology 98*, 1983-1984.

Faude, O., Meyer, T. & Kindermann, W. (2008). ‚Schwellentraining' für jedermann. *Leichtathletiktraining 19* (1), 28-37.

Ferreira, R. L. & Rolim, R (2006). The evolution or marathon training: A comparative analysis of elite runners' training programmes. *New Studies in Athletics 21* (1), 29-37.

Geese, R. & Popovic, S. (2009). Schneller durch Reaktivkrafttraining? *Leichtathletiktraining* *20* (1), 26-29.

Gibala, M. J., Little, J. P., van Essen, M., Wilkin, G. P., Burgomaster, K. A., Safdar, A., Raha, S. & Tarnopolsky, M. A. (2006). Short-term sprint interval versus traditional endurance training: similar initial adaptations in human skeletal muscle and exercise performance. *Journal of Physiology 575* (3), 901-911.

Grosser, M., Brüggemann, P. & Zintl, F. (1986). *Leistungssteuerung in Training und Wettkampf*. München: BLV.

Hanon, C., Thomas, C., Le Chevalier, J. M., Gajer, B. & Vandewalle, H. (2002). How does O$_2$ evolve during the 800 m? *New Studies in Athletics 17* (2), 61-68.

Hanon, C., Levêque, J. M. & Thomas, C. (2007). Oxygen uptake in the 1500 metres. *New Studies in Athletics 22* (1), 15-22.

Hartmann, U. (2004). *Grundlagen der Energiebereitstellung* (Materialien zur A-Trainer-Ausbildung). Mainz: Deutscher Leichtathletik Verband.

Hollmann, W., Strüder, H. K., Predel, H.-G. & Tagarakis, C. V. M. (2006). *Spiroergometrie: Kardiopulmonale Leistungsdiagnostik des Gesunden und Kranken*. Stuttgart: Schattauer.

Incalza, P. (2007). Stride parameters in endurance runners. *New Studies in Athletics 22* (4), 41-60.

Janssen, P. G. J. M. (übersetzt von Weineck, J.). (2003). *Ausdauertraining: Trainingssteuerung über die Herzfrequenz- und Milchsäurebestimmung* (3., überarb. u. erw. Aufl.). Balingen: Spitta.

Karp, J. R. (2006). Strength training and distance running: a scientific perspective. *Modern Athlete and Coach 44* (4), 20-23.

Legaz Arese, A. Munguía Izquierdo, D. & Moliner Urdiales, D. (2005). A review of the maximal oxygen uptake values necessary for different running performance levels. *New Studies in Athletics 20* (3), 7-20.

Markworth, P. (2007). *Sportmedizin: physiologische Grundlagen* (21. Aufl.). Reinbek: Rowohlt.

Mazzeo, R. S. (2008). Physiological response to exercise at altitude: an update. *Sports Medicine 38* (1), 1-8.

Nurmekivi, A., Lemberg, H., Kaljumäe, Ü. & Maaroos, J. (2002). The relationship between marathon performance and construction of training. *Modern Athlete and Coach 40* (2), 22-26.

O'Connell, C. (1996). Environmental conditions, training systems and performance developement of Kenyan runners. *New Studies in Athletics 11* (4), 25-36.

Paavoleinen, L., Häkkinen, K., Hämäläinen, I., Numela, A. & Rusko, H. (1999). Explosive-strength training improves 5-km running time by improving running economy and muscle power. *Journal of Applied Physiology 86* (5), 1527-1533.

Regelkommissionen des DLV, FLA, ÖLV und SLV (Hrsg.). (2010). *Internationale Wettkampfregeln.* Waldfischbach: Hornberger.

Reiss, M. (1998) Hauptrichtungen des Einsatzes und der Methodik des Höhentrainings in Ausdauersportarten. *Leistungssport 28* (4), 21-28.

Schön, R. & Hommel, H. (Red.) (mit Bauer, J., Hessel, H., Jung, K., Moch, K., Neuhof, J., von Papen, H. & Sanne, M.). (1992). *Rahmentrainingsplan für das Aufbautraining Lauf* (Edition Leichtathletik, 3, 2. Aufl.). Aachen: Meyer & Meyer.

Spurs, W. R., Murphy, A. J. & Watsford, M. L. (2003). The effect of plyometric training on distance running performance. *European Journal of Applied Physiology 89* (1), 1-7.

Thibault, G. (2003). A graphical model of interval training. *New Studies in Athletics 18* (3), 49-55.

Thibault, G. & Péronnet, F. (2006). It is not lactic acid's fault. *New Studies in Athletics 21* (1), 9-15.

Tulloh, B. (1998). The role of cross-country in the development of a runner. *New Studies in Athletics 13* (4), 9-11.

Turner, A. M., Owings, M., & Schwane, J. A. (2003). Improvement in Running Economy After 6 Weeks of Plyometric Training. *Journal of Strength and Conditioning Research 17* (1), 60-67.

Von Papen, H. (2008). Leitsätze für das Training des Läufers. *Leichtathletiktraining 19* (2+3), 41-47.

Weineck, J. (2000). *Optimales Training: Leistungsphysiologische Trainingslehre unter besonderer Berücksichtigung des Kinder- und Jugendtrainings* (12. Aufl.). Balingen: Spitta.

Wilber, R. L. (2007). Application of altidute/hypoxic training by elite athletes. *Medicine and Science in Sports and Exercise 39* (9), 1610-1624.

Zacharogiannis, E., Smirniotou, A., Tziortzis, S. & Paradisis, G. (2007). The relationship of selected physiological characteristics with performance on the historic Athens marathon course. *New Studies in Athletics 22* (1), 39-48.

1.11 800 AND 1500M

1.11.1 TRIPLE WORLD RECORD RESULTING FROM INTERVAL TRAINING

Even the first modern Olympic Games in Athens in 1896 included a men's 800m and 1500m race. Women ran 800m for the first time at the Olympic Games in 1928. However, the officials and journalists present were of the opinion that the women were too exhausted after the race. Endurance loads were generally considered unphysiological for women. Thus, the 800m distance, too, was estimated to be too long for women and was removed from the Olympic programme. Only in 1960 were the women's 800m and in 1972 the women's 1500m included (again) in the Olympic competition programme.

Until today, the middle distances also include the 1000m, 1609m (the mile), and 2000m, all of which are run in competitions at events. Up to the 1950s, the mile was almost as important as the 1500m, particularly in English-speaking countries. The greatest goal was to complete the mile under four minutes, which was first achieved by the British runner Roger Bannister in 1954. Sometimes, the 3000m, which from 1983 to 1993 was run by women at world championships and Olympic Games, is also referred to as a middle-distance race.

Between 1912 and 1936, the Scandinavians, especially the Finnish

runners, dominated the Olympic races from 1500 to 10,000m. The best-known runner was Paavo Nurmi, who in 1924 won two races within 50 min, the 1500 and the 5000m, and was also victorious in the cross-country event. Four years later, he won gold over 10,000m and silver over the 5000m and the 3000m steeplechase. When the Finns won all the medals over 10,000m in 1936, the German Reich's Committee for Physical Education sent the then Secretary General of the Olympic Games, Carl Diem, to Finland to determine the reasons for the Finnish superiority on site. The Finns trained under their coach Pikhala in hilly terrain around Helsinki. Short uphill runs – almost sprints, which developed leg strength – were combined with relaxing downhill runs at a moderate pace. Pikhala called his method *terrace training* since each load was supposed to be based on the previous one just like one terrace serves as the basis of a higher terrace. After having read Diem's report, running coach Woldemar Gerschler and sports-medicine expert Herbert Reindell from the German town of Freiburg im Breisgau first attempted to answer the following question in symbiotic collaboration: How can terrace training be performed if the training ground does not have the typical rolling hills? They quickly found the answer: Medium-speed runs on a running track must be alternated with jogging intervals for recovery. The most suitable appeared to be 200m sections. Gerschler and Reindell coined the terms *rewarding rest interval* (see 232) and interval training. *Interval training* in particular has been accepted worldwide.

An outstanding interpreter of interval training was Gerschler's student Rudolf Harbig. The Rudolf Harbig Prize is awarded every year to the most successful German athletes. Even today, Harbig is regarded as one of the most important German track athletes of all time. From 1941 onwards, he simultaneously held world records over 400m (46.0 sec), 800m (1:46.6 min), and 1000m (2:21.5 min). Even the 1500m quadruple world champion and world-record holder Hicham El Guerrouj and the 800m triple world champion and world-record holder Wilson Kipketer have not achieved such a feat. The continued future development of the Kenyan 800m runner David Rudisha, who achieved the only world record at the 2012 Olympic Games in London (1:40.91 min), remains to be seen.

1.11.2   THE MOST IMPORTANT COMPETITION RULES

The following abridged and simplified International Competition Rules comprise the framework for the technique and strategy, as well as for the organisation of 800m competitions:

- The 800m race is run from a one-turn staggered start in individual lanes. The starting lines in lanes 2 to 8 are white with a 40cm wide green section in the middle.
- If there are more than eight runners in an 800m race, the lanes may be occupied by two runners.
- After the first curve of the 800m race, a green line across lanes 2 to 8 shows the point from which the runners can run to the inside lane. Small cones, prisms, or tennis balls cut in half should be placed at the intersections between the lane boundary lines and the green line.

- In smaller competitions, the 800m races may also be started from the respective arced starting line.

Otherwise, the general competition rules for running and for the middle- and long-distance races apply (see chapters II–1.1.1 and II–1.10.1).

In the (track athletics) championship programme for the U12 age group, the 800m is the only middle-distance race. In the U14 age group, the 2000m is an additional middle- (or long-) distance event; in the U16 age group, the 3000m is included. From the U18 age group onwards, the 800m, 1500m, and 3000m are run in competition. In the adult and junior age groups, the 3000m race is no longer part of the championship programme on the international, national, and state levels.

1.11.3 SPORT-SCIENCE FINDINGS, PHASE STRUCTURE, AND TECHNIQUE

The phase structure and running technique of middle- and long-distance running have already been described in general in chapter II–1.10.2. Therefore, in the following, only certain specific sport-science findings will be presented.

The prototypical middle-distance event is the 1500m. At the beginning of the 20th century, even the 400m race was considered to be a middle-distance event. However, the 800m race is now sometimes considered a long sprint. The relationship between the 400 and 800m race is not only illustrated by the very great importance of the anaerobic energy supply, but also the velocity profile shown in the strategy chapter (II–1.11.6). Kinematic studies of the running technique also confirm this close relationship. For example, the support times in the 800m race are only 120–130 msec.

It is believed that in general performance over the middle distances greatly depends on the performance over shorter distances, including (maximum sprinting) speed.

Table 1 shows the 100m mean times for middle-distance world-record holders. However, runners must be able to run or to sprint the (flying) 100m even faster especially for the second reason mentioned:

- The velocity profile of the race is irregular which means that much faster segments are included.
- Running at maximal speed is less economic than running at submaximal speed. This means that an athlete runs more economically at a given speed the greater his/her speed potential.

Table 1: **Average 100m times** *in world-record middle-distance races (see also table 1 in chapter II–1.10.2).*

800m	David Luketa Rudisha (Kenya): 1:40.91 min (9 August 2012, London)	12.61 sec
	Jarmila Kratochvilova (CSSR): 1:53.28 min (26 July 1983, Munich)	14.16 sec
1500m	Hicham El Guerrouj (Morocco): 3:26.00 min (14 July 1998, Rome)	13.73 sec
	Genzebe Dibaba (Ethiopia): 3:50.07 min (17 July 2015, Monaco)	15.34 sec

1.11.4 SUMMARY OF THE MOST IMPORTANT TECHNICAL
CHARACTERISTICS = TECHNIQUE-ANALYSIS SHEET

See chapter II–1.10.3.

*Table 2: **Requirement profile for the 800m and 1500m race:** The suggested rough estimate of the value of selected factors determining performance is based on the importance for the overall performance and the percentage of time spent training (IR: information requirements, constr.: constraints; see chapter I-1.1).*

Factors determining 800m and 1500m performance Estimate of valueNotes	Estimate of value	Notes
Coordination	+ + +	optical IR: medium, acoustic IR: medium, then low, tactile IR: low–medium, kinaesthetic IR: medium, vestibular IR: low–medium; precision constr.: high, time constr.: medium, complexity constr.: low, situation constr.: medium–high, physical stress constr.: high
Flexibility	+	no extreme movement amplitudes required
Strength		extensor loop (glutes, quadriceps, triceps surae, erector spinae), iliopsoas; hamstrings; adductors, abdominus, shoulder and upper-arm muscles
Maximal strength	+ + (+)	mainly as a basis (in the 1500m race less important)
Reactive strength	+ + +	of decisive importance for running economy even over longer distances
Speed	+ + (+)	primarily cyclic (in the 1500m race less important); acyclic aspects at the start, during compensatory movements in jostling and when attacking the finish line; speed of reaction to acoustic (at the start) and optical stimuli (running in close group)
Endurance (general dynamic) Anaerobic endurance		
Strength endurance	+ + (+)	as the basis of speed endurance (in the 1500m race less important)
Speed endurance	+ + + + (+)	since the competition speed is above the running pace corresponding with the aerobic-anaerobic threshold (see lactate diagnostics in Chapter II-1.10.7), there is a continuous increase of blood-lactate concentration throughout the race
Aerobic endurance	+ + + + +	the 800m competition speed is above the velocity when reaching maximum oxygen uptake (vVO2max; see spirometry in chapter II-1.10.7), whereas the 1500m competition speed is approximately within this range
Psychological and cognitive abilities	+ + + + +	feel for pace and correct strategy (initial pace); ability to deliberately achieve low pH values (lactate acidosis) and to tolerate them; performance-oriented thinking and behaviour (see chapter I-3.1.1)
Anthropometric and primarily genetically determined characteristics	+ + + +	connective tissue with optimal energy-storing capacities; medium body height; very low percentage of body fat

1.11.5   PHOTO SEQUENCE

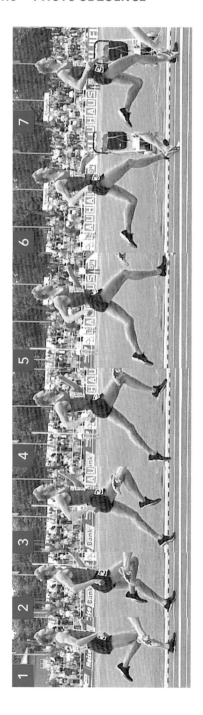

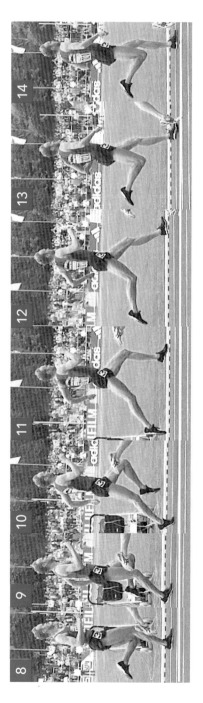

Data about the photo sequence

Athlete: Nils Schumann
(born: 20 May 1978,
Germany)
Event: 800 m
Height/weight: 1.92 m/77 kg
Performance: 1:46.08 min (7 July 2002,
Wattenscheid)
Best performance: 1:44.16 min
(30 August 2002, Brussels)
Greatest success: Olympic champion 2000,
European champion 1998

COMMENTARY

The photo sequence shows Nils Schumann 30 metres in front of the finish line at the German Athletics Championships in Wattenscheid in 2002. Still training for the European Championships in Munich, Schumann placed second. He was beaten by his successor leading the German 800m ranking list, Rene Herms, who after four additional German champion titles (2003–2006) died of virus-induced myocarditis in 2009. In 2002, more than a month after the run shown here, Schumann finished third at the European Athletics Championships behind the former world-record holder Wilson Kipketer and the Swiss André Bucher; Herms was seventh. Schumann achieved the best performance of his career three weeks later in that year. Schumann's good technique is still clearly visible even in the present photo sequence.

Schumann runs ideally with an upright or minimally bent forward body, erect and stable head position, and arm movements with good shoulder and elbow angles. However, probably due to fatigue, his shoulders swing a little too much about the longitudinal axis of his body contralaterally to his leg movements . In addition, it may

be presumed (e.g., pictures 5–7) that Schumann moves his arms back and forth not quite parallel but with slightly evasive movements to the sides.

Schumann's average stride length of 2.13m on the last 100m (due to fatigue) is slightly below the average stride length over the entire race distance (2.17m). He compensates for this, however, by increasing stride frequency (3.57 versus 3.47 strides/sec). Typically for an 800m championship race, his velocity over the last 100m is slightly higher than his average velocity for the entire race (7.59 versus 7.54 m/sec; see chapter II–1.11.6).

The good stride pattern is also obvious upon closer examination of his leg movement. Schumann places his foot with a high hip and a slightly bent knee on the ground close to the vertical projection of his CG. The foot strike takes place over the outside edge of the midfoot. In this phase of maximum fatigue, Schumann seems to lower his foot onto the entire sole. The flexion at the knee joint during the support phase also seems to be adequate for the race situation. The rear support phase results in a complete extension during push-off.

Due to the extremely erect position of the pelvis and the rapid, energetic forward movement of the thigh, Schumann can subsequently avoid an extensive rear swing phase. The minimum knee angle appears a little too large for the high speed of the 800m race. With a clearer, sprint-like heel lift under his body, he would be able to move his leg back in front of his body even faster. This would enable a slightly higher knee lift (which must, however, remain below that of a sprinter for reasons of economy) and thus an even better preparation for the subsequent touchdown of the foot. Of course, the lack of looseness during the final sprint makes this extremely difficult under conditions of the highest hyperacidity. Nevertheless, Schumann succeeds in moving his foot backward and downward in an active pulling manner before touchdown and after finishing the forward swinging movement of his lower leg during the active thigh movement.

1.11.6 STRATEGY

800M

An examination of the velocity profile in the 800m race illustrates the above-mentioned central role of the 800m run between the long sprint and the middle distances. An analysis of the two halves of the race, or 200m segments, shows that velocity in the 800m race seems to decrease continuously like in the long sprint after the start acceleration. A closer look at the average 100m split times, however, illustrates the middle-distance character of the 800m race (see figure 1) since the typical tub shape of the velocity profile becomes obvious (see chapter II–1.10.4). The faster starting phase is longer than in the 1500m race. The fact that the highest average speed is only achieved in the second 100m segment of the race is probably due to the acceleration from rest in the first segment. The actual peak velocity is probably achieved during the first 100m (see figure 2 in chapter II–1.2.2). During the last 100 metres, 800m runners usually remain below their average speed over the previous two 100m segments. It is unclear whether this is actually useful, or evidence of a final spurt that is usually started too early, or merely an expression of the fact that the race is often already decided before the last few metres.

1500M

Figures 2 and 3 show average 100m section times in the 1500m race as well as a strategic model derived from this. The latter corresponds to the typical tub shape described above (see chapter II–1.10.4). In addition to the fact that the first 100m are run significantly faster than the subsequent 100m sections and that there is an unexplained significant decrease

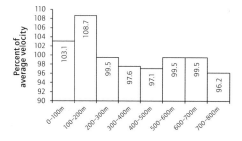

*Figure 1: **Tactical model for the 800m**, derived from an analysis of 800 races in the range of 1:42 to 1:53 min (modified on the basis of Gajer et al., 2000, p. 23): Only those performances were analysed which were not more than 1.5 sec above the personal best of the respective athlete.*

in velocity on the 7th 100m section, the following is evident: As in the 800m race, the final spurt begins on average 300m before the finish line. On the home stretch, runners are unable to accelerate any further and some of the athletes even slow down.

*Figure 2: **Average 100m segment times in the 1500m races** of 49 international and (French) national athletes in 13 different races (modified on the basis of Hanon et al., 2007, p. 16): Only those performances were analysed which were not more than 3 sec above the personal best of the respective athlete.*

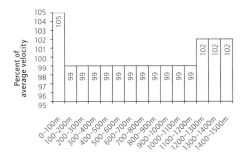

*Figure 3: **Strategic model for the 1500m**, derived from figure 2 (modified on the basis of Hanon et al., 2007, p. 17).*

CALCULATING INTERMEDIATE TIMES
The intermediate time at the half distance may be used as a rough guide in the 800m

race. As in the long sprint, a comparison with the 400m personal best and a comparison of the two 400m sections of the race are used as a guide. For the best male 800m runners in the world, the speed reserve (i.e., the difference between the time for the first lap and the personal best over 400m) is approximately 4–7 sec. The difference between the first and second half of the race should be about 2 sec (see table 3).

*Table 3: **Average time difference between the faster first and the slower second lap of an 800m race** in six different performance groups (according to Gajer et al, 2000, p. 14).*

Average finish time (min:sec) of the groups	Average time difference (sec) between the two halves of the race
1:43.57	2.37
1:45.45	2.00
1:46.86	2.64
1:48.20	2.90
1:50.17	1.67
1:52.88	1.83

In the 1500m race, the personal best over 400m can also be taken as a guide. Here, the first 400m should be run approximately 10–15 sec slower. However, it is also possible to calculate more exact individual interval or intermediate times (race plan) for each target time from the percentages presented in figures 1 and 3 by using the following formula:

$$\text{Individual 100m interval time (sec)} = \frac{100 \ (m) \bullet \text{target finish time (sec)} \bullet 100}{\text{Distance (m)} \bullet \% \text{ value from figure 1 or 3}}$$

The intermediate times aimed at in each case result from the addition of the interval times.

1.11.7 DIDACTICS: SUPERORDINATE LONG-TERM OBJECTIVES AND GENERAL METHODOLOGY

Up to and including the U14 age group, the 800 and 1000m races are the longest running distances in competitions. Training for these distances focuses primarily on aerobic endurance and cyclic speed (see chapters II–1.3.7 and II.–1.10.5). In children's athletics, this should be done almost exclusively through games and playful forms of exercise. From basic training onwards, versatile exercise forms (such as fartlek [230]) and basic endurance runs (227) are additional contents for endurance training. More specific training contents for anaerobic (speed-)endurance training, such as tempo runs (157-160), and for aerobic endurance training, such as

tempo-endurance runs (228) and long-time intervals (232), are only added in build-up training and only reach their full volume in (high-)performance training (see chapter II–1.5.7). Specific strength-endurance training begins even later, whereas general strength(-endurance) training for the trunk and feet is already started in children's athletics and in basic training. However, speed training and versatile technique training are an extensive part of middle-distance training and must not be neglected at any time of training. Until the end of basic training, they are even more important than endurance training.

1.11.8 TRAINING CONTENTS: FORMS OF GAMES AND EXERCISES

See specifically chapters II–1.3.8, II–1.5.8, and II–1.10.6.

1.11.9 SPECIAL TEST AND CONTROL PROCEDURES

	Test: Ability/skill tested	Execution/comments
T71	**Kosmin test:** Aerobic and anaerobic endurance	(See description on page 546).
T72	Middle-distance tempo-run programmes: Anaerobic and aerobic endurance	Standardised programmes may be for example: a) 5 x 1000m, rest interval: 3 min; b) LI: 2 x 5 x 400m, rest intervals: 3 min, rest intervals between sets: 6 min; c) I3: 2 x 3 x 400m, rest intervals: 8 min, rest intervals between sets: 15 min; d) I2: 3 x 400m, rest intervals: 20 min. The (average) times achieved and the post-exercise lactate values are the test criteria.

Test: Ability/skill tested		Execution/comments
T73	**3000m over-distance test:** Aerobic endurance	Maximal run under competitive conditions.
T4	**1 RPM:** Maximal strength	Squat (62), clean (63), snatch (64), hamstrings (68), quadriceps (69), arm exercises, etc. (if possible, also eccentric maximal-strength measurement).
T5	**Squat jump and T8 counter-movement and drop jump:** Two-legged speed strength and reactive strength of the extensor loop	The forward and/or backward toss of the shot (93) for distance may be performed as a simpler sport-motor test instead of counter-movement jumps.
T9	**5-stride hops with distance maximisation:** Reactive strength of the legs in comparison to one another	Test should be performed on both sides.
T10	**30m bounding run with time minimisation:** Reactive strength of the legs	
T11	**Strength-endurance tests:** Anaerobic strength endurance	squats for 1 min or 200m bounding run.
T24	**30m flying sprint:** Maximal sprinting speed	The test should also be performed in the curve.
T31	**Wingate test:** Anaerobic endurance	
T32	**Under-distance tests:** Sprinting speed and anaerobic speed endurance	150, 300, or 500m as test in training, or 200 or 400m in competition.
T61	**Standing start and acceleration:** Start acceleration without reaction speed	The test should also be performed in the curve.
T62	**Technique analysis:** Running technique	
T63	**Stride-frequency and stride-length measurement:** Technique and specific strength endurance	
T64	**Tactical analysis:** Racing strategy	
T66	**Graded field test:** Aerobic endurance	With lactate withdrawal (and spirometry), or, if this is not possible, as simple minute test (T65): e.g., Cooper test (12 min) or 30-min test (see table 4 in chapter II–1.10.7).

(continued)

455

(continued)

	Test: Ability/skill tested	Execution/comments
T2	**Flexibility tests:** General flexibility	
T3	**Body weight and body fat measurement:** Relative strength	Inappropriate upward and downward deflections should be avoided.

KOSMIN TEST

In the variation for 800m runners, athletes run twice for 60 sec with a rest interval of 3 min. In the process, the athletes try to run as far as possible. In table 4, the overall distance is assigned a corresponding 800m time. In the variation for 1500m runners, athletes run four times for 60 sec with rest intervals of 3, 2, and finally 1 min. Again, they try to run as far as possible by adding up the distances achieved in the individual runs. Table 4 again includes the 1500m times corresponding to the overall distance achieved.

*Table 4: **Result table for the Kosmin test:** For the 800m the corrected values for over-2-min runners are included in brackets (according to Kemp, 2005). On some American websites it is pointed out that for the women's 1500m 10 sec should be added to each possible time listed.*

Formulas: 800m time = 217.4 − (0.119 • distance)
(800m time) = 1451.46 − (198.54 • ln(distance))
1500m time = 500.526 − (0.162 • distance)

Distance (m)	Possible 800m time (min:sec)	Distance (m)	Possible 1500m time (min:sec)
970	1:42.0	1810	3:27.0
960	1:43.2	1800	3:28.6
950	1:44.4	1790	3:30.2
940	1:45.5	1780	3:31.9
930	1:46.7	1770	3:33.5
920	1:47.9	1760	3:35.1
910	1:49.1	1750	3:36.7
900	1:50.3	1740	3:38.3
890	1:51.5	1730	3:40.0
880	1:52.7	1720	3:41.6
870	1:53.9	1710	3:43.2

Distance (m)	Possible 800m time (min:sec)		Distance (m)	Possible 1500m time (min:sec)
860	1:55.1		1700	3:44.2
850	1:56.3		1690	3:46.5
840	1:57.4		1680	3:48.1
830	1:58.6		1670	3:49.7
820	1:59.8		1660	3:51.3
810	2:01.0	(2:01.8)	1650	3:52.9
800	2:02.2	(2:04.3)	1640	3:54.6
790	2:03.4	(2:06.8)	1630	3:56.2
780	2:04.6	(2:09.3)	1620	3:57.8
770	2:05.8	(2:11.9)	1610	3:59.4
760	2:07.0	(2:14.5)	1600	4:01.0
750	2:08.2	(2:17.1)	1590	4:02.7
740	2:09.3	(2:19.8)	1580	4:04.3
730	2:10.5	(2:22.5)	1570	4:05.9
720	2:11.7	(2:25.2)	1560	4:07.5
710	2:12.9	(2:28.0)	1550	4:09.2
700	2:14.1	(2:30.8)	1540	4:10.8
690	2:15.3	(2:33.7)	1530	4:12.4
680	2:16.5	(2:36.6)	1520	4:14.0
670	2:17.7	(2:39.5)	1510	4:15.6
660	2:18.9	(2:42.5)	1500	4:17.3
650	2:20.1	(2:45.5)	1490	4:18.9
640	2:21.2	(2:48.6)	1480	4:20.5
630	2:22.4	(2:51.7)	1470	4:22.1
620	2:23.6	(2:54.9)	1460	4:23.8
610	2:24.8	(2:58.1)	1450	4:25.4
600	2:26.0	(3:01.4)	1440	4:27.0

1.11.10 ERRORS – CAUSES – CORRECTIONS

See chapter II–1.10.8.

1.11.11 TRAINING PLANNING

The training planning for the middle distances is based on suggestions made in the general section of this book (see chapter II–3.3). Specifically, the training plans here are based on the training plans for children's and basic training presented on those pages.

BUILD-UP TRAINING INCLUDING THE STEEPLECHASE

Training for the 1500m or 2000m steeplechase is a versatile training for running which focuses on coordination, speed, and reactive strength. Training these three forms of motor stress should generally play a more important role in the build-up training of a middle-distance runner or a future long-distance runner than in later high-performance training. This means that steeplechase training must be regarded as an enhancement of running training. If possible, all middle- and long-distance runners should perform basic steeplechase training.

INCREASING VOLUME

During the transition from the basic training to the build-up training of middle- and long-distance training, the frequency of training should increase from five to six and a half sessions per week (half session = recovery session). Moreover, the individual sessions should be longer. In build-up training, there should be an annual increase in total training volume by 10–15%. This is especially true for future long-distance runners. However, for track athletics real long distances are only offered beginning with the U20 age group, and the entire range of distances is only available for adult athletes. The general increase in volume (especially for athletes who develop from young middle-distance runners to long-distance runners) is primarily due to an increase in basic aerobic endurance training.

In order to carry out an increase in mileage in high-performance training for the middle distances, two training sessions per day are suggested for the preparatory phase. One day (i.e., Sunday) remains completely free for regeneration. Furthermore, the volume within the individual training sessions is often greater than during build-up training.

COMPETITION PLANNING

Training planning includes competition planning which is geared toward the peak competition of the season (see table 5). In the middle distances, there is usually one race which covers the major distance every two or three weeks in the competition period. Moreover, there are races over longer and shorter distances, especially at the beginning of the competition period. The shorter distances may even include 100m, especially during build-up training. A planning based on competition blocks (2–4 competitions within a few days) is also used in high-performance sport to simulate the heat, semi-final, and final of a major championship.

Table 5: **Competition behaviour** of the medal winners in Rome during the 1987 World-Championship season (modified on the basis of Hirsch, 1988, pp. 312 & 314): With respect to the 800m runners, the lack of under-distance runs is unusual.

Competition frequency: 800m runners			
	Konchellah	Elliot	Barbosa
800m	22	11	15
1000m	4	2	1
1500m	–	2	–
Mile	–	4	–
2000m	–	1	–
Total	26	20	16

Competition frequency: 1500m runners			
	Bile	Gonzales	Spivey
800m	6	–	1
1000m	–	–	2
1500m	12	8	9
Mile	1	2	4
2000m	1	–	1
3000m	–	3	–
5000m	–	1	–
Total	20	13	4

Last competition before the world championships: 800m runners			
Konchellah	1000 m	2:20.49 min	6 days (22 August)
Elliot	800m	1:45.15 min	9 days (19 August)
Barbosa	800m	1:46.62 min	7 days (21 August)

Last competition before the world championships: 1500m runners			
Bile	800m	1:44.47 min	12 days (21.8.)
Gonzales	Mile	3:51.75 min	12 days (21 August)
Spivey	1000m	2:18.92 min	11 days (22 August)

MORNING RUNS

In the high-performance training plans presented in this and the following chapters, continuous runs (in the morning) are often scheduled before coordination training (e.g., ABCs of running), contrary to what was stated in chapter I–2.1. This means that these continuous runs do not constitute the main stress of the respective training day and should not be performed at a pace resulting in complete physical exhaustion. For adults, the main stress on weekdays should be primarily in the afternoon. If the focus is more on coordination training, it may be useful to perform this training before the morning runs. However, if coordination training is part of utilisation, it is always performed after the main stress (see chapter I–5.5).

*Table 6: **Training emphasis in the various mesocycles** for middle-distance training in build-up and high-performance training.*

1st mesocycle	aerobic endurance training (in varying intensity zones and using varying movement forms); strength-endurance training for the legs and the trunk; flexibility training; coordination training (during build-up training also other events as well as related to speed)
2nd mesocycle	aerobic endurance training (in varying intensity zones and using varying movement forms); anaerobic endurance training; hypertrophy-, IC- and connective-tissue-oriented maximal- and reactive-strength training for the trunk and especially for the legs; speed training; coordination training (during build-up training also other events)
3rd mesocycle	aerobic endurance training (in varying intensity zones and using varying movement forms); anaerobic endurance training; IC- and connective-tissue-oriented maximal- and reactive-strength training for the trunk and especially for the legs; speed training; coordination training
4th mesocycle	competitions and corresponding regeneration; aerobic and anaerobic endurance training at competition pace; IC- and connective-tissue-oriented maximal- and reactive-strength training for the trunk and especially for the legs; speed training; maintenance stimuli

DISCOURSE I: THE 5-PACE SYSTEM

As an alternative to the subsequent training plans, Horwill (2001) suggests the following training concept. Middle-distance runners should perform versatile endurance training by running at a 400, 800, 1500, 3000, and 5000m race pace in five consecutive training sessions. The 400m interval times calculated from the best times over the respective distance typically differ by about 4 seconds. Greater (or lesser) differences indicate specific weaknesses which require special attention in training. The sample runner in table 7 displays normal values and seems to have minor deficits in the area of basic aerobic endurance. In contrast, an athlete who runs 800m in 1:50 min (55 sec/400 m) and 1500m in 3:56 min (63 sec/400 m) tends more toward the long sprint or has clear deficits in basic aerobic endurance. Between track-session days there should be one or two days with continuous runs for 35–70 minutes. With respect to additional speed training, Horwill recommends six flying 30m sprints (132) which should be performed at the start of a training session when an athlete is still rested. The sixth (or eighth or ninth) day is a complete rest day. On the eleventh (or sixteenth) day, the microcycle of the programme begins anew.

Table 7: **Training programme according to the 5-Pace System** *by Horwill (2001).*

Day ↙ or ↘		Programme	Jogging interval	Pace	Example: Times for a 4-min 1500m runner
1 (=11)	1 (=16)	3 x 1600m	200m in 90 sec	5000m pace	4:48 min (72 sec/400 m)
3	4	4 x 800m	400m in 3 min	1500m pace	2:06 min (63 sec/400 m)
5	7	3 x 1500m	375m in 2:45 min	3000m pace	4:15 min (68 sec/400 m)
7	10	4 x 400m	400m in 3 min	800m pace	0:59 min (59 sec/400 m)
9	13	350/300/250/200m	700/600/500/400m	400m pace	48.1/41.3/34.4/27.5 (55 sec)

SUGGESTED TRAINING PLANS

Following are exemplary microcycles for the

- first mesocycle of a 17-year-old athlete in build-up training (table 8);
- first mesocycle of a 1500m runner in high-performance training (table 9); and
- third mesocycle of a 1500m runner in high-performance training (table 10).

Special 800m training plans are not presented. On the one hand, such plans can be created relatively easily as a combination of the long-sprint plans (see chapter II–1.7.10) and the training plans shown here. On the other hand, athletes who train according to the 1500m plans should be able to run fast 800m races.

Young athletes do not have to specialise in the middle distances, the steeplechase, or the long distances. The suggested training plan for the

- second mesocycle of a 17-year-old athlete in build-up training for the steeplechase (see chapter II–1.12.11); and
- third mesocycle of a 17-year-old athlete in build-up training for the long distances (see chapter II–1.13.11)

are therefore intended for the same athlete as in this chapter.

The suggested training plans for the

- second mesocycle of an athlete in high-performance training; and
- fourth mesocycle of an athlete in high-performance training

presented for the steeplechase may in some respects at least be compared to the plans presented here.

Table 8: Build-up training: Sample microcycle for a 17-year-old middle- and long-distance runner as well as steeplechaser in the first mesocycle.

Monday	Tuesday	Wednesday	Thursday	Friday	Saturday	Sunday
Trunk stabilisation exercises and abdominal crunches (20 min) with a lot of dynamic variation	Warm-up jogging (15 min)	Continuous run (30 min) first 10 min including ABCs of sprinting/jumping, arm circling, exaggerated arm actions, etc.	Cycling, swimming, inline skating, cross-country skiing or aqua jogging (40 min) alternately each week	Foot strengthening (10 min)	*Morning:* Warm-up jogging (15 min)	Rest
	Acceleration runs (3 reps) barefoot			Acceleration runs (3 reps) barefoot	Hurdle imitation and ABCs of hurdling (15 min)	
ABCs of running (15–20 run-throughs) heel kicks, pulling strides, step-overs, etc.	ABCs of jumping (15–20 run-throughs) galloping sideways, ankle jumps, skipping with two-legged landing, skipping (with one-legged landing), etc.	Strength-endurance circle (2–3 run-throughs; loading: 45 sec; rest interval: 30 sec) trunk strength, leg strength, ABCs of sprinting/jumping, hurdle Zs, arm swinging as in running with 1 kg dumbell in each hand	Contract-relax stretching (15 min) specific to the steeplechase	ABCs of running (15–20 run-throughs) runs with knees raised to half the horizontal position focusing on stride frequency, high-knee running, Can-Can exercise, etc.	Practising the hurdling technique (20 min)	*On Saturdays before the tempo runs possibly also training the techniques of one event for the quadrathlon or pentathlon*
Technique sprints (6–8 x 20–80m) coordination runs, alternating-pace sprints, slalom runs, etc.	Continuous run (60 min) flat terrain		Muscle build-up training for the trunk on apparatus, medicine-ball work, or gymnastics (30 min) e.g., goalkeeper throws, rotational throws, throws from a prone position, and tossing, using a medicine ball	Skipping and bounding runs (5 x 30m each) including variations, with correct technique	LI tempo runs (Frinolli runs: 3 x 3 x 2 laps of 120m each; rest intervals: 90 sec; rest intervals between sets: 8 min)	
Obstacle-relay competition (e.g., 5 competitions with each runner running 100m legs) over hurdle, crawling under something, jumping over a ditch, climbing over something	Contract-relax stretching (15 min) specific to the steeplechase	Fartlek and/or cross-country run (30 min) hilly terrain		Continuous run (45 min) hilly terrain	Warm-down jogging (10 diagonals on the lawn)	
Game (30 min) e.g., basketball or soccer	Foot strengthening (10 min) in the sand, with elastic band or by rope jumping		Acceleration runs (5 x 100m) over mini-hurdles placed at an arbitrary distance from one another	Acceleration runs and standing starts (e.g. 100, 80, 60, 40, and 30m) each run faster than the previous one; as utilisation	*Afternoon:* Continuous run (30 min)	
	Acceleration runs and standing starts (e.g. 100, 80, 60, 40, and 30m) each run faster than the previous one; as utilisation				Contract-relax stretching (15 min)	
					Acceleration runs and standing starts (e.g. 100, 80, 60, 40, and 30m) each run faster than the previous one; as utilisation	

Table 9: High-performance training: sample microcycle for a 1500m runner in the first mesocycle.

	Monday	Tuesday	Wednesday	Thursday	Friday	Saturday	Sunday
Morning	**Warm-up jogging** (30 min) **ABCs of jumping** (10–15 run-throughs) **Strength-endurance circle** (3–4 run-throughs; loading: 1 min; rest interval: 15 sec) trunk strength, leg strength, ABCs of sprinting, jumps, running-arm swinging with 1 kg dumbbells	**Continuous run** (45 min) first 10 min including ABCs of sprinting/jumping, arm circling, exaggerated arm actions, etc. **ABCs of running** (15–20 run-throughs) **Alternating-pace sprints** (5 x 120m) as utilisation	**Cycling, swimming, inline skating, cross-country skiing** or **aqua jogging** (40 min) alternately each week, different sport than in the afternoon	**Continuous run** (45 min) first 10 min including ABCs of sprinting/jumping, arm circling, exaggerated arm actions, etc. **ABCs of running** (10–15 run-throughs) **Technique sprints** (6–8 x 60–80m) with additional tasks	**Warm-up jogging** (30 min) **Acceleration runs** (3 reps) **ABCs of jumping** (10–15 run-throughs) **Foot strengthening** (10 min) in the sand or with elastic band **Game** (30 min) e.g., basketball or soccer	**Trunk stabilisation exercises** and **abdominal crunches** (20 min) **Acceleration runs** **Tempo runs** (e.g., 2 x 5 x 2:30 min; rest interval: 3 min; rest interval between sets: 10 min) or other programme from figure 5 in chapter II–1.10.6: 90%	Rest
Afternoon	**Warm-up jogging** (5 min) **Tempo-endurance run** (45 min) flat terrain **Warm-down jogging** (5 min) **Contract-relax stretching** (15 min) **Acceleration runs** and **standing starts** (e.g. 100, 90, 80, 70, 60, 40, and 20m)	**Rope jumping** (5 x 1 min) **Acceleration runs** (3 reps) barefoot **Tempo runs** (e.g., 3 x 6 x 2:20 min; rest interval: 2 min; rest interval between sets: 5 min) or other programme from figure 5 in chapter II–1.10.6: 85% **Acceleration runs** (5 x 80 m)	**Cycling, swimming, inline skating, cross-country skiing** or **aqua jogging** (40 min) **Contract-relax stretching** (15 min) **Muscle build-up training** for the trunk on apparatus, **medicine-ball work**, or **gymnastics** (30 min) **Acceleration runs** as utilisation	**Foot strengthening** (10 min) **Tempo-endurance run** (35 min) hilly terrain, possibly cross-country **Warm-down jogging** (5 min) **Acceleration runs** and **standing starts** (e.g., 80, 70, 60, 40, and 20m) each run faster than the previous one; as utilisation	**Continuous run** (90 min) flat terrain **Acceleration runs** and **standing starts** (e.g, 100, 90, 80, 70, 60, 40, and 20m) each run faster than the previous one; as utilisation	**Continuous run** (30 min) **Contract-relax stretching** (15 min) **Acceleration runs** and **standing starts** (e.g., 80, 70, 60, 40, and 20m) each run faster than the previous one; as utilisation	

Table 10: High-performance training: sample microcycle for a 1500m runner in the third mesocycle.

	Monday	Tuesday	Wednesday	Thursday	Friday	Saturday	Sunday
Morning	Maximal-eccentric strength training (15 min) trunk stabilisation, lifting opposite upper and lower limbs while in prone position, belly punches with tense abdominals, raising the foot/toes ABCs of sprinting (10–15 run-throughs) Acceleration runs Flying sprints (3 x 30m + 30m run-up)	Warm-up jogging (30 min) Acceleration runs Strength training at high intensity (40 min) snatch, hamstrings, quadriceps, adductors/abductors, quarter split squat Alternating-pace sprints (5 x 120m) as utilisation	Continuous run (45 min) first 10 min including ABCs of sprinting/jumping, arm circling, exaggerated arm actions, etc. Acceleration runs (3 reps) ABCs of jumping (10–15 run-throughs) Tuck jumps (2 x 4 run-throughs over 8 hurdles)	Cycling, swimming, inline skating, cross-country skiing or aqua jogging (45 min) alternately each week, different sport than in the afternoon	Warm-up jogging (30 min) Acceleration runs (3 reps) barefoot Standing starts (30, 40, 50, 40, and 30m) at maximal pace, against each other Skipping, bounding runs, and rhythm jumps (3 x 50m each)	Warm-up jogging (15 min) ABCs of sprinting (8–10 run-throughs) Acceleration runs (3 reps) l3 tempo runs (3 sets of 150, 150, and 500m each; walking interval: 5, 5, and 15 min each) Warm-down jogging (10 diagonals on the lawn)	Rest
Afternoon	Warm-up jogging (20 min) Acceleration runs (3 reps) barefoot Uphill and downhill sprints and jumps (e.g., 3 x 5 x 150m; rest interval: walking back [rapidly]; rest interval between sets: 6 min) varying programmes Game (20 min) e.g., basketball or soccer	Foot strengthening (10 min) Technique sprints (6–8 x 60–80m) coordination runs, slalom runs, stride-length training Tempo-endurance run (35 min) flat terrain Warm-down jogging (5 min) Acceleration runs and standing starts (e.g., 60, 50, 40, 30, and 20m)	Warm-up jogging (10 min) Acceleration runs (3 reps) Tempo runs (e.g., 4 x 2:30 min; rest interval: 5 min) or other programme from figure 5 in chapter II–1.10.6: 100% Warm-down jogging (10 min) Acceleration runs (5 x 80m)	Cycling, swimming, inline skating, cross-country skiing or aqua jogging (30 min) Contract-relax stretching (15 min) Strength training for the trunk or gymnastics (15 min) Acceleration runs and standing starts	Warm-up jogging (10 min) Fartlek (30 min) hilly terrain Maximal-eccentric strength training (15 min) hamstrings, quadriceps, adductors/ abductors, etc. Pull-resisted runs (5 x 80m with 2.5 kg)	Continuous run (30 min) Acceleration runs and standing starts (e.g., 60, 50, 40, 30, and 20m) each run faster than the previous one; as utilisation	

1.11.12 BIBLIOGRAPHY

Gajer, B., Hanon, C., Marajo, J. & Vollmer, J. C. (2000). *Le 800 mètres: Analyse descriptive et entraînement.* Paris: Institut National de Sport et de l'Education Physique.

Gohlitz, D., Hermann, D. & Müller, K. (2003). Die optimale 800-m-Lauftechnik. *Leichtathletiktraining 14* (4), 18-21.

Hanon, C., Thomas, C., Le Chevalier, J. M., Gajer, B. & Vandewalle, H. (2002). How does O_2 evolve during the 800 m? *New Studies in Athletics 17* (2), 61-68.

Hanon, C., Levêque, J. M. & Thomas, C. (2007). Oxygen uptake in the 1500 metres. *New Studies in Athletics 22* (1), 15-22.

Horwill, F. J. (2001). The system the Led to 12 World Records in 4 Years. *Track and Field Coaches Review 74* (3+4), 23-24.

Kemp, T. (2005). Creating a Kosmin test for 2:00+ 800m runners. *Track Coach* (170), 5437-5438.

Regelkommissionen des DLV, FLA, ÖLV und SLV (Hrsg.). (2008). *Internationale Wettkampfregeln.* Waldfischbach: Hornberger.

Skof, B. & Stuhec, S. (2004). Kinematic analysis of Jolanda Ceplak's running technique. *New Studies in Athletics 19* (1), 23-31.

Thibault, G. (2003). A graphical model of interval training. *New Studies in Athletics 18* (3), 49-55.

Vanden Eynde, E. (1982). Die modernen 800 m – Fünfzehn Jahre später. *Lehre der Leichtathletik 33* (19), 741-742

1.12 3000M STEEPLECHASE

1.12.1   KENYA'S STANDARD GOLD MEDAL

It is reported that in the 16th and 17th centuries in Germany, bar running (*Barrlaufen*), an obstacle race, was popular. The English term *steeplechase* reveals the origin of the modern event. In the 1820s, the first organised races in England were carried out from church tower (steeple) to church tower, over fences, streams, etc. Around 1850, students at Oxford and Cambridge performed runs over obstacles that were similar to steeplechase races with horses.

The first Olympic obstacle races over 2500m and 4000m took place in 1900. Four years later, only 2590m were run until the distance was increased to 3200m (approx. 2 miles) in 1908. In subsequent Olympic Games, there were no obstacle races. However, in 1912, 1920, and 1924, cross-country races between 8km (1920) and 12km (1912) were performed. The modern 3000m steeplechase distance was run for the first time in 1920. However, only in 1953 the IAAF first established the exact distances between the obstacles and the specifications of the obstacles.

In a heat at the 1928 Olympic Games, Paavo Nurmi fell into the water when trying to clear the first water jump. The Frenchman Lucien Duquesne, who followed Nurmi, unselfishly helped him out of the water. The two superior runners quickly caught up with and overtook the other runners and were many metres ahead of them on the last lap. On the final straight, Nurmi was clearly in the lead ahead of Duquesne. However, just before the finish line he slowed down to let Duquesne win. But Duquesne also slowed his pace so as not to be granted the victory. Finally, both runners broke through the finishing tape together.

Today, the Kenyans have dominated the steeplechase for more than three decades and constitute the majority of each of the 50 best athletes in the other middle- and long-distance events. Although their technique is sometimes only moderate, the male Kenyan steeplechasers were unbeaten at the last nine Olympic Games and twice they even won all the medals. The first Kenyan Olympic champion was Amos Biwott in 1968. By simply clearing the obstacle in front of the water pit without placing his foot on it, he established the Kenyan Technique of clearing the water jump which even today is used by some of his fellow countrymen (see discourse I).

At times, carefree training is hardly possible in Kenya. The majority of Kenyan world-class runners live in the west of the country, in the Great Rift Valley and the city of Eldoret. Here, there are often tribal conflicts between the Kikuyu and Kalenjin. Tegla Loroupe, Kenyan ex-marathon world-record holder and UN Ambassador for Sport, is busy launching relief operations together with European sports managers to calm the restless region. The advancement of athletics in Africa is also supported by the development programme of World Athletics. Still, runners from other nations travel to Kenya to take advantage of the natural highlands and to learn from the hard, yet playful Kenyan training and running mentality.

At the Olympic debut of the 3000m steeplechase for women in 2008, Kenya had to settle for the silver medal won by Eunice Jepkorir, who nevertheless established a national record. Gulnara Galkina from Russia won the gold medal in the world-record time of 8:58.81 min. She was the first woman to break the 9-minute barrier: This was and there still is a rapid development after the first world record of 9:48.88 min was recorded by the IAAF (now, World Athletics) in 1999.

1.12.2   THE MOST IMPORTANT COMPETITION RULES

The following abridged and simplified International Competition Rules comprise the framework for the technique and strategy as well as for the organisation of steeplechase competitions:

- *3000m steeplechase:* female juniors and male juniors, women, men, male M40–55;
- *2000m steeplechase:* male U18, female and male U20, female W40 and older, male M60 and older;
- *1500m steeplechase:* female U18; no steeplechase competitions are carried out up to and including the U16 age group.
- Figures 1–3 show the set-up and dimensions of the obstacles.

- In the 3000 and 1500m steeplechase, the segment from the start to the first passage of the finish has no obstacles; in the 2000m steeplechase, the first 100m section has no obstacles.
- Runners must clear all obstacles. They can do this in any manner. However, a runner is disqualified if he/she steps beside the water pit when clearing the water jump or if his/her foot or leg is below the horizontal plane of the top of any obstacle at the instant of clearance.

Otherwise, the general competition rules for running and for the middle- and long-distance races apply (see chapters II–1.1.1 and II–1.10.1).

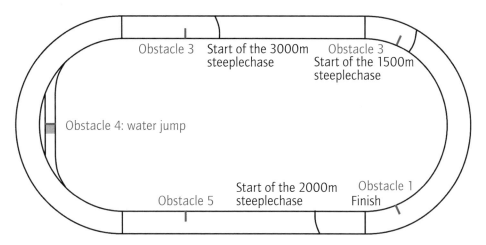

Figure 1: **Set-up of the obstacles** (modified on the basis of the Rule Commission of the DLV, FLA, ÖLV and SLV, 2010, pp. 81–82): The water jump can also be placed outside the oval track. On each lap, five obstacles must be cleared, the fourth of which is the water jump. The distance between the obstacles is a fifth of the length of the lap (i.e., close to or beyond 80m).

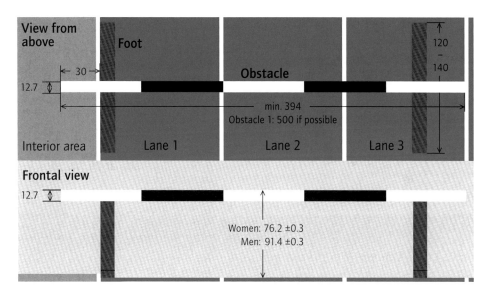

Figure 2: **Construction and dimensions of an obstacle** (all dimensions in cm; modified on the basis of the Rule Commission of the DLV, FLA, ÖLV and SLV, 2010, pp. 81–82). Every obstacle must weigh between 80 and 100 kg.

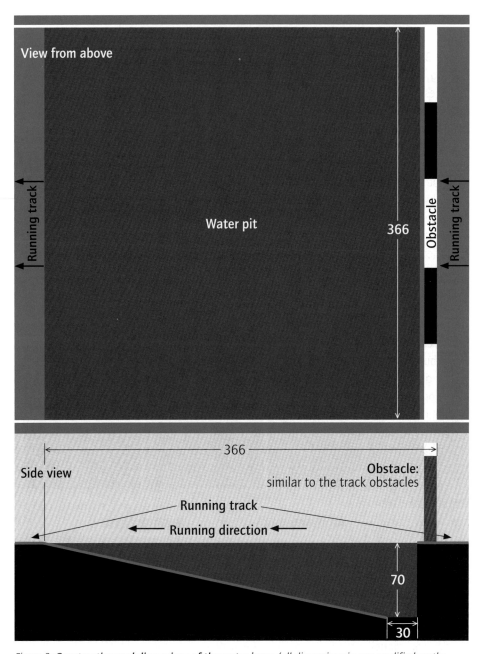

Figure 3: **Construction and dimensions of the water jump** (all dimensions in cm; modified on the basis of the Rule Commission of the DLV, FLA, ÖLV and SLV, 2010, pp. 81–82): At the start of the race, the surface of the water must be level with the surface of the track and have a maximal difference of 2cm.

1.12.3 SPORT-SCIENCE FINDINGS, PHASE STRUCTURE, AND TECHNIQUE

In the 3000m steeplechase, the natural running rhythm is interrupted a total of 35 times (i.e., 7 times by the water jump and 28 times by the other obstacles). Like the hurdle sprint, the steeplechase is a constrained run in which the running rhythm (stride frequency and stride length) must be adjusted to the distance of the next obstacle. However, unlike the short- and long-hurdle sprinter, the steeplechaser does not complete the run-up to the first obstacle and the 34 sections between the obstacles with a technically and strategically pre-planned number of strides or by using a particular stride rhythm. This is not only because of the length of the distances between the obstacles (about 80m), but especially because of running in a tight group, in which speed adjustments (e.g., for overtaking) and therefore also adjustments of the stride frequency and stride length are repeatedly necessary. This means that in terms of the running technique between the obstacles there are no fundamental differences between the steeplechase technique and the middle- and long-distance running technique described. Only in front of (and perhaps shortly behind) the obstacle are the runners forced to vary their technique. Therefore, only two technical characteristics of the steeplechase are described in the following: the clearing of the obstacles on the track (hurdle technique) and the clearing of the water jump (water-jump technique). Both techniques involve approaching and leaving the obstacle.

TECHNIQUE INDEX

As in the hurdle sprint, the quotient of the 3000m race and 3000m steeplechase times can be used as a rough guide for the development of the obstacle and water-jump techniques. Both female and male world-class steeplechasers achieve technique indexes between 0.93 and 0.96. This roughly corresponds to *running-time differences* of 20–40 sec. Some runners are reported to have even better indexes (>0.96). However, here it is likely that the runner was not in his/her best shape when running the flat time, which is certainly common among steeplechase specialists. If the index value is below 0.93, the obstacle and/or water-jump technique (or strategy) appear to be improvable.

The men's technique index for the two world records (flat versus steeplechase) is 0.936 and thus within the specified range. Due to rapid improvements of the women's 3000m steeplechase world record, the technique index for women has now almost reached the men's index. It currently is 0.927.

OBSTACLE TECHNIQUE

The technique of clearing the steeplechase obstacles is similar to the technique of clearing the identically high, but movable obstacles in the 400m hurdle race (see chapter II–1.9.3). For this reason, only major differences are described in the following. The obstacle technique can be divided into three phases:

- approach;
- obstacle stride; and
- leaving the obstacle.

PHASE 1: APPROACH

The average velocity in the 3000m steeplechase roughly corresponds to the average velocity in the 10,000m race, which is about 25% lower than in the 400m hurdle race (see table 1 in chapter II–1.10.2). It is questionable whether a steeplechaser should accelerate in front of the obstacle. Many do this (and slow down again behind the obstacle), mainly because they are accustomed to a higher approach velocity from basic training in the hurdles and because clearing the obstacle with a flatter push-off angle is easier for them. This should be avoided for reasons of economy. However, if one assumes that any displacements of the CG upward result in a decrease in horizontal velocity, then the question is only whether the steeplechaser should accelerate before or after the obstacle. If the athlete did neither, he/she would successively slow down with every obstacle. The objective must be to minimise the velocity loss at the obstacle through a good technique. Therefore, a minimal increase in velocity before the obstacle which compensates for this velocity loss and also results in a slightly flatter push-off angle is to be welcomed. In this manner, the runner will be able to resume his/her racing pace directly after the obstacle.

While approaching the obstacles, the athlete must adjust his/her stride frequency and stride length in such a way that he/she achieves a favourable push-off point in front of the obstacle. In order to accomplish this, the well-trained ability to judge distances while running is required. Moreover, the ability to sprint over obstacles (even in fatigued state) almost equally well with both legs as swing leg is an important prerequisite to make these adjustments as smooth as possible.

All of this is increasingly complicated when running in a pack. In particular, the view of the obstacle can be blocked by other runners when approaching the obstacles, especially at the beginning of the race. Moreover, runners are sometimes forced to run slightly to the side to have sufficient space or to find their own rhythm to the obstacle (see also chapter II–1.12.6).

To avoid braking forces during the front support and emphasise the forward push-off over the obstacle, the last stride is usually slightly shorter like in the hurdle sprints.

PHASE 2: OBSTACLE STRIDE

Due to the lower running velocity, the push-off is performed closer to the obstacle than in the 400m hurdles. Depending on the running velocity and the body height, men push off 1.50–1.80m in front of the obstacle, whereas some women push off somewhat closer to the obstacle. The CG is raised on average 5–10cm higher over the obstacles than over identically high hurdles in the 400m hurdles. Several reasons for this are conceivable: respect for the rigid obstacle; the fact that the flexibility and technique of most steeplechasers is rather poor; advantages in terms of movement economy (less aggressive movement of the swing and trail legs); lower running velocity means push-off point is closer to the obstacle and therefore the push-off angle is steeper, making a flatter clearance of the obstacle impossible.

The landing occurs approximately 1.0–1.2m behind the obstacle. Although the upward straightening of the trunk and the push-down of the swing leg behind the obstacle are performed less aggressively than in the hurdle sprint, the athlete nevertheless tries to land approximately on the vertical projection of the CG to generate as little braking forces as possible when landing.

The obstacle stride in the steeplechase requires a higher flexibility than would be necessary for other middle- and long-distance runs, particularly in the hamstrings and adductors. The coordination requirements, demanding special strength capacities of the hip muscles, are also more varied and must be specifically trained.

PHASE 3: LEAVING THE OBSTACLE
After clearing the obstacle, the runner should resume his/her natural running rhythm as quickly as possible. This should not require new acceleration. A prerequisite for this is a minimum acceleration in front of the obstacle and a good technique for the obstacle stride.

DISCOURSE I: SKIM TECHNIQUE

A variation of the obstacle stride which is used

- for versatile coordination training,
- by beginners,
- on the unfavourable side or side with poorer coordination,
- to clear the obstacle under high fatigue (in the final stages of a race)
- to learn the water-jump technique

is the so-called skim technique. Here, the runner places his/her swing leg on the obstacle without actually loading it and first lands with the push-off or trail leg behind the obstacle. The disadvantage of this technique is that the CG has to be lifted even higher, which means that the runner is forced to perform an even more powerful take-off in front of the obstacle and therefore loses even more horizontal speed. The main advantage of this technique is increased safety since the runner can concentrate more on the obstacle and feels the obstacle beneath him.

WATER-JUMP TECHNIQUE

The water-jump technique can be divided into four phases:

- approach,
- step on the obstacle,
- jump over the water pit, and
- leaving the pit.

PHASE 1: APPROACH

When clearing the water jump, one can lose a great deal of time by using stutter steps or having difficulties with the landing. Even worse consequences due to technical problems, such as falls or injuries, can be observed even on a world-class level. To prepare safely for the difficult clearing of the water jump, the use of an intermediate mark is often recommended. This mark is placed four, six, or eight steps in front of the water jump and the runner tries to land on it with the foot with which he pushes off on in front of the obstacle. If the athlete is slightly beyond this mark, he/she must shorten his/her steps; if the athlete is slightly in front of the mark, he/she must lengthen his/her strides slightly. However, running in the pack may significantly impede the view of the mark especially on the first laps. This shows that runners should not get too dependent on an intermediate mark and should also practice running over obstacles without an intermediate mark. Moreover, clearing the water obstacle should be practised just as often with the one (preferred) as with the other (less favoured) leg. It is the ability to clear the water jump with both legs which enables the runner to perform the clearance with only minimal changes

to his/her natural running rhythm in front of the obstacle.

Moreover, a slight acceleration in front of the water obstacle is recommended. A slight increase in horizontal velocity results in a slightly longer jump over the water pit and thus a lower loss of velocity upon landing (see phase 4). However, this acceleration should not be too fast for reasons of economy.

Since the CG must be raised more when clearing the water jump than when clearing a normal obstacle, a moderate short-long-short rhythm with a slight swing-leg squat can be observed during the final strides (for definitions of terms see chapter II-2.1.2). However, due to the attempt to achieve a tall running position and a sufficiently long distance to the obstacle, this squatting action should only be relatively slight.

PHASE 2: STEPPING ONTO THE OBSTACLE

The push-off occurs approximately 1.50–1.80m in front of the water jump; some women push-off even closer to the obstacle. The step onto the obstacle is initially very similar to the attack of a hurdle: push-off extension, forward lean of the upper body and lift of the swing leg (jackknife movement), forward movement of the opposite arm, etc. The shoulder and pelvic axis should also be kept square to the running direction throughout the water-jump clearance. Then, however, the foot of the swing leg, which is still bent at the knee joint, is placed onto the front upper edge of the obstacle beam with

*Figure 4: **Water-jump technique.***

the region between the heel and mid-foot (see figure 4). The placement should be performed gently (i.e., with as little force exertion against the beam as possible) and with a yield of the knee joint to lose only very little horizontal speed.

When the calf of the leg on the beam reaches the vertical, the thigh should be perpendicular to the lower leg (i.e., horizontal). If in addition to this the upper body is also significantly tilted forward at this moment (about 45°), the runner has succeeded in keeping his/her CG low over the obstacle. Although an even smaller knee-joint angle at this moment would result in an even flatter curve of the CG, it would also represent a less favourable position for the following push-off extension.

PHASE 3: JUMP OVER THE WATER PIT

During contact with the beam, the foot performs a rolling action so that the runner can finally push-off from the rear upper edge of the beam with the spike plate of his/her shoes (see figure 5).

To push off from the beam, the swing leg (which previously was the push-off leg in front of the obstacle) is moved forward at an acute angle. The contralateral arm

swing, which due to the forward lean of the upper body takes place in front of the body for the most part, is used to compensate for the occurring rotational momentum. During the push-off, the trunk is slowly straightened, even though the runner leaves the beam with a still noticeable forward lean of his/her trunk. The push-off should lead to an extension of the foot, knee, and hip of the push-off leg as complete as possible. The swing leg, whose knee is now approximately rectangular, and the opposite arm act as swinging elements (see chapter II–2.1.2).

The runner must wait to perform the push-off until his/her CG has moved far enough over the beam to not take off from the bar

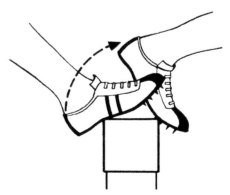

*Figure 5: **Rolling off of the foot on the beam for the water jump.***

upward, but to push off from the bar flatly forward (see figure 6). Economy of movement is also crucial when jumping over the water pit. First, it is important to avoid a passive push-off from the bar. This leads to a landing in deeper water, and the second ground contact would also possibly occur in the water and on the slope. Both would result in a loss of horizontal speed. In addition, this could lead to a fall forward since the lower body in particular is slowed down a great deal. However, the runner should also try to avoid a too high and/or a too far jump (possibly onto the flat and dry track). The acceleration needed in front of the obstacle, the force applied to the obstacle, and/or the stress when absorbing the landing would be too energy consuming.

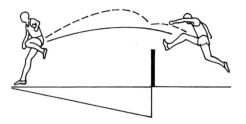

*Figure 6: **Economic** (solid line) **and uneconomic path** (dashed line) **of the CG at the water jump.***

The steeplechaser directs his/her view to the landing spot at the end of the water pit when he/she is on the obstacle beam. The prior push-off leg in front of the obstacle which is the swing leg on the obstacle becomes the landing leg and is therefore extended forward and downward (while performing a slightly grasping movement). A slight backward rotation about the

DISCOURSE II: KENYAN TECHNIQUE

Some world-class Kenyan steeplechasers clear the water jump like the obstacles on the track without placing their foot onto the beam. The advantages of this technique are that the runner can run lower over the obstacle. Therefore, he/she has to take off less in front of the obstacle and thereby loses less horizontal velocity. Moreover, he/she does not lose horizontal velocity when placing his/her foot on the beam and does not have to exert any energy to compensate for this loss when pushing off from the bar. In addition, the drop height upon landing in the pit is lower (at least when assuming that the landing spot is identical). However, this type of obstacle clearing also has some disadvantages. Due to the lack of push-off from the beam, the runner may land too far in the deep area of the pit and may not reach the flat and dry track with his/her second ground contact. This would result in a large loss of velocity during landing. In order to avoid this, the runner must usually accelerate more in front of the obstacle than the runner who uses the conventional technique. This requires additional energy. Moreover, the long jump into the water requires enormous courage and high coordination skills—two things which subside with increasing fatigue.

DISCOURSE III: SEX DIFFERENCES

Since 2002, the water pit has been identical for women and men. This is a disadvantage for women because of the natural differences in relative strength between men and women. This disadvantage is increased due to women's lower average speed. On the one hand, women must raise their CG less to jump onto the obstacle in front of the water pit, which is significantly lower in relation to their average body height. This means that their take-off is less powerful so that they lose less horizontal velocity. On the other hand, they lack the take-off height when jumping over the pit so that they are forced to take off more upward from the obstacle beam. To manage this relatively long jump, female steeplechasers often accelerate more in front of the obstacle than male steeplechasers, which means additional energy expenditure. Even some good female steeplechasers do not succeed in making the second ground contact on the flat and dry track (at the end of the race).

transverse axis of the body is initiated by raising the upper body when pushing off from the beam. This enables the athlete to land in an almost upright position on approximately the vertical projection of his/her CG while his/her view is directed forward. The knee of the landing leg is in a slightly bent position before the ground contact to absorb the landing. If possible, the tip of the foot should contact the ground approximately 20–50cm before the end of the water pit. The still contralaterally moving arms are often lifted slightly sideways to absorb the landing and to keep one's balance upon landing.

PHASE 4: LEAVING THE WATER PIT
During the first ground contact, the hip extension on the landing leg side is continued. The movement of the swing leg (former push-off leg on the beam), which is acutely angled at the knee joint, is delayed during the flight phase, but moved quickly and actively forward and upward upon landing. This movement is supported by an energetic first arm swing. The clearance of the obstacle is good when the runner succeeds in placing the second ground contact on the track (or on dry land). The shoulder-pelvis separation and the acceleration needed to reach race pace should be low. The runner should succeed in resuming his/her natural running rhythm as quickly as possible.

Overall, special speed, reactive-strength, endurance, and coordination skills are required for running onto the obstacle, the leap from the beam, and the landing in the pit, far exceeding the demands made on the runner in the middle- and long-distances on flat courses.

*Table 1: **Requirement profile for the 3000m steeplechase:** The suggested rough estimate of the value of selected factors determining performance is based on the importance for the overall performance and the percentage of time spent training (IR: information requirements, constr.: constraints; see chapter I–1.1).*

Factors determining 3000m steeplechase performance	Estimate of value	Notes
Coordination	+ + + +	optical IR: high, acoustic IR: medium, then low, tactile IR: medium–high, kinaesthetic IR: high, vestibular IR: medium; precision constr.: high, time constr.: medium–high, complexity constr.: medium–high, situation constr.: high, physical stress constr.: high
Flexibility	+ + (+)	the men's obstacles require a little higher flexibility
Strength		extensor loop (glutes, quadriceps, triceps surae, erector spinae), iliopsoas; hamstrings; special significance of the adductors and abductors of the trail leg as well as the abdominal muscles; shoulder and upper-arm muscles
Maximal strength	+ +	mainly as a basis
Reactive strength	+ + +	of decisive importance at the (water jump) obstacles as well as for running economy even over longer distances
Speed	+ +	primarily as a basis as well as to be able to quickly react in front of the obstacles if required
Endurance (general dynamic) Anaerobic endurance		
Strength endurance	+ + +	as a basis of speed endurance and specifically for clearing the obstacles
Speed endurance	+ + +	the interval-like loads at higher intensity (at the (water jump) obstacles and during the final spurt) also make specific demands on anaerobic metabolism and lactate metabolism
Aerobic endurance	+ + + + +	the average competition speed is similar to the 10,000m speed and corresponds approximately with the running speed at the aerobic-anaerobic threshold (see lactate diagnostics in chapter II-1.10.7)
Psychological and cognitive abilities	+ + + + +	feel for pace and correct strategy (initial pace); courage, in particular when clearing the water jump; performance-oriented thinking and behaviour (see chapter I-3.1.1)
Anthropometric and primarily genetically determined characteristics	+ + + +	connective tissue with optimal energy-storing capacities; medium body height; very low percentage of body fat

1.12.4 SUMMARY OF THE MOST IMPORTANT TECHNICAL CHARACTERISTICS = TECHNIQUE-ANALYSIS SHEET

OBSTACLE TECHNIQUE

APPROACH

- Early and slight adjustment of stride frequency and stride length to land on the optimal push-off point in front of the obstacle; slight acceleration.
- Attack of the obstacle from a high running position (high hips) and with an upright trunk.
- Slightly shorter last stride.
- Foot touchdown close to the vertical projection of the CG (a short front support results in an only slight bracing action).

OBSTACLE STRIDE

Push-off

- Push-off point far in front of the obstacle (results in a flat push-off; approx. 60% of the obstacle stride in front of the obstacle).
- Emphasised push-off into the obstacle with extension of the foot, knee, and hip joint of the push-off leg.
- The thigh of the swing leg is raised up to the horizontal.
- Straight-line foot movement in the running direction or with inward sickle action.
- The knee of the swing leg is still held at an acute angle.
- Beginning forward lean of the trunk at the end of the push-off.

Flight

- Further raising and extension of the swing leg and lowering of the trunk: jackknife movement (less (dynamic) than in the (short) hurdle sprint.
- The arm on the trail-leg side is extended in the direction of the swing-leg foot, while the other arm is kept at the side of the body.
- Due to the hip flexion and abduction, the knee of the trail leg is moved outward and upward.

- Downward movement of the trail leg and straightening of the trunk after the swing-leg foot has cleared the obstacle (less dynamic than in the hurdle sprint).
- At the same time, the backswing of the counter-arm is started in an outer circle around the trail leg.
- The calf of the trail leg is almost horizontal during obstacle clearance although the knee is always higher than the foot.
- The foot of the trail leg is pronated during obstacle clearance.
- The forward swing of the arm on the side of the swing leg is started.
- During the complete obstacle stride, the shoulder and pelvic axis are kept in a position as frontal as possible.
- The upward straightening of the trunk and the downward and backward movement of the swing leg lead to the grasping touchdown of the foot.
- The trail leg is moved forward and inward in the direction of the high-knee running position, while the counter-arm is moved backward and inward.

Landing

- Upon touchdown, the CG is as close to the vertical over the tip of the foot as possible.
- At the end of the first ground contact behind the obstacle, the thigh of the trail leg points almost horizontally in the running direction; the knee joint angle is approx. 90°.
- The landing leg is extended at the knee and hip joint.

LEAVING THE OBSTACLE

- If possible, no shoulder-hip separation.
- If possible, no new acceleration is necessary.
- Rapid resumption of the natural running technique.

WATER-JUMP TECHNIQUE

APPROACH

- Early and slight adjustment of stride frequency and stride length; slight acceleration on the last 10–15m; possibly landing on an intermediate mark 4, 6, or 8 steps before the push-off.
- Attacking the obstacle from a high running position (high hips) and with upright trunk.

- Slight short-long-short rhythm with swing-leg squat.
- Foot touchdown close to the vertical projection of the CG (a short front support results in an only slight bracing action).

STRIDE ONTO THE OBSTACLE

- Push-off point far in front of the obstacle (approx. 1.40–1.80m).
- Emphasised push-off into the obstacle with extension of the foot, knee, and hip joint of the push-off leg.
- The thigh of the swing leg is raised up to the horizontal (initially at an acute angle, then opened during the flight phase).
- The foot of the swing leg is moved on a straight line in the running direction for a soft placement (yielding the knee joint) on the front edge of the beam.
- Forward lean of the trunk; contralateral arm swing with a forward movement of the counter-arm.
- When the lower leg has reached a vertical position on the beam, the upper leg should be horizontal, and the trunk should be leaned forward by approx. 45°.
- The frontal position of the shoulder and pelvic axis is maintained throughout the clearance of the water jump.

JUMP OVER THE WATER PIT

- The foot rolls over the beam so that the runner can push off from the rear upper edge of the beam with the spike plate of his/her shoes.
- The runner directs his/her view to the landing spot 30–50cm in front of the end of the water pit.
- Late flat push-off with (almost) complete extension of the foot, knee, and hip joint.
- Upward straightening of the trunk (at the end of the push-off still with a slight forward lean of the trunk).
- Forward movement of the trail leg which is initially at a sharp angle under the body and then at the end of the push-off, approximately rectangular at the knee joint.
- Contralateral arm swing (a little in front of the body; arms and swing leg are used as swing elements).

- Further straightening up of the trunk and pushdown of the front leg, which becomes the landing leg.
- Slight raising of the arms sideways (within the contralateral arm swing) for keeping balance.
- Landing with slightly flexed leg approximately on the vertical projection of the CG (view is directed to the front).

LEAVING THE OBSTACLE

- Continuation of the hip extension and active forward movement of the swing leg for the second ground contact.
- Second ground contact on the flat and dry track.
- Active first arm swing(s).
- As little shoulder-hip separation as possible.
- Only a slight acceleration is required to resume racing pace.

1.12.5   PHOTO SEQUENCES

OBSTACLE TECHNIQUE

WATER-JUMP TECHNIQUE

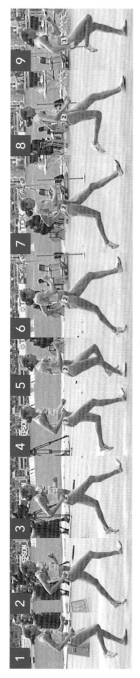

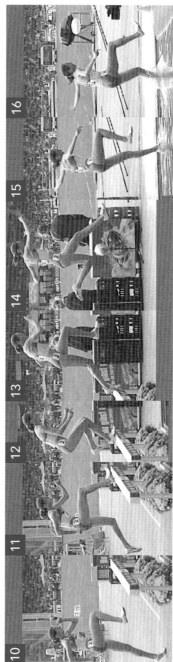

Data about the photo sequences

Athlete:	Gulnara Galkina (born: 9 July 1978, Russia)
Height/weight:	1.75 m/56 kg
Performance:	9:21.73 min (13 September 2008, Stuttgart)
Best performance:	8:58.81 min (17 August 2008, Beijing, world record)
Greatest success:	Olympic champion 2008

COMMENTARY

Before the 3000m steeplechase was included in the international championship programme for women, Gulnara Galkina (maiden name Samitowa), had achieved top-ten rankings on the flat distances: seventh place over 5000m at the 2003 World Championships, third place over 1500m at the 2004 Indoor World Championships, and sixth place over 5000m at the 2004 Olympic Games. During these years she already established her first 3000m steeplechase world record (9:08.35 min in 2003, and 9:01.59 min in 2004). In 2005, when the 3000m steeplechase was included in the women's world-championship programme for the first time, Galkina did not compete at all due to exhaustion. In 2006 she returned to the track before she placed seventh over the 3000m steeplechase at the 2007 World Championships. At the Olympic debut of this event at the 2008 Olympics, she won in world-record time. The photo sequences presented here were made one month after this highlight of the season. They show Galkina at an obstacle on the penultimate lap and at the water jump on the last lap. Her superior performance is attributed primarily to her superior times over the flat distances (see table 2). Her

technical errors are due to her relatively late turning toward the steeplechase. As expected, these errors become particularly obvious when she is tired at the later stages of the race as can be seen in the photo sequences.

*Table 2: **Galkina's best times over the flat distances** (according to the IAAF, 2010): Since the athlete's focus is on competing in her/his special event in the phases of the season in which the athlete is in top shape, some of these best times are achieved in preparatory races.*

800m	1500m	3000m	5000m
2:00.29 min	4:01.29 min	8:42.96 min	14:33.13 min

Galkina runs toward the track obstacle with a very low position of her CG. Signs of this are the touchdown of the entire sole of the foot, the noticeable amortisation of the support leg, the flat movement curve of her swing-leg foot, and the touchdown for the push-off over the obstacle, which is performed with a marked bracing action far in front of the vertical projection of her CG. The last feature is associated with running too close to the obstacle, which results in an outward sickle movement of the swing leg and an upward directed push-off which slows her down too much so that the clearance of the obstacle is too high. This may also be associated with deficits in her trail-leg technique, which is characterised by the knee being moved forward too low and below the height of the foot (picture 8). Galkina's high obstacle clearance results in a hard landing behind the obstacle. Upon her first contact with the ground, which is well under her CG, she lowers her foot from the tip of her foot onto the entire sole. Subsequently, she drops lower on the second ground contact, during which she reaches the lowest CG position with the extremely bent knee of her support leg. Her upper body and arm movements in front of and above the obstacle seem to be ideal. However, Galkina is forced to perform a very wide arm swing behind the obstacle to compensate for the angular momentum of her trail leg opened too early at the knee joint.

During the approach to the water jump, Galkina has similar problems as with the track obstacle. After two very short strides, she once again pushes off too close to the obstacle and with a too marked bracing action. Due to the resulting path of her CG, which is a little too high, her upper body is not very low during the clearance of the obstacle. However, Galkina's leg actions during obstacle clearance appear

nearly optimal: push-off extension, swing leg above the horizontal, grasping rolling-off of the foot on the beam, approximately right angle at the knee of the support leg at the moment when the leg is perpendicular to the beam, and a swing leg which is quickly moved forward at an acute angle. Whether she achieves a complete push-off extension between pictures 13 and 14 is not visible. In any case, Galkina achieves a wide leap over the water pit, and upon landing she succeeds in making her second ground contact on the flat track. By performing more controlled contralateral arm actions starting in the flight phase and ultimately resembling the flight phase of the running-jump technique of long jumping, she could improve her landing even more. The extremely powerful and dynamic exit from the water pit gives evidence to Gulnara Galkina's outstanding athletic abilities.

1.12.6 STRATEGY

A too fast starting pace is even less favourable for a steeplechaser than for a flat middle- and long-distance runner. If the runner produces too much lactate at an early stage, he/she is not only forced to slow his/her pace, but it may be almost impossible for him/her to clear the water jump. Therefore, a well-trained feel for pace, a good self-assessment under various racing conditions, and practising the correct initial pace are all of upmost importance. When comparing lap times, a 3000m steeplechase race should also

have the tub shape described in chapter II–1.10.4. Whether the runner maintains a uniform, economic race pace can be controlled even better by measuring the obstacle interval times. If, for example, the time is taken at the moment of push-off in front of the obstacle, only the interval before the water jump should be slightly faster, while the interval after the water jump should be slightly slower.

As in all middle- and long-distance races, the running path is the shortest when running on the inside of the inside lane. However, in the steeplechase, this also ensures that the runner must not run in an arced path in front of the obstacles. Since most runners run somewhat to the outside in order to have enough room in front of the obstacle, runners who do not run on the inside of the lane are often forced to run in an even longer arc. Nevertheless, so that steeplechasers are able to find their own rhythm in front of the obstacle, they should not get too close to the runner in front of them. However, due to the longer distance on the outside path, runners have the freedom of running at their individually optimal running pace and rhythm (before the obstacles) and responding to changing race situations.

1.12.7 DIDACTICS: SUPERORDINATE LONG-TERM OBJECTIVES AND GENERAL METHODOLOGY

Steeplechase competitions are only offered beginning with the U18 age group (i.e., beginning with build-up training). In children's athletics and in basic training, the steeplechase is prepared by teaching the long jump and hurdle sprint as well as through aerobic endurance training. Particularly versatile runs and sprints over various obstacles (183), long jumps from slightly elevated take-off spots (274), and cross-country fartlek runs (230) are important preparatory training forms for the steeplechase. Cross-country runs (see chapter II–1.10.5) train strength endurance, fighting spirit, the willingness to take risks, courage and perseverance, the ability to run at a certain rhythm, the ability to judge distances, and anticipation.

From the beginning, the clearing of the hurdle, obstacle, and water jump should be practised bilaterally. Falls and fear hinder the development of an optimal hurdle and obstacle technique. Therefore, running over rigid, immobile obstacles is introduced relatively late, and the coach should explicitly point out the difference to hurdle sprinting. To illustrate this difference, athletes may initially be told to use the skim technique. The obstacles (long benches, two-piece gym boxes, flat balance beam, etc.) should initially be lower than the hurdles already mastered in hurdling practice. Special (simplified) exercises should also be used to practise the clearance of the water jump at an early stage (245–246).

Trial runs over 800m obstacle courses are recommended as the first form of competition for U12 and U14 athletes. Here, children and adolescents must clear 50cm high rigid obstacles and the water pit without an obstacle in front of them. The water jump is an especially great challenge. However, here, as in the first real obstacle competitions in the U18 age group, the following applies: *An athlete may only take part in a competition after having been adequately prepared for the specific loads.* In particular, landing in the water pit and clearing the rigid obstacles at competition height while running in a pack must be practised in advance. Here, the official rules reduce the above-mentioned methodological requirement for relatively low rigid obstacles to absurdity: The obstacles for male U18 athletes are of the same height as the hurdles in the short hurdle sprint and higher than in the 400m hurdles. The obstacles for female U18 athletes are of the same height as the hurdles in the short and long hurdle sprint.

Landing in the water pit requires not only technical and coordination skills, but also special reactive-strength and endurance capabilities. These are trained at an early stage through versatile exercises from the ABCs of jumping and later through reactive multiple jumps. The landing in the water pit after jumping down from an obstacle is such a strain that it clearly should be limited in terms of its frequency per workout and training week. In basic training (after the take-off from the track without an obstacle) and at the beginning of build-up training (after push-off from an obstacle), only a maximum of four landings in the water pit should be performed per leg and per workout. Up to the peak of high-performance training, this number should only be increased very gradually to a maximum of 10 landings per leg in one training session with a maximum of two such training sessions per week. However, when landing in the sand (246), 20 landings per leg and per workout may be performed. Due to the risk of slipping, landings in the water pit should always be practised wearing spikes.

After proper (technical) basic training, a good steeplechaser must be an especially good (3000 and 5000m) runner. In addition, a steeplechaser in (high-)performance training performs considerably more strength, jumping-strength, and specific flexibility training than a comparable flat-distance runner.

1.12.8 TRAINING CONTENTS: FORMS OF GAMES AND EXERCISES

Steeplechase training includes all forms of games and exercises mentioned in connection with middle- and long-distance running (see chapter II–1.10.6) and 400m hurdles (see chapter II–1.9.8; including those games and exercises referred to in these chapters). The ABCs of jumping and multiple reactive jumps are also very important for the steeplechase (78–92 and 261–270).

241 ▨ **Obstacle relays**

Possible objectives: Obstacle and water-jump technique; aerobic and/or anaerobic endurance; versatile strength training.

Execution/variations: As pendulum, return, or lap relay; in the lap relay, the winner of the

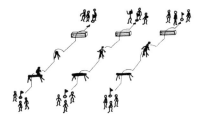

previous run-through must run on the outside lane, the loser on the inside lane; also as an endless relay; running over obstacles or skim technique; slalom runs; crawling through the middle element of a gym box; climbing over the parallel bars; leapfrogs; side vaults (or in another way) over a laterally placed vaulting horse or big gym box; higher obstacles (e.g., parallel bars) must be padded with mats; first run-through for getting acquainted with the exercise, possibly not yet in the form of a competition.

Typical load standards: Several run-throughs with rest short intervals ; vary setup and/or tasks; fun should be maintained.

242 Pursuit race over obstacles

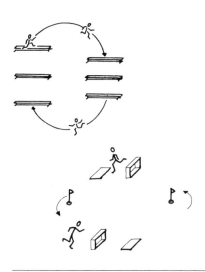

Possible objectives: Obstacle and water-jump technique; aerobic and/or anaerobic endurance.

Execution: Two or more runners start at the same distance from each other and try to catch up with the runner in front of them.

Variations: Athletes must be told to perform the exercise with both legs and/or to use the skim technique: a box element placed on its long side must not fall over when using the skim technique (no push-off); as pursuit relay or in the form of a six-days race (172); see also 241.

Typical load standards: See 241; in form of a tournament (elimination system, or, even better, using the league system); high volume (no sprints).

243 Running across an obstacle course

Possible objectives: Obstacle and water-jump technique; aerobic and/or anaerobic endurance; training in a small area (e.g., in a gym).

Execution: Athletes must be told to perform the exercise with both legs; the focus should be on

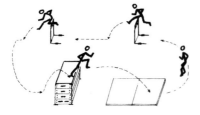

a flat push-off from the (imitated) water-jump obstacle.

Variations: Over a balance beam at low height, a long bench or small gym boxes (using the skim technique); with distance markers (see 185); as a relay (162 and 173) or a pursuit race (242).

Typical load standards: The running velocity should be similar to the competition velocity in the steeplechase; therefore, for example, relatively long courses, pre-set lap times, many laps, or the like (no sprints!).

---

244 **Cross-country runs**

Possible objectives: Aerobic and anaerobic (strength) endurance.

Execution/variations: Athletes should run as little as possible on sealed paths, but rather over uneven meadows or forest grounds; he/she should look for every obstacle (transverse tree trunks, tree stumps, benches, small ditches, etc.) to jump or run over; often uphill and downhill.

Typical load standards: In the form of a continuous run (227), tempo-endurance run (228), or fartlek (230).

---

245 **Water jump without obstacle**

Possible objectives: Water-jump technique (in particular landing technique), alternative long-jump training.

Execution: The water pit is cleared without an obstacle in front; not too fast run-up velocity to prevent falling forward on landing; the take-off leg should be moved forward during the flight phase so that the landing first occurs on the swing leg.

Variations: From a run-up or within a run on a circle (on the lawn or on the track; see 800m steeplechase competition in chapter II–1.12.7); bilateral practice

Typical load standards: Initially not more than 3-4, later 5–6 landings per leg and training session.

246 Water-jump training

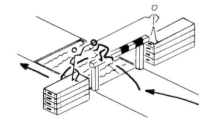

Possible objectives: Water-jump technique; reactive strength of the legs.

Execution/variations: Push-off for distance from the obstacle on the track, on the lawn, in front of the sand pit; in each case with distance marker (at 2.80–3.30m): up to a line in the sand pit, over gym mat, onto mat (also for reducing the strain of landing); initially with lateral landing when training at the water jump (see line drawing); to demonstrate the flat curve of the CG under a band (see line drawing; also at the sand pit, etc.) or with a slight touch of the hands on the beam; practising running over the obstacle also in a tight group; possibly also using an individually suitable mark in front of the obstacle which is either pre-set or must be established.

Typical load standards: Not more than 5–10 landings per leg and training session; The pace of the run-up should correspond as much as possible to the competition pace (i.e., neither with a run-up that is too fast , nor in slower endurance sessions):

a) 2 sets of 6 reps (3 with one leg, 3 with the other leg) from an 80m run-up – water jump – 80m run to the coach – brief correction by the coach – 80m run-up, etc.

b) (primarily before competitions) rather in intensive than in extensive tempo-run series (see table 3).

247 **Short obstacle series**

Possible objectives: Obstacle technique; reactive strength; flexibility, speed endurance.

Execution: Running over obstacles at competition height at significantly shorter distances and

a) at arbitrary and irregular distances (due to bilateral training the changes of the natural running rhythm are as slight as possible) or

b) at regular uneven distances (requires bilaterality) or even distances; at competition pace or slightly faster.

Variations: Running in a tight group; also in the curve; see also hurdle exercises in chapters II–1.8.8 and II–1.9.8.

Typical load standards: for example, 2–3 sets of 6–10 reps each of 100m with 4 obstacles, rest intervals: jog back, rest intervals between sets: 5 min.

248 **Tempo runs over obstacles**

Possible objectives: Aerobic and anaerobic endurance, obstacle (and water-jump) technique.

Execution/variations/***typical load standards:*** Generally, all tempo-run sessions mentioned in chapters II–1.5.8, II–1.9.8, and II–1.10.6 can be performed over 4 obstacles per lap (the water-jump technique is normally practised separately [246] or only practised additionally in very specific workouts of a competition-like character); it is especially recommended to perform such intervals over obstacles with the running pace resembling competition pace (intervals between 800 and 2000m, 3 to 8 reps); more seldom also faster intervals between 400 and 500m with lap times 4–5 sec faster than the lap times in competition; in total, 30–50% of the interval training should be performed over obstacles; see also table 3.

Table 3: **Training for specific competition preparation** *("Training which makes the competition appear easy," according to Benson, 1993, p. 18) over ten laps without a rest interval; for steeplechasers with a personal best between 8:20 and 8:40 min.*

	1st lap	2nd lap	3rd lap	4th lap	5th lap	6th lap	7th lap	8th lap	9th lap	10th lap
	each lap over 4 obstacles and the water jump			around the outside of the obstacles	each lap over 4 obstacles and the water jump			around the outside of the obstacles	each lap over 4 obstacles and the water jump	
8:20	70 sec	60 sec	70 sec	80-90 sec	70 sec	60 sec	70 sec	80-90 sec	70 sec	60 sec
8:30	75 sec	60 sec	75 sec	90-100 sec	75 sec	60 sec	75 sec	90-100 sec	75 sec	60 sec
8:40	75 sec	65 sec	75 sec	90-100 sec	75 sec	65 sec	75 sec	90-100 sec	75 sec	65 sec

1.12.9   SPECIAL TEST AND CONTROL PROCEDURES

	Test: Ability/skill tested	Execution/comments
T81	**1200m obstacle test:** a) Running technique, obstacle technique, and water-jump technique; b) all factors determining performance	Maximal run under competition conditions (obstacle height, distances, etc.; leave out only first obstacle): a) assessment by means of technique analysis sheets (see chapters II–1.10.3 and II–1.12.4), possibly with the assistance of video (T1) and photo sequences made thereof; and b) under-distance test with the time achieved as test criterion.
T82	**4000m obstacle test:** All factors determining performance	Maximal run under competition conditions (obstacle height, distances, etc.; leave out only first obstacle); perform obstacle over-distance tests only with high-performance athletes.
T4	**1 RPM:** Maximal strength	Squat (62), clean (63), snatch (64), hamstrings (68), quadriceps (69), etc. (if possible, also eccentric maximal-strength measurement).
T5	**Squat jump and T8 counter-movement and drop jump:** Two-legged speed strength and reactive strength of the extensor loop	The forward and/or backward toss of the shot (93) for distance may be performed as a simpler sport-motor test instead of counter-movement jumps.
T9	**5-stride hops with distance maximisation:** Reactive strength of the legs in comparison to one another	Test should be performed on both sides.

(continued)

(continued)

	Test: Ability/skill tested	Execution/comments
T10	**30m bounding run with time minimisation:** Reactive strength of the legs	
T11	**Strength-endurance tests:** Anaerobic strength endurance	for example, squats for 1 min or 200m bounding run.
T24	**30m flying sprint:** Maximal sprinting speed	The test should also be performed in the curve.
T31	**Wingate test:** Anaerobic endurance	
T51	**Tests over the flat course:** Obstacle technique and aerobic endurance	a) Over the same distance as in the steeplechase competition (to calculate the technique index see chapter II–1.12.3); b) over under- and over-distances.
T61	**Standing start and acceleration:** Start acceleration without reaction speed	The test should also be performed in the curve.
T62	**Technique analysis:** Running technique	
T63	**Stride-frequency and stride-length measurement:** Technique and specific strength endurance	
T64	**Tactical analysis:** Racing strategy	
T66	**Graded field test:** Aerobic endurance	With lactate withdrawal (and spirometry), or, if this is not possible, as simple minute test (T65): e.g., Cooper test (12 min) or 30-min test (see table 4 in chapter II–1.10.7).
T72	**Middle-distance tempo-run programmes:** **Anaerobic and aerobic endurance**	for example, 5 x 1000m, 2 x 5 x 400m (low intensity), or 2 x 3 x 400m (I3).
T2	**Flexibility tests:** General flexibility and flexibility specific to the steeplechase	for example, using exercises 203–205.
T3	**Body weight and body fat measurement:** Relative strength	Inappropriate upward and downward deflections should be avoided.

1.12.10 ERRORS – CAUSES – CORRECTIONS

Error	Causes	Corrections
Too much acceleration in front of the obstacle.	• Insufficient effort to achieve economic technique and strategy. • Too high velocity when running over obstacles in isolated exercises during training.	✔ Focusing on economy as a topic of discussion. ✔ Focusing on maintaining the competition velocity during training exercises.
Noticeable stutter steps or lengthening of strides in front of the (water-jump) obstacle, mostly in combination with a reduction of pace.	• Under-developed bilaterality (the runner always chooses the same push-off and swing leg). • No intermediate mark in front of the water jump or overlooking the mark when running in a tight group; too much dependence on the intermediate mark. • Being locked in or running too close behind the runner in front impairs one's own rhythm. • Fear of the obstacle for beginners (insufficient preparation). • Poor vision-based distance estimation.	✔ In practice, 50(–60)% of the obstacle clearances should be performed with the weak side. ✔ Introduction of an intermediate mark in front of the water jump; but also deliberate practice without intermediate mark. ✔ More frequent practice of the water-jump and obstacle technique while running in a tight group (possibly also more preparatory competitions). ✔ Versatile practice of the obstacle technique over high movable (hurdles) and lower rigid obstacles; in the process, focusing on a competition-appropriate approach velocity. ✔ Versatile practice of water-jump technique (with simplifications; 246). ✔ Unspecific practice of vision-based distance estimation during cross-country runs (244).
High jump over or onto an obstacle with great loss of velocity at the push-off and possibly placing the push-off foot onto the ground over the heel.	• Long last stride, backward lean of the upper body, bracing push-off too close in front of the obstacle. • Poor vision-based distance estimation. • Stutter steps and its causes (see above).	✔ Running over obstacles using distance markers (185). ✔ See corrections of stutter steps in front of the obstacle.
Long jump over or onto the obstacle with loss of velocity on landing (behind or on the obstacle).	• Push-off point too far away from the obstacle. • Poor vision-based distance estimation. • Lengthening of strides in front of the obstacle and its causes (see above).	✔ See corrections of lengthening of strides in front of the obstacle.
Bracing against the beam while placing the foot onto the water-jump obstacle (including loss of velocity).	• The swing leg is insufficiently bent when being placed on the obstacle. • Too much tension of the knee extensors of the swing leg. • Too flat push-off angle in front of the obstacle. • Long jump over or onto the obstacle and its causes (see above).	✔ Versatile practice of the water-jump technique (246) and focusing on relaxed and bent swing leg when placing it onto the obstacle. ✔ See corrections of long jump over or onto the obstacle.

(continued)

Track & Field

(continued)

Error	Causes	Corrections
Upright upper body and/or generally too high CG curve during the support on the beam of the water-jump obstacle.	• High jump over or onto the obstacle and its causes (see above). • Bracing against the beam and its causes (see above). • Fear of the water-jump clearance for beginners. • Insufficient strength of the support leg.	✔ Versatile practice of the water-jump technique (246) initially made easier by means of lower obstacles. ✔ Clearance of the obstacle under a cord or by touching the obstacle beam with one's hands (246). ✔ Strengthening of the leg extensors (49 and 62-64).
The smallest knee-joint angle of the support leg on the beam is under 90°.	• Too flat push-off onto the obstacle.	✔ Versatile practice of the water-jump technique (246) and corresponding corrections.
Slipping of the foot from the beam when placing the foot onto the beam or pushing off from the beam (at the water-jump obstacle).	• Insufficient or faulty rolling off of the foot over the beam. • Wrong shoes.	✔ Versatile practice of the water-jump technique (246) and focusing on correct rolling off of the foot over the beam. ✔ Practising the water-jump technique only wearing spikes which are suitable for the steeplechase.
Too high flight curve (of the CG) when clearing the water jump.	• The push-off from the beam occurs to soon and too far upward. • Wrong direction of view. • Upright upper body and/or too high CG curve even during the support on the beam and its causes (see above).	✔ Versatile practice of the water-jump technique (246) and direction of view to the target mark in the sand, on the lawn, or on the mat, or to the last 30-50 cm of the water pit. ✔ See corrections of upright upper body.
The runner jumps beyond the water pit.	• Too much acceleration when approaching the water jump. • Too high CG curve when jumping over the water pit and its causes (see above).	✔ See corrections of too much acceleration in front of the water pit. ✔ See corrections of too high CG curve when jumping over the water pit.
The runner lands too deep or too early in the water pit.	• Insufficient push-off due to bad starting position: the smallest knee angle of the support leg on the beam is below 90° and its causes (see above). • Velocity loss at the push-off in front of the obstacle or when placing the foot onto the obstacle and its causes (see above). • Too weak extensor muscles of the leg pushing off from the beam. • Very steep push-off upward from the beam.	✔ Versatile practice of the water-jump technique (246) and corresponding corrections (which also address causes earlier in the water jump technique). ✔ Strength training for extensor muscles of the legs (49 and 62-64).

496

Error	Causes	Corrections
Excessive velocity loss on landing in the water pit.	• Too much shoulder-hip separation due to a lack of compensatory contralateral arm actions or lateral evasion of swing leg on the beam. • Too high flight curve when jumping over the water pit and its causes (see above). • The runner lands too deep or too early in the water pit and its causes (see above).	✔ Versatile practice of the water-jump technique (246) and focusing on the shoulder and hip axis remaining as frontal as possible (if necessary, correction of the arm and leg movements during the clearance). ✔ See corrections of too high flight curve when jumping over the water pit and the runner lands too deep or too early in the water pit.
Significant decrease in velocity on the last lap or laps.	• Too high initial pace. • Uneconomic obstacle technique.	✔ Checking the racing strategy by means of the technique index and the obstacle interval times. ✔ Discussion and practice of an economic obstacle and water-jump technique (246–248, etc.).
Excessive increase in velocity on the last lap.	• Too slow initial pace. • Fear of not being able to clear the obstacles in the event of great fatigue. • Insufficient strength endurance as a justified reason for the fear mentioned.	✔ Checking the racing strategy by means of the technique index and the obstacle interval times. ✔ Training reactive strength endurance (knee and hip extensors, hip flexors, trunk muscles, etc.)

With respect to the technique of clearing the obstacles placed on the track, the errors mentioned in connection with the short hurdles should also be considered (see chapter II–1.8.10). In terms of running before and after the obstacles, the errors, causes, and corrections listed in the general chapter on running should be considered (see chapter II–1.10.8).

1.12.11 TRAINING PLANNING

Compared to pure middle-distance training (see chapter II–1.11.11), steeplechase training must be supplemented by specific water-jump and obstacle training. On the one hand, the clearance of hurdles, obstacles and the water jump are improved through versatile technique training. On the other hand, aerobic and anaerobic endurance training is performed over various obstacles. In the third and fourth mesocycle, athletes should run over obstacles only at the desired competition pace.

SUGGESTED TRAINING PLANS

Following are exemplary microcycles for the

- second mesocycle of a 17-year-old athlete in build-up training (table 5);
- second mesocycle of an athlete in high-performance training (table 6); and
- fourth mesocycle of an athlete in high-performance training (table 7).

Young athletes do not have to specialise on the middle distances, the steeplechase, or the long distances. The suggested training plans for the

- first mesocycle of a 17-year-old athlete in build-up training for the middle distance (see chapter II–1.11.11); and
- third mesocycle of a 17-year-old athlete in build-up training for the long distances (see chapter II–1.13.11)

are therefore intended for the same athlete as in this chapter.

The suggested training plans for the

- first mesocycle of an athlete in high-performance training; and
- third mesocycle of an athlete in high-performance training

presented for the middle and long distances may in some respects be compared to the plans presented here.

Table 4: **Training emphasis in the various mesocycles** *for steeplechase training in high-performance training.*

1st mesocycle	aerobic endurance training (in varying intensity zones and using varying movement forms); strength-endurance training for the legs and the trunk; flexibility training; coordination training (ABCs of sprinting/jumping) and technique training specific to the steeplechase
2nd mesocycle	aerobic endurance training (in varying intensity zones and using varying movement forms); IC- and connective-tissue-oriented maximal- and reactive-strength training for the trunk and especially for the legs; flexibility training specific to the steeplechase; coordination training (ABCs of sprinting/jumping) and technique training specific to the steeplechase
3rd mesocycle	aerobic and anaerobic endurance training (more and more frequently at competition pace and using varying movement forms); IC- and connective-tissue-oriented maximal- and reactive-strength training for the trunk and especially for the legs; speed training; flexibility training specific to the steeplechase; coordination training (ABCs of sprinting/jumping) and technique training specific to the steeplechase
4th mesocycle	competitions and corresponding regeneration; aerobic and anaerobic endurance training (frequently at competition pace); IC- and connective-tissue-oriented maximal- and reactive-strength training for the trunk and especially for the legs; technique training specific to the steeplechase; maintenance stimuli

Table 5: Build-up training: sample microcycle for a 17-year-old middle- and long-distance runner as well as a steeplechaser in the second mesocycle.

Monday	Tuesday	Wednesday	Thursday	Friday	Saturday	Sunday
Trunk stabilisation exercises and abdominal crunches (20 min) with a lot of dynamic variation	Warm-up jogging (15 min)	Continuous run (30 min) first 10 min including ABCs of sprinting/jumping, arm circling, exaggerated arm actions, etc.	Cycling, swimming, inline skating, cross-country skiing or aqua jogging (40 min) alternately each week	Foot strengthening (10 min)	*Morning:* Warm-up jogging (15 min)	Rest
ABCs of running (10–15 run-throughs) heel kicks, pulling strides, step-overs, etc.	Acceleration runs (3 reps) barefoot	Muscle build-up training (70 min) deep squat and clean (the coach must continue to check technique attentively), hamstrings, adductors and abductors, bench press, lat pull, as well as possibly additional varying exercises	Contract-relax stretching (15 min)	Acceleration runs (3 reps) barefoot	Hurdle imitation and ABCs of hurdling (15 min)	On Saturdays before the hurdles possibly also training the techniques of one event for the quadrathlon or pentathlon
Flying sprints (3 x 30m + 20–30m run-up; rest intervals: 10 min) at maximal pace through light barriers	ABCs of jumping (15–20 run-throughs) galloping sideways, ankle jumps, skipping with two-legged landing, skipping with one-legged landing), etc.	Technique sprints (5–6 x 100m) coordination runs, alternating-pace sprints, slalom runs, etc.	Muscle build-up training for the trunk on apparatus and/or for the arms, medicine-ball work, or gymnastics (30 min) e.g., goalkeeper throws, rotational throws, throws from a prone position, and tossing, using a medicine ball	ABCs of running (10–15 run-throughs) running with knees raised to half the horizontal position and high stride frequency, high-knee run, Can-Can exercise, etc.	Practising the hurdling technique (15 min)	
Practising the water-jump technique (20 min) 5–6 landings per leg on lawn or in the sand pit	Continuous run (60 min) flat terrain		Acceleration runs (5 x 100m) over mini-hurdles at arbitrary distance	Skipping and bounding runs (4 x 40m each) including variations, technically correct	Hurdle Zs (2 sets of 4 Zs each of 2 run-throughs of 60m each) varying rhythms and swing legs, low hurdles	
Game (30 min) e.g., basketball or soccer	Contract-relax stretching (15 min) primarily specific to the steeplechase			Fartlek and/or cross-country run (30 min) hilly terrain	Warm-down jogging (10 diagonals on the lawn)	
	Foot strengthening (10 min) in the sand, with elastic band, or by rope jumping			Acceleration runs and standing starts (100, 80, 60, 40, and 30m) each run faster than the previous one; as utilisation	*Afternoon:* Continuous run (30 min)	
	Acceleration runs and standing starts (100, 80, 60, 40, and 30m) each run faster than the previous one; as utilisation				Contract-relax stretching (15 min)	
					Acceleration runs and standing starts (100, 80, 60, 40, and 30m) each run faster than the previous one	

Table 6: High-performance training: sample microcycle in the second mesocycle of the summer season (second macrocycle).

	Monday	Tuesday	Wednesday	Thursday	Friday	Saturday	Sunday
Morning	Continuous run (40 min) as on Friday morning Acceleration runs (3 reps) Water-jump training (2 x 10 x approx. 150m laps on the lawn; rest intervals: 30–60 sec for correction; rest intervals between sets: 5 min) 1 obstacle per lap	Continuous run (50 min) flat terrain Acceleration runs (3 reps) barefoot ABCs of running (15–20 run-throughs) Technique sprints (6–8 x 60–80m) coordination runs, slalom runs, varying arm actions, etc.	Warm-up jogging (30 min) Acceleration runs (3 reps) Ankle jumps or skipping with two-legged landing (5 x 20 jumps) ABCs of jumping (10–12 run-throughs) Game (30 min) e.g., basketball or soccer	Cycling, swimming, inline skating, cross-country skiing or aqua jogging (50 min) alternately each week, different sport than in the afternoon	Continuous run (50 min) first 10 minutes including ABCs of sprinting/jumping, arm circling, etc. Acceleration runs (3 reps) barefoot Skipping, bounding runs, and rhythm jumps (4 x 40m each) Alternating-pace sprints (5 x 120m)	Warm-up jogging (30 min) Acceleration runs (3 reps) Hurdle imitation, ABCs of hurdling, and hurdle preparation (30 min) Hurdle Zs (3 sets of 4 Zs each of 3 run-throughs of 80m each) varying rhythms and swing legs Warm-down jogging (10 min)	Rest
Afternoon	Foot strengthening (10 min) Trunk stabilisation exercises and abdominal crunches (20 min) Fartlek (40 min) hilly terrain Contract-relax stretching (15 min) Acceleration runs over mini-hurdles	Warm-up jogging (30 min) LI tempo runs (8 x 1000m over 4 track obstacles; jogging interval: 3 min) slower than competition pace, in tight group Warm-down jogging (20 min) Acceleration runs and standing starts (100, 80, 60, 40, and 30m) each run faster than the previous one	Continuous run (90 min) flat terrain Acceleration runs (6 x 100m) over mini-hurdles at arbitrary distance; as utilisation	Cycling, swimming, inline skating, cross-country skiing or aqua jogging (30 min) Contract-relax stretching (15 min) Muscle build-up training for the trunk on apparatus and/or for the arms, medicine-ball work, or gymnastics (30 min) Acceleration runs	Warm-up jogging (10 min) Acceleration runs (3 reps) Muscle build-up training (25 min) clean and deep squat Maximal-eccentric strength training (15 min) hamstrings, quadriceps, adductors/abductors, etc. Tempo-endurance run (40 min) hilly terrain Acceleration runs	Continuous run (30 min) Contract-relax stretching (15 min) primarily specific to the steeplechase Acceleration runs (6 x 100m) over mini-hurdles at arbitrary distance; as utilisation	

Table 7: High-performance training: sample microcycle in the fourth mesocycle of the summer season (second macrocycle).

	Monday	Tuesday	Wednesday	Thursday	Friday	Saturday	Sunday
Morning	**Warm-up jogging** (10 min) **Maximal-eccentric strength training** (15 min) trunk stabilisation, lifting opposite upper and lower limbs in prone position, belly punches, raising the foot/toes **ABCs of sprinting** (10–15 run-throughs) **Acceleration runs** **Flying sprints** (3 x 30m + 30m run-up)	**Continuous run** (60 min) flat terrain **Technique sprints** (6–8 x 60–80m) coordination runs, slalom runs, varying arm actions, etc.	**Continuous run** (50 min) first 10 min including ABCs of sprinting/jumping, arm circling, etc. **Strength training** for the trunk, **medicine-ball work,** or **gymnastics** (30 min)	**Continuous run** (60 min) flat terrain **Game** (15 min) e.g., basketball or soccer	**Warm-up jogging** (30 min) **Acceleration runs** (3 reps) barefoot **ABCs of sprinting/ jumping** (12–15 run-throughs)	*Preparatory competition* • **Warm-up** jogging (20 min) • Inciting of trunk and foot muscles • 2 acceleration runs • **ABCs of** sprinting/ running • 5 acceleration runs over 80–200m **3000m (steeplechase) competition**	**Cycling, swimming, inline skating, cross-country skiing** or **aqua jogging** (45 min) alternately each week **Acceleration runs and standing starts** (100, 80, 60, 40, and 30m) each run faster than the previous one; as utilisation
Afternoon	**Warm-up jogging** (20 min) **Acceleration runs** (5 reps) barefoot **ABCs of jumping** (8–12 run-throughs) **Depth jumps** (5 x 6) from box to box **Bounding runs** (5 x 50m) alternatively: rhythm jumps **Alternating-pace sprints** (5 x 80m)	**Warm-up jogging** (5 min) **Tempo-endurance run** or **fartlek** (30 min) hilly terrain **Warm-down jogging** (5 min) **Contract-relax stretching** (15 min) specific to the steeplechase **Acceleration runs** (6 x 100m) over mini-hurdles at arbitrary distance	**Warm-up jogging** (20 min) **ABCs of hurdling** (15 min) **Acceleration runs** (3 reps) barefoot **Practising the steeplechase technique** (3 x 800m; rest intervals: 3 min) at competition pace over all obstacles **Warm-down jogging** (20 min) **Acceleration runs**	In the competition phase, the training plan must be adapted to the (irregular) competition calendar. In this plan, it may be assumed that the athlete took part in a preparatory competition (e.g., over 5000m) on the previous Saturday. If there are no other competitions for one and a half weeks (or more) between two preparatory competitions, the athlete should perform more training and his/her training should be of a more basic nature. Before the main competition, the athlete should not take part in any competition for two weeks and should train less than shown here.			

1.12.12 BIBLIOGRAPHY

Benson, T. (1993). Steeplechasing – the art of interrupted running. *Modern Athlete and Coach 31* (1), 15-18.

Dimova, A. (1999). The 2000 m Steeplechase for women. *New Studies in Athletics 14* (3), 29-34.

Farwell, P. (1998). Steeplechase workouts. Combined barrier/flat intervals. *Track and Field Coaches Review 98*, 33-34.

International Association of Athletics Federations (2010). *Biographies: Gulnara Galkina.* Zugriff am 31.10.2010 unter http://www.iaaf.org/athletes/biographies/letter=0/athcode=193819/index.html

Monz-Dietz, L. (2003a). Frauen-Hindernislauf: Wohin führt der Weg? *Leichtathletiktraining 14* (11), 5-11.

Monz-Dietz, L. (2003b). Frauen-Hindernislauf – So wird trainiert! *Leichtathletiktraining 14* (12), 31-37.

Monz-Dietz, L. (2005a). Deutschlands bester Hindernis-Nachwuchs. *Leichtathletiktraining 15* (1), 18-25.

Monz-Dietz, L. (2005b). Hindernisse in den Weg stellen! *Leichtathletiktraining 15* (6), 4-9.

Monz-Dietz, L. (2006). Jedes Hindernis nehmen. *Leichtathletiktraining 16* (2+3), 16-20.

Monz-Dietz, L. (2009). Die erste Hindernis-Olympiasiegerin. *Leichtathletiktraining 20* (5), 30-35.

Regelkommissionen des DLV, FLA, ÖLV und SLV (Hrsg.). (2010). *Internationale Wettkampfregeln*. Waldfischbach: Hornberger.

Stolley, S. (1996). Coaching the steeplechase. *Track and Field Coaches Review 96* (2), 38-44.

Von Papen, H. (2008). Leitsätze für das Training des Läufers. *Leichtathletiktraining 19* (2+3), 41-47.

1.13 5000M, 10,000M, MARATHON

1.13.1   PEOPLE'S SPORT NO. 1

"We have won!" Legend has it that after the battle of Marathon in 490 B.C., the messenger Pheidippides ran the distance from Marathon to Athens to announce the victory of the Athenians over the Persians with these words. In the course of time, runs over very long distances were performed among the native peoples of Australia, Africa, Asia, South America, and Mexico. Historical records show that around the turn of the 19th century in the Sierra Madre, in northern Mexico, the tribal people of the Tarahumara enthusiastically performed runs over 273km without interruption.

In England at the beginning of the 19th century and afterwards, runners competed against one another over distances of 3–30 miles (4.83 to 48.27km) to entertain spectators, some of whom bet on their favourite runners. Even today, the IAAF lists world records over many non-Olympic distances: 15, 20, 25, 30 and 100km, half marathon, and runs over one hour.

After having been forgotten for a long time, the legend of Pheidippides' run was revived in the years prior to 1896 and was taken as the model for the first marathon race in history at the first modern Olympic Games. The distance was 40km. In 1904, the marathon runner Fred Lorz was disqualified because he covered a large part of the distance in an automobile. The

now classic distance of 42.195 km was first run in London in 1908. The British royal family at that time insisted the race should start in front of Windsor Castle and should finish in front of the Royal Box at the Olympic Stadium.

Women ran the Olympic marathon for the first time in 1984. The fact that women were allowed to run the marathon was mainly due to the efforts of the German sports physician Ernst von Aaken, who argued that women had a great capacity for endurance. In 1967, he made sure that two women secretly participated in a marathon for the first time. At the 1988 Olympics, there was the first women's 10,000m race and at the 1996 Olympics the first 5000m race for women followed. However, since 1912 there have always been 5000 and 10,000m races for men at the Olympics. At the interim Olympic Games in 1906 and at the Olympic Games in 1908, a run over 5 miles (8047m) was held.

The methods by which athletes and their coaches were successful during the past hundred years differed entirely from those of modern times. For example, Lasse Viren, the double Olympic champion over 5000 and 10,000m in 1972, is said to have covered up to 844 km per month primarily in long runs. However, he later confessed to blood doping. Emil Zatopek, who in

1952 was the first and only runner to win the 5000 and 10,000m races as well as the marathon, is said to have completed up to sixty 400m intervals in training. Still other runners favoured more intense intervals.

Today endurance running may be described as people's sport number one and is popular in almost all countries around the world. The marathon runs in New York, Boston, Chicago, London, Sao Paulo, Seoul, etc. are mass events with tens of thousands of runners and an audience of millions along the course of the race. All official world men's world records have been run in Berlin. In 2018 the Kenian Eliud Kipchoge ran the very flat course in Germany in 2:01:39 hours. His marathon in 1:59:40 in Vienna in 2019 does not count as an official world record because it was run with many pacemakers, who were frequently replaced. The official women's world record was run in the US in Chicago, Illinois. In 2019 the Kenian Brigid Kosgei needed 2:14:04 hours for the marathon.

The Ethiopian Haile Gebreselassie may be called the most successful long-distance runner of the modern era. He set nine world records, four over 5000m, three over 10,000m, and two in the marathon. In addition, he set several world records over non-Olympic distances and won nine medals (including six gold medals) at the Olympics and world championships. His successor as the 5000 and 10,000m world record holder, Kenenisa Bekele, is also from Ethiopia. Like his female compatriot Tirunesh Dibaba, he won two gold medals at the 2008 Olympic Games. In international meetings, marathon events and championships, the North African runners from Morocco, Kenya, and Ethiopia, mostly divide up the prizes and medals over (middle and) long distances among themselves. Only occasionally runners of Caucasian and Asian descent are successful in breaking this phalanx. Two examples are the former British marathon world record holder Paula Radcliffe and the German Dieter Baumann, who won the Olympic 5000m race in Barcelona in 1992.

1.13.2   THE MOST IMPORTANT COMPETITION RULES

The most important competition rules for the 5000 and 10,000m races have been presented almost completely in the general rule chapters on running and the middle and long distances (see chapters II–1.1.1 and II–1.10.1). It should be added that in the younger age groups only the middle distances are part of the competition programme of track athletics.

The 2000m may be run beginning with the U12 age group. In the U18 and U16 category, the 3000m is the longest championship course. In the U20 age group, the longest race is the 5000m, which may be run competitively by both girls and boys beginning at the age of 15. Beginning with the female and male junior category, the 10,000m is also a part of the championship programme. The 10,000m may be run beginning with the U18 category. The 3000m is no longer run at championships for adults or juniors.

Cross-country and forest runs may have a length of up to 1.5km for the U10 age group and up to 2km in the U12 age group. At regional championships, the distances for U14 athletes may be up to 4km. The possible distances increase to 5km in the U16 age group, to 8km in the U18 age group, and to 10km in the U20 age group.

Road races may be even longer (i.e., up to 5km even in the U10 age group). The distances increase to 10km in the U16 age group, 25km in the U18 age group, marathon in the U20 age group, and 24-hour running for adult athletes. In general, however, road-running championships are only conducted beginning with the U20 age category for 10km. For adults, there are also half-marathons, marathons, and 100km championships. For road races, the following special rules apply:

- The marathon distance is 42.195km. The course must be measured along the shortest possible route that an athlete could follow within the section of the road permitted for use in the race. The line indicating this route should be highlighted in colour. The actual length of the route must not differ from the intended distance by more than 0.1% (i.e., 42.20m).

- Circuit courses are allowed. The minimum length of one lap is 10km in the marathon (5km in half-marathon races).
- The distance in kilometres on the route must be displayed to all athletes.
- The difference in altitude between start and finish should not exceed 1m per kilometre run (i.e., 42.20m in total).
- The races must be run on established roads (if necessary, also on bicycle paths or footpaths) which during the competition are blocked for motor traffic. Soft ground such as turf is not allowed. Start and finish may be in an athletics stadium.
- Runners who shorten the distance to be covered are disqualified.
- At the start and finish of all road races, water and other suitable refreshments must be provided. In road races longer than 10km, catering stations must be established at intervals of approximately 5km. In addition, approximately midway between these stations, there must be refreshment stations where water and sponges are available (there must only be refreshment stations at distances of 2–3km for all events shorter than 10km).
- Refreshments and catering may be provided by the organiser or the runner himself/herself and may be taken only at the appropriate points (possibly served by a designated person).

1.13.3   SPORT-SCIENCE FINDINGS, PHASE STRUCTURE, AND TECHNIQUE

See the middle- and long-distance chapter (II–1.10.2) for the phase structure and technique in general. Therefore, only some discipline-specific features are dealt with below.

FOOT TOUCHDOWN

While many middle-distance runners, like sprinters, are off the ground with the heel during the entire support phase, long-distance runners run by rolling over the entire foot. The first ground contact occurs (from supinated position) between the front end of the heel and the middle foot on the outer edge of the foot before the foot moves inward (pronates) and is placed flatly on the ground. Then, the foot rolls off and the push-off is performed with the ball of the foot. While the foot is supinated again, the toes are the last to break contact with the ground. Before the touchdown of the foot, the toes are raised to stretch the arch. Apart from the arch of the foot, the inward bending (pronation movement) of the foot flatly onto the ground is a significant damping and energy storage mechanism. A foot touchdown over the rear of the heel not only impairs this mechanism, but is usually also associated with a foot touchdown further ahead of the vertical projection of the CG. This results in the development of a higher braking force during the front support phase and therefore in significantly less economic running. Even in long-distance running, the backward acceleration of the foot before the foot touchdown and a short distance between the point of touchdown

and the vertical projection of the CG are characteristic features of a good running technique.

FAT METABOLISM

The marathon and the 50km walking distance are covered (almost) exclusively using aerobic energy supply. In these long distances, the aerobic fat metabolism is also important. The lowering of the respiratory quotient during a marathon race or long walking race indicates the depletion of the carbohydrate stores and an increasing fat metabolism. Therefore, a part of the training in these disciplines should be performed at that pace which is associated with the highest fat metabolisation. In the marathon, this pace is slightly below race pace (whereas in the 50km race walk it is approximately identical with race pace).

Long-distance runners have very little subcutaneous fat. But even in thin runners, the energy stored in fat is almost inexhaustible. In terms of a better load-force ratio, a low percentage of body fat results in economic running and reduces the impact on the passive musculoskeletal system during the foot strike. In addition, the increase of body temperature is a limiting factor of marathon performance. The evaporative heat loss is crucial to heat dissipation, resulting from perspiration on the skin. If there is only little subcutaneous fat tissue, the transport of heat to the outside is facilitated.

Table 1: Requirement profile for the 5000m, 10,000m, and the marathon: The suggested rough estimate of the value of selected factors determining performance is based on the importance for the overall performance and the percentage of time spent training (IR: information requirements, constr.: constraints; see chapter I–1.1).

Factors determining 5000m, 10,000m, and marathon performance	Estimate of value	Notes
Coordination	+ + +	optical IR: low, acoustic IR: low, tactile IR: low, kinaesthetic IR: medium, vestibular IR: low; precision constr.: high, time constr.: medium, complexity constr.: low, situation constr.: low–medium, physical stress constr.: high
Flexibility	+	no extreme movement amplitude required
Strength		xtensor loop (glutes, quadriceps, triceps surae, erector spinae), iliopsoas; hamstrings; adductors, abdominal muscles, shoulder and upper-arm muscles
Maximal strength	+	as basis at the most
Reactive strength	+ +	of decisive importance for running economy even over longer distances
Speed	+	as a basis at the most
Endurance (general dynamic) Anaerobic endurance		
Strength endurance	+	as a basis of speed endurance at the most
Speed endurance	+ (+)	(in the track events) of a certain importance for the final spurt
Aerobic endurance	+ + + + +	while in the 5000 and 10,000m race the competition speed is approximately identical with the running speed corresponding with the aerobic-anaerobic threshold, the speed in the marathon is lower; in particular, in the marathon the energy provision through fat metabolism as well as the management of the heat accumulation in the body are very important
Psychological and cognitive abilities	+ + + + +	feel for pace and correct strategy; maintenance of the motivation for long running at the limit (at the aerobic-anaerobic transition) in the 5000 and 10,000m race or in terms of general fatigue resistance in the marathon; performance-oriented thinking and behaviour (see chapter I-3.1.1)
Anthropometric and primarily genetically determined characteristics	+ + + +	high percentage of slow muscle fibres; connective tissue with optimal energy-storing capacities; medium (with increasing distance rather small) body height; very low percentage of body fat

1.13.4 SUMMARY OF THE MOST IMPORTANT TECHNICAL CHARACTERISTICS = TECHNIQUE-ANALYSIS SHEET

See chapter II–1.10.3.

1.13.5   PHOTO SEQUENCE

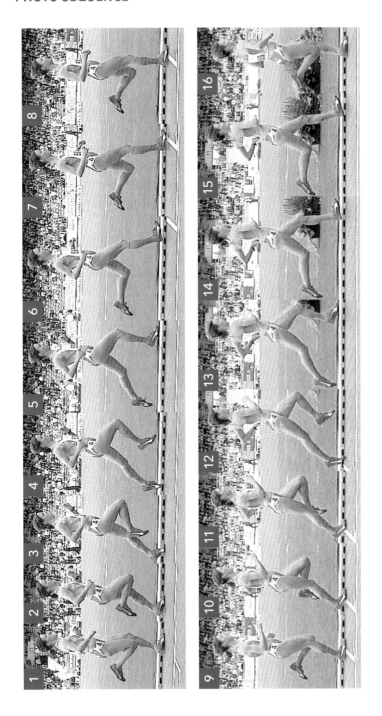

Data about the photo sequence

Athlete:	Sabrina Mockenhaupt (born: 6 December 1980, Germany)
Height/weight:	1.56 m/45 kg
Performance:	15:20.82 min (10 July 2007, Brunswick)
Best performance:	14:59.88 min (20 May 2009, Koblenz)
Greatest success:	more than 20-time German Champion over 5000m, 10,000m and in cross-country, European cross-country vice-champion in 2005

COMMENTARY

The photo sequence shows Mockenhaupt at the 2004 German Championships, which she narrowly won ahead of her permanent rival Irina Mikitenko. Figure 1 shows the velocity profile of the race and the time when the photos of this sequence were taken. The velocity development shows that it is a typical championship race with strategic variations of pace and an overall increasing running velocity toward the finish. Therefore, the final time was more than 17 sec slower than Mockenhaupt's best performance at this time. Mockenhaupt achieved her average velocity between 3900 and 4000m with an average stride length of 1.66m and a stride frequency of 3.37 strides/sec.

Mockenhaupt's effort to achieve a foot touchdown close to the vertical projection of the CG may be seen in pictures 8 and 16. She performs the touchdown over the outer edge of her foot with only a slightly bent knee. Subsequently, she lowers her foot briefly onto the entire sole while her knee joint is bent only very slightly. In the rear support phase, the push-off is performed with the ball of the foot through a powerful extension of her foot, knee, and hips. The push-off seems to be perfectly flat so that in combination with the relatively extended knee joint during the support phase, there is only a slight variation of the CG height.

During the swing phase, Mockenhaupt's knee-joint flexion is very noticeable for a long-distance runner. Therefore, she is able to bring her swing leg in front of her

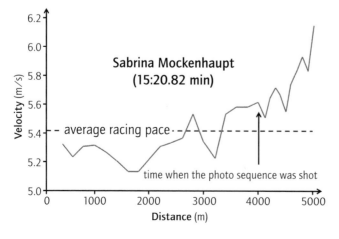

Figure 1: *Velocity profile of the race presented in the photo sequence.*

body early and to prepare a pulling foot touchdown after finishing the relaxed forward pendulum movement of her lower leg. The knee lift is approximately 35° below the horizontal. This is beneficial for long-distance running in terms of economy since a higher knee lift (as in the sprint) would result in higher energy consumption. A lower knee lift would make a pulling preparation of the next foot touchdown impossible.

Mockenhaupt runs with a typical long-distance arm swing. The elbows are bent at an angle below 90° and her hand swings

neither behind the body nor to shoulder height. The noticeable swing of the arms (especially the right) to the opposite side in front of the body is less ideal. There is also a relatively marked shoulder rotation about the longitudinal axis of the body. The upper body and head remain perfectly upright and are kept in a still position. The slight swayback posture with slightly forward-pointing pelvis is demonstrated by many long-distance runners. However, the noticeable lateral tilting of the pelvis, which is especially apparent during the support phase of the left leg, is unusual (pictures 1 and 16).

1.13.6 STRATEGY

VELOCITY CONTROL

The velocity profile in long-distance running also corresponds to the tub shape described in chapter II–1.10.4). For example, this means that the last kilometre is usually the fastest in a 10,000m race, while the first kilometre is the second fastest, and the seventh or eighth kilometre is the slowest. Nevertheless, runners try to achieve a race pace as uniform as possible for much of the race. For good long-

distance runners, the coefficient of velocity variation is 1–5% (see figure 2). However, in the marathon, the profile of the course also affects the velocity variation. World records are therefore run only on flat courses, for example in London or Berlin.

An individual timetable with interval and split times for a race as uniform as possible may be calculated using the simple formula below (see also table 2).

$$\text{Individual interval time (sec)} = \frac{\text{desired length of the interval (m)} \cdot \text{target finishing time (sec)}}{\text{length of the total distance (m)}}$$

The desired split times result from the addition of the interval times.

Table 2: *Calculating interval times in long-distance running.*

		Interval times		Racing distances	
100m (sec)	400m (min:sec)	1km (min:sec)	5km (min:sec)	10km (min:sec)	Marathon (h:min:sec)
15.1	1:00.4	2:31.1	12:35.36[1]		
15.7	1:02.8	2:37.1	13:05.5	26:11.00[2]	
16.3	1:05.2	2:43.0	13:35.0	27:10.0	
16.9	1:07.7	2:49.3	14:06.62[4]	28:13.2	
17.3	1:09.2	2:53.0	14:24.9	28:49.8[5]	2:01:39[3]
18.2	1:12.8	3:02.0	15:10.0	30:20.0	2:07:59
19.1	1:16.3	3:10.6	15:53.2	31:46.4	2:14:04[6]
20.5	1:22.0	3:25.0	17:05.0	34:10.0	2:24:10
22.0	1:28.0	3:40.0	18:20.0	36:40.0	2:34:43
25.0	1:40.0	4:10.0	20:50.0	41:40.0	2:55:49
30.0	2:00.0	5:00.0	25:00.0	50:00.0	3:30:59

[1] Men's 5000m world record   (Joshua Cheptegei, Uganda, 14 August 2020, Monaco)
[2] Men's 10,000m world record   (Joshua Cheptegei, Uganda, 7 October 2020, Valencia)
[3] Men's marathon world record   (Eliud Kipchoge, Kenia, 16 September 2018, Berlin)
[4] Women's 5000m world record   (Letesenbet Gidey, Ethiopia; 7 October 2020, Valencia)
[5] Corresponds roughly with the Women's 10,000m world record: 29:17.45
                                                  (Almaz Ayana, Ethiopa, 12 August 2016, Rio de Janeiro)
[6] Women's marathon world record   (Brigid Kosgei, Kenia, 13 October 2019, Chicago)

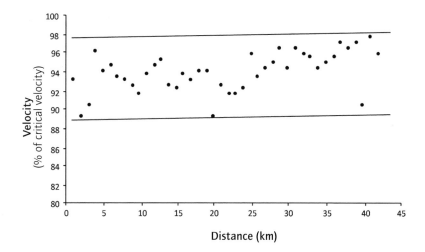

Figure 2: **Velocity profile of Paul Tergat's world-record marathon** *in 2:04:55 h in 2003 (modified on the basis of Billat, 2005, p. 32): Tergat's wave-like velocity profile is striking. Nevertheless, Tergat's coefficient of velocity variation was only 2.2%.*

FLUID INTAKE IN THE MARATHON AND OTHER STRATEGIC ASPECTS OF ROAD RACING

In long endurance races (marathon, 20 and 50km walk), the fluid loss, which is mainly caused by the production of sweat, must be counteracted by drinking during the race. However, athletes should not drink as much as possible, but only between 400 and 800 ml per hour. The actual amount depends on the individual absorption capacity and increases with the outdoor temperature, the runner's body weight, and the running speed. Fluid intake should be adjusted to the conditions and must be planned (see chapter II–1.13.2). Moreover, competition preparation in the marathon should include a check of the course or at least the course profile, studying the weather and similar factors, as well as making proper strategic decisions.

1.13.7   DIDACTICS: SUPERORDINATE LONG-TERM OBJECTIVES AND GENERAL METHODOLOGY

In long-distance running and especially in the marathon, athletes should take part in competitions only at the end of a long development process. Good long-distance runners develop from young middle-distance runners. It is assumed that aerobic endurance, contrary to basic speed, may still be improved even at a significantly older age. This is why athletes switch to continuously longer running distances and often do not run the marathon before reaching a relatively older age for competitive athletes.

The amount of track training for long-distance runners must be carefully planned throughout the year. If a 400m track is available nearby and easy to

DISCOURSE I: MARATHON FOR EVERYBODY?

Frequently, there are reports in the news of runners who suffer a cardiac arrest during a marathon. Although the risk of this is only 0.5–0.8 out of 100,000, these reports are still a haunting reminder that a marathon race should not be run by everyone or at least not by everyone at any time. The health benefits of endurance sports are undisputed and by far outweigh the risks if the exercise is well controlled. However, a marathon race is an extreme load for the cardiovascular system (especially for the elderly) and for the active and passive musculoskeletal system. Apart from the aforementioned dramatic case, this load may lead to additional temporary and permanent damage. Therefore, a marathon should be run only after a medical examination and long-term preparation (at least half a year) under the guidance of an experienced coach.

use, the temptation is great to run on it all too frequently. This easily results in a (premature) emphasis on training intensity to the disadvantage of training volume. Moreover, track training quickly leads to one-sided stress due to always running in the same direction through curves, and consequently to imbalances, complaints, and injuries. Track training should be used less for building up shape in the general preparation, and more for maintaining shape in the special preparation of a 5000 or 10,000m runner. Even the most intense running loads of long-distance runners can usually be performed in time-controlled training in the forest, on roads, etc.

1.13.8   TRAINING CONTENTS: FORMS OF GAMES AND EXERCISES

See chapter II–1.10.6.

1.13.9   SPECIAL TEST AND CONTROL PROCEDURES

	Test: Ability/skill tested	Execution/comments
T91	**Tempo-run programmes for the long distances:** (Anaerobic and) aerobic endurance	Standardised programmes, for example: a) LI: 3 x 3000m, rest intervals: 3 min; b) LI: 5 x 1000m, rest intervals: 3 min; c) LI: 2 x 5 x 400m, rest intervals: 3 min, rest intervals between sets: 6 min. The (average) times achieved and the post-exercise lactate values are the test criteria.
T92	**Under-distance tests for the long distances:** Aerobic endurance at increased velocity	1500 or 3000m for 5000m runners, 3000 or 5000m for 10,000m runners, 10,000m or half marathon for marathon runners as training test or preparatory competition
T8	**Drop jump:** Two-legged reactive strength of the extensor loop	
T9	**5-stride hops with distance maximisation:** Reactive strength of the legs in comparison to one another	Test should be performed on both sides.
T10	**30m bounding run with time minimisation:** Reactive strength of the legs	
T11	**Strength-endurance tests:** Anaerobic strength endurance	for example, 200m bounding run.

Test: Ability/skill tested	Execution/comments
T31 **Wingate test:** Anaerobic endurance	
T62 **Technique analysis:** Running technique	
T63 **Stride-frequency and stride-length measurement:** Technique and specific strength endurance	
T64 **Tactical analysis:** Racing strategy	
T66 **Graded field test:** Aerobic endurance	With lactate withdrawal (and spirometry), or, if this is not possible, as a simple minute test (T65): e.g., Cooper test (12 min) or 30-min test (see table 4 in chapter II–1.10.7).
T2 **Flexibility tests:** General flexibility	
T3 **Body weight and body fat measurement:** Relative strength	Inappropriate upward and downward deflections should be avoided. Due to the specific requirement profile, speed, speed-endurance, as well as speed-strength and maximal-strength tests (see disciplines in the previous chapters) are less relevant although they may be used in specific situations (e.g., when switching to a shorter distance).

1.13.10   ERRORS – CAUSES – CORRECTIONS

See chapter II–1.10.8.

1.13.11   TRAINING PLANNING

VOLUMES

The long distances and especially the marathon are the running disciplines with the highest training volume as one may expect. Within heterogeneous groups, there is a relationship between (weekly) training volume and marathon performance. But of course, not only the high number of training kilometres is important. An analysis of the training plans of internationally successful marathon runners in the 1990s results in the values shown in table 3a.

INTENSITIES

There are also numerous studies on training intensity. However, percentages based on the total amount of kilometres run may be misleading as an intensive workout with fewer kilometres may often require the same or even more recovery time than an extensive workout with many kilometres. Moreover, very intense runs are often performed in interval form. Therefore, due to the rest intervals, percentages on the basis of the (training) time invested would provide a different picture.

Often, a distinction is made in aerobic training below the aerobic-anaerobic threshold, aerobic-anaerobic training at the threshold, and anaerobic training above the threshold. In marathon training, the vast majority of kilometres is completed in the aerobic zone (80–90%). Approximately 10% is completed at the threshold, and only about 5% above the threshold. As expected, 10,000m runners and in particular 5000m runners perform a greater part of their training at higher intensities. In terms of training plans, a distinction is sometimes made between a threshold model, in which there is a focus on aerobic-anaerobic training, and a polarised model. The latter emphasises strictly aerobic training and clearly supra-threshold anaerobic training. However, the objective in long-distance running should also ultimately be holistic and versatile training. The guidelines should be the old coaching wisdom that the mere variation of loads implies sufficient recovery at the same time. Furthermore, the runners' subjective perception must be observed to avoid monotony and overloading.

COMPETITION PLANNING

Training plans include competition planning geared to the highlight of the season. To combine training and preparatory competitions, there is often an alternation of blocks of 3–4 competitions (often over shorter distances) with hardly any training and a competition-free period of 2–3 weeks. In the latter phase, the focus

*Table 3: **Kilometres per week in marathon training.***

*a: of world-class runners (according to Ferreira & Rolim, 2006, p. 34): 12 coaches from Brazil, Spain, Italy, Mexico, and Portugal were interviewed; the duration of the **phases** varies depending on the coach.*

b: of American female under-2:40 runners or male under-2:15 runners (according to Karp, 2008, p. 33): If the training volume is measured on the basis of training distance, men usually train much more than women. If it is measured on the basis of training duration, the percentage difference is smaller or even the other way round due to the lower running velocity of the women.

	General preparation phase	Special preparation phase	Competition phase
a	Min.: 150 Max.: 220 Ø: 185	Min.: 190 Max.: 240 Ø: 215	Min.: 170 Max.: 265 Ø: 217.5
b	Women: Max.: 145.8 Ø: 135.8		Men: Max.: 203.3 Ø: 155.6

may be on repeating the aerobic endurance base for example. Table 4 provides some further clues to the competition planning of successful 5000 and 10,000m runners. Marathon runners usually do not complete more than two or three maximum-intensity marathons per year.

SUGGESTED TRAINING PLANS

On the next pages, there are exemplary microcycles for the

- third mesocycle of a 17-year-old athlete in build-up training (table 6);
- first mesocycle of a 10,000m runner in high-performance training (table 7); and
- third mesocycle of a 10,000m runner in high-performance training (table 8).

Special 5000m or marathon training plans are not presented. 5000m plans would look very similar although they would include a slightly higher percentage of interval training. However, training for marathon runners would include more long continuous runs (up to 3 hours).

Young athletes do not have to specialise in middle distances, the steeplechase, or long distances. The suggested training plans for the

- first mesocycle of a 17-year-old athlete in build-up training for the middle distance (see chapter II–1.11.11); and
- second mesocycle of a 17-year-old athlete in build-up training for the steeplechase (see chapter II–1.12.11)

are therefore intended for the same athlete as in this chapter.

The suggested training plans for the

- second mesocycle of an athlete in high-performance training; and
- fourth mesocycle of an athlete in high-performance training

presented for the steeplechase may be compared in some respects at least to the plans presented here.

517

Table 4: **Competition behaviour** of the medal winners in Rome during the 1987 world-championship season (modified on the basis of Hirsch, 1988, pp. 312 & 314).

Competition frequency: 5000m runners			
	Aouita	Castro	Buckner
800m	3	-	-
1000m	1	-	-
1500m	4	1	2
Mile	2	-	2
2000m	1 (WR)	-	-
2 miles	1 (WR)	-	1
3000m	-	1	1
3000m steeple	1	-	-
5000m	6 (WR)	10	4
10,000m	-	2	-
Total	19; 15 up to Rome	14	10

Competition frequency: 10,000m runners			
	Kipkoech	Panetta	Kunze
1500m	-	-	1
2000m	-	1	-
3000m	-	2	-
3000m steeple	-	4	-
5000m	4	1	
10,000m	4	2	2
Total	6	13	4

Last competition before the world championships: 5000m runners			
Aouita	5000m	13:21.95 min	29 days (5 August)
Castro	5000m	13:18.59 min	15 days (19 August)
Buckner	2 miles	8:30.55 min	9 days (26 August)

Last competition before the world championships: 10,000m runners			
Kipkoech	5000m	13:36.32 min	16 days (12 August)
Panetta	5000m	13:28.37 min	9 days (19 August)
Kunze	5000m	13:24.00 min	7 days (21 August)

Table 5: **Training emphasis in the various mesocycles** for long-distance training in build-up and high-performance training.

1st mesocycle	aerobic endurance training (in varying intensity zones and using varying movement forms); strength-endurance training for the legs and the trunk; flexibility training; coordination training
2nd mesocycle	aerobic endurance training (in slightly higher intensity zones as before and using varying movement forms); IC- and connective-tissue-oriented (reactive-) strength training for the trunk and the legs; coordination training
3rd mesocycle	aerobic endurance training (in slightly higher intensity zones as before and using varying movement forms); anaerobic endurance training; IC- and connective-tissue-oriented (reactive-)strength training for the trunk and especially for the legs; coordination training
4th mesocycle	competitions and corresponding regeneration; aerobic endurance training at competition pace; IC- and connective-tissue-oriented (reactive-)strength training for the trunk and especially for the legs; maintenance stimuli

Table 6: Build-up training: sample microcycle for a 17-year-old middle- and long-distance runner as well as a steeplechaser in the third mesocycle.

Monday	Tuesday	Wednesday	Thursday	Friday	Saturday	Sunday
Warm-up jogging (15 min)	**Foot strengthening** (10 min)	**Continuous run** (30 min) first 10 min including ABCs of sprinting/jumping, arm circling, exaggerated arm actions, etc.	**Cycling, swimming, inline skating, cross-country skiing** or **aqua jogging** (40 min) alternately each week	*Morning:* **Warm-up jogging** (15 min)	*Morning:* **Warm-up jogging** (15 min)	Rest
Maximal-eccentric strength training (15 min) trunk stabilisation, lifting opposite upper and lower limbs in prone position, belly punches raising the foot/toes	**Acceleration runs** (3 reps) barefoot	**Strength training** (50 min) according to the pyramid principle or possibly maximal-eccentrically: hamstrings, quadriceps, abductors/adductors, quarter split squat, bench press, and lat pull	**Contract-relax stretching** (15 min) specific to steeplechase	**Acceleration runs** (2 reps) barefoot	**Acceleration runs** (3 reps)	
Acceleration runs (3 reps)	**Skipping and bounding runs** (4 x 30m each) including variations, high intensity	**Acceleration runs** (3 reps)	**Muscle build-up training** for the trunk on apparatus, practising a **throwing technique,** or **gymnastics** (30 min) e.g., abdominal machine, back exercises on box, hip-shoulder twists, and lumborum	**ABCs of running** (10–15 run-throughs) heel kicks, pulling strides, step-overs with grasping foot movement, etc.	**Water-jump training** (2 x 6 x approx. 150m; rest intervals: 30–60 sec for correction; rest intervals between sets: 5 min) at competition pace on the lawn, 1 obstacle per lap with flat and wide push-off and landing in the long-jump pit, with alternating the push-off leg	
ABCs of hurdling (10 min)	**Technique sprints** (4 x 200m) coordination runs, alternating-pace sprints, slalom runs, varied arm actions, etc.	**Skipping** (3 reps) for height	**Acceleration runs** (5 x 100m) over mini-hurdles at arbitrary distance	**Ankle jumps** (5 x 20) high intensity		
Practising the short-hurdling technique (40 min) after specific warm-up: 3x up to the first hurdle, 6–8x up to the 2nd–5th hurdle, distance shortened by 1–2 feet; as alternative also training the long- or high-jump technique	**Tempo-endurance run** (30 min) hilly terrain	**Tempo runs over obstacles** (1500m steeplechase: 3 x 600m, 2000m steeplechase: 3 x 800m; rest intervals: 5–8 min) competition pace over all obstacles		**Flying sprints** (3 x 30m + 20–30m run-up; rest intervals: 10 min) at maximal pace through light barriers	**Warm-down jogging** (10 diagonals on the lawn)	
Game (20 min) e.g., basketball or soccer	**Warm-down jogging** (5 min)			**Fartlek** (30 min) including uphill and downhill sprints at maximal pace	*Afternoon:* **Continuous run** (30 min)	
	Acceleration runs and standing starts (100, 80, 60, 40, and 30m) each run faster as utilisation				**Contract-relax stretching** (15 min)	
					Acceleration runs and standing starts (100, 80, 60, 40, and 30m)	

Table 7: High-performance training: sample microcycle for a 10,000m runner in the first mesocycle.

	Monday	Tuesday	Wednesday	Thursday	Friday	Saturday	Sunday
Morning	**Continuous run** (40 min) flat terrain **Acceleration runs** (3 reps) barefoot **Strength-endurance circuit** (3–4 run-throughs, loading: 1 min; rest intervals: 15 sec) trunk strength, leg strength, ABCs of sprinting, jumps, running-arm swinging with 1 kg dumbbells	**Continuous run** (60 min) first 10 min including ABCs of sprinting/jumping, arm circling, exaggerated arm actions, etc. **ABCs of running** (10–15 run-throughs) **Technique sprints** (6–8 x 60–80m) with additional tasks	**Warm-up jogging** (30 min) **Acceleration runs** (3 reps) barefoot **ABCs of jumping** (15–20 run-throughs) galloping sideways, ankle jumps, skipping with two-legged landing, skipping (with one-legged landing), etc. **Game** (30 min) e.g., basketball or soccer	Cycling, swimming, inline skating, cross-country skiing or aqua jogging (40 min) alternately each week, different sport than in the afternoon	**Continuous run** (60 min) first 10 min including ABCs of sprinting/jumping, arm circling, exaggerated arm actions, etc. **Foot strengthening** (10 min) in the sand or using an elastic band **Alternating-pace sprints** (5 x 120m)	**Trunk stabilisation exercises** and **abdominal crunches** (20 min) **Acceleration runs** (3–5 reps) **LI tempo runs** (2 x 10 x 200m; jogging intervals: 2 min; rest intervals between sets: 5 min) **Warm-down jogging** (15 min)	Rest
Afternoon	**Continuous run** (100 min) flat terrain **Acceleration runs** and **standing starts** (100, 90, 80, 70, 60, 40, and 20m) each run faster than the previous one; as utilisation	**Rope jumping** (5 x 1 min) **Tempo-endurance run** (45 min) hilly terrain, possibly cross-country **Warm-down jogging** (5 min) **Contract-relax stretching** (15 min) **Acceleration runs** (5 x 80m) as utilisation	**Continuous run** (120 min) flat terrain **Acceleration runs** and **standing starts** (100, 90, 80, 70, 60, 40, and 20m) each run faster than the previous one; as utilisation	Cycling, swimming, inline skating, cross-country skiing or aqua jogging (30 min) **Contract-relax stretching** (15 min) **Muscle build-up training** for the trunk on apparatus and/or for the arms, **medicine-ball work**, or **gymnastics** (30 min) **Acceleration runs**	**Continuous run** (80 min) hilly terrain **Acceleration runs** and **standing starts** (100, 90, 80, 70, 60, 40, and 20m) each run faster than the previous one; as utilisation	**Continuous run** (30 min) **Contract-relax stretching** (15 min) **Acceleration runs** and **standing starts** (100, 80, 60, 40, and 30m) each run faster than the previous one; as utilisation	

Table 8: *High-performance training: sample microcycle for a 10,000m runner in the third mesocycle.*

	Monday	Tuesday	Wednesday	Thursday	Friday	Saturday	Sunday
Morning	Continuous run (60 min) first 10 min including ABCs of sprinting/jumping, arm circling, exaggerated arm actions, etc. ABCs of sprinting (10–15 run-throughs) Technique sprints (6–8 x 60–80m) coordination runs, slalom runs, etc.	Warm-up jogging (5 min) Tempo-endurance run (40 min) flat terrain Warm-down jogging (5 min) Alternating-pace sprints (5 x 120m) as utilisation	Continuous run (60 min) first 10 min including ABCs of sprinting/jumping, arm circling, exaggerated arm actions, etc. ABCs of sprinting (10–15 run-throughs) Pull-resisted sprints (5 x 80m with 2.5 kg)	Cycling, swimming, inline skating, cross-country skiing or aqua jogging (45 min) alternately each week, different sport than in the afternoon	Continuous run (40 min) first 10 min including ABCs of sprinting/jumping, varied arm actions, etc. Acceleration runs (3 reps) barefoot Tuck jumps (2 x 3 run-throughs over 8 hurdles each) Skipping and bounding runs (3 x 50m each)	Warm-up jogging (30 min) Acceleration runs (3 reps) Tempo runs (4 x 800m; rest intervals: 3 min) 1500m pace, possibly with simulation of competition situations Warm-down jogging (20 min)	Rest
Afternoon	Warm-up jogging (10 min) Maximal-eccentric strength training (15 min) trunk and foot Uphill and downhill sprints and jumps (e.g. 3 x 5 x 150m; rest interval: walking back (rapidly); rest interval between sets: 6 min) Game (20 min) e.g., basketball or soccer	Continuous run (90 min) flat terrain Acceleration runs and standing starts (100, 90, 80, 70, 60, 40, and 20m) each run faster than the previous one; as utilisation	Warm-up jogging (30 min) Acceleration runs (3 reps) barefoot Tempo runs (4 x 3000m; rest interval: 3 min) competition pace, possibly with simulation of competition situations Warm-down jogging (10 min) Acceleration runs (5 x 80m) as utilisation	Cycling, swimming, inline skating, cross-country skiing or aqua jogging (30 min) Contract-relax stretching (15 min) Strength training for the trunk, or gymnastics (30 min) Acceleration runs and standing starts (100, 90, 80, 70, 60, 40, and 20m)	Warm-up jogging (10 min) Fartlek (35 min) hilly terrain Maximal-eccentric strength training (15 min) hamstrings, quadriceps, adductors/abductors, etc. Acceleration runs (5 x 60m) as utilisation	Continuous run (30 min) Acceleration runs and standing starts (100, 80, 60, 40, and 30m) each run faster than the previous one; as utilisation	

1.13.12 BIBLIOGRAPHY

Arcelli, E. (1996). Marathon and 50km walk race: physiology, diet and training. *New Studies in Athletics 11* (4), 51-58.

Benson, T. (2001). Ground contact in distance running. *Modern Athlete and Coach 39* (3), 35-37.

Billat, V. (2005). Current perspectives on performance improvement in the marathon: From universalisation to training optimisation. *New Studies in Athletics 20* (3), 21-39.

Brisswalter, J., Fougeron, B. & Legros, P. (1998). Variability in energy cost and walking gait during race walking in competitive race walkers. *Medicine and Science in Sports and Exercise 30* (9), 1451-1455.

Ferreira, R. L. & Rolim, R (2006). The evolution or marathon training: A comparative analysis of elite runners' training programmes. *New Studies in Athletics 21* (1), 29-37.

Gohlitz, D. & Ernst, O. (2006). Lange laufen – aber richtig! *Leichtathletiktraining 17* (2+3), 34-38.

Hirsch, L. (1988). Entwicklung und Tendenzen im Mittel- und Langstreckenlauf der Männer nach der WM Rom 1987. *Lehre der Leichtathletik 27* (7), 277-282 & (8), 311-314.

Karp, J. R. (2008). Training characteristics of US Olympic Marathon Trials qualifiers. *New Studies in Athletics 23* (2), 31-37.

Legaz Arese, A., Munguía Izquierdo, D. & Serveto Galindo, J. R. (2006). Physiological Measures Associated with Marathon Running Performance in High-Level Male and Female Homogeneous Groups. *International Journal of Sports Medicine 27* (4), 289-295.

Maron, B. J., Poliac, L. C. & Roberts, W. O. (1996). Risk for sudden cardiac death associated with marathon running. *Journal of the American Colloge of Cardiology 28* (2), 428-431.

Noakes, T. & Martin, D. E. (2002). IMMDA-AIMS Advisory statement on guidelines for fluid replacement during marathon running. *New Studies in Athletics 17* (1), 15-24.

Redelmeier, D. A. & Greenwald, J. A. (2007). Competing risks of mortality with marathons: retrospective analysis. *British Medical Journal 335* (7633), 1275-1277.

Regelkommissionen des DLV, FLA, ÖLV und SLV (Hrsg.). (2008). *Internationale Wettkampfregeln*. Waldfischbach: Hornberger.

Zacharogiannis, E., Smirniotou, A., Tziortzis, S. & Paradisis, G. (2007). The relationship of selected physiological characteristics with performance on the historic Athens marathon course. *New Studies in Athletics 22* (1), 39-48.

1.14 RACE WALKING: 20 AND 50KM

1.14.1 DOUBT IS A PERMANENT WALKING COMPANION

Race walking has its origins in marches lasting several days in 18th-century England. In 1866 track competitions were held in national championships over seven miles. At the end of the 19th century in Germany, there were contests over distances of 100km and more. Walking events have been a part of the Olympic programme since 1908 or since the interim Olympics in 1906 (see table 1). Women have been walking at Olympic Games since 1992 and have been covering the same distances as the men since 2017.

The short walking distances have disappeared from the Olympic programme since there is a critical speed above which a regular walking technique is no longer possible. But even the walking speeds in the 20km race-walking event are continuously approaching the running speed in the marathon (see table 1 in chapter II–1.10.2). Time and again, slow motion recordings show that the required constant ground contact is often not maintained. Instead of a double-contact phase, there is a flight phase. In order to support the judges in race walking, the addendum "visible to the human eye" was included in the rules. A walker is only disqualified if three different race-walking judges decide that the walking style does not conform to the rules. Nevertheless, the decision to disqualify one race-walker or not disqualify another is always subjective

to some extent. The doubt about whether the winner was successful primarily because of his/her skill or whether he/she was simply lucky is always present in the only athletics discipline with technical judges.

The superiority of African runners from 800m up to the marathon is often attributed to the great importance of running in local people's daily lives.

Table 1: **Change of the race-walking events at the Olympic Games** (T: track walking, R: road walking).

Year(s)	Distance(s)
1906	♂: T: 1500 and 3000m
1908	♂: T: 3500m and 10 miles
1912	♂: T: 10km
1920	♂: T: 3 and 10km
1924	♂: R: 10km
1928	-
1932 and 1936	♂: R: 50km
1948 u and 1952	♂: T: 10km and S:50km
1956-1972	♂: R: 20 and 50km
1976	♂: R: 20km
1980–1988	♂: R: 20 and 50km
1992 and 1996	♀: R: 10km ♂: S R: 20 and 50km
2000-2016	♀: R:20km ♂: R: 20 and 50km
Since 2020	♀ + ♂: R: 20 and 50km

However, the dominance of these natural runners actually seems to be limited to the running events. So far, no African athlete has won a medal in a race-walking event of similar duration at world championships or Olympic Games. Race-walking events are dominated by walkers from the former Eastern Bloc countries, especially Russia; from Italy; and from Spanish-speaking countries. Between 1964 and 1988 in particular, there were also many walkers from (primarily East) Germany. The most successful race-walkers in the recent past included the Polish quadruple Olympic champion Robert Korzeniowski (3 x 50km, 1 x 20km), Olga Kaniskina (Russia, 2007, 2008, 2009, and 2011), and Jefferson Pérez (Ecuador, 1996, 2005 2007, and 2009), each with an Olympic gold medal and three world championship titles over 20km.

1.14.2 THE MOST IMPORTANT COMPETITION RULES

The following abridged and simplified International Competition Rules comprise the framework for the technique and strategy, as well as for the organisation of race-walking competitions:

- Race walking is a progression of steps so taken that the walker makes contact with the ground, so that (to the human eye) no visible loss of contact occurs. The advancing leg must be straightened (i.e., not bent at the knee) from the moment of first contact with the ground until the vertical upright position.
- Compliance with this rule is monitored by six (up to nine) race-walking judges including a chief judge.
- Walkers must receive a warning if they are in danger of violating the rule mentioned above due to the nature of their movement style. As a warning, they are shown a yellow paddle with the symbol of the offence (no ground contact or no knee extension) on each

side. An athlete cannot be shown a second yellow paddle by the same judge for the same offence.
- When a race-walking judge observes an athlete failing to comply with the rule mentioned above, he/she must send a red card to the chief judge for this walker. The chief judge himself/herself or his/her assistant makes sure that this red card is made visible to the respective walker on one or more display panel(s) on the route and near the finish. The nature of the violation is also made visible through the symbols.
- If three different race-walking judges send a red card for the same walker, the walker will be disqualified. The chief judge or one of his/her assistants must inform the walker by showing him a red paddle. The disqualified walker must leave the competition immediately. Alternatively, it can be determined that a walker must first pause once for

a penalty time (in a penalty box). Only in the case of another red card will he/she be disqualified. The penalty time is calculated according to the following formula:

$$penalty \ [min] = \frac{walking \ distance \ [km] \bullet 1 \ min}{10 \ km}$$

- Walkers who shorten the distance to be covered are disqualified.
- Road competitions must take place on a 1–2.5km (at international championships 2–2.5km) long circuit, which during the competition is blocked for motor traffic. For events which start and finish in the stadium, the circuit should be located as close as possible to the stadium. The competition must take place in daylight.
- In the start and finish areas of all walking events, water and other suitable refreshments must be provided. In walking events longer than 10km, catering stations must be established at intervals. In addition, approximately midway between these stations, there must be refreshment stations where water and sponges are available (for all events shorter than and including 10km, and only if the weather conditions warrant

such provisions, there must only be refreshment stations at adequate intervals).

- Refreshments and catering may be provided by the organizer or the walker himself/herself and may be taken only at the appropriate spots (possibly served by a designated person).

Otherwise, the general competition rules for running and middle- and long-distance running apply (see chapters II–1.1.1 and II–1.10.1). Table 2 shows the competition distances used in Germany. U16 athletes compete at regional championships over 3000m on the track and 5km on the road.

Table 2: **Competition distances** at German Championships on the track (T) and on the road (R)

	50km	30km	20km	10km	5km	3km
Men	R		R	T		
Women			R		T	
Male juniors		R	R	T		
Female juniors			R		T	
m. U 20				R, T		
f. U 20				R	T	
m. U 18				R	T	
f. U 18					R	T

1.14.3   SPORT-SCIENCE FINDINGS, PHASE STRUCTURE, AND TECHNIQUE

PHASE STRUCTURE AND TECHNIQUE OF THE WALKING MOTION

DOUBLE SUPPORT OR FLIGHT PHASE?

As defined in the rules, the phase structure of the walking motion is different from the phase structure of the running stride (see chapter II–1.1.2 for comparison). In (everyday) walking, the front support phase of one leg overlaps the rear support phase of the other leg. There is a two-legged or so-called double support phase in which the heel of the front leg and the toes of the rear leg touch the ground. However, scientific studies show that in walking at competition speed, there are flight phases of 10–60 msec between the alternating one-legged support phases instead of a double support phase (see figure 1). In spite of the extension of the walking distances and the associated reduction of competition speeds, this has not changed (see table 1). This phase structure in which the rear swing phase of one leg overlaps the front swing of the other leg is similar to the phase structure of running. Studies have shown that every athlete has two individual speed barriers

at which coordination thresholds occur. If the treadmill speed exceeds the first threshold, there are flight phases between the support phases. During competition, this is initially tolerated by most race-walking judges (even officially sanctified by the addendum to the rules as visible to the human eye During competition, this is initially tolerated by most race-walking judges). Whereas the flight phases increase almost linearly with the walking speed after their first appearance, the coordination thresholds may be clearly distinguished on the basis of knee extension during foot touchdown. At each of the two thresholds, significant increases in the average deviation from the 180° knee extension may be seen (see figure 2). At the second threshold, the walker starts running and is disqualified.

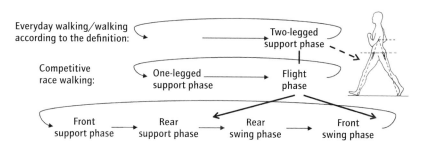

*Figure 1: **Phase structure of the walking motion** (the picture above on the right modified on the basis of Whitlock, 1957, p. 15).*

Foot touchdown on the ground	Vertical projection of the CG crosses the touchdown point	Lifting of the foot from the ground	Centre of mass of the leg crosses the vertical projection of the CG	(Foot touchdown on the ground)

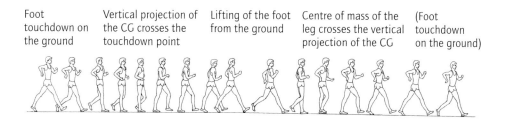

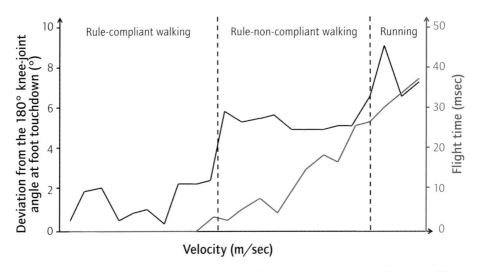

*Figure 2: **Coordinative thresholds** of a young female walker during a graded treadmill test (modified on the basis of Neumann, 2005, p. 133).*

Another study has shown that there is a reduction of the knee extension at touchdown even at constant speed due to increasing fatigue, while the duration of the flight phase increases. This means that there is a decrease in the coordinative threshold, so to speak. This explains why most disqualifications are announced only at the end of a race.

STRIDE LENGTH AND STRIDE FREQUENCY
Figure 4 provides information about the stride length and stride frequency of race walkers. The stride length is limited by the stride technique required by the rules. If a walker tries to extend his/her stride length beyond this limit, there are either (too great) flight phases or the knee extension is lost. Therefore, according to the formula in chapter II–1.1.2, the stride frequency is of decisive importance for the regulation of pace during the race. In particular, this

applies to intermediate and final spurts. Female athlete 3 in figure 4 was able to win the German Junior Championships in 2005 with a significant increase in stride frequency.

HIP ROTATION
In order to achieve a long stride and increase the push-off forward in accordance with the rules, walkers rotate their pelvis about the longitudinal body axis. The hip on the respective side is brought forward in the swing phase and is moved backward together with the leg in the support phase. To achieve an effective and energy-saving propulsion, the pelvis also rotates about the sagittal axis (i.e., the hips move up and down alternately). During the swing phase, the hip is lowered and reaches its lowest point during the first ground contact with the heel of the extended front leg. As a result, the hip is

lifted up again to its highest point during the vertical support (i.e., the transition between the front and rear support phase). The overlapping of these two rotation movements results in the typical rolling or paddling movement of the hips (see figure 3a). Moreover, the rotation about the longitudinal axis enables the walker to place down his/her feet on a line (see figure 3b).

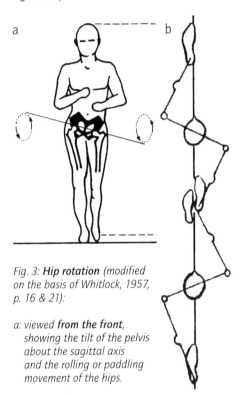

Fig. 3: **Hip rotation** *(modified on the basis of Whitlock, 1957, p. 16 & 21):*

a: viewed **from the front**, *showing the tilt of the pelvis about the sagittal axis and the rolling or paddling movement of the hips.*

b: viewed **from above***: schematic presentation of the points of foot touchdown (the left foot in the middle is in the air and illustrates how closely the feet are swung past each other), as well as the head, the line connecting the two hip joints and the legs (bulge = knee) in the widest spread position.*

ADDITIONAL FEATURES OF THE LEG MOVEMENT

In order to save energy, the walker only slightly lifts his/her leg during the swing phase. The knee is bent only slightly (passively). The foot is moved flatly and closely past or around the support leg. In the forward swing phase, the walker must not swing his/her leg too far forward to avoid flight phases and to walk economically. In order to avoid braking forces, the foot should be placed on the ground relatively close to the vertical projection of the CG (as in sprinting and running). Some authors even speak of a grasping foot touchdown (as in running). In any case, the walker subsequently (i.e., during the following front support phase) moves his/her body over the touchdown point through hip rotation and extension. In the rear support phase, the ankle is also extended while maintaining knee extension and continuing hip extension. The strong push-off should be performed in a flat direction, since by doing so flight phases are avoided. During the support phase, there is a rolling movement of the foot, which starts at the heel and then continues over the outside of the foot to the toes.

TRUNK AND ARMS

The trunk should be upright when walking, which can be facilitated by a view directed into the distance. The pelvis should be erect and hyperlordosis should be avoided. Even if each hip rotation results in shoulder-hip separation, the shoulder axis should be kept at right angles to the walking direction.

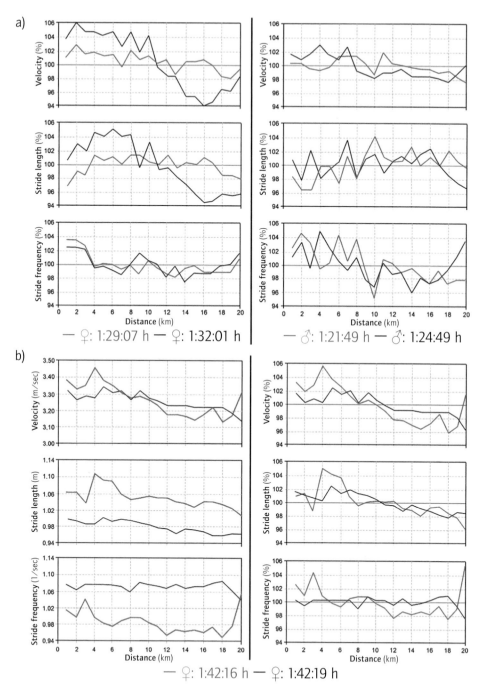

*Figure 4: **Velocity curve and its contributing factors (stride length and stride frequency)** over the 20km distance at the 2005 German Championships (modified on the basis of Neumann et al., 2005, p. 14–15): Men and women (a) as well as absolute and relative values (b) in comparison.*

The arm actions appear energetic since the strong rotational momentum of the legs and hips must be counteracted. In particular, the backswing should be emphasised to support the backward rotation of the hip on the other side of the body. Contrary to earlier recommendations, modern race walkers usually do not swing their hands in front of their body beyond the midline (sagittal plane). In addition, the athlete's hands should be raised in front of his/her body not beyond the height of the sternum. His/her arms should be swung back only to the extent that the hands are slightly behind the hips. The athlete's arms should be moved forward and backward rather than up and down to avoid vertical impulses and thus flight phases.

A relaxed face, shoulders, neck, and hands are crucial factors for movement economy (see chapter II−1.1.2).

PHASE STRUCTURE OF RACE-WALKING COMPETITIONS

As in long-distance running, the velocity profile of race walking is also determined by strategy. The course profile is of less importance on road circuits which have a maximum length of 2.5km. In races with a strategic focus on the best possible race time, the split or interval times should be as uniform as possible (see chapter II−1.13.6). However, all top-level national women (n = 4) and men (n = 4) studied by Neumann et al. (2005) completed the second half of the race of a 20km competition slower than the first half (see figure 4). Among the women, the differences tended to be higher (up to 3:25 min), whereas for the

fastest man it was only 17 seconds. If 1000m intervals are analysed, the fastest woman as well as the fastest man show a wave-shaped velocity curve, for both athletes with a maximum difference of 3% between the average speed during a 1000m interval and the average speed over the entire race. In particular, if athletes start the race too fast, the following (main) phases may be distinguished:

- development of racing speed;
- racing speed; and
- fatigue.

PHASE 1: DEVELOPMENT OF RACING SPEED

In this phase, the athlete must not only accelerate from zero velocity and move into the pack of walkers, but he/she must also develop his/her rolling stride. This coordinative adjustment usually takes a bit longer than pure acceleration. In compliance with the rules, athletes must find their optimal stride length. The phase is shorter the better an athlete is trained and warmed-up and should be completed within a few hundred metres.

PHASE 2: RACING SPEED

This phase is characterised by a relatively constant speed with a constant stride length. The better an athlete is trained and the more optimal his/her initial pace, the longer he/she will be able to walk at this pace.

PHASE 3: FATIGUE

This phase can be further divided into the following three sections, sub-phases, or levels of fatigue:

- compensated fatigue;
- decompensated fatigue; and
- exhaustion.

In the phase of compensated fatigue, an athlete can keep up his/her pace despite fatigue-induced reduction of stride length by increasing his/her stride frequency. During the sub-phase of decompensated fatigue, the increase in stride frequency is not sufficient to compensate for the loss in stride length. If an athlete is exhausted,

*Table 3: **Requirement profile for 20 and 50km race walking:** The suggested rough estimate of the value of selected factors determining performance is based on the importance for the overall performance and the percentage of time spent training (IR: information requirements, constr.: constraints; see chapter I–1.1).*

Factors determining 20 and 50km race-walking performance	Estimate of value	Notes
Coordination	+ + +	optical IR: low, acoustic IR: low, tactile IR: low, kinaesthetic IR: medium, vestibular IR: low; precision constr.: high, time constr.: medium, complexity constr.: low–medium, situation constr.: medium, physical stress constr.: high
Flexibility	+ +	special flexibility of the lower back and the hips
Strength		extensor loop (glutes, quadriceps, triceps surae, erector spinae), iliopsoas; hamstrings; adductors, abdominal muscles, shoulder and upper-arm muscles
Maximal strength	+	as basis at the most
Reactive strength	+	as basis at the most
Speed	+	walking as fast as possible as coordinative basis
Endurance (general dynamic) Anaerobic endurance		
Strength endurance	+	of the walking-specific muscles as the basis of the other endurance capacities
Speed endurance	+	in walking, as the basis of intermediate and final spurts
Aerobic endurance	+ + + + +	special importance of energy provision through fat metabolism as well as of the management of the heat accumulation in the body
Psychological and cognitive abilities	+ + + + +	feel for pace and correct strategy; maintenance of the motivation in terms of general fatigue resistance; performance-oriented thinking and behaviour (see Chapter I-3.1.1)
Anthropometric and primarily genetically determined characteristics	+ + + +	high percentage of slow muscle fibres; rather small body height; very low percentage of body fat

there is a significant reduction of velocity, stride length, and stride frequency. No race walker should reach this stage during competition.

However, the individual profiles of the three variables mentioned show that this profile is not typical for all athletes.

1.14.4   SUMMARY OF THE MOST IMPORTANT TECHNICAL CHARACTERISTICS = TECHNIQUE-ANALYSIS SHEET

FRONT SUPPORT PHASE

- Foot touchdown on the heel; all touchdowns on a straight line in the walking direction.
- The knee is straight.
- Beginning of the forward swing of the arm on the same side of the body; beginning of the powerful backswing of the opposite arm.
- Placing of the sole of the foot flatly onto the ground; the load is on the outside of the foot.
- The active hip extension results in the raising of the hip.
- Rearward movement of the hip (on the side of the support leg) by rotating the pelvis about the longitudinal axis of rotation.

REAR SUPPORT PHASE

- Powerful, flat push-off by straightening the ankle; continuation of hip extension; pelvic rotation and long retention of knee extension.
- Rolling of the foot onto the toes.
- Continuation of the arm swing up to the reversal point (in front of the body, not higher than up to the sternum; in the back, to the level of the hip or slightly behind).

REAR SWING PHASE

- Breaking contact with the ground.
- Beginning the forward swing of the leg by flexing the hip.
- A slight (passive) bending of the knee joint leads to a flat forward swing.

- Raising the toes.
- Beginning the powerful backswing of the arm on the same side of the body; beginning the forward swing of the opposite arm.
- Lowering the hips.
- Forward movement of the hip (on the side of the swing leg) by rotating the pelvis about the longitudinal axis of rotation.

FRONT SWING PHASE

- Moderate knee lift.
- Forward pendulum movement of the lower leg.
- The tip of the foot remains in a raised position.
- Continuation of the rotation of the pelvis about the longitudinal axis and of the lowering of the hips.
- Toward the end of the front swing phase, the hip extension is initiated to prepare for the touchdown of the foot close to the vertical projection of the CG (to develop only moderate braking forces in the subsequent front support phase).
- Continuation of the arm swing up to the reversal point (in front of the body, not higher than up to the sternum; behind the body, to the level of the hip or slightly further).

IN GENERAL

- Upright trunk; the view is directed straight into the distance; erect pelvis.
- No, or very little, shoulder rotation contralateral to the hip rotation.
- Arms at right angles at the elbow joints; the movement direction is rather back and forth than up and down.

1.14.5 PHOTO SEQUENCE

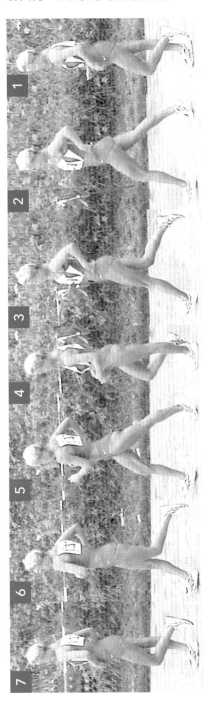

Data about the photo sequence

Athlete:	Olimpiada Ivanova (born: 26 August 1970, Russia)
Height/weight:	1.68 m/54 kg
Event:	20km race walking
Performance:	1:26:42 h (7 August 2002, Munich)
Best performance:	1:24:50 h (4 March 2001, Adler, world record)
Greatest success:	World champion in 2001 and 2005, European champion in 2005, silver medallist at the 2004 Olympic Games

COMMENTARY

The photo sequence shows Ivanova in her winning race at the European Championships in 2002. She was successful thanks to her round economic technique. She walks with an ideal upright and almost motionless upper body. In pictures 3 and 4, one can see a slight tilt of her head to the side. She swings her arms, bent acutely at the elbows, flatly back and forth with only a slight rotation of her shoulder axis. She swings her hands backward until they are next to her waist and forward until they are diagonally in front of her body (particularly on the left side).

Picture 1 shows Ivanova during the medium support on her right leg which is extended while she pulls it backward. The swing leg is bent up to approximately 90°, which is in accordance with the model technique, and swung forward with a slightly lowered hip. In picture 2, Ivanova's support leg hip is fully extended; she has rolled on her right foot up to the toe, and her right knee begins to flex. The slightly declining course seems to result in a flight phase, which may be assumed between pictures 2 and 3, and in a slightly bracing foot touchdown. The next pictures show Ivanova powerfully pulling through her extended left leg with high hip and rolling off her foot from the heel over the entire sole up to the tip of the foot. Between pictures 5 and 6 another flight phase may be assumed during which the touchdown of the ideally extended right leg is prepared.

1.14.6 STRATEGY

The relevant strategic aspects have been presented almost entirely in chapters II-1.10.4 and II-1.13.6. Figure 4 shows how velocity, stride length, and stride frequency may also vary due to strategy in a competition race.

An unfair strategy, which may be observed at the beginning of race-walking competitions, is hiding in the pack. By doing so, race walkers hope to be able to use a less perfect walking technique, which may not be detected, and thus to save energy. However, this is risky since race-walking judges also detect rule violations through circumstantial evidence, such as up-and-down movements of the head, and the race walker may easily fail to get into his/her race rhythm in time.

1.14.7 DIDACTICS: SUPERORDINATE LONG-TERM OBJECTIVES AND GENERAL METHODOLOGY

Like all track and field athletes, up-and-coming race walkers should also undergo the process of children's athletics and basic training with its emphasis on the combined events. Even at this stage, rule-compliant walking and versatile walking variations (e.g., with arm circling or only on the heels) should be a sporadic part of the games and playful forms of exercise. Children who are prompted to walk continuously faster and show a good natural technique are quickly identified as talented athletes. For these talented children, the first regular walking-specific training sessions are conducted during the second part of basic training when the first priority is established. These training sessions first focus on the development of the technique of race walking in contrast to everyday walking. The versatile training of technique, which should first be performed at slow speeds (perhaps sporadically interspersed with some faster 50m segments), must primarily ensure that athletes adhere to the rules. Only after the athletes have mastered the technique may hip rotation gradually be introduced. First (training) competitions over non-standard distances from 800 to 2000m serve to make training more fun and are the first medium-length loads at a higher pace.

Subsequently in build-up training, the percentage of specific race-walking sessions increases from year to year, with a stronger focus on specific endurance. However, aerobic endurance training should continue to be performed in a variety of movement forms (running, cycling, inline skating, sports games, etc.). Moreover, in this age group the focus is also on the development of walking speed and strength. Over shorter distances, talented young athletes should reach the competition speeds (approximately 4 min per km for males and approximately 4:30 min per km for female adolescents) which are required for adults already during late adolescence. The competition courses offered (see table 2) clearly show that the 20km distance should not be tackled before leaving adolescence and the 50km distance not before leaving the junior category.

DISCOURSE I: WALKING AS A HEALTHY SPORT FOR THE MASSES: NORDIC WALKING

In particular for the elderly, endurance novices, overweight people, and runners with poor running techniques or misaligned joints, the health benefits of running may be outweighed by excessive strain and subsequent problems. In this event, so-called Nordic walking is a good alternative. The name reflects the similarity between the technique of Nordic walking with the classic technique of (Nordic) cross-country skiing. While walking rapidly in normal running shoes, the athlete pushes himself/herself off from the ground with two walking sticks. The energetic contralateral arm movements ensure that a great proportion of body muscle mass is involved in the forward propulsion and that almost as many calories are burned as during slow running with much lower strain on the joints.

1.14.8   TRAINING CONTENTS: FORMS OF GAMES AND EXERCISES

Apart from the fact that race walkers perform a part of their training by running, many forms of games and exercises mentioned in connection with (sprinting and) running may be performed while walking. For example, the following forms of play are particularly suitable:

- shadow running or walking (101);
- collecting cards (153; in small teams);
- six-day race (172);
- other (endless) relays (154, 162, and 173);
- square runs or walks (155);
- estimating time (221);

- traffic policeman (222); and
- "The last overtakes the others!" (223).

Many exercise forms described in the chapters about running can also be performed while walking or modified in a manner specific to walking. The numbers listed in brackets refer to the comparable forms of running exercises:

- ankle jumps (84; as part of the ABCs of walking and for strengthening the calf muscles; with hip rotation and contralateral arm actions; 3–6 sets of 20–50 reps each);
- acceleration walking (129; up to the maximal velocity that can be mastered);
- versatile walking (130: in slalom, in circle, through the curve; on sand, lawn, forest floor, etc.);
- walking with varied arm actions (131; for variations refer to the respective section of the book; as a part of the ABCs of walking; in particular with hands on the hips or stick on shoulders with extended arms on the stick to emphasise the hip rotation and shoulder-hip separation);
- alternating pace walking (133);
- walking at particularly high stride frequency or with long strides (135–136; also in combination with acceleration walking [129] and alternating pace walking [133]);
- pull-resisted and uphill walking (137–138; as specific strength-endurance or stride-length training, also over longer distances; moderate resistance [≤2.5 kg] or incline [≤10%]; also against the wind; possibly also walking while wearing a weighted vest);
- downhill walking (140; as specific strength[-endurance] and frequency training);
- warm-up, warm-down, and regenerative walking (226);
- continuous walking (227; in 50km training up to 35km);
- tempo-endurance walking (228);
- tempo-endurance walking at alternating pace (229; e.g., with 10 intermediate spurts of 100m each, or as acceleration walking with a (significant) increase in intensity toward the end);
- fartlek (230; at varying intensities, but also switching to running and sprinting);
- tempo walking (depending on age or competition distances, race walkers perform all tempo runs mentioned in chapters II–1.5.8 and II–1.10.6 while walking, in 20 and 50km training, however, extensive interval forms clearly dominate); and
- under-distances at competition pace (233).
- Moreover, the variations of walking described in connection with strength training (51) are often included in the ABCs of walking to increase versatility.

251 **ABCs of walking: Imitations while standing**

Possible objectives: (Learning correct) walking technique.

Execution: Weight shift from one leg to the other leg with extension of the loaded leg and flexion of the deloaded leg (or knee); view straight ahead.

Variations: First without, then with arm action; first slow, then fast; also with transition to walking.

Typical load standards: 2–5 reps of 20–30 sec each.

252 **ABCs of walking: Transition from walking to running**

Possible objectives: Teaching the rules; feeling the personal speed limit.

Execution: Acceleration walking (129) up to the moment when the race walker is no longer able to walk technically correct and is forced to run.

Variations: Also with repeated slowing down and transition to walking, repeated acceleration and transition to running, etc.; in a group, in a row, side by side.

Typical load standards: 3–6 reps of 50–100m each.

253 ABCs of walking: Ankling with rolling off over the entire foot

Possible objectives: Rolling off of the foot; flexion and extension of the ankle joint.

Execution: The race walker concentrates on placing down his/her heel and rolling off over the outer side of his/her foot up to the big toe while performing strides of only approximately one foot length and flexing his/her knee more than is usual (for a race walker) during the swing phase.

Variations: More running (with flight phases) or more walking (no flight phases); focusing on frequency.

Typical load standards: 2–5 reps of 20–50m each.

254 ABCs of walking: Walking on a line

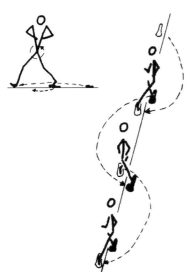

Possible objectives: Training of hip rotation.

Execution: See picture on the left; walking on the boundary line of a lane.

Variations: As over-correction also crosswise beyond the line (see picture on the right).

Typical load standards: Several times 40–100m, also while walking continuously, to distract from the monotonous movement.

255 **ABCs of walking: Trunk variations**

Possible objectives: Walking variations in terms of differential learning.

Execution/variations: forward and backward lean of the trunk while walking; exaggerated contralateral rotation of the shoulders about the longitudinal axis of the body (possibly in combination with varied arm actions [see above and 131]).

Typical load standards: Several times 40–100m, also while walking continuously, to distract from the monotonous movement.

256 **Walking sprints**

Possible objectives: Walking speed; correct technique at the personal speed limit.

Execution/variations: Walking with correct technique at the highest possible velocity that the athlete is able to master while adhering to the rules.

Typical load standards: Up to 10 x 50–200m.

1.14.9 SPECIAL TEST AND CONTROL PROCEDURES

Racer walkers should perform the test and control procedures described in connection with long-distance running while walking (and running; see chapter II–1.13.9). Sprint and jump tests are not necessary.

1.14.10 ERRORS - CAUSES - CORRECTIONS

In race walking, *technical errors* and *technical deficits* may be distinguished. Technical errors result in disqualification.

Technical deficits should be eliminated to improve performance.

Technical deficit	Causes	Corrections
Deviation of the hip (and the shoulder) to the side (see figure 5f).	• The athlete makes no effort to walk economically, in particular there is no rolling action of the hip.	✔ Corrections and advice; imitation (251), versatile walking (130), and walking on a line (254).
Lacking hip action.	• Forward lean of the trunk or not erect pelvis (hollow back; possibly caused by shortened iliopsoas). • Lacking flexibility and/or relaxation of the lower back and/or hip joints. • Insufficient automation of the target technique; the hip action is not yet performed automatically.	✔ Stretching, mobilisation and limbering up (of the iliopsoas) using exercises 22-28 and 203-205. ✔ Imitation (251), walking on a line and crosswise beyond the line (254). ✔ Frequent advice and corrections also during endurance training.
Lack of push-off extension.	• Too early flexion of the knee joint (see figure 5b). • Lack of specific strength abilities. • Backward lean of the trunk (see figure 5d).	✔ Pull-resisted walking, walking against the wind (137), and walking uphill (138) while trying to maintain a straight knee. ✔ Trunk variations (255). ✔ Deliberate correction of the backward lean of the trunk.
Too short strides (too high stride frequency).	• Lack of push-off extension and its causes (see above). • Lack of hip action and its causes (see above).	✔ See corrections of lack of push-off extension and lack of hip action. ✔ Technique training while adhering to the rules.
Too long strides (too low stride frequency).	• Too high lift of the knee during the (front) swing phase (see figure 5c). • Lack of walking speed. • Exaggerated (amplitude of) arm work.	✔ Stride-frequency training (135) while focusing on a flat and short forward swing, walking downhill (140), and walking sprints (256), and walking at alternating pace (133) while focusing on stride frequency. ✔ Correction and variation of arm work (131).
Too great bracing effect (braking forces) in the front support phase, together with a lowering of the CG in the double-support phase (see figure 5g).	• Too long strides (while adhering to the rules) and its causes (see above).	✔ See corrections of too long strides. ✔ An increase in stride frequency will quickly lead to an increase in walking speed.

Technical error	Causes	Corrections
Lack of knee extension during the front support (soft knees).	• Forward lean of the trunk (see figure 5e). • Too high velocity which cannot be mastered while walking. • Too long strides (too low stride frequency) and its causes (see above and figure 5a). • Lack of flexibility of the knee-joint flexors. • For beginners: insufficient automation of the correct walking technique.	✔ Correction and variation of the trunk position (255). ✔ In competition: Increase of stride frequency and shortening of stride length or the reduction of velocity. ✔ See corrections of too long strides above. ✔ Flexibility training of the knee-joint flexors. ✔ Introduction and training of rule-compliant walking technique.
Jumping stride (flight phases which can be seen by the naked eye; indication: up and down movements of the head).	• Too high velocity which cannot be mastered while walking. • Too long strides (too low stride frequency) and its causes (see above). • Too steep push-off angle (due to too early or too powerful ankle extension). • Exaggerated up-and-down movements of the arms. • Pulling upward of the shoulders according to the stride rhythm.	✔ In competition: Increase in stride frequency and shortening of stride length or the reduction of velocity. ✔ See corrections of too long strides above. ✔ The athlete should feel a correct rolling-off movement and a constant height of his/her CG (possible use of the contrast method: initial increase of the error). ✔ Correction and variation of arm work (131). ✔ Walking sprints while adhering to the rules (256) and walking at varying pace (133).

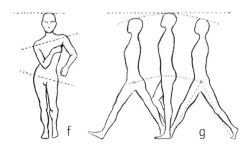

*Figure 5: **Technical errors and deficits** (modified on the basis of Whitlock, 1957).*

1.14.11 TRAINING PLANNING

BUILD-UP TRAINING

Training planning for young athletes is based on the common competition distances at that age. While for general basic training, a training frequency of five training sessions per week is prescribed (see chapter I–3.3.4), six and a half training sessions are suggested here for the first half of build-up training. Individual workouts should become longer. Although there is now a clear training focus on walking, training should still be versatile at that age and there should be an emphasis on coordination. Athletes should also participate in combined-event competitions (see Mondays). Special combined walking events may include middle distances to be walked for example. A walking triathlon (e.g., swimming, cycling, and walking, or walking, cycling, and running) may render endurance training more versatile.

Even in build-up training, the training volume for race walkers (e.g., the duration for continuous walking or continuous running) is slightly higher than the training volume in middle- and long-distance running due to the longer competition distances. In the build-up training and early high-performance training of walking (also called follow-up training), the training volume should be gradually increased by about 15% per year. This goes hand in hand with an extension of the competition courses.

HIGH-PERFORMANCE TRAINING

In the preparatory phases, high-performance race walkers ultimately perform two daily training sessions six days per week. One day (here Sunday) remains completely free for physical and psychological recovery.

Table 4: **Training emphasis in the various mesocycles** for race-walking training in build-up and high-performance training.

1st mesocycle	aerobic endurance training (in varying intensity zones and using varying movement forms); strength-endurance training for the legs and the trunk; flexibility training; coordination training (ABCs of jumping, other techniques, games, etc.) and technique training (ABCs of walking, acceleration walking, etc.)
2nd mesocycle	aerobic endurance training (in slightly higher intensity zones than before and using varying movement forms); walking-specific strength-endurance training (walking uphill and pull-resisted walking); coordination and technique training
3rd mesocycle	aerobic endurance training (in slightly higher intensity zones than before, particularly when walking, but also when performing other movement forms); walking-specific strength-endurance training (walking uphill and pull-resisted walking); coordination and technique training
4th mesocycle	competitions and corresponding regeneration; aerobic endurance training at competition pace; walking speed (walking sprints); maintenance stimuli

DISCOURSE II: HOW MUCH RUNNING TRAINING DOES RACE-WALKING TRAINING INCLUDE?

There is a consensus that walkers should perform a part of their training through running (and other forms of exercise such as swimming, cycling, inline skating, cross-country skiing, etc.). However, there is no or inconsistent information on the percentage of non-walking training. Vallence (2007) provides detailed information on the training schedule of the internationally successful Australian junior race walkers J. Tallent (then 20.5 years old) and A. Rutter (then 19.3 years old). Tallent completed 18% of his average 113 (maximum: 168) kilometres per week by running. Rutter ran 17% of his 74 (maximum: 125) weekly kilometres. Tallent performed 13.7% of his walking kilometres at race pace (Rutter: 14.3%). According to Pathus (2003), the ratio of walking to running should be 3:1 in young race walkers between 14 and 17 years of age.

It is assumed that it is somewhat easier to achieve high cardiopulmonary stress through running rather than walking. However, particularly during the competition phase, running is regarded as problematic since there may be negative transfer effects on the walking technique at a high speed.

SUGGESTED TRAINING PLANS
Following are exemplary microcycles for the

- second mesocycle of a 17-year-old athlete in build-up training (table 5);
- first mesocycle of a 20km race walker in high-performance training (table 6); and
- third mesocycle of a 20km race walker in high-performance training (table 7).

Special 50km training plans have not been presented. They would primarily be characterised by higher volumes (e.g., continuous loads of up to three hours duration).

The suggested training plans for the

- first mesocycle of a 17-year-old athlete in build-up training for the middle distance (see chapter II–1.11.11);
- third mesocycle of a 17-year-old athlete in build-up training for the long distance (see chapter II–1.13.11);
- second mesocycle of a 17-year-old athlete in high-performance training for the steeplechase (see chapter II–1.12.11); and
- fourth mesocycle of an athlete in high-performance training for the steeplechase.

may be compared to the plans presented here in some respects. Attention should be paid to the higher volume of walking due to the longer competition distances.

Table 5: Build-up training: sample microcycle for a 17-year-old athlete in the second mesocycle.

Monday	Tuesday	Wednesday	Thursday	Friday	Saturday	Sunday
Trunk stabilisation exercises and belly crunches (20 min) with a lot of dynamic variation	Warm-up walking (15 min)	Continuous walking (30 min) first 10 min including ABCs of walking, with arm circling, exaggerated arm actions, etc.	Cycling, swimming, inline skating, cross-country skiing or aqua jogging (50 min) alternately each week	Foot strengthening (10 min)	*Morning:* Warm-up walking (10 min)	Rest
Acceleration runs (5 reps) barefoot	ABCs of walking (10–15 run-throughs) ankling, upper-body variations, varied arm actions, etc.		Contract-relax stretching (15 min)	Acceleration runs (5 reps) barefoot	ABCs of walking (10–15 run-throughs)	
ABCs of sprinting (10–15 run-throughs) heel kicks, pulling strides, step-overs, etc.	Continuous walking (80 min) flat terrain	Muscle build-up training (40 min) hamstrings, adductors/abductors, bench press, lat pulls, as well as other varying exercises	Muscle build-up training for the trunk on apparatus, medicine-ball work, or gymnastics (30 min) e.g., goalkeeper throws, rotational throws, throws from a prone position, and tossing, using a medicine ball	ABCs of jumping (10–15 run-throughs) sideways galloping, ankle jumps, skipping with two-legged landing, etc.	Acceleration walking (5 reps)	*On Saturdays prior to tempo walking and tempo running possibly also training the technique for a throwing event*
	Contract-relax stretching (15 min)			Skipping and bounding runs (4 x 40m each) including variations, technically correct	LI tempo walking and running (10 x 200m walking and 10 x 200m running; walking or jogging intervals: 90 sec; rest intervals between sets: 6 min)	
Technique training for other events (45 min) flat sprints, hurdle sprints, steeplechase, long or high jump	Foot strengthening (10 min) in the sand, with elastic band, or by rope jumping	Game (30 min) e.g., basketball or soccer	Contract-relax stretching (15 min)	Tempo-endurance walking or running (30 min) alternately each week, hilly terrain	Warm-down jogging (10 min)	
Fartlek (30 min) including walking, running and sprinting; hilly terrain	Tempo walking at alternating pace (4 x 100m) focusing on good technique, as utilisation		Walking sprints (5 x 60m) as utilisation	Tempo walking at alternating pace (4 x 100m) focusing on good technique, as utilisation	*Afternoon:* Continuous walking (30 min)	
					Contract-relax stretching (15 min)	
					Walking sprints (5 x 60m) as utilisation	

Table 6: High-performance training: sample microcycle for a 20km race walker in the first mesocycle.

	Monday	Tuesday	Wednesday	Thursday	Friday	Saturday	Sunday
Morning	Continuous walking (40 min) flat terrain Acceleration walking (3 reps) barefoot Strength-endurance circuit (3–4 run-throughs, 1 min loading, rest interval: 15 sec) trunk strength, leg strength; ABCs of sprinting, jumps, walking arm swing	Continuous walking (60 min) first 10 min including ABCs of walking, with arm circling, exaggerated arm actions, etc. ABCs of walking (15–20 run-throughs) ankling, upper-body variations, etc. Rope jumping (5 x 1 min)	Warm-up jogging (30 min) Acceleration runs (3 reps) barefoot ABCs of jumping (15–20 run-throughs) sideways galloping, ankle jumps, skipping with two-legged landing, skipping variations, etc. Game (30 min) e.g., basketball or soccer	Cycling, swimming, inline skating, cross-country skiing or aqua jogging (80 min) alternately each week, different sport than in the afternoon	Continuous walking (60 min) first 10 min including ABCs of walking ABCs of walking (15–20 run-throughs) Foot strengthening (10 min) in the sand or with elastic band Pull-resisted walking (8 x 100m with 2.5 kg)	Trunk stabilisation exercises and abdominal crunches (20 min) Acceleration walking LI tempo walking and running (10 x 200m walking, 10 x 200m running, and 10 x 200m walking; rest intervals: 90 sec; rest intervals between sets: 5 min) Warm-down walking (15 min)	Rest
Afternoon	Continuous running (100 min) flat terrain Tempo walking at alternating pace (6 x 100m) focusing on good technique, as utilisation Acceleration runs (7 x 80m) focusing on good technique, as utilisation	Tempo-endurance walking (45 min) hilly terrain Warm-down walking (5 min) Contract-relax stretching (15 min)	Continuous walking (150 min) flat terrain Walking sprints (8 x 60m) as utilisation	Cycling, swimming, inline skating, cross-country skiing or aqua jogging (40 min) Contract-relax stretching (15 min) Muscle build-up training for the trunk on apparatus, medicine-ball work, or gymnastics (30 min) Acceleration walking	Continuous walking (100 min) flat terrain Tempo walking at alternating pace (6 x 100m) focusing on good technique, as utilisation	Continuous walking (40 min) Contract-relax stretching (15 min) Walking sprints (8 x 60m) as utilisation	

547

Table 7: High-performance training: sample microcycle for a 20km race walker in the third mesocycle.

	Monday	Tuesday	Wednesday	Thursday	Friday	Saturday	Sunday
Morning	Continuous running (60 min) flat terrain, including ABCs of running ABCs of running (10–12 run-throughs) Acceleration runs (3 reps) barefoot ABCs of jumping (10–12 run-throughs) Game (20 min) e.g., basketball or soccer	Warm-up walking (10 min) ABCs of walking (10–15 run-throughs) Acceleration walking (3 reps) Walking sprints (5 x 100m) Tempo-endurance walking or running (40 min) alternately each week, flat terrain Warm-down walking (5 min)	Continuous walking (60 min) first 10 min including ABCs of walking, with arm circling, exaggerated arm actions, etc. ABCs of sprinting (10–15 run-throughs) Pull-resisted runs (8 x 200m with 2.5 kg)	Cycling, swimming, inline skating, cross-country skiing or aqua jogging (80 min) alternately each week, different sport than in the afternoon	Continuous walking (60 min) first 10 min including ABCs of walking, arm circling, etc. ABCs of walking (15–20 run-throughs) ankling, upper-body variations, varied arm actions, etc.	Warm-up walking (10 min) Acceleration walking (3 reps) barefoot Tempo walking (2 x 10 x 400m; rest intervals: 2 min; rest intervals between sets: 6–8 min) walking uphill, in total 3–4 times also downhill Warm-down walking (10 min)	Rest
Afternoon	Warm-up walking (10 min) Maximal-eccentric strength training (15 min) trunk stabilisation, lifting opposite upper and lower limbs in prone position, belly punches raising the foot/toes Fartlek (40 min) walking, hilly terrain Walking sprints (8 x 60m) as utilisation	Continuous walking (100 min) flat terrain Tempo walking at alternating pace (6 x 100m) focusing on good technique, as utilisation	Warm-up walking (10 min) Acceleration walking (3 reps) barefoot Tempo walking (8 x 3km or 5 x 5km; rest intervals: 3–5 min) 20km competition pace Warm-down walking (10 min) Walking sprints (8 x 60m) as utilisation	Cycling, swimming, inline skating, cross-country skiing or aqua jogging (40 min) Contract-relax stretching (15 min) Strength training for the trunk, or gymnastics (30 min) Acceleration walking (7 x 80m)	Continuous walking (30 min) flat terrain Tempo-endurance walking (30 min) flat terrain Maximal-eccentric strength training (15 min) hamstrings, quadriceps, adductors/abductors, etc. Tempo walking at alternating pace (6 x 100m)	Continuous walking (40 min) Walking sprints (8 x 60m) as utilisation	

1.14.12 BIBLIOGRAPHY

Hedge, R. (2002). First steps in racewalking. *Modern Athlete and Coach 40* (1). 27-29.

Morozov, V. (1998). About the development of young race walkers. *Modern Athlete and Coach 36* (1), 19-22.

Neumann, H. F. (2005). Koordinative Schwelle – kritische Geschwindigkeit zwischen Regelkonformität und Disqualifikation im sportlichen Gehen. *Leipziger sportwissenschaftliche Beiträge 46* (2), 130-135.

Neumann, H. F. (2007). Einfluss zunehmender Beanspruchung auf die Bewegungskoordination von Gehern – Anforderungen an die Methodenentwicklung für eine Einzelzyklusanalyse. *Leipziger sportwissenschaftliche Beiträge 48* (1), 125-129.

Neumann, H. F., Gohlitz, D. & Ernst, O. (2005). Wettkampfanalyse zur Erhöhung der Zielgerichtetheit des Kraft- und Techniktrainings im sportlichen Gehen. *Zeitschrift für angewandte Trainingswissenschaften 12* (2), 7-20.

Pathus, H.-J. (2002). Gehen – eine Frage der Technik. *Leichtathletiktraining 13* (9), 35-39.

Pathus, H.-J. (2003). Das Gehen rechtzeitig vorbereiten: Grundsätze für den langfristigen Leistungsaufbau und der Technik beim Gehen. *Leichtathletiktraining 14* (1), 30-37.

Pathus, H.-J. (2004). Der Gang zum Olympiasieg: Robert Korzeniowsky, mehrfacher Olympiasieger im Gehen, gibt Einblicke in seine Trainingsplanung aus der Saison 1999/2000. *Leichtathletiktraining 15* (4), 36-39.

Regelkommissionen des DLV, FLA, ÖLV und SLV (Hrsg.). (2008). *Internationale Wettkampfregeln*. Waldfischbach: Hornberger.

Scholich, M. (1992). Mittel- und Langstreckenlauf/Gehen. In K.-H. Bauersfeld & G. Schröter (Hrsg.), *Grundlagen der Leichtathletik* (S. 121-135). Berlin: Sportverlag.

Simon, G., Schmidt, A., Lim, W.-K. & Kannenberg, B. (1992). Sportartspezifische Leistungsdiagnostik bei Gehern auf dem Laufbandergometer. *Deutsche Zeitschrift für Sportmedizin 43* (10). 428-434.

Vallence, B. (2007). Junior to Senior transition in racewalking. *Modern Athlete and Coach 45* (2), 20-23.

Whitlock, H. H. (1957). *Race Walking*. Eastbourne: Amateur Athletic Association

2 JUMPING

2.1 COMMON FEATURES AND A COMPARISON OF THE DISCIPLINES

2.1.1 THE MOST IMPORTANT GENERAL COMPETITION RULES

The expression *technical disciplines* encompasses all jumping and throwing events. The following abridged and simplified International Competition Rules comprise the framework for the techniques and strategy, as well as the organisation of competitions in technical disciplines:

- At the competition venue and before the beginning of the event, each athlete may participate in practice trials. When the competition begins, competition equipment and the competition site may no longer be used for practice trials.
- If a runway is used, markers may be placed alongside it, except for the high jump where the markers may be placed on the runway. The markers must be supplied or approved by the organiser. Athletes may use adhesive tape, but not chalk or a similar substance nor anything which leaves indelible marks. No personal markers may be placed in or beside the landing area (for the throwing device or the competitor).
- Except for the high jump and pole vault, each athlete (in the final) must first be allowed three trials, and after this the eight athletes with the best

performances must be allowed three additional trials (final round).

- Before the final, there may be a qualifying (round) with a maximum of three trials. Once an athlete has achieved the qualifying standard, he/she is not allowed to continue in the qualifying competition. If fewer than 12 athletes achieve the pre-set qualifying standard, the group of finalists is expanded to that number by adding athletes according to their performances in the qualifying competition. The results achieved in the qualification are not considered part of the actual competition.
- The practice and competition trials take place in the order drawn by lot. If there is a qualifying round, there is a fresh drawing of lot for the final. The final round is conducted in the reverse order of placement after the first three trials of the final. At major championships, the order may be re-adjusted after the fifth trial.
- A competitor may forgo a trial. If a competitor is hindered in his/her trial, the referee has the authority to award him/her a substitute trial. Valid trials are indicated by a white flag, invalid trials by a red flag.

- Each competitor has one minute time to begin his trial (however, see high jump and pole vault in chapters II–2.4.2 and II–2.5.2). The period begins when the competition site is ready and this is signalled to the competitor (e.g., by calling). The remaining time is shown by means of a clock. A referee indicates with a yellow flag, or through other means, that the remaining 15 seconds have begun.

- Each competitor is credited with the best of all his/her trials. In the event of a tie, the second-best performance initially decides who is the best; if the tie remains, even the third best performance decides, etc. If the athletes involved are still in a tie following application of this rule, they are awarded an additional trial until a decision has been reached (however, see vertical jumps in chapter II–2.4.2).

2.1.2 SPORT-SCIENCE FINDINGS, PHASE STRUCTURE, AND TECHNIQUE

The specific techniques of the four jumping disciplines may be divided into the following major phases:

- run-up;
- take-off;
- flight; and
- landing.

The triple jump includes three take-off and flight phases. In the pole vault, there is an additional major phase; between the take-off and the flight, there is the pole phase.

PHASE 1: RUN-UP
The run-up has three objectives:

- generation of kinetic energy;
- run-up precision; and
- take-off preparation.

While the first two objectives are pursued throughout the run-up, the third objective may be assigned to the fourth of the following sub-phases or segments of the run-up:

- start of the run-up;
- start acceleration;
- pick-up acceleration; and
- take-off preparation.

Due to the specific arm actions, the take-off preparation and the take-off in the pole vault must be discussed together with the planting preparation and the planting activity itself. The high jump plays a special role due to the shortness and the curved form of the run-up as well as the clearly submaximal speed (see chapter II–2.4.3).

GENERATION OF KINETIC ENERGY
During the run-up, the jumper increases his/her horizontal run-up velocity (v). Therefore, at the end of the run-up, his/her body of mass m has a specific momentum ($p = m \cdot v$) or a specific kinetic energy [$E_{kin} = (m \cdot v^2)/2$]. Since, precisely stated, energy cannot be generated, but only converted, it is actually chemical energy

taken in through nutrition which is converted into kinetic energy in the muscles.

RUN-UP PRECISION

The goal of the entire run-up is to land on the optimum take-off point as accurately as possible. Jumpers test the optimal run-up length in training and competition and measure it (in metres or foot lengths) in order to start the run-up in all trials from the correct distance. In a competition trial, the jumper always tries to start the run-up using the same stride length and stride frequency. However, the notion that jumpers are able to perfect their run-ups to the extent that it is always of the same length without (peripheral) sight control may be considered obsolete. Different competition sites (e.g., flat or slightly sloping), daily form, effects of the weather, mental state, and inevitable variations in coordination from trial to trial result in varying stride patterns. In studies it has been observed that the variation in stride length decreases during the last four strides. It is likely that the jumper receives the key visual information to adjust stride length at an earlier point. Getting the feeling that it is just right as early as possible in the run-up is a skill which jumpers (must) acquire in training (e.g., through arbitrary run-up lengths).

The difference between tailwind and headwind may necessitate an adjustment of the run-up length by up to three feet. Due to the lack of performance pressure in training, many jumpers are not able to run up with such high intensity in training as in competition. Therefore, they are forced to shorten the run-up in training. In particular, in high-jump and pole-vault competitions in which the height continuously increases, the athlete often requires an increasingly long run-up although the number of his/her strides remains the same. It is primarily an increase in motivation which leads to a more dynamic run-up and longer strides. The increasing run-up speed due to higher motivation may also require taking off further from the zero line. Therefore, it is not uncommon for the run-up to be extended by a few feet in length in the course of the competition.

START OF THE RUN-UP

The jumper may start his/her run-up from a standing position, from a walk-on, or from a few stutter steps. The run-up from a standing position is attributed with the greatest running accuracy. In particular, the preliminary stutter steps may lead to more relaxation and specific advantages in the high jump (see chapter II–2.4.3). However, if the athlete is especially motivated in competition, he/she may perform the walk-on or the stutter steps at the start of the run-up a bit too fast. The first real run-up strides may then become too long and the result is often a take-off behind the take-off board or too close to the bar. If the athlete is not already standing at the marker which indicates the start of the run-up with tip of his/her front foot, he/she will try to land on it with the last of his/her preliminary strides. If the athlete performs stutter steps at the beginning of the run-up, the start of the run-up and the start acceleration will overlap each other.

START ACCELERATION

The designations start acceleration and pick-up acceleration are intentionally adopted from the short sprint. Much like a sprinter, the jumper first sprints or accelerates using the toe push-off technique. However, too much forward lean of the (upper) body is problematic both in the pole vault and especially in the high jump (see chapters II–2.4.3 and II–2.5.3). Since the length of the run-up (within the limits of the rules) can be chosen individually, the jumper does not need to accelerate maximally. In general, submaximal acceleration is recommended. Maximal acceleration would be too strenuous and would distract the jumper from technically precise performance, thus causing inaccuracies in run-up length and take-off preparation. However, a too gradual acceleration results in an excessively long run-up, which also requires too much energy.

PICK-UP ACCELERATION

The jumper increases the length and frequency of his/her strides gradually, straightens his/her trunk more and more, and assumes a grasping/pulling sprint stride (see chapter II–1.3.3). For some jumpers, an abrupt change in technique and rhythm may also be observed after a certain number of strides. In connection with the upright trunk, which is important for take-off preparation, some coaches often teach their athletes to place a little more emphasise on the knee lift during pick-up acceleration than in the flat sprint. This is supposed to lead to an upright pelvis.

Pick-up acceleration and take-off preparation should overlap each other if possible. The objective is to increase horizontal velocity continuously up to the take-off. Before take-off, the jumper should achieve an optimal (not necessarily maximal) speed which enables him/her to take off effectively and achieve maximal jumping results.

TAKE-OFF PREPARATION

Depending on one's perspective, take-off preparation begins 2–7 strides before the take-off. At this point it is time to raise one's view in good time to continue sprinting with an erect head and trunk. In the long and high jump, the take-off leg is actually placed down with a moderate backward lean of the trunk (backward reclining take-off position).

An intermediate marker is often placed 4–7 strides before the take-off. However, it is not so much the athlete who should look at this marker during the performance of the jump, but the marker rather makes it easier for the coach to check the performance of the run-up to this exact point. If the athlete looks (peripherally) at this marker, he/she does so not in order to land on it exactly, but rather to deliberately emphasise his/her stride frequency beginning at this point.

During the last two strides, the jumper lowers his/her centre of gravity (CG) to achieve the bracing effect described in phase 2. Specifically, this happens during the third last support phase, during the flight phase of the penultimate run-up stride, during

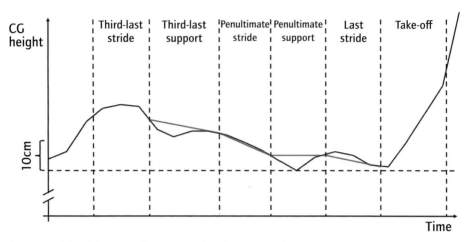

*Figure 1: **Height of the CG during a 7.40m long jump** by Jackie Joyner-Kersee (modified on the basis of Ramlow & Romanautzky, 1997): While in studies in which only the moments of contact with the ground and leaving the ground are analysed a continuous lowering of the CG until the touchdown of the take-off leg is found (see blue line), these authors locate the lowest point of the CG curve during the penultimate support. The movements of all sub-segments of the body are of crucial importance for the CG curve. Consequently, the incomplete raising of the heel of the take-off leg during the final swing phase of this leg and (in the long and high jump) of the swing leg during its swing phase from the third last support up to the penultimate support are greatly responsible for the lowering of the CG.*

the penultimate support phase, and/or during the flight phase of the last stride. The greatest part of the lowering of the CG should occur during the penultimate stride (see figure 1). The greater the lowering of the CG during the last stride, the larger the change of movement direction during the take-off to achieve a particular departure angle (see figure 8). The degree of lowering the CG depends on the event, individual technical variation, and the desired departure angle. Faster run-up velocities and lower departure angles are usually associated with less CG lowering.

The lowering of the CG is achieved through a short-long-short rhythm inter alia. This means that the penultimate stride of most jumpers is longer than the third to last

one and especially the last one. However, even among world-class jumpers, there are deviations from this behaviour (see chapters II–2.2.3 and II–2.4.3). Within the short-long-short rhythm there is the swing-leg squat during the penultimate support phase. This means that during this ground contact the leg which will be the swing leg in the take-off is bent more at the knee joint than during the previous sprinting strides and that the entire sole often touches the ground. The push-off during the penultimate ground contact is very flat and is often performed using an incomplete knee extension.

PHASE 2: TAKE-OFF

The completed lowering of the CG enables the jumper to place down his/her nearly

Figure 2: **Visualisation of the velocities relevant to the take-off** *(modified on the basis of Störmer & Rolf, 1993, p. 155):*

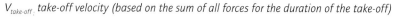

CG: centre of gravity

h_0: *height of departure*

α: *angle of departure*

$V_{run\text{-}up}$: *run-up velocity*

$V_{take\text{-}off}$: *take-off velocity (based on the sum of all forces for the duration of the take-off)*

$V_{departure}$: *velocity of departure*

V_y: *vertical velocity of departure*

V_x: *horizontal velocity of departure*

V_{xloss}: *loss of horizontal velocity upon take-off* $(= V_{run\text{-}up} - V_x)$

extended leg well before the vertical projection of the CG. Subsequently, he/she tries to bend his/her leg as little as possible (see figure 4). Through this action, which is called bracing, the jumper tries to lever himself/herself upward. He/she intends to convert some of his/her horizontal run-up velocity (or run-up momentum) into vertical velocity of departure (or vertical departure momentum; see figure 2 and 3). In addition to the behaviour of the take-off leg, it is the trunk position in particular (backward reclining take-off position) which influences the bracing angle. This angle is measured between the vertical and the line connecting the CG and the heel at the moment of the touchdown of the take-off leg (see figure 7).

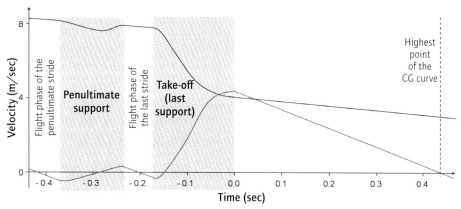

Figure 3: **Conversion of horizontal run-up velocity into vertical velocity of departure in the men's high jump** *(modified on the basis of Isoletho et al., 2007).*

After the involuntary flexion (amortisation), the push-off extension of the feet, knees, hips and trunk is brought about by the muscles of the extensor loop. It enhances the acceleration in the vertical direction. With low departure angles, the push-off is performed so flat and forward that toward the end of the extension a small part of the horizontal velocity which was lost through the bracing action may be recovered. The vertical acceleration is also reflected in the fact that the previously lowered CG is raised considerably during take-off (see figure 4).

The extensor muscles of the take-off leg work reactively and powerfully. During the eccentric phase of the stretch-shortening cycle, monosynaptic reflexes are triggered and kinetic energy is stored in the form of strain energy in the elastic structures of the muscle-tendon unit, which in combination result in an increased power output in the concentric phase. The extensor muscles

may thus be considered as a spring which first absorbs and then releases energy.

FOOT TOUCHDOWN

The hip extension in the take-off leg already starts during the front swing phase. As a result, the take-off foot moves backward (and downward) relative to the body's centre of gravity before touchdown. Therefore, as in the sprint, it is possible to speak of a pulling foot strike also in the jumps. The shifting forward of the hip already during take-off preparation and the start of the powerful hip extension before foot touchdown are prerequisites for the rapid continuation of the hip extension after foot touchdown and the athlete's quick (pulling) movement across the point of touchdown.

However, since a bracing action is intentional especially in the long and high jump, in contrast to the sprint, one cannot speak strictly of a grasping foot strike. Although the jumper tries to place his/her take-off foot actively onto the board from above, the heel and knee lift before touchdown remain incomplete as compared to the sprint. The foot is placed on the ground with a relatively flat foot-movement curve and active extension of the knee-joint (kick of the lower leg). There is a more grasping preparation of the foot strike during the take-offs in the triple jump (see chapter II–2.3.3).

In contrast to the sprint, the foot touchdown during the jump take-offs is usually performed over the entire foot. Athletes are taught that the foot should

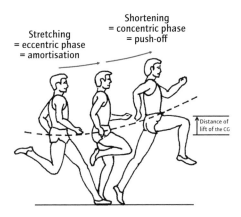

*Figure 4: **Stretch-shortening cycle and lifting path of the CG** (= vertical acceleration path) in take-offs.*

be placed down with the entire sole. A touchdown over the ball of the foot with subsequent lowering of the entire sole is regarded as a technical error. When taking off, very few jumpers touch the ground with only the ball of the foot. This requires extremely strong calf muscles and is perhaps only possible in the pole vault. High jumpers often place their take-off foot down first with the outside of the heel and only then place the foot quickly and flatly onto the ground. In the other jumping events, placing down the heel first is regarded as a technical error since it is often associated with a touchdown too far in front of the body and an excessive loss of horizontal velocity. In the diagram of the ground reaction forces, a flat foot strike may be identified through a bipartite impact force peak (see chapter II–1.1.2).

In any case, the foot strike should be active. This means that the jumper should raise the tip of his/her foot before the touchdown, especially the inside of the tip of the foot (slight supination). Raising the toes, especially the big toe, results in a pre-tension of the arch of the foot. Then the extension of the ankle (plantar flexion)

begins already before the touchdown. The idea that the push-off from the ankle begins even before the touchdown and is interrupted only by force through amortisation is helpful (see figure 5).

SWING ELEMENTS

The non-take-off leg (also called the free leg or swing leg) and the arms— including the shoulders, which are often pulled up at the end of the take-off (shrug)—are called swing elements. Despite individual and discipline-specific differences (e.g., contralateral or double arm swing) and additional functions (rotation compensation or triggering), the two fundamental functions of the swing elements are as follows.

At the beginning of the take-off movement, the swing elements are moved upward—or more precisely, the muscles exert a force (F) so that the mass (m) of the swing elements is accelerated upward (a = F/m). According to Newton's 3rd law (action = reaction), a downward directed force (or acceleration) acts on the rest of the body. When standing on a (mechanical) scale with legs extended and the arms pulled upward using a double arm swing, one sees that the pointer first deflects in the direction of a higher weight. Therefore, by using the swing elements, the load on the extensor muscles of the take-off leg is increased. This means that a more powerful use of swing elements requires specific strength capacities in the take-off leg. Therefore, it may occur that a young female jumper in particular, who is instructed to use her swing leg more actively, collapses

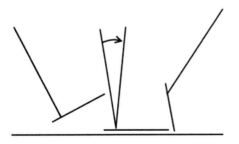

*Figure 5: **Foot touchdown during take-offs** (cf. figure 15 in chapter II–1.3.3).*

on her take-off leg. Due to the resulting compression forces, she is forced to bend her knee during the amortisation to such an extent that she is not able to achieve an extension during the subsequent take-off.

The reversal of movement between reaching out and using the swing elements during the take-off already occurs towards the end of the flight phase of the last run-up stride. However, when performing a double arm swing in the high jump for example, the arms first move downward and are accelerated upward only shortly after the touchdown of the foot.

At the end of the take-off movement, the swing elements are decelerated. This is identical with an acceleration downward. On the basis of the same physical laws described above, the remainder of the body and the CG are accelerated upward. This is also understandable on the basis of the self-test on the scale described above. One becomes lighter by slowing down the swing elements. This means that the deceleration of the swing elements results in an increase in the velocity of departure. This is also known as momentum transfer. The upward momentum of the swing elements ($p_{SE} = m_{SE} \cdot v_{SE}$) increases along with mass (m_{SE}) and speed (v_{SE}). It is transmitted to the entire body through the equally high braking impulse ($p_{SE} = \Delta p_{body}$). Thus, the velocity of the body increases relatively to the masses of the body and the swing elements ($\Delta v_{body} = v_{SE} \cdot m_{SE}/m_{body}$). The gain in the vertical velocity of departure is therefore greater the more mass and the faster this

mass is previously moved upward. In the double arm swing (e.g., in the high jump), the mass which is moved upward is greater than in the contralateral arm swing.

The importance of the swing elements for vertical velocity of departure may only be estimated indirectly. In studies, values between 7 and 25% have been found.

In the long jump and pole vault as well as in the hop take-off, the swing leg is swung forward in a sprint-like manner with an acute angle at the knee joint. If, as in the step and jump of the triple jump and in particular in the power-flop variation of the high jump, the change in direction and thus the take-off duration (see below) is greater, the knee-joint angle in the swing leg is also slightly larger. To be able to provide the decisive impulse upward, the thigh is abruptly stopped in a horizontal position. If the swinging movement of the thigh exceeds the horizontal, the result is a backward rotation of the pelvis and thus an incomplete extension of the trunk and knee of the take-off leg.

The effect of the swing leg (and a double arm swing) on the horizontal velocity component is comparable. If the extremities are accelerated forward, they slow down the forward movement of the remainder of the body. If this movement is slowed down again, the horizontal velocity of the body increases.

TRUNK MUSCLES AND STEERING BY THE HEAD

As in the sprint, the trunk muscles have a stabilising and performance-determining effect (see chapter II–1.1.2). Natural forced breathing ensures their maximum tension. During the take-off, the head is aligned with the trunk and thus controls the correct use of the trunk muscles. The head position is in turn controlled by the direction of the view.

TAKE-OFF POSITION

The position which the jumper takes at the moment when he/she breaks contact with the ground is called the take-off position. This position, which coaches use to check the athlete's technique (see errors – causes – corrections in the individual events), is very similar in all jumping events (see figure 6). The following features are characteristic of a good take-off position:

- upright trunk;
- the completely extended (i.e., at the hip slightly over-extended) take-off leg points back to the take-off spot;
- three right angles in the swing leg (possibly more acute knee-joint angle).

FORWARD ROTATION

When the take-off foot is placed on the ground, the lower body is decelerated. The translational movement of the run-up becomes a rotational movement to some extent (see figure 7). In the pole vault, the increasing resistance of the pole counteracts the forward rotation and ultimately leads to a reverse rotation (see chapter II–2.5.3). In the high jump, forward rotation is necessary for effective bar clearance (see chapter II–2.4.3). In the long and triple jump, the rotation about the lateral axis should be minimised to achieve an effective landing or an effective new take-off. This is achieved through a fast forward movement of the pelvis (hyperextension of the hip on the side of the take-off leg), a certain holding back of the shoulders, as well as certain movements during the flight phase (see chapters II–2.2.3 and II–2.3.3). The somersault long jump technique, which

Figure 6: *Take-off position in various jumping events.*

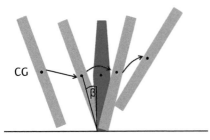

*Figure 7: **Model of imagining the jumper as a bouncing pole** (β: bracing angle).*

could possibly have used the rotation in a positive manner, was banned for safety reasons.

IMPACT VELOCITY, CHANGE OF DIRECTION, AND VELOCITY OF DEPARTURE

Even every single sprinting stride may be considered as a jump. This becomes evident, for example, when looking at the ground reaction forces. They are almost qualitatively (i.e., in terms of their appearance) identical in the sprint and jump. Quantitatively, however, significantly higher forces act on the body during take-offs (chapter II–1.1.2).

Therefore, the table of take-off parameters (table 1) also includes the sprint. It becomes obvious that there is an interrelation between movement task, horizontal velocity, and departure angle. To include the repeated take-offs in the triple jump in this system, the angle of impact must also be considered. In the jumps from a run-up, the angle of impact to the horizontal is virtually zero. The change of direction means the sum of the angle of impact and departure angle (see figure 8 and take-off preparation above). The impact velocity is defined as the velocity resulting from the vertical and horizontal velocity of the CG before take-off.

*Table 1: **Comparison of the biomechanical parameters of the jumps of top athletes** (based on data by Arampatzis et al., 1999; Brüggemann & Arampatzis, 1999; Isoletho et al., 2007, Killing et al. 2008, pp. 22, 46, 126–127; Panoutsakopoulos & Kollias, 2007; Schade et al., 2007): *In the pole vault, the departure angle (as understood in the other events) is difficult to determine since the jumper is also drawn upward by the pole.*

	Horizontal velocity directly before take-off (m/sec)		Ground contact time upon take-off (sec)	Take-off angle (degrees)
	Women	Men		
100 m (Phase 3)	up to 11.0	up top 12.0	0.08-0.09	approx. 3
Hurdle stride (110m hurdles)	higher than 8.5	higher than 9.0	0.11-0.13	approx. 15
Pole vault	7.7-8.3	9.0-9.6	0.10-0.12	16–18*
Triple jump: hop	9.1-9.5	10.2-10.6	0.10-0.13	♀: 15-17, ♂: 13-16
Triple jump: step	8.3-8.7	9.5-10.0	0.14-0.16	♀: 10-13, ♂: 11-14
Triple jump: jump	7.5-7.9	8.5-9.0	0.14-0.17	18-23
Long jump	9.2-9.7	10.3-11.0	0.10-0.13	19-22
High jump	6.0-7.5	7.0-8.5	0.14-0.19	40-55

If the departure velocity were independent of the change of direction, larger departure angles than presented in table 1 would be useful in all jumping disciplines from a mechanical point of view (see phase 3). However, biomechanically the departure velocity and the change of direction are not independent of one another.

As described, in the take-offs in athletics the change of direction occurs in the form of a bouncing deflection. In order to obtain a larger deflection (change of direction), the athlete must brace more, which means that the spring-like take-off leg must store more energy by developing more force contrary to the direction of motion to subsequently release this energy again in the desired direction of motion. Although the bracing angle remains the same, the spring-like take-off leg must store more energy if

- the (impact or) run-up velocity increases;
- the jumper's body weight is higher; and
- the swing elements are more accelerated upward.

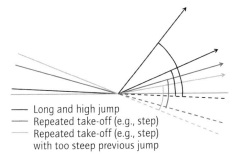

— Long and high jump
— Repeated take-off (e.g., step)
— Repeated take-off (e.g., step) with too steep previous jump

*Figure 8: **Change of direction in different take-offs** (not true to scale).*

In all these cases, the following two points have a limiting effect:

- The elastic structures of the take-off leg in which the strain energy is stored can only tolerate certain forces, strains, and stresses if not damaged. If the load is too great, there will be either injury or subconsciously triggered protective reactions. These protective responses include reducing the run-up speed, the reduction of the bracing and departure angles, insufficient push-off extension due to a softening of the muscles or breaking off the jump as is often observed in the step take-off of the triple jump.
- The spring-like take-off leg is not an ideal spring. Some of the energy is lost. For example, in the long-jump take-off, the mechanical energy after the jump is 10–15% less than before. The energy loss increases the greater the amount of energy that is stored. This means that more energy is lost if a jumper increases his/her bracing angle (while his/her run-up velocity does not change) in order to achieve a greater change of direction. Therefore, an excessive loss of horizontal velocity upon the take-off does not result in a corresponding increase in the vertical departure velocity.

Conversely, a low energy loss is identical with greater jumping power. The ability to produce greater vertical departure velocity with the same run-up speed and the same loss of horizontal velocity is equivalent to superior jumping power.

In fact, the energy loss in the eccentric phase of the ground contact upon take-off is even greater than the 10–15% mentioned above. These percentages occur only in measurable balance after the jumper was able to add mechanical energy through active muscle work in the concentric phase. However, the ability to increase departure velocity by means of an active force impulse (p = F • t) is severely limited through the short duration (t) of the take-off and in particular the concentric phase.

An excessive (lowering of the CG and) bracing is often described as a technical error. Nevertheless, there is also the opposite situation: Too little (lowering of the CG and) bracing results in too small departure angles. Visually, this appears as if running across the take-off point. The energy loss upon take-off is then too low although this may sound paradoxical. This means that the bracing angle, angle of departure, and energy loss follow an optimum curve, which, however, may be individually different (see figure 9).

The interaction of impact velocity and change of direction described thus explains the following phenomena:

- In table 1, high impact velocities are associated with small changes in direction and vice versa. During ground contact in the sprint there is the smallest, whereas in the high jump there is the greatest change in direction.
- In the triple jump, the change in direction becomes larger from jump to jump since the impact velocity is reduced through the energy losses from jump to jump.

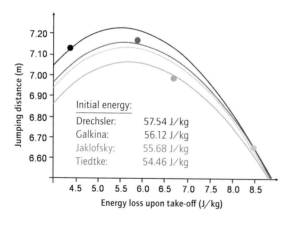

Initial energy:

Drechsler:	57.54 J/kg
Galkina:	56.12 J/kg
Jaklofsky:	55.68 J/kg
Tiedtke:	54.46 J/kg

*Figure 9: **Optimum energy loss upon take-off for optimum flight distance in the long jump** (modified on the basis of Arampatzis et al, 1999, p 122.): Due to her superior run-up speed and thus high initial energy, Drechsler would have been able to achieve the farthest jump (up to 7.22m). However, her effective jumping distance (7.13m) was shorter due to a loss of energy that was too great and thus a departure angle (16.9°) that was too small. Galkina took optimum advantage of her lower initial energy and jumped farther (7.17m). Jaklofsky's energy loss in particular was much too large. Her departure angle (20.2°) which is still not very large shows that there is no (corresponding) additional increase in this angle above the optimum energy loss. Tiedtke, whose run-up velocity or initial energy was lower, jumped farther despite suboptimal energy loss.*

- The angle of impact of one partial jump affects the departure angle of the subsequent partial jump in the triple jump since only a certain change in direction is possible for the jumper (without losing too much horizontal velocity; see figure 8).

In addition, the ground contact time changes as a part of the interaction between movement task, impact velocity, and desired change in direction (see table 1). Due to higher horizontal velocity, the jumper moves faster across the take-off support. However, a comparison of the long jump and the 100m sprint shows that a larger departure angle is associated with longer ground contact. This in turn is associated with the lowering of the CG and the bracing angle. The larger these two quantities, the longer the distance the CG must travel during the support. A longer path of support alone would require a longer support time. Furthermore, the CG is slowed more by an increased bracing upon take-off.

PHASE 3: FLIGHT

JUMPING MEANS THROWING ONESELF
The flight of a jumper follows the physical laws of an oblique throw. *As soon as the jumper leaves the ground, he/she follows a throwing parabola like a throwing device and is no longer able to change the trajectory of his/her centre of mass.* In the pole vault, the jumper has not yet left the ground completely during the pole phase since he/she is still able to exchange forces with the ground via the pole.

Only through air resistance, which in the simple laws of the oblique throw described below is not taken into account, can the jumper affect his trajectory during the flight phase. However, no flight technique in the jumps is designed to minimise drag. Attempting to do so would provide too few benefits or too great disadvantages with respect to other technical requirements.

The major factors influencing the shape of the throwing parabola are departure velocity and angle or the horizontal and vertical velocity of departure as a result of the run-up and take-off (see figure 2). In the vertical direction, the gravitational acceleration departure (g ≈ 9.81 m/sec² in local latitudes at sea level) due to gravitational force of the mass of the Earth and the CG height at departure (h_0) are included in the calculation. The following applies:

- *The maximum height of flight of the centre of gravity (h_{max}) and the flight duration (t_{flight}) are determined by vertical departure velocity (v_y)* (since the height of departure is only slightly changeable within the rules and for a given body height).

$$\gg\ h_{max} = \frac{v_y^2}{2g} + h_0$$

$$\gg\ t_{flight} = \frac{2v_y}{g}$$

applies if the height of the CG of the flying object (jumper or throwing device) at departure and upon the

Track & Field

first contact with the ground are identical. However, both in athletics throws and jumps, the height of departure (h_0) and the landing height (hland) are not identical. Therefore the following applies:

» $t_{flight} = t_{rise} + t_{drop}$

$$= \frac{v_y}{g} + \sqrt{\frac{2(h_{max} - h_{landing})}{g}}$$

- Gravitational acceleration decreases with the square of the radius to the centre of Earth. Due to the shape of the Earth (flattening at the poles), acceleration due to gravity decreases toward the equator where it is 0.5% less than at the poles. At a competition venue at an altitude of 5000 m, it is also approximately 0.15% less. For the same vertical departure velocity, the height and duration of flight would be correspondingly greater there. This effect is enhanced by the reduced air resistance at high altitude and the effect of centrifugal forces due to the rotation of the Earth. The centrifugal forces acting on a body moving with the Earth are directed away from the axis of rotation passing through the north and south poles. This force is greater the further the body is removed from the axis.
- The vertical departure velocity is based on the (average) acceleration in the vertical direction (a_y) for the duration of the take-off ($t_{take-off}$): $v_y = a_y \cdot t_{take-off}$.

This acceleration in turn is based on the (average) force exerted by the jumper in the vertical direction (F_y) to move the mass of his/her body (m) in this direction: $a_y = F_y/m$. If substituted in the above equation for h_{max}, the result is as follows:

» $h_{max} = \dfrac{F_y^2 \cdot t_{take-off}^2}{m^2 \cdot 2g} + h_0$

This formula illustrates the importance of body weight or load-force ratio for the flight height of the CG. If standard values for the high jump are used in this formula, then the reduction of body weight by 1 kg results in the increase of flight height by more than 3 cm if all other values, in particular the force mustered by the jumper, remain the same. Therefore, it is important to not only avoid unnecessary body mass (arm muscles, fat, etc.) but also to consider the athlete's health. To a certain extent, an increase in the mass of the working muscles leads to an improvement in relative strength capacities. While for female high jumpers a 3:1 ratio of height (in cm) to body weight (in kg) is assumed to be ideal, the ideal ratio for male long jumpers is 5:2.

- If the CG is at its highest point, the jumper has achieved his/her greatest potential energy (position energy, E_{pot}).

» $E_{pot} = m \cdot g \cdot h_{max} - h_0$

564

- *Flight distance (d) is determined by the horizontal departure velocity (v$_x$) and the flight duration (t$_{flight}$) which is based on the vertical departure velocity as described:*

  » $d = v_x \bullet t_{flight}$

- Based on the task, **horizontal** (long jump and triple jump) **and vertical jumps** (high jump and pole vault) are distinguished in athletics. The equations show that in the high jump the primary objective is the maximisation of the vertical departure velocity. Nevertheless, the high jumper requires a certain horizontal velocity during the flight to move across the bar. In the long jump and triple jump, the equations indicate the required optimum ratio of the vertical and horizontal velocity of departure. Matters are more complicated in the pole vault (see chapter II–2.5.3). According to the take-off parameters in table 1, the pole vault is more a horizontal jump.
- In the simplest case of the oblique throw, the aforementioned optimum

ratio between the horizontal and vertical departure velocity for achieving maximum flight distance is 1:1. This corresponds to an **optimum angle** of departure of 45°. However, this only applies if departure and landing heights are identical and the aerodynamic characteristics of the flying object (jumper or throwing device) are not taken into account (see chapters II–3.1.2, II–3.2.3, and II–3.3.3). If the landing surface is lower, as is the case in athletics throws and jumps, a flatter angle of departure results in an optimum result. However, the restriction mentioned in phase 2, namely that horizontal run-up velocity cannot be converted to vertical take-off velocity to an arbitrary extent upon take-off, has a significantly greater effect on athletics jumps.

PHASE 4: LANDING

In vertical jumps, the landing no longer determines performance; safety aspects are more important here. In horizontal jumps, the objective is also to minimise loss upon landing, which determines performance (see chapter II–2.2.3).

2.1.3 THE ROLE OF STRATEGY IN THE TECHNICAL DISCIPLINES

Beginning competitions with valid trials provides security. If these trials are also good, this may impress the opponents and may possibly have a negative effect on their performance. Although this behaviour could be called strategy, in general it plays a minor role in the technical disciplines.

The omission of trials may be called real strategy. If an athlete is well placed, slightly injured (in an important competition), or if the number of participants is small, he/she possibly can forgo one or more trials to be able to regenerate longer or to minimise stress. Moreover, a jumper or thrower may deliberately take a risk instead of first trying to perform safe trials. Therefore, a strategy section is only included in the chapter on the high jump as being representative of the vertical jumps since strategic options are a little greater here due to the rules.

2.1.4 THE SPECIFICITY IN JUMPING TRAINING: GENERAL ASPECTS OF DIDACTICS AND TRAINING PLANNING

TRAINING JUMPS WITH A SHORT RUN-UP?

Training the technique of jumping disciplines and of isolated take-offs in pop-up jumps (268) is usually started with short run-ups. This is true both for the long-term development of the beginner and for the medium-term course of the season, even for advanced athletes. The reduced sprinting speed due to the shorter run-up should facilitate the technically correct execution of take-off preparation and the take-off itself, reduce physical stress, and thus increase the possible number of repetitions.

Despite these advantages, it is important to consider the following: With decreasing speed, the character of the jump also changes. Visual impressions are different (e.g., in controlling the stride length and stride frequency for landing on the take-off board or reaching the necessary distance to the bar or to the planting box). The duration of the take-off (ground contact time) is prolonged since the jumper does not move so rapidly across the point of take-off. The importance of the eccentric phase decreases, while that of the concentric phase increases. The take-off becomes less dependent on reactive power and more dependent on maximum strength. It is possible to lower one's CG more and to achieve greater bracing and departure angles. This provides more time for the movements during the flight in the horizontal jumps; however, in vertical jumps there is inevitably less time due to lower initial energy. The coordinate (time) programme, which ingrains itself in the CNS, is different in terms of space and time. The muscles are innervated according to a different pattern. The jumper will ultimately learn a different movement.

Many problems in training which occur when switching from short to long run-ups may be explained on the basis of this background information (e.g., an excessive lowering of the CG in the long or triple jump or running too far under the pole during the pole-vault take-off).

In children's athletics or basic training, it makes no sense to have athletes jump from a run-up which is so fast that they are not able to control it. Much more serious errors would become ingrained. On the contrary, the run-ups observed during the competitions of younger athletes are often far too long. The run-up length and velocity should be in the range of the controllable maximum and should exceed this only now and then for a short time.

Particularly in jumps with a rather horizontal take-off (long jump, triple jump, and pole vault), the movement tasks and instructions should be aimed at minimising those velocity adjustments that later become errors. Therefore, coaches should instruct athletes to lower their CG only slightly even when they jump from a short run-up.

In build-up and high-performance training, it may be questioned whether it is useful to plan a period during the preparation in which no jumps from a full run-up are performed. In any case, the number of jumps from a short run-up should be reduced and the number of jumps from a long run-up should be increased early enough. In high-performance training, some coaches and athletes experiment with pull-assistance (290) to keep run-up velocity high or even to achieve supramaximal run-up velocity. In any case, however, knowledge of the velocity-dependent changes of jump coordination helps athletes and coaches to deal with problems which are not completely avoidable.

JUMPS ON SOFT GROUND?

To protect the passive musculoskeletal system (bones, joints, etc.) particularly of children and young people, (multiple) jumps are often performed on soft ground to increase the amount of take-offs performed by a single athlete, and to deliberately perform sensorimotor training. Instead of artificial surfaces,

asphalt or concrete, jumps are performed with increasing cushioning effect on felt mats, wet and hard sand, grass, woodchip jogging trails, mat tracks, soft and dry sand, or on soft floor mats. It should be considered, however, that this leads to a change in the characteristics of the jumping technique. The ground contact times become longer, and the importance of reactive strength decreases, whereupon the central nervous system responds with a different movement programme. The same is true for jumps with additional weights (291; e.g., with a weighted vest).

Soft grounds are non-specific with respect to the target motion and the desired adaptation not only in terms of neural adaptations, but also in terms of the passive structures of the muscle-tendon unit. The harder the ground, the greater the stress on the connective tissue and elastic intracellular filament structures. These structures are substantially involved in the development of force during take-offs. After appropriate preparation, they require loads at reduced volume and high intensity which are more specific in terms of the competition movement.

With respect to jumps on soft ground, it may be concluded that they should be minimised during the competition phase and its immediate preparation period although they are generally useful. It should also be considered that even though foot stability should be trained by using wobbly grounds, the risk of twisting one's ankle is initially increased when performing one-legged take-offs and landings on such grounds. In any case, an athlete must be rested and highly concentrated when performing such training.

JUMPS FROM AN ELEVATED, LOWERED, OR ELASTIC TAKE-OFF AREA?

To increase the duration of flight and to practise flight and landing technique, jumps may be performed from an elevated or elastic take-off area. Both lead to extended ground contact time. An elevated take-off area also results in less CG lowering during the penultimate stride because the CG is already low relative to the take-off area. In addition, the bracing angle and thus the departure angle are thereby increased. If the elevation and run-up velocity are too high, the jumper will be unable to achieve a take-off extension. In the long jump, for example, the take-off area should only be elevated by a maximum of 10cm. In any case, however, the movement and its coordinative control will change.

An extended flight phase without altered take-off technique may be achieved through the elevation of both the run-up and take-off area. However, the facilities required for this purpose are only available at a few locations. A slightly lower take-off point may be achieved through a run-up on gym mats and take-off from the floor. Such a take-off has the opposite effect to an elevated take-off point and may be a useful supplement.

In general, all these types of training should neither be performed too long nor too often.

2.1.5 BIBLIOGRAPHY

Arampatzis, A., Brüggemann, G.-P. & Walsch, M. (1999). Long Jump. In G.-P. Brüggemann, D. Koszewski & H. Müller (Hrsg.), *Biomechanical Research Project Athens 1997: Final Report* (S. 82-113). Oxfort: Meyer & Meyer.

Brüggemann, G.-P. & Arampatzis, A., (1999). Triple Jump. In G.-P. Brüggemann, D. Koszewski & H. Müller (Hrsg.), *Biomechanical Research Project Athens 1997: Final Report* (S. 82-113). Oxfort: Meyer & Meyer.

Isoletho, J., Virmavirta, M., Kyröläinen, H., Komi, P. (2007). Biomechanical analysis oft he high jump at the 2005 IAAF World Championships in Athletics. *New Studies in Athletics 22* (2), 17-27.

Killing, W., Bartschat, E., Czingon, H., Knapp, U., Kurschilgen, B. & Schlottke K. (2008). *Jugendleichtathletik: Offizieller Rahmentrainingsplan des Deutschen Leichtathletik-Verbandes für die Sprungdisziplinen im Aufbautraining.* Münster: Philippka.

LeBlanc, S. (2001). The role of active landings in the horizontal jumps. *Track coach* (157), 5019-5020.

Lees, A., Rojas, J., Cepero, M., Soto, V., Gutierrez, M. (2000). How the free limbs are used by elite high jumpers in generating vertical velocity. *Ergonomics 43* (10), 1622-1636.

Madella, A. (1996). Speed in the horizontal jumps: Muscular properties or cognitive treatment. *New Studies in Athletics 11* (2/3), 127-132.

Maraj, B. (1999). Evidence for Programmed and Visually Controlled Phases of the Triple Jump Approach Run. *New Studies in Athletics 14* (1), 51-56.

Panoutsakopoulos, V. & Kollias, I. (2007). Biomechanical analysis of sub-elite performers in the women's long jump. *New Studies in Athletics 22* (4). 19-28.

Ramlow, J. & Romanautzky, R. (1997). Das Absenken des Körperschwerpunkts vor dem Absprung beim Weitsprung – nicht nur eine Frage der Schrittlängengestaltung. *Leistungssport 27* (6), 44-47.

Regelkommissionen des DLV, FLA, ÖLV und SLV (Hrsg.). (2008). *Internationale Wettkampfregeln.* Waldfischbach: Hornberger.

Schade, F., Isoletho, J., Arampatzis, A., Brüggemann, G.-P. & Komi, P. (2007). Biomechanical analysis of the pole vault at the 2005 IAAF World Championships in Athletics: Extracts from the Final Report. N*ew Studies in Athletics 22* (2), 29-45.

Störmer, I. & Rolf, U. (1993). *Lehr- und Lehrhilfen: Leichtathletik: eine Anleitung für die Übungsleiter-Ausbildung, Übungsleiter, Trainer und für den Aktiven selbst.* Emden: OBW.

2.2 LONG JUMP

2.2.1 A LEAP INTO THE NEXT CENTURY

There are moments in athletics that seem to be made for eternity. After the first 8m jump by Jesse Owens in 1935 (8.13m), which remained the world record for 25 years, there was once again such a moment on 18 October 1968. The U.S. athlete Bob Beamon achieved something unbelievable in the Olympic long-jump final. At the end of his fast run-up, he took off for an enormously high leap and flew farther than could be registered by the optical measurement device. A steel measuring tape had to be fetched to measure the spectacular jumping distance of 8.90m, which was 55cm further than the previous world record. The jump of superlatives was called a leap into the next century.

So far, only two athletes have jumped farther. In the best long-jump competition of history at the 1991 World Championships in Tokyo, the Americans Mike Powell and Carl Lewis fought a duel. Although Lewis, unbeaten since 1981, achieved the best series of jumps of all time (8.68m, invalid, 8.83m, wind-aided 8.91m, 8.87m, and 8.84m), Powell established the world record of 8.95m which is still valid today. Powell became world champion again in 1993, but Lewis was the only long jumper who was able to repeat his Olympic victory. He even achieved four consecutive Olympic victories (1984–1996) and was also world champion in 1983 and 1987.

He was followed by the Cuban Iván Pedroso, who in 1995 supposedly set a new world record at the high altitude of Sestriere. The wind gauge showed a permissible 1.2 m/sec during his leap of 8.96m, but video recordings showed that an Italian judge had blocked the wind gauge.

At the Olympic Games from 1900 to 1912, there was a standing long jump competition for the men. In addition, the long jump from a run-up has been a part of the Olympic competition programme since 1896 with almost unchanged rules. However, the method of taking off from the narrow board and the methods of measuring have long been disputed. The take-off from the take-off area as in the U14 and younger age groups is under discussion. The absolute jumping distance of the jumper could be detected using modern measurement methods. A disadvantage would be the loss of excitement in the competition since hitting the take-off board with a high run-up speed has always been an established part of the requirements in the long jump.

When women started taking part in the German championships for the first time in 1920, they competed over 100m, 4 x 100m, in the shot put, and the long jump. The long jump for women became an Olympic discipline in 1948. One of the most important female athletes was the German long jumper Heike Drechsler who retired in 2005. She was the world champion in 1983 and 1993, won the Olympic gold medal in 1992 and 2000, and was awarded four consecutive European titles from 1986 to 1998. Her German record is 7.48m. This is the third best long-jump result ever achieved behind the world record of the Russian Galina Tschistjakowa with 7.52m (1988) and the result of 7.49m achieved by the American heptathlete Jackie Joyner-Kersee. The former East German athlete Heike Drechsler also won international medals in the 100 and 200m sprint when she was young and established a junior world record in the heptathlon. When she competed in the heptathlon 13 years later, as she had done only once, she achieved the best performance for the year 1994.

2.2.2 THE MOST IMPORTANT COMPETITION RULES

The following abridged and simplified International Competition Rules comprise the framework for the techniques and strategy, as well as the organisation of long-jump competitions:

- Figure 1 shows the construction and specifications of a long- (and triple-) jump area.
- The surface of the take-off board, which is sunk and fixed in the ground, is level with the runway and the surface of the landing area. Immediately beyond the take-off line, a plasticine indicator board must be inserted in the take-off board. The take-off board must be white and made of wood or other suitable rigid materials. The plasticine indicator board, also made of wood or other suitable materials, must be of another colour and the plasticine must be of a third contrasting colour if possible.
- The pit should be filled with soft, damp sand.

- The shoe sole may be up to 13 mm thick. Otherwise, the rules mentioned in connection with running (see chapter II–1.1.1) apply.
- The wind velocity is measured for a period of 5 seconds from the beginning of the run-up. The wind gauge is placed 20m from the take-off board and not more than 2m away from the runway. Otherwise, the rules mentioned in connection with the sprint (see chapter II–1.2.1) apply.
- An athlete fails if:
  » he/she touches the ground beyond the take-off line with any part of his/her body while taking off;
  » he/she runs through without jumping;
  » he/she takes off from outside either end of the board, whether beyond or before the extension of the take-off line;
  » he/she touches the ground between the take-off line and the jumping pit;

» he/she employs any form of somersaulting whilst running up or in the act of jumping;

» in the course of landing, he/she touches the ground outside the landing area closer to the take-off line than the nearest break made in the sand; or

» while leaving the landing area, he/she makes his/her first contact

a)

b)

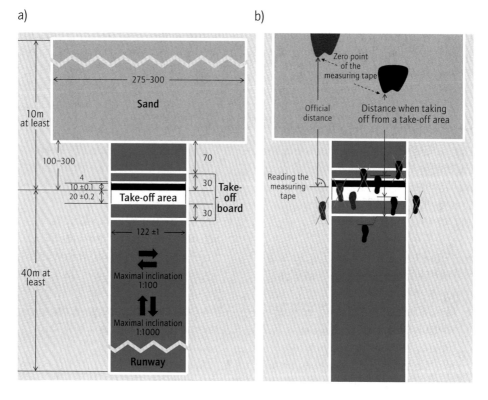

c)

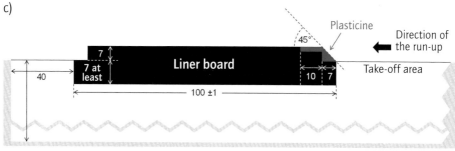

*Figure 1a: **Long-jump area viewed from the top** (specifications in cm, unless otherwise stated)
b: **Measurement, valid and invalid trials in the long jump,** c: **liner board and take-off board from the
side-view** (specifications in mm; modified on the basis of the Rule Commissions by the DLV, FLA, ÖLV
and SLV, 2010, pp. 99-102): The boundary lines of the runway, take-off area, and pit are 5cm wide.*

by foot outside the landing pit closer to the take-off line than the first break in the sand during the landing.
- An athlete does not fail if:
  - » he/she runs outside the white lines marking the runway at any point;
  - » he/she walks back through the landing area after having left the landing area in accordance to the rules; or
  - » he/she takes off before reaching the board.
- All jumps are measured from the nearest break in the landing area made by any part of the body, or anything that was attached to the body at the time it made a mark, to the take-off line, or take-off line extended. The measurement shall be taken perpendicular to the take-off line or its extension. Distances must be recorded to the nearest 0.01m

below the distance measured if the distance measured is not a whole centimetre. A break in the sand is also regarded as such if it is caused by loss of balance.
- In the competitions of U14 and younger age groups a take-off area is allowed (see figure 1b). If the take-off board is more than 1m away from the pit, the 80cm take-off area may be marked on the runway without inclusion of the take-off board. The measurement is performed from the toe of the take-off foot. An athlete does not fail if he/she takes off in front of the take-off area. However, measurement then takes place from the beginning of the take-off area.

Otherwise, the general competition rules for the technical disciplines apply (see chapter II–2.1.1).

2.2.3 SPORT-SCIENCE FINDINGS, PHASE STRUCTURE, AND TECHNIQUE

The introduction to the phase structure and important general comments on the biomechanics and technique of the jumps can be found in chapter II–2.1.2. Therefore, in the following there are only discipline-specific additions.

PHASE 1: RUN-UP

START OF THE RUN-UP
The run-up of top long jumpers is 20–23 strides long, so that the start of the run-up is marked approximately 40–50m in front of the take-off line. For younger athletes,

the following formula may be useful as a rough guide:

Number of strides = age in years + 2.

Some authors recommend a shorter run-up for women by two strides (i.e., number of strides = age in years) due to their lower speed before taking off. Other authors determine the optimal length of the run-up on the basis of specific sprinting times (see table 1).

Table 1: **Length of the run-up depending on sprinting times** *(according to Popov, 1996, p. 18).*

40m time	100m time	Optimal number of strides	
		Women	Men
4.6	10.4		22
4.8	10.9	22	20
5.0	11.3	20	18
5.2	12.0	18	16
5.4	12.5	16	14
5.7	13.0	14	12

START AND PICK-UP ACCELERATION

Carl Lewis (former world record holder over 100m and in the long jump with the second best jump of all time) performed the fastest run-up in the history of the long jump. He is said to have reached a horizontal velocity of 11.8 m/sec during the flight phase of his penultimate stride (table 2 below and table 1 in chapter II–2.1.2 provide further information on run-up velocity).

Run-up velocity is the most important factor affecting long-jump performance. Correlation studies show that run-up velocity explains about 70% of the long-jump performance in groups with heterogeneous ability. However, various athletes achieve both different jumping distances using identical run-up velocities and identical jumping distances using different run-up velocities. In figure 2, single jumps marked by a point would therefore not only lie on the two curves but would also be distributed around them. This means that specifically the take-off, flight, and landing capabilities

are also of crucial importance. Therefore, the relationship described between the run-up velocity and the jumping distance achieved in groups of very homogeneous ability (e.g., among the participants in an Olympic final) is significantly lower and often no longer detectable in several trials of one and the same long jumper. Although the highest run-up velocities are achieved in the long jump as compared to the other jumping events, the general claim that athletes should run up at an optimum velocity for the best possible jumping result is particularly true for young athletes. This is not necessarily the maximum run-up velocity possible.

TAKE-OFF PREPARATION

The take-off preparation of most athletes is characterised by the already-described short-long-short rhythm (see table 3, figure 3, and chapter II–2.1.2).

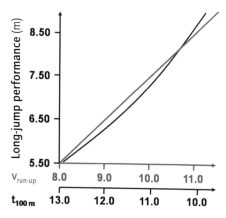

Figure 2: **Relationship between long-jump distance and run-up velocity** *(v_run-up (m/sec); modified on the basis of Killing et al., 2008, p. 125) or the 100m time (t_100 m (sec); according to the equation by Hegner, 2003: long-jump performance = 523 • t_100 m^{-1.78}).*

*Table 2: **Average take-off parameters in the long jump** (according to Killing et al., 2008, p. 126).*

	Target performance (m)	Run-up velocity (m/sec)	Contact time (sec)	Departure angle (degrees)	Vertical departure velocity (m/sec)	Loss of horizontal velocity (m/sec)	Swing-leg velocity (degrees/ sec)
Women	6.00	8.7	0.12	19.9	2.7	1.2	748
	6.35	9.0	0.12	20.0	2.8	1.2	759
	6.70	9.4	0.12	21.1	3.1	1.3	776
Men	7.00	9.7	0.12	19.6	2.9	1.3	762
	7.50	10.0	0.12	20.3	3.1	1.4	812
	8.00	10.4	0.11	20.9	3.3	1.5	840

*Table 3: **Normal range of stride-length ratios between the last strides** (according to the Frankfurt Olympic Training Centre, quoted from Knapp, 2008, p. 11).*

	Third last to penultimate stride	Penultimate stride to last stride
Women	102–110 %	87–97 %
Men	104–112 %	88–96 %

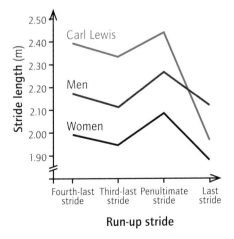

*Figure 3: **Lengths of the run-up strides at the 1987 World Championships in Rome** (modified on the basis of the IAF, 1988).*

However, there are very good jumpers who deviate from this. Bob Beamon, for example, is said to have achieved his world-record jump described in the introduction with a final stride which was much longer than the penultimate stride (penultimate stride: 2.40m; final stride: 2.60m). In general, the take-off preparation which is described in more detail below seems to have considerable room for individual variations.

In the third-last contact with the ground, the jumper pushes off forward powerfully with his later take-off leg. The result of this is not only a typically extended stride, but the fact that in most cases the jumper reaches the peak of his/her run-up velocity in the flight phase of the penultimate stride. However, the maximum knee extension is often slightly reduced during this push-off compared to maximum sprint. On the one hand, this results in a very flat push-off and the first lowering of the CG. On the other hand, this enables the athlete to move his/her take-off forward and upward early.

When the athlete's foot is placed down on the penultimate ground contact, the knee of the take-off leg should only be slightly behind or even beside or in front of the knee of the supporting leg. This allows the take-off leg to be placed down quickly from above despite the short final stride.

The touchdown of the foot during the penultimate ground contact (swing-leg squat) is usually performed from an incomplete heel lift. The development of braking forces during the front support should also be minimised during the penultimate ground contact. Since the CG is already lowered during the penultimate stride, the leg must be placed down with a little more flexion than in the free sprint to still be able to land as close to the vertical projection of the CG as possible. However, the touchdown of the foot is usually further ahead of the CG than in the free sprint (see figure 4). Although most athletes demonstrate a touchdown with the entire foot, some authors favour a support on only the ball of the foot with greater knee flexion, as was demonstrated by Ivan Pedroso.

The amortisation of the knee joint takes longer during the penultimate ground contact than in normal sprint strides. While the jumper extends (shifts forward) his/her hips, the knee is kept flexed until the foot of the take-off leg overtakes the support leg. This results in the maintenance of the low CG position (or further lowering) and the straightening (backward rotation) of the trunk into the backward reclining take-off position. This is followed by another flat

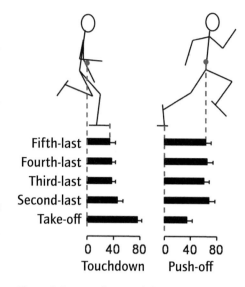

Figure 4: **Average foot touchdown and push-off relative to the vertical projection of the CG during the last five ground contacts of 20 long jumpers on the national level** (modified on the basis of Hay, 1995).

push-off with incomplete knee extension in the rear support phase. All this is usually accompanied by a slight loss of horizontal velocity. However, a loss of more than 0.3 m/sec from the penultimate stride to the last stride is a sign of a technical error. (The unusual stride pattern demonstrated by Bob Beamon perhaps results in a better push-off into the take-off and thus in a smaller loss of velocity.)

Figure 5: **Last run-up stride: from the swing-leg squat to the touchdown of the take-off leg.**

Some jumpers increase the lowering of their CG by placing their foot to the outside during the penultimate touchdown (see figure 6). The extent of the complete lowering of the CG from the sprint position to the touchdown of the take-off leg follows an optimum trend (see figure 9 in chapter II–2.1.2). In general, the CG is lowered by 5-10cm.

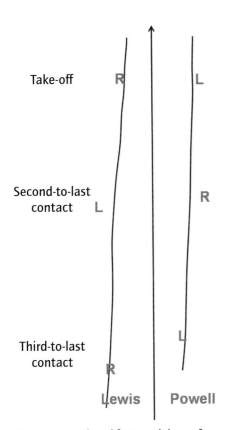

Figure 6: **CG path and foot touchdown of two long jumpers from above** (Carl Lewis: 8.72m; Mike Powell: 8.95m; according to Pozzo & Schlarb, 1997): Besides placing the penultimate contact to the outside, it is also striking that the take-off foot is placed slightly on the wrong side of the CG for stabilising the take-off.

PHASE 2: TAKE-OFF

Table 2 shows some biomechanical parameters of the long jump take-off (see also table 1 in chapter II–2.1.2). In the long jump, the distance of lift of the CG during take-off is approximately 15–20 cm. The vertical velocity of departure explains 25–42% of the long-jump performance (with correlation coefficients of 0.50 to 0.65).

During the amortisation, the knee of the take-off leg is bent to an angle of 140–150°. This is based on ground reaction forces (see chapter II–1.1.2) which even during the impact of a 6m jump briefly exceed the long jumper's body weight (or the weight force) by more than 11 times. For good female athletes, the average force in the vertical direction over the entire duration of the take-off is about four times the weight force, while for male athletes it is approximately six times the weight force. Figure 7 gives an idea of the

Figure 7: **Ground reaction forces during the takeoff** (not to scale): If there are forces whose lines of action do not run through the CG, a rotation is initiated. At the start of the take-off, a forward rotation is triggered, which may be counteracted slightly toward the end of the take-off.

magnitude and direction of the (ground reaction) forces and thus also explains the forward rotation occurring during the take-off.

When placing the take-off leg on the ground, the trunk is leaned backward by about 5–10° from the vertical (backward reclining take-off position). If the shoulders are further forward when placing the foot down, the forward rotation is greater; if they were and still remained further backward, even a reverse rotation could be initiated. The induced forward rotation of the entire body is indicated by the slight forward rotation of the trunk during the take-off (standard values measured at the Frankfurt Olympic Training Centre: 2–6° for females, 4–8° for men). The head remains upright with the view directed straight to the front during the take-off and the subsequent flight.

In general, the take-off in the long jump is accompanied by a contralateral arm swing. The motion is similar to that in the sprint. The fingertips of the front hand should not swing above eye level, while the rear hand should swing maximally to just behind the hip. The double-arm swing is very rare in world-class athletes. It is regarded as disadvantageous since it is extremely difficult in terms of coordination to change from the contralateral arm swing to the double-arm swing at (nearly) maximum running velocity. Often, when placing the foot on the ground to take off, the shoulder on the swing-leg side is a little further forward than the shoulder on the side of the take-off leg (slight shoulder-

hip separation). As a result, a powerful arm swing is performed during the take-off leading to an opposite slight twist (the shoulder on the side of the take-off leg is a little further forward than the swing-leg shoulder). The arm swing counteracts the rotational momentum of the swing leg about the longitudinal axis.

PHASE 3: FLIGHT

Figure 8 shows the partial distances which constitute the officially measured competition distance. The take-off position distance is approximately 40cm (depending on body height). The ultimate goal in the long jump is the initiation of the longest possible CG flight distance (DFI) upon take-off.

Three flight techniques are used:

* stride jump;
* hang jump; and
* running jump.

None of the flight techniques can affect the CG flight distance. Three functions of the flight phase can be distinguished which the jumper performs roughly in the following order regardless of his/her flight technique:

* continuation of the take-off;
* reduction of forward rotation; and
* landing preparation.

STRIDE JUMP

The stride-jump technique is considered to be the target technique for beginners (see figure. 9). In this technique, the

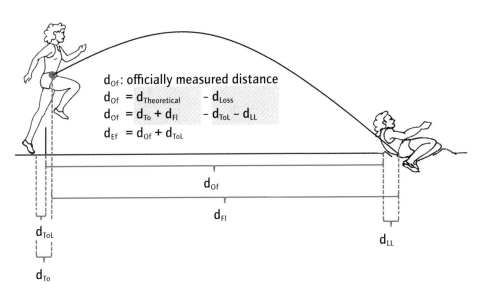

d_{Of}: officially measured distance

$$d_{Of} = d_{Theoretical} - d_{Loss}$$

$$d_{Of} = d_{To} + d_{Fl} - d_{ToL} - d_{LL}$$

$$d_{Ef} = d_{Of} + d_{ToL}$$

*Figure 8: **Simple model of the partial distances of the long jump** (modified on the basis of Arampatzis et al., 1999).*

d_{To}: Take-off position distance: from the tip of the take-off foot to the vertical projection of the CG at the moment of leaving the ground

d_{Fl}: CG flight distance: from the vertical projection of the CG at the moment of leaving the ground to the theoretical point of impact of the CG in the sand

d_{ToL}: Take-off loss: from the tip of the take-off foot to the take-off line

d_{LL}: Landing loss: from the first break made by the jumper in the sand behind the take-off line to the theoretical landing point of the CG in the sand. (The former is always in front of the latter in the jumping direction. If the jumper places his/her feet beyond the landing point of the CG, he/she inevitably falls backward. Even by actively grasping the sand, the first break in the sand cannot be shifted behind the theoretical landing point of the CG [see phase 4]).

d_{Ef}: Effective jumping distance

take-off is continued to the extent that athletes are generally taught to maintain the take-off position shortly after leaving the ground. On the one hand, this is supposed to prevent the jumper from giving up his/her take-off extension too early even during ground contact. On the other hand, the extended posture reduces the jumper's forward rotation. Since the rotational momentum initiated upon the take-off remains the same, the rotational velocity is smaller if the masses of the body segments move on a larger radius about the rotational axis through the CG. An example of this is an ice skater who during a pirouette presses his/her arms close to his/her body to rotate faster. This principle is used with all flight techniques alike.

Figure 9: **Stride-jump technique.**

Later, in the stride jump, the take-off leg is moved forward to the swing leg. While doing so, it is bent at the knee (to reduce the required torque) and moved either under the body or to the front similar to the trail leg in the hurdles sprint. The arm on the swing-leg side, which is kept behind the body during the take-off position, is moved contralaterally to the movement of the take-off leg, first backward and upward and then forward over the head to a position alongside the other arm. Finally, both legs are extended at the knee joint, the hips are bent in a jackknife position, and the hands are moved forward to a position next to the feet.

HANG JUMP

If the jumping distance is 5m or longer, the jumper has enough time for the hang jump (see figure 10). Here jumpers are also recommended to maintain the take-off position for a short time. Thereafter, the arm on the side of the take-off leg and the swing leg are lowered synchronously and are moved alongside the respective other limb. While doing so, the swing leg is extended and moved backward (see running jump for justification), while the jumper pushes his/her pelvis forward. The arms, which are now extended, are moved in a semi-circular motion behind the body and then over the head. The hang

Figure 10: **Hang-jump technique.**

*Figure 11: **Running-jump technique with 1½ strides in the air.***

position has been reached. Depending on the flight distance or duration, there is some delay in the hang position. From this hyperextension, the jackknife movement is performed vigorously. To facilitate the movement, the legs are bent at the knee joint while they are brought forward and then they are extended again to prepare for the landing. The arms continue their circular swing until they are next to the feet. This circular swing counteracts the forward rotation initiated upon take-off. Since the rotational momentum of the entire body remains the same during the flight phase, the rest of the body rotates backward opposite to the arms.

RUNNING JUMP

There are two versions of the running jump: Figure 11 shows the simpler version with 1½ strides in the air, which may be carried out if the jumping distance is 5.50m at least. The more complex version, which requires a minimum jumping distance of approximately 7.50m and is therefore almost exclusively used by men, includes 2½ steps. (An exception was the relatively small Russian 7.33m jumper Tatyana Lebedeva.)

DISCOURSE I: DO YOU COUNT IN ENGLISH OR IN GERMAN?

When Germans speak about the most complex running-jump technique, they talk about a jump consisting of 3½ strides. However, English speakers that mean the same jump call it the two-step running-in-the-air style or the two-step hitch-kick. Germans count how often the legs, while in the air, are spread in one direction and then back again in the other direction. From this point of view, the take-off position is the first stride. English speakers count the movement cycles after the take-off. At the end of the contralateral running motion, the rear leg must be brought forward to the other leg for landing. In order to describe this movement, ½ is often added in both terminologies. According to the German method of counting, the stride jump is therefore a running jump consisting of 1½ strides.

Without maintaining the take-off position, the running-style jumper tries to continue his/her running motion, initiated by the hips, while in the air. In contrast to the hang jump, the take-off leg is not kept behind the body, but is moved forward and upward contralaterally to the lowering of the swing leg. Again, the athlete reaches a stride position which is reverse to the previous one. In the running jump with 2½ strides, the athlete continues his/her running motion to switch to the first stride position again. In both cases, the legs are moved backward with the knee joint extended and moved forward and with the knee joint flexed. As described in the sprint, the lower leg follows primarily the thigh and its own inertia.

The backward movement of the straight leg and the forward movement of the bent leg counteract the forward rotation initiated upon take-off. Due to the larger radius of the leg segments around the pivot point, the rotational momentum, which is necessary for the equally fast backward movement, is greater than the rotational momentum required for the forward swing. The backward movement is identical to a forward rotation, so that the rest of the body rotates backward according to the law mentioned above (see figure 12).

During the strides in the air, the jumper pushes his/her hips forward as is the case in the hang jump to prepare for moving into the jackknife position from hyperextension. The leg which is behind at the end of the contralateral movement is

*Figure 12: **Testing the described biomechanical principle:** If the athlete, who is lying on a rotatable platform, makes running motions with his legs, his upper body will turn backward*

brought forward for landing similar to the stride jump. The extended arms are swung contralaterally to the leg actions on a semi-circle from behind the body over the head to the front of the body during each forward swing of the respective opposite leg. Correspondingly, the arms are swung in a semi-circle downward and behind the body during the backward swing of the leg on the respective opposite side of the body. In the running jump with 2½ strides, two semi-circular swings more than in the hang jump counteract the forward rotation initiated upon take-off (see figure 13).

Movement of the arms
during the
forward swing

of
the
respective
opposite
leg

backward swing

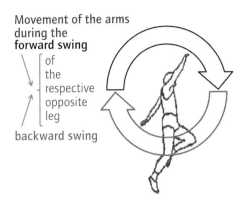

Figure 13: **Arm actions during the running jump**
(modified on the basis of Tidow, 2007, p. 15).

DISCOURSE II: ADVANTAGES AND DISADVANTAGES OF THE HANG AND RUNNING JUMP

The primary objective of the hang-jump technique is the preparation of the landing. The reactive force created through the hyperextension results in a particularly exaggerated hip and trunk flexion and ultimately in a good landing with very little loss of distance upon landing. However, with beginners, there is the risk that the hang position will become an end in itself and that the landing will be prepared much too late so that there will be a loss of distance upon landing. Even for advanced athletes, the hang jump may have an adverse impact on the take-off. In anticipation of the hang position, either the swing leg is raised not actively enough, or the athlete assumes a hollow-back posture even upon take-off. This relaxation of the abdominal muscles not only increases the load on the spine, but also impairs the development and transmission of force during the take-off.

In contrast, the supposed advantage of the running jump is the best possible transition from the run-up to the flight phase. The take-off extension and slowing down of the swing leg are performed as a continuous, natural movement. The described anti-rotational effect of the running and arm movement also favours an active, aggressive take-off forward. Since the running jump (especially its 2½-stride version) requires more time during the flight phase than the hang jump, it may easily occur that the athlete is unable to perform a technically correct landing, mainly because his limbs are brought to a parallel position very late. Nevertheless, it is recommended for athletes to use the running jump, provided the flight duration is long enough for both flight techniques, since the take-off (i.e., the generation of the longest possible CG trajectory) should be the focus of attention in the long jump.

PHASE 4: LANDING

The objective of the landing movement is the minimisation of loss upon landing (see figure 8). To achieve this, the jumper tries to place down his/her heels closed side by side as far as possible from the take-off board and to land with his/her buttocks also equally distant from the board. The landing technique should be largely independent of the flight technique.

Beginners are first taught to relax their knees (soft knees) and to let their buttocks fall on or next to the heels. The target technique for advanced athletes is more complex.

It begins from a jackknife position in which the legs are approximately horizontal and the hands are approximately next to the feet (see figure 14). Shortly before landing, the hip angle is opened again causing the legs to be lowered for the first ground contact in the sand. When they reach the sand, the heel-hip line is at approximately a 30° angle to the ground and the upper body is nearly upright again. The jumper tries to actively pull himself/herself forward into the sand by extending his/her hips and actively flexing his/her knees. In combination with the resistance of the sand, the landing movement leads to a backward rotation of the trunk. The tension of the hip and trunk flexors must then prevent the jumper from falling backward into the sand.

There are many individual variations in respect to the arm movement (see figures 9–11). In most cases, it is recommended that the arms continue their circular swing downward and backward during the first ground contact. Touching the sand with a hand or arm should be avoided when it occurs closer to the take-off board than the breaks caused by the feet or pelvis. According to Newton's third law (action = reaction), the arm swing backward leads to a forward shift of the pelvis, which should land exactly in the hole made by the feet or equidistant from the take-off board alongside that hole. A lateral landing is often caused by moving the rear leg forward at the end of a stride or running jump as is the case with the trail leg in the hurdles. The movement around the outside results in the rotation of the trunk in the opposite direction about the longitudinal axis.

Figure 14: **Landing movement.**

*Table 4: **Requirement profile for the long jump:** The suggested rough estimate of the value of selected factors determining performance is based on the importance for the overall performance and the percentage of time spent training (IR: information requirements, constr.: constraints; see chapter I–1.1).*

Factors determining the long-jump performance	Estimate of value	Notes
Coordination	+ + + +	optical IR: high, acoustic IR: low, tactile IR: low, kinaesthetic IR: medium, vestibular IR: medium; precision constr.: high, time constr.: high, complexity constr.: medium–high, situation constr.: low, physical stress constr.: low
Flexibility	+ +	no extreme movement amplitudes required
Strength		articular significance of the extensor loop (glutes, quadriceps, triceps surae, erector spinae), iliopsoas, hamstrings, abdominal muscles, adductors, shoulder and upper-arm muscles
Maximal strength	+ + + +	as a decisive basis
Reactive strength	+ + + + +	mainly of the extensor loop
Speed	+ + + + +	mainly cyclic; acyclic aspects during take-off preparation, take-off, flight, and landing
Endurance (general dynamic) Anaerobic endurance		
Strength endurance	+	as a basis at the most
Speed endurance	+ +	as a basis to be able to perform nine trials (practice and competition trials) at the same level of performance
Aerobic endurance	+ +	only as a basis for training (regeneration ability)
Psychological and cognitive abilities	+ + + + +	concentration ability (on the point); performance-oriented thinking and behaviour (see chapter I-3.1.1)
Anthropometric and primarily genetically determined characteristics	+ + + + +	high percentage of the fastest muscle fibres; connective tissue with optimal energy storage capacities; rather above-average body height; low percentage of body fat

2.2.4 SUMMARY OF THE MOST IMPORTANT TECHNICAL CHARACTERISTICS = TECHNIQUE-ANALYSIS SHEET

RUN-UP

START OF THE RUN-UP

- Run-up length with top athletes: approx. 20–23 strides (40–50m); with younger athletes: number of strides = age in years (with male youths possibly plus 2 strides); or on the basis of sprinting times.
- Start of the run-up usually from a standing position.

START AND PICK-UP ACCELERATION

- Rapid but not maximal acceleration to optimal velocity for taking off and achieving a maximum jumping distance.
- First toe push-off, then grasping/pulling sprint with high knees and erect trunk and pelvis.
- Landing on the intermediate marker 4–7 strides in front of the take-off board.
- Subconscious adjustment of stride length to hit the take-off board optimally.

TAKE-OFF PREPARATION

- Direction of view away from the take-off board straight forward parallel to the ground.
- Emphasis on stride frequency.
- Lowering of the CG of the body particularly between the third-last and penultimate support.
- Normally by using a short-long-short rhythm with a powerful, flat push-off during the third-last support with an incomplete extension of the knee joint.
- After an incomplete lifting of the heel, the bent leg is placed down for the penultimate support (swing-leg squat) as close as possible to the vertical projection of the CG; often the entire sole of the foot is placed on the ground.
- Prolonged amortisation at the knee joint and forward shift of the pelvis; maintenance of the low position of the CG (or further lowering), backward rotation of the trunk and incomplete knee-joint extension during the push-off.

TAKE-OFF

- After a slightly reduced knee lift and a flat curve of foot movement, the (almost) straight take-off leg is actively placed on the take-off board from above while performing a backward pulling movement.
- Touchdown of the entire foot sole.
- The position of the foot in front of the vertical projection of the CG and the trunk angle (5–10° behind the vertical) during the touchdown of the foot determine the bracing angle; the optimal bracing angle results in an optimal departure angle.
- Little flexion at the knee joint during amortisation (up to approx. 145°).
- Powerful push-off extension of the foot, knee, hip, and trunk.
- The shoulders are kept back to minimise the forward rotation (forward rotation of the trunk by 2–8° during take-off).
- Rapid raising and deceleration of the swing elements (swing leg is moved into the three 90° position; contralateral arm swing).

FLIGHT

STRIDE JUMP

- Short holding of the take-off position: the trunk is upright, the extended take-off leg points backward to the take-off spot, the swing leg is at the three-90°-angles position.
- The take-off leg is acutely angled at the knee joint and is brought alongside the swing leg either under the body or by using a movement similar to the trail-leg movement in the hurdles.
- The rear arm is swung contralaterally far behind the body, then over the head and alongside the other arm.
- Hip flexion; knee extension and further movement of both hands forward until they are alongside the feet.

HANG JUMP

- After take-off, the take-off leg is extended, the swing leg and the front arm are moved contralaterally downward and backward until they are alongside the respective other limb.
- Forward shift of the hips and swing of the extended arms over the head until the hang position is reached.
- Bending of both knees; bending of the hips.
- Extension of the knees and further movement of both hands forward until they are alongside the feet in the jackknife position.

RUNNING JUMP

- Continuation of the running movement in the air: 1½ or 2½ running strides in the air.
- The extended arms are swung contralaterally; each arm swings in a semi-circle from behind the body over the head to the front of the body while the bent leg on the respective opposite side of the body swings forward; from the front, each arm swings in a semi-circle downward and behind the body while the extended leg on the respective opposite side of the body swings backward.
- Forward shift of the hips.
- After the (last) running stride: The athlete takes the jackknife position (as in the stride jump).

LANDING

- The hip angle is opened and the knee-joint flexion is initiated shortly before landing, resulting in an active landing with grasping heels.
- The continuation of the arm swing downward and backward results in a forward shift of the hips; the athlete should avoid sand contact with his/her hands too early.
- The heels and the buttocks should land in the sand at equal distance from the take-off board: the buttocks should possibly land slightly beside the heels.

2.2.5 PHOTO SEQUENCES

HANG JUMP

Data about the photo sequence

Athlete:	Bianca Kappler (born: 8 August 1977, Germany)
Height/weight:	1.80 m/63 kg
Performance:	6.73 m (10 August 2007, Leverkusen)
Best performance:	6.90 m (7 July 2007, Bad Langensalza)
Greatest success:	Fifth at the 2007 World Championships, multiple German champion

COMMENTARY

The photo sequence was made in Bianca Kappler's best year which she crowned with a 6.81m jump at the world championships. As is often observed in high-performance athletes, she significantly improved her performances following parental leave (2006). Although her last jump at the European Indoor Championships in 2005 was measured as 6.96m, Kappler was certain that she could not jump so far. She told this to the judges, who after detailed video analyses equated her with the third placed athlete (6.59m). For her conduct, she was awarded the Fair Play Trophy by the International Olympic Committee.

In the illustrated jump, Kappler achieves her highest measured run-up velocity until that point (see table 5), which is due not only to her superior sprinting technique, but also to her significantly improved basic performances (see table 6). After having been behind her intermediate mark by approximately 15cm with her fifth-last ground contact, Kappler lands on the take-off board almost perfectly after a relatively long penultimate stride. Her short-long-short rhythm includes a relatively marked swing-leg squat (picture 4). From there, she places her almost extended take-off leg in an active pulling manner on the take-off board (pictures 7 and 8) and achieves a relatively noticeable backward reclining take-off position although it is still within the normal range (longitudinal axis of the trunk 8° and line between the CG and the rear of the heel 25° behind the vertical). Nevertheless, she is subsequently able to achieve an optimum take-off extension after only little amortisation (minimum knee angle = 153°). The take-off position of the swing elements is also optimal: the thigh of the swing leg is horizontal and the contralateral arm movements are active. Subsequently, the lowering and extension of the swing leg and the backward and upward movement of the arms lead to the typical hang position (picture 11). Kappler's back lands 7cm closer to the take-off board than the first break in the sand made by her heels (0cm would be optimal). Upon the first contact with the sand, Kappler's knees are relatively straight and her upper body is bent considerably forward. It is difficult to tell whether the relatively noticeable forward rotation of the trunk (8°) during take-off and/or the somewhat early taking of the jackknife position (picture 13) have led to too much forward rotation or whether Kappler should have opened her hip angle earlier before landing. In general, however, a little more active landing with a dynamic pull-though of the arms, grasping the sand, and forward pushing of the hips seems possible.

Table 5: **Biomechanical measuring values of the jump presented** *(according to Knapp, 2008, p. 11).*

Distances (m)		Stride lengths (m)			Velocities (m/sec)					CG lowering (m)	Take-off duration (sec)	Angle of departure (°)	Angular velocity of the swing-leg hip (°/sec)
					horizontal			vertical					
official	effective	third last	penultimate	last	third last	penultimate	last	after take-off					
6.73	6.75	2.21	2.45	2.16	9.41	9.58	9.43	8.12	2.83	0.10	0.12	19.2	801

Table 6: **Test values of Bianca Kappler in the year 2007** *(according to Knapp, 2008, p. 11).*

Tests	Results
30m flying	3.21 sec
100m competition	11.88 sec
Long jump from 11 run-up strides	6.28m
Jumping tests	
5-stride bounding run (from a run-up)	20.01m
3-stride hop (from a run-up)	12.11m
triple take-off test with one intermediate stride (from a run-up)	18.15m
triple take-off test with three intermediate strides (from a run-up)	27.60m
standing long jump	3.07m
Strength tests	
snatch	55 kg
clean	75 kg
deep frontal squat	85 kg
half squat	155 kg
tossing the shot forward	20.45m
tossing the shot backward	21.30m

Table 7: **Biomechanical measuring values of Iván Pedroso's jump presented in the following** *(according to Arampatzis et al., 1999, pp. 90-92).*

Distances (m)					Stride lengths (m)			Velocities (m/sec)		Angle of departure (°)
								horizontal	vertical	
official	effective	theoretical	take-off loss	landing loss	third last	penultimate	last	before take-off	after take-off	
8.42	8.50	8.67	0.08	0.17	2.28	2.43	2.16	10.82	8.72 (-2.1) 3.86	23.9

RUNNING JUMP

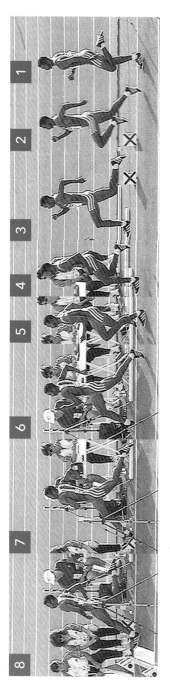

Data about the photo sequence
Athlete:	Iván Pedroso (born: 17 December 1972, Cuba)
Height/weight:	1.76 m/70 kg
Performance:	8.42 m (5 August 1997, Athens)
Best performance:	8.71 m (18 July 2007, Salamanca)
Greatest success:	World champion 1995, 1997, 1999, and 2001, Olympic winner 2000

COMMENTARY

The photo sequence shows Pedroso's winning jump, which was his first trial, at the 1997 World Championships, with which he won his second of four consecutive world champion titles.

The video, which is the basis of this photo sequence, shows that Pedroso takes off from a highly rhythmic run-up. After three relaxed skipping strides he initiates the start acceleration: seven high-frequency strides with marked forward lean and view directed to the ground. The eighth stride is a slight jump and leads over to a toe push-off run with long strides. During the subsequent twelve strides, Pedroso increases his stride frequency and raises his trunk only very gradually. He significantly increases his stride frequency only during the last three strides, straightens his trunk completely, and achieves the active knee lift which is seen in picture 3. Table 7 shows that he takes off from the typical short-long-short rhythm. In pictures 4 and 5 it is striking how early his take-off leg overtakes his support leg during the swing-leg squat. This helps him to perform an active pulling touchdown on the board. In picture 8—Pedroso has not yet placed

his take-off foot on the board—it is clearly visible that the hip on the side of the take-off leg is much more extended than in picture 7, which helps him to move his take-off foot under his body with his leg extended.

The biomechanical analysis shows that Pedroso's departure angle was the largest of all investigated jumps of the finalists. However, this alone is not a sufficient explanation of his success. What made him a winner was the fact that he achieved the highest vertical departure velocity from one of the highest run-up velocities while losing relatively little horizontal velocity. In addition to a good technique, superior strength capacities are required to bear the compression forces during the amortisation and to achieve the ideal push-off extension demonstrated in picture 10.

Picture 11 illustrates the first switch of legs of his running-jump technique. The extended swing leg is moved backward, while the bent take-off leg is moved forward. In picture 12, the first running stride in the air has almost been completed. The former swing leg is behind the body, while the take-off leg is in front of the body. The contralateral forward circling of the arms is clearly visible. Picture 13 shows the end position of the second running stride. The arms and legs are in a position which is an almost exact reversal of the position shown in picture 12. The rotation of the limbs has well counteracted the forward rotation initiated upon take-off. The slight forward lean of the trunk during the take-off position has turned into a slight backward lean of the trunk.

Picture 14 shows an asymmetrical jackknife position, as is quite often seen in running-style jumpers. Often, their landing does not appear very active either, so there

doesn't seem to be an active touchdown of the heels or forward shifting of the hips. However, with a landing loss of 17cm between the calculated landing point of the CG in the sand and the actual break in the sand, Pedroso is still among the top half of the finalists.

2.2.6 DIDACTICS: SUPERORDINATE LONG-TERM OBJECTIVES AND GENERAL METHODOLOGY

The long jump is one of the classical athletics disciplines which is introduced first to young athletes. In special competitions for children, the jumping distances achieved are often divided into zones. Jumpers are awarded a certain number of points depending on the zones they land in (e.g., 30cm long). In the zone long jump, the sum of three jumps is often counted instead of the longest jump. There is also a wide variety of games and exercises forms including jumps for distance, distance plus height, over an object, and onto an object (sometimes in the form of relays). Rarely, and only with proper safety precautions and few repetitions, are athletes asked to jump down from an object since the stress on the not yet fully grown musculoskeletal system is very high in this case.

Forms of games and exercises with two-legged take-offs improve coordination in a versatile manner and have a strengthening effect. However, special emphasis should be placed on one-legged jumps from a run-up with both the right and the left leg being used as take-off legs. These jumps are used for practising the most important

element of athletics jumps: the one-legged take-off with take-off extension and the use of the swing elements after appropriate take-off preparation. Learning the stride-jump technique is also aimed at this objective.

Although in basic training the jumping strength is usually not sufficient for a (hang or) running jump, meaning athletes keep using the stride jump, the (hang and) running jump should nevertheless already be prepared. This may be done by performing occasional jumps from an elevated (run-up and) take-off which leads to a longer flight phase. A take-off from a resilient springboard may also be used for a short term (see, however, chapter II-2.1.4).

However, flight and landing techniques are only of secondary importance. In addition to take-off training, the training of sprinting speed is of decisive importance even in children's athletics (see chapter II-1.3.7). Run-up accuracy is also of only secondary importance. Jumps are often performed from a free run-up and take-off.

In some exercises, the obstacles or the use of a take-off zone require the athletes to control their run-up length automatically.

Simple and varied forms of multiple jumps, especially skipping (87), should also be learned beginning with children's athletics. They may be used in the form of games as an alternative to running. If they are performed as exercise forms, the focus should be on the development of the correct technique. Beginning with build-up training, they are increasingly performed as reactive-strength training at maximum effort. High-intensity forms of jumping are not introduced until late in training. Therefore, things like downhill jumps (92), continuous one-legged jumps from a run-up (89), and jumps from a supramaximal run-up (290) are reserved for (high-)performance training. They require good technical fundamentals and strength capacities.

SAFETY ASPECTS

The landing area must be smooth and even. Therefore, the sand should be raked after each jump. Prolonged phases of non-use or rain may require digging and thorough raking of the sand. The sand should be free of objects such as rocks or glass. Soft-floor mats should neither be so hard that the jumper's impact upon landing is too high nor so soft that the jumper hits the ground below the mat. Large drop heights, in particular in the case of landing on one leg and soft ground, may lead to twisting one's ankle and therefore require at a minimum appropriate concentration. Particularly when taking off in running shoes from artificial tracks, the take-off zone must not be wet or slippery due to sand. If the take-off is performed from an elevation, this must not slide off. Indoors, the top elements of gym boxes may be prevented from sliding off by means of gym mats, for example.

2.2.7 TRAINING CONTENTS: FORMS OF GAMES AND EXERCISES

Due to the great importance of sprinting speed for the long jump, all training forms presented in connection with the 100m sprint (see chapter II–1.3.8) are also used in long-jump training. For training the ability to establish rhythm, (particularly frequency-oriented) hurdle sprints are a general part of long-jump training (see chapter II–1.8.8, e.g. 190). Moreover, the exercises of the ABCs of jumping and multiple jumps described in connection with the general forms of strength training (see chapter I–5.4.6) are an important part of long-jump training.

261 ▌ Shadow jumping

Possible objectives: Jumping technique; (reactive) strength and speed; specific warm-up.

Execution: Two partners run behind one another; the runner behind must imitate the jumping forms performed by the front runner; change of tasks; change of partners.

Variations: Integration of ABCs of jumping.

Typical load standards: 5 min at most; frequent changes of tasks and partners.

262 ▌ Jumping garden

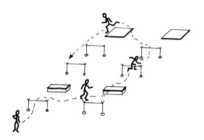

Possible objectives: Jumping technique; (reactive) strength and speed; specific warm-up.

Execution: Athletes run criss-cross through the garden and jump over the set-up objects in the order they like.

Variations: Use broad and/or high objects; athletes may be asked to take off from both legs, to run faster, to land on the swing or take-off leg or on both legs; possibly the take-off points may be marked by gymnastics hoops.

Typical load standards: 5 min at most; walking intervals; change of tasks.

263 ▌ "Who is afraid of the evil man/woman?"

Possible objectives: Sprinting and jumping technique; (reactive) strength and (reaction) speed.

Execution: For set-up, see picture; the catcher shouts: "Who is afraid of the evil man/woman?"; the teammates answer: "Nobody!"; catcher: "And if he comes?"; the teammates answer: "Then we'll run!" and try to run to the other mat without being touched by the catcher and to save themselves by jumping over the obstacle; teammates who

are nevertheless touched by the catcher will be additional catchers in the next round; if the majority are catchers, the remaining players are declared winners and a next run-through is started with only one catcher.
Variations: May also be performed as pure sprinting game.
Typical load standards: 3–5 run-throughs.

---

264  **Fishing net**

Possible objectives: Jumping technique; (reactive) strength and speed.
Execution: Two children, the fishers, run through the gym with a stretched elastic cord, while the others must jump over it.
Variations: Vary pace.
Typical load standards: Each child is a fisherman 1–3 times.

---

265 **Jump variations**

Possible objectives: Versatile jumping technique; (reactive) strength and speed; differential learning.
Execution/variations: After a (two-legged or) one-legged take-off, the jumper performs the following movements in the air: tuck, straddle, pike, strong contortion, touching heels, rotation about the longitudinal axis of the body, etc.; children invent movement variations (somersaults are forbidden).
Typical load standards: Until the children run out of new ideas.

266 **Pendulum relay with jumps over obstacles**

Possible objectives: Jumping technique; (reactive) strength and speed.
Execution: See 111.
Variations: See 262; over gym mat, banana boxes, etc.
Typical load standards: Not more than 2 or 3 times over the same setup.

267 **Jumping in a square**

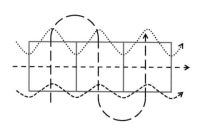

Possible objectives: Jumping technique; (reactive) strength and speed.
Execution: Streamers are stretched at 50–100cm height to mark squares as shown in the picture; the dashed lines indicate various running and jumping routes.
Variations: Jumps from a diagonal run-up are used particularly for preparing the high jump; possibly in groups of two synchronously or against each other for time.
Typical load standards: Each path no more than 2–3 times.

268 **ABCs of jumping: pop-up jump**

Possible objectives: Jumping technique; (reactive) strength and speed.
Execution: One-legged take-off from run-up with maintenance of the take-off position.
Variations: First from a short run-up (5–8 strides), then from a medium run-up (9–14 strides), and finally from a long run-up (more than 14 strides) or full competition run-up; from a high-knee run with high stride frequency (112) or step-overs (117); over obstacles (banana boxes, foam blocks, mini-hurdles, etc.); rather for distance than for

height; with orientation point to look at straight far behind the pit or with eyes closed; with orientation for height: the head is supposed to touch a band stretched over the pit, for example; from a short run-up with telemark landing (see line drawing) in the pit to prompt the athlete to maintain the take-off position.

Typical load standards: 3 to 6 times per leg and run-up length.

---

269 ▮▮▮▮▮ **ABCs of jumping: pop-up jumps onto gym boxes**

Possible objectives: Jumping technique (the box requires raising one's swing leg and keeping it in a high position, and taking off upward); (reactive) strength and speed.

Execution: Jump onto a high gym box with 2–4 elements; when running down from the box, the touchdown is absorbed by a gym mat or (even better) a small box; the trunk is kept upright, the take-off in front of the box should be performed actively by placing the foot on the ground from above.

Variations: With distance marker to enforce the take-off forward; with double-arm swing (for the high jump); with different distances between the boxes; bilateral practice.

Typical load standards: 2–4 times per leg and task.

---

270 ▮▮▮▮▮ **ABCs of jumping: pop-up jumps landing on the swing leg**

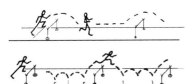

Possible objectives: Jumping technique; (reactive) strength and speed.

Execution: Like 268, but with landing and continuation of the run on the swing leg and repeated take-off (see picture).

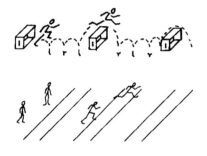

Variations: First by using mainly the 3- and 5-stride rhythm (take-off always from the same leg, in the subsequent run-through from the other leg), then also at 4- or 6-stride rhythm, later also at 1- or 2-stride rhythm; also at progressive distances and therefore with increasing speed (1-, 3-, 5-, 7-stride rhythm); without or over obstacles at individual distances (the main objective of the obstacles is to define the rhythm: they shall be not too high so that the take-off leg is not bent too early); more for distance or more for height; last jump possibly with landing in the pit; bilateral practice; also without obstacles and with eyes closed; (see also 343).

Typical load standards: 3–6 run-throughs of 3–5 take-offs each per leg and rhythm.

271 Imitation of take-off preparation

Possible objectives: Creation of an idea of the movement, strength training.

Execution: From the standing position, powerful, flat push-off from the third-last support, swing-leg squat, straightening (backward rotation) of the trunk, touchdown of the straight take-off leg from above in front of the body; imitation of the take-off and swing-leg action upon take-off.

Variations: Also from a walk-on, jogging, high-knee run or run-up; with and without arm action; without and with additional load (advanced athletes may carry 10–20 kg on their shoulders); with and without subsequent take-off; bilateral practice.

Typical load standards: 5–20 times per leg (depending on the objective).

72  Pop-up jump with exaggerated short-long-short rhythm

Possible objectives: Illustration of the rhythm for jumpers with insufficient lowering of the CG; differential learning.

Execution/variations: Penultimate stride over gym mat; prescription of stride length (e.g., by gymnastics hoop); also from longer run-ups; bilateral practice.

Typical load standards: 5–10 times per leg.

273  Pop-up jump with reduced short-long-short rhythm

Possible objectives: Prevention of an exaggerated rhythm for jumpers with too deep lowering of the CG; differential learning.

Execution: Prescription of constant, slightly shortened stride length by means of markers (gymnastics hoops, hurdle boards, foam blocks, etc.); bilateral practice.

Typical load standards: 5–10 times per leg.

274  Jumps from an elevated and/or elastic take-off area

Possible objectives: Extension of the flight phase for training the flight technique and landing; differential learning.

Execution/variations: As shown in the picture, either the complete run-up or the take-off point may be elevated by means of the top element of a gym box or a springboard (no-one-legged take-offs from a trampette; note the remarks made in chapter II–2.1.4).

Typical load standards: 3–6 times per leg, run-up length, and/or task.

275 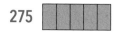 **Pop-up jumps from a lowered take-off area**

Possible objectives: Powerful take-off in spite of short take-off duration; as compensation for the previously mentioned exercise; differential learning.

Execution: run-up on a mat path, take-off behind the mats.

Variation: Pop-up jumps are also possible with the last two ground contacts being performed on lower ground.

Typical load standards: 3–6 times per leg and run-up length.

276 **Landing on a soft-floor mat**

Possible objectives: Flight technique and landing preparation.

Execution: Feet and buttocks touch the mat simultaneously.

Variations: Also on a flat mat (caution: no backward lean or backward rotation during the flight); flight and landing exercises may also be performed jumping into a foam block pit if available (as is used by gymnasts); in combination with exercises 272–275, 278, 282, and 285; also from longer run-ups; bilateral practice; with eyes closed (close eyes 2–3 strides before the take-off and open them again only after the landing).

Typical load standards: 3–6 times per leg and run-up length.

277 **Landing behind an elastic cord or sand wall**

Possible objectives: Landing technique; motivation for a good jump.

Execution/variations: An elastic cord is placed at an individual distance in the sand, or a small sand wall is shaped with a rake transverse to the

direction of jump; the jumper is supposed to lift his/her legs over the wall and pull himself/herself over the wall after touchdown of his/her feet; the pelvis lands equidistant from the board as the heels; also from longer run-ups; bilateral practice; exercises may also be performed by landing in zones (several transversely placed jumping ropes, etc. are used to mark the zones); then the exercise is called zone jumping.
Typical load standards: 3–6 times per leg and run-up length.

---

278 | | | ■ ■ ■ | **Hand toward the height marker**

Possible objectives: Arm swing in the stride, hang, and running jump.
Execution/variations: Stride jump: the athlete swings his/her rear arm upward behind his/her body and touches the height marker over his/her head; hang jump: the athlete swings both his/her arms upward behind his/her body and touches the height marker over his/her head; running jump: the focus is on the front arm, which after take-off reverses its direction of movement and touches the height marker over the head.
Typical load standards: 5–10 reps.

---

279 | | | ■ ■ | **Toward the hang/running jump: imitation in standing position**

Possible objectives: Learning the hang or running-jump technique; creating an idea of the movement.
Execution/variations: While the athlete is standing on his/her take-off leg, he/she imitates the movement of the swing leg and the arms; caution: note differences in the arm actions between the hang and running jump (see chapter II–2.2.3); increase speed of movement; every now

and then with the other side.

Typical load standards: 5–15 times until the movement is coherent in terms of space and time.

---

280 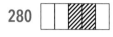 **Toward the hang jump: standing long jump through the hang position**

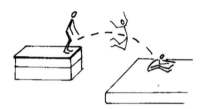

Possible objectives: Learning the hang-jump technique.

Execution: Take-off; forward shift of the hip; after the take-off, the extended arms are swung downward, behind the body and then over the head; jackknife movement.

Variations: Usually from a slightly elevated position (see picture); to the sitting position on the soft-floor mat (see 276) or with landing in the long-jump pit according to the target technique; first with two-legged take-off from the parallel position, then from the stride position with swing-leg action and initially with contralateral arm action.

Typical load standards: 5–10 reps.

---

281 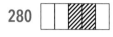 **Toward the hang jump: rudimentary hang jump from skipping**

Possible objectives: Learning the hang-jump technique.

Execution: While skipping, the athlete takes off powerfully and drops his/her swing leg and front arm; the arms are swung upward behind the body; landing in standing position, with hands over the head; every now and then with the other side.

Typical load standards: 5–10 reps.

282 Toward the hang jump: hip toward hand

Possible objectives: Learning the hang-jump technique.
Execution: After take-off with powerful swing-leg action, the athlete tries to touch his/her partner's outstretched hand or a foam block held by his/her partner with his/her hips.
Variations: Landing in the sitting position on the soft-floor mat (see 276), or with landing in the long-jump pit according to the target technique; for a short time with elevated (run-up and) take-off area or with elastic take-off area (274; note chapter II-2.1.4); also with longer run-ups; every now and then with the other side.
Typical load standards: 5–10 reps per side.

283 Toward the running jump: fleeting run over a box

Possible objectives: Learning the running-jump technique.
Execution: The athlete takes off in front of the top element of a gym box or small box with a powerful use of his/her swing leg, lowers his/her swing leg, touches the box with the stretched swing leg or gently takes off from it again; the previous take-off leg is quickly moved forward and upward and becomes the landing leg behind the box.
Variations: Distance marker to find the right distance of take-off in front of the box.
Typical load standards: 5–10 reps per side.

284 Toward the running jump: pop-up jump with early switch of legs

Possible objectives: Learning the running-jump technique.
Execution: As in exercise 268, the athlete

also lands on his/her swing leg, but instead of maintaining his/her take-off position he/she immediately continues the running motion after a vigorous use of his/her swing leg; upon landing on the extended swing leg, the thigh of the take-off leg is in front of the body horizontally; care should be taken that the arm movement is performed according to the target technique.

Variations: Telemark landing: after switching legs, the landing is performed with the take-off leg in front of the body and the swing leg behind the body.

Typical load standards: 5–10 reps per side.

---

285 | | ▨▨▨ **Toward the hang/running jump: kicking the target backward**

Possible objectives: Learning the hang or running-jump technique.

Execution: After the take-off, the athlete lowers his/her take-off leg and kicks a target backward.

Variations: The behaviour of the swing leg and arms differs from one another depending on the flight technique (see chapter II–2.2.3); the target may be a stick held by a partner, a mini-hurdle, a fitness ball lying on the floor, or a foam block placed on the front edge of the soft-floor mat (see 276); for a short term also with (run-up and) take-off from an elevated position or with elastic take-off area (274; note chapter II–2.1.4); in the running jump, the landing may be performed on the take-off leg, otherwise the landing is performed in the long sitting position on the soft-floor mat or in the pit according to the target technique; every now and then with the other side.

Typical load standards: 5–10 reps per side.

286 **Run-ups with landing on the take-off board and free run-ups**

Possible objectives: Visual adjustment of the run-up length.

Execution/variations: A (take-off) line is marked on the sprinting straight, which the athlete is supposed to land on from various or arbitrary distances (without or with rudimentary take-off); landing on lines at regular distances, every 5–6 strides; races over hurdles at various and arbitrary distances of about 20m (213); pop-up jumps (268) with landing on the board from various and arbitrary distances; in any case, only a slight change in stride length should be visible from the outside; the timely raising of the view can be prompted by a (hand) sign from the coach behind the pit which the athlete must identify.

Typical load standards: 5–10 reps per side.

287 **Determination of run-up length**

Possible objectives: Age-adequate determination of run-up length.

Execution/variations: Beginners and children determine their run-up length by positioning themselves at the take-off line, performing their run-up in the opposite direction, and imitating a take-off after 15–25 m; a partner marks the location of the tip of the foot upon take-off; the jumper now starts his/her run-up at this point (with the same foot as before); advanced athletes memorise their run-up length and measure it by lengths of feet or by means of a measuring tape to be able to start the run-up from the same distance in the next training session (see also table 1); an extension of the run-up by two strides corresponds approximately to an extension by 13 lengths in feet.

288  **Run-up controls**

Possible objectives: Run-up accuracy.

Execution/variations: Always with take-off (pop-up jump 268, or as competition-like jump 289); with deliberate knee lift, upright trunk and increased stride frequency during the last run-up strides; in competition only two markers may be used according to the rules; in training, however, several intermediate markers may be used which are controlled by the coach; under different conditions: headwind, tailwind, sun, rain, etc.

Typical load standards: 4–8 reps.

---

289  **Competition-adequate long jump**

Possible objectives: Execution of the target technique.

Execution: Even in training, the athlete should try to perform the target technique at a correspondingly high intensity.

Variations: Despite maximal effort, the competition run-up of some athletes must be shortened by 1–3 lengths in feet in training; every now and then, the run-up may be shortened by 2–4 strides or extended by 2 strides to make training more variable; without take-off board (i.e. in the triple jump area); with eyes closed (close eyes 2–3 strides before the take-off and do not open them until after landing).

Typical load standards: 3–6 reps.

---

290  **Jumps with pull support or run-up downhill**

Possible objectives: Supramaximal run-up velocity or more take-offs at nearly maximum velocity without exhausting long run-ups.

Execution/variations: See also 139; the athlete is pulled by a pulley or a rubber band fixed to

a belt around his/her hips; the band should be released about 6 strides before the take-off; the athlete tries to keep his/her speed and takes off actively (after an only slight lowering of his/her CG); in some locations there are also facilities which allow jumps from a downhill run-up.

Typical load standards: 3–10 reps depending on the variant used.

291 □□□□■ **Jumping (-strength) training with additional load**

Possible objectives: Hypergravity training.

Execution/variations: The athlete wears a weighted vest (5–10% of his/her body weight) in daily life and when performing sprinting and jumping exercises; caution: this causes increased strain on the periosteum of the shin bone (athletes should possibly wear the vest initially only in daily life but not in training), also note the remarks made in chapter II–2.1.4; not in the competition period.

Typical load standards: The volume tends to be slightly reduced depending on the chosen contents.

In (maximal-)strength training, long jumpers perform primarily exercises 41–52, 60–64, and 66–96.

2.2.8 SPECIAL TEST AND CONTROL PROCEDURES

	Test: Ability/skill tested	Execution/comments
T101	**Technique analysis:** Long-jump technique	Maximum competition jump from full run-up; evaluation on the basis of the technique analysis sheet (see chapter II–2.2.4), possibly using a video (T1) and photo sequences made thereof.
T102	**Long jump from short run-up:** Specific speed and reactive strength (for comparison of sides)	Maximum long jump from 5, 10, and 15 run-up strides; test criterion: effective jumping distance (DEf); test should be performed on both sides.
T103	**Take-off test:** Specific reactive strength	6–10 strides for run-up; three approx. 30–70cm high obstacles are placed increasingly further apart (the last obstacle remains in the pit approx. 1m behind the front edge); the first two obstacles are cleared by performing a pop-up jump; the third obstacle is cleared almost in accordance with the target technique: a) landing on the swing leg, 1 stride, take-off; or b) landing on the swing leg, 3 strides, take-off. *Test criterion:* distance between obstacles or total distance; test should be performed on both sides.
T104	**Horizontal-jump endurance test:** Specific speed endurance	9 sprints as fast as possible from standing start over 60 m with 8 min rest intervals; test criterion: the sum of the 9 times (possibly also short-sprint tempo-run programmes as test, T26).
T4	**1 RPM:** Maximal strength	Squat (62), clean (63), snatch (64), hamstrings (68), quadriceps (69), arm exercises, etc. (if possible also eccentric maximal strength measurement).
T5	**Squat jump, and T8 counter-movement and drop jump:** Two-legged speed strength and reactive strength of the extensor loop	The counter-movement jump may be replaced by the simpler test of tossing the shot forward and/or backward (93) for distance.
T9	**5-stride hops with distance maximisation:** Reactive strength of the legs in comparison to one another	Hop test should be performed on both sides.
T10	**30m bounding run with time minimisation:** Reactive strength of the legs	
T21	**60m analysis:** Sprint technique	See technique analysis sheet in chapter II–1.5.4.

	Test: Ability/skill tested	Execution/comments
T24	**30m flying sprint:** Maximum sprinting speed	Possibly only 20m.
T25	**20m frequency test:** Cyclic speed	
T61	**Standing start and acceleration up to 20m:** Start acceleration	
T66	**Graded field test:** Aerobic endurance	With lactate withdrawal (and spirometry; for young athletes also Cooper test, T65, which is easy to perform but inaccurate).
T2	**Flexibility tests:** General flexibility	
T3	**Body weight and body fat measurement:** Relative strength	Inappropriate upward and downward deflections should be avoided (see also chapter II-2.1.2: phase 3).

Moreover, in all jumping disciplines, additional sports-medicine tests (e.g., blood tests), as well as biomechanical, sport-psychology, nutritional tests, etc. may be necessary to answer specific questions.

Table 8: **Basic performances of long jumpers** (according to Killing et al., 2008, p. 232).

		Women		Men	
Age group		w17	w19	m17	m19
Best performance	(m)	**5.70**	**6.00**	**6.60**	**7.30**
Long jump in training	(m)	5.30	5.75	6.20	6.95
Long jump from 9 run-up strides	(m)	5.00	5.25	5.90	6.40
Long jump with the other leg	(m)	5.20	5.40	6.00	6.60
5-stride bounding run from 5m run-up	(m)	15.00	16.50	17.50	19.00
10m flying sprint	(sec)	1.13	1.10	1.00	0.95
30m flying sprint	(sec)	3.35	3.25	3.00	2.90
30m sprint from standing position	(sec)	4.35	4.25	3.95	3.85
100m sprint from standing position	(sec)	12.50	12.30	11.60	11.20
Tossing the shot (women: 3 kg; men: 4 kg)	(m)	13.50	14.50	15.00	18.50
Snatch	(kg)		30		45
Squat	(kg)		40		65

2.2.9 ERRORS – CAUSES – CORRECTIONS

In all disciplines, coaches should not stand too close to the action and should vary their observation point and angle of view to actually detect all errors effectively. Errors and their detection are always individual. Nevertheless, some errors can be identified which are particularly common or important for beginners. Of these errors, up to six are highlighted in blue for each discipline.

Error	Causes	Corrections
Take-off frequently behind or in front of the take-off board (or even stutter steps before take-off or take-off with the wrong leg).	• Insufficient training of the competition run-up and its rhythm. • Poor visual adaptation abilities. • Due to insecurity, the jumper still looks toward the take-off board even during his/her last strides (the jumper's poor estimation of his/her own stride length at high velocity then often results in taking off behind the board instead of in the desired correct take-off). • Inaccuracies during the run-up, in particular caused by different walk-ons or stutter steps at the beginning of the run-up. • No intermediate mark.	✔ More training of longer run-ups (289). ✔ More training of free run-ups (286). ✔ More hurdle training to improve stride rhythm. ✔ Jumps with orientation point to look at behind the pit. ✔ Possibly switch to run-up from standing position. ✔ Introduction of an intermediate mark (in training athletes should possibly work with several intermediate marks, see 288). ✔ Note: Correcting the run-up length includes observing the run-up. Much too often, coaches tell athletes who took off behind the board to lengthen their run-up although the athlete looked at the board and therefore lengthened his/her strides, for example. Instead it would be better to recommend to these athletes to raise their view, to increase their stride frequency, and to reduce their run-up length.
Too slow run-up velocity before taking off.	• Too long or too short run-up. • Insufficient speed training. • Cruising and its causes (see below).	✔ Adjustment of run-up length according to the principles mentioned in chapters II–2.1.2 and II–2.2.3. ✔ More speed training (see chapter II–1.3.8). ✔ See corrections of cruising.
Loss of velocity (cruising) during the last run-up strides.	• Uncertainty with respect to the technical performance of the take-off preparation and the take-off (in particular at high speed). • Too many practice jumps with a short run-up. • Insufficient jumping-strength capacities for the high run-up velocity.	✔ More jumps from medium to long run-ups focusing on good take-off preparation in spite of continuous acceleration and high velocity. ✔ More reactive-strength training.

Error	Causes	Corrections
Exaggerated backward lean of the trunk upon touchdown for take-off.	• Too long penultimate or last stride. • Too little knee extension during the penultimate support. • The jumper puts his/her head back.	✔ Versatile practice of take-off preparation and take-off using exercises (268–273 and others) while instructing the athlete to keep his/her body upright. ✔ Possibly controlling the viewing direction as described in 268.
Forward lean of the trunk upon touchdown for take-off.	• The jumper looks at the board during his/her last strides (with his/her head on his/her chest). • Insufficient short-long-short rhythm with too straight knee during the third-last and penultimate push-off. • The jumper is forced to shorten his/her last strides before take-off (trunk overtakes legs).	✔ Versatile practice of take-off preparation and take-off using exercises (268–273 and others) while instructing the athlete to lift his/her knees and keep his/her body upright. ✔ More run-ups with landing on the take-off board and free run-ups (286), possibly controlling the direction of view as described in 268. ✔ Pop-up jumps with emphasised short-long-short rhythm (272). ✔ Possibly backward shifting of the starting marker.
Initiation of backward rotation (or no forward rotation) about the transverse axis upon take-off.	• Exaggerated backward lean of the trunk during foot touchdown for the take-off and its causes (see above). • Insufficient extension of the knee joint upon take-off.	✔ See corrections of exaggerated backward lean of the trunk upon touchdown for take-off. ✔ Versatile practice of take-off preparation and take-off using exercises (268–273 and others) while instructing the athlete to concentrate on active push-off extension.
Initiation of too much forward rotation about the transverse axis upon take-off.	• Forward lean of the trunk upon touchdown for take-off and its causes (see above). • Insufficient hip extension upon take-off.	✔ See corrections of forward lean of the trunk upon touchdown for take-off. ✔ Versatile practice of take-off preparation and take-off using exercises (268–273 and others) while instructing the athlete to concentrate on active push-off extension.

(continued)

(continued)

Error	Causes	Corrections
Exaggerated bracing upon take-off (often associated with a touchdown over the heel).	• Too large bracing angle (i.e., the foot is placed on the ground too far in front of the vertical projection of the CG) due to » too deep lowering of the CG before take-off (caused by too many jumps from short run-ups), often associated with exaggerated short-long-short rhythm; » exaggerated backward lean of the trunk during foot touchdown for the take-off and its causes (see above); or » too long last stride(s): the jumper tries to reach the board. • No active pulling movement (hip extension) before touchdown of the take-off leg.	✔ The jumper should rather have the feeling of » running through the take-off; and » take off less powerfully or with less impact of the take-off leg. ✔ More pop-up jumps or competition-like jumps (268 and 289) from medium and primarily long run-ups while instructing the athlete to lift his/her knees, to concentrate on stride frequency, and to keep his/her body upright. ✔ Pop-up jumps with reduced short-long-short rhythm (273). ✔ See corrections of exaggerated backward lean of the trunk upon touchdown for take-off. ✔ Possibly forward shifting of the starting marker. ✔ Skipping (87), bounding runs (88), pop-up jumps (268 and 270) with pulling foot touchdown on the entire sole of the foot.
Insufficient bracing upon take-off.	• Too small bracing angle caused by » too little lowering of the CG before the take-off, often associated with insufficient short-long-short rhythm; » insufficient backward lean of the trunk during the touchdown of the take-off leg; or » too short last stride: the jumper wants to avoid taking off behind the board. • Touchdown on the ball of the foot upon take-off.	✔ Imitation of take-off preparation (271). ✔ Pop-up jumps with emphasised short-long-short rhythm (272) and powerful take-off upward. ✔ Possibly backward shifting of the starting marker or earlier emphasis on sprinting at high stride frequency during the run-up. ✔ Skipping (87), bounding runs (88), pop-up jumps (268 and 270) with deliberate touchdown of the entire foot.
Collapsing of the take-off leg during the amortisation of the take-off resulting in insufficient take-off extension of the knee joint.	• Exaggerated bracing upon take-off and its causes (see above). • Insufficient reactive force of the extension muscles of the take-off leg. • Unusually powerful action of the swing leg.	✔ See corrections of exaggerated bracing upon take-off. ✔ Eccentric- and reactive-strength training of the extension muscles (e.g., using exercises 77 and 84–92). ✔ The athlete must be instructed to maintain a powerful swing-leg action but to lower his/her CG less and brace less.

Error	Causes	Corrections
Insufficient push-off extension of the hip joint (hip bend).	• Too much concentration on landing: the jumper initiates the jackknife position already upon take-off. • Insufficient forward shift of the hips (beginning hip extension) before placing down the take-off leg. • Insufficient stretchability of the hip flexors on the take-off-leg side. • Exaggerated bracing upon take-off and its causes.	✔ Versatile take-off exercises (e.g., 268 and 270) with actively pulling foot touchdown and keeping of the take-off position (the foot points back to the take-off point). ✔ Stretching of the hip flexors (25). ✔ See corrections of exaggerated bracing upon take-off.
Insufficient use of the swing elements (arms and swing leg) upon take-off.	• Insufficient automation of the use of the swing legs in accordance with the target technique. • Hang jump (negative transfer from the flight to the take-off technique). • Insufficient strength of the hip flexors of the swing leg. • Insufficient reactive strength of the extension muscles of the take-off leg (this means that this error may be regarded as a relief technique). • Exaggerated bracing and its causes (see above): more powerful use of the swing elements would result in the collapse of the take-off leg (relief technique). • Possibly also weight increase (relief technique).	✔ Imitations and versatile take-offs (e.g., using exercises 87, 268, and 270) and deliberately powerful use of the swing elements. ✔ Exercises for the improvement of the swing-leg action during the hang jump or switch to the stride or running jump. ✔ Strengthening of the hip flexors using exercises 73, 87, and 112 (also with ankle weights). ✔ Eccentric- and reactive-strength training of the extension muscles (e.g., using exercises 77, and 84–92). ✔ See corrections of exaggerated bracing upon take-off. ✔ Control of body weight.
Too high flight curve (too much loss of horizontal velocity upon take-off).	• Exaggerated bracing upon take-off and its causes (see above). • Flight technique too complex: the jumper tries to gain time by performing a steeper take-off.	✔ See corrections of exaggerated bracing upon take-off. ✔ Possibly return to simpler flight technique.
Too flat flight curve.	• Insufficient bracing upon take-off and its causes (see above). • Collapse of the take-off leg and its causes (see above).	✔ See corrections of insufficient bracing upon take-off and collapse of the take-off leg.
Restless arm and/or leg movements in the air (e.g., uncoordinated leg movements instead of running movement, or bent arms, and/or leg moved backward in a bent position).	• Insufficient automation of the desired target technique and its timing. • The flight technique is too complex for the short duration of the flight.	✔ More technique training using exercises 279–285. ✔ Return to a simpler flight technique.

(continued)

(continued)

Error	Causes	Corrections
The jumper is unable to initiate the landing movement in time or to prepare it correctly (e.g., insufficient jackknife position).	• Too flat flight curve and its causes (see above). • The intended flight technique is too complex (in spite of a useful departure angle the duration of the flight is too short for the intended flight technique). • Insufficient jackknife position due to too weak trunk and hip flexors or insufficient flexibility of the trunk and hip extensors.	✔ See corrections of too flat flight curve. ✔ Possibly return to a simpler flight technique. ✔ Strength training of the abdominals (41, 44, and 67) and hip flexors (73); stretching of the lower back muscles (23) and hip extensors (24 and 27).
Landing too far to the side.	• Evasion to the side upon take-off.	✔ Versatile jumps focusing on a straight take-off; the coach checks the movement from a position in front of the athlete.
Landing with staggered legs (the heels do not land the same distance from the board).	• Landing too far to the side and its causes (see above). • The jumper is unable to initiate his/her landing movements in time and to prepare them correctly and its causes (see above). • Insufficient concentration on the landing or insufficient practice of landing.	✔ See corrections of landing too far to the side and jumper is unable to initiate his/her landing movements in time and to prepare them correctly. ✔ More practice of landing using exercises 276-277 and focusing on bringing the feet close together before landing.
The pelvis (or the remaining trunk) land closer to the board than the heels.	• Initiation of backward rotation (or no forward rotation) about the transverse axis upon take-off and its causes (see above). • Late or no opening of the hip angle before landing. • Blocking of the knee joints during landing.	✔ See corrections of initiation of backward rotation about the transverse axis upon take-off. ✔ Practising an actively grasping landing using exercise 277.
The pelvis (or the remaining trunk) land farther from the board than the heels, or the jumper remains standing, or even falls forward.	• Initiation of too much forward rotation about the transverse axis upon take-off and its causes (see above). • Too early or exaggerated opening of the hip angle before the heels are placed on the ground. • The jumper is unable to initiate the landing movement in time or to prepare it correctly and its causes (see above).	✔ See corrections of initiation of too much forward rotation about the transverse axis upon take-off above. ✔ If the athlete has sufficient jumping strength, he/she should switch from the stride to the hang or running jump with 1½ strides or from these to the running jump with 2½ strides to be able to counteract the forward rotation during the flight better and to introduce the landing later. ✔ See corrections of jumper is unable to initiate the landing movement on time or to prepare it correctly.

See also the "Errors – Causes – Corrections" chapter in the 100m section (chapter II–1.3.10).

2.2.10 TRAINING PLANNING

Training planning for long jumpers is done in accordance with recommendations in the general part of this book (see chapter I–3.3). In particular, the training plans suggested here are based on the training plans for children's athletics and basic training presented in chapter I–3.3. The statements made in connection with the 4 x 100m training plans (see chapter II–1.6.11) about volume and intensity as well as the differences between build-up and high-performance training in terms of contents also apply to the long jump.

SUGGESTED TRAINING PLANS

Below, there are exemplary microcycles for the

- first mesocycle of a 17-year-old athlete in build-up training (table 10);
- first mesocycle of an athlete in high-performance training (table 11); and
- third mesocycle of an athlete in high-performance training (table 12).

It is assumed that long jumpers, triple jumpers, and short sprinters have not yet definitely specialised by the age of 17 and that a switch to the long sprint is even still possible (see Saturday). The sample microcycle presented in connection with the triple jump (see chapter II–2.3.10) for the third mesocycle of a 17-year-old athlete in build-up training is therefore intended for the same athlete as here in table 10. The sample microcycle presented in connection with the 4 x 100m relay (see chapter II–1.6.11) for the second mesocycle of a 17-year-old athlete in build-up training could be included in this series after only a few changes.

With the exception of technique training, long and triple-jump training are very similar even in high-performance training. In addition to the training plans mentioned here, the triple-jump chapter therefore includes a sample microcycle for the

- second mesocycle of an athlete in high-performance training; and
- fourth mesocycle of an athlete in high-performance training.

Table 3: **Training emphasis in the various mesocycles** *for long-jump training in build-up and high-performance training.*

1st mesocycle	basic aerobic and anaerobic endurance training; hypertrophy-oriented maximal-strength training especially for the legs and the trunk; basic reactive-strength training for the legs; flexibility training; general (e.g., hurdle training, games, etc.), and special (e.g., ABCs of sprinting/jumping, technique training from short to medium-length run-ups) coordination training
2nd mesocycle	basic anaerobic (speed-) endurance training; hypertrophy-, IC- and connective-tissue-oriented maximal- and reactive-strength training especially for the legs and the trunk; sprinting-speed training; special coordination training (e.g., ABCs of sprinting/jumping, technique training from medium-length run-ups)
3rd mesocycle	special speed-endurance training at high intensity; IC- and connective-tissue-oriented maximal- and reactive-strength training especially for the legs and the trunk; sprinting-speed and acceleration training at maximum intensity; special coordination training (long run-ups)
4th mesocycle	competitions and corresponding regeneration; IC- and connective-tissue-oriented maximal- and reactive-strength training especially for the legs and the trunk; speed and acceleration training at maximum intensity; technique training; maintenance stimuli

Table 10: Build-up training: sample microcycle for a 17-year-old long and triple jumper in the first mesocycle.

Monday	Tuesday	Wednesday	Thursday	Friday	Saturday	Sunday
Trunk stabilisation exercises and abdominal crunches (20 min) with a lot of dynamic variation	Foot strengthening (10 min) little jumps on gym mats	Warm-up jogging (6 min)	Continuous run (40 min)	LI runs (6 x 80m, rest intervals: 20 sec) for warming up	Baton handovers (25 min) while sitting/standing, jogging, and sprinting at submaximal speed	Rest
Acceleration runs (2 reps) barefoot	Acceleration runs (2 reps) barefoot	Acceleration runs (2 reps)	Contract-relax stretching (15 min)	ABCs of jumping (8–10 run-throughs)	ABCs of sprinting/jumping (15–20 run-throughs)	
ABCs of sprinting (10–15 run-throughs) emphasis: grasping/pulling	ABCs of jumping (15–20 run-throughs) sideways galloping, ankle jumps, and skipping with two-legged landing, skipping variations, etc.	ABCs of hurdling and specific warm-up using hurdles (25 min)	Two out of the following:	Practising the triple-jump technique (30 min) technical development of rhythm jumps	Acceleration runs (2 reps)	
Acceleration runs (2 reps)	Acceleration runs (2 reps)	Hurdle Zs (2 sets of 4 Zs each of 2 run-throughs over 4 hurdles each; rest intervals: 3 min; rest intervals between sets: 10 min) e.g., out in 3-stride rhythm with the weak side, back with the strong side	Muscle build-up training for the trunk on apparatus and/or for the arms, medicine-ball work, gymnastics, technique training for the throwing events, boxing, etc. (30 min each) e.g., goalkeeper throws, rotational throws, throws from the prone position, and tossing, using a medicine ball	Muscle build-up training (45 min) hamstrings, quadriceps, adductors, abductors, hip flexors and extensors	LI tempo runs (3 x 300m, 4 x 200m, and 3 x 300m; rest intervals: 3, 3, 6–8, 2, 2, 2, 6–8, 3, and 3 min) in running shoes, 200m runs possibly as endless relay	
Practising the long-jump technique (40 min) short run-ups, pop-up jumps with the left and right leg as take-off leg, additional tasks (e.g., learning the running-jump technique)	Muscle build-up training (30 min) full squat and clean (coach must continue to carefully supervise the technique), possibly abdominal exercises in between	Contract-relax stretching (15 min)	Tappings (8 x 5 sec) or	Foot strengthening (10 min) in the sand or with elastic band	Contract-relax stretching (15 min)	
Technique sprints (4–6 reps) e.g., sprints with additional tasks such as varying arm actions, pre-set stride lengths, etc.	Game (30 min) e.g., basketball or handball	Warm-down jogging (10 diagonals on the lawn)	Frequency coordination (10 min) over foam blocks as utilisation	Alternating-pace sprints (4 x 60m) as utilisation	Warm-down jogging (10 diagonals on the lawn)	
		Bounding runs and pop-up jumps (3 run-throughs each) as utilisation			Standing starts (3 x 30m) as utilisation	

Table 11: High-performance training: sample microcycle in the first mesocycle.

	Monday	Tuesday	Wednesday	Thursday	Friday	Saturday	Sunday
Morning	Trunk stabilisation exercises and abdominal crunches (20 min) Acceleration runs (3 reps) ABCs of jumping (12–15 run-throughs) Practising the long-jump technique (45 min) short to medium run-up lengths, additional tasks		Foot strengthening (10 min) ABCs of hurdling (15 min) Hurdle sprints (30 min) versatile Muscle build-up training (45 min) abductors, quadriceps, hip flexors, and full squat Pop-up jumps		LI runs (6 x 100m, rest intervals: 30 sec) for warming up ABCs of jumping (12–15 run-throughs) Skipping, pop-up and squat-extension jumps (5–7 run-throughs each) or start jumps, or jumps onto boxes Tappings (8 x 5 sec)	Warm-up jogging (10 min) Acceleration runs (3 reps) LI tempo runs (3 x 5 x 200m; rest intervals: 1.5–2 min; rest intervals between sets: 6–8 min) in running shoes, possibly as endless relay Contract-relax stretching (15 min)	Rest
Afternoon	Rope jumping (5 min) ABCs of sprinting (10–12 run-throughs) Technique sprints (4–6 reps) Muscle build-up training (50 min) hamstrings, adductors, hip/back extensors, and clean High-knee run (5 x 20 sec)	LI runs (8 x 80m; rest intervals: 20 sec) as warm-up ABCs of jumping (6–8 run-throughs) Bounding runs and/or rhythm jumps (3 x 4 x 50m) Medicine ball work (30 min) Game (30 min) e.g., basketball or handball	Warm-up jogging (8 min) Acceleration runs I3 tempo runs (4 x 5 x 60m; rest intervals: walk back; rest intervals between sets: 6–8 min), possibly including pull-resisted sprints, uphill or hurdles Contract-relax stretching (15 min) Warm-down jogging (15 min) Standing starts	Continuous run (40 min) Contract-relax stretching (15 min) Muscle build-up training (35 min) trunk on apparatus plus (35 min) arms Frequency coordination (10 min) over foam blocks as utilisation	Warm-up jogging (8 min) Acceleration runs ABCs of sprinting (12–15 run-throughs) Muscle build-up training (45 min) hamstrings, adductors and lunges Foot strengthening (15 min) in the sand Alternating-pace sprints (6 x 80m)	Bounding runs (3–5 run-throughs) as utilisation	

Table 12: High-performance training: sample microcycle in the third mesocycle.

Monday	Tuesday	Wednesday	Thursday	Friday	Saturday	Sunday
Warm-up jogging (6 min)	LI runs (6 x 100m; rest intervals: 30 sec) as warm-up	Warm-up jogging (6 min)	Warm-up jogging (6 min)	Foot strengthening (10 min)	Warm-up jogging (6 min)	Rest
Maximal-eccentric strength training (15 min) trunk stabilisation, lifting opposite upper and lower limbs while in prone position, belly punches with tense abdominals, raising the foot/toes	Tuck jumps (3 x 3 run-throughs over 5 hurdles each)	Strength training for the trunk, medicine-ball work, or gymnastics (45 min) e.g., abdominal machine, shoulder-hip twist, lumborum, hip/back extensors	High-intensity strength training (15 min) snatch	Acceleration runs (2 reps)	Acceleration runs (3 reps)	
Acceleration runs (3 reps)	Acceleration runs (3 reps)	High-intensity strength training (45 min) bench press, lat pull, and 2 more varying arm exercises	Acceleration runs (3 reps)	ABCs of sprinting (8–10 run-throughs)	Depth jumps (5 x 10) from box to box; or ankle jumps with a partner pushing downward for 5 jumps and then lifting upward for 5 jumps	
ABCs of sprinting (8–10 run-throughs)	Pull-assisted sprints (2–3 reps) with pulley, release of the cable 10 m in front of the second light barrier		ABCs of jumping (8–10 run-throughs)	Standing starts (2–3 reps)	One-legged jumps (hops) (4–5 run-throughs of 20m each) and/or rhythm jumps, high intensity	
Practising the long-jump technique (40 min) long run-up, as in competition	Flying sprints (1–2 x 20m + 30-40m run-up) through light barriers		Practising the long-jump technique (40 min) medium run-up lengths, additional tasks	Pull-resisted runs and crouch starts alternately (40–50 min; altogether 8–12 sprints of 10-40m each) against each other; the shorter the distance, the higher the sled loading (up to 60 kg)	12 tempo runs (80, 120, 150, 120, and 80m; rest intervals: 8, 12, 15, and 12 min)	
High-intensity strength training (25 min) clean and quarter-split squat	Pop-up jumps (3 x 3 run-throughs with 4 take-offs and 5 intermediate strides)		Jumping test (15 min) a different test each week (e.g., 10-stride bounding run or maximal long jump from 10 run-up strides, possibly before technique training)	Maximal-eccentric strength training (30 min) hamstrings, adductors, etc.		
Frequency coordination (10 min) as utilisation				Alternating-pace sprints (3–4 x 60m)		

2.2.11 BIBLIOGRAPHY

Arampatzis, A., Brüggemann, G.-P. & Walsch, M. (1999). Long Jump. In G.-P. Brüggemann, D. Koszewski & H. Müller (Hrsg.), *Biomechanical Research Project Athens 1997: Final Report* (S. 82-113). Oxfort: Meyer & Meyer.

Balius, X., Roig A., Turró, C. Escoda, J. & Álvarez, J. C. (2000). Enhancing Measurement Acuity in the Horizontal Jumps: The DTL Project and The Rieti '99 experience. *New Studies in Athletics 15* (2), 21-27.

Čoh, M., Kugovnik, O. & Dolenec, A. (1997). Kinematisch-dynamische Analyse der Absprungaktion beim Weitsprung. *Leistungssport 27* (2), 47-49.

Čoh, M. (2000). Kinematic And Dynamic Model Of The Long Jump. *Track coach* (150), 4789-4795.

Fleischmann, R. (2004). Mit Methode weit springen. *Leichtathletiktraining 15* (1+2), 37-41.

Florczak, U. (2008). Deutsche Weitenjäger im Technikcheck. *Leichtathletiktraining 19* (8), 28-33.

Hay, J. G. (1995). Aktuelle Erkenntnisse zur Biomechanik des Weitsprungs. *Die Lehre der Leichtathletik 34* (24), 129-136.

Hegener, P. (2003). Weitsprung und 100 m-Zeit – eine biomechanische Untersuchung. *Leistungssport 33* (6), 36-39.

Hilliard, C. (2007). Technical preparation & coaching drills for the long jump. *Modern Athlete and Coach 45* (3), 7-9.

IAF. (1988). *Scientific report on the second IAAF World Championships in Athletics, Rome 1987.* London

Jones, M. (2008). The last three-to-five strides in the long jump approach. *Track coach* (182), 5814-5817.

Katzenbogner, H. (2007). Vielfältige Weitsprünge in einer Einheit. *Leichtathletiktraining 18* (6), 4-11.

Killing, W., Bartschat, E., Czingon, H., Knapp, U., Kurschilgen, B. & Schlottke K. (2008). *Jugendleichtathletik: Offizieller Rahmentrainingsplan des Deutschen Leichtathletik-Verbandes für die Sprungdisziplinen im Aufbautraining.* Münster: Philippka.

Klimmer, H. (1999). A single-stride long jump leads to the hitch-kick. *Modern Athlete and Coach 37* (2), 24-28.

Knapp, U. (2008). Weite Sätze in die Grube. *Leichtathletiktraining 19* (1), 10-15.

Mendoza, L. & Nixdorf, E. (2006). Angewandte Leistungdiagnostik in den Sprungdisziplinen. In W. Steinmann & N. Müller (Hrsg.), *Trainingslehre und Methodik der Leichtathletik: Im memoriam Berno Wischmann* (Mainzer Studien zur Sportwissenschaft, 22, S. 125-146). Niedernhausen: Schors.

Mendoza, L., Nixdorf, E. & Isele, R. (2006). Gesetzmäßigkeiten des Horizontalsprungs. *Leichtathletiktraining 17* (5), 26-29.

Miladinov, O. (2006). New aspects in perfecting the long jump technique. *New Studies in Athletics 21* (4), 7-25.

Moura, N. A. & Fernandes de Paula Moura, T. (2001). Training principles for jumpers: implications for special strength development. *New Studies in Athletics 16* (4), 51-61.

Moura, N. A., Fernandes de Paula Moura, T. & Borin, J. B. (2005). Approach speed and performance in the horizontal jumps: What do Brazilian athletes do? *New Studies in Athletics 20* (3), 43-48.

Panoutsakopoulos, V. & Kollias, I. (2007). Biomechanical analysis of sub-elite performers in the women's long jump. New Studies in Athletics 22 (4). 19-28.

Popov, V. (1996). How to improve run-up speed and precision. *Modern Athlete and Coach 34* (2), 18-21.

Pottel, R. (2001). Kofi-Amoah Prah im Vergleich zu Pedroso und Taurima. *Leichtathletiktraining 12* (5), 18-23.

Pozzo, R. & Schlarb, H. (1997). 3-dimensionale kinematische Analyse von Spitzenleistungen im Weitsprung. *Forschung – Innovation – Technologie: das F.I.T.-Wissenschaftsmagazin der Deutschen Sporthochschule Köln* (2), 22-27.

Regelkommissionen des DLV, FLA, ÖLV und SLV (Hrsg.). (2010). *Internationale Wettkampfregeln.* Waldfischbach: Hornberger.

Schulek, A. (2002). Long jump with supramaximal and normal speed. *New Studies in Athletics 17* (2), 37-43.

Störmer, I. (1999). *Weitsprung: Anleitungen für Übungsleiter, Sportlehrer, Trainer und für den Aktiven selbst* (3. Aufl). Emden: OBW.

Tidow, G. (2007). The Long Jump. *Modern Athlete and Coach 45* (3), 10-18.

2.3 TRIPLE JUMP

2.3.1 THE FIRST OLYMPIC CHAMPION: A TRIPLE JUMPER

The only jump discipline in ancient Greece, the long jump, was probably five consecutive squat jumps from a standing position. This is supported by the following four facts: First, the take-off was performed from a type of threshold (bater) adjacent to the skamma, a 50-foot-long area (over 16m) of loosened soil for better detection of the footprints. Some athletes are said to have jumped beyond the skamma. Secondly, the athletes carried swing weights (halteres) in their hands, which are only of advantage when jumping from a standing position. Third, the long jump was part of the ancient pentathlon, in which the number five was otherwise also very important (e.g., five trials in the javelin and discus throw). Fourth, the jumps were probably accompanied by music to set their rhythm.

A similar standing triple jump was part of the modern Olympic Games in 1900 and 1904. The best jumper, Raymond Ewry, achieved a distance of approximately 10.50m with a two-legged first jump and a one-legged second and third jump.

The Irish triple jump with the three partial jumps being performed on the same leg also originates long before the birth of Christ. In the era of Friedrich Ludwig Jahn, the father of gymnastics, (1778–1852), the German triple jump was developed with the partial jumps being performed as (triple-jump) steps (left-right-left, or right-left-right). For the Olympic triple jump, the IAAF ultimately prescribed the jumping sequences left-left-right, or right-right-left (hop-step-jump).

In fact, the triple jump was the first competition in the first modern Olympic Games in 1896. The winner was James Connolly, an American of Iranian descent, who achieved 13.71m. He was also second in the high jump (1.65m) and third in the long jump (5.84m). The winners and the second-placed athletes were honoured on the final day in pouring rain. The silver medal and olive branches were awarded to the winner, bronze and olive branches for second place. Gold medals were only introduced at the Olympic Games in 1904.

Since then, Australians (Winter and Metcalfe), Japanese (Oda, Nambu, and Tajima), Russians (particularly Sanejew, and others), and Brazilians (da Silva, and Oliveira) have established triple jump world records. The Polish athlete Schmidt, the Italian Gentile, the Cuban Perez, and the American Banks also deserve mention. Sweden also has a great tradition in the triple jump with three Olympic medallists (Lindblom in 1912, Ahman in 1948, and Olsson in 2004).

Although the 18m barrier was already surpassed in Barcelona in 1992 by the

American Mike Conley, who won the Olympic gold medal, his world record of 18.17m was not recognised due to a strong tailwind. In the 1995 World Championships in Gothenburg, however, Jonathan Edwards from Great Britain was the first to jump 18.16m and then 18.29m, which is still the current world record.

Women competed in the triple jump as early as the beginning of the 20th century. The unofficial world record of 11.66m established in 1939 was only surpassed in 1981 by the American Terri Turner, who jumped 12.43m. Since 1991, there have been female triple jumpers at the world championships and since 1996 at the Olympic Games. The women's triple jump at the 2008 Olympic Games went down in history as the best women's triple jump competition ever: Six women jumped a total of ten times over 15m. Francoise Mbango Etone from Cameroon was ultimately able to defend her title from 2004 with a jump of 15.39m. But only in 2021 was Yulimar Rojas from Venezuala able to break Inessa Kravets's 26-year world record of 15.50m. In the Olympic stadium in Tokyo, she jumped 15.67m.

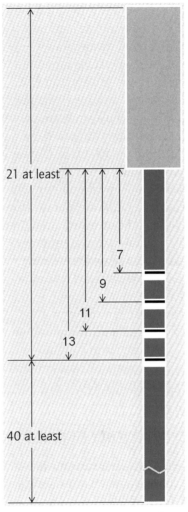

Figure 1: **Triple-jump area viewed from the top** (specifications in m; all other specifications correspond to those in figure 1 in chapter II–2.2.2; modified on the basis of the Rule Commissions by the DLV, FLA, ÖLV and SLV, 2010, pp. 99–102).

2.3.2 THE MOST IMPORTANT COMPETITION RULES

The following abridged and simplified International Competition Rules comprise the framework for the techniques and strategy, as well as the organisation of triple-jump competitions:

- Figure 1 shows the construction and specifications of a triple-jump area.
- For international competitions, it is recommended that the take-off line for women is not less than 11m and for men not less than 13m from the front edge of the pit. In any other competition, this distance should be adjusted to the respective performance level of the athletes. Frequently, an 11m take-off board for men as well as a 9m and not so often a 7m take-off board are provided. The landing and take-off zone between the take-off board and the landing pit must provide firm and consistent support.
- The triple jump is made up of a hop, a step, and a jump in that respective order. The three jumps must be performed in a left-left-right or right-left-right sequence.

- The rules for the long jump take-off also apply to the take-off for the hop. The landings and take-offs between the hop and step, and between the step and jump, are performed on the landing and take-off zone between the take-off board and the landing pit.
- An athlete does not fail if
  » he/she touches the ground with his/her swing leg while jumping; or
  » he/she lands outside the marked track during the hop and/or step.

Otherwise, the general competition rules for the technical disciplines and the long jump apply (see chapters II–2.1.1 and II–2.2.2).

At championships, the triple jump is only contested beginning with the w/m15 age group.

2.3.3 SPORT-SCIENCE FINDINGS, PHASE STRUCTURE, AND TECHNIQUE

The introduction to the phase structure and general comments on the biomechanics and technique of the jumps are to be found in chapter II–2.1.2. Therefore, in the following there are only discipline-specific additions.

MAIN OBJECTIVE
The special features of the triple jump are the repeated take-offs. The velocity and the angle of departure of one partial jump determine the impact velocity and the impact angle of the subsequent partial jump. In the event of identical

departure and landing heights, the departure angle and the impact angle of a jump are approximately the same. Due to air resistance, the landing angles are actually a little larger. A take-off can only be evaluated correctly if the entire change of direction (impact angle plus departure angle) is taken into account. Each take-off leads to a loss of horizontal velocity (see figure 2 and table 1). Small changes in direction are associated with small losses in horizontal velocity and energy, while big changes are associated with great losses (see chapter II–2.1.2).

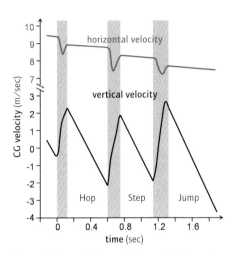

Figure 2: **Curve of the vertical and horizontal velocity in the triple jump** *(modified on the basis of Fukashiro et al., 1981).*

The effective triple-jump distance (D_{Ef}; see figure 3) increases with the mean horizontal velocity and the duration of the entire jump:

$$distance = duration \cdot velocity.$$

However, the total duration and horizontal velocity are not independent of one another, but influence each other negatively. Athletes who want to fly longer must take off in a more upward fashion, which means that they must achieve greater changes in direction upon take-off. Athletes who want to be faster must take off in a less upward fashion. The respective changes in direction must therefore be optimal: great enough to allow for sufficient flight duration and to have enough time in the hop for switching strides, and small enough to minimise losses of energy and speed. This **triple-jump economy** is described in chapter II–2.3.8.

Another possibility to achieve a high average horizontal velocity during the jump is to increase the run-up velocity. However, the physical stress and the loss of energy and horizontal velocity upon the take-offs increase with the extent of the change of direction and the impact velocity. If the departure angles (in particular in the hop) are not correspondingly flat, the loss tends to exceed the advantages of the higher starting velocity. A very fast run-up requires perfect jumping strength and technique.

In summary, the maintenance of horizontal velocity through relatively small departure angles in the first two partial jumps may be designated as the major objective of the triple jump.

Moreover, the triple jump places enormous demands on balance. During the short ground contacts, in which the jumper must develop enormous force, and during the flight phases, rotations about three body axes must be controlled. This becomes more difficult as performance improves since the proportion of flight phases (75–82% of the triple-jump duration), in which the rotations initiated upon take-off may have an effect, increases compared to the support phases (18–25%).

The three take-off points and the landing should be aligned if possible, as the official distance is measured perpendicular to the take-off line. However, the possible loss caused solely by the deviation from the straight jump direction is low (up to approx. 3cm). However, in most cases the

*Table 1: **Average biomechanical parameters for certain performance groups** (Killing et al., 2008, p. 159).*

	Run-up velocity (m/sec) Total distance (m)		Ground contact time of the take-off (sec)	Partial distances (m)	Horizontal departure velocity (m/sec)	Vertical departure velocity (m/sec)
Women	8.5	Hop:	0.12	4.62 (36%)	7.9 (-0.57)	2.08
		Step:	0.14	3.62 (28%)	7.3 (-0.67)	1.44
	12.80	Jump:	0.16	4.56 (36%)	6.2 (-1.04)	2.08
	8.8	Hop:	0.12	4.91 (36%)	8.2 (-0.65)	2.21
		Step:	0.14	3.83 (29%)	7.5 (-0.65)	1.50
	13.50	Jump:	0.16	4.76 (35%)	6.4 (-1.15)	2.13
	9.1	Hop:	0.11	5.15 (36%)	8.4 (-0.71)	2.39
		Step:	0.15	4.15 (29%)	7.8 (-0.57)	1.52
	14.30	Jump:	0.15	5.00 (35%)	6.5 (-1.29)	2.39
Men	9.4	Hop:	0.11	5.37 (36%)	8.9 (-0.53)	2.18
		Step:	0.14	4.17 (28%)	8.1 (-0.75)	1.42
	14.90	Jump:	0.16	5.36 (36%)	6.8 (-1.30)	2.28
	9.7	Hop:	0.12	5.81 (36%)	9.1 (-0.65)	2.33
		Step:	0.15	4.66 (29%)	8.1 (-0.97)	1.85
	16.00	Jump:	0.17	5.53 (35%)	6.9 (-1.16)	2.33
	10.2	Hop:	0.12	6.16 (36%)	9.5 (-0.70)	2.46
		Step:	0.15	5.13 (30%)	8.5 (-0.98)	1.78
	17.10	Jump:	0.15	5.81 (34%)	7.1 (-1.45)	2.66

$$d_{Of} = d_{Ef} - d_{LL}$$
$$d_{Ef} = d_H + d_S + d_J$$
$$d_{Ef} = d_{To\_H} + d_{Fl\_H} + d_{To\_S} + d_{Fl\_S} + d_{To\_J} + d_{Fl\_J} - d_{LL}$$

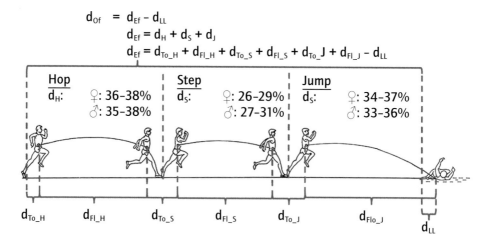

*Figure 3: **Simple model of partial distances as well as the average percentage of partial distances of the triple jump** (H: hop, S: step, J: jump; for further explanation of the abbreviations see figure 8 in chapter II–2.2.3).*

deviation from the straight jump direction goes hand in hand with tilting to the side during the flight or a lateral deflection of the hip or shoulder during the ground contacts. This impairs maximum force development during the take-offs and must therefore be absolutely minimised (see figure 4).

PHASE 1: RUN-UP

START OF THE RUN-UP

For similar skill levels and age, the triple-jump run-up is approximately two strides shorter than the long-jump run-up due to the slightly reduced run-up velocity before the take-off (see chapter II–2.2.3).

START AND PICK-UP ACCELERATION

The horizontal velocity before take-off (in the flight phase of the last stride) of triple jumpers is slightly reduced on average in comparison to that of long jumpers (see table 1 in chapter II–2.1.2). Even an athlete who starts in both disciplines usually runs up slower in the triple jump than in the long jump. A faster run-up speed results

*Figure 4: **Optimal upright body position** from the front view: no deviation to the side or tilting during the support or flight phases.*

in a higher load especially during the take-off for the step. Therefore, a reduction in speed seems to be caused not least by the (subconscious) fear of being unable to withstand these loads. However, the German record holder Ralf Jaros (17.66m) is reported to have reached his maximum sprinting speed only in front of the triple-jump take-off board. He is said to have not reached a corresponding velocity either in training or in tests or in sprint competitions.

The fastest run-up velocities in triple-jump history were achieved by Mike Conley at the Olympic Games in 1992. In five jumps, Conley achieved run-up velocities of 11.0–11.3 m/sec (Ø 11.1 m/sec). He was able to achieve this increase in velocity compared to previous jumps only because he performed a significantly flatter hop and was therefore able to reduce the loads mentioned in phases 2 and 4 (see below).

Overall, there is less correlation between the run-up velocity and jumping distance in the triple jump than in the long jump (however, see figure 5). The influence of jumping strength and technique is therefore greater in the triple jump than in the long jump. In homogeneous ability groups (such as the finalists in international championships) or in various trials of a single jumper, frequently no correlation between run-up velocity and the triple-jump result can be found.

However, the ability to achieve high maximum velocity makes it possible to run up at submaximal speed. This could

DISCOURSE I: HOP- OR JUMP-DOMINATED OR ACTUALLY FOCUSED ON THE STEP?

Hay (1999) distinguishes three triple-jump techniques: the hop-dominated technique with the hop being at least 2% longer than the jump, the jump-dominated technique with the jump being at least 2% longer than the hop, and the intermediate balanced technique. The hop-dominated and the balanced versions are observed similarly often. The jump-dominated version is rare.

Even at world-class level there is evidence that athletes who frequently use the hop-dominated technique achieve their best attempts with a more balanced distribution of effort. The world records by da Silva and Banks as well as Conley's best jumps were jump-dominated. The fact that a long hop is a high hop at the same time results in a significant increase in load during the step take-off. There is the danger of an excessive loss of velocity upon the step take-off, a rather flat and short step, and a worse overall performance.

The objective of many considerations about technique and available reactive strength is to achieve a good step. This partial jump in particular is often (much) too short for less advanced athletes. Since a) the horizontal velocity before the hop take-off is higher than before the step take-off, b) the step is a repeated take-off contrary to the hop, and c) the jump landing is performed with a significantly lower CG position, the step cannot be as long as the other partial jumps. But since precisely the step is often identified as a key point of the triple jump, a good triple-jump technique can be described as focused on the step. However, there are marked individual differences even on the world-class level. Men are able to jump 17m after a hop of at least 6m and step distances of 4.60–5.40m. Hay's system may therefore be expanded as follows:

	short step		long step
Hop-dominated:	38:27:35	37:29:34	36:31:33
Balanced:	37:27:36	36:29:35	35:31:34
Jump-dominated:	35:27:38	34:29:37	33:31:36

(the figures refer to the partial distances of the individual jumps as a percentage of the total jumping distance)

Comparing the percentage partial distances, women achieve slightly shorter step distances on average than men. The most likely reason for this might be the different relative strength ratios: Muscle mass constitutes a smaller percentage of the total body mass in women.

facilitate the coordination control of the hop take-off and could thus improve it. This means that the highest possible expression of maximum sprint speed is desirable in any case – either to jump with a better technique or faster.

TAKE-OFF PREPARATION

During the last (two) strides of the triple jump run-up, there are fewer deviations from normal sprint technique than in the long jump (see figure 6). This is due to the desired small departure angle in the hop. Short-long-short rhythm, CG lowering, and swing-leg squat should be less marked (or as little as possible). As a result, many triple jumpers achieve an even higher horizontal velocity in the final stride than in the penultimate stride in contrast to long jumpers.

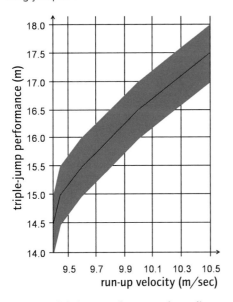

*Figure 5: **Triple-jump performance depending on the run-up velocity** between 6 and 1m in front of the take-off board (according to data by Hutt, 1990).*

*Figure 6: **Last two run-up strides.***

PHASE 2: HOP TAKE-OFF

It is the objective of the triple jumper to accelerate across the take-off board, which means to run over it. The foot touchdown is performed from a more marked heel lift, higher knee lift (thigh nearly horizontal) and more emphasised grasping action than in the long jump. The foot is placed down with the entire sole closer to the vertical projection of the CG. The backward lean of the trunk (backward reclining take-off position) and thus the bracing angle as well as the resulting amortisation (i.e., the eccentric bending of the knee of the take-off leg) are smaller. The complete push-off extension of the ankle, knee, and hip joint is also more clearly directed forward than in the long jump.

It is difficult to deter athletes from a high hop for two psychological reasons:

- If athletes want to jump far in total, they are reluctant to restrain themselves during the first jump.
- They know that they require time to switch legs in the air (see phase 4).

Therefore, E. Hutt, the former German national coach for the triple jump clearly stated that the hop is a part of the run-up.

DISCOURSE II: WHICH LEG SHOULD BE CHOSEN AS THE HOP-STEP LEG?

If a triple jumper has a strong leg and a weak leg, then it is natural to use the strong leg for two take-offs and to perform only one jump with the weak leg. However, it is also obvious that a triple jumper should have two equally strong take-off legs if possible. If this is the case, it often makes sense to choose the long-jump take-off leg as the jump leg since the athlete is accustomed to taking off with a steeper and more bracing action of this leg than would be useful for the triple-jump hop. The fast run across the take-off board described is therefore often more successfully performed with the other leg which is perhaps slightly weaker. The long-jump take-off leg may then set an even more powerful impulse for the jump at a lower horizontal velocity and initiate the flight and landing phase which is similar to the long jump. To answer the question posed in the title for each individual athlete, both variants (left-left-right and right-right-left) should be frequently practiced in training and test exercise.

ARM ACTIONS

Some world class jumpers (e.g., Sanejew, Olsson, Claye, and Taylor) have successfully performed a hop-take-off with double-arm swing. This has quite a few advantages:

- Upon take-off, a larger mass is swung forward and upward.
- The twisting of the trunk is reduced by the double-arm swing. The double-arm swing is therefore intended to contribute to the stabilisation of the pelvis.

*Figure 7: **Hop take-off.***

- The jumper does not need to change from the contralateral to the double-arm swing during the subsequent flight phase(s).

However, during the hop the double-arm swing also has two disadvantages:

- It is difficult to compensate for the rotational momentum about the longitudinal body axis caused by the swing leg.
- The jumper must switch from the contralateral to the double-arm swing during the take-off preparation. Due to the high speed of movement, this is extremely difficult in terms of coordination and may disrupt the flow of movement and lead to a reduction in run-up velocity.

The latter might also be the main reason why the double-arm swing has been used in the hop so infrequently. However, the slightly slower run-up velocity in the triple jump and its lower significance in comparison to the long jump (see phase 1) enables a few jumpers to master this movement task and to use its benefits.

In any case, the following rule, which was mentioned for the long jump, also applies to the triple jump: The athlete's fingertips should not be raised above eye level in front of the body, and, when using the contralateral arm swing, the other hand should be swung only to just behind the hip.

PHASE 3: FLIGHT PHASE OF THE HOP
Similar to the running long-jump technique, the triple jumper moves his/her take-off leg forward in the flight phase of the hop. It is moved forward with an acute angle at the knee joint until the thigh reaches the horizontal. Top athletes move their swing leg backward with a straight knee. If the vertical velocity of departure is lower and thus the flight duration shorter, particularly in younger or female jumpers, it may be necessary to move the swing leg backward in a bent position. The reduced distance between the mass of the leg and the pivot point (hip) allows a higher angular velocity. However, this behaviour counteracts the forward rotation triggered upon take-off less than a straight leg.

The torso should remain upright during the hop. The take-off leg is moved upward until a clear knee lift is achieved (thigh

*Figure 8: **Flight phase of the hop.***

is horizontal). From there, the grasping/pulling preparation of the next take-off is prepared. In the process, some jumpers straighten their leg very early to nearly the horizontal. Other jumpers straighten their leg at the knee joint only after the start of the hip extension, approximately when the leg is at an angle of 45° to the ground. Due to the different distances between the mass of the leg and the pivot point (hip), the early extension counteracts more strongly the forward rotation about the transverse axis of the body, while the late extension leads to an increased velocity of touchdown. After switching legs, the swing leg initially remains behind the body and begins its forward motion only shortly prior to the foot touchdown.

ARM ACTIONS
There are at least four versions of arm actions during the flight phase of the hop:

- The arms swing contralaterally as in the sprint. Only the elbows are often extended a little more. This is the simplest technique, which is also possible with less advanced athletes with relatively short flight duration.
- The arms are swung forward in a semicircle as in the running-jump technique of the long jump and thus

counteract the forward rotation about the transverse axis of the body triggered upon take-off. The rear arm is moved over the head.

- The athlete switches to the double-arm swing by moving both arms behind his/her body.

Athletes who have already begun with a double-arm swing continue this movement and move their almost outstretched arms in a semi-circular swing backward behind their body. In the process, they also counteract the forward rotation.

PHASE 4: STEP TAKE-OFF

The step take-off is also referred to as hop-step transition which is supposed to emphasise the unity of the take-off preparation during the flight phase of the hop, hop landing, and step take-off. It represents the most challenging part of the triple jump. This applies to the coordination and strength requirements. The addition of the vertical fall and departure velocity results in velocity changes which in top male athletes may exceed 5 m/sec. For women, it may be more than 4 m/sec. The short ground contact time (see table 1) is

an indication of the acceleration and forces required for this. Figure 9 shows how many times the force peaks exceed one's own body weight.

Upon the foot touchdown for the step take-off, the jumper again tries to place down his/her (almost) straight leg relatively close to the vertical projection of his/her CG. He/she places down his/her foot in an almost hitting manner on the entire sole of his/her foot. The jumper tries to extend his/her hip as fast as possible and to move it (and thus his/her complete body) across the touchdown point of his/her foot. All this serves to reduce braking forces during the front support, which, however, is still

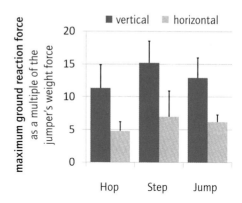

Figure 9: **Maximum ground reaction forces in the triple jump** (according to data by Perttunen et al., 2000; 4 men, 3 women, jumping distances from 11.37 to 15.24m; Ø13.25 ± 1.32m.): Since the horizontal and the vertical force peaks occur at the same time just after foot touchdown, a maximum resultant force can be calculated for the step in the group average. This force is higher than 16.7 times the body weight. With respect to the vertical force peak, Amadio (1985) found a mean value of 18.2 times the body weight in better athletes; the maximum value was 22.3 times the body weight.

Table 2: **Average, minimum and maximum of the rearward horizontal velocity of the take-off foot relative to the CG immediately prior to foot touchdown in** 16 athletes with jumping distances from 15.55–17.95m (Koh & Hay, 1990).

	Grasping velocity (m/sec)
Hop	6.93 (4.93–8.94)
Step	6.43 (2.91–9.10)
Jump	5.13 (2.32–7.10)

*Figure 10: **Step take-off.***

*Figure 11: **Flight phase of the step.***

limited by the fact that a slight bracing is required for the generation of a sufficient vertical impulse.

Although the jumper tries to achieve as little amortisation as possible, he/she is forced to yield to a knee angle of 126–137° at his/her knee joint due to the forces described above. Subsequently, a new complete take-off extension is performed. The swing leg, which is bent relatively little at the knee joint, is moved forward into a (nearly) horizontal thigh position.

ARM ACTIONS
Based on the preparation during the flight phase of the hop (see phase 3), the step is accompanied by a contralateral arm swing or double-arm swing (see phase 2 for the respective advantages and disadvantages).

PHASE 5: FLIGHT PHASE OF THE STEP
During the flight phase of the step, the jumper initially remains in the take-off position. The rear knee is slightly bent, which results in a slight lift of the rear foot. However, lifting the foot above hip level indicates an excessive forward rotation initiated upon take-off. The front knee is raised further to slightly above hip level. The upper body remains upright or

is perhaps only slightly bent forward to compensate for the movement of the front leg. The shoulder-hip separation should also remain slight. From this position, the grasping/pulling preparation of the next take-off is performed. The jumper moves his foot downward and backward as late as possible, but at maximum speed. Again, an early extension of the knee of the take-off leg (split in the air) and a late knee extension may be distinguished (see phase 3). The rear leg is held back for a long time.

ARM ACTIONS
During the flight phase of the step, three main forms of arm work may be distinguished in various jumpers:

- Jumpers who have already switched to the double-arm swing normally continue this movement and move their arms in a wide semi-circular swing downward and behind their body. In the process, they also counteract the forward rotation.
- The final position of the previous contralateral arm swing is roughly maintained and leads to the next contralateral arm swing. This is the simplest technique.
- To switch from the contralateral arm swing to the double-arm swing, the

front arm is moved backward. Due to the advantages mentioned, most top jumpers strive to achieve a double-arm swing during the jump take-off.

PHASE 6: JUMP TAKE-OFF

The jump take-off is also referred to as step-jump transition, thus stressing the unity of the take-off preparation during the flight phase of the step, the landing of the step, and the take-off for the jump. The jump is the only one of the three partial jumps of the triple jump, in which the objective is to maximise rather than to optimise the jumping distance. The jumper tries to make best use of the remaining horizontal speed and to achieve the optimum combination of horizontal and vertical departure velocity to achieve a maximum jumping distance (see chapter II–2.1.2). The effort to preserve horizontal velocity in the hop and step as well as the effort to perform an optimal jump take-off are successful if the loss of horizontal

DISCOURSE III: FLIGHT DURATIONS AND RHYTHM

Not only the flight distance but also the flight duration of the step is often shorter than that of the hop. Since the departure height and the landing height are almost identical in these two partial jumps, the short duration of the flight may already be read from the vertical departure velocities presented in table 1. Nevertheless, in terms of triple-jump economy, the distribution of jumping durations of 31% : 31% : 38% required by Hutt (1990) should be the objective. This means that the hop and step should be of approximately the same duration. This requires a very flat hop. Even in the case of approximately the same vertical departure velocity, the jump would take longer than the hop and step since the height of the CG is lower in the jump landing.

The foot touchdowns for the three take-offs are audible. Therefore, the rhythm of a triple jump may be used by the coach and the athlete himself/herself for acoustic jump analysis. In the case of an equally long hop and step, the rhythm is uniform: "tap – tap – tap" instead of "tap – ta–tapp" (see also chapter II–2.3.8).

Even the jumper himself or herself has the impression that the triple-jump movement is characterised by a certain rhythm and succinct rhythmic changes: The take-off and flight phase of the hop must be performed fluently. The step take-off is extremely powerful but nevertheless fast. The flight phase of the step is characterised by rather freezing the movement and waiting. The jump take-off is aggressive and powerful again, and the subsequent flight phase and landing also have a rhythm of their own depending on the flight technique. Athletes must learn these changes.

*Figure 12: **Jump take-off.***

velocity upon the jump take-off is larger than in the previous two take-offs.

The characteristics of technique are similar to the step take-off:

- almost hitting foot touchdown with high backward directed touchdown velocity;
- not very noticeable backward reclining take-off position and small bracing angle (slightly larger than in the hop and step, but smaller than in the long jump);
- as little amortisation as possible (minimum knee-joint angle: 128–140°);
- rapid movement of the body across the point of support; and
- swing leg bent only up to approximately 90° as a medium-long pendulum.

ARM ACTIONS

According to the preparation during the flight phase of the step (see phase 5), the jump is accompanied by a contralateral arm swing or a double-arm swing (for the respective advantages and disadvantages see phase 2).

PHASE 7: FLIGHT PHASE OF THE JUMP

In world-class athletes, the vertical departure velocity and thus the duration of the flight of the jump particularly among men is sufficient for all three flight techniques mentioned in connection with the long jump. A running jump (with a maximum of 1½ strides) is still rare, since the jump is usually performed with a double-arm swing contrary to the long jump. This is easier to combine with a stride or hang jump. Only after the take-off, the arms are moved further upward, and subsequently they are moved forward and downward to the feet.

*Figure 13: **Flight phase of the jump.***

PHASE 8: LANDING

The landing of the jump is basically identical with the long-jump landing. However, due to the lower horizontal velocity and the steeper landing approach angle, the timing

*Figure 14: **Landing in the sand.***

is different. For example, the athlete cannot place down his/her heels so far ahead of his/her centre of gravity as in the long jump without falling back.

*Table 3: **Requirement profile for the triple jump:** The suggested rough estimate of the value of selected factors determining performance is based on the importance for the overall performance and the percentage of time spent training (IR: information requirements, constr.: constraints; see chapter I–1.1).*

Factors determining the triple-jump performance	Estimate of value	Notes
Coordination	+ + + + +	optical IR: high, acoustic IR: low, tactile IR: low, kinaesthetic IR: high, vestibular IR: high; precision constr.: high, time constr.: high, complexity constr.: medium–high, situation constr.: low, physical stress constr.: medium–high
Flexibility	+ +	hardly any extreme movement amplitudes are required
Strength		particular significance of the extensor loop (glutes, quadriceps, triceps surae, erector spinae) and trunk muscles, iliopsoas, hamstrings, adductors, shoulder and upper-arm muscles
Maximal strength	+ + + + +	particularly relative maximal strength
Reactive strength	+ + + + +	mainly of the extensor loop
Speed	+ + + + +	mainly cyclic; as well as in the acyclic movements involved in the three partial jumps
Endurance (general dynamic) Anaerobic endurance		
Strength endurance	+	as a basis at the most
Speed endurance	+ +	as a basis to be able to perform nine trials (practice and competition trials) at the same level of performance
Aerobic endurance	+ +	only as a basis for training (regeneration ability)
Psychological and cognitive abilities	+ + + + +	concentration ability (on the point); intelligent distribution of jumps (flat hop) performance-oriented thinking and behaviour (see chapter I-3.1.1)
Anthropometric and primarily genetically determined characteristics	+ + + + +	high percentage of the fastest muscle fibres; connective tissue with optimal energy storage capacities; medium up to above-average body height (particularly in women); low percentage of body fat

2.3.4 SUMMARY OF THE MOST IMPORTANT TECHNICAL CHARACTERISTICS = TECHNIQUE-ANALYSIS SHEET

RUN-UP

START OF THE RUN-UP

- Run-up length with top athletes: approx. 18–23 strides (35–50m); with younger athletes: number of strides = age in years (with girls possibly minus 2 strides); or on the basis of sprinting times.
- Start of the run-up usually from a standing position.

START AND PICK-UP ACCELERATION

- Rapid but not maximal acceleration to optimal velocity for taking off and achieving a maximum jumping distance.
- First toe push-off, then grasping/pulling sprint with emphasis on high knees and erect trunk and pelvis.
- Landing on the intermediate marker 4–7 strides in front of the take-off board.
- (Subconscious) adjustment of stride length for an optimum landing on the take-off board.

TAKE-OFF PREPARATION

- Direction of view away from the take-off board straight ahead parallel to the ground.
- Emphasis on stride frequency.
- (Hardly noticeable) lowering of the CG and swing-leg squat; (hardly noticeable) short-long-short rhythm.
- Continued acceleration up to the take-off board.

TAKE-OFF AND FLIGHT PHASE OF THE HOP

- After grasping/pulling preparation, the (nearly) extended take-off leg is actively placed on the take-off board from above; the ground contact is made with the entire sole of the foot.
- The touchdown of the foot in front of the vertical projection of the CG and the trunk angle (as vertical as possible) determine the bracing angle; a small bracing angle results in a small departure angle and optimal running across the take-off board.
- As little flexion at the knee joint during amortisation as possible.
- The body moves quickly across the support point, the hip is quickly extended.
- Flat and complete push-off extension of the foot, knee, hip, and trunk.
- The shoulders are kept back to minimise the forward rotation (during the take-off, the trunk rotates forward by 2–8°).
- Rapid raising and slowing down of the swing elements (the swing leg is moved forward at an acute angle at the knee joint; when the jumper breaks contact with the ground, it reaches the three 90° position; usually with a contralateral arm swing).
- Switching stride in the air: the acutely angled take-off leg is moved forward until the thigh is horizontal, the swing leg is moved backward with a straight knee if possible.
- Four variations of arm movement: 1. contralateral, 2. semi-circular forward swing, 3. backward movement of the front arm to perform a double-arm swing, or 4. backward movement of both arms to perform a new double-arm swing.
- Grasping/pulling preparation of the next take-off: hip extension and forward pendulum movement of the lower swing leg; the tip of the foot is raised.

TAKE-OFF AND FLIGHT PHASE OF THE STEP

- After the grasping/pulling preparation, the same leg as in the hop is actively placed on the ground from above in (an almost) extended position; the ground contact is made with the entire sole of the foot.
- The bracing angle is small enough to lose as little horizontal velocity as possible and large enough to generate sufficient vertical velocity of departure.
- The knee of the support leg is bent as little as possible.
- The body moves quickly across the support point; the hip is quickly extended.
- Flat and complete push-off extension.
- During ground contact, the upper body is moved from a minimal backward lean to a slight forward lean; too much forward rotation and/or shoulder-hip separation should be avoided.
- The swing leg is quickly moved forward and upward (usually only bent at a right angle); when leaving the ground, the thigh is often still slightly below the horizontal.
- After the contralateral arm swing, the end position is maintained, or the front arm is moved backward to prepare a double-arm swing; after the double-arm swing, both arms are moved downward and backward behind the body.
- During the flight: The knee of the swing leg is raised further up to slightly above hip height; the take-off leg is kept behind the body for a long time, the lower leg continues its swinging movement backward and upward (not above hip height).
- Grasping/pulling preparation of the next take-off; hip extension and forward swinging movement of the lower take-off leg; the tip of the foot is raised.

TAKE-OFF AND FLIGHT PHASE OF THE JUMP

- After the grasping/pulling preparation, the leg not used in the step take-off is actively placed on the ground from above in an (almost) extended position; the ground contact is made with the entire sole of the foot.
- The bracing angle is a little larger as in the hop and step but smaller than in the long jump.
- As little amortisation as possible.
- The body moves quickly across the support point.
- Powerful and complete push-off extension, a bit further upward than in the hop and step.
- During the ground contact, the upper body is moved from a minimal backward lean to a slight forward lean; too much forward rotation should be avoided.
- The swing leg is quickly moved forward and upward (in most cases only bent at approximately a right angle); if possible, up to the horizontal.
- In most cases double-arm swing (contralateral arm swing is also possible).
- Stride- or hang-jump technique (see chapter II–2.2.4).

LANDING

- Opening the hip angle from the jackknife position and beginning the knee-joint flexion shortly before landing, leading to active landing with grasping heels.
- The continuation of the arm swing downward and backward results in a forward shift of the hips; too early sand contact with the hands should be avoided.
- The heels and the buttocks should land in the sand at equal distance from the take-off board; the buttocks are possibly placed into the sand in a slightly lateral position.

2.3.5 PHOTO SEQUENCES

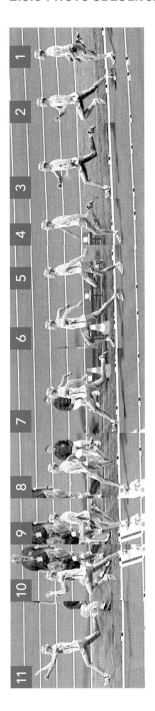
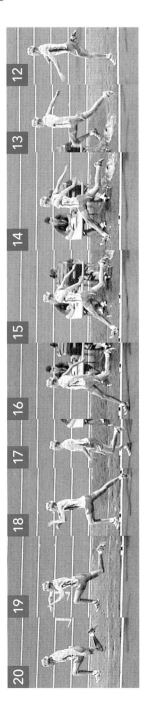
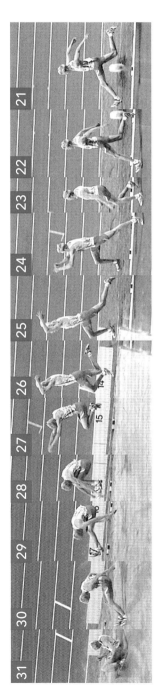

Data about the photo sequence

Athlete:	Christian Olsson (born: 25 January 1980, Sweden)
Height/weight:	1.92 m/73 kg
Performance:	17.53 m (wind: ± 0.0 m/sec; 8 August 2002, Munich)
Best performance:	17.79 m (wind: +1.4 m/sec; 22 August 2004, Athens)
Greatest success:	Olympic champion 2004; World champion 2003

COMMENTARY

In 1995, the 15-year-old Christian Olsson watched Jonathan Edwards establish a triple-jump world record at the World Championships in Olsson's hometown of Gothenburg. At that time, Olsson discovered his love for this discipline, but also participated in the high jump. In 1999, he jumped over 2.21m and won the gold medal in the high jump at the Junior European Championships; in the triple jump, he was only second with 16.18m. Nevertheless, he achieved his later successes exclusively in the triple jump. The photo sequence shows his winning jump at the European Championships in 2002, where he defeated his role model Jonathan Edwards for the first time. The biomechanical parameters presented in table 4 help in the analysis of the photo sequence.

The most striking aspect of Olsson's triple jump technique is his unusual arm action in the hop. Long before reaching the take-off board, he switches to parallel arm movements. He performs the hop like a high jumper with a distinct double-arm swing. It cannot be determined whether the fact that he exhibited the slowest run-up velocity of the three medallists is related to this double-arm swing or to his sprint abilities. The higher run-up velocities of Friedek and Edwards result in shorter ground-contact phases on the take-off board and in a longer hop. Olsson, however, is more successful in maintaining his lower initial horizontal velocity throughout the three partial jumps. He loses less velocity in each take-off than his competitors and is therefore eventually significantly faster than they are in the jump. In the short ground contact phase, he converts less horizontal velocity to vertical velocity and thus takes off more flatly.

Olsson sprints to the take-off board with upright torso, high knee lift, and high hips. He lowers his CG only slightly (picture 5). He avoids excessive bracing (picture 8) and achieves a perfect, flat take-off extension (picture 10). Then he performs an exemplary switch of legs in the flight phase of the hop with the swing leg swinging far backward in straight position, the take-off leg moved forward in an acutely angled position, and an upright trunk. The arms are moved downward and backward in a straight position. The step take-off is performed from an actively grasping/pulling movement (while the trunk is again kept stable through a powerful double-arm swing) and leads after minor amortisation (picture 17) to a very good push-off extension (picture 18). The knee of the swing leg is moved further over the horizontal and the take-off leg is kept back. Olsson then performs the grasping/pulling jump take-off which is characterised by the same qualities as the previous take-offs. The jump is performed using the hang technique and is completed with an appropriate landing.

Table 4: **Biomechanical parameters** of the best jumps of the top three finishers at the European Championships in Munich in 2002 (according to Killing, 2002).

Athlete (trial)	official distance = effective distance - loss of distance (m)	stride lengths (m; as well as for partial jumps in %)					horizontal velocity during flight (m/sec)				
		penultimate stride	last stride	hop	step	jump	penultimate stride	last stride	hop	step	jump
Olsson (5)	17.53 = 17.57 - 0.04	2.60	2.41	6.16 (35)	5.15 (29)	6.26 (36)	10.05	10.01	9.50	8.57	7.67
Friedek (2)	17.33 = 17.47 - 0.14	2.48	2.20	6.50 (37)	5.30 (30)	5.67 (32)	10.40	10.36	9.56	8.41	6.85
Edwards (2)	17.32 = 17.45 - 0.18	2.44	2.38	6.48 (37)	4.84 (28)	6.14 (35)	10.65	10.68	9.75	8.83	7.04

Athlete (trial)	take-off: ground contact time (sec/100), loss of horizontal velocity, and vertical velocity of departure (m/sec), as well as angle of departure (°)											
	hop				step				jump			
Olsson (5)	12	0.52	2.31	14	15	0.92	1.85	12	17	0.90	2.28	17
Friedek (2)	11	0.80	2.55	15	14	1.15	2.05	14	17	1.56	2.33	19
Edwards (2)	09	0.94	2.61	15	12	0.92	1.75	11	14	1.79	3.02	23

2.3.6 DIDACTICS: SUPERORDINATE LONG-TERM OBJECTIVES AND GENERAL METHODOLOGY

In children's athletics and in basic training, the triple jump is prepared in particular by using the sprint, the long jump, and by learning reactive multiple jumps. Gradually, bounding runs (toward the end of basic training), rhythm jumps (more toward the end of build-up training), and one-legged jumps are introduced. In each case, technical development must precede maximum efforts in reactive-strength training. During the development of technique, aids are used which are later rejected at least in certain phases: soft surfaces (e.g., lawn.), slower velocities, etc.

(see chapter II–2.1.4). In winter, before a young athlete changes to the w/m15 age group, he/she probably performs rhythm jumps on a mat path for the first time. However, he/she is already able to perform a technically correct bounding run at high speed on an artificial track. The objective is to achieve a continuous increase in load, which at no time leads to overloading the tissue structures used in the exercise.

Technique jumps in training (and competition) should be performed from the highest possible, but still controllable run-up speed. This means that beginners should initially perform a triple jump from a standing position and soon thereafter from a 3- or 5-stride run-up. If a certain run-up length or velocity is mastered using a proper technique, the athlete switches to the next higher length or velocity. For advanced athletes, frequent jumping from short run-ups should be avoided. This would too easily lead to a too high hop and (even if the hop were not too high) to problems with the maximal reactive force generation during the hop-step transition (see chapter II–2.1.4).

After a comprehensive introduction, the focus of the triple-jump technique training in build-up training is especially on the hop and the step take-off. The main objectives include running over the take-off board to achieve a flat hop, an active step, and maintaining an upright body position. Due to prior long-jump experience, it is usually not necessary to practise the jump so often. However, it is absolutely necessary to use both legs as take-off legs: The hop and the step are performed equally often with the actual jump leg.

The variety of possible techniques of arm movement makes it difficult to work on them in practical training. One possibility is initially not to deal with them in specific technique training and to leave them to the jumper's intuition. At the same time, one should require athletes to also perform

versatile skipping, bounding runs, and rhythm jumps (possibly even long jumps) with a double-arm swing early in training. Alternative arm movements may then be deliberately tested in specific triple-jump training at a later time.

TRIPLE JUMPER ≠ SLOW LONG JUMPER

Friedek (2008) expressed the fear that those who are fast enough for international success in the triple jump may be satisfied with national success in the 100m sprint and the long jump. At the regional level, the negative selection even begins at the U16 and U18 age groups. Coaches (and parents) of faster athletes want to maximise success in the sprint or long jump through special training content at an early stage. The slower athletes switch to the triple jump. Therefore, future success in the triple jump would depend on general improvement in the sprint or renunciation of negative selection. A possible solution could be independent of all this: The (short) sprint and horizontal jump may be considered as a single group of disciplines in which all athletes benefit from comprehensive and versatile training of reactive multiple jumps. If athletes are well prepared, they should probably start in all disciplines in this group until the end of adolescence.

(See also the comments on the safety aspects of the long jump in chapter II–2.2.6.)

2.3.7 TRAINING CONTENTS: FORMS OF GAMES AND EXERCISES

Due to the relatively late introduction of the triple jump in the course of age, no forms of games are mentioned below. However, all forms of games and exercises (see chapter II–1.3.8 and II–2.2.7) mentioned in connection with the 100m sprint and the long jump are also preparation for the triple jump. In particular, the jump is prepared by means of long jumps with the good leg and the bad leg. For training the ability to establish rhythm, (frequency-oriented) hurdle sprints in particular are a general component of triple-jump training (see chapter II–1.8.8, e.g., 190). A key content of triple-jump training is the multiple jumps described in connection with the general forms of strength training (see chapter I–5.4.6). In particular, bounding runs (88), rhythm jumps, and later one-legged jumps (89) are extensively varied:

- with deliberate grasping/pulling foot touchdown
- from a standing position, slow or fast run-up
- for height, distance, and/or speed
- with an increase in height, distance, and/or speed
- deliberately flat at high speed
- with contralateral or double-arm swing

- athletes should learn to experiment with movement and to vary grasping, height, distance, speed and the arm swing even within one run-through (e.g., every now and then individual jumps that are particularly high or long)
- with or without final landing in the pit
- on flat ground, on stairs, uphill, and downhill (the last variety only with adult athletes)
- rhythm jumps in all possible variations:
  l-l-r-r-l-l-r-r-..., or: r-r-l-l-l-l-r-r-r-l-l-l-...,
  l-l-r-r-r-l-l-r-r-r-..., or: r-r-l-l-l-r-r-l-l-l-...,
  l-r-r-l-r-r-..., or: r-l-l-l-r-l-l-l-...,
  r-r-l-r-r-l-..., or: l-l-r-l-l-r... (triple-jump rhythm; possibly with the step being performed over an obstacle)

- non-specific to increase volume on cinder track, grass, mat path, forest floor, or sand; during the competition period only on the artificial track
- non-specific barefoot or wearing running shoes, during the competition period primarily wearing spikes
- non-specific with adults possibly with additional weight

---

301 | | ▮ | **Triple jump using markers**

Possible objectives: Holistic introduction of the triple jump; correct distribution of jumps (triple-jump economy).

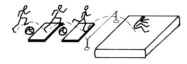

Execution: After explanation of the rules (sequence of foot contacts), take-off points are indicated by markers (e.g., mats or traffic cones; see pictures), and the triple jump is performed initially from a standing position, then from a short run-up (2–8 strides); the markers should encourage submaximal jumps.

Variations: It is particularly important that athletes are asked early to perform the step over objects (e.g., banana box); different markers depending on the level of performance (e.g., 35% – 30% – 35%.):

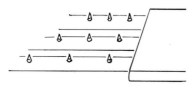

7m	= 2.45m + 2.10m	+ 2.45m
8m	= 2.80m + 2.40m	+ 2.80m
9m	= 3.15m + 2.70m	+ 3.15m
10m	= 3.50m + 3.00m	+ 3.50m
11m	= 3.85m + 3.30m	+ 3.85m
12m	= 4.20m + 3.60m	+ 3.85m

(Toe – toe – toe – heel); even with advanced athletes with marker for the hop so that it does not become too long (e.g. foam block in front of which the step take-off must be performed); when jumping without obstacles, also with eyes closed: initially one's eyes should be closed only for a part of the triple jump, then one's eyes should be closed 2–3 strides before the take-off and should be opened only after landing in the sand.

Typical load standards: 5–10 reps per side.

302  **High-knee run/step-overs + hop**

Possible objectives: Run-up organisation, little lowering of the CG, running over the board; switching strides during the flight phase of the hop.

Execution: On the sprinting straight (to avoid a too high hop): after a high-knee run or step-overs with the focus on stride frequency, the athlete takes off for the hop, switches legs in the air, lands on the take-off leg, and continues running.

Variations: Preventing or reducing short-long-short rhythm by using rings or foam blocks on the ground (273); after a submaximal run-up, the athlete switches to the high-knee run or step-overs on call or at a marker; later also followed by step and jump take-off into the pit; with advanced athletes also with eyes closed.

Typical load standards: 3-10 reps per side.

303   Hop + rudimentary step take-off

Possible objectives: Switching strides in the air and active grasping preparation of the step take-off.

Execution: The athlete performs the hop take-off in front of the pit, switches strides, and places his/her take-off leg in the sand in a hitting manner.

Variations: From gradually increasing run-up length.

Typical load standards: 3–6 reps per side, thereafter with real step take-off.

304   Hop + step take-off + telemark landing

Possible objectives: Maintenance of the take-off position throughout the step.

Execution/variations: The hop with subsequent step take-off is performed with short to medium-length run-ups; the athlete maintains the take-off position and lands in the telemark position in the sand.

Typical load standards: 3–6 reps per side.

305   Hop + jump

Possible objectives: Flat hop and active step.
Execution: The athlete performs the hop from the

highest controllable speed (see chapter II–2.3.7) and subsequently takes off (with the same leg) for a maximally long jump into the pit; the stride-jump technique is used since this jump shall improve the actual step.

Variations: As a competition or a test with a measurement of the distance; with additional hops before the take-off as 3-stride or 5-stride hop (see one-legged jumps (89), and T9)

Typical load standards: 3–8 reps per side.

306 Hop + step onto or over an object

Possible objectives: Flat hop and active step.

Execution: The athlete performs a flat hop and steeper step from the highest controllable speed (see chapter II–2.3.7); the landing after the step takes place on a longitudinally placed one- or two-element gym box.

Variations: With and without take-off for the jump from the box; a longitudinally placed mat (with adolescents also transversely positioned) over which the hop is performed, and a transversely positioned mat in front of the box may help with orientation; subsequently, the box may be omitted and the jump may be performed after an equally high hop and step from the track.

Typical load standards: 3–6 reps per side and task.

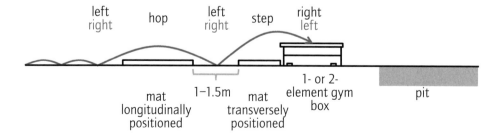

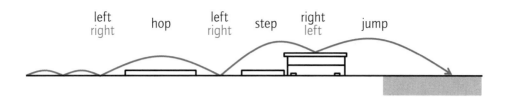

| left right | hop | left right | step | right left | jump |

---

307 **Hop + step + rudimentary jump take-off**

Possible objectives: Actively grasping preparation of the jump take-off.

Execution: The athlete performs the hop and step take-off in front of the pit and places the jump take-off leg in the sand in a hitting manner.

Variations: From gradually increasing run-up length.

Typical load standards: 3–6 reps per side, thereafter with real jump take-off.

---

308 **Competition-like triple jump**

Possible objectives: Execution of the target technique.

Execution: Even in training, the athlete should try to perform the target technique at correspondingly high intensity.

Variations: Despite maximal effort, some athletes are forced to reduce their run-up in training by 1–3 feet in length; to achieve a varied workout, the run-up may be shortened by 2–4 strides or extended by 2 strides every now and then.

Typical load standards: 3–6 reps.

---

309 **Double triple jump and similar variations**

Possible objectives: Variation of multiple-jump training at maximum intensity; practice of the landing at reduced velocity (as compared to the long jump).

Execution/variations: In each case from the highest controllable run-up velocity and with final landing in the pit; also as a test; double triple jump: l-l-r-l-l-r or r-r-l-r-r-l (i.e., hop + step + step + hop + step + jump), or extra hop: l-l-l-r- or r-r-r-l (i.e., hop + hop + step + jump), or German triple jump: l-r-l or r-l-r (i.e., step, step, jump).
Typical load standards: 3–6 reps per side.

310 Hop while kicking a ball backward

Possible objectives: Stretched backward movement of swing leg during the hop.
Execution/variations: The athlete takes off for the hop in front of a football, kicks the ball backward by moving his/her stretched swing leg backward during the flight phase, and then takes off for the step (and jump); with medium-length run-ups.
Typical load standards: 5–8 reps per side.

311 Hop from an elevation (one-legged depth jumps)

Possible objectives: Competition-like drop height during the hop-step transition.
Execution: The hop is performed from the top element of a gym box for example, while the repeated take-off is performed from the track.
Variations: The repeated take-off may be a jump (305) or a step followed by a jump; if the jump is performed only after the step, it may be performed from the track or from an elevation (the latter is very difficult); from a standing position, from a walk-on, or from short or medium-length run-ups.
Typical load standards: 3–6 reps per side and task.

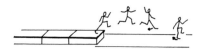

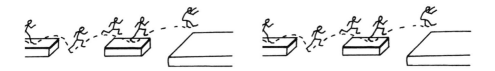

312  **Jump over obstacle**

Possible objectives: Correction of a too flat jump (rare); practice landing at reduced velocity (as compared to the long jump).

Execution/variations: The triple jump is performed with a jump over different height markers from the highest controllable run-up velocity; with subsequent landing.

Typical load standards: 3–6 reps.

2.3.8 SPECIAL TEST AND CONTROL PROCEDURES

Test: Ability/skill tested	Execution/comments
T111 Technique analysis: Long-jump technique	Maximal competition jump from full run-up; evaluation on the basis of the technique analysis sheet (see chapter II–2.2.4), possibly using a video (T1) and photo sequences made thereof.
T112 Analysis of triple-jump duration, duration of the partial jumps, partial distances, etc.: Triple-jump technique	The duration of the triple jump on the whole and the partial jumps may be relatively easily seen from simple video recordings (see next page, and discourse III); in high-performance sport, computerised video analysis allows additional biomechanical analysis (stride lengths of the last strides, partial distances [see discourse I], partial velocities, etc.).
T113 Triple jump from short run-up: Specific speed and reactive strength	Maximum triple jump from 5, 10, and 15 run-up strides; test should be performed on both sides (i.e., both r-r-l and l-l-r); test criterion: effective jumping distance (Deff).
T114 Double triple jump: Specific speed and reactive strength	Maximum multiple jump from long run-up; test should be performed on both sides (i.e., both r-r-l-r-r-l and l-l-r-l-l-r); test criterion: effective jumping distance (Deff).

(continued)

(continued)

	Test: Ability/skill tested	Execution/comments
T115	**Long jump:** Specific speed and reactive strength	Maximum long jump from full run-up; test should be performed on both sides.
T4	**RPM:** Maximal strength	Squat (62), clean (63), snatch (64), hamstrings (68), quadriceps (69), arm exercises, etc. (if possible also eccentric maximal strength measurement).
T5	**Squat jump, and T8 counter-movement and drop jump:** Two-legged speed strength and reactive strength of the extensor loop	The counter-movement jump may be replaced by the simpler test of tossing the shot forward and/or backward (93) for distance.
T9	**5-stride hops with distance maximisation:** Reactive strength of the legs in comparison to one another	Possible triple-jump performance according to figure 16).
T10	**30m bounding run with time minimisation:** Reactive strength of the legs	
T21	**60m analysis:** Sprint technique	See technique analysis sheet in chapter II–1.5.4.
T24	**30m flying sprint:** Maximum sprinting speed	Possibly only 20m.
T25	**20m frequency test:** Cyclic speed	
T61	**Standing start and acceleration up to 20m:** Start acceleration	
T66	**Graded field test:** Aerobic endurance	With lactate withdrawal (and spirometry; for young athletes also Cooper test, T65, which is easy to perform but inaccurate).
T104	**Horizontal-jump endurance test:** Specific speed endurance	
T2	**Flexibility tests:** General flexibility	
T3	**Body weight and body fat measurement:** Relative strength	Inappropriate upward and downward deflections should be avoided (see also chapter II–2.1.2: phase 3).

ANALYSIS OF TRIPLE-JUMP DURATION

The measurement of the duration of a triple jump may be performed relatively easily using digital video recordings. The time code and the single-frame function usually allow a sufficiently accurate measurement. If the time code is not accurate enough, checking the video settings of your tablet, etc., can help to find out how much time passes between two frames (30 frames per second => 0.0333 sec, 60 fps => 0.01666 sec, etc.). Thus, counting frames leads to the time passed between to events.

As the transition between the run-up and the hop, one may select the frame in which both thighs are parallel for example. The first contact of the heel with the sand may be defined as the end of the jump.

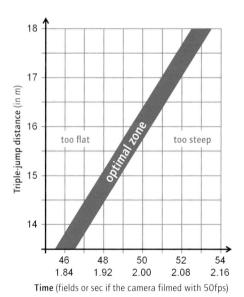

The mean horizontal velocity ($v_x = d/t$) of the entire jump may be calculated from the duration (t) of the entire jump together with the distance (d) achieved. If possible, the effective distance (i.e., the measured competition distance plus the [estimated] take-off loss) should be used for calculation. The method is scientifically not quite exact, since, for example, the behaviour of the jumper after touching the sand with his heels also affects the distance. Nevertheless, the method is sufficiently accurate for the findings desired.

Figure 15 shows that there is an optimal jumping duration for each jumping distance. The basis of this is that in terms of triple-jump economy an optimal ratio of triple-jump duration and triple-jump velocity must be the goal (major objective). If there are jumps which are off the optimum range, there are specific opportunities for improvement. Athletes who are right from the optimum range, jump too steep (i.e., with large departure angles; especially in the hop and jump). In the future, these athletes should try to perform a flatter take-off, to maintain more velocity throughout the jumps, and possibly to perform a faster run-up. Jumps to the left of the optimum range are too flat. If the simple effort to achieve a steeper departure angle is not helpful, more concentration should be placed on improving jumping strength and technique.

*Figure 15: **Optimal relationship between triple-jump distance and triple-jump duration** (modified on the basis of Hutt, 1990): The measurement of the duration is performed using the method described in the text.*

Through an analysis of fields, the duration of the three partial jumps may also be estimated accurately enough. Again, the frame in which both thighs are parallel may be selected as the transition between the partial jumps. Based on this calculation, the durations of the three partial jumps should have a percentage ratio of 31:31:38 (according to Hutt, 1990; see discourse III).

POSSIBLE TRIPLE-JUMP PERFORMANCE

As an approximation, the possible triple-jump performance may be estimated using the following rule of thumb:

Triple-jump distance = long-jump distance · 225%

Hutt (1990) calculates the possible triple-jump performance by means of three tests:

- Test exercise 1: 5-stride hop with take-off from the jump leg from run-up (T9);
- Test exercise 2: 5-stride hop with take-off from the hop-step leg from run-up (T9);
- Test exercise 3: 30m flying sprint (T24).

Figure 16 shows a nomogram by which the possible triple-jump performance may be determined graphically from these three test exercises.

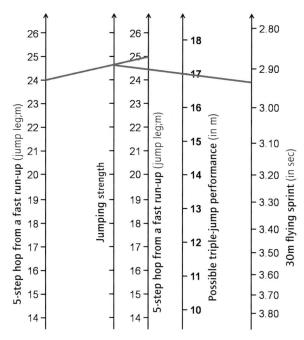

Figure 16: **Nomogram for determining potential triple jump performance** *(modified on the basis of Hutt, unpublished): The results of the three test exercises are marked on the respective scales. Subsequently, the two points for the jump results are connected by a straight line and the point of intersection with the scale for jumping strength is marked. This point is connected to the point for the sprint result. The intersection of this line with the remaining scale indicates the potential triple-jump performance. The example plotted is a potential 17m jumper.*

Table 5: **Basic performances of triple jumpers** (according to Killing et al., 2008, p. 232).

		Women		Men	
Age group		w17	w19	m17	m19
Best performance	(m)	12.20	13.00	14.00	15.30
Long jump in training	(m)	11.50	12.20	13.00	14.20
Long jump from 9 run-up strides	(m)	5.10	5.40	6.20	6.60
Long jump with the other leg	(m)	4.90	5.20	5.90	6.20
5-stride bounding run from 5m run-up	(m)	16.50	17.60	18.50	20.00
5-stride hop from 5m run-up, good leg/ poor leg	(m)		15.50/15.40		18.50/18.30
100m bounding run from a standing position	(jumps)	38	35	33	31
10m flying sprint	(sec)	1.16	1.13	1.05	1.00
30m flying sprint	(sec)	3.35	3.25	3.00	2.95
40m sprint from a standing position	(sec)	5.60	5.45	5.20	5.00
100m sprint from a standing position	(sec)	13.00	12.60	11.90	11.35
Tossing the shot (women: 3 kg; men: 4 kg)	(m)	13.00	15.00	16.00	20.00
Snatch; squat	(kg)		35; 40		55; 65

2.3.9 ERRORS – CAUSES – CORRECTIONS

Error	Causes	Corrections
Run-up too slow.	• Fear of stress during the step take-off. • The athlete always performs a too high hop (for causes see below). • Double-arm swing during the hop (makes it difficult to develop a high run-up velocity).	✔ In many cases, an increase in run-up velocity goes hand in hand with a reduction in the departure angle of the hop to keep the stress during the step take-off roughly the same and therefore tolerable. ✔ See corrections of too high hop below. ✔ Possibly switch to contralateral arm swing during the hop.
Excessive bracing during the hop take-off.	• Excessive lowering of the CG during take-off preparation through too marked short-long-short rhythm and too distinct swing-leg squat. • Negative transfer from the long jump or too many jumps from short run-up. • Too long last step; possibly due to inaccuracies during the run-up: performing a long stride to reach the board. • Backward lean of the trunk.	✔ Increased practice of flat hops from a fast run-up with the least possible take-off preparation and upright torso throughout the take-off (e.g., by means of exercises 306), possibly predefinition of uniform stride length by means of gymnastics hoops (see 273). ✔ Possibly switching to the non-take-off leg in the long jump as the hop and step leg. ✔ Adjustment or increased practice of the competition run-up (e.g., using exercises 288 and 308).
Hop too high.	• Excessive bracing during the hop and its causes (see above). • The athlete makes no effort to achieve triple jump economy, and excessive motivation (the jumper wants to jump very far). • The jumper knows (subconsciously) that he/she needs time to switch legs in the air.	✔ See corrections of excessive bracing during the hop above. ✔ Focusing on the significance of a flat hop and running across the take-off board as a topic of discussion ("The hop is a part of the run-up"). ✔ In the case of low performance ability, the switch of stride should be performed deliberately with a bent swing leg.
Balance problems: forward, backward, or sideward lean, zig-zag jump, evasion or twisting of hip and/or shoulder.	• Lack of jumping experience. • Lack of trunk strength and stability. • Incorrect or unsuitable arm actions. • The cause of visible rotations is often found in prior movements (for example, athletes who exhibit a forward lean of the trunk during the jump take-off trigger a forward rotation during the step take-off, which may possibly be associated with a too high hop).	✔ Versatile (multiple) jumps on various surfaces, at different speeds, with different objectives, with additional tasks (e.g., eyes closed), etc.; while focusing on the correct jumping technique (upright and frontally aligned upper body, straight arm actions, etc.). ✔ Strengthening the trunk muscles (e.g., using exercises 41–47 and 66–67). ✔ Possibly switching from the contralateral to the double-arm swing or vice versa.

Error	Causes	Corrections
Step too short or breaking off the trial upon the step take-off.	• The height of the hop exceeds the athlete's strength capacities (the athlete is not able to absorb the falling height to initiate the necessary change in direction; see above for the causes of an excessive hop). • Balance problems and their causes (see above). • Too few jumps at competition intensity. • Beginners: lack of preparation for performing the step in competition.	✔ See corrections of hop too high above. ✔ Technique jumps with deliberately short hop (predefinition of length by means of gymnastics hoops, for example) and long step (e.g., over an object). ✔ Maximal- and reactive-strength training for the lower extremities (e.g., using exercises 62–64, 75-77, and 79–92). ✔ See corrections of balance problems above. ✔ More jumps from a long run-up (308–309). ✔ Triple-jump competitions require long-term preparation.
Excessive bracing during the repeated take-offs (upon touchdown, the foot is too far ahead of the vertical projection of the CG).	• The touchdown of the foot is too far ahead of the body (the CG is lowered too much). • The jumper wants to make the previous jump too long; he/she initiates the grasping/pulling preparation of the next take-off too late. • The athlete makes no effort to maintain high horizontal velocity.	✔ More multiple jumps at competition intensity, with deliberately flat and fast repeated take-offs (e.g., within exercises 305–309 and 311). ✔ Focusing on the significance of high average velocity for triple-jump economy as a topic of discussion.
Too much loss of velocity during the three take-offs.	• Excessive bracing during the hop take-off and during the repeated take-offs and its causes (see above). • Too low grasping velocity backward (technique and/or strength deficits; possibly caused by too slow switching of strides during the hop). • Too high hop and its causes (see above).	✔ See corrections of excessive bracing above. ✔ More practice with multiple jumps (88–92), also from run-up, with deliberate grasping/pulling foot touchdown. ✔ Strength training for the hip extensors (62–64 and 72). ✔ Practice switching strides during the hop (e.g., using exercise 310); athletes of low performance ability should perform the switching strides with a bent leg. ✔ See corrections of too high hop above. ✔ Focusing on the significance of high average velocity for triple-jump economy as a topic of discussion.

(continued)

(continued)

Error	Causes	Corrections
Incomplete push-off extension of the take-off leg during the repeated take-offs.	• The jumper is so compressed that his/her strength is not sufficient to straighten the leg again during the period in which the body moves across the support point due to its horizontal velocity » compression due to horizontal velocity in the case of excessive bracing (for causes see above); or » compression due to falling velocity or vertical velocity after too high previous jump (see "too high hop" and its causes above).	✔ See corrections of excessive bracing above. ✔ See corrections of too high hop above. ✔ More maximal- and reactive-strength training for the legs and the trunk (using exercises 41–49, 62–64, 66–72, 75–77, and 79–92).
Jump too short.	• Hop and step too long or too high. • Too much velocity loss during the repeated take-offs and their causes (see above). • Jump leg too weak.	✔ See corrections of too high hop above. ✔ Predefinition of economic partial distances by means of markers (301). ✔ See corrections of too much velocity loss during the repeated take-offs above. ✔ Making sure that in maximal- and reactive-strength training both legs are equally stressed. ✔ More complete triple jumps (308).

See also the errors, causes, and corrections mentioned in connection with the sprint (see chapter II–1.3.10) and particularly those in connection with the run-up, flight phase and landing in the sand in the long jump (see II–2.2.9).

2.3.10 TRAINING PLANNING

As discussed in chapter II–2.3.6, the short sprint and the horizontal jumps may be regarded as a single group of disciplines, for which the training may be organised in a uniform manner far into build-up training, regardless of the subsequent special discipline. The preliminary observations made in connection with the 4 x 100m relay and the long jump (see chapter II–1.6.11 and 2.2.10–II) therefore also apply to the triple jump.

SUGGESTED TRAINING PLANS

Below, there are exemplary microcycles for the

• third mesocycle of a 17-year-old athlete in build-up training (table 7);
• second mesocycle of an athlete in high-performance training (table 8); and
• fourth mesocycle of an athlete in high-performance training (table 9).

As mentioned above, it is assumed for build-up training that there is not yet definitive specialisation. The sample microcycle presented in connection with the long jump for the first mesocycle of a 17-year-old athlete in build-up training is therefore intended for the same athlete as in table 7 in this chapter. The sample microcycle presented in connection with the 4 x 100m relay for the second mesocycle of a 17-year-old athlete in build-up training could be included in this series after only a few changes.

With the exception of technique training, long and triple-jump training are very similar even in high-performance training. In addition to the training plans mentioned here, the long-jump chapter therefore includes a sample microcycle for the

- first mesocycle of an athlete in high-performance training; and
- third mesocycle of an athlete in high-performance training.

*Table 6: **Training emphasis in the various mesocycles** for triple-jump training in build-up and high-performance training.*

1st mesocycle	basic aerobic and anaerobic endurance training; hypertrophy-oriented maximal-strength training especially for the legs and the trunk; basic reactive-strength training for the legs; flexibility training; general (e.g., hurdle training, games, etc.), and special (e.g., ABCs of sprinting/jumping, technique training from short to medium-length run-ups) coordination training
2nd mesocycle	basic anaerobic (speed-) endurance training; hypertrophy-, IC- and connective-tissue-oriented maximal- and reactive-strength training especially for the legs and the trunk; sprinting-speed training; special coordination training (e.g., ABCs of sprinting/jumping, technique training from medium-length run-ups)
3rd mesocycle	special speed-endurance training at high intensity; IC- and connective-tissue-oriented maximal- and reactive-strength training especially for the legs and the trunk; sprinting-speed and acceleration training at maximum intensity; special coordination training (long run-ups)
4th mesocycle	competitions and corresponding regeneration; IC- and connective-tissue-oriented maximal- and reactive-strength training especially for the legs and the trunk; speed and acceleration training at maximum intensity; technique training; maintenance stimuli

Table 7: Build-up training: sample microcycle for a 17-year-old long and triple jumper in the third mesocycle.

Monday	Tuesday	Wednesday	Thursday	Friday	Saturday	Sunday
Warm-up jogging (6 min)	Foot strengthening (10 min)	Warm-up jogging (10 min)	Warm-up jogging (6 min)	Warm-up jogging (6 min)	I1 runs (6 x 80m, rest intervals: 20 sec) for warming up	Rest
Maximal-eccentric strength training (15 min) trunk stabilisation, lifting opposite upper and lower limbs in prone position, belly punches, raising the foot/toes	Acceleration runs (2 reps) barefoot	Two of the following: Strength training for the trunk on apparatus and/or for the arms, medicine-ball work, gymnastics, technique training for the throwing events, boxing, etc. (30 min each) e.g., goalkeeper throws, rotational throws, throws from a prone position, and tossing, using a medicine ball	Acceleration runs (2 reps) barefoot	ABCs of jumping (8–10 run-throughs)	Tuck jumps (3 x 2 run-throughs over 5 hurdles each)	*On Saturdays before the tempo runs possibly also training the technique of one event of the quadrathlon or pentathlon*
Acceleration runs (2 reps) barefoot	ABCs of jumping (8–10 run-throughs) sideways galloping, ankle jumps, skipping with two-legged landing, skipping variations, etc.		ABCs of sprinting (8–10 run-throughs)	Acceleration runs (3 reps)	or	
ABCs of sprinting (8–10 run-throughs)	Acceleration runs (2 reps)		Standing starts (2 reps)	Pop-up jumps (2 x 2 run-throughs per leg of 4 take-offs each at 5-stride rhythm)	Depth jumps (5 x 6 from box to box)	
Acceleration runs (2 reps) wearing spikes	Practising the long-jump technique (40 min) with medium run-up lengths with the weaker leg as take-off leg, with long run-up length with the better leg as take-off leg	Tappings (8 x 5 sec) or frequency coordination (10 min) over foam blocks at 1m distance	Crouch starts (20, 20, 30, 40, 50, 40, and 30m; rest intervals: 4, 4, 6, 8, 10, and 8 min) 2 practice starts, then at maximum pace against each other	Strength training (40 min) according to the pyramid principle (e.g., quarter-split squat); as well as maximal-eccentric strength training: hamstrings, adductors, etc.	Acceleration runs (3 reps)	
Flying sprints (3 x 30m + 20–30m run-up; rest intervals: 10 min) at maximal pace through light barriers	I1 tempo runs (2 x 100m, rest interval: 15 min)		Practising the triple-jump technique (35 min) with medium or long run-ups, individual tasks and corrections	Alternating-pace sprints (3–4 x 60m) as utilisation	I2 tempo runs (80, 150, 120, and 80m; rest intervals: 8, 15, and 12 min)	
Bounding runs and/ or rhythm jumps (4–6 run-throughs) with double-arm swing						

Table 8: *High-performance training: sample microcycle for the second mesocycle.*

	Monday	Tuesday	Wednesday	Thursday	Friday	Saturday	Sunday
Morning	Trunk stabilisation exercises and abdominal crunches (20 min) ABCs of sprinting (12–15 run-throughs) Acceleration runs (3 reps) Flying sprints or crouch starts (5 x 30m flying or 20, 30, 40, 50, 40, 30, and 20m from the block) ABCs of endurance (5 x 20 sec)		LI runs (8 x 80m) ABCs of jumping (8–10 run-throughs) Tuck jumps (5 x 2 run-throughs over 10 hurdles each) Rhythm jumps (approx. 10 x 40m) versatile; double-arm swing Pop-up jumps (e.g., 3 run-throughs per leg using 1-stride rhythm)		LI runs (6 x 100m) Ankle jumps or skipping with two-legged landing (5 x 15 jumps) Acceleration runs Practising the triple-jump technique (45 min) medium run-up lengths (e.g., long jump with the weak leg as the take-off leg or hop-jump)	Warm-up jogging (6 min) Acceleration runs (3 reps) barefoot ABCs of sprinting/ jumping (10–12 run-throughs) I3 tempo runs (80, 100, 120, 150, 180, 150, 120, 100, and 80m; rest intervals: 2, 3, 4, 5, 10, 6, 5, and 4 min)	Rest
Afternoon	Warm-up jogging (6 min) ABCs of jumping (12–15 run-throughs) Acceleration runs (3 reps) Practising the triple-jump technique (45 min) e.g., double triple jump with short run-up or step-jump following hop from elevation	Foot strengthening (10 min) Acceleration runs (5 reps) barefoot Strength training (60 min) according to the pyramid principle: clean (or snatch), hamstrings, quadriceps, adductors/abductors, hip flexors and extensors Game (20 min) e.g., basketball or handball	Warm-up jogging (6 min) Acceleration runs (3 reps) ABCs of sprinting (12–15 run-throughs) I2 tempo runs (3 x 3 x 60m; rest interval: 3 min; rest intervals between sets: 10–12 min) possibly including slight pull-resisted sprints or hurdle sprints	Continuous run (30 min) Contract-relax stretching (15 min) Strength training for the trunk on apparatus or medicine-ball work (35 min) Frequency coordination (10 min) as utilisation	Warm-up jogging (8 min) Acceleration runs (5 reps) Maximal-eccentric strength training (30 min) hamstrings, adductors, etc. Strength training (15 min) pyramid principle: primarily full squat Alternating-pace sprints (4 x 60m)	Contract-relax stretching (15 min) Warm-down jogging (10 diagonals on the lawn) Bounding runs (3–5 run-throughs) as utilisation	

Table 9: *High-performance training: sample microcycle for the fourth mesocycle.*

Monday	Tuesday	Wednesday	Thursday	Friday	Saturday	Sunday
Warm-up jogging (6 min)	**LI runs** (8 x 80m, rest intervals: 20 sec) for warming up	**Warm-up jogging** (6 min)	Rest	**Warm-up jogging** (6 min)	Rest	*Preparatory competition* • Warm-up jogging or LI runs
Maximal-eccentric strength training (15 min) trunk stabilisation, lifting opposite upper and lower limbs while in prone position, belly punches with tense abdominals, raising the foot/toes	**ABCs of jumping** (8–10 run-throughs)	**ABCs of sprinting** (8–10 run-throughs)		**Belly punches with tense abdominals** (4 x 5 sec)		• Inciting (trunk and foot) • 2 acceleration runs • ABCs of sprinting/jumping
Acceleration runs (3 reps)	**Practising the triple-jump technique** (30–40m) medium to long run-ups, last individual fine-tuning	**Depth** or **tuck jumps** (approx. 20 jumps)		**High-intensity strength training** (15 min) snatch		• 2 standing starts • Rhythm jumps • 1–3 run-up checks • 1–2 x full-length run-up plus hop-step
High-intensity strength training (45 min) clean and quarter split squat, bench press, lat pull, double-arm swing with dumbbells		**Acceleration runs** (3 reps)		**Acceleration runs** (2 reps)		• 2–3 short run-up, jump-leg take-off, landing
Alternating-pace sprints (4 x 60m) as utilisation		**Flying sprints** (2 x 20m with individual run-up length; rest interval: 10 min) at maximum pace through light barriers		**Rhythm jumps** (approx. 3–4 run-throughs) at high intensity		**Triple-jump competition** (6 trials)
		12/11 tempo runs (2 x 120m; rest interval: 12 min) first run at submaximal pace, second run at maximal pace		**Standing starts** (2 reps)		
				Run-ups with landing on the take-off point (3 reps) the competition run-up is measured on the sprinting straight and the athlete tries to land on the take-off point		

In the competition phase, the training plan must be adapted to the (irregular) competition calendar. In this plan, it may be assumed that the athlete took part in a preparatory competition over 100m (2 runs) and long jump (3 trials with the right leg, 3 trials with the left leg) on the previous Sunday. Due to the enormous impact loads, triple-jump competitions require relatively long recovery periods: A complete day off plus an additional day with only few impact loads (see Monday) and only submaximal technique training in the subsequent week may be necessary. If there are no other competitions for one and a half weeks (or more) between two competitions, the athlete should perform more training and his/her training should be of a more basic nature. Before the main competition, the athlete should train even less than shown here.

2.3.11   BIBLIOGRAPHY

Amadio, A. C. (1985). *Biomechanische Analyse des Dreisprungs.* Dissertation, Deutsche Sporthochschule Köln.

Brüggemann, G.-P. & Arampatzis, A., (1999). Triple Jump. In G.-P. Brüggemann, D. Koszewski & H. Müller (Hrsg.), *Biomechanical Research Project Athens 1997: Final Report* (S. 82-113). Oxfort: Meyer & Meyer.

Cruise, B. (2003). Triple Jump. *Modern Athlete and Coach 41* (1), 26-28.

Czingon, H. (mit Adamczewski, H., Dickwach, H., Elbe, J., Gehrke, K., Hutt, E., Jeitner, G., Killing, W., Kruber, D., Metzler, U., Simon, B. & Veldmann, B.). (1994). *Rahmentrainingsplan für das Aufbautraining Sprung* (Edition Leichtathletik, 4, 3. Aufl.). Aachen: Meyer & Meyer.

Elbe, J. (1998). Beschreibung der Lehrbildreihe Nr. 1153, Dreisprung, Jonathan Edwards. *Die Lehre der Leichtathletik 37* (33), 77-79.

Friedek, C. & Hess, S. (2008). Der Traum vom perfekten Sprung. *Leichtathletiktraining 19* (8), 34-39.

Fukashiro, S., Imoto, Y., Koboyashi, H. & Miyashita, M. (1981). A biomechanical study of the triple jump. *Medicine and Science in Sports and Exercise 13*, 233-237.

Hay. J. G. (1992). The biomechanics of the the triple jump: a review. J*ournal of Sports Sciences 10* (4), 343-378.

Hay, J. (1996). Ein Plädoyer für eine jump-orientierte Dreisprungtechnik. *Die Lehre der Leichtathletik 35* (8), 17-18, (9), 19.

Hay, J. G. (1999). Effort distribution and performance of Olympic triple jumpers. *Journal of applied biomechanics 15* (1), 36-51.

Hutt, E. (1990). Dreisprung für Praktiker. *Die Lehre der Leichtathletik 29* (4), 15-17, (5), 15-18 & (6), 19-21.

Hutt, E. (1992). Dreisprung für Praktiker II: Das Training. *Die Lehre der Leichtathletik 31* (21), 15-18, (23), 15-18 & (24), 15-16.

Hutt, E. (1998). Dreisprung: Technikbeschreibung eines Rekordsprungs. *Leichtathletiktraining 9* (6), 18-24.

Johnson, C. (1996). The elastic strength development of Jonathan Edwards. *New Studies in Athletics 11* (2-3), 63-69.

Jonath, U., Krempel, R., Haag, E. & Müller, H. (1995). *Leichtathletik 2*: Springen. Reinbek: Rowohlt Taschenbuch.

Jürgens, A. (1998). Biomechanische Untersuchung des Hop-Step-Übergangs. *Die Lehre der Leichtathletik 37* (31), 73-74, (32) 75-76, (33), 77.

Jürgens, A. (2008). Mit Tempo in die Grube. *Leichtathletiktraining 19* (5), 10-16.

Killing, W. (2002). Die Sprünge von München: Die Dreispringer der EM von München unter der biomechanischen Lupe. Teil 2. *Leichtathletiktraining 13* (12), 30-39.

Killing, W., Bartschat, E., Czingon, H., Knapp, U., Kurschilgen, B. & Schlottke K. (2008). *Jugendleichtathletik: Offizieller Rahmentrainingsplan des Deutschen Leichtathletik-Verbandes für die Sprungdisziplinen im Aufbautraining.* Münster: Philippka.

Koh, T. J. & Hay, J. G. (1990). Landing leg motion and Performance in the horizontal jumps II: The triple jump. *International Journal of Sports Biomechanics 6*, 361-73.

Moura, N. A., Fernandes de Paula Moura, T. & Borin, J. B. (2005). Approach speed and performance in the horizontal jumps: What do Brazilian athletes do? *New Studies in Athletics 20* (3), 43-48.

Niessen, M., Hartmann, U. & Jürgens, A. (2005). Bewegungsanalyse und Bewegungssteuerung im Dreisprung. In Bundesinstitut für Sportwissenschaften (Hrsg.), *BISp-Jahrbuch 2004.* Bonn: Bundesinstitut für Sportwissenschaften.

Ognyan, M. & Bonov, P. (2004). Individual approach in improving the technique of triple for women. *New Studies in Athletics 19* (4), 27-36.

Perttunen, J., Kyröläinen, H., Komi, P. V. & Heinonen, A. (2000). Biomechanical loading in the triple jump. *Journal of Sports Sciences 18* (5), 363-370.

Regelkommissionen des DLV, FLA, ÖLV und SLV (Hrsg.). (2010). *Internationale Wett-kampfregeln.* Waldfischbach: Hornberger.

2.4 HIGH JUMP

2.4.1 SIMPLER, FASTER, HIGHER – (FOSBURY) FLOP

In order to become men, East African Watusi boys must jump higher than their own body height. The high jump is also rooted in the historical tradition of the Celts. Many of the rules which are still valid today were formulated in England in 1865 (three trials, one-legged take-off, etc.). According to these rules, the high jump was also a part of the competition programme of the first modern Olympic Games in 1896. When women took part in the Olympic Games for the first time in 1928, they also performed the high jump. Between 1900 and 1912 the two-legged high jump from a standing position was also a part of the Olympic Games. Raymond Ewry, the Human Frog, dominated the competition (world record: 1.65m with a type of scissors jump). Even today, the jump from a standing position is a training exercise (336).

There is no other jumping discipline with as many technique variations as the high jump. Until 1936, athletes had to clear the bar feet first. In 1968, coaches and athletes around the world studied slow motion films of the Russian world record holder Valerie Brumel (2.28m). Many experts considered his straddle technique as the best style to clear the bar. During the same period, a 1.93m tall student from Oregon attracted attention at the US Olympic trials: Richard Douglas "Dick" Fosbury varied the well-known scissors jump in such a way that

he cleared the bar with his head first and then fell onto the mat backward. This flop style of jumping had only been made possible shortly before through the introduction of soft floor mats. Before that time, high jumpers had landed on a hill of sand. Arm and wrist fractures were among the most common high jump injuries. Experts initially laughed at this new technique, saying that it had no chance of success, and that it was too dangerous. But on the day of the Olympic high jump final on 20 October 1968, spectators in the Mexican National Stadium could not help but be amazed at the new technique. While one straddle jumper after the other failed, Fosbury cleared all six heights up to 2.22m in the first attempt. The backward jumper finally cleared 2.24m in the third attempt and won the gold medal. The triumph of the flop was unstoppable, leading to the women's world record of 2.09m established by the Bulgarian Stefka Kostadinova (1987) and the men's world record of 2.45m established by the Cuban Javier Sotomayor (1993).

However, the straddle was long thought to have the same potential: Using this technique, East German Rosemarie Ackermann was the first woman to jump over 2m in 1977. The Russian Vladimir Yashchenko jumped highest with this technique: 2.35m, a new indoor world record in 1978. In 1988, East German

Christian Schenk achieved by far the highest height in the decathlon using the straddle: 2.27m.

The triumph of the flop is not least attributed to the fact that it is easier to learn. Therefore, German Ulrike Meyfarth, only 16 years old, was able to establish a world record of 1.92m and win the gold medal at the Olympic Games in Munich in 1972 using the new flop technique. Following the world records established by Ackermann, in 1982 Meyfarth became world-record holder again, improved the record to 2.03m in 1983, and became the Olympic Champion again in 1984. The image of Germany as a high-jump nation was complete with Dietmar Mögenburg (world record of 2.35m in 1980 and Olympic Champion in 1984), Carlo Thränhardt (world indoor record of 2.42m 1988), Heike Henkel (world champion with 2.05m 1991, indoor world record of 2.07m in 1992, and Olympic Champion in 1992), Martin Buss (world champion in 2001), and Ariane Friedrich (2.06m) as the final champion until today.

2.4.2 THE MOST IMPORTANT COMPETITION RULES

The following abridged and simplified International Competition Rules comprise the framework for the techniques and strategy, as well as the organisation of high-jump competitions:

VERTICAL JUMPS (HIGH JUMP AND POLE VAULT)

- The crossbar must be made of fibreglass or another suitable material, but not of metal. Figure 1 shows the specifications of the bar and its end pieces. The flat surfaces of the end pieces must be hard and smooth. They must not be covered with rubber or any other material which has the effect of increasing the friction between them and the supports.
- The jumping height is measured in whole centimetres and perpendicularly from the ground to the lowest part of the upper side of the bar. The bar may not have a bias.
- Before the start of the competition, the chief judge shall announce the starting height and the further heights to the athletes. The increment of raising of the bar should never increase. However, if a competitor has already been established as the winner, he/she may choose the increase in jumping height as he/she likes. (This does not apply in the combined events.)
- A competitor may commence at any jumping height previously announced and may jump at his/her own discretion at any subsequent height. Three consecutive failures, regardless of the height at which any of such failures occur, disqualify the jumper from further jumping. If an athlete forgoes a trial at a certain height, he/she may not make any subsequent trial at that height.

- An athlete fails if after the jump, the bar does not remain on the supports because of the action of the athlete whilst jumping. An athlete does not fail if the bar rotates due to contact and does not remain resting on its usual support surfaces.
- If it is clear that the bar did not fall due to an action by the competitor (e.g., through a gust of wind), the trial must either be regarded as valid or a new trial must be granted.
- If according to the rules described, all competitors are eliminated and there is a tie, the procedure must be as follows: The competitor who at the critical height had fewer failed attempts is better placed. If the athletes are still equal, the athlete with the lowest total number of failed attempts throughout the competition, up to and including the height last cleared, is awarded the better place. If the tie persists, it is only resolved by means of a jump-off if it concerns the first place. (This does not apply to the combined events.) During the jump-off, all equal athletes initially perform a trial for the next height above the highest height which they cleared. If one jumper fails or several jumpers fail in the jump-off while other jumpers clear (or one athlete clears) the height, the athlete(s) who has/have failed are eliminated and is/are assigned the appropriate place. If several jumpers clear a height in the jump-off, the bar is raised in the high jump by 2cm and in the pole vault by 5cm. If all remaining jumpers fail at a certain height, the bar is lowered by the same amount. In both cases, all remaining jumpers are granted another trial. The procedure is continued in this manner until the winner is determined.

HIGH JUMP

- Figure 1 shows the construction and specifications of a high-jump area.
- The front side of the zero line is vertically below the front side of the bar.
- The crossbar supports are designed so that the bar may fall forward and backward. The bar may weigh up to 2 kg, and may have a maximum sag of 2cm. If a weight of 3 kg is attached to the centre of the bar, the bar may sag no more than 7cm.
- The time available until the start of the trial is
  - » 1 min with more than three competitors,
  - » 1.5 min with two or three competitors,
  - » 2 min in successive trials of one competitor, or
  - » 3 min if there is only one athlete left in the competition (in the combined events 2 min).
- In the high jump, shoe spikes may be up to 12mm long (subject to any restrictions set by the organisers). The heel may be up to 19mm thick, and the remaining sole up to 13mm.
- The take-off is performed with one foot.
- An athlete fails if he/she touches the ground including the landing area beyond the vertical plane through the nearer edge of the crossbar without having before jumped over the bar.

An athlete does not fail if he/she, touches the landing area with his/her foot while jumping, and in the opinion of the judge, no advantage is gained.

Otherwise, the general competition rules for the technical disciplines apply (see chapter II–2.1.1).

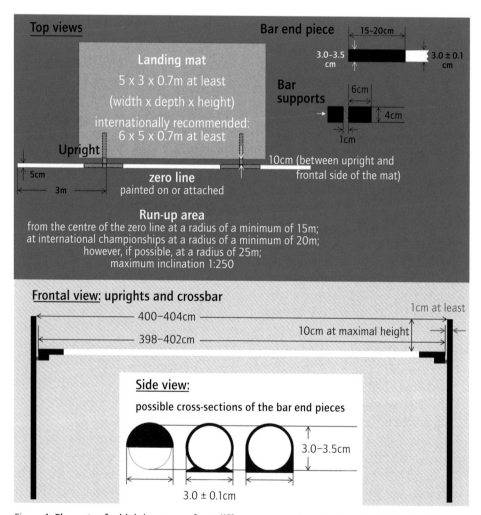

Figure 1: *Elements of a high-jump area from different perspectives (modified on the basis of the Rule Commissions by the DLV, FLA, ÖLV and SLV, 2010, pp. 92–95).*

2.4.3 SPORT-SCIENCE FINDINGS, PHASE STRUCTURE, AND TECHNIQUE

The introduction to the phase structure and general comments on the biomechanics and technique of the jumps can be found in chapter II–2.1.2. Therefore, in the following there are only additional comments pertaining to the discipline.

DIFFERENCES BETWEEN THE TECHNIQUES
Figure 2 shows that the official jumping height (bar height) can be divided into three or four partial heights. Figure 3 shows the development of technique and explains that it is primarily based on the improvement of clearance height (HClear). However, there are also many other reasons for the performance development shown in the top row: improved training methods and competition facilities, professionalism, possibly doping, etc.

Figure 5 shows the straddle technique that has long been considered to be equivalent to the flop technique. However, only in the flop is it theoretically possible to clear the bar while pushing the CG through under the top edge of the bar. The CG is a theoretical point which may be outside the body in an extreme bridge position (see figure 4). This means that the flop technique enables the athlete to clear the bar more effectively so that the bar may be higher although the maximal height of the CG is the same as in the straddle.

Additionally, the following advantages of the flop technique are mentioned in the literature in comparison with the straddle:

- The flop technique is known as the more natural movement
  - » since upon take-off a forward rotation about the transverse axis of the body is initiated as in all other take-offs (in athletics; see phase 2). In the straddle, a backward rotation about the transverse axis of the body is initiated upon take-off. It is difficult to generate backward rotation during a one-legged take-off from the run-up, resulting in a more ineffective utilisation of run-up speed, and
  - » since the swing leg is usually moved upward in a bent knee position as with all other one-legged take-offs. In the straddle, the swing leg is raised in a straight position and very high. This requires very well-trained flexibility.
- A natural movement is much easier to learn than one that differs greatly from the usual patterns of movement.
- The curved run-up and forward rotation allow for higher run-up speed.
- The curved run-up in the flop technique has more specific advantages (see phases 1 and 2). The straddle is performed from a straight run-up, which is performed in the direction of the frontal side of the mat at an angle of 20–45°.
- The flop technique offers various individual possibilities of variation and is therefore suitable for a wide range of jumpers (see discourse I).

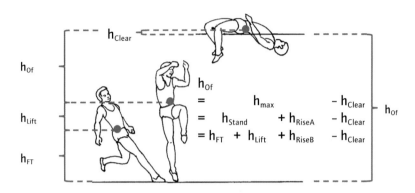

Figure 2: **Partial height model of the high jump:**

h_{Of}:   Official jumping height (bar height)

h_{max}:   Maximal (flight) height of the centre of gravity

h_{Clear}:   Clearance height: difference between the flight height of the CG and the height of the bar
(in some studies the maximally possible bar height is determined by means of light barriers
above the bar, and clearance height is defined as the difference between the flight height
of the CG and the maximally possible bar height)

h_{Stand}:   CG height when standing with arms hanging down (see table 1)

H_{RiseA}:   Rising height of the CG up to the highest point of the CG flight curve
(as compared to the CG height when standing)

h_{FT}:   CG height upon touchdown of the foot for take-off

h_{Lift}:   Distance of lift of the CG during the take-off (between foot touchdown and leaving the ground)

h_{RiseB}:   Rising height of the CG up to the highest point of the flight curve of the CG
(as compared to the CG height when leaving the ground)

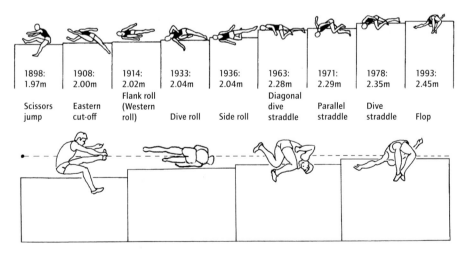

1898: 1.97m	1908: 2.00m	1914: 2.02m	1933: 2.04m	1936: 2.04m	1963: 2.28m	1971: 2.29m	1978: 2.35m	1993: 2.45m
Scissors jump	Eastern cut-off	Flank roll (Western roll)	Dive roll	Side roll	Diagonal dive straddle	Parallel straddle	Dive straddle	Flop

Figure 3: **Development of the men's world record and differences in the possible crossbar heights
with identical CG flight height.**

*Figure 4: **Shifting the CG to the outside of the body** in extreme bridge position.*

*Table 1: **CG height while standing** (h_{Stand}, according to Killing et al., 2008, p. 44, and Killing, 2009a, p. 190).*

		h_{Stand} (cm)	
		Women	Men
Average in world-class athletes		103.9	111.3
Body height (cm)	170	95.2	96.9
	180	100.8	102.6
	190	106.4	108.3
	200		114.0

SIGNIFICANCE OF PARTIAL HEIGHTS

Although the better clearance height is the main advantage of the flop, there is only a very slight correlation between the clearance height and the competition results among good flop jumpers. If one compares several jumps of one and the same jumper (the CG height in a standing position is then identical), the correlation is slightly closer, but still relatively low.

In table 1 it is evident that men and taller athletes are at an advantage in terms of the model of partial heights. Therefore, it seems that tall people in particular choose the high jump. In a group of high-performance high jumpers, it was discovered that the men (n=72; best performance: 214.7 ± 11.79cm) had an average body height of 1.92m, while the women (n = 72; 182.2 ± 8.01cm) were 1.80m tall on average. However, in the group of flop jumpers there is hardly any or no correlation between performance and body height or CG height when standing. For world-class male high jumpers, the CG height when standing represents a smaller percentage of the maximal flight height of the CG than for world-class female high jumpers: 48.4% in the male group compared to 53.6% in the female group. Therefore, the CG height when standing affects the high jump performance of women by about 12%, whereas the corresponding value for men is only approximately 2%.

*Figure 5: **Straddle technique** (above: parallel straddle; below: dive straddle).*

The rising height, which is dependent on jumping abilities, is of paramount importance for the competition performance in the (flop) high jump. For both men and women, the competitive performance depends 80% on h_{RiseA} (correlation coefficient r = 0.9). The influence is even greater in longitudinal studies of a single jumper, i.e. with constant CG height when standing.

PHASE 1: RUN-UP

The high jump run-up can also be divided into the sub-phases used in the previous chapters. However, the following flop-specific division of the usual J-shaped run-up is more common:

- start of the run-up;
- straight segment of the run-up;
- arched segment of the run-up; and
- take-off preparation.

START OF THE RUN-UP

An athlete who uses his/her left leg for the flop take-off places his/her marker on the right side of the run-up area (looking in the direction of the high-jump facility) to indicate the start of the run-up and vice versa, since the flop take-off is performed with the leg distant to the bar. (On the contrary, the straddle take-off is performed with the leg closer to the bar.)

The run-up in the high jump is initiated more frequently than in the other jumping events from several stutter steps. This is justified as follows: To get into the clearly backward reclining take-off position described in phase 2, the athlete must run up very erectly. Many athletes who start from a standing position assume the forward lean of the body which is typical of the toe push-off acceleration at the beginning of the run-up (see chapter II–1.3.3). Due to the shortness of the run-up, they do not succeed in straightening up their trunk early and far enough. A pre-acceleration with several stutter steps and deliberately upright running after hitting the marker may be helpful in this situation. Alternatively, the run-up from a standing position may also be extended by two strides to give the athlete more time to straighten himself/herself up. Both alternatives (but especially the former) increase the inaccuracy of the run-up length since there are more possibilities for deviations.

The high jump run-up of top athletes (possible preliminary stutter steps not counted) includes 8–12 strides. Younger athletes sometimes use 7 or even fewer strides.

STRAIGHT SEGMENT OF THE RUN-UP

Flop jumpers usually start from a straight run-up segment. The extension of the line on which the jumper is running is either perpendicular to the extension of the zero line or already points slightly to the facility (see figure 6). In this segment of the run-up, the jumper performs the major part of his/her acceleration work.

Many, but by no means all, top jumpers perform 2–3 exceptionally powerful strides before beginning the curved segment of the run-up. Sometimes, these strides appear more like a bounding run (88) than a sprint run. In most cases, an increase in the pre-activation of the jumping muscles is mentioned as the reason for this. For less advanced athletes such a run-up pattern is not recommended.

ARCHED SEGMENT OF THE RUN-UP

Beginners run the last three strides in a curve; world-class athletes the last 5–6 strides. To make the transition to the curved run as smooth as possible, some coaches recommend starting the curve with the take-off leg. A start with the leg outside to the curve too easily results in a step to the outside which causes the CG to tilt suddenly inward. Speed and rhythm are disturbed. At the beginning of the curve or shortly afterward, some jumpers use an intermediate or turn-around marker. This marker shows the running direction to the jumper, who looks at it at the beginning of the run-up. It may also help the coach to check the accuracy of the run-up. However, an athlete should lift his/her view early from the ground, so as not to run with an excessive forward lean of his/her trunk.

To counteract the centrifugal forces occurring in the curve,

- the jumper should incline his/her body and thus his/her CG inside. Figures 6 and 8 illustrate the inward lean into the curve, which is typical of the flop technique;
- the jumper should place his/her feet on a uniformly curved line. Thus, even the leg inside of the curve may exert force in the direction of the centre of

the circle (point M in figure 6; for the reduction of stride width during the curve run see also chapter II–1.4.3); and

- the jumper emphasises stride frequency. The flight phases, during which the jumper is driven to the outside, are thus shortened.

The radius of curvature should increase with run-up velocity. If the radius remained constant, the athlete would be forced to increase his/her inward lean and to exert steadily increasing force in the direction of the centre of the circle. If the radius is larger, the length of the curve and the number of strides required to cover this distance will also increase together with the velocity of the run-up. Due to their greater strength

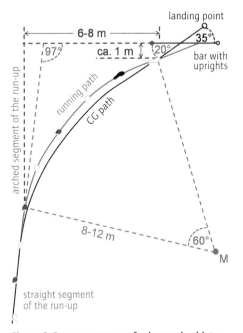

Figure 6: **Run-up pattern of advanced athletes** (modified on the basis of Tidow, 2007; see also figure 9).

capability, men are able to maintain a more pronounced inward lean. Therefore, the curve radii run by women and young athletes (despite their lower velocity) are often similarly large to those of men.

High jumpers usually reach their highest run-up velocity during the penultimate stride. The noticeable lowering of the CG prevents further acceleration into the last run-up stride (see figure 7). Table 1 in chapter II–2.1.2 shows the run-up velocities of top jumpers. The run-up velocities of younger jumpers are correspondingly slower. A comparison with other jumping events shows that the horizontal velocity before the take-off in the high jump may be regarded as clearly submaximal. This is due to the fact that in the high jump only the vertical component of the departure velocity is crucial. The jumper runs up only at that velocity which he/she can convert in vertical velocity upon take-off by means of his/her reactive-strength capability. However, studies of heterogeneous groups as well as some longitudinal studies of individual athletes show that the run-up velocity increases with performance. However, on the basis of the logic described, an increase in run-up velocity depends on a corresponding improvement in reactive-strength upon take-off.

TAKE-OFF PREPARATION

In the penultimate run-up stride, the athlete reaches his/her greatest inward lean into the curve, which may be up to 30° especially for men. This alone results in a lowering of the CG (see figure 8). As illustrated by the approximation of the light blue and the black lines in figures 6 and 9, the jumper then already begins to straighten from the inward lean. By doing so, he/she initiates a rotation about the sagittal axis which continues in the flight phase (see phase 2 and figure 11).

The stride length pattern throughout the high jump run-up is (individually and among individuals) characterised by significantly greater diversity than in the other jumping disciplines or in the sprint. Most high jumpers perform the last two run-up strides by using the typical long-short rhythm. However, in several cases a uniform or reverse (short-long) pattern may be observed. In the process, the CG is additionally lowered through the swing-leg squat and the total lowering is more significant than in any other jumping event in athletics. In one study, the average minimum knee-joint angle in the penultimate support is approx. 128° for men and 137° for women. At this moment, and not during the ground contact upon

*Figure 7: **Lowering the CG due to the inward lean** during the last two run-up strides as well as the lift of the CG upon take-off.*

take-off, the jumper reaches his/her lowest CG position. Viewed from the centre of the curve, the swing-leg squat is characterized by the following positions: ground contact of the entire sole of the foot, knees side by side, torso and lower support leg perpendicular to the ground.

Toward the take-off, the athlete leans his/her trunk backward and shifts his/her hips forward. The take-off foot is placed further in front of the CG than in any other jumping event (see figure 7). At the moment of foot touchdown, the trunk and the straight take-off leg almost form a line (backward reclining take-off position). Due to the incomplete knee extension during the push-off upon the penultimate ground contact, the low CG position, and the forward reaching movement of the take-off leg, the last stride is not necessarily short in terms of distance (points of foot touchdown) but very short in terms of time (see figure 9).

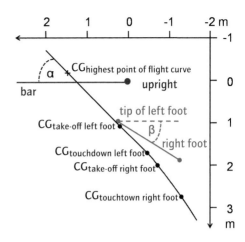

Figure 9: **Path of the centre of gravity viewed from above** during the winning jump (2.32m) by Krymarenko at the 2005 World Championships (modified on the basis of Isolehto et al., 2007): For the average of all finalists,

- the flight phase of the last stride was only about half as long as the previous ones. For the finalists, the time between the release of the penultimate support and placement of the last ground contact was 58 ± 14 msec (compare the values for the sprint in chapter II–1.3.3);

- the distance between the tip of the toe upon take-off and the zero line was 1.02 ± 0.3m, while the distance of the tip of the toe from the upright (in the direction of the centre of the zero line) was 8.6 ± 0.4cm;

- the CG passed over the bar at a distance of 1.78 ± 0.08m from the upright on the run-up side;

- the highest point of the CG trajectory was 6.34 ± 0.03cm behind the bar. This is only partly a sign that the take-off point was often too close to the bar; and

- α was 31.7 ± 0.2° and β was 28.6 ± 4.3° (the values deviate from the values suggested by Tidow in figure 6).

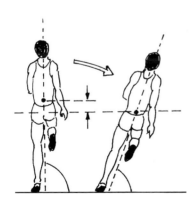

Figure 8: **Lowering of the CG due to the inward lean** during the run-up of the flop technique of high jumping.

677

DISCOURSE I: SPEED AND POWER FLOP

Two main variations of the flop technique can be primarily distinguished: the speed and the power flop. More specifically, these variations are two sides of one spectrum, in the middle of which both variations seamlessly merge. At one end of the spectrum, there is the jumper who takes off from a run-up at maximum velocity, while at the other end there is the jumper who takes off from a standing position. Both extremes are impractical. Nevertheless, on the one hand, there are high jumpers who prefer to utilise their superior reactive-strength capability to convert their run-up velocity into height. On the other hand, there are high jumpers who rather try to utilise their higher concentric maximal and explosive strength (see table 2).

*Table 2: **Differences between speed and power flop** (modified on the basis of Reid, 1984).*

	Speed flop	Power flop
Physique	small and light	tall and heavy
Run-up length	rather long	rather short
Run-up velocity	fast	slow
Curve radius	large	small
CG lowering before take-off	little	much
Distance between take-off foot and bar	long	short
Ground-contact time upon take-off	short	long
Minimal knee-joint angle	large	small
Use of swinging elements	narrow-ranging	wide-ranging
Departure angle	flat	steep

In recent years, there has been a trend toward the speed flop. For example, at the 2005 World Championships, the highest average run-up velocity of all finalists was measured so far. Ultimately, the fact that one is a speed or power flop jumper is primarily a matter of predisposition. However, in spite of that, every jumper should plan on improving his/her reactive-strength capability and technique to such an extent that the highest possible run-up velocity is converted into a maximum jump height for each jumper.

PHASE 2: TAKE-OFF

During the take-off (and flight) of the high jump, there are also more individually distinct forms of technique than in other disciplines (see discourses I and IV). Even for one athlete, there are still clear variations (only some of which are deliberately planned): fewer on one day, more at points of measurement that are further apart. The variations demonstrate the compensatory nature which is typical for athletic movements. For example, if an athlete takes off closer to the bar, he/she must jump at a steeper angle.

*Table 3: **Distance of the tip of the foot from the zero line** (according to Killing, 2009a, p. 137).*

Group (n = 36 each) average competition performance ± standard deviation	Distance from the bar Average ± standard deviation (min.-max.)
Men (225.0 ± 5.80cm)	94.78 ± 14.81cm (66-126cm)
Men (204.3 ± 5.32cm)	82.42 ± 13.54cm (47-105cm)
Women (189.1 ± 3.34cm)	82.56 ± 15.22cm (59-116cm)
Women (175.4 ± 4.68cm)	69.67 ± 11.39cm (47-98cm)

TAKE-OFF POINT

The take-off should be performed in the first third of the bar. This pertains to the lateral localisation of the take-off point in the direction of the zero line. While beginners often take off too far in the direction of the opposite upright, top high jumpers place their take-off foot almost directly in front of the upright on the run-up side (see figure 9). Table 3 provides information about the distance perpendicular to the zero line. As the jumping height increases, the jumper is also forced to take off further away from the bar.

The take-off point, the departure angle, and the velocity of departure should be coordinated in such a way that (the CG of) the jumper passes the bar at its middle section. This is where the bar is lowest because of its slight bend. Moreover, a safe landing is assured this way and contact with the upright is avoided. It is also assumed that the take-off point, angle of departure, and the velocity of departure should be chosen in such a way that the peak of the CG trajectory are just above the bar, i.e., neither before nor behind the bar.

BRACING AND DEPARTURE ANGLE

Due to the desired large departure angle in the high jump, the bracing angle (or the backward reclining take-off position) is greater than in all other jumping events in athletics. The bracing angle in the high jump is determined by the backward position and inward position of the body. The backward lean of the finalists at the 2005 World Championships in Athletics was 36.8 ± 2.1°. (Other authors do not calculate the position angle of the line connecting the tip of the toe and the CG, but rather the line connecting the ankle joint and the CG and arrive at correspondingly smaller angles.) At the moment of foot touchdown, the inward lean is only 2–14°. (Some authors calculate the bracing angle as a single parameter.)

DISCOURSE II: PLANTING THE TAKE-OFF FOOT IN THE RUNNING DIRECTION

A key requirement of the target technique—especially from a health perspective—is planting the foot of the take-off leg in the running direction. As is illustrated in figure 6, the take-off foot should point toward the mat at about a 20° angle to the zero line. For beginners in particular, the take-off foot often points away from the bar (sometimes significantly). This is due to the short flight duration over low heights which leaves less time for rotation in the air. Moreover, these athletes often have a false idea of movement. They already perform the rotation about the longitudinal axis before the jump. However, even top-level jumpers sometimes demonstrate a foot touchdown parallel to the zero line. It sometimes seems as if they even use the ligaments on the inside of the foot for energy storage. It is therefore not surprising that after correcting the foot touchdown, there is initially a decrease in performance and that athletes therefore have difficulties with readjustment. However, accidents in competition, such as the foot fracture of the top German jumper Eike Onnen, which was caused by this technical error, show the high and dangerous forces which are generated in the foot as a result of this error. The foot is stressed in a non-physiological way and is bent to the inside. Therefore, when training with beginners, coaches should always require a proper foot touchdown through appropriate exercises and advice at all times. To prevent torsion injuries, special high-jump shoes with spikes on the heel should also be avoided in this age group.

At the moment of breaking contact with the ground, the backward and inward lean should equal zero. Figure 9 shows that at this moment the CG is or should be just above the jumper's toe. To prevent too early, too much, or too fast rotation about the sagittal axis, jumpers are advised to keep their shoulder axis away from the bar for as long as possible (the corresponding coaching cue is to jump away from the bar). However, at the moment of breaking contact with the ground, one can see that the head, arm(s), and shoulders (lowering of the shoulder closer to the bar) of all jumpers are already directed to the bar. The thigh of the swing leg should reach the horizontal and the hip nearer to the bar is lifted in comparison to the other hip.

The resulting angle of departure to the horizontal is smaller than intuitively expected by many people. For the finalists at the 2005 World Championships, the angle of departure was 45.1 ± 3.5°. A departure angle of 45° means that the vertical and horizontal departure velocity are equal. The horizontal departure velocity was 4.31 ± 0.49 m/sec, while the vertical

Table 4: **Knee joint angle upon the flop take-off** *among male world-class jumpers (according to Isoletho et al., 2007): A less noticeable flexion of the knee joint is (at least in the high jump) no indication of better performance. On the contrary: For women, increased performance is associated with a greater change of the knee-joint angle. Even in one and the same person, this knee flexion varies considerably from jump to jump.*

Foot plant	168.14 ± 3.73°
Maximum flexion	143.72 ± 8.26°
Leaving the ground	173.93 ± 3.40°

departure velocity was 4.30 ± 0.15 m/sec (see chapter II–2.1.2). Angle α in figure 9 must also be optimised. If an athlete jumps too frontally toward the bar (too large), he/she does not have enough time to switch from hip hyperextension to hip flexion behind the bar. There is the risk of knocking off the bar through delayed hip hyperextension or hip flexion. At least, there is the risk of ineffective bar clearance. If the athlete takes off too parallel to the bar (α too small), he/she must take off closer to the bar and moves very slowly over the bar. The jumper must

Figure 10: **Take-off for the flop.**

maintain his/her hyperextension for a very long period of time. The margin between already knocking off the bar during the rise on the one hand and during the fall behind the bar on the other hand is very small.

INITIATION OF ROTATION

To be able to clear the bar perfectly, an athlete must initiate optimal rotation about all three body axes upon take-off. Since flop jumpers pass the bar in a backward position, beginners often think that they must generate a backward rotation upon take-off. This is a misconception. Upon the flop take-off, a forward rotation about the transverse axis of the body is initiated. The following applies to the foot plant, take-off direction, and rotation: ***The flop includes a forward take-off like all other jumps in athletics.***

The jumper reaches the backward position and backward rotation about the transverse axis of the body above the bar through the rotation about the longitudinal axis, which is also initiated upon take-off. This is directed away from the bar. Jumpers who take off with the left leg rotate to the left, whereas jumpers who take off with the right leg rotate to the right. In addition, there is a rotation about the sagittal axis toward the bar due to straightening from the inward lean. The following applies to all three components of the rotation: The greater the jumping height, the lower the induced angular momentum must be. This is due to the fact that the higher the jump height, the longer the flight phase, i.e., the time during which the angular momentum is effective.

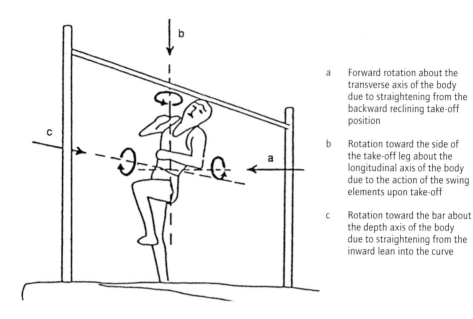

	a	Forward rotation about the transverse axis of the body due to straightening from the backward reclining take-off position
	b	Rotation toward the side of the take-off leg about the longitudinal axis of the body due to the action of the swing elements upon take-off
	c	Rotation toward the bar about the depth axis of the body due to straightening from the inward lean into the curve

*Figure 11: **Rotations initiated upon the high-jump take-off** (modified on the basis of Dapena, 1980).*

The forward rotation occurs naturally in all take-offs from a run-up (see figure 7 in chapter II–2.1.2). The rotation about the longitudinal axis is initiated by the actions of the trunk and swing elements during the take-off. The lower the jumping height and the shorter the flight duration, the more the jumper must move his swing elements away from the bar.

DISTANCE OF LIFT OF THE CG

The male finalists at the 2005 World Championships in Athletics lifted their CG upon take-off by 45 ± 5cm (from 0.93 ± 0.05m to 1.37 ± 0.05m, body height: 1.92 ± 0,05m). There was a correlation coefficient of r = -0.70 between the vertical departure velocity and the CG position upon the foot touchdown for the take-off. The more noticeable the lowering of the CG before the take-off, the higher the velocity of departure. Table 5 also shows that the distance of lift of the CG during ground contact increases with performance.

*Table 5: **Performance parameters according to the performance development of a 1.90m tall man** (according to Killing et al., 2008, p. 53): The ground contact time is less dependent on the performance than on the type of the athlete. Note the difference between h_{RiseA} and h_{RiseB}. h_{RiseB} was 0.94 ± 0.07m on average in the best trials of all finalists at the 2005 World Championships.*

Jumping height	CG flight height	Rising height	Distance of lift of the CG	Contact time
(m)	(m)	(h_{RiseA}; m)	(cm)	(sec)
1.90	2.03	0.90	33.0	0.161
2.00	2.08	0.97	37.0	0.161
2.10	2.16	1.03	41.0	0.162
2.20	2.24	1.09	43.0	0.160

DISCOURSE III: IS THE ARCHED RUN-UP REALLY NECESSARY?

A rotation about the sagittal axis is not necessary to fly backward over the high jump bar in a bridge position. Too early or excessive rotation about the sagittal axis toward the bar even prevents the athlete from jumping through the point upon take-off. Therefore, one could also do without the arched run-up. Double Olympic Champion Ulrike Meyfarth temporarily experimented with a straight run-up. The problems upon foot planting mentioned in the previous discourse could probably be avoided. In some biomechanical studies, only very little or no inward lean is calculated at the moment of foot touchdown for the take-off. Some experts in biomechanics note that they could find no empirical evidence for the benefit of the arched run-up.

For those who are not satisfied with the exclusive use of the arched run-up as evidence of its efficiency, there are some plausibility statements, which speak for the arched run-up:

- Without inward lean into the curve, the lowering of the CG and the bracing angle must be generated solely through the swing-leg squat and the backward lean of the body. This could interfere with run-up velocity and swing-leg movement.
- Some authors suggest that the inward lean into the curve improves the functioning of the hip abductor muscles of the take-off leg. It is assumed that due to the arched run-up they are able to contribute even more power to the development of the vertical departure velocity.
- Generating rotation about the sagittal axis from a straight run-up (leaning to the side) would be detrimental to generating vertical departure velocity. Without rotation about the sagittal axis, the athlete must produce more rotation about the longitudinal axis to pass the bar in supine position. This could also be detrimental to the generation of vertical departure velocity.

However, this does not seem to be so much a question of technique as force. Only by means of superior (reactive) strength does an athlete succeed in straightening himself/herself up completely from a larger bracing angle subsequent to a greater lowering of the CG.

The height of the CG upon foot touchdown and upon leaving the ground also depends greatly on the use of the swing elements. A distinct double-arm swing results in a greater distance of lift of the CG. Although the high position of the swing elements at the end of the take-off increases the height of the CG at the moment of breaking contact with the ground, this is useless if it has a negative effect on the departure velocity and thus the rising height (which is to be feared when using the arm-relief technique described below, for example).

ARM ACTIONS

During the take-off preparation, take-off and the flight phase of the flop jump, high jumpers demonstrate a variety of techniques using their arms. Although certain advantages and disadvantages of one or the other techniques may be listed, similar heights were achieved with all techniques in the past (with the exception of the relief technique).

For men, the double-arm swing is the most common technique. The advantage of this technique is that a great deal of mass (two arms) is accelerated upward and that this mass is in a high position at the end of the take-off. A *short* and a *long double-arm swing* can be distinguished. In the short double-arm swing, the arm closer to the bar remains behind the body during the last stride. In the long double-arm swing, the arm closer to the bar remains in front of the body during the penultimate stride and during the last run-up stride both arms are swung behind the body (more or less parallel). The long double-arm swing disturbs the run-up more, results in a greater loss of horizontal velocity than the short double-arm swing, and is therefore more suitable for power floppers. If the acceleration path actually becomes longer due to the long double-arm swing, this may lead to a higher terminal velocity of the swing elements. Some jumpers intuitively

develop an even longer double-arm swing, such as the butterfly technique of the South African double world champion (2001 and 2003) Hestrie Cloete (best performance: 2.06m). She moves her arms to the front of her body in the third-last stride and then swings them for a long time in a straight position backward over her head and behind her body. Despite the success achieved with this technique, it does not seem sensible for other jumpers to use this or other very long double-arm swings because they lead to a severe deterioration of the run-up.

Only very few jumpers, however, including the inventor of flop technique, Dick Fosbury, demonstrate a *contralateral arm swing*. The running motion is not disturbed in the process and a very fast speed-flop take-off with a short but powerful arm swing is possible. The distance of lift of the CG during take-off and the mass accelerated upward are reduced.

The *lead-arm technique* is most frequent in women, whereas in men this technique is between the double-arm and contralateral-arm technique in terms of frequency. In this technique, there is also no (or little) deviation from the contralateral arm swing, which is typical of the running motion up to the take-off. The arm closer to the bar, which upon the foot touchdown for take-off is in front of the body, is moved further upward in the direction of the bar. For some jumpers, the leading arm (comparable to the relief technique) is already lifted very high at the moment of the foot touchdown for take-off. The disadvantage of the lead-arm technique is the reduced swinging momentum.

For some young jumpers in particular, a kind of *relief technique* can be observed regarding the arm actions. This means that the arms are raised very early on, even beginning during the penultimate contact with the ground. Upon the foot touchdown for the take-off, the arms are then already above the shoulders. This results in a reduction of (a) the peak force in the take-off leg at the start of the take-off (impact), (b) the swing momentum, and (c) the distance of lift of the CG during take-off. The position of the CG at the end of the take-off is still high, and the take-off is short but not very powerful. The relief technique is therefore observed most frequently in fast young female jumpers. Sometimes, jumpers who increase their body weight disproportionately to their jumping strength also develop this technique intuitively to avoid collapsing during impact.

Regardless of the arm actions, the jumper keeps looking at the bar over his/her shoulder closer to the bar during take-off.

PHASE 3: FLIGHT

Upon take-off, the velocity of departure, the angle of departure, and the rotational momentum are determined. If these parameters are sufficient, it is the objective of the flight phase that the body segments are moved in such a manner that the bar is cleared without touching it. The flight phase of the flop technique may be divided into the following three sub-phases:

- rising phase,
- bar clearance, and
- falling away from the bar.

RISING PHASE

In the rising phase, the jumper initially maintains his/her take-off position more or less. By keeping many parts of his/her body away from the fulcrum (CG), he/she rotates slowly. In most cases, the swing leg remains initially lifted or parallel to

Figure 12: Flight phase during the flop.

the bar. It is moved beside the other knee only with the beginning (over-)extension of the hips. An early lowering of the swing leg accelerates the rotation about the longitudinal axis and slows down the rotation about the transverse axis. During the rising phase, the jumper looks at the bar over his/her shoulder closer to the bar.

BAR CLEARANCE

The objective of the actions of the jumper during the clearance of the bar is not to touch the bar. If the athlete's bar clearance is good, the height of the bar may be higher for a given flight height of the CG than in the event of a poor bar clearance (see table 6).

To avoid contact with the bar, the jumper must take on a pronounced bridge position (see figure 12). For top jumpers, the angle between the lines connecting the shoulder and the hip as well as the knee and the hip is approximately 220–230° for a short time. For better jumpers or jumps, there is a trend toward more hyperextension than for poorer jumpers or jumps. The bridge

Table 6: **Assessment of bar clearance** (according to Killing et al, 2008, p. 45). On the basis of the best trials of all male finalists at the 2005 World Championships, the average clearance height was 5.1 ± 0.33cm.

Clearance height at max. jumping height	Assessment of bar clearance
-3–2cm	acrobatic
3–6cm	well
7–10cm	average
more than 11cm	bad

position is initiated primarily by turning one's eyes away from the bar and throwing one's head back. Other authors also speak alternatively or additionally of an initiation of the movement through the leading arm, through the deliberate hyperextension of the hip and/or through a flexion at the knee joints. Moving the knees apart (abduction at the hips) facilitates the hyperextension of the hips, slows down the rotation about the longitudinal axis, and enhances the rotation about the transverse axis. If the athlete continues looking at the bar along the backside of his/her shoulder (or even with his/her head on the chest) the result is often less hyperextension but a better control of bar clearance.

With respect to arm movement above the bar, there are three main variations with many intermediate forms:

- The arm closer to the bar may be extended headways or sideways both from the double-arm swing and from the lead-arm technique while the other arm is placed alongside the body. If an arm is placed alongside one's body, this should be done at the side instead of at the front of the belly to keep the arm as low as possible.
- The athlete may place both arms at his/her sides from a short double-arm or contralateral arm swing. Contrary to the aforementioned variation, the arms are relatively high in relation to the CG in this variation. However, particularly in the case of an extreme hyperextension of the hips and a noticeable backward movement of the

DISCOURSE IV: SIT-AND-KICK FLOP

Most jumpers initiate the overextension of their hips above the bar directly from the extended take-off position. For some jumpers, however, a significant hip flexion may be seen between the push-off extension and the hyperextension above the bar (see figure 13). Due to this flexion, the shoulder closer to the bar is moved away from the bar during the rise, which may be interpreted as a preliminary counter-movement to initiate the subsequent hyperextension. So far, this technique has only been observed in world-class male jumpers due to their longer rising phase. It is extremely complex in terms of coordination and tends to result in more failed attempts.

Take-off leg

Figure 13: Sit-down and running
movement during the sit-and-kick flop.

For few world-class jumpers (e.g., Detchenique and Thomas), the sit-down movement is combined with a running movement of the legs similar to the running-jump technique in long jumping. The take-off leg is moved upward in an acutely angled position, while the swing leg is moved downward in a straight position (see figure 13). This results in an accelerated rotation about the bar (lowering of the head). Likewise, certain body parts can also generate opposed movements in other parts of the body during the flight (e.g., rotation about the longitudinal axis of the hip caused by arm rotation).

heels, the body parts are as close as possible to the CG and the velocity of the rotation about the bar increases.

- The jumper may extend both arms headways or at least sideways from a double-arm swing or from the relief technique. By shifting his/her arms downward, he/she achieves a very high hip position relative to the position of his/her CG. The disadvantage is that the mass of the arms is thereby shifted far away from the CG and the jumper rotates about the bar more slowly. He/she runs the risk of knocking the bar down with his/her heels.

FALLING AWAY FROM THE BAR

To avoid touching the bar with the lower leg and to prepare for the landing, the jumper bends his/her trunk and hips and extends his/her knee joints. Again the head, which is moved onto the chest, has a control function. The jumper finally reaches the L position.

PHASE 4: LANDING

In the high jump, an athlete should land on his/her upper back. In the event of very high jumps, the athlete often lands in such a way that his/her head and neck touch the mat first when there is too much initial rotation upon take-off, or when the athlete makes himself/herself very small behind the bar. Although this does not normally result in injuries due to the modern soft floor mats, it should be avoided. The hands and arms are moved to the sides to make the landing area larger (see figure 14). The head remains on the chest. To avoid the face from being hit with one of the knees, the knees should be opened or remain so (as during bar clearance).

It is also possible to use the landing position as an indicator of the quality of the take-off, for example, whether the direction of flight, the angle of departure, and the initiation of rotation were correct (see 331). Top male high jumpers fly up to 4m (horizontal distance) during the flop jump.

*Figure 14: **Landing position.***

Table 7: **Requirement profile for the high jump:** The suggested rough estimate of the value of selected factors determining performance is based on the importance for the overall performance and the percentage of time spent training (IR: information requirements, constr.: constraints; see chapter I–1.1).

Factors determining high-jump performance	Estimate of value	Notes
Coordination	+ + + + +	optical IR: high, acoustic IR: low, tactile IR: low, kinaesthetic IR: high, vestibular IR: high; precision constr.: high, time constr.: high, complexity constr.: medium–high, situation constr.: low, physical stress constr.: medium–high
Flexibility	+ +	hardly any extreme movement amplitudes required (hyper-extension above the bar requires sufficient flexibility)
Strength		particular significance of the extensor loop (glutes, quadriceps, triceps surae, erector spinae) and trunk muscles, iliopsoas, hamstrings, adductors, shoulder and upper-arm muscles
Maximal strength	+ + + + +	particularly relative maximal strength
Reactive strength	+ + + + +	mainly of the extensor loop
Speed	+ + +	cyclic; acyclic aspects during take-off preparation, take-off, flight, and landing
Endurance (general dynamic) Anaerobic endurance		
Strength endurance	+	as a basis at the most
Speed endurance	+ +	as a basis to be able to perform 12–15 trials (practice and competition trials) at a high level of performance
Aerobic endurance	+	only as a basis for training (regeneration ability)
Psychological and cognitive abilities	+ + + + +	concentration ability (on the point); full concentration not only in the third trial; correct strategy; performance-oriented thinking and behaviour (see chapter I–3.1.1)
Anthropometric and primarily genetically determined characteristics	+ + + + +	high percentage of the fastest muscle fibres; connective tissue with optimal energy storage capacities; above-average body height (particularly in women); very low percentage of body fat

2.4.4 SUMMARY OF THE MOST IMPORTANT TECHNICAL CHARACTERISTICS = TECHNIQUE-ANALYSIS SHEET

RUN-UP

START OF THE RUN-UP AND STRAIGHT SEGMENT OF THE RUN-UP

- Start of the run-up from stutter steps, walk-on, or from a standing position.
- Run-up length for top athletes: 8–12 strides (possibly plus walk-on and preliminary stutter steps); in younger athletes sometimes fewer strides (5 strides at least).
- Straight run-up at an angle of approximately 90° in the direction of the extension of the zero line (possibly even slightly in the direction of the high-jump facility).
- Rapid, but not maximum acceleration to the optimal speed for take-off and achievement of a maximum jumping height.
- Initially toe push-off sprinting, then grasping/pulling sprinting with noticeable knee lift and upright trunk and pelvis; only top athletes should possibly perform a few jumping strides.
- Possibly stepping on an intermediate or turn-around marker 3–5 strides before taking off.

ARCHED SEGMENT OF THE RUN-UP

- Smooth transition to the arched segment of the run-up.
- 3–6 strides for the arched run-up segment.
- The radius of curvature should be adapted to the jumper's run-up velocity and strength, and the jumper should achieve a corresponding inward lean into the curve.
- The emphasis should be placed on stride frequency.
- (Subconscious) adjustment of stride length for hitting the optimal take-off point.
- Final run-up direction approx. 30° to the bar or zero line.

TAKE-OFF PREPARATION

- The jumper should look at the bar.
- Lowering of the CG particularly during the penultimate run-up stride through inward lean and swing-leg squat.
- (Short-)long-short rhythm of the last strides (at least in terms of time, mostly also in terms of space).
- Powerful and flat push-off from the third-last support with slightly incomplete knee extension.
- After an incomplete heel lift, the bent leg is placed down for the penultimate support (swing-leg squat) as close to the vertical projection of the CG as possible; often the entire foot sole is placed on the ground.
- Extended amortisation in the knee joint and forward shifting of the pelvis; maintenance of the low CG position, backward rotation of the upper body (taking of the backward reclining take-off position), and incomplete knee extension during the push-off from the penultimate support.
- The straightening movement from the inward lean is already started during the last stride.

TAKE-OFF

- After a slightly reduced knee lift and a flat curve of the foot movement, the take-off leg is actively placed on the ground from above in an (almost) extended position using a backward pulling movement; initially, the touchdown is often performed over the outside of the heel, and then on the entire sole of the foot; the foot points toward the high-jump facility at an angle of approximately 20°.
- The take-off is performed close to the first upright (i.e., in the first third of the bar); distance from the tip of the foot to the zero line: 60–110cm, depending on the athlete's level of performance and the technique variation used.
- The position of the foot in front of the vertical projection of the CG and the trunk angle (backward reclining take-off position) during the foot touchdown determine the bracing and departure angles.

- After a short amortisation, there is a powerful push-off extension of the foot, knee, hip, and trunk.
- The swing elements are rapidly lifted and then decelerated (swing leg is moved into the three -90 position; double-arm swing or lead-arm technique).
- Initiation of an appropriate rotation in order to clear the bar optimally: forward rotation about the transverse axis of the body (straightening from the backward reclining take-off position), rotation about the longitudinal axis toward the side of the take-off leg (by moving the swing elements away from the bar), only little rotation about the sagittal axis toward the bar (straightening from the inward lean).
- Upright body position at the moment of leaving the ground.

FLIGHT

- Maintenance of the take-off position.
- For taking the bridge position above the bar: The knee of the swing leg is moved beside the other knee, the thighs are spread, the head is thrown backward, the hips are over-extended, the knees are bent.
- The arms should be kept low and should be used to control the flight phase.
- The highest point of the flight curve is at the middle of the bar as well as neither in front of nor behind the bar.
- To take the L position when falling away from the bar the head should be taken onto the chest, the trunk and hips should be bent, and the knee joints should be extended.

LANDING

- The jumper lands on his/her upper back.
- The athlete's head remains on his/her chest.
- The arms are extended sidewards away from the trunk.
- The athlete's legs remain in a spread position.

2.4.5 PHOTO SEQUENCE

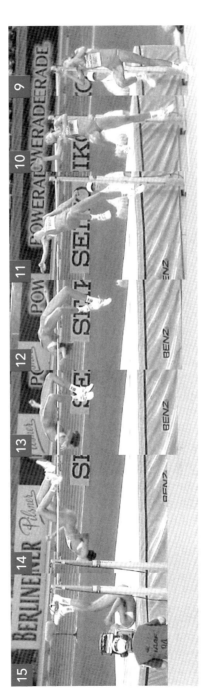

Data about the photo sequence

Athlete:	Blanka Vlasic (born: 8 November 1983, Croatia)
Height/weight:	1.93 m/66 kg
Performance:	2.04 m (20 August 2009, Berlin)
Best performance:	2.08 m (31 August 2009, Zagreb)
Greatest success:	World champion 2007 and 2009, second place at the 2011 World Championships, European Champion 2010

COMMENTARY

The photo sequence shows Vlasic's winning jump at the 2009 World Championships, less than two weeks before the highest-ever jump in her career. To date, only the world-record holder Stefka Kostandinova has jumped higher outdoors than Vlasic. At the 2009 World Championships there was the expected duel of two very different jumpers: the relatively small German Ariane Friedrich and the much taller Blanka Vlasic. When standing, Vlasic's CG height was 9cm higher than that of Friedrich's, which means that Vlasic was able to clear the same height without having to use her jumping strength to lift her CG over this distance. However, Vlasic's taller body height meant more body mass. Therefore, she would have had to generate correspondingly higher forces upon take-off to achieve the same rising height as Friedrich, who was 9 kg lighter.

In fact, the run-up velocity of both athletes was identical, although Vlasic's run-up looks slower due to her body height and longer strides. Nearly 7 m/sec are not an exceptionally high run-up velocity. In particular, picture 2 illustrates Vlasic's powerful run-up with active knee lift, noticeable inward lean and upright upper body. However, her tendency toward a slight swayback posture can also be seen, which in the backward reclining take-off position (picture 6) causes her hips to remain behind a bit. This could also be caused by her relatively long (or only slightly shortened) last run-up strides. In the meantime, her arms are preparing for a short double-arm swing.

The initiation of the rotation about the longitudinal axis (due to turning the side of her body which is closer to the bar away from the bar during the take-off) has already begun by shifting forward her right shoulder between pictures 4 and 5. Vlasic plants her take-off foot almost parallel to the bar. The result of this is the lifting of the outer shoe sole, which can be seen in picture 8 (see discourse II). The distance to the bar and accordingly the steepness of her jump as well as the contact time show middle range values which are typical for the women's high jump. Vlasic moves her

*Table 8: **Biomechanical measuring values of the jump shown in the photo sequence** (according to Killing, 2009b, p. 31; CG heights are explained in figure 2).*

Jumping height (m)	CG heights (m)						Stride lengths (m)			Run-up velocity (m/sec)	Distance to bar (m)	Hyperextension (°)
	h_{max}	h_{FT}	h_{Lift}	h_{Stand}	h_{RiseA}	h_{Clear}	third-last	penultimate	last			
2.04	2.07	0.97	0.30	1.10	0.97	0.03	2.19	2.17	2.12	6.95	0.69	236

acutely angled swing leg rapidly to the horizontal position, which is reached at the moment of breaking contact with the ground, while she turns her knee further away from the bar. Finally, she reaches her full take-off extension between pictures 9 and 10.

Vlasic's bar clearance includes the following overlapping movements: moving the right arm first over then below the bar, moving the left arm first to the front and then to the side of the body, throwing her head backward, lowering her swing leg, and a relatively noticeable hyperextension of her hips while bending her knees at the same time. The rotation about the bar, which was initiated upon the take-off and is obviously very suitable, results in a very noticeable lowering of her head behind the bar. To avoid knocking down the bar with her heels and prepare for the landing, Vlasic takes her head onto her chest, flexes her hips and straightens her knee joints.

2.4.6 STRATEGY IN THE VERTICAL JUMPS

The special feature of competitions in the vertical jump is their increasing character. Runners (with the exception of the heats and semi-finals in the sprint) must provide top performances in the first (and only) trial. Throwers and horizontal jumpers have more trials, but must provide top performances from the first trial on. This does not apply to vertical jumpers. Some jumpers deliberately forego one to two trials during warm-up jumping and start the competition one or two heights lower to specifically prepare again immediately before the decisive heights. This approach is particularly useful for good jumpers in heterogeneous and large fields of participants, who have long breaks between warm-up jumping and competition.

However, it seems to make sense in terms of economy not to perform too many competition jumps and to enter the competition only at a height as high as possible. Moreover, the jumper adjusts his/her technique consciously or unconsciously for reasons of economy. In general, jumpers save energy during the competition trials with lower heights to give their best only in the decisive trials.

The most obvious element of the strategy in the vertical jump is the omission of trials or the selection of the jumping heights. For example, a jumper may forego one or more of the subsequent heights after having cleared a lower height all too easily (this strategy is again based on the principle of economy). If a jumper does not jump to achieve a maximum height, but to win the competition or to reach a good placement, it may make sense to forego heights or trials at the higher heights. If a jumper cannot improve his/her placement through a successful jump in an upcoming trial due to the failed-attempt rule, it may make sense to forego this height (see table 9).

The fact that a vertical jumper usually finishes his/her competition with three invalid attempts poses particular challenges to the psyche of high jumpers and pole-vaulters.

2.4.7 DIDACTICS: SUPERORDINATE LONG-TERM OBJECTIVES AND GENERAL METHODOLOGY

Versatile long and high jumps are already performed in children's athletics. At the beginning of basic training at the latest, young athletes should jump in the high-jump area over a height marker. At first, this may be an elastic cord. By means of the methodical sequence included in the collection of exercises presented below, the flop technique is developed. This should be done in a special training phase with the emphasis placed on the high jump in several sessions. Initially, the focus of attention should be on the run-up, the take-off, and the initiation of rotation. Special exercises for practising the specific bar clearance of the flop (e.g., flop from a standing position) are used only after mastering the rough form of the movement. Due to the many degrees of freedom (individual possibilities of variation) of the flop technique, athletes are given a number of varied tasks in terms of differential learning soon after mastering the rough form (see exercises 338–340).

Table 9: **Example of competition strategy in the high jump** (P = placement)

Example 1	1.85 m	P	1.90 m	P	1.93 m	P	1.96 m	P
Jumper A	XO	2	O	1	O	1	XXX	2
Jumper B	O	1	XXO	2	–	2	XXO	1

Due to the competition order, jumper A jumps each time before jumper B. Up to a height of 1.85 both have not failed an attempt. After the first trials over 1.85m, jumper B is ahead of jumper A. At this height, jumper A decides to continue jumping to get herself three new trials. Jumper B makes the same decision after the first trials over 1.90m. Except for jumper A and B, all other jumpers were eliminated at 1.90m. Therefore, jumper B makes a different decision at 1.93m than at 1.90m. The second place is secure for her and her placement and the number of available trials over 1.96m would not change as a result of a successful jump over 1.93 m. Her strategy proves successful since she is the only one to clear 1.96m.

Example 2	2.20 m	P	2.23 m	P	2.26 m	P	2.28 m	P
Jumper X	XO	2	X-	2	X-	2	X	2
Jumper Y	O	1	O	1	O	1	XXX	1

Due to the competition order, jumper X jumps each time before jumper Y. After the height of 2.20, jumper Y is ahead of jumper X due to a failed attempt by jumper X. After the first trials over 2.23 m, jumper X cannot do anything about this at this height. All other jumpers have already been eliminated and jumper X knows that the second place is secure for him. Since he realises that his strength is fading, he decides against getting three new trials through a successful trial over 2.23m. He keeps the remaining two trials for the next height(s). After the first attempts by both jumpers over 2.26m, he makes a comparable decision and risks everything over 2.28m. But his strategy does not work: 2.28m was just too high.

A controversial topic is the role of the scissors jump, which is often introduced as an alternative high-jump technique even before the flop technique (mostly even from an arched run-up). Although most children find it easy to learn this technique, switching to the different take-off for the flop may lead to problems later on.

High-jump training should be complemented early on through gymnastics for practising rotations in three-dimensional space. Moreover, in gymnastics clearing the bar may be practised in combination with related movements which include an active hyperextension of the hips (14). However, special flexibility training, in particular static holding exercises (bridge), should be integrated into build-up training only much later.

While the basic training of future high jumpers is based primarily on the combined events, build-up training is characterised by increased specialisation. Now there is an increase in the percentage of (maximal) strength training and reactive (multiple) jumps in particular as is also the case in the other jumping events.

Both female and male high jumpers are often early developers who often demonstrate amazing performances even in (early) adolescence. For female jumpers in general, but especially for female high jumpers, even the most talented ones, there is frequently a stagnation or even decrease of performance during (late) adolescence. This is due to the great importance of body weight in the high jump and the natural development from girls to women. This development is associated with an increase in subcutaneous fat and a stagnation or decrease in relative strength or the load-force ratio. This normal development should be discussed with athletes early on to prepare them. The problematic years should be used for specific technique refinement and an introduction to strength training in order to subsequently achieve a positive development of the load-force ratio again.

SAFETY ASPECTS

The high jump mat should be large and high enough. It should neither be too hard nor too soft (to avoid the risk of hitting the ground). The mat should be close enough to the zero line and the uprights. The methodology should be geared toward the jumper clearing the bar in the middle, so that he/she lands neither on the outer edge of the mat nor on its front edge due to a take-off too parallel to the bar. The take-off surface must provide sufficient support (i.e., should not be covered with sand, worn off or slippery). In particular, if beginners and younger athletes do not yet wear special high-jump shoes with heel spikes, the surface should be dry.

2.4.8 TRAINING CONTENTS: FORMS OF GAMES AND EXERCISES

All forms of games and the forms of exercise not directly used for improving the flight and landing techniques which were mentioned in connection with the long jump (see chapter II–2.2.7) are also part of high-jump training. Moreover, almost all training forms for the 100m sprint (see chapter II–1.3.8) are of significance for the high jump as well. Hurdle sprints (particularly using the 1-stride rhythm, 193) are also important preparatory exercises for the high jump (see chapter II–1.8.8).

321 **Aerobatic pilot**

Possible objectives: Training the curved run-up of the flop; versatile running; warm-up.

Execution: Running in curves, in slalom, circle, etc.; the arms are stretched to the side and tilted according to the inward lean into the curve.

Variations: As shadow running (101) with a partner or in a group; with coordination tasks; on marked lines in the gym or on a cinder court; the children fly figures or letters.

Typical load standards: 15–45 sec per task.

322 **Scissors jump chasing game and other chasing games in which the children being chased may rescue themselves by jumping**

Possible objectives: Versatile sprinting and high jumping, learning the scissors-jump technique.

Execution/variations: Initially one, then two or three catchers try to tag the other players in a limited field; in the middle of the field, there is an obstacle (e.g., long bench with medicine balls on it.); the children being chased may rescues themselves from the catchers by means of a scissors jump over the obstacle since the catchers are not allowed to jump over the obstacle; the tagged children must leave the field and possibly perform exercises specific to the high jump; the last one caught is the winner.

Typical load standards: 2–5 run-throughs (as long as the children have fun).

323   ▮▮▮▮▮   Alternative high-jump techniques

Possible objectives: Versatile high jumping and flying.

Execution: For example, over an elastic cord in the long-jump or high-jump area; the children are told to invent and test many different jumping techniques (somersaults are only allowed at the high-jump facility).

Variations: If the children have no more ideas, the coach may give tips which suggest new directions or may demonstrate historic techniques (e.g., the straddle or the Hay technique: somersault forward over the bar after one-legged take-off); the run-up direction may be freely chosen or is prescribed (e.g., frontal jump after run-up perpendicular to the bar); possibly the two-legged take-off may be allowed (e.g., two-legged flop with run-up).

Typical load standards: Until no new variations are presented by the children or the children are no longer having fun.

324   ▮▮▮▮▮   Handball jump throw

Possible objectives: Versatile high jumping and throwing.

Execution: Handball-typical jump throw.

Variations: Over an obstacle (partner); also as shot toward the goal; also with goalkeeper; bilateral practice; also within handball game.

Typical load standards: 5–20 reps per side and task (depending on the task).

325 | Lay-up shot

Possible objectives: Versatile high jumping with height marker.

Execution: Basketball-typical lay-up shot, often by using the 2-line lay-up drill (shooting line and rebounding line).

Variations: In basketball game; even without ball at the basket, "Who can touch the net/rim?", "How high can you touch the backboard?"; bilateral practice.

Typical load standards: 5–20 reps per side and task (depending on the task).

326 | Pop-up jump with height marker

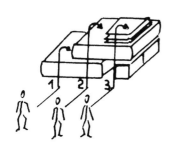

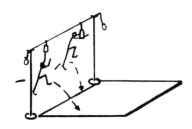

Possible objectives: Jumping high after run-up using a height marker.

Execution/variations: Run-up, take-off, and placing the swing leg onto the elevation (see upper picture); caution: if the landing area is too high, the athlete will bend his/her trunk toward the swing leg; however, this may happen only after take-off (maximum hip extension upon take-off); with double-arm swing; gymnastic rings may also be useful alternative height markers; also from arched run-up in the high-jump area with the leading arm touching a bar placed high or a stick which is held by the coach standing on the mat; bilateral practice.

Typical load standards: 5–10 reps per side and task (depending on the task).

327 | Curve, slalom, and figure-eight runs

Possible objectives: Training the curved run-up for the flop; specific warm-up.

Execution/variations: Marking the slalom, circle, figure eight, etc. (e.g., by means of cones); when

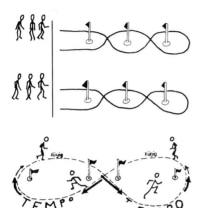

running the figure eight, crossing the running paths in the middle is an additional coordination task (peripheral vision) if there are many athletes; also as high-knee run (112), step-over (117), or skipping (87); also with interspersed pop-up jumps (268); bilateral practice.

Typical load standards: With changing tasks 2–4 reps each (depending on the objective), or within tempo-run programmes (see 143–145).

 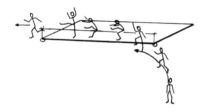

---

328 ▮▮▮ **Scissors jump**

Possible objectives: Simplified jumping technique in children's athletics; straight-line foot touchdown upon take-off; initiation of a vertical take-off momentum as great as possible; run-up corrections; specific warm-up.

Execution: Take-off with the leg distant to the bar, while lifting the acutely angled swing leg; take-off direction approx. 30° to the zero line (or bar); extending the swing leg, and forward and downward lean of the trunk; pushing down the swing leg and raising the take-off leg as a contralateral scissors movement; placing the swing leg onto the mat, straightening the trunk, and continuing running on the mat.

Variations: From straight or flop-typical curved run-up (with turn-around markers); bilateral practice.

Typical load standards: 5–15 reps per leg (depending on the objective).

329   Introduction of the flop: falling exercises

Possible objectives: Preparation of backward landing on the high-jump mat; reduction of fear; versatile coordination; stabilisation.

Execution: See picture; the athlete should fall backward onto the mat like a board.

Variations: With arms placed at the sides of the body or extended sidewards; (forward and) backward rolls (7) as well as judo rolls should also be a part of the established exercise repertoire in children's training.

Typical load standards: 5–10 reps per exercise.

330 Introduction of the flop: pop-up jump from 5-stride arched run-up

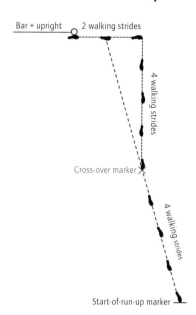

Possible objectives: Development of the flop technique; introduction of the arched run-up.

Execution: See pop-up jump (268), about two strides straight and three strides in a curve.

Variations: Possibly marking the running path by means of cones or a rope placed on the ground; caution: such a prescription may be problematic for larger heterogeneous groups since it may not be suitable for all children; an individual marker for the start of the run-up should possibly be used even here; the picture on the left shows one method of finding such a marker; bilateral practice.

Typical load standards: 3–6 reps per leg.

---

331 | ▯▮▯▯ | **Introduction of the flop: pop-up jump with initiation of rotation**

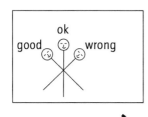

Possible objectives: Development of the flop technique; introduction of the flop-typical rotation.

Execution: As above (330); upon take-off, the jumper should initiate the flop-typical rotation and land on the high-jump mat on his/her back; during the flight, he/she should try to maintain his/her take-off position.

Variations: Possibly marking the landing point and direction on the mat; the partner/coach should check the position of the take-off foot; bilateral practice.

Typical load standards: 5–10 reps per leg.

---

332 Introduction of the flop: pop-up jump with initiation of rotation over a low cord

Possible objectives: Development of the flop technique; getting accustomed to an obstacle.

Execution: An elastic cord is initially stretched extremely low (upper edge of the mat); the jumper is told not to do anything different than before (331); the height of the cord is gradually increased.

Variations: The jumper should be told to straighten himself/herself upon take-off and to maintain his/her straight position; the partner/coach should check the position of the take-off foot; bilateral practice.

Typical load standards: 5–15 reps per leg.

333 Introduction of the flop: flop jumps from short and medium run-up

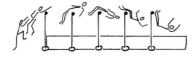

Possible objectives: Development of the flop technique; first test of the target technique; later, the reduced intensity (due to the short run-up) is used to increase volume.

Execution: Due to increasing the height of the cord, the previous exercise (332) automatically develops into the first form for the flop jump.

Variations: As soon as beginners master the initial rudimentary movement of the flop, the exercises below (334-336) may be included according to the whole-part-whole method; however, they should always try to integrate the skills learned into the overall movement; additional corrections of detailed movements may always be made (e.g., active swing leg; hyperextension, etc.); subsequently, the complete movement is expanded by extending the run-up to seven strides; bilateral practice; only rarely from an elevated or elastic take-off surface to extend the flight phase to facilitate learning the flight technique.

Typical load standards: 5-15 reps per leg; when training with advanced athletes focusing on volume, even significantly more repetitions are possible; also as rather specific speed-endurance or strength-endurance training (e.g., as up to 60 jumps with jogging interval; caution: significant changes compared to the target technique).

DISCOURSE V: SHORT, MEDIUM, AND LONG RUN-UP IN THE HIGH JUMP

A run-up preparation specific to the flop with an arched segment of the run-up and inward lean into the curve is not possible from less than five run-up strides. Therefore, the 5-stride run-up (from a standing position) is the shortest run-up length used in training. What may be called a medium run-up length depends on the competition run-up (= long run-up). Some competition run-ups consist of only 8 strides. Therefore, a medium run-up length may consist of 6 or 7 strides (see also chapter II–2.1.4).

334 ▢▢▢▢▢ Take-off in front of a barrier

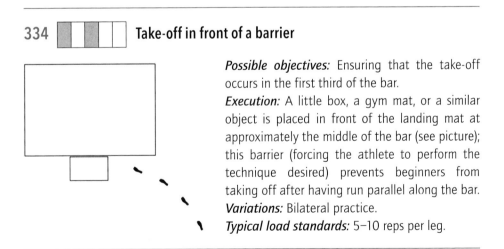

Possible objectives: Ensuring that the take-off occurs in the first third of the bar.

Execution: A little box, a gym mat, or a similar object is placed in front of the landing mat at approximately the middle of the bar (see picture); this barrier (forcing the athlete to perform the technique desired) prevents beginners from taking off after having run parallel along the bar.

Variations: Bilateral practice.

Typical load standards: 5–10 reps per leg.

335  Jump onto a pile of mats

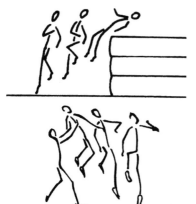

Possible objectives: Prevention of leaning toward the bar too early; reaching a horizontal flight position at the highest point of the trajectory; maintenance of the extended take-off position; lowering of the swing leg.

Execution: The height of a normal high-jump mat is increased by means of additional soft floor mats; the athlete lands on the top mat in a lying position.

Variations: The variation shown on the left is only possible from a very short run-up; bilateral practice.

Typical load standards: 5–10 reps per leg.

336  Standing flop

Possible objectives: Improvement of the hyperextension above the bar.

Execution: To achieve a similar flight height as in the high jump, the athlete jumps from a small box or big two-element gym box; using a two-legged squat-extension jump (82), the athlete jumps backward over the bar; he/she tries to first achieve an obvious hyperextension and then quickly the L position; legs are open.

Variations: Also as competition or test form; also with one leg from a lateral starting position with preliminary swing of the swing leg; for advanced athletes, the head and eye movement during the flop from a standing position (and during the flop from run-up) may be improved by a person standing behind the high-jump facility and giving a sign; the jumper is supposed to look at this person during the hyperextension and to be able to tell after the jump whether this person lifted his/her arm or not.

Typical load standards: 5–15 reps.

337  High-jump oxer

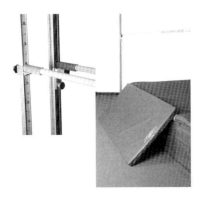

Possible objectives: If the jumper braces too much, jumps too steeply, or makes too little use of his/her run-up velocity, this exercise is supposed to help to change the technique for the development of a high and long jump with the focus on velocity.

Execution: Using a second pair of uprights, two bars (or two elastic cords) are placed at the same height 10–20cm apart.

Variations: The disadvantage of markers on the ground is that control of the view and the head may be disturbed; it is therefore more useful to lean a gym mat against the landing mat frontally and at an angle.

Typical load standards: 5–15 reps.

338  Run-up variations

Possible objectives: ABCs of sprinting/jumping specific to the high jump; differential learning; estimation of the distance to the bar.

Execution/variations: Run-up as high-knee run or step-overs; skipping run-up (take-off without interruption of the rhythm); galloping sideways (through the curve), then two run-up strides and take-off; rotation about the longitudinal axis during the run-up; starting the run-up with eyes closed, eyes remain closed until the coach claps his hands; jumps from a very fast or very relaxed run-up; with narrow or wide curve, etc.

Typical load standards: Only 1–3 reps per task; 4–6 tasks (e.g., during special warm-up or 2–3 tasks during the major part of the training session).

339 Take-offs with various arm actions

Possible objectives: Demonstration of different possibilities of arm actions; differential learning.

Execution/variations: Jumping without arm actions, with contralateral arm actions, (short or long) double-arm swing or lead-arm technique (possibly also relief technique with premature (exaggerated) lifting of arms or butterfly technique).

Typical load standards: 5–15 reps.

340 Variations of the flight phase

Possible objectives: Differential learning; contrast method

Execution/variations: With deliberately bent-over flying posture or very long maintained hyperextension; with head on the chest or thrown backward; with early or later lowered swing-leg; with varying arm position; with knees spread or closed, etc.

Typical load standards: Only 1–3 reps per task.

The following gymnastics exercises are particularly suitable for high jumpers: 8, 10, and 14.

341 Bridge

Possible objectives: Special flexibility and idea of technique.

Execution: (See picture).

Variations: From handstand to bridge position; handspring and backflip (14).

Typical load standards: Holding the position 3-6 x for 10–30 sec each.

342 ▏█▎ **Competition-like high jump**

Possible objectives: Performance of target technique.

Execution: Even in training, the athlete should try to perform the target technique at high intensity.

Variations: Despite maximal effort, some athletes must shorten the competition run-up by 1-3 feet in training; to make training more variable, the run-up may be extended by 2 strides now and then.

Typical load standards: 6–12 reps.

In high-jump training, the ABCs of jumping, pop-up jumps, and multiple jumps (see chapters I–5.4.6 and II–2.2.7) are also frequently performed in the curve. In general, these exercises must first be developed in terms of coordination before they are used specifically in reactive-strength training. Unlike long jumpers, who perform pop-up jumps by landing on the swing leg (270), high jumpers more often perform the following exercise:

343 ▏█▎ **ABCs of jumping: pop-up jumps landing on the take-off leg**

Possible objectives: High-jump technique; (reactive) strength and speed.

Execution: One-legged take-off from a run-up while holding the take-off position, landing on the take-off leg, resuming running and repeating take-off.

Variations: Over obstacle (e.g., mini-hurdles; only so high that the take-off leg may remain extended during flight); with four or six strides between the take-offs; also through the curve; with contralateral arm swing or double-arm swing or rudimentary lead-arm technique (see also pop-up jumps while landing on the swing leg 270); bilateral practice; also with eyes closed (without obstacles).

Typical load standards: 3–6 run-throughs with 3–5 take-offs each per leg.

With respect to strength training, high jumpers primarily perform the following exercises: 41–52, 61–64, 66–67, and 69–96.

The tempo-run programmes for jumpers presented especially in chapter II–1.3.8 are frequently performed in the curve (in both directions).

2.4.9 SPECIAL TEST AND CONTROL PROCEDURES

	Test: Ability/skill tested	Execution/comments
T121	**Technique analysis:** High-jump technique	Maximal competition jump from full run-up; evaluation on the basis of the technique analysis sheet (see chapter II–2.2.4), possibly using a video (T1) and photo sequences made thereof; in high-performance sport, a computer-supported biomechanical evaluation of the video recordings made by at least 2 cameras enables a more detailed observation of jumping techniques.
T122	**High jump from shortened run-up:** Specific speed and reactive strength	Maximal high jump from 5 and 7 run-up strides.
T123	**Standing flop:** Speed strength of the extensor loop of the legs and bar clearance	Standing flop (336) from a standardised elevation (e.g., small gym box, or large, two-element gym box).
T124	**5+1 test:** Specific reactive-strength endurance and general jumping agility	(See description below.)
T125	**Jump-and-reach test:** Specific reactive-strength	Test criterion: difference between reaching a height while standing and reaching a height with a one-legged jump with a run-up while touching an increasingly higher target object.
T3	**Body weight and body fat measurement:** Relative strength	Inappropriate upward and downward deflections should be avoided (see also chapter II–2.1.2: phase 3).
T4	**1 RPM:** Maximal strength	Squat (62), clean (63), snatch (64), hamstrings (68), quadriceps (69), hip flexors (73), etc. (if possible also eccentric maximal strength measurement).
T5	**Squat jump, and T8 counter-movement and drop jump:** Two-legged speed strength and reactive strength of the extensor loop	The counter-movement jump may be replaced by the simpler test of tossing the shot forward and/or backward (93) for distance.

	Test: Ability/skill tested	Execution/comments
T9	**5-stride hops with distance maximisation:** Reactive strength of the legs in comparison to one another	Hop test should be performed on both sides.
T10	**30m bounding run with time minimisation:** Reactive strength of the legs	See technique analysis sheet in chapter II–1.5.4.
T21	**60m analysis:** Sprint technique	
T24	**30m flying sprint:** Maximum sprinting speed	Possibly only 20m.
T61	**Standing start and acceleration up to 20m:** Start acceleration	
T103	**Take-off test:** Specific reactive strength	Test should be performed on both sides.
T115	**Long jump:** Specific speed and reactive strength	Test should be performed on both sides.
T2	**Flexibility tests:** General flexibility	

5+1-JUMP TEST ACCORDING TO KILLING

The suggested multiple high-jump competition is both a versatile and volume-focused technique and jumping-strength training as well as a good test specifically for the high jump. Within one training session, the athlete performs one competition each using the following jumping techniques:

- scissors jump from the usual take-off leg;
- scissors jump from the other leg;
- frontal jump from the usual take-off leg;
- two-legged flop with short run-up from the usual run-up side; and
- flop from the other leg.

The jumps are performed with a medium-length run-up (5–7 strides). During each repetition of the test, the run-up length should be identical. The starting height should be low in order to accurately adjust the length of the run-up and to become accustomed to each new technique. In each case, the height is increased by 5cm, initially perhaps even by 10cm. To limit the number of trials, the jumper gets only two trials instead of the usual three. Thus, the jumper performs 8–10 jumps for each technique and a total of 40–50 jumps in one session (however, only 16–20 one-legged take-offs per leg).

The "+1" represents the result in the flop from the competition run-up. This test is

711

performed in another training session or in competition (close in time). Killing's (1997) standard values for the 5+1 test are presented in table 10.

Due to the shortened run-up and the high number of jumps, the 5+1 test is no longer performed in the competition phase (exception: possibly as the last session before the transition period).

*Table 10: **Standard values for the 5(+1)-jump test** (according to Killing, 1998): As the comparison with table 9 shows, best performance should be interpreted here as best performance in training.*

Best flop performance	Starting height in the test	Target performance in the 5-jump test	Target performance in the 5+1-jump test
1.50m	0.80m	6.00m	7.45m
1.60m	0.90m	6.50m	8.05m
1.70m	1.00m	6.95m	8.60m
1.80m	1.10m	7.40m	9.15m
1.90m	1.20m	7.90m	9.70m

*Table 11: **Basic performances of high jumpers** (according to Killing et al., 2008, p. 232)*

Age group		Women		Men	
		w17	w19	m17	m19
Best performance	(m)	1.65	1.80	1.90	2.10
Flop in training	(m)	1.53	1.65	1.75	1.95
Scissors jump	(m)	1.35	1.50	1.65	1.75
5-jump test	(m)	6.00	6.75	7.50	8.00
Long jump from 9 run-up strides	(m)	5.00	5.30	6.20	6.60
5-stride bounding run from 5m run-up	(m)	10.50	11.50	13.00	14.50
Standing flop from two-element gym box	(m)	1.55	1.75	1.85	2.00
20m flying sprint	(sec)	2.35	2.30	2.25	2.15
30m sprint from a standing position	(sec)	4.40	4.35	4.05	3.95
Snatch	(kg)		30		45
Squat	(kg)		40		65

2.4.10   ERRORS – CAUSES – CORRECTIONS

Error	Causes	Corrections
Frequent inaccuracies during the run-up (highly variable stride pattern from run-up to run-up; take-off too close to or too far away from the bar).	• The athlete does not use a marker for the start of the run-up. • Irregular stutter steps or walk-on at the beginning of the run-up in connection with insufficient feel for the movement and insufficient adaptation to the visual impressions. • Too long run-up. • Insufficient run-up rhythm. • Too few jumps from long run-ups.	✔ Use of markers for the start of the run-up. ✔ Possibly switching to starting the run-up from a standing position or shortening the run-up by (one or) two strides. ✔ Training the ability to establish rhythm, e.g., by means of frequency coordination (135) or hurdle sprints. ✔ Arched run-ups or imitations with subsequent pop-up jump (e.g., 327–328, and 330). ✔ More competition-like jumps even in training (342).
Too wide run-up arc (final run-up direction parallel to the bar). (This also includes the error described as step to the side during the penultimate ground contact. Due to a run-up which is a little too short, the jumper is forced to adjust his/her run-up direction and to ensure his/her inward lean by performing a step to the side.)	• The jumper wants to take off sideways or even backward. • Run-up a little too short (the jumper is forced to adjust his/her run-up direction to avoid taking off below the bar).	✔ Repetition of the methods to learn the flop used with beginners (330–333). ✔ Explanation of the flop technique and the rotations initiated as part of this technique. ✔ Possibly slight lengthening of the run-up or advising the jumper to run through the curve using a higher stride frequency. ✔ Use of intermediate markers or markers to run around or run across so that the athlete runs toward the bar on a straighter path.
Run-up too straight toward the bar (final run-up direction too frontal toward the bar).	• Run-up a little too long (the jumper wants to shorten the path). • Athlete makes insufficient effort to achieve an inward lean.	✔ Possibly slight shortening of the run-up. ✔ Use of intermediate markers, run-around markers, or run-across markers so that the athlete runs toward the bar using a wider arc. ✔ Jumps while focusing on the inward lean (328, 330, 333, 335, and 342).

(continued)

(continued)

Error	Causes	Corrections
Run-up as straight – angle – straight (instead of straight – curve).	• Stepping to the side with the leg on the outside of the curve results in an abrupt change in direction. • Too late start of the curved segment of the run-up. • Coordination or strength problems while running with an inward lean or taking off from the inward lean.	✔ The athlete should start the curved segment of the run-up one stride earlier using the leg on the inside of the curve (possible use of an intermediate marker). ✔ Use of markers to run around or run across. ✔ Imitation exercises (327), ABCs of sprinting/jumping while running through the curve (e.g., 87, 112, and 117) and take-offs while running through the curve (e.g., 328 and 330). ✔ Emphasis on stride frequency and knee lift while running through the curve.
Run-up as curve – straight (instead of straight – curve).	• Beginner stage. • Athlete makes insufficient effort to achieve an inward lean immediately before take-off.	✔ Use of intermediate markers or markers to run around or run across. ✔ Imitation exercises (327) ✔ Jumps while focusing on the inward lean (328, and 330)
Insufficient inward lean.	• Too slow run-up velocity. • Run-up too straight to the bar (too wide radius of the curve) and its causes (see above). • Coordination or strength problems while running with an inward lean or taking off from the inward lean.	✔ Possible increase of run-up velocity. ✔ See corrections of run-up too straight toward the bar. ✔ Imitation exercises (327), ABCs of sprinting/jumping while running through the curve (e.g., 87, 112, and 117) and take-offs while running through the curve (e.g., 328 and 330). ✔ Flop jumps (333 and 342) with the instruction to maintain a noticeable inward lean over a long period. ✔ More strength training (specifically for the trunk and foot muscles).
Athlete straightens himself/herself too early from the inward lean.	• Run-up as straight – angle – straight or curve – straight and its causes (see above). • To high run-up velocity. • Too small radius of the curve (the jumper cannot maintain his/her inward lean). • Coordination or strength problems while running with inward lean or take-off from the inward lean.	✔ See corrections of run-up as straight – angle – straight or curve – straight. ✔ Possible reduction of run-up velocity or increasing the radius of the curve. ✔ Imitation exercises (327), ABCs of sprinting/jumping while running through the curve (e.g., 87, 112, and 117) and take-offs while running through the curve (e.g., 328 and 330). ✔ Flop jumps (333 and 342) with the instruction to maintain a noticeable inward lean. ✔ More strength training (specifically for the trunk and foot muscles).

Error	Causes	Corrections
No backward lean of the trunk (backward reclining take-off position) upon foot touchdown for take-off.	• Too late switch from toe push-off to grasping/pulling sprinting due to a short run-up from a standing position. • Insufficient forward shift of the hips during the last run-up stride due to insufficient hip extension and too powerful knee extension when pushing off from the penultimate support. • Athlete makes insufficient effort to perform a bracing pop-up jump upward.	✔ Extension of the run-up by two strides or switching to start the run-up from stutter steps. ✔ Imitation exercises (327) and versatile pop-up (324-326), scissors (328), and flop jumps for height (333 and 342) with corresponding advice for correction.
Take-off point not in the first third of the bar or not close to the first upright.	• Not yet established run-up leads to stutter steps (possibly two strides too many). • The jumper wants to take off sideways or even backward.	✔ Use of intermediate marker(s), as well as marker(s) to run around or run across. ✔ Repetition of the methods to teach the flop to beginners (330–335).
During the ground contact for take-off, the take-off foot is parallel to the zero line or is even directed away from it.	• Turning the shoulders (and hips) too early: the shoulder closer to the bar is turned away from the bar already during the take-off preparation (the jumper wants to anticipate the rotation about the longitudinal axis). • Too wide run-up arc and its causes (see above). • Positive experiences in terms of energy storage (see discourse II).	✔ One scissors jump (328) from arched run-up and one flop (333 and 342) alternately with reference to correct foot and trunk position and deliberate fast and short take-off. ✔ See corrections of too wide run-up arc. ✔ Focusing on injury risk as a topic of discussion.
Insufficient use of the swing elements (arms and swing leg) upon take-off.	• See chapter II–2.2.9. • Insufficient swing-leg action due to anticipating the bar clearance position. • Contralateral arm swing or relief technique instead of lead-arm technique or double-arm swing.	✔ See Chapter II–2.2.9. ✔ More pop-up (268–270, 326, 330, and 343) and scissors jumps (328) as well as flops (333, 340, and 342) without dropping the swing leg. ✔ Change of arm technique only if necessary.
Too large knee-joint angle of the swing leg or even straight swing leg.	• Too slow run-up and take-off. • Jumping technique with too much emphasis on strength.	✔ Change of technique in the direction of the speed flop as part of exercise 342. ✔ Deliberately angled swing leg in the ABCs of jumping and during multiple jumps (e.g., 87 and 343).

(continued)

Track & Field

(continued)

Error	Causes	Corrections
Sideward lean to the bar during take-off.	• The inward lean is not very noticeable or the athlete prematurely straightens himself/herself from the inward lean and its causes (see above). • Too wide run-up arc (final run-up direction parallel to the bar) and its causes (see above; the athlete is forced to jump sideways). • Incorrect movement of the arm closer to the bar (directed toward the bar too early). • Take-off point too far away (run-up a little too long; the jumper wants to reach the mat).	✔ See corrections of inward lean is not very noticeable or athlete straightens himself/herself from the inward lean too early. ✔ See corrections of too wide run-up arc. ✔ Imitation of correct arm actions (e.g., within exercise 330). ✔ Slight shortening of the run-up and advising the jumper to run through the curve using a higher stride frequency.
Jump too long (the jumper is not able to translate his/her run-up velocity into height; often in combination with an ineffective bar clearance).	• Run-up too fast. • Sideward lean to the bar during take-off and its causes (see above). • Run-up too straight to the bar and its causes (see above). • Insufficient bracing and its causes (see chapter II–2.2.9). • No backward lean upon foot touchdown for take-off and its causes (see above).	✔ Athlete should possibly run up in a more controlled manner and focus on a powerful take-off upward, possibly initially in the form of a pop-up and scissors jump. ✔ See corrections of sideward lean to the bar during take-off. ✔ See corrections of run-up too straight to the bar. ✔ See corrections of insufficient bracing in chapter II–2.2.9. ✔ See corrections of no backward lean upon foot touchdown for take-off.
Jump too steep (the jumper risks knocking off the bar both during the rising and falling behind the bar).	• Running too close to the bar (run-up a little too short). • Too much bracing and its causes (see chapter II–2.2.9). • High-jump technique with too much emphasis on strength. • Too low run-up velocity.	✔ Slight extension of the run-up. ✔ See corrections of too much bracing in chapter II–2.2.9. ✔ Change of technique in the direction of the speed flop with faster run-up and short take-off for a high-long jump.
Jump too parallel to the bar (the jumper risks knocking off the bar both during the rising and falling behind the bar).	• Too wide run-up arc (final run-up direction too parallel to the bar) and its causes (see above).	✔ See corrections of too wide run-up arc. ✔ Correction of take-off by means of landing on a specified point (marker) on the mat.
The jumper reaches the highest point of the flight trajectory behind the bar or even knocks off the bar while rising.	• Take-off point too close to the zero line. • With correct take-off point: • Jump too long and its causes (see above). • Sideward lean to the bar during take-off and its causes (see above).	✔ Slight lengthening of the run-up or advising the jumper to run through the curve using higher stride frequency. ✔ See corrections of jump too long. ✔ See corrections of sideward lean to the bar during take-off.

716

Error	Causes	Corrections
The jumper reaches the highest point of the flight trajectory in front of the bar or knocks off the bar while falling.	• Take-off point too far from the zero line. • With correct take-off point: • Jump too steep and its causes (see above). • Jump too parallel to the bar and its causes (see above).	✔ Slight shortening of the run-up or advising the jumper to run more powerfully at the beginning of the run-up. ✔ See corrections of jump too steep. ✔ See corrections of jump too parallel to the bar.
Insufficient hyperextension over the bar.	• Insufficient push-off extension upon take-off due to too much bracing (in relation to the available reactive-strength abilities; see chapter II-2.2.9). • Insufficient experience with the movement. • Incorrect eye and head control (possibly out of fear). • Incorrect timing: too early release of the hyperextension and initiation of the hip flexion (possibly due to too frequent jumping from short run-ups).	✔ See corrections of too much bracing in chapter II-2.2.9. ✔ Standing flops with correct eye and head control (336; possibly using a marker to look at behind the mat) as well as jumps onto the mat pile (335). ✔ Gymnastic exercises with active (hyper) extension of the body (e.g., 8, 10, and 14). ✔ Competition-like flop jumps (342) with deliberately long maintenance of the hyperextension: "Try to knock off the bar with your feet!"
Frequent knocking off of the bar with the lower legs.	• Incorrect timing: too late hip flexion and extension of the knee joints. • Jump too long and its causes (see above); as a result of this, there is not enough time for the switch from hyperextension to L-position. • Too slow rotation about the bar (no diving action of the head behind the bar) due to • insufficient rotation about the (sagittal and/or) transverse axis upon take-off, • insufficiently making oneself small during the flight.	✔ Standing flops (336) with correct eye and head control, noticeable heel movement toward the buttocks with subsequent extension of the knee joints, and at least one arm placed close to the body. ✔ Development or practice of back flip (14). ✔ See corrections of jump too long. ✔ Flop jumps (342) while trying to achieve a tighter radius of the curve and a more noticeable inward lean ✔ Rapid straightening from the inward and backward lean upon take-off (rapid movement of shoulders across the support).
Tilted position above the bar (swing-leg hip lower than take-off leg hip).	• Insufficient rotation about the longitudinal axis due to • Insufficient initiation of rotation upon take-off, • lack of control (through arms) in the air.	✔ Imitation exercises (331) and flop jumps with deliberate movements of the swing elements away from the bar. ✔ Active lowering of the leading arm behind the bar and turning outward of the swing leg to initiate bar clearance. ✔ The respective opposites of the two aforementioned causes of error (i.e., excessive rotation about the transverse axis or longitudinal axis) are extremely rare and are therefore not discussed in detail. As expected, the corrections would also be opposite.

(continued)

(continued)

Error	Causes	Corrections
Landing on one's head.	• Too excessive making oneself small behind the bar. • Too low mat.	✔ After clearing the bar, the athlete should keep his/her legs extended and should not bend his/her hips too much. ✔ Increasing the height of the mat.
The hands first touch the mat for support (risk of injury).	• Incorrect idea by a beginner about what is safe. • Not accustomed to landing on one's back.	✔ Focusing on injury risk as a topic of discussion and practising landing on one's back using falling exercises (329) and standing flops (336).

See also the errors, causes, and corrections in the sprint chapter (II–1.3.10)

2.4.11 TRAINING PLANNING

Compared to horizontal jumps, run-up velocity is of minor importance in the high jump (see chapter II–2.4.3) and accordingly must be practised less (see for comparison chapter II–2.2.10). This means that for high-performance training a lower total training volume than in the long jump and triple jump is suggested: eight training sessions per microcycle in the first two mesocycles. In build-up training, this additional training time is filled primarily by specific and versatile contents. The suggested training plan below for 17-year-olds therefore includes:

• A gymnastics module for practising handsprings and backflips with typical (trunk) hyperextension for improving bar clearance.
• A javelin module, since throwing the javelin has a certain affinity with the high jump with respect to stride rhythm, bracing, arched back, etc. It is no coincidence that combined athletes who are good high jumpers are usually also quite good javelin throwers.
• A long-jump module as an alternative speed and jumping-strength training. (However, in the subsequent third mesocycle, even a 17-year-old high jumper would perform two technique sessions in his/her special discipline.)

The athlete should continue to be able to complete a quadrathlon or pentathlon (i.e., the first day of a heptathlon or decathlon).

Even in high-performance training, high jumpers do a great deal of hurdling. This is good for the development of rhythm, the ability to visually estimate distances, hip and trunk flexibility, and the ability to perform a number of quick take-offs (when running at a 1-stride rhythm).

Table 12: **Training emphasis in the various mesocycles** *for high-jump training in build-up and high-performance training.*

1st mesocycle	anaerobic endurance training; hypertrophy-oriented maximal-strength training especially for the legs and the trunk; basic reactive-strength training for the legs; flexibility training; general (e.g., hurdle training, gymnastics, etc.), and special coordination training (e.g., ABCs of sprinting/jumping, technique training from short run-ups)
2nd mesocycle	speed-(endurance) training; IC- and connective-tissue-oriented maximal- and reactive-strength training especially for the legs and the trunk; general (e.g., hurdle training, gymnastics, etc.) and special coordination training (e.g., ABCs of sprinting/jumping, technique training from medium run-ups)
3rd mesocycle	IC- and connective-tissue-oriented maximal- and reactive-strength training especially for the legs and the trunk; sprinting-speed and acceleration training at maximum intensity; special coordination training (long run-ups)
4th mesocycle	competitions and corresponding regeneration; IC- and connective-tissue-oriented maximal- and reactive-strength training especially for the legs and the trunk; speed and acceleration training at maximum intensity; technique training; maintenance stimuli

SUGGESTED TRAINING PLANS

Below, there are exemplary microcycles for the

- second mesocycle of a 17-year-old athlete in build-up training (table 13);
- first mesocycle of an athlete in high-performance training (table 14); and
- third mesocycle of an athlete in high-performance training (table 15).

The sample microcycles presented in connection with the long and triple jump (see chapter II–2.2.10 and II–2.3.10) for the

- first mesocycle of a 17-year-old athlete in build-up training;
- third mesocycle of a 17-year-old athlete in build-up training;
- second mesocycle of an athlete in high-performance training; and
- fourth mesocycle of an athlete in high-performance training

provide ideas for the training plans not presented here.

Table 13: Build-up training: sample microcycle for a 17-year-old athlete in the second mesocycle.

Monday	Tuesday	Wednesday	Thursday	Friday	Saturday	Sunday
Trunk stabilisation exercises and belly crunches (20 min)	Foot strengthening (10 min)	Warm-up jogging (6 min)	Continuous run (30 min)	Ll runs (6 x 80m; rest intervals: 20 sec) for warming up	Warm-up jogging (6 min)	Rest
Acceleration runs 3 reps)	Acceleration runs (2 reps) barefoot	Acceleration runs (3 reps)	Contract-relax stretching (15 min)	ABCs of sprinting (8–10 run-throughs)	Acceleration runs (3 reps)	
ABCs of jumping (10–15 run-throughs) galloping sideways, ankle jumps, skipping with two-legged landing, skipping variations, etc.	ABCs of sprinting (15–20 run-throughs)	ABCs of jumping (8–10 run-throughs)	Strength training for the trunk on apparatus, medicine-ball work, or boxing, etc. (30 min each) e.g., goalkeeper throws, rotational throws, throws from a prone position, and tossing, using a medicine ball	Practising the long-jump technique (30 min) medium to long run-up, as alternative speed-strength and jumping-strength training	ABCs of hurdling (20 min)	
Practising the high-jump technique (40 min) medium run-up length, scissors and flop jumps, additional tasks	Acceleration runs (2 reps)	Skipping and pop-up jumps (2 x 2 run-throughs each per side) through the curve over low obstacles, also with a double-arm swing; skipping: emphasis on one take-off leg; pop-up jumps: at 4-stride rhythm, landing on take-off leg		Strength training (40 min) according to the pyramid principle: hamstrings, quadriceps, abductors, adductors, and full squats	Hurdle sprints (20 min) versatile	
Technique sprints (4–6 reps) sprints with additional tasks such as varied arm actions, with pre-set stride lengths, etc.	Gymnastics (30 min) improvement of front handspring, backflip, etc.	Bounding runs (4 run-throughs of 30m each)	Tappings (8 x 5 sec) or	Foot strengthening (10 min) in the sand	Hurdle Zs (2 sets of 3 Zs each of 2 run-throughs over 4 hurdles each; rest intervals: 3 min; rest intervals between sets: 10 min) e.g., out at 3-stride rhythm with the weak side, back with the strong side	
	Strength training (30 min) according to the pyramid principle: clean and snatch (the coach must continue to supervise the technique attentively), possibly interspersed with abdominal exercises	Practising the javelin-throw technique (30 min) medium run-up lengths	Frequency coordination (10 min) over foam blocks at 1m distance as utilisation	Slalom sprints (3 reps) as utilisation	Contract-relax stretching (15 min)	
	Game (20 min) e.g., basketball or handball	Alternating-pace sprints (6 x 60m)			Warm-down jogging (10 diagonals on the lawn)	
					Pop-up jumps (3–4 run-throughs) as utilisation	

Table 14: High-performance training: sample microcycle in the first mesocycle.

	Monday	Tuesday	Wednesday	Thursday	Friday	Saturday	Sunday
Morning		Rope jumping (5 min)	Foot strengthening (10 min) small jumps on gym mats	Warm-up jogging (6 min)	LI runs (6 x 100m; rest intervals: 30 sec) for warming up	Warm-up jogging (10 min)	Rest
		Acceleration runs	Acceleration runs	Game (30 min)	ABCs of jumping (12–15 run-throughs)	Acceleration runs (3 reps)	
		ABCs of hurdling (15 min)	ABCs of sprinting (10–15 run-throughs)	Contract-relax stretching (15 min)	Skipping, pop-up and squat-extension jumps (5–7 run-throughs each) or start jumps, or jumps onto boxes	I3 tempo runs (4 x 5 x 60m; rest intervals: walking back; rest intervals between sets: 6–8 min) possibly including pull-resisted runs, slalom sprints, uphill or over hurdles	
		Hurdle sprints (40 min) versatile, primarily 1-stride rhythm	Technique sprints (4–6 reps)	Muscle build-up training (40 min) for the trunk on apparatus, or gymnastics	Tappings (8 x 5 sec)	Contract-relax stretching (15 min)	
		Contract-relax stretching (10 min)	Muscle build-up training (50 min) hamstrings, adductors, hip/back extensors, and clean	Frequency coordination (10 min) as utilisation			
Afternoon	Trunk stabilisation exercises and belly crunches (20 min)	LI runs (8 x 80m; rest intervals: 20 sec) for warming up	Pop-up jumps (3–5 run-throughs per side) e.g., at 4-stride rhythm with landing on take-off leg, through the curve, as utilisation		Warm-up jogging (8 min)	Warm-down jogging (10 diagonals on the lawn)	
	Acceleration runs (3 reps)	ABCs of jumping (12–15 run-throughs)			Acceleration runs	Pop-up jumps (3 run-throughs per side) at 1-stride rhythm, as utilisation	
	Practising the high-jump technique (45 min) shortened run-up, during rest intervals: gymnastics	Bounding runs and/or rhythm jumps (3 x 4 x 50m)			ABCs of sprinting (12–15 run-throughs)		
	Muscle build-up training (30 min) step-ups, calf exercise, and full squat	Medicine-ball work (30 min)			Strength training (45 min) according to the pyramid principle: abductors, quadriceps, hip flexors, and quarter split squat		
	Acceleration runs as utilisation	High-knee run (5 x 20 sec) with ankle weights			Foot strengthening (10 min) in the sand		
					Alternating-pace sprints (6 x 80m)		

Table 15: *High-performance training: sample microcycle in the third mesocycle.*

Monday	Tuesday	Wednesday	Thursday	Friday	Saturday	Sunday
Warm-up jogging (6 min)	**LI runs** (6 x 100m, rest intervals: 30 sec) for warming up	**Warm-up jogging** (6 min)	**Warm-up jogging** (6 min)	**Foot strengthening** (10 min)	**Warm-up jogging** (6 min)	Rest
Maximal-eccentric strength training (15 min) trunk stabilisation, lifting opposite upper and lower limbs in prone position, belly punches, raising the foot/toes	**Tuck jumps** (3 x 3 run-throughs over 3 hurdles each)	**Gymnastics** (30 min) improvement of front handspring, backflip, etc.	**High-intensity strength training** (15 min) snatch	**Acceleration runs** (2 reps)	**Acceleration runs** (3 reps)	
Acceleration runs (3 reps)	**Acceleration runs** (3 reps)	**Strength training** for the trunk, or **medicine-ball work** (40 min) e.g., abdominal machine, shoulder-hip twist, lumborum, and hip/back extensors	**Acceleration runs** (3 reps)	**ABCs of sprinting** (8–10 run-throughs)	**ABCs of jumping** (8–10 run-throughs)	
ABCs of sprinting (8–10 run-throughs)	**Pull-assisted sprints** (2–3 reps) with pulley, release of the assistance 10 m in front of the second light barrier		**ABCs of jumping** (8–10 run-throughs)	**Standing starts** (2–3 reps)	**Depth jumps** (3 x 10) from box over hurdle; alternatively: ankle jumps with a partner pushing downward on 5 jumps and then lifting upward on 5 jumps	
Practising the high-jump technique (40 min) long run-up, competition-like	**Flying sprints** (1–2 x 20m + 30m run-up)		**Practising the high-jump technique** (40 min) medium run-up lengths, additional tasks	**Pull-resisted sprints** and **standing starts** alternately (25–35 min; altogether 6–8 sprints of 10–30m each) against each other, the shorter the distance, the higher the sled loading (up to 60 kg)	**One-legged jumps (hops)** (4–5 x 2 run-throughs of 20m each) maximum intensity; alternatively: rhythm jumps	
High-intensity strength training (25 min) clean and quarter-split squat	**Pop-up jumps** (3 x 3 run-throughs with 4 take-offs) landing on take-off leg, with 4 intermediate strides through the curve		**Jumping test** (15 min) a different test each week (e.g., maximal flop/scissors jump from 7 run-up strides, jump-and-reach test with one-legged take-off from run-up; possibly before technique training)	**Maximal-eccentric strength training** (30 min) quadriceps, glutes, etc.	**I2 tempo runs** (3 x 3 x 60m; rest intervals: 3 min; rest intervals between sets: 10–12 min) possibly including slalom sprints	
Frequency coordination (10 min) as utilisation				**Alternating-pace sprints** (3–4 x 60m) as utilisation		

2.4.12 BIBLIOGRAPHY

Ae, M., Nagahara, R., Ohshima, Y., Koyama H., Takamoto, M. & Shibayama, K. (2008). Biomechanical analysis of the top three male high jumpers at the 2007 World Championships in Athletics. *New Studies in Athletics 23* (2), 45-52.

Antekolovic, L., Blazevic, I., Mejovsek, M. & Coh, M. (2006). Longitudinal follow-up of kinematic parameters in the high jump – A case study. *New Studies in Athletics 21* (4), 27-37.

Dapena, J. (1980). Mechanics of rotation in the Fosbury-flop. *Medicine and Science in Sports and Exercise 12* (1), 45-53.

Dapena, J. (1996). Die Rotationen über der Latte beim Fosbury-Flop. *Die Lehre der Leichtathletik 35* (16), 39-40, (17), 43-46 & (18) 50.

Geese, R. (2000). Der Doppelarmeinsatz beim Flop – ein vernachlässigtes Element der Sprungtechnik! *Leistungssport 30* (5), 15-18.

Greig, M. P. & Yeadon, M. R. (2000). The influence of touchdown parameters on the performance of a high jumper. *Journal of applied biomechanics 16* (4), 367-378.

McEwen, F. (2007). High jump: Teaching the Fosbury flop. *Modern Athlete and Coach 45* (4), 10-14.

Isoletho, J., Virmavirta, M., Kyröläinen, H., Komi, P. (2007). Biomechanical analysis oft he high jump at the 2005 IAAF World Championships in Athletics. *New Studies in Athletics 22* (2), 17-27.

Killing, W. (1998). Hochsprung-Trainerfortbildung: Mainz, 18.10.1997. *Die Lehre der Leichtathletik 37* (1), 1-4, (2), 5-6.

Killing, W. (2009a). *Trainings- und Bewegungslehre des Hochsprungs* (2. unveränd. Aufl.). Köln: Sportverlag Strauß.

Killing, W. (2009b). Zweimal Bronze für Deutschlands Höhenjäger. *Leichtathletiktraining 20* (10+11), 26-35.

Killing, W., Bartschat, E., Czingon, H., Knapp, U., Kurschilgen, B. & Schlottke K. (2008). *Jugendleichtathletik: Offizieller Rahmentrainingsplan des Deutschen Leichtathletik-Verbandes für die Sprungdisziplinen im Aufbautraining.* Münster: Philippka.

Lees, A., Rojas, J., Cepero, M., Soto, V., Gutierrez, M. (2000). How the free limbs are used by elite high jumpers in generating vertical velocity. *Ergonomics 43* (10), 1622-1636.

Mühlbach, T. (2007). Bausteine für das richtige Floppen. *Leichtathletiktraining 18* (8), 20-27.

Patrick, S. (2001). High jump: Technical aspects. *Track Coach* (155), 4938-4940.

Regelkommissionen des DLV, FLA, ÖLV und SLV (Hrsg.). (2010). *Internationale Wettkampfregeln.* Waldfischbach: Hornberger.

Ritzdorf, W. (2009). Approaches to technique and technical training in the high jump. *New Studies in Athletics 24* (3), 31-34.

Schiffer, J. (2009). The high Jump. *New Studies in Athletics 24* (3), 9-22.

Tidow, G. (2007). The flop high jump: Model technique analysis sheet. *Modern Athlete and Coach 45* (4), 31-40.

2.5 POLE VAULT

2.5.1 THE FIBREGLASS REVOLUTION

For thousands of years, people of various cultures have jumped with poles. The Frisians jumped over drainage ditches using pullstocks. The Celts used poles to perform long jumps. In Crete, jumping over bulls with the help of poles was a test of courage. In ancient Greek literature, jumping with the assistance of a lance is mentioned. The pioneer of German Physical Culture, Friedrich GutsMuths (1759–1839), regarded jumping with a pole as a part of military training and therefore included it in his programme of exercises. In 1850, Scottish immigrants introduced pole vaulting in America. However, the exercise they performed was more climbing up the pole than jumping with it. In 1889, this technique was banned in America. Climbing up the pole was also banned when the pole vault was included in the competition programme of the first modern Olympic Games in Athens in 1896, using poles made of ash or hickory. In 1900, the planting box and lighter bamboo poles were introduced. The last world record using a bamboo pole was established by the American Cornelius Warmerdam in 1942 (4.77m). It was not until 1957 that this record was surpassed by one centimetre by Warmerdam's fellow countryman Robert Gutowski who used an aluminium pole. In the same year, Gutowski even cleared 4.82m. However, at that time the jump was declared invalid since the pole fell forward below the bar.

In 1960, it was again an American, Don "Tarzan" Bragg, who established the next official world record of 4.80m (this time using a steel pole) and won the Olympic gold medal. Steel poles were considered to be bad for the back and required a somewhat different vaulting technique and constitution of the pole-vaulter than is the case today.

The year 1961 marked a revolution in the pole vault. Already shortly after the Second World War, pole-vaulters, who initially had been looking for lighter and still durable poles, experimented with a material from the aerospace industry: epoxy resin reinforced by glass fibre. Quite by accident they discovered that higher grip heights were possible with these new bendable poles. In both the U.S. and the U.S.S.R., pole-vaulters started to look for the best poles to use for this discipline of athletics which is most dependent on material. Again, American pole-vaulters improved the world record with the new poles. The first one was John Davies, who vaulted over 4.83m on 20 May 1961. In the subsequent three years, the world record was improved by almost 50cm. The first world-record holder coming from the Eastern bloc was the East German Wolfgang Nordwig (1970: 5.46m; 1972: Olympic champion).

At the first world championships (1983), the unexpected winner was a young unknown Ukrainian. But eventually Sergei Bubka also won the next five world-championship titles and the gold medal at the 1988 Olympic Games in Seoul. Bubka established his first world record in 1984 with 5.85m. In subsequent years until 1994, he improved this record to 6.14m (6.15m indoors) by using the piecemeal approach. Since he did not have to fear being overtaken by anyone, he regularly improved the world record by only 1cm. In each case of course, he was rewarded handsomely. When he jumped over 6.01m at the 1997 World Championships, his maximum CG height was measured as 6.50m—enough for a bar height of 6.30m. The same strategy was used by his female counterpart, Yelena Isinbayeva (Russia), twenty years later. Only since 1995 has the IAAF been keeping a world-record list for women, who since 2000 have also competed in the pole vault at the Olympic Games. In 2009, Isinbayeva established a world record of 5.06m in Zurich.

After Frenchmen Renaud Lavillenie set the world record of 6.16 indoors, the world was recently amazed by a young Swede. In 2020, at the age of 20, Armand Duplantis cleared 6.18 indoors. At the World Championships in 2022, he cleared 6.21m outdoors.

2.5.2 THE MOST IMPORTANT COMPETITION RULES

The following abridged and simplified International Competition Rules comprise the framework for the techniques and strategy, as well as the organisation of pole-vault competitions:

- Figure 1 shows the construction and specifications of a pole-vault facility.
- The crossbar must rest with its ends on the pegs so that if it is touched by an athlete or his/her pole, it will fall easily to the ground in the direction of the landing area. The bar is allowed to weigh up to 2.25 kg and to have a maximum sag of 3cm. If a weight of 3 kg is attached to the centre of the bar, the bar may sag no more than 11cm.
- The front side of the zero line must be in line with the rear upper edge of the planting box and with its lateral extension. The zero line is marked both on the ground and on the mat.
- The facility is in zero position when the front side of the bar is perpendicular above the front edge of the zero line. From there, the athlete may have the crossbar moved up to 80cm in the direction of the landing area. Before the competition starts, he/she must inform the appropriate official of the position of the crossbar he/she requires for his/her first trial.
- The bar is raised after each height by at least 5cm until an athlete has won.
- If the performance capacity of the competitors is very heterogeneous, a neutralisation height may be determined before the competition,

Frontal views

Cross section through front mats

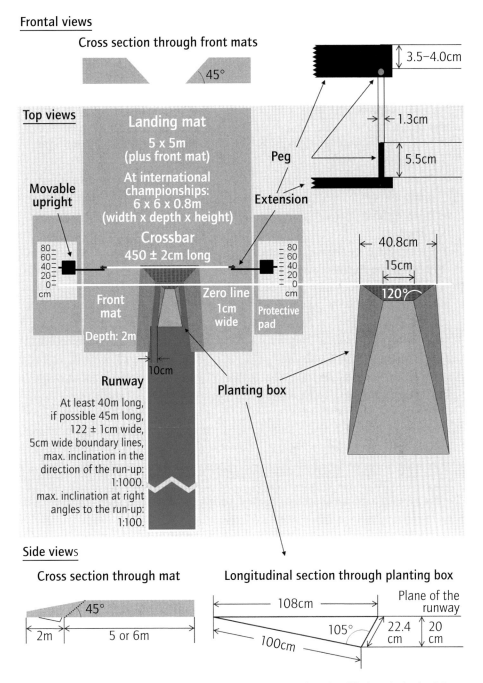

Figure 1: *Elements of a pole vault facility from various perspectives* (modified on the basis of the Rule Commissions by the DLV, FLA, ÖLV and SLV, 2010, pp. 96–98).

at which the competition is interrupted and the athletes who have not yet entered the competition are allowed to perform practice jumps at the competition facility.

- The time available until the start of a trial is
  » 1 min if there are more than three competitors,
  » 2 min if there are two to three competitors,
  » 3 min with successive trials of one competitor, or
  » 5 min if there is only one competitor (3 min in the combined events).
- Athletes may use their own poles. No athlete is allowed to use any other athlete's pole except with the consent of the owner. The vaulting pole may be of any length or diameter, but the basic surface must be smooth. The pole may have protective layers of tape at the grip end and at the bottom end.
- Athletes may, during the competition, place a substance on their hands or on the pole in order to obtain a better grip. However, they must not use a bandage on their hands or fingers, unless this is necessary to cover an open wound.
- An athlete fails if
  » he/she touches the landing area or the ground beyond the zero line with any part of his/her body or with the pole, without first clearing the crossbar, or if the pole is not placed in the planting box upon take-off;
  » after leaving the ground, he/she places his/her lower hand above the upper one or moves the upper hand higher on the pole;
  » during the vault, he/she steadies or replaces the bar with his/her (hand(s); or
  » he/she touches the pole after its release before it has fallen away from the bar, and the referee is of the opinion that, were it not for the intervention, the crossbar would have been knocked off.
- If, in making a trial, an athlete's pole breaks, it is not counted as a failure.

Otherwise, the general competition rules for the technical disciplines and the vertical jumps apply (see chapter II–2.1.1 and II–2.4.2).

2.5.3 SPORT-SCIENCE FINDINGS, PHASE STRUCTURE, AND TECHNIQUE

The introduction to the phase structure and general comments on the biomechanics and technique of the jumps can be found in chapter II–2.1.2. Therefore, in the following there are only discipline-specific additions.

PARTIAL HEIGHT MODELS
Coaches often divide the competition height as follows:

Competition height
= net grip height
+ excess height above the upper hand.

Grip height is the distance between the bottom end of the pole and the centre of the upper hand (with extended pole). Grip height may be estimated at any time during a workout or competition simply by using the length of the pole. When speaking of net grip height, the 20cm depth of the planting box is deducted. Relative grip height is the difference between the athlete's vertical reaching height and his grip height. As grip height increases, it becomes increasingly difficult to straighten the pole to the vertical. A higher grip height (and thus also a longer distance of the take-off foot from the zero line) is therefore associated with higher run-up velocity and superior or improved planting and take-off performances (although grip height is not independent of the behaviour during the pole phase). According to the formula above, excess height is the vertical difference between the height of the bar and the upper hand on the upright pole. World-class male pole-vaulters reach excess heights of 90–120cm, whereas female pole-vaulters have so far reached values of up to 85cm (see table 2). A higher excess height above

the upper hand is interpreted primarily in terms of improved performance during the pole and flight phase (although it is not independent of run-up, take-off, and plant).

Older biomechanical models of partial heights divide the pole vault similar to the high jump in accordance with the partial movement phases used below (see formula below).

A biomechanical model which does not divide the pole vault into sub-phases, but considers the pole-vaulter's mechanical energy in certain phases has led to a deeper understanding of the pole vault. Mechanical energy is the sum of kinetic energy (i.e., the movement energy determined by the pole-vaulter's velocity) and potential energy (i.e., the position energy determined by the pole-vaulter's height). The pole-vaulter's initial energy during the flight phase of the last stride as well as the energy at the moment of maximum pole bend and at the moment of the maximum flight height of the CG are of particular interest here.

Competition height (h_{of})
= height of the CG upon foot touchdown for take-off
+ lift of the CG during the take-off (until leaving the ground)
+ rising height of the CG during the bending phase of the pole (up to the maximum pole bend)
+ rising height of the CG during the extension phase of the pole (until release of the pole)
+ rising height of the CG during flight (up to the maximum height of the CG)
− clearance height (difference between the maximum CG height and the bar height)

MAJOR OBJECTIVE AND ENERGY TRANSFER

As in the high jump, the major objective of the pole vault is to reach a high flight height or potential energy (combined with skilful bar clearance). To achieve this, the elastic vaulting pole is used similar to the take-off leg which works in a bracing and reactive manner (see chapter II–2.1.2). The kinetic energy at the end of the run-up is converted into potential energy through the pole either directly (redirective function) or indirectly (spring function).

REDIRECTIVE FUNCTION

Even rigid vaulting poles are used to change the pole-vaulter's direction. The pole-vaulter uses the pole to redirect his/

her velocity from the horizontal to the vertical. The pole-vaulter has often been described as a pendulum on a pendulum (or as a lever on a lever). One pendulum is the pole which turns into an upright position, while the other pendulum is the pole-vaulter hanging with his/her hands on the pole and swinging forward with his/her feet.

SPRING FUNCTION

Figure 2a shows that the flexible pole absorbs some of the kinetic energy generated during the run-up and returns it to the pole-vaulter. Furthermore, figure 2b illustrates the curves of the pole-vaulter's potential and kinetic energy.

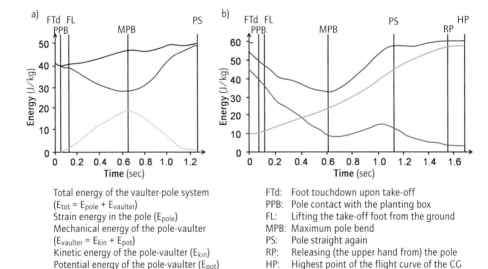

Total energy of the vaulter-pole system ($E_{tot} = E_{pole} + E_{vaulter}$)
Strain energy in the pole (E_{pole})
Mechanical energy of the pole-vaulter ($E_{vaulter} = E_{kin} + E_{pot}$)
Kinetic energy of the pole-vaulter (E_{kin})
Potential energy of the pole-vaulter (E_{pot})

FTd: Foot touchdown upon take-off
PPB: Pole contact with the planting box
FL: Lifting the take-off foot from the ground
MPB: Maximum pole bend
PS: Pole straight again
RP: Releasing (the upper hand from) the pole
HP: Highest point of the flight curve of the CG

*Figure 2a: **Energy transfer to the pole and back to the pole-vaulter** (modified on the basis of Schade, 2008); b: **Kinetic and potential energy curves** from Nick Hysong's winning jump over 5.90m at the 2000 Olympics (modified on the basis of Schade et al., 2004).*

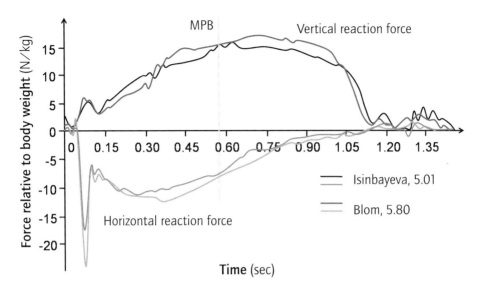

*Figure 3: **Vertical and horizontal reaction forces in the planting box** during the two winning jumps at the 2005 World Championships (modified on the basis of Schade, 2007; MPB = maximum pole bend).*

The spring effect enables pole-vaulters to grip a flexible vaulting pole approx. 90cm higher than a rigid pole. This can be explained as follows:

- While the vault with a flexible pole is similar to what in physics is called an elastic collision, the vault using an (almost) rigid pole has more characteristics of an inelastic collision. The difference may be illustrated for example by dropping an orange and a hard rubber ball onto the ground. During the inelastic collision of the orange with the ground, the kinetic energy wears off due to internal friction and deformation. During the elastic (or resilient) impact of the rubber ball, the movement is redirected in a different direction at a nearly identical velocity.

As mentioned, the pole-vaulter uses the pole to redirect his/her direction of motion. When using a rigid pole, the direction of the CG movement must change quickly and significantly (see figure 4). His/her hands are decelerated very suddenly and sharply and his/her arms, shoulders, and torso are loaded accordingly and abruptly. Under these circumstances, the strained biomaterials have relatively poor elastic properties. As in the orange, a great part of the kinetic energy from the run-up wears off in these biomaterials.

If, however, a flexible pole is used, energy storage must not only take place in the muscles, tendons, ligaments, etc., but a great amount of energy is stored in the pole.

DISCOURSE I: STRESS ON THE SPINAL CORD

Despite reduced stress due to the use of flexible poles, problems in the lumbar spine are among the most common complaints and injuries of pole-vaulters even today. Due to the pole and the ground contact, the hands and the foot are decelerated during the take-off while the trunk is continuously and actively moved forward. The lower arm must be well trained and should be fixed at the elbow joint, and abdominal muscles must be tight to prevent an excessive hyperextension and overloading of the spine during penetration.

The change in direction of the CG or the conversion of kinetic energy from the run-up and take-off into the strain energy of the pole and the potential energy of the pole-vaulter take place more gradually. The blow to the upper body is significantly lower, and the lower peak forces also improve the energy storage properties of the muscles, tendons, ligaments, etc. This means that during the plant and the subsequent phases, much less energy is lost in a flexible than in a rigid pole. Actually, energy loss is reduced if the pole is softer. However, the obvious decision to jump with poles as soft as possible would be short-sighted since a too soft pole would not only possibly break, but would also straighten too slowly or too late (i.e., far beyond the vertical). Therefore, the goal should be to find the best compromise between softness during the initial bending of the pole, the straightening velocity, and the grip height (see discourse VI and table 9 for further information). This description also explains why

pole-vaulters with high initial energy at the end of the run-up gain less energy during the interaction with the pole than pole-vaulters with low initial energy at the end of the run-up. Higher run-up velocity and harder poles result in a greater blow to the chest and a correspondingly greater energy loss during the planting of the pole. An indication of this is found in Rens Blom's higher force peak in the horizontal reaction force curve at the moment of the plant in figure 3. The energy gained during the subsequent interaction with the pole (see below) must first compensate for the initial energy loss.

- To reduce the impact load on the upper body while jumping with a rigid pole, the athlete himself/herself must achieve a maximum change of direction, which means that his/her take-off must be very steep. However, the stronger bracing action of the take-off leg associated with a larger departure angle also results in an increased loss of energy from the run-up. The more gradual change in direction during the jump with a flexible pole allows a flat departure angle and thus a lower energy loss in the take-off leg. The flatter departure angle and the lower impact load to the upper body may also result in the pole-vaulter being more confident to run up and to take off as quickly as possible.

- When vaulting with a flexible pole, the initial position after the take-off and penetration is more favourable to supply the vaulter-pole system with more energy (see discourse II and phase 3). Instead of swinging passively forward after take-off as on the rigid pole, the pole-vaulter may begin his/her active swing-up movement from the largely vertical hang position. Furthermore, the geometry of the arms with the much more extended lower arm on the flexible pole may promote a more

effective use of muscles for energy generation and a fast swing-up.

- Figure 2b shows that the strain energy stored in the pole is not exclusively converted directly into potential energy (jumping height) of the pole-vaulter. The kinetic energy (upward directed velocity) of the pole-vaulter initially also increases again after reaching the point of the maximum pole bend. The pole-vaulter is shot upward by the pole (catapulting effect). Due to this pre-acceleration (relief), which does not occur on the rigid pole, the pulling and pushing movement into the ultimate single-arm handstand on the pole is easier for the athlete. Again, the result is an increased energy generation and a gain in jumping height.

During a vault with a flexible pole, the chord of the pole (i.e., the connecting line between the upper hand and the bottom end of the pole) shortens up to 30% (see figure 4 and table 5). In the past, this phenomenon was often said to be primarily responsible for the higher grip height which is possible on the flexible pole. However, if on a rigid pole an identical energy balance were possible with identical grip height, the shortening of the chord of the pole would only result in a faster angular velocity about the pivotal point in the planting box due to the mass of the pole-vaulter getting closer to the pivot point.

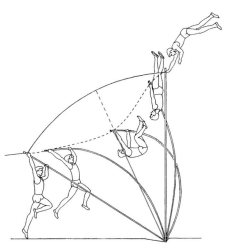

*Figure 4: **Path** (and change of direction) **of the upper hand while jumping with a rigid and bent pole as well as shortening the chord of the pole at the moment of maximum pole bend.***

DISCOURSE II: ADDITIONAL ASPECTS OF ENERGY BALANCE

No material, not even for the most modern vaulting pole, is perfectly elastic, which means that it would release exactly the same amount of energy again as it was loaded with. Approximately 7–10% of the energy transferred to the pole is ultimately lost in the form of thermal energy through internal friction, external friction in the planting box, and kinetic energy not transferred back to the pole-vaulter. Nevertheless, the total energy of the vaulter-pole system in figure 2a increases during the course of the vault. This is because the active sub-system, the pole-vaulter, is able to continuously supply the complete vaulter-pole system with mechanical energy through muscle work during the pole phase. Contrary to the other jumping events, the pole-vaulter is still able to change the path of his/her CG and thus the mechanical energy stored in him/her when he/she is airborne. During the pole phase, he/she remains connected to the ground and can exchange forces with it.

With respect to kinetic energy, translational movements of the CG and rotational movements about the CG must be observed. If the pole-vaulter's legs swing forward passively and quickly after the take-off, a great deal of energy remains in his/her body. With respect to energy transfer and the ability to generate more energy, the athlete has, however, possibly wasted his/her potential. Coaches therefore recommend moving the shoulders forward upon take-off for a subsequently more active swing-up. Pole-vaulters who do not completely reach the I-position (see figure 10) and instead push their feet in the direction of the bar too early are a different case. This results in a conversion of the strain energy of the straightening pole into a rotational motion instead of into a translational motion upward. Only the upper body is accelerated upward, while the feet are quickly moved downward.

PHASE 1: RUN-UP

GRIPPING AND CARRYING THE POLE

Apart from the selection of a pole and a suitable distance of the uprights from the zero line, a convenient manner of gripping the pole determines whether the vault will be successful even before the beginning of the run-up. In the pole vault, the manner of gripping the pole and the selection of the take-off leg depend on the pole-vaulter's preferred hand. Right-handers grip the pole so that the right hand is at the top and take off with the left leg – even if they take off with the right leg in the long and high jump. The only prominent known exception to this rule is the former German record holder Annika Becker (4.77m). It is often argued that this is the reason why she demonstrated a very good plant and take-off, but only a relatively poor pole phase.

The description below refers to right-handers or pole-vaulters who take off with their left leg. The pole-vaulter should concentrate on correct

- grip height,
- grip width, and
- pole rotation.

In general, as grip height increases, it becomes increasingly difficult to move the pole to the vertical. This effect is reduced with flexible vaulting poles since such a pole becomes softer as the grip height increases and thus enables a better energy balance.

Grip width is the distance between the upper edge of the upper hand and the upper edge of the lower hand. It varies between approx. 40cm for the smallest women to 70cm for the tallest men.

DISCOURSE III: NARROW OR WIDE GRIP?

The rules of thumb with respect to grip width vary between a lower arm length, shoulder width, and an arm length.

A relatively narrow or wide grip on the pole each have both advantages and disadvantages, which is why coaches and athletes are successful with different approaches. A wide grip

Figure 5: **Possible general rules for grip width.**

- makes it easier to carry and control the pole during the run-up because it is easier to counteract the forward and downward directed pitching moment of the pole;
- makes the preparation of the plant more difficult; either the left arm must be brought far ahead of the body and must be extended at the elbow, which makes the pressure movement of the arm upward more difficult, or the shoulder axis must be rotated far away from the frontal position while lifting the pole, which complicates the forward movement of the right shoulder upon take-off;
- facilitates the pre-bending of the pole and the transfer of energy to the pole (increased bending moment; see discourse IV); and
- makes the forward movement of the shoulder into the C position more difficult since the pressure direction of the lower arm is directed forward rather than upward, and the subsequent work on the pole is also made more difficult.

However, in addition to height and arm length, an athlete's individual technique variation also determines grip width.

The pole-vaulter must take the pole in his/her hands in such a way that during the take-off the pre-bend (see discourse VI) points in the direction in which he/she wants to bend the pole.

Figure 6: **Holding the pole** viewed from the side and from the front and possible differences in gripping the pole with the upper hand (i.e., with the lower hand while carrying it): The grip variation on the right requires a high mobility and may otherwise result in a tense arm and shoulder posture. As the figure shows, the pole should be carried so high (upper hand on the iliac crest) that the upper arm is significantly bent at the elbow. The bottom hand (i.e., the upper hand while carrying the pole) is in front of the sternum so that the pole is diagonally in front of the body with the tip of the pole laterally in front of the pole-vaulter.

Before the pole-vaulter starts to run, he/she raises the tip of the pole. Figure 6 illustrates the correct starting position. It is no problem when the tip of the pole is located a little left to the pole-vaulter. Most modern pole-vaulters prefer carrying the pole at a relatively steep angle at the beginning of the run-up (65–75° to the horizontal). This gives the pole-vaulter the impression that the pole is lighter since he/she must exert less force to counteract the forward directed pitching moment of the pole.

START OF THE RUN-UP

Most pole-vaulters start the run-up from a resting position. Usually, an even number of strides is chosen since the corresponding starting position is perceived as more comfortable while carrying the pole.

The run-up of top pole-vaulters is usually 16–20 strides long so that the start marker is placed approximately 35–45m in front of the zero line. The run-up of women is often 2 strides shorter than that of comparable men. For young athletes, table 1 may serve as a guideline. Alternatively, the optimal run-up length may also be determined on the basis of sprinting times (see table 2).

Table 1: **Length of the competition run-up according to training age** (according to Czingon, 2004a).

Beginner (U14 or U16)	8 run-up strides
After one year (U14 or U16)	10 run-up strides
In the 2nd/3rd year (m/w 15 or 18)	12 run-up strides
In the 3rd/4th year (U18 or U19)	12–14 run-up strides

START AND PICK-UP ACCELERATION

A pole carried at a steep angle (see above) prevents a significant forward lean of the (upper) body during toe push-off sprinting. The disadvantage that the start acceleration is thereby made more difficult may be easily compensated for by extending the run-up by two strides.

Until the beginning of the plant preparation, the pole is only minimally lowered to an angle of 50–60° to the horizontal. The pole should be carried steadily and with loose shoulders and arms. This leads to a slight accompanying movement of the arms and shoulders, but not of the pole, according to the rhythm of running. Table 2 in this chapter as well as table 1 in chapter II–2.1.2 provide information on the final run-up velocities in the pole vault. The pole-vaulters with the fastest run-ups, like Svetlana Feofanova or Sergei Bubka, reach velocities of up to 8.6 (Feofanova)

*Table 2: **Relationship between run-up velocity, run-up length, and vaulting height** (according to Petrov, 2004)*

100m time (sec)	Final run-up velocity (m/sec)	Number of strides	Grip height (m)	Possible vaulting height (m)
10.2–10.5	9.8–10.0	20–22	5.15–5.20	6.15–6.25
10.6–10.9	9.6–9.7	18–20	5.05–5.10	5.90–6.05
11.0–11.4	9.2–9.4	16–18	4.85–4.95	5.50–5.70
11.5–12.0	8.8–9.0	14–16	4.70–4.80	5.20–5.40
12.1–12.5	8.3–8.4	12–14	4.50–4.65	4.80–5.10
12.6–12.9	8.0–8.1	10–12	4.25–4.40	4.30–4.60
13.0–13.5	7.5–7.6	10	4.00–4.20	4.00–4.20

and 9.9 m/sec (Bubka) in the segment between 10 and 5m in front of the zero line. In this 5m segment, the pole-vaulters achieve an average velocity which is 0.0–0.4 m/sec faster than in the previous 5m segment. The maximum run-up velocity is approximately 1.00–1.25 m/sec slower than the maximum sprinting speed without a pole.

More than 80% of the energy for reaching the maximum flight height of the CG is generated during the run-up. An increase in run-up velocity by 0.1 m/sec results in a performance improvement of about 5–8cm. However, a study of more than 700 vaults of various female and male pole-vaulters showed that the run-up velocity determines competition performance by only 35–56% (correlation coefficient: 0.59–0.75). The comparison of several jumps of one and the same pole-vaulter also shows that the fastest run-up velocities do not necessarily lead to the highest vaults. On the one hand, this emphasises the importance of the pole phase. On the other hand, it is clear that a run-up which is as fast as possible but still controllable must also be the objective in the pole vault, especially with respect to the aforementioned sudden load on the upper body upon the plant and take-off.

PLANT AND TAKE-OFF PREPARATION

The entire run-up and in particular the preparation of the plant are characterised by an upright trunk and a noticeable knee lift. The preparation of the plant begins six strides before the take-off. From here, the pole-vaulter begins to lower the tip of the pole for the plant. The lowering of the pole is performed primarily by raising the right hand. During the entire run-up, the left hand remains approximately at the same height in front of the chest until the beginning of its upward pressure movement. It represents the pivot point about which the pole rotates while it is being lowered. In order to have an optimal starting point for the pressure movement, the left elbow remains below the left hand throughout the run-up. The right hand at first moves slowly, then faster and faster upward at the side of the body. In order to be able to move the hand upward close to the body, the elbow must point backward while the shoulder is passed. During the third-last ground contact or at the latest during the subsequent flight phase, the pole should pass through the horizontal at chest to shoulder height. In this process, a slight forward shift of the left hand and a slight opening of the shoulder axis to the right are almost inevitable. However, an excessive forward shift of the left hand hinders the subsequent pressure movement of the left arm (see below). An excessive opening of the shoulders interferes with the running rhythm and the energy transfer to the pole if the shoulder is not frontally aligned again before take-off.

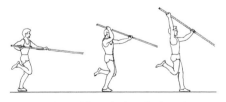

*Figure 7: **Pole positions during the last three ground contacts**. (The grip width seems to be very large; see discourse III.)*

The pressure movement of both arms upward begins above shoulder height. When the pole-vaulter's CG is above the support of the right leg (penultimate ground contact), the pole should already be above the height of the head. This leads to an active and fast last step.

A timely early plant guarantees that the pole-vaulter can further accelerate even during the preparation for the plant. In order not to lose much energy during the take-off, the desired departure angle in the pole vault should remain relatively flat (see table 1 in chapter II–2.1.2). The stride rhythm (short – long – short), the lowering of the CG, and the bracing action are accordingly not very noticeable.

PHASE 2: PLANT AND TAKE-OFF

During the take-off, the pole-vaulter's arms continue their upward pushing movement. The pole-vaulter tries to maximise the acceleration of his/her arms and the pole upward and to establish a distance as great as possible between his/her body and the pole before the pole makes contact with the planting box. At the moment of pole contact, the right arm should reach its full vertical extension. This also leads to a planting angle between the pole and the runway which is as large as possible (approx. 30° for top pole-vaulters). The left arm is straightened until an obtuse angle has been reached, but there is no full extension. The palm of the left hand is located under the pole. The shoulder axis is aligned square to the direction of movement. The pelvis and shoulders (or the trunk) are actively accelerated forward.

DISCOURSE IV: FREE TAKE-OFF

Another objective of the run-up is to reach an optimum take-off point. After Bubka's success, the free take-off was regarded as the ideal technique for a long time. According to the narrowest definition, the free take-off is a take-off in which the pole touches the back wall of the planting box, is loaded and starts bending only after the pole-vaulter has left the ground. The angle between the pole and the ground at the moment of contact with the planting box is as large as possible. The pole-vaulter can take off freely without the movement of his/her trunk being slowed down. Similar to a triple jumper during the hop, the pole-vaulter jumps onto the pole at the highest possible velocity (and with slight forward rotation). The possibility to actively move the shoulders forward and to keep the pelvis and legs far away from the pole creates optimal conditions for the pole-vaulter's subsequent pendulum movement (reverse rotation).

A prerequisite for the free take-off is that the upper hand at the moment of leaving the ground is vertically above the tip of the foot. In practice, coaches compare the theoretical point of take-off while standing with the actual point of take-off (see figure 8). If the tip of the foot is closer to the planting box, one speaks of running under the pole. The opposite (i.e., staying behind the pole) is extremely rare. The criterion hand above the tip of the foot may be achieved even with slight running under the pole if the take-off is dynamic enough. With a more noticeable running under the pole, this is not possible because the hands are slowed down too much by the pole.

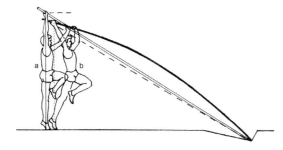

*Figure 8: Criterion **hand above tip of the toe**:*
a: with static measuring of the take-off point, and
b: with dynamic take-off and slight running under the pole.

Recently, there have also been some scientific findings which emphasise the advantages of the non-free take-off while running (slightly) under the pole:

* During the take-off, the pole-vaulter does not gain velocity (see chapter II–2.1.2), and the redirection of the movement path of the CG is caused by the pole to a large extent. This means that in the event of a take-off while running under the pole and a correspondingly early contact of the pole with

the planting box, the energy transfer to the pole only takes place earlier and already starts during ground contact.

- The pole can be bent in two ways: with the right hand (compression forces, 65–85% of the bend is based on this) and with the left hand (bending moment). Possible disadvantages with respect to the compression caused by the run-up velocity could be compensated for by improved force transfer through the left hand, since, as long as the take-off foot is on the ground, the pole-vaulter has an abutment against which he/she may exert force upward while pressing with his/her left hand. Proponents of the free take-off reject the argument, referring to the short take-off time and other disadvantages in terms of the sequence of movements (see discourse V).
- While the free take-off demands a great deal of courage by the pole-vaulter, early pole contact possibly allows for better control of the vault and may provide security. The pole-vaulter feels the resistance of the pole early and may influence it during the take-off.

A truly free take-off is extremely rare. Many athletes are successful despite running under the pole. The question as to which technique is superior must remain unanswered. Scientific studies have not provided any evidence that there is a relationship between the moment of pole contact with the planting box and energy balance. Moreover, individual deviations of a pole-vaulter's take-off point of ± 8cm should have no effect on the height of the vault.

Trunk and head remain upright. Until the end of the penetration, the head is moved toward the left elbow.

The take-off is flat and quick. A slightly late swing-leg action is relatively common in the pole vault. At the moment of leaving the ground, the knee-joint angle is acute, and the thigh is still well below the horizontal.

In addition, the pole-vaulter should focus on a straight take-off. If upon take-off the pole-vaulter's CG is not directly behind the bar, the athlete will vault to the side and will not only vault lower, but might land

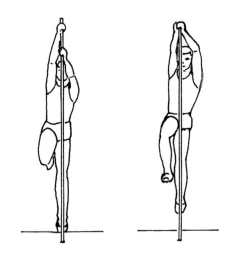

Figure 9: *Straight-line take-off.*

beside the mat or collide with the upright. The head and the take-off point should be located directly behind the pole. Both shoulders are level (see figure 9).

PHASE 3: POLE PHASE

The pole phase may be divided into the following sub-phases:

- penetration;
- swing-up;
- extension along the pole; and
- pull, turn, and push.

The transitions between these phases are the C, L, and I positions respectively (see figure 10). However, these transitions should not be understood as statically held positions, but are rather used by the coach as visual control points in a continuous motion. The coach may thereby want to see whether the previous phase was successful.

During the pole phase, the pole-vaulter tries to shift his/her CG upward in relation to his/her hands, and thus fulfils two functions: First, he/she tries to reach a good position for the subsequent flight phase; second, he/she provides the pole-vaulter system with more energy. According to the law of action = reaction, raising the legs results in downward directed pressure on the pole which the pole-vaulter tries to develop as extensively and constantly as possible. These additional compression forces increase the bending of the pole until the moment of maximum pole bend, and the subsequent extension of the pole is delayed.

PENETRATION

Since penetration may only be partially described as a distinct phase, it has been placed in parentheses in figure 10. In the jumps, leaving the ground traditionally

DISCOURSE V: SIGNIFICANCE OF THE LEFT ARM

The pole and the arms form the tension triangle. Proponents of the free take-off argue for a submaximal extension of the left arm during take-off, since according to their theory the bending of the pole should be primarily transmitted to the pole by compression (see discourse IV). A fully extended left arm would cause the shoulders to stay behind during take-off and penetration. This would result in an incomplete take-off and insufficient stretching of the front of the body, which would be an unfavourable starting point for the swing-up. Through the abrupt deceleration of the shoulders, the lower body would first swing quickly and passively forward. However, the pole-vaulter would not be able to continue his/her swing-up movement effectively. Accordingly, the pole-vaulter should increase the pressure of his/her left arm only after the take-off to move his/her shoulder axis away from the pole again and to shift the axis of transverse rotation from the upper hand to the shoulders.

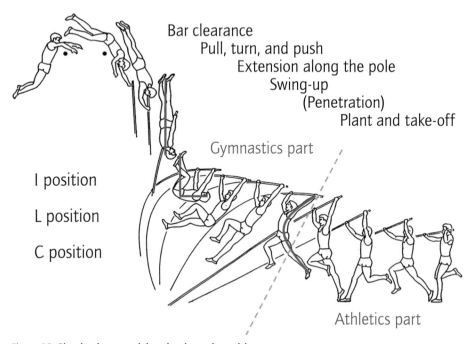

Bar clearance
Pull, turn, and push
Extension along the pole
Swing-up
(Penetration)
Plant and take-off

Gymnastics part

I position

L position

C position

Athletics part

*Figure 10: **Simple phase model and pole vault positions.***

characterises the end of the take-off phase. Afterward, there is a distinct phase to be observed in good pole-vaulters in which the hyperextension of the body increases further until the C position is reached. While the trunk remains as upright as possible, the left hand moves up to above the pole-vaulter's head with the elbow fixed at an obtuse angle. Only then is the direction of the movement reversed in the shoulders and the right hip. This segment of the motion is traditionally referred to as penetration into the pole or the hang phase. However, the penetration is more the result of an active take-off than a newly intended movement by the pole-vaulter after take-off. In the pole-vaulter's mind, the swing-up usually follows

immediately after an active take-off. It just takes a little time until the pole-vaulter's muscle force overcomes the inertia of the body and until a reduction in the arm-torso angle, thigh-trunk angle, and trunk hyperextension becomes visible.

SWING-UP

The swing-up is performed reactively and powerfully from the hyperextension after penetration. The stretched muscles at the front of the body are now contracted.

With an already fully extended right arm and an extending left arm, the pole-vaulter tries to reduce the angle between his/her upper arm and trunk and to move his/her hands in a semi-circle motion to his/

DISCOURSE VI: A SHORT LESSON ON VAULTING POLES

Modern vaulting poles are made of fibreglass. Some poles, which are identifiable by their darker colour, contain up to approximately 20% carbon fibres. These are lighter than glass fibre, but also more brittle, which is the reason why their percentage is limited in poles. High-quality poles are tested before delivery for significantly greater bending (up to 120°) than actually occurs in the pole vaulting. Moreover, the material hardly ages. This means that high-quality vaulting poles do not break unless there is previous damage. This may occur, for example, if one steps on a pole lying on the ground with spikes or if the pole falls on the edge of an object.

Modern vaulting poles are not completely straight, but rather slightly pre-bent (deviation of 4–5cm from the straight line on half the length of the pole). Due to the pre-bending and other special features of its structure, the pole has a soft side which specifies the direction in which it may be deflected and bent more easily (see figure 11). Poles with even greater pre-bending (banana poles), which were temporarily used by some pole-vaulters, were difficult to handle during the plant and take-off.

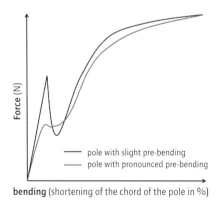

bending (shortening of the chord of the pole in %)

Figure 11: **Reduction of the peak force to be generated by the pole-vaulter after take-off for deflecting the pole from the extended position due to the pre-bending of the pole** (modified on the basis of Czingon, 2004b).

Vaulting poles are designed so that they have optimum bending properties if the upper hand grips the pole not more than 30cm away from the upper end of the pole. Poles primarily differ in their length and stiffness (flexibility).

Not only longer, but also stiffer poles are heavier since more material is used in the walls of the poles that are hollow. These poles usually also have a slightly larger diameter. The stiffness of the poles is indicated by the flex number. This number describes how many cm the pole flexes downward when it is horizontally suspended at its ends, and a standard weight is hung from its centre. This means that stiffer poles have smaller flex numbers. To facilitate distinction, certain flex number ranges are assigned kilogram or pound values. Since these are a mere translation of the pole stiffness, they correspond to the pole-vaulter's body weight only to a limited extent. Consequently, the weight indications on poles for beginners are below their body weight, whereas they are above the body weight for advanced pole-vaulters. The warning on the poles by some manufacturers that the pole should only be used when one's body weight does not exceed the weight indicated on the pole is unrealistic for beginners and seems to be only a matter of legal protection for the manufacturer.

Figure 12: **Example of a marking carved into the top end of a pole by the manufacturer**; first line: length in cm (430) and weight in kilograms (73); second line: length in feet (14) and inches (0), and weight indication in pounds (160); third line: production year (09), flex number (18.2), production month (May), and production day (15).

The flex numbers and weights of different poles are initially only comparable if the lengths (and the manufacturers) of the poles are identical. Table 3 is an attempt to put the flex numbers of poles of different length in relation to one another. The flex numbers of adjacent poles must not differ too much from one another to enable pole-vaulters to always vault with the most appropriate pole. If a pole becomes too soft at the low and middle level of performance, a flex-number difference of about 1.0 is sufficient to ensure an easy transition to the next higher pole. However, the range of poles used by top pole-vaulters usually includes poles with significantly smaller stiffness gradations. On his/her way from novice to expert (see also table 4), a pole-vaulter needs at least 30 different poles. When keeping in mind that a high-quality pole costs between 500 and 1000 Euros, it becomes clear how expensive pole vaulting is. The necessary poles, facilities, and qualified coaches are often available only in certain centres in a few countries.

her hip. The straight take-off leg is swung forward and upward. Since the mass is kept far away from the pivotal points in the hip and shoulder, greater muscle force is necessary to reduce the angle between the leg and trunk on the one hand, while the vaulter-pole system is supplied with more energy through this (increased) work on the other hand. During the swing-up, the angle between the thigh of the swing leg and the trunk remains approximately constant. Right-handers (or pole-vaulters taking off with their left leg) swing their legs on the right side of the pole forward and upward.

Table 3: **Interrelationships between various degrees of pole stiffness and various pole lengths** *for facilitating the transition to the next longer pole (according to Czingon, 2004c).*

Stiffness of the pole (kg)

| Pole lengths (cm) | | | | | | | | |
350	370	400	415	430	445/460	475	490	510/520
35								
40								
45								
50								
55	50							
...	54	50						
	59	54						
	63	57						
	66	59	57					
	...	61	59					
		63	61	57				
		66	63	59				
		68	66	61				
		70	68	63				
		73	70	66	57			
		...	73	68	59			
			75	70	61	59		
			77	73	63	61		
			80	75	66	63	61	
			...	77	68	66	63	61
				80	70	68	66	63
				84	73	70	68	66
				86	75	73	70	68
				...	80	75	73	70
					82	77	75	73
					84	80	77	75
					86	82	80	77
					...	84	82	80
						86	84	82
						...	86	84
							88	86
							91	88
							...	91
								...

Table 4: Stiffness of the poles used by 6m pole-vaulters (as of March 2004, according to Petrov, 2004).

Name	Best performance (m)	Height (m)	Weight (kg)	Run-up velocity (m/sec)	Flex number (520 pole)
Bubka	6.15	1.83	80	9.94	10.6
Tarasov	6.05	1.94	81	9.75	11.2
Markov	6.05	1.81	80	9.84	11.8
Hartwig	6.03	1.94	92	9.73	10.8
Gataulin	6.02	1.90	81	9.75	11.4
Trandenkov	6.01	1.90	78	9.47	11.7
Brits	6.01	1.96	88	9.74	11.0
Lobinger	6.01	1.90	82	9.62	11.4
Ecker	6.00	1.93	78	9.71	11.7
Galfion	6.00	1.84	82	9.68	11.9

Approximately when the right hand, the shoulders, hips, and the left foot form one line again, this line crosses the chord of the pole. The previous sub-phase is sometimes called the long pendulum swing, while the subsequent phase is called the rockback. Usually, both sub-phases are based on only one intended movement by the pole-vaulter. The pole-vaulter reaches the L position roughly at the moment of maximum pole bend. In this position, the pole-vaulter's trunk is parallel to the ground (see figure 10).

EXTENSION ALONG THE POLE

The direction of motion in the hips changes approximately in the L position. The pole-vaulter begins to extend his/her hips again and moves both legs in such a way that they are side by side. First, the lower legs are moved to above the top end of the pole before they are finally extended in the direction of the chord of the pole. Meanwhile, the arms continue their semi-circular swing to bring the hands close to the hips. At the end of this movement, the left arm is bent again. In this process, the left elbow is supposed to pass the pole on its right side since the extension along the pole would be hindered if the pole-vaulter trapped the pole under his/her armpit.

To be catapulted optimally upward from the pole, the athlete should reach the extended inverted hang of the I position even before the pole has reached its full extension. In this phase, the pole-vaulter should try to stay close to the pole and align his/her body with the direction in which the pole is extending (see figure 13).

Thus, the energy of the extending pole may be optimally transferred back to the pole-vaulter.

The extension along the pole merges into the pull, turn, and push. Many pole-vaulters begin the rotation about the longitudinal axis of their bodies toward the end of their extension along the pole.

PULL, TURN, AND PUSH

There are many names for the pull, turn, and push phase of the pole vault: pull, rotation, and push; pull-and-turn; pull-up and turn, etc. This is due to the impossibility to express all the overlapping sub-phases of this complex movement with only one term.

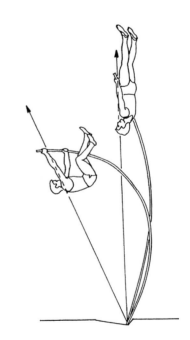

Figure 13: **Positioning of the body into the line of pole extension.**

The pole-vaulter should look away from the bar at the latest at the start of the pull, turn, and push. By turning his/her gaze to the left and downward in the direction of the planting box, he/she initiates the rotation about his/her longitudinal axis. The pole-vaulter turns his/her stomach toward the pole and bar. In the process, he/she keeps his/her outstretched legs close together to enable a rapid rotation about his/her longitudinal axis. The pole-vaulter now tries to bend his/her right elbow for the first time during the pole phase. He/she tries to pull himself/herself upward with both hands and to continue to exert force on the pole in the direction of the planting box in the process.

Approximately when the pole is extended again, the pulling movement is converted into a pushing movement, which ultimately leads to a one-armed handstand on the pole. After the vertical reaction forces in the planting box have been reduced to zero approximately at the moment of pole extension, a renewed increase of the vertical forces may subsequently be observed in good pole-vaulters (see figure 3).

Table 5: **Biomechanical measurements** of the best trials of the top three finishers as well as the average values of all finalists with a valid trial at the 2005 World Championships in Helsinki (according to Schade et al., 2007): The results for the men were relatively poor due to unfavourable weather conditions. Isinbayeva's vault was the new world record at that time.

Pole-vaulter	Bar height (m)	Velocity[1] 16/15–11/10 m (m/sec)	Velocity[1] 11/10–6/5 m (m/sec)	Grip height[2] (m)	Take-off distance[3] (m)	Maximum CG height (m)	Depth[4] (m)	Shortening of the pole chord (%)
Isinbayeva	5.01	8.10	8.31	4.37	3.41	5.19	0.66	31.7
Pyrek	4.60	7.80	8.01	4.24	3.46	4.80	0.61	21.6
Hamackova	4.50	7.60	7.72	4.29	3.19	4.54	0.57	31.1
Average values of all **women** (n=10)	4.47 ± 0.22	7.80 ± 0.26	7.96 ± 0.28	4.21 ± 4.21	3.35 ± 0.13	4.63 ± 0.24	0.62 ± 0.12	26.1 ± 3.6
Blom	5.80	9.01	9.04	4.81	3.75	5.91	0.61	28.3
Walker	5.75	9.16	9.26	4.94	3.93	5.89	0.73	25.4
Gerasimov	5.65	8.77	8.87	4.95	4.24	5.79	0.48	26.4
Average values of all **men** (n=10)	5.57 ± 0.14	9.00 ± 0.235	9.13 ± 0.185	4.89 ± 0.05	4.07 ± 0.24	5.78 ± 0.09	0.72 ± 0.16	27.7 ± 1.7

[1] Average run-up velocity in the 5m interval presented (women: 15–10m and 10–5m; men: 16–11m and 11–6m).
[2] From the centre of the upper hand to the lowest point in the planting box with the pole extended again (no net grip height).
[3] Not exactly specified in this source; usually defined as the horizontal distance between the tip of the take-off foot upon take-off and the zero line.
[4] Horizontal distance between the CG and the zero line at the moment of maximum CG height.
[5] One pole-vaulter is not included in the calculation since his velocities could not be measured.

This muscular work may lead to a gain of height of about 14cm. When the arms are straight, they release the pole, first the left one, then the right one.

Toward the end of the pull, turn and push, the pole-vaulter must also control the falling direction of the pole. Less advanced pole-vaulters with poles which are so long that they are higher than the height of the bar must make sure that the pole does not fall in the direction of the bar and knock it down. More advanced pole-vaulters must prevent their falling pole from passing under the bar so that they do not fall on it after bar clearance.

PHASE 4: FLIGHT

The flight phase starts as soon as the upper hand has released the pole. Similar to the high jump, the flight phase may be divided into the following sub-phases:

- rising phase;
- bar clearance; and
- flyaway from the bar.

RISING PHASE

A rising phase during the flight is actually only observed in very good (male) pole-vaulters. During the rising phase, the hips remain only slightly bent until the legs have crossed the bar far enough. Less good pole-vaulters are not catapulted high enough by the pole to demonstrate a rising phase without support. In poor pole-vaulters, the support on the pole and the clearance of the bar even overlap each other.

BAR CLEARANCE

Like high jumpers, pole-vaulters also try to pass over the bar in such a manner that the clearance height is as low as possible (see partial-height models). Since the flight path of the CG cannot be changed during bar clearance, the pole-vaulter tries to lift his/her body parts which are above the bar and to keep the other parts of the body either low or to lower them. This is especially evident in the flexing of the hips and trunk. As soon as the legs have crossed the bar far enough, the pole-vaulter tries to lower his/her feet behind the bar.

The clearance of the bar also shows whether the pole-vaulter has chosen a correct setting of the uprights prior to the vault. Whether the vault will be valid depends on the run-up velocity, pole stiffness, grip height, penetration action, and work on the pole. Otherwise, the pole-vaulter, in spite of possibly sufficient CG height, will either fall onto the bar when descending or his/her vault will be too good and he/she will knock down the bar on the ascent. Due to the many possible variations, pole-vaulters often perform compensatory movements (e.g., with the arms) when they are above the bar.

FLYAWAY FROM THE BAR

As soon as the pole-vaulter's trunk has crossed the bar far enough, the athlete flexes his/her knees, extends his/her hips and trunk, and moves his/her arms backward and upward. As a result, the pelvis is moved forward while the feet, head, and hands are moved backward.

PHASE 5: LANDING

Before landing, the pole-vaulter flexes his/her hips and trunk slightly again, while holding his/her body relatively straight at the same time in order not to rotate about the transverse axis of his/her body too quickly. A safe landing is on the back. The jumper should pay attention to the falling direction of the pole so that he/she is able to catch the pole with his/her hands if it falls onto him/her.

The landing should normally not take place in a standing position even with beginners as well as during preliminary exercises and vaults over low heights. If he/she cannot

Table 6: *Requirement profile for the pole vault:* The suggested rough estimate of the value of selected factors determining performance is based on the importance for the overall performance and the percentage of time spent training (IR: information requirements, constr.: constraints; see chapter I–1.1).

Factors determining pole-vault performance	Estimate of value	Notes
Coordination	+ + + + +	optical IR: high, acoustic IR: low, tactile IR: high, kinaesthetic IR: high, vestibular IR: high; precision constr.: high, time constr.: high, complexity constr.: high, situation constr.: low, physical stress constr.: medium–high
Flexibility	+ + +	special flexibility of the shoulders required
Strength		nearly all muscles of the body; particular significance of the retroversion muscles of the shoulders and the flexion muscles of the trunk and hips
Maximal strength	+ + + + +	particularly relative maximal strength
Reactive strength	+ + + + +	of the legs and arms
Speed	+ + + +	mainly cyclic; acyclic aspects during plant and take-off preparation, take-off, pole phase, flight, and landing
Endurance (general dynamic) Anaerobic endurance		
Strength endurance	+ +	only as a basis, for example for gymnastics training
Speed endurance	+ +	as a basis to be able to perform 12–15 trials (practice and competition trials) at a high level of performance
Aerobic endurance	+ +	only as a basis for training (regeneration ability)
Psychological and cognitive abilities	+ + + + +	concentration ability (on the point, full concentration not only in the third trial); courage when jumping into the pole, when performing gymnastics in the inverted hang on an "unstable device", etc.; correct strategy; performance-oriented thinking and behaviour (see chapter I–3.1.1)
Anthropometric and primarily genetically determined characteristics	+ + + + +	high percentage of the fastest muscle fibres; connective tissue with optimal energy storage capacities; rather above-average body height; low percentage of body fat

avoid landing on the mat with his/her feet first, the pole-vaulter should stress his/her feet as little as possible and let himself/herself fall on his/her back to avoid twisting his/her ankle or falling from the mat when trying to remain standing.

2.5.4 SUMMARY OF THE MOST IMPORTANT TECHNICAL CHARACTERISTICS = TECHNIQUE-ANALYSIS SHEET

(Description for a right-hander)

RUN-UP

START OF THE RUN-UP

- Suitable distance of the uprights from the zero line, appropriate stiffness and length of the pole (distance between upper hand and top end of the pole not more than 30cm), and grip height.
- The right hand grips the pole at the top, the left hand grips the pole between an arm's length and a lower-arm's length below; the pre-bend of the pole must be turned in the correct direction.
- Run-up length of top athletes: approx. 16–20 strides (35–45m); with younger athletes, the length of the run-up depends on training experience, technical abilities, or sprinting speed (see tables 1 and 2).
- Start of the run-up from a standing position; the pole is held 65–75° to the horizontal; left hand is in front of the sternum, elbow is kept low; right hand next to the hip, elbow flexed; trunk relatively upright.

START ACCELERATION AND PICK-UP ACCELERATION

- Rapid but not maximal acceleration with only minimal lowering of the pole (down to 50–60°).
- Landing on the intermediate marker (6 strides in front of the take-off point).
- (Subconscious) adjustment of stride length to land on the optimal take-off point.
- Grasping/pulling sprinting; noticeable knee lift.

PLANT AND TAKE-OFF PREPARATION

- The lowering of the tip of the pole begins six strides before the take-off by moving the right hand upward on the side of and close to the body; the left hand remains at chest height; the shoulder axis is kept as square as possible.
- During the third-last ground contact, the pole is horizontal approximately at shoulder height (or slightly below the shoulder); the right elbow points backward.
- Upward pressure movement of both arms; during the penultimate ground contact the right hand is already above the head.
- At the moment of pole contact with the planting box, the right arm reaches a vertically extended position.
- Take-off preparation and take-off are similar to the take-off for the hop in the triple jump.

PLANT AND TAKE-OFF

- Short, flat take-off (little bracing) with the left leg.
- Straight-line take-off (head and take-off foot are behind the pole; no lateral deviation in the shoulders or hips).
- Upon pole contact with the planting box or when leaving the ground, the right hand should be above the tip of the left foot (or the pole-vaulter runs only slightly under the pole).
- Active forward movement of the upright trunk and head, particularly of the shoulders, which are held square to the movement direction and are approximately identically high.

- For most pole-vaulters, the thigh of the swing leg is below the horizontal with an acute knee-joint angle when leaving the ground.
- The pole-vaulter looks away from the planting box and directs his/her view gradually to the bar.

POLE PHASE

PENETRATION AND SWING-UP

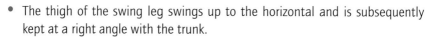

- Increase of hyperextension until the C position has been reached; abdominal muscles are contracted.
- The trunk remains initially upright.
- The left hand moves over the head.
- The thigh of the swing leg swings up to the horizontal and is subsequently kept at a right angle with the trunk.
- The swing-up is performed by decreasing the angle between arm and trunk and between the thigh of the take-off leg and the trunk; the right arm and the take-off leg remain straight.
- Extension of the left elbow.
- When passing the chord of the pole, the right hand, shoulders, pelvis, and the left foot are on one line.
- The feet pass the pole on the right side.
- The L position is reached at the moment of maximum pole bend.

EXTENSION ALONG THE POLE, AND PULL, TURN, AND PUSH

- Further decreasing of the angle between the arm and the trunk; the right arm is kept long; the left arm is flexed, its elbow passes the pole on the right side.
- Beginning hip extension; the legs are moved into a side-by-side position; first, the lower legs are moved to above the top end of the pole, then the body is extended close along the pole in the direction of the chord of the pole; the I position is reached even before the pole is straight.

- The pole-vaulter looks away from the bar to the left and downward in the direction of the planting box and initiates the rotation about the longitudinal axis with his/her belly turning toward the pole and the bar.
- Approximately at the moment of pole straightening, the pulling movement of both arms changes to a pushing movement of both arms.
- The falling direction of the pole must be checked.
- The hands are released one after the other as soon as the respective elbows are straight.

FLIGHT PHASE

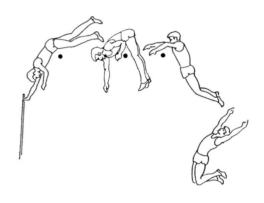

- The extended position of the body is maintained until the legs have passed over the bar far enough; then the hips and trunk are quickly flexed.
- The knees are subsequently flexed, the hips and the trunk are extended, and the arms are moved backward and upward.

LANDING

- The hips and the trunk are flexed to land safely on the back.
- The falling direction of the pole must be watched.

2.5.5 PHOTO SEQUENCE

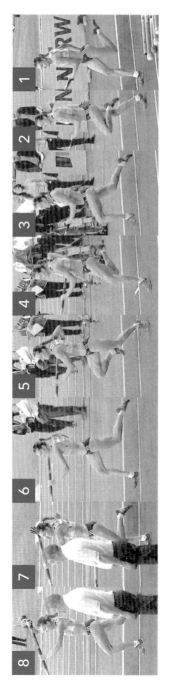

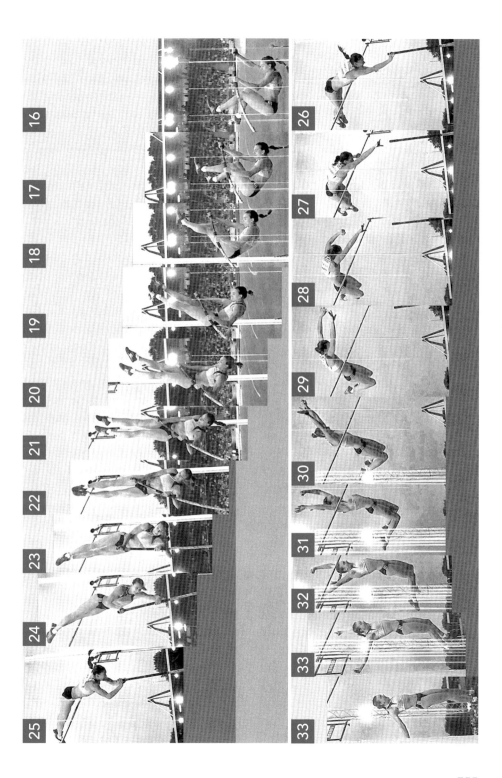

Data about the photo sequence

Athlete: Yelena Isinbayeva
                        (born: 3 June 1982, Russia)
Height/weight: 1.74 m/65 kg
Performance: 5.00 m (22 June 2005,
                        London, world record)
Best performance: 5.06 m (28 August 2009,
                        Zurich, world record)
Greatest success: Olympic champion 2004
                        and 2008, world champion
                        2005 and 2007)

COMMENTARY

The vault presented (time interval between frames: 0.08 sec) holds an exceptional position among Yelena Isinbayeva's more than 15 outdoor world records because it was the first vault by a female pole-vaulter over five metres. After she had improved the world record by the usual one centimetre, she did not end the competition on that day, but had the bar set 4cm higher. Apart from financial incentives, the reason for this decision was perhaps that Isinbayeva, who normally had no rival, was not the only athlete trying to improve the 4.96m world record on that day. The Polish pole-vaulter Anna Rogowska seemed to have had a definite, although small chance to clear that height. Perhaps Isinbayeva subsequently wanted to make sure that she would be the first woman to break the 5m barrier.

Like many pole-vaulters, and female pole-vaulters in particular, Isinbayeva comes from the field of artistic gymnastics. However, she demonstrates excellent skills both in the gymnastics and athletics part of the pole vault. After 16 strides, she achieves a run-up velocity of 8.7 m/sec which makes her one of the fastest runners in women's pole vaulting. The first pictures illustrate her good sprinting technique with only a minimal forward lean of the body, acutely angled swing leg, high knee lift, high hips, active touchdown with the balls of her feet, etc. She increases her stride frequency before the take-off so that her stride length is relatively short in comparison to her body height. For this jump she used an intermediate marker for the seventh last ground contact, which was 15.30m in front of the zero line.

Isinbayeva grips her 4.45m long pole (80 kg) at the top, which is why she was often advised to change to a 4.60m long pole. Her grip width is relatively narrow. She keeps her right hand open and moves it upward close to her body. In pictures 2 and 7, one can see the black, extremely sticky substance which is used by most Russian pole-vaulters for a firmer grip. Isinbayevas planting motion may be described as perfectly early, with the pole passing through the horizontal position at shoulder height upon the third last ground contact. The withdrawal of the right shoulder is very short. The left elbow is low already in the carrying position and is brought under the pole early. Isinbayeva rotates the pole in her left hand, which she temporarily opens (picture 5), while the pole is kept in the fork formed by the thumb and index finger.

Isinbayeva performs her last two ground contacts on the entire sole. Pictures 9 and 10 show that she runs approximately one foot in length under the pole (the tip of the toe is approx. 3.60 in front of the zero line), she withdraws her head slightly, and she does not stretch out her right arm completely. There may actually be potential for a more aggressive take-off with these three aspects. Nevertheless, Isinbayeva jumps onto the pole with much drive forward, so that her body is moved under her left hand and she achieves a noticeable C position (picture 11).

From there, Isinbayeva performs an ideal swing-up with her swing leg kept high and her take-off leg performing a long swinging movement. The swing-up is continued through the L position (picture 16) smoothly into the extension movement along the pole, while the angle between the arm and trunk becomes consecutively smaller. The legs are stretched out and moved to above the top of the pole (picture 19). The I position, which is perfectly close to the pole and completely vertical, is achieved well before the pole is straight (pictures 21–22). Isinbayeva starts the pull, turn, and push into a handstand on the pole (pictures 26–27) and then clears the bar. Although Isinbayeva appears to bend her knees a little early, this movement leads to a useful increase in her rotational velocity resulting in a rotation of her trunk away from the bar (distance of the uprights from the zero line: 70cm).

2.5.6 DIDACTICS: SUPERORDINATE LONG-TERM OBJECTIVES AND GENERAL METHODOLOGY

The pole vault and its preparatory exercises guarantee that the fun factor in children's and basic training, which is geared toward the combined events, is high. Beginning in children's athletics, the pole vault is prepared through versatile forms of jumps and exercises such as swinging on ropes and rings (35), brachiating (37), climbing (17 and 19), etc. Subsequently, the development of good sprint and long-jump techniques as well as of versatile and pole-vault-specific gymnastic skills are crucial pre-requisites for pole vaulting. The actual practice of the pole vault (technique) begins in basic training. The combined event for male U16 athletes, which consists of nine disciplines, also includes the pole vault. However, for safety reasons athletes should not take part in competitions before the technique of the event is sufficiently mastered. Czingon (2004d) suggests the following exercise sequence:

- depth jumps with poles;
- long jumps with poles;
- vaulting with a rigid pole;
- vaulting with a bent pole; and
- vaulting with a run-up of more than 8 strides.

The first three terms may refer to both the take-off and the landing height as well as the movement task (see 356–362). In accordance with the whole-part-whole method, the learning steps are supplemented by special run-up, penetration, swing-up, etc. exercises. The first three learning steps at least shall begin with vaults leading to landings in the witches-ride position (357). This is the best guarantee for a straight-line jump, which is a prerequisite for safe pole vaulting. If the landing does not take place in a line with the run-up at any time, it is absolutely necessary for the athlete to return to this exercise. The bend is only introduced when the vaults with the rigid pole are technically correct.

SAFETY ASPECTS

There are always reports of serious accidents in the pole vault. However, these accidents are not due so much to the fact that the discipline is fundamentally dangerous, but rather to insufficient landing mats, poor pole material, and a lack of methodical preparation. If the following safety precautions are taken, the pole vault is a relatively safe sport.

The landing mat should be at least 5 x 6.5m (better: 6 x 8m) in size. If the technique of the jumpers is still unstable, additional mats should be placed around the landing mat and the uprights. When practising, the distance between the uprights and the

zero line should be 80cm (at least). This is to ensure a sufficient depth of the vault (= vertical projection of the highest point of the CG in the direction of the run-up) and a safe landing in the middle of the mat. Only with experienced athletes who want to find their maximum grip height and pole stiffness may the distance of the uprights be reduced a little, but it should never be less than 50cm. If the bar supports are not used in training, they should be adjusted to a great height out of reach of the practising athlete.

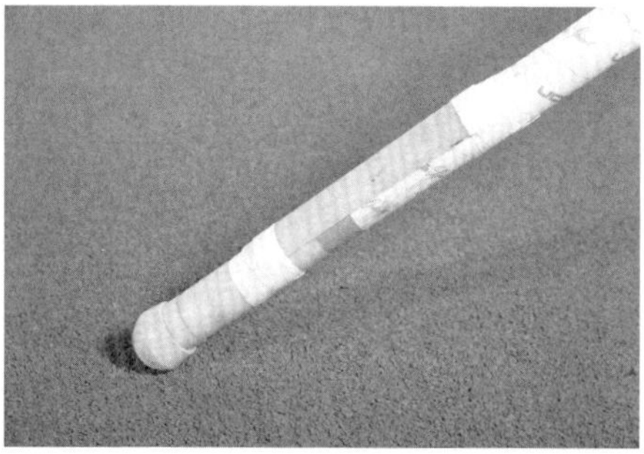

Poles should be checked for damage before use. If there is a scratch on them—especially if there are white stains around the scratch—these poles should be no longer used. Poles should never be placed on the ground as to prevent damage caused by spikes. There should be no sharp edges in the area around the landing mat and on the uprights. A training partner should catch the pole after the jump. To protect the pole from making contact with the upper edge of the planting box, there should be a suitable protection attached to the lower end of the pole (see figure 14).

Helmets, which are used only by few athletes, are likely to provide pole-vaulters with a false sense of security. They may interfere with the movement and do not protect against injuries to the (neck) spine, which are arguably the greatest danger.

Figure 14: **Protection at the bottom end of the pole.**

2.5.7 TRAINING CONTENTS: FORMS OF GAMES AND EXERCISES

All game and exercise forms mentioned in connection with the 100m sprint and nearly all forms mentioned in connection with the long jump (see chapters II–1.3.8 and II–2.2.7) are also part of pole-vault training. In addition, all gymnastic exercises mentioned in chapter I–5.2.2 as well as some exercises for the hurdle sprint are also important for pole-vaulters. Moreover, the forms of the ABCs of jumping and multiple jumps described in chapter I–5.4.6 are a crucial part of pole-vault training.

351 **Over the shark pool, Board the ship, etc.**

Possible objectives: Playful preparation for the pole vault; basics of coordination and strength for swinging in the hang position and the swing-up.

Execution/variations: See examples in the pictures; in the context of a story (e.g., about pirates), with always changing setup of apparatus; only swinging, with swing-up or even turn and push; later also over a band; focusing on an arm position which is appropriate for pole-vaulters and on a straight upper arm; bilateral practice.

Typical load standards: As long as it's fun.

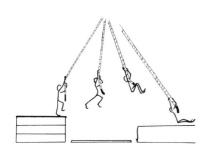

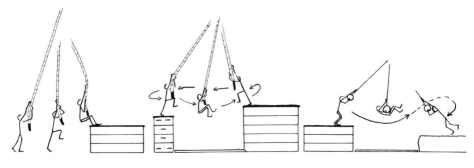

352 **Pole roundabout, pole clock, etc.**

Possible objectives: Familiarisation with the pole; playful teaching of the grip technique and arm extension upward during penetration.

Execution/variations: Pole roundabout: Children form a circle as presented in the figure above and

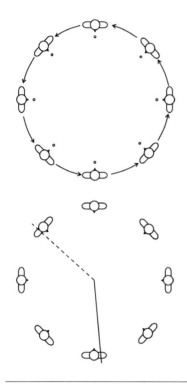

hold a pole which is as vertical as possible in front of their body; the grip width is appropriate for the pole vault; on a command, they release their own pole and try to reach the pole to the right (or left or the second pole to the right or left) before it falls; the circle should be slowly enlarged.

Pole clock: Children form a circle (see picture below); right-handers hold the pole above their right shoulder; the tip of the pole is in the centre of the circle; then the player pushes the pole upward so that the tip of the pole remains in the centre of the circle and the pole reaches a vertical position; when the pole tips over, the next player catches it; possibly also balancing of poles, etc.

Typical load standards: As long as it's fun.

---

353 Knights tournament: jousting, ring jousting, etc.

Possible objectives: First playful familiarisation with running while carrying the pole.

Execution/variations: Jousting: players should knock down balls or other objects placed at different heights with the pole; (caution: as this exercise may provoke a false technique of carrying the pole, it should not be performed too often); the pole-carrying relay, which is a pendulum relay in which the pole is carried as in the pole vault and the receiver grips the pole at the opposite end, unfortunately prompts all too often an incorrect horizontal technique of carrying the pole; ring jousting: children should hold the pole above their head and hit a ring lying on the floor (best with the ring sliding on the floor of the gym); as part of a story (knights tournament); more of the introductory exercises presented below may also be packed into this story: Across the moat (356), Storming the castle wall (361), etc.; bilateral practice.

Typical load standards: As long as it's fun.

---

354 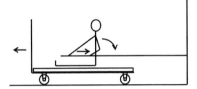 Mat transporter rally

Possible objectives: Playful familiarisation with extension along the pole.

Execution/variations: The player pushes himself/herself off a wall with the pole while sitting on a mat transporter; against each other ("Who gets the farthest?"); bilateral practice.

Typical load standards: As long as it's fun.

---

355  Medical assistant, human horizontal bar, etc.

Possible objectives: Trust the fibreglass pole (The pole doesn't break); gymnastic skills.

Execution/variations: Ensure that the feet of the carriers are shoulder-width apart, their knees and hips bent slightly, back straight; initially only jumping into the hand-supported position on the horizontal bar, then upswing; initially with uprights close together, then further apart, with more pole bending.

Typical load standards: Each child once in each position; as long as it's fun.

356 Pole vaulting from an elevation

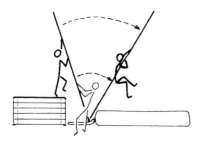

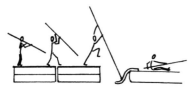

Possible objectives: Trust the pole (The pole will carry me); technique of and strength for the take-off, plant and pole phase (holding strength, grip technique, staying behind the pole, etc.).

Execution: (See exemplary illustrations; also from a hill into the long-jump pit, etc.); for right-handers the following applies: the athlete steps to the front of the box, grips the pole with his/her right hand just below reaching height and with his/her left hand in front of his/her face; he/she maintains the grip, places the pole on his/her right shoulder, walks to the end of the box; right foot forward, one dynamic stride with the left leg while extending the right arm, take-off with the left leg.

Variations: The coach initially secures the pole (see picture above; too much assistance by the coach results in the athlete not taking off); as part of a story (e.g., Over the (castle) moat); initially into witch-ride landing (357), then with swing-up into the sitting position, lying position, side position, prone position (361), and finally for height (362); later even with bending the pole (370–371; an elevated run-up enables many vaults with bending without long approach run); bilateral practice.

Typical load standards: 5–10 reps per task.

In all vaults using a rigid pole, an active take-off, as well as the moving of the pole forward and upward are the first crucial steps in learning—also in terms of health safety in order to avoid back problems, for example. For the coach, the movement of the pole from the run-up to the pole phase should appear smooth and continuous; the athlete should prevent the pole from stopping and remaining in one position during the take-off.

357 **Moving the rigid pole through the vertical position into the witch-ride landing**

Possible objectives: Straight-line take-off; plant technique; run-up control for vaults with the rigid pole.

Execution: After the take-off, the pole-vaulter initially stays in the take-off position, remains behind the pole and swings his/her left leg to the left and his/her right leg to the right of the pole (witch ride) only shortly before the landing; the active extension of the right arm and the movement of the chest forward to the pole during the take-off (passive left arm) prevents the painful contact of the pole with the crotch.

Variations: Initially from an elevated position (365), then as pole walking (358), then from 2–6 run-up strides into the long-jump pit (359, see picture), and finally at the pole-vault facility; bilateral practice; in the event of problems initially with both legs from a standing position (see picture below; caution: the athlete should not become accustomed to the two-legged vault); later also with swinging past the pole (but no complete swing-up) and landing in a standing position in the direction of the run-up, or with keeping the take-off leg back and landing in prone position on the pole.

Typical load standards: 5–10 reps per task.

358 **Pole walking**

Possible objectives: Plant and take-off technique; special warm-up.

Execution: Starting position for a right-hander: stride position with left foot in front, the right hand grips approx. two hand's width above reaching height, usual grip width, pole horizontal at shoulder height, right hand next to right

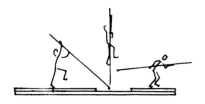

shoulder, right elbow points to the rear, left elbow low, shoulder axis as square as possible; two dynamic run-up strides with active extension of the right arm upward; take-off with the left leg; placing of the tip of the pole only a short distance in front of the left foot; with witch-ride landing (357) or lateral swing past the pole into a standing position in the direction of the run-up. *Variations:* In the gym, the tip of the pole should be placed onto a gym mat or onto a synthetic surface while possibly holding the pole upside down to prevent it from sliding away (however, a sliding away is prevented by the correct technique: passive left arm, active right arm, placing the pole onto the ground only after leaving the ground if possible, loading of the pole only close to the vertical); possibly along a line to help him/her to perform a straight-line vault; bilateral practice; in the event of problems initially from two walk-on strides instead of two run-up strides (grip height roughly identical to reaching height); later also from three or four run-up strides: in the starting position the pole points upward, right hand below shoulder height with fingers pointing downward, the grip should be a little higher.
Typical load standards: 5–10 reps per task.

359 Pole vaulting into the long-jump pit

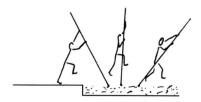

Possible objectives: When vaulting into the long-jump pit, the run-up and plant are easier since the planting point is not fixed; introduction of the pole vault even if a vaulting facility is not available.
Execution/variations: As vaults with a rigid pole and witch-ride landing (357), or with slight swing-up over a low cord (362); 2–6 run-up strides (the longer the run-up, the steeper the pole in the starting position; see previous exercise); later or in the event of problems (e.g., if the planting

movement is performed forward instead of upward), the planting point should be indicated by a hoop placed in the sand.

Typical load standards: 5–10 reps per task.

Table 7: **First rough determination of run-up length on the basis of body height** *(according to Johnson, 2001).*

Body height	1.52m	1.68m	1.83m	1.91m
6 stride run-up	9.14m	10.06m	10.67m	11.28m
Extension of the run-up by 2 strides each	3.05m	3.35m	3.66m	3.81m

360 Single-arm exercise

Possible objectives: Active take-off with rapid extension of the right arm; hanging from the extended right arm.

Execution: The tip of the pole is on the ground, the right arm is flexed, the pole is held at a short distance above the right shoulder; 4–6 run-up strides; the tip of the pole is pushed over the ground into the planting box; active take-off extension; the chest is moved forward; maintenance of the take-off position.

Variations: Usually with witch-ride landing (357), possibly also while keeping the take-off leg back and landing in prone position on the pole.

Typical load standards: 5–10 reps.

361 Swing-ups

Possible objectives: Technique and strength for the swing-up, extension along the pole, and pull, turn, and push.

Execution: Combination of plant and take-off and swing-up (as well as extension along the pole and pull, turn, and push) in accordance with the target technique.

Variations: Initially landing in sitting position, then in supine position, later in sideward position after a quarter turn toward the pole or in prone position after a half turn toward the pole; initially, a rigid pole is used (4–6 run-up strides); when the athlete is able to perform Jagodins (370) swing-ups can also be done with a bent pole (8 and more run-up strides); the band may be fixed so high that the pole-vaulter just misses reaching it with his/her feet.

Typical load standards: 5–10 reps per task.

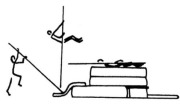

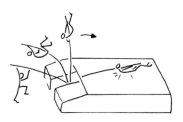

362   **Complete movement on the rigid pole**

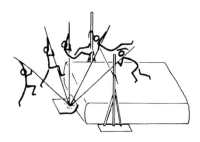

Possible objectives: Pole-vault technique; (reactive) strength; high volume due to short run-ups.

Execution: Plant and take-off, swing-up, extension along the pole, pull, turn, and push, and bar clearance; mostly over band or bar; landing on the back (landing on the feet only if performed with children into the long-jump pit (359)).

Variations: With beginners also possible at a self-made facility (see picture).

Typical load standards: 5–15 reps.

363 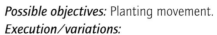 Plant imitations

Possible objectives: Planting movement.

Execution/variations:

a) In a standing position: grip height as in competition or higher; dropping of the tip of the pole, right hand straight upward, left hand with only little movement, shoulders square (in the end, the right shoulder is moved forward).

b) When walking (with noticeable knee lift): slow imitation of the complete movement or only imitation of the turning movement of the hand (on the left leg: right hand shortly below the shoulder, fingers downward, pole approximately horizontal; on the right leg: right hand above head height, brief ground contact with the tip of the pole and while walking forward back to the starting position on the left leg).

c) As part of the ABCs of sprinting (e.g., while running with knees raised to half the horizontal position [113] or performing step-overs [117]), or while running or sprinting: with pre-set number of strides or at the end of an acceleration run; with continuation of running or with rudimentary take-off; running with knees raised to half the horizontal position for example with ground contacts in rings on the floor (possibly different colour for the third-last contact).

d) With short pole or pole gripped at the centre, without placing the tip of the pole on the ground; or a medicine ball, a light bar, or a similar object is moved upward in front of the body.

Bilateral practice.

Typical load standards: 5–10 reps per task.

364 **ABCs of sprinting/jumping with pole**

Possible objectives: Correct technique of carrying the pole; technique of sprinting while carrying the pole; plant and take-off (preparation); trunk stability, etc.

Execution/variations:

a) ABCs of sprinting/jumping while carrying the pole;

b) emphasised skipping while moving the pole upward and downward: the pole is gripped at the centre using the usual grip width; the pole is carried with bent arms above the head; the arms are simultaneously extended while performing a powerful take-off with the left leg, then the arms are bent again during the take-off with the right leg (the pole should be shifted in a parallel manner, which means that neither the top nor the bottom end is moved more upward or downward than the other end); also while performing a (slow) high-knee run (extension when the left foot is on the ground, flexion when the right foot is on the ground);

c) step-overs (117) with the pole and extended arms above the head: with the pole in the running direction and with pole-vault-appropriate grip at the centre, or with the longer end backward and upward; with the pole square to the running direction while gripping the pole at the centre or at one of the two ends;

etc. (see also 363c).

Typical load standards: 1–3 reps per task.

365 **Sprints with the pole**

Possible objectives: Correct technique of carrying the pole; technique of sprinting while carrying

the pole; plant and take-off (preparation); trunk stability, etc.

Execution/variations: acceleration and tempo runs (129 and 143-144); later also pull-resisted and pull-assisted sprints (137 and 139); without or with plant imitation at the end (see 363).

Typical load standards: Depending on the training form.

---

366  **Swing-ups on rings, ropes, trapeze, horizontal bar, parallel bars, etc.**

Possible objectives: Strength for the swing-up and extension along the pole.

Execution/variations: Beginners must initially learn to keep themselves in the inverted hanging position (in spite of moving rings), which means that they begin with simple backward rotation and return (40); only then may the swing-up within the complete movement be performed (see pictures); the movement is easiest on the rings or in the space between the bars since then there is nothing between an athlete's hands which hinders the movement of the legs; initially from the extended hanging position, then from the take-off position; the swing-up should be started from a counter-swing (trunk forward and feet/foot backward, then shoulders backward and feet/foot forward and upward); the arms remain extended; the head is aligned with the trunk; the athlete should focus on the simultaneous decrease of the angle between the arm and trunk and the angle between thigh and trunk (not only lifting the feet while keeping the shoulders extended); also on diagonal bar or diagonally held rope; also after a previous jump from a short run-up onto the horizontal bar or rope; possibly also on bungee rope (see line drawing below); advanced athletes

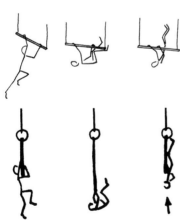

continue the movement with a pulling action of their arms (pull, turn, and push); top athletes reach the support and handstand position in the process (with assistance).

Typical load standards: The variation and amount of performing the exercise must be increased depending on the athlete's abilities.

Swing-up   Cloud shifter

---

367 | | **Cloud shifter**

Possible objectives: Strength for the extension along the pole.

Execution/variations: In basic training repeated extension from the angled inverted hanging position to the extended inverted hanging position on the rings; later as shown in the picture (first left, later right variation).

Typical load standards: The variation and amount of performing the exercise must be increased depending on the athlete's abilities.

---

368 | | **Gymnastic exercises for the pull, turn, and push, as well as bar clearance**

Possible objectives: Technique of and strength for the pull, turn, and push, as well as the bar clearance.

Execution/variations: In basic training first simple backward roll (7), handstand (8), and cartwheel (roundoff, 9); later backward roll into a fleeting handstand and push-off over the bar and roundoff with support on stepwise increasing elevation (upper box elements or later small boxes) over a bar.

Typical load standards: The variation and amount of performing the exercise must be increased depending on the athlete's abilities.

  369 Maintained bending position

Possible objectives: Introduction of vaulting with a bent pole; technique of take-off and penetration.

Execution/variations: Plant without actually moving of the pole to the vertical; while standing, from a walk-on, or with the assistance presented in the pictures from a short run-up (max. 4 strides); possibly also with two assistants (combination of the assistance presented in the two lower pictures).

Typical load standards: 3–6 reps (e.g., alternating with Jagodins [370]).

 370 Jagodins

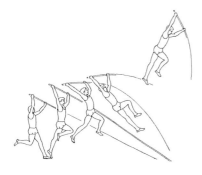

Possible objectives: Introduction of the vault with bent pole; concentration on active take-off (chest forward) and active left arm after take-off; run-up check.

Execution/variations: After active take-off, the pole-vaulter maintains the bend of the pole through active action of his/her lower arm, but does not swing up.

Typical load standards: 3–15 reps depending on the objective of the exercise.

371 Complete movement on the bent pole

Possible objectives: Technique of the target movement; (reactive) strength and speed.

Execution: Mostly over band or bar to provide the pole-vaulter with an orientation; the run-up length should be increased depending on the athlete's ability; the change to competition run-up length should be made early enough.

Variations: As training competition, possibly with additional challenges (maximally 6 trials and/or only two trials per height).

Typical load standards: 5–15 reps.

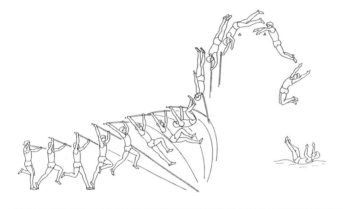

372 Slide box

Possible objectives: Improvement of the run-up as well as the plant and take-off without the risk of the vault.

Execution/variations: Run-up and plant into the slide box; with take-off (or continuation of running); from medium to long run-up; checking the take-off point and technique (there is the risk of learning an incorrect technical pattern); bilateral practice.

Typical load standards: 5–10 reps.

373 | | | | ▨ ▮ | **Backward somersault using a rigid pole**

> *Possible objectives:* Exaggeration of the swing-up movement; versatility.
>
> *Execution/variations:* The pole-vaulter continues the swing-up movement into a backward somersault, passing the pole on the right side.
>
> *Typical load standards:* 5–10 reps.

---

374 | | | | ▨ ▮ | **Full twist using a bent pole**

> *Possible objectives:* Exaggerated pull-turn and push movement; versatility.
>
> *Execution/variations:* The pole-vaulter exaggerates the longitudinal rotation toward the pole and even continues the rotation about the longitudinal axis after leaving the pole while (approximately) lying horizontally in the air; after a full twist he/she finally lands on his/her back.
>
> *Typical load standards:* 3–6 reps.

---

375 | | | | ▨ ▮ | **Forward somersault on a bent pole**

> *Possible objectives:* Exaggeration of the push with the lower arm; versatility.
>
> *Execution/variations:* In a Jagodin exercise (370), the athlete keeps on pushing with the left arm even when the pole is straightening again, thus initiating a forward somersault.
>
> *Typical load standards:* 5–10 reps.

In (high-)performance training, pole-vaulters try to continuously improve their gymnastic and jumping abilities on the trampoline. In gymnastics, the free circle and giant circle (on the horizontal bar) in particular are target exercises which are specific to the pole vault. All strength-training exercises mentioned in chapter I–5.4 (35–96) may be used in pole-vault training although the emphasis placed on them may be different.

2.5.8 SPECIAL TEST AND CONTROL PROCEDURES

	Test: Ability/skill tested	Execution/comments
T131	**Technique analysis:** Pole-vault technique	Maximal competition jump from full run-up; evaluation on the basis of the technique analysis sheet (see chapter II–2.5.4), possibly using a video (T1) and photo sequences made thereof; in high-performance sport, the computer-supported biomechanical evaluation of the video recordings made by several cameras enables a more detailed (e.g., energetic) observation of vaulting technique.
T132	**Relative grip height and excess height:** As factors determining performance	(See description in chapter II–2.5.3.)
T133	**Pole vault from shortened run-up:** Specific speed and reactive strength	Maximum pole vault from 6 run-up strides using a rigid pole, and from 8 and 12 run-up strides using a bent pole.
T134	**Tests of specific strength and gymnastic skills:** Strength and gymnastic skills	While in gymnastics the athlete's level of performance is only determined by whether he/she masters or does not master a specific exercise, some specific strength capacities are tested for example on the basis of the maximum number of repetitions which the athlete is able to perform without rest (e.g., cloud shifters, swing-ups, etc.).
T135	**Pole-vault endurance test:** Specific speed endurance	5 sets of 3 sprints each as fast as possible from a standing start over 60 m with 5 min rest interval between repetitions and 10 min rest interval between sets; test criterion: sum of the individual times (possibly also short-sprint tempo-run programmes as test, T26).
T4	**1 RPM:** Maximal strength	Inclined bench press (54), pull-overs (57), squat (62), clean (63), snatch (64), lat pull (65), abdominal machine (66) hamstrings (68), quadriceps (69), etc. (if possible also eccentric maximal strength measurement).
T5	**Squat jump, and T8 counter-movement and drop jump:** Two-legged speed strength and reactive strength of the extensor loop	The counter-movement jump may be replaced by the simpler test of tossing the shot forward and/or backward (93) for distance.
T9	**5-stride hops with distance maximisation:** Reactive strength of the legs in comparison to one another	Hop test should be performed on both sides.

	Test: Ability/skill tested	Execution/comments
T10	**30m bounding run with time minimisation:** Reactive strength of the legs	
T21	**60m analysis:** Sprint technique	See technique analysis sheet in chapter II–1.5.4.
T24	**30m flying sprint:** Maximum sprinting speed	Possibly only 20m; with and without pole.
T25	**20m frequency test:** Cyclic speed	With and without pole.
T61	**Standing start and acceleration up to 20m:** Start acceleration	With and without pole.
T66	**Graded field test:** Basic aerobic endurance	With lactate withdrawal (and spirometry; for young athletes also Cooper test, T65, which is easy to perform but inaccurate).
T115	**Long jump:** Specific speed and reactive strength	Test should be performed on both sides.
T2	**Flexibility tests:** General flexibility	
T3	**Body weight and body fat measurement:** Relative strength	Inappropriate upward and downward deflections should be avoided.

Table 8: **Basic performances of pole-vaulters** (according to Killing et al., 2008, p. 233).

		Women		Men	
Age group		w17	w19	m17	m19
Best performance	(m)	3.80	4.20	4.80	5.20
Difference = grip height – reaching height	(m)	1.9	2.0	2.0	2.1
Difference = pole stiffness – body weight (4.30m pole)	(kg)	5.0	10.0	6.0	12.0
Excess height above the upper hand	(cm)	0	30	50	80
Long jump from 6 run-up strides	(m)	45	50	50	55
Standing long jump	(m)	2.55	2.75	2.80	3.00
Long jump from 6 run-up strides	(m)	4.80	5.00	5.20	5.60
Long jump from competition run-up	(m)	5.40	5.60	6.00	6.40
10-stride bounding run from a standing position	(m)	24.00	26.00	26.00	28.00
Number of swing-ups into straight inverted hang within 60 sec		18	21	18	21
Pull-ups	(number)	10	15	12	18
Bench press	(% of body weight)	80	100	90	120
Tossing of the shot (women: 3 kg; men: 4 kg)	(m)	12.50	14.00	16.00	19.00
Snatch	(% of body weight)	60	80	60	80
Mastered gymnastic exercises on the horizontal bar		Support – handstand, upward circle forward handstand		like women + floating upstart – handstand, giant circle	
Mastered gymnastic exercises on the floor		Front handspring, forward somersault		like women + back flip, backward somersault, combinations	

2.5.9 ERRORS – CAUSES – CORRECTIONS

Error	Causes	Corrections
Unsteady pole carriage and/or too much movement of the elbows and/or shoulders.	• Insufficient automation of useful pole-carrying technique and smooth (not jerky) planting movement. • Upper body too tense.	✔ Frequent imitation of the pole-carrying technique and planting motion while standing, walking, and with increasing running velocity (363). ✔ Frequent ABCs of sprinting and acceleration runs (364) while carrying the pole and corresponding corrections.
Too early or too late lowering of the tip of the pole.	• Insufficient automation of smooth plant preparation. • Too much concentration on other run-up and plant elements.	✔ Frequent imitation of the pole-carrying technique and planting motion while standing, walking and with increasing running velocity (363). ✔ Run-up as well as plant and take-off using a slide box (372). ✔ Use of intermediate markers.

Error	Causes	Corrections
Too late and/or too slow upward planting movement of the arms.	• Lack of planting practice. • Too many take-offs from a short run-up (with a short run-up the stride frequency and the planting movement are slower; with a long run-up the arms cannot follow the faster leg movement).	✔ Frequent imitation of the planting movement while standing, walking and with increasing running velocity (363), and while running with knees raised to half the horizontal position at high stride frequency (113), or during fast high-knee running (112); also with assisting device (pole filled with sand, medicine ball, etc.), and with stride-length limitations (hoops, foam blocks, etc.). ✔ Run-up and planting movement using a slide box (372), and vaults at the pole-vault facility (371), more often and earlier in the season from a long run-up. ✔ Use of intermediate markers.
Too early plant preparation: The pole-vaulter performs even the last 2–3 strides with the pole above his/her head and must interrupt the planting movement accordingly.	• Fear of not being able to raise the pole in time before the contact with the planting box. • Too early lowering of the tip of the pole and its causes (see above). • Too many vaults from short run-ups: When using a longer run-up, the pole-vaulter starts lowering the tip of the pole (by raising his/her hands) after the same number of strides as when using a shorter run-up.	✔ Frequent imitation of the planting movement while standing, walking, and with increasing running velocity (363). ✔ Run-up and planting movement using a slide box (372) and vaults at the facility (371), more often and even early in the season from long run-up. ✔ Use of intermediate markers.
The pole is held approximately horizontally at the height of the hip for a short time (may possibly be tolerated in advanced athletes as individual technical variation if the plant and take-off is otherwise smooth).	• Too early lowering of the tip of the pole and its causes (see above). • Insufficient automation of modern pole-carrying technique and plant preparation. • The elbow of the lower arm is held over the pole right from the beginning.	✔ See corrections of too early lowering of the tip of the pole. ✔ With corresponding verbal corrections: "Let the pole fall", "your right hand lowers the tip of the pole", "keep your left elbow low", "your left hand acts as a high pivotal point in front of your chest", etc.
During the plant, the left hand is pushed forward so much that the left arm is temporarily straight at the elbow when the pole is approx. horizontal.	• Too wide grip (see also discourse III). • The pole-vaulter pushes the pole forward to establish contact with the planting box: fear of free take-off.	✔ Possibly more narrow grip. ✔ Frequent imitation of the planting movement while standing, walking, and with increasing velocity (363). ✔ Initially vaults (358-362) with a short run-up without the unnecessary additional movement of pushing the pole forward, then using a slide box (372), and finally during vaults from a long run-up (371).

(continued)

(continued)

Error	Causes	Corrections
Too long final run-up strides or sometimes even jumping run-up strides.	• The run-up is somewhat too long. • Fear of free take-off (the coach has sent the jumper, who permanently runs under the pole, farther and farther back). • Too late and/or too slow planting movement of the arms and their causes (see above): The legs must wait for the arms. • Too early planting movement and its causes (see above).	✔ Depending on the cause, shortening the run-up by one or more feet in length or exercises to learn the free take-off ✔ Learning the free take-off initially with short run-ups (hands forward and upward, chest forward, foot stays behind); ✔ Use of distance markers during the take-off (e.g., 0.5–1 cm thick, solid foam mat: provides tactile feedback when stepping on it without risk of injury; should be used only for a short time). ✔ See corrections of too late and/or too slow planting movement.
Too short (stutter) steps before taking off (almost only in absolute beginners; possibly in combination with a change of grip height (sliding downward) during take-off and/or with take-off with the wrong leg).	• Lack of trust in the pole. • The run-up is not automated. • Great problems with the plant and take-off movement.	✔ Exercises for establishing trust in the pole (e.g., 355–357). ✔ Vaults into the long-jump pit with variable planting point. ✔ The vault should initially be performed with a short run-up (360–362) to reduce the possibilities of deviations. ✔ Frequent imitation of the planting movement while standing, walking, and with increasing running velocity (363).
Excessive lowering of the CG during the penultimate ground contact.	• Negative influence of the long and high jump. • Too many vaults with the rigid pole (the pole-vaulter wants to take-off too much upward; when vaulting with a flexible pole, the take-off should be flatter).	✔ Imitation exercises, such as deliberately flat take-offs into the long-jump pit with plant imitation (363; e.g., gripping a short gymnastic stick at its centre). ✔ More vaults with a long run-up or long run-ups earlier in the season. ✔ Corresponding corrections also in connection with vaults from a short run-up.
Loss of velocity during the last run-up strides.	• Too long run-up. • Too much concentration on the planting movement. • Too long final run-up strides or sometimes even jumping run-up strides and its causes (see above). • Too early preparation of the plant and its causes (see above). • Fear of a blow to the arm, shoulder, and back during the take-off (for causes see below). • Excessive lowering of the CG during the penultimate ground contact and its causes (see above).	✔ Possibly shortening of the run-up by two strides. ✔ Slide-box exercise (372) and vaults from a long run-up (371) while focusing on continuous increase in velocity. ✔ See corrections of too long final run-up strides or sometimes even jumping run-up strides. ✔ See corrections of too early preparation of the plant. ✔ See corrections of the movement of pole stops at the moment of contact with the planting box. ✔ See corrections of excessive lowering of the CG during the penultimate ground contact.

Error	Causes	Corrections
Lack of upward extension movement of the arms during the plant and take-off.	• Fear of the blow to the arm, shoulder, and back although paradoxically a better extension movement would reduce precisely this blow (for the causes of the blow see below). • Insufficient automation of the plant and take-off technique. • The left hand is pushed forward so much that the left arm is temporarily straight at the elbow and its causes (see above).	✔ Frequent imitation of the planting movement while standing, walking, and with increasing running velocity (363). ✔ Planting and take-off exercises using a rigid pole (357), flexible pole (Jagodins, 370), and a slide box (372), with corresponding corrections. ✔ See corrections for when the left hand is pushed forward so much that the left arm is temporarily straight at the elbow.
The athlete runs too far under the pole during take-off.	• Run-up somewhat too short. • Too long final run-up strides or sometimes even jumping run-up strides (see above). • Too many vaults from short run-ups result in (visual) familiarisation with a certain take-off point.	✔ Depending on the cause, lengthening or shortening of the run-up by one or more feet in length. ✔ See corrections of too long final run-up strides or sometimes even jumping run-up strides. ✔ Early switch to longer run-ups and taking into account the duration of the phase of adjustment.
Backward lean of the trunk before and during the take-off.	• The athlete makes no effort to actively bring forward his/her shoulders at the moment of take-off, often due to mental anticipation of the swing-up (the pole-vaulter wants to swing up already upon take-off). • Negative effect of familiarisation to frequent and too far running under the pole during take-off (for causes see above).	✔ The pole-vaulter should initially vault from short and then increasingly longer run-ups with deliberately active forward movement of his/her shoulders; initially isolated with pole walking (358), when moving the rigid pole through the vertical position into the witch-ride landing (357), or as Jagodins (370), then with subsequent reversal of the movement direction at the shoulder joint into the swing-up movement (362 and 371). ✔ Imitation (e.g., while jumping onto the rope and subsequent swing-up [351]). ✔ See corrections of running too far under the pole during take-off.
Shoulders not square to the running direction upon take-off.	• Too much opening of the shoulder axis when the right hand passes the height of the shoulder approx. 2 strides before taking off, and subsequently insufficient forward movement of the right shoulder, possibly due to too large grip width. • Negative effect of familiarisation to too frequent blow to the arm, shoulder, and back (for causes see below).	✔ Frequent imitation of the planting movement while standing, walking, and with increasing running velocity (363) with corresponding corrections. ✔ Pole vaults (361–362 and 370–371) with corresponding corrections. ✔ Possibly reduction of grip width. ✔ See corrections for when the movement of the pole stops at the moment of contact with the planting box.

(continued)

(continued)

Error	Causes	Corrections
Insufficient take-off forward and upward.	• Insufficient jumping strength. • Running too far under the pole during take-off and its causes (see above). • Backward lean of the trunk before and during take-off and its causes (see above). • Shoulders not square to the running direction upon take-off and its causes (see above).	✔ Reactive-strength training for the lower extremities (e.g., 87–88, 268, and 270). ✔ See corrections of running too far under the pole during take-off. ✔ See corrections of backward lean of the trunk before and during take-off. ✔ See corrections of shoulders not square to the running direction upon take-off.
The movement of the pole stops at the moment of contact with the planting box and the pole does not move smoothly forward and upward (the pole-vaulter often has the impression of receiving a heavy blow to his/her upper arm, shoulder, and back; associated with a great loss of velocity and energy).	• Too stiff pole. • Insufficient upward extension movement of the arms and its causes (see above). • Insufficient forward and upward take-off and its causes (see above).	✔ Possibly switching to a softer pole. ✔ See corrections of insufficient upward extension movement of the arms. ✔ See corrections of insufficient forward and upward take-off.
Insufficient penetration: The trunk does not remain upright, the lower body swings passively forward too early (particularly beginners seem to swing up quickly at first, but are then not able to continue this movement up to the extension along the pole).	• Backward lean of the trunk before and during take-off and its causes (see above). • Shoulders not square to the running direction upon take-off and its causes (see above). • Stiff and completely straight left arm hinders the forward movement of the shoulders during take-off and penetration, possibly due to too large grip width and/or too stiff pole.	✔ See corrections of backward lean of the trunk before and during take-off. ✔ See corrections of shoulders not square to the running direction upon take-off. ✔ Possibly reduction of grip width. ✔ More upward and less forward pressure movement of the arms in combination with simultaneously active forward movement of the shoulders upon take-off (e.g., initially isolated in Jagodins [370]), possibly initially using a softer pole and with the left arm only fixed at an obtuse angle.

Error	Causes	Corrections
Too slow swing-up and extension along the pole (often only lifting the legs without sufficient reduction of the arm-trunk angle or flexion of the take-off leg immediately after the take-off and tight curling of the trunk to prevent an even slower swing-up).	• Insufficient strength capacities (primarily of the shoulder and trunk muscles). • Drop of the swing-leg after take-off. • The head is thrown back or bent onto the chest. • Fear (e.g., "Do I have enough depth?") or insufficient orientation.	✔ More isolated practice of the swing-up and extension along the pole as a strength training and imitation exercise (e.g., swing-ups (366) from the take-off position; the swing-leg knee is kept high and the head is aligned with the trunk; simultaneous reduction of the angles between the arm and trunk and between the thigh of the take-off leg and the trunk). ✔ Swing-ups on the rigid pole or on the flexible pole from a relatively short run-up (361). ✔ Additional strengthening exercises for the shoulder and trunk muscles (e.g., 367) ✔ Expansion of the repertoire of related gymnastic exercises. ✔ Backward somersault on the rigid pole (373). ✔ Focusing on fears as a main topic and reduction of fears through positive experience.
The pole-vaulter rotates during the swing-up about the longitudinal axis of the pole.	• No straight-line take-off (often as a part of the following complex of errors: view past the left side of the pole, right shoulder significantly higher than the left one, laterally inclined trunk, take-off point too far to the right).	✔ Versatile forms of pole vaulting into the witch-ride landing (357; the straight take-off resulting from this correction should then also be transferred to other forms of vaulting). ✔ Imitations. ✔ Use of a marker to the right of the optimal take-off point (the pole-vaulter is not allowed to step on this marker; should only be used for a short time).
Too early tilting of the legs toward the bar.	• Too slow swing-up and extension along the pole and its causes (see above). • The pole-vaulter wants to push his/her feet over the bar instead of extending the feet toward the sky and to approach the upper grip hand with his/her hips. • Too early bending (pulling movement) of the right arm. • Incorrect control of view (the pole-vaulter's view is directed too long to the bar).	✔ See corrections of too slow swing-up and extension along the pole. ✔ Swing-up toward the height marker (361); with corresponding corrections of the movement of the right arm and view control (the pole-vaulter should look at the height marker, but look away before the feet come close to the height marker). ✔ Corresponding corrections also in connection with other exercises of technique training.

(continued)

(continued)

Error	Causes	Corrections
In the I position and during the pull, turn, and push the pole-vaulter's CG is (too early) too far away from the pole.	• Too early tilt of the legs toward the bar and its causes (see above). • Insufficient orientation. • Insufficient automation of the target technique.	✔ Imitations (possibly on special appropriate devices). ✔ Swing-ups into the prone position, with active pulling movement on the pole. ✔ Expansion of the repertoire of related gymnastic exercises.
Incomplete or too late rotation about the longitudinal axis of the body toward the pole and to the bar (only in beginners and not very advanced athletes).	• Incorrect control of view. • Insufficient automation of the appropriate bar clearance technique. • Breaking-off the vault due to other severe errors at an earlier stage during the vaulting process (e.g., the aforementioned rotation about the pole and its causes).	✔ Practicing the correct turn of the head and control of view during imitations on a rope and vaults from short run-ups. ✔ Swing-ups into the side and later the prone position (361) on a rigid and on a flexible pole from a short run-up, possibly with feet first toward the height marker. ✔ Complete pole vaults using a rigid pole (362; also for height). ✔ Full twist using a flexible pole (374).

Table 9 includes information on errors and corrections with respect to the depth of the vault and the extent of pole bending.

Toward the end of the pole phase, beginners often try to push off from the pole at a right angle by pushing away the pole in the direction of the runway while lying approximately horizontally in the air. Due to the small mass of the pole, this is an impossible undertaking, which accelerates the body only imperceptibly toward the mat. The coach must teach the athlete that (with the same grip height and width and with an identical pole), he/she may only increase the depth of his/her vault through higher run-up velocity, improved plant and take-off, as well as better work on the pole (i.e., development of pressure in the direction of the planting box).

Error	Causes	Corrections
The pole-vaulter does not land in line with the run-up direction (usually only in beginners).	• No straight-line take-off: For example, the pole-vaulter wants to jump past the pole instead of onto the pole (possibly due to a lack of trust in the pole). • Severe irritation due to wind.	✔ Versatile forms of pole vaulting into the witch-ride landing (357) with corresponding corrections. ✔ Exercises for developing trust in the pole (e.g., 355–356). ✔ In the event of too much crosswind, possibly break-off training or competition.

Table 9: **Decision guidance with respect to grip height and pole stiffness** (according to Linthorne, 1989): It may possibly be a part of the considerations that a more narrow grip width makes the pole feel stiffer, whereas a wider grip makes the pole feel softer (see also discourse III).

		Depth of the vault		
		In spite of a short distance between the uprights and the zero line, the pole-vaulter falls onto the bar from above or might even land in the planting box or not pass the vertical	Good	In spite of an 80cm distance of the uprights, the pole-vaulter knocks off the bar while rising
Pole bend	Slight	Lower grip height on softer pole	Identical grip height on softer pole	Higher grip height on identical pole
	Good	Lower grip height on identical pole	Optimal grip height and pole stiffness	Higher grip height on identical pole
	Too much	Lower grip height on identical pole	Identical grip height on stiffer pole	Higher grip height on stiffer pole

Numerous errors, causes, and corrections mentioned in connection with the sprint should also be considered (see chapter II–1.3.10). Some errors, causes, and corrections listed for the long jump (e.g., too bracing take-off or insufficient swing-leg action) may also apply to the pole vault in a slightly modified manner (see chapter II–2.3.9).

2.5.10 TRAINING PLANNING

In the pole vault, technical workouts are usually longer than in the other jumping events (see chapter II–2.3.10). Due to this and the greater importance of trunk strength and gymnastics, the total amount of training is significantly greater in the pole vault than in horizontal jumps and the high jump. The training plans for high-performance training presented below include 10 training sessions per week in the 1st–3rd mesocycle. For the build-up training for a 17-year-old athlete, six training sessions are still suggested although they are considerably longer than in the other disciplines and in basic training. The coach should ensure that the interval between arm-strength training and technique training is as long as possible (3 days) since tired arm muscles could hinder technique training.

SUGGESTED TRAINING PLANS
Below, there are exemplary microcycles for the

- second mesocycle of a 17-year-old athlete in build-up training (table 11);

- first mesocycle of an athlete in high-performance training (table 12); and
- third mesocycle of an athlete in high-performance training (table 13).

The exemplary microcycles for the

- first mesocycle of a 17-year-old athlete in build-up training;
- third mesocycle of a 17-year-old

athlete in build-up training;
- second mesocycle of an athlete in high-performance training; and
- fourth mesocycle of an athlete in high-performance training

presented for the long and triple jump (chapters II–2.2.10 and II–2.3.10) provide ideas for the organisation of the training plans not presented below.

Table 10: **Training emphasis in the various mesocycles** for pole-vault training in build-up and high-performance training.

1st mesocycle	basic aerobic and anaerobic endurance training; hypertrophy-oriented maximal-strength training for the arms, legs, and the trunk; basic reactive-strength training; flexibility training; general (e.g., gymnastics, hurdle training, games, etc.), and special (e.g., ABCs of sprinting/jumping, technique training from short- to medium-length run-ups) coordination training
2nd mesocycle	basic anaerobic (speed-)endurance training; hypertrophy-, IC- and connective-tissue-oriented maximal- and reactive-strength training for the arms, legs, and the trunk; sprinting-speed training; special coordination training (e.g., gymnastics, ABCs of sprinting/jumping, technique training from medium-length run-ups)
3rd mesocycle	special speed-endurance training at high intensity; IC- and connective-tissue-oriented maximal- and reactive-strength training; sprinting-speed and acceleration training at maximum intensity; special coordination training (gymnastics and technique training from long run-ups)
4th mesocycle	competitions and corresponding regeneration; IC- and connective-tissue-oriented maximal- and reactive-strength training; speed and acceleration training at maximum intensity; technique training; maintenance stimuli

Table 11: Build-up training: sample microcycle for a 17-year-old athlete in the second mesocycle.

Monday	Tuesday	Wednesday	Thursday	Friday	Saturday	Sunday
Foot strengthening (10 min)	Warm-up jogging (6 min)	Continuous run (30 min)	Ll runs (6 x 80m, rest intervals: 20 sec) with pole	Trunk stabilisation exercises and abdominal crunches (20 min) with a lot of dynamic variation	Warm-up jogging (6 min)	Rest
ABCs of sprinting (15–20 run-throughs)	Acceleration runs (3 reps)	Contract-relax stretching (15 min)	ABCs of sprinting (8–10 run-throughs)	Strength training (40 min) according to the pyramid principle: bench press, lat-pull, pull-overs and two further varying arm exercises, as well as hamstrings, quadriceps, adductors, abductors, and full squat.	Acceleration runs (3 reps)	
Acceleration runs (3 reps) with pole	ABCs of jumping (8–10 run-throughs)	Strength training for the trunk on apparatus, or medicine-ball work (40 min) e.g., goalkeeper throws, rotational throws, throws from a prone position, and tossing, using a medicine ball	Practising the pole-vaulting technique (50 min) plant imitations, pole walking, swing-ups from short to medium-length run-up, slide-box take-offs, etc.		ABCs of jumping (15–20 run-throughs) galloping sideways, ankle jumps, skipping with two-legged landing, skipping variations, etc.	
Practising the pole-vaulting technique (60 min) e.g., Jagodins and complete vaults from medium-length run-up	Pop-up jumps (Approx. 5 run-throughs per leg) using 5-stride rhythm with plant imitation using a short plastic stick				Bounding runs (e.g., 5 x 30m)	
Gymnastics (30 min) primarily strength elements such as swing-ups, cloud shifters, rope climbing, moving forward in the arm-support position and swinging on parallel bars, etc.	Strength training (30 min) according to the pyramid principle: clean and snatch (careful check of technique)	Foot strengthening (10 min) in the sand	Gymnastics (45 min) primarily technical elements such as handsprings and backflips, upstarts (kips) on the parallel bars and horizontal bar, somersaults on the trampoline, inverted hang and somersault dismount on the swinging rings, etc.	Game (30 min) e.g., basketball or handball	I3 tempo runs (100, 150, 200, 180, 120, and 80m; rest intervals: 3, 5, 7, 6, and 4 min)	
	Hurdle Zs or technique sprints (6–8 Zs or runs of approx. 80m each) alternately each week; also alternating-pace sprints	Tappings (8 x 5 sec) or frequency coordination (10 min) over foam blocks at 1m distances			Contract-relax stretching (15 min)	
					Warm-down jogging (10 diagonals on the lawn)	
					Standing starts (3 x 30m) maximal, as utilisation	

Table 12: High-performance training: sample microcycle in the first mesocycle.

	Monday	Tuesday	Wednesday	Thursday	Friday	Saturday	Sunday
Morning	Warm-up jogging (6 min) ABCs of sprinting (10–15 run-throughs) Acceleration runs (5 reps) with pole Practising the pole-vault technique (60 min) medium run-up length, e.g., complete vaults using a rigid pole, Jagodins, etc.	LI runs (8 x 80m with pole) ABCs of jumping (12–15 run-throughs) Bounding runs or rhythm jumps (3 x 4 x 50m) Muscle build-up training (45 min) abductors, quadriceps, hip flexors, and full squat Tappings	Continuous run (40 min) Contract-relax stretching (15 min) Muscle build-up training (40 min) e.g., abdominal machine, shoulder-hip twist, lumborum, and hip/back extensors Frequency coordination (10 min) over foam blocks, as utilisation	Foot strengthening (10 min) Acceleration runs (3 reps) ABCs of jumping (12–15 run-throughs) Practising the pole-vault technique (60 min) plant imitations, swing-ups from short run-up, with backward somersault, etc.	Morning LI runs with pole (6 x 100m) ABCs of hurdling (15 min) Hurdle sprints (30 min) versatile Muscle build-up training (40 min) bench press, lat pull, pull-overs, and two additional varying arm exercises	Trunk stabilisation exercises and abdominal crunches (20 min) Acceleration runs (3 reps) ABCs of sprinting (12–15 run-throughs) LI tempo runs (3 x 5 x 200m; rest interval: 1.5–2 min; rest interval between sets: 6–8 min) in running shoes, possibly as endless relay	Rest
Afternoon	Rope jumping (5 min) Gymnastics (85 min) technical elements (horizontal bar, floor, trampoline) and strength exercises (swing-ups, cloud shifters, etc.) as muscle-build-up training for the trunk and supplementary exercises on apparatus Game (30 min)	Warm-up jogging (6 min) Technique sprints (4–6 reps) I3 tempo runs (4 x 5 x 60m; rest interval: walk back; rest interval between sets: 6–8 min) possibly including pull-resisted runs, uphill runs, runs over hurdles or with pole Warm-down jogging Contract-relax stretching Standing starts		Warm-up jogging (6 min) Gymnastics (60 min) technical elements such as free circle, giant circle, handsprings, backflips, and somersaults Skipping, pop-up jumps, and squat-extension jumps (5 run-throughs each) alternatively start jumps and jumps onto a box High-knee run (5 x 20 sec)	Warm-up jogging (6 min) Medicine-ball work (30 min) Muscle build-up training (45 min) hamstrings, adductors, clean, and lunges Foot strengthening (15 min) in the sand Alternating-pace sprints (6 x 80m)	Contract-relax stretching (15 min) Warm-down jogging (10 diagonals on the lawn) Pop-up jumps (4–6 run-throughs) with plant imitation with short plastic stick as utilisation	

Table 13: *High-performance training: sample microcycle in the third mesocycle.*

	Monday	Tuesday	Wednesday	Thursday	Friday	Saturday	Sunday
Morning	Warm-up jogging (6 min) ABCs of jumping (8–10 run-throughs) Acceleration runs (3 reps) with pole Practising the pole-vault technique (60 min) Jagodins and complete vaults from long run-up	LI runs (6 x 100m) with pole Tuck jumps (3 x 3 run-throughs over 5 hurdles each) ABCs of sprinting Acceleration runs Pull-assisted sprints (2–3 reps) Flying sprints (1–2 x 20m + 30m run-up)	Foot strengthening (15 min) Strength training for the trunk or Medicine-ball work (45 min) e.g., abdominal machine, shoulder-hip twist, lumborum, and hip/back extensors Game (15 min) e.g., basketball or handball	Warm-up jogging (6 min) High-intensity strength training (15 min) snatch Acceleration runs (3 reps) with pole Practising the pole-vault technique (60 min) medium-length run-up, individual additional tasks	Warm-up jogging (6 min) Acceleration runs ABCs of sprinting (8–10 run-throughs) Standing starts Pull-resisted runs and standing starts with pole alternately (40–50 min: 8–12 sprints in total, 10–40m each) additional load up to 20 kg	Warm-up jogging (6 min) Maximal-eccentric strength training (15 min) trunk stabilisation, lifting opposite upper and lower limbs while in prone position, belly punches with tense abdominals, raising the foot/toes Acceleration runs (3 reps)	Rest
Afternoon	Warm-up jogging (6 min) Gymnastics (90 min) technical elements (horizontal bar, floor, trampoline) and strength exercises (swing-ups with subsequent pull and press up into the handstand as high-intensity strength training for the upper body and supplementary exercises on apparatus	Warm-up jogging (6 min) Acceleration runs Pop-up jumps (3 x 2 run-throughs per side) over mini-hurdles, with plant imitation using a short stick High-intensity strength training (30 min) clean and quarter-split squat Standing starts (3 x 30m) at maximum intensity		Warm-up jogging (6 min) Acceleration runs ABCs of jumping (8–10 run-throughs) Jumping test (15 min) each week a different one, e.g., maximum long jump from 10 run-up strides Gymnastics (60 min) development/improvement of free circle, giant circle, handsprings and backflips, somersaults	Warm-up jogging (6 min) Maximal-eccentric strength training (30 min) hamstrings, adductors, etc. High-intensity strength training (45 min) bench press, lat pull, pull-overs, and two varying arm exercises Alternating-pace sprints (3–4 x 60m) as utilisation	Depth jumps (3 x 10) from box to box; alternatively ankle jumps with a partner pushing downward on 5 jumps and then lifting upward on 5 jumps One-legged jumps (hops) (4–5 run-throughs of 20m each) alternatively rhythm jumps 12 tempo runs (100, 150, 120, and 80m; rest intervals: 10, 15, and 12 min)	

2.5.11   BIBLIOGRAPHY

Adamczweski, H. & Dickwach, H. (1991). Block Sprung. In Deutscher Leichtathletikverband (Hrsg.), *Aktuelle Trainingsgrundlagen des Hochleistungstrainings.* Darmstadt.

Adamczewski, H. & Perlt, B. (1997). Run-up velocities of female and male pole vaulting and some technical aspects of women's pole vault. *New Studies in Athletics 12* (1), 63-76.

Adamczewski, H. & Perlt, B. (2005). Auswertung der Leichtathletik-Europameister-schaften U23 in Erfurt vom 14.-17.7.2005 im Stabhochsprung der Männer und Frauen. *Zeitschrift für angewandte Trainingswissenschaft 12* (2), 21-40.

Bussabarger, D. (2004). Analysing Tommy Skippers vault technique. *Track Coach* (169), 5394-5397.

Czingon, H. (2004a). Sicher zum Einstichkasten: Zur Optimierung der Anlaufgestaltung im Stabhochsprung. *Leichtathletiktraining 15* (1+2), 26-29.

Czingon, H. (2004b). Biegen, aber nicht brechen! Was macht den Stab beim Stabhochsprung so einzigartig und was ist das Besondere an den verschiedenen Stäben? Teil 1. *Leichtathletiktraining 15* (6), 32-39.

Czingon, H. (2004c). Biegen, aber nicht brechen! Was macht den Stab beim Stabhochsprung so einzigartig und was ist das Besondere an den verschiedenen Stäben? Teil 2. *Leichtathletiktraining 15* (7), 36-39.

Czingon, H. (2004d). *Stabhochsprung* (unveröffentlichte Materialien zur DLV-A-Trainer-Ausbildung). Mainz: DLV-Trainerschule.

Czingon, H. (2005). Die erste Frau über fünf Meter! *Leichtathletiktraining 16* (8), 35-39.

Grabner, S. (2004). Technical and conditioning aspects of the women's pole vault. *New Studies in Athletics 19* (3); 43-54.

Jennemann, V. (2004). Das fliegende Klassenzimmer. *Sportpraxis 45* (4), 36-42.

Johnson, J. (2001). Beginning pole vaulting progressions and formulas. *Track coach* (157), 5008-5010.

Killing, W., Bartschat, E., Czingon, H., Knapp, U., Kurschilgen, B. & Schlottke K. (2008). *Jugendleichtathletik: Offizieller Rahmentrainingsplan des Deutschen Leichtathletik-Verbandes für die Sprungdisziplinen im Aufbautraining.* Münster: Philippka.

Linthorne, N. (1989). The fiberglass pole. *Modern Athlete and Coach 27* (1), 15-18 & (2), 43.

Linthorne, N. (2000). Energy loss in the pole vault take-off and the advantage of the flexible pole. *Sports Engineering 3* (4), 205-218.

McGinnis, P. M. (1997). Mechanics of the pole vault take-off. *New Studies in Athletics 12* (1), 43-46.

Petrov, V. (2004). Pole vault – the state of the art. *New Studies in Athletics 19* (3), 23-32.

Regelkommissionen des DLV, FLA, ÖLV und SLV (Hrsg.). (2010). *Internationale Wettkampfregeln.* Waldfischbach: Hornberger.

Schade, F., Arampatzis, A., Brüggemann, G.-P. & Komi, P. V. (2004). Comparison of the men´s and the women´s pole vault at the 2000 Sydney Olympic Games. *Journal of Sports Sciences 22*, 835-842.

Schade, F., Arampatzis, A. & Brüggemann, G.-P. (2004). A new way of looking at the biomechanics of the pole vault. *New Studies in Athletics 19* (3), 33-42.

Schade, F., Isoletho, J., Arampatzis, A., Brüggemann, G.-P. & Komi, P. (2007). Biomechanical analysis of the pole vault at the 2005 IAAF World Championships in Athletics: Extracts from the Final Report. *New Studies in Athletics 22* (2), 29-45.

Schade, F. (2008). *Biomechanics of the Pole Vault* (Präsentation, 3rd European Polevault Conference, Köln, 25.-27.04.2008). Zugriff am 15.09.2009 unter www.stabhochsprung. com.

Schade, F. & Arampatzis, A. (2012). Influence of pole plant time on the performance of a special jump and plant exercise in the pole vault. *Journal of Biomechanics 45*, 1625-1631.

Young, M. A. (2002). A technical model for pole vault success. *Track Coach* (161), 5129-5133.

3 THROWING

3.1 COMMON FEATURES AND COMPARISON OF THROWING DISCIPLINES

3.1.1 THE MOST IMPORTANT GENERAL COMPETITION RULES

The following abridged and simplified International Competition Rules comprise the framework for the techniques and strategy, as well as the organisation of throwing events:

- Competition implements (throwing devices) must be provided by the organiser. Competitors may be permitted to use their own implements when they meet the standards and have been checked and marked by the organiser. Each competition implement must be made available to all competitors. No modifications may be made to any implement during the competition.
- Supporting devices (e.g., gloves [exception: hammer throw], weights attached to the body, taping of two or more fingers together) are not allowed. It is permitted to use a suitable substance in order to obtain a better hand grip, on the neck in the shot put, and on gloves in the hammer throw.
- The (landing) sector consists of cinders, grass, and other suitable materials on which the implement makes an imprint upon landing. The sector is marked with 5-cm-wide lines.

The overall slope of the sector in the put/throw direction must not be greater than 1:1000.

- The competitor is allowed to interrupt a trial once started, to lay down the implement, and/or to leave the circle or runway, provided he/she does not violate another rule (e.g., timeout).
- It is a failure if the shot, the discus, the hammer head, or the javelin head touch the sector line or the ground outside the sector line when contacting the ground upon first landing.
- The athlete must not leave the circle or runway before the implement has touched the ground. The athlete must leave the circle or runway (even when the trial is interrupted) behind the white lines which extend at least 0.75m on either side of the circle or runway.
- Measuring each put or throw must be made immediately after each valid trial. Distances are recorded to the nearest 0.01m below the distance measured if the distance measured is not a whole centimetre.
- After each throw, implements must be carried back to the area next to the circle or the runway and never be thrown back.

CONCERNING THE PUT AND THROW FROM THE CIRCLE

- The rim of the circle must be made of band iron, steel, or other suitable materials. It should be at least 6mm thick and white. The top of the ring must be flush with the ground outside. The ground surrounding the circle may be concrete, asphalt, or synthetic. The interior of the circle may be constructed of concrete, asphalt, or some other firm, but not slippery material. The surface of this interior shall be level and 20mm ± 6mm lower than the upper edge of the rim of the circle.
- The angle between the two lines delimiting the sector is 34.92°. This angle is achieved as follows: Form an equilateral triangle (3 tape measures). The third side is shorter than the two equal sides by a factor of 0.6. The equal sides are the sector lines which (in theory) meet at the centre of the throwing circle. (Example: Two points located 20m from the centre of the circle on the two sector lines must have a distance of 12m.)
- An athlete is neither allowed to spray nor spread any substance in the circle or on his shoes nor to roughen the surface of the circle.
- In putting/throwing competitions from the circle, a competitor may use only one marker. This may be placed on the ground immediately behind the circle or adjacent to it. It may only be placed there for the duration of the competitor's trial and must not affect the view of the referee.
- The competitor begins his/her trial from a motionless starting position.
- During his/her trial, the athlete is allowed to touch the inside edge of the circle, but he/she must not touch the top of the rim of the circle or the ground outside it.
- The measurement of each throw is made from the nearest mark made by the fall of the shot, discus, and hammer head to the inside of the circumference of the circle along a straight line to the centre of the circle.

Otherwise, the general competition rules for the technical disciplines apply (see chapter II-2.1.1).

3.1.2 SPORT-SCIENCE FINDINGS, PHASE STRUCTURE, AND TECHNIQUE

As the jumping events, the throwing events may also be divided into four major phases each:

- preliminary movements;
- pre-acceleration;
- delivery movement; and
- recovery (reverse) and flight of the implement.

However, the specific techniques of each throwing event differ from each other much more significantly than the four jumping events especially pertaining to the first two phases.

Similarities are particularly evident in the delivery motion in the javelin throw, discus throw, and shot put. The two-

DISCOURSE I: THE SHOT PUT: A THROWING DISCIPLINE?

In the shot put, throwing is prohibited by definition. Nevertheless, the shot put is considered a throwing event. This is supported by two reasons:

- One might describe the shot put as a pushing movement, whereas the other throwing events are pulling movements. But the shot put is characterised by the typical features of the throwing motion described in this chapter (e.g., pre-acceleration of the thrower, benefit of a long acceleration path, pressure leg and bracing leg, shoulder-hip separation, arc position, and kinematic chain). Due to the common features of the throwing motion, the classic methodical series for learning the techniques are also structured in a very similar way in these disciplines (see chapter II-313).
- The flight of the shot also follows the laws of the oblique throw in physics.

For reasons of simplification, the term *throw* is sometimes used in this chapter meaning throws and shot puts.

handed reverse delivery in hammer throwing deviates to some extent from these one-handed forward deliveries. Many of the similarities between the javelin throw, discus throw, and shot put may be expanded to other athletic movements. They occur rather similarly in hitting movements (tennis forehand, clear in badminton, swinging a baseball bat, etc.) and other throwing movements (e.g., in sport games like handball, baseball, cricket, etc.).

PHASE 1: PRELIMINARY MOVEMENTS

In the discus throw, shot put, and the hammer throw from the pendulum swings, the athlete performs a preliminary movement that is directed opposite to the movement direction of the pre-acceleration. Since the cyclic run-up segment of the javelin and the arm-circle swings of the hammer throw are performed in the main direction of the movement, they must be regarded as the first part of the pre-acceleration phase. The hammer throw, provided it is performed from the initial pulling movement (exploxive pick-up), and the javelin throw may therefore be performed without preliminary movements.

PHASE 2: PRE-ACCELERATION

Although the specific techniques differ greatly among these disciplines, the common feature of all throwing events is that the athlete's body and the throwing implement are pre-accelerated before the delivery motion. The importance of the pre-acceleration becomes clear when comparing the throw from a standing position with the competition throw. For example, in the javelin throw the throwing performance from a standing position is approximately one-third under the competition performance. To simplify matters, one could assume that the implement is accelerated during the delivery motion by a fixed amount of velocity (no matter whether it is a standing throw or throw using the competition technique). Then, when using the competition technique including pre-acceleration, the higher velocity of the implement at the beginning of the delivery motion alone would lead to a higher velocity of departure than a standing throw without pre-acceleration. However, the kinetic energy which is transmitted to the athlete's body during pre-acceleration is also especially important. In the delivery motion, this kinetic energy is converted into a high departure velocity of the implement as skilfully as possible. The kinetic energy of the thrower-implement system at the end of pre-acceleration may be available in the form of translational and/or rotational velocity.

PHASE 3: DELIVERY MOVEMENT

The delivery motion includes two ground contacts. The rear leg in the throwing direction is referred to as the pressure leg, while the front leg is referred to as the bracing leg.

LONG PATH OF ACCELERATION

To provide a body or an implement with maximum final velocity, its acceleration path should be as long as possible. This general biomechanical principle is explained by the law of linear momentum ($m \cdot v = F \cdot t$). To provide a mass (m) with the highest possible velocity (v), a mean force (F) as large as possible must be applied to this body over a period of time (t) as long as possible. With the available path of acceleration, the acceleration time also increases. However, this results only in an increase in momentum if the force development in the throwing direction is not reduced too much. If the mean force decreases to the same or even greater extent than the path and time increase, the momentum generated is ultimately less despite the longer acceleration path.

It is primarily the delivery motion which determines the velocity of departure of a throwing implement. This is why the delivery motion is also called the main acceleration phase. In order to achieve an acceleration path as long as possible in this phase, javelin throwers, discus throwers, and shot putters take similar starting positions before the foot touchdown which introduces the delivery motion. The legs and feet are more in front of the body in the throwing direction. The pressure leg is placed on the ground with the knee flexed at about the vertical projection of the CG. The shoulders and the head remain behind the CG in the throwing direction. The implement and the throwing arm are far behind the body so that they may pass

DISCOURSE II: SIGNIFICANCE OF BODY MASS

As in the runs and jumps, relative maximum strength (i.e., strength related to body weight) also plays an important role in the throwing events since the athlete must not only accelerate the throwing implement, but also himself/herself as described above. While it is a hindrance to an athlete's acceleration that a greater force (F) is required to accelerate a greater mass (m) to the same extent (a = F / m), a greater inertia of the athletes is helpful in accelerating the throwing implement. For example, if an athlete pushes a shot with a certain force away from himself/herself, then the shot pushes the athlete by itself with the same force (action = reaction). The mass difference between the two objects (athlete and shot) decides how much the two objects are accelerated in opposite directions. Similarly, in the hammer throw for example, the weight of the implement pulls in one direction and the athlete in the other direction. In general, a heavier athlete is a better abutment for the implement.

Since there is more or less adequate space and time available for the pre-acceleration of athletes, and since the ultimate objective is the acceleration of the implement, the absolute maximum strength plays a much more important role in the throwing events than in the jumping and sprinting events. The highest possible (absolute) strength values are achieved by great muscle hypertrophy resulting in a corresponding increase in body weight. However, the size of the muscle must not restrict movement technique and the elastic properties of the muscle-tendon units. This is especially true when the implement is light as in the javelin throw and the velocity of the movement is therefore high. In this event, passive mass (fat) is also disruptive. However, passive mass may also be a hindrance in the other throwing disciplines. For example, a negative correlation is assumed between abdominal fat and maximum shoulder-hip separation. In spite of this, world-class performances appear to be possible in these disciplines even with relatively large (passive) body masses.

through the largest possible amplitude of movement during the delivery.

FOOT TOUCHDOWN

The delivery motion in the javelin throw, discus throw, and the shot put begins with the placement of the pressure leg on the ball of the foot. Shortly thereafter, the bracing leg touches down, usually on the inside of the foot or on the entire sole of the foot (in the javelin throw sometimes also on the heel). Figure 1 shows the similar foot touchdown positions in the three throwing disciplines. Depending on the foot touchdowns, the delivery movements of the three throwing disciplines may be divided in the following two sub-phases:

- placement of the pressure leg until the placement of the bracing leg; and
- placement of the bracing leg until the implement leaves the thrower's hand.

ACTION OF THE PRESSURE LEG

The acceleration of the javelin, discus, and shot during the delivery motion begins with the rotation and extension movement of the rear leg (i.e., the action of the pressure leg). The extension of the ankle, knee, and hip joint is overlapped by the rotation of the knee of the pressure leg and the pelvis in the throwing direction. In particular, this results in a rapid forward movement of the hip on the side of the throwing hand. While the rotation of the

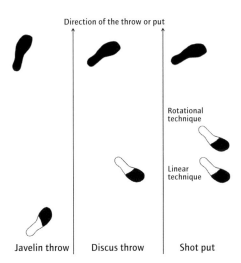

Figure 1: **Comparable foot position in three throwing events** performed by a right-hander; in the javelin throw at the moment of the respective foot touchdown, in the discus throw during the backward reclining position of delivery (or striking position; moment of touchdown of the bracing leg): The bracing leg is placed slightly to the left so that the hip on the side of the pressure leg may be brought forward.

foot of the pressure leg is most noticeable in the discus throw and the rotational shot put, the glide technique of shot putting also includes a variation in which the push-off is performed more over the inner edge of the foot with less foot rotation. In the javelin throw, the spikes require a more frontal touchdown of the foot. While the foot is rolled from the heel over the ball of the foot onto the top of the foot and the knee must be turned less inwardly, the pelvis still rotates approximately 90° about its longitudinal axis during the delivery movement.

ACTION OF THE BRACING LEG

As in the jumps, bracing in the throws also means the touchdown of a (nearly) straight leg well ahead of the vertical projection of the centre of gravity (CG). Also as in the jumps, the athlete tries to bend his/her bracing leg after touchdown as little as possible in the knee and then to stretch it as quickly as possible in a reactive and powerful manner. This action of the bracing leg has the following three functions:

- deceleration of the horizontally directed translational velocity of the thrower to avoid fouling;
- re-direction of translational velocity from the horizontal to the vertical to achieve an optimal height of departure and a sufficiently large angle of departure; and
- conversion of translational into rotational velocity to accelerate the throwing implement.

Due to the deceleration of the lower part of the body and the opposite side, the athlete's upper body and throwing-hand side rotate forward. With each rotation, the most external part of the body, in this case the throwing hand holding the implement, achieve the highest velocity.

SHOULDER-HIP SEPARATION

Shoulder-hip separation is the temporary twisting of the hip and shoulder axis. It is measured as the angle between the line running through both hip joints (hip axis) and the line running through both shoulder joints (shoulder axis) in a horizontal plane (top view). In the discus throw in particular, this angle may be up to 90° for a brief time.

While the throwing implement is held back, the actions of the pressure leg and bracing leg lead to the rotation of the pelvis about the longitudinal axis of the body. This may result in even more noticeable shoulder-hip separation. However, the rotation of the pelvis and an already existing shoulder-hip separation primarily lead to an effective and rapid transmission of the rotation to the shoulder axis. The oblique muscles and the connective tissue of the trunk transmit the force of the legs to the thorax and the shoulders. Through their contraction, the trunk muscles are involved in the acceleration of the shoulders and the throwing arm. The shoulder on the side of the throwing hand is brought forward as quickly as possible so that the chest finally points in the direction of the throw.

ARC POSITION

The holding back of the implement, the hip rotation due to the actions of the bracing and pressure leg, and the shoulder rotation due to dissolving the shoulder-hip separation result in the arc position. In the javelin throw, the arc position is most obvious since the arc includes the throwing arm. However, the legs and trunk also pass through a very similar position (see figure 2) in the other throwing disciplines.

Since the athlete continues to hold the throwing implement back contrary to the throwing direction, the arc position leads to a strain on the shoulder muscles and the straight abdominal muscles, including the connective tissue. This results in the transmission of the force of the legs and the trunk to the throwing arm, the dissolution of the arc position, and the acceleration of the throwing arm, throwing hand, and the throwing implement.

Finally, the muscle tendon units and connective tissue structures spanning the elbow joint and the joints of the hand are involved in the acceleration of the implement to a different degree depending on the discipline-specific technique.

Figure 2: **Arc position in the javelin throw and comparable positions in the discus throw and shot put.**

BLOCKING THE OPPOSITE SIDE

The non-throwing arm initially supports the late opening of the shoulder axis. Since the non-throwing arm begins its movement as late as possible, the shoulder axis remains turned out of the frontal position (closed) for a long time and the throwing hand is also kept back for a long time. Then, at least for a brief moment, the extended opposite arm points in the throwing direction. While in the javelin throw it is often held in this position even during the acyclic part of the run-up, it passes through this position in a circular motion in the discus throw and shot put. From this (forward and upward) position, the opposite arm is bent backward and downward and is brought to the body. The active backward movement toward the axis of rotation supports the rotation about the longitudinal axis of the upper body. An additional effect is that the chest and frontal shoulder muscles are stretched in the process (breast tension) and that thereby the power output during the subsequent contraction is increased. The slight lowering of the opposite shoulder associated with this arm movement results in a lift of the shoulder on the side of the throwing arm, thus increasing the height of departure. Further effects of the lateral inclination of the shoulder axis associated with this in the javelin throw are discussed in discourse II in chapter II–3.2.3.

KINEMATIC CHAIN AND DELAY OF THE THROW

The movement process described is a kinematic chain. When examining the velocity-time curves of various body segments on the side of the throwing arm, it becomes clear how these are accelerated in chronological order to increasing top velocities and are then slowed down again (see figure 3). The acceleration takes place from bottom to top and from proximal (close to the centre of the body) to distal (far from the centre of the body). The long holding back of the implement previously described, resulting in late acceleration of the implement, is also referred to as delay of the throw or the use of the whip principle.

PHASE 4: RECOVERY

Recovery techniques differ in the four throwing disciplines. However, the objectives are identical:

- discharge of the remaining kinetic energy of the thrower;
- avoidance of fouling.

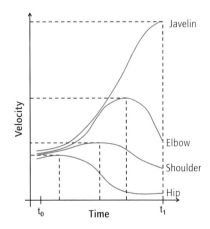

*Figure 3: **Kinematic chain** in the javelin throw (modified on the basis of Menzel, 1988; see also the respective diagrams in the individual event chapters): Another examination confirms that the wrist may be positioned between the elbow and the javelin.*

FLIGHT OF THE IMPLEMENT

The laws of the oblique throw have already been described in connection with the jumping events (see chapter II–2.1.2). While the calculation was primarily performed by using the components horizontal and vertical velocity of departure, the formula shown in figure 4 calculates the distance of flight (d_{FL}) using the velocity of departure (v), the angle of departure (α), and the height of departure (h_0), as well as the gravitational acceleration (g), which

does not vary much on earth. Although the mass of the implement plays a role in its acceleration, this is not the case after it has left the thrower's hand.

VELOCITY OF DEPARTURE

Achieving a maximum velocity of departure is the main objective of all athletics throws. Since it is the only parameter which is squared in the formula, it represents the most important parameter of delivery. This is true at least as long as one uses

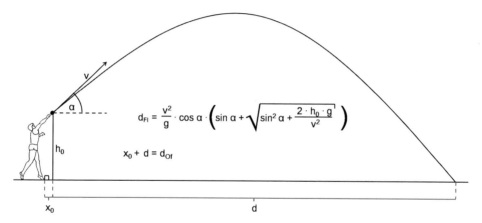

$$d_{FI} = \frac{v^2}{g} \cdot \cos \alpha \cdot \left(\sin \alpha + \sqrt{\sin^2 \alpha + \frac{2 \cdot h_0 \cdot g}{v^2}} \right)$$

$$x_0 + d = d_{Of}$$

Figure 4: **Calculation of the throwing distance** (d_{FL}) and competition performance (d_{Of}) while neglecting air resistance (for explanation of abbreviations see main text).

Table 1: **Example calculations of the throwing distance** using the formula in figure 4 for estimating the significance of the parameters of departure.

Velocity of departure (v):	12 m/sec		v:	24 m/sec	
Angle of departure (α):	40°	Flight distance: 16.54m	α:	40°	Flight distance: 60.12m
Height of departure (h_0):	2.0m		h_0:	2.0m	
Velocity of departure (v):	12 m/sec	Flight distance: 15.55m	v:	24 m/sec	Flight distance: 54.10m
Angle of departure (α):	30°	Distance loss:	α:	30°	Distance loss:
Height of departure (h_0):	2.0m	−0.99m (−6.0 %)	h_0:	2.0m	−6.02m (−10.0 %)
Velocity of departure (v):	12 m/sec	Flight distance: 16.06m	v:	24 m/sec	Flight distance: 59.56m
Angle of departure (α):	40°	Distance loss:	α:	40°	Distance loss:
Height of departure (h_0):	1.5m	−0.48m (−2.9 %)	h_0:	1.5m	−0.56m (−0.9 %)

real and not theoretical extreme values for the delivery parameters. For example, if the angle of departure were 90°, the velocity of departure would be completely irrelevant to the distance of the flight (which would always be 0 m). Table 1 illustrates the influence of the velocity of departure on the throw. In the shot put and hammer throws, the correlations between the velocity of departure and competitive performance are very high. They reach a highly significant value of r = 0.87 even in the very homogeneous performance group of the ten finalists at the 2007 World Championships. If aerodynamics is of greater importance (javelin and discus), the correlations between the velocity of departure and the distance achieved decrease. In large groups with widely varying performances (heterogenous performance group), the correlation coefficients remain relatively high so that the velocity of departure is still the major difference between good and poor throwers. Homogeneous performance groups such as the finalists at international championships are often able to achieve similar, very high velocities of departure. In this case, the skilful use of the other parameters of departure has a greater impact on the thrower's success in competition.

ANGLE OF DEPARTURE

The second objective of a good delivery is achieving an optimal angle of departure. In the normal oblique throw in physics, the optimal angle of departure is 45°. However, since the height of departure in the athletics throws is higher than the landing height, the optimal angle of departure is slightly lower. Due to the aerodynamic characteristics of the javelin and the discus (see below) which provide lift to the implement, there is a further decrease in the optimal angle of departure in these disciplines. In addition, motion-specific limitations in the individual disciplines are held responsible for smaller angles of departure. Deviations of ± 3° from the theoretically optimal angle of departure result in relatively small changes in throwing distance. In shot puts of approximately 22m, there are deviations of less than 20cm. However, greater deviations from the optimal angle of departure have an increasing negative impact on the distance achieved.

HEIGHT OF DEPARTURE

The achievement of a maximum height of departure has relatively little impact on the throwing distance. Because of rule limitations and the fact that the technique needs to be effective with respect to the velocity and angle of departure, the height of departure can be changed maximally by only a few centimetres. The flight distance would change by approximately the same number of centimetres. In the event of a relatively short throwing distance (i.e., in the shot put), this results in the greatest difference in percentage of distance.

POINT OF DEPARTURE AND LATERAL DIRECTION OF DEPARTURE

The position-of-delivery distance (x_0) is the difference between the distance measured according to the rules (d_{of}) and the actual horizontal distance between the point of departure and the landing point (d_{FI}; see figure 4). This difference partly results from the fact that javelin throwers, for example, release the implement well in front of the scratch line, while the shot usually leaves the athlete's hand beyond the vertical projection of the inner edge of the rim of the circle. Secondly, the difference results from the fact that there may be an angle between the straight line along which the measurement is performed and the straight line between the point of departure and the landing point. For example, the departure point of the hammer head is clearly beside the ring. In the javelin throw, one can often observe that a right-hander releases the javelin far on the left side of the runway and the javelin lands close to the right boundary of the landing sector. This leads to an angle between the aforementioned straight lines and a slight loss of distance since the official distance is measured along the right sector boundary. Similar to the height of departure, there is only little room to optimise the position-of-delivery distance through effective technique. However, the position-of-delivery distance may determine the outcome of a competition as the example described in connection with the javelin photo sequence shows (see chapter II-3.2.5).

AERODYNAMICS

The formula presented in figure 4 applies only in a vacuum. Under real conditions, air resistance must be taken into consideration. Air resistance depends on the shape of the implement and the direction and velocity of the upstream flow. The front surface (i.e., the surface of the implement at right angles to the direction of the upstream flow) is of crucial importance. Air resistance increases with the square of upstream flow velocity. The direction of the upstream flow is the result of the magnitude and direction of the flight velocityof the implement and the force and direction of the wind. Due to the higher velocity of departure and the longer duration of flight (= duration of effect), air resistance is of greater importance in the long throws. Figure 5 shows that back wind results in a lower velocity of upstream flow and a larger angle of upstream flow. The effects of headwind are the opposite.

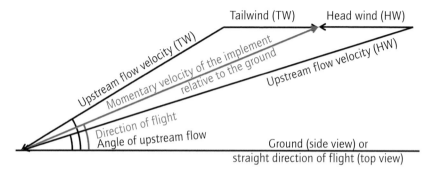

*Figure 5: **Changing the angle and velocity of upstream flow for tailwind and head wind.***

Since the mass (m) of the shot and the hammer is relatively large, the force (F) exerted through the air resistance leads only to a slight deceleration (a = F/m) of these implements. Moreover, the air resistance of shots is always the same, no matter from which direction the air comes. The javelin and discus are not only lighter, but have special aerodynamic features with respect to their shape. Their position and rotation at the moment of delivery (and resulting from this in flight) have a significant impact on the distance of the throw.

For better illustration, the three-dimensional position angle of these implements is described by two two-dimensional position angles. From the side view, the angle of attack is crucial for flight behaviour. It results from the position angle (angle of attitude) and the direction of flow (see figure 6). The exact shape of the implement and the angle of attack determine the magnitude of the frontal drag force relative to the normal force, acting at a right angle to it at any time during the flight. The absolute magnitude

of the forces is determined by the velocity of the upstream flow. The frontal resistance reduces the flight velocity of the implement. The vertical component of the normal force (i.e., lifting force) acts against gravity. The magnitude of the lifting force compared to the normal force depends on the angle of the upstream flow. Due to the decline of the flight curve caused by gravitation, the angle of upstream flow becomes smaller and eventually negative during flight. If the implement flies horizontally in the area of maximum altitude (angle of upstream flow = 0°), the normal force is directed entirely upward and is identical with the lifting force. Since frontal drag force and lifting force cannot be changed independently of each other, the objective should be to find the optimum compromise of the smallest possible frontal drag and the greatest possible lifting force. Where this optimum can be found is described in connection with the disciplines themselves.

The position of the javelin and the discus from the (top or) rear view is also of crucial

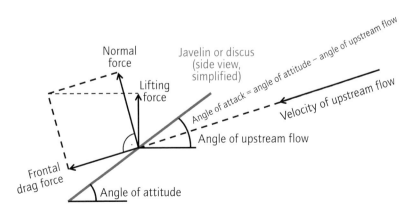

*Figure 6: **Frontal resistance and lift during the javelin and discus throw from the side-view.***

importance to their flight features. The tilt angle in the javelin throw and the angle of lateral inclination in the discus throw result in a force acting perpendicular to both frontal drag force and normal force. The implement is thereby deflected from its direction of movement to the side.

3.1.3 GENERAL ASPECTS OF THE DIDACTICS OF THE THROWING DISCIPLINES

Potential throwers should also undergo a combined event-oriented basic training in children's athletics and in basic training. Learning the basic forms of running and jumping is an important prerequisite to subsequently practise throws.

It is one objective of children's athletics to create many and varied opportunities to gain experience in the throws. To perform a great number of throws seems to be particularly important for many girls. Due to their gender-specific education, girls still have much less throwing experience than boys.

After a playful holistic and versatile introduction, the throws are generally developed by first teaching the last phase, the final delivery movement. Classic methodical series for learning the shot put, the javelin throw and discus throw begin with throws or puts from a frontal position with the chest being already turned in the direction of the throw. Subsequently, shoulder and hip rotation, footwork and pre-acceleration are added successively.

The similarities mentioned in chapter II-3.1.2 represent a particular challenge to teaching and learning throws. It is often said that beginners want to accelerate the implement too early; others speak of the necessity to separate the upper and lower parts of the body. All this means that successively performing the partial movements while holding the throwing implement back for as long as possible is the most important teaching and learning objective in practising the throws with beginners.

Studies indicate that bilateral practice not only prevents muscle imbalances, but also accelerates the learning of throwing techniques from the very beginning.

Similar to the jumps, the coach should ensure that advanced athletes do not perform too many standing throws or puts since this simplification results in a significant modification of the movement in particular in terms of central nervous control (see chapter II–2.1.4). Only with appropriate pre-acceleration, will the typical rhythm of the overall movement and elements of the technique like the arc position be fully achieved, used, and practised.

The interaction between strength and technique (see chapter I–3.1.2) and thus between the weight of the implements and the technique should be observed in the learning process. The lighter weights of the competition implements prescribed by the rules is supposed to reduce the stress on the musculoskeletal system and to facilitate learning the technique and to prevent excessive, strength-induced deviations from the target technique. Even with athletes who come from other disciplines or who have started athletics training too late, the initial use of lighter weights may accelerate learning the throwing technique. However, in high-performance training throws with light weights are a method of specific speed training. Contrary to this, throws with weights which are heavier than the competition implement are the most special form of speed-strength training.

SAFETY PRECAUTIONS

Being hit by a throwing implement may cause serious injury and may be life-threatening. It is therefore necessary to comply with strict rules to ensure risk-free training:

- Before throwing, the thrower must assure that the landing area for the implement is free. This is quickly forgotten when throwing from the circle due to the athlete's starting position with his/her back to the direction of the throw.
- In group training, the implements should never be retrieved directly after the throw, but always together on the command of the coach or teacher after all implements have been thrown

and are now lying in the landing area. Before entering the landing sector to retrieve the implement, athletes must make sure that nobody is throwing.

- Implements should never be thrown back to the point of delivery, but should always be carried back.
- Additional safety measures mentioned in connection with the individual disciplines should also be observed.

3.1.4 BIBLIOGRAPHY

Kühl, L. & Hommel, H. (Red.) (mit Bartonietz, K., Becker, M., Becker, S., Böttcher, G., Deyle, M., Gaede, E., Hartmann, W., Losch, M., Rapp, E., Thomas, B., Wollbrück, R. & Zöllkau, H.). (1997). *Rahmentrainingsplan für das Aufbautraining Wurf* (Edition Leichtathletik, 5, 3. Aufl.). Aachen: Meyer & Meyer.

Maurer, H. (2005). Beidseitiges Üben sportmotorischer Fertigkeiten. *Zeitschrift für Sportpsychologie 12* (3), 93-99.

Menzel, H.-J. (1988). Biomechanical analysis of the javelin throw. In IAF (Hrsg.), *Scientific report on the II. World Championships in Athletics.* London.

Regelkommissionen des DLV, FLA, ÖLV und SLV (Hrsg.). (2008). *Internationale Wettkampfregeln.* Waldfischbach: Hornberger.

Wank, V. (2006). Biomechanik und leistungsrelevante Parameter der leichtathletischen Wurfdisziplinen. In K. Wohlgefahrt & S. Michel, *Beiträge zur speziellen Trainings- wissenschaft Leichtathletik: Symposium der dvs-Kommission Leichtathletik vom 10.-11.10.2002 in Bad Blankenburg* (Schriften der Deutschen Vereinigung für Sportwissschaft, 153, S. 132-144). Hamburg: Czwalina.

3.2 JAVELIN THROW

3.2.1 A DISCIPLINE FOR INVENTORS

In the mid-1990s, eight spears made of spruce wood were discovered in Schöningen near the German town of Braunschweig. They are estimated to be 400,000 years old and are considered the oldest spears made by humans known to date. Since that time a variety of spears have been used by many peoples as hunting and war weapons. Evidence for this and references to the importance of spears are provided by the mythologies of various cultures. Gungnir, the spear of Odin (the supreme god of Germanic and Norse mythology), never missed its target and always came back to its master. In Greek mythology, Heracles was considered a superior javelin thrower. It is assumed that for the first time in 708 B.C. the javelin throw was a competition at the Olympic Games of Ancient Greece as a discipline in the pentathlon. In throwing for distance and to a target, the throwers wrapped a cord (ankyle) around the back of the spear which they held by a loop in their throwing hand. This improved the force transmission and the rotation of the spear about its longitudinal axis. Likewise, rifle bullets also rotate in a barrel to keep their trajectory. In modern times, the flutter of the javelin, which is considered a technical error even today, has been minimised primarily by using stiffer materials which ultimately brought about modern carbon javelins.

The freestyle javelin throw was part of the Olympic Games for the first time in 1906 (interim Olympic Games) and in 1908. In 1908, the javelin throw with grasp of the javelin at its centre was introduced as a discipline of its own. This technique is still used today. At the 1912 Olympics, there was also a two-handed javelin throw competition. Women have thrown the javelin at the Olympic Games since 1932.

By increasing its diameter, American Bud Held improved the javelin's aerodynamic properties. Using his "flying cigar," he was the first to throw over 80m on 8 August 1953. This hollow javelin not only ended the era of the Finnish javelins made of birch wood, but also the 50-year-old Finnish-Swedish dominance in the javelin throw. Eight years later, the IAAF banned the thickened spear, but the world records established with it remained valid.

In 1956, the IAAF became aware of a javelin technique similar to the discus throw. Its inventor was the then over 50-years-old former Spanish discus thrower Felix Erausquin. Soft soap was applied to the tail of the javelin. Then the javelin was brought back and wrapped around the body so that the tail was across one's back. The thrower gripped the javelin with wet hands at its binding, rotated around his/her longitudinal body axis, and let the tail of the javelin slip through his/her fingers during the delivery. Using this technique, Erausquin threw 83.40m in 1956, surpassing Held's world record. His Finnish imitator Saarikoski even achieved 98.40m. Considerably longer distances seemed possible. The technique was supposed to be the secret weapon of the Spaniards at the 1956 Olympics in Melbourne. However, after Erausquin's compatriot Salcedo had demonstrated it at a meeting in Paris, this technique was banned by the IAAF and the records achieved by using it were cancelled. In addition to a radical change in the nature of the discipline, larger stadiums and safety cages would have been necessary.

However, a few years later, stadiums were too small even for javelin throws with the traditional technique. In 1984, the javelin thrown by East German Uwe Hohn landed only a very short distance in front of the artificial surface on the other side of the stadium. The scoreboard showed 04.80m since it was not designed to record distances over 100m. In order to obtain more valid results, the IAAF had already been thinking about the forward displacement of the centre of gravity of the javelin. The change in the men's javelin specifications with a shift of the centre of gravity forward by 4cm went into effect beginning on 1 April 1986. As desired, this resulted in poorer gliding characteristics (less dynamic lift) and the tip of the javelin nearly always sticking in the ground in landings. Moreover, changes to the surface of the javelin were prohibited in 1992. The world record with the new javelin is still held since 1996 by Czech Jan Zelesny with 98.48m. Until 1999, the 600g javelin, which is used by youth athletes and women, led to many invalid attempts since the tip of the javelin did not descend early enough, particularly when the duration of flight was short. Finally, the women's world record of exactly 80m set by East German Petra Felke was established for all time by also shifting the centre of gravity of the women's javelin 3cm forward. The new world record of 72.28m (2008) is held by Czech double Olympic champion Barbora Špotáková. With five athletes each in the men's and women's all-time top-20 list, Germany is the top nation with the modern javelin. The most prominent athletes are Johannes Vetter (second place in the all-time best list with 97.76m, Word Champion 2017); Thomas Röhler (third place in the all-time best list with 93.90m, Olympic Champion 2016); and the World Champions Steffi Nerius (2009), Matthias de Zordo (2011), Christina Obergföll (2013), and Katharina Molitor (2015).

3.2.2 THE MOST IMPORTANT COMPETITION RULES

The following abridged and simplified International Competition Rules comprise the framework for the technique and strategy, as well as the organisation of javelin competitions:

- Table 1 describes the javelins to be used. The javelin must not have any mobile parts or other apparatus which during the throw could change its centre of gravity or throwing properties. The javelin consists of three parts: a shaft, a head, and a cord grip. All three parts constitute a fixed and integrated whole. The cross section of the javelin must be circular throughout. The maximum diameter of the shaft must be immediately in front of the cord grip. From the cord grip, the javelin must taper uniformally to the tip at the front and to the tail at the rear.
- The shaft may be solid or hollow and must be constructed of metal or other suitable material. The surface of the shaft must be smooth and uniform throughout.
- The head of the javelin must be constructed completely of metal. It must also be smooth and uniform along the whole of its surface. The angle of the tip must not exceed 40°.
- The grip, which must cover the centre of gravity of the javelin, must not exceed the diameter of the shaft by more than 8mm. It must have a regular non-slip pattern surface, but without thongs, notches, or

indentations of any kind. The grip must be of uniform thickness.
- Figure 1 describes the layout of a javelin throw runway and landing sector.
- The angle between the two boundary lines of the sector is 29°. This angle is achieved as follows: Form an equilateral triangle (three tape measures). The third side is shorter than the two equal sides by a factor of 0.5. The equal sides form the sector

Table 1: **Minimum weight, diameter of the shaft at its thickest point, and length of the javelins** for the various age groups in the German Athletics Federation (see Rule Commissions by the DLV, FLA, ÖLV and SLV, 2010, pp. 120–121): The rules provide many other specifications for the construction of javelins (e.g., length of the metal head, width of the cord grip, position of the centre of gravity, and diameter at various points).

Age groups		Weight, diameter, length
Female U14, male U14	w60 and older, m80 and older	400g, 2.0-2.3cm, 185-195cm
Female U16 and 18	w50-55, m70-75	500g, 2.0-2.4cm, 200-210cm
Female U20, women, male U16	w40-45, m60-65	600g, 2.0-2.5cm, 220-230cm
Male U18	m50-55	700g, 2.3-2.8cm, 230-240cm
Male U20, men	m40-45	800g, 2.5-3.0cm, 260-270cm

lines which (in theory) meet at a point that is 8m from the delivery arc (see point A in figure 1). (Example: Two points located 50m from point A on the two sector lines must have a distance of 25m).

- In the javelin throw, the spikes on the sole of the shoes may be up to 12mm long (subject to possible restrictions set by the organisers).
- The javelin must be held at the grip and must be thrown over the shoulder or upper part of the throwing arm and must not be slung or hurled. Until the javelin has been thrown, an athlete must not turn completely around at any time so that his/her back is entirely toward the throwing arc. Unorthodox throwing styles are not allowed.
- If the javelin breaks during a throw or while in the air, it is not considered a failure, provided no other rule was violated. In this case the athlete must be awarded a new trial.
- It is a failure
  » if an athlete in the course of his/her trial touches the lines marking the runway or the ground outside these lines with any part of his/her body; or
  » if the javelin does not first strike the ground with the tip of the metal head.
- The measurement of each throw must be made from where the head of the javelin first struck the ground to the inside edge of the arc, along a straight line to point A (see figure 1). Otherwise, the general competition rules for the technical disciplines and throwing apply (see chapters II–2.1.1 and II–3.1.1).

(ROUNDERS) BALL THROW

For (rounders) ball throwing competitions the following applies:

- Table 2 describes the (rounders) balls to be used. They may be made of filled leather or rubber.
- Figure 2 describes the layout of a (rounders) ball-throwing area as well as the measurement method to be used.
- If an athlete touches the scratch line or the ground beyond it (in the direction of the throw) with any part of his/her body, the trial is not valid.

Below, the two disciplines are summarised under the term *ball throw*.

Table 2: **Minimum weight and allowed diameter of** (rounders) **balls** *for the various age groups in the German Athletics Federation (see Rule Commissions by the DLV, FLA, ÖLV and SLV, 2010, p. 123).*

	Age groups	Weight, diamete
Rounders ball throw	U8, 10, and 12	70-85g, 6.0-6.7cm
Ball throw	U14 and 16	200g, 7.5-8.5cm

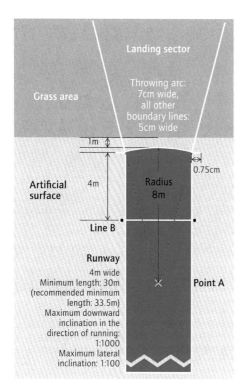

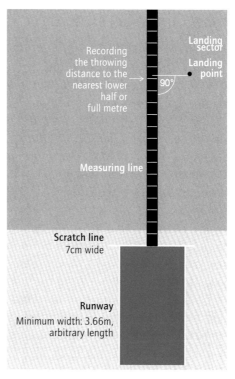

Figure 1: **Javelin runway and landing sector** *(modified on the basis of the Rule Commissions by the DLV, FLA, ÖLV and SLV, 2010, p. 106): The throwing arc is the section of a circle around point A which is also the point where the extensions of both sector boundaries intersect. During measurement, the measuring tape is drawn in a straight line from the point of landing across point A. After the landing of the implement, it is also considered leaving the competition area if an athlete steps back on or behind line B which must be painted or indicated by markers outside the runway.*

Figure 2: **(Rounders) ball-throwing area** *(modified on the basis of the Rule Commissions by the DLV, FLA, ÖLV and SLV, 2010, p. 124): The zero point of the measuring line (e.g., rolled out measuring tape) coincides with the edge of the scratch line on the side of the runway.*

3.2.3 SPORT-SCIENCE FINDINGS, PHASE STRUCTURE, AND TECHNIQUE

The javelin throw may be divided into the following four phases:

- cyclic part of the run-up;
- acyclic part of the run-up;
- delivery movement; and
- recovery and flight of the javelin.

PHASE 1: CYCLIC PART OF THE RUN-UP

HOLDING THE JAVELIN

All three methods of holding the javelin (see figure 3) have in common that two fingers are placed at the rear end of the 8mm thick cord grip. By placing the fingers behind the cord grip, an effective force transmission is to be ensured during the explosive pull of the javelin in the delivery. The thumb-and-index-finger grip (American grip) is the most common type of grip. Although this grip ensures optimal force transmission to the javelin by using the two strongest fingers, it may easily lead to an erroneous deviation of the head of the javelin during delivery. The thumb-and-middle-finger grip (Finnish grip) is supposed to provide for a better steering of the javelin. The V-grip (claw grip) is considered a healthy grip. However, it may lead to problems in the transmission of force to the javelin and reduce the rotation of the javelin about its longitudinal axis (see phase 4).

POSITION AT THE START OF THE RUN-UP

The run-up of top javelin throwers begins 25–35m in front of the throwing arc. Some beginners and less advanced athletes choose significantly shorter run-ups. Some beginners leave out the cyclic part of the run-up completely and begin with an already withdrawn javelin in a lateral starting position (see phase 2).

As in the jumps, the javelin run-up may be started from a standing position, walk-on, or from some stutter steps. At the beginning of the run-up, the pelvis,

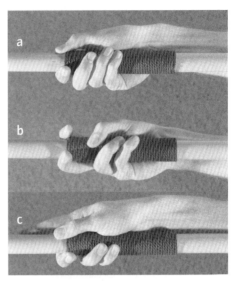

Figure 3: **Techniques of gripping the javelin** viewed from the top; a: thumb-and-index-finger grip (American grip), b: V-grip (claw grip), c: thumb-and-middle-finger grip (Finnish grip).

chest, and head are square to the running direction. The throwing hand is higher than ear level vertically above the shoulder. The back of the hand faces outward. The elbow of the throwing arm points approximately in the running direction. The javelin is in a horizontal position or is inclined slightly to the ground.

ACCELERATION

Most of the pre-acceleration of the athlete takes place in the cyclic part of the run-up. This part of the run-up is ultimately only cyclic to some extent since it is an acceleration run with increasing stride length and stride frequency. The cyclic part of the run-up is 8–12 strides long for most top throwers. For less advanced athletes who learn the cyclic run-up for the first time, this part of the run-up includes 4–5 strides.

During acceleration, the method of carrying the javelin and the alignment of the upper body remain the same as at the start of the run-up. The degree of the sprint-like forward lean of the trunk during the first run-up strides (toe push-off sprinting) depends on the individual variation of technique. At the end of the cyclic part of the run-up, the trunk should be upright. The throwing arm remains relaxed, but relatively motionless, whereas the free arm is used as in running.

The accuracy of the cyclic part of the run-up is usually controlled by an intermediate marker. Due to the submaximal running velocity during the cyclic part of the run-up, the intermediate marker may also be used by the athlete to correctly find the transition from the cyclic to the acyclic part of the run-up by looking peripherally to the marker. In this case, it is neither necessary to count strides nor to estimate the correct point to withdraw the javelin solely from the visual distance to the scratch line or to the 8m point.

PHASE 2: ACYCLIC PART OF THE RUN-UP

The acyclic part of the run-up consists of the **5-stride rhythm**. Some high-performance throwers also use a 7- or 9-stride rhythm which is lengthened by one or even two crossover strides.

WITHDRAWAL OF THE JAVELIN AND CROSSOVER STRIDE(S)

At the beginning of the acyclic part of the run-up, the javelin is withdrawn (also called the drawback of the javelin or the power reach). The withdrawal of the javelin is accompanied by a 90° rotation of the upper body about the longitudinal axis of the body and results in the position characterised as follows:

- The shoulder axis points in the direction of the throw. The hip axis is also rotated considerably out of the frontal position, with slight variations from stride to stride.
- The opposite arm is raised in the throwing direction in front of the thrower's body. The back of the hand is turned upward.
- The thrower's view is still directed in the throwing direction. The chin of the upright head is near the front shoulder.
- The throwing arm is straight and points backward. The throwing hand is at shoulder level or slightly above. The back of the hand is turned downward.

Figure 4: *Body position during the third-last stride of the run-up.*

- The tip of the javelin is close to the thrower's temple. The position of the javelin is still nearly horizontal or it points slightly upward.

The thrower achieves the position described and illustrated in figure 4 during the third stride of the 5-stride rhythm (at the latest). There are distinct differences in how this position may be achieved. A distinction is made between the Swedish, which is the most common form, and the Finnish and Russian methods of withdrawing the javelin. In the Swedish method of javelin withdrawal, the hand is moved backward on a direct path, sometimes after a slight counterswing forward. The Finnish method of javelin withdrawal is performed by using a circular movement, first forward and downward, then backward and upward. The Russian method of withdrawal is also performed in the form of an arc, but upward and backward.

Moreover, the withdrawal may be performed rather gradually using 2–3 strides or almost completely during only one stride. Usually, a quick withdrawal is recommended since this does not result in too much loss of velocity. Such a withdrawal may be performed in the form of an ambling movement during the first stride of the 5-stride rhythm or using conventional crossover coordination particularly during the second stride. While the latter variation is considered natural and is often performed intuitively, the first variation mentioned also has advantages. In this variation, the first stride including the withdrawal is most often performed as

a long toe push-off stride or quick and flat jump. This results in a deliberate and clear transition from the cyclic to the acyclic part of the run-up and enables the athlete to focus early on the impulse stride, bracing stride, and delivery motion.

Every second step is performed as a crossover stride (in front of the supporting leg). The swing leg crosses in front of the athlete's laterally aligned body in the direction of running. The foot touchdowns are significantly less turned away from the frontal position than the hip and shoulder axis. They deviate by approximately 20–45° from the frontal position. The javelin thrower tries to further accelerate (by approx. 0.2–0.4 m/sec) by performing pulling foot strikes (see chapter II-1.3.3). Since there are even some top-level throwers who do not succeed in this, the maintenance of velocity is considered a minimum requirement.

IMPULSE STRIDE AND BRACING STRIDE
During the flight phase of the penultimate stride within the 5-stride rhythm (i.e., during the impulse stride), female world-class throwers reach a velocity of 5–7 m/sec, whereas male world-class throwers reach 6–8 m/sec. Within the heterogeneous performance group described in Table 3, there is a clearly positive correlation between run-up velocity and throwing distance. Table 4 shows average run-up velocities of different age groups. During their run-up, javelin throwers achieve approximately 70% of their maximum sprinting speed. This means that maximum sprinting performance does not limit performance.

Table 3: **Correlations between biomechanical parameters and throwing distance** *for 57 men with throwing distances between 45.25 and 87.17 m (according to Murakami et al., 2006): In a longitudinal study of nine trials for one person, there was a correlation between the acceleration path and the throwing distance of even r=0.73 (Böttcher & Kühl, 1996).*

Parameter	Correlation with throwing distance
Run-up velocity during the flight phase of the impulse stride	$r = 0.742$; $p < 0.001$
Acceleration path during the delivery movement	$r = 0.426$; $p < 0.01$
Duration of acceleration during the delivery movement	$r = -0.418$; $p < 0.01$
Elbow angle at the moment of delivery	$r = -0.484$; $p < 0.001$
Abduction angle of the shoulder at the moment of delivery	$r = -0.474$; $p < 0.001$
Forward lean of the trunk in relation to the vertical at the moment of delivery	$r = 0.463$; $p < 0.001$
Knee-joint angle at the moment of delivery	$r = 0.319$; $p < 0.05$

Table 4: **Run-up velocities** *11–6 m (men) or 10–5 m in front of the scratch line, measured by means of light barriers (according to Adamczewski & Perlt, 2003).*

Age group	Number of throws analysed	Run-up velocity (m/sec)
Male U18	82	5.97 ± 0.42
Male U 20	141	6.08 ± 0.46
Men	161	6.27 ± 0.56
Female U18	93	5.40 ± 0.33
Female U20	166	5.52 ± 0.38
Women	217	5.74 ± 0.36

The impulse stride is usually the longest stride of the 5-stride rhythm (see table 5 and figure 5). The length of this stride, which is related to the athlete's body height and run-up velocity, increases with increasing age and level of proficiency. The correlations between the length of the impulse stride and the throwing distance vary greatly in different studies, but appear to higher for women. The impulse stride is the final preparation of the delivery motion.

According to the jump-like nature of the impulse stride, the leg is placed down in a pulling manner on the entire sole of the foot before the push-off for the impulse stride is performed. A touchdown with the heel first should be avoided since this is usually associated with a touchdown of the foot well ahead of the vertical projection of the CG and a take-off which is directed too much upward. The impulse stride should be performed flatly and rapidly in order to maintain a high run-up velocity and not to be forced to first compensate for a high velocity of fall at the beginning of the pressure leg support.

During the flight phase of the impulse stride (0.20–0.30 sec), the legs overtake the lower part of the body. In order to achieve a long path of acceleration in the following main acceleration phase, the shoulders stay behind the hips. This backward or sideward rotation was already initiated by the thrower during the third-last stride. When placing down the pressure leg, the longitudinal axis of the trunk deviates from the vertical by 10–30°

(ε, see figure 6 and table 5). However, there is a trend toward recommending athletes not to lean backward too much (i.e., not to extend the acceleration path at any cost). If the athlete leans back too much, the result is too great emphasis on the eccentric phase at the beginning of the action of the pressure leg and thereby a loss of velocity even before the touchdown of the bracing leg.

When viewed from behind in the running direction, the trunk is straight, which means that it is neither inclined to the right nor to the left side of the runway. The thrower's buttocks must not be stretched out to the

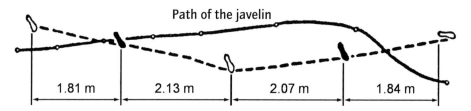

Path of the javelin

| 1.81 m | 2.13 m | 2.07 m | 1.84 m |

*Figure 5: **Path of the feet and javelin during the last four strides of a 94.44m throw**, viewed from the top (modified on the basis of Harnes, 1985).*

*Table 5: **Mean values of selected parameters of javelin throws** between 1992 and 2000 (according to Adamczewski & Perlt, 2003; for the weights of javelins see also table 1): Böttcher and Kühl (1998) recommend for a 1.78m woman bracing stride lengths corresponding to the run-up velocity during the impulse stride: 6.0 m/sec: 2.00m, 6.5 m/sec: 2.15m, and 7.0 m/sec: 2.30m. In each case, the third-last stride should be shorter by a factor of 0.91, the bracing stride should be shorter by a factor of 0.77.*

	Age group		Number of analysed throws	Throwing distance (m)	Impulse stride length (m)	Bracing stride length (m)	Impulse stride/bracing stride ratio	Backward lean of the trunk upon touchdown of the pressure leg (ε)
Specialists	Male U18	(600 g)	82	64.9	1.95	1.70	1.16	26°
	Male U 20	(800 g)	141	64.0	2.17	1.75	1.25	24°
	Men	(800 g)	161	78.1	2.26	1.87	1.22	23°
	Female U 18	(600 g)	93	45.7	1.69	1.47	1.17	26°
	Female U 20	(600 g)	166	48.4	1.72	1.51	1.15	26°
	Women	(600 g)	217	57.3	1.87	1.56	1.20	26°
Combined-event athletes	Male U18	(600 g)	17	52.8	1.65	1.52	1.10	28°
	Male U20	(800 g)	25	52.9	1.80	1.54	1.18	27°
	Men	(800 g)	59	57.3	1.85	1.64	1.13	25°
	Female U18	(600 g)	15	38.1	1.63	1.33	1.25	25°
	Female U20	(600 g)	21	39.7	1.68	1.41	1.21	24°
	Women	(600 g)	44	42.8	1.87	1.46	1.31	25°

side of the runway. Beginners should try to achieve a straight delivery and should make sure that the arm and tail of the javelin point straight backward. Among top-level throwers, the English athletes Backley and Hill were known for the straightness of their throwing techniques. However, to increase the tension in the chest and front shoulder muscles as well as to extend the acceleration path, many top throwers take their throwing arm further back (see figure 5) so that when viewed from behind, the tail of the javelin clearly points to the side. This over-rotation reaches its maximum at the moment of placing down the pressure leg. This means that when viewed from above, the javelin, shoulder, and hip axis may significantly deviate from each other at the moment of placing down the pressure leg (see table 6). However, when viewed from the side, the three axes should appear parallel (see figure 6).

Table 6: **Extent of the rotation out of the frontal position** *(0°) viewed from above for the male finalists at the 1995 World Championships (according to Morris et al., 1997): The results of seven finalists at the 1999 World Championships according to Campos et al. (2004) are less uniform. This means that for four throwers there was an increase in the shoulder-hip separation (difference between the hip axis and shoulder axis) from the touchdown of the pressure leg up to the touchdown of the bracing leg.*

Thrower	Throwing distance (m)	Shoulder axis (SA)			Hip axis (HA)			Difference = SA – HA		
		Touchdown of the pressure leg	Touchdown of the bracing leg	Delivery	Touchdown of the pressure leg	Touchdown of the bracing leg	Delivery	Touchdown of the pressure leg	Touchdown of the bracing leg	Delivery
Zelezny	89.06	105°	53°	-35°	68°	29°	-31°	37°	24°	-4°
Backley	86.30	86°	45°	-45°	50°	20°	-31°	36°	25°	-14°
Henry	86.08	98°	54°	-31°	62°	38°	-20°	36°	16°	-11°
Hecht	83.30	92°	61°	-28°	57°	29°	-21°	35°	32°	-7°
Wennlund	82.04	77°	47°	-38°	58°	22°	-40°	19°	25°	2°
Hill	81.06	92°	55°	-27°	51°	24°	-19°	41°	31°	-8°
Rybin	79.54	79°	34°	-31°	61°	19°	-38°	18°	15°	7°
Linden	79.72	79°	34°	-35°	63°	27°	-38°	17°	7°	3°
Parviainen	79.58	99°	47°	-18°	61°	23°	-10°	38°	24°	-8°
Moruyev	79.14	89°	42°	-24°	30°	18°	-32°	59°	24°	8°
Räty	78.76	97°	46°	-33°	40°	16°	-34°	47°	30°	1°
Hakkarainen	78.16	96°	46°	-33°	66°	27°	-37°	30°	19°	4°
Average	81.90	90.8	47.0	-31.5	55.6	24.3	-29.3	34.4	22.7	-2.3
Standard dev.	± 3.54	± 9.0°	± 8.1°	± 6.9°	± 11.2°	± 6.1°	± 9.5°	± 12.3°	± 7.3°	± 7.3°

*Figure 6: **Impulse stride with illustration of the backward lean and the parallelism of axes.***

In order to optimally prepare for the final stride of the 5-stride rhythm (bracing stride), the thrower performs a double scissor movement of the legs during the impulse stride. During the push-off into the impulse stride, the pressure leg swings flatly and rapidly forward past the supporting leg. However, even before the pressure leg is placed down, the bracing leg is again brought in front of the pressure leg. The further the foot of the bracing leg is in front of the pressure leg before this leg is placed on the ground, the faster the bracing leg may subsequently be placed on the ground. The bracing stride itself should rather be seen as a part of the delivery motion since the main acceleration phase starts with the action of the pressure leg before the bracing leg is placed down.

PHASE 3: DELIVERY MOVEMENT

From the moment of the touchdown of the pressure leg to the javelin leaving the hand, the javelin is accelerated over a distance of 3.0–3.5m for top-level male throwers. During the 0.28–0.38 sec required for this, the javelin is accelerated from its velocity during the run-up, which corresponds approximately to that of the athlete, to its departure velocity. Table 3 shows that longer throwing distances are associated with a longer acceleration path and a shorter acceleration time.

From a pulling motion backward, the pressure leg is placed down approximately on the vertical projection of the CG with a slight flexion at the knee joint. This flexion is described as "sitting on the pressure leg", "soft knee", and "soft step". A soft touchdown minimises the braking forces at the beginning of the pressure leg support. In addition, the touchdown of the bracing leg well ahead of the body is only made possible by the bent knee and the resulting slight lowering of the CG.

An increasing number of top athletes place down the pressure leg only with the ball of the foot, particularly when the backward lean of their trunk is not very noticeable, without briefly lowering the foot onto the entire sole. However, in spite of this, a touchdown of the foot with the entire sole is frequent. The touchdown direction of the foot should be less than 45°

to the direction of the throw and not exceed this value. The thrower tries to actively push himself/herself forward as soon as possible after the touchdown. In the process, the foot of the pressure leg is rolled from the ball of the foot over the tip of the toes to the back of the foot, which is then dragged along the ground (sliding contact). The knee and hip of the pressure leg are rotated forward and accelerated.

Figure 7: **Bracing stride**, from the touchdown of the pressure leg until the touchdown of the bracing leg: In the right picture, the backward reclining position of delivery (striking position) is presented.

Figure 8: **Delivery motion** from the backward reclining position (striking position) to the release (side view).

Figure 9: **Delivery motion** (rear view).

In many cases, the bracing stride is ultimately a walking stride since the bracing leg is placed down before the pressure leg leaves the ground. However, some top throwers perform the action of the pressure leg so actively that the back of the foot already slides over the ground when the bracing leg is placed down. The foot of the bracing leg is placed down with the entire sole approximately in the running direction. Sometimes, a slight inward rotation of the foot toward the throwing-arm side with a touchdown using the inner edge of the foot first is also recommended. A heel-first touchdown is also common.

A short interval of time between the touchdown of the pressure leg and the touchdown of the bracing leg is an indicator of high run-up velocity, an adequate backward lean of the trunk, an active action of the pressure leg, and an effective touchdown of the bracing leg. In top throwers, the duration of this phase is 0.14–0.26 sec. Even top throwers do not always succeed in increasing their CG velocity in this phase so that the reduction in the loss of velocity becomes the minimum objective.

The bracing stride, which should be as flat as possible, is shorter by about 10–30% than the impulse stride (see table 5) and generally the shortest stride of the whole 5-stride rhythm. Similar to the stride pattern in the jumps, there are large individual differences. The analysis of Jan Zelesny's world-record throw showed that the ratio of his last two strides was 0.97, which means that his bracing stride was slightly longer.

For younger and less-skilled throwers, the bracing stride is shorter. In addition to body height and run-up velocity, a lower strength capacity of the knee extensors of the bracing leg might be the cause of this. Therefore, they must place down the foot of the bracing leg closer to the vertical projection of the CG since otherwise the strain on the bracing leg would be too high. The angle between the bracing leg and the ground becomes larger (see table 7), whereas the reduction of the velocity of the CG becomes smaller. This means that less translational run-up velocity is transferred to the rotation of the body during delivery.

For the same bracing angle, the strain on the bracing leg also increases with run-up velocity. Therefore, an increase in run-up velocity is not very useful without improving the load tolerance of the bracing leg.

In top male javelin throwers, the time between the touchdown of the bracing leg and the moment when the javelin leaves the hand is between 0.11 and 0.14 sec. In this period, the CG velocity of top female and male throwers is reduced through the action of the bracing leg by 50–70% to 1.5–3.5 m/sec. In order to achieve an effective braking effect, the bracing leg should only be bent slightly if possible. This results in a considerable impact load on the bracing leg and the lower trunk region for which the javelin thrower must continuously prepare through years of training. The minimum knee angles of the combined-event athletes with shorter throwing distances in table 7 are correspondingly smaller. However, there are also world-class athletes who bend their knee joints up to 135°.

Many features of the delivery motion have already been described in connection with the common characteristics of the throwing events (see chapter II-3.1.2). Shortly

Table 7: **Mean values of selected parameters of javelin throws between** 1992 and 2000 (according to Adamczewski & Perlt, 2003; for detailed group description see table 5): The finalists of the 2002 European Championships demonstrated touchdown angles of 45.6° (women) and 41.7° (men). For some top-level throwers larger elbow angles were found.

	Age group	Elbow angle upon touchdown of the bracing leg	Angle of touchdown between the bracing leg and the ground	Minimal knee angle in the bracing leg
Specialists	Male U18	136°	48.2°	146°
	Male U20	139°	46.3°	147°
	Men	140°	44.6°	153°
	Female U18	134°	49.4°	148°
	Female U20	137°	48.1°	148°
	Women	137°	46.3°	147°
Combined-event athletes	Male U18	130°	52.8°	144°
	Male U20	133°	53.6°	143°
	Men	132°	51.3°	142°
	Female U18	126°	54.1°	143°
	Female U20	128°	53.7°	142°
	Women	136°	50.1°	143°

the wrist provides the javelin with the last acceleration impulse. Figures 5 and 15 illustrate the path of the javelin in this phase from the top view; figure 11 shows the path of the javelin from the side view.

The delay of the throw may be measured for example using the elbow angle at the moment of placing down the bracing leg. It is striking that specialists as well as older and more powerful athletes are more successful in keeping the throwing arm stretched out with the javelin behind their body for a longer time (see table 7). According to another criterion in respect to the delay of the javelin throw, the javelin should not have yet reached 40% of its final maximum velocity in the middle between the touchdown of the bracing leg and leaving the hand. This means that for top throwers more than 60% of the kinetic energy of the javelin at the moment of release is transmitted to the javelin only during the last 0.05 sec (see table 8). Less qualified throwers do not succeed in achieving this.

Depending on the extent of the aforementioned over-rotation during the impulse stride, the lateral movement of the javelin transverse to the direction of the run-up also changes during the delivery motion. Despite similar throwing distances, it can vary between 10 and 70cm. Throws with marked over-rotation and lateral movement rather result in throws along the sector boundaries and larger tilt angles (see phase 4).

The positive relationship between the forward lean of the body at the moment of

before the touchdown of the bracing leg, the hip of the throwing-arm side reaches its maximum velocity (see table 8) before it is slowed down through the action of the bracing leg. This is followed by the acceleration and deceleration of the shoulder of the throwing-arm side and the inward rotation of the throwing arm associated with the acceleration of the elbow forward and upward. The back of the throwing hand is now turned outward. The forearm is almost parallel to the shaft of the javelin. Finally, the elbow is slowed down by the extension of the elbow joint (forearm whip) before the extension of release and throwing distance in table 3 may be interpreted as an indication of the importance of a high forward rotational velocity of the upper body. This rotational velocity is based on the action of the bracing leg and the active forward movement of the shoulders due to the contraction of the anterior trunk muscles.

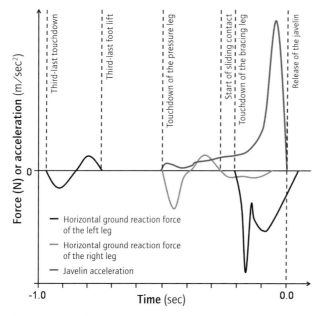

Figure 10: *Exemplary curve of javelin acceleration and ground reaction forces in the direction of the run-up during the throw of a right-hander with full run-up (modified on the basis of Adamczewski, 1995).*

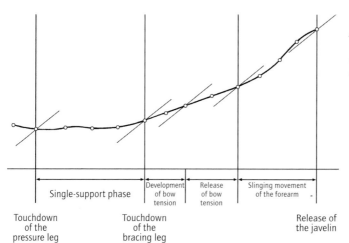

Figure 11: **Path of the javelin from the side view** *(modified on the basis of Bauersfeld & Schröter, 1998, p. 329).*

Table 8: **Average biomechanical parameters** *of better and weaker javelin throwers at the 2004 German Championships (according to Lehmann, 2005): For the seven male world-class javelin throwers examined by Campos et al. (2004), the hip on the side of the throwing arm reached its highest velocity 0.13 ± 0.01 sec before the delivery, while the respective value for the shoulder on the side of the throwing arm was 0,09 ± 0,02 sec and for the elbow on the side of the throwing arm 0,06 ± 0,01 sec.*

	Weaker women (n = 4)	Better women (n = 4)	Weaker men (n = 4)	Better men (n = 5)
Mean official distance (m)	55.57	61.22	77.38	82.58
Time from the touchdown of the bracing leg until reaching maximum hip velocity (sec)	-0.09	-0.12	-0.08	-0.10
Time from the touchdown of the bracing leg until reaching maximum shoulder velocity (sec)	0.02	0.01	0.02	0.00
Time from the touchdown of the bracing leg until reaching maximum elbow velocity (sec)	0.05	0.05	0.06	0.06
Time from the touchdown of the bracing leg until the maximum increase in velocity of the javelin (sec)	0.08	0.08	0.07	0.05
Mean CG velocity from the touchdown of the pressure leg until the touchdown of the bracing leg (m/sec)	4.78	5.77	6.26	6.11
Mean CG velocity from the touchdown of the bracing leg until the release of the javelin (m/sec)	3.58	4.33	4.64	4.16
Maximum elbow velocity (m/sec)	10.53	11.33	11.83	12.17
Maximum shoulder velocity (m/sec)	6.57	7.68	8.27	7.96
Maximum hip velocity (m/sec)	5.44	6.22	6.85	6.53
Velocity of the javelin when placing down the pressure leg (m/sec)	4.94	5.67	6.05	5.94
Velocity of the javelin when placing down the bracing leg (m/sec)	8.2	9.4	9.73	10.21
Velocity of the javelin at the time of the maximum increase in acceleration (m/sec)	9.77	10.77	10.08	11.05
Velocity of the javelin at the time of the maximum increase in velocity of the javelin (m/sec)	14.82	16.72	18.13	17.57
Maximum increase in velocity of the javelin = maximum acceleration of the javelin (m/sec^2)	117.3	129.7	162.9	175.1
Maximum increase in acceleration (m/sec^3)	0.647	0.689	1.300	1.446

DISCOURSE I: BALL THROW

The ball throw and the javelin throw are described as **straight throws**. The technique of the ball throw is simpler than that of the javelin throw since the aerodynamic properties of the flying implement do not matter. Therefore, the ball throw (even as a form of competition) is introduced at an earlier age than the javelin throw. However, the technique of the ball throw should be based on that of the javelin throw right from the start.

*Figure 12: **Technique of gripping the ball.***

PHASE 4: RECOVERY AND FLIGHT OF THE JAVELIN

POINT OF RELEASE AND RECOVERY MOVEMENT

When the javelin leaves the athlete's hand, both the throwing hand and the toe of the bracing leg are located about 2m in front of the scratch line in the horizontal direction. Table 9 shows hardly any performance-based differences, only slight gender-based differences with respect to the point of release. However, for the finalists at the 2002 European Championships, slightly greater distances were measured (women: 2.14m; men: 2.57m). The optimisation of the point of release in terms of a maximum measured distance of the throw, primarily by changing the point of starting the run-up, must in no way hamper the forward directed delivery movement which should be as explosive as possible.

At the moment of release, the CG should not have exceeded the touchdown point of the bracing leg. Therefore, maintaining a stretched bracing leg after the javelin has left the hand represents the first part of the recovery movement. As soon as the javelin thrower has moved across the bracing leg, he/she takes another stride to absorb his/her remaining horizontal velocity. The foot is placed correspondingly clearly ahead of the vertical projection of the CG. The bracing leg stays behind the body to keep the CG behind the touchdown point. Some top throwers, including world record holder Želesný, have experimented with a delivery technique in which they initiate such a strong forward rotation of the upper body during the delivery motion so that they must support themselves with their hands or even land in a prone position during the recovery.

DISCOURSE II: DISCUSSION OF SELECTED ASPECTS OF THE DELIVERY MOTION

Slinging movement of the forearm

In classical descriptions of technique, the slinging movement of the forearm is performed as an explosive elbow extension after bringing forward the elbow. Two findings give reason to expand on this idea. Böttcher and Kühl (1996) note that longer throws are associated with less bending at the elbow during the delivery (r = 0.82) and identify 90° as the optimal smallest angle at the elbow. Murakami et al. (2006) note that longer throws are associated with less elbow extension at the moment of delivery (see table 3). For the World Championship finalists examined by Campos et al. (2004), the elbow angle at the moment when the javelin leaves the hand is also between 150° and 160°. This means that with 60–70° there is only relatively little extension of the elbow. Therefore, Murakami et al. (2006) suggest in terms of the slinging movement of the forearm that it is more a rapid inward rotation of the shoulder joint at a relatively constant elbow angle. In the case of a rotation whose axis of rotation passes through the upper arm, the largest radius (lever) between the axis of rotation and the javelin is established by an elbow angle of 90° to best translate the rotation into javelin velocity.

Freedom of the throwing side

When observing javelin throwers during the delivery from the front or back, it is striking that they incline their trunk to the side of the bracing leg (see figure 13). This phenomenon may not only be observed in all javelin throwers, but also in handball players or in servers in tennis. However, if there is too much lateral lean of the trunk in the javelin throw, this is regarded as an error. In any case, a correlation between the degree of lateral bending and the throwing distance could not be found. Justifications for bending the trunk to the side or for reducing such a movement are rare in the literature.

The term *freedom of the throwing side* which is used for this phenomenon seems to indicate that by bending the trunk to the side the acceleration path does not become so much of a circular path and may be straighter. However, there is another reason which seems more likely:

In order to transmit the greatest possible acceleration force onto the javelin, the athlete must use large muscle groups. Such a muscle group is the pectoralis (pectoral muscle). It can cause a powerful anteversion (forward movement) and inward rotation at the shoulder joint. These functions are performed more powerfully with smaller abduction at the shoulder joint. Accordingly, a correlation analysis (Murakami et al., 2006) shows that the throwing distance increases with a decreasing angle of abduction. The average lateral lean at an abduction angle of approximately 90° seems to be an optimal prerequisite for effective muscle work, a maximum angle of delivery, and a sufficient height of delivery.

Another possible reason for the lateral bending could be that the thrower's CG is thereby shifted behind the bracing leg and the bracing effect is improved.

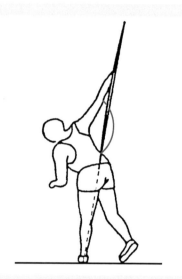

Figure 13: *Javelin thrower with relatively marked freedom of the throwing side and illustration of the throwing diagonal and the abduction angle of the shoulder.*

Figure 14: *Recovery movement.*

VELOCITY, ANGLE, AND HEIGHT OF DEPARTURE

For top-level male javelin throwers, the velocity of departure is 28–32 m/sec (101–119 km/h); women achieve 24–28 m/sec (86–101 km/h). With a correlation coefficient of up to r = 0.9, the velocity of departure determines about 80% of the variation in the throwing distance.

Theoretical considerations and experiments with the javelin gun, which shoots javelins at attitude and tilt angles of 0°, speak in favour of departure angles of 40–45°. The actual values are significantly lower (see table 9). For seven finalists at the 1999 World Championships, these angles varied between 27.7° and 40.1°. The standard deviations of the specialists in table 9 remained below 3°. The average values show no gender-, age-, or performance-related tendencies.

The difference between a theoretically and a practically optimal angle of departure results from the interaction with the velocity of departure. If the javelin thrower tries to release the javelin at a steeper angle, he/she will not be able to accelerate his/her trunk and arm forward so much and thereby will lose departure velocity. Therefore, the objective is to achieve the optimum combination of the greatest possible angle of departure and the greatest possible velocity of departure.

For male elite athletes, the height of delivery is between 1.7 and 2.1m and is statistically not related to the throwing distance. Women achieve delivery heights averaging 105% of their body height.

ANGLE OF ATTACK AND ANGLE OF TILT

The term and the importance of the angle of attack have already been introduced in connection with the common features of the throwing events (see chapter II–3.1.4). In the javelin throw, an attack angle of 0–2.5° theoretically ensures that there is an optimum relationship between frontal drag and lift. For top throwers, positive values up to 10° and very small negative angles were measured (see table 9).

*Table 9: **Mean values of selected delivery parameters** of javelin throws between 1992 and 2000 (according to Adamczewski & Perlt, 2003): In respect to the 600g javelin, throws with both the old and the new javelin were considered. This explains the slightly larger angles of attitude and angles of attack for throws with 600g javelins. At the time of the examination, male U18 athletes still threw the 600g javelin, while today they throw the 700g javelin. Note the larger attitude and attack angles and smaller tilting angles in the combined-event athletes. While the larger attitude and attack angles are interpreted as a performance reserve in the combined-event athletes, the smaller tilting angles are understood as a different technical solution which is typical for this group of athletes. Brunner et al. (1996) found significantly (p <0.01) smaller tilting angles (3.27 ± 3.07°) in elite throwers (>70 m; n = 6) than in beginners (n = 6; 9.64 ± 4.90°).*

	Age group		Number of investigated throws	Throwing distance (m)	Angles of departure	Angles of attitude	Angles of attack	Angles of tilt	Point of delivery (m)
Specialists	Male U18	(600 g)	82	64.9	34.3°	40.7°	6.4°	14.5°	-2.05
	Male U20	(800 g)	141	64.0	33.3°	37.5°	4.2°	13.3°	-2.06
	Men	(800 g)	161	78.1	34.3°	35.4°	1.1°	11.7°	-2.18
	Female U18	(600 g)	93	45.7	34.3°	41.1°	6.8°	14.7°	-1.80
	Female U20	(600 g)	166	48.4	34.5°	42.0°	7.5°	14.5°	-1.83
	Women	(600 g)	217	57.3	34.2°	40.5°	6.3°	13.1°	-1.85
Combined-event athletes	Male U18	(600 g)	17	52.8	32.9°	44.8°	11.9°	10.9°	-2.09
	Male U20	(800 g)	25	52.9	34.2°	41.7°	7.5°	9.5°	-2.11
	Men	(800 g)	59	57.3	33.9°	40.5°	6.6°	5.9°	-2.23
	Female U18	(600 g)	15	38.1	31.0°	43.5°	12.5°	11.9°	-2.02
	Female U20	(600 g)	21	39.7	33.7°	45.1°	11.4°	13.6°	-1.83
	Women	(600 g)	44	42.8	31.7°	44.4°	12.7°	11.0°	-1.83

The angle of attitude (= angle of departure + angle of attack) must be set correctly by the thrower at an early stage. There are correlation coefficients of r = 0.9 between the angle of attitude at the moment of release and the angle of attitude when placing the bracing leg onto the ground, and of approximately r = 0.6 between the angle of attitude at the moment of release and at the moment when placing the pressure leg onto the ground. Changes in the angle of attitude even during the delivery movement often occur as an unfavourable upward deflection of the head of the javelin. This error, which is often demonstrated by female throwers, is often caused by a bending of the wrist. In this case, a small error may have a great effect. As soon as the axis of the javelin is deflected from the movement direction of the javelin, the grip behind the centre of gravity of the javelin increases the rotation of the javelin. If the head of the javelin and thus the centre of gravity are deflected upward from the movement path of the hand, one speaks of throwing below the point.

The angle of tilt describes how far the shaft of the javelin is deflected from the direction of flight when viewed from above (or from behind; see figure 15). The angle of tilt should be as small as possible to minimise frontal drag. However, table 9 shows values which significantly differ from 0°. The reason for this is the described turning of the javelin out of the throwing direction during the impulse stride. During the subsequent explosive acceleration, even top throwers no longer

succeed in aligning the axis of the javelin with the direction of the throw. They seem to accept this since their objective is the development of maximum force to achieve a higher velocity of departure. If the javelin is tilted upon delivery, it will be driven off to the side according to the same principle applying to the lift.

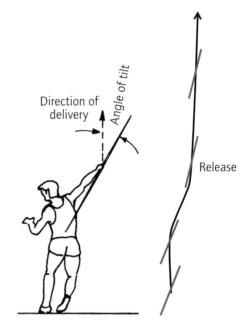

*Figure 15: **Tilt angle viewed from the rear as well as from above.***

ROTATION OF THE JAVELIN

On the one hand, it is possible that the thrower will set the javelin in rotation about an axis transverse to its longitudinal axis upon release. Such rotation about the transverse axis, which is often caused by throwing below the point mentioned above, should be avoided. On the other hand, the mere position of the javelin in relation to the airflow acting on it causes it to rotate about its transverse axis.

The centre of pressure of the drag force is located in the volume centre of the javelin. However, this is not identical with the centre of gravity of the javelin. If one imagines figure 16 as a view from the side, it is clear that the eccentric impulse of air resistance leads to a rotation about the centre of mass which results in a lowering of the head of the javelin.

Through rule changes for the men's javelin in 1986 and the women's javelin in 1999, which were mentioned in the introduction, the centre of gravity of the javelin was shifted further toward the head of the javelin. Thus, the distance between the centre of pressure and the centre of mass of the javelin was enlarged. This larger radius results in greater torque so that the head of the javelin tilts downward more rapidly and the dynamic lift is reduced.

Since an increase in the diameter of the front part of the javelin or a reduction in the diameter of the tail of the javelin could also shift the centre of pressure of the javelin forward, which would again result in a reduction of the radius, the maximum and minimum diameter of the javelin at specific locations were exactly specified. Due to the shift of the centre of gravity, the distances achieved by men were reduced by about 7m, while the women's distances were reduced by only 1–3m. Furthermore, the new javelins have led to more valid trials.

If one throws a javelin without an angle of attack (i.e., angle of attitude = angle of delivery), there is initially no drag force setting the javelin in rotation. However, due to the gravity-induced decrease in the angle of upstream flow and the corresponding increase in the angle of attack, the tilt of the head of the javelin is subsequently triggered anyway. This

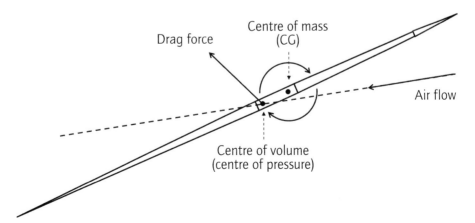

*Figure 16: **Rotation of the javelin** (viewed from the side: lowering of the head of the javelin; viewed from above: reduction of the tilt angle).*

reduction in the angle of attitude in turn counteracts the increase in the angle of attack.

Like the angle of attack, the angle of tilt also leads to a rotation of the javelin. If figure 16 is taken as a view of the javelin from above, it becomes clear that the airflow results in a rotation about the vertical axis which initially reduces the tilt angle (before it increases again in the opposite direction).

Biomechanical studies have shown that javelin throwers also set the javelin in a rotation about the longitudinal axis. The javelin should rotate about its own axis up to 20 times per second. Since this rotation acts as resistance to deflections, the flight stability of the javelin increases and the two rotations mentioned above are slowed down.

VIBRATION OF THE JAVELIN

Figures 5, 11, and 15 show that the acceleration of the javelin does not take place on a completely straight path. Due to this, as well as to their own inertia, even modern stiff javelins are set in vibration with the head and the tail of the javelin swinging in one direction and the centre of gravity swinging in the opposite direction.

DISCOURSE III: THROWING THROUGH THE POINT

Studies have shown that longer rather than shorter throws frequently and clearly remain below the theoretical distance calculated on the basis of the formula for the throwing parabola. First, this is due to the fact that air resistance (which is not included in the formula) increases quadratically with the velocity of departure which must be higher in longer throws. Second, the long path of acceleration and the great efforts of strength which are necessary to achieve a high velocity of departure have a negative influence on the other parameters of departure (unfavourable angle of tilt, excessive vibration, etc.). The javelin with its many (flight) properties seems to be a device that does not compensate for many errors, especially if the athlete wants to "pull on" the javelin too powerfully. Again and again, (even) top javelin throwers make statements such as: "My longest throw was actually the most relaxed one." The feel for the lightest throwing implement in athletics, which results in throwing through the point, sometimes seems to be more important than sheer strength.

Other throwers and even jumpers also speak of correctly throwing or jumping through the point. Phrases like this express the spatiotemporal fine-tuning of the partial movements which is difficult to put into words, but results in significant differences in measurable performances without many visible external changes in movement.

Impressive high-speed recordings show that the javelin is temporarily bent like a banana and winds through the air in a snake-like manner. This increases the frontal resistance of the spear during flight.

The stiffer the javelin, the greater its resistance to vibration, a resistance which is transmitted to the elbow. If a mediocre thrower throws an unusually stiff carbon javelin with high pulling velocity but with an incorrect technique, this may lead to excessive strain and injury to the elbow.

Table 10: **Requirement profile for the javelin throw:** *The suggested rough estimate of the value of selected factors determining performance is based on the importance for the overall performance and the percentage of time spent training (IR: information requirements, constr.: constraints; see chapter I–1.1).*

Factors determining javelin-throw performance	Estimate of value	Notes
Coordination	+ + + + +	optical IR: medium, acoustic IR: low, tactile IR: low, kinaesthetic IR: medium, vestibular IR: medium; precision constr.: high, time constr.: high, complexity constr.: high, situation constr.: low, physical stress constr.: low
Flexibility	+ + + +	primarily of the throwing-arm shoulder
Strength		primarily anteversion and inward-roation muscles of the shoulder (pectoralis, etc.), elbow extensors (triceps), extension loop (glutes, quadriceps, triceps surae, erector spinae), hip and trunk flexors and rotators (iliopsoas, abdominus, etc.)
Maximal strength	+ + +	as one of the most important basics, primarily as high relative strength
Speed strength	+ + + + +	as the most important factor; primarily of the upper body
Reactive strength	+ + + +	primarily of the legs
Speed	+ + + + +	primarily acyclic aspects of the delivery motion; cyclic aspects are of less significance
Endurance (general dynamic) Anaerobic endurance		
Strength endurance	+ +	as a basis to be able to perform 6 trials plus practice trials at a high level of performance
Speed endurance	+	as a basis
Aerobic endurance	+	as a basis
Psychological and cognitive abilities	+ + + + +	concentration ability (on the point); performance-oriented thinking and behaviour (see chapter I–3.1.1)
Anthropometric and primarily genetically determined characteristics	+ + + +	high percentage of the fastest muscle fibres; connective tissue with optimal energy storage capacities; rather above-average body height (There are, however, throwers with very different body proportions successful.)

3.2.4 SUMMARY OF THE MOST IMPORTANT TECHNICAL CHARACTERISTICS = TECHNIQUE-ANALYSIS SHEET

CYCLIC PART OF THE RUN-UP

GRIP

- Thumb-and-index-finger grip (American grip), thumb-and-middle-finger grip (Finnish grip), V-grip (claw grip; see figure 3).

START OF THE RUN-UP

- Run-up length for top athletes approximately 25–35m, 8–12 strides of which are for the cyclic part of the run-up; less advanced athletes perform only 5 strides; beginners leave out the cyclic part of the run-up and the javelin withdrawal.
- The run-up is normally started from a stride position.

ACCELERATION

- The throwing hand is kept relaxed and motionless at a perpendicular angle over the shoulder above the height of the ear; the back of the hand is turned outward; the javelin points horizontally in the running direction or slightly downward.
- The free arm is moved in a sprint-like manner; the shoulder and hip axis are kept square to the running direction; at the end of the cyclic part of the run-up, the trunk is upright.
- The athlete should only accelerate to a velocity which he/she is at least able to maintain during the acyclic part of the run-up.
- Landing on the intermediate marker at the transition to the acyclic part of the run-up.

ACYCLIC PART OF THE RUN-UP

WITHDRAWAL OF THE JAVELIN AND CROSSOVER STRIDE(S)

- Withdrawal of the javelin during 1–2 stride(s) at the beginning of the 5- (or 7-) stride rhythm; if the withdrawal takes place upon the first stride, it is performed mostly with a flat transitional jump; the withdrawal is performed mostly in the form of a straight backward movement of the javelin.
- The trunk is turned outward during the withdrawal of the javelin: The shoulder axis and hip axis are turned in the throwing direction, while the face and view remain in the throwing direction.
- The throwing arm is extended backward, the hand is at or slightly above shoulder height, the back of the hand is turned downward; the javelin is directed horizontally or slightly upward, the tip of the javelin is at eye level; the free arm is in front of the body.
- Every second stride is performed as a crossover stride in front of the body; pulling foot touchdowns; the feet are turned out of the throwing direction by not more than 45°.
- The athlete should try to continue his/her acceleration.

IMPULSE STRIDE

- Longest stride of the acyclic part of the run-up (quick and flat jump).
- The pulling touchdown of the entire sole leads over to a powerful push-off into the impulse stride.
- The pressure leg swings flatly and rapidly forward past the supporting leg; however, the bracing leg is already brought in front of the body before the touchdown of the pressure leg.
- Side view: Taking a slight backward lean of the trunk (10–30°); rear view: trunk upright.

- The throwing arm remains behind in a stretched-out position and is sometimes even twisted further against the throwing direction ("over-rotation").
- The athlete reaches a position with his/her hip axis, shoulder axis, and the javelin axis being parallel when viewed from the side; he/she maintains this position until the pressure leg is placed on the ground.
- No loss of velocity if possible.

DELIVERY MOVEMENT

BRACING STRIDE: FROM THE TOUCHDOWN OF THE PRESSURE LEG TO THE TOUCHDOWN OF THE BRACING LEG

- Pulling touchdown of the pressure leg near the vertical projection of the CG; touchdown with the ball of the foot or the entire sole of the foot; the touchdown direction of the foot should be ≤45° in relation to the throwing direction; the knee joint is slightly bent.
- Quick start of an active pressure movement forward with rolling of the foot and forward acceleration of the knee and the hip on the side of the throwing arm.
- Short duration and no loss of velocity until the bracing leg is placed on the ground.
- The throwing hand is held back with the elbow as extended as possible.
- The head of the javelin remains at eye level for a long time; the throwing hand is at the height of the throwing shoulder (early setting of an optimal angle of departure and attitude).

FROM THE TOUCHDOWN OF THE BRACING LEG (BACKWARD RECLINING OR STRIKING POSITION) TO THE RELEASE

- The extended bracing leg is placed down at a flat angle of touchdown; subsequently, it is bent as little as possible and quickly straightened again; the touchdown is performed with the entire sole of the foot and in the direction of the throw or turned slightly toward the side of the throwing hand.
- The actions of the pressure and bracing leg lead to a rotation of the hip, separation of the hip and shoulder axis, transmission of the rotation to the shoulder axis, bow tension, tension of the chest muscles, and transmission of the acceleration to the upper arm.
- The throwing hand is kept backward for a long time; the arm is turned inward (the elbow is moved forward and upward, the forearm is moved close to the javelin, the back of the hand is turned a little outward, the wrist is kept straight for a long time).
- Extension of the elbow and subsequently of the wrist; release of the javelin out of the hand.
- Highest possible although late acceleration of the javelin to the highest possible velocity of departure using an optimal angle of departure, a positive angle of attack as small as possible, an angle of tilt as small as possible, as little rotation about the transverse axis as possible, as little vibration as possible, and a height of departure as high as possible.

RECOVERY (REVERSE)

- The maximisation of the throwing distance through an optimal point of departure must not hinder the maximal and dynamic delivery and the necessary recovery.
- The bracing leg must be kept extended; subsequently, the athlete should perform an additional stride to absorb his/her remaining horizontal velocity; the parts of the body should be kept behind the point of touchdown if possible.

Track & Field

3.2.5 PHOTO SEQUENCE

Data about the photo sequence
Athlete: Steffi Nerius
                      (born: 1 July 1972, Germany)
Height/weight: 1.78 m/72 kg
Performance: 67.30 m (18 August 2009,
                      Berlin)
Best performance: 68.34 m (31 August 2008,
                      Elstal)
Greatest success: World champion 2009,
                      Olympic vice-champion
                      2004, European champion
                      2006)

COMMENTARY

The photo sequence shows Nerius' longest throw at the 2009 World Championships, with which she shocked her competitors during the first trial and won the competition. In her long career, which she finished immediately after the 2009 World Championships, this throw was her second-longest throw using the type of javelin which the rules have prescribed since 1999.

Steffi Nerius throws from a 13-stride run-up with a final 7-stride rhythm, during which she withdraws the javelin primarily during the second stride (from left to right) contralaterally to the action of her legs. Picture 2 shows Nerius in a perfect position during the last stride before the impulse stride. Her view is directed in the throwing direction, while her head and trunk are upright. Her throwing arm is stretched backward in such a manner that the javelin is almost parallel to her shoulder axis with its tip at her right temple. Until the backward reclining (or striking) position (pictures 9–10) is achieved, the position of the javelin hardly changes relative to the shoulder axis. Her opposite arm points in the direction of the throw with the back of her hand turned upward and the opposite shoulder close to the chin. When viewed from behind, it becomes clear that Nerius throws relatively straight (i.e., with only slight over-rotation during the impulse stride). The touchdown of her foot before the impulse stride is performed in an active pulling manner with an almost straight leg (picture 3). Subsequently, Nerius performs a scissor movement of her legs, which run ahead of her body, while she takes the typical backward reclining position. Picture 6 shows Nerius' effort to touch down with her pressure-leg foot inthe running direction, while she simultaneously tries to keep her shoulder axis closed. After moving the opposite arm in front of her body during the impulse stride, the opening of the opposite arm introduces her active action of the pressure leg (hip forward, knee to the floor, foot turning onto its back) which leads to turning her chest in the direction of the throw. The touchdown of the nearly straight bracing leg is very flat (<45°), which in conjunction with the subsequently only slightly yielding knee of the bracing leg results in a very great bracing effect. While the hip and shoulder axis rotate about the longitudinal axis of her body, she keeps her throwing arm back for a long time (see picture 10). By bringing her elbow to the javelin late (picture 11) and through the subsequent explosive forearm whip (pictures 12 and 13), she achieves a late, but very high final acceleration of the javelin. After releasing the javelin, Nerius continues her bracing action to completely slow down her remaining horizontal velocity after a single additional stride.

*Table 11: **Biomechanical measuring values** of the throw presented (according to Lehmann, 2010, p. 13).*

Result	Velocity of departure	Angle of departure	Angle of attitude	Angle of tilt	Impulse and bracing stride length		Point of delivery	Duration of impulse stride	Duration of bracing stride	Duration until release
(m)	(m/sec)	(°)	(°)	(°)	(m)		(m)	(sec)	(sec)	(sec)
67.30	25.6	33.6	40.5	12.2	1.81	1.49	1.90	0.26	0.18	0.10

The biomechanical parameters of the best trials of all finalists show the complexity of the javelin throw. Nerius (see table 11) achieved only the fourth-fastest velocity of departure. With the exception of Barbora Spotakova (second place: 66.42m; 38.8°) and Mariya Abakumova (third place: 66.06m; 36.3°), all finalists achieved an angle of departure of 33.2–33.9°. Nerius' attack angle of 6.9° appears relatively large and this angle was smaller for five finalists. Her angle of tilt was even the seventh smallest. Her point of delivery was the fifth-closest to the scratch line. However, Spotakova's and Abakumova's points of delivery were an additional 1.10 and 1.00 m behind. This means that Spotakova's throw was actually longer than Nerius' throw. In total, Nerius succeeded in combining all parameters in the best possible manner on that day.

3.2.6 DIDACTICS: SUPERORDINATE LONG-TERM OBJECTIVES AND GENERAL METHODOLOGY

The ball throw is a preliminary form of the javelin throw and is one of the classic athletics disciplines which are first included in competitions for children. Ball throw competitions are offered up to the U16 age group. However, beginning with the U14 age group, and especially in the U16 age group, the focus is on the transition to the javelin throw.

At the beginning of the playful lessons on the straight throw, the focus is on various target-throw games. If the starting position is prescribed, a rough form of technique often develops on its own. Children should learn a variable throwing technique not only through forms of games specific to athletics, but also in traditional games such as dodgeball, rounders, handball, etc. In recent years, children's athletics has produced a variety of throwing devices, which are distinguished by their challenging characteristics. These range from homemade flutter balls (tennis balls with fluttering ribbon) to relatively expensive Aero howlers. Throwing missiles and soft javelins are also a preparation for the javelin throw since these devices encourage children to use techniques which are specific to the javelin throw.

Learning a correct technique is of crucial importance in the javelin throw, not only in terms of performance, but also for reasons of health. Overload injuries occur particularly frequently at the elbow joint (tennis or thrower's elbow). For example, they may be the result of too frequent and excessive lowering of the throwing hand, followed by a pulling arm movement at shoulder height. In addition to proper technique, a gentle increase in load and the early development of the necessary strength skills are crucial to avoid overstrain. For example, well-developed abdominal muscles protect against hyperlordosis during the arc position. Single-arm throws with balls or javelins that are slightly heavier than the competition device should be performed only in performance training. For top adult athletes, 1.5–2 kg (women) or 2–2.5 kg (men) are the absolute maximum limits for single-arm overhead throws. However, the following applies: the higher the pre-acceleration, the lower the maximum weight.

SAFETY PRECAUTIONS

The javelin is still forbidden in American high schools because of the associated risks. In addition to the safety precautions mentioned in connection with common features in the throwing events (see chapter II–3.1.3), the following should be observed when throwing the javelin:

- In general, javelin training should take place in an appropriate area. Preliminary exercises may be performed with athletes standing in a row side by side. It is important that no athlete steps forward out of the row and that no one retrieves his/her javelin before the athlete next to him/her has thrown his/her javelin. There are only few auxiliary devices (e.g., soft balls) which may be thrown toward a partner while standing in two rows with the athletes facing each other.
- When retrieving the javelins, the athletes should walk, not run or race, toward them from the the side instead of from the direction of delivery since the javelins usually stick in the ground with their sharp ends pointing backward in a flat angle in the direction of the delivery.
- Javelins which are not thrown should always be carried vertically. Whoever imitates the withdrawal must make sure that nobody is behind him/her within an area of approximately 3 metres.

3.2.7 TRAINING CONTENTS: FORMS OF GAMES AND EXERCISES

All training forms mentioned in connection with the 100m sprint (see chapter II–1.3.3) may also be used for the javelin throw in terms of reactive-strength and speed-strength training. In addition, hurdle sprints are a general part of javelin-throw training for the improvement of flexibility and coordination (ability to establish rhythm; see chapter II–1.8.8). Moreover, forms of the ABCs of jumping and multiple jumps (see chapter I–5.4.6) are an important part of javelin-throw training.

381 Keep your field free

Possible objectives: Strength (endurance) of the throwing muscles (as many throws as possible).

Execution: An equal number of throwing devices (which must be soft and light; if possible more throwing devices than players) are placed on two equally large fields; upon command, two equally large teams try to keep their field free by throwing the devices into the opponent's field; after a certain time (which the athletes do not know in advance), the game is suddenly stopped by a signal; the winner is the team with the fewest devices in their field.

Typical load standards: 2–4 run-throughs of 30 sec to 3 min each.

382 Various target-throw games

a:

b:

c:

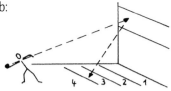

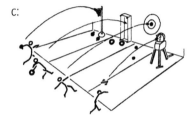

Possible objectives: Technique of the straight throw in its variety; strengthening of the throwing muscles; possibly also reaction speed and catching.

Execution/variations: a: against the wall; b: with additional emphasis on throwing strength; c: toward different targets and with different devices; d: as a combined throwing event or as a throwing biathlon (see 224); e and f: toward mobile targets (possibly gymnastic hoops hanging from rings); g: as team games (here: driving the ball); g-i: toward increasingly higher targets; j: in many throwing and hit-off games (here dodgeball, but also rounders [103], handball [1 and 324] or Zombie ball: each player may hit off anybody else; players who have been hit off must leave the field until that player is hit off who hit off him/her); throwing in outdoors, with stones, fir cones, snow balls, etc.

d:

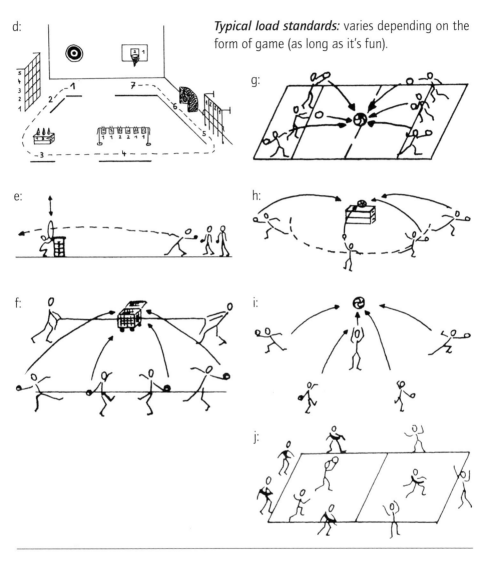

Typical load standards: varies depending on the form of game (as long as it's fun).

g:

e:

h:

f:

i:

j:

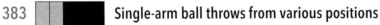

383 ▮▮▮ **Single-arm ball throws from various positions**

Possible objectives: Technique of the straight throw (slinging movement of the forearm); strength (endurance) of the throwing muscles; specific warm-up.

Execution/variations: Throw (e.g., from the positions presented) with tennis balls, rounders balls, and handballs, later also with nocken balls

(claw grip with the pin between the index and middlefinger) and with balls or shots that are heavier than the competition device.

Typical load standards: 5–20 reps per side, depending on the objective and age; if performed as throwing-strength training, even more reps may be performed.

384 ▮▮▮ **Versatile circling of arms, forearms, and hands**

Possible objectives: Specific warm-up for the throws; mobilisation; dynamic flexibility training.

Execution/variations:

a) Circling of arms: both arms forward or backward, parallel circles or with the arms pointing in opposite directions; one arm forward, the other arm backward.

b) Circling of forearms: upper arms stretched out to the sides, forearms circle in opposite directions or same direction.

c) Circling of hands: either separate or folded in prayer position.

Change of circling direction; slow or fast; in combination with running, ABCs of sprinting/jumping, or turns around the longitudinal body axis.

Typical load standards: 2–3 reps of 5–20 circular swings.

385  Frontal throw

Possible objectives: Technique of the straight throw (slinging movement of the forearm); specific warm-up.

Execution: The legs and hips are already square to the throwing direction; the shoulder is either already square (with the elbow turned inward) or is kept backward in the position of shoulder-hip separation; from one of the starting positions described: bending the trunk and successive acceleration of the throwing-arm shoulder, elbow, hand, and the javelin.

Variations: Throw horizontal to the ground (with ball) or downward (with javelin so that it sticks in the ground); bilateral practice.

Typical load standards: 3–10 reps per side.

386  Standing throw

Possible objectives: Technique of the straight throw; strength endurance of the throwing muscles; specific warm-up.

Execution: From the positions presented successive acceleration and deceleration of the hip, shoulder, and elbow of the throwing-hand side, as well as of the throwing hand itself.

Variations: With tennis balls, softballs, baseballs, rounders balls, handballs, etc.; possibly after taking the ball from far behind (e.g., from a box or from the hand of a partner); possibly often and in rapid succession; for demonstrating a straight-line throwing movement: throwing sticks or tennis rings which rotate vertically, or throwing tennis rings or balls which after landing roll forward in a straight line; with throwing missiles, Aero howlers, soft javelins, etc. to introduce the javelin throw; later with javelins: first forward and downward with the javelin sticking in the ground, then with

larger angles of departure; now also with nocken balls, and finally with javelins and balls which are a little heavier than the competition device; along a wall to demonstrate the freedom of the throwing side; if the athlete leans excessively to the side of the bracing leg, the wall should be on the other side; bilateral practice.

Typical load standards: 5–20 reps per side, depending on objective and age.

---

387   Throw with bracing stride

Possible objectives: Technique of the straight throw (placement of the bracing leg, continuous action of the pressure leg); strength (endurance) of the throwing muscles; specific warm-up.

Execution/variations: In the starting position, the bracing leg is either placed in front of the

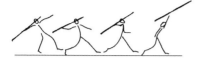

body in a shortened backward reclining (or striking) position, or beside the body, or slightly behind the pressure leg; with beginning action of the pressure leg, the bracing leg is placed flatly forward and then the javelin is delivered; various devices (see 386); bilateral practice.

Typical load standards: 5–20 reps per side, depending on objective and age.

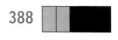

388 **ABCs of sprinting/jumping/running: lateral crossover strides**

Possible objectives: Versatile running coordination; preparation of the acyclic part of the run-up.

Execution/variations: Crossover strides in front of or behind the supporting leg, hip and shoulder axis in running direction, arms lifted to shoulder height in running direction; feet square to or in the direction of running.

Typical load standards: 1–3 run-throughs of 20–30m each.

389 **Throw from the 3-stride rhythm**

Possible objectives: Technique of the straight throw (shortest run-up with impulse stride); (reactive) strength of the throwing muscles; specific warm-up.

Execution: Throw in accordance with the target technique while only performing the last three strides of the run-up.

Variations: Initially 3-stride rhythm while walking; performance of the impulse stride over a drawn or marked ditch (rhythm: "leeeft – right-left" or "riiight – left-right"); different devices (see 386); also as flat throws with the javelin sticking into a hill; bilateral practice.

Typical load standards: 5–20 reps per side, depending on objective and age.

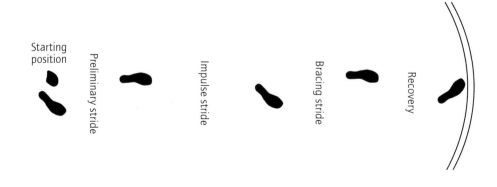

---

390 | ▨█ | **Throw from the 5- (or 7-) stride rhythm**

Possible objectives: Technique of the straight throw (without withdrawal of the javelin); strength of the throwing muscles; specific warm-up.

Execution: Lateral starting position with the javelin withdrawn; rhythm: "left – right – left – right-left", or the other way round; delivery in accordance with the target technique.

Variations: 7- or even 9-stride rhythm from a lateral starting position; impulse stride over a drawn or marked ditch; various devices (see 386); bilateral practice.

Typical load standards: 5–20 reps per side, depending on objective and age.

391  Two-arm overhead throws

Possible objectives: Strength capacities specific to the javelin throw; technique: the elbow leads the delivery action.

Execution/variations: Primarily using medicine balls, but also as two-arm shot throws; against a wall or to a partner; while sitting with and without back support, from a one- or two-legged knee-stand position, from a frontal or lateral standing position, from a walk-on or run-up; when sitting or kneeling, the athlete receives the medicine ball from a partner who throws it with more or less power; in the other positions with or without circular swinging movement of the arms; upward or downward.

Typical load standards: 1–5 sets of 5–20 reps, depending on the objective.

In addition, the medicine-ball throws mentioned in the general part (93–96) are part of javelin-throw training.

392 Flexibility training and mobilisation specific to the javelin throw

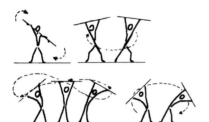

Possible objectives: Flexibility specific to the javelin throw; mobilisation and strengthening of the trunk and the arms.

Execution/variations: Initially slow, then rapid movement execution.

Typical load standards: See chapter I–4.2.

In addition, primarily 20, 21, and 28 are important stretching exercises for the javelin throw.

393 ▭ Delivery imitations

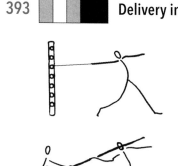

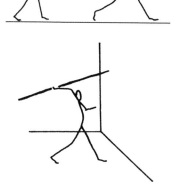

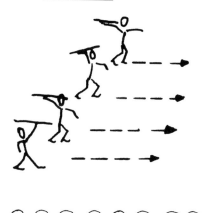

Possible objectives: Technique of the straight throw (movement idea).

Execution/variations: Slow execution of the delivery motion taking into consideration the correct coordination of the partial movements (action of the pressure leg, shoulder-hip separation, bow tension, holding back of the throwing hand, etc.); free or against resistance (e.g., an elastic band); also with a partner or the coach supporting certain parts of the movement (e.g., by holding back the long throwing arm or pushing forward the hips), possibly as a puppet exercise (all movements of the thrower are guided by a partner); bilateral practice.

Typical load standards: 3–5 reps, alternated with throws.

394 ▭ Run-up imitations

Possible objectives: Technique of the javelin run-up (movement idea).

Execution/variations: Initially, the cyclic and acyclic part of the run-up are performed by walking (only the impulse stride is performed as a quick and flat jump); then at slow running pace; later the run-up is also performed at a normal pace with and without delivery without scratch line or far in front of the scratch line; prescription of stride length by means of hoops or similar devices (the impulse stride and possibly the flat transitional jump are extended); establishment of the intermediate marker; bilateral practice.

Typical load standards: 3–6 reps per task.

395 **Javelin runs and series of crossover or impulse strides**

Possible objectives: Technique of the acyclic part of the run-up.

Execution/variations: Acceleration and coordination runs (129) while carrying the javelin as in the cyclic part of the run-up; several successive crossover or impulse strides while holding the trunk and arms as well as carrying the javelin in the manner which is typical of the acyclic part of the run-up; the direction of the foot touchdown must be observed; bilateral practice.

Typical load standards: 2–4 reps each; significantly more reps when performed as speed-endurance training.

396 **Isolated javelin withdrawals**

Possible objectives: Improvement of javelin withdrawal.

Execution/variations: The javelin is withdrawn while standing, walking, running slowly and finally while running faster; several uninterrupted repetitions: withdrawal, some crossover strides, and then return to running with the trunk square to the running direction while holding the javelin high, then the next withdrawal, etc.; bilateral practice.

Typical load standards: 3–10 reps each.

397 **Throw from a full run-up**

Possible objectives: Development of the target technique.

Execution: See chapter II–3.2.3.

Variations: In performance training also with heavier and lighter loads; finding the individually optimal intermediate marker during the transition from the cyclic to the acyclic part of the run-up;

also as simulated competition; bilateral practice.
Typical load standards: 5–12 reps, in high-performance training sometimes more.

398   Impulse stride depth jumps

Possible objectives: Reactive-strength training using a technique specific to the javelin throw.
Execution: Athletes perform the impulse stride from a box which is maximally 30cm high; depth jump followed by throw.
Variations: Short acyclic part of the run-up on a longer elevation.
Typical load standards: 1–5 sets of 3–10 reps each.

399   Javelin strength-training device

Possible objectives: (Speed-)strength training using a technique specific to the javelin throw.
Execution: The weighted sled is released forward with maximum body or trunk effort, caught, and then released again.
Variations: Single- and two-arm throws while standing or sitting; exercises using a cable pulley may also be performed as an alternative (possibly a special pulley with a brake may be used which prevents the cable from bouncing back or delays the bounce).
Typical load standards: 1–5 sets of 3–15 reps each (see chapter I–4.3).

In addition, the following exercises are important elements of the strength training of javelin throwers: 35–47, 49–59, 61–67, 69–72, 77–88, and 91–96.

Strength training which is very similar to the technique of the javelin throw for example is the performance of the action of the pressure leg with a bar placed on the shoulders or throwing the javelin while wearing a weighted vest.

3.2.8 SPECIAL TEST AND CONTROL PROCEDURES

	Test: Ability/skill tested	Execution/comments
T141	**Technique analysis:** Javelin technique	Maximal competition throw from a full run-up; evaluation on the basis of the technique analysis sheet (see chapter II–3.2.4), possibly using a video (T1) and photo sequences made thereof; in high-performance sport, also computer-supported 3D analysis based on at least two simultaneous video recordings.
T142	**Javelin throw with a short run-up:** Specific speed strength as well as laterality differences	Throwing distance in the javelin throw: • from a standing position; • from one stride (placement of the bracing leg); • from 3-stride rhythm; • from 5-stride rhythm (without javelin withdrawal); • from 7-stride rhythm (without javelin withdrawal); • with the weaker side from the run-ups mentioned.
T143	**Throwing a different device or weight:** Specific speed strength as well as laterality differences	Throwing distance in the ball, shot, and javelin throw: • with lighter weight; • with heavier weight; • with the weaker side and changed device.
T144	**General throwing tests for the javelin throw:** Specific strength endurance	Throwing distance: • two-hand overhead throw from the stride position; • two-hand overhead throw from the run-up with circular arm swing; • tossing forward or backward (93).
T145	**Javelin-throw endurance test:** Specific speed endurance	The total distance achieved in 10 throws with a fixed run-up and in pre-set time.
T4	**1 RPM:** Maximal strength	Press (54), pull-over (57), squat (62), clean (63), snatch (64), lat-pull (65), hip-shoulder twist (67), quadriceps (69), arm exercises, etc. (if possible also eccentric maximal strength measurement).
T5	**Squat jump, and T8 counter-movement and drop jump:** Two-legged speed strength and reactive strength of the extensor loop	
T9	**5-stride hops with distance maximisation:** Reactive strength of the legs in comparison to one another	Hop test should be performed on both sides.

	Test: Ability/skill tested	Execution/comments
T10	**30m bounding run with time minimisation:** Reactive strength of the legs	
T21	**60m analysis:** Sprint technique	See technique analysis sheet in chapter II–1.5.4.
T24	**30m flying sprint:** Maximum sprinting speed	Test should be performed on both sides.
T115	**Long jump:** Specific speed and reactive strength	
T2	**Flexibility tests:** General flexibility	
T3	**Body weight and body fat measurement:** Relative strength	Inappropriate upward and downward deflections should be avoided.

In high-performance sport, additional tests are possible (e.g., the direct measurement of the velocity of departure, measurements on the javelin strength-training device, throws with special javelins which enable the measurement of acceleration) as well as performing last ground contacts on force-measurement plates. In all throwing disciplines, additional sports-medicine tests (e.g., blood tests), sport psychology, nutritional tests, etc. may be necessary to answer specific questions.

Table 12: *Basic performances of javelin throwers (according to Kühl & Hommel, 1997, pp. 233–234): The values for women are related to the old javelin (before 1999).*

		Women					Men			
Target distance in the javelin throw	(m)	39.0	45.0	54.0	60.0	65.0	57.0	68.0	72.0	76.0
Two-hand overhead throw of a 4kg weight	(m)			11.5	12.8	13.5				
Throw of the 900g javelin	(m)						47.0	59.0	63.0	68.0
Throw of the hockey ball	(m)	65.0	70.0							
Throw of the 500g javelin	(m)	43.0	48.0	57.0	63.0	68.0				
Throw of the 600g javelin	(m)						63.0	75.0	79.0	83.0
Forward throw of the 4kg shot	(m)	11.0	12.5	13.2	14.0	15.0	16.0	17.5	18.5	19.5
Backward throw of the 4kg shot	(m)	12.8	14.5	15.2	16.0	17.0	17.5	19.5	21.0	24.0
30m flying sprint	(sec)	3.75	3.65	3.55	3.45	3.35	3.30	3.20	3.10	3.05
3-stride hops	(m)	7.50	7.80	8.20	8.30	8.40	8.80	9.20	9.40	9.80
5-stride bounding run	(m)		15.0	15.8	16.5	17.5	17.0	18.0	19.0	20.0
Snatch	(kg)	40	47.5	55	65	80	70	80	92.5	105
Bench press	(kg)	45	55	60	70	75	75	–	–	–

3.2.9 ERRORS – CAUSES – CORRECTIONS

In all disciplines, coaches should not stand too close to the action and should vary their observation point and angle of view to actually detect all errors effectively. Errors and their detection are always individual. Nevertheless, some errors can be identified which are particularly common or important for beginners. Of these errors, up to six are highlighted in blue for each discipline.

Error	Causes	Corrections
Unfavourable method of carrying the javelin during the cyclic part of the run-up (e.g., due to the wrist being bent, the tip of the javelin points outward or upward; the throwing hand is too low; the throwing hand is moved too much to and fro or up and down, etc.)	• Insufficient automation of carrying the javelin in accordance with the target technique which enables the athlete to withdraw the javelin as easily as possible and to smoothly change to the acyclic part of the run-up.	✔ Focusing on a correct, fixed, and relaxed method of carrying the javelin. ✔ Run-up imitations (394), runs while carrying the javelin (395), and javelin withdrawals (396).
Loss of velocity during the acyclic part of the run-up.	• The cyclic part of the run-up is too long and/or too fast. • Too high transitional jump between the cyclic and acyclic part of the run-up. • Too slow or too late javelin withdrawal and its causes (see below.), • Coordination problems while running sideways with withdrawn javelin and its causes (see below).	✔ Reduction of the length of the cyclic part of the run-up or performing it at a lower velocity. ✔ Practising the smooth transition between the parts of the run-up using a flatter or less pronounced transitional jump through versatile imitations (394 and 395) and isolated javelin withdrawals (396). ✔ See corrections of too slow or too late withdrawal of the javelin and coordination problems while running sideways with withdrawn javelin.
Too slow or too late withdrawal of the javelin.	• Insufficient stride rhythm. • Automation of an incorrect movement pattern with respect to the timing of the javelin withdrawal during the 5-stride rhythm. • Coordination problems while running sideways with withdrawn javelin and its causes (see below).	✔ Possible introduction of a transitional jump. ✔ Focusing on the correct timing as a topic of discussion, imitation (396), and practice (397): withdrawal of the javelin during the first two strides; the athlete must reach the lateral position of his/her shoulder and the stretched back position of his/her arm during the third stride of the 5-stride rhythm at the latest. ✔ See corrections of coordination problems while running sideways with withdrawn javelin.

Error	Causes	Corrections
Coordination problems while running sideways with withdrawn javelin (e.g., shoulder axis not in running direction, feet square to the running direction, rather sideways galloping than crossover strides, unfavourable direction of view, etc.).	• Insufficient automation of the unnatural running posture with twisted body during the acyclic part of the run-up, with both feet as well as the view and the shoulder axis pointing in the direction of the run. • Exercises such as sideways galloping (83) and lateral crossover strides (388) are too often performed with the feet square to the movement direction.	✔ Crossover and impulse-stride series (395) with deliberately pulling foot touchdowns, as well as with correct foot, shoulder, arm, head, and javelin position. ✔ The exercises of the ABCs of sprinting/running/jumping (83 and 388) should be performed with the feet square to the running direction as well as specific to the javelin with the feet in the running direction.
Too high impulse stride (in combination with loss of horizontal velocity during the push-off into the impulse stride and touchdown of the pressure leg).	• Too high run-up velocity (the thrower uses the impulse stride for slowing down). • Beginners deliberately perform a (high) jump. • The swing leg (which subsequently becomes the pressure leg) is lifted too high during the push-off into the impulse stride. • The thrower wants to perform a too long impulse stride.	✔ Focusing on the objective of maintaining a maximal horizontal velocity until the bracing leg is placed on the ground. ✔ Practising and imitation of an active, flat push-off with flat swing-leg movement over a not too broad ditch using a 3- or 5-stride rhythm or a full run-up (389, 390, 394, 395, and 397).
Insufficient backward lean of the trunk upon touchdown of the pressure leg.	• Due to a too short impulse stride there is not enough time for the legs to overtake the trunk. • The intended angle of delivery is too small; often in combination with the direction of view too much downward (to the landing point). • Too early release activity (forward movement of the throwing shoulder); usually caused by insufficient effort of the thrower to achieve a long path of acceleration after the touchdown of the pressure leg.	✔ Slow imitations (394) during which the throwing hand is held back by a partner or an elastic rope. ✔ Faster imitations (394) and throws (389, 390, and 397) with impulse stride over a ditch and deliberate taking of an appropriate backward lean. ✔ Focusing on an optimal angle of delivery and checking whether it is achieved by the athlete; through target throws (e.g., with a ball into a defined area on a wall) and appropriate orientation point to look at (also in the javelin throw area). ✔ Focusing on the importance of a late acceleration of the javelin on a long path as a topic of discussion.

(continued)

(continued)

Error	Causes	Corrections
Too much backward lean of the trunk upon touchdown of the pressure leg.	• Too high (or too long) impulse stride and its causes (see above). • The intended angle of delivery is too large; often in combination with the direction of view too much upward. • Insufficient effort of the thrower to continue the fast action of his/her pressure leg.	✔ Rapid and flat impulse strides series (395) with less backward lean of the trunk. ✔ Imitations (394) and throws (389, 390, and 397) with deliberate checking of the backward lean and fast and active continuation of the action of the pressure leg leading to the touchdown of the bracing leg. ✔ Focusing on an optimal angle of delivery and checking whether it is achieved by the athlete; through target throws (e.g., with a ball into a defined area on a wall) and appropriate orientation point to look at (also in the javelin throw area).
At the beginning of the delivery movement, the throwing hand is (clearly) below shoulder height. (If there is an additional bending of the wrist, the tail of the javelin touches the ground.) (The opposite error, raising the throwing hand too high is very rare.)	• Too low throwing hand after the withdrawal of the javelin. • Too much backward lean of the trunk upon touchdown of the pressure leg and its causes (see above). • If the thrower demonstrates a too slow or decelerating run-up, a clear falling movement of the hand, and a delayed action of the pressure leg, then he/she wants to perform a wide backswing to perform a particularly powerful delivery.	✔ Run-up imitations, crossover and impulse-stride series (394 and 395) with the correct carrying of the javelin. ✔ See corrections of too much backward lean of the trunk upon touchdown of the pressure leg. ✔ Delivery imitations (393) with the correct movement path of the hand. ✔ Throws from an accelerated 3-, 5-, 7-stride rhythm and finally with full run-up (389, 390, and 397) with high hand, and appropriate orientation point to look at and continuation of the fast action of the pressure leg. ✔ Throw rather fast than powerful.

Error	Causes	Corrections
Upon touchdown of the pressure leg, the shoulder axis does not point in the direction of the throw and/ or insufficient extension of the elbow of the throwing arm upon touchdown of the pressure leg.	• Too slow or too late withdrawal of the javelin and its causes (see above). • Insufficient effort of the thrower to achieve a long path of acceleration during the delivery movement (no active withdrawal of the throwing hand). • Insufficient forward movement (closing) of the opposite arm. • Anticipation of the delivery movement: The thrower initiates the rotation of his/ her shoulder axis (opening) too early. • Coordination problems while running sideways with withdrawn javelin and their causes (see above).	✔ See corrections of too slow or too late withdrawal of the javelin. ✔ Focusing on the importance of a long path of acceleration as a topic of discussion. ✔ Illustration of the correct positions of the throwing arm through slow run-up and delivery imitations (393 and 394): holding back the throwing hand by a partner or an elastic rope. ✔ Run-up imitations (394) including the backward reclining position of delivery with correct movement of the opposite arm (stay closed, opposite shoulder to chin). ✔ Subsequently, throws with increasing run-up velocity (389–390 and 397) and focus on correct arm and shoulder positions. ✔ See corrections of coordination problems while running sideways with withdrawn javelin.
Passive action of the pressure leg.	• Touchdown of the pressure-leg foot square to the running direction (more than 45° to the running direction); due to coordination problems while running sideways with withdrawn javelin and their causes (see above), the previous foot touchdowns are usually also turned too much to the side. • The pressure-leg knee is too straight at the moment of touchdown. • Too high run-up velocity.	✔ Delivery and run-up imitations (393 and 394), first by focusing on the correct action of the pressure leg; then the correct action of the pressure leg is integrated into the entire movement process which is performed at increasingly faster velocity. ✔ Throws from the 3-, 5-, 7-stride rhythm and finally with full run-up (389, 390, and 397) while focusing on correct foot touchdowns, appropriate run-up velocity and active action of the pressure leg. ✔ See corrections of coordination problems while running sideways with withdrawn javelin.
Flight phase during the bracing stride (only with beginners).	• Too high movement of the bracing leg. • Too long bracing stride. • Insufficient effort of the thrower to continue the fast action of the pressure leg against the bracing leg.	✔ Standing throws (386) and throws with placement of the bracing leg (387), throws with correct pressure and bracing leg action. ✔ Throws from the 3- and 5-stride rhythm (389 and 390) with fast placement of the bracing leg.

(continued)

(continued)

Error	Causes	Corrections
Insufficient holding back of the throwing hand upon touchdown of the bracing leg.	• Insufficient flexibility of the shoulder joint. • Insufficient extension of the elbow of the throwing arm upon touchdown of the pressure leg and its causes (see above).	✔ Flexibility training of the shoulder muscles (21 and 392). ✔ Many standing throws and throws with a short run-up with deliberate holding back of the throwing hand (late acceleration of the javelin). ✔ See corrections of insufficient extension of the elbow of the throwing arm upon touchdown of the pressure leg.
Insufficient action of the bracing leg (insufficient bracing effect).	• Too large bracing angle (between the leg and the horizontal) due to a too short bracing stride. • Too much yielding at the knee joint of the bracing leg due to too small bracing angle and too long bracing stride. • Touchdown of the bracing leg with the ball of the foot or with bent knee. • Insufficient extension force in the bracing leg. • Too high run-up velocity. • Insufficient backward lean of the trunk upon touchdown of the pressure leg and its causes (see above).	✔ Imitations of correct bracing leg action (393 and 394) as well as practising throws with increasing run-up velocity (387, 389, 390, and 397). ✔ Maximal- and reactive-strength training for the bracing leg using exercises 49, 62–64, 69, 82, and 84–92, or pop-up jumps (368) and long jump with the bracing leg as take-off leg. ✔ See corrections of insufficient backward lean of the trunk upon touchdown of the pressure leg.
Insufficient bow tension.	• Passive action of the pressure leg and its causes (see above). • Insufficient action of the bracing leg and its causes (see above). • Insufficient holding back of the throwing hand and its causes (see above).	✔ See corrections of passive action of the pressure leg, insufficient action of the bracing leg, and insufficient holding back of the throwing hand.
Too low path of the throwing hand (the frequent result is a very arched path of acceleration around the outside, may lead to overstrain symptoms at the elbow joint, etc.).	• The elbow is not brought forward and upward and the throwing arm is not rotated inward (during the delivery movement the elbow is sometimes moved below shoulder height).	✔ Delivery imitations (393) from pressure-leg action to bow tension, with correct path of the elbow and hand of the throwing arm, against the resistance of a partner or an elastic rope. ✔ Subsequently, throws with correct path of the hand and increasing run-up velocity (386, 387, 389, 390, and 397).
Insufficient slinging action of the forearm (insufficient final acceleration of the javelin).	• Too low path of the throwing hand and its causes (see above). • Too early release due to an incorrect technique of gripping the javelin. • Insufficient (reactive) strength of the elbow extensors.	✔ See corrections of too low path of the throwing hand. ✔ Check of the gripping technique. ✔ Frontal throws (385) with emphasis on the slinging action of the forearm. ✔ Strength training for the triceps brachii using exercises 38, 39, 54, 56, 57, and 391.

Error	Causes	Corrections
Considerable evasive movements which can be seen from the rear (e.g., running path of the last strides; forward or backward lean of the trunk during the preparation of the delivery or during the delivery itself).	• Insufficient effort of the thrower to achieve a straight-line delivery movement.	✔ Throws from a standing position and from the 3- or 5-stride rhythm (386, 387, 389, and 390) along the wall, with the wall being alternately at the side of the bracing and pressure leg.
Too steep angle of delivery.	• Insufficient forward acceleration of the trunk, elbow, and hand. • Too much backward lean of the trunk upon touchdown of the pressure leg and its causes (see above). • At the beginning of the delivery movement, the throwing hand is below shoulder height and its causes (see above).	✔ Imitations (393 and 394) and throws with increasing run-up velocity (386, 387, 389, 390, and 397), focusing on a more noticeable forward acceleration of the shoulders, elbow, and hand. ✔ Ball throws toward a low target on a wall, as well as javelin throws toward targets on the ground. ✔ See corrections of too much backward lean of the trunk upon touchdown. ✔ See corrections of at the beginning of the delivery movement, the throwing hand is below shoulder height.
Too flat angle of delivery.	• Too much effort to achieve a high velocity of departure to the disadvantage of the angle of departure (too much forward bending of the trunk). • Insufficient backward lean of the trunk upon touchdown of the pressure leg and its causes (see above). • Too low path of the throwing hand and its causes (see above).	✔ Throws toward high targets or over height markers. ✔ See corrections of insufficient backward lean of the trunk upon touchdown of the pressure leg. ✔ See corrections of too low path of the throwing hand.
Too steep angle of attitude. (The opposite error, a too flat angle of attitude, is very rare.)	• The tip of the javelin is moved away from the temple too early due to a bending of the wrist and/or throwing below the point (the path of the point of grip is below the path of the centre of mass of the javelin) which is caused by a too low path of the throwing hand and its causes (see above).	✔ Throws while focusing on keeping the tip of the javelin at eye level for a very long time; as an over-correction, the tip of the javelin should initially be held at the height of the mouth or chin. ✔ Demonstration of video freeze frames since throwers frequently do not notice the early evasion of the tip of the javelin. ✔ See corrections of too low path of the throwing hand.

(continued)

(continued)

Error	Causes	Corrections
The javelin lands on the side of the throwing hand outside the landing sector (since/and/or the angle of tilt is too large). (The opposite error is very rare.)	• Too much over-rotation during the acyclic part of the run-up. • The tip of the javelin is not held close to the temple but at a lateral distance from it. • Not enough freedom of the throwing side, in combination with lateral delivery movement (see also too low path of the throwing hand).	✔ Throws along a wall for emphasising the straightness of the throwing movement. ✔ Run-up imitations (394), as well as crossover and impulse-stride series (395) with the tip of the javelin held close to the temple and with less over-rotation. ✔ Delivery imitations (393) with useful freedom of the throwing side and high path of the throwing hand against the resistance of a partner or an elastic rope; subsequently, corresponding throws with increasing run-up velocity (386, 387, 389, 390, and 397).
Stepping over the scratch line after the delivery.	• The point of delivery is too close to the scratch line due to » incorrect run-up marker (the distance to the scratch line is too short); or » higher run-up velocity and longer strides in competition due to excessive motivation. • Insufficient action of the bracing leg and its causes (see above). • Lack of concentration during the recovery movement, possibly due to too frequent practice throws with running through. • Beginners sometimes extend the run-up unknowingly by two strides.	✔ Moving the marker back. ✔ If the athlete's run-up velocity is too high, he/she should be instructed to start the run-up in a relaxed manner. ✔ See corrections of insufficient action of the bracing leg. ✔ Even during practice, stepping over the scratch line should be forbidden or even punished more often by having the athlete perform additional tasks (e.g., retrieval of the javelins of all training partners). ✔ Verbal accompaniment of the run-up rhythm by a partner, intermediate markers (e.g., hoops or similar devices for each ground contact), or instructing the athlete to count his/her strides better.
Waste of run-up distance upon delivery (the recovery movement is finished clearly in front of the throwing arc).	• Incorrect run-up marker (too far away from the scratch line). • Too short strides due to too slow run-up velocity. • Insufficient propelling of the body across the bracing leg due to » too slow run-up velocity; or » passive action of the pressure leg and its causes (see above). • Beginners sometimes shorten the run-up unknowingly by two strides.	✔ Moving the marker forward. ✔ Increasing the run-up velocity. ✔ Throws with increasing run-up length and velocity (389, 390, and 397), by actively moving the body over the bracing leg. ✔ Verbal accompaniment of the run-up rhythm by a partner, intermediate markers (e.g., hoops or similar devices for each ground contact), or instructing the athlete to count his/her strides better.

3.2.10 TRAINING PLANNING

The training planning for throwers is done in accordance with recommendations in the general part of this book (see chapter I-3.3). In particular, the training plans suggested here are based on the training plans for children's athletics and basic training presented in chapter I-3.3.

AMOUNT OF TRAINING AND INTENSITY

As the age of the athlete increases, the training frequency also increases and the individual training sessions become longer. For the build-up training of a 17-year-old, six training sessions per week are assumed. To ensure that the individual sessions are not too long and certain training modules can be performed with the athlete as rested and focused as possible, ten training sessions per microcycle (= week) are suggested for the first two mesocycles of high-performance training. Since one day remains completely free for regeneration (usually Sunday) as in build-up training, the athlete performs two daily sessions on four days of the week. In high-performance training, especially in the first mesocycles, the amount of training performed within individual training modules (e.g., in strength training) tends to be greater than during build-up training.

In the third and fourth mesocycles of high-performance training, there is not only a reduction in the amount of training within individual workouts and training modules, but training frequency is also reduced. The main reason for this is the very high intensity which javelin throwers want to

Table 13: _Training emphasis in the various mesocycles_ for javelin-throw practice in build-up and high-performance training.

1st mesocycle	basic aerobic and anaerobic endurance training; strength-endurance, hypertrophy-oriented maximal-strength, speed-strength, and reactive-strength training (also using a heavy throwing implement); flexibility training; general (sprinting, hurdling, jumping, games, etc.), and javelin-specific (short- to medium-length run-ups) coordination training
2nd mesocycle	(speed-)endurance training; hypertrophy-, IC- and connective-tissue-oriented maximal-strength, speed-strength, and reactive-strength training (also using a heavy throwing implement); speed training (sprint and specific using a light device); flexibility training; general (sprinting, hurdling, jumping, games, etc.), and javelin-specific coordination training (short to long run-ups)
3rd mesocycle	IC- and connective-tissue-oriented maximal-strength, speed-strength, and reactive-strength training; speed training (sprint and specific using a light device); technique training (medium to long run-ups); maintenance stimuli
4th mesocycle	competitions and corresponding regeneration; IC- and connective-tissue-oriented maximal-, speed- and reactive-strength training; sprinting-speed training; technique training (primarily long run-ups); maintenance stimuli

achieve which is only possible in a rested state. During a week with a competition (in the fourth mesocycle), there is even less training than during the third mesocycle, both in build-up and high-performance training. A model microcycle in the competition period will be described in the discus throw chapter (see chapter II–3.3.10).

DIFFERENCES BETWEEN BUILD-UP AND HIGH-PERFORMANCE TRAINING IN TERMS OF CONTENTS

The training plan for high-performance athletes is based on the assumption that specialisation in the javelin throw is completed. Young javelin throwers in build-up training should certainly still be able to also participate in combined-event competitions. The training plan presented includes (apart from the other throwing events and the hurdles) in particular the high jump as a general content. Due to many similarities in terms of movement structure (organisation of the final strides, bracing action, etc.), there are many synergies between the high jump and the javelin throw, so that young athletes often achieve similarly good results in both disciplines. In high-performance training, these general contents are reduced in favour of more extensive and also intensive strength training. The strength training for the trunk is already relatively extensive in build-up training.

DIFFERENCES TO THE SHOT PUT AS WELL AS THE DISCUS AND HAMMER THROW

Unlike shot putters, and discus and hammer throwers, most javelin throwers cannot withstand more than two pure technique sessions per week even during the phases of the most extensive technique training due to the great stress on the throwing arm. However, young javelin throwers often specialise somewhat earlier, whereas shot putters and discus throwers in particular often compete in both disciplines for a longer time. In the training plans presented below, the great importance of speed and reactive strength for javelin throwers (in high-performance training) is expressed for example through

- reduced training frequency in the third mesocycle (see chapter II–3.3.10),
- reduced amount of muscle build-up training particularly in the third mesocycle, and
- increased amount of jumping and sprinting loads.

SINGLE OR DOUBLE PERIODISATION?

For reasons of better comparability, the training plans presented for the throwing events are based on double periodisation. In fact, in the long throws (javelin, discus, and hammer throw), there is often either no winter competition period at all or the winter competition period is of significantly less importance.

SUGGESTED TRAINING PLANS

Below, there are exemplary microcycles for the

- second mesocycle of a 17-year-old athlete in build-up training (table 14);
- first mesocycle of an athlete in high-performance training (table 15); and the
- third mesocycle of an athlete in high-performance training (table 16).

The exemplary microcycles presented in connection with the discus and hammer throws (see chapters II–3.3.10 and II–3.5.10) for the

- first mesocycle of a 17-year-old athlete in build-up training; and the
- third mesocycle of a 17-year-old athlete in build-up training

may be used for further orientation taking into account the statements made above. Similar aspects apply to the exemplary microcyles presented in connection with the discus throw for the

- second mesocycle of an athlete in high-performance training; and the
- fourth mesocycle of an athlete in high-performance training.

Table 14: Build-up training: sample microcycle for a 17-year-old athlete in the second mesocycle.

Monday	Tuesday	Wednesday	Thursday	Friday	Saturday	Sunday
Trunk stabilisation exercises and abdominal crunches (20 min) with a lot of dynamic variation	**LI runs** (6 x 80m, rest intervals: 20 sec) for warming up	**Foot strengthening** (10 min) e.g., versatile small jumps on gym mats	**Warm-up jogging** (6 min) including circling of the (fore) arms, etc.	**Warm-up jogging** (6 min) including backward and sideways running, etc.	**Warm-up jogging** (6 min) including picking up, carrying, and forward throwing of a ball	Rest
Warm-up specific to the javelin throw (20 min) e.g., arm circling, javelin mobilisation, and relaxed ball throws against a wall	**ABCs of sprinting/jumping** (12–15 run-throughs) heel kicks, high-knee run, lateral crossover strides, galloping sideways, skipping, etc.	**Practising the shot-put, discus-throw, or hammer-throw technique** (50 min) alternately each week; including specific warm-up	**Game** (30 min) e.g., handball, hockey, or tennis	**Warm-up specific to the javelin throw** (10 min) e.g., arm circling, ball throws, and (delivery) imitations (against resistance)	**ABCs of sprinting/jumping/hurdling** (15–20 run-throughs)	
Practising the javelin-throw technique (30 min) throws with medium-length run-ups, imitation of the competition run-up	**Acceleration runs** (3 reps)	**Medicine-ball throws** (30 min) e.g., goalkeeper throws, rotational throws, throws from a prone position, tossing, and overhead throws	**Contract-relax stretching** (15 min)	**Practising the javelin-throw technique** (40 min) short and medium run-up lengths, with different balls and javelins, bilateral practice	**Acceleration runs** (2 reps)	
Strength training (40 min) according to the pyramid principle: snatch, flies, reverse flies, pull-overs, lat pull with underhand grip	**Practising the high-jump technique** (30 min) scissors and flop jumps with medium and long run-up, bilateral practice	**Strength training** (25 min) according to the pyramid principle: clean and full squats	**Gymnastics** (30 min) versatile rotational movements depending on the athlete's level of skill	**Muscle build-up training** (50 min) for arms and legs on apparatus	**Hurdle Zs** (2 sets of 4 Zs each of 2 run-throughs over 4 low hurdles each; rest intervals: 3 min; rest intervals between sets: 10 min) out at 3-stride rhythm with the weak side, back with the strong side	
Ball throws (10 reps) light ball	**Technique sprints** (2 x 4 x 60m) sprints with additional tasks such as varied arm actions, alternating-pace sprints, pre-set stride lengths, etc.	**Acceleration runs** (4 x 60m)	**Muscle build-up training** (30 min) abdominal machine, shoulder-hip twists, lumborum, hip/back extensors using a big box	**Foot strengthening** (10 min) in the sand	**Contract-relax stretching** (15 min)	
			Skipping and bounding runs (4 x 30m each)	**Versatile throws** (10–20 reps) discus, (medicine) ball, stick, etc.	**Warm-down jogging** (10 diagonals on the lawn)	
					Skipping with two-legged landing (4 x 20m)	

862

Table 15: High-performance training: sample microcycle in the first mesocycle using double periodisation.

	Monday	Tuesday	Wednesday	Thursday	Friday	Saturday	Sunday
Morning	Trunk stabilisation exercises and abdominal crunches (20 min) Warm-up specific to the javelin throw (20 min) Practising the javelin-throw technique (50 min) short to medium run-up lengths, normal and heavy javelin	Warm-up jogging (15 min) with additional tasks ABCs of jumping and ABCs of javelin (15–20 run-throughs) e.g., sideways galloping, crossover strides, and impulse strides Pop-up jumps and bounding runs (2x 5 x 30 m) Alternating-pace sprints (4 x 60m)	Rope jumping (5 min) Medicine-ball work (45 min) e.g., overhead throws from a sitting position, (one-legged) knee-stand position, standing position, and with run-up; goalkeeper throws; chest pass; rotational throws; throws from a prone position; and tossing	Continuous run (30 min) Contract-relax stretching (15 min) Walking and skipping over hurdles and gymnastics (30 min) versatile combinations, rotations about all body axes	Warm-up jogging (6 min) Warm-up specific to the javelin throw (10 min) Practising the javelin-throw technique (60 min) e.g., differential learning; from a standing position, with short and medium run-up; normal and light balls and javelins	Warm-up jogging (6 min) including arm circling, backward and sideways running, rotations, etc. ABCs of sprinting (12–15 run-throughs) Muscle build-up training (30 min) step-ups and dead-lifts Acceleration runs (3 reps)	Rest
Afternoon	Foot strengthening (10 min) little jumps Game (30 min) e.g., handball Contract-relax stretching (15 min) Muscle build-up training (30 min) e.g., pull-overs, bench press, and lat pull Handball throws (3 x 10 reps per side)	Warm-up jogging (6 min) Acceleration runs (3 reps) I3 uphill runs (2 x 4 x 100m; rest intervals: 4–5 min) Muscle build-up training (60 min) hamstrings, quadriceps, adductors and abductors, clean, and lunges Ankle jumps (3 x 6 reps)	Muscle build-up training (50 min) e.g., shoulder press, flies, reverse flies, pull-overs Ball throws (3 x 6 reps per side) light weight, against a wall	Warm-up jogging (6 min) Acceleration runs (3 reps) Strength-endurance circle (60 min) including full squat, jumps onto a box, ABCs of sprinting/jumping, and many trunk-strengthening exercises Skipping with two-legged landing (3 x 20m) as utilisation	Warm-up jogging (6 min) Technique sprints (6 x 60m) pre-set stride lengths Foot strengthening (15 min) in the sand Speed-strength-endurance training (50 min) arms: light weight, rapid movement reversals, many exercises; also javelin strength-training device	LI tempo runs (3 x 4 x 150m; rest intervals: 1.5–2 min; rest intervals between sets: 6–8 min) Contract-relax stretching (15 min) Warm-down jogging (10 diagonals on the lawn) Ankle jumps (3 x 6 reps)	

863

Table 16: High-performance training: sample microcycle in the third mesocycle using double periodisation.

	Monday	Tuesday	Wednesday	Thursday	Friday	Saturday	Sunday
Morning	Morning: **Foot strengthening** (10 min) **Maximal-eccentric strength training** (15 min) trunk and foot **Practising the javelin-throw technique** (60 min) including specific warm-up, imitations, throws from medium and long run-ups with the competition javelin	**LI runs** (8 x 60m, rest intervals: 15 sec) for warming up **ABCs of sprinting** (8–10 run-throughs) **Standing starts** (4 x 30m) at maximum intensity **Strength training** (40 min) according to the pyramid principle: e.g., hamstrings, quadriceps, adductors and abductors, calves, and snatch (starting position of the barbell: at the hips) with jump into the lunge position **Imitations** of the competition run-up and **ball throws** (15 min) from a standing position; as utilisation	**Warm-up jogging** (15 min) including arm circling, backward and sideways running, rotations, etc. **Strength training** (40 min) according to the pyramid principle: e.g., abdominal machine, shoulder-hip twists, lumborum, hip/back extensors, and rockbacks	**Warm-up jogging** (6 min) **ABCs of jumping** (8–10 run-throughs) **Tuck jumps** (5 x 5 hurdles) **Bounding runs** (2 x 2 x 20m) **Practising the javelin-throw technique** (60 min) warm-up, medium and short run-ups, light and normal javelin	**Warm-up jogging** (6 min) **Medicine-ball work** (45 min) reactive overhead throws from a sitting position, overhead throws with run-up, goalkeeper throws, chest pass, rotational throws, throws from a prone position, and tossing **Strength training** (50 min) according to the pyramid principle: e.g., pull-overs, bench press, and lat-pull, flies, and reverse flies **Ball throws** (3 x 5 per side)	**LI runs** (8 x 60m) **Contract-relax stretching** (15 min) specific to the javelin **ABCs of sprinting and ABCs of javelin** (12–15 run-throughs) **Depth jumps** (5 x 10 reps) **Crouch starts** (30, 20, and 10m) and **pull-resisted sprints** (30, 20, and 10m) alternately; high pulling load **High-intensity strength training** (30 min) snatch and split squat **Pop-up jumps** (2 x 2 x 30m per side)	Rest
Afternoon	**Warm-up jogging** (6 min) **ABCs of jumping** (8–10 run-throughs) **Depth jumps** (5 x 10 reps) **Pop-up jumps** (2 x 2 x 30m per side) **High-intensity strength training** (40 min) reactive pull-overs, reactive bench press, etc. **Handball throws**		**Acceleration runs** (3 reps) **12 tempo runs** (80, 120, 150, 120, and 80m; rest intervals: 8, 12, 15, and 12 min)	**Warm-up jogging** (6 min) **Skipping over hurdles** (15 min) **Rhythm sprints** (5 x 40m) at maximum intensity, over mini-hurdles **Strength training** (30 min) according to the pyramid principle: clean (from the ground) and ¼ squat **Skipping with two-legged landing** (3 x 20m)			

3.2.11 BIBLIOGRAPHY

Adamczewski, H. (1995). Untersuchungen am Messplatz Speerwurf. *Die Lehre der Leichtathletik 34* (17), 97-100, (18), 101-104 & (19) 105-108.

Adamczewski, H. & Perlt, B. (2003). Zu ausgewählten Problemen der Technik im Speerwurf von Spezialisten und Mehrkämpfern. *Zeitschrift für angewandte Trainingswissenschaft 10* (2), 44-74.

Bartonietz, K. (2008). Nach der Wurfsaison ist vor der Wurfsaison. *Leichtathletiktraining 19* (2+3), 32-39.

Bartonietz, K. (2009). Unterschiedliche Geräte zum Fliegen bringen. *Leichtathletiktraining 20* (5), 4-11

Bergström, A. (2000). The development of the javelin. *New Studies in Athletics 15* (3/4), 25-28.

Böttcher, J & Kühl, L. (1996). Untersuchungen zum Speerwurf. *Die Lehre der Leichtathletik 35* (31), 81-82, (32), 84-85 & (33) 86-88.

Böttcher, J & Kühl, L. (1998). The technique of the best female javelin throwers in 1997. *New Studies in Athletics 13* (1), 47-61.

Brunner, F., Morris, C., Bartlett, R., Müller, E. & Lindinger, S. (1996). Three-dimensional evaluation of the kinematic release parameters of javelin throwers of different skill levels. *Journal of applied biomechanics 12* (1), 58-71.

Campos, J., Brizuela, V. & Ramon, V. (2004). Three-dimensional kinematic analysis of elite javelin throwers at the 1999 IAAF World Championships in Athletics. *New Studies in Athletics 19* (2), 47-57.

Harnes, E. (1985). *Speerwurftraining im Nachwuchsbereich.* Unveröffentlichtes Manuskript.

Kühl, L. & Hommel, H. (Red.) (mit Bartonietz, K., Becker, M., Becker, S., Böttcher, G., Deyle, M., Gaede, E., Hartmann, W., Losch, M., Rapp, E., Thomas, B., Wollbrück, R. & Zöllkau, H.). (1997). *Rahmentrainingsplan für das Aufbautraining Wurf* (Edition Leichtathletik, 5, 3. Aufl.). Aachen: Meyer & Meyer.

Lehmann, F. (2005). Zum technikorientierten Krafttraining in den leichtathletischen Wurfdisziplinen am Beispiel des Speerwurfs. *Zeitschrift für angewandte Trainingswissenschaften 12* (1), 28-38.

Lehmann, F. (2010). Javelin Throw. In Deutscher Leichtathletikverband (Hrsg.), *Biomechanical Analysis of selected events at the 12th IAAF World Championships in*

Track & Field

Athletics, Berlin 15-23 August 2009. Zugriff am 20.04.2010 unter http://www.iaaf. org/mm/Document/Development/research/05/64/50/20100415080101_ httppostedfile_8-BiomechanicsReportWCBerlin2009_Throws_19909.pdf.

Morriss, C. & Bartlett, R. (1996). Biomechanical factors critical for performance in the men's javelin throw. *Sports medicine 21* (6), 438-446.

Morriss, C., Bartlett, R. & Fowler, N. (1997). Biomechanical analysis of the men's javelin throw at the 1995 World Championships in Athletic. *New Studies in Athletics 12* (2-3), 31-41.

Murakami, M., Tanabe, S., Ishikawa, M., Isolehto, J., Komi, P. V. & Ita, A. (2006). Biomechanical analysis of the javelin at the 2005 IAAF World Championships in Athletics. *New Studies in Athletics 21* (2), 67-80.

Regelkommissionen des DLV, FLA, ÖLV und SLV (Hrsg.). (2010). *Internationale Wettkampfregeln.* Waldfischbach: Hornberger.

Salo, A. & Viitasalo, J. T. (1995) Vergleich kinematischer Merkmale des Speerwurfs bei Werfern internationalen und nationalen Niveaus und bei Zehnkämpfern. *Leistungssport 25* (5), 40-44.

Wank, V., Falck, O. & Friedrichs, A. (1996). Leistungsdiagnostik im Speerwurf – Zur Relevanz ausgewählter Parameter. In A. Gollhofer, *Integrative Forschungsansätze in der Bio & Mechanik: 3. Symposium der dvs-Sektion Biomechanik vom 6.-8.4.1995 in Herzogenhorn/Schwarzwald* (S. 287-296). St. Augustin: Academia.

Wank, V. (2006). Biomechanik und leistungsrelevante Parameter der leichtathletischen Wurfdisziplinen. In K. Wohlgefahrt & S. Michel, *Beiträge zur speziellen Trainingswissenschaft Leichtathletik: Symposium der dvs-Kommission Leichtathletik vom 10.-11.10.2002 in Bad Blankenburg* (Schriften der Deutschen Vereinigung für Sportwissschaft, 153, S. 132-144). Hamburg: Czwalina.

3.3 DISCUS THROW

3.3.1 LONG DISCUS CAREERS

In the past, many discus throwers have been successful over a long period of time. It is not uncommon to find careers of 20 years in the top international range and peak performances achieved by athletes older than 30.

In Olympic history, the success of American Al Oerter is unique. He beat the world-record holder Fortune Gordien at the Olympic Games in Melbourne in 1956 and was Olympic champion for the first time although he was a rank outsider at 20 years of age. In 1960 in Rome, Oerter also remained calm and won against the new world-record holder Richard Babka (USA). In 1962, he set a world record for the first time by throwing 61.10m. Therefore, his third Olympic gold medal in 1964 in Tokyo was no surprise. However, his repeated success in Mexico City in 1968 was a sensation. He had already been written off as an old man and barely managed to qualify for the U.S. Olympic Team. Oerter's secret to success: great nerves, concentration, and few competitions for which he prepared in a calm and composed manner.

In the recent past, some German athletes have similarly long and successful careers: Lars Riedel, eighth in the all-time world list with 71.70m, was five-time world champion: four times in succession from 1991 to 1997, and in 2001. The triple world champion Franka Dietzsch was victorious in 1999, 2005, and 2007. Robert Harting, Olympic champion in 2012 and triple world champion of 2009, 2011, and 2013, was succeeded as Olympic champion by his brother Christoph in 2016.

The two current world-record holders also come from Germany. Since the discus throw is the throwing discipline in which the difference in weight between the women's throwing device and the men's device is the greatest in terms of percentage, the best throwing distance achieved by a woman is longer than that achieved by a man. East German athlete Gabriele Reinsch threw 76.80m in Neubrandenburg on 7 September 1988. Two years earlier, her compatriot Jürgen Schult threw almost 3 metres shorter (74.08m) also in Neubrandenburg. Jürgen Schult, who subsequently became the German national coach, also had a very long career. After he was world champion in 1987 and Olympic champion in 1988, he won a silver medal at the 1999 World Championships at the age of 39. Schult's world record is the oldest of men's Olympic athletics.

Before Schult, eight other athletes in addition to Al Oerter managed to establish more than three world records each: Jadwiga Waiss (Poland), Gisela Mauermayer, Liesel Westermann (both from Germany), Tamara Press, Faina

Melnik (both from the U.S.S.R.), and Fortune Gordien, Jay Silvester and Mac Williams (all from the U.S.A.). Some of these athletes also achieved long careers at the highest level. Jay Silvester's first and last world records were separated by seven years and eight metres, while there were five years and six metres between Faina Melnik's first and eleventh world record.

The origins of discus throwing are found in Greek antiquity. Beginning in 708 B.C., the discus throw was part of the Olympic pentathlon. The discuses weighed up to 5.7 kg, their diameter was up to 34cm, and they were often illustrated with religious drawings. It is therefore also assumed that they are of religious origin or were used for military purposes.

At the first modern Olympic Games in 1896, the discus was thrown from a 60 x 70cm large podium according to the ancient model. The throwing circle, which is common today, was used for the first time at the Olympic Games in 1920. Women have been participating in the discus throw since the 1928 Olympic Games.

3.3.2 THE MOST IMPORTANT COMPETITION RULES

The following abridged and simplified International Competition Rules comprise the framework for the technique and strategy, as well as the organisation of discus competitions:

- Figure 1 illustrates the design of a discus. In addition, table 1 describes the discuses to be used. The body of the discus may be solid or hollow and shall be made of wood, or other suitable materials. Circular plates are set flush into the centre of the sides. The diameter of these circular plates is from 5.0–5.7cm. At its outside, the discus must be provided with a circular metal rim, whose outer edge must be rounded in a true circular fashion having a radius of approximately 6mm. From the beginning of the curve of the metal rim, the thickness of the discus increases regularly up to the upper and lower circular plates. The upper and lower side of the discus must be identical; the discus must also be symmetrical in terms of rotation around the Y axis. Each side of the discus must be made without indentations, projections, or sharp edges.
- Figure 2 describes the layout of the discus (and hammer) throwing area. All discus throws must be made from a protective enclosure or cage to ensure the safety of spectators, officials, and all athletes in the stadium.
- It is not considered a failure if the discus strikes the cage after release provided that no other rule is infringed.

Otherwise, the general competition rules for technical disciplines and throwing apply (see chapters II–2.1.1 and II–3.1.1).

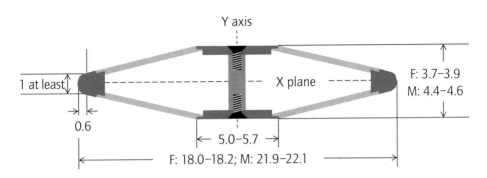

Figure 1: **Cross-sectional picture of a discus** *(M = men, F = women; all specifications in cm; modified on the basis of the Rule Commissions by the DLV, FLA, ÖLV and SLV, 2010, p. 111).*

Table 1: **Minimum weight, outer diameter, and thickness in the centre of the discuses** *for the different age groups in the German Athletics Federation (see Rule Commissions by the DLV, FLA, ÖLV and SLV, 2010, p. 112). The diameter of the flat upper and lower plates, as well as the thickness of the metal rim, measured 6 mm from the edge, are specified in more detail in the rules.*

Age groups		Weight, diameter, thickness
Female U14, male U14	w80 and older	**750 g,** 16.6–16.8cm, 3.3–3.5cm
Female U16, 18, and 20, male U16, women	w40–75, m60 and older	**1000 g,** 18.0–18.2cm, 3.7–3.9cm
Male U18	m50–55	**1500 g,** 20.0–20.2cm, 3.8–4.0cm
Male U20		**1750 g,** 21.0–21.2cm, 4.1–4.3cm
Men	m40–45	**2000 g,** 21.9–22.1cm, 4.4–4.6cm

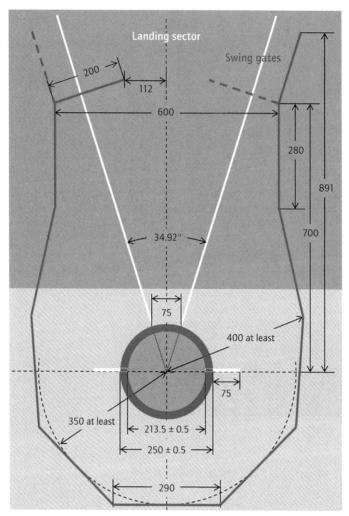

Figure 2: **Combined discus and hammer throw area with protective cage** *(all specifications in cm, modified on the basis of the Rule Commissions by the DLV, FLA, ÖLV and SLV, 2010, p. 118). For the discus throw, the blue coloured insert ring is removed. Swing gates are not necessary for the discus throw. If present, they are both fully open. The sector boundary lines and the two marker strips which are attached to the sides of the ring are 5cm wide.*

3.3.3 SPORT-SCIENCE FINDINGS, PHASE STRUCTURE, AND TECHNIQUE

The technique of throwing the discus used today is known as a throw from 1½ rotations. This description fits the thrower's pelvis best. When looking at the discus path in figure 3, two rotations can be identified. Between the end of the backswing and the release, the shoulders perform approximately 1¾ rotations. With

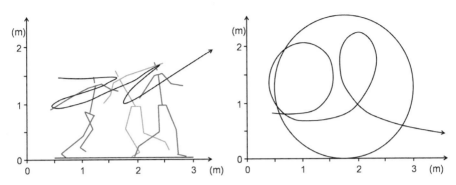

*Figure 3: **Trajectory of the discus** from the turning point at the end of the preliminary swings to the flight (modified on the basis of Wank, 2006, p. 139).*

respect to the connecting line between the feet there are only 1¼ rotations. Experiments with more rotations (1¾ or 2½) did not lead to an increase in throwing distance. Despite the longer total acceleration path, no higher velocity of departure was achieved.

This technique may be divided into the following four main phases:

- preliminary swing;
- turn;
- delivery motion; and
- recovery and flight of the discus.

PHASE 1: PRELIMINARY SWING

GRIPPING THE DISCUS
Figure 4 illustrates how the discus is gripped. The athlete's hand is located approximately in the middle of the discus. The outer sections of the long fingers (not the outer section of the thumb) hold the edge of the discus. The wrist is bent slightly inward (palmarflexed) to achieve a suitable angle of tilt upon release (see

phase 4). During the turn and the delivery motion, the thrower's hand is on the discus. This means that without the rotational movement of the thrower, the discus would fall out of his/her hand. The discus is not held between fingers and forearm. It is pressed against the outer sections of the fingers only by the centrifugal forces so that it remains in the thrower's hand.

STARTING POSITION
At the beginning of the throw, the athlete positions himself/herself in a kind of quarter squat (62) at the rear rim of the circle with his/her back square to the

*Figure 4: **Technique for gripping the discus:** The tilted position of the discus with hanging outside edge, which is important for an optimal delivery, is clearly visible.*

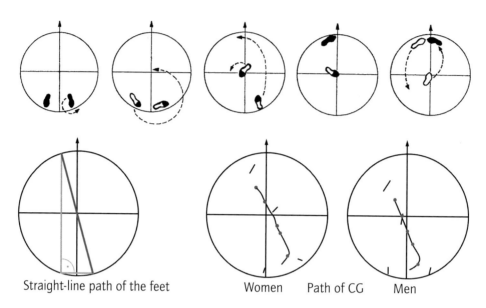

Straight-line path of the feet   Women   Path of CG   Men

*Figure 5: **Foot action and path of CG** (path of CG modified on the basis of Hay & Yu, 1996): According to the authors, the illustrated paths of the CG represent two typical examples. The blue dots indicate the transitions between the partial phases: end of the two-legged starting phase, the one-legged starting phase, the supportless phase, the one-legged delivery phase, and the two-legged delivery phase. It is noticeable that the male athlete does not fully exploit the ring.*

DISCOURSE I: ENTERING THE THROWING CIRCLE

According to Schult (2006), the technique of discus throwing already begins when entering the throwing circle. Once the athlete has focused outside of the circle, he/she steps forward in the direction of the rear circular edge using a regular stride rhythm. In the process, he/she deliberately shifts his/her weight to the respective foot touchdowns. His/her CG moves in serpentine lines. The trunk and limbs remain loose and follow the rhythmic movements of the legs. This deliberate entering of the throwing circle leads directly (i.e., without breaks and extra movements) to the preliminary swing (no repeated swinging movements). The rhythm of the weight shifts remains unchanged all the way from entering the circle, through the shift of weight to the leg on the side of the throwing hand during the preliminary swing, up to the shift of weight to the opposite leg during the two-legged starting phase.

direction of the throw. The athlete's feet, whose entire soles are placed on the ground, are slightly further apart than shoulder width. For less advanced athletes, a somewhat narrower foot position during the two-legged starting phase facilitates shifting the weight to the supporting leg of the one-legged starting phase. The wide starting position of advanced athletes results in a clearer shift of weight during the preliminary phase and the two-legged starting phase and subsequently to a wider circular swing of the free leg. In the starting position, the centre line of the throwing sector is either exactly between the legs or the leg on the side of the throwing hand is a little closer to it. Figure 5 illustrates the starting position and the subsequent foot movements. The knees are bent at an obtuse angle (>90°) and shifted slightly forward. The straight upper body is upright or slightly bent forward.

PRELIMINARY SWING
At approximately shoulder height, the discus is swung on a wide circular path against the subsequent direction of rotation behind the body (see figure 6). Right-handed throwers shift the greater part of their body weight to the right leg (see figure 7), which remains on the ground with the entire sole of the foot, while the left leg is rotated inward on the ball of the foot toward the right leg. While some throwers keep looking contrary to the throwing direction, others look backward up toward the left boundary line of the landing sector. Right-handers swing the discus with extended arm backward up to approximately above their left foot. Thus,

Figure 6: **Backswing movement.**

when viewed from above, the throwing arm is brought behind the shoulder axis (the axis running through both shoulder joints) which leads to a separation of this axis from the hip axis (axis through both hip joints). Subsequently, the thrower tries to hold his/her throwing hand behind his/her shoulder axis and the shoulder on the side of the throwing arm behind the hip on the side of the throwing arm. This is called trailing of the discus and separation of the shoulder and hip axis. To support both these movements, the opposite arm should meanwhile not be brought behind the shoulder axis, but it should remain approximately at shoulder height sideways in front of the body. However, the trailing and the shoulder-hip separation reach their greatest range of movement only at the beginning of the delivery movement (see phase 3).

To prevent the discus from falling out of his/her hand, the discus thrower opens his/her hand a little at approximately the point of reversal through an external rotation at the shoulder joint (see picture on the right in figure 6). During the subsequent turn, he/she closes his/her hand again by turning his/her hand back over the discus.

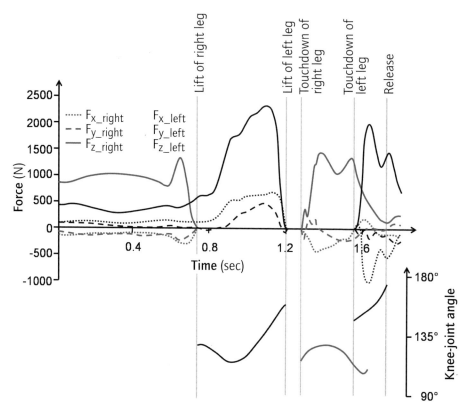

*Figure 7: **Ground reaction forces and knee angles of a top-level discus thrower performing a standing delivery**, with illustration of the transitions between the partial phases (simplified terminology for a right-hander; FX: horizontally in the throwing direction; FY: horizontally square to the throwing direction; FZ: vertically; modified on the basis of Dickwach & Knoll, 2003).*

PHASE 2: TURN

The turn may be divided into three partial phases:

- two-legged starting phase;
- one-legged starting phase; and
- supportless phase (leg reversal).

TWO-LEGGED STARTING PHASE

Right-handers start the turn by turning the left leg outward on the ball of the foot. The knee and foot are turned outward through an outward rotation at the knee and hip joint (see figures 5 and 8). By pushing himself/herself off with the right leg, the thrower shifts his/her weight to the left leg and initiates the rotation of the upper body which is counterclockwise when viewed from above. Figure 5 shows that in this process the CG is not completely moved to above the point of support of the left leg. However, coaches often ask their athletes to shift their weight more to the left leg. This is supposed to prevent an early falling into the centre of the circle and/or an excessive backward tilt to the left side of the ring (viewed in the direction of the throw). This also corresponds with the instruction that the start of the turn should be performed in a calm and controlled instead of in an overhasty manner. The CG is kept relatively low or is lowered somewhat. The right leg has completed its push-off when the left foot reaches a position square to the throwing direction and is lifted from the ground via the ball and the tip of the foot (see picture on the right in figure 8).

ONE-LEGGED STARTING PHASE

During the one-legged starting phase, the right-handed discus thrower continues his/her rotation on the ball of the left foot. After the thrower has tried to keep the right foot on the ground for a long time, it is now swung in a wide and flat circle around the supporting leg beyond the rim of the ring. However, some throwers also perform a lifting movement of the heel of the free leg. They bend their knee joint to about 90° so that the foot is lifted up to knee height. Such a lift of the heel is followed by a kicking motion of the lower leg (knee extension) during the push-off with the supporting leg. This kicking action of the free leg represents

a swing element (see chapter II–2.1.2) which supports the push-off in the throwing direction and the rotation. In no event should the thigh of the later pressure leg be raised up to the horizontal.

Approximately when the foot and knee of the supporting leg point in the throwing direction, the powerful push-off in the throwing direction begins (see figure 7 and middle picture in figure 9). In this process, the extension of the knee remains incomplete. The reasons for this are threefold:

- The incomplete extension of the knee results in a flat push-off so that the thrower does not first have to compensate for a high falling velocity after the leg reverse.
- It prevents a too wide leg reverse since there is only limited space available for the thrower in the 2.50m large circle. He/she must use this space optimally.
- In combination with the hip extension, the incomplete knee extension introduces a rotation about the transverse body axis. Viewed from the side, the legs subsequently overtake the upper body so that

*Figure 8: **Two-legged starting phase.***

*Figure 9: **One-legged starting phase.***

after the leg reverse the shoulders remain significantly behind. While the arm-trunk angle hardly changes, the increasing inclination of the body or longitudinal axis of the trunk is responsible for the more noticeable high-low movement of the discus during its second loop (see figure 3).

During the push-off from the rear rim of the circle, various trunk postures may be observed. Some athletes try to achieve an almost complete hip extension to hold back their shoulders during the leg reverse (see figure 10). The axis of rotation about the longitudinal axis then corresponds approximately to the longitudinal axis of the trunk. However, the position shown in the right picture of figure 10 may also be achieved with a significant bend of the hip and a forward lean of the trunk. Then, the axis of rotation deviates from the trunk axis in such a way that the shoulders are on the side of the axis of rotation opposite the pelvis.

SUPPORTLESS PHASE (LEG REVERSE)

The flight phase of the leg reverse is relatively short (about 0.06–0.08 sec, see also figure 7). Only very few world-class athletes work completely without a flight phase. During the leg reverse, the touchdown of the pressure leg and the subsequent rapid continuation of rotation are prepared by an extreme inward rotation of the foot and the entire pressure leg. At the moment of touchdown, the foot of the pressure leg should already point backward (see figure 5). In addition, the foot of the pressure leg, when viewed

from the side, is again moved toward the rear rim of the circle to reduce the braking forces upon touchdown. Due to the push-off from the rear rim of the circle, which should be as powerful as possible, and this active placement in the centre of the circle, some American authors also speak of sprinting through the circle. The objective is a touchdown with the ball of the foot approximately in the centre of the circle.

During the leg reverse, the staying behind of the shoulder against the throwing direction continues.The athlete rotates about a horizontal axis square to the direction of the throw. Accordingly, the pressure leg is placed down slightly in front of the vertical projection of the CG (see picture on the right in figure 10).

The rotation about the longitudinal axis of the body also continues. The rotational velocity increases when masses are shifted closer to the axis of rotation. Therefore, during the leg reverse and the first part of the one-legged delivery phase, the thrower tries to bring forward his/her bracing leg closely past the pressure leg (knee next to knee). Viewed from the side, the foot of the bracing leg overtakes the pressure

Figure 10: **Supportless phase** (leg reverse).

*Table 2: **Distance between the ground contacts of the feet during the leg reverse and during the backward reclining position of delivery** in four male top athletes (according to IAT Leipzig, quoted from Schult, 2008).*

Throwing distance achieved	65.93 ± 4.46m
Distance between the foot contacts of the leg reverse	1.21 ± 0.12m
Distance between the foot contacts during the backward reclining position of delivery	0.88 ± 0.14m

leg approximately when the pressure leg is placed on the ground. Some throwers also move their counterarm closer to the axis of rotation. In the process, the arm is moved against the direction of rotation to the front of the chest, constituting a counterrotation to the rotation of the lower part of the body and resulting in an increase in both the lower body's rotation in the direction of the throw and the shoulder-hip separation.

World-class discus throwers (n=6, performance: 66.34–68.86m) accelerate the discus up to the end of the one-legged starting phase to path velocities between 7.8 and 9.1 m/sec. There may subsequently be a slight reduction of path velocity before the start of the main acceleration phase of the delivery movement not only through air resistance and the braking forces during the touchdown subsequent to the leg reverse, but also through an active holding back of the throwing shoulder and hand. At this time, the initial velocity of the device is somewhat slower for women than for men (see table 3). Although a maximal initial velocity (pre-acceleration) is theoretically useful, this is not the case if, for example, the technically correct main acceleration, which should be as large as possible, is affected for example by the release of the shoulder-hip separation. Therefore, a large increase in velocity during the leg reverse or shortly afterwards is not useful.

PHASE 3: DELIVERY MOVEMENT

The delivery movement may be divided into two sub-phases:

- one-legged delivery phase; and
- two-legged delivery phase.

*Table 3: **Path velocities of the discus at the phase transitions and the changes of velocity within the sub-phases** for women (competition performance: 57.90 ± 7.51m) and men (59.07 ± 4.43m; simplified terminology for a right-hander; measurements in m/sec; Hay & Yu, 1995).*

	Upon lift of the right foot	Change	Upon lift of the left foot	Change	Upon touchdown of the right foot	Change	Upon touchdown of the left foot	Change	Upon release
Women (n = 15)	4.85 ± 1.26	2.18 ± 1.46	7.03 ± 0.78	-0.44 ± 1.52	6.59 ± 1.48	1.30 ± 1.15	7.89 ± 1.30	15.34 ± 1.39	23.22 ± 1.49
Men (n = 14)	5.09 ± 0.89	3.09 ± 1.09	8.18 ± 0.86	-0.63 ± 1.06	7.56 ± 0.77	0.08 ± 1.39	7.64 ± 1.63	16.16 ± 1.57	23.80 ± 0.99

Track & Field

ONE-LEGGED DELIVERY PHASE

After placing the ball of the pressure leg in the centre of the circle the thrower attempts to

Figure 11: **One-legged delivery:** *In the right picture, the athlete has achieved the backward reclining position of delivery.*

- place the bracing leg quickly and flatly onto the ground;
- still hold back his/her throwing hand and shoulder (trailing and shoulder-hip separation); and
- continue and accelerate the fast rotation of the foot, knee, and hip of his/her pressure leg on the ball of the foot in the direction of throwing. Placing the heel on the ground and sticking out the buttocks to the side of the ring should to be avoided.

With respect to the rotation and extension movement of the pressure leg, which is typical of the throws, it is striking that the knee angle of the pressure leg increases slightly only at the beginning (see figure 7). Contrary to what might be expected, it becomes smaller again before the touchdown of the bracing leg. Overall, the changes of the knee-joint angle in the pressure leg remain relatively slight (approx. 25°). The vertical ground reaction forces of the pressure leg, which are shown

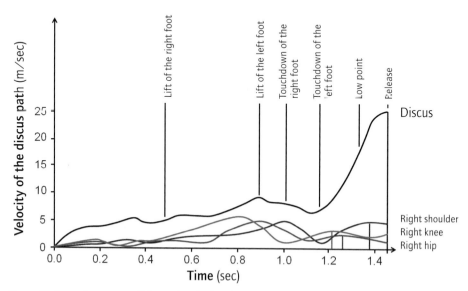

Figure 12: **Exemplary curve of the path velocity of the discus and certain points of the body** *in relation to the transitions between the partial phases (modified on the basis of Wank, 2006; simplified terminology for a right-hander): The kinematic chain which is explained in more detail in chapter II–3.1.2 is visible.*

*Table 4: **Percentage durations of the partial phases** (according to Schlüter & Nixdorf, 1984): 100% corresponds to the period from the turning point at the end of the preliminary swing until the moment when the discus leaves the hand.*

Two-legged starting phase	One-legged starting phase	Supportless phase	One-legged delivery phase	Two-legged delivery phase
40 %	29 %	6 %	13 %	12 %

in figure 7, hardly exceed the weight of this top athlete. In respect to the horizontal ground reaction forces, there is initially a slight development of force against the direction of the throw. Only shortly before the delivery, there is force development in the pressure leg in the direction of the landing sector which is, however, even slighter. All this might be due to the fact that the thrower should not push himself/ herself too far upward and forward if he/she wants to avoid falling forward or

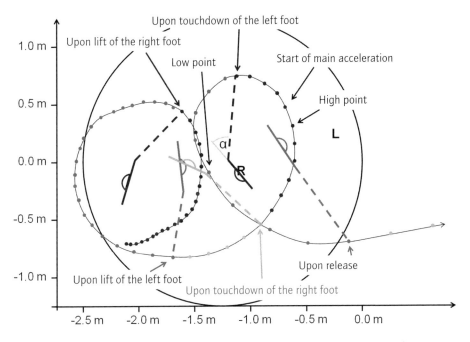

*Figure 13: **Positions of the axis through both shoulder joints** (solid bars) **and the throwing arm** (interrupted bars) **at the transition points between the partial phases, discus path, and position of the right** (R) **and left** (L) **tip of the foot in the backward reclining position of delivery** from the top view (simplified terminology for a right-hander; modified on the basis of Dickwach & Knoll, 2003): Between the points, there are identical time intervals. The increasing spatial distance between the points illustrates the acceleration. For men, the high point of the second loop is approximately 0.35–0.50cm above 60% of body height. The low point of the second loop is 0.35–0.50cm below the 60% level of body height.*

stepping over the scratch line. Instead, he/she attempts to maximise his/her rotational velocity.

The discus reaches the high point of the second loop approximately when the throwing arm of the thrower exceeds the centre line of the landing sector (12-o'clock position; see figures 3 and 13). The pelvis and the CG move across the support point of the pressure leg. The upper body is leaned backward against the direction of the throw and passes through the position in which the chest is turned against the direction of the throw.

The final increase in the path velocity of the discus toward delivery already begins in the single-support phase after the high point of the discus path (see figures 12 and 13). The prerequisites for a long acceleration path in the main acceleration phase (whose length corresponds to the athlete's physique) to achieve a high

maximum value of acceleration and for the optimal utilisation of the kinematic chain (see figure 12) are a noticeable trailing of the discus (see figure 13) and a shoulder-hip separation of up to 90° at the beginning of the increase in discus velocity. Figure 14 illustrates the differences in trailing and in shoulder-hip separation. When the bracing leg touches the ground, the throwing arm should not yet have exceeded the 9-o'clock position and the trailing and shoulder-hip separation should have reached their maximum.

Coaches often use the cue, "Look back at your watch!" to provoke a noticeable trailing action and good shoulder-hip separation. To delay the forward and upward swing of the counterarm and thus to keep the left side of the body (in the case of right-handers) closed, the discus thrower should look back at the wrist of the non-throwing arm during the one-legged delivery phase (see middle image in figure 11).

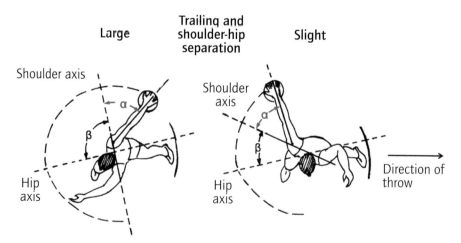

*Figure 14: **Differences in the backward reclining position of delivery in terms of trailing (α) and shoulder-hip separation (β)** with corresponding effects on the path of acceleration.*

TWO-LEGGED DELIVERY PHASE

By placing the bracing leg on the ground, the backward reclining position of delivery is reached. The two-legged delivery phase begins. With 0.16 to 0.24 sec, this phase from the touchdown of the bracing leg until releasing the discus from the hand is usually slightly longer than the one-legged delivery phase with 0.14 to 0.20 sec. However, there are also special male throwers who exhibit the opposite tendency, which means that the one-legged delivery phase is longer. When comparing various trials of one athlete, individual technical solutions lead to relatively constant phase lengths. Significant correlations between the phase lengths (see also table 4) and the throwing distance cannot be found.

The bracing leg is placed down close to the front rim of the circle somewhat to the bracing-leg side. The touchdown is performed on the inner edge of the foot, which is then placed flatly on the ground, with an already relatively large knee angle. The knee of the bracing leg and especially its hip must subsequently not move beyond the foot of the bracing leg. In order to achieve an optimal bracing effect and to lift the CG and ultimately the discus, the knee of the bracing leg is further extended (see figure 7). While the pressure leg continues its rotation and extension movement, the fixed bracing-leg side represents the abutment and approximately the rotational axis about which the right side of the body rotates forward (see figure 16 and chapter II–3.1.2 for the action of the counterarm).

More than 60% of the velocity of departure is transmitted to the discus only during the two-legged delivery phase. The thrower reaches the highest acceleration values (i.e., the fastest increase in path velocity of the device) in the area of the low point of the discus path behind his/her body (see figures 3, 13, and 15). For top male athletes (n = 6, performance: 66.34–68.86m), these values are between 86–114 m/sec^2. After reaching maximum acceleration, the acceleration values decrease again. It becomes apparent that a lower maximum acceleration may be compensated for by a longer acceleration

Figure 15: Two-legged delivery phase.

path. Here it is not the total path of acceleration that is important, which for elite throwers may even vary between 7 and 11m, but rather the acceleration path during the final increase in velocity. For the male group, this was between 3.56 and 4.63m. This corresponds to an angular distance of 264 ± 30°, which, when viewed from the top, is covered by the straight throwing arm during the main acceleration phase. From the beginning of the increase in velocity up to the delivery, the male group described reached an increase in velocity of 15.2–17.3 m/sec. With lower initial velocities (see phase 2) and similar velocities of departure (see phase 4), some female discus throwers achieve an increase in velocity of beyond 18 m/sec (see also table 3).

As exemplified in figure 7, there is a significant decrease in the force development of the pressure leg at the beginning of the two-legged delivery phase. Sometimes, the pressure leg is only dragged along the ground clearly before the delivery (resulting in negative horizontal ground reaction forces). Depending on whether the thrower performs a standing delivery or a jump delivery, there may also be a single support or support-free phase shortly before the discus leaves the athlete's hand. Both the standing and jumping delivery are practised in the world rankings although the standing delivery is slightly more common, at least among women. Therefore, the two technique variants are considered equally good. The standing delivery is assumed to lead to a calmer and more controlled movement

Figure 16: **Fixed left side of the body:** From the backward reclining position of delivery until the release, the foot, knee, hip and shoulder are approximately in one line.

performance, more effective bracing-leg action, a safe delivery position with a better abutment for the final discus acceleration, and stronger horizontal force development. It is often performed with a slightly wider backward reclining position of delivery than the jumping delivery. The advantages of the jump delivery are said to be an early high rotational velocity of the overall system and the more active extension of both legs (vertical force development) and a slightly higher height of departure.

At the end of the delivery movement, the thrower sets the discus in rotation about its axis of symmetry (see Y-axis in figure 1). For this purpose, he/she lets the discus roll off his/her index finger so that, viewed from the top, the discus rotates clockwise (with right-handers). When the discus is released from the hand,

- it is approximately at the thrower's shoulder level;

DISCOURSE II: VARIATIONS OF THE HEAD AND TRUNK POSITION DURING THE DELIVERY

Beginning at approximately the low point of the discus path, many throwers demonstrate a more or less noticeable throwing-back movement of their head. This may support the bow tension and its utilisation. In addition, some throwers exhibit a tilt of their head to the side of the throwing hand. This is associated with bending the trunk to the side of the throwing hand, as is demonstrated by the world champion Robert Harting for example. Some authors favour this technique and point out that the result may be an increased radius of the discus in relation to its axis of rotation. However, this would only be an advantage if the angular velocity of the rotation about the longitudinal axis remained unaffected by it. Still, it is not certain that there is such an increase in the angular momentum of the entire system. If the height of release and the position of the throwing arm remain unchanged during the delivery, there will also be an increase in the angle of shoulder abduction with the increasing lateral tilt of the trunk. This could be detrimental to the development of power during the anteversion at the shoulder joint.

Lars Riedel is an example of the fact that a long throw is possible without the tilt of the trunk to the side of the throwing hand (see picture sequence in chapter II–3.3.5). From the rear view, his head is upright and his trunk is slightly inclined to the opposite side when the discus leaves his hand.

- the chest is square to the direction of the throw or has already slightly exceeded this position; and
- the still straight throwing arm overtakes the shoulder axis (see figure 13).

PHASE 4: RECOVERY AND FLIGHT OF THE DISCUS

RECOVERY

The recovery considerably differs depending on the technique of delivery used by the thrower. The leg reverse, after which the previous pressure leg is in front (see figure 17), is not very dynamic with throwers using a standing delivery. The triple world champion Franka Dietzsch, for example, did not use a leg reverse at all. She only moved her pressure leg next to her supporting leg and finished her trial standing with both feet side by side at the front rim of the circle and watched the discus fly. However, discus throwers using a jump delivery sometimes demonstrate acrobatic recovery movements with multiple pirouettes on the previous pressure leg before they come to rest. In the process, the thrower must try to avoid the CG from exceeding the point of support in the direction of the throw.

*Figure 17: **Recovery** (leg reverse).*

VELOCITY, ANGLE, HEIGHT, AND POINT OF DEPARTURE

Currently, the best male discus throwers in the world throw only a few metres further than the world's top female throwers. The velocities of departure achieved are therefore similar and range from 23–26 m/sec. In groups of heterogeneous ability, the correlations with the throwing distance may reach a correlation coefficient of $r = 0.91$. This means that approximately 80% ($= r^2 \cdot 100$) of the variance of the throwing distance may be explained by the velocity of departure. In groups of homogeneous ability, such as the finalists at international championships, the correlation coefficients may fall below $r = 0.5$. In such groups, the objective rather seems to be to control the discus and achieve a flight attitude as stable as possible despite an optimal velocity of departure.

Figure 18 provides detailed information on the optimal angle of departure which ultimately must always be viewed in connection with the velocity of departure, the angle of attitude, the angle of lateral tilt, the wind conditions, and the shape and weight of the discus. The optimal angle of departure may vary within a range of 3–5° without the throwing distance changing by more than 0.5 m. The actual angles of departure measured among the World Cup finalists in 1997 varied between 27.0° in a 65.48m throw and 42.8° in a 64.30m throw (range of all throws examined: 59.16–66.80m).

In the discus throw, the official distance is measured along a line through the centre

DISCOURSE III: THROWING THE SLING BALL

A wide variety of sling balls is used in different games around the world. Moreover, distance throwing with the sling ball is a sport performed at gymnastics festivals. The ball is thrown with a run-up similar to the javelin throw. Two different techniques are used: the Frisian technique with frontal run-up and backward circle of the arm in a vertical plane, and a technique similar to the discus throw with one or sometimes two turns about the longitudinal axis of the body. The women's record distance is over 60m using a sling ball weighing 1 kg, while the men's record distance is over 85m using a sling ball weighing 1.5 kg. However, the current best performances achieved at German Gymnastics Festivals are only 50 (women) or 60 metres (men).

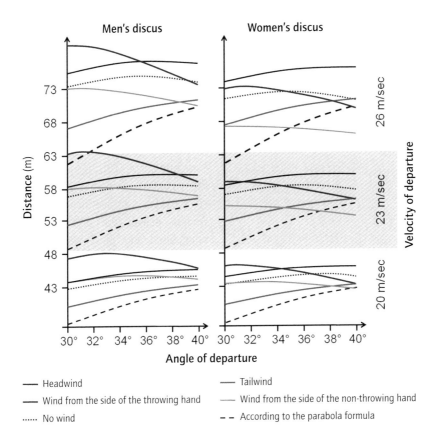

*Figure 18: **Simulated flight distances of a men's and women's discus** with three different velocities of departure depending on the angle of departure and a wind velocity of 5 m/sec from different directions (with an optimal angle of attitude and lateral tilt in each case) compared to the distance as calculated using the formula for the trajectory parabola (modified on the basis of Hildebrand & Dickwach, 2003, p. 62): The diagram also shows that in the case of crosswinds during the competition there are disadvantages for right- or left-handers.*

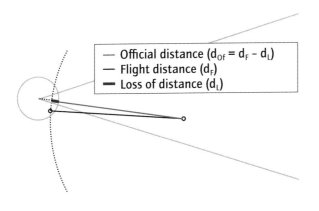

*Figure 19: **Difference between flight distance and officially measured competition distance in the discus throw.***

*Table 5: **Loss of distance and height of departure in the discus throw** (according to Hay & Yu, 1995).*

		Women	Men
Number of athletes		14	15
Body height	(m)	1.80 ± 0.06	1.92 ± 0.05
Official distance	(m)	57.90 ± 7.51	59.07 ± 4.43
Loss of distance	(m)	0.58 ± 0.22	0.45 ± 0.21
Height of release	(m)	1.51 ± 0.17	1.65 ± 0.17
Height of release	(% of body height)	84	86

of the throwing circle and is read at the front edge of the rim of the circle. When viewed from above, the point of delivery is lateral to this line on the side of the throwing hand. Moreover, the landing point is further away from the point of delivery than from the front edge of the rim of

the circle (see figure 19). Table 5 provides details on the loss of distance resulting from this and on the height of departure. Although the possible differences are relatively small, differences in the loss of distance may decide competitions. However, it is amazing that in a group of female throwers there is a significant correlation (r = 0.66, p < 0.01) between the increasing loss of distance and the competition distance achieved. Perhaps women deliver the discus in a more uninhibited and active way if they have more space for the recovery movement.

ROTATION AND LATERAL TILTING OF THE DISCUS, ANGLE OF LATERAL TILT, AND ANGLE OF ATTACK

A discus should always be thrown in such a manner that during the entire flight there is the smallest possible frontal drag and the greatest possible lift. Figure 20 illustrates how much longer a discus may fly, which rotates correctly about its axis of symmetry and whose attitude of flight

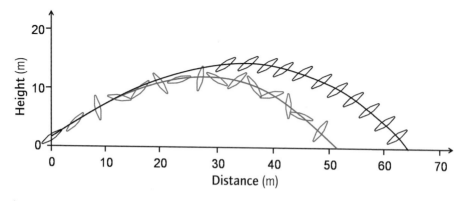

*Figure 20: **Flight path of two discuses with identical velocity of departure, but one of them rotating about the axis of symmetry and with a stable flying position, and the other flying without stable rotation** (modified on the basis of Soong, 1982, quoted from Wank, 2006, p. 134).*

is favourable, than a discus flying in an uncontrolled manner. In the latter case, there is higher frontal resistance and no lift is created. With a favourable attitude of flight, the discus may fly farther than calculated using the formula for the trajectory parabola since this formula does not take into account the aerodynamic properties (see figure 18 above and figure 6 in chapter II–3.1.2). The throwers described in tables 3 and 5 increased distances by 4.05 ± 3.15m (women) and 2.42 ± 3.29m (men). The difference between men and women is not significant and therefore cannot lead to the conclusion that the gain in distance is greater with the women's discus. Although the ratio of size (diameter or surface exposed to the air stream) and weight is more favourable with the women's discus, the men's discus, however, maintains a more stable flight attitude (see the following).

For a long time, it has been neglected that the discus changes its spatial position during the flight. Due to its shape, the discus should actually raise its front edge upwards when being streamed at from the front and from below. However, instead of rotating about this horizontal axis of rotation, which is square to the direction of the throw, the rotation of the discus about its axis of symmetry causes a deviating rotation about a third axis which is perpendicular to the other two axes. The lateral tilt of the discus changes in such a manner that the discus, which (if thrown by a right-hander) rotates clockwise (viewed from above) and is streamed at from the front and from below, tilts

downward on the left side (viewed by the thrower). Due to this lateral tilting, the lift is reduced until the symmetry axis of the discus is horizontal and no lifting forces of air resistance act on the discus anymore.

There are three possibilities to delay the tilt of the discus:

• The discus should be released with a slightly negative angle of attack (angle of attitude < angle of upstream flow; see chapter II–3.1.2). This results in the discus being streamed at from above at the beginning of its flight, whereby the right side of the discus (thrown by a right-hander viewed from behind) first tilts downward a little. Due to the flattening of the trajectory, which is caused by gravitation, the angle of upstream flow decreases and the angle of attack becomes positive. Now, the discus is streamed at from below and its left side tilts downward. By being streamed at from above, the discus is subjected to a negative lift at the beginning of its flight which has a negative effect on the flight distance. However, above an angle of attack of 25° the airflow around the discus becomes turbulent, the lifting force also decreases sharply, while the frontal resistance increases significantly. A small angle of attitude or initially negative angle of attack also results in the angle of attack of 25° being reached later during the falling part of the trajectory. The lift is maintained for longer and the flight distance increases. This means that due to a small angle of attitude, the phase of lift is shifted backward. The fact that in the case of small positive angles of attack the effect of lift is more noticeable than the effect of the increased frontal resistance results in the discus flying farther than calculated on the basis of its trajectory (see figure 18).

- Right-handers can release the discus in such a manner that upon release its right side is tilted downward. The thrower can achieve this (contrary to some former descriptions of the target technique) through a smaller angle of abduction of the throwing shoulder (hand slightly below shoulder level) and/or a slight bending of the wrist (palmar flexion). A lateral tilt deviating from 0° reduces the forces (negative or positive) of the lift. However, if the left side of the discus tilts downward as described above, the lateral tilt up to the position of 0° becomes initially more favourable. It is only thereafter that in the process of the continued tilting, the lift decreases due to the increasing lateral tilt. There is an overall increase in the effect of the lift.

  Due to the change of the side streamed at and the lateral tilt, it may well occur that the discus flies in a zigzag manner when viewed from behind or from above. If a right-hander releases the discus with a negative angle of attack and with its right side tilted downward, the discus is first driven off to the left. If now the direction of airstream changes to the bottom of the discus, while its right side is still tilted downward, the discus is driven off to the right. If the discus now exceeds the lateral tilt of 0° and while its left side tilts downward, it is driven off again to the left.

- How fast the discus tilts to the side during its flight depends on its rotational velocity, its mass, and on the distribution of this mass in the discus. The faster the discus rotates about its axis of symmetry, the slower it tilts sideward. For top throwers, the rotational velocity of the discus is approximately eight revolutions per second. Due to the fact that the men's discus is double the weight of the women's discus, it is also twice as difficult for the discus to be deflected from its starting attitude of flight. Since, however, women and men achieve (not only similar throwing distances but also) similar throwing durations, the tilting of the discus is a bigger problem for women. Therefore, women more frequently use the first two strategies identified above: the negative angle of attack, and the downward tilt of the distal edge of the discus during the release. According to the regulations, the mass does not have to be distributed evenly in the discus. The more mass is stored away from the axis of rotation, i.e. at the edge of the discus, the greater the moment of inertia that counters the tilting of the discus. However, the farther the mass of the discus is shifted to the edge of the discus, the more difficult it is to set the discus in rotation.

Table 6 provides a guideline for optimal angles of departure, attitude, and lateral tilt. Compared to a throw in which the difference between the angle of release and the angle of attack as well as the angle of lateral tilt are equal to 0°, a gain in distance of up to more than 6m may be achieved by optimising the angle of attack and lateral tilt of the men's discus released at high velocity in the event of headwind or wind coming from the side of the throwing arm.

*Table 6: **Optimal angles of departure, differences between the angle of departure and angle of attitude, as well as angle of lateral tilt** in the case of different wind directions (5 m/sec) and velocities of departure, partly divided up into the men's and women's discus, in a simulation in which there is a variation of the angle of departure between 30° and 40°, a variation of the above mentioned difference between 0° and −10°, and a variation of the angle of lateral tilt between 0° and 30° (downward tilted outer side) (according to Hildebrand & Dickwach, 2003, p. 68).*

	Velocity of departure (m/sec)	No wind		Wind coming from the side of the throwing arm		Headwind		Wind coming from the side of the non-throwing arm		Tailwind	
		Men	Women	Men	Women	Men	Women	Men	Women	Men	Women
Angle of departure	20 ↓ 26	34-38°		34-40°		34° ↓ 30°	30° ↓ 32°	36° ↓ 30°	30-34°	approx. 40°	
Optimal difference: angle of departure – angle of attitude	20 ↓ 26	−10°		−4° ↓ −10°	−6°	−10°		−10°		−4° ↓ −10°	(−8°)– (−10°)
Angle of lateral tilt	20 ↓ 26	20° ↓ 30°	30°	0°	0° ↓ 30°	30°		30° ↓ 20°	30°	0° ↓ 30°	25° ↓ 30°

*Table 7: **Requirement profile for the discus throw:** The suggested rough estimate of the value of selected factors determining performance is based on the importance for the overall performance and the percentage of time spent training (IR: information requirements, constr.: constraints; see chapter I–1.1).*

Factors determining discus-throw performance	Estimate of value	Notes
Coordination	+ + + + +	optical IR: medium, acoustic IR: low, tactile IR: low, kinaesthetic IR: medium, vestibular IR: high; precision constr.: high, time constr.: high, complexity constr.: high, situation constr.: low, physical stress constr.: low
Flexibility	+ +	primarily of the throwing-arm shoulder
Strength		primarily anteversion muscles of the shoulder (pectoralis, deltoideus, etc.), extension loop (glutes, quadriceps, triceps surae, erector spinae), and trunk muscles (primarily rotatory muscles: abdominus obliqui, etc.)

(continued)

(continued)

Factors determining discus-throw performance	Estimate of value	Notes
Maximal strength	+ + + +	as the most important basis
Speed strength	+ + + + +	as the most important factor; primarily of the upper body
Reactive strength	+ + +	primarily of the legs
Speed	+ + + +	acyclic speed
Endurance (general dynamic) Anaerobic endurance		
Strength endurance	+ +	as a basis to be able to perform 6 trials plus practice trials at a high level of performance
Speed endurance	+	as a basis at most
Aerobic endurance	+	as a basis at most
Psychological and cognitive abilities	+ + + + +	concentration ability (on the point); performance-oriented thinking and behaviour (see chapter I–3.1.1)
Anthropometric and primarily genetically determined characteristics	+ + + +	high percentage of the fastest muscle fibres; connective tissue with optimal energy storage capacities; rather above-average body height and arm spread

3.3.4 SUMMARY OF THE MOST IMPORTANT TECHNICAL CHARACTERISTICS = TECHNIQUE-ANALYSIS SHEET

Description for a right-hander:

PRELIMINARY SWING

GRIP

- The hand is located on the middle of the discus; the tips of the fingers hold the edge of the discus; the wrist is bent slightly inward (palmarflexed).

STARTING POSITION

- Quarter squat at the rear rim of the circle; the back is square to the direction of the throw; the legs are

slightly further apart than shoulder width; the centre line of the throwing sector is approximately in the middle between the feet; the upper body is bent slightly forward or upright.

PRELIMINARY MOVEMENT

- The thrower swings the discus with an extended arm approximately at shoulder level to behind his/her body.
- The weight is shifted to the right leg and the left leg is turned inward in the direction of the right leg.
- The point of reversal of the discus is approximately above the left foot; at the point of reversal, the hand is slightly opened to prevent the discus from falling downward.

TURN

TWO-LEGGED STARTING PHASE

- The counterclockwise rotation is started by turning the left leg outward on the ball of the foot; the outward rotation leads over into the rotation of the pelvis about the longitudinal axis; then the shoulder axis and the trailing throwing arm are also turned while the shoulder-hip separation is maintained.
- The push-off with the right leg results in a shift of the CG nearly to above the left foot and supports the initiation of the turn.
- The throwing hand is again placed over the discus.
- The counter-arm remains in front of the body and supports the shoulder-hip separation.
- The right leg remains on the ground for a long time which results in the creation of pre-tension in the right hip.

ONE-LEGGED STARTING PHASE

- The right foot is released from the ground at approximately the moment when the left knee points toward the side.

- Turn on the ball of the left foot; flat circular swing of the right foot on a wide arc around the supporting leg.
- Possible lift of the heel of the swing leg with subsequent kicking movement.
- As soon as the knee of the supporting leg points in the direction of the throw, the thrower performs a powerful, flat push-off with incomplete knee extension.
- Maintenance of the shoulder-hip separation and the trailing of the throwing arm.

SUPPORTLESS PHASE (LEG REVERSE)

- Short (in respect to time) and flat reverse of legs.
- The right thigh remains clearly below the horizontal.
- The legs overtake the trunk (while the shoulders stay behind).
- Inward rotation of the right leg so that the foot points (sideward and) backward already upon touchdown; before the touchdown, the foot is accelerated in the direction of the rear rim of the circle.
- The left leg (and arm) are moved toward the axis of rotation.
- Maintenance of the shoulder-hip separation and the trailing of the throwing arm.

DELIVERY MOVEMENT

ONE-LEGGED DELIVERY PHASE

- Touchdown of the leg, which is bent at the knee joint at an obtuse angle, slightly in front of the vertical projection of the CG, approximately in the centre of the circle.
- Rapid and uninterrupted continuation of the rotation of the right leg on the ball of the foot and consequently also the pelvis and trunk.
- The CG moves across the point of support.
- The discus reaches its highest point approximately when the throwing arm points in the direction of the throw.
- The athlete looks back at the back of his/her counter-arm hand.
- The trunk is leant backward against the direction of the throw and passes through the position in which the chest is turned against the direction of the throw.
- The shoulder-hip separation and the trailing of the throwing arm reach their

maximum due to the active holding back of the throwing hand and the action of the pressure leg.

- The bracing leg is moved flatly and rapidly in the direction of the front rim of the circle.

TWO-LEGGED DELIVERY PHASE (TOUCHDOWN OF THE BRACING LEG UP TO THE RELEASE OF THE DISCUS)

- Upon the touchdown of the bracing leg, the throwing arm has not yet crossed the right angle to the centre line of the landing sector when viewed from above.
- The bracing leg is placed down with the inner edge of the foot and is then placed flatly on the ground, when viewed from the rear somewhat left to the centre line of the landing sector and the right leg; the knee, which was already very much extended upon touchdown, is extended even further; the knee and hip stay behind the foot.
- The counter-arm, which is bent at an obtuse angle, is initially swung forward and upward before it is drawn backward and downward toward the body.
- The rotation of the pressure leg on the ball of the foot is continued; the discus reaches its lowest point when the right knee already points approximately in the direction of the throw and when the throwing arm points backward.
- The action of the pressure and bracing legs result in the continuation of the rotation of the hip and consequently of the shoulder until they are square to the direction of the throw; release of the shoulder-hip separation and the trailing of the throwing arm (the throwing arm is brought forward).
- The trunk is straightened up into the delivery.
- The discus is rolled off the index finger (high rotational velocity in the clockwise direction); release from the hand at shoulder height, with slightly negative angle of attitude and optimal angle of lateral tilt (hanging outer edge).
- Standing or jumping delivery.

RECOVERY

- The standing delivery is sometimes performed without leg reverse.
- In the jumping delivery, the legs are reversed and the turn is sometimes continued on the right leg.
- The CG is kept behind the point of support to avoid stepping over the frontal rim of the circle.
- The thrower leaves the circle through its back half.

3.3.5 PHOTO SEQUENCE

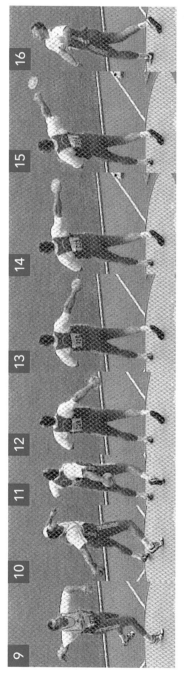

Data about the photo sequence

Athlete:	Lars Riedel (born: 28 June 1967, Germany)
Height/weight:	1.99 m/110 kg
Performance:	65.67 m (29 July 2000, Braunschweig)
Best performance:	71.50 m (3 May 1997, Wiesbaden)
Greatest success:	Olympic champion 1996, World champion 1991, 1993, 1995, 1997, and 2001)

COMMENTARY

The photo sequence shows Lars Riedel's winning throw for one of his eleven German national titles. Nearly two months later, he won second place at the Olympic Games in Sydney with a throw of 68.50m, 80cm behind his constant rival Virgilijus Alekna from Lithuania.

In the starting position, Riedel's feet are slightly wider apart than shoulder width. As a right-hander, he is standing more on the right side of the circle (viewed in the direction of the throw). From picture 1 to picture 2, the preliminary swing is accompanied by a shift in body weight from the left toward the right leg. However, in the process, he is far from relieving his left leg completely. The reversal point of the discus is at shoulder height approximately vertically above the left foot. His view and counter-arm, which other throwers turn more in the direction of the preliminary swing, remain directed opposite to the throwing direction. At the beginning of the turn (outward turning of the left foot and knee), there is a significant shift of weight to the left leg due to pushing off with the right leg. After a very upright position, the knee joint is now bent down

to about 110° and the hip is also pushed back slightly. There was the criticism that Riedel initiates his turn by first significantly turning his head. In spite of this, picture 4 illustrates very well that he tries to keep the discus trailing behind his body and his shoulder and hip separated. The swing leg knee is bent sharply, and the heel is raised up to the height of his buttocks. From there, it is swung in a wide radius around the supporting leg and performs an active kicking motion. When releasing his supporting leg, which is not fully extended as prescribed by the model technique, Riedel moves his swing leg, which is now bent more again, into a distinct high-knee position. From there, he places this leg very actively onto the ground contrary to the direction of the throw, while he moves his counter-arm close to his body to accelerate his rotation. In the process, he turns his right foot so far inward that upon touchdown it already points backward. This enables Riedel to continue his rapid rotation on the pressure leg, thus developing a high degree of shoulder-hip separation and trailing of the discus. While Riedel continues his rotation on the right leg, he moves his left leg close to, but slightly lifted around the pressure leg. On the one hand, some authors have described the touchdown direction of the foot of the bracing leg as a little too frontal, which means that the foot could point somewhat more to the right side of the circle. On the other hand, Riedel creates maximum space for the unobstructed forward movement of his right hip by doing so. Moreover, the virtually unchanged position of the left side of the body, which is shown from the rear in pictures 11–15, illustrates the good bracing and blocking function of the left half of his body. Meanwhile, Riedel brings forward his right hip, shoulder, and finally his extended throwing arm. Riedel's slight bending at the hip to the left, which is associated with a tilt of his head to the left, may not necessarily be a disadvantage in the process (see discourse II). The last pictures show that Riedel is the prototype of a thrower performing a standing delivery. Only after the delivery does Riedel pull his right leg forward to the edge of the rim and then reverses his legs. Without continuing his rotation about the longitudinal axis of his body, he follows the flying discus with his eyes.

3.3.6 DIDACTICS: SUPERORDINATE LONG-TERM OBJECTIVES AND GENERAL METHODOLOGY

Compared to other disciplines, there are relatively few game forms which may be used to prepare for the discus throw. This may be due to the fact that rotary and slinging throws are rather unnatural movements which are not necessarily tried intuitively by children. Secondly, the throwing direction is relatively difficult to control in these throws, which may be dangerous in itself, so that such throws are not encouraged by coaches and educators. Accordingly, rotational throws are not part of the combined events for children and young adolescents. In the women's combined events, the rotary throw is not even part of the competitions for the adult age groups, which further inhibits teaching it.

However, the further development of children's and playful athletics has also brought forth new ideas and assistive devices with respect to the teaching of rotary throws. As in the javelin throw, the first introduction to the discipline for children takes place using target throws.

For this purpose, old and therefore free bicycle tyres, which are not very dangerous, may be used. Soft light discuses reduce the risk of injury and allow an early approach to the target technique. The same applies to special discuses for children which are easy to grip and set in rotation. In addition, sling balls, which are available at many schools, may often be used for teaching novices the discus throw.

After the general non-specific introduction of rotary throws in children's athletics, the teaching of specific techniques begins in basic training. In this process, the individual methodological steps (frontal throw, standing throw, throw with a single turn, throw with 1½ turns) are usually initially imitated without equipment and are developed using assistive devices (light sling balls held short, 600g nocken ball, etc.) before they are performed using the (children's) discus.

In Germany, most discus throwers favour the standing delivery. This may be related to the fact that coaches want to avoid a too early leg reversal during the delivery motion since this is regarded as a typical technical error with young athletes. However, since the jumping delivery is equally popular on an international level, it may be advisable to try to practice both variations by using the contrast method before the athlete chooses one variation.

In the combined-event-oriented basic training, not only technical principles, but also the foundations for strength are established for the discus throw. Here, for example, general trunk-strength training and general throws (e.g., tossing [93], which may also be performed from a lateral position) are important. However, strength training, in particular special strength training, becomes more significant in build-up training. The contents of the combined events are reduced and there is an increasing specialisation on throws and finally the discus throw.

SAFETY PRECAUTIONS
In addition to the safety precautions mentioned in connection with the common features of the throwing events (see chapter II–3.1.3), the following aspects must be observed in the discus throw:

- In general, the discus throw should be practised from a protective cage. Moreover, the athletes waiting outside the cage must be far enough away from the net.

- Some preliminary exercises with assistive devices and without the turn may be performed side by side using the V-formation (see figure 21). Here, it must be ensured that the V-form is followed precisely. No-one should be allowed to stand on the side of the thrower's throwing-hand. The coach takes his/her observation position inside the V.

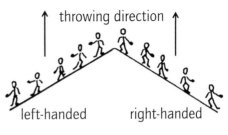

*Figure 21: **V-formation.***

3.3.7 TRAINING CONTENTS: FORMS OF GAMES AND EXERCISES

All the training forms mentioned in connection with the 100m sprint (see chapter II-1.3.3) may also be used for preparing the discus throw in terms of reactive-strength and speed-strength training. For the same reason, the forms of the ABCs of jumping and multiple jumps (see chapters I–5.4.6 and II–2.2.7) described in connection with the general training forms of strength training and the long jump are an important part of discus-throwing training.

401 **Target-throw game using the rotary throwing technique**

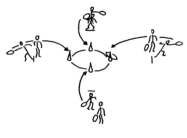

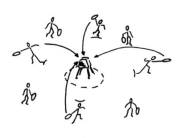

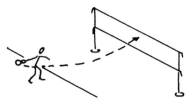

Possible objectives: Playful introduction of the rotary throw.

Execution/variations: Slinging throws from a standing position or with a single turn to a target; gymnastic hoops or bicycle tyres are thrown over poles, cones, or similar objects (3 points) or touch these objects at least (1 point), in circle formation (e.g., centre circle of the soccer field) or safe formation in rows; later also window throws (see picture below) using tennis rings, (shortly held) sling balls, soft discuses, children's discuses, etc.; throws from a suitable distance through the field goal (American football/rugby), into a marked target zone on a wall, etc.; counting hits or points; bilateral practice.

Typical load standards: As long as it's fun.

402 **Chasing the ball**

Possible objectives: Strength training of the oblique trunk muscles; orientation in spite of head rotation.

Execution: The players position themselves in a circle (looking outward); two (medicine) balls are given to two players who are standing on opposite sides of a circle; a passing direction is defined; the players pass the ball from player to player as fast as possible and try to catch up with the respective other ball.

Variations: The technique should not be prescribed initially, then without movements of the feet, with trunk rotation and arms stretched out forward; change passing direction; with one ball circling in one direction and the other ball circling in the opposite direction; circle formation with looking inward; using more balls.

Typical load standards: Depending on the variation, the load duration should be only relatively short; in combination with other games or exercise forms in the circle formation.

In addition, pirouettes and rotational jumps (3; also with eyes closed) and other rotations about one's longitudinal axis (6) may be used for preparing learning the discus technique

403   Versatile rotational throws without detailed technique prescription

Possible objectives: Testing technique and its variations; orientation in space and balance.

Execution/variations: From a standing position, with a run-up, with a single and double turn; frequently with a sling ball, but also with other devices; bilateral practice; also as throwing and walking: each subsequent throw is performed from the landing point of the first throw (e.g., who can achieve the longest distance with three throws?); notice: for safety reasons, all other athletes must wait behind the thrower.

Typical load standards: As long as it's fun.

404 Familiarisation with the discus

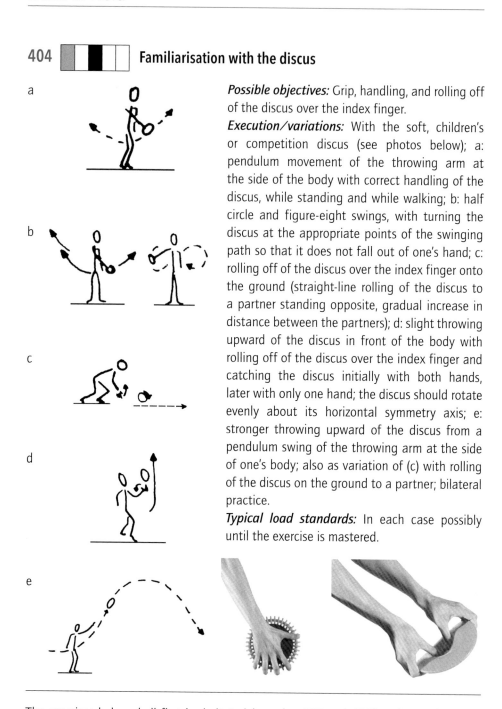

a

b

c

d

e

Possible objectives: Grip, handling, and rolling off of the discus over the index finger.

Execution/variations: With the soft, children's or competition discus (see photos below); a: pendulum movement of the throwing arm at the side of the body with correct handling of the discus, while standing and while walking; b: half circle and figure-eight swings, with turning the discus at the appropriate points of the swinging path so that it does not fall out of one's hand; c: rolling off of the discus over the index finger onto the ground (straight-line rolling of the discus to a partner standing opposite, gradual increase in distance between the partners); d: slight throwing upward of the discus in front of the body with rolling off of the discus over the index finger and catching the discus initially with both hands, later with only one hand; the discus should rotate evenly about its horizontal symmetry axis; e: stronger throwing upward of the discus from a pendulum swing of the throwing arm at the side of one's body; also as variation of (c) with rolling of the discus on the ground to a partner; bilateral practice.

Typical load standards: In each case possibly until the exercise is mastered.

The exercises below shall first be imitated (see also 407 and 408) and may then also be performed using assisting devices with aerodynamics playing no role (shortly held sling ball ball with appropriate weight, tennis ring, etc.). Only when a soft, children's, or competition discus is thrown does the handling of the discus have to be developed first through familiarisation exercises (404).

---

405 ▮▮▮▮▮ Frontal throw

Possible objectives: Technique of the delivery movement (during the delivery, the chest must be square to the throwing direction).

Execution: The starting position, the area of the reversal point, and the phase of release are illustrated below.

Variations: First parallel, then stride position (the lateral distance between the feet should also be maintained in the stride position: the feet should not be directly behind each other in the throwing direction); various throwing devices (the holding loop of a sling ball should usually be folded in half [possibly by wrapping it with tape] and gripped close to the ball); advanced athletes may also perform the throws in the frontal sitting position with stretched legs; bilateral practice.

Typical load standards: 5–10 reps per side.

from a standing position with feet side by side

from a stride position

---

406 ▮▮▮▮▮ Standing throw

Possible objectives: Technique of the delivery movement; special throwing strength; special warm-up.

Execution: In the backward reclining position of delivery, the discus is swung back up to approximately above the foot of the bracing leg; the reversal of movement is performed from this clear shoulder-hip separation with subsequent acceleration of the discus, first from the lower extremities, then from the upper body.

Variations: With lighter and heavier discuses, shots, batons, etc.; the movement should possibly be imitated one or two times from the point of reversal to the low point (hip movement); then the discus should be swung back again without interruption of the movement followed by a standing throw; over a height marker; bilateral practice.

Typical load standards: Depending on the training goal and state, between 5 and 30 reps per side.

---

407 **Imitation of the delivery movement**

Possible objectives: Technique of the delivery movement, in particular the succession of partial movements.

Execution/variations: Slow execution of the delivery movement without a device or with the strap discus (since the strap fixes the hand to the discus, the discus does not fall in spite of the lack of centrifugal forces; only for imitation); the

hips should be shifted forward while the throwing arm points backward; the throwing arm (and/or counter-arm) is either fixed by an elastic band (e.g., to wall bars) or is held back by a partner; with a stick placed on the shoulders, the hip is brought from the backward reclining position of delivery up to the frontal position, while the throwing hand is moved to the low point (the stick is supposed to demonstrate the position of the shoulder; in performance sport, the stick may be replaced by a barbell); release of the sling ball without much effort with the hand being initially held back by a partner and released only when the thrower has brought his/her hip forward; bilateral practice.

Typical load standards: 3–6 reps each, alternating with standing throws (406).

---

408 Imitation: versatile turns specific to the discus throw

Possible objectives: Versatile preparation of the turning movements on the leg opposite to the throwing hand (forward, wide, and controlled) and on the leg on the side of the throwing hand (backward, tight, and fast).

Execution/variations: 1/4, 1/2, 3/4, full, 5/4, etc. turn on the leg opposite to the throwing hand with an initial outward turn of the supporting leg; 1/2 turn on the leg on the side of the throwing hand, with the shoulders and the throwing hand trailing behind; also with continuous alternation of legs, with breaks or uninterrupted, slowly or as dynamic leg reversal with a flat jump onto the pressure leg (continuous leg reversals); always with corresponding shift of the weight onto the supporting leg and turn on the ball of the foot; on a suitable surface (no running track), on a line, on a gymnastic bench (upside down), or in the throwing circle; bilateral practice, now and then,

the exercise may be performed backward.
Typical load standards: 5–10 reps per task.

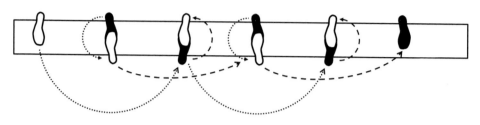

---

409 | | | Throws with the pressure leg already forward (3/4-4/4 turn)

Possible objectives: Second part of the turn, in particular by moving the bracing leg closely past the pressure leg and flat placement of the bracing leg.

Execution: The thrower swings the discus backward and upward to the position shown and pushes himself/herself off powerfully with his/her rear leg, the pressure leg continues its turn on the ball of the foot, the discus is trailed, the bracing leg is brought forward closely past the supporting leg and placed down at the front rim of the circle, and then a delivery movement is performed in accordance with the target technique.

Variations: The movement is initially imitated without discus or with strap discus; as imitation only into the backward reclining position of delivery and back again; by throwing suitable balls, throwing batons, shortly gripped sling balls, etc., finally by throwing the discus; possibly with slight lifting and active placement of the pressure leg at the beginning of the movement; bilateral practice.

Typical load standards: 6–15 reps.

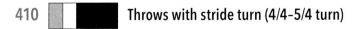

410   Throws with stride turn (4/4–5/4 turn)

Possible objectives: Technique of the delivery with leg reverse (simplified first part of the turn); powerful push-off from the rear rim of the circle.

Execution: Less advanced athletes initially begin from the starting position presented above, while more advanced athletes begin from the starting position presented below; the movement is introduced by swinging the discus backward and upward to the position presented; then the thrower slightly pushes himself/herself off with the leg on the side of the throwing arm, followed by a powerful push-off with the other leg in the direction of the centre of the circle; then the thrower performs a flat leg reverse with trailed discus and finally a delivery movement in accordance with the target technique.

Variations: First as imitation (possibly with a stick between the hands for holding back the throwing arm), then with assistive devices, and finally with the discus (see 409); possibly with leg reverse over a ditch and/or with orientation point to look at (after the leg reverse); bilateral practice.

Typical load standards: 6–15 reps.

411   Imitations: Starting the turn

Possible objectives: Preliminary movement and two-legged starting phase, in particular shift of weight and outward turn of the leg opposite the throwing hand.

Execution: The technique of the discus throw is performed only up to the end of the two-legged starting phase.

Variations: Without discus, with strap discus, ball or shot of suitable weight, or with closely gripped sling ball; if performed with throwing implement also with release of the leg on the side of the throwing hand and subsequent placement of the swing leg in the starting position for exercise 410, thereafter either back to the starting position or repeated backswing of the implement and execution of exercise 410; entering the throwing circle, taking the starting position, and the preliminary turn should be performed without interruption (see discourse I); the partner holds his/her hand above the thrower's left heel (right-hander), the thrower shall touch this hand at the end of the backswing; bilateral practice.

Typical load standards: 3–6 reps alternating with other exercises (e.g., 410, 412, and 413).

412 Imitations: First part of the turn

Starting position (photo taken in the direction of the throw)

Possible objectives: Correct turn up to the one-legged starting phase.

Execution: The turn should be performed until the swing leg points toward the centre of the circle; however, the thrower should not yet perform an active push-off with his/her supporting leg; the swing leg must be placed in the centre of the circle and should rest in double support; the shoulder should stay behind.

Variations: Various devices (see 411); knocking down a (traffic) cone or a similar object with the swing leg to initiate a wide movement of the swing leg; possibly also from the starting position for exercise 410; the exercise should also be performed from the end position backward up to the reversal point of the discus and from there the

turn should be started anew; the end position is the starting position of exercise 409, which may be added after having checked the position and a repeated backswing of the discus.

Typical load standards: 3–6 reps alternating with other exercises (e.g., 410, 411, and 413).

End position (photo taken from the side)

413   Imitations: turn up to the backward reclining position of delivery

Possible objectives: Discus-throw technique, in particular maximum trailing and shoulder-hip separation in the backward reclining position of delivery.

Execution: Turn and leg reverse with continuation of the turn on the pressure leg into the backward reclining position of delivery; holding back of the throwing hand (objective: placement of the foot of the bracing leg under the throwing hand).

Variations: Various devices (see 411); also with stick or (in performance training) with a barbell placed on the shoulders (or a stick between the hands, see 410); possibly only from the starting positions of exercises 409 or 410; also as running in (410) while holding the opposite hand (see photo); possibly with marker to look at (see 410; the thrower first looks backward, then in the direction of the throw, then backward (or at the back of his/her hand), and then in the direction of the throw again); also by knocking down a (traffic) cone (see 410); possibly with a gym mat placed behind the side of the throwing hand to avoid a premature backward tilt toward the centre of the circle (see photos below); the end position is the starting position of exercise 406 which may be added after having checked the position and a repeated backswing of the discus; bilateral practice.

Typical load standards: 3–6 reps alternating with other exercises (e.g., 406 and 414).

414 Throws with full turn (6/4 turn)

Possible objectives: Target technique.

Execution: See description in chapter II–3.3.3.

Variations: With (lighter) balls, shortly gripped sling balls, in performance training also with shots or throwing batons, which are heavier than the competition device (according to a study, the optimum range of weight for men is 1.5–3 kg and the optimum length of the throwing batons is 35–80cm); in the course of the season, initially heavier, then lighter devices should be used; maximal throws should be alternated with easy technical throws (e.g., focusing on the correct placing of the discus in the air or wind); athletes should practice even in bad weather and in different wind conditions; possibly also with the verbal accompaniment "tuuuuurn – and throw" to emphasise a slow start; bilateral practice.

Typical load standards: Between 6 and 40 reps depending on the athlete's performance ability and the training objective.

415 Special gymnastic exercises and strengthening

Possible objectives: Flexibility and strength training as well as imitation of technique.

Execution/variations: Trunk twist (see top picture on the left); flag waving (see bottom picture on the left), as well as delivery motion with barbell discs while standing or lying; first slow, then fast.

Typical load standards: 2–3 series of 5–15 reps each.

The medicine-ball throws mentioned in the general part (see chapter I–5.4.7) are already used for preparing the discus throw in basic training. It is absolutely necessary to perform tossing (93) also laterally or diagonally backward (from next to the left knee to above the right shoulder and vice versa). Many of the medicine-ball throws used for the other throwing disciplines are also used in practising the discus throw (e.g., 391, 426, and 428).

416 　　Special throws focusing on strength

Possible objectives: (Speed-)strength training using a technique specific to the discus throw.

Execution/variations: The exercises presented should be performed with a partner throwing the ball to the exercising athlete in an appropriate manner.

Typical load standards: 3–5 sets per exercise of 6–15 reps each.

The hand should be brought behind the ball at the reversal point.

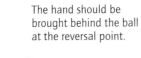

417 　　　　■ Discus strength-training device

Possible objectives: (Speed-)strength training using a technique specific to the discus throw.

Execution/variations: This special device, which is available only at a few training centres, enables the performance of delivery motions with a slide being accelerated along a circular and inclined rail.

Typical load standards: Varies depending on the training objective and athlete's state of performance.

In addition, the following exercises are important elements of the strength training of discus throwers: 38, 41–47, 49–55, 58, 61–64, 66–67, 69–72, 77–88, and 90–96.

3.3.8 SPECIAL TEST AND CONTROL PROCEDURES

	Test: Ability/skill tested	Execution/comments
T151	**Technique analysis:** Discus technique	Maximal competition throw; evaluation on the basis of the technique analysis sheet (see chapter II–3.3.4), possibly using a video (T1) and photo sequences made thereof; in high-performance sport, also computer-supported 3D analysis based on at least two simultaneous video recordings.
T152	**Discus throw with reduced pre-acceleration:** Specific speed strength as well as laterality differences	Throwing distance in the discus throw: • from a sitting position square to the direction of the throw with extended legs (416); • from a standing position (406); • with the pressure leg already brought forward (409); • with running in (410); • with the weaker side using the methods of pre-acceleration mentioned.
T153	**Throwing a different device and/or weight:** Specific speed strength as well as laterality differences	Throwing distance in the shot, baton, and discus throw: • using a weight lighter than the competition discus; • using a weight heavier than the competition discus; • with the weaker side and changed device.
T154	**General throwing tests for the discus throw:** Speed strength	Throwing distance in: • tossing forward, backward, and sideward (93); • the rotational throw while sitting (95).
T155	**Discus-throw endurance test:** Specific strength endurance	The total distance achieved in 10 throws in a pre-set time counts.
T4	1 RPM: Maximal strength	Bench press (54), butterfly (55), squat (62), clean (63), snatch (64), hip-shoulder twist (67), quadriceps (69), etc.
T5	**Squat jump, and T8 counter-movement and drop jump:** Two-legged speed strength and reactive strength of the extensor loop	
T9	**5-stride hops with distance maximisation:** Reactive strength of the legs in comparison to one another	Test should only be performed if it is not too stressful due to the bodyweight; both legs should be tested.
T10	**30m bounding run with time minimisation:** Reactive strength of the legs	Only if it is not too stressful due to the bodyweight.

(continued)

(continued)

	Test: Ability/skill tested	Execution/comments
T61	**20m sprint from a standing start:** (Sprint) acceleration	
T2	**Flexibility tests:** General flexibility	
T3	**Body weight and body fat measurement:** Relative strength	Inappropriate upward and downward deflections should be avoided.

In high-performance sport, additional tests are possible (e.g., measurement installations at the discus strength-training device, and throws with ground contacts on force-measurement plates).

Table 8: **Basic performances of discus throwers** *(according to Kühl & Hommel, 1997, pp. 231–232).*

		Women					Men				
Discus weight and	(kg)	1.0	1.0	1.0	1.0	1.0	1.5	1.5	1.5	1.75	2.0
target distance in the discus throw	(m)	31.0	37.0	43.0	52.0	58.0	42.0	48.0	52.0	55.0	55.0
Discus weight when	(kg)	0.75	0.75	0.75	0.75	0.75	1.0	1.0	1.0	1.5	1.75
throwing a lighter discus	(m)	35.0	41.0	48.0	57.0	62.0	49.0	56.0	60.0	58.0	58.0
Discus weight when	(kg)	–	–	1.5	1.5	1.5	–	–	–	2.0	–
throwing of a heavier discus	(m)			32.0	40.0	46.0				50.0	
Sideward toss of a 3kg weight	(m)	–	–	–	–	–	–	–	–	28.0	30.0
Shot weight when	(kg)	3.0	3.0	4.0	4.0	4.0	–	–	–	–	–
throwing the shot forward	(m)	11.0	12.0	13.5	14.0	16.0					
Shot weight when	(kg)	3.0	3.0	4.0	4.0	4.0	4.0	4.0	4.0	6.26	7.26
throwing the shot backward	(m)	12.0	13.5	15.0	16.0	18.0	16.5	18.5	18.5	18.0	18.5
30m flying sprint	(m)	3.90	3.75	3.65	3.55	3.50	3.50	3.30	3.30	3.20	3.10
3-stride hop	(m)	6.90	7.50	7.80	8.30	8.60	8.20	8.80	8.80	9.30	9.70
Extension jump	(m)	–	0.50	0.55	0.58	0.62	0.60	0.65	0.68	0.70	0.75
Two-legged long jump	(m)	–	–	–	–	–	–	–	–	2.90	3.00
Bench press	(kg)	–	55	70	80	90	80	95	100	110	135
Clean and jerk	(kg)	–	–	60	75	95	65	80	90	100	125
Snatch	(kg)	–	45	55	65	75	65	75	80	90	100
Full squat	(kg)	–	65	85	95	110	100	120	125	135	150

3.3.9 ERRORS – CAUSES – CORRECTIONS

Error	Causes	Corrections
Placing backward the leg opposite the throwing hand in the direction of the throw at the start of the turn (beginner's error).	• Still insufficient mastering of the shift of weight to the opposite leg: The thrower thinks that the backward placing of the leg is necessary to reach the centre of the circle with the pressure leg. • Overhasty start of the turn.	✔ Versatile practice of turn and the start of the turn (411–414) while instructing the thrower to start slowly and to shift his/her weight to the left leg.
Falling backward toward the centre of the circle at the start of the turn.	• Insufficient shift of weight onto the supporting leg during the one-legged starting phase in connection with » insufficient push-off with the leg on the side of the throwing hand; » overhasty start of the turn.	✔ Improvement of the introduction of the turn and shift of weight through imitations (411–413): for example, knocking down a cone with the swing leg or with a gym mat behind one's back. ✔ The thrower should be instructed to start the turn slowly and in a controlled manner (throwing the discus is like an acceleration run).
Insufficient outward turn of the leg opposite the throwing hand during the two-legged starting phase.	• Incorrect introduction of the turn by » bringing forward the throwing arm, » opening the opposite arm, » turning the head and the trunk, and/or » insufficient effort of the thrower to let his/her leg(s) introduce the movement.	✔ Improvement of introducing the turn through the legs by means of imitation (411–413). ✔ Concentration on a correct introduction of the turn when throwing assistive devices.
Too close movement of the swing leg around the supporting leg during the turn.	• Falling backward toward the centre of the circle at the start of the turn and its causes (see above). • Feet are too close together in the starting position. • (Premature lift and) drawing the swing leg to the axis of rotation.	✔ See corrections of falling backward toward the centre of the circle. ✔ Stationary turns (3/4, 4/4, 5/4) (3 and 408) as well as turns with subsequent leg reverse (412–414), while shifting weight to the supporting leg and wide movement of the swing leg; also knocking down a cone with the swing leg.
Insufficient trailing and shoulder-hip separation during the turn.	• Insufficient backward swing of the throwing arm during the preliminary movement; possibly due to insufficient control of the discus. • The foot on the side of the throwing hand is involved in the preliminary movement (i.e., does not remain standing; no tension development). • Insufficient outward turn of the leg opposite the throwing hand during the two-legged starting phase and its causes (see above).	✔ Exercises to get familiarised with the discus (404). ✔ Practising the preliminary movement (411): instruction of the thrower to open and close his/her hands at the point of reversal; touching the hand of a partner at the point of reversal. ✔ Instructing the thrower to place his/her foot firmly on the ground, possibly temporary fixing the foot by a partner. ✔ See corrections of insufficient outward turn of the leg opposite the throwing hand.

(continued)

913

(continued)

Error	Causes	Corrections
Too short leg reverse (too stationary turn).	• Too close movement of the swing leg around the supporting leg and its causes (see above). • Insufficient push-off at the end of the one-legged starting phase. • Insufficient acceleration of the swing leg in the direction of the throw (the thigh and/or the lower leg are not brought forward enough; insufficient kicking movement of the lower leg).	✔ See corrections of too close movement of the swing leg around the supporting leg and its causes. ✔ Continuous leg reversals (408) with powerful push-off, active movement of the swing leg, and wide and flat leg reverse. ✔ Imitations and throws with wide and flat leg reverse over a ditch (e.g., 408). ✔ Testing and possible reinforcement of the lower-leg kick.
Too far leg reverse	• Excessive motivation of a tall and advanced thrower. • Upward directed push-off with fully extended knee and/or • The swing leg (thigh) is brought up too high (into the horizontal position).	✔ Versatile imitations and throws (412-414) with controlled turn and powerful but flat push-off into the leg reverse
Passive foot touchdown and insufficient continuation of the rotation of the pressure leg during the one-legged delivery phase.	• Insufficient velocity of rotation about the longitudinal axis (already before the touchdown). • Insufficient inward rotation of the pressure leg before the touchdown. • No acceleration of the foot against the direction of the throw immediately before the touchdown, possibly due to insufficient bending of the knee (touchdown too early). • Touchdown on the entire sole of the foot. • No active rotational work (insufficient rotation of the pelvis and extension of the hip).	✔ Continuous leg reversals (408), imitations and throws (410 and 414) with active initiation of the rotation during the push-off for the leg reverse, deliberate inward rotation of the swing leg, active placement of the pressure leg on the ball of the foot and more rapid turning action.
Upright trunk and CG too far in the direction of the throw upon touchdown of the pressure leg (the shoulders are already above the point of touchdown or even farther in the direction of the throw).	• Insufficient holding back of the shoulders during the one-legged starting phase and during the leg reverse due to » falling backward toward the centre of the circle at the start of the turn and its causes (see above); » excessive hip flexion at the start of the turn; or » excessive knee extension during the push-off with the supporting leg toward the end of the one-legged starting phase.	✔ See corrections of falling backward toward the centre of the circle at the start of the turn and its causes. ✔ Imitation and throws (412-414) focusing on an upright trunk at the beginning, the knee not being fully extended, and the legs and the pelvis overtaking the trunk.

Error	Causes	Corrections
Touchdown of the bracing leg too far on the side of the throwing hand.	• Balance problems during the turn. • Touchdown of the pressure leg not in the centre of the circle (too far to the right or the left). • Too early touchdown (the athlete has not yet turned on his/her pressure leg far enough). • Insufficient continuation of the rotation of the pressure leg during the one-legged delivery phase and its causes (see above).	✔ Rotational jumps, pirouettes (3), turns and continuous leg reversals (408). ✔ Imitations and throws (411–414) with slow and controlled start of the turn and with control of the points of foot touchdown (but without sight control by the athlete during movement execution: "Don't look at your feet"). ✔ See corrections of insufficient continuation of the rotation of the pressure leg during the one-legged delivery phase.
Placement of the bracing leg too far outside on the bracing-leg side.	• Balance problems during the turn. • Turn too far during the one-legged start phase: placement of the pressure leg too far on the side of the bracing leg. • Starting position too far on the side of the throwing hand (too diagonal path of the points of foot touchdown).	✔ Rotational jumps, pirouettes (3), turns and continuous leg reversals (408). ✔ Imitations and throws (411–414) while checking the foot touchdown points (but without sight control by the athlete during movement execution: "Don't look at your feet").
Insufficient trailing and shoulder-hip separation in the backward reclining position of delivery.	• Insufficient trailing and shoulder-hip separation during the turn and their causes (see above). • Too early delivery action of the trunk instead of active holding back of the throwing arm during the leg reverse and the one-legged delivery phase. • Insufficient continuation of the rotation of the pressure leg during the one-legged delivery phase and its causes (see above).	✔ See corrections of insufficient trailing and shoulder-hip separation during the turn. ✔ Imitations and throws (409–414) with deliberate holding back of the throwing arm; imitation (e.g., with stick between the hands or on the shoulders). ✔ See corrections of insufficient continuation of the rotation of the pressure leg during the one-legged delivery phase.

Lacking effect of the bracing leg.	• Placement of the bracing leg too far outside on the bracing-leg side and its causes (see above).
	• No active extension of the bracing leg, possibly due to a lack of reactive strength.
	• The vertical projection of the CG is already too near to the touchdown point of the bracing leg due to
	  » CG too far in the direction of the throw when placing the pressure leg and its causes (see above); or
	  » too early delivery activity of the upper body.
		✔ See corrections of placement of the bracing leg too far outside on the bracing-leg side, and CG too far in the direction of the throw upon touchdown of the pressure leg.
		✔ Throws and imitation initially from a standing position (406 and 407), then with increasing pre-acceleration (409, 410, and 414) focusing on the trunk staying behind and an active extension of the bracing leg.
		✔ Reactive-strength training for the legs (e.g., 64).

(continued)

(continued)

Error	Causes	Corrections
Insufficient bringing forward of the hip on the side of the throwing hand.	• Insufficient continuation of the rotation of the pressure leg during the one-legged delivery phase and its causes (see above). • Upright trunk upon touchdown of the pressure leg and its causes (see above). • Touchdown of the bracing leg too far on the side of the throwing hand and its causes (see above). • Lacking effect of the bracing leg and its causes (see above). • Too early delivery activity of the upper body. • Passive action of the pressure leg.	✔ See corrections of insufficient continuation of the rotation of the pressure leg during the one-legged delivery phase, of upright trunk upon touchdown of the pressure leg, of touchdown of the bracing leg too far on the side of the throwing hand, and of lacking effect of the bracing leg. ✔ Development of starting the delivery activity with active action of the pressure leg while throwing from a standing position (406) and maintenance of the active action of the pressure leg with increasing pre-acceleration (409, 410, and 414), as well as consolidation of the active action of the pressure leg by means of appropriate imitation exercises.
Throwing out of the trouser pocket (too small angle of abduction of the shoulder of the throwing arm during the delivery motion).	• Too small angle of abduction even during the turn. • Excessive lowering of the discus after the high point during the one-legged delivery phase, possibly due to the thrower assuming that he/she should achieve a larger angle of delivery.	✔ Imitations and throws (409–414) focusing on a large angle of abduction already during the preliminary swing and the turn. ✔ Making the athlete understand that the high-low movement of the discus is rather caused by the lean of his/her trunk than by changing the angle of abduction of the shoulder of the throwing arm; corresponding imitations and throws while standing (406 and 407).
Stepping over the frontal rim of the circle during the delivery.	• Too far leg reverse and its causes (see above) • Lack of effect of the bracing leg and its causes (see above). • Excessive forward lean of the trunk during the delivery. • Insufficient recovery movement, possibly due to frequent stepping over during practice. • Jumping delivery.	✔ See corrections of too far leg reverse and lack of effect of the bracing leg. ✔ Focus on the maximal velocity of the rotation of the trunk during the delivery while actively holding the opposite shoulder back and drawing the opposite arm backward and downward toward one's body. ✔ Avoidance of invalid throws even during practice. ✔ Possibly (temporary) replacement of the jumping delivery by the standing delivery which is more controlled.

Error	Causes	Corrections
Soon after delivery, the discus tilts downward laterally (the axis of symmetry is shifted to the horizontal which happens more quickly with lighter discuses).	• Too small angle of lateral tilt (no hanging outer edge) and/or too large angle of attitude due to an unfavourable technique of gripping the discus and/or too large angle of abduction at the shoulder joint of the throwing arm. • Unfavourable wind (see chapter II–3.3.3: phase 4).	✔ Initially in standing throws (406), later in throws with increased pre-acceleration (409, 410, and 414), the athlete should focus on the followings points: the back of the hand is turned upward, the wrist is slightly bent (palmarflexed), the discus is released not above the height of the shoulder.
The discus flutters.	• In most cases, the athlete has an insufficient feel for the discus due to a lack of experience.	✔ Exercises to get familiarised with the discus (404); subsequently, the control of the discus during standing throws (405 and 406) should be improved, and the pre-acceleration (409, 410, and 414) should be increased only when the problem does no longer occur in standing throws.
The discus lands on the side of the throwing hand outside the landing sector or in the net.	• The fingers of the throwing hand are too close together. • The discus is rolled off over the middle instead of over the index finger. • Touchdown of the bracing leg too far on the side of the throwing hand and its causes (see above). • Insufficient bringing forward of the hip on the side of the throwing hand and its causes (see above).	✔ Checking the technique of gripping the discus: The fingers should possibly be a bit more apart and the rim of the discus should possibly be better gripped by the tips of the fingers (in particular with the tip of the index finger). ✔ See corrections of touchdown of the bracing leg too far on the side of the throwing hand and insufficient bringing forward of the hip on the side of the throwing hand.
The discus lands on the bracing-leg side outside the landing sector or in the net.	• Fingers of the throwing hand too far apart. • Placement of the bracing leg too far outside on the bracing-leg side and its causes (see above).	✔ Checking the technique of gripping the discus: The fingers should possibly be a bit closer together. ✔ See corrections of placement of the bracing leg too far outside on the opposite side.

3.3.10 TRAINING PLANNING

Many introductory statements on training planning made in connection with the javelin throw (see chapter II–3.2.10) also apply equally to the discus throw.

Since in the throwing events, contrary to sprinting and jumping events, not only relative strength (i.e., strength related to body weight) but also absolute maximum strength plays a crucial role, muscle build-up training is of greater importance in the throwing events than in the sprinting and jumping events. This applies both to the arms and to the trunk and legs. Moreover, the importance of absolute maximum strength and muscle mass for the competition result increases with the weight of the device. Therefore, hypertrophy-oriented strength training increases from the javelin, via the discus throw, to the shot put and is also a training focus for a longer part of the preparatory period. The first mesocycle is characterised by the greatest amount of general athletic training during the course of the season, the second mesocycle is characterised by the greatest amount of maximum-strength training, the third mesocycle by the greatest expenditure of time for technique training, and the fourth mesocycle by a general reduction in the amount of training.

SUGGESTED TRAINING PLANS

Below, there are exemplary microcycles for the

- first mesocycle of a 17-year-old athlete in build-up training (table 10);
- second mesocycle of an athlete in high-performance training (table 11); and
- fourth mesocycle of an athlete in high-performance training (table 12).

It is assumed that 17-year-old shot putters, discus throwers, and hammer throwers have not yet specialised. The exemplary microcycles presented in connection with the shot put and hammer throw (see chapters II–3.4.10 and II–3.5.10) for the

- second mesocycle of a 17-year-old athlete in build-up training;
- third mesocycle of a 17-year-old athlete in build-up training

are therefore intended for the same athlete.

Even in high-performance training, the non-technical training for the discus throw and shot put are similar. Therefore, as a supplement to the training plans presented here, the chapter on the shot put includes an exemplary microcycle for the

- first mesocycle of an athlete in high-performance training; and
- third mesocycle of an athlete in high-performance training.

Table 9: **Training emphasis in the various mesocycles** *for discus-throw practice in build-up and high-performance training.*

1st mesocycle	basic aerobic and anaerobic endurance training; strength-endurance, hypertrophy-oriented maximal-strength, speed-strength, and reactive-strength training (also using a heavy throwing implement); flexibility training; general (sprinting, jumping, games, etc.), and discus-specific coordination training
2nd mesocycle	(speed-)endurance training; hypertrophy-, IC- and connective-tissue-oriented maximal-, speed-, and reactive-strength training (also using a heavy throwing implement); speed training (sprint and specific use of a light device); general (sprinting, jumping, games, etc.), and discus-specific coordination training
3rd mesocycle	hypertrophy-, IC- and connective-tissue-oriented maximal-, speed- and reactive-strength training; speed training (sprint and specific use of a light device); technique training
4th mesocycle	competitions and corresponding regeneration; IC- and connective-tissue-oriented maximal-, speed- and reactive-strength training; sprinting-speed training; technique training; maintenance stimuli

Table 10: Build-up training: sample microcycle for a 17-year-old thrower (discus, shot, and hammer) in the first mesocycle.

Monday	Tuesday	Wednesday	Thursday	Friday	Saturday	Sunday
Trunk stabilisation exercises and abdominal crunches (20 min) with a lot of dynamic variation	Warm-up jogging (6 min) including backward and sideward running	Foot strengthening (10 min)	Continuous run (30 min) or cycling, swimming, inline skating, etc.	Warm-up jogging (6 min) including rolls, turns, cartwheels, etc.	Warm-up jogging (6 min) including picking up, carrying on the left or right side, and forward throwing of a ball or other device	Rest
Warm-up specific to the shot put (15 min) e.g., arm circling, tossing, and chest pass from a squatting position	ABCs of sprinting (8–10 run-throughs) heel kicks, high-knee run, etc.	Warm-up specific to the discus throw (15 min) e.g., arm circling, rotational jumps, and passing the medicine ball with turning the trunk	Contract-relax stretching (15 min)	Practising the hammer-throw technique (50 min) including specific warm-up: e.g., arm circling, standing throws, turn imitations, throws using normal and heavy devices	ABCs of sprinting/ jumping (15–20 run-throughs)	
Practising the shot-put technique (40 min) differential learning: frontal puts and standing puts, also using a medicine ball, stone, heavy shot, etc.	Acceleration runs (2 reps)	Practising the discus-throw technique (40 min) many frontal throws and standing throws, also with heavier discuses, shots, and batons; turn imitations (e.g., on a gymnastic bench)	Gymnastics (30 min) versatile rotational movements depending on the athlete's level of skill	Muscle build-up training (50 min) for arms and legs on apparatus	Acceleration runs (2 reps) barefoot	
Muscle build-up training (40 min) bench press, bench pull, shoulder press, lat pull, clean	ABCs of jumping (8–10 run-throughs) e.g., galloping sideways, ankle jumps, and skipping with two-legged landing	Strength-endurance circuit (50 min) including full squat, medicine-ball throws, abdominal crunches, ABCs of sprinting/jumping, etc.	Muscle build-up training (30 min) e.g., abdominal machine, shoulder-hip twists, lumborum, and hip/ back extensors using a big box	Foot strengthening (10 min) in the sand	LI tempo runs (3 x 4 x 150m; rest intervals: 2 min; rest intervals between sets: 6 min) in running shoes	
Medicine-ball putting (10 reps) as utilisation	Alternating-pace sprints (2 reps)	Standing starts (3 x 30m) as utilisation	ABCs of jumping (6 run-throughs) as utilisation	Discus throws (10 reps) using a light shot as utilisation	Contract-relax stretching (15 min)	
	Skipping and bounding runs (8–12 run-throughs) many variations				Warm-down jogging (10 diagonals on the lawn)	
	Game (30 min) e.g., handball, field hockey, or soccer				Squat-extension jumps (10 reps) plus one ankle jump each and short rest intervals, as utilisation	
	Contract-relax stretching (15 min)					

Table 11: High-performance training: sample microcycle in the second mesocycle using double periodisation.

	Monday	Tuesday	Wednesday	Thursday	Friday	Saturday	Sunday
Morning	Trunk stabilisation exercises and abdominal crunches (20 min) Warm-up specific to the discus throw (20 min) e.g., arm circling and standing throws Practising the discus-throw technique (50 min) imitations and 6/4 turn	Foot strengthening (10 min) small jumps Walking and skipping over hurdles (20 min) Rhythm sprints (6 x 60 m) e.g., over mini-hurdles Muscle build-up training (30 min) snatch and full squat	Warm-up jogging (6 min) Shot and baton throws (50 min) including specific warm-up, heavy implement, throws with 4/4 to 6/4 turn Speed-strength and muscle build-up training (50 min) for the trunk and the arms; using a medicine ball, on the strength-training device, exercises using a technique specific to the discus throw (e.g., delivery motion with barbell discs and flag waving) and less specific on apparatus. Discus throws (10 reps per side) light device; as utilisation	Warm-up jogging (6 min) ABCs of jumping (12–15 run-throughs) Bounding runs (4 x 30m) Jumps onto a box (5 x 10 reps) Pirouettes, rotational jumps, and gymnastics (30 min) versatile variations	Warm-up jogging (6 min) Warm-up specific to the discus throw (25 min) throws with the weak hand, etc. Practising the discus-throw technique (45 min) e.g., imitation of movement segments and 4/4 to 5/4 turn	Warm-up jogging (6 min) with additional tasks ABCs of sprinting (12–15 run-throughs) Acceleration runs (3 reps) I3 tempo runs (2 x 3 x 150m; rest intervals: 3 min; rest intervals between sets: 10 min)	Rest
Afternoon	Warm-up jogging (6 min) ABCs of jumping (12–15 run-throughs) Skipping and bounding runs (2 x 4 x 30m) Muscle build-up training (50 min) e.g., flies, reverse flies, bench press, deltoideus and biceps curl Shot throws (10 reps per side) light device	Warm-up jogging (6 min) Acceleration runs ABCs of sprinting (12–15 run-throughs) I1 tempo runs (2 x 5 x 100m; rest intervals: 1.5–2 min; rest intervals between sets: 6 min) Contract-relax stretching (15 min) Warm-down jogging Ankle jumps		Warm-up jogging (6 min) Game (30 min) e.g., soccer or field hockey Muscle build-up training (60 min) hamstrings, quadriceps, adductors/abductors, and clean Skipping with two-legged landing (3 x 20m) as utilisation	Warm-up jogging (6 min) Strength training (70 min) according to the pyramid principle and maximal-eccentric: for the trunk and the arms (e.g., flies, bench pull, bench press, shoulder press) Foot strengthening (15 min) in the sand Shot throws (10 reps per side) light weight	Contract-relax stretching (15 min) Strength training (40 min) maximal-eccentric and according to the pyramid principle: for the legs squats, etc. Ankle jumps (3 x 6 reps)	

Table 12: *High-performance training: sample microcycle in the fourth mesocycle using double periodisation.*

Monday	Tuesday	Wednesday	Thursday	Friday	Saturday	Sunday
Warm-up jogging (6 min)	Warm-up jogging (6 min)	Warm-up jogging (6 min)	Warm-up jogging (6 min)	Warm-up jogging (6 min)	Rest	*Preparatory competition*
Maximal-eccentric strength training (15 min) trunk stabilisation, lifting opposite upper and lower limbs in prone position, belly punches, raising the foot/toes	Practising the discus-throw technique (50 min) including specific warm-up, imitations, throws using competition technique, final individual fine-tuning	ABCs of sprinting (8–10 run-throughs)	Practising the discus-throw technique (40 min) including specific warm-up, imitations, throws using competition technique, final individual fine tuning	ABCs of sprinting/ jumping (8–10 run-throughs)		• Warm-up jogging • Inciting the trunk and foot muscles • Two acceleration runs • Squat-extension jumps and reactive push-ups for inciting
Acceleration runs (2 reps)	High-intensity strength training (40 min) e.g., flies, reverse flies, inclined bench press, and lat pull	Acceleration runs (2 reps)	Strength training (40 min) according to the pyramid principle: special exercises for the trunk and arms (e.g., delivery motion with barbell discs)	Acceleration runs (2 reps)		• Imitations • Practice throws from a standing position and from a turn • Imitations before every throw
Tuck jumps (5 x 3 hurdles)	Discus throws (10 reps per side) light shot, as utilisation	Pull-resisted sprints (2 x 20m) heavy weight	Discus throws (10 reps per side) light discus, as utilisation	Depth jumps (3 x 5) from box to box		Discus competition (6 trials)
Bounding run (2 x 2 x 30m)		Standing starts (3 x 30m) maximal		Crouch starts (3 x 30m) maximal		
High-intensity strength training (30 min) clean and quarter-split squat		Jumps onto a box or tossing (5 x 3 reps)		High-intensity strength training (15 min) snatch		
Ankle jumps (3 x 6 reps) as utilisation		Strength training (40 min) according to the pyramid principle: e.g., standing throw imitations using a barbell, squats, etc.				
		Ankle jumps				

In the competition phase, the training plan must be adapted to the (irregular) competition calendar. In this plan, it can be assumed that the athlete took part in a preparatory competition on the previous Sunday. At these competitions, the athlete should also now and then take part in other events, such as the shot put or the 100m sprint. If between two preparatory competitions there are no other competitions for one and a half weeks (or more), the athlete should perform more training and his/her training should be of a more basic nature. Before a major competition, the athlete should train even less than shown here.

3.3.11   BIBLIOGRAPHY

Bartonietz, K. (2000). Die Wurfdisziplinen bei der WM ´99. *Leichtathletiktraining 11* (4), 24-29.

Böttcher, G. (2000). Technik-Varianten im Diskuswurf. *Leichtathletiktraining 11* (9+10), 31-37.

Böttcher, G. (2005). Spezielle Kraft für das Diskuswerfen. *Leichtathletiktraining 16* (2+3), 40-47.

Dickwach, H. & Knoll K. (2003). Zur Technik des Diskuswerfens auf der Grundlage von 3-D-Videobild- und -Bodenreaktionskraftmessung. *Zeitschrift für angewandte Trainingswissenschaft 10* (2), 95-103.

Dickwach, H. & Knoll, K. (2004). Zur Bewegungsstruktur der Trainingsübungen Kugel- und Stabwurf im Vergleich zum Diskuswurf. *Zeitschrift für angewandte Trainingswissenschaft 11* (1), 60-71.

Hay, J. & Bing, Y. (1995). Critical characteristics of technique in throwing the discus. *Journal of Sport Sciences 13* (2), 125-140.

Hay, J. & Bing, Y. (1996). Weight shift and foot placement in throwing the discus. *Track coach (135)*, 4297-4300.

Hildebrand, F. & Dickwach, H. (2003). Flugverhalten des Diskus und Weiten in Abhängigkeit von unterschiedlichen Windbedingungen. *Zeitschrift für angewandte Trainingswissenschaft 10* (1), 56-59.

Knicker, A. (1994). Kinematic analyses of the discus throwing competitions at the IAAF World Championships in athletics, Stuttgart 1993. *New Studies in Athletics 9* (3), 9-16.

Knicker, A. (1999). Discus Throw. In G.-P. Brüggemann, D. Koszewski & H. Müller (Hrsg.), *Biomechanical Research Project Athens 1997: Final Report.* Oxfort: Meyer & Meyer.

Kühl, L. & Hommel, H. (Red.) (mit Bartonietz, K., Becker, M., Becker, S., Böttcher, G., Deyle, M., Gaede, E., Hartmann, W., Losch, M., Rapp, E., Thomas, B., Wollbrück, R. & Zöllkau, H.). (1997). *Rahmentrainingsplan für das Aufbautraining Wurf* (Edition Leichtathletik, 5, 3. Aufl.). Aachen: Meyer & Meyer.

Neighbour, B. (2009). The discus technique. Part 1. *Modern Athlete and Coach 47* (1), 20-22.

Oltmanns, K. (2005). Grundlagentraining = Lerntraining! – Beispiel: Diskuswerfen. *Leichtathletiktraining 16* (2+3), 52-62.

Regelkommissionen des DLV, FLA, ÖLV und SLV (Hrsg.). (2010). *Internationale Wettkampfregeln.* Waldfischbach: Hornberger.

Salomon, H. (2008). Drehwürfe leicht gemacht. *Leichtathletiktraining 19* (11), 18-21.

Schlüter, W. & Nixdorf, E. (1984). Kinematische Beschreibung und Analysen der Diskuswurftechnik. *Leistungssport 14* (6), 17-22.

Schult, J. (2006). Harting und Wierig im internationalen Check. *Leichtathletiktraining 17* (8), 18-27.

Schult, J. (mit Ständner, M. & Lang, T.). (2008). Weite Würfe mit der Scheibe. *Leichtathletiktraining 19* (7), 30-39.

Schult, J. (2008). Methodik zur Verbesserung der Diskustechnik. In Deutscher Leichtathletikverband (Hrsg.). *Kongress 2008: Leichtathletik mit Perspektiven* (Kongress-CD). Münster: Philippka.

Tidow, G. (1994). Model technique analysis sheets Part IX: The discus throw. *New Studies in Athletics 9* (3). 47-68.

Wank, V. (2006). Biomechanik und leistungsrelevante Parameter der leichtathletischen Wurfdisziplinen. In K. Wohlgefahrt & S. Michel, *Beiträge zur speziellen Trainingswissenschaft Leichtathletik: Symposium der dvs-Kommission Leichtathletik vom 10.-11.10.2002 in Bad Blankenburg* (Schriften der Deutschen Vereinigung für Sportwissschaft, 153, S. 132-144). Hamburg: Czwalina.

3.4 SHOT PUT

3.4.1 DEVELOPMENT OF TECHNIQUES

Since ancient times, people have probably pitted their strength against each other by putting heavy objects (e.g., stones). Even today, a 15kg iron stone is put at gymnastics festivals and as part of outdoor strength sports. The shot put is said to have its origin in the strength competitions of Swiss shepherds of the 13th century. Stone putting is also a discipline in the Scottish Highland Games. These games were first conducted in the early Middle Ages and their purpose was to help the Celtic kings to find their strongest men.

In the 14th century, when cannons became increasingly popular, cannonballs were used more and more as putting devices. The weight of the modern shot equalling 16 English pounds was established in 1860. The shot put was initially performed from a square with a side length of 7 feet. With these general requirements, the shot put became a discipline in the Olympic Games in 1896. Since the 1906 intermediate Olympic Games, the shot put has been performed from a 7-foot circle which is still used today. In 1926, the Women's Sports Federation established their shot weight at 4 kg. However, it was not before 1948 that the women's shot put became an Olympic discipline.

It is typical of the shot put that in the course of history various techniques have developed. Athletes experimented with various preliminary movements from a starting position standing sideways in respect to the throwing direction. In 1953, Parry O'Brien established his first world record of exactly 18m. O'Brien is considered the inventor of the most common technique today. It is referred to the glide or linear technique of shot putting, or the O'Brien technique. O'Brien was known as a shot-put fanatic. He always had a shot in his car, and he often stopped somewhere, got out, and practised for hours. Therefore, by 1959 he had established nine world records (19.30m). O'Brien was an American just like all the world-record holders from 1934–1976.

Unexpectedly, a Russian established a new world record with a completely new technique. Using the spin or rotational shot-put technique, Soviet Alexander Baryshnikov achieved exactly 22m on 6 October 1976. However, the linear shot-put technique remained competitive. Using this technique, Udo Beyer, Ulf Timmermann (both from the GDR), and Alessandro Andrei (Italy) continuously improved the world record until Timmermann was the first to reach 23m in 1988. However, the rotational shot-putter Randy Barnes took the world record back to the USA in 1990. With 23.12m he overtook Timmermann's world record achieved with the linear technique by only 6cm. It took 31 years for Barnes's record to be broken, and again it was broken by an American. Shortly before his second Olympic title in 2021, Ryan Crouser achieved 23.37m using the rotational technique.

Since 1936, when German Gerhard Stöck won a medal in two Olympic throwing events, this has never been achieved by an athlete again. After achieving third place in the shot put, Stöck was victorious in the javelin throw. However, a double success seemspossible due to the discus-like rotational technique of shot putting. For example, Rutger Smith from the Netherlands was fourth in the discus throw and third in the shot put at the 2007 World Championships.

After the turn of the millennium, two German women achieved distances over 20m using another technique which

had been known for decades, but had temporarily been forgotten. Due to an injury, the Olympic champion and triple world champion Astrid Kumbernuss experimented with the scissor-step technique. Petra Lammert, who placed fifth at the 2007 World Championships, achieved her greatest success using this technique, which is characterised by the shot putter beginning virtually on the wrong leg compared with the linear technique of shot putting.

The cartwheel technique performed by some shot-putters with a gymnastics background was less promising in terms of biomechanics, but highly entertaining. In this technique, which has now been banned, the backward reclining position of delivery was reached after performing a one-armed cartwheel on the free hand.

3.4.2 THE MOST IMPORTANT COMPETITION RULES

The following abridged and simplified International Competition Rules comprise the framework for the technique and strategy as well as the organisation of shot-put competitions:

- Table 1 describes the shots to be used. Each shot must be made of solid iron, brass, or another metal that is not softer than brass, or a shell of such metal filled with lead or other solid material. It must be spherical in shape and its surface must be completely smooth.
- Figure 1 describes the layout of a

shot-put area. The stop board must be white and made of wood or other suitable material in the shape of an arc so that the inner surface aligns with the inner edge of the rim of the circle and is perpendicular to the surface of the circle. It must be firmly fixed to the ground.

- The shot must be put from the shoulder with only one hand. When an athlete takes a stance in the circle to commence a put, the shot must touch or be in close proximity to the athlete's neck or chin. During the action of putting, the hand must not be dropped below this position and the shot must not be taken behind the line of the shoulders. Cartwheeling techniques are not permitted.

- It is a failure if an athlete in the course of a trial:
  - » releases the shot other than as permitted under the rules (e.g., throws or drops it); or
  - » touches any part of the stop board other than its inner side with any part of his/her body.

Otherwise, the general competition rules for the technical disciplines and throwing apply (see chapters II–2.1.1 and II–3.1.1).

*Table 1: **Minimum weight and outer diameter of the shots** for the different age groups (see Rule Commissions by the DLV, FLA, ÖLV and SLV, 2010, p. 110).*

Age groups		Weight, diameter, thickness
Female U14, 16, and 18, male U14	w50 and older, m80 and older	3.000 kg, 8.5–10.0cm
Female U20, women, male U16	w40–45, m70–75	4.000 kg, 9.5–11.0cm
Male U18	m60–65	5.000 kg, 10.0–12.0cm
Male U20	m50–55	6.000 kg, 10.5–12.5cm
Men	m40–45	7.260 kg, 11.0–13.0cm

3.4.3 SPORT-SCIENCE FINDINGS, PHASE STRUCTURE, AND TECHNIQUE

In the shot put, there are three techniques to pre-accelerate the thrower and the device:

- the linear (or glide) technique;
- the scissor-step technique; and
- the rotational (or spin) technique.

With all three techniques, comparable putting distances may be achieved (see chapter II–3.4.1 as well as discourse III) and the main acceleration is also similar. Correspondingly, the first two of the four main phases presented below are described for the three techniques separately before the two additional main phases are presented for all three techniques together:

- preliminary movement;
- pre-acceleration;
- delivery; and
- recovery and flight of the shot.

In the linear technique, the pre-acceleration phase is called the glide, in the scissor-step technique it is called scissor step, and in the rotational technique it is called the turn.

PHASE 1 OF THE LINEAR TECHNIQUE: PRELIMINARY MOVEMENT

GRIPPING AND POSITIONING THE SHOT ON THE NECK

Figure 2 illustrates the grip and positioning of the shot. Pressure from the shot is on the basic joints of the long fingers. The

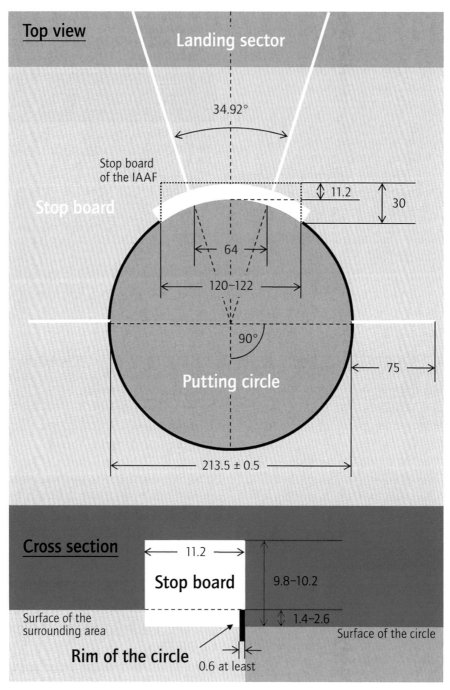

Figure 1: **Shot-put area** (all specifications in cm, modified on the basis of the Rule Commissions by the DLV, FLA, ÖLV and SLV, 2010, p. 110). The white boundary lines are 5 cm wide.

thumb and little finger support the shot at the sides. The shot is positioned in the pit of the collarbone (supraclavicular fossa) and is pressed toward the neck laterally from the front. The shot is in contact with both the chin and collarbone. The wrist is extremely bent (dorsiflexion). The forearm is pronated so that the fingers are not on the shot, but behind it. The index finger of the putting hand is near the collarbone. The upper arm is abducted from the body. The elbow position or the position of the putting arm may vary. For beginners, it is best to position the arm so that the forearm already points in the direction of the throw, or the abducted elbow points contrary to the direction of the put. For advanced athletes, the putting arm is often raised more toward the side and upward. The release is performed more from a rotational movement in which the elbow must first be brought behind the shot. The result is that in this ideal position, force transmission to the shot (hitting the shot) is more difficult in terms of coordination than in the starting position used by beginners. However, the path of acceleration, the shoulder-hip separation, and the tension of the chest muscles may also be positively affected.

STARTING POSITION AND PRELIMINARY MOVEMENT

In the starting position, the linear shot putter stands at the rear rim of the circle with his/her back turned to the direction of the throw. He/she stands on the leg of the side of the putting hand, whose foot is placed on the imaginary and extended centre line of the landing sector. The tip of

*Figure 2: **Positioning of the shot on the neck.***

the toe touches the rear rim of the circle and points opposite the direction of the put. In order to maintain balance better, the load is initially on the entire sole of the foot.

At the end of the preliminary movement, the shot putter reaches a crouching position, which is characterised by the upper body being approximately horizontal, and the knee of the supporting leg being bent at nearly 90°. The shift of the shot to the back and downward contrary to the putting direction leads to a long path of acceleration. For beginners and less advanced athletes, the forward lean of the upper body and the bend of the supporting leg are less distinct since their strength is not sufficient to subsequently raise the shot from such a low bent position quickly and effectively. To shift the CG of the putter-shot system as far to the back as possible, the weight of the advanced athlete now rests on the ball of the foot. The foot of the free leg is placed near the foot of the supporting leg. The shoulder and the hip axis are aligned parallel to the rear rim of the circle. The shot putter looks at a point just beyond the circle and continues to do so at least until he/she reaches the backward reclining position of delivery.

The preliminary movement (i.e., taking the crouch position) is characterised by many individual variations. As an important difference, the **dynamic and static preliminary movement** may be distinguished. In the dynamic preliminary movement, the subsequent push-off and swing-leg movement is performed reactively and powerfully without a break after taking the crouch position. In the static preliminary movement, the linear shot putter remains briefly in the crouch position. Whereas in the dynamic preliminary movement there is probably a more powerful push-off from the rear rim of the circle by using the stretch-shortening cycle, the static preliminary movement is said to allow a higher degree of control since it is easier to maintain balance using this variation.

For some athletes taking the crouch position involves some very complex preliminary movements. The preliminary movement of the linear shot-put world-record holder Ulf Timmermann, who has found many imitators, may be described as follows:

- standing position on the entire sole of the extended push-off leg; forward bending of the trunk and contralateral lift of the swing leg to the horizontal balance position (T-position; according to some sources, this position is supposed to convey a sense of one's body position at the end of the push-off);
- pulling the swing leg to the bracing leg and simultaneously bending the knee of the supporting leg, sometimes with rounded back; usually, the swing leg is not fully brought to the supporting leg and the foot of the swing leg should by no means swing past the supporting leg;
- shifting the weight to the ball of the foot so that the shot is positioned as far as possible outside of the circle; simultaneous lifting of the centre of gravity by extending the knee and ankle; and
- from there bending the supporting leg to the crouch position with dynamic transition to the push-off.

However, in the static preliminary movement in particular, the taking of the crouch position may be performed in a more

Figure 3: **Taking the crouch position through the horizontal balance position** as a possible preliminary movement in the linear technique of shot putting.

direct way (e.g., without an intermediate horizontal balance position and/or the multiple rhythmic bending and stretching of the supporting leg). There is no evident connection between the preliminary movement and the putting performance. Thus, the forward lean of the upper body and the bending of the supporting leg may be sufficient while the foot of the swing leg stays next to the foot of the supporting leg. The preliminary movement is often associated with inhaling and subsequent holding one's breath. Using the technique of forced breathing, the shot putter holds his/her breath until the shot leaves his/her hand.

PHASE 2 OF THE LINEAR TECHNIQUE OF SHOT PUTTING: GLIDE

The glide can be divided into two sub-phases:

- push-off with the later pressure leg; and
- supportless phase.

PUSH-OFF WITH THE LATER PRESSURE LEG

In the transition from the preliminary movement to the push-off, the linear shot putter shifts his/her body weight backward through the active extension of the ankle of his/her supporting leg. The vertical projection of the CG of the shot-putter and the shot is no longer over the foot of the supporting leg, but is shifted toward the stop board. During this action, the active backswing of the free leg, the maximally powerful push-off with the supporting leg, and the slight raising of the upper body are

Figure 4: *Push-off with the later pressure leg in the linear technique of shot putting.*

initiated. The knee and hip of the swing leg are extended. In respect to the push-off with the supporting leg, athletes are often recommended to initially lift the ball of their foot from the ground and to provide the final application of force with the heel (see figure 4). However, a push-off with the entire foot or with the ball of the foot while the heel is raised may be acceptable especially for tall athletes. While the knee of the supporting leg is (almost) fully extended, the hip is only extended up to approximately 90°. In the process, the knee of the swing leg usually reaches its extension slightly before the push-off leg. The position achieved after the push-off leg has left the ground has many different names in athletics literature. The legs of the shot-putter form an inverted V or the A-position. Along with the upper body, this position is also called the T-position (which is now tilted; see horizontal balance position above).

While the shoulder axis still remains parallel to the rear rim of the circle, a shoulder-hip separation is developed by turning the hip axis to the side in accordance with the leg movement. Additionally, the swing leg is rotated somewhat to the outside so that the foot is eventually parallel to the

DISCOURSE I: VARIATIONS OF THE ACTION OF THE COUNTER-ARM WHEN PUSHING OFF FROM THE REAR RIM OF THE CIRCLE

In respect to the action of the counter-arm performed by (scissor-step and) linear shot putters, at least three variations may be distinguished:

- From the beginning of the movement, the counter-arm is actively held back against the rotational movement during the delivery and/or is brought to the front of the body (from the point of view of the shot-putter). The hand of the counter-arm is sometimes moved up to near the elbow of the putting arm to keep the opposite side closed for a long time or to avoid turning the opposite side in the direction of the throw too early.
- In the starting position, the counter-arm hangs down loosely or is held backward and downward. From there, it is initially (slightly) moved as a swing element in the direction of the put and is only subsequently moved backward during the flight phase as described above. The backward movement, which is more noticeable then, provides a counter-movement to the rotation of the lower part of the body (rotation compensation). Since the rotation of the body is stronger in the scissor-step technique, this kind of counter-arm movement is also more common and more pronounced in the scissor-step technique.
- Some top German shot-putters have experimented with another counter-arm movement (e.g., Oliver Sven Buder and Ralf Bartels) to keep the opposite side closed for a long time. They swing the counter-arm backward and to the front of the body using a pendulum movement which begins beside the trunk when the push-off and the swing leg movement are initiated.

ground and pointing outward. The upper body and the shot are still kept relatively low in order to ensure a long acceleration path in the main acceleration phase.

SUPPORTLESS PHASE

The backward shift of the CG at the beginning of the push-off, the push-off with the heel, the effort to keep the upper body low, as well as the resulting direction of the push-off are supposed to lead to an extremely flat flight phase. The term glide is used to indicate that during the flight phase the pressure leg in particular, as well as the bracing leg, are moved extremely flat over the ground. However, the foot of the pressure leg should not trail on the ground to avoid braking forces and to be able to turn inward by 45–90°. This movement is therefore ultimately a flat one-legged jump backward. Although the term jump in this context is avoided in athletics literature since it could create the idea of a push-off which is directed too far upward, it may be quite helpful for beginners. With right-handed beginners, the term jump flatly from right to right(-left) is probably better suited to create the idea of a push-off as powerful as possible rather than the term glide.

During the flight phase, the linear shot-putter bends the previous push-off leg again and moves it quickly under his/her body so that it can act effectively as the pressure leg (see figure 5). He places it down at the end of the flight phase in nearly the centre of the circle approximately on the vertical projection of the CG of the shot putter and the shot. How far exactly the foot of the pressure leg is moved during the flight phase depends on various factors. Assuming that all (advanced) athletes exploit the putting circle to the fullest, which means that in the initial position they touch the rear rim of the circle with the tip of their foot and in the backward reclining position of delivery they touch the stop board with their

bracing leg, the point of touchdown of the pressure leg is determined by the width of the backward reclining position of delivery. The most important factors influencing the width of the backward reclining position of delivery are supposedly the body height and leg strength of the athlete. The taller and the stronger the athlete, the wider the backward reclining position of delivery should be. Whereas beginners should move their pressure leg beyond the centre of the circle, most world-class linear shot-putters place down their pressure leg somewhat in front of the centre of the circle (see figure 6).

At the moment of placing down the pressure leg, the almost straight bracing leg has also nearly reached its touchdown point. The upper body continues its movement and is raised a little further. The shoulder axis is still as parallel with the rear rim of the circle as possible.

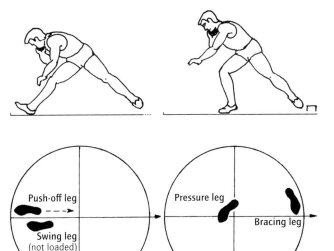

Figure 5: *Supportless phase in the linear technique of shot putting.*

Figure 6: *Foot positions in the linear technique of shot putting* before and after the glide.

PHASE 1 OF THE SCISSOR-STEP TECHNIQUE: PRELIMINARY MOVEMENT

The gripping and the positioning of the shot on the neck in the scissor-step technique are equal to the linear technique of shot putting. The starting position and the preliminary movement are also similar to the linear technique. However, the crucial difference is that the weight of the athlete rests on the later bracing leg. Since as yet there are only few female world-class athletes who have used this technique, not much can be said about variations of the starting position and the preliminary movement. At the beginning of the preliminary movement, the aforementioned female athletes take a position of horizontal balance on the push-off leg, during which they lean their upper body so far downward that the fingertips of the downward hanging free arm touch the ground. Then they lower their free leg until the foot is close to the foot of the supporting leg. At the same time, they raise their slightly rounded upper body again a little, while the supporting leg is extended. Subsequently, they bend their supporting leg while their upper body is horizontal and reach a backward crouch position at the rear rim of the circle, which—apart from the supporting leg—is equal to the corresponding position in the linear technique of shot putting.

PHASE 2 OF THE SCISSOR-STEP TECHNIQUE: SCISSOR STEP

The scissor step may be divided in two sub-phases:

- push-off with the later bracing leg; and
- supportless phase.

PUSH-OFF WITH THE LATER BRACING LEG

The push-off from the rear rim of the circle also resembles the linear technique of shot putting. The athlete shifts his/her CG backward by extending the ankle of his/her supporting leg and starts the backswing of the swing leg and the simultaneous extension of the push-off leg. The shoulders are only slightly raised so that the upper body remains nearly horizontal. The shoulder and pelvic axis remain parallel to the rear rim of the circle. The aforementioned female athletes perform the push-off with the entire foot, not with the heel.

SUPPORTLESS PHASE

When the push-off leg breaks contact with the ground, the swing leg has also finished its movement in the direction of the put. The push-off leg is fully extended at the knee joint, while the swing leg is not. The foot of the swing leg is clearly moved beyond the centre of the circle and is located about a foot in length above the ground. Now the scissor movement of legs begins. After a short delay, the foot of the swing leg changes its direction of movement and is moved backward and downward contrary to the direction of throw. It is placed down as the pressure leg approximately in the centre of the circle (see figure 7). At the same time, the push-off leg is moved toward the stop board in order to become the bracing leg. It is brought forward quickly and flatly and

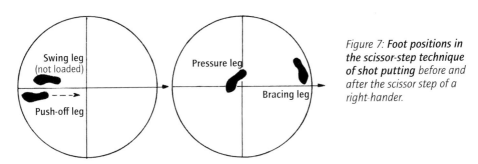

*Figure 7: **Foot positions in the scissor-step technique of shot putting** before and after the scissor step of a right-hander.*

with a slightly bent knee. At the moment of the touchdown of the pressure leg, the knee of the bracing leg should already have overtaken the pressure leg when viewed from the side. The position of the upper body still remains virtually unchanged. With this technique, the athlete should also keep his/her eyes fixed on a point behind the ring at least until reaching the backward reclining position of delivery.

PHASE 1 OF THE ROTATIONAL TECHNIQUE: PRELIMINARY MOVEMENT

The rotational technique of shot putting resembles the technique of discus throwing (see chapter II–3.3.3). Therefore, in particular the shot-put-specific characteristics of the preliminary movement and the turn are described below.

In the rotational technique, the gripping and positioning of the shot on the neck are basically the same in the linear technique of shot putting. However, the shot is often placed somewhat further to the side on the neck, but never behind the ear. This means that during the turn, it can be fixed in such a way that the shot putter can better act against the centrifugal forces. The upper part of the putting arm is positioned in the extension of the shoulder axis. It is

frequently raised not quite up to a 90° angle to the trunk.

In the smaller shot-put circle, there is less room available for the turn or the diagonal sprint through the circle than in the discus-throw circle. This has an effect on the starting position. In most athletics literature sources, a shoulder-wide and thus slightly narrower stance than in the discus throw is recommended. This leads to the athlete standing as far back in the circle as possible and not running through the circle too diagonally. If the athlete

*Figure 8: **Preliminary movement in the rotational technique of shot putting**: The backswing is sometimes performed somewhat farther back than presented here and with an inward turning of the left knee. However, the shoulder-hip separation achieved is frequently not as big as with most discus throwers.*

chooses a wider starting position in order to be able to initiate a wide movement of the swing leg, it is rather the foot on the side opposite the putting hand which is placed closer to the imaginary and extended centre line of the landing sector. The extent of the knee and hip flexion varies at least as much as in the discus throw. It is usually recommended to keep one's trunk almost upright and the knees slightly bent and pushed forward.

The preliminary movement (i.e., the rotation against the direction of the later turn) is often less noticeable than with discus throwers. The weight is less clearly shifted to the leg on the side of the putting hand and the shoulder-hip separation is also less noticeable.

PHASE 2 OF THE ROTATIONAL TECHNIQUE: TURN

As in the discus throw, the turn may be divided in three sub-phases:

- two-legged starting phase;
- one-legged starting phase; and
- supportless phase (leg reverse).

During the one- and two-legged starting phases, the shot passes through a path of acceleration which is approximately half to three quarters of a circle when viewed from above. The radius of this circle varies significantly even with top athletes. While a larger radius has theoretical advantages in terms of a longer path of acceleration, a smaller radius facilitates the control of the device. The radius depends on the athlete's height, the width of the stance in the starting position, the forward lean of the trunk, the amount of weight shifted to the leg on the side of the putting hand during the preliminary movement and then to the supporting leg of the one-legged starting phase.

Due to the smaller circle compared to the discus throw, rotational shot-putters

DISCOURSE II: SPIRAL TECHNIQUE

The variation of the rotational technique described above and used by most modern shot putters is called spin technique by Paish (2005). However, he emphasises that in the past many rotational shot putters were very successful with a different technique during the turn which he describes as the *spiral technique*. Examples of athletes demonstrating this technique are Aleksander Baryshnikov (22.00m) and Brian Oldfield (22.84m). During the first quarter to half turn of the one-legged starting phase, these athletes raised the foot of their swing leg (almost) up to hip level far outside the circle while bending their knee up to 90°. After a type of pause, they sprinted from this position through the circle with the foot of the swing leg passing the foot of the supporting leg at a relatively close distance.

try to especially emphasise the rotatory pre-acceleration. Athletes try to achieve a high rotational speed while keeping their body mass far away from the axis of rotation. In this case this involves the extended opposite arm and the swing leg which is moved in a wide circle around the supporting leg. An increase in the translational acceleration in the direction of the put results all too easily in placing the pressure leg too close to the stop board. A comparison of the fourth and fifth picture from the left in figure 9 illustrates quite well the relatively low degree of

knee extension in the supporting leg and the flat movement of the swing leg when pushing off from the rear rim of the circle. The push-off should be performed mainly from the ankle.

By supporting the rotation with the counter-arm, there is already a continuous decrease in the initial shoulder-hip separation during the starting phase which is completely eliminated during the flight phase. However, a visible overtaking of the hip axis by the shoulder axis should be avoided. Then, toward the end of the

Figure 9: **The turn in the rotational technique of shot putting.**

Figure 10: **The leg reverse in the rotational technique of shot putting viewed from the rear.**

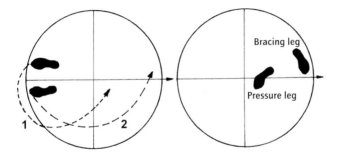

Figure 11: **Foot positions in the rotational technique of shot putting before and after the turn.**

Bracing leg

Pressure leg

one-legged start through the flight phase up to the one-legged delivery phase, the rotational shot-putter once again develops a shoulder-hip separation. This process is again initiated by the counter-arm which is brought to the front of the chest. The counter-arm and the shoulder axis stay behind or rotate against the rotational direction of the entire body so that the lower part of the body rotates faster in the direction of the overall angular momentum.

Figure 9 shows that the foot of the swing or pressure leg is moved back again contrary to the direction of the put before being placed onto the ground. The objective of this action is not only the achievement of a sufficiently wide backward reclining position of delivery, but also the avoidance of braking forces upon touchdown and enabling the athlete to continue the work of his/her pressure leg. Nevertheless, the touchdown of the pressure leg takes place

in front of the vertical projection of the CG and closer to the stop board than in the other two techniques. With rotational shot putters, the width of the backward reclining position of delivery eventually is only about 73% when compared to linear shot-putters.

When viewed from the side, the bracing leg is mostly still behind or maximally next to the pressure leg at the moment of the touchdown of the pressure leg. The athlete strives to move it flatly, closely, and thus quickly past the other leg to the front.

During the one-legged starting phase, the path velocity of the shot is higher than the path velocity of the CG of the shot-putter. During the leg reverse and the one-legged delivery phase, it is the other way round: The CG of the shot putter moves faster than the CG of the shot. He/she passes under and around the shot.

DISCOURSE III: POPULARITY AS WELL AS ADVANTAGES AND DISADVANTAGES OF THE DIFFERENT TECHNIQUES OF SHOT PUTTING

In respect to the popularity of the three shot-put techniques described, there are significant differences. In recent years, there were both rotational and linear shot putters among the male finalist at the world championships and the Olympic Games who were successful. Today, there is even a slight majority of rotational shot putters. However, there are hardly any rotational shot putters among female world-class shot putters, but there are some women who use the scissor-step technique of shot putting. In the men's combined events, the rotational technique is less common than with specialists. Moreover, there are significant regional differences. While the United States may currently be described as a typical country of rotational shot putters, Germany must be considered as the country of linear shot putters. (This may certainly be seen as a parallel to the discus throw with Germany being the country of the standing-delivery throwers.) The gender and combined-event-specific as well as regional differences are strongly prejudiced and to some extent attributed to the same cause: The rotational technique often leads to more invalid trials and there is a wider distribution of distances achieved in the valid trials than in the linear technique (or scissor-step technique). Finding the correct time and point to release the shot in the rotational movement is considered more difficult in terms of coordination. This means that rotational shot putters are more prepared to take risks, whereas linear shot putters are more safety conscious.

Depending on the sources, opinions vary as to whether the rotational technique is particularly suitable for small and fast athletes or whether it is more useful for taller athletes since it enables them to deal better with the putting circle which is actually too small. According to table 3, there seems to be more evidence that the first opinion is true. However, there are also successful examples which seem to prove that both views are valid. In any case, a feel for rotational movements, good balance, and a more rotational release technique (which in some cases is also observable in the linear technique) are crucial for potential rotational shot-putters. On the contrary, it is argued that the linear technique in particular is potentially successful only for tall and strong athletes due to the limited path of acceleration. The rotational technique, however, enables a wider range of athletic types to achieve peak performances.

In the linear technique of shot putting, the acceleration path is shorter (up to 3m) than in the rotational technique (up to 4m). It is too great a simplification to interpret this in terms of an advantage of the rotational technique according to the principle of the ideal acceleration path since the shorter path of acceleration in the linear technique is more of a straight line. Accelerating forces on the shot which are not aimed in the direction of the put are thereby significantly reduced. In fact, in a rotational shot put the path velocity of the shot at the beginning of the main acceleration phase is usually slower or there is a larger reduction in path velocity than in a linear shot put (see figure 12). Furthermore, the important path of acceleration during the final increase in velocity is shorter for rotational shot putters due to their narrower and more upright backward reclining position of delivery. But this can also not be regarded as an indisputable advantage of the linear technique of shot putting since at the beginning of the main acceleration phase the overall kinetic energy of the putter-shot system is more important than the speed of the shot. In the rotational technique, the rotational speed must be added to the translational velocity in the direction of the stop board, which is similar to the translational velocity in the linear shot put. But even this supposed advantage of the rotational technique may be countered by offering the following argument: When the main acceleration phase begins, it is not only necessary that the greatest possible pre-acceleration of the putter-shot system has been achieved, but also that the athlete should also have positioned his/her body parts optimally for maximum final acceleration. The wider backward reclining position of delivery of the linear shot-putter seems to enable the athlete to develop more force to accelerate the device.

The scissor-step technique may, in many respects, be regarded as an intermediate technique between the linear and rotational techniques of shot putting. The scissor-step technique is sometimes even seen as a transitional technique when changing from the linear to the rotational technique. As in the rotational technique, the push-off from the rear rim of the circle is performed with the later bracing leg. However, an athlete begins in a starting position which is similar to the linear technique. The rotation of the lower part of the body in the supportless and one-legged delivery phase is greater than in the linear technique and lower than in the rotational technique. When placing down the pressure leg, the bracing leg is far less advanced toward the stop board than in the linear technique, but is closer to the stop board than in the rotational technique. This is also reflected in the times between placing the pressure leg and placing the bracing leg on the ground. The action of the swing leg when pushing off from the rear rim of the circle tends to be weaker than in the linear technique since the pressure leg must reverse its direction of movement early enough for the touchdown in the centre of the circle. The touchdown of the pressure leg with a significant pre-acceleration against the direction of the put is regarded as a main advantage of the scissor-step technique when compared with the other two techniques. This should lead to an active and rapid force development of the pressure leg in the direction of the put. Furthermore, the scissor-step technique is supposed to help to keep the left side closed, which means that the pelvis and shoulder axis are turned in the direction of the put only late. The scissor-step technique is also regarded as a good alternative for linear shot putters who frequently put the shot from a too wide backward reclining position of delivery. Moreover, the scissor-step technique is assumed to be more natural and therefore easier to learn since it is performed at a normal stride rhythm (left-right-left or right-left-right; therefore also referred to as 2-step technique). The last three benefits might make the scissor-step technique particularly attractive for combined-event athletes who have less time to practise the shot put and are used to alternate leg actions.

Even though sufficient scientific data concerning the scissor-step technique is still lacking, it may be concluded that all three techniques appear equivalent and that the selection is based more or less on personal preferences.

*Table 2: **Phase lengths** at the 2008 World Indoor Championships (WIC 08) and the 2007 World Championships (WC 07).*

Championship: source	Technique	One-legged starting phase	Supportless phase	One-legged delivery phase	Two-legged delivery phase	Second one-legged delivery phase	Supportless delivery phase
WIC 08: Gutiérrez-Davila et al., 2009	Linear shot putters (2 men, 7 women)	0.30 ± 0.13*	0.15 ± 0.03	0.13 ± 0.05	0.16 ± 0.03	0.04 ± 0.02	0.03 ± 0.02
	Rotational shot putters (6 men, 1 woman)	0.46 ± 0.04	0.06 ± 0.03	0.21 ± 0.03	0.16 ± 0.04	0.02 ± 0.01	0.03 ± 0.02
WC 07: Byun et al., 2008	Linear shot putters (4 men)		0.12-0.14	0.06-0.14		0.20-0.30	
	Rotational shot putters (6 men)		0.00-0.08	0.20-0.28		0.18-0.22	

*Gutiérrez-Davila et al. (2009) define the start of this phase for linear shot-putters as the start of the acceleration of the swing leg in the direction of the stop board. The mean value is influenced by one outlier. The German shot-putter Christina Schwanitz took only 0.09 sec for this phase. Without her, the mean value is 0.33 ± 0.11.

PHASE 3: DELIVERY MOVEMENT

The delivery movement can be divided into two sub-phases:

- one-legged delivery phase; and
- two-legged delivery phase.

ONE-LEGGED DELIVERY PHASE

The linear technique of shot putting allows for the shortest one-legged delivery phase. Although coaches often instruct athletes (in respect to all three techniques) to place down the bracing leg quickly and actively, the simultaneous touchdown of the pressure leg and the bracing leg is rejected even for the linear technique of shot putting (see phase lengths in table 2). A slightly delayed touchdown seems to ensure the longest possible acceleration path of the shot during the delivery movement, an optimally wide backward reclining position of delivery, and the best working angles in the joints of the muscles involved. At the beginning of the contact of the pressure leg, the linear shot-putter tries to bend his/her knee joint only slightly (amortisation). He/she tries to accelerate the knee of his/her pressure leg and through its extension also the hip on the side of the putting hand in the direction of the put. During this phase, a first, although still slight rotation of the shoulders about the longitudinal axis of the body can be observed, which is initiated by the action of the pressure leg and the beginning forward and upward swing of the counter-arm. The actions of the scissor-step technique are very similar to those of the linear technique although the path of the bracing leg is slightly longer.

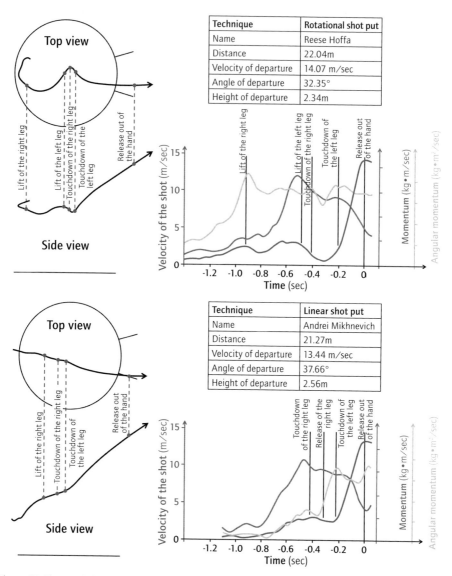

Figure 12: *Shot path (left), departure parameters, development of the path velocity of the shot, of the momentum of the CG of the putter-shot system, and of the angular momentum about this CG for the first- and third-placed athletes (both right-handers) at the 2007 World Championships in Osaka (modified on the basis of Byun et al., 2008): A division of the impulse into a lateral, horizontal, and vertical component shows how horizontal velocity is converted to vertical velocity in both techniques through the bracing leg. Mikhnevich's acceleration path is noticeably straight. For other world-class linear shot putters, the flattening of the curve during the supportless and one-legged delivery phase, which is observable from the side view and which is due to the shot putter's attempt to keep his/her trunk and the shot low for a long time, is more conspicuous. From the top view, one can also see other acceleration paths during the two-legged delivery phase which are more curved due to a more rotational delivery.*

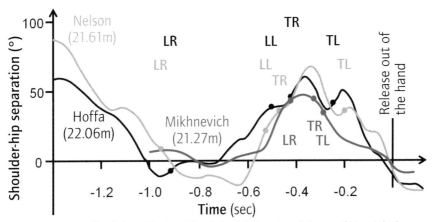

LR, LL, TR, TL = Lift of the right leg, lift of the left leg, touchdown of the right leg, touchdown of the left leg

Figure 13: **Shoulder-hip separation** *in a linear shot putter (Mikhnevich) and two rotational shot putters (all right-handers; modified on the basis of Byun et al., 2008): Due to the complexity of evaluation, similar studies also show the complete course of the shoulder-hip separation only for selected athletes. Generalisations are therefore difficult. Although contrary statements can be found in athletics literature, the reference quoted here confirms other sources according to which the rotational technique is characterised by a more noticeable shoulder-hip separation. The linear shot putter already achieves his/her maximum shoulder-hip separation in the flight phase, whereas the rotational shot putter does so during the one-legged delivery phase. For rotational shot putters, the initial shoulder-hip separation is completely released during the turn on the left leg and is developed again only during the forward swing and touchdown of the right leg.*

The amortisation of the knee of the pressure leg and the entire one-legged delivery phase are longer in the rotational put. The rotational shot-putter tries to continue the turn on the ball of the foot of the pressure leg so that the foot of the pressure leg as well as the hip and shoulder axis continue their rotation by approximately 90° about the longitudinal axis. The CG of the putter-shot system exceeds the touchdown point of the pressure leg and the bracing leg continues its flat movement to the stop board. Toward the end of the one-legged delivery phase, the rotational shot-putter also begins the forward and upward swing of the counter-arm to initiate the dissolution of the shoulder-hip separation.

Figure 14: **One-legged delivery phase in the linear technique** *(above)* **and the rotational technique of shot putting** *(below): The respective right picture depicts the backward reclining position of delivery.*

DISCOURSE IV: CONCERNING THE FOOT TOUCHDOWN DURING THE ACTION OF THE PRESSURE LEG

Like rotational shot putters and discus throwers, some world-class linear shot putters place their pressure leg on the ground only with the ball of the foot. The advantage of this variation is that the rotational movement of the pressure leg is facilitated. In fact, however, there is only a slight rotation of the foot of the pressure leg to be observed in many representatives of this variation. Accordingly, Kollark (2007) calls the action of the pressure leg in the linear technique of shot putting an extension and rotation movement, opposed to the rotation and extension movement in the discus throw and the rotational technique of shot putting. This means that at the beginning of the action of the pressure leg in the linear and scissor-step technique, the focus is on a maximally powerful extension movement. In the process, it may be useful to eliminate the action of the ankle joint as the weakest joint of the leg. Therefore, many linear and scissor-step shot-putters place down the foot of their pressure leg (temporarily) on the entire sole. Then, the push-off with the pressure leg is sometimes performed with the inner side of the foot instead of with the ball of the foot.

In all techniques, there may be a reduction in the velocity of the shot during the supportless phase and at the beginning of the single-support phase due to an active holding back of the shot and braking and frictional forces during the touchdown of the pressure leg. Then, the final increase in the velocity of the shot until its release already begins in the one-legged delivery phase regardless of the technique used. However, the increase in velocity achieved up to the touchdown of the bracing leg is only slight. The greatest percentage of the velocity increase occurs in the two-legged delivery phase. An examination of the linear shot-put technique leads to the conclusion that an increase in velocity should begin only briefly before the touchdown of the bracing leg. Upon the touchdown of the bracing leg, the velocity of the shot should be identical with or only 0.2 m/sec faster than the 2.1–2.8 m/sec upon the touchdown of the pressure leg. A decrease in velocity during this period is an indication of an excessive holding back of the shot and/or a passive touchdown of the bracing leg, whereas a more noticeable increase in velocity is an indication of the premature delivery activity of the upper body. In the rotational technique, there is already an increase in velocity of 1–2 m/sec from the touchdown of the pressure leg to the touchdown of the bracing leg. Nevertheless, here too, an increase in velocity should be neither minimal nor maximal but optimal.

*Table 3: **Biomechanical measuring values** of the best trials of the finalists at the 2008 World Indoor Championships in Valencia (according to Gutiérrez-Davila et al., 2009): The correlations listed were calculated for the total group.*

		Male linear shot-putters (n=2)	Male rotational shot-putters (n=6)	Female linear shot-putters (n=7)	Female rotational shot-putter (n=1)
a	Body height (m)	2.03 ± 0.01	1.91 ± 0.06	1.80 ± 0.08	1.76
b	Velocity of the shot upon the touchdown of the bracing leg (m/sec)	2.74 ± 0.68	1.75 ± 0.56	2.66 ± 0.33	3.06
c	Height of the CG upon the touchdown of the bracing leg (m)	0.95 ± 0.00	0.93 ± 0.04	0.81 ± 0.05	0.89
d	Height of the CG upon the touchdown of the bracing leg (% of body height)	46.8 ± 0.3	49.0 ± 1.6	45.0 ± 2.5	50.6
e	Height of the shot upon the touchdown of the bracing leg (m)	1.27 ± 0.01	1.30 ± 0.07	1.10 ± 0.08	1.26
f	Height of the shot upon the touchdown of the bracing leg (% of body height)	62.4 ± 0.8	68.1 ± 2.8	61.0 ± 4.0	71.6
g	Angle of the line connecting the feet upon the touchdown of the bracing leg (the centre points between the heel and the tip of the toe were connected;°)	23 ± 6	14 ± 20	13 ± 7	19
h	Angle of the hip axis upon the touchdown of the bracing leg (°)	10 ± 1	–30 ± 13	–39 ± 9	–19
i	Angle of the shoulder axis upon the touchdown of the bracing leg (°)	–58 ± 11	–72 ± 25	–61 ± 10	–31
j	Shoulder-hip separation upon the touchdown of the bracing leg (= h – j; °)	68 ± 11	42 ± 15	22 ± 8	14
k	Angular velocity of the hip axis in the horizontal plane upon the touchdown of the bracing leg (°/sec)	134 ± 168	496 ± 297	280 ± 170	531
l	Angular velocity of the shoulder axis in the horizontal plane upon the touchdown of the bracing leg (°/sec)	299 ± 167	626 ± 241	404 ± 115	200
m	Acceleration path of the shot from the touchdown of the bracing leg to the release of the shot out of the hand (m); correlated with a (r=0.63; p<0.01)	1.82 ± 0.04	1.54 ± 0.10	1.54 ± 0.11	1.14
n	Acceleration path of the shot from the touchdown of the bracing leg to the release of the shot out of the hand (% of body height); correlated with d (r=-0.53; p<0.05) and with f (r=-0.60; p<0.05)	89.4 ± 1.1	80.6 ± 7.4	85.4 ± 3.4	64.8
o	Average acceleration of the shot from the touchdown of the bracing leg to the release of the shot out of the hand (m/sec²); correlated with m (r=-0.74; p<0.005)	43.46 ± 0.12	55.35 ± 7.46	45.40 ± 5.66	70.29
p	Angle of the hip axis upon the release of the shot out of the hand (°)	91 ± 1	98 ± 12	74 ± 16	103
q	Angle of the shoulder axis upon the release of the shot out of the hand (°)	107 ± 1	112 ± 10	89 ± 10	105
r	Angular velocity of the hip axis in the horizontal plane upon the release of the shot out of the hand (°/sec)	573 ± 154	731 ± 186	498 ± 322	1016
s	Angular velocity of the shoulder axis in the horizontal plane upon the release of the shot out of the hand (°/sec)	602 ± 33	872 ± 219	712 ± 356	912

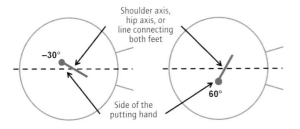

Explanation of the angles mentioned in the table using two examples

Figure 15: **The backward reclining position of delivery from the rear view.**

Table 4: **Measuring values** (in italics) **and guiding values for the linear technique of shot putting**, *based on the 3-D analysis of 5 women (performance: 18.19 ± 1.19m) and 6 men (performance: 19.28 ± 0.96m; according to Dickwach, 2006). The values provided by Luhtanen et al. (1997) for a rotational shot-putter indicate that the knee-joint angles are similar in this technique. The values provided by Dickwach et al. (1997) indicate that in the scissor-step technique the width of the backward reclining position of delivery is narrower than in the linear technique and greater than in the rotational technique.*

The **backward reclining position of delivery** is achieved when the bracing leg is placed on the ground. This position, which is very similar in all techniques, has been described by many studies. The data presented in tables 3 and 4 may be commentated as follows:

- The touchdown of the foot of the bracing leg takes place at and parallel to the stop board. The foot is placed down either over the inner side of the foot or with an initial contact of the ball of the foot and is finally bent down so that the entire sole of the foot is on the ground.
- When looking in the direction of the put, the foot of the pressure leg is placed further on the putting-hand side of the circle than the foot of the bracing leg. This is necessary so that the hip of the pressure leg has enough space to rotate forward.
- During the shoulder-hip separation and backward recline, the spine should be straight. For rotational shot putters, the backward reclining position of delivery is narrower and more upright than for linear shot-putters.

a	Knee joint angle of the pressure leg upon the touchdown of the pressure leg	105–123°
b	Minimal knee joint angle of the pressure leg during the ground contact of the pressure leg	98–120°
c	Knee joint angle of the pressure leg upon the touchdown of the bracing leg	98–128°
d	Knee joint angle of the pressure leg upon the lift of the bracing leg	125–150°
e	Extension angle of the pressure leg (difference between d and b)	15–40°
f	Knee joint angle of the bracing leg upon the touchdown of the bracing leg	128–167°
g	Minimal knee joint angle of the bracing leg during the ground contact of the bracing leg	126–137°
h	Flexion angle of the bracing leg (difference between f and g)	(-)2–21°
i	Maximal knee joint angle of the bracing leg during the ground contact of the bracing leg	167–178°
j	Extension angle of the bracing leg (difference between i and g)	31–44°
k	Angle between the trunk and the horizontal upon the touchdown of the bracing leg	45–55°
l	Distance of holding back the shot upon the touchdown of the pressure leg (relative to the foot of the pressure leg)	35–20cm
m	Distance of holding back the shot upon the touchdown of the bracing leg (relative to the foot of the pressure leg)	15–0cm
n	Width of the backward reclining position of delivery (distance between the centre points of the balls of the feet relative to body height)	54–53 %
o	Lateral distance between the balls of the feet in the backward reclining position of delivery	10–35cm

TWO-LEGGED DELIVERY PHASE

The importance of the two-legged delivery phase for the shot-put performance is illustrated by the fact that even world-class shot-putters reach approximately 90% of their competition performance when performing a standing put from a starting position resembling the backward reclining position of delivery (of linear shot-putters).

After an active touchdown, the bracing leg should be bent at the knee joint as little as possible and should be extended again as soon as possible (see table 4). As described in the chapter on the common features of the throwing events (chapter II–3.1.2), the action of the pressure and bracing legs result in the (acceleration of the) hip rotation and, via the shoulder-hip separation, in the (acceleration of the) shoulder rotation. Although the pelvis is accelerated forward and upward, it is not moved beyond the foot of the bracing leg to prevent stepping over the stop board after delivery. The actions of the pressure leg and bracing leg result in the trunk straightening and the lift of the CG and the shot.

The shot putter passes through a position in which the upper half of the putting arm, the shoulder axis, and the counter-arm point approximately in the direction of the angle of departure. Shortly afterwards, the lower half of the putting arm reaches the position in which it points approximately in the direction of the angle of departure. Beginning with this moment, the direction of the forearm remains almost unchanged.

Like a billiard cue, it points in the intended direction of the put. Therefore, the shot must eventually be moved away from the neck. Through the forward and upward movement of the upper arm and the elbow extension, the shot is further accelerated until the departure.

The shoulder axis rotates faster than the hip axis so that the shoulder-hip separation is resolved (0°) at the latest at the moment when the shot leaves the hand. For the rotational technique of shot putting in particular, the shoulder axis has usually already overtaken the hip axis. At the moment of departure, the shoulder axis and the hip axis are approximately square to the direction of the put. The upper body reaches the vertical position.

As a result of an active and effective extension movement of both legs, there is another one-legged and/or supportless phase even before the shot leaves the athlete's hand, regardless of the technique used by top-lever shot-putters. Nevertheless, no shot putter lifts one of his/her feet from the ground earlier than 0.08 sec before the shot leaves his/her hand.

*Figure 16: **Two-legged delivery phase of a linear shot putter** (above) **and a rotational shot putter** (below).*

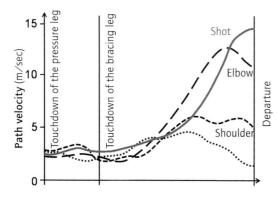

*Figure 17: **Kinematic chain during a put using the linear technique** (modified on the basis of Hinz, 1991, quoted from Wank, 2006): The figure shows the path velocities on the side of the putting hand. The shoulder of the opposite side should reach its maximum velocity before the hip and shoulder on the side of the putting hand. The hip on the side of the putting hand as well as the hip and shoulder on the opposite side are decelerated in most cases to below 2 m/sec until the moment of departure.*

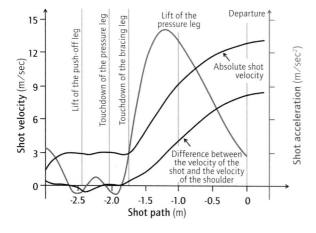

*Figure 18: **Acceleration as well as absolute and relative velocity of the shot** during a 20.56m trial by Yuriy Bilonog using the linear technique (modified on the basis of Dickwach, 2006): It is obvious that the final path of acceleration has been calculated to be approximately 2m. As in this example, there should be a continuous increase in acceleration, which means that there should be no dip in the curve of acceleration. The maximum acceleration is typically reached shortly before the release of the pressure leg. In the example given, the arm activity is responsible for 64% of the velocity of departure.*

948

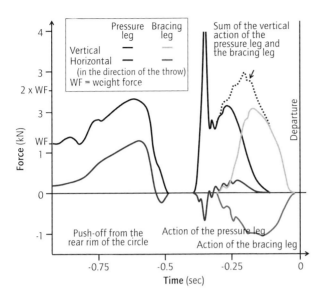

Figure 19: **Vertical and horizontal ground reaction forces** during a 19.15m put of a male linear shot putter (modified on the basis of Dickwach et al., 2006). In respect to the ground reaction forces of Astrid Kumbernuss presented by Dickwach et al. (1997), it is striking that the supportless phase and the single-support phase are somewhat longer in the scissor-step technique than in the linear technique and that the horizontal ground reaction force upon the touchdown of the pressure leg is initially characterised by a positive force peak.

PHASE 4: RECOVERY AND FLIGHT OF THE SHOT

RECOVERY

The recovery movement (see figure 20) is the inevitable result of an active delivery movement. As mentioned above, the shot putter already achieves a new supportless phase shortly before the shot has finally left his/her hand through the active extension of his/her legs. The rotation about the longitudinal axis of the body is continued and the shot-putter tries to place the nearly straight former pressure leg onto the ground as quickly as possible. The shot-putter succeeds in keeping the vertical projection of his/her CG behind his/her supporting leg and the stop board and thereby avoids stepping over the stop board only if the action of the bracing leg has led to a sufficient reduction of the horizontal velocity in the direction of the throw.

Figure 20: **Recovery movement of a linear shot putter** (above) **and a rotational shot putter** (below).

Linear and scissor-step shot putters usually come to rest on the leg on the side of the putting arm without rotating again fully about the longitudinal axis so that they are able to leave the circle in a controlled manner through the back half. For some rotational shot putters, the remaining rotational energy is so great that they rotate several times on the supporting leg before reaching a controlled standing position.

VELOCITY, ANGLE, HEIGHT, AND POINT OF DEPARTURE

Table 5 provides information on the departure parameters of world-class athletes. Table 6 shows among other things the maximum flight distances (which should not be confused with the competition results in which the point of departure is also of crucial importance) which are possible with a certain velocity of departure. A comparison of the two tables shows that the theoretically optimal angles of departure clearly deviate from the actual average mean values. Similar to the javelin throw, this is due to an interaction between the velocity and the angle of departure. Larger angles of departure are associated with lower velocities of departure. Due to gravity, it is significantly more difficult to generate vertical velocity of departure than to generate horizontal velocity of departure. In order to achieve a larger angle of departure, the athlete would have to focus more on lifting the shot and would not be able to accelerate his/her putting arm and shoulder forward so aggressively. Moreover, due to anatomical conditions, the decisive chest and shoulder muscles can exert greater force if the arm is not raised so high. To understand this, one must only think of the differences in the maximum loads that can be overcome in the bench press and the inclined bench press. It is also reported that there is a negative association between the height of departure and the velocity of departure. The greater the height of departure, the lower the velocity of departure. This is already to be expected from the interaction between the velocity of departure and the angle of departure mentioned above, since at the moment when the shot leaves the

Table 5: *Departure parameters at the 2008 World Indoor Championships in Valencia (according to Gutiérrez-Davila et al., 2009): The table includes the average and standard deviation of the best trials of the finalists. Byun et al. (2008) identified a higher height of departure of 2.33 ± 0.16m for 10 male World Championship finalists with a similar average performance (20.82 ± 0.71m). Schaa (2010) did not discover any clear differences between linear and rotational shot-putters.*

	Number	Distance (m)	Weight (kg)	Height (m)	Height of departure (m)	Height of departure (% of body height)	Distance of departure (m)	Distance of departure (% of body height)	Velocity of departure (m/sec)	Angle of departure (°)
Men	8	20.75 ± 0.58	125.6 ± 12.6	1.94 ± 0.08	2.17 ± 0.07	112.1 ± 2.9	0.11 ± 0.06	5.5 ± 2.9	13.64 ± 0.28	37.38 ± 2.26
Women	8	18.78 ± 0.95	94.0 ± 15.5	1.80 ± 0.07	1.98 ± 0.17	109.9 ± 5.9	0.07 + 0.09	3.5 ± 4.8	12.92 ± 0.35	38.88 ± 2.95

Table 6: **Theoretically optimal angles of departure for optimal flight distances with different velocities of departure** and a height of departure of 2.00m (according to Wank, 2006): The maximum values are in bold. The exact theoretically optimal angle of departure is sometimes located between the values presented. The angles of departure of the best puts by male finalists at the 2007 World Championships (30.77–37.66°) are significantly lower than the theoretically ideal values (see explanation in the main text).

		Angle of departure					
		36°	38°	40°	42°	44°	46°
Velocity of departure	10 m/sec	11.93m	12.00m	**12.03m**	12.01m	11.95m	11.85m
	11 m/sec	14.03m	14.14m	**14.19m**	**14.19m**	14.13m	14.02m
	12 m/sec	16.32m	16.46m	16.54m	**16.56m**	16.51m	16.40m
	13 m/sec	18.79m	18.97m	19.08m	**19.12m**	19.09m	18.97m
	14 m/sec	21.44m	21.68m	21.82m	**21.89m**	21.86m	21.74m
	15 m/sec	24.29m	24.54m	24.76m	**24.85m**	24.83m	24.71m

hand, the arm points approximately in the direction of the departure angle and is thus directed more upward if a larger departure angle is achieved. Accordingly, a larger angle of departure correlates with a shorter horizontal distance of the point of the departure beyond the rim of the circle.

AERODYNAMICS AND ENVIRONMENTAL INFLUENCES (INCLUDING THE HAMMER THROW)

Contrary to the javelin and the discus throws, aerodynamics plays a subordinate role in the shot put and the hammer throw. Compared to the distance calculated on the basis of the trajectory formula, the loss of distance due to air resistance is only approximately 15cm in puts over 20m using a shot of 12cm diameter. If a shot with a diameter of 13cm is used, the loss of distance is approximately 19cm. In the hammer throw, air resistance may cause a loss of distance of more than 4.5m under normal conditions compared to

the vacuum. Differences in hammer head size may lead to differences in throwing distance of up to 0.5m.

Assuming that there had been no wind when the men's world record in the shot put was established, a tailwind of 2 m/sec would have led to an increase in distance of 3cm, whereas an equally strong headwind would have resulted in a loss of distance of 10cm. If the same calculation were made for the hammer throw, there would be a wind-related increase of 62 and a loss of 66cm.

If the men's hammer-throw world record had been established at the equator, the same departure parameters would have resulted in a 45cm shorter official distance at the North or South Poles; for the men's shot-put world record, the loss of distance would have been 11cm. Assuming that the world record had been achieved in Athens (38° north latitude) at sea level, a competition venue in the same location at an altitude of 1,000m would have led to a 55cm longer hammer throw. If the same calculation were applied to the men's shot-put world record, there would be an improvement of only 2cm (for a more detailed explanation of these effects see chapter II–2.1.2).

In respect to the men's world records, the slope of the landing sector, allowed according to the rules, would result in possible differences in throwing distances of about ± 9cm for the hammer throw and of ± 2cm for the shot put.

*Table 7: **Requirement profile for the shot put:** The suggested rough estimate of the value of selected factors determining performance is based on the importance for the overall performance and the percentage of time spent training (IR: information requirements, constr.: constraints; see chapter I–1.1).*

Factors determining shot-put performance	Estimate of value	Notes
Coordination	+ + + + (+)	optical IR: low-medium, acoustic IR: low, tactile IR: low, kinaesthetic IR: medium, vestibular IR: medium-high; precision constr.: high, time constr.: high, complexity constr.: medium-high, situation constr.: low, physical stress constr.: low
Flexibility	+	primarily of the shoulder and the adductors of the hip on the side of the putting arm
Strength		primarily anteversion muscles of the shoulder (pectoralis, etc.), elbow extensors (triceps brachii), extension loop (glutes, quadriceps, triceps surae, erector spinae), and trunk muscles (primarily rotatory muscles: abdominus obliqui, etc.)
Maximal strength	+++++	the most important influencing factor in combination with maximal strength
Speed strength	+++++	the most important influencing factor in combination with speed strength
Reactive strength	+ +	rather as a basis; primarily of the legs
Speed	+ + + +	acyclic speed
Endurance (general dynamic) Anaerobic endurance		
Strength endurance	+ +	as a basis to be able to perform 6 trials plus practice trials at a high level of performance
Speed endurance	+	as a basis at most
Aerobic endurance	+	as a basis at most
Psychological and cognitive abilities	+ + + + +	concentration ability (on the point); performance-oriented thinking and behaviour (see chapter I-3.1.1)
Anthropometric and primarily genetically determined characteristics	+ + + +	high percentage of fast muscle fibres; connective tissue with optimal energy storage capacities; rather above-average body height and arm spread

Changes in air density and therefore air resistance caused by weather or temperature and air pressure may also affect the flight distance. In respect to the men's hammer-throw world record, a rise in temperature of 10° would lead to a gain in distance of 17cm, whereas an increase in air pressure of 2 kPa would lead to a loss in distance of 8cm if the other parameters remain constant.

3.4.4 SUMMARY OF THE MOST IMPORTANT TECHNICAL CHARACTERISTICS = TECHNIQUE-ANALYSIS SHEET

(Description for right-handers)

PRELIMINARY PHASE: LINEAR TECHNIQUE

GRIPPING THE SHOT

- The shot rests on the basic joints of the fingers; the thumb and little finger provide side support; the shot touches the chin, the anterior neck and the clavicle.
- Putting arm: wrist dorsiflexed, forearm pronated, elbow bent at an acute angle and abducted from the trunk.

STARTING POSITION

- The shot putter stands on his/her right leg at the rear rim of the circle, his/her back is square to the direction of the put; the foot is placed on the centre line of the landing sector with the entire sole of the foot on the ground and pointing contrary to the direction of the put.

PRELIMINARY MOVEMENT

- The method of taking the crouch position varies: frequently through the horizontal balance position, sometimes by performing rhythmic bending and stretching movements of the supporting leg.
- Crouch position: upper body horizontal, supporting leg bent up to 90° (beginners more upright); shoulder and hip axis square to the direction of the put; weight on the ball of the foot; foot of the swing leg near the foot of the supporting leg; inhaled for forced breathing.
- Short static phase or dynamic transition from bending the supporting leg to the glide.

GLIDE

PUSH-OFF FROM THE LATER PRESSURE LEG

- Shift of weight toward the stop board by extending the ankle of the supporting leg.
- Simultaneous rapid, powerful, and complete extension of the push-off and swing leg; flat push-off over the heel; flat movement of the swing leg over the ground toward the stop board.
- The shoulder remains parallel to the rear rim of the circle; the hip axis follows the leg movement; this leads to the development of shoulder-hip separation and in combination with the external rotation of the swing leg to a horizontal position of the foot of the swing leg.
- Only slight lift of the upper body including the shot; the trunk and swing leg form a line.
- The counter-arm is either held back or initially used as a swing element before it is moved backward, or it is moved backward using a pendulum movement from next to the trunk.

SUPPORTLESS PHASE

- Flat and short flight phase.
- The pressure leg is flatly and rapidly pulled under the body, bent and turned inward, without dragging the foot over the ground.
- Touchdown of the pressure leg in the centre of the circle or a little further away from the stop board (beginners sometimes place their pressure leg closer to the stop board), approximately on the vertical projection of the CG of the shot putter and the shot.
- Only slight further lifting of the upper body and the shot; the shoulder axis is still parallel to the rear rim of the circle; the trunk and swing leg are still aligned; the bracing leg is still moving flatly toward the stop board.
- The shot putter looks backward and downward at least until he/she places his/her bracing leg on the ground.

PRELIMINARY PHASE: SCISSOR-STEP TECHNIQUE

GRIPPING THE SHOT

- The shot rests on the basic joints of the fingers; the thumb and little finger provide side support; the shot touches the chin, the anterior neck and the clavicle.
- Putting arm: wrist dorsiflexed, forearm pronated, elbow bent at an acute angle and abducted from the trunk.

STARTING POSITION

- The shot putter stands on his/her left leg at the rear rim of the circle, his/her back is square to the direction of the put; the foot is placed on the centre line of the landing sector with the entire sole of the foot on the ground and pointing contrary to the direction of the put.

PRELIMINARY MOVEMENT

- The method of taking the crouch position varies: frequently through the horizontal balance position, sometimes by performing rhythmic bending and stretching movements of the supporting leg.
- Crouch position: the upper body is horizontal, the supporting leg is bent up to 90° (beginners more upright); the shoulder and hip axis are square to the direction of the put; the weight is on the ball of the foot; the foot of the swing leg is near the foot of the supporting leg; the athlete has inhaled for forced breathing.
- Short static phase or dynamic transition from bending the supporting leg to the scissor step.

SCISSOR STEP

PUSH-OFF WITH THE LATER BRACING LEG

- Shift of weight toward the stop board by extending the ankle of the supporting leg.
- Rapid, powerful, and flat push-off in the direction of the stop board by extending the supporting leg; mostly using a push-off with the entire foot.
- Simultaneous backswing of the swing leg; the foot of the swing leg swings far beyond the centre of the circle and is lifted up to one foot in length above the ground.

- The hip and shoulder axis remain parallel to the rear rim of the circle.
- Only slight lift of the upper body including the shot.
- The counter-arm is moved as a swing element in the direction of the throw.

SUPPORTLESS PHASE

- Contralateral scissor movement of the legs and rotation of the lower part of the body:
- After a short delay, the movement direction of the foot of the swing leg is reversed, and the swing leg is moved backward and downward in a bent position and placed on the ground approximately in the centre of the circle where it acts as the pressure leg; the foot of the pressure leg is turned inward so that the foot is turned only 90–135° out of the direction of the throw; the foot is placed down approximately on the vertical projection of the CG of the shot-putter and the shot.
- The push-off leg is moved flatly and closely next to the pressure leg; when the pressure leg is placed on the ground, the later bracing leg should have already overtaken the pressure leg.
- The rotation of the hip, which follows the movement of the legs, leads to the shoulder-hip separation; the counter-arm is actively moved backward.
- The upper body and the shot are lifted only a bit further; the shoulder axis is still parallel to the rear rim of the circle.
- The shot putter looks backward and downward at least until he/she places his/her bracing leg on the ground.

PRELIMINARY PHASE: ROTATIONAL TECHNIQUE

GRIPPING THE SHOT

- The shot rests on the basic joints of the fingers; the thumb and little finger provide side support; the shot is placed on the neck next to the ear.
- Putting arm: the wrist is dorsiflexed, the forearm is pronated, the elbow is bent at an acute angle, the upper arm is approximately aligned with the shoulder axis and is abducted from the trunk at an angle slightly below 90°.

STARTING POSITION

- Quarter squat at the rear rim of the circle: the back is square to the direction of the throw; the legs are approximately shoulder-width apart; the centre line of the landing sector is approximately in the middle between the feet; the upper body is slightly leant forward or upright; the right foot is placed on the ground with the entire sole.

PRELIMINARY MOVEMENT

- The shoulder axis is turned clockwise until the shoulder axis points (approximately) in the throwing direction; in the process, the weight is shifted onto the right leg and the left leg is turned inward in the direction of the right leg.

TURN

TWO-LEGGED STARTING PHASE

- The counterclockwise turn begins with the outward turn of the left leg on the ball of the foot; the outward turn leads to the rotation of the pelvis about the longitudinal axis; the shoulder axis as well as the putting arm and the shot follow with shoulder-hip separation.
- The push-off with the right leg results in shifting the CG in the direction of the left foot and supports the introduction of the turn.
- The extended counter-arm is used as a swing element.
- The CG is lowered.
- By keeping the right leg on the ground for a long time, the shot putter creates a pre-tension in his/her right hip.

ONE-LEGGED STARTING PHASE

- The right foot is released approximately when the left knee points to the side.
- Turn on the left ball of the foot; flat swinging movement of the right foot in a wide circle around the supporting leg.
- Possibly slight lift of the heel of the swing leg with subsequent kicking movement.

- High rotational velocity.
- As soon as the knee of the support leg points in the direction of the throw, the shot putter performs a flat push-off movement from his/her ankle joint with incomplete extension of the knee joint and flat movement of the swing leg.
- The shoulder-hip separation is completely released, but the shoulder axis does not overtake the hip axis.

SUPPORTLESS PHASE: LEG REVERSE

- Short, flat reverse of legs.
- The body moves around and under the shot; the legs run ahead.
- Inward rotation of the right leg, upon touchdown, the foot points (outward and) backward; before being placed down, the foot is accelerated toward the rear rim of the circle; the touchdown occurs slightly beyond the centre of the circle and in front of the shot-putter's CG.
- Creation of a shoulder-hip separation by keeping back the shoulder and swinging the counter-arm in front of the body, while the lower part of the body continues its turn.
- The left leg is moved close to the axis of rotation; the bracing leg overtakes the pressure leg at the moment of touchdown.

DELIVERY MOVEMENT

Rotational technique of shot putting (RT)

Linear technique of shot putting (LT)

ONE-LEGGED DELIVERY PHASE

- Short amortisation in the pressure leg.
- LT and scissor-step technique (SST): Maximally rapid initiation of the extension and turning movement of the pressure leg, the foot of the pressure leg remains on the ball or is lowered down on the entire foot; slight but still gradual lift of the shot and trunk; the beginning forward and upward swing of the counter-arm introduces the rotation of the shoulder axis.
- RT: Rapid and uninterrupted continuation of the turn on the ball of the foot; the CG moves across the point of touchdown; the shot-putter looks back at the back of his/her hand of the counter-arm in order to hold his/her shoulder-hip separation very long or even to twist more; shortly before the touchdown of the bracing leg, the forward and upward swing of the counter-arm starts.
- The bracing leg is moved flatly and quickly in the direction of the stop board; it is placed down in an almost extended position and further to the left than the pressure leg; the foot is parallel to the stop board and is placed down with the inner edge of the foot first.
- Upon the touchdown of the bracing leg, the shot should still be behind the foot of the pressure leg.

TWO-LEGGED DELIVERY PHASE (TOUCHDOWN OF THE BRACING LEG UP TO RELEASE OF THE SHOT)

- The amortisation in the knee of the bracing leg is as short as possible and the full extension of this leg is achieved as quickly as possible.
- Continuation of the extension and rotation movement (LT and SST) or rotation and extension movement (RT) of the pressure leg.
- The actions of the pressure and bracing leg result in a further rotation of the hip and then the shoulder until they are square to the direction of the throw; the shoulder-hip separation is released.
- An additional effect of the actions of the pressure and the bracing leg is that the pelvis is moved forward and upward but not beyond the foot of the bracing leg; the trunk is straightened (and vertical when the shot is released) so that the CG and the shot are lifted.
- The counter-arm is swung forward and upward; the shot putter passes through a position in which the counter-arm, the shoulder axis, and the upper part of the throwing arm point in the direction of the throw; from the moment when the elbow has reached a position behind the shot, the forearm remains directed approximately in the direction of departure.
- The shot is moved away from the neck, and the putting arm is extended in

the direction of departure; the counter-arm is simultaneously moved backward and downward toward the body.

- The active extension of the legs already leads to the single-support phase and/or to the supportless phase shortly before the shot is released out of the hand.

RECOVERY

- The shot putter reverses his/her legs so that his/her right leg is in front, and he/she tries to balance himself/herself (LT and SST), or sometimes he/she performs several turns on his/her right leg (RT).
- The shot putter keeps his/her CG behind the point of support to avoid stepping over the stop board.
- The shot putter leaves the circle through its back half.

3.4.5 PHOTO SEQUENCES

LINEAR TECHNIQUE OF SHOT PUTTING

Data about the photo sequence

Athlete:	Ralf Bartels (born: 21 February 1978, Germany)
Height/weight:	1.86 m/145 kg
Performance:	20.58 m (6 August 2002, Munich)
Best performance:	21.44 m (13 March 2010, Doha, indoors)
Greatest success:	Bronze medal at the 2005 and 2009 World Championships, European Champion in 2006 and 2011 (indoors)

COMMENTARY

As may be seen from the rain protection for the judges, camera, and microphone in this photo sequence, the shot-put final at the 2002 European Championships took place under difficult weather conditions. Despite the cold and wet weather, the linear shot putter Ralf Bartels, whose personal best at that time was 20.85m, was less than 30cm short of that distance. The winner was another linear shot putter (Juri Belonog, 21.37m), followed by a rotational shot putter (Joachim Olson, 21.16m, see photo sequence below).

Ralf Bartels puts from a dynamic preliminary movement (not shown here). His crouch position with approximately horizontal upper body is not too low (relatively large knee angle). For a

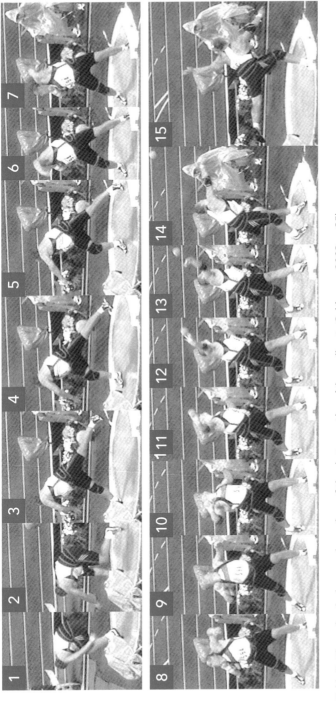

Table 8: Biomechanical measuring values of the shots mentioned (according to Goldmann, 2003, p. 35).

Name	Distance (m)	Shot velocities (m/sec) upon			Angle of departure	Shot heights (m) upon			Main acceleration path (m)	Width of the backward reclining position of delivery (m)	Percentage of the departure velocity due to the motion of the arm
		Right touchdown	Left touchdown	Departure		Right touchdown	Left touchdown	Departure			
Juri Belonog	21.37	2.6	2.8	13.8	36.4°	1.04	1.28	2.33	2.02	1.04	78%
Joachim Olsen	21.16	1.6	2.4	13.7	39.4°	0.77	1.25	2.13	1.83	0.77	64%
Ralf Bartels	20.58	2.3	3.1	13.6	34.9°	1.13	1.19	2.18	2.24	1.13	70%

long time, the typical feature of Ralf Bartel's glide was a backward pendulum movement of his free arm contrary to the putting direction at the beginning of the push-off at the rear rim of the circle (pictures 1 and 2). Later, he switched to a vertically downward hanging position of his arm which is moved slightly in the direction of the put as a swing element at the beginning of the glide before he moves it back again to the front of his body (see discourse I). In accordance with the target technique, the push-off from the rear rim of the circle leads to an extension of both legs. It is possibly due to the wet weather that the push-off is somewhat too far upward. The shoulders and the foot of the swing leg are lifted a little too high, resulting in a relatively short glide path of the right leg and thus in a wide backward reclining position of delivery (61% of the body height). During the supportless phase, Bartels moves his counter-hand backward and upward. The flower in the background shows that the hand remains behind, while the body continues to move (pictures 4 and 5).

In the main acceleration phase (touchdown of the right leg to the release of the shot), Bartels achieves a very long path of acceleration when one considers his body height. He achieves this due to his wide backward reclining position of delivery and his good release technique in spite of his relatively upright upper body at the start. The main acceleration phase begins with an active and long forward and upward push of his pressure leg. The opening movement of the counter-arm prepares the

action of his trunk. After the touchdown of his pressure leg, Bartels places his swing leg, which was initially a little too high, quickly onto the ground. The duration of 0.10 sec between the touchdown of the right leg and the touchdown of the left leg is in the middle of the normal range. As a result, Bartels forms a fixed abutment with the left side of his body and hardly bends the knee of his bracing leg. Due to the active work of his legs and counter-arm as well as a long holding back of his putting arm, Bartels achieves a very good development of tension of the front side of his body (pictures 9 and 10). Then he pushes his arm explosively to the front and bends his wrist outward. Due to his relatively upright trunk at the beginning of the main acceleration phase, Bartels achieves only a relatively flat angle of departure. Approximately at the moment of the release of the shot, the bracing leg is also released from the ground, followed by a rapid reverse of legs so that the right leg is in front.

SCISSOR-STEP TECHNIQUE OF SHOT PUTTING

Data about the photo sequence

Athlete:	Petra Lammert (born: 3 March 1984, Germany)
Height/weight:	1.77 m/78 kg
Performance:	19.34 m (10 June 2007, Schönebeck)
Best performance:	20.04 m (26 May 2007, Zeven)
Greatest success:	Fifth place at the 2007 World Championships, third place at the 2006 European Championships, European Indoor Champion in 2009

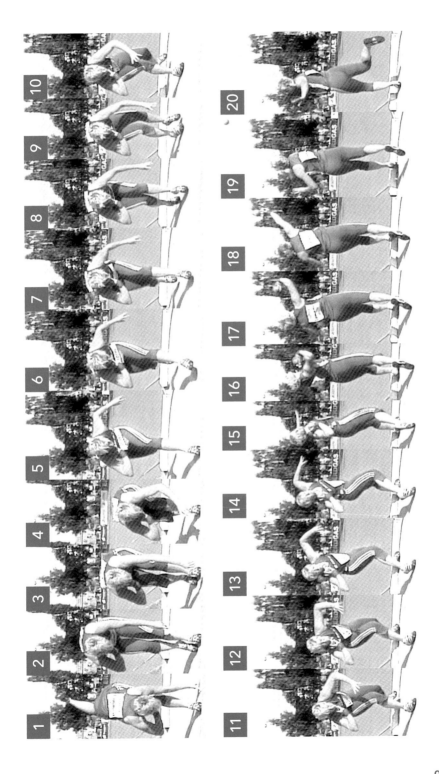

COMMENTARY

According to her coach Dieter Kollark, Petra Lammert switched to the scissor-step technique since there was a fundamental error in her linear technique. When placing her right foot on the ground in the centre of the circle, she turned this foot too early (more like a discus thrower) in the direction of the put so that she was unable to actively use her pressure leg. In the scissor-step technique, this error no longer appeared so obviously and often. In Kollark's opinion, the position of the pressure leg also improved. It is now not so far on the pressure leg side, but more behind the bracing leg.

The photo sequence was filmed about two weeks after Petra Lammert had achieved her current best distance using the scissor-step technique. In 2010, Petra Lammert returned to the linear technique, but was unable to improve her personal best by using this technique.

Lammert's preliminary movement includes a horizontal balance position with a very low upper body. Her free hand touches the ground. The highly raised right leg is bent at the knee joint (picture 1). Then, the previously slightly bent left leg is extended again, the trunk is raised slightly above the horizontal, and the right leg is lowered next to the support leg and now only bent slightly (picture 2). Subsequently, the rhythmic and dynamic preliminary movement is continued by bending both legs and lowering the shoulders slightly again below hip height. In the process, the foot of the swing leg remains laterally behind the foot of the pressure leg (picture 3). From there, the rapid and powerful push-off with the left leg is started which is fully straightened at the knee joint through the push-off, and the entire sole of the foot is released from the ground approximately at the moment of full extension (pictures 4–6). At the same time, the right leg performs its swinging movement toward the stop board. In accordance with the target technique, it is not fully straightened at the knee joint in the process (contrary to the swing leg during the glide). However, by extending her right hip more actively, Lammert would be able to perform a more dynamic movement of her swing leg with her right foot getting closer to the stop board (which cannot be seen in the photo taken from the rear). During the push-off from the rear rim of the circle, Lammert uses her free arm as a swing element, moves it in the direction of the put, and lifts her shoulders only slightly above hip height.

However, she pushes herself off in such a way that during the flight she lowers her shoulders again to approximately hip height (pictures 6–9). She now moves her free arm actively backward against the direction of the put. Due to the somewhat passive action of the swing leg, there is an early backward movement of the right leg during the flight phase. The point of touchdown of the right foot is therefore significantly behind the centre of the circle, which eventually leads to a very wide backward reclining position of delivery. After landing on the ball of her right foot, Lammert bends this foot flatly onto the ground at an angle of approximately 135° to the centre line of the landing sector (picture 10). Together with the action of her pressure leg, she begins to lift her upper body quickly and vigorously and to open her counter-arm (beginning with picture 10). It would be ideal if the opening of the counter-arm started later, in that case, however, also with an active rotation of the head. Although the bracing leg is placed on the ground in a not completely straight position, it yields very little and is then actively extended (beginning with picture 12). Pictures 13–15 reveal Lammert's main problem mentioned above.

She does not extend her pressure leg fully and turns it in the direction of the put too early. Ultimately, the too wide backward reclining position of delivery and the lacking action of the pressure leg (possibly in combination with fear of invalid trials) result in Lammert not getting close enough to the stop board (although the action of her putting arm is perfect). A leg reverse is hardly necessary.

ROTATIONAL TECHNIQUE OF SHOT PUTTING

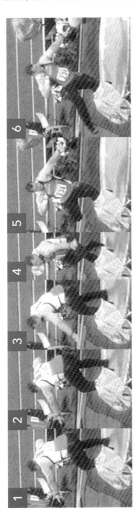

Data about the photo sequence

Athlete:	Joachim Olsen (born: 31 May 1977, Denmark)
Height/weight:	1.84 m/120 kg
Performance:	21.16 m (6 August 2002, Munich)
Best performance:	21.61 m (13 June 2007, Copenhagen)
Greatest success:	Bronze medal at the 2004 Olympic Games, European vice-champion in 2002

COMMENTARY

As already mentioned in connection with Ralf Bartels, the weather conditions were very difficult during the shot-put final at the 2002 European Championships. Rotational shot putters are said to have greater problems with a wet circle than linear shot putters. On that day, Joachim Olsen remained only 41cm behind his personal best at the time and was defeated only by the linear shot putter Juri Belonog (21.37m). Olsen started out as a discus thrower and linear shot putter. While he was studying history at the University of Idaho in the USA, the country of rotational shot putters, he switched from the linear to the rotational technique and quickly made significant progress.

The typical positioning of rotational shot-putters with a high and abducted elbow is clearly visible. Olsen initially holds his counter-arm in a constant position slightly in front of his shoulder axis. When looking in the direction of the put, Olsen, who is a right-hander, seems to stand slightly offset to the left side of the circle in the starting position although this is difficult to assess from the perspective chosen in the photo sequence. His feet are approximately shoulder-width apart and his upper body is clearly bent forward (picture 1). Although he straightens slightly during the start of the turn, he still maintains a significant forward lean of his trunk. The outward turn of Olson's left leg does not start before the turn of his trunk. He shifts his weight clearly toward his left leg. When pushing off from his right leg, he tries to leave this leg standing on the ground for a long time (pictures 2–4). After a slight lift of the heel of this leg, he moves it around the supporting leg on a wide circle while performing a kicking movement. After finishing the movement of the swing leg in a knee-lift position below the horizontal, Olsen tries to place down his pressure leg quickly after only a short flight phase. The push-off with the left leg is performed out of the ankle joint (not visible here) and with only minor knee extension (pictures 5–7). In combination with a flat movement of the swing leg and Olsen's visible effort to place his pressure leg down on the ground quickly, this results in a flat and short flight phase and in a point of touchdown of the pressure leg which is favourable for rotational shot-putters because it is not too close to the stop board (picture 8). Even if the right foot only points approximately to the left side of the circle upon touchdown, Olsen succeeds in quickly continuing his turn on the ball of his pressure leg. He holds his counter-arm close to his body to increase his rotational velocity and his shoulder-hip separation even more so to delay the release of the shot as long as possible. Olsen moves his bracing leg flatly and closely past his pressure leg to the stop board (pictures 9–11). Now the actual forward and upward rotation-extension movement of the pressure leg starts. At the same time, the action of the already largely straightened bracing leg increases the rotation about the longitudinal axis of the body and the acceleration upward. In the process, Olsen's bracing leg is extremely stable and there is hardly any bending of the knee joint (pictures 12 and 13). Simultaneously with the start of the rotation and extension movement of the pressure leg, the counter-arm also performs an opening movement forward and upward and thus initiates the action of the upper body. Subsequently, the counter-arm is moved further to the left and downward toward the body to tighten the chest muscles. As a result of the leg action, the chest is turned into the frontal position. Just before this is achieved, the shot leaves the neck to be finally released (pictures 14–17). In the process, the explosive leg extension results in Olsen leaving the ground well before releasing the shot. He is just able to avoid the trial from becoming invalid by performing an acrobatic leg reverse so that the straight right leg is in front (pictures 18–20).

3.4.6 DIDACTICS: SUPERORDINATE LONG-TERM OBJECTIVES AND GENERAL METHODOLOGY

The U14 is the youngest age group in which the shot put is an official competition discipline. However, in younger age groups it should be prepared in practice by performing one- and two-handed putting and pushing passes in versatile forms of games and exercises. Sufficiently heavy (although not overly heavy) devices (e.g., 2–3 kg in the U14 age group) and the prescription of an appropriate starting position and of the (rather vertical) putting direction ensure that the athlete indeed performs a putting and not a(n overhead) throwing movement. When putting, the elbow remains behind the device during the arm action.

In basic training, which focuses on learning techniques, the question soon arises about which technique to choose. On the one hand, the focus should be on learning a good technique for the standing put. On the other hand, in terms of differential learning, athletes should experiment with various techniques of pre-acceleration. Here it is well possible that beginners use quite different techniques than the rotational, linear, or scissor-step techniques of shot putting (even in competition). Right-handers, for example, frequently use various more or less frontal, lateral, or backward walk-on or hop-on techniques with a left-right-left stride rhythm. At a later stage, all three advanced techniques should also be mastered in their rough form and tested in competition before making a first preliminary decision regarding the technique to be preferred in competition. In respect to the rotational and scissor-step technique, synergies with the discus throw should be used. However, the discus throw and the rotational technique of shot putting should not be practised together in one training session due to existing differences. Even after the first preliminary decision to use a specific technique, the remaining techniques should be used as important training exercises.

In the shot put it is particularly evident how the weaker strength of less advanced athletes inevitably results in a different technical model. In both the starting position and the backward reclining position of delivery, younger and weaker athletes do not succeed in effectively accelerating the shot out of the low position which is observable in world-class athletes. Therefore, they should choose a path for the shot which is higher in relation to their own body height.

Even for shot putters, speed and explosive strength are decisive factors determining performance. Therefore, they benefit from basic training which is geared toward the combined events. Although there is usually a first emphasis on the discipline group including the discus throw, shot put, and hammer throw at the end of the training for the U16 age category, young athletes should still take part in combined-event competitions during build-up training. Sometimes, the discus throw and shot put are competed at the same time up to the

point of (high-)performance training.

SAFETY PRECAUTIONS

In addition to the safety precautions mentioned in connection with the common features of the throwing events (see chapter II–3.1.3), the following requirements must be observed in the shot put:

- The rotational technique results in a wide scatter in the direction of delivery.
- Preliminary exercises using medicine balls (but not with shots) may well be performed in face-to-face line-up. However, the distance between the two rows must be greater than the putting distance of the best athletes. Moreover, the athletes on one side should put the medicine ball simultaneously to their respective partners on the other side on the command of the coach. The waiting partners should look toward the athlete putting the ball. This prevents an athlete (e.g., in a rear starting position) from being hit by an approaching ball.
- Athletes should not play around carelessly with the shots in order to prevent the balls from falling on their own or other athletes' feet.

3.4.7 TRAINING CONTENTS: FORMS OF GAMES AND EXERCISES

All training forms mentioned in connection with the 100m sprint (see chapter II–1.3.3) may also be used for preparing the shot put

in terms of reactive-strength and speed-strength training. For the same reason, the forms of the ABCs of jumping and multiple jumps (see chapters I–5.4.6 and II–2.2.7) described in connection with the general training forms of strength training and the long jump are an important part of shot-put training. The forms of games and exercises mentioned in connection with the discus throw (see chapter II–3.3.7) especially foster the development of the rotational technique of shot putting.

421 ▢ Target and skilfulness puts

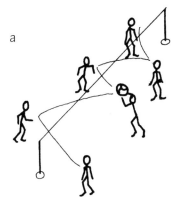

a

Possible objectives: Playful introduction to putting; experiencing the versatile coordination of (vertical) putting; strengthening the putting muscles; specific warm-up.

Execution: a: Ball over the cord (like volleyball, with the exception that the players are allowed to catch the ball) or a push-pass relay (while sitting, kneeling, standing); b: putting the ball toward a partner through a ring, only throws without touching the ring count; increase in height and distance; c: putting against a wall, with a partner or by catching the ball that bounces off the wall oneself ("Who manages the most trials without the ball falling on the ground?" or "Who throws the farthest distance to the wall?"); d: putting from various positions (sitting, kneeling, standing) over a height marker while catching one's own ball; e: putting toward a high target; f: boccia using the shot-putting movement: "Which team puts the most devices into the inner circle or achieves the most points?"

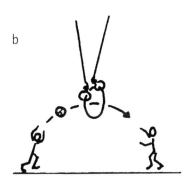

b

Variations: One-handed (left and right alternately) or two-handed put (chest pass, 426) of a medicine ball, shot, stone, etc.

Typical load standards: Only as long as it's fun.

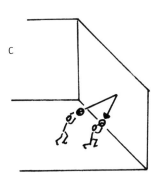

c

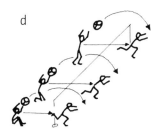

d

e 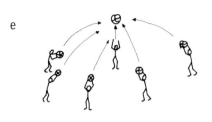   f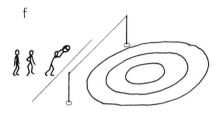

422 ◼️ Putting into zones

Possible objectives: Competitive putting game; putting technique; strengthening the putting muscles.

Execution: A height marker should be used to encourage a put (instead of a throw); to quickly identify the distance, the ranges should be divided into zones which are assigned points.

Variations: One-handed (left and right alternately) or two-handed put (chest pass, 426) from a sitting, kneeling, or standing position using a medicine ball, shot, stone, etc.; as an individual competition ("Who gets the most points with five puts?") or team competition ("Which team gets the most points?"); a cord may be spread diagonally so that the athletes can choose their individual height.

Typical load standards: Only as long as it's fun.

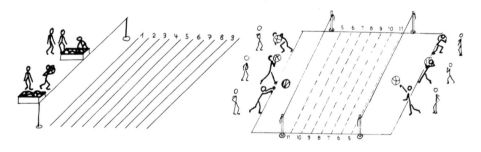

423 **Putting and walking**

> *Possible objectives:* Competitive putting game; putting technique; strengthening of the putting muscles.
>
> *Execution:* Each subsequent put is performed from the landing point of the first put ("Who reaches the furthest distance with five puts?").
>
> *Variations:* Also as golf putting: "Who manages to put across the field (e.g., into the goal) with the least puts?" (See also 422.)
>
> *Typical load standards:* Only as long as it's fun.

424 **Vertical putting**

> *Possible objectives:* Competitive putting game; putting technique; strengthening of the putting muscles.
>
> *Execution/variations:* On command, all athletes perform a vertical put from a squat: "Which ball/ shot lands last?" (See also 422.)
>
> *Typical load standards:* Only as long as it's fun.

425 **Putting for speed**

> *Possible objectives:* Competitive putting game; putting technique; strengthening of the putting muscles.
>
> *Execution/variations:* "Who is the first to take 10 medicine balls from a box behind himself/herself and put them over a height marker placed at a distance (e.g., of 3m)?"
>
> *Typical load standards:* Only as long as it's fun.

426  **Chest pass (two-handed put)**

Possible objectives: Putting technique (frontal final position, arm action); speed-strength and reactive-strength training of the putting muscles; specific warm-up.

Execution: Putting the medicine ball forward and upward from the position presented; extension of the elbow joints and palmar flexion of the wrists so that the fingers point outward in the end.

Variations: In a sitting, knee-stand, standing position, from a full squat, from an arched back position, from a stride position, with a walk-on or run-up; also as a reactive-strength exercise while standing a short distance from the wall (a rebounding ball is required), or toward a partner: catching a fast ball, point of reversal shortly in front of the chest and fast return of the ball using a pushing movement.

Typical load standards: 2–5 x 8–20 reps depending on the execution, objective and performance ability.

427 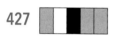 **Becoming accustomed to the shot**

Possible objectives: Developing a feel for the weight of the shot; controlling the shot; specific warm-up.

Execution/variations: Rotating the shot around the hips, the lower legs, and the head, as well as figure eights around and through slightly split legs (in both directions); gripping the shot with one hand from above, without dropping it, then gentle throwing up the shot and gripping it again from above; throwing the shot gently from one hand to the other behind one's back; gently throwing the shot with the wrists from hand to hand in front of the chest, only the fingers and the basic joints of the fingers touch the shot;

gently putting the shot above the shoulder and catching it with the same hand.

Typical load standards: 10–20 reps depending on the exercise.

The following exercises should first be introduced using a medicine ball. If a shot is used, one should become accustomed to the shot first. This should especially be the case before a shot is used for the first time, but also before each training session.

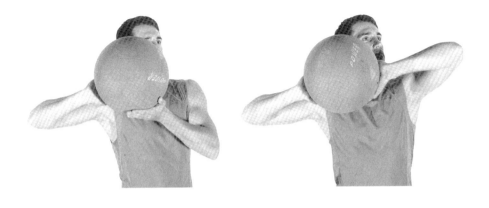

---

428   **Puts from various positions**

Possible objectives: Reduction of the kinematic chain (isolation of the motion of the upper body); specific speed-strength training of the upper body; if performed while standing up from a knee stand: also demonstration of the movement direction from low to high.

Execution/variations: From a sitting position (with stretched legs), a knee-stand, or while standing up from a one-legged knee-stand; using a medicine ball or shot; with a height marker; bilateral practice.

Typical load standards: 1–3 x 5–20 reps depending on age, objective and performance ability.

429 **Frontal put**

From a parallel position

From a stride position

Possible objectives: Technique of the delivery movement (while releasing the shot, the chest must be square to the direction of the put); specific warm-up.

Execution: The photos show the respective starting position, the point of movement reversal, as well as the approximate moment when the shot leaves the hand.

Variations: Initially from a parallel position, then from a stride position; using a medicine ball or shot; particularly for beginners, the shot should be lighter than the competition device; over a height marker; also in rapid succession against a wall; bilateral practice.

Typical load standards: 5–10 reps

430  Standing put

Specific to the linear shot put:

Specific to the rotational shot put:

Possible objectives: Technique of the delivery movement from the backward reclining position; specific speed strength; specific warm-up.

Execution: The starting position and execution are very much identical with the put from a backward reclining position; the weight is initially on the pressure leg; the bracing leg is hardly loaded.

Variations: Corresponding with the linear or scissor-step technique (relatively wide backward reclining position of delivery, rather linear acceleration of the upper body and the shot from the rear and from below to the front and upward) or the rotational technique (relatively narrow backward reclining position of delivery, rather rotational acceleration of the shot with more upright trunk, extreme shoulder-hip separation and wide circular swinging movement of the extended counter-arm); from a static starting position (possibly with slight lift of the bracing leg and subsequent active touchdown) or with dynamic, reactive, and powerful preliminary movement (moving down to the starting position and rapid movement reversal); for beginners, the starting position is more upright depending on the athlete's strength abilities; for beginners initially without, later also with subsequent leg reverse; using a medicine ball or shot, especially for beginners, the shot should be lighter than the competition device; in performance sport also with a weight heavier than the competition device; over a height marker; along a wall (wall on the left or on the right); with a cord at a height of 1 m or higher shortly in front of the stop board, the hip should be brought forward and upward toward the cord; (see also table 9).

Typical load standards: 6–20 reps.

*Table 9: **Possible variations as a part of the differential learning of the two-legged delivery phase** (modified on the basis of Beckmann et al., 2008; see chapter I–4.1 on the theory of differential learning).*

Movement geometry	a) Knee angle of the pressure leg at the beginning of the two-legged delivery phase 90°, 180°, <90°, … b) Trunk inclination: Forward lean, backward lean, lean to the right/left c) Change of the foot position and/or the distance between the feet in or square to the direction of the throw d) Putting with the right or left arm e) …
Movement velocity	f) Fast or slow
Movement acceleration	g) Becoming faster or slower during the (partial) movement
Movement rhythm	h) Fast pre-acceleration, slowly performed delivery phase i) Slow action of the legs, fast performance of the trunk and arm movement j) Fast leg movement, slow opening of the trunk, rapid arm extension k) …
Ancillary conditions of the movement	l) Change of the putting direction: (diagonally) to the left, right, upward and downward m) Glide, scissor step or turn on declining or inclining surface or with a lateral inclination to the left or to the right n) …
Movement combinations	Combinations of a-n

431 ▢▢■ Standing put imitations

Possible objectives: Technique of the delivery movement, particularly the succession of partial movements; specific warm-up; strength training.

Execution/variations: Imitation of movement details (e.g., action of the pressure leg, action of the bracing leg, raising the trunk, action of the counter-arm, remaining behind the putting arm with development of tension in the chest, position of the forearm, etc.); with or without device; possibly while holding the partner's hand with the counter-arm; standing put in two phases: initially inward rotation of the pressure leg and opening of the counter-arm until the shoulder points in the direction of the put, rest, and continuation from there with delivery of the shot; with a stick or

(advanced athletes) with a barbell on the shoulder. *Typical load standards:* 1–5 x 5–10 reps depending on the objective.

---

432 **Puts from the 3-stride rhythm**

Possible objectives: Versatile putting experiences with high pre-acceleration (a and c); alternative competition technique for less advanced athletes (b).

Execution: Right-handers put with left-right-left stride rhythm.

Variations: Outside the circle, with running into the circle, or in the circle; walking or running with more or less noticeable rhythmisation and with a flat jump from left to right (comparable to the impulse stride in the javelin throw)

a) frontal starting position (right-handers stand in stride position with the right foot in front): with more or less noticeable twist of the shoulder from the frontal position and lowering of the CG before taking the backward reclining position of delivery

b) lateral starting position: either similar to the standing put position with the left leg already moved forward (picture in the middle) or with the left leg next to the right one (picture at the bottom)

c) starting position with the back turned in the direction of the put and walking backward to prepare the scissor-step technique

using a medicine ball or shot, also with weight (above or) below the weight of the competition device; over a height marker; bilateral practice.

Typical load standards: 5–10 reps per variation.

433   Linear shot-put technique: glide imitations

Possible objectives: Technique of the glide.

Execution/variations:

a) shot twist: standing position on the pressure leg, trunk bent forward, swing leg extended to the rear; hopping on the pressure leg while turning this leg during one hop from the position before the glide to the position after the glide, and during the next hop back to the position before the glide, etc.; the hip slightly rotates together with the pressure leg, the shoulder axis remains unchanged; on the spot or while moving backward;

b) limping snake: the members of the group stand one behind the other and hold the swing-leg foot of the athlete in front with the counter-arm ("Which group can hop backward the fastest?"); also as a form of competition for children;

c) glide imitations into the backward reclining position of delivery (and not further: shoulder axis still parallel to the rear rim of the circle, foot of the pressure leg turned inward): without shot, with the shot held low with extended arms, with a stick on the shoulders,

arms stretched out to the side (flyer), or with the shot on the neck (delivery only after a rest and check of the backward reclining position of delivery, if at all); glide possibly over a ditch or under a cord; in performance training also with a bar on the shoulders;

d) while being led by a partner: the partner holds both hands or (if performed with a shot) only the counter-arm (by means of an elastic band) and ensures that the push-off is powerful and directed toward the stop board and that the upper body stays behind and is kept closed;

e) glide without swing leg: the swing leg is already stretched backward, powerful push-off with the supporting leg into the backward reclining position of delivery;

f) swing-leg exercise: a ball is placed behind the swing leg and is kicked away powerfully during the glide;

g) slide and step (see pictures below): the swing leg slides over the ground, then the pressure leg is placed into the centre of the circle; also with subsequent delivery;

bilateral practice; also with eyes shut.

Typical load standards: 3–10 reps per variation.

434  **Linear technique of shot putting: putting from the glide**

Possible objectives: Target technique; specific speed-strength and reactive-strength training.
Execution: According to the target technique (see chapter II-3.4.3).
Variations: The starting position, direction of the put, rhythm, etc. may be changed in terms of differential learning; the distance of the glide should be adjusted individually; initially without, then with subsequent leg reverse; using a light weight or (with advanced athletes) a heavy weight; with a marker to look at; bilateral practice; in high-performance training also wearing a weighted vest.
Typical load standards: 5–30 reps depending on age, performance ability, training period, etc.

435 **Scissor-step and rotational technique: putting from the switch of legs**

Possible objectives: Rotation of the lower part of the body to take the backward reclining position of delivery.
Execution: The left foot is placed on the spot where the right one would be placed in the backward reclining position of delivery, while the right one is placed on the spot where the left one would be placed; the feet and the upper body are directed to the rear rim of the circle; the trunk is bent backward; the shot is delivered after the feet have simultaneously switched their position (the athlete should not jump too much) into the backward reclining position of delivery (the turning direction should be in accordance with the target technique).
Variations: Swing of the counter-arm against the direction of the put during the switch of legs; in terms of differential learning also with incorrect

turning direction.
Typical load standards: 3–10 reps per variation.

---

436 Scissor-step technique: scissor-step imitations

Possible objectives: Technique of the scissor step.
Execution/variations: The variations listed in connection with exercise 433 (b–e) may also be performed using the scissor-step technique; walking scissor step: placement of the leg on the side of the putting arm backward into the centre of the circle, while the other leg is still in contact with the rear rim of the circle, then the bracing leg is placed backward into the backward reclining position of delivery; also with subsequent delivery of the shot.
Typical load standards: 3–10 reps per variation.

---

437 Scissor-step technique: put from the scissor step

Possible objectives: Target technique; specific speed-strength and reactive-strength training.
Execution: According to the target technique (see chapter II–3.4.3).
Variations: Change of the starting position, direction of the put, rhythm, etc. in terms of differential learning; initially with and then without subsequent leg reverse; using a light weight or (with advanced athletes) a heavy weight; with a marker to look at; bilateral practice.
Typical load standards: 5–30 reps depending on age, performance ability, training period, etc.

Rotational technique of shot putting: The method of teaching the turn corresponds with the method described for the discus throw, by increasing the turn gradually by ¼ turn each:

- 2/4 turn = put from the (walking) scissor-step technique (436);
- 3/4 to 4/4 turn (409): In the starting position, the pressure leg is already placed in

the centre of the circle, the leg on the non-putting side is at the rear rim of the circle, the shoulder axis is square to the direction of the put (4/4), or the putting shoulder is pointing in the direction of the put (3/4);

- 4/4 to 5/4 turn (410): In the starting position, the leg on the non-putting side is placed in the centre of the circle, while the leg on the side of the putting arm is placed on the ground outside the circle, the shoulder axis is either square to the direction of the put (4/4), or the shoulder on the non-putting side is pointing in the direction of the put (5/4).

The individual steps are initially imitated without a device or with a device up to the backward reclining position of delivery before they are performed with the release of a medicine ball or shot and without a break. In addition, the athletes should perform the corresponding turns (408) and turn imitations described in connection with the discus throw (411–413).

---

438  **Rotational shot-put technique: put from the turn**

Possible objectives: Target technique; specific speed-strength and reactive-strength training.

Execution: According to the target technique (see chapter II–3.4.3).

Variations: Change of the starting position, direction of the put, rhythm, etc. in terms of differential learning; initially with and then without subsequent leg reverse; using a light weight or (with advanced athletes) a heavy weight; with a marker to look at; bilateral practice.

Typical load standards: 5–30 reps depending on age, performance ability, training period, etc.

439 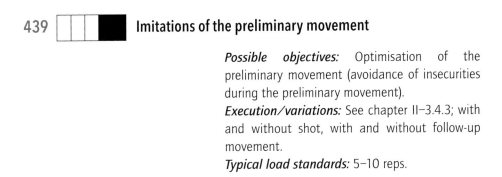 **Imitations of the preliminary movement**

Possible objectives: Optimisation of the preliminary movement (avoidance of insecurities during the preliminary movement).

Execution/variations: See chapter II–3.4.3; with and without shot, with and without follow-up movement.

Typical load standards: 5–10 reps.

In addition to the throws presented in the general chapter on strength (93–96), the medicine-ball exercises presented in connection with the javelin throw (391 and 416) are also important contents of the speed-strength training of shot-putters.

In strength training, the delivery movement may be practised relatively specifically by using the one-armed inclined bench press with a dumbbell (54). In addition, the following exercises are important elements of the strength training of shot-putters: 38, 39, 41–47, 49–57, 59, 61–64, 66, 69–72, 77–88, and 90–96.

3.4.8 SPECIAL TEST AND CONTROL PROCEDURES

Test: Ability/skill tested	Execution/comments
T151 **Technique analysis:** Discus technique	Maximal competition throw; evaluation on the basis of the technique analysis sheet (see chapter II–3.3.4), possibly using a video (T1) and photo sequences made thereof; in high-performance sport, also computer-supported 3D analysis based on at least two simultaneous video recordings.
T152 **Discus throw with reduced pre-acceleration:** Specific speed strength as well as laterality differences	Throwing distance in the discus throw: • from a sitting position square to the direction of the throw with extended legs (416); • from a standing position (406); • with the pressure leg already brought forward (409); • with running in (410); • with the weaker side using the methods of pre-acceleration mentioned.

(continued)

(continued)

Test: Ability/skill tested	Execution/comments
T161 **Technique analysis:** Shot-put technique	Maximal competition put; evaluation on the basis of the technique analysis sheet (see chapter II–3.4.4), possibly using a video (T1) and photo sequences made thereof; in high-performance sport, also computer-supported 3D analysis based on at least two simultaneous video recordings.
T162 **Shot put with reduced or shortened pre-acceleration:** Specific speed strength as well as laterality	Distance achieved in the shot put: • from a sitting position square to the direction of the throw with extended legs or from the knee-stand (428); • from a parallel standing position (429); • from the backward reclining position of delivery (430); • from the 3-stride rhythm (432); • using the linear technique of shot putting (434); • using the scissor-step technique of shot putting (437); • from the 4/4 (409), 5/4 (410), or 6/4 (414) turn; and • with the weak side from the pre-accelerations mentioned.
T163 **Shot put using a different weight:** Specific speed strength as well as laterality	Shot-put distance: • using a weight lighter than the competition shot; • using a weight heavier than the competition shot; and • with the weaker side and changed device.
T164 **General throwing tests for the shot put:** Speed strength	Throwing distance in: • tossing forward, backward, and sideward (93); • the overhead throw using both hands (391); and • the rotational throw while sitting (95).
T165 **Shot-put endurance test:** Specific strength endurance	The total distance achieved in 10 puts in a pre-set time counts.
T4 **1 RPM:** Maximal strength	Bench press (54), shoulder press (56), squat (62), clean and jerk (63), snatch (64), hip-shoulder twist (67), quadriceps (69), etc.
T5 **Squat jump, and T8 counter-movement and drop jump:** Two-legged speed strength and reactive strength of the extensor loop	

Test: Ability/skill tested		Execution/comments
T9	**5-stride hops with distance maximisation:** Reactive strength of the legs in comparison to one another	Test should only be performed if it is not too stressful due to the bodyweight; both legs should be tested.
T10	**30m bounding run with time minimisation:** Reactive strength of the legs	Only if it is not too stressful due to the bodyweight.
T61	**20m sprint from a standing start:** (Sprint) acceleration	
T2	**Flexibility tests:** General flexibility	
T3	**Body weight and body fat measurement:** Relative strength	Inappropriate upward and downward deflections should be avoided.

In high-performance sport, additional tests are possible (e.g., performance of the ground contacts on force-measurement plates).

Table 10: **Basic performances of (young) shot-putters** *(according to Kühl & Hommel, 1997, pp. 229–230). Today, male U20 athletes put the 6.0 instead of the 6.26kg shot.*

		Women				Men				
Shot weight and	(kg)	4.0	4.0	4.0	4.0	5.0	5.0	6.26	7.26	7.26
target distance in the shot put	(m)	**13.0**	**15.5**	**17.0**	**19.0**	**14.0**	**16.0**	**17.0**	**17.0**	**18.5**
Shot weight when	(kg)	3.0	3.0	3.0	3.0	4.0	4.0	5.0	6.26	6.26
putting a lighter shot	(m)	15.0	16.5	19.0	21.0	15.5	17.5	18.5	18.3	20.0
Shot weight when	(kg)	5.0	5.0	5.0	5.0	–	–	7.26	–	–
putting a heavier shot	(m)	11.0	13.5	15.0	17.0			15.5		
Forward throw of a 4 kg shot	(m)	12.0	14.2	15.8	17.5	15.0	17.0	–	–	–
Shot weight when	(kg)	4.0	4.0	4.0	4.0	4.0	4.0	6.26	7.26	7.26
throwing the shot backward	(m)	13.5	16.2	17.8	19.5	16.5	18.5	19.0	19.0	19.0
30m flying sprint	(sec)	3.75	3.58	3.50	3.45	3.50	3.30	3.10	3.10	3.10
3-stride hop	(m)	7.50	8.30	8.60	8.80	8.20	8.80	9.30	9.60	9.70
Extension jump	(cm)	50	60	65	68	60	65	75	77	79
Two-legged long jump	(m)	2.10	2.30	2.50	2.70	–	2.80	2.90	3.00	3.10
Bench press	(kg)	55	80	95	115	80	95	130	150	160
Clean and jerk	(kg)	50	70	85	105	65	80	110	130	150
Snatch	(kg)	45	65	75	90	65	75	85	105	115
Squat (full, barbell behind the neck)	(kg)	65	95	110	130	100	120	140	160	180

3.4.9 ERRORS – CAUSES – CORRECTIONS

LT = linear technique of shot putting; SST = scissor-step technique of shot putting; RT = rotational technique of shot putting

Error	Causes	Corrections
Primarily LT/SST: Insecurities during the preliminary movement.	• The athlete stands only on the ball of one foot too early and/or for too long. • Insufficient practice of a routine-like preliminary movement.	✔ The push-off leg should initially be placed on the ground with the entire sole of the foot; beginners should not lift themselves on the ball of the foot. ✔ Finding, establishing, and practising the individually optimal preliminary movement.
LT/SST: Too upright position at the beginning of the push-off from the rear rim of the circle (knee and hip angle too large).	• Insufficient effort of the shot-putter to achieve a functionally straight and long path of acceleration and optimal angle of departure. • Insufficient force of the extension loop or the technique is not adapted to the increased strength conditions.	✔ Glide or scissor step under a cord. ✔ Practising the preliminary movement for taking an optimal crouch position. ✔ Strength training for the extensor loop (e.g., 62–64).

Error	Causes	Corrections
LT/SST: *Too much lift of the upper body during the glide or scissor step.*	• Crouch position too low in relation to the athlete's strength abilities. • Insufficient effort by the shot-putter to achieve a functionally long path of acceleration in the phase of delivery.	✔ The starting position and preliminary movement should be changed so that the position at the beginning of the push-off is more upright. ✔ Strength training for the extensor loop, particularly for the back extensors, (62, especially good mornings). ✔ Glide or scissor step under a cord as well as variations and corrections of the backward reclining position of delivery during standing puts (430).
LT/SST: *Jump-like and too long glide or scissor step in terms of time (and distance: the CG is raised too high with or without too much horizontal movement of the CG).*	• Powerful push-off, but insufficient shift of weight in the direction of the stop board (in LT possibly due to a push-off with the ball of the foot instead of with the heel). • The action of the swing leg is directed too far upward. • The athlete tries to achieve a too narrow backward reclining position of delivery. • Beginners must cover too much distance with the glide or the scissor step (because they are placed too close to the rear rim of the circle). • Too much lift of the upper body during the glide or scissor step and its causes (see above).	✔ Imitation and practise of the push-off from the rear rim of the circle with initiation of the shift of the CG through extension of the ankle joint; in LT including the subsequent lifting of the tip of the foot and push-off with the heel. ✔ Practising a flat action of the swing leg (433 and 436). ✔ Puts using a flat glide or scissor step into differently wide backward reclining positions of delivery until the optimal width has been found. ✔ Beginners should try to find a suitable starting position closer to the stop board; as the technique and strength are increasing, the starting position should be shifted again to the rear rim of the circle. ✔ See corrections of lift of the upper body is raised too high during the glide or scissor step.

(continued)

(continued)

Error	Causes	Corrections
LT/SST: *Too short glide or scissor step in terms of distance (and time: insufficient horizontal movement of the CG with or without too little lift of the CG).*	• Insufficient shift of weight in the direction of the stop board. • The action of the swing leg is too passive. • The athlete tries to achieve a too wide backward reclining position of delivery. • The athlete' starting position is too close to the stop board. • Insufficient extension force in the push-off leg, possibly due to a too large or too small knee-joint angle in the crouch position; staying in the crouch position for too long may also result in a loss of force.	✔ Imitation and practise of the push-off from the rear rim of the circle by initiating the shift of the CG through extension of the ankle joint. ✔ Glide and scissor-step imitations while kicking away a ball with the swing leg. ✔ Puts using a flat glide or scissor step into differently wide backward reclining positions of delivery until the optimal width has been found. ✔ Choice of a starting position closer to the rear rim of the circle. ✔ Strength training for the extensor loop (e.g., 62-64). ✔ The athlete should possibly experiment with different knee-joint angles in the crouch position. ✔ The athlete should avoid a long static phase in the crouch position; the concentration phase should take place before the start of the preliminary movement (i.e., before taking the crouch position).

Many errors mentioned in connection with the discus throw (see chapter 3.3.9), particularly in respect to the turn, as well as their causes and corrections also apply to the rotational technique of shot putting and are therefore not mentioned here again.

Error	Causes	Corrections
RT: *Turn too far (the pressure leg is placed too close to the stop board).*	• Too much emphasis on the translatory acceleration in the direction of the stop board. • The push-off into the supportless phase is performed too much from the knee joint (and too little from the ankle joint; too much extension of the knee joint). • The swing leg is too high. • Too early movement of the upper body in the direction of the put. • Negative transfer from the discus throw in which a longer step during the turn is useful. • Excessive motivation.	✔ Optimisation of the technique of the turn in respect to the rotational acceleration (wide movements of the swing elements, incomplete extension of the knee joint, flat swing leg, staying behind of the upper body, shift of weight to the supporting leg of the one-legged starting phase, etc.) and improvement through imitation (411-413). ✔ The discus throw and the shot put should not be practised together in one session. ✔ Focus on a controlled start of the turn also in competition.

Error	Causes	Corrections
LT/SST/RT: *Insufficient inward turn of the foot of the pressure leg before the touchdown (usually in combination with an insufficient development of shoulder-hip separation).*	• Insufficient turn of the hip axis or the lower part of the body during or shortly before the supportless phase. • Insufficient rotation of the counter-arm contrary to the direction of rotation of the hip axis. • Insufficient inward rotation of the pressure leg.	✔ Imitation of the glide (433), scissor step (436), or turn (412–413) while checking the position of the feet; the remaining behind of the shoulder axis and the action of the counter-arm; objective: Upon touchdown, the foot of the pressure leg is turned only 90–135° out of the direction of the put (LT/SST) or already points almost opposite the direction of the put (RT).
LT/SST/RT: *Too wide backward reclining position of delivery.*	• Passive, late, and/or incorrectly aligned touchdown of the bracing leg, usually in combination with a too long one-legged delivery phase during which the body moves relatively passively across the point of touchdown; possibly to compensate for a too short glide or scissor step and its causes (see above) or a turn too much on the spot and its causes LT: • Insufficient drawing of the pressure leg under the CG. SST: • Insufficient action of the swing leg or too far backward movement of the swing leg against the direction of the put before it is placed on the ground as the pressure leg.	✔ Imitation and puts while trying to achieve an early forward movement of the bracing leg and a touchdown of the bracing leg as soon as possible after the touchdown of the pressure leg. ✔ The athlete should experiment with different wide backward reclining positions of delivery. ✔ See corrections of too short glide or too short scissor step, or too short leg reverse in chapter 3.3.9. LT: ✔ Imitation (433) and puts (434) with active drawing (and inward turn) of the pressure leg. SST: ✔ Imitation (436) and puts (437) while focusing on an optimal scissor movement of the legs.
LT/SST/RT: *Too narrow backward reclining position of delivery.*	LT/SST: • (Spatially) too long glide or scissor step and its causes (see above). • Choice of a starting position too close to the stop board. • The backward reclining position of delivery is not adapted to the (increased) strength conditions. RT: • In most cases, exclusively due to a too wide turn and its causes (see above).	✔ See corrections of jump-like and too long glide or scissor step. ✔ The athlete should choose a starting position closer to the rear rim of the circle. ✔ The athlete should experiment with differently wide backward reclining positions of delivery. ✔ See corrections of turn too far.
LT/SST/RT: *Insufficient lateral displacement of the feet in the backward reclining position of delivery (or the bracing leg is even farther on the side of the putting hand than the pressure leg).*	• Insufficient rotation of the lower part of the body before the touchdown of the bracing leg RT: • Loss of balance and/or touchdown of the pressure leg too far to the left or to the right from the centre.	✔ Imitations while checking the points of touchdown (caution: the athlete should not look at his feet while performing the movement). ✔ Use of overcorrection and the contrast method.

(continued)

(continued)

Error	Causes	Corrections
Primarily RT: *Too much lateral displacement of the feet in the backward reclining position of delivery.*	• The athlete has chosen a starting position in which the supporting leg of the one-legged starting phase is too far away from the centre line of the landing sector (the feet are placed on a line passing too diagonally through the circle). • Too far turn during the one-legged starting and/or delivery phase. • Balance problems during the turn.	✔ Rotational jumps, pirouettes (3), turns and successive leg reversals (408). ✔ Imitations and puts (409, 410, and 412–414) while checking the points of touchdown of the feet (but without looking at the feet while performing the movements).
LT/SST/RT: *Too upright backward reclining position of delivery (the angles at the knee and at the hip of the pressure leg are too large).*	• Insufficient development of shoulder-hip separation and its causes (see above). LT/SST: • Too upright position at the beginning of the push-off from the rear rim of the circle and its causes (see above). • Too much lift of the upper body during the glide or scissor step and its causes (see above). RT: • Insufficient remaining behind of the shoulders during the turn.	✔ See corrections of insufficient development of shoulder-hip separation, too upright position at the beginning of the push-off from the rear rim of the circle, and too much lift of the upper body during the glide or scissor step. ✔ Imitations of the turn up to the backward reclining position of delivery with noticeable running ahead of the legs.
Primarily LT/SST: *Too low backward reclining position of delivery (in relation to the athlete's strength capacities).*	• Insufficient raising during the glide or the scissor step (emphasis on a long path of acceleration to the disadvantage of optimal working angles of the muscles). • Jump-like glide (see above), passive yielding touchdown of the pressure leg, and delayed touchdown of the bracing leg result in a noticeable upward-downward-upward movement of the shot.	✔ The athlete should experiment with different degrees of raising himself/herself during puts from the glide or scissor step, as well as with standing puts from different starting positions. ✔ See corrections of jump-like glide. ✔ Imitations and puts while focusing on the almost simultaneous touchdown of the pressure leg and bracing leg, the fast transition to an active work of the pressure and bracing leg, and the continuous upward movement of the shot.

Error	Causes	Corrections
Primarily LT/SST: *Insufficient extension of the pressure leg.*	• The CG has already moved too far across the point of touchdown of the pressure leg due to » a too wide backward reclining position of delivery and its causes (see above), » a (too long and) passive yield of the pressure leg upon touchdown. • Insufficient extension force of the pressure leg. • Too early lift of the pressure leg.	✔ See corrections of too wide backward reclining position of delivery. ✔ Imitations (431) and puts (430) from the backward reclining position of delivery while focusing on the active work of the pressure leg; including versatile variations (see table 9). ✔ Imitations and puts from pre-acceleration while focusing on the almost simultaneous touchdown of the pressure leg and bracing leg and the fast transition to an active and long extension of the pressure leg (possibly use of overcorrection and contrast method). ✔ Strength training for the extensor loop (e.g., 62–64).
LT/SST/RT: *Insufficient bracing effect of the front leg.*	• The CG moves forward so much that it is above the point of touchdown of the bracing leg due to the passive yield of the bracing leg after its touchdown and subsequent insufficient extension, possibly due to the insufficient extension force of the bracing leg or the touchdown of the bracing leg only with the ball of the foot.	✔ Puts from pre-acceleration while focusing on the foot touchdown and a rapid, reactive and powerful upward extension of the bracing leg (possibly use of overcorrection and contrast method). ✔ Strength training for the extensor loop (e.g., 62–64).
LT/SST/RT: *Too early release of the shoulder-hip separation.*	• Too early delivery activity of the upper body, which means that the shoulder axis is not kept closed long enough due to opening the counter-arm and directing one's eyes to the front too early (the athlete wants to accelerate the shot too early). • Insufficient extension of the pressure leg and its causes (see above). • Insufficient bracing effect of the front leg and its causes (see above).	✔ Imitations of the preliminary movement and the pre-acceleration and then stop in the backward reclining position of delivery with keeping the counter-side closed (the shoulder axis remains directed to the rear rim of the circle, possibly supported by a partner holding back the counter-arm). ✔ Imitations (431, the delivery begins with the work of the pressure leg), as well as standing puts (430) with active extension of both legs and late activity of the upper body. ✔ See corrections of insufficient extension of the pressure leg and insufficient bracing action of the front leg.

(continued)

(continued)

Error	Causes	Corrections
LT/SST/RT: *Throwing the shot.*	• Insufficient automation of the difference between the put (push) and the throw (pull). • In the starting position, the shot is too far back on the neck. • In the starting position, the middle fingers are not placed behind the shot, but over the shot. • The elbow is not abducted enough from the trunk or lowered during the two-legged delivery phase. • The shot is moved away from the neck too early.	✔ Vertical upward puts (424 and 427). ✔ Check the starting position: the athlete should place the shot far (or farther) forward on his/her neck, pronate his/her forearm, keep his/her index finger (close) to the collarbone, abduct his/her forearm from the trunk, hold his/her elbow not too far at the side, and possibly more at the front of his/her body. ✔ The athlete should press the shot actively against his/her neck during pre-acceleration. ✔ Imagination aids: "The forearm should be like a billiards cue," or "the forearm is moved upward on a diagonal rail pointing in the direction of departure."
RT: *The athlete loses his/her control of the shot.*	• Incorrect holding of the shot (e.g., insufficient abduction of the elbow). • Too high centrifugal forces (possibly due to the trunk bent too far forward during the turn).	✔ Check the method of holding the shot; active pressing of the shot against one's neck during the turn. ✔ Imitations and puts while keeping one's trunk upright.
LT/SST/RT: *At the moment of departure, the shoulder axis is not square to the direction of the put.*	• Insufficient bringing forward of the hip on the side of the putting hand due to. » insufficient inward turn of the foot of the pressure leg before touchdown and its causes (see above); » insufficient extension of the pressure leg and its causes (see above); » insufficient bracing action of the front leg and its causes (see above); » RT: Lowering the foot of the pressure leg onto the entire sole.	✔ See corrections of insufficient inward turn of the foot of the pressure leg before touchdown, insufficient extension of the pressure leg, and insufficient bracing action of the front leg. ✔ LT/SST: Imitations of the preliminary movement and pre-acceleration into the backward reclining position of delivery plus the subsequent start of the work of the pressure leg while holding back the shoulder girdle. ✔ RT: Imitations of preliminary movement and pre-acceleration into the the backward reclining position of delivery (413) and puts from varying pre-accelerations with active continuation of the turn on the ball of the foot (409, 410, and 414).

992

Error	Causes	Corrections

LT/SST/RT:
At the moment of departure, the upper body is not upright.
	• Insufficient forward and upward movement of the pelvis during the delivery movement due to
	  » insufficient extension of the pressure leg and its causes (see above); or
	  » excessive action of the bracing leg;
	• Excessive or insufficient forward rotation of the upper body during the delivery movement.
		✔ See corrections of insufficient extension of the pressure leg.
		✔ Puts in the direction of a suitable height marker.
		✔ Placing a cord at hip height, approx. one foot in length behind the stop board and moving the pelvis toward this cord during the delivery (430).
		✔ Variation and optimisation of the forward acceleration of the shoulders, especially of the right shoulder, during standing puts and puts from pre-acceleration.

LT/SST/RT: *Significant deviation in the direction of the CG path from the direction of the put (when viewed from the rear; e.g., the body of a right-hander moves in the direction of the left sector boundary; the shot lands close to the right sector boundary).*	• Incorrect starting position (too far on the side of the putting hand when viewed in the direction of the put) or direction of movement (too far in the direction of the bracing-leg side) already at the beginning of pre-acceleration. • The counter-arm is not drawn to the body, but continues its swing backward and downward resulting in an excessive bending of the trunk to the bracing-leg side.	✔ Variation or change of the starting position. ✔ Puts along a wall (see the exercise presented for the javelin throw, 386) or obstacles on the side of the bracing leg (e.g., a cone that is knocked over when the bracing leg is placed too far to the outside). ✔ Target puts. ✔ Standing puts (430) and corresponding imitations (431) with correct action of the counter-arm; then also with pre-acceleration.
LT/SST/RT: *Too early leg reverse to recover.*	• Insufficient coordination of the partial movements. • Insufficient effort by the shot-putter to achieve an abutment for the acceleration of the shot through the ground contact. • Fear of stepping over the stop board.	✔ All exercises for practising a technically correct delivery movement (429–431). ✔ Puts for distance with the leg reverse being forbidden. ✔ The athlete should try to find the border zone between a valid put and stepping over.

LT/SST/RT:
No leg reverse to recover.
	• Altogether passive pre-acceleration and delivery movement with various previous errors:
	  » passive release of the shoulder-hip separation;
	  » LT/SST: Insufficient extension of the pressure leg and its causes (see above);
	  » primarily RT: insufficient pre-acceleration (during the turn).
		✔ Imitation of a leg reverse which is correct both technically and in terms of the temporal sequence and its translation into the put from pre-acceleration.
		✔ See corrections of insufficient extension of the pressure leg.
		✔ Puts at maximum intensity.

(continued)

(continued)

Error	Causes	Corrections
LT/SST/RT: Too flat angle of departure of the shot (usually in combination with too low height of departure).	• Insufficient bracing action of the front leg and its causes (see above). • Too early and/or excessive forward rotation of the upper body.	✔ See corrections of insufficient bracing action of the front leg. ✔ Imitations and puts from a standing position and pre-acceleration, while focusing on beginning the delivery motion with the active extension of the legs (while holding back the shoulders). ✔ Focusing on the optimal angle of departure as a topic of discussion.
LT/SST/RT: Too steep angle of departure.	• Insufficient forward rotation of the upper body during the delivery motion. • Excessive orientation at the theoretically optimal angle of departure of 42° while neglecting a maximal velocity of departure.	✔ Imitations and puts from a standing position and pre-acceleration while focusing on the forward acceleration of the right shoulder. ✔ Focusing on the optimal angle of departure as a topic of discussion.
LT/SST/RT: Stepping over the stop board.	• Insufficient bracing action of the front leg and its causes (see above). • Too frequent putting while stepping over the stop board in practice. • Lack of concentration or excessive motivation in competition, especially in the rotational technique.	✔ See corrections of insufficient bracing action of the front leg. ✔ The athlete should be required to perform valid puts even in practice and to concentrate until having left the circle according to the rules. ✔ RT: Controlled start of the turn.

3.4.10 TRAINING PLANNING

Many introductory statements on training planning made in connection with the javelin throw and the discus throw (see chapters II–3.2.10 and II–3.3.10) also apply to the shot put.

As for other throwing events, suggestions for training plans are provided here which focus on arm loads on some days and leg loads on other days not only in strength training (split principle, see chapter I–4.3), but also in general training. This is to ensure a sufficient regeneration of the loaded structures.

The relatively normal heavy weight of adult shot-putters may make certain running and jumping loads problematic since this could lead to too great stress on the joints and other passive structures. In particular, running loads to improve overall endurance, speed, and strength may often be properly replaced by alternative loads (e.g., on a bike or in water).

SUGGESTED TRAINING PLANS

Below, there are exemplary microcycles for the

- second mesocycle of a 17-year-old athlete in build-up training (table 12);
- first mesocycle of an athlete in high-performance training (table 13); and

- third mesocycle of an athlete in high-performance training (table 14).

It is assumed that 17-year-old shot-putters, discus, and hammer throwers have not yet finally specialised. The exemplary microcycles presented in connection with the discus and hammer throw (see chapters II–3.3.10 and II–3.5.10) for the

- first mesocycle of a 17-year-old athlete in build-up training; and
- third mesocycle of a 17-year-old athlete in build-up training

are therefore intended for the same athlete.

Even in high-performance training, the non-technique training for the discus throw, shot put, and hammer throw are similar. Therefore, as a supplement to the training plans presented here, the chapters on the discus and hammer throw include exemplary microcycles for the

- second mesocycle of an athlete in high-performance training; and the
- fourth mesocycle of an athlete in high-performance training.

Table 11: **Training emphasis in the various mesocycles** for shot-put practice in build-up and high-performance training.

1st mesocycle	basic aerobic and anaerobic endurance training; strength-endurance, hypertrophy-oriented maximal-, speed-, and reactive-strength training (also using a heavy throwing implement); flexibility training; general (sprinting, jumping, games, etc.) and specific coordination training for the shot put
2nd mesocycle	(speed-)endurance training; hypertrophy-, IC- and connective-tissue-oriented maximal-, speed-, and reactive-strength training (also using a heavy throwing implement); speed training (sprint and specific use of a light device); general (sprinting, jumping, games, etc.) and specific coordination training for the shot put
3rd mesocycle	hypertrophy-, IC- and connective-tissue-oriented maximal-, speed- and reactive-strength training; speed training (sprint and specific use of a light device); technique training
4th mesocycle	competitions and corresponding regeneration; IC- and connective-tissue-oriented maximal-, speed- and reactive-strength training; sprinting-speed training; technique training; maintenance stimuli

Table 12: Build-up training: sample microcycle for a 17-year-old thrower (discus, shot, and hammer) in the second mesocycle.

Monday	Tuesday	Wednesday	Thursday	Friday	Saturday	Sunday
Trunk stabilisation exercises and abdominal crunches (20 min) with a lot of dynamic variation	**LI runs** (6 x 80m; rest intervals: 20 sec) as a warm-up	**Foot strengthening** (10 min)	**Warm-up jogging** (15 min) including arm circling, sideways running, etc.	**Warm-up jogging** (6 min) including rolls, turns, cartwheels, etc.	**Warm-up jogging** (6 min) including picking up, carrying on the left or right side, and throwing an object forward	Rest
Practising the hammer-throw technique (50 min) including specific warm-up	**ABCs of sprinting/ jumping** (12–15 run-throughs) heel kicks, high-knee run, galloping sideways, skipping, etc.	**Warm-up specific to the shot put** (15 min) becoming accustomed to the shot, tossing, frontal puts	**Game** (30 min) e.g., handball, field hockey, or soccer	**Warm-up specific to the discus throw** (10 min) arm circling, rotational jumps, etc.	**ABCs of sprinting/ jumping/hurdling** (15–20 run-throughs)	
	Acceleration runs (3 reps)	**Practising the shot-put technique** (40 min) linear, scissor-step, and rotational technique alternately each week	**Contract-relax stretching** (15 min)	**Practising the discus-throw technique** (40 min) throws from a standing position and with (shortened) turn using a heavy, normal-weight, and light device; imitations	**Acceleration runs** (2 reps)	
Muscle build-up training (40 min) snatch, flies, reverse flies, inclined bench press, lat pull with underhand grip	**Practising the long-jump technique** (30 min) pop-up jump series, jumps with a short and medium run-up	**Medicine-ball throws** (25 min) goalkeeper throws, rotational throws, throws from a prone position, tossing, chest pass	**Gymnastics** (30 min) versatile rotational movements depending on the athlete's level of skill	**Muscle build-up training** (50 min) for arms and legs on apparatus	**Hurdle Zs** (2 sets of 4 Zs each of 2 run-throughs over 4 low hurdles each; rest intervals: 3 min; rest intervals between sets: 10 min) out at 3-stride rhythm with the weak side, back with the strong side	
Standing puts (10 reps) using a light medicine ball	**Technique sprints** (2 x 4 x 60m) sprints with additional tasks such as varied arm actions, alternating-pace sprints, pre-set stride lengths, etc.	**Muscle build-up training** (25 min) clean and full squat	**Muscle build-up training** (30 min) abdominal machine, shoulder-hip twists, lumborum, hip/back extensors using a big box	**Foot strengthening** (10 min) in the sand	**Contract-relax stretching** (15 min)	
		Acceleration runs (4 x 60m)	**ABCs of jumping** (6 run-throughs) as utilisation	**Discus throws** (10 reps) using a light shot	**Warm-down jogging** (10 diagonals on the lawn)	
					Squat-extension jumps (10 reps) always followed by one ankle jump each and short rest intervals	

Table 13: High-performance training: sample microcycle in the first mesocycle using double periodisation.

	Monday	Tuesday	Wednesday	Thursday	Friday	Saturday	Sunday
Morning	Trunk stabilisation exercises and abdominal crunches (20 min) Warm-up specific to the shot put (20 min) Practising the shot-put technique (50 min) linear, scissor-step, and rotational technique alternately each week	Warm-up jogging (15 min) with additional tasks ABCs of jumping (12–15 run-throughs) Skipping and bounding runs (2 × 4 × 30m) Pirouettes, rotational jumps, and gymnastics (30 min) versatile variations	Rope jumping (5 min) Medicine-ball work (45 min) frontal and standing puts, chest passes, goalkeeper throws, rotational throws; throws from a prone position, and tossing; alternatively: boxing	Continuous run (30 min) Contract-relax stretching (15 min) Walking over hurdles and skipping over hurdles (30 min) possibly also in combination with forward or backward rolls and/or rotations about the longitudinal axis between the hurdles	Warm-up jogging (6 min) Warm-up specific to the shot put (20 min) shot habituation and tossing Practising the shot-put technique (50 min) differential learning, standing put, and competition technique	Warm-up jogging (6 min) including arm circling, sideways and backward running, rotations, etc. ABCs of sprinting (12–15 run-throughs) Muscle build-up training (30 min) step-ups and deadlifts Acceleration runs (3 reps)	Rest
Afternoon	Foot strengthening (10 min) little jumps Game (30 min) e.g., soccer Contract-relax stretching (15 min) Muscle build-up training (50 min) inclined bench press, flies, reverse flies, and dips Chest passes (3 × 10 reactive reps)	Warm-up jogging (6 min) Acceleration runs (3 reps) 13 uphill runs (6 × 100m; rest intervals: 4–5 min) Muscle build-up training (60 min) hamstrings, quadriceps, adductors and abductors, clean, and lunges Ankle jumps (3 × 6 reps)	Strength-endurance training (45 min) bench press, bench pull, shoulder press, and lat pull Frontal puts (10 reps per side) light weight; as utilisation	Warm-up jogging (6 min) Acceleration runs (3 reps) Strength-endurance circle (60 min) including full squat, jumps onto a box, ABCs of sprinting/jumping, and many trunk-strengthening exercises Skipping with two-legged landing (3 × 20m) as utilisation	Warm-up jogging (6 min) Technique sprints (6 × 60 m) e.g., alternating-pace sprints Foot strengthening (15 min) in the sand Muscle build-up training (50 min) triceps, deltoideus, one-armed bench press with dumbbells, etc. Sandbag boxing	13 tempo runs (2 × 5 × 100m; rest intervals: 1.5–2 min; rest intervals between sets: 6–8 min) Contract-relax stretching (15 min) Warm-down jogging (10 diagonals on the lawn) Ankle jumps (3 × 6 reps) as utilisation	

Table 14: *High-performance training: sample microcycle in the third mesocycle using double periodisation.*

	Monday	Tuesday	Wednesday	Thursday	Friday	Saturday	Sunday
Morning	**Warm-up jogging** (6 min) **Maximal-eccentric strength training** (15 min) trunk and feet **Practising the shot-put technique** (60 min) including specific warm-up, puts using competition technique as well as with light and normal-weight device	**Foot strengthening** (10 min) **ABCs of sprinting** (8–10 run-throughs) **Acceleration runs** (2 reps) **Standing starts** (3 x 20m) **Skipping over hurdles** (10 min) **Rhythm sprints** (3 x 40m) at maximum intensity, over mini-hurdles	**Warm-up jogging** (6 min) with additional tasks **Practising the shot-put technique** (50 min) including specific warm-up (e.g., tossing following a depth jump), few puts at high intensity and using the competition device **Muscle build-up training** (45 min) bench press, bench pull, shoulder press, and lat pull	**Warm-up jogging** (6 min) **Acceleration runs** ABCs of jumping (8–10 run-throughs) **Tuck jumps** (5 x 5 hurdles) **Bounding runs** (2 x 3 x 20m) up stairs **Pirouettes, rotational jumps and gymnastics** (30 min)	**Warm-up jogging** (6 min) **Practising the shot-put technique** (60 min) including specific warm-up, puts using competition technique, as well as using a light and normal-weight device **LI tempo runs** (5 x 100m; rest intervals: 1.5–2 min)	**Warm-up jogging** (6 min) including arm circling, sideways and backward running, rotations, etc. **ABCs of sprinting** (8–10 run-throughs) **Acceleration runs** (2 reps) **Crouch starts** (20, 30, 20, and 10m) and **Pull-resisted sprints** (20, 30, 20, and 10m) alternately; high pulling load	Rest
Afternoon	**Warm-up jogging** (6 min) **ABCs of jumping** (8–10 run-throughs) **Depth jumps and jumps onto a box** (40 jumps altogether) individually or in combination **Strength training** (50 min) according to the pyramid principle: inclined bench press, flies, reverse flies, and dips **Reactive chest passes**	**Warm-up jogging** (6 min) **Contract-relax stretching** (15 min) **Strength training** (60 min) according to the pyramid principle: hamstrings, quadriceps, adductors, abductors, calf, and clean **Imitations** (10 min) competition technique	**Frontal puts** (10 reps per side) light shot; as utilisation		**Warm-up jogging** (6 min) **Muscle build-up training** (70 min) abdominal machine, shoulder-hip twists, lumborum, and hip/back extensors; snatch, and full squat **Shot puts** (6 x per side) light shot; as utilisation	**Warm-up jogging** (6 min) **High-intensity strength training** (40 min) including specific warm-up, reactive bench press, etc. **Medicine-ball work** (40 min) overhead throws, goalkeeper throws, rotational throws; throws from a prone position, and tossing **Sandbag boxing**	**High-intensity strength training** (30 min) clean and jerk into the lunge position, and split squat **Ankle jumps** (3 x 6 reps) as utilisation	

3.4.11 BIBLIOGRAPHY

Alexander, M. J., Lindner, K. J. & Whalen, M. T. (1996). Structural and biomechanical factors differentiating between male and female shot put athletes. *Journal of Human Movement Studies 30* (3), 103-146.

Bakarynov, Y., Goldmann, W., Ivanov, A., Kvitkov, A., Palokangas, J., Sherstyuk, V., Tschiene, P. & Winch, M. (1997). NSA round table 35: Shot put – rotational technique. *New Studies in Athletics 12* (4), 9-22.

Beckmann, H., Welminski, D. & Schöllhorn, W. (2008). Differentielles Lernen in der Leichtathletik – Techniktraining in der Leichtathletik. In D. Lühnenschloß & P. Wastl. (Hrsg.), *Quo vadis olympische Leichtathletik?: Probleme, Bilanzen, Perspektiven: Symposium der dvs-Kommission Leichtathletik vom 8.-9. September 2006 in Magdeburg* (Schriften der Deutschen Vereinigung für Sportwissenschaft, 181, S. 195-207). Hamburg: Czwalina.

Byun, K. O., Fujii, H., Murakami, M., Endo, T., Takesako, H., Gomi, K. & Tauchi, K. (2008). A biomechanical analysis of the men's shot put at the 2007 World Championships in Athletics. *New Studies in Athletics 23* (2), 53-62.

Čoh, M., Supej, M. & Štuhec, S. (2007). Biodynamic analysis of the rotational shot put technique. *Track Coach* (181), 5769-5775.

Dickwach, H. (mit Perlt, P., Wiese, G. & Rabich G.). (2006). Zur Angleittechnik im Kugelstoßen auf der Grundlage der biomechanischen Wettkampfanalysen und leistungsdiagnostischer Untersuchungen. In K. Wohlgefahrt & S. Michel, *Beiträge zur speziellen Trainingswissenschaft Leichtathletik: Symposium der dvs-Kommission Leichtathletik vom 10.-11.10.2002 in Bad Blankenburg* (Schriften der Deutschen Vereinigung für Sportwissschaft, 153, S. 145-158). Hamburg: Czwalina.

Dickwach, H., Hildebrand, F. & Perlt, B. (1997). Vergleich zweier Technikvarianten im Kogelstoßen – Analyse aus dem Angleiten und aus der Wechselschritttechnik von Astrid Kumbernuss. *Zeitschrift für angewandte Trainingswissenschaft 4* (1), 90-109.

Goldmann, W. (2003). Männer-Kugel: Die Top-Drei von München. *Leichtathletiktraining 14* (9+10), 34-39.

Goldmann, W. (2005). Die Kugel richtig beschleunigen: Die Angleit- und Drehstoßtechnik im Aufbautraining – grundsätzliche Überlegungen und eine Übungsauswahl zum Erlernen der Technik. *Leichtathletiktraining 16* (2+3), 12-21.

Goss-Sampson, M. A. & Chapman, M. (2003). Temporal and kinematic analysis of the rotational shot put technique. *Journal of Sport Sciences 21* (4), 237-238.

Gutiérrez-Davila, M., Rojas, J., Campos, J., Gámez, J. & Encarnación, A. (2009). Biomechanical analysis of the shot put at the 12th IAAF World Indoor Championships. *New Studies in Athletics 24* (3), 45-61.

Hommel, H. & Schrader, A. (2008). Wechselschritt: ‚ja oder nein?' *Leichtathletiktraining 19* (4), 20-26.

Hubbard, M., de Mestre, N. J. & Scott, J. (2001). Dependence of release variables in the shot put. *Journal of Biomechanics 34*, 449-456.

Kollark, D. (2007). Eine wirkliche Alternative zum Angleiten. *Leichtathletiktraining 18* (12), 21-25.

Kühl, L. & Hommel, H. (Red.) (mit Bartonietz, K., Becker, M., Becker, S., Böttcher, G., Deyle, M., Gaede, E., Hartmann, W., Losch, M., Rapp, E., Thomas, B., Wollbrück, R. & Zöllkau, H.). (1997). *Rahmentrainingsplan für das Aufbautraining Wurf* (Edition Leichtathletik, 5, 3. Aufl.). Aachen: Meyer & Meyer.

Linthorne, N. P. (2001). Optimum release angle in the shot put. *Journal of Sports Sciences 19* (5), 359-372.

Luhtanen, P., Blomqvist, M. & Vänttinen, T. (1997). A Comparison of two elite shot putters using the rotational shot put technique. *New Studies in Athletics 12* (4), 25-33.

Mizera, F. & Horvath, G. (2002). Influence of environmental factors on shot put and hammer throw range. *Journal of Biomechanics 35* (6), 785-796.

Oltmanns, K. (1999). Die Rückenstoßtechnik im Übergang zum Aufbautraining. *Leichtahtletiktraining 10* (10+11), 58-65.

Oltmanns, K. (2007). Bereit für das Angleiten. *Leichtathletiktraining 18* (5), 28-33.

Oesterreich, R., Bartonietz, K. & Goldmann, W. (1997) Drehstoßtechnik: Ein Modell für die langjährige Vorbereitung von jungen Sportlern. *Die Lehre der Leichtathletik 36* (38), 81-82, (39), 83-84 & (40), 86.

Paish, W. (2005). Coaches in a spin – an appraisal of shot putting. *Track Coach* (170), 5435-5436 & 5438.

Regelkommissionen des DLV, FLA, ÖLV und SLV (Hrsg.). (2010). *Internationale Wettkampfregeln*. Waldfischbach: Hornberger.

Salzer, P. (2007). Von der Wechselschritt- zur Drehstoßtechnik. *Leichtathletiktraining 18* (12), 4-11.

Schaa, W. (2010). Shot put. In Deutscher Leichtathletikverband (Hrsg.), *Biomechanical Analysis of selected events at the 12th IAAF World Championships in Athletics, Berlin 15-23 August 2009*. Zugriff am 20.04.2010 unter http://www.iaaf.org/ mm/Document/Development/research/05/64/50/20100415080101_ httppostedfile_8-BiomechanicsReportWCBerlin2009_Throws_19909.pdf.

Terzis, G., Karampatsos, G. & Georgiadis, G. (2007). Neuromuscular control and performance in shot-put athletes. *Journal of sports medicine and physical fitness 47* (3), 284-290.

Terzis, G., Stratakos, G., Manta, P. & Georgiadis, G. (2008). Throwing performance after resistance training and detraining. *Journal of Strength and Conditioning Research 22* (4), 1198-1204.

Tidow, G. (1990). Model technique analysis sheets for the throwing events. Part IV: The shot put. *New Studies in Athletics 5* (1), 44-60.

Tsirakos, D. K., Bartlett, R. M. & Kollias, I. A. (1995). A comparative study of the release and temporal characteristics of shot put. J*ournal of Human Movement Studies 28* (5), 227-242.

Wank, V. (2006). Biomechanik und leistungsrelevante Parameter der leichtathletischen Wurfdisziplinen. In K. Wohlgefahrt & S. Michel, *Beiträge zur speziellen Trainings-wissenschaft Leichtathletik: Symposium der dvs-Kommission Leichtathletik vom 10.-11.10.2002 in Bad Blankenburg* (Schriften der Deutschen Vereinigung für Sportwissschaft, 153, S. 132-144). Hamburg: Czwalina.

Young, M. (2007). Biomechanics of the glide shot put. *Track Coach* (180), 5743-5754.

Young, M & Li, L. (2005). Determination of Critical Parameters among Elite Female Shot Putters. *Sports Biomechanics 4* (2). 131-148.

Zatsiorsky, V. M. (1990). The biomechanics of shot putting technique. In G.-P. Brüggemann & J. K. Rühl (eds.). *Techniques in Athletics – The first International Conference – Cologne, 7-9 June 1990: Conference Proceedings: Volume 1: Main Conference: Keynote Symposia* (S. 118-125). Köln: Sport & Buch Strauß.

3.5 HAMMER THROW

3.5.1 WEARING A KILT AND THROWING A SLEDGEHAMMER

Like stone putting, which was mentioned in connection with the shot put, the hammer throw is a part of the Scottish Highland Games. Nowadays, athletes who wear kilts compete against each other in such exotic disciplines like the weight throw over a bar or caber tossing. As early as the 12th century, Scotsmen and Irishmen are said to have pitted their strength against each other by throwing a stone hammer with a wooden handle. Later, they used an iron sledgehammer. Even today, an iron weight attached to a rigid wooden handle is thrown at the Highland Games.

In modern athletics, this hammer was transformed into a steel sphere fixed to a steel wire with a handle. The total weight of this device was set at 16 pounds, which was the weight used in the shot put in England in 1887. The overall length of the hammer was also limited to four feet, which is the length still prescribed today. Until 1909, the hammer was also thrown from a nine-foot circle. Since then, athletes have had to accelerate the device from a smaller circle of seven feet in diameter.

As in many other disciplines, there were also resourceful hammer throwers who tried to perfect their throwing devices to the last detail. To increase the radius to the centre of mass of the hammer in spite of the prescribed total length, they experimented with longer wires and smaller hammer heads made of metals with a higher specific density (e.g., tungsten). Or these materials were placed in a hammer head with normal size in such a manner that its centre of gravity was shifted away from the centre of the sphere (away from the handle). Today, this is no longer allowed.

Whereas the hammer throw is performed at the Highland Games after a few overhead swings from a standing position, hammer throwers in athletics have extended their path of acceleration by up to four rotations about the longitudinal axis of their bodies. In the process, control of the throwing direction is a major challenge. In the past, this led to some tragic accidents. The result was that the hammer throw became an event peripheral to the competition programme. To improve the security in stadiums and to enable the hammer throw to become a central event again, the IAAF (now World Athletics) implemented a number of steps in recent years: in the shot put, discus throw and hammer throw, the landing sector was reduced from 40° to 34.92°, the protective cages were enlarged and are now closed on one side in the landing area.

Since 1900, the hammer throw has been an Olympic discipline for men. After initial American dominance, Soviet athletes in particular have shaped the development of the hammer throw since the World War

II. The world record by Russian Jury Sedych (86.74m) established in 1986 is still valid today. Women have been throwing the hammer at world championships since 1997 and at Olympic Games since 2000. Again, many Russian women have improved the world record. However, the last world record was established by Anita Wlodarczyk (82.98m, 2016) from Poland.

3.5.2 THE MOST IMPORTANT COMPETITION RULES

The following abridged and simplified International Competition Rules comprise the framework for the technique and strategy, as well as the organisation of hammer-throw competitions:

- Table 1 describes the hammers to be used. A hammer consists of three parts: hammer head, wire, and handle.

*Table 1: **Minimum weight (including the handle and wire), diameter of the head and length** (measured from the inner side of the handle) of the hammers for the different age groups in the German Athletics Federation (see Rule Commissions by the DLV, FLA, ÖLV and SLV, 2010, p. 116)*

Age groups		Weight, diameter, thickness
Female U14, 16, and 18, male U14	w50 and older, m80 and older	**3.000kg,** 8.5-10.0cm, 116.0-119.5cm
Female U20, women, male U16	w40-45, m70-75	**4.000kg,** 9.5-11.0cm, 116.0-119.5cm
Male U18	m60-65	**5.000kg,** 10.0-12.0cm, 116.0-120.0cm
Male U20	m50-55	**6.000kg,** 10.5-12.5cm, 117.5-121.5cm
Men	m40-45	**7.260kg,** 11.0-13.0cm, 117.5-121.5cm

- The hammer head must be made of solid iron or another metal that is not softer than brass, or it consists of a shell of brass filled with lead or another solid material. The centre of gravity of the head must not be more than 6mm from the centre of the hammer head. If a filling is used, this must be inserted in such a manner that it is immovable.
- The handle must be rigid and without hinging joints of any kind (see figure 1). The handle may have a curved or straight grip.
- The wire must be a single unbroken and straight length of steel wire not less than 3mm in diameter and must be such that it cannot stretch noticeably during the turn. The wire must be connected to the head by means of a swivel. The wire must be connected to the handle by a loop. No swivel is permitted here.
- Figure 1 describes the layout of the hammer-throw area. The hammer may by thrown out of a discus circle, provided the diameter of the circle is reduced to 213.5cm by placing a circular ring inside it (18.25cm wide).
- Figure 2 in chapter II-3.3.2 describes the protective cage used for the discus

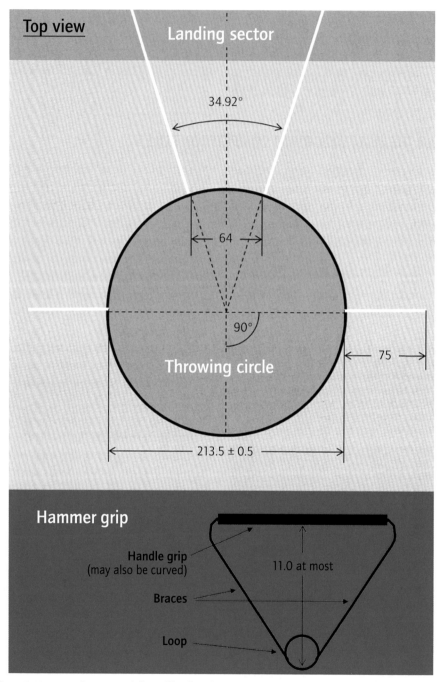

Figure 1: **Hammer-throw area** (all specifications in cm, modified on the basis of the Rule Commissions by the DLV, FLA, ÖLV and SLV, 2010, pp. 105 and 115); for the protective cage see figure 2 in chapter II–3.3.2.

and hammer throws. For the hammer throw, the last 2m of the protective cage must consist of movable swing gates which are 10m high. If a thrower turns counterclockwise, the left gate is swung into the sector, whereas the right gate is swung into the sector if the thrower turns clockwise.

- Wearing gloves is allowed. They must be smooth on the front and back, and the tips of the glove fingers, other than the thumb, must be open.
- An athlete, in his/her starting position prior to the preliminary swings or turns, is allowed to put the head of the hammer onto the ground inside or outside the throwing circle.

- Provided no other rule is violated, it is not considered a failure if
  - » the head of the hammer touches the ground inside or outside the circle during the swings or the turns (An athlete may stop and begin the throw again.);
  - » the hammer breaks during a throw or while in the air (The athlete must be awarded a new trial.); or
  - » a part of the hammer hits the protective cage after the delivery.

Otherwise, the general competition rules for the technical disciplines and throwing apply (see chapters II–2.1.1 and II–3.1.1).

3.5.3 SPORT-SCIENCE FINDINGS, PHASE STRUCTURE, AND TECHNIQUE

The hammer throw may be divided into the following four phases:

- preliminary movements and circular arm swings;
- turns;
- delivery movement; and
- recovery and flight of the hammer.

PHASE 1: PRELIMINARY MOVEMENTS AND CIRCULAR ARM SWINGS

GRIPPING THE HAMMER
The hammer is first gripped with the non-dominant hand (for right-handers with the left hand). The hammer handle rests on the respective second phalanges of the long fingers. Since enormous forces act on these phalanges during the throw, hammer throwers wear special gloves.

Subsequently, the long fingers of the dominant hand embrace the long fingers of the inner hand. It is the other way round with the thumbs: The thumb of the inner hand is placed over the one of the outer hand (see figure 2). Alternatively, the thumbs may also be placed parallel to each other. Some athletes begin the

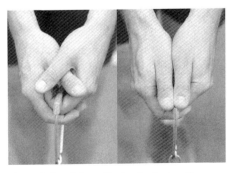

*Figure 2: **Possible methods of gripping the hammer.***

preliminary movements with one arm and only grip the handle with their dominant hand just before the start of the circular arm swings.

STARTING POSITION

At the beginning of the rotations, the thrower stands with his/her back turned in the throwing direction at the rear rim of the circle. The athlete's feet are approximately shoulder width or slightly wider apart. The imaginary, extended centre line of the throwing sector is located between the feet. The tips of the feet point slightly outward. The upper body is upright. The knees are only slightly bent. There is a distinction between the pivot leg and the rotational leg. During the turns, the *pivot leg* keeps continuous contact with the ground and alternates between ball and heel touchdown (see phase 2). For right-handers, who rotate counter-clockwise when viewed from above, the left leg is the pivot leg. The other leg, which is lifted in each turn and circulates around the pivot leg is referred to as the *rotational leg*. To ensure a correct positioning of the low and high points of the later hammer orbit, the shoulder on the side of the rotational leg is a little further withdrawn in throwing direction. In order to facilitate the initial pendulum movements, men in particular also start with the rotational leg being somewhat offset from the rear edge in the direction of the throw. Only with the beginning of the final circular arm swing is the rotational leg placed in the described starting position at the rear rim of the circle and thus enhances the shoulder-hip separation during the transition to the turns.

PRELIMINARY PENDULUM SWINGS OR EXPLOSIVE PICK-UP

There are several variations of transition to the circular arm swings. The preliminary pendulum swings are the variation in which the hammer is initially moved like a pendulum from between the legs or from the side of the pivot leg contrary to the direction of the throw and then to the side of the rotational leg behind the body to start from there the first circular arm swing by reversing the movement path of the hammer. The circular arm swings are performed without preliminary movements if they are started by means of the "explosive pick-up" of the hammer from the ground. Here, the thrower, whose trunk is slightly bent and somewhat twisted (shoulder-hip separation), puts the hammer down on the ground behind himself/herself on the side of the rotational leg inside or outside the ring. World champion Betty Heidler uses an intermediate technique by placing the hammer on the ground in front of herself and behind the circle, swinging it from there to the side of her rotational leg behind her body, and beginning the circular arm swings from this position.

CIRCULAR ARM SWINGS

The main purpose of circular arm swings is the generation of the horizontal rotation velocity of the hammer. Figure 3 shows that at the end of the circular arm swings or at the beginning of the first one-leg support, the hammer head has already reached slightly more than half of its departure velocity. The velocity is even greater when only three turns are used (about 65%). Contrary to all other athletics throwing events, in the hammer throw the main acceleration of the device does not occur in the delivery phase, but already during pre-acceleration.

The horizontal rotation speed about a vertical axis can be produced almost exclusively during the double support phases. Figure 4 illustrates the underlying principle.

To keep from falling (i.e., to keep the CG of the thrower-hammer system over the supportarea) the thrower moves his/her pelvis in the opposite direction of the hammer. This contrary rotation of the hips is called countering. The upper body remains more or less upright. To achieve a wide movement radius, the thrower

slightly rotates his/her shoulders together with the hammer.

To describe the motion of the thrower relative to the position of the hammer, the azimuth angle is used. This angle describes the direction in which the hammer points when projected on a horizontal plane. 0° corresponds to a direction parallel to the imaginary extended centre line of the sector contrary to the throwing direction. From there, the angle increases in the rotational direction of the hammer (see figure 5).

In order to primarily produce horizontal acceleration about a vertical axis, the path of the hammer should be kept as flat as possible. However, since the hammer must be swung over the athlete's head,

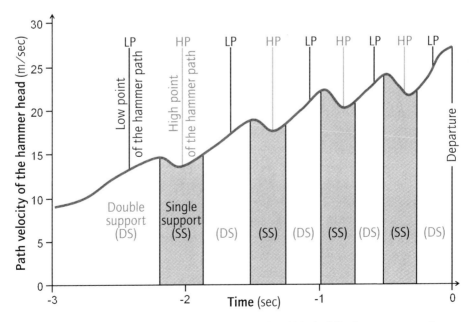

*Figure 3: **Velocity curve of the hammer head** in a throw, for which the following parameters of departure were measured: Velocity of departure: 27.16 m/sec, angle of departure: 38.26°, height of departure: 1.73m (modified on the basis of Murofushi et al., 2005).*

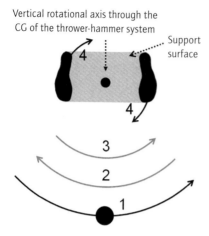

Figure 4: **Generating horizontal rotational velocity** *(according to Maheras, 2009): A right-hander rotates the hammer and his/her arms counter-clockwise (while rotating his/her pelvis contralaterally) (1). If he/she were in a swivel chair for example, the rest of his/her body (and the swivel chair) would turn clockwise (2). To compensate for this rotation (3), the athlete pushes with his/her left foot forward against the ground and with his/her right foot backward (4).*

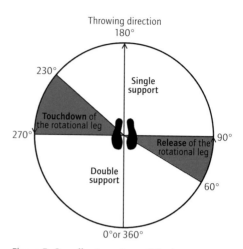

Figure 5: **Coordinate system of the hammer throw** *(modified on the basis of Ständner, 1999a): The figure shows the action of the legs during the turns in relation to the direction in which the hammer (wire) points during the turns when viewed from above (azimuth angle).*

there is inevitably a high-low movement of the hammer. During the final circular arm swing, the high point should be at an azimuth angle of 140–150° and approximately at head height (in the event of three turns also slightly higher). During the transition to the first turn, the low point of the hammer should be located at 320–330° and 30–40cm above the ground. When swinging the hammer over his/her head, the hammer thrower lifts his/her upper arms up to a vertical position and bends his/her elbow sharply. When the hammer is in the area of the high point, the thrower performs a short pressing action with his/her pivot leg (contrary to the direction illustrated in figure 4). The heel of the pivot leg is slightly raised, the weight is shifted somewhat to the rotational leg, the hip on the side of the rotational leg is moved slightly back in the direction of the throw, whereas the corresponding shoulder is moved back more distinctly. In the process, a slight shoulder-hip separation is developed. This enables the thrower to straighten his/her arms rapidly to the side. This action is referred to as grasping the hammer. Subsequently, the hammer is swung at a wide radius in front of the body to the other side with arms stretched forward and not so far downward (following the principle shown in figure 4). The heel of the pivot leg is lowered again, the weight is again evenly distributed on both feet, the pelvis is returned to the starting position, and the shoulder-hip separation is released.

An athlete must accelerate the hammer to optimal velocity. Most throwers do so by using two circular arm swings, but some use three. If the velocity is too slow, it is impossible to make up for this deficit during the turns. An excessively high velocity during the transition to the turns may result in a loss of control during the turns and prevent the continuous increase in velocity of the hammer head up to the departure. Therefore, the circular arm swings are often described as relaxed and controlled despite the already significant development of velocity.

During the transition to the turns, the thrower bends his/her knees and thus lowers his/her centre of gravity. When the hammer has reached its low point, the athlete's knees have taken an angle of approximately 120–130° with which they begin to turn. In order to achieve a wide movement radius as well as a good push-off into the turns, the weight is placed more on the rotational leg and is shifted in the direction of the pivot leg while lowering the centre of gravity of the body (pushing toward the left leg).

PHASE 2: TURNS

Most hammer throwers turn four times about the longitudinal axis of their body before they deliver the hammer. However, very good performances are also possible with only three turns (see figure 6) as the men's world record impressively proves. The five turns made by Wladyslaw Piskunov, the bronze medal winner at the 1999 World Championships (and two-time doping offender), were an absolute exception.

The rotations can be divided into

- double-support phases; and
- single-support phases; as well as
- phases of the downward movement of the hammer head from the high to the low point; and
- phases of the upward movement of the hammer head from the low to the high point.

Figure 3 shows that the velocity of the hammer head increases especially in the double-support phases and in the phases of downward movement. However, this may not lead one to the conclusion that

Figure 6: **Three turns** from the end of the circular arm swings to the start of the double-support phase upon delivery.

the thrower generates the kinetic energy for the rotation of the thrower-hammer system primarily in these phases. The velocity of the hammer head in the fixed external coordinate system is based on three different accelerations and velocities:

- translatory movement of the thrower through the circle;
- acceleration due to earth's gravity; and
- rotation of the thrower-hammer system.

THE MOVEMENT OF THE THROWER THROUGH THE CIRCLE

The thrower lifts the ball of his/her pivot-leg foot approximately when the hammer has reached its low point. Both feet are now turned in the direction of the rotation. The pivot leg is turned on the heel, whereas the rotational leg is turned on the ball of the foot. When the hammer has reached an azimuth angle of 60–90° and the foot of the pivot leg also points in the 90° direction, the rotational leg has completed its push-off and is lifted from the ground (see figure 5). During the single support, the foot of the pivot leg continues to turn on the heel. When it points approximately in the direction of the high point of the hammer, it is rolled over the outside of the foot onto the ball of the foot. Now it continues to be turned in the same direction on the ball of the foot. When the hammer has reached an azimuth angle of 220–270° and the direction of the foot of the pivot leg has already exceeded this directional line, the rotational leg is placed onto the ground (see table 2). The

rotational leg is usually placed onto the ground directly with the ball of the foot. However, some coaches and athletes try to place the heel down first and then roll the foot off onto the ball during the first turns. At the moment of touchdown, the tip of the foot of the rotational leg is approximately 10cm farther in the direction of the throw than the tip of the foot of the pivot leg (see figures 7 and 8) and points in a 270–300° direction. Then, both feet continue to be turned as quickly as possibly on their balls. In particular, the heel of the pivot-leg foot should be turned rapidly and flatly under the body. When the foot of the pivot leg points approximately contrary to the direction of the throw (≈0°), it is briefly placed down on the entire sole. Then, when the hammer reaches its low point, it switches again to turning on the heel.

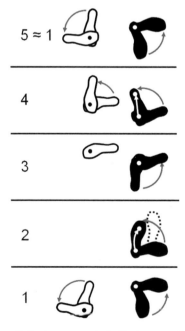

Figure 7: Foot movements in the hammer throw.

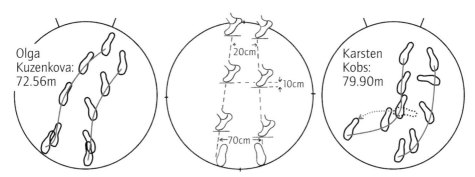

*Figure 8: **Optimal conical path of foot movement** (centre) **and two examples** from the 1999 World Championships (modified on the basis of Bartonietz, 1991 & 2000): In each case it is a thrower, whose left leg (which in each picture is on the right) is the pivot leg. As in the examples, a movement toward the side of the pivot leg can frequently be observed. Whether this makes sense when considering that the hammer must be thrown through the narrow opening of the cage must remain unanswered. Karsten Kobs demonstrates the variation mentioned in connection with the circular arm swings. He initially places his rotational leg backward (see dotted lines).*

*Table 2: **Position of the hammer head upon lift and touchdown of the rotational leg and upon release of the hammer** relative to the CG of the thrower-hammer system (azimuth angle) in the respectively best, analysable trials of the top 7 women (minus the athlete in fifth place) and of the top 6 men at the 1999 World Championships in Sevilla (according to Gutiérrez et al., 2002): A comparison with figure 5 shows that the values presented there apply especially to women. The position upon the touchdown of the foot moves toward 270°, while no clear trend can be seen in respect to the position upon lift of the foot. Since with world-record holder Sedych the azimuth angle was relatively constant below 230° upon touchdown, the moving azimuth angle, evident in many throwers, is sometimes described as an error. Some authors even suggest decreasing touchdown angles as an objective.*

Group (average competition distance analysed)	zeroth double-support phase	first single-support phase	first double-support phase	second single-support phase	second double-support phase	third single-support phase	third double-support phase	fourth single-support phase	fourth double-support phase (departure of the hammer)
					End of the …				
Women (67.78 ± 4.40m)	87 ± 24°	237 ± 8°	89 ± 20°	252 ± 15°	73 ± 27°	259 ± 16°	72 ± 13°	271 ± 13°	121 ± 12°
Men (79.06 ± 0.64m)	58 ± 20°	207 ± 30°	53 ± 14°	237 ± 17°	53 ± 14°	243 ± 14°	54 ± 18°	257 ± 24°	109 ± 15°

Thus, during one turn the thrower moves twice the distance between the pivot point below the heel and the pivot point below the ball of the foot of the pivot leg. If the thrower performs four turns and has a large shoe size and even more so if he/she uses five rotations, the 2.135m large hammer-throw circle may be too small. Therefore, some throwers perform the first turn exclusively on the ball of the foot without gaining much space like discus throwers.

The described movement of the thrower through the circle has an effect on the measurable velocity of the hammer head through space. If an object rotates about a point at a velocity of 20 m/sec and at a constant radius and this point simultaneously moves parallel to the rotation plane on a straight line through space at a velocity of 2 m/sec, then the absolute velocity of the object varies in space by 4 m/sec. The object moves at 18 m/sec at the moment when it moves contrary to the direction of movement of the rotational centre (20 − 2), and at 22 m/sec when it moves in the same direction (20 + 2). Actually, when viewed from above, the common centre of gravity of the thrower and the hammer moves on an almost straight line through the circle. However, the plane of the hammer rotation is not parallel to the path of movement of the CG, but tilted against it with a varying angle.

THE EFFECT OF GRAVITY

During rotation, gravity acts on the hammer. It accelerates the downward movement and decelerates the upward movement. This explains part of the increase in velocity during the downward movement and the loss of velocity during the upward movement in figure 3. Figures 9 and 10 show that the tensile force acting on the hammer wire is highest at each low point when the influence of gravity must be overcome. If one eliminates the translation of the thrower through the circle and the influence of gravity from the calculation of the velocity profile of the hammer head, there is an almost linear increase in path velocity for some throwers (i.e., a more or less constant acceleration of the hammer head). For others, a lesser form of the original pattern remains. Nevertheless, the claim made that rotational acceleration occurs almost exclusively in the double-support phases due to the absolute curve cannot be supported.

The higher ground reaction forces generated by both legs together in the double-support phases (see figure 10) cause the CG of the overall thrower-hammer system to be accelerated upward during the double-support phases. In the single-support phases, the ground reaction forces are below the weight force so that the system is accelerated downward. The amount of fluctuation of the common CG of the thrower and the hammer is approximately 10cm. The high and low points are reached just before the hammer reaches its high and low points.

HORIZONTAL ROTATION OF THE THROWER-HAMMER SYSTEM

The total rotation of the thrower-hammer system can be divided into two partial

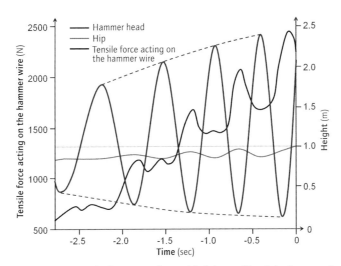

*Figure 9: **Tensile force acting on the hammer wire and height profile of the hammer head** in a 64m throw (according to Brice et al., 2008), complemented by a trajectory of the hip as expected to be ideal according to Otto (1990a & b): The trajectory of the thrower's CG is very similar (see Murofushi et al., 2007). According to Dapena (1986), the CG of eight world-class throwers reaches its high point (low point) only after the hammer has passed its low point (high point) and has moved through an additional azimuth angle of 60°.*

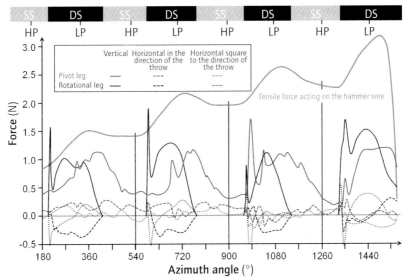

*Figure 10: **Ground reaction forces and tensile force acting on the hammer wire** (modified on the basis of Murofushi et al., 2007): The thrower had to perform the throw in such a manner that the rotational leg remained in one half of the circle (on a force plate) and the rotational leg was placed down in the other half of the circle (on another force plate). In spite of this, the thrower, whose best performance is 83.47m, achieved a remarkable velocity of departure of 27.2 m/sec (angle of departure: 38.3°, height of departure: 1.73m; body height: 1.865m; body weight: 97.9kg) (SS = single support, DS = double support, HP = high point, LP = low point)*

DISCOURSE I: SLINGING THROWS

The hammer and discus throws are also known as slinging throws. In these throws, the device is accelerated by the thrower on a looped path (see figure 11 below and figure 3 in chapter II–3.3.3). The thrower and the device rotate about a moving axis of rotation. The radius between the centre of mass of the device and the instantaneous axis of rotation is determined by the device (diameter of the discus and length of the hammer), the physique of the athlete (especially his/her arm length), and his/her posture. The radius (r) and the angular velocity (ω), with which the thrower and the device rotate, result in the path velocity of the device ($v_p = r \cdot \omega$). The thrower tries to maximise all three parameters through his/her technique and optimum acceleration impulses before releasing the device. Then the device continues its flight at its current (path) velocity tangentially to the previous circle-like path.

Since the radius is limited by the athlete's physique, it is particularly important to maximise angular velocity. This is especially difficult with the heavy and moving hammer, which, relative to its weight (and the weights and departure velocities of the other throwing devices used in athletics), is accelerated to a very high velocity of departure. The acceleration can only be generated by many little impulses (torque impulses) over a long acceleration path (i.e., a long acceleration time).

During the rotations, the sling thrower must counteract the centrifugal forces of the device (with the mass mdevice). This becomes more difficult as the rotational velocity increases, since the centrifugal forces ($F_{centrifugal} = m_{device} \cdot r \cdot \omega^2$) increase quadratically with rotational velocity. This can be measured through the tensile forces acting on the hammer wire (see figures 9 and 10). In a world-record throw using the men's hammer, these forces may exceed 3,000 N (approximately the weight force of a mass of 300kg).

rotations: rotation in a horizontal plane about a vertical axis and rotation in a vertical plane about a horizontal axis, which is approximately parallel to the centre line of the landing sector.

The generation of horizontal rotational velocity about a vertical axis during the turns is much more difficult than during the circular arm swings. During the single-support phases only one leg is on the ground, which can help to develop effective rotational forces. If an athlete does not want to tip over, the CG of the thrower-hammer system must also be located over the touchdown point. The vertical axis of rotation then passes through the point of touchdown, which makes the generation

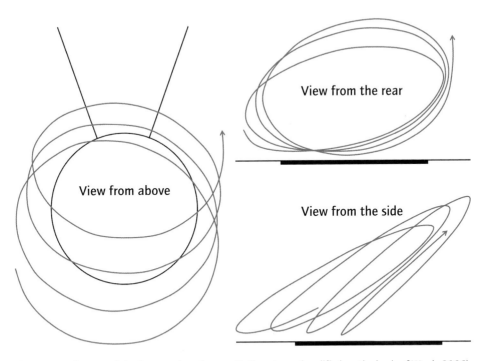

*Figure 11: **Trajectory of the hammer** in a throw with three turns (modified on the basis of Wank, 2006).*

of eccentric impulses that have an effect on rotation impossible. (However, it is argued below that an athlete should actually keep the vertical projection of his/her CG next to (not directly above) the point of touchdown and use the tipping over to support the rotation in an effective manner.)

During the double-support phases of the rotations, the generation of horizontal acceleration about a vertical axis is also difficult. Due to the direction from which the rotational leg is placed on the ground, it first develops a braking force (see figure 10). This force acts contrary to the direction desired for the rotational acceleration (see figure 4). Subsequently, the thrower must

first compensate for this loss before he/she is able to accelerate the rotation of the entire thrower-hammer system again. This becomes increasingly difficult in the ever shorter double-support phases. Therefore, a single-support phase as short as possible and a double-support phase as long as possible are frequently recommended. The athlete should therefore release the rotational leg as late as possible and, more importantly, place it onto the ground early. Due to the assumed importance of the double-support phases for the acceleration of the hammer, the touchdown of the rotational leg is equated to the grasping of the hammer. Short single-support phases may for example be achieved by moving the rotational leg very closely and flatly around the pivot leg. By keeping the mass of the rotational leg close to the axis of rotation, the rotational velocity is increased and the necessary path of the foot is shortened. However, this also leads to a very narrow width of support during the double-support phases, making it difficult to generate rotation about the vertical axis. The generated torque is minor due to the small radius of the touchdown points to the rotation axis. The superiority of the shortest possible single-support phases and the double-support phases as long as possible cannot be proved on the basis of biomechanical data.

A closer look reveals that the thrower uses the following strategies to increase or to maintain the angular momentum about the vertical axis during the rotations and to accelerate the hammer head. The thrower tries to slightly drag the hammer during the entire rotation if possible (positive angle of traction) or at least to keep the hammer perpendicular to his/her shoulder axis (angle of traction = 0°, see figure 12). If the angle of traction becomes negative, the hammer head is slowed down. One speaks of overtaking, running away, or running ahead of the hammer head.

Toward the end of the double-support phases, the thrower pushes himself/herself vigorously off with his/her rotational leg so that his/her lower body turns faster than his/her upper body and the hammer. This leads to a shoulder-hip separation, which is greatest just before or at the moment of the touchdown of the rotational leg. At the beginning of

the double-support phase, the shoulder-hip separation is released until a position of -5° to + 10° has been reached. The minimum is reached between the azimuth angle of 0° and the lift of the rotational leg. The reasons for this are (1) the braking forces described, and (2) the active release of the shoulder-hip separation by the thrower to accelerate the device. If the thrower places his/her rotational leg without or with too little shoulder-hip separation, it would be impossible for him/her to maintain a positive angle of traction and to accelerate the hammer.

For the modern hammer throwing technique, the maximum shoulder-hip separation is only 30–50°, and the hammer is dragged only slightly. A more noticeable staying behind of the hammer would result in a shortening of the radius of the hammer trajectory, which would be deemed negative. The hammer thrower

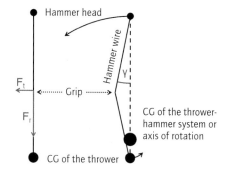

*Figure 12: **Angle of traction** (γ), **tangential** (Fₜ), **and radial force** (Fᵣ; modified on the basis of Hildebrand, 1994): The left part of the figure shows an angle of traction of 0°, while in the right part of the figure a positive angle of traction is presented. If the hammer handle were on the other side of the dotted line, the angle of traction would be negative.*

forms with his/her stretched out arms and his/her shoulder axis an isosceles triangle and keeps his/her eyes directed toward the head of the hammer. If the view and thereby the head is turned ahead in the direction of rotation, this easily results in

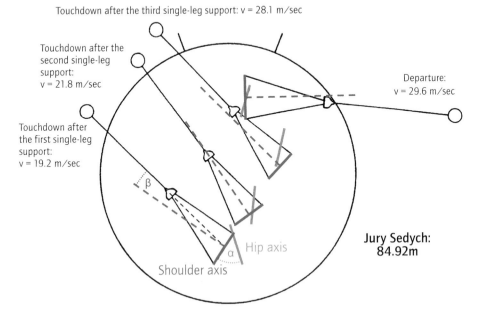

Figure 13: **Shoulder-hip separation** *(α)* **and trailing** *(β) of the hammer for a world-record holder (according to Bartonietz, 1990).*

Table 3: **Shoulder-hip separation and trailing of the hammer in a women's world record** *(according to Isele et al., 2010).*

Anita Wlodarczyk: 77.96m (world record)	zeroth double-support phase	first single-support phase	first double-support phase	second single-support phase	second double-support phase	third single-support phase	third double-support phase	fourth single-support phase	fourth double-support phase (departure of the hammer)
Shoulder-hip separation	27°	51°	5°	17°	49°	29°	17°	36°	12°
Trailing: Staying of the hammer wire behind the perpendicular to the shoulder axis	-19°*		14°		-8°*		7°		-11°*
		4°		30°		33°		20°	

*A negative value indicates that the hammer has overtaken the perpendicular to the shoulder axis (see figure 13).

'a pre-turn of the shoulders and thus in an insufficient development of the shoulder-hip separation. This eventually also leads to a negative angle of traction. Furthermore, a pre-turn of the view may adversely affect the planned maximum parallelism of the hip and shoulder axis to the ground.

During the turns, the thrower must keep a complex dynamic equilibrium (see figure 14). Strong forced breathing is necessary to withstand the high forces that must be mustered by the trunk muscles to prevent the thrower's shoulders from being pulled in the direction of the hammer head. To keep the movement radius large enough, the thrower tries to keep his/her shoulders close to the axis of rotation and to move his/her pelvis away from the rotational axis. The keeping away of the pelvis from the hammer head during the turns is also called countering (see circular arm swings). The opposite (i.e., bringing the hip forward

and moving the shoulders backward) results in a reduction of the radius and is not completely avoidable at the end of the turns when the plane of rotation becomes increasingly steeper. Ultimately, there is no statistical correlation between the radius and the velocity of departure, which indicates the greater importance of rotational velocity (see discourses 1 and 2).

VERTICAL ROTATION OF THE THROWER-HAMMER SYSTEM

To throw the hammer at an angle of departure of almost 45°, there must be a vertical velocity of departure which is almost as great as the horizontal velocity (see chapter II-2.1.2 and II-3.1.2). It is primarily this vertical velocity which is generated during the turns and which leads to an increase in overall velocity. This results in the plane of rotation, in which the hammer moves, becoming steeper by 4–5° per rotation when viewed from the

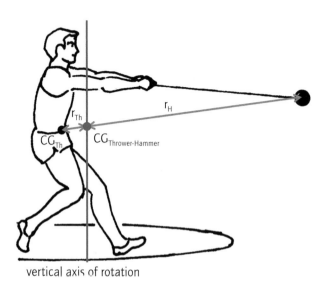

vertical axis of rotation

*Figure 14: **Dynamic equilibrium during the turns** (modified on the basis of Dapena, 1986): The centrifugal forces of the thrower's CG correspond to the centrifugal forces of the hammer (larger radius, smaller mass). The forces acting against the ground, which ensure the acceleration of the system, have a disturbing effect. The fact that the radius rH does not run along the hammer wire is a sign of the great strength requirements made on the back muscles.*

DISCOURSE II: THE INTERACTION OF HAMMER-HEAD VELOCITY, TANGENTIAL FORCE, RADIAL FORCE, ANGLE OF TRACTION, AND PATH RADIUS

As mentioned, the hammer thrower tries to maintain a positive angle of traction to accelerate the hammer. However, this is only possible if the rotational velocity of the thrower increases continuously, and he/she is thus able to maintain a tangential force in the direction shown in figure 12. Therefore, coaches identify a uniformly increased rhythm of the turns as a crucial criterion of technique. At a constant rotational velocity or decreasing acceleration (slower increase in velocity), the centrifugal forces cause the angle of traction to become smaller and eventually negative. The athlete is now pulling the hammer virtually in the wrong direction and thus slows it down.

However, the angle of traction is also affected by the thrower's radial force. If the radius of the hammer is reduced by increasing the tensile force acting in the direction of the wire in the event of an angle of traction of 0° and a constant rotational velocity, the hammer head is accelerated and the angle of traction becomes negative. The resulting running ahead of the hammer head means that the velocity just gained is lost again. Similarly, an increase in radius results in a reduction in hammer-head velocity, but also in a positive impact on the angle of traction. The tensile force acting in the direction of the hammer wire is briefly reduced before it rises even more to slow down the drift of the hammer head to the outside again. Therefore, hammer throwers keep the path radius relatively constant with relatively little inter- and intra-individual variation (see table 4). Figure 15 shows that the thrower fails to keep (or that it is not possible to keep) the angle of traction constantly positive. But it is crucial that the positive area under the curve is larger than the negative area and that this difference is as large as possible.

side (see figure 11). The high points get higher, while the low points get lower (see figure 9). Figure 16 explains how the thrower increases the velocity of rotation about the horizontal axis and shows that he/she can continue to do so during the single-support phase. Therefore, the single-support phases should not necessarily be as short as possible, as is often assumed, but they should be in optimal relationship to the double-support phases in terms of time.

The contralateral (phase-shifted by 180°) movement of the trunk on the other side of the axis of rotation leads to a rhythmic and increasing raising and lowering of the

*Table 4: **Phase duration, mean radius between the hammer head and the CG of the thrower-hammer systems, and the mean rotational momentum of the hammer** in each of the respectively best, analysable trials of the top 6 men (M: average competition distance analysed: 79.06 ± 0.64m) and the top 7 women (minus the athlete in fifth place; F: average competition distance analysed: 67.78 ± 4.40m) at the 1999 World Championships in Sevilla (according to Gutiérrez et al., 2002): The table includes mean values and standard deviations.*

Parameter	Gender	First single-support phase	First double-support phase	Second single-support phase	Second double-support phase	Third single-support phase	Third double-support phase	Fourth single-support phase	Fourth double-support phase	1	2	3	4
				Phases defined by the rotational leg							**360° turns of the hammer (regardless of phases)**		
Duration (sec)	F	0.31 ± 0.04	0.36 ± 0.03	0.27 ± 0.01	0.25 ± 0.02	0.26 ± 0.02	0.22 ± 0.02	0.27 ± 0.02	0.25 ± 0.03	0.67 ± 0.04	0.54 ± 0.03	0.48 ± 0.02	0.45 ± 0.01
	M	0.30 ± 0.02	0.35 ± 0.12	0.27 ± 0.02	0.23 ± 0.04	0.24 ± 0.03	0.22 ± 0.02	0.25 ± 0.03	0.24 ± 0.02	0.66 ± 0.13	0.50 ± 0.05	0.44 ± 0.01	0.42 ± 0.01
Mean radius of the hammer (m)	F	1.77 ± 0.04	1.70 ± 0.03	1.70 ± 0.02	1.67 ± 0.03	1.69 ± 0.04	1.65 ± 0.02	1.69 ± 0.04	1.90 ± 0.06	1.73 ± 0.02	1.68 ± 0.03	1.68 ± 0.03	1.69 ± 0.04
	M	1.73 ± 0.04	1.67 ± 0.03	1.67 ± 0.04	1.64 ± 0.02	1.64 ± 0.04	1.62 ± 0.02	1.64 ± 0.02	1.89 ± 0.11	1.70 ± 0.03	1.66 ± 0.03	1.63 ± 0.03	1.64 ± 0.06
Mean angular momentum of the hammer (kg/m/sec)	F	105 ± 8	119 ± 9	125 ± 8	139 ± 7	142 ± 8	150 ± 6	152 ± 9	191 ± 10	113 ± 8	133 ± 7	147 ± 7	160 ± 10
	M	190 ± 34	215 ± 32	238 ± 23	258 ± 19	267 ± 15	281 ± 9	285 ± 10	357 ± 27	204 ± 32	249 ± 21	274 ± 13	292 ± 15

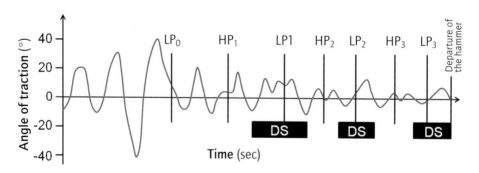

*Figure 15: **Variations of the angle of traction during three turns** (modified on the basis of Hildebrand, 1994; LP = low point, HP = high point, DS = double support).*

trunk (see figure 9). Thus, the knee of the pivot leg is bent the most in the area of the high point (genuflection) and extended the most, but never completely, around the low point. With variations from turn to turn, the minimum knee-joint angle is about 90°, while the maximum knee-joint angle is about 150°. While the hammer is over the CG of the thrower, the thrower is virtually hanging on to the hammer which he/she accelerates downward.

The reduction of the duration of a rotation (see tables 4 and 5) can be explained by the higher overall velocity of rotation or by a reduction of the radius when considering the vertical axis (see figure 17). A change of the angular momentum about the vertical axis is not necessary in the process.

The thrower's acceleration work results in a movement of the low and high points of the hammer trajectory from their position during the circular arm swings in the direction of an azimuth angle of 0° or 180° (see figure 18). To achieve an optimal direction of departure and maximum final acceleration, the thrower must be careful

The CG of the thrower and the hammer or the horizontal axis of rotation

*Figure 16: **Generation of vertical rotational velocity in the double and single-support phases** (modified on the basis of Maheras, 2009): By keeping the CG of the thrower-hammer system to the left of his/her pivot leg or closer to the rotational leg during the double-support phases and by possibly pushing himself/herself off more powerfully with his/her pivot leg during the double-support phases (1), the thrower generates a rotational momentum which actually should result in a tilt of his/her upper body to the left (2). However, this is compensated for by the counter-clockwise acceleration of the hammer and the arms (3), which actually should result in a clockwise rotation of the body (4).*

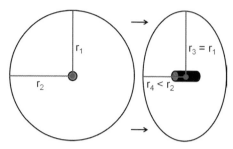

Figure 17: **Change of the radius in respect to the vertical axis of rotation** *(blue dot) with inclined total axis of rotation (black and gray dot or cylinder).*

The thrower tries to keep his/her trunk more or less upright despite the increasing gradient of the hammer trajectory. Therefore, he/she must increasingly raise his/her extended arms from the initial ideal arm-trunk angle of 90° when approaching the high point and must move them to his/her trunk when approaching the low point. Only so is the thrower able to maintain his/her balance and the radius of the hammer, which decreases only slightly, to overcome the high tensile forces against gravity at the low point, to avoid placing the hammer head on the ground in the delivery motion, and to effectively accelerate the hammer.

that the 0° or 180° direction is not reached too early and that subsequently the high and low points do not move too much beyond this direction.

Table 5: **Hammer-head velocity and its basic parameters as well as angle of departure** *in each of the respectively best, analysable trials of the finalists at the 2009 World Championships in Berlin (according to Isele et al., 2010): The table includes mean values and standard deviations. The end of each double support and the departure were chosen as the phase transitions between the turns. The performance level of the men was relatively poor, whereas the performance level of the women was very high (world record by Anita Wlodarczyk: 77.96m; German record by Betty Heidler: 77.12m).*

Group		Distance analysed (m)	Starting velocity (m/sec)	Acceleration path Duration Increase in velocity First turn	Second turn	(m) (sec) (m/sec) Third turn	Fourth turn	Total path Total duration Velocity of departure	Angle of departure (°)
Women	Four turns (n=6)	74.01 ± 2.94	16.2 ± 1.4	10.3 ± 0.4 0.59 ± 0.04 3.8 ± 1.0	10.5 ± 0.7 0.49 ± 0.04 2.2 ± 0.4	10.1 ± 0.7 0.43 ± 0.03 1.0 ± 0.2	12.3 ± 0.6 0.49 ± 0.03 3.9 ± 0.4	43.1 ± 1.2 1.99 ± 0.11 27.2 ± 0.6	40.7 ± 1.4
	Three turns (n=2)	73.07 ± 2.43	16.4 ± 1.6	9.8 ± 0.1 0.58 ± 0.03 4.0 ± 1.1	10.5 ± 1.1 0.48 ± 0.06 2.3 ± 0.8	13.2 ± 0.8 0.54 ± 0.03 4.6 ± 0.3		33.5 ± 0.2 1.60 ± 0.06 27.1 ± 0.6	38.1 ± 0.7
Men	Four turns (n=7)	77.27 ± 1.87	15.9 ± 0.8	10.5 ± 0.5 0.62 ± 0.03 3.6 ± 0.9	10.6 ± 0.6 0.51 ± 0.03 2.1 ± 0.5	10.5 ± 0.4 0.45 ± 0.02 1.4 ± 0.3	12.7 ± 0.5 0.51 ± 0.02 4.5 ± 0.3	44.2 ± 1.0 2.09 ± 0.07 27.5 ± 0.4	41.2 ± 1.8
	Three turns (n=1)	78.09	17.9	10.8 0.60 3.1	10.7 0.48 2.0	13.9 0.56 4.6		35.3 1.64 27.6	42.3

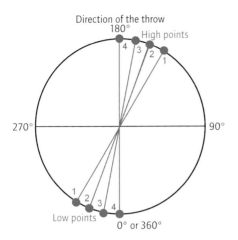

*Figure 18: **Movement of the azimuth angle of the low and high points** of the hammer trajectory (according to data provided by Murofushi et al., 2007, for example).*

PHASE 3: DELIVERY MOTION

The delivery motion begins with the last touchdown of the rotational leg. Although the frequently required early touchdown of the rotational leg cannot necessarily extend the previous double-support phases (since the lift also happens sooner then), it results in a longer double-support phase during the delivery motion. As mentioned, the thrower has a better opportunity to develop power and therefore to accelerate the hammer in a double-support phase.

Although the hammer has already reached 80–90% of its velocity of departure at the beginning of the delivery motion, the final acceleration of the device is nevertheless crucial. The delivery motion is an ongoing continuation of the previous movement. Once again it is necessary to overcome centrifugal forces and gravity and to actively accelerate the hammer. In the process, the thrower must resist the maximum tensile forces acting on the hammer wire (i.e., he/she must apply such forces; see figures 9 and 10).

Shortly after the highest of the high points, the athlete's legs are at an extremely bent position at the start of the double-support phase of the delivery. Contrary to the previous turns, the thrower actively straightens his/her body beyond the low point. The athlete's view and head are turned somewhat forward in the direction of rotation. Both feet initially continue their turn on the balls; as before, the touchdown of the pivot leg switches to the heel until the leg is placed down on the entire sole of the foot when it points in the direction of an azimuth angle of 90°. The hip of the rotational leg is pushed in the direction of

*Figure 19: **Delivery motion.***

rotation and upward until the hip axis is pointed in the direction of the throw. The weight is shifted to the side of the pivot leg, and the part of the body on the side of the pivot leg is fixed to establish a block. When the hip axis points in the direction of the throw, it cannot be turned further due to the foot position. In addition, the final slinging motion of the arms functions as a counter-rotation which results in the abrupt deceleration of the hip axis.

When approaching the delivery, the athlete's head and shoulders are taken somewhat back so that upon delivery the head is over the heel of the rotational leg. Releasing the hammer in a hollow-back position with the head and the shoulders moved further backward is avoided in the modern hammer throw technique since it may result in flubbing the throw.

The final acceleration is performed by the active raising of the stretched arms. Due to the upward acceleration of the hammer, the athlete is pushed against the ground. There is no upward jump. The angle of departure is usually a bit steeper than the line connecting the last high and low points. This is an indication of the acceleration work in the vertical direction during the delivery motion. The hammer leaves the athlete's hands approximately at shoulder height at an azimuth angle of approximately 90°. In the process, the correct timing of opening the hand is crucial to ensure that the hammer is thrown in the right direction and does not land in the net. In continuation of the delivery, the hands are subsequently swung far over the thrower's head.

PHASE 4: RECOVERY AND FLIGHT OF THE HAMMER

RECOVERY

The fact that hardly any kinetic energy is left in the athlete's body and that the athlete is not in danger of falling down are signs of technically successful turns and a good delivery. Therefore, a recovery motion is hardly necessary. Some athletes drag their rotational leg a short distance across the ground in the direction of the

Table 6: **Parameters of departure** at the moment of releasing the hammer in each of the best throws by the male finalists at the 2007 World Championships in Osaka (according to Umegaki et al., 2009): The table includes mean values and standard deviations.

Competition result		81.28 ± 1.29m
Point of departure:		
Position of the hammer head from the centre of the circle	to the side	1.83 ± 0.20m
	to the front	0.98 ± 0.22m
Height of departure:		
Position of the hammer head above the ground		1.49 ± 0.19m
Angle of departure:		
Angle between the trajectory of the hammer head and the horizontal (viewed from the side)		40.2 ± 2.0°
Direction of departure:		
Angle between the trajectory of the hammer head and a parallel to the centre line of the landing sector (viewed from the top; when turning counter-clockwise and releasing the hammer from the right side of the circle: positive angle = to the right, negative angle = to the left)*		-0.7 ± 4.9°

*The authors show that due to a change in the rules (closing the cage on the side opposite the landing sector) the direction of departure has changed to the desired straighter delivery in comparison to the 1991 World Championships (direction of departure: -8.7 ± 6.5°).

Table 7: **Requirement profile for the hammer throw:** *The suggested rough estimate of the value of selected factors determining performance is based on the importance for the overall performance and the percentage of time spent training. (IR: Information requirements, constr.: constraints; see chapter I–1.1).*

Factors determining hammer-throw performance	Estimate of value	Notes
Coordination	+ + + + +	optical IR: medium-low, acoustic IR: low, tactile IR: medium, kinaesthetic IR: medium-high, vestibular IR: high; precision constr.: high, time constr.: high, complexity constr.: high, situation constr.: low, physical stress constr.: low
Flexibility	+	primarily of the shoulder area
Strength		primarily trunk muscles (erector spinae, rotatory parts: oblique abdominal muscles, etc.), shoulder and shoulder girdle muscles (primarily backward muscles: trapezius, rhomboideus, deltoideus, latissimus dorsi, etc.), and extension loop (glutes, quadriceps, triceps surae)
Maximal strength	+ + + + +	the most important influencing factor in combination with speed strength
Speed strength	+ + + + +	the most important influencing factor in combination with maximal strength
Reactive strength	+ +	rather as a basis
Speed	+ + + +	acyclic speed
Endurance (general dynamic) Anaerobic endurance		
Strength endurance	+ +	as a basis to be able to perform 6 trials plus practice trials at a high level of performance
Speed endurance	+	as a basis at most
Aerobic endurance	+	as a basis at most
Psychological and cognitive abilities	+ + + + +	concentration ability (on the point); performance-oriented thinking and behaviour (see chapter I–3.1.1)
Anthropometric and primarily genetically determined characteristics	+ + + +	high percentage of fast muscle fibres; rather above-average body height and arm spread (moreover, some experts favour short legs and a long trunk)

turn or perform a slight reverse of their legs resulting in a switch of leg position.

VELOCITY, ANGLE, HEIGHT, POINT, AND DIRECTION OF DEPARTURE

Table 5 provides information on the velocities of departure achieved by world-class athletes. For the men's world record, a velocity of departure of about 30 m/sec is required. Table 6 provides information on the other parameters of departure.

Due to the height of departure, which is only slightly higher than the landing height in relation to the distance of the flight, the theoretically optimal angle of departure in the hammer throw is only slightly below 45° (i.e., approximately 44°). With an identical velocity of departure, an angle of departure which is 5° smaller results in a reduction of the flight distance by about 1m. The average angles of departure achieved in the hammer throw are also somewhat below the theoretically optimal angles. A larger angle of departure requires a larger angle for the plane of rotation of the hammer to the horizontal during the turns and during the delivery. This results in more elevated high points and lower low points, which may result in the hammer head touching the ground at the low point (see figures 9, 11, and 19). To avoid this, smaller athletes in particular must choose a somewhat flatter hammer orbit and therefore a smaller angle of departure. Moreover, a steeper hammer orbit also results in an increase in the peak force which the thrower must apply against gravity at the low point of the hammer orbit. This means that, in addition to body height, the athlete's strength may limit the gradient of the hammer orbit.

The chapter on the shot put (II–3.4.3) also includes some information on the aerodynamics of the hammer.

3.5.4 SUMMARY OF THE MOST IMPORTANT TECHNICAL CHARACTERISTICS = TECHNIQUE-ANALYSIS SHEET

(Description for right-handers)

PRELIMINARY MOVEMENTS AND CIRCULAR ARM SWINGS

GRIPPING THE HAMMER

- The hammer handle rests on the respective second phalanges of the long fingers of the left hand; the right hand embraces the left one; the left thumb is placed over the right one, or the thumbs are parallel to each other.

STARTING POSITION

- Both feet are placed at the rear rim of the circle; possibly, the rotational leg (right foot) is initially placed somewhat backward in the direction of the throw before it takes its starting position at the rear rim of the circle at the beginning of the last circular arm swing.
- The feet are shoulder width or slightly wider apart; the toes point approximately opposite to the direction of the throw, but slightly away from one another; the knees are slightly bent; the trunk is upright; the back is turned approximately

in the direction of the throw; however, the right shoulder is taken somewhat farther back to achieve the correct position of the low and high points.

PENDULUM SWINGS OR EXPLOSIVE PICKING UP OF THE HAMMER

- The hammer is initially moved like a pendulum between the legs or on the side of the pivot leg (the left side from the thrower's point of view), before it is swung backward to the side of the rotational leg at the beginning of the circular arm swings; or
- the thrower places the hammer onto the ground on the right side behind his/her body and picks it up from there explosively to start the circular arm swings; or
- as a mixed form: the thrower places the hammer in front of his/her body on the ground, picks it up from there explosively, and swing it backward to the side of his/her rotational leg.

CIRCULAR ARM SWINGS (2 OR 3)

- Reversal of movement or lifting of the hammer to swing it to the front of the body and upward over the head on the side of the pivot leg.
- Lifting the upper arms to the vertical and bending downward of the forearms to the horizontal to move the hammer flatly and with a low high point over the head.
- In the area of the high point, the right shoulder is taken back (development of shoulder-hip separation) as early as possible to be able to straighten the arms (first the left arm) in front of the chest (grasping the hammer).
- The hammer is first swung downward with extended arms and on a wide path of movement in front of the feet (release of the shoulder-hip separation), before it is swung upward again to the other side; high low point.
- The pelvis moves in the direction which is respectively opposite the direction of the hammer (countering).
- The high point is located on the left side behind the thrower (from his/her point of view), whereas the position of the low point is to the right and in front of the thrower.
- Controlled optimal pre-acceleration of the hammer (neither too fast nor too slow).
- During the transition to the first rotation: The feet are turned in the direction of rotation (on the right side on the ball of the foot, on the left side on the heel or also on the ball of the foot in the case of four turns), the CG is lowered (bending of the knees), and the weight is shifted from the right to the left leg.

TURNS (3 OR 4)

- When the hammer points toward 40–90° during its upward movement and the foot of the rotational leg, which rotates on the heel, points approximately in the direction of 90°, the rotational leg has completed its push-off and is lifted from the ground.
- During the single-support phase, the rotational leg is moved closely and flatly around the rotational leg; the legs rotate faster than the upper body and the hammer; a maximum shoulder-hip separation of 30–50° is developed before the touchdown of the rotational leg.
- When the foot of the rotational leg points in a 120–180° direction in the area of the high point of the hammer path, its point of touchdown switches over the outer edge to the ball; the hammer reaches its high point at 150–180°.
- The rotational leg is placed on the ground with the ball of the foot at a hammer azimuth angle of 220–270° and the feet point approximately in the direction of 270° (during the first turns, the foot may also be rolled off rapidly over its heel); it is placed approximately 10 cm further in the direction of the throw than the pivot leg; the distance between the feet becomes closer from turn to turn.
- Subsequently, both feet continue their fast turn on the balls; the pivot leg is turned a little faster: its foot is placed on the ground with the entire sole when it points approximately in the 0° direction, and the touchdown or pivot point is shifted to the heel approximately when the hammer reaches its low point.
- The shoulder-hip separation has nearly been released when the hammer has reached its low point at 330–360°.
- At the beginning of the turns, the upper body is upright or leaned slightly forward; with increasing centrifugal forces, the shoulders are taken back until the thrower has reached a slight backward lean; the body moves up and down contralaterally to the hammer.
- The arms remain straight, and the thrower's view is directed to the hammer.
- The rhythm of the turns gradually increases.

DELIVERY MOTION

- After the turns, the movement is continued without interruption.
- The rotational leg is placed on the ground early with considerably bent legs.
- Subsequently, the legs are extended beyond the low point of the hammer up to its departure.
- The hammer is accelerated further, while the shoulder-hip separation is released.
- Both feet are turned further up to the 90° position, while the hip axis is turned accordingly until it points in the direction of the throw.
- The pivot leg is placed on the ground with the entire sole of the foot; the side of the pivot leg is fixed and a block is established.
- The head and the shoulders are slightly taken back.
- The hammer is released using the extended arms.
- The departure of the hammer occurs at shoulder level when the wire points toward 90°.

RECOVERY

- The thrower remains standing; some throwers drag their rotational leg a short distance toward the pivot leg or reverse their legs, resulting in a switch of leg position.
- The CG is kept behind the support point in order to avoid stepping over.
- The thrower leaves the circle through its rear half.

3.5.5 PHOTO SEQUENCE

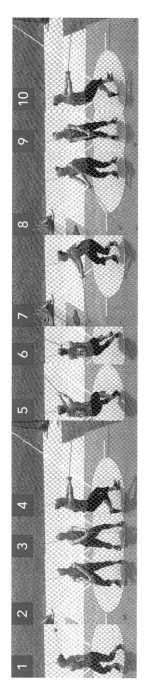
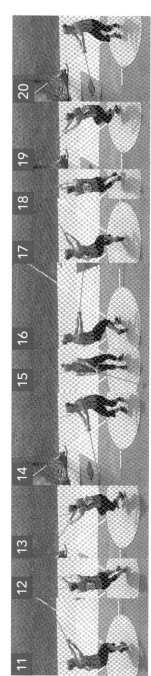
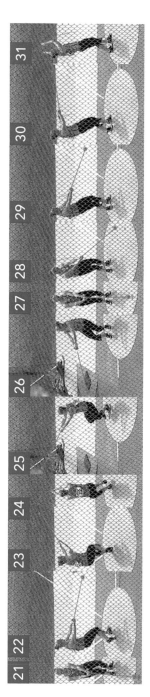

Data about the photo sequence

Athlete:	Betty Heidler (born: 14 October 1983, Germany)
Height/weight:	1.75m/81kg
Performance:	70.24m (22 May 2004, Halle)
Best performance:	79.42m (21 May 2011, Halle, world record)
Greatest success:	World champion in 2007, world vice-champion in 2009, Olympic bronze medal in 2012, European champion in 2010

COMMENTARY

The photo sequence shows the future world champion and world-record holder at a young age. A little more than three months after this throw, Heidler was fourth at the Olympic Games in Athens with a throw of 72.73m (her best performance until then).

In the starting position, Heidler stands at the centre of the rear rim of the circle. The tip of the foot of her pivot leg touches the rim of the circle. Her right foot is somewhat set back in the direction of the throw (picture 1). She initially places the head of the hammer onto the ground in front of her. Then she picks it up explosively and swings it to the right side of her body. From there, she begins the first of three circular arm swings which gradually increase in velocity. She takes her right shoulder far back so that the shoulder axis points approximately in the direction of the throw (picture 1). The pelvis and the slightly bent legs remain stable in the process. With the women's lighter hammer, there is often significantly less countering.

The photo sequence begins with the transition to the first turn. It is clearly visible how Heidler accelerates the hammer out of the range of the high point in the direction of the low point by releasing the shoulder-hip separation (pictures 1 and 2). In the process, the low point is at an optimal position in front of her right foot. During this slinging movement, the CG is lowered and shifted slightly over the right foot for a short time. Approximately when the hammer has reached its low point, the push-off with the right leg, the shift of the body weight to the left leg, and the outward turn of the left foot on the heel begin (pictures 2–4). Heidler looks at the hammer head and continues to do so up to the delivery. By doing so, she avoids a pre-turning of her head and shoulders in an exemplary manner. The positions of the thrower and the hammer are also very good when the rotational leg is released in picture 4. As recommended, the hammer is located at an azimuth angle of 90°, the arms and the hammer wire are horizontal, and the upper body is upright. By using a somewhat more active push-off with the right leg, the CG would have been moved even a little further over the left leg. At this moment, Heidler's starting velocity (see table 8) is already quite high.

During the single-support phases (pictures 5–6, 11–13, 17–19, and 23–25), Heidler does not succeed in overtaking the hammer fast enough. Her right leg is placed onto the ground relatively late and each time a little too far in the direction of the rear rim of the circle. Accordingly, she is only able to turn her left heel under her body and accelerate the hammer rather late during the double-support phases

Table 8: **Biomechanical parameters** for the throw in the photo sequence (according to Deyle, 2005, p. 39): Starting velocity = velocity of the hammer head upon the lift of the right foot moving into the first turn.

Distance (m)	Angle of departure (°)	Velocities of the hammer head (m/sec)		Path of the hammer head (m)	Turns
		Departure	Start		
70.24	37.9	27.0	17.9	40.9	4

(pictures 7–10, 14–16, and 20–22). In the language of hammer throwers this means: "She grasps the hammer too late". After the beginning of the turns, this error can hardly be corrected and remains. This could be remedied by an earlier and more rapid outward turn of the left foot on the heel and a more active push-off with the right leg, which sets the athlete's body in rotation rather than the hammer.

In this throw, the error described also affects the delivery movement (pictures 26–30) in which she also accelerates the hammer too late. Moreover, moving her head onto her chest prevents a full extension upon delivery and an active arm stroke. This results in a slightly too shallow angle of departure.

3.5.6 DIDACTICS: SUPERORDINATE LONG-TERM OBJECTIVES AND GENERAL METHODOLOGY

Rotations about the longitudinal axis of the body which are as versatile as possible are used to prepare the hammer throw (as well as the discus throw and the rotational technique of shot putting) as early as in children's athletics. Initially, hammer-throw-like throws with auxiliary devices are performed at the beginning of basic training. When throwing from a standing position, the device should be located at shoulder height at an azimuth angle of approximately 270°. For this purpose, rigid devices like a broom(stick), a baseball bat, a medicine ball, or a sling ball placed on an elevation may be used. Throws with acceleration of the device from the bottom and the outside next to the knee

of the rotational leg convey an incorrect impression of the technique of delivery. However, standing throws and throws from circular arm swings should represent only relatively short intermediate learning steps before the turns are learned. The number of turns should be increased relatively rapidly from initially only one, then two turns, to three turns, even if these turns have noticeable technical defects. A rapid progression to three turns with subsequent improvement in the technique according to the whole-part-whole method has proven more effective than a slower progression. Only in this way can the athlete develop a feel for centrifugal forces, rotation, movement rhythm, actual velocities, and working angles, etc. Learning the technically correct action of the lower drives during the turns is crucial to an effective hammer-throw technique. In the process, lighter auxiliary devices such as (extended) sling balls are initially used.

A possible switch to four rotations may take place soon enough in build-up training. Here, more use is made of the competition device as well as heavier auxiliary devices such as round weights (kettlebells) or heavier hammers.

SAFETY PRECAUTIONS

In addition to the safety precautions mentioned in connection with the common features of the throwing events (see chapter II–3.1.3), the following requirements must be observed in the hammer throw:

- Hammer throws should be practised only in the appropriate area (i.e., from a throwing cage). The athletes and the coach waiting outside the cage must be far enough away from the net.
- Since there are very few stadiums with several hammer-throw cages next to each other, and since only few preparatory exercises (without a hammer, without turns, and/or without delivery) can be performed simultaneously without a cage, the hammer throw is hardly possible with larger groups. If auxiliary devices are thrown outside the cage, other athletes, coaches, and bystanders may only stand directly opposite the desired direction of the throw.
- The moving parts of the hammer should be checked before use. Worn wires and kinks in the wire are potential breaking points. Straightening a kink results in an increased risk of breakage. Therefore, a kinked wire should be replaced.
- A hammer-throw facility requires a landing sector that is not used for football, for example. Performance-oriented hammer practice would destroy any (grass) football field.

3.5.7 TRAINING CONTENTS: FORMS OF GAMES AND EXERCISES

Sprints, exercises from the ABCs of jumping, and multiple jumps (see chapter I–5.4.6, II–3.1.8, and II–2.2.7) are also used in the speed-strength and reactive-strength training of hammer throwers. Versatile pirouettes and rotational jumps (3), rolls (6 and 7, in particular about the longitudinal axis of the body), their combinations as well as the rotations of the discus throw and the rotational technique of shot putting, which are not specific to the hammer throw, (see chapters II–3.3.7 and II–3.4.7) are used for the varied training of balance during rotational movements.

441 ▮▮▯▯ Relay run with rotations

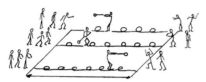

Possible objectives: Versatile training of rotations about the longitudinal axis (balance during rotations about the longitudinal axis).

Execution/variations: Age-appropriate device (e.g., medicine ball held high in front of the body or extended sling ball); short distance (e.g., 10m); possibly prescription of the number of rotations or prescription of the desired rotation by using an additional task (the ball must remain above the hip or must be swung over four obstacles, etc.)

Typical load standards: As long as it's fun.

442 ▮▮▮▮ Target throws

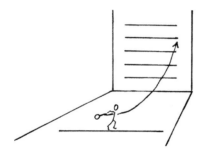

Possible objectives: Hammer-throw technique (versatile slinging throws with both hands).

Execution/variations: In children's training, there should be only few technique prescriptions: two-handed throw from a starting position with one's back turned in the direction of the throw with (something like) circular arm swings or 1–2 turns; somewhat later also with two or three sling balls held simultaneously; also with rotation in the opposite direction.

Typical load standards: As long as it's fun.

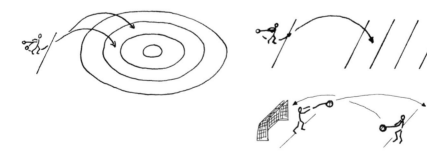

The putting and walking exercise (423) described in connection with the shot put may also be performed as throwing and walking with one turn at the most.

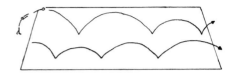

443 Windmill

Possible objectives: Versatile training of rotations about the longitudinal axis with pulling resistance (balance during rotations about the longitudinal axis).

Execution/variations: Rapid rotation with shuffles or skips about a vertical axis between two partners; in both directions alternately; with forward movement and reciprocal slinging of the partner.

Typical load standards: As long as it's fun.

444 Circling of the pelvis

Possible objectives: Dynamic flexibility training; mobilisation; specific warm-up; technique of countering.

Execution/variations: While standing or on the rings.

Typical load standards: 1–5 reps per variation of 6–10 circular movements per direction.

445 Familiarisation with the hammer

Possible objectives: Correct grip; feel for the device; specific warm-up.

Execution/variations: Pendulum swings of the hammer between the legs or at the side of the body; when using a short device also figure eight swings in front of the body (figure eight turns; e.g.,

with a barbell plate and arms stretched forward, while standing and sitting also as strength training; when performed in a standing position, the ground may be wobbly); one-armed swinging of a sling ball or hammer around the body, while switching the device from one hand to the other in front of and behind the body; rotations while performing stutter steps on the spot and with one sling ball in each hand, while holding a light hammer or round weight in both hands; rotations about the longitudinal axis with a sling ball or hammer in front of the body and fast shuffles (caution: may be counterproductive for beginners in terms of a correct turn on the heel and ball of the foot); always in both directions.

Typical load standards: Several times according to feel.

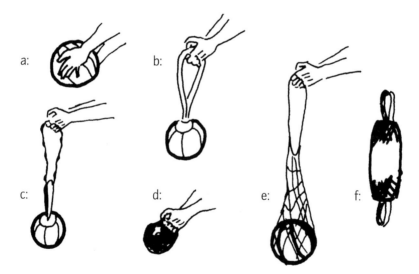

All exercises presented below may be performed by using the auxiliary devices shown (according to Jonath, Krempel, Haag & Müller, 1995) as well as by using various hammers: a: medicine ball, b: sling ball, c: extended sling ball, d: round weight (kettlebell), e: (medicine) ball in a ball net, f: sandbag. In addition, rigid devices such as a broom(stick), a baseball bat, or a hammer with a wooden handle can be used, particularly during imitations and if the throws are performed without introducing circular arm swings. Light hammers can be used for specific speed training, while heavy hammers can be used for specific speed-strength training beginning with build-up training (see table 9). Heavy hammers with normal wire length particularly increase the radial forces, while short, even heavier hammers require especially greater tangential forces. If hammers are used which are even heavier than the hammers mentioned, the strength requirements and the necessary adjustments of the throwing technique, particularly in terms of rotational velocity, become so great that overstressing and negative learning effects in respect to technique may be expected.

Table 9: **System of training devices with hammer weight and hammer length** (modified on the basis of Ständner, 1999b).

	Ultralight device	Light device	Competition device	Heavy device	Very heavy device	Short super-heavy device
Female U14	1.5–2.0kg 0.8–1.2m	2.5kg 1.1m	3.0kg 1.195m	–	–	–
Female U16	2.0kg 1.1–1.2m	2.5kg 1.1–1.2m	3.0kg 1.195m	–	–	4.0kg 0.7–0.8m
Female U18	2.0kg 1.2m	2.5kg 1.2m	3.0kg 1.195m	3.5kg 1.2m	4.0kg 1.2m	5.0–5.5kg 0.7–0.8m
Female U20	2.5kg 1.2m	3.5kg 1.2m	4.0kg 1.195m	4.5kg 1.2m	5.0kg 1.1m	6.25kg 0.7–0.8m
Women	3.0kg 1.2m	3.5kg 1.2m	4.0kg 1.195m	4.5kg 1.2m	5.0kg 1.2m	7.0–8.0kg 0.7–0.8m
Male U14	1.5–2.0kg 0.8–1.2m	2.5kg 1.1m	3.0kg 1.195m	–	–	–
Male U16	2.5kg 1.1–1.2m	3.5kg 1.1–1.2m	4.0kg 1.195m	–	–	5.0kg 0.7–0.8m
Male U18	3.0kg 1.2m	4.5kg 1.2m	5.0kg 1.215m	5.5kg 1.2m	6.25kg 1.2m	6.0–8.0kg 0.7–0.8m
Male U20	4.0kg 1.2m	5.5kg 1.2m	6.25kg* 1.215m	6.75kg 1.2m	7.26kg 1.2m	8.0–10.0kg 0.7–0.8m
Men	5.0kg 1.2 m	6.75kg 1.2m	7.26kg 1.215m	8.0kg 1.215m	9.0kg 1.1m	11–12.5kg 0.7–0.8m

*Today, male U18 athletes throw the 6kg hammer.

446 | Standing throws

Possible objectives: Technique of the delivery motion; specific strength training.

Execution/variations: With a medicine ball or a rigid device (baseball bat, broom, or a hammer with a wooden handle; the dominant hand initially holds the outer end back and upward and then slides to the other hand at the beginning of the rotation) or with a short device (sling ball, round weight, etc.) placed at shoulder level or slightly above (e.g., on a large gymnastic box) or held by the coach or a partner; in the starting position, the straight arms and feet point in a 270° direction and are located approximately at shoulder height; subsequently, the thrower performs a delivery which follows the target technique as much as possible (although throws with an acceleration of the weight from the outside next to the knee of the rotational leg seem to have a strengthening effect, they teach the thrower to use an incorrect technique of delivery); versatile combinations: rolls (6-7), rotational jumps (3), and standing throws with medicine balls thrown by a partner; bilateral practice.

Typical load standards: 1–5 x 5–10 reps depending on the training objective.

447 | Circular arm swings

Possible objectives: Technique of circular arm swings; specific warm-up, and strengthening.

Execution/variations: The movement should initially be imitated without the device; then with a light device (medicine ball, barbell plate or (extended) sling ball); also as rolling on the floor in a sitting position with extended or spread legs: using circular arm swings, the hammer is rolled in a wide circle on the floor; one-armed circular swings

with hammer, both with the left and with the right hand; with emphasis on the counter-movement of the hips and a wide path of the hammer head; use of a marker for the correct position of the low point(s); the low point(s) should be kept high by using an obstacle (small box); variation of speed; with different height of the CG or stretching and bending of the legs; the hammer is circled in both directions; sometimes slow, sometimes fast(-er than in the actual throw); also with eyes shut; also with simultaneous (forward, backward or sideways) walking, while standing on only one leg and/or on wobbly ground (e.g., on one or two balance board(s)); for advanced athletes also with a heavier hammer or even two hammers.

Typical load standards: 1–5 x 5–15 circular swings depending on the variation.

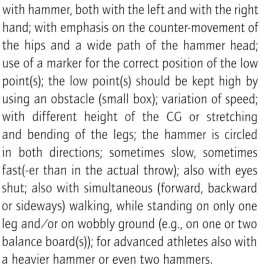

448 Circular arm swings + delivery

Possible objectives: First deliveries from pre-acceleration (the exercise is only a relatively short intermediate learning step and is performed seldom after having learned the turns).

Execution: The delivery is performed without turns from the circular arm swings; the athlete should concentrate on the correct position of the low point(s); bilateral practice.

Typical load standards: 5–15 reps.

449 Ball-heel exercises

Possible objectives: Preparation of the hammer-throw turns (versatile ball-heel switches).

Execution/variations: The athlete stands in a squatting position on the ball of one foot and on the heel of the other foot, then he/she rolls off his/her feet simultaneously to the heel and to the ball respectively, back and forth; also with sideways movement by slightly turning the feet; also while performing a 90° turn of the feet as at the beginning of the first turn in the hammer throw, but without lifting the feet back to the starting position, and again in the same direction or in the opposite direction; also barefoot.

Typical load standards: 1–3 x 5–10 reps depending on the variation.

450 Imitations: Turns without delivery

Possible objectives: Technique of the turns (foot movement, guiding the device, positions of

the low and high points, etc.), balance during rotations about the longitudinal axis.

Execution/variations: Heel-ball turn without hammer and without placing down the rotational leg, which is moved flatly over the ground; imitation of the transition to the first turn or of the double-support phase while holding the medicine ball or barbell plate in front of the body (azimuth angle: 270°–0°–90°), back on the same path and repetition of the exercise (also as strength training); turns, initially without a device and with a break after each turn or at various points to check the position, then with a medicine ball, barbell plate, baseball bat, broom(stick) held in front of the body, finally with round weight, extended sling ball, and hammer; when performing the turns while holding the three devices last mentioned, the athlete should initially perform 2–3 circular arm swings and a turn alternately, then one circular arm swing and one turn, then one circular arm swing and two turns, etc.; later also with a stick for a change, the stick being held with a wide grip and with arms stretched over the head; along a line or on a gym bench; with constant, increasing, varying, or maximal speed of rotation; with a uniform (flat) trajectory of the hammer head, or with an increasingly steeper trajectory; with a wide, narrow or an increasingly narrow foot spacing; with both arms, only with the left or only with the right hand; downhill or uphill; focusing on short single-support phases; even advanced athletes are happy about playful phases of relief (see slinging of a partner); also turn in the opposite direction; also with eyes shut; also without shoes.

Typical load standards: Beginners should perform only few turns, whereas advanced athletes should perform up to more than 10 turns per repetition; 5–10 reps.

451 **Throws from one to four turns (without circular arm swings)**

Possible objectives: Technique of the turns (simplified start of the turns), specific speed-strength training.

Execution: Only possible with a medicine ball, a barbell plate, or another rigid device (baseball bat, broom, or hammer with a wooden handle; the dominant hand initially grips the outer end backward and upward and then slides to the other hand when the turn is started).

Variations: Although beginners start with one turn, they should increase the number of turns to three relatively quickly (despite great technical errors to be expected); combinations: rotational jumps or several jumps onto a small box placed behind the circle and subsequent throw of a medicine ball from two turns; bilateral practice.

Typical load standards: 5–30 reps, in high-performance training even more; depending on the athlete's age, performance capacity, training objective and phase.

452 **Throws from circular arm swings and turns**

Possible objectives: Target technique; specific speed (light hammer) or speed-strength training (heavy hammer).

Execution: 2–3 circular arm swings according to the target technique, 3–4 turns and subsequent delivery.

Variations: Although beginners may initially perform fewer turns, they should increase the number of turns to three relatively quickly (despite great technical errors to be expected); various devices above and below the competition weight (see Tab. 9); there should be an alternation between submaximal (focus on technical details) and maximum execution; bilateral practice.

Typical load standards: 5–30 reps, in high-performance training even more; depending on the athlete's age, performance capacity, training objective and phase; if various weights are used, then mostly from heavy to light.

In versatile coordination training, there should be, for example, a combination of ankling (253) with turns about the longitudinal axis of the body while simultaneously moving forward on a straight line as well as possibly with additional circling of the arms. Pirouettes and rotational jumps (3) may also be combined with sprinting and jumping exercises:

- turns on the spot – sprint;
- two ankle jumps (84) with a half turn to the left – hurdle jump – two ankle jumps with a half turn to the right – hurdle jump, etc.;
- rotational jump (360°) – jump onto a box (91) – back again, and repetition of the exercise; and
- many other combinations.

Passing the medicine ball (392) should also be performed with knees bent at 90° as well as in combination with rotational jumps.

In the strength training of hammer throwers, the following exercises are primarily used: 35–37, 41–47, 49–53, 56, 58, 59, 61–67, 69–72, 74, 77–88, 90–96.

453 Tolling the bells

Possible objectives: Special strength training (extensor loop).

Execution: The athlete swings a round weight from between his/her legs over his/her head; while the weight moves over his/her head, he/she turns 180° about his/her longitudinal axis to catch the weight again between his/her legs and to accelerate it upward again in the opposite direction.

Variations: With both arms or only one arm.

Typical load standards: 2–5 x 6–15 reps (see chapter I–4.3).

3.5.8 SPECIAL TEST AND CONTROL PROCEDURES

	Test: Ability/skill tested	Execution/comments
T171	**Technique analysis:** Hammer-throw technique	Maximal competition throw; evaluation on the basis of the technique analysis sheet (see chapter II–3.5.4), possibly using a video (T1) and photo sequences made thereof; using the time code of the camera, not only the azimuth angle can be estimated, but the duration of the single- and double-support phases as well as the individual turns can be measured; in high-performance sport, also computer-supported 3D analysis based on at least two simultaneous video recordings.
T172	**Throwing auxiliary devices or the hammer with reduced or changed pre-acceleration:** Specific speed strength as well as laterality	Distance achieved in the throw: • from a standing position with a medicine ball or baseball bat; • from circular arm swings (448) with the hammer; • from one or two turns with a medicine ball; • from one, two, three, or four turns with the hammer; and • with the weak side from the pre-accelerations mentioned.
T173	**Hammers with different weights:** Specific speed strength as well as laterality	Hammer-throw distance: • with various lighter hammers; • with various heavier hammers; and • with the weaker side and changed device.
T174	**General throwing tests for the hammer throw:** Speed strength	Throwing distance in: • tossing the shot forward, backward, and sideward (93); • the overhead throw using both hands (391) and • the rotational throw while sitting (95).
T175	**Hammer-throw endurance test:** Specific strength endurance	The total distance achieved in 10 throws in a pre-set time counts.
T4	**1 RPM:** Maximal strength	Deltoid maschine (56), bench pull (58), squat (62), clean (63), snatch (64), hip-shoulder twist (67), etc.

	Test: Ability/skill tested	Execution/comments
T5	**Squat jump, and T8 counter-movement and drop jump:** Two-legged speed strength and reactive strength of the extensor loop	
T9	**5-stride hops with distance maximisation:** Reactive strength of the legs in comparison to one another	Test should only be performed if it is not too stressful due to the bodyweight; both legs should be tested.
T10	**30m bounding run with time minimisation:** Reactive strength of the legs	Only if it is not too stressful due to the bodyweight.
T61	**20m sprint from a standing start:** (Sprint) acceleration	
T2	**Flexibility tests:** General flexibility	
T3	**Body weight and body fat measurement:** Relative strength	Inappropriate upward and downward deflections should be avoided.

Table 10: **Basic performances of (young) hammer throwers** *(according to Ständner, 1999b).*

Women								
Competition performance	(m;	**30–40**	**40–50**	**45–53**	**53–60**	**60–65**	**65–70**	**70–75**
Hammer weight	kg)	(3)	(3)	(4)	(4)	(4)	(4)	(4)
Hammer throw, light	(m;	37–47	45–55	50–57	57–64	64–69	69–74	74–79
Length: 1.2m; weight	kg)	(2)	(2.5)	(3.5)	(3.5)	(3.5)	(3.5)	(3.5)
Hammer throw, heavy	(m;	–	35–45	41–49	49–56	52–57	57–62	62–67
Length: 1.2m; weight	kg)		(3.5)	(4.5)	(4.5)	(5)	(5)	(5)
Hammer throw, short	(m;	–	22–26	24–28	25–28	25–28	28–30	30–32
Length: 0.75m; weight	kg)		(5)	(6)	(7)	(8)	(8)	(8)
Backward tossing of the 4kg shot	(m)	9.0–10.5	10.5–12.0	12.0–13.5	13.5–15.0	15.0–16.5	16.5–18.0	18.0–19.5
Standing snatch	(kg)	–	30–40	40–50	50–60	60–72.5	72.5–85	85–97.5
Standing clean	(kg)	–	40–52.5	52.5–65	65–77.5	77.5–92.5	92.5–110	110–125
Squat (90°, barbell behind the neck)	(kg)	–	40–60	60–80	80–100	100–130	130–160	160–190
Deadlift	(kg)	–	–	90–105	105–120	120–140	140–160	160–180
Standing long jump	(m)	1.8–2.0	2.0–2.2	2.2–2.4	2.3–2.5	2.4–2.6	2.5–2.7	2.6–2.8
5 two-legged jumps	(m)	9.5–10.5	10.5–11.5	11.5–12.5	12.5–13.5	13.0–14.0	13.5–14.5	14.0–15.0
30 m from a standing start	(sec)	4.9–5.3	4.7–4.9	4.6–4.8	4.5–4.7	4.4–4.6	4.3–4.5	4.2–4.4
1000m run	(min)	4:00–4:20	3:50–4:00	3:40–3:50	3:30–3:40	3:20–3:30	3:10–3:20	3:00–3:10

Men					
Competition performance	(m;	**58–60**	**64–66**	**70–73**	**72–75**	**77–79**
Hammer weight	kg)	(5)	(5)	(5)	(6)	(6)
Hammer throw, heavy	(m;	–	–	64–67	66–69	71–73
Length: 1.2m; weight	kg)			(6)	(7)	(7)
Backward tossing of the 4kg shot	(m)	18.0–18.5	19.5–20.0	21.0–22.0	22.5–23.0	23.5–24.0
Backward tossing of the 7.26kg shot	(m)	–	–	17.5–18.0	18.5–18.7	19.0–19.2
Snatch	(kg)	70–75	80–85	90–95	105–110	115–120
Clean	(kg)	90–100	105–110	115–120	130–140	150–160
Full squat	(kg)	120–130	140–150	160–170	190–200	220–230
30m flying sprint	(sec)	3.30–3.35	3.20–3.25	3.15–3.20	3.10–3.15	<3.10
3 two-legged jumps	(m)	8.6–8.8	9.0–9.2	9.3–9.5	9.8–10.0	10.0–10.2

Table 11: **Basic performances of (young) male hammer throwers** *(modified on the basis of Kühl & Hommel, 1997, p. 235).*

Competition performance	(m;	**55**	**58**	**63**	**70**	**72**
Hammer weight	kg)	(4)	(5)	(6.26)	(6.26)	(7.26)
Hammer throw, light	(m;	60	63	70	80	79
Weight	kg)	(3)	(4)	(5)	(5)	(6.26)
Hammer throw, very light	(m;	–	–	78	–	88
Weight	kg)			(4)	(4)	
Hammer throw, heavy	(m;	–	–	56	–	62
Weight	kg)			(7.26)	(7.26)	
Throw of a 7.5kg round weight **from one turn**	(m)	15.0	16.7	–	–	–
Forward throw of a 4 kg shot	(m)	15.0	17.0	–	–	–
Backward throw of a 4 kg shot	(m)	16.5	18.5	20.5	22.0	23.5
30 m flying sprint	(sec)	3.50	3.30	3.20	3.15	3.10
3-stride hop	(m)	8.2	8.8	–	–	–
3-step two-legged jump	(m)	–	–	9.0	9.5	10.0
Clean	(kg)		100	110	120	140
Snatch	(kg)	(no 1RPM)	75	85	95	110
Full squat	(kg)		140	160	180	200

3.5.9 ERRORS – CAUSES – CORRECTIONS

Error	Causes	Corrections
No counter movement of the pelvis (stiff hip) during the circular arm swings (for women, this must not necessarily be regarded as an error; for men it often leads to balance problems).	• The athlete thinks that the circular arm swings are not a movement by the entire body. • Lack of looseness. • Extended knees. • No heel lift of the pivot leg to grasp the hammer. • Upper body not upright.	✔ Circling the hips in a standing position or on the rings (445). ✔ Initially slow, then more rapid circular arm swings while focusing on a contralateral counter movement with bent knees, upright upper body, temporarily lifted heel of the pivot leg, and loose arm movement.
No extended arms during the turns or when the hammer is in front of the thrower during the circular arms swings (shortening of the radius).	• Error in beginners due to a lack of movement security (drawing the arms to the body makes it easier to control one's balance) and lack of looseness. • Fear that the hammer will hit the ground if its trajectory is too steep.	✔ Versatile practice of the counter movement (443 and 444), the circular arm swings (447), and the turns (450), often with only one hand on the hammer; if both hands are on the hammer, the coach should possibly instruct the athlete again to stretch out his/her arms, to stay loose, to keep the trajectory flat, etc.; perhaps use of the contrast method by requiring the athlete to draw his/her arms close to his/her body. ✔ Imitation of the correct arm-shoulder position while standing and corresponding correction by the coach.
Too fast or too slow circular arm swings.	• Too much haste or excessive motivation on the one hand, and fear, reservation or excessive concentration on correct technique on the other hand.	✔ The athlete should experiment with various velocities of his/her circular arm swings in practice: Which velocity results in the highest possible pre-acceleration while it simultaneously enables the athlete to have sufficient control of the movement and to gradually increase his/her velocity during the turns? ✔ Training competitions.
Too steep trajectory of the hammer during the circular arm swings.	• Insufficient effort by the athlete to keep the low point(s) high. • Insufficient lifting of the elbow and/or insufficient bending of the elbow when the hammer is swung over the head. • The upper body does not remain upright.	✔ Circular arm swings in which the hammer is swung over a 30–40cm high obstacle placed in the area of the low point; permanent feedback by the coach about whether the high point of the hammer is approximately at the height of the athlete's head; possible use of a height marker (rope) behind the thrower. ✔ Imitation exercise focusing for example on a high elbow lift, upright upper body, etc.

Error	Causes	Corrections
The low point of the hammer trajectory during the circular arm swings is on the side of the pivot leg.	• Incorrect basic posture of the shoulder axis or no active taking back of the right shoulder to grasp the hammer (stiff trunk); possibly due to » too late lifting and bending of the arms; and » too fast circular arm swings and their causes (see above).	✔ Orientation marker for an optimal position of the low point(s) at an azimuth angle of 320–330°; however, the orientation mark should also be varied while keeping the position of the feet constant to encourage the athlete to aim for different positions of the low point(s). ✔ Imitation exercises to achieve a correct movement of the arms and the shoulder axis. ✔ See corrections of too fast circular arm swings.
The low point of the hammer trajectory during the circular arm swings is too far on the side of the rotational leg.	• No active guiding of the hammer head with stretched arms to the side of the rotational leg. • Too early lifting and bending of the arms. • The thrower only lets the hammer fall instead of accelerating it through the low point(s).	✔ Orientation marker for an optimal position of the low point(s) at an azimuth angle of 320–330°; however, the orientation mark should also be varied while keeping the position of the feet constant to encourage the athlete to aim for different positions of the low point(s). ✔ Imitation exercises and circular arm swings focusing on an active lowering of the shoulder on the side of the pivot leg after the hammer has been swung over the head and on a long acceleration of the hammer to the side of the pivot leg in combination with rotation of the shoulder axis.
Running ahead of the hammer during the transition to the first turn or to the single-support phases (the hammer has overtaken the athlete and is then decelerated).	• The athlete starts the rotation of his/her lower body to the next turn too late (the rotational leg is lifted from the ground later than at 90°); along with • the athlete wanting to accelerate the hammer too much and therefore too long. • Balance problems.	✔ All imitations, turns, and throws focusing on an early and active grasping and accelerating of the hammer during its downward movement and subsequent early and active initiation of the turning movement through the lower body, particularly through the push-off with the rotational leg. ✔ The athlete's view should be directed to the hammer head. ✔ Versatile and unspecific pirouettes, rotational jumps, and rolls (3, 6, 7) for improving balance.

(continued)

(continued)

Error	Causes	Corrections
Dragging the hammer during the transition to the first turn or to the single-support phases.	• The athlete initiates the turns not through his/her leg action but through a pre-turn of his/her view, head, and shoulders.	✔ As a main topic, focusing on the ideal position when releasing the rotational leg from the ground as well as versatile imitation and practice of the lift of the rotational leg (e.g., while holding a stick in one's hands): upper body upright, arms horizontal, hammer at shoulder height with an angle of traction of 0°, the arms, feet, and the hammer point in the direction of the 90° azimuth angle, and the athlete's view is directed to the hammer head (see figure 3).
Too late touchdown of the rotational leg (with hammer azimuth angles of >270°).	• Too late release of the rotational leg (with a hammer azimuth angle of >90°). • The upper body is not overtaken by the lower body during the single-support phase, possibly due to a too wide movement of the rotational leg around the pivot leg (discus swing leg). • Too fast circular arm swings and first turn(s) have led to a loss of control.	✔ Versatile imitations (e.g., while holding a stick in one's hands), turns and throws focusing on an early and powerful push-off with the rotational leg and close movement of the rotational leg around the pivot leg during the single-support phase. ✔ Start with somewhat slower and therefore more controlled circular arm swings and first turn(s).
Hard touchdown of the rotational leg (the athlete falls onto his/her rotational leg).	• During the single-support phases, the vertical projection of the CG is too far beside the pivot leg, for example due to the following actions which disturb the athlete's balance: » initiation on the turns through the upper body; » the rotational leg is moved around the pivot leg at too great a distance (discus swing leg) and is placed on the ground too far away from the pivot leg; and » extension of the pivot leg during the single-support phases.	✔ Versatile imitations, turns, and throws focusing on: ✔ shifting the weight to the pivot leg at the end of the double-support phases; ✔ fixation of one's view to the hammer head while simultaneously initiating the turn early and actively through the lower body (lower driving elements); ✔ moving the rotational leg closely and flatly around the pivot leg; ✔ lowering the CG during the single-support phases ("the athlete virtually hangs on to the hammer"); ✔ imitations and turns (450) on a gym bench to encourage the athlete to place down his/her foot close to the pivot foot.
The athlete moves too diagonally or curvilinearly through the circle.	• The foot of the rotational leg is turned on the heel and/or ball either more than or less than 180° (most frequently it is turned on the heel not up to the 180° direction).	✔ Imitations and turns (450) on a line or a gym bench (caution: the athlete must not be allowed to look at his/her feet during the dynamic movement execution since this would lead to an incorrect trunk posture and would disturb his/her balance).

Error	Causes	Corrections
Insufficient increase in rotational velocity.	• Too fast start. • The number of turns is too great in relation to the athlete's technical skill. • The hammer overtakes the thrower. • The rotational leg is moved around the pivot leg at too great a distance (discus swing leg) and is placed on the ground too far away from the pivot leg. • Insufficient leg work in general, as well as nearly all other errors mentioned.	Versatile imitations and throws from a turn with a noticeably slow start. ✔ In case of great problems, beginners should throw with fewer turns in competition. ✔ Athletes should throw more frequently from three and four turns in practice. ✔ Imitations and turns (450) on a gym bench to encourage a touchdown with the feet close together.
The hammer touches the ground during the final low point.	• Too steep hammer trajectory in relation to the athlete's body height. • Insufficient strength of the extensor loop: In the area of the final low point, there are generally the highest pulling forces which the thrower is not able to resist.	✔ Imitations, circular arm swings, turns, and throws focusing on a flatter hammer trajectory. ✔ Maximal-strength, speed-strength, and reactive-strength training of the extensor loop (e.g., 62–64 and 82), also by throwing various (heavy) devices.
Insufficient acceleration of the hammer during the delivery motion.	• Too late touchdown of the rotational leg and its causes. • Insufficient leg work: for example, insufficient » turn of the feet up to 90°; » knee extension; and » turn of the hip axis until it points in the throwing direction. • Insufficient final slinging motion of the arms.	✔ See corrections of too late touchdown of the rotational leg. ✔ Imitations, standing throws, and throws from initially few turns focusing on correct technique (turning and extension motion of the legs) and correct sequence of strength efforts (legs and arms).
Delivery with a hollow back: The head is thrown back and moved sideways beyond the point of touchdown of the rotational leg when viewed from the rear; there is too much weight placed on the rotational leg.	• Too early and excessive throwing back of the head. • Balancing problems (lateral inclination of the upper body) already during the final turn(s). • Too early action of the upper body. • Too early extension of the pivot leg and/or passive push-off with the rotational leg into the delivery.	✔ Imitations, standing throws, throws from fewer turns, and finally competition-like throws focusing on the correct technique and correct timing. ✔ Versatile turns (450) focusing on an upright trunk.
Too flat angle of departure (flat flight trajectory of the hammer).	• Too flat hammer trajectory during the turns or insufficient steepness of the plane of hammer rotation due to insufficient acceleration in the vertical direction. • Fear of the hammer hitting the ground.	✔ Circular arm swings and turns with varying steepness of the hammer trajectory; now and then deliberately risking that the hammer hits the ground to explore the limits of the trajectory. ✔ Throws using a height marker.

(continued)

(continued)

Error	Causes	Corrections
Stepping over.	• A thrower (with long feet) performs four turns while switching between heel and ball contact. • Loss of balance or control due to turns which are too fast in relation to the technical skills of the athlete. • Technically incorrect delivery with insufficient transfer of energy to the hammer.	✔ The first turn may be performed on the ball of the foot. ✔ The athlete should begin with somewhat slower and therefore more controlled circular arm swings and first turns. ✔ Imitations, standing throws, throws with fewer turns, and submaximal technical throws focusing on the correct technique.
The hammer lands on the side of the rotational leg in the cage or outside the sector.	• The low point of the hammer trajectory has moved too far to the side of the pivot leg and is located at an azimuth angle of >0° in the final turn. • Too late touchdown of the rotational leg and its causes (see above). • Flubbing of the throw through excessive or incorrect trunk action and/or drawing the arms to the body.	✔ Turns and throws while using a marker for the optimal positioning of the low point(s); differential learning with variable positioning of the low point(s). ✔ See corrections of too late touchdown of the rotational leg. ✔ Imitations, standing throws, throws with fewer turns, and submaximal technique throws focusing on long arms, later pulling back the head, and more upright upper body.
The hammer lands on the side of the pivot leg in the cage or outside the sector.	• Too early release of the hammer out of the hand due to a too early opening of the grip (wrong timing) or insufficient grip strength. • The low point(s) of the hammer trajectory is (are) too far on the side of the rotational leg (<360°).	✔ Differential learning while trying to aim for various directions of delivery. ✔ Training of grip strength (using exercise 53). ✔ Turns and throws with markers for the optimal positioning of the low point(s) or with variable positioning of the low point(s).

3.5.10 TRAINING PLANNING

Many introductory statements on training planning made in connection with the javelin throw, the discus throw, and the shot put (see chapters II–3.2.10, II–3.3.10, and II–3.4.10) also apply to the hammer throw.

A crucial component of the hammer throw is its movement rhythm. Therefore, when approaching the competition phase, the above-mentioned requirement to practice all throws in a competition-like manner using a quality competition technique applies especially to the hammer throw. To avoid negative adaptations of the central nervous system, throws with fewer turns, with heavy equipment, etc. should be avoided. If hammers of different weight are used in a training session in the first mesocycles, the hammers should be used from heavy to light.

The trunk muscles are of paramount importance to the hammer throw. The amount of strength training for the trunk should be even higher than for other throwing events. Unfortunately, it is not possible to fully show this in the abridged training schedules below.

SUGGESTED TRAINING PLANS

Below, there are exemplary microcycles for the

- third mesocycle of a 17-year-old athlete in build-up training (table 13); and
- second mesocycle of an athlete in high-performance training (table 14).

It is assumed that 17-year-old shot-putters, discus throwers, and hammer throwers have not yet finally specialised. The exemplary microcycles presented in connection with the discus throw and the shot put (see chapters II–3.3.10 and II–3.4.10) for the

- first mesocycle of a 17-year-old athlete in build-up training; and
- second mesocycle of a 17-year-old athlete in build-up training

are therefore intended for the same athlete.

Even in high-performance training, the non-technique training for the discus throw, shot put, and hammer throw are similar. Therefore, as a supplement to the training plans presented here, the chapters on the discus throw and the shot put include exemplary microcycles for the

- first mesocycle;
- third mesocycle; and
- fourth mesocycle

of an athlete in high-performance training.

Table 12: **Training emphasis in the various mesocycles** for hammer-throw practice in build-up and high-performance training.

1st mesocycle	basic aerobic and anaerobic endurance training; strength-endurance, hypertrophy-oriented maximal-strength, speed-strength, and reactive-strength training (also using a heavy throwing implement); flexibility training; general (sprinting, jumping, games, etc.) and specific coordination training for the hammer throw
2nd mesocycle	(speed-)endurance training; hypertrophy-, IC- and connective-tissue-oriented maximal-, speed-, and reactive-strength training (also using a heavy throwing implement); speed training (sprint and specific using a light device); general (sprinting, jumping, games, etc.) and specific coordination training for the hammer throw
3rd mesocycle	hypertrophy-, IC- and connective-tissue-oriented maximal-, speed- and reactive-strength training; speed training (sprint and specific using a light device); technique training
4th mesocycle	competitions and corresponding regeneration; IC- and connective-tissue-oriented maximal-, speed- and reactive-strength training; sprinting-speed training; technique training; maintenance stimuli

Table 13: Build-up training: sample microcycle for a 17-year-old thrower (discus, shot, and hammer) in the third mesocycle.

Monday	Tuesday	Wednesday	Thursday	Friday	Saturday	Sunday
Warm-up jogging (6 min) including rolls, turns, cartwheels, etc. **Maximal-eccentric strength training** (15 min) trunk stabilisation, lifting opposite upper and lower limbs in prone position, belly punches etc. **Practising the discus-throw technique** (45 min) including specific warm-up, primarily competition-like throws of normal-weight and light discuses **Strength training** (45 min) according to the pyramid principle: snatch, bench press, bench pull, shoulder press, and lat pull **Discus throws** (10 reps) using a light shot, as utilisation	**LJ runs** (6 x 80m; rest intervals: 20 sec) as a warm-up **Tuck jumps** (3 x 2 run-throughs over low hurdles) or **Depth jumps** (5 x 6) from box to box **Acceleration runs** (3 reps) **Flying sprints** (3 x 30m + 20–30m run-up; rest intervals: 10 min) at maximal pace through light barriers **Bounding runs** (2 x 2 x 30m) high intensity **Medicine-ball throws** (30 min) goalkeeper throws, rotational throws, throws from a prone position, tossing, chest passes	**Foot strengthening** (10 min) **Warm-up specific to the hammer throw** (25 min) e.g., rotational jumps, passing the circulating hammer in front of and behind the body, (one-armed) circular arm swings, and continuous turns on a line **Practising the hammer-throw technique** (35 min) relatively few competition-like throws using a normal-weight and a light device **Strength training** (30 min) according to the pyramid principle: clean and full squat **Alternating-pace sprints** (4 x 60m) as utilisation	**Warm-up jogging** (6 min) including backward and sideways running **ABCs of hurdling** (20 min) walking and skipping over hurdles, etc. **Acceleration runs** (3 reps) **Practising the hurdling technique** (30 min) primarily over low hurdles using a 3-stride rhythm **Contract-relax stretching** (15 min) **Strength training** (30 min) according to the pyramid principle: abdominal machine, shoulder-hip twists, lumborum, and hip and back extensors **ABCs of jumping** (6 run-throughs) as utilisation	**Warm-up jogging** (6 min) including rolls, turns, cartwheels, etc. **Warm-up specific to the shot put** (15 min) e.g., forward and backward tossing **Practising the shot-put technique** (35 min) determination of the competition technique, competition-like puts using a normal-weight and light device **Strength training** (50 min) according to the pyramid principle and/or maximal-eccentric strength training: for arms and legs on apparatus **Standing puts** (10 reps) using a light medicine ball, as utilisation	**Warm-up jogging** (6 min) including picking up, carrying, and forward throwing of various devices **ABCs of jumping** (10–12 run-throughs) e.g., galloping sideways, ankle jumps, skipping with two-legged landing, and skipping **Acceleration runs** (3 reps) **Crouch starts** (20, 30, 40, 50, 40, 30, and 20m, long rest intervals) 2 x focusing on technique, then at maximum intensity against each other or **Practising the long-jump technique** (35 min) including specific warm-up, medium-length up to long run-ups	Rest

Table 14: High-performance training: sample microcycle in the second mesocycle using double periodisation.

	Monday	Tuesday	Wednesday	Thursday	Friday	Saturday	Sunday
Morning	Trunk stabilisation exercises and abdominal crunches (20 min) Warm-up specific to the hammer throw (20 min) e.g., circular arm swings and turns Practising the hammer-throw technique (50 min) normal-weight and light device	Foot strengthening (10 min) little jumps Walking and skipping over hurdles (20 min) Rhythm sprints (6 x 60 m) e.g., with hoops for ground contact Muscle build-up training (30 min) snatch and deadlift	Warm-up jogging (6 min) Round-weight throws (35 min) including specific warm-up, from 1–3 turns Speed-strength and muscle build-up training (50 min) for trunk and arms; using a medicine ball, round weight (e.g., tolling of the bells) and on apparatus, specific and general exercises	Warm-up jogging (6 min) ABCs of jumping (12–15 run-throughs) Jumps onto a box (5 x 10 reps) Pirouettes, rotational jumps, and gymnastics (40 min) versatile variations, combinations, and imitations	Warm-up jogging (6 min) Warm-up specific to the hammer throw (25 min) versatile foot exercises, etc. Practising the hammer-throw technique (45 min) imitation and throws of a normal-weight and heavy device	Warm-up jogging (6 min) with additional tasks ABCs of sprinting (12–15 run-throughs) Muscle build-up training (30 min) clean and full squats Acceleration runs (3 reps) I3 tempo runs (2 x 3 x 150m; rest intervals: 3 min; rest intervals between sets: 10 min)	Rest
Afternoon	Warm-up jogging (6 min) ABCs of jumping (12–15 run-throughs) also with turns Muscle build-up training (60 min) e.g., bench pull, bench press, deltoideus and various trunk exercises Hammer-throw-like medicine-ball throws (10 reps per side) light device	Warm-up jogging (6 min) Acceleration runs ABCs of walking/sprinting (12–15 run-throughs) LI runs (2 x 5 x 100m; rest intervals: 1.5–2 min; rest intervals between series: 6 min) Contract-relax stretching (15 min) Warm-down jogging Ankle jumps (3 x 10 reps)	Hammer throws (10 reps) light weight; as utilisation	Warm-up jogging (6 min) Game (30 min) e.g., soccer or field hockey Muscle build-up training (60 min) hamstrings, quadriceps, adductors, abductors, and clean Skipping with two-legged landing (3 x 20m) as utilisation	Warm-up jogging (6 min) Muscle build-up training (80 min) e.g., bench pull, shoulder press, and lat pull; abdominal machine, shoulder-hip twists, lumborum, hip and back extensors Foot strengthening (15 min) in the sand Medicine-ball throws (2 x 10 reps)	Contract-relax stretching (15 min) Ankle jumps (3 x 10 reps)	

3.5.11 BIBLIOGRAPHY

Bartonietz, K. (1990). Biomechanical analysis of throws with hammers of various weight and length as basis for an effective training. In G.-P. Brüggemann & J. K. Rühl (eds.). *Techniques in Athletics – The first International Conference – Cologne, 7-9 June 1990: Conference Proceedings: Volume 2: Main Conference: Free Communication Sessions* (S. 542-551). Köln: Sport & Buch Strauß.

Bartonietz, K. (2002). Weit Werfen will gelernt sein. *Leichtathletiktraining 13* (10+11), 22-29.

Brice, S. M., Ness, K. F., Rosemond, D., Lyons, K. & Davis, M. (2008). Development and validation of a method to directly measure the cable force during the hammer throw. *Sports Biomechanics 7* (2), 274-287.

Dapena, J. (1986). A kinematic study of center of mass motions in hammer throwing. *Journal of Biomechanics 19* (2), 147-158.

Dapena, J. (1989). Some biomechanical aspects of hammer throwing. *Athletics Coach 23* (3), 12-19.

Dapena, J., Gutiérrez-Dávila, M., Soto, V. M. & Rojas, F. J. (2003). Prediction of distance in hammer throwing. *Journal of Sports Sciences 21* (1), 21-28.

Deyle, M. (2005). Deutschlands beste Hammerwerferinnen. *Leichtathletiktraining 16* (2+3), 30-39.

Deyle, M. (2007). Hammerwerfen bis zur Perfektion. *Leichtathletiktraining 18* (6), 28-39.

Deyle, M. & Lipske, J. (2009). Drehen mit dem Hammer will gelernt sein. Teil 1. *Leichtathletiktraining 20* (2+3), 12-19.

Deyle, M. (2009). Drehen mit dem Hammer will gelernt sein. Teil 2. *Leichtathletiktraining 20* (5), 22-29.

Gutiérrez, M., Soto, V. M. & Rojas, F. J. (2002). A biomechanical analysis of the individual techniques of the hammer throw finalists in the Seville Athletics World Championship 1999. *New Studies in Athletics 17* (2), 15-26.

Hildebrand, F. (1994). Eine biomechanische Analyse des Hammerwerfens. In D. Schmidtbleicher & A. F. Müller (Hrsg.), *Leistungsdiagnostische und präventive Aspekte der Biomechanik: 2. Symposium der dvs-Sektion Biomechanik vom 15.-17.4.1993 in Frankfurt/Main* (Schriften der Deutschen Vereinigung für Sportwissenschaften, 59, S. 86-93). Sankt Augustin: Academia.

Isele, R., Nixdorf, E. & Mendoza, L. (2010). Biomechanical Analysis of the Hammer Throw. In Deutscher Leichtathletikverband (Hrsg.), *Biomechanical Analysis of selected events at the 12th IAAF World Championships in Athletics, Berlin 15-23 August 2009.* Zugriff am 20.04.2010 unter http://www.iaaf.org/mm/Document/Development/ research/05/64/50/20100415080101_httppostedfile_8-BiomechanicsReportWC Berlin2009_Throws_19909.pdf.

Judge, L. W. & McAtee, G. (1999). Tips for technical improvement in the hammer throw. *Modern Athlete and Coach 37* (3), 15-19.

Kühl, L. & Hommel, H. (Red.) (mit Bartonietz, K., Becker, M., Becker, S., Böttcher, G., Deyle, M., Gaede, E., Hartmann, W., Losch, M., Rapp, E., Thomas, B., Wollbrück, R. & Zöllkau, H.). (1997). *Rahmentrainingsplan für das Aufbautraining Wurf* (Edition Leichtathletik, 5, 3. Aufl.). Aachen: Meyer & Meyer.

Maheras, A. V. (2009). Reassessing velocity generation in hammer throwing. *New Studies in Athletics 24* (4), 71-80.

Murofushi, K., Sakurai, S., Umegaki, K. & Kobayashi, K. (2005). Development of a System to Measure Radius of Curvature and Speed of Hammer Head during Turns in Hammer Throw. *International Journal of Sport and Health Science 3*, 116-128.

Murofushi, K., Sakurai, S., Umegaki, K. & Takamatsu, J. (2007). Hammer acceleration due to thrower and hammer movement patterns. *Sports Biomechanics 6* (3), 301-314.

Otto, R. M. (1990a). Kinematic analysis of the world record in the hammer throw – Juri Sedych throws 86.74 m. In G.-P. Brüggemann & J. K. Rühl (eds.). Techniques in Athletics – The first International Conference – Cologne, 7-9 June 1990: Conference Proceedings: Volume 2: Main Conference: Free Communication Sessions (S. 523-531). Köln: Sport & Buch Strauß.

Otto, R. M. (1990b). Biomechanical analysis of the hammer throw – Athens 1986 and Rome 1987. In G.-P. Brüggemann & J. K. Rühl (eds.). *Techniques in Athletics – The first International Conference – Cologne, 7-9 June 1990: Conference Proceedings: Volume 2: Main Conference: Free Communication Sessions* (S. 561-570). Köln: Sport & Buch Strauß.

Regelkommissionen des DLV, FLA, ÖLV und SLV (Hrsg.). (2010). *Internationale Wettkampfregeln.* Waldfischbach: Hornberger.

Riedel, B. (2002). Auf den Übergang kommt es an! *Leichtathletiktraining 13* (10+11), 37-45.

Ständner, M. (1999a). Hammerwurf – schwierig aber faszinierend: Teil 1. *Leichtathletiktraining 10* (5), 4-11.

Ständner, M. (1999b). Hammerwurf – schwierig aber faszinierend: Teil 2. *Leichtathletiktraining 10* (6), 20-26.

Umegaki, K., Murofushi, K., Murofushi, S., Sakurai, S., Seki, Y. & Kimura, Y. (2009). Reducing the dead zone in the hammer landing sector. *New Studies in Athletics 24* (2), 35-41.

Wank, V. (2006). Biomechanik und leistungsrelevante Parameter der leichtathletischen Wurfdisziplinen. In K. Wohlgefahrt & S. Michel, *Beiträge zur speziellen Trainingswissenschaft Leichtathletik: Symposium der dvs-Kommission Leichtathletik vom 10.-11.10.2002 in Bad Blankenburg* (Schriften der Deutschen Vereinigung für Sportwissschaft, 153, S. 132-144). Hamburg: Czwalina.

4 COMBINED EVENTS

4.1 HEPTATHLON AND DECATHLON

4.1.1 THE KINGS OF ATHLETES

The pentathlon of ancient Greece consisted of a stadium run over 192 meters, a multi-jump for distance, a discus throw, and a final wrestling competition. In the Middle Ages, there were combined events for common people which consisted of different numbers of the most varied disciplines. In modern times, exercises on (gymnastics) apparatuses were also added. Even today, there are combined events in gymnastics which include disciplines from various sports. At the Olympic Games, the decathlon with today's disciplines was contested for the first time in Stockholm in 1912. At that time, Swedish King Gustav V called the winner Jim Thorpe (USA) the king of the athletes. In recognition of their impressive versatile performances, this title of nobility for combined-event athletes has survived to this day.

Women have competed in the athletics combined events since 1928. Due to concern about whether women could be expected to withstand the stress of the combined events, the women's pentathlon only became an Olympic discipline in 1964. The heptathlon with today's

Table 1: Past combined-event competitions and combined-event competitions in gymnastics.

Decathlon (men's) at the 1904 OG	100 yards, shot put, high jump, 880 yards race walking, hammer throw, pole vault, 120-yard hurdles, weight throw, long jump, 1 mile	
Pentathlon (men's) at the 1906 OG	Standing long jump, discus throw, javelin throw, 192m, wrestling	
Pentathlon (men's) at the 1912–1924 OG	Long jump, javelin throw, 200m, discus throw, 1500 m	
Pentathlon (women's)	Since 1928	1st day: shot put, long jump; 2nd day: 100m, high jump, javelin throw
	Since 1949	1st day: shot put, high jump, 200m; 2nd day: 80m hurdles, long jump
	Since 1961	1st day: 80m hurdles, shot put, high jump; 2nd day: long jump, 200m
	Since 1969	1st day: 100m hurdles, shot put, high jump; 2nd day: long jump, 200m
	Since 1977	100m hurdles, shot put, high jump, long jump, 800m
Jahn-Enneathlon	Jump, (uneven) bars, floor; 100m, long jump, shot put; 100m freestyle, 25m underwater swimming, springboard diving (1m or 3m board)	
German octathlon	Jump, (uneven) bars, floor, balance beam/horizontal bar; 100m, long jump, shot put, sling-ball throw	
Frisian pentathlon	Shooting; shot put, 1000m; 100m freestyle; épéé fencing	
Pentathlon	100m, long jump, shot put, sling-ball throw, 2000m	

disciplines was introduced in 1981. The current sequence of the disciplines was established in 1983. The fact that women still do not compete in the decathlon at major events is justified by the IAAF by the high cost of the pole vault which would make it impossible for many women in poor countries to take part. In 2004–2008, the IAAF tentatively kept a world-record list for the women's decathlon.

The USA is by far the most successful nation in the decathlon. All too often, American winners at Olympic Games and World Championships have been superior to athletes from Germany, which can be considered the second strongest nation with many Olympic champions, world champions, and world record holders in the combined events. There have been only six world records in the decathlon since the current scoring tables were introduced in 1985. Czech Tomáš Dvořák came close to

Table 2: *Disciplines of the outdoor combined events and world-record performances.*

	Heptathlon (women)		Decathlon (women)		Decathlon (men)	
	Discipline	J. Joyner-Kersee	Discipline	A. Skujytė	Discipline	K. Mayer
First Day	100m hurdles	12.69 sec	100m	12.45 sec	100m	10.55 sec
	High jump	1.86m	Discus throw	46.19m	Long jump	7.80m
	Shot put	15.80m	Pole vault	3.10 m	Shot put	16.00m
	200m	22.56 sec	Javelin throw	48.78 m	High jump	2.05m
			400m	57.19 sec	400m	48.42 sec
Second Day	Long jump	7.27m	100m hurdles	14.22 sec	110m hurdles	13.75 sec
	Javelin throw	45.66m	Long jump	6.12m	Discus throw	50.54m
	800m	2:08.51 min	Shot put	16.42m	Pole vault	5.45m
			High jump	1.78m	Javelin throw	71.90m
			1500m	5:15.86 min	1500m	4:36,11 min
	Total points	7291	Total points	8358	Total points	9126

Table 3: *Disciplines of the indoor combined events and world-record performances.*

	Indoor pentathlon (women)		Indoor heptathlon (men)	
	Discipline	N. Dobrynska	Discipline	A. Eaton
First Day	60m hurdles	8.38 sec	60m	6.79 sec
	High jump	1.84m	Long jump	8.16 m
	Shot put	16.51m	Shot put	14.56m
	Long jump	6.57m	High jump	2.03m
	800m	2:11.15 min		
Second Day			60m hurdles	7.68 sec
			Pole vault	5.20m
			1000m	2:32.77 min
	Total points	5013	Total points	6645

the mark of 9000 points (8994 points in 1999), which was only just surpassed in 2001 by his compatriot Roman Šebrle (9026 points). The current record was set in 2018 by Frenchman Kevin Mayer (9126 points), after American Ashton Eaton reached 9045 points in 2015.

The heptathlon world record is still held by Jackie Joyner-Kersee (7291 points), who is also second on the all-time best list with 7.49 m in the long jump. Between 2002 and 2007, Sweden's Carolina Klüft dominated the international competitions. She is still second in the all-time best list

with 7032 points and once declared, I want to find out how far I can go, and it's worth the pain." This statement is typical of the attitude of all-around athletes, who prefer to compete with each other rather than against each other. A confirmation of this attitude is the mutual support in competition despite the striving for maximum performance and the final victory lap of all athletes. One can see this before international championships when the family of combined athletes meets every year in Götzis, Austria. No other city has seen so many all-time best performances in the combined events.

4.1.2 THE MOST IMPORTANT COMPETITION RULES

The following abridged and simplified International Competition Rules comprise the framework for the technique and strategy, as well as the organisation of combined-event competitions:

- See tables 2, 3, and 4 for disciplines with their sequence and distribution in two days. The first day of the heptathlon or decathlon is called quadrathlon or pentathlon, respectively.
- There should be an interval of at least 30 minutes between the time one event ends and the next event begins. The period of time between the finish of the last event on the first day and the start of the first event on the second day should be at least 10 hours.

- The rules for each event constituting the competition apply with the following exceptions:
  - » In the long jump and each of the throwing events, each athlete is allowed only three trials.
  - » The incremental raising of the bar in the high jump and pole vault remains the same between all jumping heights. At international championships, the increments are 3cm in the high jump and 10cm in the pole vault.
  - » In the running events, only one false start per race is allowed without the disqualification of the athlete(s) responsible for the false start. Any athlete responsible for further false starts in the race is disqualified.

- Any athlete failing to proceed to the start in one of the events is not allowed to take part in the subsequent events and is considered to have abandoned the competition.
- The performances are translated into points (see below). The scores must be announced separately for each event and as a cumulative total to all athletes after the completion of each

Table 4: **Combined events in the lower age groups:** *The sequence of disciplines is not prescribed for young athletes; beginning with U18, it is only prescribed which disciplines are performed on which of the two competition days.*

Up to national level:	
Female U18: Heptathlon	1st day: 100m hurdles, high jump, shot put, 100m; 2nd day: long jump, javelin throw, 800m
Female U16: Heptathlon	1st day: 100m, high jump, shot put, long jump; 2nd day: 80m hurdles, javelin throw, 800m
Male U16: Enneathlon	1st day: 100m, long jump, shot put, high jump; 2nd day: 80m hurdles, discus throw, pole vault, javelin throw, 1000m
U16: Block competitions:	
Sprint/jump	100m, 80m hurdles, long jump, high jump, javelin throw
Run	100m, 80m hurdles, long jump, ball throw, 2000m
Throw	100m, 80m hurdles, long jump, shot put, discus throw
Primarily at the regional level:	
U14 and 16: Quadrathlon	75/100m, long jump, high jump, shot put
U14: Block combined event	75m, 60m hurdles, long jump, ball throw, 2000m
U12, 14 and 16: Triathlon	50/75/100m, long jump, (rounders) ball throw

event. The athletes shall be placed in the order of the total number of points obtained. If two or more athletes achieve an equal number of points, the athlete who has won more events is awarded the higher place. If the athletes are tied following the application of this rule, the athlete who has the highest number of points in any one event shall be awarded the higher place. If the athletes are still equal following the application of this rule, the athlete who has the highest number of points in a second event, etc. shall be awarded the higher place.

THE SCORING TABLES

According to the World Athletics Combined-Event Scoring Tables, the number of points (S) awarded for a performance (P) in one discipline of the combined events is calculated (by means of a computer programme) using the following formula:

$$S = a \cdot (P - b)^c.$$

Since lower numerical values correspond to better performances in the running events, P and b have been transposed. Moreover, the correction for electronic timing must be added in the sprints:

$$> 400\ m: \quad S = a \cdot (b - P)^c$$
$$400\ m: \quad S = a \cdot (b - (P + 0.14))^c$$
$$100/200\ m: \ S = a \cdot (b - (P + 0.24))^c.$$

P must be specified in sec for the runs, in cm for the jumps, and in m for the throws.

DISCOURSE I: THE CONSTANT DISCUSSION ABOUT THE SCORING TABLES

Since the first scoring table for the decathlon in 1912, the table was changed in 1920, 1936, 1952, 1964, and most recently in 1985. The reasons for the changes were the orientation on the world records in the individual disciplines (which at the beginning were awarded 1,000 points and are worth approximately 1,200 points today), different performance developments in the disciplines, over- or under-valuations in the decathlon in connection with this, and the question of whether the points should increase linearly with the performances or not. Progressive scoring tables (i.e., greater point increases with greater achievements) reward outstanding individual performances more, whereas regressive scoring tables (i.e., smaller point increases with greater achievements) reward all-round athletes more. Today's scoring tables are slightly progressive (see constant c). But even today, it is striking that combined-event athletes are awarded fewer points in the throws and middle distances than in the sprints and jumps. This is mainly due to the fact that top performances in the throws require a higher body mass, whereas top performances in the running events require a lower body mass. However, neither the one nor the other extreme is useful for combined-event athletes due to the requirements of the other disciplines. To enhance the value of the throwing and running disciplines, it is therefore recommended to use top performances in the combined events (instead of top performances in the individual events) as the basis of the scoring tables. In each discipline, for example, the average of the all-time top 50 could be taken as the basic value for the table. Moreover, the progression of the points tables should be adjusted (by a statistical normalisation).

Table 5: Constants a, b, and c for calculating the points in the combined events.

	Women			Men		
	a	b	c	a	b	c
100m	17.857	21.0 sec	1.81	25.4347	18.00 sec	1.81
200m	4.99087	42.5 sec	1.81	5.8425	38.00 sec	1.81
400m	1.34285	91.7 sec	1.81	1.53775	82.00 sec	1.81
800m	0.11193	254.0 sec	1.88			
1500m	0.02883	535 sec	1.88	0.03768	480.00 sec	1.85
100/110m hurdles	9.23076	26.7 sec	1.835	5.74352	28.50 sec	1.92
Long jump	0.188807	210cm	1.41	0.14354	220cm	1.40
High jump	1.84523	75cm	1.348	0.8465	75cm	1.42
Pole vault	0.44125	100cm	1.35	0.2797	100cm	1.35
Javelin throw	15.9803	3.8m	1.04	10.14	7.0m	1.08
Discus throw	12.3311	3.0m	1.10	12.91	4.0m	1.10
Shot put	56.0211	1.5m	1.05	51.39	1.5m	1.05

Table 6: **Excerpt from the women's scoring tables** *(if there is no performance for the exact number of points indicated in the list, the next-best performance is chosen; BP, WP, 2BP, 2WP, etc.: best, worst, second best, second worst, etc. performance in heptathlons with at least 6,598-points [for each athlete, only the best competition was counted]; status: end of 2021).*

Points	100m hurdles	High jump	Shot put	200m	Long jump	Javelin throw	800m
1200	12.50 sec	1.98m	20.02m	21.82 sec	7.09m	67.41m	1:54.76 min
1100	13.16 sec	1.90m	18.54m	22.79 sec	6.79m	62.30m	2:01.06 min
1000	13.85 sec	1.82m	17.07m	23.80 sec	6.48m	57.18m	2:07.63 min
900	14.56 sec	1.74m	15.58m	24.86 sec	6.17m	52.04m	2:14.52 min
800	15.32 sec	1.66m	14.09m	25.97 sec	5.84m	46.87m	2:21.77 min
700	16.12 sec	1.57m	12.58m	27.14 sec	5.50m	41.68m	2:29.47 min
600	16.97 sec	1.49m	11.07m	28.40 sec	5.15m	36.46m	2:37.70 min
500	17.89 sec	1.39m	9.55m	29.75 sec	4.78m	31.21m	2:46.60 min
400	18.90 sec	1.30m	8.01m	31.23 sec	4.39m	25.92m	2:56.38 min
BP	12.54 sec	1.98m	17.31m (2BP:16.45m)	22.56 sec (4BP: 23.06 sec)	7.27m (2BP: 6.95m)	59.32m (5BP: 54.74m)	2:04.20 min
WP	14.05 sec	1.73m	12.61m	25.43 sec	5.98m	39.42m	2:20.59 min

Table 7: **Excerpt from the men's scoring tables** *(explanations: see above; decathlons of at least 8539 points; status: end of 2021).*

Points	100m	Long jump	Shot put	High jump	400m	110m hurdles	Discus throw	Pole vault	Javelin throw	1500m
1100	9.98 sec	8.16m	20.15m	2.31m	44.23 sec	13.05 sec	60.89m	5.60m	83.67m	3:40.78 min
1000	10.30 sec	7.76m	18.40m	2.21m	46.17 sec	13.80 sec	56.17m	5.29m	77.19m	3:53.79 min
900	10.82 sec	7.36m	16.79m	2.11m	48.19 sec	14.59 sec	51.40m	4.97m	70.67m	4:07.42 min
800	11.27 sec	6.95m	15.31m	2.00m	50.32 sec	15.41 sec	47.59m	4.64m	64.09m	4:21.77 min
700	11.75 sec	6.51m	13.53m	1.89m	52.58 sec	16.29 sec	41.72m	4.30m	57.45m	4:36.96 min
600	12.26 sec	6.06m	11.89m	1.77m	54.98 sec	17.23 sec	37.79m	3.94m	50.74m	4:53.20 min
500	12.81 sec	5.59m	10.24m	1.65m	57.57 sec	18.25 sec	31.78m	3.57m	43.95m	5:10.73 min
400	13.41 sec	5.09m	8.56m	1.52m	60.40 sec	19.38 sec	26.68m	3.18m	37.05m	5:29.96 min
BP	10.12 sec (3BP: 10.31)	8.24m (5BP: 8.02)	17.32m (2BP: 16.94m)	2.18m	45.00 sec (2BP: 46.21 sec)	13.46 sec (3BP: 13.69 sec)	55.22m (2BP: 53.22)	5.45m (7BP: 5.20m)	79.057.42m (3BP: 72.42m)	4:12.61 min (5BP: 4:19.60)
WP	11.24 sec	7.15m	13.60m	1.91m (2WP: 1.97)	50.44 sec	14.87 sec	39.63m (2WP: 43.25m)	4.40 m (2WP: 4.60m)	53.61m	4:59.43 min (5WP: 4:50.97)

4.1.3 SPORT-SCIENCE FINDINGS, PHASE STRUCTURE, AND TECHNIQUE

COMBINED-EVENT ATHLETES AND SPECIALISTS

If the performances of specialists are assigned points and compared with the results of the combined-event athletes, the result is that heptathletes are closer to the performances of specialists than decathletes. On average, world-class heptathletes achieve approximately 79–81% of the performances of top specialists, whereas decathletes achieve only approximately 72–73%. This is attributed to the more versatile performance requirements of the decathlon.

TYPES OF COMBINED-EVENT ATHLETES

Among decathletes, the sprinter-jumper type and the jumper-thrower type can be distinguished. The former is characterised in particular by good reactive-strength capabilities of the lower extremities and high sprinting speed, which also helps him/her to achieve good results over the hurdles as well as in the long jump and in the pole vault. Compared to the sprinter-jumper type, the jumper-thrower type is characterised by good coordination and superior maximum strength of the upper extremities. Maximal strength is not only positive for the throws, but also for the pole vault. Athletes who have more talent for the running or throwing events have no chance due to the great importance of sprinting speed (see discourse I).

Frequently, first-day and second-day types can also be distinguished. This is attributed to the fact that the disciplines on the second day are believed to place greater emphasis on coordination and are often introduced at a later age. Specifically, athletes who have switched to the combined events relatively late or only recently often have problems with these disciplines.

Ultimately, combined-event athletes must of course be all-rounders. Specialists who achieved above-average performances in only one or two disciplines and were often favoured by earlier scoring tables, have no chance in the decathlon today.

This is not the case in the women's heptathlon. The heptathlon seems to require a similar athletic profile as the long jump. Many athletes give evidence to this claim: Jackie Joyner-Kersee was not only the Olympic champion in the heptathlon, but also in the long jump. Long-jump double Olympic champion Heike Drechsler achieved the world's best heptathlon performance in 1994, and Carolina Klüft specialised in the long jump after her combined-events career. It does not seem possible to achieve a very good heptathlon performance without a good long-jump performance. Running, throwing, and upper-body strength seem to be required less in the heptathlon than in the decathlon.

KEY DISCIPLINES

Identifying key disciplines is not easy since various approaches produce different

Table 8: Correlation between the performances in the individual disciplines and the total performance in the best competitions of eight Czech decathletes with an average best performance of 8,461 points (Wang & Lu, 2007): An investigation of 50 of the best youth decathletes shows that the superior athletes are primarily those who received early training in the disciplines on the second competition day which are very demanding in terms of coordination. Highly significant correlations with the total decathlon performance were found for the 110m hurdles, the discus throw, the pole vault, and the javelin throw (Wentz & Engelhardt, 1997). The table below suggests that the advantage of early training is later lost to a certain extent (however, this is not an absolute argument against early training).

	100m	Long jump	Shot put	High jump	400m	hurdles	Discus throw	Pole vault	Javelin throw	1500m
Percentage correlation	46%	56%	1%	51%	4%	80%	17%	79%	-9%	5%
(correlation coefficient)	(0.679)	(0.749)	(0.076)	(0.711)	(0.207)	(0.892)	(0.414)	(-0.300)	(0.887)	(0.222)
Significance (p)	0.032	0.016	0.429	0.024	0.311	0.001	0.154	0.235	0.002	0.298
Order of rank ($p < 0.05$)	5	3		4		1			2	

results. In the above comparison of combined-event athletes with specialists, the long jump has been identified as a key discipline of the heptathlon. The 100m (or 200m) sprint can be rightly considered a key discipline since sprinting speed is also a prerequisite for many other disciplines. Coaches often regard the hurdles as well as the pole vault in the decathlon and the javelin throw in the heptathlon as key disciplines. These disciplines are believed to place very high demands on coordination and this alone requires an enormous training effort. Moreover, the training for the hurdle sprints is said to have many beneficial effects on the other disciplines. The speed and reactive strength acquired in the hurdles, the necessary flexibility and agility, the ability to establish movement rhythm etc. also have a positive effect on nearly all other disciplines. The gymnastics training specific to the pole vault may at the same time be regarded as strength training for the throws. The javelin throw is the individual discipline whose movement structure is most different from the movement structure of the other disciplines in the heptathlon. (A good example is the world-record holder Jackie Joyner-Kersee whose javelin performance is farthest from the performances of specialists; see table 2.)

Statistical analyses arrive at even different conclusions. Although the correlation analysis between the overall performance and the individual performance in table 8 also gives evidence to the leading role of the hurdles in the decathlon, it proves that there is even a tendency of a negative correlation between the pole vault and overall performance. (This could mean that some athletes concentrate too much on the pole vault in training at the expense of other disciplines or that a long pole-vault competition has a negative effect on the subsequent two disciplines.) Another study examined which disciplines have the greatest point differences among the

Table 9: Significant differences between the average score in the individual disciplines of the top ten athletes and the following 40 athletes in the all-time world-ranking list (AWL) and the 2007 world-ranking list (WL) for the heptathlon and decathlon (according to Dickwach et al., 2008).

			Significant difference between places 1-10 and 11-50
Women	AWL	p<0.001:	Long jump
		p<0.01:	200m, javelin throw
		p<0.05:	100m hurdles
	WL	p<0.001:	High jump
		p<0.01:	–
		p<0.05:	100m hurdles, shot put, long jump, 800m
Men	AWL	p<0.001:	Long jump
		p<0.01:	–
		p<0.05:	400m, javelin throw
	WL	p<0.001:	Shot put, high jump, 110m hurdles, pole vault
		p<0.01:	400m
		p<0.05:	100m

world's 50 best athletes. In the decathlon, it is the last three (or four) disciplines in particular. In the heptathlon, it is the long jump, high jump, shot put, and especially the javelin throw. A new scoring table (see discourse I) could lead to changes here.

In addition to these general reflections, individual considerations may lead to the determination of one's own key disciplines (see chapter II–4.1.6).

CONCERNING THE TECHNIQUES OF THE DISCIPLINES

In the long term, combined-event athletes should try to achieve the same model techniques as the specialists. In the short term, combined-event athletes should try to develop an effective competition technique. Momentary simplifications may be necessary for this. For example, in the javelin throw the athlete may start the movement with an already withdrawn javelin and may throw using only the 5-stride rhythm if this makes it easier for him/her to improve on important key elements of the delivery. A study of the javelin throw showed that the angle of attitude upon delivery is too steep for many combined-event athletes. The correction of this error should be given priority.

In the shot put, the linear or scissor-step technique should be preferred to the rotational technique. The former mentioned techniques lead to fewer failures, and the distances achieved in the valid trials are more constant. Some experts recommend taking a higher position of the CG since the maximal forces during the backward reclining position of delivery are lower.

The switch from the hurdles sprint to the discus throw is frequently described as the most difficult transition between two disciplines. Particularly in the discus throw, many decathletes remain far behind the results they are able to achieve in individual discus competitions. This is attributed especially to the difference between the linear and the rotational movement as well as the different movement rhythm. (This is an additional reason for not using the rotational shot-putting technique in the decathlon since the transition after the 100m race and the long jump might be similarly difficult). Prior to the discus throw, an athlete should perform a lot of imitations and other rotations about the longitudinal axis to manage the transition. Moreover, repeated mental rehearsal of the movement may facilitate the adjustment to the respective next discipline.

Due to its ease in learning and the possibility to better utilise the athlete's speed potential, the flop has very quickly replaced the straddle in the combined events.

Table 10: **Requirement profile for the combined events:** *The suggested rough estimate of the value of selected factors determining performance is based on the importance for the overall performance and the percentage of time spent training.*

Factors determining combined-events performance	Estimate of value	Notes
Coordination	+ + + + +	See individual disciplines
Flexibility	+ +	Some disciplines (e.g., hurdles, high jump, and javelin throw) require special flexibility
Strength		Nearly all muscles of the body
Maximal strength	+ + + +	primarily of the extensor loop
Reactive strength	+ + + + +	rather as a basis
Speed	+ + + +	cyclic and acyclic aspects in the jumps and throws
Endurance (general dynamic) Anaerobic endurance		
Strength endurance	+ +	as a basis
Speed endurance	+ + + +	particularly for the 200m and 800m or 400m
Aerobic endurance	+ + +	as an important basis as well as for the 800m and 1500m
Psychological and cognitive abilities	+ + + + +	(see individual disciplines); in addition, the athlete should be able to maintain his/her concentration for the two competition days and to positively process the results of the individual disciplines
Anthropometric and primarily genetically determined characteristics	+ + + +	high percentage of fastest muscle fibres; connective tissue with optimal energy storage capacities; rather above-average body height (men: mostly 185–195cm; body weight (kg) ≈ body height in cm – 100); low percentage of body fat

4.1.4 SUMMARY OF THE MOST IMPORTANT TECHNICAL CHARACTERISTICS = TECHNIQUE-ANALYSIS SHEET

See the respective individual disciplines.

4.1.5 PHOTO SEQUENCES

See the respective individual disciplines.

4.1.6 STRATEGY AND COMPETITION BEHAVIOUR

STRATEGY

Strategy in the combined events is important even when planning training. Which disciplines deserve special attention? The key disciplines? The disciplines with the greatest possible point increases? Are these the weak or the strong disciplines? Although ultimately all disciplines must be practised, various emphases are conceivable.

In the technical disciplines, the athlete must weigh the risk. Normally, the first trial is a deliberately safe performance which means that in the first long jump a loss of distance is accepted in front of the board. If the first trial is valid, the athlete can then attack in the second and third trials. However, an athlete can also take a risk in the first trial in order to increase his/her chances of achieving an ideal jump. In the high jump and the pole vault, an athlete may choose a low initial height and to jump over all the following heights, or he/she may save energy and start later or forego certain heights. Moreover, it is important to clear each height in the first trial if possible in order to save energy. However, due to the small number of possible combined-event competitions per year and the devastating effect of not scoring in a discipline, combined-event athletes should take less risk than individual-event athletes.

The final middle-distance runs are established according to the score achieved up to that point and not according to the potential 1500m performance. In addition to specifying the intended intermediate times, it is therefore helpful to know the 1500m performance of the other runners, especially one's immediate opponents in the ranking. Trying to keep pace with an opponent who is similar to oneself in ranking is only sensible if performance abilities are similar. If this opponent is a clearly better 1500m runner, such behaviour may have very negative effects on the running time.

COMPETITION BEHAVIOUR

INCLUDING USEFUL TIPS FOR SPECIALISTS

Correct competition behaviour begins with waking up early enough. An athlete should get up about four hours before the start of the first discipline and soon after have a wholesome breakfast. Many combined-event athletes go for a short run before breakfast to get their circulation going and especially on the second day their tired muscles. Breakfast should be finished no later than two hours before the start of the competition. The actual warm-up begins approximately one hour before the first discipline of the day. On the second day, the warm-up should be more extensive although the athlete might feel differently.

Between two disciplines, athletes must not only cope with the positive and negative experiences of the previous discipline(s), but they must also choose the right balance between rest and preparation for the next discipline. On the one hand, an athlete must save energy, on the other hand he/she must prepare ideally for the next discipline. To avoid rush, he/she must measure the run-up early enough and begin with the practice jumps or throws. Before the first trial, an athlete should certainly perform one or two test trials in competition attire (i.e., without a tracksuit). Throughout the day, the athlete should consume some carbohydrate food and especially drink enough between the disciplines. The athlete should bring his/ her own food and should eat it especially during the competition breaks before the throwing events. In addition, extra clothing for any type of weather, an umbrella or a parasol, a blanket, and a sleeping pad should also be part of the competition luggage. For the various disciplines, combined-event athletes often need up to eight pairs of shoes.

The first day in particular should end with a long warm-down jog and an extensive high-carbohydrate meal immediately after the competition. Massages and adequate sleep help regeneration.

4.1.7 DIDACTICS: SUPERORDINATE LONG-TERM OBJECTIVES AND GENERAL METHODOLOGY

General basic training which is versatile in terms of coordination and thus geared to the combined events provides the basis for any subsequent specialisation in athletics (see chapters I-3.1.1 and I-3.3.4). Ultimately, the subsequent special discipline may also be the decathlon or heptathlon. This concept is important for the methods of combined-event training. Ultimately, the decathlon does not consist of ten disciplines, but should be regarded as one independent discipline. It would not be useful to train for ten disciplines with one tenth of the training time devoted to each discipline. It is therefore important to identify core elements and training forms in terms of coordination, strength, speed, endurance, and flexibility. In respect to coordination, this means that over the years and within each macrocycle sprinting techniques, the ability to establish movement rhythm, and the common features of the jumping and throwing disciplines should primarily be developed. Of the other major types of motor stress, sprinting speed and the strength of the extensor loop are of great importance in many disciplines in particular.

In recent years, alternative forms of competition for children have become increasingly more popular. Competitions for children are generally designed as combined-event and often as team competitions (see table 11). More and more children start in classic athletics disciplines only at a later age and during the transition to basic training.

Due to the high number of training hours and the diverse forms of stress, the combined events are among the sports with the highest injury rates for both youths and adults. An athlete's weak points are revealed. A study of 50 of Germany's best youth decathletes showed that there is an average incidence of 0.81 injuries per year. For adult men, the incidence is even as high as 0.97. Stress injuries (lumbar spine problems, patellar tendon irritation, etc.) are particularly common. These stress injuries also include a great number of ligament ruptures at the ankle, which are often caused by a lack of concentration resulting from physical and mental fatigue. In addition to preventive strength training (trunk strengthening, sensorimotor training, etc.) and a proper technique (e.g., in the pole vault), the rule of thumb should be to reduce the load when in doubt. "Better undertrain than overtrain" is a saying in the USA.

Due to the lack of time, the risk of overtraining, and the fact that the requirements of some of the individual disciplines conflict with one another (see discourse I), the objective of combined-event training can only be the optimal, and not the maximal development of the performance prerequisites. Decision must be made on the basis of a a cost-benefit relation (see training planning in chapter II–4.1.11).

*Table 11: **Examples of combined events for children**: The programme by the Federal Youth Games for schools (see www.bundesjugendspiele.de) also includes an alternative athletics combined-event competition for teams for each of the various age groups.*

Children's decathlon (according to Schulz, 2003) for 7- to 9-year-old children; in each discipline, the children can win 0, 1, 2, or 3 points	
10-second sprint	Who can run around a cone placed at a distance of 10, 15 or 20m and back to the starting point in 10 seconds?
Zone long jump	1 point: 1.60-2.30m; 2 points: 2.30-3.00m; 3 points: >3.00m
Putting a medicine ball into zones	800g ball; 0 points: <4m or no put; 1 point: 4-6m; 2 points: 6-9m; 3 points: >9m
Jump- and-reach test with one-legged take-off	with run-up; by touching a band stretched at a height of 1.70m, 2.00m, or 2.30m
30-second run on a 30m lap	as many laps as possible; 1 point for each lap started
Sprint over/around banana boxes placed in a lane on the track	8m approach to the first box, then the distance between the boxes is 5.50m; over or in a slalom around the boxes, after 30m around a turning mark and back in a free adjacent lane; 0 points: >16 sec; 1 point: 15-16 sec; 2 points: 14-15 sec; 3 points: <14 sec
Throw a bicycle tyre toward a target	Several javelins stick in the ground at a slight angle; the children are told to throw the tyres over the javelins using a rotational throw; 3 trials, 1 point per exact throw
Pole flying	From an elevation for distance; the coach provides pushing assistance to the child on the pole; the scoring depends on the facility used; landing with one's feet in a zone as far in the back half of the mat as possible
Throw an Aero howler toward a target	Using an Aero howler or rounders ball; from a distance of 5m through a bicycle tyre hanging from the crossbar of a football goal post; 3 trials, 1 point per exact throw
400 m	0 points: >3:20 min; 1 point: 2:30-3:20 min; 2 points: 1:40-2:30 min; 3 points: <1:40 min

Kids' Athletics (according to www.kidsathletics.de) For 8- to 9-year-old children (group 1), 10- to 11-year-old children (group 2), and 12- to 13-year-old children (group 3); team competitions: sprint as a relay, in the throws and jumps, the sum of the individual results counts; teams of identical size are required (e.g., 5 girls + 5 boys); the rankings achieved by the teams in the individual disciplines are added and the team with the lowest total score is the winner, etc.; also possible as an indoor competition	
Sprint/hurdles (groups 2 and 3)	Both the 40m hurdle distance and the 40m flat distance are started with a forward roll on a gym mat; half of the group begins with the hurdle distance, while the other half begins with the flat distance; the first runner runs over the hurdles, around the turning marker, and changes over to the second runner who runs the flat distance, around the turning marker, and exchanges with the third runner who runs over the hurdles, etc. until all runners have run the hurdle and the flat distance once each
Sprint/slalom (group 3)	Like sprint/hurdles, but using a slalom course instead of a hurdles course
Formula 1 (groups 1–3)	Relay on a versatile 80m lap with sprinting segments, slalom segments, obstacles, etc.
Continuous run (groups 1–3)	The teams start from different points on a versatile 90m lap; each child runs at his/her own pace for 8 min and collects cards from a referee for each finished lap; which team collects the most cards?
Pole flying (groups 2 and 3)	Pole vaulting for distance into landing zones; 3-stride run-up from a standing position with feet together and two-legged landing are obligatory; the best trial of 2 is counted
Rope jumping (groups 1 and 3)	How often can the athlete jump over the rope in 15 sec?; group 1: two-legged (2 trials); group 3: one-legged (1x left, 1x right)
Leaping like a frog (groups 1 and 2)	The first child performs a squat-extension jump for distance and lands on two legs; the next child takes off from the landing point, etc.; which teams gets the furthest (2 trials)?
Jumping for speed (groups 1 and 2)	the child jumps sideways over an approximately 20cm high obstacle; how many jumps does he/she make in 15 sec?; two trials per child
Running through a grid with knees raised to half the horizontal position (group 3)	5m course with very flat, thin obstacles placed at a distance of 40 cm (coordination grid); standing start from a cone, running through the grid with knees raised to half the horizontal position (113), the cone must be touched with one's hand at the end, running back through the grid with knees raised to half the horizontal position; the time is taken at the moment when the cone is touched; which team achieves the lowest overall time?
Target throw (groups 1 and 2)	A flutter ball, Aero howler, soft javelin or a similar device is thrown from a distance of 5m (group 1) or 7m (group 2) from a stride position toward a target at a height of at least 2.50m; 2 trials per child; which team achieves the most exact throws?
Javelin throw (groups 1–3)	Throwing a soft javelin or Turbo-Jav for distance using a measuring tape placed on the ground; the distance is estimated for an accuracy of 25cm; 2 trials
Throw-in from a knee-stand position (group 1)	Two-handed overhead throw of a 1kg ball from a knee-stand position on a gym mat or on the lawn; falling forward after delivery is permitted; measurement as in the javelin throw
Backward toss (group 3)	Tossing backward (93); measurement as in the javelin throw
Rotational throw (groups 2 and 3)	Rotational throw from a lateral standing position (e.g., bicycle tyres toward 3 vertical target zones at a distance of 5m); for right-handers: right target zone 3 points, centre 2 points, and left 1 point; 2 trials

4.1.8 TRAINING CONTENTS: FORMS OF GAMES AND EXERCISES

In general, all games and exercises forms mentioned in connection with the individual disciplines may be used in the combined events. However, as previously discussed, the focus should be on identifying the most important exercises.

4.1.9 SPECIAL TEST AND CONTROL PROCEDURES

In general, all tests and control procedures mentioned in connection with the individual disciplines may be used in the combined events. However, in terms of economy it is important to focus on certain essential tests as in the forms for games and exercises. In tables 12 and 13 respective suggestions have been presented.

*Table 12: **Basic and competition performances for certain target scores in the heptathlon** (according to Vindusková, 2003).*

Target score:	4800	5500	6200
60m	8.20 sec	7.80 sec	7.50 sec
100m	12.90 sec	12.30 sec	11.80 sec
150m (standing start)	20.2 sec	19.2 sec	18.2 sec
600m (standing start)	1:49.0 min	1:43.0 min	1:37.0 min
5-stride bounding run from a standing position	13.00m	14.00m	15.00m
Overhead throw with a 4kg shot	11.80m	12.90m	15.20m
Bench press (1RPM)	45 kg	55 kg	70 kg
Standing put of a 4kg shot	9.30m	10.40m	12.70m
Shot put using 3kg shot	11.50m	12.70m	15.00m
100m hurdles	15.60 sec	14.50 sec	13.80 sec
High jump	1.60m	1.70m	1.80m
Shot put	10.50m	11.70m	14.00m
200m	26.80m	25.50m	24.50m
Long jump	5.30m	5.75m	6.20m
Javelin throw	35.00m	40.00m	45.00m
800m	2:30.00 min	2:24.00 min	2:15.00 min

*Table 13: **Typical competition and basic performances of a male decathlete** with a best performance between 8,300 and 8,500 points (according to Gehrke et al., 1994, pp. 186–188).*

100m	10.85–10.90 sec	30m from a crouch start	4.19–4.31 sec
Long jump	7.70–7.80 m	30m flying	2.92–2.98 sec
Shot put	14.40–15.00m	150m from a standing start	15.4–16.4 sec
High jump	2.04–2.08m	300m from a standing start	32.9–34.1 sec
400m	48.30–49.20 sec	5-stride hop with run-up	21.2–23.0m
110m hurdles	14.30–14.50 sec	Shot put from a standing position	13–14m
Discus throw	41–45m	Javelin throw from a standing position	47.50–50.00m
Pole vault	4.70–4.90m	Bench press	128–140 kg
Javelin throw	58–60m	Backward toss of 4kg shot	21.90–23.30m
1500m	4:29–4:35 min	Full squat	130–145 kg

4.1.10   ERRORS – CAUSES – CORRECTIONS

See respective individual events.

4.1.11   TRAINING PLANNING

The training plans for combined-event athletes are based on remarks made in the general section (see chapter I–3.3). In particular, the training plans suggested here are joined with the training plans for children's athletics and the basic training presented in chapter I–3.3.

COMPETITIONS

One of the first steps in planning training is to specify the major scheduled competitions. In the past, combined-event athletes were only able to start in their special discipline in the summer season. Therefore, the plan was often based on single periodisation or double periodisation with only a very rudimentary winter competition season. The winter competition season was enhanced by the introduction of indoor combined-event competitions. Nevertheless, the highlight of the competition year is still in the summer (since athletics is mainly an outdoor sport).

Combined-event athletes usually participate in two to five combined-event competitions per year. Heptathletes may take part in one or two competitions more than decathletes. The total stress of a decathlon is significantly higher and requires an extended period of regeneration and rehabilitation before the next combined-event competition.

In addition, there are the preparatory competitions in which athletes often start in about three disciplines. Most heptathletes or decathletes prefer starting in their strong disciplines. Although this may be quite important for the athlete's self-confidence, coaches should also ensure that the athletes test themselves in their weak, unloved, technically demanding and shaky disciplines in competition. Shaky disciplines are those in which the competition results were subject to strong fluctuations in the past.

MAXIMAL TOTAL TRAINING VOLUME

It is characteristic of the combined events that the demands placed on athletes are extremely diverse. Training for the combined events is appropriately versatile and extensive. The total training volume is the greatest when compared to the other disciplines of athletics. Therefore, it is necessary to avoid overloading by ensuring that the switch to another load results in a recovery of the previously stressed structures at the same time (first legs, then arms; first jumping, then throwing; first sprinting, then running; first relaxed technique training, then stressful strength training, etc.).

The total amount of training should rise very gradually by increasing training frequency and the duration of training sessions. In respect to the build-up training of a 17-year-old athlete, seven training sessions per week are assumed here. Twelve training sessions per microcycle (= week) are suggested for high-performance training so that the individual sessions are

not too long and specific training modules may be carried out in a state as rested and focused as possible. The fact that one day is completely free for regeneration (usually Sunday) means that during build-up training athletes perform two training sessions on school-free Saturdays, while athletes in high-performance training train twice a day on six days of the week. Although in the course of the season there is the usual shift from volume-oriented and fundamental training sessions to intensity- and technique-oriented training sessions, training frequency is only significantly reduced in the competition period.

TECHNIQUE TRAINING

There are very different perspectives about the question how often certain techniques should be practised. On the one hand, some coaches from former Eastern Bloc countries claim that elite athletes should practise every technique twice a week without specifying the mesocycle. However, it seems impossible, at least in the general preparatory period of build-up training, to practise each of the approximately nine techniques of the decathlon (three jumping disciplines, three throwing disciplines, hurdles, crouch start and toe push-off sprinting, as well as grasping/pulling sprinting), even once per week due to the many other required training contents. On the other hand, some coaches and athletes report that they do not train for certain disciplines. For example, Frank Busemann is said not to have practised the long jump before his impressive 8m leap at the 1996 Olympic Games. He had already internalised a sufficiently good technique, had avoided the extreme loads of the take-off because of ankle problems, and had adequately prepared himself through general sprint and jump training. Similar information is provided on the javelin training of the Czech world-record holders and 70m throwers Dvorák and Šebrle.

In search of a solution, some authors point out overlapping elements of technique. Apart from the common features of the throwing and jumping events and the importance of the sprint for the hurdles and the jumps, the following is meant for example: practising the hurdle sprint also results in an improvement of the stride rhythm in the long jump and vice versa. High-jump and javelin practice have a mutually positive effect on stride rhythm, backward lean of the trunk, bracing foot touchdown, and bow tension.

Some coaches experiment with a two-week microcycle in which all disciplines are dealt with. When using one-week microcycles, the general and individual key disciplines (see chapters II–4.1.3 and II–4.1.6) are practised throughout the general preparation phase. In build-up training, they are practised each week and in high-performance training possibly several times per week. The other disciplines are practised alternately. Accordingly, the training plan for a 17-year-old decathlete contains a hurdle session, a pole-vault session, and an additional jumping and throwing session besides general training contents for sprinting and jumping coordination. In the jumping session, there

is an alternation of the long and high jump, while in the throwing session there is an alternation of the shot put, discus, and javelin throw. Instead of a weekly alternation, block training is also possible. This means that in the throwing session the first weeks should be devoted to the shot put, the next few weeks to the discus throw, and the final weeks to the javelin throw. Due to the overlapping elements of the high jump and javelin throw (see above), the javelin throw belongs together with the long jump in one week, while the high jump is practised with one of the other two throwing events. Coordination training is usually followed by strength or endurance training in the same training session.

During the special preparation or competition period, it often occurs that all techniques are practised in one week. Coupled training, which is now frequently used, refers to practising several techniques in one training session according to the sequence of the combined-event disciplines. For example, the following disciplines are trained one after the other for a short time each:

- Heptathlon:
  » hurdles, high jump, (shot put);
  » high jump, shot put;
  » long jump, javelin throw;
- Decathlon:
  » crouch start, long jump, (shot put);
  » shot put, high jump;
  » hurdles, discus throw, (pole vault);
  » pole vault, javelin throw.

Table 14: **Training emphasis in the various mesocycles** for combined-event practice in build-up and high-performance training.

1st mesocycle	aerobic endurance training, anaerobic (strength- and speed-)endurance training; hypertrophy-oriented maximal-strength and reactive-strength training; flexibility training; general coordination training and technique training for the key disciplines
2nd mesocycle	aerobic endurance training, anaerobic (speed-)endurance training; hypertrophy-, IC- and connective-tissue-oriented maximal- and reactive-strength training; (sprinting-)speed training; flexibility training; general coordination training and technique training primarily for the key disciplines
3rd mesocycle	anaerobic (speed-)endurance training; IC- and connective-tissue-oriented maximal- and reactive-strength training; speed training (also in the technical disciplines); technique training; maintenance stimuli
4th mesocycle	competitions and corresponding regeneration; IC- and connective-tissue-oriented maximal- and reactive-strength training; speed training; technique training; maintenance stimuli

In high-performance training, a maximum of three disciplines are practised in one training session, while in build-up training only two disciplines are usually practised.

SUGGESTED TRAINING PLANS

Following are the exemplary microcycles for the

- second mesocycle of a 17-year-old decathlete in build-up training (table 15);
- first mesocycle of a decathlete in high-performance training (table 16); and
- third mesocycle of a heptathlete in high-performance training (table 17).

The training plans presented in connection with the other disciplines, particularly for the fourth mesocycle in the triple jump (see chapter II–2.3.10), provide direction for the training in the mesocycles not presented here.

Table 15: Build-up training: sample microcycle for a 17-year-old decathlete in the second mesocycle.

Monday	Tuesday	Wednesday	Thursday	Friday	Saturday	Sunday
Trunk stabilisation exercises and abdominal crunches (20 min) with a lot of dynamic variation	Foot strengthening (10 min) little jumps	LI runs (5 x 100m; rest intervals: 30 sec)	Continuous running, cycling, aqua-jogging, cross-country skiing, etc. (30 min)	Warm-up jogging (6 min)	*Morning:* LI runs (6 x 80m; rest intervals: 20 sec)	Rest
ABCs of sprinting (10–15 run-throughs) grasping/pulling	Acceleration runs (3 reps) barefoot	Acceleration runs (2 reps)	Contract-relax stretching (30 min)	Acceleration runs (3 reps) barefoot	Bounding runs and/or rhythm jumps (2 x 4 x 30m)	
Acceleration runs (3 reps)	Practising the pole-vault technique (60 min) after a specific warm-up, example.g., planting exercises, swing-ups, Jagodins, and complete vaults from medium run-up lengths are practiced	ABCs of jumping (10–15 run-throughs) e.g., galloping sideways, ankle jumps, and skipping with two-legged landing	Medicine-ball work (40 min) goalkeeper throws, rotational throws, throws from a prone position, tossing, chest passes, frontal putting, and overhead throws	ABCs of jumping (10–15 run-throughs)	Gymnastics (80 min) development of new techniques as well as trunk and arm exercises focusing on strength	
Flying sprints (3 x 30m with 20m run-up; rest intervals: 10 min) at maximal pace through light barriers		Pop-up jumps (4 run-throughs of 4 jumps per side, each using a 3-stride rhythm)		Practising a jumping technique (40 min) e.g., learning the running-jump technique from medium run-up lengths	*Afternoon:* Warm-up jogging (15 min)	
Practising a throwing technique (40 min) e.g., the javelin throw: after specific warm-up, throws with various devices from a standing position and with short run-up	Strength training (30 min) according to the pyramid principle: clean and snatch (carefully checking the technique)	ABCs of hurdling and warm-up specific to the hurdles (20 min)	Muscle build-up training (30 min) bench press, lat-pull, and two additional varying exercises for the arms and/or shoulders	Strength training (45 min) maximal-eccentric strength training and/or according to the pyramid principle: hamstrings, quadriceps, adductors/abductors, hip flexors and hip extensors	ABCs of sprinting (12–18 run-throughs)	
	I3 tempo runs (3 x 600m; rest intervals: 5 min)	Hurdle Zs (2 sets of 4 Zs each of 2 run-throughs over 4 hurdles each; rest intervals: 3 min; rest intervals between sets: 10 min) out at 3-stride rhythm with the weak side, back with the strong side			Acceleration runs	
Game (20 min) e.g., soccer or basketball	Warm-down jogging (10 diagonals on the lawn)	Warm-down jogging	Tappings (8 x 5 sec) as utilisation	Foot strengthening (10 min) in the sand or using an elastic band	I3 tempo runs (150, 180, 220, 250, 200, 150, and 100m; rest intervals: 3, 4, 5, 7, 6, and 5 min)	
	Ankle jumps (5 x 6 reps) as utilisation	Frequency coordination (3 run-throughs) as utilisation		Alternating-pace sprints (4 x 60m) as utilisation	Contract-relax stretching (15 min)	
					Warm-down jogging	
					Standing starts	

Table 16: High-performance training: sample microcycle for a decathlete in the first mesocycle.

	Monday	Tuesday	Wednesday	Thursday	Friday	Saturday	Sunday
Morning	Trunk stabilisation exercises and abdominal crunches (20 min) Acceleration runs Practising the pole-vault technique (60 min) imitations, rigid pole, short run-ups Muscle build-up training (30 min) for the arms	Foot strengthening (10 min) little jumps on mats Acceleration runs (3 reps) barefoot ABCs of hurdling (20 min) Hurdle sprints (20 min) specific warm-up, then versatile (e.g., even and varying rhythms)	LI runs (8 x 80m; rest intervals: 20 sec) Practising a throwing technique (50 min) e.g., the shot put, versatile standing puts and alternative pre-accelerations Acceleration runs, skipping, and pop-up jumps (5 x 50m each) many variations	Warm-up jogging (6 min) with arm circling, rotations, etc. Gymnastics (80 min) technical and strength-oriented elements for the pole vault, high jump, and the throws; high strength loads primarily for the arms	LI runs (6 x 100m; rest intervals: 30 sec) ABCs of jumping (12–15 run-throughs) Practising a jumping technique (40 min) e.g., the high jump: scissors jump and flop with a short and medium-length run-up Technique sprints (6 x 60–80m) e.g., alternating-pace sprints	Rope jumping (5 min) Practising a throwing technique (50 min) e.g., the discus throw: standing throws, imitations and throws with 4/4 to 5/4 turn LI tempo runs (2 x 5 x 400m; rest intervals: 3 min; rest intervals between sets: 10 min)	Rest
Afternoon	Warm-up jogging (6 min) ABCs of jumping (10–15 run-throughs) Bounding runs and rhythm jumps (2 x 5 x 50m) Muscle build-up training (50 min) hamstrings, adductors, hip and back extensors and cleans Game (30 min)	Warm-up jogging (15 min) ABCs of sprinting (15–20 run-throughs) I3 tempo runs (5 x 60m, 4 x 80m, 5 x 60m, 4 x 80m, rest intervals: walking back; rest intervals between sets: 6–8 min) possibly including pull-resisted, uphill, or slalom sprints Contract-relax stretching (15 min) Warm-down jogging Skipping with two-legged landing	Warm-up jogging (6 min) Acceleration runs (3 reps) Muscle build-up training (40 min) abductors, quadriceps, hip flexors, and full squats Fartlek (30 min) Frequency coordination (10 min) over foam blocks as utilisation	Continuous run (50 min) Contract-relax stretching (15 min) Muscle build-up training (30 min) for the trunk on the apparatus, taking the morning programme into account Tappings (8 x 5 sec) as utilisation	Warm-up jogging (6 min) Acceleration runs ABCs of sprinting (12–15 run-throughs) Strength-endurance circle (45 min) ABCs of sprinting/jumping endurance, jumps onto a box, lunges, etc. Foot strengthening (15 min) in the sand or using an elastic band Standing starts	Continuous running, cycling, aqua-jogging, cross-country skiing, etc. (30 min) Contract-relax stretching (15 min) Frequency coordination (10 min) over mini-hurdles Muscle build-up training (30 min) for the arms Medicine-ball work (40 min) for the trunk and arms	

Table 17: *High-performance training: sample microcycle for a heptathlete in the third mesocycle.*

	Monday	Tuesday	Wednesday	Thursday	Friday	Saturday	Sunday
Morning	**Warm-up jogging** (6 min) **Maximal-eccentric strength training** (15 min) trunk and foot **Practising the long-jump technique** (45 min) in a competition-appropriate manner **Practising the javelin-throw technique** (45 min) in a competition-appropriate manner	**LI runs** (10 x 60m; rest intervals: 15 sec) **ABCs of sprinting** (8–10 run-throughs) **Tuck jumps** (3 x 3 run-throughs over 5 hurdles each) **Pull-assisted sprints** (2–3 reps) using a pulley **Flying sprints** (1–2 x 30m plus 25-30m run-up)	**Warm-up jogging** (6 min) **Practising the shot-put technique** (45 min) including specific warm-up, imitations, competition-like puts **Gymnastics** (30 min) for the high jump as well as versatile rotational movements	**LI runs** (8 x 80m; rest intervals: 20 sec) **Practising the hurdling technique** (45 min) after specific warm-up 2–3 x in a competition-like manner up to the 1st, 3rd, and 5th hurdle each, as well as 1 x up to the 11th hurdle **Practising the high-jump technique** (45 min) including specific warm-up, competition-like run-up	**Warm-up jogging** (6 min) **ABCs of sprinting** (8–10 run-throughs) **Acceleration runs** (3 reps) **Depth jumps** (5 x 10) from box to box **Pull-resisted sprints and crouch starts alternately** (12 sprints of 10–40m each) high additional load	**Warm-up jogging** (6 min) **ABCs of jumping** (8–10 run-throughs) **Acceleration runs** **Rhythm jumps/ one-legged jumps or bounding run** (2 x 4 x 20m) high intensity **Medicine-ball work** (40 min) for the trunk and putting/ throwing	Rest
Afternoon	**Warm-up jogging** (15 min) with arm circling, touching the ground on the left and right side, etc. **High-intensity strength training** (40 min) bench press, lat pull, and shoulder press **Game** (30 min) e.g., basketball or handball	**Warm-up jogging** (6 min) **ABCs of jumping** (8–10 run-throughs) **Acceleration runs** **Pop-up jumps** (2 x 2 run-throughs per leg) 5-stride rhythm **High-intensity strength training** (30 min) snatch and quarter-split squat **I1 tempo runs** (80, 250, and 150m; rest intervals: 8 and 20 min)	**Continuous run** (30 min) **Contract-relax stretching** (15 min) **Strength training** (45 min) according to the pyramid principle: abdominal machine, shoulder-hip twists, lumborum, hip and back extensors **Frequency coordination** (10 min) as utilisation	**Foot strengthening** (10 min) **Strength training** (45 min) according to the pyramid principle: pull-overs, inclined bench press, flies, and reverse flies **LI tempo runs** (3 x 4 x 200m; rest intervals: 90 sec; rest intervals between sets: 8 min) **Warm-down jogging** **Standing starts** (3 x 30m)	**LI runs** (6 x 100m; rest intervals: 30 sec) **Strength training** (45 min) maximal-eccentric and according to the pyramid principle: hamstrings, adductors, cleans, etc. **Accelerations** (3 reps) barefoot **I2 tempo run** (600m) 800m pace	**Warm-up jogging** (15 min) including backward and sideways running, touching the ground, rotations, etc. **ABCs of sprinting** (8–10 run-throughs) grasping/pulling **Acceleration runs** (3 reps) **I2 tempo runs** (80, 120, 150, 120 and 80m; rest intervals: 8, 12, 15, and 12 min)	

4.1.12   BIBLIOGRAPHY

Dickwach, H., Schleichhardt, A. & Wagner, K. (2008). Das Niveau der Einzelleistungen im Zehn- und Siebenkampf. *Leichtathletiktraining 19* (5), 17-23.

Geese, R. (2004). Ist eine Revision der internationalen Mehrkampfwertung überfällig? *Leistungssport 34* (5), 9-12.

Panteleyev, V. (1998). Preperation of decathletes. *Modern Athlete and Coach 36* (3), 35-38.

Regelkommissionen des DLV, FLA, ÖLV und SLV (Hrsg.). (2008). *Internationale Wettkampfregeln*. Waldfischbach: Hornberger.

Schäfer, G. (2004). Dos and Don'ts der Trainingsplanung. *Leichtathletiktraining 15* (8), 4-9.

Schulz, D. (2003). Zehnkampf für Kinder – einfach und schnell. *Leichtathletiktraining 14* (5), 24-30.

Ushakov, A. (1997). Some aspects influencing decathlon training. *Modern Athlete and Coach 35* (2), 25-29.

Vindusková, J. (2003). Training women for the Heptathlon – A brief outline. *New Studies in Athletics 18* (2), 27-45.

Wang, Z. & Lu, G. (2007). The Czech Phenomenon of Men´s Decathlon development. *International Journal of Sports Science and Engineering 1* (3), 209-214.

Wentz, S. & Engelhardt, M. (1997). Verletzungsanalyse und Leistungsparameter bei Jugendzehnkämpfern. *Deutsche Zeitschrift für Sportmedizin 48* (10), 389-394.

Westera, W. (2006). Decathlon: Towards a balanced and sustainable performance assessment method. *New Studies in Athletics 21* (1), 39-50.

ABOUT THE AUTHORS

Strüder, Univ.-Prof. Dr. Heiko K.
President of the German Sport University Cologne and head of the Institute of Movement and Neurosciences; chair of Training and Movement Theory in Individual Sports (Athletics – Swimming – Gymnastics).

Jonath, Ulrich
Long-time head of the division for athletics at the German Sport University Cologne; Lecturer at the local Coaches' Academy; World Athletics coach educator and national coach of the German Athletics Federation (DLV); coach and lecturer on an international level; author of numerous textbooks and educational films.

Scholz, Kai
German graduate degree in Sport Science; secondary school teacher; A-level coach of the German Athletics Federation (DLV); lecturer on athletics at the German Sport University Cologne.

In cooperation with:
Hollmann, Univ.-Prof. mult., Dr. med. Dr. h.c. mult. Wildor
Founder and long-time head of the Institute for Cardiovascular Research and Sports Medicine at the German Sport University Cologne; Chair of Cardiology and Sports Medicine (emeritus); honorary president of the International Federation of Sports Medicine (FIMS) and the German Society of Sports Medicine and Prevention.

Knicker, Dr. Axel
Lecturer on athletics, biomechanics, and training science in the Institute of Movement and Neurosciences at the German Sport University Cologne; author of numerous research papers on muscular fatigue, the biomechanics of throws, and the specificity of strength training.

Ritzdorf, Dr. Wolfgang
Instructor of athletics in the Institute of Movement and Neurosciences at the German Sport University Cologne; former coach of the women's high jump for the German Athletics Federation (DLV); World Athletics (WA) coach educator for jumping events and head-coordinator for the Coach Education and Certification System; director of the former WA World High Jump Centre in Cologne.

Schiffer, Dr. Jürgen
Secondary school teacher for sports and English; former assistant head of the Central Library of Sports Sciences at the German Sport University Cologne; author of a bilingual dictionary on athletics; co-editor (1987-1999) of the German magazine "Lehre der Leichtathletik" ("Theory of Athletics"); co-editor and documentation editor of the World Athletics technical quarterly "New Studies in Athletics."

Stein, Dr. Norbert

Instructor of athletics at the German Sport University Cologne; former DLV coach for the women's high jump; lecturer of training science at the Coaches' Academy of the German Olympic Sports Federation; former coach of the German Athletics Federation (DLV) and IAAF coach educator; director of the former ATC Cologne Training Centre.

INDEX

1103